A SELECT LIBRARY

OF THE

NICENE AND POST-NICENE FATHERS

OF

THE CHRISTIAN CHURCH

EDITED BY

PHILIP SCHAFF, D.D., LL.D.,

PROFESSOR OF CHURCH HISTORY IN THE UNION THEOLOGICAL SEMINARY, NEW YORK.

IN CONNECTION WITH A NUMBER OF PATRISTIC SCHOLARS OF EUROPE AND AMERICA

VOLUME XIII

SAINT CHRYSOSTOM:

HOMILIES ON GALATIANS, EPHESIANS, PHILIPPIANS, COLOSSIANS, THESSALONIANS, TIMOTHY, TITUS, AND PHILEMON.

WM. B. EERDMANS PUBLISHING COMPANY
GRAND RAPIDS   MICHIGAN

ISBN 0-8028-8111

Reprinted, May 1976

PHOTOLITHOPRINTED BY CUSHING - MALLOY, INC.
ANN ARBOR, MICHIGAN, UNITED STATES OF AMERICA

CONTENTS.

ST. CHRYSOSTOM AS A HOMILIST.

BY THE AMERICAN EDITOR OF THE HOMILIES ON PHILIPPIANS, COLOSSIANS,
AND THESSALONIANS.

THESE Homilies are often less complete in exposition than those on earlier books of the New Testament, and in literary excellence will not compare with the Homilies on the Statues, and many other discourses given at Antioch. But to the student of preaching, they are quite as instructive, if not really more so. Here at Constantinople the great preacher was burdened with administrative details, and harassed by Court intrigues, so that his sermons were often given with far less than his earlier careful preparation, and seem to have been generally left afterwards to the mercy of shorthand reporters, and of editors who sent them forth when he was in banishment or in the grave. Any minister who has winced to see an unwritten sermon or other address of his own in the morning paper, with the accumulated and interlaced mistakes of reporter, compositor, and proof-corrector, can sympathize with the situation. But in fact the preacher thus appears in undress, and his methods may be in some respects the subject of a more profitable inspection. You see the sermon in about as imperfect, and sometimes distorted, a condition as it is seen in the actual delivery by many of the congregation. You see the frequent questions, the abrupt turns of phrase, the multiplied repetitions, by which a skilled and sympathetic preacher, keenly watching his audience, strives to retain attention and to insure a more general comprehension. You are drawn near to him, and almost stand by his side.

John of the Golden Mouth is, upon the whole, our very best example, — most richly instructive and fruitfully inspiring, — in respect of expository preaching, which is of late beginning to be more highly valued and more frequently attempted in our country than ever before. We have many good models in Scotland, some in England, and a few at home. Nor should the student ever forget Luther, or fail to profit by the peculiar methods of some recent Germans; but one who is reasonably endowed with historical sympathy can learn most from Chrysostom. The study of an ancient preacher is in this respect like the study of the Greek and Latin classics, that it demands sympathy with ideas and persons far away from ourselves, thus broadening the intellect, invigorating the imagination, and deepening in us a true feeling for all that is human. One who is at first without interest in Chrysostom, perhaps even repelled by the extravagant expressions, the heaped-up imagery, the frequent bad taste (at least, according to our standards), of this eminently representative Asiatic Greek, is precisely the man that ought to read Chrysostom, if he wishes to educate himself in the broadest and highest sense. Study the great preacher till you can thoroughly appreciate and heartily enjoy him. This will be much aided, of course, by reading a biography, as that by Stephens, or the long article in Smith's Dictionary of Christian Biography, or the introductory biographical sketch in the ninth volume of this series. You very soon find that he is profoundly in earnest, and all alive. Christianity is with him a living reality. He dwells always in its presence and companionship. We may discern what seem to us grave errors of doctrinal opinion, but we feel the quickening pulses of genuine Christian love and zeal. And how fully he sympathizes with his hearers! He thoroughly knows them, ardently loves them, has a like temperament, shares not a little in the faults of his age and his race, as must always be the case with a truly inspiring orator or poet. Even when severely rebuking, when blazing with indignation, he never seems alien, never stands aloof, but throws himself among them, in a very transport of desire to check, and rescue, and save. Is there, indeed, any preacher, ancient or modern, who in these respects equals John Chrysostom?

His homilies are not directly a model for us, as regards the construction of discourse. The early Christians disliked to hear, or make, a smoothly symmetrical and elegantly finished oration like those of the secular orators. They wished for familiar and free addresses, such as we call a prayer-meeting *talk;* and this was precisely the meaning of their words "homily" and "sermon." The preacher took up his passage of Scripture — usually somewhat extended — in a familiar way, sentence by sentence, with explanations and remarks, as he saw occasion; sometimes we find Chrysostom actually returning to go over the passage again, that it may suggest further remarks. At length, he would be apt to seize upon some topic of doctrine or practice which the text had directly or remotely suggested, and discuss that by way of conclusion, not infrequently wandering far off into the thoughts which one after another occurred. Now, modern taste requires much more system and symmetry in building a discourse. The Schoolmen taught their pupils to analyze and arrange,[1] and modern preaching has taken the corresponding form, for good and for ill. An expository sermon of to-day must be much more systematic in its explanations, and much more regular in its entire construction, than those of the ancient preachers. Admirable models in this direction are furnished in Scotland. But while conforming to modern taste as to structure, one may learn much, very much, from the preachers of the early centuries, especially from Chrysostom, in respect of freedom, versatility, and skill in practical application. The modern careful preparation and orderly arrangement, combined (*mutatis mutandis*) with the ancient freedom and directness, and reduced to harmony and vital symmetry by zealous practice, might constitute the best type of expository preaching.

And it may be repeated that Chrysostom is not least helpful in these expository talks on the shorter epistles of Paul. Though often appearing fragmentary, they lay bare his habitual processes and reveal his most vigorous powers, and are not wanting in passages that burst into passion or shine in splendor.

Their value is increased rather than lessened for thoughtful readers by the restoration of the true text. The Oxford translation of the Homilies on these Epistles was published (1843) before the appearance of the corresponding volume of Field's critical edition of the Greek text (1855). The translation was based, for Philippians, on the edition of Chrysostom's Works by the English scholar Savile (1612), with some comparison of the Benedictine edition by Montfaucon (1718), and the Paris or Second Benedictine edition (1834–1839); and for Colossians and Thessalonians, on the Paris edition, with comparison of Savile. There was also occasional use of some collations from one MS. for Philippians, and one or two more for Thessalonians. Field has pointed out that the Benedictine and the Paris, and other editions, including that of Migne (1863), really followed, with slight alteration, the text of Savile. But the earliest edition of Chrysostom's Homilies on the Epistles of Paul, published at Verona in 1529, presents a very different text; and Field's careful study of collations from four MSS. for Philippians, six for Colossians, and five for Thessalonians, together with the Catena, satisfied him that the Verona edition had in general given the true text, and he has reproduced it, with such alterations as the MSS. generally agreeing with it appeared, in his judgment, to require. The American editor was at first inclined to think that Field had been unduly influenced by the Catena, which would naturally abridge its extracts, particularly in drawing from an author so efflorescent and repetitious as Chrysostom, and which had often appeared to do so when he was studying it throughout the Gospel of Matthew. But after going through Philippians with the construction of a composite text, which was felt to be

---

[1] How this came about, the editor has sought to explain in his "Lectures on the History of Preaching" (New York, Armstrong), p. 103 f.

inconsistent and unsatisfactory, like that of the Oxford translator and that of Migne, the editor was not far advanced in Colossians before he saw clearly that the Verona text as rewrought by Field was, beyond question, generally correct and greatly to be preferred. Accordingly the whole of this portion, Philippians as well as the rest, has been conformed to Field's text, except in occasional passages, where Field's own MSS. were thought to indicate otherwise, and these have been pointed out in the foot-notes if they possessed the least importance. The foot-notes also present some few specimens of the numerous enlargements and explanatory changes or transitional additions by which the altered text printed by Savile and his followers sought to piece out and smooth into literary propriety the rough, fragmentary, and sometimes obscure expressions of the true text.[1] It was only when nearly all this work had been done that the editor observed that some other portions of the Oxford translation were originally based on Field's text, which for those portions had appeared in time for the purpose. Thus his part of the work has in fact become assimilated to the American edition for Matthew, and for Acts and Romans.

The *translation* of the Oxford edition shows general excellence, and frequent felicity of English expression. Besides the numerous cases of differences in text, the translation has been altered where the syntax seemed to be misunderstood, where the passion for variety of rendering (as often in the common or authorized English version of the Bible) had obscured the verbal connection of passages, &c. It is possible that the American editor, in his love for Chrysostom's freedom and downrightness, has sometimes gone to the opposite extreme from that of the translators in England, and become too baldly literal.

The foot-notes in square brackets are from the editor. The others are from the Oxford translators, being retained except where they were superseded by the change of text or of translation, or for some other reason appeared to be no longer useful. Their references to other volumes of the Oxford edition have been conformed in the paging to the American edition for Matthew, Acts, and Romans, and the Statues ; elsewhere the pages were simply omitted.

J. A. B.

---

[1] Persons interested in text-criticism may care to know that Field's volume for the Homilies on these Epistles, with a digest of various readings, would strikingly illustrate for them, in different material, the scientific principles and methods of Westcott and Hort. In the Homilies on Colossians they will find (out of six MSS. collated for Field, viz., A B C D E H), a well-marked and singularly uniform group of three, viz., B C H, presenting the peculiarities of the altered text, adopted in many passages by Savile and followers, but in many others not adopted. The " internal evidence of groups," as described by Westcott and Hort in vol. ii., Schaff's Companion to the Bible, or Warfield's Textual Criticism, may be here applied with great ease and assured results. In Thessalonians (out of five MSS., B C I K L) B and C are the same documents as before, but C here presents marked differences of text. B K, with or without one or two other MSS., will be found very generally wrong, with the peculiarities of the altered text. C sometimes joins them, but oftener stands aloof, frequently uniting with I or L in giving the true text, and sometimes standing alone for the right. In Philippians (out of four MSS., C E F G) C G will quite frequently give the altered text, but there is not such uniformity as in the Homilies on the other Epistles. It may be added that (as Field also remarks) the alterations throughout the Homilies on these Epistles show a marked family likeness, and doubtless came from the same early critical editor, who, however, altered much more freely in some Homilies (as on Philippians) than in others (as on 2 Thess.). The altered text sometimes places Chrysostom among the supporters of a " Syrian" reading of the New Testament, where his real text is not so, but the instances observed in these Homilies are not so numerous as to affect his general position. It is to be hoped that other MSS. of Chrysostom will be collated, and more complete materials be at hand for future critics to settle details now remaining uncertain, and perhaps to throw light on the origin of the altered or Savilian text; but the superiority of the Verona type, as given by Field, is not at all likely to be ever again otherwise than clear and assured.

THE COMMENTARY

AND

HOMILIES OF ST. JOHN CHRYSOSTOM,

ARCHBISHOP OF CONSTANTINOPLE,

ON THE

EPISTLES OF ST. PAUL THE APOSTLE

TO THE

GALATIANS AND EPHESIANS.

The Oxford Translations Revised, with Additional Notes, by

REV. GROSS ALEXANDER, D.D.,

PROFESSOR OF NEW TESTAMENT GREEK IN VANDERBILT UNIVERSITY, NASHVILLE, TENN.

CONTENTS.

COMMENTARY ON GALATIANS.

HOMILIES ON EPHESIANS.

PREFACE.

St. Chrysostom's Commentary on the Epistle to the Galatians is continuous, according to chapter and verse, instead of being arranged in Homilies, with a moral or practical application at their close, as in his exposition of other Epistles. It was written at Antioch, as Montfaucon infers from a reference which the Author, makes upon Chap. i., ver. 16 (p. 20) to other of his writings, which certainly were written about the same time in that city. Vid. *Hom. de Mutal. Nom.*, Tom. III., p. 98, Ed. Ben. The year is uncertain, but seems not to have been earlier than A.D. 395.

The Homilies on the Epistle to the Ephesians have been by some critics assigned to the Episcopate at Constantinople, in consequence of certain imperfections in their composition, which seemed to argue absence of the comparative leisure which he enjoyed at Antioch. There is a passage too in Homily XI., pp. 231, 232, which certainly is very apposite to the Author's circumstance in the court of Eudoxia. Yet there are strong reasons for deciding that they too were delivered at Antioch. St. Babylas and St. Julian, both saints at Antioch, are mentioned familiarly, the former in Homily IX., p. 205, the latter in Homily XXI., pp. 342, 343. Monastic establishments in mountains in the neighborhood are spoken of in Homily VI., p. 165, and XIII., p. 248 ;[1] and those near Antioch are famous in St. Chrysostom's history. A schism too is alluded to in Homily XI., p. 230, as existing in the community he was addressing, and that not about a question of doctrine ; circumstances which are accurately fulfilled in the contemporary history of Antioch, and which are more or less noticed in the Homilies on 1 Corinthians, which were certainly delivered at Antioch.[2]

Moreover, he makes mention of the prevalence of superstitions, Gentile and Jewish, among the people whom he was addressing, in Homily VI., fin., p. 166, Homily XII., fin., p. 240, which is a frequent ground of complaint in his other writings against the Christians of Antioch : *vid.* in Gal. p. 15 ; in 1 Cor., Homily XII., §§ 13, 14 ; in Col., Homily VIII., fin. ; *Contr. Jud.* I., pp. 386–388.

Since Evagrius, the last Bishop of the Latin succession in the schism, died in A.D. 392, these Homilies must have been composed before that date.

As to the Translations, the Editors have been favored with the former by a friend who conceals his name ; and with the latter, by the Rev. William John Copeland, M.A., Fellow of Trinity College, Oxford.

J. H. NEWMAN.

---

[1] Vid. also XXI., p. 338. [2] Vid. also Preface to Translation of Homilies on 1 Cor., p. xiii.

COMMENTARY[1] OF ST. JOHN CHRYSOSTOM,

ARCHBISHOP OF CONSTANTINOPLE,

ON THE

EPISTLE OF ST. PAUL THE APOSTLE

TO THE

GALATIANS.

CHAPTER I

VERSE 1–3.

"Paul, an Apostle, (not from men, neither through man, but through Jesus Christ and God the Father, who raised Him from the dead ;) and all the brethren which are with me, unto the Churches of Galatia : Grace to you and peace from God the Father, and our Lord Jesus Christ."

THE exordium[2] is full of a vehement and lofty spirit, and not the exordium only, but also, so to speak, the whole Epistle. For always to address one's disciples with mildness, even when they need severity is not the part of a teacher but it would be the part of a corrupter and enemy. Wherefore our Lord too, though He generally spoke gently to His disciples, here and there uses sterner language, and at one time pronounces a blessing, at another a rebuke. Thus, having said to Peter, " Blessed art thou, Simon Barjona," (Matt. xvi : 17.) and having promised to lay the foundation of the Church upon his confession, shortly afterwards He says, "Get thee behind Me, Satan : thou art a stumbling block unto Me." (Matt. xvi : 23.) Again,

on another occasion, " Are ye also even yet without understanding ? " (Matt. xv : 16.) And what awe He inspired them with appears from John's saying, that, when they beheld Him conversing with the Samaritan woman, though they reminded Him to take food, no one ventured to say, " What seekest Thou, or why speakest thou with her ? " (John iv : 27.) Thus taught, and walking in the steps of his Master, Paul hath varied his discourse according to the need of his disciples, at one time using knife and cautery, at another, applying mild remedies. To the Corinthians he says, " What will ye ? shall I come unto you with a rod, or in love, and in a spirit of meekness ? " (I Cor. vi : 21.) but to the Galatians, "O foolish Galatians." (Gal. iii : 1.) And not once only, but a second time, also he has employed this reproof, and towards the conclusion he says with a reproachful allusion to them, " Let no man trouble me ; " (Gal. vi : 17). but he soothes them again with the words, " My little children, of whom " I am again in travail : " (Gal. iv : 19.) and so in many other instances.

Now that this Epistle breathes an indignant spirit, is obvious to every one even on the first perusal ; but I must explain the cause of his anger against the disciples. Slight and unimportant it could not be, or he would not have used such vehemence. For to be exasperated by common matters is the part of the little-

[1] [Properly so-called. His other works on the Scriptures are in the form of homilies, or expository sermons, with the exception of his continuous commentary on the first six chapters of Isaiah. But as Schaff says "his homilies are expository and his commentaries are homiletical."—G. A.]

[2] "The two threads which run through this Epistle—the defence of the Apostle's own authority, and the maintenance of the doctrine of grace—are knotted together in the opening salutation. By expanding his official title into a statement of his direct commission from God, he meets the personal attack of his enemies ; and by dwelling on the work of redemption in connection with the name of Christ (v. 4) he resists their doctrinal errors."—Lightfoot.—G. A.]

I

minded, morose, and peevish ; just as it is that of the more indolent and sluggish to lose heart in weighty ones. Such a one was not Paul. What then was the offence which roused him ? it was grave and momentous, one which was estranging them all from Christ, as he himself says further on, " Behold, I Paul say unto you, that if ye receive circumcision, Christ will profit you nothing ; " (Gal. v : 2.) and again, " Ye who would be justified by the Law, ye are fallen away from Grace." (Gal. v : 4.) What then is this ? For it must be explained more clearly. Some of the Jews who believed, being held down by the preposessions of Judaism, and at the same time intoxicated by vain-glory, and desirous of obtaining for themselves the dignity of teachers, came to the Galatians, and taught them that the observance of circumcision, sabbaths, and new-moons, was necessary, and that Paul in abolishing these things was not to be borne. For, said they, Peter and James and John, the chiefs of the Apostles and the companions of Christ, forbade them not. Now in fact they did not forbid these things, but this was not by way of delivering positive doctrine, but in condescension to the weakness of the Jewish believers, which condescension Paul had no need of when preaching to the Gentiles ; but when he was in Judæa, he employed it himself[1] also. But these deceivers, by withholding the causes both of Paul's condescension and that of his brethren, misled the simpler ones, saying that he was not to be tolerated, for he appeared but yesterday, while Peter and his colleagues were from the first,— that he was a disciple of the Apostles, but they of Christ,—that he was single, but they were many, and pillars of the Church. They accused him too of acting a part ; saying, that this very man who forbids circumcision observes the rite elsewhere, and preaches one way to you and another way to others.

Since Paul then saw the whole Galatian people in a state of excitement, a flame kindled against their Church, and the edifice shaken and tottering to its fall, filled with the mixed feelings of just anger and despondency, (which he has expressed in the words, " I could wish to be present with you now, and to change my voice,"—Gal. iv : 20.)he writes the Epistle as an answer to these charges. This is his aim from the very commencement, for the underminers of his reputation had said, The others were disciples of Christ but this man of the "Apostles." Wherefore he begins thus, " Paul, an Apostle not from men, neither through man." For these deceivers, as I was saying before, had said

that this man was the last of all the Apostles and was taught by them, for Peter, James, and John, were both first called, and held a primacy among the disciples, and had also received their doctrines from Christ Himself ; and that it was therefore fitting to obey them rather than this man ; and that they forbad not circumcision nor the observance of the Law. By this and similar language and by depreciating Paul, and exalting the honor of the other Apostles, though not spoken for the sake of praising them, but of deceiving the Galatians, they induced them to adhere unseasonably to the Law. Hence the propriety of his commencement. As they disparaged his doctrine, saying it came from men, while that of Peter came from Christ, he immediately addresses himself to this point, declaring himself an apostle " not from men, neither through man." It was Ananias who baptized him, but it was not he who delivered him from the way of error and initiated him into the faith ; but Christ Himself sent from on high that wondrous voice, whereby He inclosed him in his net. For Peter and his brother, and John and his brother, He called when walking by the seaside, (Matt. iv : 18.) but Paul after His ascension into heaven. (Acts. ix : 3, 4.) And just as these did not require a second call, but straightway left their nets and all that they had, and followed Him, so this man at his first vocation pressed vigorously forward, waging, as soon as he was baptized, an implacable war with the Jews. In this respect he chiefly excelled the other Apostles, as he says, "I labored more abundantly than they all;"(1Cor. xv : 10.) at present, however, he makes no such claim, but is content to be placed on a level with them. Indeed his great object was, not to establish any superiority for himself, but, to overthrow the foundation of their error. The not being "from men" has reference to all alike for the Gospel's root and origin is divine, but the not being "through man" is peculiar to the Apostles ; for He called them not by men's agency, but by His own.[2]

But why does he not speak of his vocation rather than his apostolate, and say, " Paul " called " not by man ? " Because here lay the whole question ; for they said that the office of a teacher had been committed to him by men, namely by the Apostles, whom therefore it behooved him to obey. But that it was not entrusted to him by men, Luke declares in the

---

[1][As is narrated, for example, in Acts xxi : 20–26, which was, Baur and his Tübingen critics to the contrary notwithstanding, in accordance with Paul's principle and practice, as announced in 1 Cor. ix : 20.—G. A.]

[2] " Not from men as an ultimate, nor through man as a mediate authority."—Ellicott.

" In the first clause, 'from men,' he distinguishes himself from the false apostles who did not derive their authority from God at all ; in the second, 'through man,' he ranks himself with the twelve who were commissioned directly from God. The singular is used in second clause, 'through man,'because offices which emanate from a body of men are conferred by their single representative."—Lightfoot.

[" Paul has in second clause used the singular because the contrast is 'through Jesus Christ.'"—Meyer.—G. A.]

words, "As they ministered to the Lord, and fasted, the Holy Ghost said, Separate me Barnabas and Saul." (Acts xiii: 2.)

From this passage it is manifest [1] that the power of the Son and Spirit is one, for being commissioned by the Spirit, he says that he was commissioned by Christ. This appears in another place, from his ascription of the things of God to the Spirit, in the words which he addresses to the elders at Miletus: "Take heed unto yourselves, and to all the flock, in the which the Holy Ghost hath made you bishops."(Acts xx: 28.) Yet in another Epistle he says, "And God hath set some in the Church, first Apostles, secondly prophets, thirdly teachers." (1 Cor. xii: 28.) Thus he ascribes indifferently the things of the Spirit to God, and the things of God to the Spirit. Here too he stops the mouths of heretics, by the words "through Jesus Christ and God the Father;" for, inasmuch as they said this term "through" was applied to the Son as importing inferiority, see what he does. He ascribes it to the Father, thus teaching us not to prescribe laws to the ineffable Nature, nor define the degrees of Godhead which belong to the Father and Son. For to the words "through Jesus Christ" he has added, "and God the Father;" for if at the mention of the Father alone he had introduced the phrase "through whom," they might have argued sophistically that it was peculiarly applicable to the Father, in that the acts of the Son were to be referred to Him. But he leaves no opening for this cavil, by mentioning at once both the Son and the Father, and making his language apply to both. This he does, not as referring the acts of the Son to the Father, but to show that the expression implies no distinction of Essence. [2] Further, what can now be said by those, who have gathered a notion of inferiority from the Baptismal formula,—from our being baptized into the name of the Father, Son, and Holy Spirit? [3] For if the Son be inferior because He is named after the Father, what will they say seeing that, in the passage before us, the Apostle beginning from Christ proceeds to mention the Father?—but let us not even utter such a blasphemy, let us not swerve from the truth in our contention with them; rather let us preserve, even if they rave ten thousand times, the due measures of reverence. Since then it would be the height of madness and impiety to argue that

the Son was greater than the Father because Christ was first named, so we dare not hold that the Son is inferior to the Father, because He is placed after Him in the Baptismal formula. "Who raised Him from the dead."

Wherefore is it, O Paul, that, wishing to bring these Judaizers to the faith, you introduce none of those great and illustrious topics which occur in your Epistle to the Philippians, as, "Who, being in the form of God, counted it not a prize to be on an equality with God," (Phil. ii: 6.) or which you afterwards declared in that to the Hebrews, "the effulgence of his glory, and the very image of His substance;" (Heb. i: 3.) or again, what in the opening of his Gospel the son of thunder sounded forth, "In the beginning was the Word, and the Word was with God, and the Word was God;" (John i: 1.) or what Jesus Himself oftentimes declared to the Jews, "that His power and authority was equal to the Father's?" (John v: 19, 27, &c.) Do you omit all these, and make mention of the economy of His Incarnation only, bringing forward His cross and dying? "Yes," would Paul answer. For had this discourse been addressed to those who had unworthy conceptions of Christ, it would have been well to mention those things; but, inasmuch as the disturbance comes from persons who fear to incur punishment should they abandon the Law, he therefore mentions that whereby all need of the Law is excluded, I mean the benefit conferred on all through the Cross and the Resurrection. To have said that "in the beginning was the Word," and that "He was in the form of God, and made Himself equal with God," and the like, would have declared the divinity of the Word, but would have contributed nothing to the matter in hand. Whereas it was highly pertinent thereto to add, "Who raised Him from the dead," for our chiefest benefit was thus brought to remembrance, and men in general are less interested by discourses concerning the majesty of God, than by those which set forth the benefits which come to mankind. Wherefore, omitting the former topic, he discourses of the benefits which had been conferred on us.

But here the heretics insultingly exclaim, "Lo, the Father raises the Son!" For when once infected, they are wilfully deaf to all sublimer doctrines; and taking by itself and insisting on what is of a less exalted nature, and expressed in less exalted terms, either on account of the Son's humanity, or in honor of the Father, or for some other temporary purpose, they outrage, I will not say the Scripture, but themselves. I would fain ask such persons, why they say this? do they hope to prove the Son weak and powerless to raise *one* body?

---

[1] This digression, and others which follow, were occasioned by the controversies of the day; the Arians and Macedonians denying the co-equality and consubstantiality of FATHER, SON, and HOLY GHOST.

[2] ["To urge this use of διὰ in connection with Son and the Father as direct evidence for the ὁμοουσία of the Father and the Son (as Chrysostom and Theod.)may perhaps be rightly deemed precarious. Yet there is something *very* noticeable in this use of a common preposition with both the first and second persons of the Trinity by a writer so cumulative and yet for the most part so exact in his use of prepositions as St. Paul."—Ellicott.—G. A.]

[3] [That is, from the order of the three names.—G. A.]

Nay, verily, faith in Him enabled the very shadows of those who believed in Him, to effect the resurrection of the dead. (Acts. v : 15.) Then believers in Him, though mortal, yet by the very shadows of their earthly bodies, and by the garments which had touched these bodies, could raise the dead, but He could not raise Himself? Is not this manifest madness, a great stretch of folly? Hast thou not heard His saying, " Destroy this Temple, and in three days I will raise it up?" (John ii : 19.) and again, " I have power to lay down my life, and I have power to take it again? " (John x : 18.) Wherefore then is the Father said to have raised Him up, as also to have done other things which the Son Himself did? It is in honor of the Father, and in compassion to the weakness of the hearers.

" And all the brethren which are with me."

Why is it that he has on no other occasion in sending an epistle added this phrase? For either he puts his own name only or that of two or three others, but here has mentioned the whole number and so has mentioned no one by name.

On what account then does he this?

They made the slanderous charge that he was singular in his preaching, and desired to introduce novelty in Christian teaching. Wishing therefore to remove their suspicion, and to show he had many to support him in his doctrine, he has associated with himself " the brethren," to show that what he wrote he wrote with their accord.[1]

" Unto the Churches of Galatia."

Thus it appears, that the flame of error had spread over not one or two cities merely, but the whole Galatian people. Consider too the grave indignation contained in the phrase, " unto the Churches of Galatia : " he does not say, " to the beloved " or " to the sanctified," and this omission of all names of affection or respect, and this speaking of them as a society merely, without the addition " Churches of God," for it is simply " Churches of Galatia," is strongly expressive of deep concern and sorrow. Here at the outset, as well as elsewhere, he attacks their irregularities, and therefore gives them the name of " Churches," in order to shame them, and reduce them to unity. For persons split into many parties cannot properly claim this appellation, for the name of " Church " is a name of harmony and concord.

" Grace to you and peace from God the Father, and our Lord Jesus Christ."

This he always mentions as indispensible, and in this Epistle to the Galatians especially ; for since they were in danger of falling from grace he prays that they may recover it again, and since they had come to be at war with God, he beseeches God to restore them to the same peace.

" God the Father."

Here again is a plain confutation of the heretics, who say that John in the opening of his Gospel, where he says " the Word was God," used the word Θεὸς without the article, to imply an inferiority in the Son's Godhead ; and that Paul, where he says that the Son was " in the form of God," did not mean the Father, because the word Θεὸς is without the article. For what can they say here, where Paul says, ἀπὸ Θεοῦ Πατρος, and not ἀπὸ τοῦ Θεοῦ? And it is in no indulgent mood towards them that he calls God, " Father," but by way of severe rebuke, and suggestion of the source whence they became sons, for the honor was vouchsafed to them not through the Law, but through the washing of regeneration. Thus everywhere, even in his exordium, he scatters traces of the goodness of God, and we may conceive him speaking thus : " O ye who were lately slaves, enemies and aliens, what right have ye suddenly acquired to call God your Father ? it was not the Law which conferred upon you this relationship ; why do ye therefore desert Him who brought you so near to God, and return to your tutor ?[2]

But the Name of the Son, as well as that of the Father, had been sufficient to declare to them these blessings. This will appear, if we consider the Name of the Lord Jesus Christ with attention ; for it is said, " thou shalt call His Name Jesus ; for it is He that shall save His people from their sins ; " (Matt. i : 21.) and the appellation of " Christ " calls to mind the unction of the Spirit.

Ver 4. " Who gave himself for our sins." [3]

Thus it appears, that the ministry which He undertook was free and uncompelled ; that He was delivered up by Himself, not by another. Let not therefore the words of John, " that the Father gave His only-begotten Son " (Jo. iii : 16.) for us, lead you to derogate from the dignity of the Only-begotten, or to infer therefrom that He is only human. For the Father is said to have given Him, not as implying that the Son's ministry was a servile one, but to teach us that it seemed good to the Father, as Paul too has shown in the immediate context: " according to the will of our God, and Father." He says not

---

[1] [Meyer agrees with Lightfoot and Ellicott in the view that πάντες means not all the Christians of the place where he was (probably Ephesus), but only his traveling companions ; but he differs from them in holding that " the impressive effect of the epistle could not but be strengthened by indicating that these brethren collectively desired to address the very same instructions, warnings and exhortations to the Galatians."—G. A.]

[2] [The word is παιδαγωγός, the same that is used in Gal. 3 : 24, 25, and translated ' school-master ' in the A. V., but ' tutor ' in the Rev. Ver.—G. A.]

[3] [" The Galatians had practically ignored the atoning death of Christ ; compare ii : 21 and v : 4."—Lightfoot.—G. A.]

"by the command," but "according to the will," for inasmuch as there is an unity of will in the Father and the Son, that which the Son wills, the Father wills also.

"For our sins,"[1] says the Apostle; we had pierced ourselves with ten thousand evils, and had deserved the gravest punishment; and the Law not only did not deliver us, but it even condemned us, making sin more manifest, without the power to release us from it, or to stay the anger of God. But the Son of God made this impossibility possible for he remitted our sins, He restored us from enmity to the condition of friends, He freely bestowed on us numberless other blessings.

Ver. 4. "That He might deliver us out of this present evil world."

Another class of heretics[2] seize upon these words of Paul, and pervert his testimony to an accusation of the present life. Lo, say they, he has called this present world evil, and pray tell me what does "world" [age] αἰών mean but time measured by days and seasons? Is then the distinction of days and the course of the sun evil? no one would assert this even if he be carried away to the extreme of unreasonableness. "But" they say, "it is not the 'time,' but the present 'life,' which he hath called evil.'" Now the words themselves do not in fact say this; but the heretics do not rest in the words, and frame their charge from them, but propose to themselves a new mode of interpretation. At least therefore they must allow us to produce our interpretation, and the rather in that it is both pious and rational. We assert then that evil cannot be the cause of good, yet that the present life is productive of a thousand prizes and rewards. And so the blessed Paul himself extols it abundantly in the words, "But if to live in the flesh, if this is the fruit of my work, then what I shall choose I wot not;" (Phil. i: 22.) and then placing before himself the alternative of living upon earth, and departing and being with Christ, he decides for the former. But were this life evil, he would not have thus spoken of it, nor could any one, however strenuous his endeavor, draw it aside into the service of virtue. For no one would ever use evil for good, fornication for chastity, envy for benevolence. And so, when he says, that "the mind of the flesh is not subject to the law of God, neither indeed can it be, (Rom. viii: 7.) he means that vice, as such, cannot become virtue; and the expression, "evil world," must be understood to mean evil actions, and a

depraved moral principle. Again, Christ came not to put us to death and deliver us from the present life in that sense, but to leave us in the world, and prepare us for a worthy participation of our heavenly abode. Wherefore He saith to the Father, "And these are in the world, and I come to Thee; I pray not that Thou shouldest take them from the world, but that Thou shouldest keep them from the evil," (Jo. xvii: 11, 15.) i. e., from sin. Further, those who will not allow this, but insist that the present life is evil, should not blame those who destroy themselves; for as he who withdraws himself from evil is not blamed, but deemed worthy of a crown, so he who by a violent death, by hanging or otherwise, puts an end to his life, ought not to be condemned. Whereas God punishes such men more than murderers, and we all regard them with horror, and justly; for if it is base to destroy others, much more is it to destroy one's self. Moreover, if this life be evil, murderers would deserve a crown, as rescuing us from evil. Besides this, they are caught by their own words, for in that they place the sun in the first, and the moon in the second rank of their deities, and worship them as the givers of many goods, their statements are contradictory. For the use of these and the other heavenly bodies, is none other than to contribute to our present life, which they say is evil, by nourishing and giving light to the bodies of men and animals and bringing plants to maturity. How is it then that the constitution of this "evil life is so ministered to by those, who according to you are gods? Gods indeed they are not, far from it, but works of God created for our use; nor is this world evil. And if you tell me of murderers, of adulterers, of tomb-robbers, these things have nothing to do with the present life, for these offences proceed not from that life which we live in the flesh, but from a depraved will. For, if they were necessarily connected with this life, as embraced in one lot with it, no man would be free or pure from them, for no man can escape the characteristic accidents of humanity, such as, to eat and drink, to sleep and grow, to hunger and thirst, to be born and die, and the like; no man can ever become superior to these, neither sinner nor just man, king nor peasant, We all are subject to the necessity of nature. And so if vice were an essential element of this life, no one could avoid it, any more than the things just mentioned. And let me not be told that good men are rare, for natural necessity is insuperable by all, so that as long as one virtuous man shall be found, my argument will in no wise be invalidated. Miserable, wretched man! what is it thou sayest? Is this life evil, wherein we have learnt to know God, and meditate on

---

[1] ["The idea of satisfaction is implied not in the preposition ὑπέρ, but the whole nature of the case."—Meyer.—G.A.]

[2] That is, the Manichees, who considered matter intrinsically evil, and paid divine honors to the sun, moon, and stars. Vid. Epiph. *Hær.* lxvi. [On Mani and the Manichean heresy see Schaff, *Church History*, Vol. II. pp. 498-508 where a full account of the literature is given also.—G. A.]

things to come, and have become angels instead of men, and take part in the choirs of the heavenly powers? What other proof do we need of an evil and depraved mind?

"Why then," they say, "does Paul call the present life evil?" In calling the present world [age] evil, he has accommodated himself to our usage, who are wont to say, "I have had a bad day," thereby complaining not of the time itself, but of actions or circumstances. And so Paul in complaining of evil principles of action has used these customary forms of speech; and he shows that Christ hath both delivered us from our offences, and secured us for the future. The first he has declared in the words, "Who gave Himself for our sins;" and by adding, "that He might deliver us out of this present evil world," he has pronounced our future safety. For neither of these did the Law avail, but grace was sufficient for both.

Ver. 4. "According to the will of our God and Father." [1]

Since they were terrified by their notion that by deserting that old Law and adhering to the new, they should disobey God, who gave the Law, he corrects their error, and says, that this seemed good to the Father also: and not simply "the Father," but "our Father," which he does in order to affect them by showing that Christ has made His Father our Father.

Ver. 5. "To whom be the glory for ever and ever. Amen."

This too is new and unusual, for we never find the word, "Amen" placed at the beginning of an Epistle, but a good way on; here, however, he has it in his beginning, to show that what he had already said contained a sufficient charge against the Galatians, and that his argument was complete, for a manifest offence does not require an elaborate crimination. Having spoken of the Cross, and Resurrection, of redemption from sin and security for the future, of the purpose of the Father, and the will of the Son, of grace and peace and His whole gift, he concludes with an ascription of praise.

Another reason for it is the exceeding astonishment into which he was thrown by the magnitude of the gift, the superabundance of the grace, the consideration who we were, and what God had wrought, and that at once and in a single moment of time. Unable to express this in words, he breaks out into a doxology, sending up for the whole world an eulogium, not indeed worthy of the subject, but such as was possible to him. Hence too he proceeds to use more vehement language; as if greatly kindled by a sense of the Divine benefits, for having said,

"To whom be the glory for ever and ever, Amen," he commences with a more severe reproof.

Ver. 6. "I marvel that ye are so quickly[1] removing[2] from Him that called you in the grace of Christ, unto a different Gospel."

Like the Jews who persecuted Christ, they imagined their observance of the Law was acceptable to the Father, and he therefore shows that in doing this they displeased not only Christ, but the Father also, for that they fell away thereby not from Christ only, but from the Father also. As the old covenant was given not by the Father only, but also by the Son, so the covenant of grace proceeded from the Father as well as the Son, and Their every act is common: "All things whatsoever the Father hath are Mine." (John xv: 16.) By saying that they had fallen off from the Father, he brings a twofold charge against them, of an apostasy, and of an immediate apostasy. The opposite extreme a late apostasy, is also blameworthy, but he who falls away at the first onset, and in the very skirmishing, displays an example of the most extreme cowardice, of which very thing he accuses them also saying: "How is this that your seducers need not even time for their designs, but the first approaches suffice for your overthrow and capture? And what excuse can ye have? If this is a crime among friends, and he who deserts old and useful associates is to be condemned, consider what punishment he is obnoxious to who revolts from God that called him." He says, "I marvel," not only by way of reproof, that after such bounty, such a remission of their sins, such overflowing kindness, they had deserted to the yoke of servitude, but also in order to show, that the opinion he had had of them was a favorable and exalted one. For, had he ranked them among ordinary and easily deceived persons, he would not have felt surprise. "But since you," he says, "are of the noble sort and have suffered, much, I do marvel." Surely this was enough to recover and lead them back to their first expressions. He alludes to it also in the middle of the Epistle, "Did ye suffer so many things in vain? if it be indeed in vain." (Gal. iii: 4.) "Ye are removing;" he says not, "ye are removed," that is, "I will not believe or suppose that your seduction is complete;" this is the language of one about to recover them, which further on he expresses yet more clearly in the words, "I have confidence to you-ward in the Lord that ye will be none otherwise minded." (Gal. v: 10.)

"From Him that called you in the grace of Christ."

---

[1] ["And not by our own merits. cf. τοῦ καλέσαντος, v. 6."—Lightfoot.
"The salvation was willed by God to whom Christ was obedient (Phil. ii: 9)."—Meyer.—G. A.]

[2] [This note of time helps to fix the date of the Epistle as being about 56 or 57 during Paul's two years' stay at Ephesus (Ac. 19:10). So most modern expositors, though Lightfoot and some others put it later.—G. A.]

The calling is from the Father, but the cause of it is the Son. He it is who hath brought about reconciliation and bestowed it as a gift, for we were not saved by works in righteousness: or I should rather say that these blessings proceed from Both ; as He says, "Mine are Thine, and Thine are Mine." (John xvii: 10.) He says not "ye are removing from the Gospel" but "from God who called you,"a more frightful expression, and more likely to affect them. Their seducers did not act abruptly but gradually, and while they removed them from the faith in fact, left names unchanged. It is the policy of Satan not to set his snares in open view ; had they urged them to fall away from Christ, they would have been shunned as deceivers and corrupters, but suffering them so far to continue in the faith, and putting upon their error the name of the Gospel, without fear they undermined the building employing the terms which they used as a sort of curtain to conceal the destroyers themselves. As therefore they gave the name of Gospel to this their imposture, he contends against the very name, and boldly says, "unto a different Gospel,"—

Ver. 7. "Which is not another Gospel."

And justly, for there is not another.[1] Nevertheless the Marcionites[2] are misled by this phrase, as diseased persons are injured even by healthy food, for they have seized upon it, and exclaim, "So Paul himself has declared there is no other Gospel." For they do not allow all the Evangelists, but one only, and him mutilated and confused according to their pleasure. Their explanation of the words, "according to my Gospel and the preaching of Jesus Christ," (Rom. xvi: 25.) is sufficiently ridiculous ; nevertheless, for the sake of those who are easily seduced, it is necessary to refute it. We assert, therefore, that, although a thousand Gospels were written, if the contents of all were the same, they would still be one, and their unity no wise infringed by the number of writers. So, on the other hand, if there were one writer only, but he were to contradict himself, the unity of the things written would be destroyed. For the oneness of a work depends not on the number of its authors, but on the agreement or contradictoriness of its contents. Whence it is clear that the four Gospels are one Gospel ; for, as the four say the same thing, its oneness is preserved

by the harmony of the contents, and not impaired by the difference of persons. And Paul is not now speaking of the number but of the discrepancy of the things spoken. With justice might they lay hold of this expression, if the Gospels of Matthew and Luke differed in the signification of their contents, and in their doctrinal accuracy ; but as they are one and the same, let them cease being senseless and pretending to be ignorant of these things which are plain to the very children.

Ver. 7. "Only there are some that trouble you, and would pervert the Gospel of Christ."

That is to say, ye will not recognize another Gospel, so long as your mind is sane, so long as your vision remains healthy, and free from distorted and imaginary phantoms. For as the disordered eye mistakes the object presented to it, so does the mind when made turbid by the confusion of evil thoughts. Thus the madman confounds objects ; but this insanity is more dangerous than a physical malady, for it works injury not in the regions of sense, but of the mind ; it creates confusion not in the organ of bodily vision, but in the eye of the understanding.

"And would[3] pervert the Gospel of Christ."

They had, in fact, only introduced one or two commandments, circumcision and the observance of days, but he says that the Gospel was subverted, in order to show that a slight adulteration vitiates the whole. For as he who but partially pares away the image on a royal coin renders the whole spurious, so he who swerves ever so little from the pure faith, soon proceeds from this to graver errors, and becomes entirely corrupted. Where then are those who charge us with being contentious in separating from heretics, and say that there is no real difference between us except what arises from our ambition ? Let them hear Paul's assertion, that those who had but slightly innovated, subverted the Gospel. Not to say that the Son of God is a created Being, is a small matter. Know you not that even under the elder covenant, a man who gathered sticks on the sabbath, and transgressed a single commandment, and that not a great one, was punished with death ? (Num. xv: 32, 36.) and that Uzzah, who supported the Ark when on the point of being overturned, was struck suddenly dead, because he had intruded upon an office which did not pertain to him ? (2 Sam. vi: 6, 7.) Wherefore if to transgress the sabbath, and to touch the falling Ark, drew down the wrath of God so signally as to deprive the offender of even a momentary respite, shall he who corrupts unutterably awful doctrines find excuse and par-

---

[1] [The Revised version brings out the difference of the words for "another." The first is ἕτερον, "a different kind of" gospel, the second is ἄλλο, "another," simply. " To a different sort of gospel,—nay, it is not another gospel. There cannot be two gospels. Only certain men are troubling you and trying to pervert the gospel of Christ. But a perverted gospel is no gospel at all."—G. A.]

[2] Marcion flourished about A. D. 120—130. His doctrine was a compound of various preceding theologies, chiefly the Gnostic. He received only a part of St. Luke's Gospel. Tertull. *in Marc.* iv. 2—4. He it was who on asking Polycarp to "acknowledge" him, received for answer, "I acknowledge thee as the first-born of Satan."

[3] [θέλοντες : On this word Jerome aptly says, *Volunt sed non valent.* The troubling of the Galatians, however, did actually take place.—G. A.]

don? Assuredly not. A want of zeal in small matters is the cause of all our calamities; and because slight errors escape fitting correction, greater ones creep in. As in the body, a neglect of wounds generates fever, mortification, and death; so in the soul, slight evils overlooked open the door to graver ones. It is accounted a trivial fault that one man should neglect fasting; that another, who is established in the pure faith, dissembling on account of circumstances, should surrender his bold profession of it, neither is this anything great or dreadful; that a third should be irritated, and threaten to depart from the true faith, is excused on the plea of passion and resentment. Thus a thousand similar errors are daily introduced into the Church, and we are become a laughing-stock to Jews and Greeks, seeing that the Church is divided into a thousand parties. But if a proper rebuke had at first been given to those who attempted slight perversions, and a deflection from the divine oracles, such a pestilence would not have been generated, nor such a storm have seized upon the Churches. You will now understand why Paul calls circumcision a subversion of the Gospel. There are many among us now, who fast on the same day as the Jews, and keep the sabbaths in the same manner; and we endure it nobly or rather ignobly and basely. And why do I speak of Jews seeing that many Gentile customs are observed by some among us; omens, auguries, presages, distinctions of days, a curious attention to the circumstances of their children's birth, and, as soon as they are born, tablets with impious inscriptions are placed upon their unhappy heads, thereby teaching them from the first to lay aside virtuous endeavors, and drawing part of them at least under the false domination of fate.[1] But if Christ in no way profits those that are circumcised, what shall faith hereafter avail to the salvation of those who have introduced such corruptions? Although circumcision was given by God, yet Paul used every effort to abolish it, because its unseasonable observance was injurious to the Gospel. If then he was so earnest against the undue maintenance of Jewish customs, what excuse can we have for not abrogating Gentile ones? Hence our affairs are now in confusion and trouble, hence have our learners being filled with pride, reversed the order of things throwing every thing into confusion, and their discipline having been neglected by us their governors, they spurn our reproof however gentle. And yet if their superiors were even more worthless and full of numberless evils, it would not be right for the disciple to disobey. It is said

of the Jewish doctors, that as they sat in Moses' seat, their disciples were bound to obey them, though their works were so evil, that the Lord forbad His disciples to imitate them. What excuse therefore is there for those who insult and trample on men, rulers of the Church, and living, by the grace of God, holy lives? If it be unlawful for us to judge each other, much more is it to judge our teachers.

Ver. 8, 9. "But though we, or an angel from heaven, should preach unto you any Gospel other than that which we preached unto you, let him be anathema."

See the Apostle's wisdom; to obviate the objection that he was prompted by vainglory to applaud his own doctrine, he includes himself also in his anathema; and as they betook themselves to authority, that of James and John, he mentions angels also saying, "Tell me not of James and John; if one of the most exalted angels of heaven corrupt the Gospel, let him be anathema." The phrase "of heaven" is purposly added, because priests are also called angels. "For the priest's lips should keep knowledge, and they should seek the law at his mouth: for he is the messenger [angel] of the Lord of hosts." (Mal. ii: 7.) Lest therefore it should be thought that priests are here meant by the term "angels," he points out the celestial intelligences by the addition, "from heaven." And he says not, if they preach a contrary Gospel, or subvert the whole of the true one, let them be anathema; but, if they even slightly vary, or incidentally disturb, my doctrine. "As we have said before, so say I now again." That his words might not seem to be spoken in anger, or with exaggeration, or with recklessness he now repeats them.[2] Sentiments may perhaps change, when an expression has been called forth by anger, but to repeat it a second time proves that it is spoken advisedly, and was previously approved by the judgment. When Abraham was requested to send Lazarus, he replied, "They have Moses and the Prophets; let them hear them: if they hear them not, neither will they be persuaded, if one rise from the dead." (Luke xvi: 31.) And Christ introduces Abraham thus speaking, to show that He would have the Scriptures accounted more worthy of credence, even than one raised from the dead: Paul too, (and when I say Paul, I mean Christ, who directed his mind,) prefers them before an angel come down from heaven. And justly, for the angels, though mighty, are but servants and ministers, but the Scriptures were all written and sent, not by servants, but

---

[1] [There is an eloquent passage on this same subject of foolish and sinful superstitions among Christians in Homily xii. on Ephesians, near the end.—G. A.]

[2] [Though this view of Chrysostom, that the προειρήκαμεν refers to what immediately precedes is held by many others, it is not tenable for two reasons; 1. St. Paul would have used the singular προείρηκα, as he does in λέγω, immediately following. 2. The πρό in composition, and the καί ἄρτι, both, mark some greater distinction of time than this would allow.—G. A.]

by God the Lord of all. He says, if "any man" preach another Gospel to you than that which we have preached,—not "if this or that man:" and herein appears his prudence, and care of giving offence, for what needed there still any mention of names, when he had used such extensive terms as to embrace all, both in heaven and earth? In that he anathemized evangelists and angels, he included every dignity, and his mention of himself included every intimacy and affinity. "Tell me not," he exclaims, "that my fellow-apostles and colleagues have so spoken; I spare not myself if I preach such doctrine." And he says this not as condemning the Apostles for swerving from the message they were commissioned to deliver; far from it, (for he says, whether we or they thus preach;) but to show, that in the discussion of truth the dignity of persons is not to be considered.

Ver. 10. "For [1] am I now persuading men or God?" or am I seeking to please men? if I were still pleasing men, I should not be a servant of Christ."

Granting, says he, that I might deceive you by these doctrines, could I deceive God, who knows my yet unuttered thoughts, and to please whom is my unceasing endeavor? See here the Apostolical spirit, the Evangelical loftiness! So too he writes to the Corinthians, "For we are not again commending ourselves unto you, but speak as giving you occasion of glorying;" (2 Cor. v: 12.) and again, "But with me it is a very small thing that I should be judged of you, or of man's judgment." (1 Cor. iv: 3.) For since he is compelled to justify himself to his disciples, being their teacher, he submits to it; but he is grieved at it, not on account of chagrin, far from it, but on account of the instability of the minds of those led away and on account of not being fully trusted by them. Wherefore Paul now speaks, as it were, thus:—Is my account to be rendered to you? Shall I be judged by men? My account is to God, and all my acts are with a view to that inquisition, nor am I so miserably abandoned as to pervert my doctrine, seeing that I am to justify what I preach before the Lord of all.

He thus expressed himself, as much with a view of withstanding their opinions, as in self-defence; for it becomes disciples to obey, not to judge, their master. But now, says he, that the order is reversed, and ye sit as judges, know that I am but little concerned to defend myself before you; all, I do for God's sake, and in order that I may answer to Him concerning my doctrine. He who wishes to persuade

men, is led to act tortuously and insincerely, and to employ deceit and falsehood, in order to engage the assent of his hearers. But he who addresses himself to God, and desires to please Him, needs simplicity and purity of mind, for God cannot be deceived. Whence it is plain that I have thus written to you not from the love of rule, or to gain disciples, or to receive honor at your hands. My endeavor has been to please God, not man. Were it otherwise, I should still consort with the Jews,[2] still persecute the Church. I who have cast off my country altogether, my companions, my friends, my kindred, and all my reputation, and taken in exchange for these, persecution, enmity, strife, and daily-impending death, have given a signal proof that I speak not from love of human applause. This he says, being about to narrate his former life, and sudden conversion, and to demonstrate clearly that it was sincere. And that they might not be elevated by a notion that he did this by way of self-vindication to them, he premises, "For do I now persuade men?" He well knew how, on a fitting occasion, to correct his disciples, in a grave and lofty tone: assuredly he had other sources whence to demonstrate the truth of his preaching,—by signs and miracles, by dangers, by prisons, by daily deaths, by hunger and thirst, by nakedness, and the like. Now however that he is speaking not of false apostles, but of the true, who had shared these very perils, he employs another method. For when his discourse was pointed towards false apostles, he institutes a comparison by bringing forward his endurance of danger, saying, "Are they ministers of Christ? (I speak as one beside himself) I more; in labors more abundantly, in prisons more abundantly, in stripes above measure, in deaths oft." (2 Cor. xi: 23.) But now he speaks of his former manner of life and says,

Ver. 11, 12. "For[3] I make known to you, brethren, as touching the Gospel which was preached by me that it is not after man. For neither did I receive it from man, nor was I taught it, but it came to me through revelation of Jesus Christ."

You observe how sedulously he affirms that he was taught of Christ, who Himself, without human intervention, condescended to reveal to him all knowledge. And if he were asked for his proof that God Himself thus immediately revealed to him these ineffable mysteries, he would instance his former manner of life, arguing that his conversion would not have been so

---

[1] ["I speak thus strongly, for my language shall not be misconstrued. Will any one now say that careless of winning the favor of God, I seek to ingratiate myself with men?" Lightfoot.—G. A.]

[2] ["χριστοῦ δοῦλος should not be taken in an historical sense, as Chrysostom. This would be feeble and lacking in depth of thought. No, it is to be taken in its ethical character."—Meyer.—G. A.]

[3] [The reading γάρ (Rev. Ver. W. H.) gives a reason for what is implied in the sentence preceding, while δέ, an inferior reading, means 'but,' (now to enter more particularly on the subject of my letter) "I make known to you."—So Meyer.—G. A.]

sudden, had it not been by Divine revelation. For when men have been vehement and eager on the contrary side, their conviction, if it is effected by human means, requires much time and ingenuity. It is clear therefore that he, whose conversion is sudden, and who has been sobered in the very height of his madness, must have been vouchsafed a Divine revelation and teaching, and so have at once arrived at complete sanity. On this account he is obliged to relate his former life, and to call the Galatians as witnesses of past events. That the Only-Begotten Son of God had Himself from heaven vouchsafed to call me, says he, you who were not present, could not know, but that I was a persecutor you do know. For my violence even reached your ears, and the distance between Palestine and Galatia is so great, that the report would not have extended thither, had not my acts exceeded all bounds and endurance. Wherefore he says,

Ver. 13. "For[1] ye have heard of my manner of life in time past in the Jews' religion, how that beyond measure I persecuted the Church of God, and made havoc of it."

Observe how he shrinks not from aggravating each point; not saying simply that he "persecuted" but "beyond measure," and not only "persecuted" but "made havoc of it," which signifies an attempt to extinguish, to pull down, to destroy, to annihilate, the Church.

Ver. 14. "And I advanced in the Jews' religion beyond many of mine own age among my countrymen, being more exceedingly zealous for the traditions of my fathers."

To obviate the notion that his persecution arose from passion, vain-glory, or enmity, he shows that he was actuated by zeal, not indeed "according to knowledge," (Rom. x: 2.) still by a zealous admiration of the traditions of his fathers. This is his argument;[2]—if my efforts against the Church sprung not from human motives, but from religious though mistaken zeal, why should I be actuated by vain-glory, now that I am contending for the Church, and have embraced the truth? If it was not this motive, but a godly zeal, which possessed me when I was in error, much more now that I have come to know the truth, ought I to be free from such a suspicion. As soon as I passed over to the doctrines of the Church I shook off my Jewish prejudices, manifesting on that side a zeal still more ardent; and this is a proof that

my conversion is sincere, and that the zeal which possesses me is from above. What other inducement could I have to make such a change, and to barter honor for contempt, repose for peril, security for distress? none surely but the love of truth.

Ver. 15, 16. "But when it was the good pleasure of God, Who separated me, even from my mother's womb, and called me through His grace, to reveal His Son in me, that I might preach Him among the Gentiles, immediately I conferred not with flesh and blood."

Here his object is to show, that it was by some secret providence that he was left for a time to himself. For if he was set apart from his mother's womb to be an Apostle and to be called to that ministry, yet was not actually called till that juncture, which summons he instantly obeyed, it is evident that God had some hidden reason for this delay. What this purpose was, you are perhaps eager to learn from me, and primarily, why he was not called with the twelve. But in order not to protract this discourse by digressing from that which is more pressing, I must entreat your love not to require all things from me, but to search for it by yourselves, and to beg of God to reveal it to you. Moreover I partly discussed this subject when I discoursed before you on the change of his name from Saul to Paul; which, if you have forgotten, you will fully gather from a perusal of that volume.[3] At present let us pursue the thread of our discourse, and consider the proof he now adduces that no natural event had befallen him,—that God Himself had providentially ordered the occurrence.

"And called me through His grace."

God indeed says that He called him on account of his excellent capacity, as He said to Ananias, "for he is a chosen vessel unto Me, to bear my name before the Gentiles, and kings," (Acts ix: 15.) that is to say, capable of service, and the accomplishment of great deeds. God gives this as the reason for his call. But he himself everywhere ascribes it to grace, and to God's inexpressible mercy, as in the words, "Howbeit for this cause I obtained mercy," not that I was sufficient or even serviceable, but "that in me as chief might Jesus Christ show forth all His long-suffering, for an ensample of them which should hereafter believe on Him unto eternal life." (1 Tim. i: 16.) Behold his overflowing humility; I obtained mercy, says he, that no one might despair, when the worst of men had shared His bounty. For this is the force of the words, "that He might show forth all His long-suffering for an ensample of them which should hereafter believe on Him."

"To reveal His Son[4] in me."

---

[1] ["He begins here the *historical proof* that he was indebted for his gospel to the *revelation* he had mentioned."—Meyer.
"My early education was such that no human agency could have brought the change (from Judaism to Christianity). It required a direct interposition from God."—Lightfoot.—G. A.]
[2] [Chrysostom's interpretation of this passage is hardly sustained by the context. It is not a proof of his sincerity that he is adducing ; he is continuing and completing the statement that his former manner of life was proof that he could not have received the Gospel from man.—G. A.]

[3] [Vid. *Hom. de Mut. Nom.* t. iii. p. 98. Ed. Ben.—G. A.]
[4] ["In his pre-Christian blindness Paul had known Christ κατὰ σάρκα, 2 Cor. v: 16."—Meyer.—G. A.]

Christ says in another place, "No one knoweth who the Son is, save the Father; and who the Father is, save the Son, and he to whomsoever the Son willeth to reveal Him." (Luke x: 22.) You observe that the Father reveals the Son, and the Son the Father; so it is as to Their glory, the Son glorifies the Father, and the Father the Son; "glorify Thy Son, that the Son may glorify Thee," and, "as I have glorified Thee." (John xvii: 1, 4.) But why does he say, "to reveal His Son in me," and not "to me?" it is to signify, that he had not only been instructed in the faith by words, but that he was richly endowed with the Spirit; —that the revelation had enlightened his whole soul, and that he had Christ speaking within him.[1]

"That I might preach Him among the Gentiles."

For not only his faith, but his election to the Apostolic office proceeded from God. The object, says he, of His thus specially revealing Himself to me, was not only that I might myself behold Him, but that I might also manifest Him to others. And he says not merely, "others," but, "that I might preach Him among the Gentiles," thus touching beforehand on that great ground of his defence which lay in the respective characters of the disciples; for it was necessary to preach differently to the Jews and to the heathen.

"Immediately I conferred not with flesh and blood."

Here he alludes to the Apostles, naming them after their physical nature; however, that he may have meant to include all mankind, I shall not deny.[2]

Ver. 17. "Neither went I up to Jerusalem to them which were Apostles before me."

These words weighed by themselves seem to breath an arrogant spirit, and to be foreign to the Apostolic temper. For to give one's suffrage for one's self, and to admit no man to share one's counsel, is a sign of folly. It is said, "Seest thou a man wise in his own conceit? there is more hope of a fool than of him;" (Prov. xxvi: 12.) and, "Woe unto them that are wise in their own eyes, and prudent in their own sight!" (Isa. v: 21.) and Paul himself in another place, "Be not wise in your own conceits." (Rom. xii: 16.) Surely one who had been thus taught, and had thus admonished others, would not fall into such an error, even were he an ordinary man; much less then Paul himself. Nevertheless, as I said, this expression nakedly considered may easily prove a snare and offence to many hearers. But if the cause of it is subjoined, all will applaud and admire the speaker.

This then let us do; for it is not the right course to weigh the mere words, nor examine the language by itself, as many errors will be the consequence, but to attend to the intention of the writer. And unless we pursue this method in our own discourses, and examine into the mind of the speaker, we shall make many enemies, and every thing will be thrown into disorder. Nor is this confined to words, but the same result will follow, if this rule is not observed in actions. For surgeons often cut and break certain of the bones; so do robbers; yet it would be miserable indeed not to be able to distinguish one from the other. Again, homicides and martyrs, when tortured, suffer the same pangs, yet is the difference between them great. Unless we attend to this rule, we shall not be able to discriminate in these matters; but shall call Elijah and Samuel and Phineas homicides, and Abraham a son-slayer; that is, if we go about to scrutinize the bare facts, without taking into account the intention of the agents. Let us then inquire into the intention of Paul in thus writing, let us consider his scope, and general deportment towards the Apostles, that we may arrive at his present meaning. Neither formerly, nor in this case, did he speak with a view of disparaging the Apostles or of extolling himself, (how so? when he included himself under his anathema?) but always in order to guard the integrity of the Gospel. Since the troublers of the Church said that they ought to obey the Apostles who suffered these observances, and not Paul who forbade them, and hence the Judaizing heresy had gradually crept in, it was necessary for him manfully to resist them, from a desire of repressing the arrogance of those who improperly exalted themselves, and not of speaking ill of the Apostles. And therefore he says, "I conferred not with flesh and blood;" for it would have been extremely absurd for one who had been taught by God, afterwards to refer himself to men. For it is right that he who learns from men should in turn take men as his counsellors. But he to whom that divine and blessed voice had been vouchsafed, and who had been fully instructed by Him that possesses all the treasures of wisdom, wherefore should he afterwards confer with men? It were meet that he should teach, not be taught by them. Therefore he thus spoke, not arrogantly, but to exhibit the dignity of his own commission. "Neither went I up," says he, "to Jerusalem to them which were Apostles before me." Because they were continually repeating that the Apostles were before him, and were called before him, he says, "I went not up to them." Had it been needful for him to communicate with them, He, who revealed to him his commission, would have given him this injunction.

---

[1] ["Εν ἐμοί means 'in my mind,' 'in my consciousness.' 2 Cor. iv: 6," in opposition to Lightfoot who says, " 'In me' means, as the context shows, not a revelation made inwardly to himself, but through him to others."—G. A.]

[2] ["Flesh and blood" is twice used elsewhere (Mat. 16: 17 and Eph. 6: 12,) to denote "weak human nature," "feeble man."—G. A.]

Is it true, however, that he did not go up thither?[1] nay, he went up, and not merely so, but in order to learn somewhat of them. When a question arose on our present subject in the city of Antioch, in the Church which had from the beginning shown so much zeal, and it was discussed whether the Gentile believers ought to be circumcised, or were under no necessity to undergo the rite, this very Paul himself and Silas[2] went up. How is it then that he says, I went not up, nor conferred? First, because he went not up of his own accord, but was sent by others; next, because he came not to learn, but to bring others over. For he was from the first of that opinion, which the Apostles subsequently ratified, that circumcision was unnecessary. But when these persons deemed him unworthy of credit and applied to those at Jerusalem he went up not to be farther instructed, but to convince the gainsayers that those at Jerusalem agreed with him. Thus he perceived from the first the fitting line of conduct, and needed no teacher, but, primarily and before any discussion, maintained without wavering what the Apostles, after much discussion, (Acts xv: 2, 7.) subsequently ratified. This Luke shows by his own account, that Paul argued much at length with them on this subject before he went to Jerusalem. But since the brethren chose to be informed on this subject, by those at Jerusalem, he went up on their own account, not on his own. And his expression, " I went not up," signifies that he neither went at the outset of his teaching, nor for the purpose of being instructed. Both are implied by the phrase, " Immediately I conferred not with flesh and blood." He says not, " I conferred," merely, but, " immediately; " and his subsequent journey was not to gain any additional instruction.

Ver. 17. " But I went away into Arabia."

Behold a fervent soul! he longed to occupy regions not yet tilled, but lying in a wild state. Had he remained with the Apostles, as he had nothing to learn, his preaching would have been straitened, for it behooved them to spread the word every where. Thus this blessed man, fervent in spirit, straightway undertook to teach wild barbarians,[3] choosing a life full of battle and labor. Having said, " I went into Arabia," he adds, " and again I returned unto Damascus." Here observe his humility; he speaks

not of his successes, nor of whom or of how many he instructed. Yet such was his zeal immediately on his baptism, that he confounded the Jews, and so exasperated them, that they and the Greeks lay in wait for him with a view to kill him. This would not have been the case, had he not greatly added to the numbers of the faithful; since they were vanquished in doctrine, they had recourse to murder, which was a manifest sign of Paul's superiority. But Christ suffered him not to be put to death, preserving him for his mission. Of these successes, however, he says nothing, and so in all his discourses, his motive is not ambition, nor to be honored more highly than the Apostles, nor because he is mortified at being lightly esteemed, but it is a fear lest any detriment should accrue to his mission. For he calls himself, " one born out of due time," and, " the first of sinners," and " the last of the Apostles," and; " not meet to be called an Apostle." And this he said, who had labored more than all of them; which is real humility; for he who, conscious of no excellence, speaks humbly of himself, is candid but not humble; but to say so after such trophies, is to be practised in self-control.

Ver. 17. " And again I returned unto Damascus."

But what great things did he not probably achieve in this city? for he tells us that the governor under Aretas the king set guards about the whole of it, hoping to entrap this blessed man. Which is a proof of the strongest kind that he was violently persecuted by the Jews. Here, however, he says nothing of this, but mentioning his arrival and departure is silent concerning the events which there occurred, nor would he have mentioned them in the place I have referred to, (2 Cor. xi: 32.) had not circumstances required their narration.

Ver. 18. " Then after three years I went up to Jerusalem[4] to visit Cephas."

What can be more lowly than such a soul? After such successes, wanting nothing of Peter, not even his assent, but being of equal dignity with him, (for at present I will say no more,) he comes to him as his elder and superior. And the only object of this journey was to visit Peter; thus he pays due respect to the Apostles, and esteems himself not only not their better but not their equal. Which is plain from this journey, for Paul was induced to visit Peter by the same feeling from which many of our brethren sojourn with holy men: or rather by a humbler feeling for they do so for their own benefit, but this blessed man, not for his own instruction or correction, but merely for the sake of

---

[1] [Paul here simply means he did not go to Jerusalem before he began preaching.—G. A.]

[2] Of those who were sent with St. Paul from Antioch to Jerusalem, Barnabas is the only one named in Acts xv : 2, and it would rather seem from Ver. 22, that Silas was then at Jerusalem, and did not accompany St. Paul till his return from thence.

[3] [" This journey is to be looked upon not as having for its object a quiet preparation, but as a first experiment of extraneous ministry."—Meyer, Farrar, *Life and Work of Paul.* Ch. xi. takes the opposite view and says. " No one, I think, who reads this passage attentively can deny that it gives the impression of an intentional retirement from human intercourse." So also Schaff, who says it was a sort of substitute for the three years intercourse with Jesus enjoyed by the other Apostles. *Ap. Ch.* 236.—G. A.]

[4] [First visit to Jerusalem, Acts ix: 26. For a reconciliation of the two accounts of this visit see *Handy Com. on Gal.* Excursus A (by Sanday).—G.A.]

beholding and honoring Peter by his presence. He says, " to visit Peter ; " he does not say to see, ($\iota\delta\epsilon\tilde{\iota}\nu$,) but to visit and survey, ($\iota\sigma\tau\sigma\rho\tilde{\eta}\sigma\alpha\iota$,) a word which those, who seek to become acquainted with great and splendid cities, apply to themselves. Worthy of such trouble did he consider the very sight of Peter ; and this appears from the Acts of the Apostles also. (Acts xxi: 17,18 etc.) For on his arrival at Jerusalem, on another occasion, after having converted many Gentiles, and, with labors far surpassing the rest, reformed and brought to Christ Pamphylia, Lycaonia, Cilicia, and all nations in that quarter of the world, he first addresses himself with great humility to James, as to his elder and superior. Next he submits to his counsel, and that counsel contrary to this Epistle. " Thou seest, brother, how many thousands there are among the Jews of them which have believed ; therefore shave thy head, and purify thyself." (Acts xxi: 20 f.) Accordingly he shaved his head, and observed all the Jewish ceremonies ; for where the Gospel was not affected, he was the humblest of all men. But where by such humility he saw any injured, he gave up that undue exercise of it, for that was no longer to be humble but to outrage and destroy the disciples.

Ver. 18. " And tarried with him fifteen days."

To take a journey on account of him was a mark of respect ; but to remain so many days, of friendship and the most earnest affection.[1]

Ver. 19. " But other of the Apostles saw I none, save James,[2] the Lord's brother."

See what great friends he was with Peter especially ; on his account he left his home, and with him he tarried. This I frequently repeat, and desire you to remember, that no one, when he hears what this Apostle seems to have spoken against Peter, may conceive a suspicion of him. He premises this, that when he says, "I resisted Peter," no one may suppose that these words imply enmity and contention ; for he honored and loved his person more than all and took this journey for his sake only, not for any of the others. " But other of the Apostles saw I none, save James." " I saw him merely, I did not learn from him," he means. But observe how honorably he mentions him, he says not "James" merely, but adds this illustrious title, so free ishe from all envy. Had he only wished to point out whom he meant, he might have shown this by another

appellation, and called him the son of Cleophas, as the Evangelist does. [3] But as he considered that he had a share in the august titles of the Apostles, he exalts himself by honoring James ; and this he does by calling him " the Lord's brother," although he was not by birth His brother, but only so reputed. Yet this did not deter him from giving the title ; and in many other instances he displays towards all the Apostles that noble disposition, which beseemed him.

Ver. 20. " Now touching the things which I write unto you, behold, before God, I lie not."

Observe throughout the transparent humility of this holy soul ; his earnestness in his own vindication is as great as if he had to render an account of his deeds, and was pleading for his life in a court of justice.

Ver. 21. " Then I came into the regions of Syria and Cilicia."[4]

After his interview with Peter, he resumes his preaching and the task which lay before him, avoiding Judæa, both because of his mission being to the Gentiles, and of his unwillingness to "build upon another man's foundation." Wherefore there was not even a chance meeting, as appears from what follows.

Ver. 22, 23. " And I was still unknown by face unto the Churches of Judæa ; but they only heard say, he that once persecuted us now preacheth the faith of which he once made havoc."

What modesty in thus again mentioning the facts of his persecuting and laying waste the Church, and in thus making infamous his former life, while he passes over the illustrious deeds he was about to achieve ! He might have told, had he wished it, all his successes, but he mentions none of these and stepping with one word over a vast expanse, he says merely, " I came into the regions of Syria and Cilicia ; " and, " they had heard, that he, which once persecuted us, now preacheth the faith of which he once made havoc." The purpose of the words, " I was unknown to the Churches of Judæa," is to show, that so far from preaching to them the necessity of circumcision, he was not known to them even by sight.

Ver. 24. " And they glorified God in me."

See here again how accurately he observes the rule of his humility ; he says not, they admired me, they applauded or were astonished at me, but ascribes all to Divine grace by the words, " they glorified God in me."

---

[1] [And yet it was not long enough to have allowed his receiving his doctrine and Gospel from Peter. Besides he had already been preaching three years.—G. A.]

[2] " Thus this James is distinguished from the circle of the twelve (1 Cor. xv. 8.) to which Peter belonged but included in the number of Apostles in the wider sense, which explains the merely supplementary mention of this Apostle."—Meyer.

[3] [Compare John xix: 25 with Matt. xxvii: 56. But see Lightfoot's learned and exhaustive essay on " The Brethren of the Lord, Com. on Gal. pp. 88—127, and Schaff, Church History, I, 272–275.—G.A.]

[4] [Compare Acts ix : 30, where Luke says the brethren took Paul to Caesarea, and thence despatched him to Tarsus (in Cilicia.–G. A.]

CHAPTER II

" Then after the space of fourteen years,[1] I went up again to Jerusalem with Barnabas, taking Titus also with me. And I went up by revelation."

His first journey was owing to his desire to visit Peter, his second, he says, arose from a revelation of the Spirit.

Ver. 2. "And I laid before them the Gospel which I ·preach among the Gentiles, but privately before them who were of repute, lest by any means I should be running or had run, in vain."

What is this, O Paul! thou who neither at the beginning nor after three years wouldest confer with the Apostles, dost thou now confer with them, after fourteen years are past, lest thou shouldest be running in vain? Better would it have been to have done so at first, than after so many years; and why didst thou run at all, if not satisfied that thou wert not running in vain? Who would be so senseless as to preach for so many years, without being sure that his preaching was true? And what enhances the difficulty is, that he says he went up by revelation; this difficulty, however, will afford a solution of the former one. Had he gone up of his own accord, it would have been most unreasonable, nor is it possible that this blessed soul should have fallen into such folly; for it is himself who says, " I therefore so run, as not uncertainly ; so fight I, as not beating the air." (I Cor. ix: 26.) If therefore he runs, "not uncertainly," how can he say, "lest I should be running, or had run, in vain?" It is evident from this, that if he had gone up without a revelation, he would have committed an act of folly. But the actual case involved no such absurdity ; who shall dare

to still harbor this suspicion, when it was the grace of the Spirit which drew him? On this account he added the words " by revelation," lest, before the question was solved, he should be condemned of folly ; well knowing that it was no human occurrence, but a deep Divine Providence concerning the present and future. What then is the reason of this journey of his? As when he went up before from Antioch to Jerusalem, it was not for his own sake, (for he saw clearly that his duty was simply to obey the doctrines of Christ,) but from a desire to reconcile the contentious; so now his object was the complete satisfaction of his accusers, not any wish of his own to learn that he had not run in vain. They conceived that Peter and John, of whom they thought more highly than of Paul, differed from him in that he ommitted circumcision in hiᴤ preaching, while the former allowed it, and they believed that in this he acted unlawfully, and was running in vain. I went up, says he, and communicated unto them my Gospel, not that I might learn aught myself, (as appears more clearly further on,) but that I might convince these suspicious persons that I do not run in vain. The Spirit forseeing this contention had provided that he should go up and make this communication.

Wherefore he says that he went up by revelation,[2] and, taking Barnabas and Titus as witnesses of his preaching, communicated to them the Gospel which he preached to the Gentiles, that is, with the omission of circumcision. " But privately before them who were of repute." What means " privately?" Rather, he who wishes to reform doctrines held in common, proposes them, not privately, but before all in common ; but Paul did this privately, for his object was, not to learn or reform any thing, but to cut off the grounds of those who would fain deceive. All at Jerusalem were offended, if the law was transgressed, or the use of circumcision forbidden ; as James says, " Thou seest, brother, how many thousands there are among the Jews of them which have believed ; and they

---

[1] [" The Acts mention five such journeys after his conversion : (1.)-ix : 23 (Comp. Gal. i : 18.) (2.)-xi : 30 ; xii : 25. (3.)-xv : 2, the journey to the Apostolic Council, A. D. 50 or 51. (4.)-x viii :22, the journey in 54. (5.)- xxi : 15 (Comp. Ro. 15 : 25 ff.) the last journey when he was made a pardoner and sent to Caesarea in 58. The first of these journeys cannot be meant on account of Gal. i : 18. The second is excluded by the chronoligical date of Gal. ii : 1, for as it took place during the famine of Palestine in the year of Herod's death, A. D 44, it would put the commission of Paul back to the year 30, which is much too early. There is no good reason, why Paul should have mentioned this second journey. The fifth journey cannot be meant for it took place after the composition of Epistle to Galatians and after dispersion of Apostles. Nor can we think of the fourth journey which was transient, nor was Barnabas with him on that journey, Acts xv : 39. So the journey here mentioned is the same as that of Acts xv : 2. This took place 50 or 51, i. e., fourteen years after his conversion, 37.—Schaff in Pop. Com. —G. A.]

14

[2] [" In St. Luke's narrative (Acts xv : 2.) he is said to have been sent by the Church at Antioch. The revelation either prompted or confirmed the decision of the Church."—Lightfoot.—G. A.]

are informed of thee, that thou teachest to forsake the law." (Acts xxi: 20, et seq.) Since then they were offended he did not condescend to come forward publicly and declare what his preaching was, but he conferred privately with those who were of reputation before Barnabas and Titus, that they might credibly testify to his accusers, [1] that the Apostles found no discrepancy in his preaching, but confirmed it. The expression, "those that were of repute," (τοῖς δοκοῦσιν) does not impugn the reality of their greatness; for he says of himself, "And I also seem (δοκῶ) to have the Spirit of God," thereby not denying the fact, but stating it modestly. And here the phrase implies his own assent to the common opinion.

Ver. 3. "But not even Titus, who was with me, being a Greek, [2] was compelled to be circumcised."

What means, "being a Greek?" Of Greek extraction, and not circumcised; for not only did I so preach but Titus so acted, nor did the Apostles compel him to be circumcised. A plain proof this that the Apostles did not condemn Paul's doctrine or his practice. Nay more, even the urgent representations of the adverse party, who were aware of these facts, did not oblige the Apostles to enjoin circumcision, as appears by his own words,—

Ver. 4. "And that because of the false brethren, privily brought in."

Here arises a very important question, Who were these false brethren? [3] If the Apostles permitted circumcision at Jerusalem, why are those who enjoined it, in acccordance with the Apostolic sentence, to be called false brethren? First; because there is a difference between commanding an act to be done, and allowing it after it is done. He who enjoins an act, does it with zeal as necessary, and of primary importance; but he who, without himself commanding it, alloweth another to do it who wisnes yields not from a sense of its being necessary but in order to subserve some purpose. We have a similar instance, in Paul's Epistle to the Corinthians, in his command to husbands and wives to come together again. To which, that he might not be thought to be legislating for them, he subjoins, "But this I say by way of permission, not of commandment." (1 Cor. vii: 5.) For this was not a judgment

authoritatively given butan indulgence to their incontinence; as he says, "for your incontinency." Would you know Paul's sentence in this matter? hear his words, "I would that all men were even as I myself,"(1 Cor. vii: 7.) in continence. And so here, the Apostles made this concession, not as vindicating the law, but as condescending to the infirmities of Judaism. Had they been vindicating the law, they would not have preached to the Jews in one way, and to the Gentiles in another. Had the observance been necessary for unbelievers, then indeed it would plainly have likewise been necessary for all the faithful. But by their decision not to harass the Gentiles on this point, they showed that they permitted it by way of condescension to the Jews. Whereas the purpose of the false brethren was to cast them out of grace, and reduce them under the yoke of slavery again. This is the first difference, and a very wide one. The second is, that the Apostles so acted in Judæa, where the Law was in force, but the false brethren, every where, for all the Galatians were influenced by them. Whence it appears that their intention was, not to build up, but entirely to pull down the Gospel, and that the thing was permitted by the Apostles on one ground and zealously practiced by the false brethren on another.

Ver. 4. "Who came in privily to spy out our liberty, which we have in Christ Jesus, that they might bring us into bondage."

He points out their hostility by calling them spies; for the sole object of a spy is to obtain for himself facilities of devastation and destruction, by becoming acquainted with his adversary's position. And this is what those did, who wished to bring the disciples back to their old servitude. Hence too appears how very contrary their purpose was to that of the Apostles; the latter made concessions that they might gradually extricate them from their servitude, but the former plotted to subject them to one more severe. Therefore they looked round and observed accurately and made themselves busybodies to find out who were uncircumcised; as Paul says, "they came in privily to spy out our liberty," thus pointing out their machinations not only by the term "spies," but by this expression of a furtive entrance and creeping in.

Ver. 5. "To whom we gave place in the way of subjection, no, not for an hour."[4]

Observe the force and emphasis of the phrase; he says not, "by argument," but, "by subjection,"for their object was not to teach good doctrine, but to subjugate and enslave them.

---

[1] [That is, that Barnabas and Titus as witnesses of the proceedings might testify to the Judaizing teachers everywhere, &c.–G.A.]

[2] [Being "a Greek:" Lightfoot says this is a "causal" participial clause giving the "reason" why Titus was not circumcised; *because* he was a Greek and not a Jew or part Jew as Timothy was. Schaff makes it a "concessive" clause; *although* he was a Greek, that is, a heathen. Farrar in *Life and Work of Paul*(233-6)claims that Titus *was* circumcised but not compelled to be. This however cannot be held in view of the context and the position of the words in the sentence.—G. A.]

[3] [These were formerly Pharisees (Acts xv: 5.) and were still so in spirit although they professed Christianity and were baptized." Schaff in *Pop. Com.*—G. A.]

[4] ["Had we consented to the suggestion to circumcise Titus, we should thereby have yielded to the false brethren standing in the background, who declared the circumcision of Gentile Christians to be necessary (Acts xv: 5.) ; but this did not at all take place."—Meyer.—G. A.]

Wherefore, says he, we yielded to the Apostles, but not to these.

Ver. 5. "That the truth of the Gospel might continue with you." [1]

That we may confirm, says he, by our deeds what we have already declared by words,—namely, that the "old things are passed away, behold they are become new;" and that "if any man is in Christ he is a new creature;" (2 Cor. v: 17.) and that "if ye receive circumcision, Christ will profit you nothing." (Gal. v: 2.) In maintaining this truth we gave place not even for an hour. Then, as he was directly met by the conduct of the Apostles, and the reason of their enjoining the rite would probably be asked, he proceeds to solve this objection. This he does with great skill, for he does not give the actual reason, which was, that the Apostles acted by way of condescension and in the use of a scheme, ($\delta\iota\varkappa o\nu o\mu\iota\alpha$) as it were; for otherwise his hearers would have been injured. For those, who are to derive benefit from a scheme should be unacquainted with the design of it; all will be undone, if this appears. Wherefore, he who is to take part in it should know the drift of it; those who are to benefit by it should not. To make my meaning more evident, I will take an example from our present subject. The blessed Paul himself, who meant to abrogate circumcision, when he was about to send Timothy to teach the Jews, first circumcised him and so sent him. This he did, that his hearers might the more readily receive him; he began by circumcising, that in the end he might abolish it. But this reason he imparted to Timothy only, and told it not to the disciples. Had they known that the very purpose of his circumcision was the abolition of the rite, they would never have listened to his preaching, and the whole benefit would have been lost. But now their ignorance was of the greatest use to them, for their idea that his conduct proceeded from a regard to the Law, led them to receive both him and his doctrine with kindness and courtesy, and having gradually received him, and become instructed, they abandoned their old customs. Now this would not have happened had they known his reasons from the first; for they would have turned away from him, and being turned away would not have given him a hearing, and not hearing, would have continued in their former error. To prevent this, he did not disclose his reasons; here too he does not explain the occasion of the scheme, ($o\iota\varkappa o\nu o\mu\iota\alpha$) but shapes his discourse differently; thus:

Ver. 6. "But from those who were reputed to be somewhat,[2] (whatsoever they were, it maketh no matter to me, God accepteth no man's person.)"

Here he not only does not defend the Apostles, but even presses hard upon those holy men, for the benefit of the weak. His meaning is this: although they permit circumcision, they shall render an account to God, for God will not accept their persons, because they are great and in station. But he does not speak so plainly, but with caution. He says not, if they vitiate their doctrine, and swerve from the appointed rule of their preaching, they shall be judged with the utmost rigor, and suffer punishment; but he alludes to them more reverently, in the words, "of those who were reputed to be somewhat, whatsoever they were." He says not, "whatsoever they 'are,'" but "were," showing that they too had thenceforth[3] ceased so to preach, the doctrine having extended itself universally. The phrase, "whatsoever they were," implies, that if they so preached they should render account, for they had to justify themselves before God, not before men. This he said, not as doubtful or ignorant of the rectitude of their procedure, but (as I said before) from a sense of the expediency of so forming his discourse. Then, that he may not seem to take the opposite side and to accuse them, and so create a suspicion of their disagreement, he straightway subjoins this correction: "for those who were reputed to be somewhat, in conference imparted nothing to me." This is his meaning; What you may say, I know not; this I know well, that the Apostles did not oppose me, but our sentiments conspired and accorded. This appears from his expression, "they gave me the right hand of fellowship;" but he does not say this at present, but only that they neither informed or corrected him on any point, nor added to his knowledge.

Ver. 6. "For those who were reputed to be somewhat, imparted nothing to me:"

That is to say, when told of my proceedings, they added nothing, they corrected nothing, and though aware that the object of my journey was to communicate with them, that I had come by revelation of the Spirit, and that I had Titus with me who was uncircumcised, they neither circumcised him, nor imparted to me any additional knowledge.

Ver. 7. "But contrariwise."

---

[1] ["In order that by our conduct the principle of Christian freedom should not be shaken and ye should not be induced to deviate from the truth of the Gospel by mixing it up with Mosaism."—Meyer.—G. A.]

[2] [Lightfoot says, "The expression is depreciatory here, not indeed of the twelve themselves but of the extravagant and exclusive claims set up for them by the Judaizers." So also Dr. Schaff. "The addition of $\tau\iota$ $\epsilon\iota\nu\alpha\iota$ and $\delta\pi o\iota o\iota$ betrays a certain irritation in reference to the opponents who would not concede Paul an estimation given to the original Apostles."—Meyer.—G. A.]

[3] ["It is entirely in opposition to the context that Chrysostom Theophylact and Jerome refer this to the earlier teaching of the Apostles, making Paul say that whether at an earlier date they had been Judaizers or not was to him a matter of indifference."—Meyer.—G. A.]

Some hold his meaning to be, not only that the Apostles did not instruct him, but that they were instructed by him. But I would not say this, for what could they, each of whom was himself perfectly instructed, have learnt from him? He does not therefore intend this by the expression, "contrariwise," but that so far were they from blaming, that they praised him: for praise is the contrary of blame. Some would probably here reply: Why did not the Apostles, if they praised your procedure, as the proper consequence abolish circumcision?[1] Now to assert that they did abolish it Paul considered much too bold, and inconsistent with his own admission. On the other hand, to admit that they had sanctioned circumcision, would necessarily expose him to another objection. For it would be said, if the Apostles praised your preaching, yet sanctioned circumcision, they were inconsistent with themselves. What then is the solution? is he to say that they acted thus out of condescension to Judaism? To say this would have shaken the very foundation of the economy. Whereforehe leaves the subject in suspense and uncertainty, by the words, "but of those who were reputed to be somewhat; it maketh no matter to me." Which is in effect to say, I accuse not, nor traduce those holy men; they know what it is they have done; to God must they render their account. What I am desirous to prove is, that they neither reversed nor corrected my procedure, nor added to it as in their opinion defective, but gave it their approbation and assent; and to this Titus and Barnabas bear witness. Then he adds,

Ver. 7. "When they saw that I had been entrusted with the Gospel of the Uncircumcision even as Peter with the Gospel of the Circumcision[2],"—

The Circumcision and Uncircumcision; meaning, not the things themselves, but the nations known by these distinctions; wherefore he adds,

Ver. 8. "For He that wrought for Peter unto the Apostleship of the Circumcision wrought for me also unto the Gentiles."

He calls the Gentiles the Uncircumcision and the Jews the Circumcision, and declares his own rank to be equal to that of the Apostles; and, by comparing himself with their Leader not with the others, he shows that the dignity of each was the same. After he had established the proof of their unanimity, he takes courage, and proceeds confidently in his argument, not stopping at the Apostles, but advances to Christ Himself, and to the grace which He had conferred upon him, and calls-the Apostles as his witnesses, saying,

Ver. 9. "And when they perceived the grace that was given unto me, James and Cephas and John, they who were reputed to be pillars, gave to me and Barnabas the right hands of fellowship."[3]

He says not when they "heard," but when they "perceived," that is, were assured by the facts themselves, "they gave to me and Barnabas the right hands of fellowship." Observe how he gradually proves that his doctrine was ratified both by Christ and by the Apostles. For grace would neither have been implanted, nor been operative in him, had not his preaching been approved by Christ. Where it was for the purpose of comparison with himself, he mentioned Peter alone; here, when be calls them as witnesses, he names the three together, "Cephas, James, John," and with an encomium, "who were reputed to be pillars." Here again the expression "who were reputed" does not impugn the reality of the fact, but adopts the estimate of others, and implies that these great and distinguished men, whose fame was universal, bare witness that his preaching was ratified by Christ, that they were practically informed and convinced by experience concerning it. "Therefore they gave the right hands of fellowship" to me, and not to me only, but also to Barnabas, "that we should go unto the Gentiles, and they unto the Circumcision." Here indeed is exceeding prudence as well as an incontrovertible proof of their concord. For it shows that his and their doctrine was interchangeable, and that both approved the same thing, that they should so preach to the Jews, and he to the Gentiles. Wherefore he adds,

Ver. 9. "That we should go unto the Gentiles and they unto the Circumcision."[4]

Observe that here also he means by "the Circumcision," not the rite, but the Jews; whenever he speaks of the rite, and wishes to contrast it, he adds the word "uncircumcision;" as when he says, "For circumcision indeed profiteth, if thou be a doer of the law; but if thou be a transgressor of the law, thy circumcision is become uncircumcision." (Ro. ii: 25.) And again, "Neither circumcision availeth any

---

[1] [They did virtually abolish circumcision by the decree of the council at Jerusalem as is shown in the account in (Acts xv.) And the failure of the effort to have Titus circumcised shows that the account in Gal. ii has nothing inconsistent with that decree. This as to Gentiles. The question did not concern Jews, who were already circumcised in infancy except in cases like that of Timothy where circumcision had been neglected. His case Paul himself decided without any consultation with others.—G. A.]

[2] ["This passage cannot be worse misunderstood than it has been by Baur according to whom there was a special Gospel of the uncircumcision and a special gospel of the circumcision, one maintaining the necessity of circumcision, the other allowing it to drop."—Meyer.—G. A.]

[3] ["If there had been a real conflict in doctrine, the Apostles would not have given Paul their hand, and Paul would have refused them his."—G.A.]

[4] [" There was no difference of doctrine or gospel, but only a division of territory, and how little Paul considered his apostolic call to the 'Gentiles' as excluding the conversion of the Jews from his operations may be seen from such passages as 1 Cor. ix: 20; Ro. i: 16; ix: 1; xi: 14."—Meyer.—G. A.]

thing, nor uncircumcision." But when it is to the Jews and not to the deed that he gives this name, and wishes to signify the nation, he opposes to it not uncircumcision in its literal sense, but the Gentiles. For the Jews are the contradistinction to the Gentiles, the Circumcision to the Uncircumcision. Thus when he says above, "For He that wrought for Peter into the Apostleship of the Circumcision, wrought for me also unto the Gentiles;" and again, "We unto the Gentiles and they unto the Circumcision," he means not the rite itself, but the Jewish nation, thus distinguishing them from the Gentiles.

Ver. 10. "Only they would that we should remember the poor; which very thing I was also zealous to do."

This is his meaning: In our preaching we divided the world between us, I took the Gentiles and they the Jews, according to the Divine decree; but to the sustenance of the poor among the Jews I also contributed my share, which, had there been any dissension between us, they would not have accepted. Next, who were these poor persons? Many of the believing Jews in Palestine had been deprived of all their goods, and scattered over the world, as he mentions in the Epistle to the Hebrews[1]," "For ye took joyfully the spoiling of your possessions;" and in writing to the Thessalonians, (1 Thes. ii: 14.) he extols their fortitude, "Ye became imitators of the Churches of God which are in Judæa, . . . for ye also suffered the same thing of your own countrymen, even as they did of the Jews." And he shows throughout that those Greeks who believed were not under persecution from the rest, such as the believing Jews were suffering from their own kindred, for there is no nation of a temper so cruel. Wherefore he exercises much zeal, as appears in the Epistles to the Romans (Ro. xv: 25—27.) and Corinthians (1 Cor. xvi: 1—3.) that these persons should meet with much attention; and Paul not only collects money for them, but himself conveys it, as he says, "But now I go unto Jerusalem ministering unto the saints," (Ro. xv: 25.) for they were without the necessaries of life. And he here shows that in this instance having resolved to assist them, he had undertaken and would not abandon it.

Having by these means declared the unanimity and harmony between the Apostles and himself, he is obliged to proceed to mention his debate with Peter at Antioch.

Ver. 11, 12. "But when Cephas came to Antioch, I resisted him to the face, because he stood condemned. For before that certain came

from James, he did eat with the Gentiles: but when they came, he drew back and separated himself, fearing them that were of the circumcision."

Many, on a superficial reading of this part of the Epistle, suppose that Paul accused Peter of hypocrisy. But this is not so, indeed it is not, far from it;[2] we shall discover great wisdom, both of Paul and Peter, concealed herein for the benefit of their hearers. But first a word must be said about Peter's freedom in speech, and how it was ever his way to outstrip the other disciples. Indeed it was upon one such occasion that he gained his name from the unbending and impregnable character of his faith. For when all were interrogated in common, he stepped before the others and answered, "Thou art the Christ, the Son of the living God." (Mat. xvi: 16.) This was when the keys of heaven were committed to him. So too, he appears to have been the only speaker on the Mount; (Mat. xvii: 4.) and when Christ spoke of His crucifixion, and the others kept silence, he said, "Be it far from Thee." (Mat. xvi: 22.) These words evince, if not a cautious temper, at least a fervent love; and in all instances we find him more vehement than the others, and rushing forward into danger. So when Christ was seen on the beach, and the others were pushing the boat in, he was too impatient to wait for its coming to land. (John xxi: 7.) And after the Resurrection, when the Jews were murderous and maddened, and sought to tear the Apostles in pieces, he first dared to come forward, and to declare, that the Crucified was taken up into heaven. (Acts ii: 14, 36.) It is a greater thing to open a closed door, and to commence an action, than to be free-spoken afterwards. How could he ever dissemble who had exposed his life to such a populace? He who when scourged and bound would not bate a jot of his courage, and this at the beginning of his mission, and in the heart of the chief city where there was so much danger,—how could he, long afterwards in Antioch, where no danger was at hand, and his character had received lustre from the testimony of his actions, feel any apprehension of the believing Jews? How could he, I say, who at the very first and in their chief city feared not the Jews while Jews, after a long time and in a foreign city, fear those of them who had been converted? Paul therefore does not speak this against Peter, but with the same meaning in which he said, "for they who were reputed to be somewhat, whatsoever they were, it maketh no matter to me." But to remove any doubt on this point, we must unfold the reason of these expressions.

The Apostles, as I said before, permitted cir-

---

[1] [Hebrews x: 34 [This is interesting as showing that Chrysostom attributed the Epistle to the Hebrews to St. Paul, though most modern critics do not agree with him in that view.—G. A.]

[2] [ἀλλ' οὐκ ἔστι ταῦτα, οὐκ ἔστιν ἄπαγε.—G. A.]

cumcision at Jerusalem, an abrupt severance from the law not being practicable; but when they come to Antioch, they no longer continued this observance, but lived indiscriminately with the believing Gentiles which thing Peter also was at that time doing. But when some came from Jerusalem who had heard the doctrine he delivered there, he no longer did so fearing to perplex them, but he changed his course, with two objects secretly in view, both to avoid offending those Jews, and to give Paul a reasonable pretext for rebuking him.[1] For had he, having allowed circumcision when preaching at Jerusalem, changed his course at Antioch, his conduct would have appeared to those Jews to proceed from fear of Paul, and his disciples would have condemned his excess of pliancy. And this would have created no small offence; but in Paul, who was well acquainted with all the facts, his withdrawal would have raised no such suspicion, as knowing the intention with which he acted. Wherefore Paul rebukes, and Peter submits, that when the master is blamed, yet keeps silence, the disciples may more readily come over. Without this occurrence Paul's exhortation would have had little effect, but the occasion hereby afforded of delivering a severe reproof, impressed Peter's disciples with a more lively fear. Had Peter disputed Paul's sentence, he might justly have been blamed as upsetting the plan, but now that the one reproves and the other keeps silence, the Jewish party are filled with serious alarm; and this is why he used Peter so severely. Observe too Paul's careful choice of expressions, whereby he points out to

---

[1] S. Jerome adopts the interpretation given in the text, viz. that S. Peter's dissimulation was no sin, but intended as an opportunity for S. Paul to declare the freedom of the Gentiles from the Jewish Law. On the other hand, S. Austin considers that he acted through wrong motives, and sinned in dissembling. In this opinion he is supported by Tertullian, S. Cyprian S. Cyril, of Alexandria, S. Gregory and Ambrosiaster. (Hieron. *in loc, et alibi.* August. *de Bapt. contr. Donatist.* ii. 2. *de Mendacio* 8. Tertull. *de Præscript.* 23. *in Marc.* iv. 3. v. 3. Cyprian, *Ep. ad Quint.* 71. Cyril. Alex. *in Julian.* ix. fin. Gregor. *in Ezech.* ii. *Hom.* 6, 9. Ambrosiast. *in loc.*) S. Austin is influenced in his judgment of the transaction by an anxiety lest disingenuousness and duplicity should receive countenance from the apparent example of an Apostle; S. Chrysostom and S. Jerome by affectionate reverence for the memory of so great a benefactor and so exalted a saint. Vid. Justinian, *in loco.*
[In earlier life Chrysostom had himself practised such a "scheme," as that which he here attributes to Paul. In order to induce his friend Basil to be consecrated as a bishop he made on him the (false) impression that he himself had already been consecrated.] Neander (*Life of Chrysostom* p. 22.) says: "In the first book of his work on the Priesthood Chrysostom defends the principle that a falsehood is permitted for a good object. An invention which has for its sole object the advantage of another is rather an οἰκονομία (the word he uses in expounding our passage.) This lax view respecting truth was not peculiar to Chrysostom but was consonant with the prevailing spirit of the Eastern Church. There were a few exceptions however to this view, among whom were John of Lycopolis in Egypt, and Basil of Caesarea who says τοῦ κυρίον διαφορὰν ψεύδους οὐδεμαίν ἐκφήναντος. Schaff says (*Prolegomena* p. 8): "Origen, Jerome and Chrysostom explain the offense of this collision away by turning it into a theatrical and hypocritical farce, shrewdly arranged by the Apostle for a purpose. In this respect the modern standard of ethics is far superior to that of the Fathers and more fully accords with the spirit of the New Testament." [We may add that Chrysostom's view gains nothing; for to save one Apostle from the charge of unpremeditated hypocrisy, he makes both guilty of premeditated hypocrisy.—G. A.]

---

the discerning, that he uses them in pursuance of the plan, (ὀικονομίας) and not from anger.

His words are, "When Cephas came to Antioch, I resisted him to the face, because he stood condemned;" that is, not by me but by others; had he himself condemned him, he would not have shrunk from saying so. And the words, "I resisted him to the face," imply a scheme for had their discussion been real, they would not have rebuked each other in the presence of the disciples, for it would have been a great stumblingblock to them. But now this apparent contest was much to their advantage; as Paul had yielded to the Apostles at Jerusalem, so in turn they yield to him at Antioch. The cause of censure is this, "For before that certain came from James," who was the teacher at Jerusalem, "he did eat with the Gentiles, but when they came he drew back and separated himself, fearing them that were of the Circumcision:" his cause of fear was not his own danger, (for if he feared not in the beginning, much less would he do so then,) but their defection. As Paul himself says to the Galatians, "I am afraid of you, lest by any means I have bestowed labor upon you in vain:" (Gal. iv: 11.) and again, "I fear lest by any means as the serpent beguiled Eve, . . . so your minds should be corrupted." (2 Cor. xi: 3.) Thus the fear of death they knew not, but the fear lest their disciples should perish, agitated their inmost soul.

Ver. 13. "Insomuch that even Barnabas was carried away with their dissimulation."

Be not surprised at his giving this proceeding the name of dissimulation, for he is unwilling, as I said before, to disclose the true state of the case, in order to the correction of his disciples. On account of their vehement attachment to the Law, he calls the present proceeding "dissimulation," and severely rebukes it, in order effectually to eradicate their prejudice. And Peter too, hearing this joins in the feint, as if he had erred, that they might be corrected by means of the rebuke administered to him. Had Paul reproved these Jews, they would have spurned at it with indignation, for they held him in slight esteem; but now, when they saw their Teacher silent under rebuke, they were unable to despise or resist Paul's sentence.

Ver. 14. "But when I saw that they walked not uprightly according to the truth of the Gospel."

Neither let this phrase disturb you, for in using it he does not condemn Peter, but so expresses himself for the benefit of those who were to be reformed by the reproof of Peter.

Ver. 14. "I said unto Cephas before them all."

Observe his mode of correcting the others;

he speaks " before them all," that the hearers might be alarmed thereby. And this is what he says,—

Ver. 14. " If thou, being a Jew, livest as do the Gentiles, and not as do the Jews, how compellest thou the Gentiles to live as do the Jews ? "[1]

But it was the Jews and not the Gentiles who were carried away together with Peter; why then does Paul impute what was not done, instead of directing his remarks, not against the Gentiles, but against the dissembling Jews? And why does he accuse Peter alone, when the rest also dissembled together with him? Let us consider the terms of his charge; " If thou, being a Jew, livest as do the Gentiles, and not as do the Jews, how compellest thou the Gentiles to live as do the Jews ? " for in fact Peter alone had withdrawn himself. His object then is to remove suspicion from his rebuke; had he blamed Peter for observing the Law, the Jews would have censured him for his boldness towards their Teacher. But now arraigning him in behalf of his own peculiar disciples, I mean the Gentiles, he facilitates thereby the reception of what he has to say; which he also does by abstaining from reproof of the others, and addressing it all to the Apostle. " If thou," he says, " being a Jew, livest as do the Gentiles, and not as do the Jews ;" which almost amounts to an explicit exhortation to imitate their Teacher, who, himself a Jew, lived after the manner of the Gentiles. This however he says not, for they could not have received such advice, but under color of reproving him in behalf of the Gentiles, he discloses Peter's real sentiments. On the other hand, if he had said, Wherefore do you compel these Jews to Judaize ? his language would have been too severe. But now he effects their correction by appearing to espouse the part, not of the Jewish, but of the Gentile, disciples; for rebukes, which are moderately severe, secure the readiest reception. And none of the Gentiles could object to Paul that he took up the defense of the Jews. The whole difficulty was removed by Peter's submitting in silence to the imputation of dissimulation, in order that he might deliver the Jews from its reality. At first Paul directs his argument to the character which Peter wore, " If thou, being a Jew : " but he generalizes as he goes on, and includes himself in the phrase,[1]

Ver. 15. " We being Jews by nature, and not sinners of the Gentiles."[2]

These words are hortatory, but are couched in the form of a reproof, on account of those Jews. So elsewhere, under cover of one meaning he conveys another ; as where he says in his Epistle to the Romans, " But now I go unto Jerusalem, ministering unto the saints." (Rom. xv : 25.) Here his object was not simply to inform them of the motive of his journey to Jerusalem, but to excite them to emulation in the giving of alms. Had he merely wished to explain his motive, it would have sufficed to say, "I go to ministering unto the saints ; " but now observe what he says in addition ; " For it hath been the good pleasure of Macedonia and Achaia to make a certain contribution for the poor among the saints that are at Jerusalem. Yea, it hath been their good pleasure and their debtors they are." And again, " For if the Gentiles have been made partakers of their spiritual things, they owe it to them, also to minister unto them in carnal things." (Rom. xv : 26, 27.)

Observe how he represses the high thoughts of the Jews ; preparing for one thing by means of another, and his language is authoritative. " We being Jews by nature, and not sinners of the Gentiles." The phrase, " Jews by nature," implies that we, who are not proselytes, but educated from early youth in the Law, have relinquished our habitual mode of life, and betaken ourselves to the faith which is in Christ.

Ver. 16. " Knowing that a man is not justified by the works of the Law, save through faith, in Jesus Christ, even we believed on Christ Jesus."

Observe here too how cautiously he expresses himself; he does not say that they had abandoned the Law as evil, but as weak. If the law cannot confer righteousness, it follows that circumcision is superfluous ; and so far he now proves; but he proceeds to show that it is not only superfluous but dangerous. It deserves especial notice, how at the outset he says that a man is not justified by the works of the Law ; but as he proceeds he speaks more strongly;

Ver. 17. " But if, while we sought to be justified in Christ, we ourselves also were found sinners is Christ a minister of sin ? "

If faith in Him, says he, avail not for our justification, but it be necessary again to embrace the Law, and if, having forsaken the Law for Christ's sake, we are not justified but condemned for such abandonment,—then shall we find Him, for whose sake we forsook the Law and went over to faith the author of our condemnation.[3] Observe how, he has

---

[1]. [For the bearing of this passage upon the Tübingen theory of Baur, "the most important of recent theological controvrrsies" see Lightfoot's *Commentary on Galatians, Excursus on St. Paul and the Three,* pp. 191 ff., and Fisher's *Supernatural Origin of Christianity,* pp. 205-ff.—G. A.]

[2] [Schaff says : "The following verses to the end of the chapter are a summary report or dramatic sketch of Paul's address to Peter." So also Meyer who gives four good reasons for this view. So also Schmoller (in Lange) and Ellicott. Others think that vv. 15-21 are addressed to the Galatians.—G. A.]

[3] ["Thus to be justified in Christ, it was necessary to sink to the level of Gentiles, to become 'sinners' in fact. But are we not thus making Christ a minster of sin ? Away with the profane thought ! No, the guilt is not in abandoning the Law, but in seeking it again when abandoned. Thus alone we convict ourselves of transgression. On the other hand in abandoning the Law we did but follow the promptings of the Law." Lightfoot.—G. A.]

resolved the matter to a necessary absurdity. And mark how earnestly and strongly he argues. For if, he says, it behooved us not to abandon the Law, and we have so abandoned it for Christ's sake, we shall be judged. Wherefore do you urge this upon Peter, who is more intimately acquainted with it than any one? Hath not God declared to him, that an uncircumcised man ought not to be judged by circumcision; and did he not in his discussion with the Jews rest his bold opposition upon the vision which he saw? Did he not send from Jerusalem unequivocal decrees upon this subject? Paul's object is not therefore to correct Peter, but his animadversion required to be addressed to him, though it was pointed at the disciples; and not only at the Galatians, but also at others who labor under the same error with them. For though few are now circumcised, yet, by fasting and observing the sabbath with the Jews, they equally exclude themselves from grace. If Christ avails not to those who are only circumcised, much more is peril to be feared where fasting and sabbatizing are observed, and thus two commandments of the Law are kept in the place of one. And this is aggravated by a consideration of time: for they so acted at first while the city and temple and other institutions yet existed; but these who with the punishment of the Jews, and the destruction of the city before their eyes,[1] observe more precepts of the Law than the others did, what apology can they find for such observance, at the very time when the Jews themselves, in spite of their strong desire, cannot keep it? Thou hast put on Christ, thou hast become a member of the Lord, and been enrolled in the heavenly city, and dost thou still grovel in the Law? How is it possible for thee to obtain the kingdom? Listen to Paul's words, that the observance of the Law overthrows the Gospel, and learn, if thou wilt, how this comes to pass, and tremble, and shun this pitfall. Wherefore dost thou keep the sabbath, and fast with the Jews? Is it that thou fearest the Law and abandonment of its letter? But thou wouldest not entertain this fear, didst thou not disparage faith as weak, and by itself powerless to save. A fear to omit the sabbath plainly shows that you fear the Law as still in force; and if the Law is needful, it is so as a whole, not in part, nor in one commandment only; and if as a whole, the righteousness which is by faith is little by little shut out. If thou keep the sabbath, why not also be circumcised? and if circumcised, why not also offer sacrifices? If the Law is to be observed, it must be observed as a whole, or not at all. If omitting one part

makes you fear condemnation, this fear attaches equally to all the parts. If a transgression of the whole is not punishable, much less is the transgression of a part; on the other hand, if the latter be punishable, much more is the former. But if we are bound to keep the whole, we are bound to disobey Christ, or by obedience to Him become transgressors of the Law. If it ought to be kept, those who keep it not are transgressors, and Christ will be found to be the cause of this transgression, for He annulled the Law as regards these things Himself, and bid others annul it. Do you not understand what these Judaizers are compassing? They would make Christ, who is to us the Author of righteousness, the Author of sin, as Paul says, "Therefore Christ is the minister of sin." Having thus reduced the proposition to an absurdity, he had nothing further to do by way of overthrowing it, but was satisfied with the simple protestation,

Ver. 17. "God forbid:" for shamelessness and irreverence need not be met by processes of reasoning, but a mere protest is enough.

Ver. 18. "For if I build up again those things which I destroyed, I prove myself a transgressor."[2]

Observe the Apostle's discernment; his opponents endeavored to show, that he who kept not the Law was a transgressor, but he retorts the argument upon them, and shows that he who did keep the Law was a transgressor, not merely of faith, but of the Law itself. "I build up again the things which I destroyed," that is, the Law; he means as follows: the Law has confessedly ceased, and we have abandoned it, and betaken ourselves to the salvation which comes of faith. But if we make a point of setting it up again, we become by that very act transgressors, striving to keep what what God has annulled. Next he shows how it has been annulled.

Ver. 19. "For I[3] through the Law died unto the Law."

This may be viewed in two ways; it is either the law of grace which he speaks of, for he is wont to call this a law, as in the words, "For the law of the Spirit of life made me free:" (Rom. viii: 2.) or it is the old Law, of which he says, that by the Law itself he has become dead to the Law. That is to say, the Law itself has taught me no longer to obey itself, and therefore if I do so, I shall be transgressing even its teaching.[4]

---

[1] [The Epistle to the Galatians was written in the year A. D. 56 or 57 and the destruction of Jerusalem occurred in A. D. 70.-G. A.]

[2] ["I myself (Paul now politely chooses the first person but means Peter) stand convicted of transgression if I build again (as thou dost now at Antioch) the very law of Moses which I pulled down (as thou didst at Cæsarea by divine command and at first at Antioch) and thus condemn my own former conduct."—Schaff in *Pop. Com.*—G. A.]

[3] ['ἐγὼ γὰρ—In my case the process has been this, using his own experience.—G. A.]

[4] ["This second interpretation of Chrysostom is undoubtedly the correct one (though he errs in elucidating the relation of διὰ by referring to Deut. xviii: 15.) comp. Rom. vii: 4, 6; The law itself led him to Christ, by developing the sense of sin and the need of redemption."—Schaff in *Pop. Com.*—G. A.]

How, in what way has it so taught? Moses says, speaking of Christ, "The Lord God will raise up unto thee a Prophet from the midst of thee of thy brethren, like unto me; unto Him shall ye hearken." (Deut. xviii: 15.) Therefore they who do not obey Him, transgress the Law. Again, the expression, "I through the Law died unto the Law," may be understood in another sense: the Law commands all its precepts to be performed, and punishes the transgressor; therefore we are all dead to it, for no man has fulfilled it. Here observe, how guardedly he assails it; he says not, "the Law is dead to me;" but, "I am dead to the Law;" the meaning of which is, that, as it is impossible for a dead corpse to obey the commands of the Law, so also is it for me who have perished by its curse, for by its word am I slain. Let it not therefore lay commands on the dead, dead by its own act, dead not in body only, but in soul, which has involved the death of the body. This he shows in what follows:

Ver. 19, 20. "That I might live unto God,[1] I have been crucified with Christ."

Having said, "I am dead," lest it should be objected, how then dost thou live? he adds the cause of his living, and shows that when alive the Law slew him, but that when dead Christ through death restored him to life. He shows the wonder to be twofold; that by Christ both the dead was begotten into life, and that by means of death. He here means the immortal life, for this is the meaning of the words, "That I might live unto God I am crucified with Christ."[1] How, it is asked, can a man now living and breathing have been crucified? That Christ hath been crucified is manifest, but how canst thou have been crucified, and yet live? He explains it thus;

Ver. 20. "Yet[2] I live; and yet no longer I, but Christ liveth in me."

In these words, "I am crucified with Christ," he alludes to Baptism,[3] and in the words "nevertheless I live, yet not I," our subsequent manner of life whereby our members are mortified. By saying "Christ liveth in me," he means nothing is done by me, which Christ disapproves; for as by death he signifies not what is commonly understood, but a death to sin; so by life, he signifies a delivery from sin. For a man cannot live to God, otherwise than by dying to

sin; and as Christ suffered bodily death, so does Paul a death to sin. "Mortify," says he "your members which are upon the earth; fornication, uncleanness, passion;" (Col. iii: 5.) and again, "our old man was crucified,"(Rom. vi: 6.) which took place in the Bath.[3] After which, if thou remainest dead to sin, thou livest to God, but if thou let it live again, thou art the ruin of thy new life. This however did not Paul, but continued wholly dead; if then, he says, I live to God a life other than that in the Law, and am dead to the Law, I cannot possibly keep any part of the Law. Consider how perfect was his walk, and thou wilt be transported with admiration of this blessed soul. He says not, "I live," but, "Christ liveth in me;" who is bold enough to utter such words? Paul indeed, who had harnessed himself to Christ's yoke, and cast away all worldly things, and was paying universal obedience to His will, says not, "I live to Christ," but what is far higher, "Christ liveth in me." As sin, when it has the mastery, is itself the vital principle, and leads the soul whither it will, so, when it is slain and the will of Christ obeyed, this life is no longer earthly, but Christ liveth, that is, works, has mastery within us. His saying, "I am crucified with Him" "I no longer live," but "am dead," seeming incredible to many, he adds,

Ver. 20. "And that life which I now live in the flesh, I live in faith, the faith which is in the Son of God."

The foregoing, says he, relates to our spiritual life, but this life of sense too, if considered, will be found owing to my faith in Christ. For as regards the former Dispensation and Law, I had incurred the severest punishment, and had long ago perished, "for all have sinned, and come short of the glory of God." (Rom. iii: 23.) And we, who lay under sentence, have been liberated by Christ, for all of us are dead, if not in fact, at least by sentence; and He has delivered us from the expected blow. When the Law had accused, and God condemned us, Christ came, and by giving Himself up to death, rescued us all from death. So that "the life which I now live in the flesh, I live in faith." Had not this been, nothing could have averted a destruction as general as that which took place at the flood, but His advent arrested the wrath of God, and caused us to live by faith. That such is his meaning appears from what follows. After saying, that "the life which I now live in the flesh, I live in faith," he adds,

Ver. 20. "In the Son of God, Who loved me, and gave Himself up for me."

How is this, O Paul! why dost thou appropriate a general benefit, and make thine own what was done for the whole world's sake? for

---

[1] ["That I might live unto God " is not to be joined to "I have been crucified with Christ " as Chrysostom, for it belongs to the completeness of the thought introduced by γαρ ver. 19.—Meyer.—G. A.]

[2] [This is the rendering of the Rev. Ver. though the American Committee has, " And it is no longer I that live ; " and correctly so. For as Dr. Schaff says, The reading of the Rev. Ver. (and the Author. Ver. too) conveys a beautiful and true idea, but it is grammatically incorrect, since the original has no "nevertheless" and no "yet." Pop. Com. on Gal. and Companion to the Greek Testament, p. 453.—G. A.]

[3] [Chrysostom held baptismal regeneration.—G. A.]

he says not, "Who loved us," but, "Who loved me." And besides the Evangelist says, "God so loved the world;" (John iii: 16.) and Paul himself, "He that spared not His own Son, but delivered Him up, not for Paul only, but, "for us all;" (Rom. viii: 32.) and again, "that He might purify unto himself a people for his own possession, (Tit. ii: 14.) But considering the desperate condition of human nature, and the ineffably tender solicitude of Christ, in what He delivered us from, and what He freely gave us, and kindled by the yearning of affection towards Him, he thus expresses himself. Thus the Prophets often appropriate to themselves Him who is God of all, as in the words, "O God, thou art my God, early will I seek Thee." (Psalm lxiii: 1.) Moreover, this language teaches that each individual justly owes as a great debt of gratitude to Christ, as if He had come for his sake alone, for He would not have grudged this His condescension though but for one, so that the measure of His love to each is as great as to the whole world. Truly the Sacrifice was offered for all mankind,[1] and was sufficient to save all, but those who enjoy the blessing are the believing only. Nevertheless it did not deter Him from His so great condescension, that not all would come; but He acted after the pattern of the supper in the Gospel, which He prepared for all, (Luke xiv: 16.) yet when the guests came not, instead of withdrawing the viands, He called in others. So too He did not despise that sheep, though one only, which had strayed from the ninety and nine. (Mat. xviii: 12.) This too in like manner St.

Paul intimates, when he says, speaking about the Jews, "For what if some were without faith, shall their want of faith make of none effect the faithfulness of God? God forbid: yea let God be found true, but every man a liar." (Rom. iii: 3, 4.) When He so loved thee as to give Himself up to bring thee who wast without hope to a life so great and blessed, canst thou, thus gifted, have recourse to things gone by? His reasoning being completed, he concludes with a vehment asseveration, saying,

Ver. 21. "I do not make void the grace of God."[3]

Let those, who even now Judaize and adhere to the Law, listen to this, for it applies to them.

Ver. 21. "For if righteousness is through the Law, then Christ died for naught."

What can be more heinous than this sin?[4] what more fit to put one to shame than these words? Christ's death is a plain proof of the inability of the Law to justify us; and if it does justify, then is His death superfluous. Yet how could it be reasonable to say that has been done heedlessly and in vain which is so awful, so surpassing human reason, a mystery so ineffable, with which Patriarchs travailed, which Prophets foretold, which Angels gazed on with consternation, which all men confess as the summit of the Divine tenderness? Reflecting how utterly out of place it would be if they should say that so great and high a deed had been done superfluously, (for this is what their conduct came to,) he even uses violent language against them, as we find in the words which follow.

CHAPTER III

VERSE I.

"O foolish Galatians,[2] who did bewitch you, before whose eyes Jesus Christ was openly set forth, crucified?"

HERE he passes to another subject; in the former chapters he had shown himself not to be an Apostle of men, nor by men, nor in want of Apostolic instruction. Now, having established his authority as a teacher, he proceeds to discourse more confidently, and draws a comparison between faith and the Law. At the outset he said, "I marvel that ye are so quickly removing;" (Gal. i: 6.) but here, "O foolish Galatians;" then, his indignation was in its

---

[1] ["Chrysostom teaches that God foreordained all men to holiness and salvation and that Christ died for all and is both willing and able to save all, but not against their will."—Schaff, *Proleg.* p. 20.—G. A.]

[2] [" Paul addresses himself again directly to the Galatians with an expression of indignant surprise at their relapse into Judaism and passes from the historical to the doctrinal part of the Epistle, from the apology of his apostolic authority to the defense of his apostolic teaching."—Schaff in *Pop. Com.*—G. A.]

[3] ["Negative side of the life which Paul (from ver. 19) has described as his own. By this negative, with the grave reason assigned for it in the latter part of the verse, the perverse conduct of Peter is completely condemned."—Meyer.—G. A.]

[4] [" This blasphemous inference gives the finishing stroke to the false Judaizing gospel.

"This collision between Peter and Paul furnished material to the Ebionites for an attack upon Paul, to the Gnostics for an attack upon the Jewish apostles and to Porphyry for an attack upon Christianity itself [as well as to Baur and the Tübingen school for an attack in modern times from a different standpoint]. But Christianity has surveyed all these attacks and gains new strength from every conflict."—Schaff.—G. A.]

birth, but now, after his refutation of the charges against himself, and his proofs, it bursts forth. Let not his calling them "foolish" surprise you; for it is not a transgression of Christ's command not to call one's brother a fool, but rather a strict observance of it. For it is not said simply, "Whosoever shall say to his brother, Thou fool," (Mat. v: 22.) but, whosoever shall do so, "without a cause."[1] And who more fittingly than they could so be called, who after so great events, adhered to past things, as if nothing else had ever happened? If on this account Paul is to be called a "reviler," Peter may likewise, on account of Annanias and Sapphira, be called a homicide; but as it would be wildness to do so in that case, much more in this. Moreover it is to be considered, that this vehemence is not used at the beginning, but after these evidences and proofs, which, rather than Paul himself, might now be held to administer the rebuke. For after he had shown that they rejected the faith, and made the death of Christ to be without a purpose, he introduces his reproof, which, even as it is, is less severe than they merited. Observe too how soon he stays his arm; for he adds not, Who has seduced you? who has perverted you? who has been sophistical with you? but, "Who hath cast an envious eye on you?" thus tempering his reprimand with somewhat of praise. For it implies that their previous course had excited jealousy,[2] and that the present occurrence arose from the malignity of a demon, whose breath had blasted their prosperous estate.

And when you hear of jealousy in this place, and in the Gospel, of an evil eye, which means the same, you must not suppose that the glance of the eye has any natural power to injure those who look upon it. For the eye, that is, the organ itself, cannot be evil; but Christ in that place means jealousy by the term. To behold, simply, is the function of the eye, but to behold in an evil manner belongs to a mind depraved within. As through this sense the knowledge of visible objects enters the soul, and as jealousy is for the most part generated by wealth, and wealth and sovereignty and pomp are perceived by the eye, therefore he calls the eye evil; not as beholding merely, but as beholding enviously from some moral depravity. Therefore by the words, "Who hath looked enviously on you," he implies that the persons in question acted, not from concern, not to sup-

ply defects, but to mutilate what existed. For envy, far from supplying what is wanting, subtracts from what is complete, and vitiates the whole. And he speaks thus, not as if envy had any power of itself, but meaning, that the teachers of these doctrines did so from envious motives.

Ver. 1. "Before whose eyes Jesus Christ was openly set forth, crucified."

Yet was He not crucified in Galatia, but at Jerusalem. His reason for saying, "among you,"[3] is to declare the power of faith to see events which are at a distance. He says not, "crucified," but, "openly set forth crucified," signifying that by the eye of faith they saw more distinctly than some who were present as spectators. For many of the latter received no benefit, but the former, who were not eye-witnesses, yet saw it by faith more clearly. These words convey both praise and blame; praise, for their implicit acceptance of the truth; blame, because Him whom they had seen, for their sakes, stripped naked, transfixed, nailed to the cross, spit upon, mocked, fed with vinegar, upbraided by thieves, pierced with a spear; (for all this is implied in the words, "openly set forth, crucified,")[4] Him had they left, and betaken themselves to the Law, unshamed by any of those sufferings. Here observe how Paul, leaving all mention of heaven, earth, and sea, every where preaches the power of Christ, bearing about as he did, and holding up His cross: for this is the sum of the Divine love toward us.

Ver 2. "This only would I learn from you, Received ye the Spirit by the works of the Law, or by the hearing of faith?"

As ye do not attend, says he, to long discourses, nor are willing to contemplate the magnitude of this Economy, I am desirous, (seeing your extreme ignorance,) to convince you by concise arguments and a summary method of proof. Before, he had convinced them by what he said to Peter; now, he encounters them entirely with arguments, drawn not from what had occurred elsewhere, but from what had happened among themselves.[5] And his persuasives and proofs are adduced, not merely from what was given them in common with others, but from what was especially conferred on themselves. Therefore he says, "This only would I learn from you, Received ye the Spirit by the works of the Law, or by the hearing of faith." Ye have received, he says, the Holy Spirit, ye

---

[1] [The word εἰκῆ, 'without a cause,' occurs in the *textus receptus* on inferior authority in connection with the words 'whosoever shall be angry with his brother' (without a cause), but no where with the words, 'whosoever shall say, Thou fool,' as Chrys. here connects them.—G. A.]

[2] [" The word means 'to bewitch by words, to enchant,' and is not to be explained with Chrysostom, 'who has envied you?' that is, your previous happy condition?"—Meyer.—G. A.]

[3] [Εν ὑμῖν is spurious, being omitted by Aleph. A. B. C. versions, Fathers, and Rev. Ver. as well as by W. and H.—G. A.]

[4] [" This signifies the life-like pictorial vivacity and effectiveness of Paul's preaching of Christ and Him crucified. The Greek verb is used of placarding public notices and proclamations."—Schaff. —G. A.]

[5] [" See how effectually he treats the topic from (their own) experience."—Luther, quoted by Meyer. G. A.]

have done many mighty works, ye have effected miracles in raising the dead, in cleansing lepers, in prophesying, in speaking with tongues,—did the Law confer this great power upon you? was it not rather Faith, seeing that, before, ye could do no such things? Is it not then the height of madness for these who have received such benefits from Faith, to abandon it, and desert back to the Law which can offer you nothing of the same kind?

Ver. 3. "Are ye so foolish? having begun in the Spirit, are ye now perfected in the flesh?"

Here again he seasonably interposes a rebuke; time, he says, should have brought improvement; but, so far from advancing, ye have even retrograded. Those who start from small beginnings make progress to higher things; ye, who began with the high, have relapsed to the low. Even had your outset been carnal, your advance should have been spiritual, but now, after starting from things spiritual, ye have ended your journey in that which is carnal; for to work miracles is spiritual, but to be circumcised is carnal. And after miracles ye have passed to circumcision, after having apprehended the truth ye have fallen back to types, after gazing on the sun ye seek a candle, after having strong meat ye run for milk. He says, "made perfect,"[1] which means not "initiated" merely, but "sacrificed," signifying that their teachers took and slew them like animals, while they resigned themselves to suffer what those teachers pleased. As if some captain, or distinguished man, after a thousand victories and trophies, were to subject himself to infamy as a deserter, and offer his body to be branded at the will of others.

Ver. 4. "Did ye suffer so many things in vain?[2] if it be indeed in vain."

This remark is far more piercing than the former, for the remembrance of their miracles would not be so powerful as the exhibition of their contests and endurance of sufferings for Christ's sake. All that you have endured, says he, these men would strip you of, and would rob you of your crown. Then, lest he should dismay and unnerve, he proceeds not to a formal judgment, but subjoins, "if it be indeed in

vain;" if you have but a mind to shake off drowsiness and recover yourselves, he says, it is not in vain. Where then be those who would cut off repentance[3]? Here were men who had received the Spirit, worked miracles, become confessors, encountered a thousand perils and persecutions for Christ's sake, and after so many achievements had fallen from grace; nevertheless he says, if you have the purpose, ye may recover yourselves.

Ver. 5. "He therefore that supplieth to you the Spirit, and worketh miracles among you, doeth he it by the works of the law, or by the hearing of faith?"

Have ye been vouchsafed, he says, so great a gift, and achieved such wonders, because ye observed the Law, or because ye adhered to Faith? plainly on account of Faith. Seeing that they played this argument to and fro, that apart from the Law, Faith had no force, he proves the contrary, viz., that if the Commandments be added, Faith no longer avails; for Faith then has efficacy when things from the Law are not added to it. "Ye who would be justified by the Law, ye are fallen away from grace:" (Gal. v: 4.) This he says later, when his language has grown bolder, employing the vantage-ground by that time gained; meanwhile while gaining it, he argues from their past experience. For it was when ye obeyed Faith, he says, not the Law, that ye received the Spirit and wrought miracles.

And here, as the Law was the subject of discussion, he moots another special point of controversy, and very opportunely and with much cogency introduces a notice of Abraham.

Ver. 6. "Even as Abraham believed God, and it was reckoned unto him for righteousness."

Even the miracles done by themselves, he says, declare the power of Faith, but I shall attempt if you will suffer me to draw my proofs from ancient narratives also. Then, as they made great account of the Patriarch, he brings his example forward, and shows that he too was justified by Faith.[4] And if he who was before grace, was justified by Faith, although plentiful in works, much more we. For what loss was it to him, not being under the Law? None, for his faith sufficed unto righteousness. The Law did not then exist, he says, neither does it now exist, any more than then. In disproving the need of the Law, he introduces one who was justified before the Law, lest an objection should also be made to him; for as then it was

---

[1] [This distinction between τελέω and ἐπιτελέω was not in the mind of the Apostle. The contrast with ἐναρξάμενοι, 'having begun,' shows that ἐπ τελεῖσθε simply means 'are ye made perfect,' "the compound involving the idea of bringing to a 'complete and perfect' end." (Ellicott.) There may be a slight tinge of irony in the compound word.—G. A.]

[2] ["As we know nothing of persecutions endured by Galatians, it seems preferable to take the word in a neutral sense embracing all spiritual experiences (blessings and benefits as well) of the Galatians. (Comp. v. 3 and 6.)"—Schaff. Lightfoot refers it to the persecutions endured by the Galatians from Jews citing Gal. v: 11; and says "the εἰ γε leaves a loophole for doubt which the καί, following, widens." So Ellicott. Meyer says, "It refers to everything which the false apostles in their Judaistic zeal had troubled and burdened the Galatians with. The εἰκῆ then means " and all to no profit, all in vain," if indeed it be only (καί) in vain and not to the positive risk of your Messianic salvation that ye have suffered."—G. A.]

[3] The Novatians, who said the revealed covenant of grace did not provide for the case of the lapsed.

[4] [" The answer, obvious of itself, to the preceding question, is ἐξ ἀκοῆς πίστεως, 'from the hearing of faith,' and to this Paul subjoins that great religious-historic argument for the righteousness of faith which is presented in the justification of the progenitor of the theocratic people."—Meyer.—G. A.]

not yet given, so now, having been given, it was abrogated. And as they made much of their descent from Abraham, and feared lest, abandoning the Law, they should be considered strangers to his kin ; Paul removes this fear by turning their argument against themselves, and proves that faith is especially concerned in connecting them with Abraham. He draws out this argument more at length in the Epistle to the Romans ; however he urges it also here in, the words,

Ver. 7. "Know therefore, that they which be of faith, the same are sons of Abraham."

Which he proves by ancient testimony thus:

Ver. 8. "And the Scripture,[1] foreseeing that God would justify the Gentiles by faith, preached the Gospel beforehand unto Abraham, saying, In thee shall all the nations be blessed."

If then those were Abraham's sons, not, who were related to him by blood, but who follow his faith, for this is the meaning of the words, "In thee all the nations," it is plain that the heathen are brought into kindred with him.

Hereby too is proved another important point. It perplexed them that the Law was the older, and Faith afterwards. Now he removes this notion by showing that Faith was anterior to the Law ; as is evident from Abraham's case, who was justified before the giving of the Law. He shows too that late events fell out according to prophecy ; "The Scripture," says he, "foreseeing that God would justify the Gentiles by faith, preached the Gospel beforehand unto Abraham." Attend to this point. He Himself who gave the Law, had decreed, before He gave it, that the heathen should be justified by Faith. And he says not "revealed," but, "preached the Gospel," to signify that the patriarch was in joy at this method of justification, and in great desire for its accomplishment.

Further, they were possessed with another apprehension ; it was written, "Cursed is every one that continueth not in all things that are written in the book of the Law, to do them." (Deut. xxvii: 26.) And this he removes, with great skill and prudence, turning their argument against themselves, and showing that those who relinquish the Law are not only not cursed, but blessed ; and they who keep it, not only not blessed but cursed. They said that he who kept not the Law was cursed, but he proves that he who kept it was cursed, and he who kept it not, blessed. Again, they said that he who adhered to Faith alone was cursed, but he shows that he who adhered to Faith alone, is blessed. And how does he prove all this ? for it is no common thing which we have promised ; wherefore it is

necessary to give close attention to what follows. He had already shown this, by referring to the words spoken to the Patriarch, "In thee shall all nations be blessed," (Gen. xii : 4.) at a time, that is, when Faith existed, not the Law ; so he adds by way of conclusion,

Ver. 9. "So then they which be of faith are blessed with the faithful Abraham."[2]

Then, that they might not turn round, and object that, true it was Abraham was justified by Faith, for the Law was not then given, but what instance would be found of Faith justifying after the delivery of the Law ? he addresses himself to this, and proves more than they required : namely, not only that Faith was justifying, but that the Law brought its adherents under a curse. To be sure of this, listen to the very words of the Apostle.

Ver. 10. "For[3] as many as are of the works of the Law are under a curse."

This is what he lays down, before proving it ; and what is the proof ? it is from the Law itself :—

Ver. 10, 11. "For it is written, Cursed is every one that continueth not in all things that are written in the book of the Law to do them. Now that no man is justified by the Law is evident."

For all have sinned, and are under the curse.

However he does not say this yet, lest he should seem to lay it down of himself, but here again establishes his point by a text which concisely states both points ; that no man has fulfilled the Law, (wherefore they are under the curse,) and, that Faith justifies. What then is the text ? It is in the book of the prophet Habakkuk, "The just shall live by faith," (Hab. ii : 4.) which not only establishes the righteousness that is of Faith, but also that there is no salvation through the Law. As no one, he says, kept the Law, but all were under the curse, on account of transgression, an easy way was provided, that from Faith, which is in itself a strong proof that no man can be justified by the Law. For the prophet says not, "The just shall live by the Law," but, "by faith :"

Ver. 12. "And the Law is not of faith ; but He that doeth them shall live in them."

For the Law requires not only Faith but works also, but grace saves and justifies by Faith. (Eph. ii : 8.)

---

[1] [" The Scripture personified. The only case in N. T. where the personification of Scripture goes beyond λέγει or εἶπεν," etc. —Lightfoot.—G. A.]

[2] [" After having pointed out from Scripture v. 6 and 7, that none other than believers are sons of Abraham, Paul now shows further from Scripture that none other than believers have a share in Abraham's blessing, i. e., are justified."—Meyer.—G. A.]

[3] [" Having shown by postive proof that justification is of faith, he adds the negative argument derived from the impossibility of maintaining its opposite, namely, justification by Law. This negative argument is twofold :

First, it is impossible to fulfill the requirements of the law and nonfulfillment lays us under a curse (Ver. 10) ; Secondly, supposing the fulfilment possible, still the spirit of the Law is antagonistic to faith, which is elsewhere spoken of as the source of life. (Ver. 11 and 12)."—Lightfoot.—G. A.]

You see how he proves that they are under the curse who cleave to the Law, because it is impossible to fulfill it; next, how comes Faith to have this justifying power? for to this doctrine he already stood pledged, and now maintains it with great force of argument. The Law being too weak to lead man to righteousness, an effectual remedy was provided in Faith, which is the means of rendering that possible which was "impossible by the Law." (Rom. viii: 3.) Now as the Scripture says, "the just shall live by faith," thus repudiating salvation by the Law, and moreover as Abraham was justified by Faith, it is evident that its efficacy is very great. And it is also clear, that he who abides not by the Law is cursed, and that he who keeps to Faith is just. But, you may ask me, how I prove that this curse is not still of force? Abraham lived before the Law, but we, who once were subject to the yoke of bondage, have made ourselves liable to the curse; and who shall release us therefrom? Observe his ready answer to this; his former remark was sufficient; for, if a man be once justified, and has died to the Law and embraced a novel life, how can such a one be subject to the curse? however, this is not enough for him, so he begins with a fresh argument, as follows:—

Ver. 13. "Christ redeemed us from the curse of the Law, having become a curse for us: for it is written, Cursed is every one that hangeth on a tree." [1]

In reality, the people were subject to another curse, which says, "Cursed is every one that continueth not in the things that are written in the book of the Law." (Deut. xxvii: 26.) To this curse, I say, people were subject, for no man had continued in, or was a keeper of, the whole Law; but Christ exchanged this curse for the other, "Cursed is every one that hangeth on a tree." As then both he who hanged on a tree, and he who transgresses the Law, is cursed, and as it was necessary for him who is about to relieve from a curse himself to be free from it, but to receive another instead of it, therefore Christ took upon Him such another, and thereby relieved us from the curse. It was like an innocent man's undertaking to die for another sentenced to death, and so rescuing him from punishment. For Christ took upon Him not the curse of transgression, but the other curse, in order to remove that of others. For, "He had done no violence neither was any deceit in His mouth." (Isa. liii: 9; 1 Peter ii: 22.) And as by dying He rescued from death those who were dying, so by taking upon Himself the curse, He delivered them from it.

Ver. 14. "That upon the Gentiles might come the blessing of Abraham."

How on the Gentiles? It is said, "In thy seed shall all the nations of the earth be blessed:" (Gen. xxii: 18; xxvi: 4.) that is to say, in Christ. If this were said of the Jews, how would it be reasonable that they who were themselves subject to the curse, on account of transgression, should become the authors of a blessing to others? an accursed person cannot impart to others that blessing of which he is himself deprived. Plainly then it all refers to Christ who was the Seed of Abraham, and through whom the Gentiles are blessed. And thus the promise of the Spirit is added, as Paul himself declares, "that we might receive the promise of the Spirit through faith." [2] As the grace of the Spirit could not possibly descend on the graceless and offending, they are first blessed the curse having been removed; then being justified by faith, they draw unto themselves the grace of the Spirit. Thus the Cross removed the curse, Faith brought in righteousness, righteousness drew on the grace of the Spirit.

Ver. 15. "Brethren, I speak after the manner of men; Though it be but a man's covenant, yet when it hath been confirmed, no one maketh it void or addeth thereto."

"To speak after the manner of men" means to use human examples. [3] Having founded his argument on the Scriptures, on the miracles wrought among themselves, on the sufferings of Christ, and on the Patriarch, he proceeds to common usages; and this he does invariably, in order to sweeten his discourse, and render it more acceptable and intelligible to the duller sort. Thus he argues with the Corinthians, "Who feedeth a flock, and eateth not of the milk of the flock? Who planteth a vineyard, and eateth not the fruit thereof?" (1 Cor. ix: 7.) and again with the Hebrews, "For a testament is of force where there hath been death; for doth it ever avail while he that made it liveth?" (Heb. ix: 17.) One may find him dwelling with pleasure on such arguments. In the Old Testament God does the same thing in many instances, as, "Can a woman forget her sucking child?" (Isa. xlix: 15.) and again, "Shall the clay say to him that fashioneth it, What makest thou?" (Isa. xlv: 9.) and in Hosea, He represents a husband set at nought by his wife. (Hos. ii: 5, f.) This use of human

---

[1] ["A parenthetic justification from Deut. xxi: 23 of the startling expression just used. The passage refers to those criminals who, after being stoned, were hung upon a stake, but were not permitted to remain over night lest the holy land should be desecrated. Our Saviour fulfilled the legal curse by hanging dead on the cross. This is one of the strongest passages for the doctrine of a vicarious atonement. The vicarious efficacy lies not so much in the preposition, ὑπέρ,' 'for,' as in the whole sentence."—Schaff —G. A.]

[2] ["After a wondrous chain of arguments * * the apostle comes back to the subject of verse 2: the gift of the Holy Ghost came through faith in Christ."—Ellicott.—G. A.]

[3] ["Paul now assumes a milder tone and reasons from the common dealings of men."—Schaff.—G. A.]

examples frequently occurs in types also, as when the prophet takes the girdle, (Jer. xiii : 1–9.) and goes down to the potter's house. (Jer. xviii : 1–6.) The meaning of the present example is, that Faith is more ancient than the Law, which is later and only temporary, and delivered in order to pave the way for Faith. Hence he says, "Brethren, I speak after the manner of men;" above he had called them "foolish," now he calls them "brethren," at once chiding and encouraging them. "Though it be but a man's covenant, yet when it hath been confirmed." If a man, says he, makes a covenant, does any one dare to come afterwards and overturn it, or subjoin aught to it ? for this is the meaning of "or addeth thereto." Much less then when God makes a covenant; and with whom did God make a covenant?

Ver. 16, 17, 18. "Now to Abraham were the promises spoken and to his seed. He saith not, And to seeds,[1] as of many ; but as of One, And to thy seed, which is Christ.[2] Now this I say, A covenant, confirmed before hand by God the Law, which came four hundred and thirty years after, doth not disannul, so as to make the promise of none effect. For if the inheritance is of the Law, it is no more of promise : but God hath granted it to Abraham by promise."

Thus God made a covenant with Abraham, promising that in his seed the blessing should come upon the heathen ; and this blessing the Law cannot turn aside. As this example was not in all respects appropriate to the matter in hand, he introduces it thus, " I speak after the manner of men," that nothing might be deduced from it derogatory to the majesty of God. But let us go to the bottom of this illustration. It was promised Abraham that by his seed the heathen should be blessed ; and his seed according to the flesh is Christ ; four hundred and thirty years after came the Law ; now, if the Law bestows the blessings even life and righteousness, that promise is annulled. And so while no one annuls a man's covenant, the covenant of God after four hundred and thirty years is annulled ; for if not that covenant but another instead of it bestows what is promised, then is it set aside, which is most unreasonable.

Ver. 19. "What then is the Law ? it was added because of transgressions."

This remark again is not superfluous ; observe too how he glances round at every thing, as if he had an hundred eyes. Having exalted Faith, and proved its elder claims, that the Law may not be considered superfluous, he sets right this side of the doctrine also, and proves that the Law was not given without a view, but altogether profitably. "Because of transgressions;" that is to say, that the Jews might not be let live carelessly, and plunge into the depth of wickedness,[3] but that the Law might be placed upon them as a bridle, guiding, regulating, and checking them from transgressing, if not all, at least some of the commandments. Not slight then was the advantage of the Law ; but for how long ?

Ver. 19. "Till the seed should come to whom the promise hath been made."

This is said of Christ ; if then it was given until His advent, why do you protract it beyond its natural period ?

Ver. 19. "And it was ordained through Angels by the hand of a Mediator."

He either calls the priests Angels, or he declares that the Angels themselves ministered to the delivery of the Law. By Mediator here he means Christ,[4] and shows that He was before it, and Himself the Giver of it.

Ver. 20. "Now a mediator is not a mediator of one, but God is one."[5]

What can the heretics[6] say to this? for as, according to them, the expression "the Only True God" excludes the Son from being true God, so here the phrase "God is One," excludes Him from being God in any sense. But if, although the Father is called "One God," the Son is nevertheless God, it is very plain that though the Father is called "Very God," the Son is very God likewise. Now a mediator, says he, is between two parties ; of whom then is Christ the Mediator? plainly of God and of men. Observe, he says, that Christ also gave the Law ; what therefore it was His to give, it is His to annul.

---

[3] [" This interpretation of Chrysostom must be rejected on lexical grounds. The law was in order to bring sin to light and make it appear in its true character and thus by a knowledge of the disease prepare its cure."—Ellicott and Schaff.—G. A.]
[4] [" We may reasonably wonder," says Ellicott, "how the early expositors (Basil and Theodoret excepted) could have so generally coincided in the perplexing view of Origen that the Mediator here mentioned was Christ. On the contrary it is plain that it was Moses, Deut. v : 5."—G. A.]
[5] [" This verse is counted the most difficult passage in the New Testament, and has given rise to about 300 interpretations."
That of Lightfoot seems to satisfy the context, and is thus forcibly put by him : " The law is of the nature of a contract between two parties. God on the one hand and the Jewish people on the other. It is valid only so long as both parties fulfil the terms of contract. It is therefore contingent and not absolute. Unlike the law the promise is absolute and unconditional. It depends on the sole decree of God. There are not two contracting parties. There is nothing of the nature of a stipulation. The giver is everything and the recipient nothing."—Com. in loco.—G. A.]
[6] The heretics refered to are the Anomœans, who held Arianism in its most developed form, against whom S. Chrysostom has written Homilies. For the particular objection answered in the text, vid. also Basil, in Eunom, iv. p. 294. Athan. Or in Arian, iii. 9. Greg. Naz. Orat. 36, p. 586.

---

[1] [" A difficulty arises here from the stress which Paul lays on the singular of the word 'seed,' which is a collective noun in Heb. and Greek, and includes the whole posterity. But it is not a question of grammar but of spiritual meaning. The promise refers to Christ par excellence, and to all those and only those who are truly members of His body, united to Him by a living faith. If all the single descendants of Abraham were meant, the children of Hagar and Keturah and subsequently of Esau and his descendants, would have to be included."—Schaff.—G. A.]
[2] "[Not as a single individual but as Head of the church which is His body, Eph. 1: 23. The key to the passage is in ver. 28 and 29: ' Ye are all one in Christ Jesus.' "—Schaff.—G. A.]

Ver. 21. "Is the Law then against the promises of God?"

For if the blessing is given in the seed of Abraham, but the Law brings in the curse, it must be contrary to the promises. This objection he meets, first, by a protest, in the words,

Ver. 21. "God forbid:"

And next he brings his proof;

Ver. 21. "For if there had been a law given which could make alive verily righteousness would have been of the Law."

His meaning is as follows; If we had our hope of life in the Law, and our salvation depended on it, the objection might be valid. But if it save you, by means of Faith, though it brings you under the curse, you suffer nothing from it, gain no harm, in that Faith comes and sets all right. Had the promise been by the Law, you had reasonably feared lest, separating from the Law, you should separate from righteousness, but if it was given in order to shut up all, that is, to convince all and expose their individual sins, far from excluding you from the promises, it now aids you in obtaining them. This is shown by the words,

Ver. 22. "Howbeit the scripture [1] hath shut up all things under sin, that the promise by faith in Jesus Christ might be given to them that believe."

As the Jews were not even conscious of their own sins, and in consequence did not even desire remission; the Law was given to probe their wounds, that they might long for a physician. And the word "shut up" means "convinced," and conviction held them in fear. You see then it is not only not against, but was given for the promises. Had it arrogated to itself the work and the authority, the objection would stand; but if its drift is something else, and it acted for that, how is it against the promises of God? Had the Law not been given, all would have been wrecked upon wickedness, and there would have been no Jews to listen to Christ; but now being given, it has effected two things; it has schooled its followers in a certain degree of virtue, and has pressed on them the knowledge of their own sins. And this especially made them more zealous to seek the Son, for those who disbelieved, disbelieved from having no sense of their own sins, as Paul shows;

"For being ignorant of God's righteousness, and seeking to establish their own righteousness, they did not subject themselves to the rightousness of God." (Rom. x: 3.)

Ver. 23. "But before faith came, we were kept inward under the Law, shut up unto the faith which should afterwards be revealed."

Here he clearly puts forward what I have stated: for the expressions "we were kept" and "shut up," signify nothing else than the security given by the commandments of the Law; which like a fortress fenced them round with fear and a life conformable to itself, and so preserved them unto Faith.

Ver. 24. "So that the Law hath been our tutor to bring us unto Christ, that we might be justified by faith."

Now the Tutor is not opposed to the Preceptor, but cooperates with him, ridding the youth from all vice, and having all leisure to fit him for receiving instructions from his Preceptor. But when the youth's habits are formed, then the Tutor leaves him, as Paul says.

Ver. 25, 26. "But now that faith is come which leads to perfect manhood we are no longer under a tutor [2]. For ye are all sons of God through faith in Christ Jesus."

The Law then, as it was our tutor, and we were kept shut up under it, is not the adversary but the fellow-worker of grace; but if when grace is come, it continues to hold us down, it becomes an adversary; for if it confines those who ought to go forward to grace, then it is the destruction of our salvation. If a candle which gave light by night, kept us, when it became day, from the sun, it would not only not benefit, it would injure us; and so doth the Law, if it stands between us and greater benefits. Those then are the greatest traducers of the Law, who still keep it, just as the tutor makes a youth ridiculous, by retaining him with himself, when time calls for his departure. Hence Paul says, "But after faith is come, we are no longer under a tutor." We are then no longer under a tutor, "for ye are all sons of God." Wonderful! see how mighty is the power of Faith, and how he unfolds as he proceeds! Before, he showed that it made them sons of the Patriarch, "Know therefore," says he, "that they which be of faith, the same are sons of Abraham;" now he proves that they are sons of God also, "For ye are all," says he, "sons of God through faith, which is in Christ Jesus;" by Faith, not by the Law. Then, when he has said this

---

[1] ["The Law then though differing widely from the promise is not antagonistic to it, does not interfere with it. On the contrary, we might imagine such a law as would justify and give life. This was not the effect of the law of Moses, however; on the contrary (ἀλλὰ) the Scripture (that, namely, about the curse, v. 10:) testifies that the Law condemned all alike, yet not finally and irrevocably but only as leading the way for the dispensation of faith." —Lightfoot. Meyer takes a different view of v. 21: "For if it had been opposed to the promises, the Law must have been in a position to procure life and if this were so, then would righteousness actually be from the Law, which according to the Scripture cannot be so (ver. 22)."—G. A.]

[2] ["The pædagogus or tutor, frequently a superior slave, was entrusted with the moral supervision of the child. Thus his office was quite distinct from that of the διδάσκαλος; so the word "Schoolmaster" conveys a wrong idea. As well in his inferior rank as in his recognized duty of enforcing discipline, this person was a fit emblem of the Mosaic law. There is a very complete illustration of the use which Paul makes of the metaphor in Plato (Lysis, p. 208 C)."—Lightfoot.—G. A.]

great and wonderful thing, he names also the mode of their adoption,

Ver. 27. " For as many of you as were baptized into Christ, did put on Christ."

Why does he not say, " For as many of you as have been baptized into Christ, have been born of God ? " for this was what directly went to prove that they were sons ;—because he states it in a much more awful point of view ; If Christ be the Son of God, and thou hast put on Him, thou who hast the Son within thee, and art fashioned after His pattern, hast been brought into one kindred and nature with Him.

Ver. 28. "There can be neither Jew nor Greek, there can be neither bond nor free, there can be no male and female : for ye all are one in Christ Jesus."

See what an insatiable soul ! for having said, "We are all made children of God through Faith," he does not stop there, but tries to find something more exact, which may serve to convey a still closer oneness with Christ. Having said, " ye have put on Christ," even this does not suffice Him, but by way of penetrating more deeply into this union, he comments on it thus : " Ye are all One in Christ Jesus," that is, ye have all one form and one mould, even Christ's. What can be more awful than these words ! He that was a Greek, or Jew, or bond-man yesterday, carries about with him the form, not of an Angel or Archangel, but of the Lord of all, yea displays in his own person the Christ.

Ver. 29. " And if ye are Christ's, then are ye Abraham's seed, heirs according to promise."

Here, you observe, he proves what he had before stated concerning the seed of Abraham,— that to him and to his seed the promises were given.[3]

CHAPTER IV

VERSE 1-3.

" But I say, that so long as the heir is a child, he differeth nothing from a bond-servant, though he is lord of all; but is under guardians and stewards, until the term appointed of the father. So we also when we were children, were held in bondage under the rudiments of the world."

THE word "child" in this place denotes not age but understanding;[1] meaning that God had from the beginning designed for us these gifts, but, as we yet continued childish, He let us be under the elements of the world, that is, new moons and sabbaths, for these days are regulated by the course of sun and moon.[2] If then also now they bring you under law they do nothing else but lead you backward now in the time of your perfect age and maturity. And see what is the consequence of observing days; the Lord, the Master of the house, the Sovereign Ruler, is thereby reduced to the rank of a servant.

Ver. 4, 5. " But when the fulness of the time came God sent forth His Son, born of a woman, under the Law that he might redeem them which were under the Law, that we might receive the adoption of sons."

Here he states two objects and effects of the Incarnation, deliverance from evil and supply of good, things which none could compass but Christ. They are these; deliverance from the curse of the Law, and promotion to sonship. Fitly does he say, that we might "receive," " [be paid,]" implying that it was due;[4] for the promise was of old time made for these objects to Abraham, as the Apostle has himself shown at great length. And how does it appear that we have become sons ? he has told us one mode, in that we have put on Christ who is the Son; and now he mentions another, in that we have received the Spirit of adoption.

Ver. 6, 7. " And because ye are sons, God sent forth the Spirit of His Son into your hearts, crying, Abba, Father. So that thou art no longer a bond-servant, but a son; and if a son, then an heir through God."

Had not we been first made sons, we could not have called Him Father. If then grace hath made us freemen instead of slaves, men

---

[1] [" This reference of νήπιος to mental immaturity is quite in opposition to the context.—Meyer. " The heir in his nonage represents the Jewish people and the state of the world before Christ."—Schaff. So Meyer : " The κληρονόμος νήπιος represents the Christians as a body regarded in their earlier pre-Christian condition."—G. A.]

[2] [This interpretation is rejected by Schaff, Meyer, Ellicott, Lightfoot et al. Schaff says : " ' Elements' here represents the religion before Christ as an elementary religion full of external rites and ceremonies. * * Comp. v : 10, for a specimen."—G. A.]

[3] [So Schaff : " Verse 16 must here be kept in view where Christ is declared to be the seed of Abraham. Union with Christ constitutes the true spiritual descent from Abraham and secures the inheritance of all the Messianic blessings by promise as against inheritance by law." Pop. Com. in loc.—G. A.]

[4] [" The proposition here (ἀπό) simply means to receive from or at the hands of anyone."—Meyer.—But Lightfoot holds that ἀπο λάβωμεν cannot be the same as λάβωμεν, the simple verb.—G. A.]

instead of children, heirs and sons instead of aliens, is it not utter absurdity and stupidity to desert this grace, and to turn away backwards?

Ver. 8, 9. "Howbeit at that time not knowing God, ye were in bondage to them which by nature are no gods.[1] But now, that ye have come to know God, or rather to be known of God, how turn ye back again to the weak and beggarly rudiments whereunto ye desire to be in bondage over again."

Here turning to the Gentile believers he says that it is an idolatry, this rigid observance of days, and now incurs a severe punishment. To enforce this, and inspire them with a deeper anxiety, he calls the elements "not by nature Gods." And his meaning is,—Then indeed, as being benighted and bewildered, ye lay grovelling upon the earth, but now that ye have known God or rather are known of Him, how great and bitter will be the chastisement ye draw upon you, if, after such a treatment, ye relapse into the same disease. It was not by your own pains that ye found out God, but while ye continued in error, He drew you to Himself. He says "weak and beggarly rudiments," in that they avail nothing towards the good things held out to us.

Ver. 10. "Ye observe days, and months, and seasons, and years."

Hence is plain that their teachers were preaching to them not only circumscision, but also the feast-days and new-moons.

Ver. 11. "I am afraid of you, lest by any means I have bestowed labor upon you in vain."

Observe the tender compassion of the Apostle; they were shaken and he trembles and fears. And hence he has put it so as thoroughly to shame them, "I have bestowed labor upon you," saying, as it were, make not vain the labors which have cost me sweat and pain. By saying "I fear," and subjoining the word "lest," he both inspires alarm, and encourages good hope. He says not "I have labored in vain," but "lest," which is as much as to say, the wreck has not happened, but I see the storm big with it; so I am in fear, yet not in despair; ye have the power to set all right, and to return into your former calm. Then, as it were stretching out a hand to them thus tempest-tost,[2] he brings himself into the midst, saying,

Ver. 12. "I beseech you, brethren, be as I am; for I am as you are."

This is addressed to his Jewish disciples, and he brings his own example forward, to induce them thereby to abandon their old customs. Though you had none other for a pattern, he says, to look at me only would have sufficed for such a change, and for your taking courage. Therefore gaze on me; I too was[3] once in your state of mind, especially so; I had a burning zeal for the Law; yet afterwards I feared not to abandon the Law, to withdraw from that rule of life. And this ye know full well how obstinately I clung hold of Judaism, and how with yet greater force I let it go. He does well to place this last in order : for most men, though they are given a thousand reasons, and those just ones, are more readily influenced by that which is like their own case, and more firmly hold to that which they see done by others.

Ver. 12. "Ye did me no wrong."

Observe how he again addresses them by a title of honor, which was a reminder moreover of the doctrine of grace. Having chid them seriously, and brought things together from all quarters, and shown their violations of the Law, and hit them on many sides, he gives in and conciliates them speaking more tenderly. For as to do nothing but conciliate causes negligence, so to be constantly talked at with sharpness sours a man ; so that it is proper to observe due proportion everywhere. See then how he excuses to them what he has said, and shows that it proceeded not simply because he did not like them, but from anxiety. After giving them a deep cut, he pours in this encouragement like oil; and, showing that his words were not words of hate or enmity, he reminds them of the love which they had evinced toward him, mixing his self-vindication with praises. Therefore he says, "ye did me no wrong."

Ver. 13, 14. "But ye know that because of an infirmity of the flesh I preached the Gospel unto you the first time. And that which was a temptation in my flesh ye despised not, nor rejected."

Not to have injured one is indeed no great thing, for no man whatever would choose to hurt wantonly and without object to annoy another who had never injured him. But for you, not only have ye not injured me, but ye have shown me great and inexpressible kindness, and it is impossible that one who has been treated with such attention should speak thus from any malevolent motive. My language then cannot be caused by ill-will; it follows, that it proceeds

---

[1] ["It is clear from the context that here the apostle is not speaking of the Jewish race alone but of the heathen world also before Christ. He distinctly refers to their previous idolatrous worship (v. 8) and describes their adoption of Jewish ritualism as a 'return' to the weak and beggarly discipline of childhood. * * * Heathenism had been in respect to the 'ritualistic' element, which is the meeting-point of Judaism and heathenism, a disciplinary training like Judaism. They were made up of precepts and ordinances, as opposed to 'grace' and 'promise,' and in an imperfect way they might do the same work. They might by multiplying transgression and begetting a conviction of it prepare the way for liberty in Christ."—Lightfoot.—G. A.]

[2] ["Paul in the following paragraph (ver. 12-20) interrupts his argument for a moment by an affectionate appeal to the feelings of the Galatians."—Schaff.—G. A.]

[3] ["'Εγενόμην must be supplied in the second clause and not ἤμην as Chrysostom would understand : Become as I, free from Judaism, for I also have become as you. For when I abandoned Judaism I became as a Gentile and put myself on the same footing with you."—Meyer.—G. A.]

from affection and solicitude.[1] " Ye did me no wrong; ye know that because of an infirmity of the flesh I preached the Gospel unto you." What can be gentler than this holy soul, what sweeter, or more affectionate ! And the words he had already used, arose not from an unreasoning anger, nor from a passionate emotion, but from much solicitude. And why do I say, ye have not injured me ? Rather have ye evinced a great and sincere regard for me. For " ye know," he says, " that because of an infirmity of the flesh I preached the Gospel unto you; and that which was a temptation to you in my flesh ye despised not, nor rejected." What does he mean ? While I preached to you, I was driven about, I was scourged, I suffered a thousand deaths, yet ye thought no scorn of me ; for this is meant by that which was a temptation to you in my flesh ye despised not, nor rejected."[2] Observe his spiritual skill ; in the midst of his self-vindication, he again appeals to their feelings by showing what he had suffered for their sakes. This however, says he, did not at all offend you, nor did ye reject me on account of my sufferings and persecutions; or, as he now calls them, his infirmity and temptation.

Ver. 14. " But ye received me as an Angel of God."

Was it not then absurd in them to receive him as an Angel of God, when he was persecuted and driven about, and then not to receive him when pressing on them what was fitting ?

Ver. 15, 16. " Where then is that gratulation of yourselves ? for I bear you witness, that, if possible, ye would have plucked out your eyes, and given them to me. So then am I become your enemy, because I tell you the truth ? "

Here he shows perplexity and amazement, and desires to learn of themselves the reason of their change. Who, says he, hath deceived you, and caused a difference in your disposition towards me ? Are ye not the same who attended and ministered to me, counting me more precious than your own eyes ? what then has happened ? whence this dislike? whence this suspicion ? Is it because I have told you the truth ? You ought on this very account to pay me increased honor and attention; instead of which " I am become your enemy, because I tell you the truth,"—for I can find no other reason but this. Observe too what humbleness of mind appears in his defence of himself; he proves not by his conduct to them, but by theirs to him

that his language could not possibly have proceeded from unkind feeling. For he says not; How is it supposable that one, who has been scourged and driven about, and ill-treated a thousand things for your sakes, should now have schemes against you ? But he argues from what they had reason to boast of, saying, How can one who has been honored by you, and received as an Angel, repay you by conduct the very opposite ?

Ver. 17. " They zealously seek you in no good way ; nay, they desire to shut you out that ye may seek them."

It is a wholesome emulation[3] which leads to an imitation of virtue, but an evil one, which seduces from virtue him who is in the right path. And this is the object of those persons, who would deprive you of perfect knowledge,[4] and impart to you that which is mutilated and spurious, and this for no other purpose than that they may occupy the rank of teachers, and degrade you, who now stand higher than themselves, to the position of disciples. For this is the meaning of the words " that ye may seek them." But I, says he, desire the reverse, that ye may become a model for them, and a pattern of a higher perfection : a thing which actually happened when I was present with you. Wherefore he adds,

Ver. 18. " But it is good to be zealously sought in a good matter at all times, and not only when I am present with you."

Here he hints that his absence had been the cause of this, and that the true blessing was for disciples to hold right opinions not only in the presence but also in the absence of their master. But as they had not arrived at this point of perfection, he makes every effort to place them there.

Ver. 19. "My little children,[5] of whom I am again in travail until Christ be formed in you."

Observe his perplexity and perturbation, " Brethren, I beseech you : " " My little children, of whom I am again in travail : " He resembles a mother trembling for her children. " Until Christ be formed in you." Behold his paternal tenderness, behold this despondency worthy of an Apostle. Observe what a wail he utters, far more piercing than of a woman in travail; —Ye have defaced the likeness, ye have destroyed the kinship, ye have changed the form, ye need

---

[1] [" ' Ye did me no wrong' probably means : I have no personal ground of complaint."—Schaff and Lightfoot.—G. A.]

[2] [" ' On account of some weakness of the flesh,' means he was compelled by reason of bodily weakness to make a stay there which did not form part of his plan, and during that forced sojourn he preached there."—Meyer.—G. A.]
" He was detained there by some bodily infirmity or sickness and was thus induced to preach the Gospel."—Schaff.—G. A.]

[3] [This word does not here mean " they vie with you," as Chrysostom interprets it, but " they zealously seek you or pay court to you," (1 Cor. xii : 31).—G. A.]

[4] [" They desire to shut you out" (not from a state of true knowledge, as Chrysostom interprets) but " from other teachers," anti-judaizing teachers, (according to Meyer) or from me (Paul) and so virtually from Christ Himself (according to Schaff) or from Christ (Lightfoot).—G. A.]

[5] [" A mode of address common in St. John but nowhere else found in St. Paul."—Lightfoot. " It expresses Paul's tenderness and their feebleness."—Schaff.—G. A.]

another regeneration and refashioning;[1] nevertheless I call you children, abortions and monsters though ye be. However, he does not express himself in this way, but spares them, unwilling to strike, and to inflict wound upon wound. Wise physicians do not cure those who have fallen into a long sickness all at once, but little by little, lest they should faint and die. And so is it with this blessed man; for these pangs were more severe in proportion as the force of his affection was stronger. And the offense was of no trivial kind. And as I have ever said and ever will say, even a slight fault mars the appearance and distorts the figure of the whole.

Ver. 20. " Yea, I could wish to be present with you now, and to change my voice."

Observe his warmth, his inability to refrain himself, and to conceal these his feelings; such is the nature of love; nor is he satisfied with words, but desires to be present with them, and so, as he says, to change his voice, that is, to change to lamentation, to shed tears, to turn every thing into mourning. For he could not by letter show his tears or cries of grief, and therefore he ardently desires to be present with them.

Ver. 20. " For I am perplexed about you."

I know not, says he, what to say, or what to think. How is it, that ye who by dangers, which ye endured for the faith's sake, and by miracles, which ye performed through faith, had ascended to the highest heaven, should suddenly be brought to such a depth of degradation as to be drawn aside to circumcision or sabbaths, and should rely wholly upon Judaizers? Hence in the beginning he says, "I marvel that ye are so quickly removing," and here, "I am perplexed about you," as if he said, What am I to speak? What am I to utter? What am I to think? I am bitterly perplexed. And so he must needs weep, as the prophets do when in perplexity; for not only admonition but mourning also is a form in which solicitous attention is often manifested. And what he said in his speech to those at Miletus, " By the space of three years I ceased not to warn every one... with tears," he says here also, " and to change my voice." (Acts xx: 31.) When we find ourselves overcome by perplexity and helplessness which come contrary to expectation, we are driven to tears; and so Paul admonished them sharply, and endeavored to shame them, then in turn soothed them, and lastly he wept. And this weeping is not only a reproof but a blandishment; it does not exasperate like reproof, nor

relax like indulgent treatment, but is a mixed remedy, and of great efficacy in the way of exhortation. Having thus softened and powerfully engaged their hearts by his tears, he again advances to the contest,[2] and lays down a larger propostion, proving that the Law itself was opposed to its being kept. Before, he produced the example of Abraham, but now (what is more cogent) he brings forward the Law itself enjoining them not to keep itself, but to leave off. So that, says he, you must abandon the Law, if you would obey it, for this is its own wish: this however he does not say expressly, but enforces it in another mode, mixing up with it an account of facts.

Ver. 21. " Tell me," he says, " ye that desire to be under the Law, do ye not hear the Law?"[3]

He says rightly, " ye that desire," for the matter was not one of a proper and orderly succession of things but of their own unseasonable contentiousness. It is the Book of Creation which he here calls the Law, which name he often gives to the whole Old Testament.

Ver. 22. " For it is written, (Gen. xv: 16.) that Abraham had two sons, one by the handmaid and the other by the freewoman."

He returns again to Abraham, not in the way of repetition, but, inasmuch as the Patriarch's fame was great among the Jews, to show that the types had their origin from thence, and that present events were pictured aforetime in him. Having previously shown that the Galatians were sons of Abraham, now, in that the Patriarch's sons were not of equal dignity, one being by a bondwoman, the other by a freewoman, he shows that they were not only his sons, but sons in the same sense as he that was freeborn and noble. Such is the power of Faith.

Ver. 23. " Howbeit the son by the handmaid is born after the flesh; but the son by the freewoman is born through promise."

What is the meaning of " after the flesh?" Having said that Faith united us to Abraham, and it having seemed incredible to his hearers, that those who were not begotten by Abraham should be called his sons, he proves that this paradox had actually happened long ago; for that Isaac, born not according to the order of nature, nor the law of marriage, nor the power of the flesh, was yet truly his own son. He was the issue of bodies that were dead, and of a womb that was dead; his conception was not by the flesh, nor his birth by the seed, for the womb was dead both through age and barren-

---

[1] ["I travailed with you once in bringing you to Christ. By your relapse you have renewed a mother's pangs in me."—Lightfoot.
"'Until Christ be formed in you,' is not an inversion of the metaphor he has begun with, but means, 'till you have taken the form of Christ as the embryo develops into the child.'"—Lightfoot.—G. A.]

[2] [The digression which contains his "affectionate appeal" (see note above) ends with verse 20, after which he resumes.—G. A.]
[3] [" The Apostle resumes his argument for the superiority of the Gospel over the Law and illustrates the difference of the two by an allegorical interpretation of the history of Hagar and Sarah."—Schaff.—G. A.]

ness, but the Word of God fashioned Him. Not so in the case of the bondman; He came by virtue of the laws of nature, and after the manner of marriage. Nevertheless, he that was not according to the flesh was more honorable than he that was born after the flesh. Therefore let it not disturb you that ye are not born after the flesh; for from the very reason that ye are not so born, are ye most of all Abraham's kindred. The being born after the flesh renders one not more honorable, but less so, for a birth not after the flesh is more marvellous and more spiritual. And this is plain from the case of those who were born of old time; Ishmael, for instance, who was born according to the flesh, was not only a bondman, but was cast out of his father's house; but Isaac, who was born according to the promise, being a true son and free, was lord of all.

Ver. 24. "Which things contain an allegory."[1]

Contrary to usage, he calls a type an allegory; his meaning is as follows; this history not only declares that which appears on the face of it, but announces somewhat farther, whence it is called an allegory. And what hath it announced? no less than all the things now present.

Ver. 24. "For these women" he says, "are two covenants; one from mount Sinai, bearing children unto bondage, which is Hagar."

"These:" who? the mothers of those children, Sarah and Hagar; and what are they? Two covenants, two laws. As the names of the women were given in the history, he abides by this designation of the two races, showing how much follows from the very names. How from the names?

Ver. 25. "Now this Hagar is Mount Sinai in Arabia:"

The bond-woman was called Hagar, and "Hagar" is the word for Mount Sinai in the language of that country.[2] So that it is necessary that all who are born of the Old Covenant should be bondmen, for that mountain where the Old Covenant was delivered hath a name in common with the bondwoman. And it includes Jerusalem, for this is the meaning of,

Ver. 25. "And answereth to Jerusalem that now is."

That is, it borders on, and is contiguous to it.[3]

Ver. 25. "For she is in bondage with her children."

What follows from hence? Not only that she was in bondage and brought forth bondmen, but that this Covenant is so too, whereof the bondwoman was a type. For Jerusalem is adjacent to the mountain of the same name with the bondwoman, and in this mountain the Covenant was delivered. Now where is the type of Sarah?

Ver. 26. "But Jerusalem that is above is free."

Those therefore, who are born of her are not bondmen. Thus the type of the Jerusalem below was Hagar, as is plain from the mountain being so called; but of that which is above is the Church. Nevertheless he is not content with these types, but adds the testimony of Isaiah to what he has spoken. Having said that Jerusalem which is above "is our Mother," and having given that name to the Church, he cites the suffrage of the Prophet in his favor,

Ver. 27. "Rejoice, thou barren that bearest not, break forth and cry, thou that travailest not, for more are the children of the desolate than of her which hath the husband." (Isa. liv: 1.)

Who is this who before was "barren," and "desolate?" Clearly it is the Church of the Gentiles,[4] that was before deprived of the knowledge of God? Who, "she which hath the husband?" plainly the Synagogue. Yet the barren woman surpassed her in the number of her children, for the other embraces one nation, but the children of the Church have filled the country of the Greeks and of the Barbarians, the earth and sea, the whole habitable world. Observe how Sarah by acts, and the Prophet by words, have described the events about to befal us. Observe too, that he whom Isaiah called barren, Paul hath proved to have many children, which also happened typically in the case of Sarah. For she too, although barren, became the mother of a numerous progeny. This however does not suffice Paul, but he carefully follows out the mode whereby the barren woman became a mother, that in this particular likewise the type might harmonize with the truth. Wherefore he adds

---

[1] ["The story of Hagar and Sarah has another (namely a figurative, typical) meaning besides (not instead of) the literal or historical. Paul does not deny the fact but makes it the bearer of a general idea which was more fully expressed in two covenants. He uses allegorical here in a sense similar to the word "typical" in 1 Cor x: 11."—Schaff.—G. A.]
[See on this difficult passage Schaff's *Excursus in Com.* and Lightfoot's *Excursus* xiii. *Com.* p. 368.—G. A.]
[2] [So Meyer: "In Arabia the name Hagar (τὸ Ἅγαρ) signifies Mt. Sinai." But Schaff says: "It cannot be satisfactorily proven that the name Hagar was an Arabic designation for Mt. Sinai, as the testimonies of Chrysostom and the traveler Harant are isolated and unconfirmed. The shorter reading, 'For Sinai is a mountain in Arabia' (τὸ γὰρ Σινᾶ ὄρος ἐστίν ἐν τῇ Ἀραβίᾳ) given by the Sinaitic and other MSS. and preferred by Lachmann, Tischendorf and Lightfoot (*Excursus* p. 361 of *Com.*) is quite intelligible and easily gives rise to the longer reading."—G. A.]

[3] ["This interpretation of Chrysostom is hardly the right one. The subject of συνστοιχεῖ is Hagar and not Mt. Sinai—a view which runs counter to the context. It means that Hagar belongs to the same category with the present Jerusalem, is like it in that she was a bondwoman as Jerusalem with its children is also in bondage." Meyer.—G. A.]
[4] ["Against this view of Chrysostom it may be urged that ἥτις ἐστὶ μήτηρ ἡμῶν (which is our mother) is proved by (γὰρ). The passage of the O. T. quoted in v. 27 and the ἡμῶν includes 'all' Christians."—Meyer. (See his long and good note *in loc.*)—G. A.]

Ver. 28. "Now we, brethren, as Isaac was, are children of promise."

It is not merely that the Church was barren like Sarah, or became a mother of many children like her, but she bore them in the way Sarah did. As it was not nature but the promise of God which rendered Sarah a mother, [for the word of God which said, "At the time appointed I will return unto thee, and Sarah shall have a son," (Gen. xviii: 14.) this entered into the womb and formed the babe,] so also in our regeneration it is not nature, but the Words of God spoken by the Priest,[1] (the faithful know them,) which in the Bath of water as in a sort of womb, form and regenerate him who is baptized.

Wherefore if we are sons of the barren woman, then are we free. But what kind of freedom, it might be objected, is this, when the Jews seize and scourge the believers, and those who have this pretence of liberty are persecuted ? for these things then occurred, in the persecution of the faithful. Neither let this disturb you, he replies, this also is anticipated in the type, for Isaac, who was free, was persecuted by Ishmael the bondman. Wherefore he adds,

Ver. 29, 30. "But as then he that was born after the flesh persecuted him that was born after the Spirit, even so it is now. Howbeit what saith the Scripture? (Gen. xxi: 10.) Cast out the handmaid and her son : for the son of the handmaid shall not inherit with the son of the freewoman."

What ! does all this consolation consist in showing that freemen are persecuted by bondmen ? By no means, he says, I do not stop here, listen to what follows, and then, if you be not pusillanimous under persecution, you will be sufficiently comforted. And what is it that follows? "Cast out the son of the handmaid, for he shall not inherit with the son of the freewoman." Behold the reward of tyranny for a season, and of reckleness out of season ! the son is cast out of his father's house, and becomes,

together with his mother, an exile and a wanderer. And consider too the wisdom of the remark ; for he says not that he was cast forth merely because he persecuted, but that he should not be heir. For this punishment was not exacted ׃rom him on account of his temporary persecution, (for that would have been of little moment, and nothing to the point,) but he was not suffered to participate in the inheritance provided for the son. And this proves that, putting the persecution aside, this very thing had been typified from the beginning, and did not originate in the persecution, but in the purpose of God. Nor does he say, "the son of Abraham shall not be heir," but, "the son of the handmaid," distinguishing him by his inferior descent. Now Sarah was barren, and so is the Gentile Church ;[2] observe how the type is preserved in every particular, as the former, through all the by-gone years, conceived not, and in extreme old age became a mother, so the latter, when the fulness of time is come, brings forth. And this the prophets have proclaimed, saying, "Rejoice, thou barren that bearest not ; break forth and cry, thou that travailest not ; for more are the children of the desolate than of her which hath the husband." And hereby they intend the Church ; for she knew not God, but as soon as she knew Him, she surpassed the fruitful synagogue.[3]

Ver. 31. "Wherefore, brethren, we are not children of a handmaid but of the freewoman."

He turns and discusses this on all sides, desiring to prove that what had taken place was no novelty, but had been before typified many ages ago. How then can it be otherwise than absurd for those who had been set apart so long and who had obtained freedom, willingly to subject themselves to the yoke of bondage?

Next he states another inducement to them to abide in his doctrine.

---

[1] ["Chrysostom assumes the prevailing conception of a real priesthood and sacrifice, baptismal regeneration, etc."—Schaff, *Prolegomena*, p. 8.—G. A.]

[2] [See note above on this interpretation.—G. A.]

[3] ["Before the emergence of the Christian people of God, the heavenly Jerusalem was still unpeopled, childless, στεῖρα, 'barren,' οὐ τίκτουσα 'not bearing,' and so like Sarah before she became the mother of Isaac. But with the emergence of the Christian people of God this heavenly Jerusalem has become a fruitful mother richer in children than the Jerusalem that now is."—Meyer.—G. A.]

CHAPTER V

"With freedom did Christ set us free; stand fast therefore.[1]"

HAVE ye wrought your own deliverance, that ye run back again to the dominion ye were under before? It is Another who hath redeemed you, it is Another who hath paid the ransom for you. Observe in how many ways he leads them away from the error of Judaism; by showing, first, that it was the extreme of folly for those, who had become free instead of slaves, to desire to become slaves instead of free; secondly, that they would be convicted of neglect and ingratitude to their Benefactor, in despising Him who had delivered, and loving him who had enslaved them; thirdly, that it was impossible. For Another having once for all redeemed all of us from it, the Law ceases to have any sway. By the word, "stand fast," he indicates their vacillation.

Ver. 1. "And be not entangled again in a yoke of bondage."

By the word "yoke" he signifies to them the burdensomeness of such a course, and by the word "again" he points out their utter senselessness. Had ye never experienced this burden, ye would not have deserved so severe a censure, but for you who by trial have learnt how irksome this yoke is, again to subject yourself to it, is justly unpardonable.

Ver. 2. "Behold, I Paul say unto you, that if ye receive circumcision, Christ will profit you nothing."

Lo, what a threat! reasonably then did he anathematize even angels. How then shall Christ profit them nothing? for he has not supported this by argument, but only declared it, the credence due to his authority, compensating, as it were, for all subsequent proof. Wherefore he sets out by saying, "Behold, I Paul say unto you," which is the expression of one who has confidence in what he asserts. We will subjoin what we can ourselves as to how Christ shall profit nothing them who are circumcised.

He that is circumcised is circumcised for fear of the Law, and he who fears the Law, distrusts the power of grace, and he who distrusts can receive no benefit from that which is distrusted. Or again thus, he that is circumcised makes the Law of force; but thus considering it to be of force and yet transgressing it in the greater part while keeping it in the lesser, he puts himself again under the curse. But how can he be saved who submits himself to the curse, and repels the liberty which is of Faith? If one may say what seems a paradox, such an one believes neither Christ nor the Law, but stands between them, desiring to benefit both by one and the other, whereas he will reap fruit from neither. Having said that Christ shall profit them nothing, he lays down the proof[2] of it shortly and sententiously, thus:

Ver. 3. "Yea, I testify again[3] to every man that receiveth circumcision that he is a debtor to do the whole Law."

That you may not suppose that this is spoken from ill-will[4], I say not to you alone, he says, but to every one who receiveth circumcision, that he is a debtor to do the whole Law. The parts of the Law are linked one to the other. As he who from being free has enrolled himself as a slave, no longer does what he pleases, but is bound by all the laws of slavery, so in the case of the Law, if you take upon you a small portion of it, and submit to the yoke, you draw down upon yourself its whole domination. And so it is in a worldly inheritance: he who touches no part of it, is free from all matters which are consequent on the heirship to the deceased, but if he takes a small portion, though not the whole, yet by that part he has rendered himself liable for every thing. And this occurs in the Law,

---

[1] [The text of this verse is not settled. The *textus receptus* has τῇ ἐλευθερίᾳ οὖν ᾗ χριστὸς ἡμᾶς ἠλευθέρωσε στήκετε, etc. Chrysostom has τῇ γὰρ ἐλευθερίᾳ ᾗ χριστὸς ὑμᾶς ἐξηγόρασε, στήκετε, etc. W. & H. have τῇ ἐλευθερίᾳ ἡμᾶς χριστὸς ἠλευθέρωσεν στήκετε οὖν καί, etc., with Aleph, A. B. C. Rev. Ver.
But W. & H. suspect there is some primitive error. Lightfoot joins τῇ ἐλευθερίᾳ with τῆς ἐλευθέρας of the preceding verse and retains the relative ᾗ, making it read; We are sons of the free woman with the freedom wherewith Christ freed us. *Com. in loc.* and *Excursus* p. 371.

[2] [The following verse does not introduce proof that Christ shall profit them nothing, but leads on to more detailed information and so is introduced by δέ, *autem*. So Meyer; though Lightfoot makes δέ adversative to the idea of ὠφελήσει, and so Ellicott. Rev. Ver. agrees with Meyer's view.—G. A.]

[3] [" Again refers to 'I say' in preceding sentences." Schaff, Lightfoot, Ellicott. Meyer says, "It calls to the remembrance of his readers his last presence," (second visit.)—G. A.]

[4] [" 'To every man' stands in a climactic relation to foregoing ὑμῖν remorselessly embracing all; that no one may think himself excluded. Hence Chrysostom's view is wrong."—Meyer.—G. A.]

not only in the way I have mentioned, but in another also, for Legal observances are linked together. For example; Circumcision has sacrifice connected with it, and the observance of days; sacrifice again has the observance both of day and of place; place has the details of endless purifications; purifications involve a perfect swarm of manifold observances. For it is unlawful for the unclean to sacrifice, to enter the holy shrines, to do any other such act. Thus the Law introduces many things even by the one commandment. If then thou art circumcised, but not on the eighth day, or on the eighth day, but no sacrifice is offered, or a sacrifice is offered, but not in the prescribed place, or in the prescribed place, but not the accustomed objects, or if the accustomed objects, but thou be unclean, or if clean yet not purified by proper rules, every thing is frustrated. Wherefore[1] he says, "that he is a debtor to the the whole Law." Fulfil not a part, but the whole, if the Law is of force; but if it be not of force, not even a part.

Ver. 4. "Ye are severed from Christ, ye who would be justified by the Law; ye are fallen away from grace."

Having established his point, he at length declares their danger of the severest punishment. When a man recurs to the Law, which cannot save him, and falls from grace, what remains but an inexorable retribution, the Law being powerless, and grace rejecting him?

Thus having aggravated their alarm, and disquieted their mind, and shown them all the shipwreck they were about to suffer, he opens to them the haven of grace which was near at hand. This is ever his wont, and he shows that in this quarter salvation is easy and secure, subjoining the words,

Ver. 5. "For we through the Spirit by faith wait for the hope of righteousness."[2]

We need none of those legal observances, he says; faith suffices to obtain for us the Spirit, and by Him righteousness, and many and great benefits.

Ver. 6. "For in Jesus Christ neither circumcision availeth any thing, nor uncircumcision;[3] but faith working through love."

Observe the great boldness with which he now encounters them; Let him that hath put on Christ, he says, no longer be careful about such matters. Having before said that Circumcision was hurtful, how is it that he now considers it indifferent? It is indifferent as to those who

had it previously to the Faith, but not as to those who are circumcised after the Faith was given. Observe too the view in which he places it, by setting it by the side of Uncircumcision; it is Faith that makes the difference. As in the selection of wrestlers, whether they be hook-nosed or flat-nosed, black or white, is of no importance in their trial, it is only necessary to seek that they be strong and skilful; so all these bodily accidents do not injure one who is to be enrolled under the New Covenant, nor does their presence assist him.

What is the meaning of "working through love?"[4] Here he gives them a hard blow, by showing that this error had crept in because the love of Christ had not been rooted within them. For to believe is not all that is required, but also to abide in love. It is as if he had said, Had ye loved Christ as ye ought, ye would not have deserted to bondage, nor abandoned Him who redeemed you, nor treated with contumely Him who gave you freedom. Here he also hints at those who have plotted against them, implying that they would not have dared to do so, had they felt affection towards them. He wishes too by these words to correct their course of life.

Ver. 7. "Ye were running well; who did hinder you?[5]

This is not an interrogation, but an expression of doubt and sorrow. How hath such a course been cut short? who hath been able to do this? ye who were superior to all and in the rank of teachers, have not even continued in the position of disciples. What has happened? who could do this? these are rather the words of one who is exclaiming and lamenting, as he said before, "Who did bewitch you?" (Gal. iii: 1.)

Ver. 8. "This persuasion came not of him that calleth you."

He who called you, called you not to such fluctuations, he did not lay down a Law, that you should judaize. Then, that no one might object, "Why do you thus magnify and aggravate the matter by your words; one commandment only of the Law have we kept, and yet you make this great outcry?" hear how he terrifies them, not by things present but future in these words:

Ver. 7. "A little leaven leaveneth the whole lump."

And thus this slight error, he says, if not cor-

---

[1] [Perhaps Paul's reason for his statement that every one who suffers himself to be circumcised is a debtor to keep the whole Law is this Scripture which he quotes in iii: 10: Cursed is he that continueth not in all the things that are written etc.—G. A.]

[2] [" The Holy Spirit is the divine ' agent ' and faith is the subjective ' source ' of our expectation."—Meyer,—G. A.]

[3] [" Circumcision and uncircumcision are circumstances of no effect or avail in Christianity; and yet they were in Galatia the points on which the disturbance turned,"—Meyer,—G. A.]

[4] [" How necessary it was for the Galatians that prominence should be given to the activity of faith ' in love ' may be seen from verses 15, 20, 26. The passive view of ἐνεργουμένη (wrought through love) as held by some Fathers and by Catholics is erroneous. In New Test. ἐνεργεῖσθαι is always middle:' faith 'which is operative through love."—Meyer.—G. A.]

Lightfoot says: " The words δι ἀγάπης ενεργουμένη bridge over the gulf which seems to separate the language of St. Paul and St. James. Both assert a principle of practical energy as opposed to a barren theory."—G. A.]

[5] [The words ἀληθεία μὴ πείθεσθαί are wanting in Chysostom's text.—G. A.]

rected, will have power (as the leaven has with the lump) to lead you into complete Judaism.

Ver. 10. "I have confidence to you-ward in the Lord, that ye will be none otherwise minded."

He does not say, "ye are not minded," but, "ye will not be minded;" that is, you will be set right. And how does he know this? he says not "I know," but "I trust in God, and invoking His aid in order to your correction, I am in hopes;" and he says, not merely, "I have confidence in the Lord," but, "I have confidence towards you in the Lord." Every where he connects complaint with his praises; here it is as if he had said, I know my disciples, I know your readiness to be set right. I have good hopes, partly because of the Lord who suffers nothing, however trival, to perish, partly because of you who are quickly to recover yourselves. At the same time he exhorts them to use diligence on their own parts, it not being possible to obtain aid from God, if our own efforts are not contributed.

Ver. 10. "But he that troubleth you shall bear his judgment, whosoever he be."

Not only by words of encouragement, but by uttering a curse or a prophecy against their teachers, he applies to them an incentive. And observe that he never mentions the name of these plotters, that they might not become more shameless. His meaning is as follows. Not because "ye will be none otherwise minded," are the authors of your seduction relieved from punishment. They shall be punished; for it is not proper that the good conduct of the one should become an encouragement to the evil disposition of the other. This is said that they might not make a second attempt upon others. And he says not merely, "he that troubleth," but, "whosoever he be," in the way of aggravation.

Ver. 11. "But I, brethren, if I still preach circumcision, why am I still persecuted?"

Observe how clearly he exonerates himself from the charge,[1] that in every place he judaized and played the hypocrite in his preaching. Of this he calls them as witnesses; for ye know, he says, that my command to abandon the Law was made the pretext for persecuting me. "If I still preach circumcision, why am I still persecuted? for this is the only charge which they of the Jewish descent have to bring against me. Had I permitted them to receive the Faith, still retaining the customs of their fathers, neither believers nor unbelievers would have laid snares for me, seeing that none of their own usages

were disturbed. What then! did he not preach circumcision? did he not circumcise Timothy? Truly he did. How then can he say, "I preach it not?" Here observe his accuracy; he says not, "I do not perform circumcision," but, "I preach it not," that is, I do not bid men so to believe. Do not therefore consider it any confirmation of your doctrine, for though I circumcised, I did not preach circumcision.

Ver. 11. "Then hath the stumbling block of the cross been done away."

That is, if this which ye assert be true, the obstacle, the hindrance, is removed; for not even the Cross was so great an offence to the Jews, as the doctrine that their father's customs ought not to be obeyed. When they brought Stephen before the council, they said not that this man adores the Crucified, but that he speaks "against this holy place and the Law." (Acts vi : 13.) And it was of this they accused Jesus, that He broke the Law. Wherefore Paul says, If Circumcision be conceded, the strife you are involved in is appeased; hereafter no enmity to the Cross and our preaching remains. But why do they bring this charge against us, while waiting day after day to murder us? it is because I brought an uncircumcised man into the Temple (Acts xxi : 29.) that they fell upon me. Am I then, he says, so senseless, after giving up the point of Circumcision, vainly and idly to expose myself to such injuries, and to place such a stumbling-block before the Cross? For ye observe, that they attack us for nothing with such vehemence as about Circumcision. Am I then so senseless as to suffer affliction for nothing at all, and to give offence to others? He calls it the offence of the Cross, because it was enjoined by the doctrine of the Cross; and it was this which principally offended the Jews, and hindered their reception of the Cross, namely, the command to abandon the usages of their fathers.

Ver. 12. "I would that they which unsettle you, would even cut themselves off."

Observe how bitterly he speaks here against their deceivers.[2] At the outset he directed his charge against those who were deceived, and called them foolish, once and again. Now, having sufficiently corrected and instructed them, he turns to their deceivers. And you should remark his wisdom in the manner in which he

---

[1] ["The false teachers had spread the malicious report that Paul himself preached circumcision because he practiced it in the case of Timothy. But this was a measure of expediency and charity and not a surrender of principle."—Schaff.

[2] "This calumny was sufficiently absurd to admit of his dismissing it, as he does here, with all brevity and with what a striking experimental proof!"—Meyer.—G. A.]

[2] ["The vivid realization of the doings of his opponents, who were not ashamed to resort even to such falsehood, now wrings from his soul a strong and bitterly sarcastic wish of holy indignation."—Meyer.

Paul wishes that the circumcisers would not stop with circumcision but go beyond it to mutilation (make themselves eunuchs) like the priests of Cybele. A severe irony and similar to the one in Phil. iii: 2, 3, where Paul calls the boasters of circumcision "the Concision." Self mutilation was a recognized form of heathen worship especially in Pessinus in Galatia and therefore quite familiar to the readers. Thus by their glorying in the flesh the Galatians relapsed into their former heathenism,—Schaff and Lightfoot. The Revised Version here has, "would even cut themselves off," the American Committee has, "would go beyond circumcision —G. A.]

admonishes and chastens the former as his own children, and as capable of receiving correction, but their deceivers he cuts off, as aliens and incurably depraved. And this he does, partly, when he says, "he shall bear his judgment whosoever he be;" partly when he utters the imprecation against them, "I would that they which unsettle you would even cut themselves off." And he says well "that unsettle you." For they had compelled them to abandon their own fatherland, their liberty, and their heavenly kindred, and to seek an alien and foreign one; they had cast them out of Jerusalem which is above and free, and compelled them to wander forth as captives and emigrants. On this account he curses them; and his meaning is as follows, For them I have no concern, "A man that is heretical after the first and second admonition refuse." (Tit. iii: 10) If they will, let them not only be circumcised, but mutilated. Where then are those who dare to mutilate themselves [1]; seeing that they draw down the Apostolic curse, and accuse the workmanship of God, and take part with the Manichees? For the latter call the body a treacherous thing, and from the evil principle; and the former by their acts give countenance to these wretched doctrines, cutting off the member as being hostile and treacherous. Ought they not much rather to put out the eyes, for it is through the eyes that 'desire enters the soul? But in truth neither the eye nor any other part of us is to blame, but the depraved will only. But if you will not allow this, why do you not mutilate the tongue for blasphemy, the hands for rapine, the feet for their evil courses, in short, the whole body? For the ear enchanted by the sound of a flute hath often enervated the soul; and the perception of a sweet perfume by the nostrils hath bewitched the mind, and made it frantic for pleasure. Yet this would be extreme wickedness and satanic madness. The evil spirit, ever delighting in slaughter, hath seduced them to crush the instrument, as if its Maker had erred, whereas it was only necessary to correct the unruly passion of the soul. How then does it happen, one may say, that when the body is pampered, lust is inflamed? Observe here too that it is the sin of the soul, for to pamper the flesh is not an act of the flesh but of the soul, for if the soul choose to mortify it, it would possess absolute power over it. But what you do is just the same as if one seeing a man lighting a fire, and heaping on fuel, and setting fire to a house, were to blame the fire, instead of him who kindled it, because it had caught this heap of fuel, and risen to a great height. Yet the blame

would attach not to the fire but to the one who kindled it; for it was given for the purpose of dressing food, affording light, and other like ministries, not for burning houses. In like manner desire is implanted for the rearing of families and the ensuring of life, not for adultery, or fornication, or lasciviousness; that a man may become a father, not an adulterer; a lawful husband, not a seducer; leaving heirs after him, not doing damage to another man's. For adultery arises not from nature, but from wantonness against nature, which prescribes the use not the misuse. These remarks I have not made at random, but as a prelude to a dispute, as skirmishing against those who assert that the workmanship of God is evil, and who neglecting the sloth of the soul, madly inveigh against the body, and traduce our flesh, whereof Paul afterwards discourses, accusing not the flesh, but devilish thoughts.

Ver. 13. "For ye, brethren, were called for freedom; only use not your freedom for an occasion to the flesh."

Henceforward he appears to digress[2] into a moral discourse, but in a new manner, which does not occur in any other of his Epistles. For all of them are divided into two parts, and in the first he discusses doctrine, in the last the rule of life, but here, after having entered upon the moral discourse, he again unites with it the doctrinal part. For this passage has reference to doctrine in the controversy with the Manichees.[3] What is the meaning of, "Use not your freedom for an occasion to the flesh?" Christ hath delivered us, he says, from the yoke of bondage, He hath left us free to act as we will, not that we may use our liberty for evil, but that we may have ground for receiving a higher reward, advancing to a higher philosophy. Lest any one should suspect, from his calling the Law over and over again a yoke of bondage, and a bringing on of the curse, that his object in enjoining an abandonment of the Law, was that one might live lawlessly, he corrects this notion, and states his object to be, not that our course of life might be lawless, but that our philosophy might surpass the Law. For the bonds of the Law are broken, and I say this not that our standard may be lowered, but that it may be exalted. For both he who commits fornication, and he who leads a virgin life, pass the bounds of the Law, but not in the same direction; the one is led away to the worse, the other is elevated to the better; the one transgresses the Law, the other transcends it.

---

[1] ['Αποκόπτειν ἑαυτούς. Chrysostom here, as often, "goes off at a word" into a digression on a subject which is only remotely suggested by the passage in hand.—G. A.]

[2] [This is not a digression. It is in strict continuity with the preceeding context and gives a reason for the indignant expression of the foregoing sentence.
"They are defeating the very purpose of your calling: ye were called for liberty and not for bondage."—Lightfoot.—G. A.]

[3] [On the doctrine of the Manichees see Schaff *Church History* vol. ii. p. 498–508, where a full account of the literature is given also.—G. A.]

Thus Paul says that Christ hath removed the yoke from you, not that ye may prance and kick, but that though without the yoke ye may proceed at a well-measured pace. And next he shows the mode whereby this may be readily effected; and what is this mode? he says,

Ver. 13. "But through love be servants one to another." [1]

Here again he hints that strife and party-spirit, love of rule and presumptuousness, had been the causes of their error, for the desire of rule is the mother of heresies. By saying, "Be servants one to another," he shows that the evil had arisen from this presumptuous and arrogant spirit, and therefore he applies a corresponding remedy. As your divisions arose from your desire to domineer over each other, "serve one another;" thus will ye be reconciled again. However, he does not openly express their fault, but he openly tells them its corrective, that through this they may become aware of that; as if one were not to tell an immodest person of his immodesty, but were continually to exhort him to chastity. He that loves his neighbor as he ought, declines not to be servant to him more humbly than any servant. As fire, brought into contact with wax, easily softens it, so does the warmth of love dissolve all arrogance and presumption more powerfully than fire. Wherefore he says not, "love one another," merely, but, "be servants one to another," thus signifying the intensity of the affection. When the yoke of the Law was taken off them that they might not caper off and away another was laid on, that of love, stronger than the former, yet far lighter and pleasanter; and, to point out the way to obey it, he adds;

Ver. 14. "For the whole law is fulfilled in one word, even in this; Thou shalt love thy neighbor as thyself."

Seeing that they made so much of the Law, he says, "If you you wish to fulfill it, do not be circumcised, for it is fulfilled not in circumcision but in love." Observe how he cannot forget his grief, but constantly touches upon what troubled him, even when launched into his moral discourse.

Ver. 15. "But if ye bite and devour one another, take heed that ye be not consumed one of another."

That he may not distress them, he does not assert this, though he knew it was the case,[2] but mentions it ambiguously. For he does not say, "Inasmuch as ye bite one another," nor again does he assert, in the clause following, that they shall be consumed by each other; but "take heed that ye be not consumed one of another," and this is the language of apprehension and warning, not of condemnation. And the words which he uses are expressly significant; he says not merely, "ye bite," which one might do in a passion, but also "ye devour," which implies a bearing of malice. To bite is to satisfy the feeling of anger, but to devour is a proof of the most savage ferocity. The biting and devouring he speaks of are not bodily, but of a much more cruel kind; for it is not such an injury to taste the flesh of man, as to fix one's fangs in his soul. In proportion as the soul is more precious than the body, is damage to it more serious. "Take heed that ye be not consumed one of another." For those who commit injury and lay plots, do so in order to destroy others; therefore he says, Take heed that this evil fall not on your own heads. For strife and dissensions are the ruin and destruction as well of those who admit as of those who introduce them, and eats out every thing worse than a moth does.

Ver. 16. "But I say, Walk by the Spirit, and ye shall not fulfil the lust of the flesh."

Here he points out another[3] path which makes duty easy, and secures what had been said, a path whereby love is generated, and which is fenced in by love. For nothing, nothing I say, renders us so susceptible of love, as to be spiritual, and nothing is such an inducement to the Spirit to abide in us, as the strength of love. Therefore he says, " Walk by the Spirit and ye shall not fulfil the lust of the flesh:" having spoken of the cause of the disease, he likewise mentions the remedy which confers health. And what is this, what is the destruction of the evils we have spoken of, but the life in the Spirit? hence he says, "Walk by the Spirit and ye shall not fulfil the lust of the flesh."

Ver. 17. "For the flesh lusteth against the Spirit, and the Spirit against the flesh, for these are contrary the one to the other: that ye may not do the things that ye would."

Here some make the charge that the Apostle has divided man into two parts, and that he states the essence of which he is compounded to be conflicting with itself, and that the body has a contest with the soul. But this is not so, most certainly; for by "the flesh," he does not mean the body; if he did, what would be the sense of the clause immediately following, "for it lusteth," he says, "against the Spirit?" yet the body moves not, but is moved, is not an agent, but is acted upon. How then does it

---

[1] ["An ingenious juxtaposition of 'freedom' and brotherly 'service' in that freedom."—Meyer.
Ye were called for 'freedom,' but through love make yourselves willing 'bond-servants' to each other."—.G A.]
[2] [See Lightfoot, Introduction, p. 39. Note 3.—G. A.]

[3] [" Paul returns to the warning in ver. 13, not to abuse their freedom for an occasion to the 'flesh' "—Schaff.
" In verse 13 he had warned them against using liberty for an occasion to the 'flesh'; now, ver. 16, he shows them how they are to accomplish that end and this introduces the deadly and interminable antagonism between the spirit and the flesh."—Lightfoot.—G. A.]

lust, for lust belongs to the soul not to the body, for in another place it is said, "My soul longeth," (Ps. lxxx iv: 2.) and, "Whatsoever thy soul desireth, I will even do it for thee," (1 Sam. xx: 4.) and, "Walk not according to the desires of thy heart," and, "So panteth my soul." (Ps. xlii: 1.) Wherefore then does Paul say, "the flesh lusteth against the Spirit?" he is wont to call the flesh, not the natural body but the depraved will, as where he says, "But ye are not in the flesh, but in the Spirit," (Rom. viii: 8, 9.) and again, "They that are in the flesh cannot please God." What then? Is the flesh to be destroyed? was not he who thus spoke clothed with flesh? such doctrines are not of the flesh, but from the Devil, for "he was a murderer from the beginning." (John viii: 44.) What then is his meaning? it is the earthly mind, slothful and careless, that he here calls the flesh, and this is not an accusation of the body, but a charge against the slothful soul. The flesh is an instrument, and no one feels aversion and hatred to an instrument, but to him who abuses it. For it is not the iron instrument but the murderer, whom we hate and punish. But it may be said that the very calling of the faults of the soul by the name of the flesh is in itself an accusation of the body. And I admit that the flesh is inferior to the soul, yet it too is good, for that which is inferior to what is good may itself be good, but evil is not inferior to good, but opposed to it. Now if you are able to prove to me that evil originates from the body, you are at liberty to accuse it; but if your endeavor is to turn its name into a charge against it, you ought to accuse the soul likewise. For he that is deprived of the truth is called "the natural man." (1 Cor. 11: 14.)[1] and the race of demons "the spirits of wickedness." (Eph. vi: 12.)

Again, the Scripture is wont to give the name of the Flesh to the Mysteries of the Eucharist, and to the whole Church, calling them the Body of Christ. (Col. i: 24.) Nay, to induce you to give the name of blessings to the things of which the flesh is the medium, you have only to imagine the extinction of the senses, and you will find the soul deprived of all discernment, and ignorant of what it before knew. For if the power of God is since "the creation of the world clearly seen, being perceived through the things that are made," (Rom. i: 20.) how could we see them without eyes? and if "faith cometh of hearing," (Rom. x: 17.) how shall we hear without ears? and preaching depends on making circuits wherein the tongue and feet are employed. "For how shall they preach, except they be sent?" (Rom. x: 15.) In the same way writing is performed by means of the hands. Do you not see that the ministry of the

flesh produces for us a thousand benefits? In his expression, "the flesh lusteth against the Spirit," he means two mental states. For these are opposed to each other, namely virtue and vice, not the soul and the body. Were the two latter so opposed they would be destructive of one another, as fire of water, and darkness of light. But if the soul cares for the body, and takes great forethought on its account, and suffers a thousand things in order not to leave it, and resists being separated from it, and if the body too ministers to the soul, and conveys to it much knowledge, and is adapted to its operations, how can they be contrary, and conflicting with each other? For my part, I perceive by their acts that they are not only not contrary but closely accordant and attached one to another. It is not therefore of these that he speaks as opposed to each other, but he refers to the contest of bad and good principles. (Compare Rom. vii: 23.) To will and not to will belongs to the soul; wherefore he says, "these are contrary the one to the other," that you may not suffer the soul to proceed in its evil desires. For he speaks this like a Master and Teacher in a threatening way.

Ver. 18. "But if ye are led by the Spirit, ye are not under the Law."[2]

If it be asked in what way are these two connected, I answer, closely and plainly; for he that hath the Spirit as he ought, quenches thereby every evil desire, and he that is released from these needs no help from the Law, but is exalted far above its precepts. He who is never angry, what need has he to hear the command, Thou shalt not kill? He who never casts unchaste looks, what need hath he of the admonition, Thou shalt not commit adultery? Who would discourse about the fruits of wickedness with him who had plucked up the root itself? for anger is the root of murder, and of adultery the inquisitive gazing into faces. Hence he says, "If ye are led by the Spirit, ye are not under the Law;" wherein he appears to me to have pronounced a high and striking eulogy of the Law, if, at least, the Law stood, according to its power, in the place of the Spirit before the Spirit's coming upon us. But we are not on that account obliged to continue apart with our schoolmaster. Then we were justly subject to the Law, that by fear we might chasten our lusts, the Spirit not being manifested; but now that grace is given, which not only commands us to abstain from them, but both quenches them, and leads us to a higher rule of life, what more need is there of the Law? He who has attained an exalted excel-

---

[1] [That is, the "psychical" man, from ψυχή, the soul.—G. A.]

[2] ["If you adopt the rule of the Spirit, you thereby renounce your allegiance to the Law. In this passage the Spirit is doubly contrasted; first with the flesh, and secondly, with the Law, both of which are closely allied."—Lightfoot.—G. A.]

lence from an inner impulse, has no occasion for a schoolmaster, nor does any one, if he is a philosopher, require a grammarian. Why then do ye so degrade yourselves, as now to listen to the Law, having previously given yourselves to the Spirit?

Ver. 19, 20, 21. "Now the works of the flesh are manifest,[1] which are these; fornication,[2] uncleanness, lasciviousness, idolatry, sorcery, enmities, strife, jealousies, wrath, factions, divisions, heresies, envyings, drunkenness, revellings, and such like: of the which I forewarn you even as I did forewarn you, that they which practice such things shall not inherit the kingdom of God."

Answer me now, thou that accusest thine own flesh, and supposest that this is said of it as of an enemy and adversary. Let it be allowed that adultery and fornication proceed, as you assert, from the flesh; yet hatred, variance, emulations, strife, heresies, and witchcraft, these arise merely from a depraved moral choice. And so it is with the others also, for how can they belong to the flesh? you observe that he is not here speaking of the flesh, but of earthly thoughts, which trail upon the ground. Wherefore also he alarms them by saying, that "they which practice such things shall not inherit the kingdom of God." If these things belonged to nature and not to a bad moral choice, his expression, "they practice," is inappropriate, it should be, "they suffer." And why should they be cast out of the kingdom, for rewards and punishments relate not to what proceeds from nature but from choice?

Ver. 22. "But the fruit of the Spirit is love, joy, peace."

He says not, "the work of the Spirit," but, "the fruit of the Spirit." Is the soul, however, superfluous? the flesh and the Spirit are mentioned, but where is the soul? is he discoursing of beings without a soul? for if the things of the flesh be evil, and those of the Spirit good, the soul must be superfluous. By no means, for the mastery of the passions belongs to her, and concerns her; and being placed amid vice and virtue, if she has used the body fitly, she has wrought it to be spiritual, but if she separate from the Spirit and give herself up to evil desires, she makes herself more earthly. You observe throughout that his discourse does not relate to the substance of the flesh, but to the moral choice, which is or is not vicious. And why does he say, "the fruit[3]

of the Spirit?" it is because evil works originate in ourselves alone, and therefore he calls them "works," but good works require not only our diligence but God's loving kindness. He places first the root of these good things, and then proceeds to recount them, in these words, "Love, joy, peace, long-suffering, kindness, goodness, faithfulness, meekness, temperance; against such there is no law." For who would lay any command on him who hath all things within himself, and who hath love for the finished mistress of philosophy? As horses, who are docile and do every thing of their own accord, need not the lash, so neither does the soul, which by the Spirit hath attained to excellence, need the admonitions of the Law. Here too he completely and strikingly casts out the Law, not as bad, but as inferior to the philosophy given by the Spirit.

Ver. 24. "And they that are of Christ Jesus[4] have crucified the flesh with the passions and the lusts thereof."

That they might not object, "And who is such a man as this?" he points out by their works those who have attained to this perfection, here again giving the name of the "flesh" to evil actions. He does not mean that they had destroyed their flesh, otherwise how were they going to live? for that which is crucified is dead and inoperative, but he indicates the perfect rule of life. For the desires, although they are troublesome, rage in vain. Since then such is the power of the Spirit, let us live therein and be content therewith, as he adds himself,

Ver. 25. "If we live[5] by the Spirit, by the Spirit let us also walk,"

—being governed by His laws. For this is the force of the words "let us walk," that is, let us be content with the power of the Spirit, and seek no help from the Law. Then, signifying that those who would fain have introduced circumcision were actuated by ambitious motives, he says,

Ver. 26. "Let us not be vainglorious,"[6] which is the cause of all evils, "provoking[7] one another" to contentions and strife, "envying one another," for from vainglory comes envy and from envy all these countless evils.

---

development, from their root, the Spirit."—Ellicott. So substantially Lightfoot and Schaff. But Meyer demurs and says no marked distinction is intended. He refers it to Paul's fondness for variety of expression.—G. A.]

[4] [Having now enumerated the distinctive works of the flesh and fruit of the Spirit he says, Now if you are Christ's you have decided between these, the Spirit and the flesh, and have crucified the flesh, with its passions (passive) and lusts (active).—G. A.]

[5] [Therefore if having crucified the flesh we are dead to it and live by the Spirit, let us conform our conduct to our new life, let us also walk by the Spirit.—Lightfoot, substantially.—G. A.]

[6] ["Paul works round again to the subject of ver. 15 and repeats his warning. It is clear that something had occurred which alarmed him on this point."—Lightfoot.—G. A.]

[7] ["'Provoking' (προκαλούμενοι) on the part of the strong, 'envying,' (φθονοῦντες) on the part of the weak. The strong vauntingly challenged their weaker brethren; the weak could only retaliate with envy."—Ellicott.—G. A.]

---

[1] ["Would you ascertain whether you are walking by the Spirit or the flesh? Then apply the plain practical test."—Lightfoot. —G. A.]

[2] ["The sins here mentioned seem to fall into four classes: (1) Sensual sins; fornication, uncleanness, lasciviousness; (2) Unlawful dealings in things spiritual; idolatry, sorcery; (3) Violations of brotherly love; enmities . , . . . envyings; (4) Excesses, drunkenness and revellings."—Lightfoot.—G. A.]

[3] [" Used apparently with a significant reference to the organic

CHAPTER VI

" Brethren,[1] even if a man be overtaken in any trespass."[2]

FORASMUCH as under cover of a rebuke they gratified their private feelings, and professing to do so for faults which had been committed, were advancing their own ambition, he says, " Brethren, if a man be overtaken." He said not if a man commit but if he be " overtaken " that is, if he be carried away.[3]

" Ye which are spiritual [4] restore such a one,"

He says not " chastise " nor " judge," but " set right." Nor does he stop here, but in order to show that it behoved them to be very gentle towards those who had lost their footing, he subjoins,

" In a spirit of meekness."

He says not, " in meekness," but, " in a spirit of meekness," signifying thereby that this is acceptable to the Spirit, and that to be able to administer correction with mildness is a spiritual gift. Then, to prevent the one being unduly exalted by having to correct the other, puts him under the same fear, saying,

" Looking to thyself, lest thou also be tempted."

For as rich men convey contributions to the indigent, that in case they should be themselves involved in poverty they may receive the same bounty, so ought we also to do. And therefore he states this cogent reason, in these words, " looking to thyself, lest thou also be tempted." He apologizes for the offender, first, by saying "if ye be overtaken; " next, by employing a term indicative of great infirmity [5]; lastly, by the words " lest thou also be tempted," thus arraigning the malice of the devil rather than the remissness of the soul.

Ver. 2. " Bear ye one another's burdens."

It being impossible for man to be without failings, he exhorts them not to scrutinize severely the offences of others, but even to bear their failings, that their own may in turn be borne by others. As, in the building of a house, all the stones hold not the same position, but one is fitted for a corner but not for the foundations, another for the foundations, and not for the corner, so too is it in the body of the Church. The same thing holds in the frame of our own flesh ; notwithstanding which, the one member bears with the other, and we do not require every thing from each, but what each contributes in common constitutes both the body and the building.

Ver. 2. " And so fulfil the law of Christ."

He says not " fulfil," but, "complete [6] ;" that is, make it up all of you in common,[7] by the things wherein ye bear with one another. For example, this man is irascible, thou art dull-tempered ; bear therefore with his vehemence that he in turn may bear with thy sluggishness ; and thus neither will he transgress, being supported by thee, nor wilt thou offend in the points where thy defects lie, because of thy brother's forbearing with thee. So do ye by reaching forth a hand one to another when about to fall, fulfil the Law in common, each completing what is wanting in his neighbor by his own endurance. But if ye do not thus, but each of you will investigate the faults of his neighbor, nothing will ever be performed by you as it ought. For as in the case of the body, if one were to exact the same function from every member of it, the body could never consist, so must there be great strife among brethren if we were to require all things from all.

Ver. 3. " For if a man thinketh himself to be something, when he is nothing, he deceiveth himself."

---

[1] [" I have just charged you to shun provocation and envy. I now ask you to do more—to be gentle even to those whose guilt is flagrant."—Lightfoot.—G. A.]

[2] Ἐν τινι παραπτώματι, " in a false step or slip," ommitted, in the text yet commented on.

[3] [Meyer holds the same view of this word (προλημφθῇ) and says, " If he be overtaken," means if the sin has reached him more rapidly than he could flee from it. Ellicott, however, says this view of the πρό would tend to excuse and qualify, whereas καί seems to point to an aggravation of the offense. The meaning then is " be caught before he could escape."—So Lightfoot but not Schaff. —G. A.]

[4] [" Paul leaves it with every reader to regard himself included or not."—Meyer.—G. A.]

[5] Viz., in a false step, ἐν τινι παραπτώματι·

[6] Not πληρώσατε, but ἀναπληρώσατε.

[7] [" This explanation of Chrysostom is not satisfactory. The word in all cases appears to denote a complete filling up."—Ellicott.

" By lending a hand to bear your neighbor's burden, you will fulfil the most perfect of all laws—the law of Christ. But if (ver. 3) any one asserts his superiorty, if any one exalts himself above others, he is nothing worth and is a vain self-deceiver. Nay (ver. 4) rather let each man test his own work (ἔργον being in an emphatic position) and then his boast will be his own and not depend on comparison with others."—Lightfoot. —G. A.]

Here again he reflects on their arrogance. He that thinks himself to be something is nothing, and exhibits at the outset a proof of his worthlessness by such a disposition.

Ver. 4. " But let each man prove his own work."

Here he shows that we ought to be scrutinizers of our lives, and this not lightly, but carefully to weigh our actions ; as for example, if thou hast performed a good deed, consider whether it was not from a vain glory, or through necessity, or malevolence, or with hypocrisy, or from some other human motive. For as gold appears to be bright before it is placed in the furnace, but when committed to the fire, is closely proved, and all that is spurious is separated from what is genuine, so too our works, if closely examined, will be distinctly made manifest, and we shall perceive that we have exposed ourselves to much censure.

Ver. 4. " And then shall he have his glorying in regard of himself alone and not of his neighbor."

This he says, not as laying down a rule, but in the way of concession ; and his meaning is this,[1]—Boasting is senseless, but if thou wilt boast, boast not against thy neighbor, as the Pharisee did. For he that is so instructed will speedily give up boasting altogether ; and therefore he concedes a part that he may gradually extirpate the whole. He that is wont to boast with reference to himself only, and not against others, will soon reform this failing also. For he that does not consider himself better than others, for this is the meaning of " not in regard of his neighbor, but becomes elated by examining himself by himself, will afterwards cease to be so. And that you may be sure this is what he desires to establish, observe how he checks him by fear, saying above, " let every man prove his own work," and adding here,

Ver. 5. " For each man shall bear his own burden."

He appears to state a reason prohibitory of boasting against another ; but at the same time he corrects the boaster, to that he may no more entertain high thoughts of himself by bringing to his remembrance his own errors, and pressing upon his conscience the idea of a burden, and of being heavily laden.[2]

Ver. 6. " But let him that is taught in the word communicate unto him that teacheth in all good things."

Here he proceeds to discourse concerning

Teachers, to the effect that they ought to be tended with great assiduity by their disciples. Now what is the reason that Christ so commanded ? For this law, "that they which preach the Gospel should live of the Gospel," (i Cor. ix : 14.) is laid down in the New Testament; and likewise in the Old, (Num. xxxi : 47 ; xxxv ; 1–8.) many revenues accrued to the Levites from the people ; what is the reason, I say, that He so ordained ? Was it not for the sake of laying a foundation beforehand of lowliness and love ? For inasmuch as the dignity of a teacher oftentimes elates him who possesses it, He, in order to repress his spirit, hath imposed on him the necessity of requiring aid at the hands of his disciples. And to these in turn he hath given[3] means of cultivating kindly feelings, by training them, through the kindness required of them to their Teacher, in gentleness towards others also. By this means no slight affection is generated on both sides. Were not the cause of this what I have stated it to be, why should He, who fed the dull-minded Jews with manna, have reduced the Apostles to the necessity of asking for aid ? Is it not manifest He aimed at the great benefits of humility and love, and that those who were under teaching might not be ashamed of Teachers who were in appearance despicable ? To ask for aid bears the semblance of disgrace, but it ceased to be so, when their Teachers with all boldness urged their claim, so that their disciples derived from hence no small benefit, taught hereby to despise all appearances. Wherefore he says, " But[4] let him that is taught in the word communicate unto him that teacheth in all good things," that is, let him show to him all generosity ; this he implies by the words, " in all good things." Let the disciple, says he, keep nothing to himself, but have every thing in common, for what he receives is better than what he gives,—as much better as heavenly are better than earthly things. This he expresses in another place, "If we sowed unto you spiritual things, is it a great matter if we shall reap your carnal things ? " (i Cor. ix : 11.) Wherefore he gives the procedure the name of a "communication," showing that an interchange takes place. Hereby too love is greatly fostered and confirmed. If the teacher asks merely for competency, he does not by receiving it derogate from his own dignity. For this is praiseworthy, so assidu-

---

[1] [" If any one wishes to find matter for boasting, let it be truly searched for in his own actions and not derived from a contrast of his own fancied virtues with the faults of others."—Ellicott.—G.A.]

[2] [Ellicott says, " The qualitative and humbling distinction of Chrysostom does not appear natural or probable, nor does it refer to that which will take place in every man after the examination (Meyer); but is apparently used ethically in reference to what according to the nature of things must be the case."—G. A.]

[3] [Those philosophers among the Greeks who received pay from their pupils were looked down upon, and called Sophists, vid. Xen. *Mem.* I. 6. §. 13.

[4] [Different views are held as to the connection of this with the preceding. Lightfoot says the connection is this ; "I spoke of bearing one another's burdens. There is one special application I would make of this rule ; provide for the wants of your teachers. Δέ arrests a former topic before it passes out of sight." (Compare 4 : 20.) But Ellicott takes a different view and says : "The duty of sharing their temporal blessings with their teachers is placed in contrast with the foregoing declaration of individual responsibility in spiritual matters." So also Meyer who, however, refers it to moral good.—G. A.]

ously to apply to the Word, as to require the aid of others, and to be in manifold poverty, and to be regardless of all the means of subsistence. But if he exceed the due measure, he injures his dignity, not by mere receiving, but by receiving too much. Then, lest the vice of the Teacher should render the disciple more remiss in this matter, and he should frequently pass him by, though poor, on account of his conduct, he proceeds to say,

Ver. 9. "And let us not be weary in well doing."[1]

And here he points out the difference between ambition of this kind, and in temporal affairs, by saying, "Be not deceived[2]; God is not mocked; for whatsoever a man soweth, that shall he also reap. For he that soweth unto his own flesh shall of the flesh reap corruption; but he that soweth unto the Spirit shall of the Spirit reap eternal life." As in the case of seeds, one who sows pulse cannot reap corn, for what is sown and what is reaped must both be of one kind, so is it in actions, he that plants in the flesh, wantonness, drunkenness, or inordinate desire, shall reap the fruits of these things. And what are these fruits? Punishment, retribution, shame, derision, destruction. For of sumptuous tables and viands the end is no other than destruction; for they both perish themselves, and destroy the body too. But the fruit of the Spirit is of a nature not similar but contrary in all respects to these. For consider; hast thou sown alms-giving? the treasures of heaven and eternal glory await thee: hast thou sown temperance? honor and reward, and the applause of Angels, and a crown from the Judge await thee.

Ver. 9, 10. "And let us not be weary in well-doing; for in due season we shall reap, if we faint not. So then as we have opportunity, let us work that which is good toward all men, especially toward them that are of the household of faith."

Lest any one should suppose that their Teachers were to be cared for and supported, but that others might be neglected, he makes his discourse general, and opens the door of this charitable zeal to all; nay, he carries it to such a height, as to command us to show mercy both to Jews and Greeks, in the proper gradation indeed, but still to show mercy. And what is this gradation? it consists in bestowing greater care upon the faithful. His endeavor here is the same as in his other Epistles; he discourses not merely of showing mercy, but of doing it with zeal and perseverance, for the expressions of "sowing" and of "not fainting" imply this. Then, having exacted a great work, he places its reward close at hand, and makes mention of a new and wondrous harvest. Among husbandmen, not only the sower but also the reaper endures much labor, having to struggle with drought and dust and grievous toil, but in this case none of these exist, as he shows by the words, "for in due season we shall reap, if we faint not." By this means he stimulates and draws them on; and he also urges and presses them forward by another motive, saying, "As we have therefore opportunity, let us do good." As it is not always in our power to sow, so neither is it to show mercy; for when we have been carried hence, though we may desire it a thousand times, we shall be able to effect nothing more. To this argument of ours the Ten Virgins (Mat. xxv: 1 ff) bear witness, who although they wished it a thousand times, yet were shut out from the bridegroom, because they brought with them no bountiful charity. And so does the rich man who neglected Lazarus (Luke xvi : 19.) for he, being destitute of this succor, although he wept and made many entreaties, won no compassion from the Patriarch, or any one else, but continued destitute of all forgiveness, and tormented with perpetual fire. Therefore he says, "as we have opportunity, let us work that which is good toward all men," hereby especially also setting them free from the narrow-mindedness of the Jews. For the whole of their benevolence was confined to their own race, but the rule of life which Grace gives invites both land and sea to the board of charity, only it shows a greater care for its own household.

Ver. 11, 12. "See with how large letters I have written unto you with mine own hand. As many as desire to make a fair show in the flesh, they compel you to be circumcised."

Observe what grief posesses his blessed soul. As those who are oppressed with some sorrow, who have lost one of their own kindred, and suffered an unexpected calamity, rest neither by night nor day, because their grief besieges their soul, so the blessed Paul, after a short moral discourse, returns again to that former subject which chiefly disturbed his mind, saying as follows : "see with how large letters I have written unto you with mine own hand." By this he signifies that he had written the whole letter[3]

---

[1] [Dislocated by Chrysostom. This is a part of verse 9, and is an encouragement not to become weary in below sowing to the Spirit.—Meyer.—G. A.]

[2] [Meyer, understanding "all good things" to mean every thing that is morally good, says, that this is a warning to the readers, in respect to this necessary moral fellowship not to allow themselves to be led astray (by the teachers of error or otherwise). Lightfoot and Schaff refer this warning to the consequences of failure to share their temporal blessings with their teachers. Ellicott says, "Verse 7 is a continuation of the subject in a more general and extended way but not without reference to the special command which immediately precedes."—G. A.]

[3] [Ellicott hesitatingly adopts this view also. So Alford and Riddle (in Lange). But Meyer, Schaff, Schmoller (in Lange) and Lightfoot say that ἔγραψα (Philem 19) is the epistolary aorist and marks the point at which Paul takes the pen from the amanuensis ; and that only this concluding paragraph was written with his own hand. So the American Committee also in the Rev. Ver.—G. A.]

himself, which was a proof of great sincerity. In his other Epistles he himself only dictated, another wrote, as is plain from the Epistle to the Romans, for at its close it is said, "I Tertius, who write the Epistle, salute you ;" (Rom. xvi : 22.) but in this instance he wrote the whole himself. And this he did by necessity, not from affection merely, but in order to remove an injurious suspicion. Being charged with acts wherein he had no part, and being reported to preach Circumcision yet to pretend to preach it not, he was compelled to write the Epistle with his own hand, thus laying up beforehand a written testimony. By the expression "what sized," he appears to me to signify, not the magnitude, but, the misshapen appearance[1] of the letters, as if he had said, "Although not well skilled in writing, I have been compelled to write with my own hand to stop the mouth of these traducers."

Ver. 12, 13. "As many as desire to make a fair show in the flesh, they compel you to be circumcised ; only that they may not be persecuted for the cross of Christ. For not even they who receive circumcision do themselves keep the Law ; but they desire to have you circumcised, that they may glory in your flesh."

Here he shows that they suffered this, not willingly but of necessity, and affords them an opportunity of retreat, almost speaking in their defence, and exhorting them to abandon their teachers with all speed. What is the meaning of "to make a fair show in the flesh ?" it means, to be esteemed by men. As they were reviled by the Jews for deserting the customs of their fathers, they desire, says he, to injure you, that they may not have this charged against them, but vindicate themselves by means of your flesh.[2] His object here is to show that they did not so act from respect to God ; it is as if he said, This procedure is not founded in piety, all this is done through human ambition ; in order that the unbelievers may be gratified by the mutilation of the faithful, they choose to offend God that they may please men ; for this is the meaning of, "to make a fair show in the flesh." Then, as a proof that for another reason too they are unpardonable, he again convinces them that, not only in order to please others, but for their own vain glory,[3] they had enjoined

this. Wherefore he adds, "that they may glory in your flesh," as if they had disciples, and were teachers. And what is the proof of this ? "For not even they themselves," he says, "keep the Law ;" even if they did keep it, they would incur grave censure, but now their very purpose is corrupt.

Ver. 14. "But far be it from me to glory, save in the cross of our Lord Jesus Christ."

Truly this symbol is thought despicable ; but it is so in the world's reckoning, and among men ; in Heaven and among the faithful it is the highest glory. Poverty too is despicable, but it is our boast ; and to be cheaply thought of by the public is a matter of laughter to them, but we are elated by it. So too is the Cross our boast. He does not say, "I boast not," nor, "I will not boast," but, "Far be it from me that I should," as if he abominated it as absurd, and invoked the aid of God in order to his success therein. And what is the boast of the Cross ? That Christ for my sake took on Him the form of a slave, and bore His sufferings for me the slave, the enemy, the unfeeling one ; yea He so loved me as to give Himself up to a curse for me. What can be comparable to this ! If servants who only receive praise from their masters, to whom they are akin by nature, are elated thereby, how must we not boast when the Master who is very God is not ashamed of the Cross which was endured for us. Let us then not be ashamed of His unspeakable tenderness ; He was not ashamed of being crucified for thy sake, and wilt thou be ashamed to confess His infinite solicitude ? It is as if a prisoner who had not been ashamed of his King, should, after that King had come to the prison and himself loosed the chains, become ashamed of him on that account. Yet this would be the height of madness, for this very fact would be an especial ground for boasting.

Ver. 14. "Through which the world hath been crucified unto me, and I unto the world."[4]

What he here calls the world is not the heaven nor the earth, but the affairs of life, the praise of men, retinues, glory, wealth, and all such things as have a show of splendor. To me these things are dead. Such an one it behooves a Christian to be, and always to use this language. Nor was he content with the former putting to death, but added another, saying, "and I unto the world," thus implying a double putting to death, and saying, They are dead to me, and I to them, neither can they captivate and overcome me, for they are dead once for all,

---

[1] [" The word used, πηλίκοις, denotes size not irregularity. Nor is it probable that Paul who was educated at Jerusalem and Tarsus, the great centre of Jewish and Greek learning, was ignorant and unskillful in writing Greek. The boldness of the handwriting answers to the force of the Apostle's convictions."—Lightfoot.—G. A.]

[2] [" Certain men have an 'object' in displaying their zeal for carnal ordinances. They hope thereby to save themselves from persecution for professing the cross of Christ."—Lightfoot.—G. A.]

[3] [" They advocate circumcision and yet they themselves neglect the ordinances of the Law. They could not face the obloquy to which their abandonment of the Mosaic Law would expose them. So they tried to keep on good terms with their unconverted fellow-Jews by imposing circumcision on the Gentile converts also thus getting the credit of zeal for the law."—Lightfoot.—G. A.]

[4] [" For myself, on the other hand, far be it from me, etc.: By way of contrast to the boasting of the pseudo-apostles, Paul now presents his own ground of boasting, namely, the crucifixion of Christ, by whose crucifixion is produced the result that no fellowship of life longer exists between him and the world : it is dead for him and he is dead for it."—Mever.—*Alter pro mortuo habet alterum.* (Schott.)—G. A.]

nor can I desire them, for I too am dead to them. Nothing can be more blessed than this putting to death, for it is the foundation of the blessed life.

Ver. 15, 16. " For neither is circumcision any thing, nor uncircumcision, but a new creature. And as many as shall walk by this rule, peace be upon them, and mercy, and upon the Israel of God."

Observe the power of the Cross, to what a pitch it hath raised him! not only hath it put to death for him all mundane affairs, but hath set him far above the Old Dispensation. What can be comparable to this power? for the Cross hath persuaded him, who was willing to be slain and to slay others for the sake of circumcision, to leave it on a level with uncircumcision, and to seek for things strange and marvellous and above the heavens. This our rule of life he calls " a new creature," both on account of what is past, and of what is to come; of what is past, because our soul, which had grown old with the oldness of sin, hath been all at once renewed by baptism, as if it had been created again.[1] Wherefore we require a new and heavenly rule of life. And of things to come, because both the heaven and the earth, and all the creation, shall with our bodies be translated into incorruption. Tell me not then, he says, of circumcision, which now availeth nothing; (for how shall it appear, when all things have undergone such a change?) but seek the new things of grace. For they who pursue these things shall enjoy peace and amity, and may properly be called by the name of " Israel." While they who hold contrary sentiments, although they be descended from him (Israel) and bear his appellation, have yet fallen away from all these things, both the relationship and the name itself. But it is in their power to be true Israelites, who keep this rule, who desist from the old ways, and follow after grace.

Ver. 17. " From henceforth let no man trouble me."

This he says not as though he were wearied or overpowered; he who chose to do and suffer all for his disciples' sake; he who said, " Be instant in season, out of season;" (2 Tim. iv: 2.) he who said, " If peradventure God may give them repentance unto the knowledge of the truth, and they may recover themselves out of the snare of the devil;" (2 Tim. ii: 25, 26.) how shall he now become relaxed and fall back? Wherefore does he say this? it is to gird up their slothful mind, and to impress them with deeper fear, and to ratify the laws enacted by

himself, and to restrain their perpetual fluctuations.[2]

Ver. 17. " For I bear branded on my body the marks of Jesus."

He says not, " I have," but, " I bear," like a man priding himself on trophies and royal ensigns. Although on a second thought it seems a disgrace, yet does this man vaunt of his wounds, and like military standard-bearers, so does he exult in bearing about these wounds. And why does he say this? " More clearly by those wounds than by any argument, than by any language, do I vindicate myself," says he. For these wounds utter a voice louder than a trumpet against my opponents, and against those who say that I play the hypocrite in my teaching, and speak what may please men. For no one who saw a soldier retiring from the battle bathed in blood and with a thousand wounds, would dare to accuse him of cowardice and treachery, seeing that he bears on his body the proofs of his valor, and so ought ye, he says, to judge of me. And if any one desire to hear my defence, and to learn my sentiments, let him consider my wounds, which afford a stronger proof than these words and letters. At the outset of his Epistle he evinced his sincerity by the suddenness of his conversion, at its close he proves it by the perils which attended his conversion. That it might not be objected that he had changed his course with upright intentions, but that he had not continued in the same purpose, he produces his trials, his dangers, his stripes as witnesses that he had so continued.

Then having clearly justified himself in every particular, and proved that he had spoken nothing from anger or malevolence, but had preserved his affection towards them unimpaired, he again establishes this same point by concluding his discourse with a prayer teeming with a thousand blessings, in these words;

Ver. 18. " The grace of our Lord Jesus Christ be with your spirit, brethren. Amen."

By this last word he hath sealed all that preceded it. He says not merely, " with you," as elsewhere, but, " with your spirit," thus withdrawing them from carnal[3] things, and displaying throughout the beneficence of God, and reminding them of the grace which they enjoyed, whereby he was able to recall them from all their judaizing errors. For to have received the Spirit came not of the poverty of the Law, but of the righteousness which is by Faith, and to

---

[1] [" It is a matter of indifference whether one is circumcised or uncircumcised; and the only matter of importance is that one should be created anew, transferred into a new spiritual condition of life."—Meyer.—G. A.]

[2] [" Lightfoot similarly, but more clearly; " Paul closes the epistle as he began it, with an uncompromising assertion of his authority: Henceforth let no man question my authority; let no man thwart or annoy me. Jesus is my Master and his brand is stamped on my body. I bear this badge of an honorable servitude."—G. A.]

[3] [So also Lightfoot, who says, " with your spirit" is probably in reference to the carnal religion of the Galatians, but this cannot be pressed because the same form of benediction occurs in Philem. 25; 2 Tim. iv: 22. Meyer denies there is any such allusion at all. G. A.]

preserve it when obtained came not from Circumcision but from Grace. On this account he concluded his exhoration with a prayer, reminding them of grace and the Spirit, and at the same time addressing them as brethren, and supplicating God that they might continue to enjoy these blessings, thus providing for them a twofold security. For both prayer and teaching, tended to the same thing and together became to them as a double wall. For teaching, reminding them of what benefits they enjoyed, the rather kept them in the doctrine of the Church; and prayer, invoking grace, and exhorting to an enduring constancy, permitted not the Spirit to depart from them. And He abiding in them, all the error of such doctrines as they held was shaken off like dust.[1]

[1] [Dr. Schaff strikingly says : " The last sentence of this polemic Epistle is a benediction and the last word is a word of affection, 'brethren.' (The word ἀδελφοί stands last in the true text, as the Rev. Version has it.) It takes the sting out of the severity. Thus concludes thiᴗ Epistle so full of polemic fire and zeal, yet more full of grace—free sovereign grace, justifying sanctifying grace, and full of forgiving love even to ungrateful pupils ; an Epistle for the time and an Epistle for all times."—*Popular Commentary, in loco.*—G. A.]

HOMILIES OF ST. JOHN CHRYSOSTOM,

ARCHBISHOP OF CONSTANTINOPLE,

ON THE

EPISTLE OF ST. PAUL THE APOSTLE

TO THE

EPHESIANS

THE ARGUMENT.

EPHESUS is the metropolis of Asia. It was dedicated to Diana, whom especially they worshipped there as their great goddess. Indeed so great was the superstition of her worshippers, that when her temple was burnt, they would not so much as divulge the name of the man who burnt it.

The blessed John the Evangelist spent the chief part of his time there: he was there when he was banished,[1] and there he died. It was there too that Paul left Timothy, as he says in writing to him, "As I exhorted thee to tarry at Ephesus. (1 Tim. 1: 3.)

Most of the philosophers also, those more particularly who flourished in Asia, were there; and even Pythagoras himself is said to have come from thence; perhaps because Samos, whence he really came, is an island of Ionia.[2] It was the resort also of the disciples of Parmenides, and Zeno, and Democritus, and you may see a number of philosophers there even to the present day.

These facts I mention, not merely as such, but with a view of showing that Paul would needs take great pains and trouble in writing to these Ephesians. He is said indeed to have entrusted them, as being persons already well-instructed, with his profoundest conceptions; and the Epistle itself is full of sublime thoughts and doctrines.[3]

He wrote the Epistle from Rome, and, as he himself informs us, in bonds. "Pray for me, that utterance may be given unto me, in opening my mouth to make known with boldness the mystery of the Gospel, for which I am an ambassador in chains." (Eph. vi: 19.) It abounds with sentiments of overwhelming loftiness and grandeur. Thoughts which he scarcely so much as utters any where else, he here plainly declares; as when he says, "To the intent that now unto the principalities and the powers in the heavenly places might be made known through the Church the manifold wisdom of God." (Eph. iii: 10.) And again; "He raised us up with him, and made us to sit with him in heavenly places. (Eph. ii: 6.) And again; "Which in other generations was not made known unto the sons of men, as it hath now been revealed unto His holy apostles and prophets in the Spirit, that the Gentiles are fellow-heirs, and fellow-partakers of the promise in Christ." (Eph. iii: 5.)

---

[1] [The Apocalypse already implies that he stood at the head of the churches of Asia Minor. Rev. 1: 4, 9, 11, 20. Chs. 2 and 3. This is confirmed by the unanimous testimony of antiquity. The most probable view is that he was exiled to Patmos under Nero, wrote the Apocalypse soon after Nero's death, 68 or 69 A. D., returned to Ephesus and died there after 98 A. D.—Schaff, *Ch. Hist.* I. p. 424, 429.—G. A.]

[2] [Of which Ephesus was one of the cities. G.A.]

[3] [Coleridge calls it "the divinest composition of man." Alford: "The greatest and most heavenly work of one whose very imagination is peopled with things in the heavens." Grotius: "Equalling the sublimity of its thoughts with words more sublime than any human language ever possessed."—Quoted in Schaff, *Ch. Hist.* I. p. 781.—G. A.]

HOMILY I

CHAPTER I. VERSES 1–2.

"Paul, an apostle of Christ Jesus through the will of God, to the saints which are at Ephesus,[1] and the faithful in Christ Jesus. Grace to you, and peace, from God our Father, and the Lord Jesus Christ."

OBSERVE, he applies the word "through" to the Father. But what then? Shall we say that He is inferior? Surely not.

"To the saints," saith he, "which are at Ephesus, and the faithful in Christ Jesus."

Observe that he calls saints, men with wives, and children, and domestics. For that these are they whom he calls by this name is plain from the end of the Epistle, as, when he says, "Wives, be in subjection unto your own husbands." (Eph. v: 22.) And again, "Children, obey your parents:" (Eph. vi: 1.) and, "Servants, be obedient to your masters." (Eph. vi: 5.) Think how great is the indolence that possesses us now, how rare is any thing like virtue now and how great the abundance of virtuous men must have been then, when even secular men could be called "saints and faithful." "Grace to you, and peace, from God our Father, and the Lord Jesus Christ." "Grace" is his word; and he calls God, "Father;" since this name is a sure token of that gift of grace. And how so? Hear what he saith elsewhere; "Because ye are sons, God sent forth the Spirit of His Son into our hearts, crying, Abba, Father." (Gal. iv: 6.)

"And from the Lord Jesus Christ."

Because for us men Christ was born, and appeared in the flesh.

Ver. 3. "Blessed[2] be the God," he saith, "and Father of our Lord Jesus Christ."

Observe; The God of Him that was Incarnate[3]. And though thou wilt not, The Father of God the Word.

Ver. 3. "Who hath blessed us with every spiritual blessing in the heavenly places in Christ."

He is here alluding to the blessings of the Jews[4]; for that was blessing also, but it was not spiritual blessing. For how did it run? "The Lord bless thee, He will bless the fruit of thy body;" (Deut. vii: 13.) and "He will bless thy going out and thy coming in." (Deut. xxviii: 4.) But here it is not thus, but how? "With every spiritual blessing." And what lackest thou yet? Thou art made immortal, thou art made free, thou art made a son, thou art made righteous, thou art made a brother, thou art made a fellow-heir, thou reignest with Christ, thou art glorified with Christ; all things are freely given thee. "How," saith he, "shall He not also with Him freely give us all things?" (Rom. viii: 32.) Thy First-fruits is adored by Angels, by the Cherubim, by the Seraphim! What lackest thou yet? "With every spiritual blessing." There is nothing carnal here. Accordingly He excluded all those former blessings, when He said, "In the world ye have tribulation," (John xvi: 33.) to lead us on to these. For as they who possessed carnal things were unable to hear of spiritual things, so they who aim at spiritual things cannot attain to them unless they first stand aloof from carnal things.

What again is "spiritual blessing in the heavenly places?" It is not upon earth, he means, as was the case with the Jews. "Ye shall eat the good of the land." (Isa. i: 19.) "Unto a land flowing with milk and honey." (Ex. iii: 8.) "The Lord shall bless thy land." (Deut. vii: 13.) Here we have nothing of this sort, but what have we? "If a man love Me, he will keep My word, and I and My Father will come unto him, and make our abode with him." (Jo. xiv: 23.) "Every one therefore which heareth these words of Mine, and doeth them, shall be likened unto a wise man which built his house upon the rock, and the floods came, and the winds blew, and beat upon that house, and it fell not, for it was founded upon the rock."

---

[1] [At Ephesus, Chrysostom's text has these words (ἐν Ἐφέσῳ) and he betrays no knowledge of any copies which omitted them. But they are omitted by Aleph* B. by some MSS., consulted by Basil, and apparently by Origen's text, for he interprets τοῖς οὖσιν (those who are) absolutely, as he would not have done had he read ἐν Ἐφέσῳ. The Revisers insert the words but with a marginal note. Westcott and Hort bracket them. See their discussion of the point in Appendix (vol. II. of Greek Text), p. 123. For a full discussion see Meyer's *Introduction to Ephesians*, Sec. 1, where he earnestly defends "the right of these words to a place in the text."—G. A.]

[2] [Compare Rom. ix: 5; 2 Cor. i: 3; Luke i: 68; 1 Peter i: 3.—G. A.]

[3] [Meyer holds that the genitive τοῦ κυρίου, etc. does not limit Θεὸς, but only πατήρ: "Blessed be God who at same time is Father of our Lord Jesus Christ." So also Ellicott.—G. A.]

[4] ["A contrast to the earthly benefits promised to the Jews in the Old Testament is foreign to the context."—Meyer.—G. A.]

(Mat. vii : 24, 25.) And what is that rock but those heavenly things which are above the reach of every change? "Every one therefore who," saith Christ, "shall confess Me before men, him will I also confess before My Father which is in Heaven: But whosoever shall deny Me, him will I also deny." (Mat. x : 32, 33.) Again, "Blessed are the pure in heart, for they shall see God." (Mat. v : 8.) And again, "Blessed are the poor in spirit, for theirs is the kingdom of Heaven." (Mat. v : 3.) And again, "Blessed are ye which are persecuted for righteousness sake, for great is your reward in Heaven." (Mat. v : 11, 12.) Observe, how every where He speaketh of Heaven, no where of earth, or of the things on the earth.[1] And again, "Our citizenship is in Heaven, from whence also we wait for a Saviour the Lord Jesus Christ." (Phil. iii : 20.) And again, "Not setting your mind on the things that are on the earth, but on the things which are above." (Col. iii : 3.)

"In Christ."

That is to say, this blessing was not by the hand of Moses, but by Christ Jesus: so that we surpass them not only in the quality of the blessings, but in the Mediator also. As moreover he saith in the Epistle to the Hebrews; "And Moses indeed was faithful in all his house as a servant, for a testimony of those things which were afterward to be spoken; but Christ as a Son over His house, whose house are we." (Heb. iii : 5-6.)

Ver. 4. "Even as," he proceeds, "He chose us in Him before the foundation of the world, that we should be holy and without blemish before Him in love."

His meaning is somewhat of this sort. Through whom He hath blessed us, through Him He hath also chosen us. And He, then, it is that shall bestow upon us all those rewards hereafter. He is the very Judge that shall say, "Come, ye blessed of my Father, inherit the kingdom prepared for you from the foundation of the world." (Mat. xxv : 34.) And again, "I will that where I am they will also be with Me." (John xvii : 24.) And this is a point which he is anxious to prove in almost all his Epistles, that ours is no novel system, but that it had thus been figured from the very first, that it is not the result of any change of purpose, but had been in fact a divine dispensation and fore-ordained. And this is a mark of great solicitude for us.

What is meant by, "He chose us in Him?" By means of the faith which is in Him, Christ,

he means, happily ordered this for us before we were born; nay more, before the foundation of the world. And beautiful is that word "foundation," as though he were pointing to the world as cast down from some vast height. Yea, vast indeed and ineffable is the height of God, so far removed not in place but in incommunicableness of nature; so wide the distance between creation and Creator! A word which heretics may be ashamed to hear.[2]

But wherefore hath He chosen us? "That we should be holy and without a blemish before Him." That you may not then, when you hear that "He hath chosen us," imagine that faith alone is sufficient, he proceeds to add life and conduct. To this end, saith he, hath He chosen us, and on this condition, "that we should be holy and without blemish." And so formerly he chose the Jews. On what terms? "This nation, saith he, hath He chosen from the rest of the nations." (Deut. xiv : 2.) Now if men in their choices choose what is best, much more doth God. And indeed the fact of their being chosen is at once a token of the loving kindness of God, and of their moral goodness.[3] For by all means would he have chosen those who were approved. He hath Himself rendered us holy, but then we must continue holy. A holy man is he who is a partaker of faith; a blameless man is he who leads an irreproachable life. It is not however simply holiness and irreproachableness that He requires, but that we should appear such "before Him." For there are holy and blameless characters, who yet are esteemed as such only by men those who are like whited sepulchres, and like such as wear sheep's clothing. It is not such, however, He requires, but such as the Prophet speaks of; "And according to the cleanness of my hands." (Ps. xviii : 24.) What cleanness? That which is so "in His eyesight." He requires that holiness on which the eye of God may look.

Having thus spoken of the good works of these, he again recurs to His grace. "In love," saith he, "having predestinated us." Because this comes not of any pains, nor of any good works of ours, but of love; and yet not of love alone, but of our virtue also. For if indeed of

[1] ["Such a specification of the 'sphere' and thence of the 'spiritual character' of the action would seem superfluous after the definite words preceding. · In four other passages in this Epistle the expression, 'in the heavenlies,' seems 'local' (i : 20 ; ii : 6 ; iii : 10 ; vi : 12). So the expression here must be referred as a 'local' predication to εὐλογίᾳ πνευμαηκῇ defining the 'region' whence the blessings of the Spirit come. Cf. Heb. vi : 4."—Ellicott.—G. A.]

[2] [And an argument which can hardly be considered valid, based, as it is, on the literal and etymological meaning of a word in a passage where it is plainly used metaphorically and not literally.— The word is καταβολή.—G. A.]

[3] [Τεκμήριον καὶ τῆς αὐτῶν ἀρετῆς, a proposition which will strike a Protestant reader of any denomination with surprise, to say the least. Schaff says, "Chrysostom laid great stress on free will and the co-operation of the human will with divine grace in the work of conversion. Cassian, the founder of Semi-Pelagianism, was his pupil and appealed to his authority. We may say that in tendency and spirit he was a Catholic Semi-Pelagian or Synergist before Semi-Pelagianism was brought into a system." Prolegomena p. 20. Chrysostom's exposition of this passage is inaccurate, inconsistent, illogical and untenable. If He chose us in order that we should be holy how can holiness, or "moral goodness," as Chrysostom says, be an antecedent condition of His choosing us? See note on ch. ii : 10.—G. A.]

love alone, it would follow that all must be saved; whereas again were it the result of our virtue alone, then were His coming needless, and the whole dispensation. But it is the result neither of His love alone, nor yet of our virtue, but of both. "He chose us," saith the Apostle; and He that chooseth, knoweth what it is that He chooseth. "In love,"[1] he adds, "having foreordained us;" for virtue would never have saved any one, had there not been love. For tell me, what would Paul have profited, how would he have exhibited what he has exhibited, if God had not both called him from the beginning, and, in that He loved him, drawn him to Himself? But besides, His vouchsafing us so great privileges, was the effect of His love, not of our virtue. Because our being rendered virtuous, and believing, and coming nigh unto Him, even this again was the work of Him that called us Himself, and yet, notwithstanding, it is ours also. But that on our coming nigh unto Him, He should vouchsafe us so high privileges, as to bring us at once from a state of enmity, to the adoption of children, this is indeed the work of a really transcendent love.

Ver. 4, 5. "In love,"[1] saith he, "having foreordained us unto adoption as sons through Jesus Christ unto Himself."

Do you observe how that nothing is done without Christ? Nothing without the Father? The one hath predestinated, the other hath brought us near. And these words he adds by way of heightening the things which have been done, in the same way as he says also elsewhere, "And not only so, but we also rejoice in God, through our Lord Jesus Christ." (Rom. v: 11.) For great indeed are the blessings bestowed, yet are they made far greater in being bestowed through Christ; because He sent not any servant, though it was to servants He sent, but the Only-begotten Son Himself.

Ver. 5. "According to the good pleasure," he continues, "of His will."

That is to say, because He earnestly willed it. This is, as one might say, His earnest desire.[2] For the word "good pleasure" every where means the precedent will, for there is also another will. As for example, the first will is that sinners should not perish; the second will is, that, if men become wicked, they shall perish. For surely it is not by necessity that He punishes them, but because He wills it. You may see something of the sort even in the words of Paul, where he says, "I would that all men were even as I myself." (1 Cor. vii: 7.) And

again, "I desire that the younger widows marry, bear children." (1 Tim. v: 14.) By "good pleasure" then he means the first will, the earnest will, the will accompanied with earnest desire, as in case of us, for I shall not refuse to employ even a somewhat familiar expression, in order to speak with clearness to the simpler sort; for thus we ourselves, to express the intentness of the will, speak of acting according to our resolve. What he means to say then is this, God earnestly aims at, earnestly desires, our salvation. Wherefore then is it that He so loveth us, whence hath He such affection? It is of His goodness alone. For grace itself is the fruit of goodness. And for this cause, he saith, hath He predestinated us to the adoption of children; this being His will, and the object of His earnest wish, that the glory of His grace may be displayed. "According to the good pleasure of His will," he proceeds,

Ver. 6. "To the praise of the glory of His grace,[3] which He freely bestowed on us in the Beloved."

That the glory of His grace may be displayed, he saith, which He freely bestowed on us in the Beloved. Now then if for this He hath shown grace to us, to the praise of the glory of His grace, and that He may display His grace, let us abide therein. "To the praise of His glory." What is this? that who should praise Him? that who should glorify Him? that we, that Angels, that Archangels, yea, or the whole creation? And what were that? Nothing. The Divine nature knoweth no want. And wherefore then would He have us praise and glorify Him? It is that our love towards Him may be kindled more fervently within us. He desireth nothing we can render; not our service, not our praise, nor any thing else, nothing but our salvation; this is His object in every thing He does. And he who praises and marvels at the grace displayed towards himself will thus be more devoted and more earnest.

"Which He freely bestowed on us," he saith. He does not say, "Which He hath graciously given us," (ἐχαρίσατο) but, "wherein He hath shown grace to us." (ἐχαρίτωσεν) That is to say, He hath not only released us from our sins, but hath also made us meet objects[4] of His love. It is as though one were to take a leper, wasted by distemper, and disease, by age, and poverty, and famine, and were to turn him all at once into a graceful youth, surpassing all mankind in beauty, shedding a bright lustre from his cheeks, and eclipsing the

---

[1] [These words, ἐν ἀγάπῃ, are in the Revised Version and in the text of Westcott and Hort joined with what precedes, ἁγίους καὶ ἀμώμους. So also Alford. Meyer and Ellicott, however, are in accord with Chrysostom and probably right in joining ἐν ἀγάπῃ with προορίσας, following.—G. A.]

[2] [The good pleasure of His will means, "God's free self-determination, independent of all human desert, as regulative of the προορίζειν."—Meyer.—G. A.]

[3] ["As love was the motive for the divine predestination, so is the glorifying of the divine love, here designated 'grace,' its divinely conceived ultimate aim."—Meyer.—G. A.]

[4] ["The word does not here mean 'to make love worthy,' as Chrys., referring to inherent righteousness, but 'to grant grace,' just as ver. 7 sets forth simply the work of 'pardoning grace.'"—Meyer.—G. A.]

sun-beams with the glances of his eyes; and then were to set him in the very flower of his age, and after that array him in purple and a diadem and all the attire of royalty. It is thus that God hath arrayed and adorned this soul of ours, and clothed it with beauty, and rendered it an object of His delight and love. Such a soul Angels desire to look into, yea, Archangels, and all the holy ones. Such grace hath He shed over us, so dear hath He rendered us to Himself. "The King," saith the Psalmist, " shall greatly desire thy beauty." (Ps. xlv: 11.) Think what injurious words we uttered heretofore, and look, what gracious words we utter now. Wealth has no longer charms for us, nor the things that are here below, but only heavenly things, the things that are in the heavens. When a child has outward beauty, and has besides a pervading grace in all its sayings, do we not call it a beautiful child? Such as this are the faithful. Look, what words the initiated utter! What can be more beautiful than that mouth that breathes those wondrous words, and with a pure heart and pure lips, and beaming with cheerful confidence, partaketh of such a mystical table? What more beautiful than the words, with which we renounce the service of the Devil, and enlist in the service of Christ? than both that confession which is before the Baptismal laver,[1] and that which is after it? Let us reflect as many of us as have defiled our Baptism, and weep that we may be able again to repair it.

Ver. 6. " In the Beloved,"[2] he saith, " in whom we have[3] our redemption through His Blood."[4]

And how is this? Not only is there this marvel, that He hath given His Son, but yet further that He hath given Him in such a way, as that the Beloved One Himself should be slain!

Yea, and more transcendent still! He hath given the Beloved for them that were hated. See, how high a price he sets upon us. If, when we hated Him and were enemies, He gave the Beloved, what will He not do now, when we are reconciled by Him through grace?

Ver. 7. " The forgiveness," saith he, " of our trespasses."

Again he descends from high to low: first speaking of adoption, and sanctification, and blamelessness, and then of the Passion, and in this not lowering his discourse and bringing it

down from greater things to lesser, no rather, he was heightening it, and raising it from the lesser to the greater. For nothing is so great as that the blood of this Son should be shed for us. Greater this than both the adoption, and all the other gifts of grace, that He spared not even the Son. For great indeed is the forgiveness of sins, yet this is the far greater thing, that it should be done by the Lord's blood. For that this is far greater than all, look how here again he exclaims,

Ver. 7, 8. " According to the riches of His grace, which He made to abound toward us."

The abovementioned gifts are riches, yet is this far more so. "Which,"saith he, " He made to abound toward us." They are both "riches" and "they have abounded," that is to say, were poured forth in ineffable measure. It is not possible to represent in words what blessings we have in fact experienced. For riches indeed they are, abounding riches, and He hath given in abundance riches not of man but of God, so that on all hands it is impossible that they should be expressed. And to show us how He gave it to such abundance, he adds,

Ver. 8, 9. " In all wisdom and prudence[5], having made known unto us the mystery of His will."

That is to say, Making us wise and prudent, in that which is true wisdom, and that which is true prudence. Strange! what friendship! For He telleth us His secrets; the mysteries, saith he, of His will, as if one should say, He hath made known to us the things that are in His heart. For here is indeed the mystery which is full of all wisdom and prudence. For what will you mention equal to this wisdom! Those that were worth nothing, it hath discovered a way of raising them to wealth and abundance. What can equal this wise contrivance? He that was an enemy, he that was hated, he is in a moment lifted up on high. And not this only, —but, yet more, that it should be done at this particular time, this again was the work of wisdom; and that it should be done by means of the Cross. It were matter of long discourse here to point out, how all this was the work of wisdom, and how He had made us wise. And therefore he repeats again the words,

" According to His good pleasure[6] which He purposed in Him."[7]

That is to say, this He desired, this He tra-

---

[1] Different usages were observed as regards the Baptismal Confession. In all cases there was one before Baptism. In some places it was made three times; and in some it was written after it was spoken. vid. Bingham *Antique*, xi. 7. &c.

[2] [" The designation of Christ by ὁ ἠγαπημένος makes us feel the greatness of the divine grace."—Meyer.—G. A.]

[3] [" More precise elucidation of what has been said, on the basis of experience (ἔχομεν)."Meyer.—G. A.]

[4] ["'Through His Blood' is a more precise definition of the preceding ἐν ᾧ 'in whom.' "—Meyer. "We have redemption not in His work without His Person but in His Person which with His work is a living unity."—Olshausen in *Lange*.—G. A.]

[5] [" 'In all wisdom and prudence' is not to be joined, as Chrysostom does, with 'having made known' (γνωρίσας), because it would thus denote the attribute of God operative in the γνωρίζειν, which on account of the πάσῃ, 'every,' is not admissible. Paul in making known the mystery had to set forth not the display of 'grace in itself but as revealed.' Hence some definition to the clause, 'which he made to abound toward us,' is necessary and this is the 'in all wisdom and prudence.' "—Meyer.—G. A.]

[6] [" According to His good pleasure' belongs to γνωρίσας, stating that God has accomplished the making known in pursuance of His free self-determination. cf. ver. 5."—Meyer.—G. A.]

[7] [" 'Which He purposed in Him,' in itself redundant, serves for the attaching of that which follows."—Meyer. G. A.]

vailed for, as one might say, that He might be able to reveal to us the mystery. What mystery? That He would have man seated up on high. And this hath come to pass.

Ver. 10. "Unto a dispensation of the fulness of the times to sum up all things in Christ, the things in the heavens and the things upon the earth, even in Him."

Heavenly things, he means to say, had been severed from earthly. They had no longer one Head. So far indeed as the system of the creation went, there was over all One God, but so far as management of one household went, this, amid the wide spread of Gentile error, was not the case, but they had been severed from His obedience.

"Unto a dispensation," saith he, "of the fulness of the times."

The fulness of the times, he calls it. Observe with what nicety he speaks. And whereas he points out the origination, the purpose, the will, the first intention, as proceeding from the Father, and the fulfillment and execution as effected by the agency of the Son, yet no where does he apply to him the term minister[1].

"He chose us," saith he, "in Him, having foreordained us unto adoption as sons through Jesus Christ to Himself;" and, "to the praise of the glory of His grace, in whom we have redemption through His blood,—which He purposed in Him, unto a dispensation of the fulness of the times, to sum up all things in Christ;" and no where hath he called Him minister. If however the word "in" and the word "by" implies a mere minister, look what the matter comes to. Just in the very beginning of the Epistle, he used the expression "through the will of the Father." The Father, he means, willed, the Son wrought. But neither does it follow, that because the Father willed, the Son is excluded from the willing; nor because the Son wrought, that the Father is deprived of the working. But to the Father and the Son, all things are common. "For all Mine are Thine," saith He, "and Thine are Mine." (Jo. xvii: 10.)

The fulness of the times,[2] however, was His coming. After, then, He had done everything, by the ministry both of Angels, and of Prophets, and of the Law, and nothing came of it, and

it was well nigh come to this, that man had been made in vain, brought into the world in vain, nay, rather to his ruin; when all were absolutely perishing, more fearfully than in the deluge, He devised this dispensation, that is by grace; that it might not be in vain, might not be to no purpose that man was created. This he calls "the fulness of the times," and "wisdom." And why so? Because at that time when they were on the very point of perishing, then they were rescued.

That "He might sum up" he saith.

What is the meaning of this word, "sum up?" It is "to knit together." Let us, however, endeavor to get near the exact import. With ourselves then, in common conversation, the word means the summing into a brief compass things spoken at length, the concise account of matters described in detail. And it has this meaning. For Christ hath gathered up in Himself the dispensations carried on through a lengthened period, that is to say, He hath cut them short. For "by finishing His word and cutting it short in righteousness." (Romans ix: 28.) He both comprehended former dispensations, and added others beside. This is the meaning of "summing up."

It has also another signification; and of what nature is this? He hath set over all one and the same Head, i. e., Christ according to the flesh, alike over Angels and men. That is to say, He hath given to Angels and men one and the same government; to the one the Incarnate, to the other God the Word.[3] Just as one might say of a house which has some part decayed and the other sound, He hath rebuilt the house, that is to say, He has made it stronger, and laid a firmer foundation. So also here He hath brought all under one and the same Head.[4] For thus will an union be

---

[1] E. G. of the Angels by way of contrast, "Are they not all ministering spirits, sent forth to minister," εἰς διακονίαν. Hebr. i: 14. However S. Irenæus says, "Ministral ei ad omnia sua progenies et figuratio sua, id est Filius et Spiritus Sanctus." Hær. iv: 17. And St. Justin Martyr applies to our Lord the word ὑπηρετεῖν. Tryph. 61, as scripture does the word Angel or Messenger. The distinction is obvious; our Lord may be named the Minister or Instrument of the Father in the sense in which our reason may be called the instrument of our mind, as being one with it and in it. In this sense St. Hilary calls the Son obedientem dictis Dei Deum. de Trin. v. vid. Petav. De Trin. ii. 7. §. 7.

[2] ['Which he purposed in him' (i. e. 'Christ' according to Rev. Ver. and W. and H.; but 'God' according, to Meyer and Ellicott, who have αὐτῷ) "with a design to the dispensation of the fullness of the times, i. e., the dispensation to be established at the setting in of the fulness of the times. Gal. iv: 4. Mark. i: 15."—Meyer.—G. A.]

[3] ["A distinction at variance with Scripture."—Meyer.—G. A.]
[4] ["This illustration has been again employed by Harless whose view of this passage is that the apostle speaks thus: 'The Lord and Creator of the whole body of which heaven and earth are members, has in the restoration of one member restored the whole body; and in this consists the greatest significance of the reconciliation that it is not merely a restoration of the life of earth but a bringing back of the harmony of the universe. This concedes to the τὰ ἐπὶ τοῖς οὐρανοῖς merely an indirect participation in the ἀνακεφαλαίωσις and the de facto operation of the Messianic οἰκονομία on the heavenly world is set aside,—which appears the less admissible inasmuch as the τὰ ἐπὶ τοῖς οὐρανοῖς has the precedence (in position)."—Meyer. "Heaven and earth have become places of sin (vi: 12:) indeed heaven was the first theatre of sin when a part of the angels fell into sin and away from God (1 Tim. iii: 6; 1 Jo. iii: 8; James ii: 19; 2 Peter ii: 4;) thence it came to earth (2 Cor. xi: 3; 1 Cor. x: 20, 21) Thus the state originally appointed by God and the development He wished to be without disturbance, ceased (Rom. viii: 18-24,) so that a renewing of the heavens and the earth was taken into view (2 Peter iii: 13.) The center of this renewal is Christ and His redeeming work. Here we may certainly apply what Bengel so aptly remarks on Rom. viii: 19. that pro suo quodque genus captu, 'every kind according to its capacity,' participates in this Anacephalaiosis, the evil (angels) as conquered and rejected opponents, the good angels as participating friends, the redeemed as accepted children, the rest of creation as subordinate companions."—Braune in Lange. Similarly Eadie: "Not only has harmony been restored to the universe and the rupture occasioned by sin repaired, but beings still in rebellion are placed under Christ's control, as well as the unconscious elements and spheres of nature. This summation is seen in the form of government: Jesus is universal regent."—G. A.]

effected, thus will a close bond be effected, if one and all can be brought under one and the same Head, and thus have some constraining bond of union from above. Honored then as we are with so great a blessing, so high a privilege, so great loving-kindness, let us not shame our Benefactor, let us not render in vain so great grace. Let us exemplify the life of Angels, the virtue of Angels, the conversation of Angels, yea, I entreat and conjure you, that all these things turn not to our judgment, nor to our condemnation, but to our enjoyment of those good things, which may God grant we may all attain, in Christ Jesus, our Lord, with whom to the Father, together with the Holy Ghost, be glory, strength, &c. &c.

HOMILY II.

CHAPTER I. VERSES 11–14.

"In whom also we were made a heritage, having been foreordained according to the purpose of Him who worketh all things after the counsel of his will."

PAUL earnestly endeavors on all occasions to display the unspeakable loving-kindness of God towards us, to the utmost of his power. For that it is impossible to do so adequately, hear his own words. "O! the depth of the riches both of the wisdom and knowledge of God; how unsearchable are His judgments, and His ways past tracing out." (Rom. xi: 33.) Still, notwithstanding, so far as it is possible, he does display it. What then is this which he is saying; "In whom also we were made a heritage, being predestinated?" Above he used the word, "He chose us;" here he saith, "we were made a heritage." But inasmuch as a lot is a matter of chance, not of deliberate choice, nor of virtue, (for it is closely allied to ignorance and accident, and oftentimes passing over the virtuous, brings forward the worthless into notice,) observe how he corrects this very point: "having been foreordained," saith he, "according to the purpose of Him who worketh all things." That is to say, not merely have we been made a heritage, as, again, we have not merely been chosen, (for it is God who chooses,) and so neither have we merely been allotted, (for it is God who allots,)[1] but it is "according to a purpose." This is what he says also in the Epistle to the Romans, (Rom. viii: 28–30.) "To them that are called according to His purpose;" and "whom He called, them He also justified, and whom He justified, them he also glorified." Having first used the expression, "to them that are called according to a purpose," and at the same time wishing to declare their privilege compared with the rest of mankind, he speaks also of inheritance by lot, yet so as not to divest them of free will. That point then, which more properly belongs to happy fortune, is the very point he insists upon. For this inheritance by lot depends not on virtue, but, as one might say, on fortuitous circumstances. It is as though he had said, lots were cast, and He hath chosen us;[2] but the whole is of deliberate choice. Men predestinated, that is to say, having chosen them to Himself, He hath separated. He saw us, as it were, chosen by lot before we were born. For marvellous is the foreknowledge of God, and acquainted with all things before their beginning.

But mark now how on all occasions he takes pains to point out, that it is not the result of any change of purpose, but that these matters had been thus modeled from the very first, so that we are in no wise inferior to the Jews in this respect; and how, in consequence, he does every thing with this view. How then is it that Christ Himselt saith, "I was not sent, but unto the lost sheep of the house of Israel?" (Mat. xv: 24.) And said again to his disciples, "Go not into any way of the Gentiles, and enter not into any city of the Samaritans." (Mat. x: 5.) And Paul again himself says, "It was necessary that the word of God should first be spoken to you. Seeing ye thrust it from you and judge yourselves unworthy of eternal life, lo, we turn to the Gentiles." (Acts xiii: 46.) These expressions, I say, are used with this design, that no one may suppose that this work came to pass incidentally only. "According to the purpose," he says, "of Him who worketh all

---

[1] [Meyer against the Rev. Version and many scholars makes the meaning here to be: "In whom we were allotted the inheritance." He shows that as πιστεύειν may take as subject when in passive voice the dative of the active construction, so also may κληροῦν which takes in the active a dative.—See also verse 14, κληρονομία.—G. A.]

[2] "Why calls he the grace of God by the name of lot? because in a lot there is no choice, but the will of God; for when it is said, 'a man does, he does not,' merits are regarded; and then there is a choice, not a lot. But when God found no merits of ours, He saved us by the lot of His will, because He willed, not because we were worthy. This is a lot," &c. August. in Psalm xxx. Enar. iii. 13.

things after the counsel of His will." That is to say, He had no after workings; having modeled all things from the very first, thus he leads forward all things "according to the counsel of His will." So that it was not merely because the Jews did not listen that He called the Gentiles, nor was it of mere necessity, nor was it on any inducement arising from them.

Ver. 12, 13. "To the end that we should be unto the praise of His glory, we who had before hoped[1] in Christ. In whom ye also having heard the word of the truth, the Gospel of your salvation."

That is to say, through whom. Observe how he on all occasions speaks of Christ, as the Author of all things, and in no case gives Him the title of a subordinate agent, or a minister. And so again, elsewhere, in his Epistle to the Hebrews, he says, "that God, having of old time spoken unto the Fathers in the prophets, hath at the end of these days spoken unto us in His Son," (Heb. 1 : 1.) that is "through" His Son.

"The word of truth," he says, no longer that of the type, nor of the image.

"The Gospel of your salvation." And well does he call it the Gospel of salvation, intimating in the one word a contrast to the law, in the other, a contrast with punishment to come. For what is the message, but the Gospel of salvation, which forbears to destroy those that are worthy of destruction.

Ver. 14. "In whom having also believed, ye were sealed with the Holy Spirit of promise, which is an earnest of our inheritance."

Here again, the word "sealed," is an indication of especial forecast. He does not speak of our being predestinated only, nor of our being allotted, but further, of our being sealed. For just as though one were to make those who should fall to his lot manifest, so also did God separate them for believing, and sealed them for the allotment of the things to come.

You see how, in process of time, He makes them objects of wonder. So long as they were in His foreknowledge, they were manifest to no one, but when they were sealed, they became manifest, though not in the same way as we are; for they will be manifest except a few. The Israelites also were sealed, but that was by circumcision, like the brutes and reasonless creatures. We too are sealed, but it is as sons, "with the Spirit."

But what is meant by, "with the Spirit of promise?" Doubtless it means that we have received that Spirit according to promise. For there are two promises, the one by the prophets, the other from the Son.

By the Prophets.—Hearken to the words of Joel; "I will pour out My spirit upon all flesh, and your sons and your daughters shall prophesy, your old men shall dream dreams, your young men shall see visions," (Joel ii: 28.) And hearken again to the words of Christ; "But ye shall receive power, when the Holy Ghost is come upon you, and ye shall be my witnesses both in Jerusalem, and in all Judea, and Samaria, and unto the uttermost part of the earth." (Acts. i:8.) And truly, the Apostle means, He ought, as God, to have been believed; however, he does not ground his affirmation upon this, but examines it like a case where man is concerned, speaking much as he does in the Epistle to the Hebrews; (Heb. vi: 18.) where he says, "That by two immutable things in which it was impossible for God to lie, we may have a strong encouragement." Thus here also he makes the things already bestowed a sure token of the promise of those which are yet to come. For this reason he further calls it an "earnest," (Cf. also 2. Cor. i : 22.) for an earnest is a part of the whole. He hath purchased what we are most concerned in, our salvation; and hath given us an earnest in the mean while. Why then did He not give the whole at once? Because neither have we, on our part, done the whole of our work. We have believed. This is a beginning; and He too on His part hath given an earnest. When we show our faith by our works, then He will add the rest. Nay, more, He hath given yet another pledge, His own blood, and hath promised another still. In the same way as in case of war between nation and nation they give hostages: just so hath God also given His Son as a pledge of peace and solemn treaties, and, further, the Holy Spirit also which is from Him. For they, that are indeed partakers of the Spirit, know that He is the earnest of our inheritance. Such an one was Paul, who already had here a foretaste of the blessings there. And this is why he was so eager, and yearned to be released from things below, and groaned within himself. He transferred his whole mind thither, and saw every thing with different eyes. Thou hast no part in the reality, and therefore failest to understand the description. Were we all partakers of the Spirit, as we ought to be partakers, then should we behold Heaven, and the order of things that is there.

It is an earnest, however, of what? of

Ver. 14. "The redemption of God's own possession."

---

[1] [Meyer's reference of ἡμᾶς * * * τοὺς προηλπικότας to Jewish Christians seems precarious. It seems better to make the ἡμᾶς refer to Christians in general, the προ in προηλπικότας refer to the time before the second Advent and the καὶ ὑμεῖς to the readers. So De Wette and Theophylact.—G. A.]

For our absolute redemption takes place then.[1] For now we have our life in the world, we are liable to many human accidents, and are living amongst ungodly men. But our absolute redemption will be then, when there shall be no sins, no human sufferings, when we shall not be indiscriminately mixed with all kinds of people.

At present, however, there is but an earnest, because at present we are far distant from these blessings. Yet is our citizenship not upon earth; even now we are out of the pale of the things that are here below. Yes, we are sojourners even now.

Ver. 14. "Unto the praise of His glory."

This he adds in immediate connection. And why? Because it would serve to give those who heard it full assurance. Were it for our sake only, he means to say, that God did this, there might be some room for misgiving. But if it be for His own sake, and in order to display His goodness, he assigns, as a sort of witness, a reason why these things never possibly could be otherwise. We find the same language everywhere applied to the case of the Israelites. "Do Thou this for us for Thy Name's sake;" (Ps. cix: 21.) and again, God Himself said, "I do it for Mine own sake;" (Isa. xlviii: 11.) and so Moses, "Do it, if for nothing else, yet for the glory of Thy Name." This gives those who hear it full assurance; it relieves them to be told, that whatever He promises, for His own goodness' sake He will most surely perform.

MORAL. Let not the hearing, however, make us too much at our ease; for although He doth it for His own sake, yet notwithstanding He requires a duty on our part. If He says, "Them that honor Me I will honor, and they that despise Me shall be lightly esteemed," (1 Sam. ii: 30.) let us reflect that there is that which He requires of us also. True, it is the praise of His glory to save those that are enemies, but those who, after being made friends, continue His friends. So that if they were to return back to their former state of enmity, all were vain and to no purpose. There is not another Baptism, nor is there a second reconciliation again, but "a certain fearful expectation of judgment which shall devour the adversaries." (Heb. x: 27.) If we intend at the same time to be always at enmity with Him and yet to claim forgiveness at His hand, we shall never cease to be at enmity, and to be wanton, to grow in depravity, and to be blind to the Sun of Righteousness which has risen. Dost thou not see the ray that shall open thine eyes? render them then good and sound and quicksighted. He hath showed thee the

true light; if thou shunnest it, and runnest back again into the darkness, what shall be thy excuse? What sort of allowance shall be made for thee? None from that moment. For this is a mark of unspeakable enmity. When indeed thou knewest not God, then if thou wert at enmity with Him, thou hadst, be it how it might, some excuse. But when thou hast tasted the goodness and the honey, if thou again abandonest them, and turnest to thine own vomit, what else art thou doing but bringing forward evidence of excessive hatred and contempt? 'Nay,' thou wilt say, 'but I am constrained to it by nature. I love Christ indeed, but I am constrained by nature.' If thou art under the power and force of constraint, thou wilt have allowance made; but if thou yield from indolence, not for a moment.

Now then, come, let us examine this very question, whether sins are the effect of force and constraint, or of indolence and great carelessness. The law says, "Thou shalt not kill." What sort of force, what sort of violence, is there here? Violence indeed must one use to force himself to kill, for who amongst us would as a matter of choice plunge his sword into the throat of his neighbor, and stain his hand with blood? Not one. Thou seest then that, on the contrary, sin is more properly matter of violence and constraint. For God hath implanted in our nature a charm, which binds us to love one another. "Every beast (it saith) loveth his like, and every man loveth his neighbor." (Ecclus. xiii.: 15.) Seest thou that we have from our nature seeds which tend to virtue; whereas those of vice are contrary to nature? and if these latter predominate, this is but an evidence of our exceeding indolence.

Again, what is adultery? What sort of necessity is there to bring us to this? Doubtless, it will be said, the tyranny of lust. But why, tell me, should this be? What, is it not in every one's power to have his own wife, and thus to put a stop to this tyranny? True, he will say, but a sort of passion for my neighbor's wife seizes hold on me. Here the question is no longer one of necessity. Passion is no matter of necessity, no one loves of necessity, but of deliberate choice and free will. Indulgence of nature, indeed, is perhaps matter of necessity, but to love one woman rather than another is no matter of necessity. Nor is the point with you natural desire, but vanity, and wantonness, and unbounded licentiousness. For which is according to reason, that a man should have an espoused wife, and her the mother of his children, or one not acknowledged? Know ye not that it is intimacy that breeds attachment. This, therefore, is not the fault of nature. Blame not natural desire. Natural desire was bestowed

[1] ["The final consummation of the redemption effected by the λύτρον of Christ (v. 7.) at the Parousia (Lu. xxi : 28.) when suffering, sin and death are wholly done away and in the glorifying of the body there sets in the δόξα of the children of God."—Meyer. —G. A.]

with a view to marriage; it was given with a view to the procreation of children, not with a view to adultery and corruption. The laws, too, know how to make allowance for those sins which are of necessity,—or rather nothing is sin when it arises from necessity but all sin rises from wantonness. God hath not so framed man's nature as that he should have any necessity to sin, since were this the case, there would be no such thing as punishment. We ourselves exact no account of things done of necessity and by constraint, much less would God, so full of mercy and loving-kindness.

Again, what is stealing? is it matter of necessity? Yes, a man will say, because poverty causes this. Poverty, however, rather compels us to work, not to steal. Poverty, therefore, has in fact the contrary effect. Theft is the effect of idleness; whereas poverty produces usually not idleness, but a love of labor. So that this sin is the effect of indolence, as you may learn from hence. Which, I ask, is the more difficult, the more distasteful, to wander about at night without sleep, to break open houses, and walk about in the dark, and to have one's life in one's hand, and to be always prepared for murder, and to be shivering and dead with fear; or to be attending to one's daily task, in full enjoyment of safety and security? This last is the easier task; and it is because this is easier, that the majority practise it rather than the other. Thou seest then that it is virtue which is according to nature, and vice which is against nature, in the same way as disease and health are.

What, again, are falsehood and perjury? What necessity can they possibly imply? None whatever, nor any compulsion; it is a matter to which we proceed voluntarily. We are distrusted, it will be said. True, distrusted we are, because we choose it. For we might, if we would, be trusted more upon our character, than upon our oath. Why, tell me, is it that we do not trust some, no, not on their oath, whilst we deem others trustworthy even independently of oaths.[1] Seest thou that there is no need of oaths in any case? ' When such an one speaks,' we say, ' I believe him, even without any oath, but thee, no, not with thy oaths.' Thus then an oath is unnecessary; and is in fact an evidence rather of distrust than of confidence. For where a man is over ready to take his oath, he does not leave us to entertain any great idea of his scrupulousness. So that the man who is most constant in his use of oaths, has on no occasion any necessity for using one, and he who never uses one on any occasion, has in himself

the full benefit of its use. Some one says there is a necessity for an oath, to produce confidence; but we see that they are the more readily trusted who abstain from taking oaths.

But again, if one is a man of violence, is this a matter of necessity? Yes, he will say, because his passion carries him away, and burns within him, and does not let the soul be at rest. Man, to act with violence is not the effect of anger, but of littleness of mind. Were it the effect of anger, all men, whenever they were angry, would never cease committing acts of violence. We have anger given us, not that we may commit acts of violence on our neighbors, but that we may correct those that are in sin, that we may bestir ourselves, that we may not be sluggish. Anger is implanted in us as a sort of sting, to make us gnash with our teeth against the devil, to make us vehement against him, not to set us in array against each other. We have arms, not to make us at war amongst ourselves, but that we may employ our whole armor against the enemy. Art thou prone to anger? Be so against thine own sins: chastise thy soul, scourge thy conscience, be a severe judge, and merciless in thy sentence against thine own sins. This is the way to turn anger to account. It was for this that God implanted it within us.

But again, is plunder a matter of necessity? No, in no wise. Tell me, what manner of necessity is there to be grasping: what manner of compulsion? Poverty, a man will say, causes it, and the fear of being without common necessaries. Now this is the very reason why you ought not to be grasping. Wealth so gotten has no security in it. You are doing the very same thing as a man would do, who, if he were asked why he laid the foundation of his house in the sand, should say, he did it because of the frost and rain. Whereas this would be the very reason why he should not lay it in the sand. They are the very foundations which the rain, and blasts, and wind, most quickly overturn. So that if thou wouldest be wealthy, never be rapacious; if thou wouldest transmit wealth to thy children, get righteous wealth, at least, if any there be that is such. Because this abides, and remains firm, whereas that which is not such, quickly wastes and perishes. Tell me, hast thou a mind to be rich, and dost thou take the goods of others? Surely this is not wealth: wealth consists in possessing what is thine own. He that is in possession of the goods of others, never can be a wealthy man; since at that rate even your very silk venders, who receive their goods as a consignment from others, would be the wealthiest and the richest of men. Though for the time, indeed, it is theirs, still we do not call them wealthy. And why forsooth? Because they are in possession of what belongs to

---

[1] Vid. also *Hom. ad Pop. Antioch.* vii. fin. However, in Act Apost. Hom. x. fin. he considers oaths allowable in order to convince the weak. St. Augustine says the same, *de Serm. Dom.* i. 51. thus accounting for St. Paul's expressions, Rom. i: 9. 1 Cor. xv: 31. 2 Cor. ii: 31. Gal. i. 20.

others. For though the piece itself happens to be theirs, still the money it is worth is not theirs. Nay, and even if the money is in their hands, still this is not wealth. Now, if consignments thus given render not men more wealthy because we so soon resign them, how can those which arise from rapine render them wealthy? However, if at any rate thou desirest to be wealthy, (for the matter is not one of necessity,) what greater good is it that thou wouldest fain enjoy? Is it a longer life? Yet, surely men of this character quickly become shortlived. Oftentimes they pay as the penalty of plunder and rapaciousness, an untimely death; and not only suffer as a penalty the loss of the enjoyment of their gains, but go out of life having gained but little, and hell to boot. Oftentimes too they die of diseases, which are the fruits of self-indulgence, and of toil, and of anxiety. Fain would I understand why it is that wealth is so eagerly pursued by mankind. Why surely for this reason hath God set a limit and a boundary to our nature, that we may have no need to go on seeking wealth beyond it. For instance He hath commanded us, to clothe the body in one, or perhaps in two garments; and there is no need of any more to cover us.

Where is the good of ten thousand changes of raiment, and those moth-eaten? The stomach has its appointed bound, and any thing given beyond this, will of necessity destroy the whole man. Where then is the use of your herds, and flocks, and cutting up of flesh? We require but one roof to shelter us. Where then is the use of your vast ground-plots, and costly buildings? Dost thou strip the poor, that vultures and jackdaws may have where to dwell? And what a hell do not these things deserve? Many are frequently raising edifices that glisten with pillars and costly marbles, in places which they never so much as saw. What scheme is there indeed that they have not adopted? Yet neither themselves reap the benefit, nor any one else. The desolateness does not allow them to get away thither; and yet not even thus do they desist. You see that these things are not done for profit's-sake, but in all these cases folly, and absurdity, and vainglory, is the motive. And this, I beseech you to avoid, that we may be enabled to avoid also every other evil, and may obtain those good things which are promised to them that love Him, in our Lord Jesus Christ, with whom to the Father, together with the Holy Ghost, be glory, strength, honor forever. Amen.

HOMILY III.

VERSES. 15–20.

"For this cause I also, having heard of the faith in the Lord Jesus, which is among you, and which ye show toward all the saints, cease not to give thanks for you, making mention of you in my prayers; that the God of our Lord Jesus Christ, the Father of glory, may give unto you a spirit of wisdom and revelation in the knowledge of Him: having the eyes of your heart enlightened; that ye may know what is the hope of His calling, what the riches of the glory of His inheritance in the saints, and what the exceeding greatness of His power to us-ward who believe, according to that working of the strength of His might, which He wrought in Christ, when He raised Him from the dead."

NEVER was anything equal to the yearnings of the Apostle, never anything like the sympathy and the affectionateness of the blessed Paul, who made his every prayer in behalf of whole cities and peoples, and writes the same to all,[1] "I thank my God for you, making mention of you in my prayers." Think how many he had in his mind, whom it were a labor so much as to remember; how many he made mention of in his prayers, giving thanks to God for them all as though he himself had received the greatest blessing.

"Wherefore," he says, i. e., because of what is to come,[2] because of the good things that are laid up in store for them who rightly believe and live. And it is meet then to give thanks to God both for all the things which mankind have received at His hands, both heretofore and hereafter; and meet to give Him thanks also for the faith of them that believe.

"Having heard," saith he, "of the faith in the Lord Jesus which is among you, and which ye show[3] toward all the saints."

He on all occasions knits together and combines faith and love, a glorious pair; nor does he mention the saints of that country only, but all.

---

[1] [Ro. i. 9; 1 Cor. i. 4; Phil. i. 3, 4; Col. i. 3; 1 Thes. i. 2.—G. A.]

[2] ["On the contrary this 'wherefore,' διὰ τοῦτο, refers to what precedes ver. 13, 14, 'because this is the case that ye too are in Christ and have been sealed with the Spirit.' So Theophylect."—Meyer.—G. A.]

[3] [The word 'love,' ἀγάπην, which gets into the Auth. Ver. from some inferior MSS., is omitted by Aleph. A. B. W. and H. Rev. Vers. cf. Col. i: 4.—G. A.]

"I cease not to give thanks for you, making mention of you in my prayers."

What is thy prayer, and what thy entreaty? It is

"That the God of our Lord Jesus Christ, the Father of glory, may give unto you a spirit of wisdom and revelation." [1] Two things he requires them to understand, as it is their duty to understand them; to what blessings they are called, and how they have been released from their former state. He says, however, himself, that these points are three. How then are they three? In order that we may understand touching the things to come; for from the good things laid up for us, we shall know His ineffable and surpassing riches, and from understanding who we were, and how we believed, we shall know His power and sovereignty, in turning again to Himself those who had been so long time estranged from Him. "For the weakness of God is stronger than men." (1 Cor. i: 25.) Inasmuch as it is by the self-same power by which He raised Christ from the dead, that He hath also drawn us to Himself. Nor is that power limited to the resurrection, but far exceeds it.

Ver. 21, 22. "And made Him to sit at His right hand, in the Heavenly places, far above all rule and authority, and power and dominion, and every name that is named: and He put all things in subjection under His feet, and gave Him to be Head over all things to the Church, which is His body, the fulness of Him that filleth all in all."

Vast indeed are the mysteries and secrets of which He hath made us partakers. And these it is not possible for us to understand otherwise than by being partakers of the Holy Ghost, and by receiving abundant grace. And it is for this reason that Paul prays. "The Father of glory," that is, He that hath given us vast blessings, for he constantly addresses Him according to the subject he is upon, as, for instance, when he says, "The Father of mercies and God of all comfort." (2 Cor. i: 3.) And, again, the Prophet says, "The Lord is my strength and my might." (Ps. xviii: 1.)

"The Father of glory."

He has no name by which he may represent these things, and on all occasions calls them "glory," which is in fact, with us, the name and appellation of every kind of magnificence. Mark, he says, the Father of glory; (cf. Acts vii: 2) but of Christ the God.[2] What then? Is the Son inferior to the glory? No, there is no one, not even a maniac, would say so.

"May give unto you,"

That is, may raise and wing your understanding, for it is not possible otherwise to understand these things. "For the natural man receiveth not the things of the Spirit of God; for they are foolishness unto him." (1 Cor. ii: 14.) So then, there is need of spiritual "wisdom," that we may perceive things spiritual, that we may see things hidden. That Spirit "revealeth" all things. He is going to set forth the mysteries of God. Now the knowledge of the mysteries of God, the Spirit alone comprehends, who also searcheth the deep things of Him. It is not said, "that Angel, or Archangel, or any other created power, may give," that is, confer upon you a spiritual gift. And if this be of revelation, then is the discovery of arguments consequently vain. For he that hath learned God, and knoweth God, shall no longer dispute concerning any thing. He will not say, This is impossible, and That is possible, and How did the other thing come to pass? If we learn God, as we ought to know Him; if we learn God from Him from whom we ought to learn Him, that is from the Spirit Himself; then shall we no longer dispute concerning any thing. And hence it is that he says,

"Having the eyes of your heart enlightened in the knowledge of Him." [3]

He that hath learned what God is, will have no misgiving about His promises, and disbelief about what hath been already brought to pass. He prays, then, that there may be given them "a spirit of wisdom and revelation." Yet still he also establishes it, as far as he can himself, by arguments, and from "already" existing facts. For, whereas he was about to mention some things which had already come to pass, and others which had not as yet happened; he makes those which have been brought to pass, a pledge of those which have not: in some such way, I mean, as this,

"That ye may know," saith he, "what is the hope of His calling."

It is as yet, he means, hidden, but not so to the faithful.

"And," again, "what is the riches of the glory of His inheritance in the saints."[4]

---

[1] [Chrysostom's hasty and superficial treatment of this great passage would seem to justify the language of Dr. Newman in his preface to the Oxford translation of these homilies on Ephesians. There are "imperfections in their composition which in the opinion of some critics argued the absence of that comparative leisure which he enjoyed at Antioch." Schaff also says: "His life in Constantinople was too much disturbed to leave him quiet leisure for preparation." This, however, in referring to his Homilies on Acts. *Prolegomena* p. 19.—G. A.]

[2] [Compare Mat. xxvii. 46; John xx: 17; Rev. iii: 12.—G. A.]
[3] ["The words, 'in the knowledge of Him,' ἐνέπι γνώσει αὐτοῦ, are not to be joined with the words 'having your heart enlightened,' as Chrysostom here, which entirely destroys the paralellism and symmetry of the sentence, but with the words, may give you a spirit of wisdom, etc., (in the knowledge of Him)."—Meyer and Ellicott.—G. A.]
[4] ["That ye may know what a great and glorious hope is given to the man whom God has called to the Kingdom of the Messiah; and that ye may know what is the object of that hope, namely, the riches of the glory of the inheritance which He gives; and that ye may know that by which this hope is to be realized, namely, the infinite power of God as shown in the resurrection and exaltation of Jesus Christ."—Meyer.—G. A.]

This too is as yet hidden.

But what is clear? that through His power we have believed that He hath raised Christ. For to persuade souls, is a thing far more miraculous than to raise a dead body. I will endeavor to make this clear. Hearken then. Christ said to the dead, " Lazarus, come forth," (John xi: 43.) and straightway he obeyed. Peter said, "Tabitha, arise," (Acts ix: 40.) and she did not refuse. He Himself shall speak the word at the last day, and all shall rise, and that so quickly, that "they which are yet alive, shall in no wise precede them that are fallen asleep," (1 Thess. iv: 15.) and all shall come to pass, all run together "in a moment, in the twinkling of an eye." (1 Cor. xv: 52.) But in the matter of believing, it is not thus, but how is it? Hearken then to Him again, how He saith, "How often would I have gathered thy children together, and ye would not." (Matt. xxiii: 37.) You perceive that this last is the more difficult. Accordingly, it is upon this that he builds up the whole argument; because by human calculations it is far more difficult to influence the choice, than to work upon nature. And the reason is this, it is because He would thus have us become good of our own will. Thus with good reason does he say,[1]

"The exceeding greatness of His power to us-ward who believe."

Yes, when Prophets had availed nothing, nor Angels, nor Archangels, when the whole creation, both visible and invisible, had failed, (the visible lying before us, and without any power to guide us, and much also which is invisible,) then He ordered His own coming, to show us that it was a matter which required Divine power.

" The riches of the glory,"

That is, the unutterable glory ; for what language shall be adequate to express that glory of which the saints shall then be partakers? None. But verily there is need of grace in order that the understanding may perceive it, and admit even so much as at least one little ray. Some things indeed they knew even before ; now he was desirous that they should learn more, and know it more clearly. Seest thou how great things He hath wrought? He hath raised up Christ. Is this a small thing? But look again. He hath set Him at His right hand. And shall any language then be able to represent this? Him that is of the earth, more mute than the fishes, and made the sport of devils, He hath in a moment raised up on high. Truly this is indeed the " exceeding greatness of His power." And behold, whither He hath raised Him.

" In the heavenly places ; "

He hath made Him far above all created nature, far above all rule and authority.

" Far above all rule," he saith.

Need then indeed is there of the Spirit, of an understanding wise in the knowledge of Him. Need then is there indeed of revelation. Reflect, how vast is the distance between the nature of man and of God. Yet from this vile estate hath He exalted Him to that high dignity. Nor does He mount by degrees, first one step, then another, then a third. Amazing ! He does not simply say, "above," but, "far above;" for God is above those powers which are above. And thither then hath He raised Him, Him that is one of us, brought Him from the lowest point to the supremest sovereignty, to that beyond which there is no other honor. Above "all" principality, he says, not, i. e., over one and not over another, but over all,

"Rule and authority and power, and dominion, and every name that is named."

Whatever there be in Heaven, He has become above all. And this is said of Him that was raised from the dead which is worthy of our admiration ; for of God the Word, it cannot possibly be, because what insects are in comparison of man, this the whole creation is in comparison of God. If all mankind are to be counted as spittle and were counted as the turn of a balance, consider the invisible powers as insects. But of Him that was one of us, this is great and surprising indeed. For He raised Him up from the very lowest parts of the earth. If all the nations are as a drop, how small a portion then of that drop is a single man ! Yet Him hath He made higher than all things, "not only in this world, but also in that which is to come." Therefore powers there are whose names are to us unintelligible, and unknown.

"And He put all things in subjection under His feet."

Not simply so set Him above them as to be honored above them, nor by way of comparison with them, but so that He should sit over them as His slaves. Amazing ! Awful indeed are these things ; every created power hath been made the slave of man by reason of God the Word dwelling in Him.[2] For it is possible for a man to be above others, without having others in subjection, but only as preferred before them. But here it is not so. No, " He put all things in subjection under His feet." And not simply put them in subjection, but in the most abject

---

[1] Ἔχοντας.

[2] Διὰ τὸν ἐνοικοῦντα Θεὸν Λόγον. The 'inhabitation' of the Word in our flesh, was a favorite form of speech with the Nestorians, who thereby insinuated that the Word dwelt in 'a' man, or denied Christ's unity of person. Yet the phrase is strictly orthodox, as being derived from John i[*]: 14, and is especially maintained by Cyril, the antagonist of Nestorius, in order to denote that God was in human 'nature,' vid. Cyril in Schol. 25. Theodor. Eran. ii, Ephræm. Antioch. apud Phot. 229.

subjection, that below which there can be none. Therefore he adds, "under His feet."

"And gave Him to be Head over all things to the Church."

Amazing again, whither hath He raised the Church? as though he were lifting it up by some engine, he hath raised it up to a vast height, and set it on yonder throne; for where the Head is, there is the body also. There is no interval to separate between the Head and the body; for were there a separation, then were it no longer a body, then were it no longer a head. "Over all things," he says. What is meant by "over all things?" He hath suffered neither Angel nor Archangel nor any other being to be above Him. But not only in this way hath He honored us, in exalting that which is of ourselves, but also in that He hath prepared the whole race in common to follow Him, to cling to Him, to accompany His train.

"Which is His body."

In order then that when you hear of the Head you may not conceive the notion of supremacy only, but also of consolidation, and that you may behold Him not as supreme Ruler only, but as Head of a body.

"The fulness of Him that filleth all in all" he says.

As though this were not sufficient to show the close connection and relationship, what does he add? "The fullness of Christ is the Church." And rightly, for the complement of the head is the body, and the complement of the body is the head. Mark what great arrangement Paul observes, how he spares not a single word, that he may represent the glory of God. "The complement," he says, i. e., the head is, as it were, filled up by the body, because the body is composed and made up of all its several parts, and he introduces Him as having need of each single one and not only of all in common and together; for unless we be many, and one be the hand, and another the foot, and another some other member, the whole body is not filled up. It is by all then that His body is filled up. Then is the head filled up, then is the body rendered perfect, when we are all knit together and united. Perceivest thou then the "riches of the glory of His inheritance? the exceeding greatness of His power towards them that believe? the hope of your calling?"

MORAL. Let us reverence our Head, let us reflect of what a Head we are the body,—a Head, to whom all things are put in subjection. According to this representation we ought to be better, yea, than the very angels, and greater than the Archangels, in that we have been honored above them all. God "took not hold of Angels," as he says in writing to the Hebrews, "but He took hold of the seed of Abraham."

(Heb. ii : 16.) He took hold of neither principality, nor power, nor dominion, nor any other authority, but He took up our nature, and made it to sit on His right hand. And why do I say, hath made it sit? He hath made it His garment[1], and not only so, but hath put all things in subjection under His feet. How many sorts of death supposest thou? How many souls? ten thousand? yea, and ten thousand times told, but nothing equal to it wilt thou mention. Two things He hath done, the greatest things. He hath both Himself descended to the lowest depth of humiliation, and hath raised up man to the height of exaltation. He saved him by His blood. He spoke of the former first, how that He so greatly humbled Himself. He speaks now of what is stronger than that—a great thing, the crown of all. Surely, even had we been counted worthy of nothing, it were enough. Or, had we been counted worthy even of this honor, it were enough, without the slaying of the Son. But where there are the two, what power of language must it not transcend and surpass? The very resurrection is not great, when I reflect on these things. It is of Him that he says, "The· God of our Lord Jesus Christ," not of God the Word.

Let us feel awed at the closeness of our relation, let us dread lest any one should be cut off from this body, lest any one should fall from it, lest any one should appear unworthy of it. If any one were to place a diadem about our head, a crown of gold, should we not do every thing that we might seem worthy of the lifeless jewels? But now it is not a diadem that is placed about our head, but, what is far greater, Christ is made our very Head, and yet we pay no regard to it. Yet Angels reverence that Head, and Archangels, and all those powers above. And shall we, which are His body, be awed neither on the one account nor the other? And what then shall be our hope of salvation? Conceive to yourself the royal throne, conceive the excess of the honor. This, at least if we chose, might more avail to startle us, yea, even than hell itself. For, even though hell were not, that we having been honored with such an honor, should be found base and unworthy of it, what punishment, what vengeance must not this carry with it? Think near whom thy Head is seated, (this single consideration is amply sufficient for any purpose whatever,) on whose right hand He is placed, far above all principality, and power, and might. Yet is the body of this Head trampled on by the very devils.

---

[1] Ἱμάτιον. Thus Cyril Alex. speaks of Christ as 'clothed about' with our nature. *In Success.* 2 p. 142. Vid. also Epiph. *Ancor.* §. 95. Augustine in *Psalm* 130. 10. This, as well as other theological terms, was abused by heretical disputants; as if it implied either that the manhood of Christ might be put off from His divine nature, or that it was a mere accidental and unsubstantial medium of manifesting it.

Nay, God forbid it should be thus; for were it thus, such a body could be His body no longer. Thy own head the more respectable of thy servants reverence, and dost thou subject thy body to be the sport of them that insult it? How sore punishment then shalt thou not deserve? If a man should bind the feet of the emperor with bonds and fetters, will he not be liable to the extremity of punishment? Dost thou expose the whole body to fierce monsters, and not shudder?

However, since our discourse is concerning the Lord's body, come, and let us turn our thoughts to it, even that which was crucified, which was nailed, which is sacrificed.[1] If thou art the body of Christ, bear the Cross, for He bore it: bear spitting, bear buffetings, bear nails. Such was that Body; that Body "did no sin, neither was guile found in His mouth." (1 Pet. ii: 22.) His hands did every thing for the benefit of them that needed, His mouth uttered not a word of those things which are not convenient. He heard them say, "Thou hast a devil," and He answered nothing.

Further, our discourse is concerning this Body, and as many of us as partake of that Body and taste of that Blood, are partaking of that which is in no wise different from that Body, nor separate. Consider that we taste of that Body that sitteth above, that is adored by Angels, that is next to the Power that is incorruptible. Alas! how many ways to salvation are open to us! He hath made us His own body, He hath imparted to us His own body, and yet not one of these things turns us away from what is evil. Oh the darkness, the depth of the abyss, the apathy! "Set your mind," saith he, "on the things that are above, where Christ is, seated on the right hand of God." (Col. iii: 1.) And after all this, some set their affections upon money, or licentiousness, others are carried captive by their passions!

Do ye not see, that even in our own body, when any part is superfluous and useless, it is cut off, is cut away? It is of no use that it has belonged to the body, when it is mutilated, when it is mortified, when it is decayed, when it is detrimental to the rest. Let us not then be too confident, because we have been once made members of this body. If this body of ours, though but a natural body, nevertheless suffers amputation, what dreadful evil shall it not undergo, if the moral principle should fail? When the body partakes not of this natural food, when the pores are stopped up, then it mortifies; when the ducts are closed, then it is palsied. So is it with us also, when we stop our ears, our soul becomes palsied; when we partake not of the spiritual food, when, instead

of corrupt bodily humors, evil dispositions impair us, all these things engender disease, dangerous disease, disease that wastes. And then there will be need of that fire, there will be need of that cutting asunder. For Christ cannot endure that we should enter into the bride-chamber with such a body as this. If He led away, and cast out the man that was clothed in filthy garments, what will He not do unto the man who attaches filth to the body; how will He not dispose of him?

I observe many partaking of Christ's Body lightly and just as it happens, and rather from custom and form, than consideration and understanding. When, saith a man, the holy season of Lent sets in, whatever a man may be, he partakes of the mysteries, or, when the day of the Lord's Epiphany[2] comes. And yet it is not the Epiphany, nor is it Lent, that makes a fit time for approaching, but it is sincerity and purity of soul. With this, approach at all times; without it, never. "For as often," (1 Cor. xi: 26.) saith he, "as ye do this, ye proclaim the Lord's death," i. e., "ye make a remembrance of the salvation that has been wrought for you, and of the benefits which I have bestowed." Consider those who partook of the sacrifices under the old Covenant, how great abstinence did they practise? How did they not conduct themselves? What did they not perform? They were always purifying themselves. And dost thou, when thou drawest nigh to a sacrifice, at which the very Angels tremble, dost thou measure the matter by the revolutions of seasons? and how shalt thou present thyself before the judgment-seat of Christ, thou who presumest upon His body with polluted hands and lips? Thou wouldest not presume to kiss a king with an unclean mouth, and the King of heaven dost thou kiss with an unclean soul? It is an outrage. Tell me, wouldest thou choose to come to the Sacrifice with unwashen hands? No, I suppose, not. But thou wouldest rather choose not to come at all, than come with soiled hands. And then, thus scrupulous as thou art in this little matter, dost thou come with soiled soul, and thus dare to touch it? And yet the hands hold it but for a time, whereas into the soul it is dissolved entirely. What, do ye not see the holy vessels so thoroughly cleansed all over, so resplendent? Our souls ought to be purer than they, more holy, more brilliant. And why so? Because those vessels are made so for our sakes. They partake not of Him that is in them, they perceive Him not. But we do;—

---

[1] Θυομένου.

[2] This was the great festival of the Greek Church, being in remembrance of our Lord's Baptism, and, as it would appear, of His birth inclusively. The festival of Christmas, which had been in use in the West from an earlier date, was introduced at Antioch A. D. 376, with much opposition. Chrysostom, A. D. 387, urges its due celebration in his *Hom. de Beato Philogon.* and *Serm. in Diem Natal. J. C.*

yes, verily. Now then, thou wouldest not choose to make use of a soiled vessel, and dost thou approach with a soiled soul? Observe the vast inconsistency of the thing. At the other times ye come not, no, not though often ye are clean; but at Easter, however flagrant an act ye may have committed, ye come. Oh! the force of custom and of prejudice! In vain is the daily Sacrifice,[1] in vain do we stand before the Altar; there is no one to partake. These things I am saying, not to induce you to partake any how, but that ye should render yourselves worthy to partake. Art thou not worthy of the Sacrifice, nor of the participation? If so, then neither art thou of the prayer. Thou hearest the herald,[2] standing, and saying, "As many as are in penitence, all pray."[3] As many as do not partake, are in penitence. If thou art one of those that are in penitence, thou oughtest not to partake; for he that partakes not, is one of those that are in penitence. Why then does he say, "Depart, ye that are not qualified to pray," whilst thou hast the effrontery to stand still? But no, thou art not of that number, thou art of the number of those who are qualified to partake, and yet art indifferent about it, and regardest the matter as nothing.

Look, I entreat: a royal table is set before you, Angels minister at that table, the King Himself is there, and dost thou stand gaping?"[4] Are thy garments defiled, and yet dost thou make no account of it?—or are they clean? Then fall down and partake. Every day He cometh in to see the guests, and converseth with them all. Yes, at this moment is he speaking to your conscience; "Friends, how stand ye here, not having on a wedding garment?" He said not, Why didst thou sit down? no, before he sat down, He declared him to be unworthy, so much as to come in. He saith not, "Why didst thou sit down to meat," but, "Why camest thou in?" And these are the words that He is at this very moment addressing to one and all of us that stand here with such shameless effrontery. For every one, that partaketh not of the mysteries, is standing here in shameless effrontery. It is for this reason, that they which are in sins are first of all put forth; for just as when a master is present at his table, it is not right that those servants who have offended him should be present, but they are sent out of

the way: just so also here when the sacrifice is brought forth, and Christ, the Lord's sheep, is sacrificed; when thou hearest the words, "Let us pray together," when thou beholdest the curtains drawn up,[5] then imagine that the Heavens are let down from above, and that the Angels are descending!

As then it is not meet that any one of the uninitiated be present, so neither is it that one of them that are initiated, and yet at the same time defiled. Tell me, suppose any one were invited to a feast, and were to wash his hands, and sit down, and be all ready at the table, and after all refuse to partake; is he not insulting the man who invited him? were it not better for such an one never to have come at all? Now it is just in the same way that thou hast come here. Thou hast sung the Hymn[6] with the rest: thou hast declared thyself to be of the number of them that are worthy, by not departing with them that are unworthy. Why stay, and yet not partake of the table? I am unworthy, thou wilt say. Then art thou also unworthy of that communion thou hast had in prayers. For it is not by means of the offerings only, but also by means of those canticles that the Spirit descendeth all around. Do we not see our own servants, first scouring the table with a sponge, and cleaning the house, and then setting out the entertainment? This is what is done by the prayers, by the cry of the herald. We scour the Church, as it were, with a sponge, that all things may be set out in a pure church, that there may be "neither spot nor wrinkle." (Eph. v: 27.) Unworthy, indeed, both our eyes of these sights, and unworthy are our ears! "And if even a beast," it is said, "touch the mountain, it shall be stoned." (Ex. xix: 13.) Thus then they were not worthy so much as to set foot on it, and yet afterwards they both came near, and beheld where God had stood. And thou mayest, afterwards, come near, and behold: when, however, He is present, depart. Thou art no more allowed to be here than the Catechumen is. For it is not at all the same thing never to have reached the mysteries, and when thou hast reached them, to stumble at them and despise them, and to make thyself unworthy of this thing. One might enter upon more points, and those more awful still; not however to burden your understanding, these will suffice. They who are not brought to their right senses with these, certainly will not be with more.

That I may not then be the means of increas-

---

[1] [On Chrysostom's view of the eucharistic sacrifice, see *Prolegomena*, p. 21, note.—G. A.]

[2] i. e. the Deacon, Ἀθανάσιος προστάξας διακόνῳ κηρύξαι εὐχὴν κ. τ. λ. Socr. *Hist.* ii. 11. id qu. ἀναγινώσκειν, Athan. *de fug* 24.

[3] Vid. Bingh. *Antiqu.* xiii. 2. and xiv. 5. [The text here seems to be corrupt, Field's text is, "As many as are in penitence, all pray," (δεήθητε πάντες) which is evidently inconsistent with the context. The text should probably be, "As many as are in penitence, depart; as many as are not in penitence, pray all." So Field suggests in a note saying, *Locus corruptus videtur, sic fortasse redintegrandus*: ὅσοι ἐν μετανοίᾳ ἀπέλθετε, ὅσοι μὴ ἐν μετανοίᾳ δεήθητε πάντες.—G. A.]

[4] Vid. Bingh. *Antiqu.* xv. 2.

[5] ἀμφίθυρα, curtains before the choir or altar. vid. Chrysost. *in Matt. Hom.* 84. *fin.* where, however, it has not the ecclesiastical sense, Epihan. *Epist.* 51. 9. *apud Hieron.* ed. Vallars. where the curtain had a figure of Christ or some Saint, (to which Epihanius objects.) vid. also Evagr. *Hist.* vi. 21.

[6] The Angelic Hymn, Holy, Holy, Holy, vid. Chrysost. in 2 Cor. Hom. 18. Cyril. *Hieros. Myst.* v. 6.

ing your condemnation, I entreat you, not to forbear coming, but to render yourselves worthy both of being present, and of approaching. Tell me, were any king to give command and to say, " If any man does this, let him partake of my table ; " say, would ye not do all ye could to be admitted ? He hath invited us to heaven, to the table of the great and wonderful King, and do we shrink and hesitate, instead of hastening and running to it ? And what then is our hope of salvation? We cannot lay the blame on our weakness ; we cannot on our nature. It is indolence and nothing else that renders us unworthy.

So far have I spoken of myself. But may He that pricketh the heart, He that giveth the Spirit of compunction, pierce your hearts, and plant the seeds in the depth of them, that so through His fear ye may conceive, and bring forth the spirit of salvation, and come near with boldness. For, " thy children," it is said, " are like olive plants round about thy table." (Ps. cxxviii : 3.) O, then, let there be nothing old, nothing wild, nothing harsh. For of such sort are the young plants that are fit for fruit, for the beautiful fruit, fruit I mean of the olive-tree. And thriving they are, so as all to be round about the table, and come together here, not in vain or by chance, but with fear and reverence. For thus shall ye behold with boldness even Christ Himself in heaven, and shall be counted worthy of that heavenly kingdom, which may God grant we may all attain, in Jesus Christ, our Lord with whom to the Father, together with the Holy Spirit, be glory, might, honor, now and ever, and for ages of ages. Amen.

HOMILY IV.

CHAPTER. II. VERSES 1—3.

" And you did He quicken, when ye were dead through your trespasses and sins, wherein aforetime ye walked, according to the course of this world, according to the prince of the power of the air, of the spirit that now worketh in the sons of disobedience; among whom we also all once lived, in the lusts of our flesh, doing the desires of the flesh, and of the mind; and were by nature children of wrath even as the rest."

THERE is, we know, a corporal, and there is also a spiritual, dying.[1] Of the first it is no crime to partake, nor is there any peril in it, inasmuch as there is no blame attached to it, for it is a matter of nature, not of deliberate choice. It had its origin in the transgression of the first-created man, and thenceforward in its issue it passed into a nature, and, at all events, will quickly be brought to a termination ; whereas this spiritual dying, being a matter of deliberate choice, has criminality, and has no termination. Observe then how Paul, having already shown how exceedingly great a thing it is, in so much that to heal a deadened soul is a far greater thing than to raise the dead, so now again lays it down in all its real greatness.

" And you," saith he " when ye were dead through your trespasses and sins, wherein aforetime ye walked according to the course of this world, according to the prince of the power of the air, of the spirit that now worketh in the sons of disobedience." You observe the gentleness of Paul, and how on all occasions he encourages the hearer, not bearing too hard upon him. For whereas he had said, Ye have arrived at the very last degree of wickedness, (for such is the meaning of becoming dead,) that he may not excessively distress them,[2] (because men are put to shame when their former misdeeds are brought forward, cancelled though they be, and no longer attended with danger,) he gives them, as it were, an accomplice, that it may not be supposed that the work is all their own, and that accomplice a powerful one. And who then is this? The Devil. He does much the same also in the Epistle to the Corinthians, where, after saying, " Be not deceived, neither fornicators, nor idolaters," (1 Cor. vi : 9.) and after enumerating all the other vices, and adding in conclusion, "shall inherit the kingdom of God ; " he then adds, " and such were some of you ; " he does not say absolutely, " ye were," but " some of you were," that is, thus in some sort were ye. Here the heretics attack us. They tell us that these expressions (" prince of all the power of the air," etc.) are used with reference to God, and letting loose their unbridled tongue, they fit these

---

[1] [The Commentators, except Meyer, refer the νεκρούς to spiritual death, as Chrysostom does. Meyer refers it to "eternal death, the eternal condemnation," and says the νεκρούς is proleptic. He distinctly says it does not refer to physical death, though Ellicott represents him as saying that it does.—G. A.]

[2] [Paul's motive in this passage is probably not what Chrysostom says, but, on the contrary, to show how desperately bad their state was.—G. A.]

things to God, which belong to the Devil alone. How then are we to put them to silence? By the very words they themselves use; for, if He is righteous, as they themselves allow, and yet hath done these things, this is no longer the act of a righteous being, but rather of a being most unrighteous and corrupted; and corrupted God cannot possibly be.

Further, why does he call the Devil "the prince" of the world? Because nearly the whole human race has surrendered itself to him, and all are willingly and of deliberate choice his slaves. And to Christ, though He promises unnumbered blessings, not any one so much as gives any heed; whilst to the Devil, though promising nothing of the sort, but sending them on to hell, all yield themselves. His kingdom then is in this world, and he has, with few exceptions, more subjects and more obedient subjects than God, in consequence of our indolence.

"According to the power," saith he, "of the air, of the spirit."[1]

Here again he means, that Satan occupies the space under Heaven, and that the incorporeal powers are spirits of the air, under his operation. For that his kingdom is of this age, i. e., will cease with the present age, hear what he says at the end of the Epistle; "Our wrestling is not against flesh and blood, but against the principalities, against powers, against the world rulers of this darkness;" (Eph. vi: 12.) where, lest when you hear of world-rulers you should therefore say that the Devil is uncreated, he elsewhere (Gal. i: 4.) calls a perverse time, "an evil world," not of the creatures. For he seems to me, having had dominion beneath the sky, not to have fallen from his dominion, even after his transgression.

"That now worketh," he says, "in the sons of disobedience."

You observe that it is not by force, nor by compulsion, but by persuasion, he wins us over; "disobedience" or "untractableness" is his word, as though one were to say, by guile and persuasion he draws all his votaries to himself. And not only does he give them a word of encouragement by telling them they have an associate, but also by ranking himself with them, for he says,

"Among whom we also all once lived."

"All," because he cannot say that any one is excepted.

"In the lusts of our flesh, doing the desires of the flesh, and of the mind, and were by nature children of wrath, even as the rest."

That is, having no spiritual affections. Yet,

lest he should slander the flesh, or lest it should be supposed that the transgression was not great, observe how he guards the matter,

"Doing," he says, "the desires of the flesh and of the mind."

That is, the pleasurable passions. We provoked God to anger, he saith, we provoked Him to wrath, we were wrath, and nothing else. For as he who is a child of man is by nature man, so also were we children of wrath[2] even as others; i. e., no one was free, but we all did things worthy of wrath.

Ver. 4. "But God, being rich in mercy."

Not merely merciful, but rich in mercy; as it is said also in another place; "In the multitude of thy mercies." (Ps. lxix: 17.) And again, "Have mercy upon me, according to the multitude of thy tender mercies." (Ps. li: 1.)

Ver. 4. "For His great love,[3] wherewith He loved us."

Why did He love us? For these things are not deserving of love, but of the sorest wrath, and punishment. And thus it was of great mercy.

Ver. 5. "Even when we were dead through our trespasses He quickened us together with Christ."

Again is Christ introduced, and it is a matter well worthy of our belief, because if the Firstfruits live, so do we also. He hath quickened both Him, and us. Seest thou that all this is said of Christ incarnate? Beholdest thou "the exceeding greatness of His power to us-ward who believe?" (Eph. i: 19.) Them that were dead, them that were children of wrath, them hath he quickened. Beholdest thou "the hope of his calling?"

Ver. 6. "He raised us up with Him and made us sit with Him."

Beholdest thou the glory of His inheritance?

---

[1] [" The word ἀήρ which is commonly confined to the region of the air, may be extended to all that supra-terrestrial but sub-celestial region which seems to be, if not the abode, at least the haunt of evil spirits, cf Job i: 7."—Ellicott.—G. A.]

[2] Chrysostom understands the words according to the order in which they stand in the original text, ἤμεν τέκνα φύσει ὀργῆς, "we were natural" or "genuine children of wrath," referring "by nature" not to "we were" but to "children." To say that we were by "nature" under wrath, might have seemed all one with saying that God created Adam under wrath. When then we so speak, we must take the word "nature" in S. Augustine's sense, not to mean our literal nature, but "as referring to our birth." " In eo quod dixi, 'naturâ esse malæ animæ nullo modo queunt,' si quæritur quomodo accipiamus quod ait Apostolus, 'Fuimus et nos naturâ filii iræ, &c.'" respondemus, naturam in his verbis meis me intelligi voluisse illam, quæ proprie natura dicitur, in quâ sine vitiis creati sumus. Nam ista propter originem natura appellatur, quæ origo utique habet vitium, quod est contra naturam. August. Retract. i. 15. §. 6. vid, also de Lib. Arb. iii. 54.] " That man is a born subject of wrath from birth, an object of the divine condemnation, is not at all a doctrine of the Apostle, according to whom man by his actual sin falls under the wrath of God, inasmuch as he becomes subject to and follows the inborn principle of sin in opposition to his moral will which he likewise by nature bears in himself. Certainly man is born with this natural sinful quality, i. e., with the principle of sin, by the awakening and development of which the moral will is vanquished (Rom. vii, cf. Jo. iii: 6.) It is not, however, the mere fact of this inborn presence having its basis in his flesh that in and of itself makes him a child of wrath, but he only becomes so when that constitution of his moral nature, that mingling of the two opposite principles in his natural disposition has brought about the victory of the sin-principle, which however is the case with every one."—Meyer.—G. A.]

[3] [Διὰ τὴν πολλὴν ἀγάπην αὐτοῦ : "namely, in order to satisfy it."—Meyer.—G. A.]

That "He hath raised us up together," is plain. But that He "hath made us sit with Him in the heavenly places in Christ Jesus," how does this hold? It holds as truly, as that He hath raised us together. For as yet no one is actually raised, [1] excepting that inasmuch as as the Head hath risen, we also are raised, just as in the history, when Jacob did obeisance, his wife also did obeisance to Joseph. (Gen. xxxvii: 9, 10.) And so in the same way "hath He also made us to sit with Him." For since the Head sitteth, the body sitteth also with it, and therefore he adds "in Christ Jesus." Or again, if it means, not this, it means that by the laver of Baptism He hath "raised us up with Him." How then in that case hath He made "us to sit with Him?" Because, saith he, "if we suffer we shall also reign with Him," (2 Tim. ii: 12.) if we be dead with Him we shall also live with Him. Truly there is need of the Spirit and of revelation, in order to understand the depth of these mysteries. And then that ye may have no distrust about the matter, observe what he adds further.

Ver. 7. "That in the ages to come, He might show the exceeding riches of His grace, in kindness towards us, in Christ Jesus."

Whereas he had been speaking of the things which concerned Christ, and these might be nothing to us, (for what, it might be said, is it to us, that He rose) therefore he shows that they do moreover extend to us, inasmuch as He is made one with us. Only that our concern in the matter he states separately. "Us," saith he, "who were dead through our trespasses He raised up with Him, and made us sit with Him." Wherefore, as I was saying, be not unbelieving, take the demonstration he adduces both from former things, and from His Headship, and also from His desire to show forth His goodness. For how will He show it, unless this come to pass? And He will show it in the ages to come. What? that the blessings are both great, and more certain than any other. For now the things which are said may to the unbelievers seem to be foolishness; but then all shall know them. Wouldest thou understand too, how He hath made us sit together with Him? Hear what Christ Himself saith to the disciples, "Ye also shall sit upon twelve thrones, judging the twelve tribes of Israel." (Matt. xix: 28.) And again, "But to sit on My right hand and on My left hand is not Mine to give, but it is for them for whom it hath been

prepared of My Father." (Matt. xx: 23.) So that it hath been prepared. And well saith he, "in kindness towards us in Christ Jesus," for to sit on His right hand is honor above all honor, it is that beyond which there is none other. This then he saith, that even we shall sit there. Truly this is surpassing riches, truly surpassing is the greatness of His power, to make us sit down with Christ. Yea, hadst thou ten thousand souls, wouldest thou not lose them for His sake? Yea, hadst thou to enter the flames, oughtest thou not readily to endure it? And He Himself too saith again, "Where I am, there shall also My servant be." (John. xii: 26.) Why surely had ye to be cut to pieces every day, ought ye not, for the sake of these promises cheerfully to embrace it? Think, where He sitteth? above all principality and power. And with whom it is that thou sittest? With Him. And who thou art? One dead, by nature a child of wrath. And what good hast thou done? None. Truly now it is high time to exclaim, "Oh the depth of the riches both of the wisdom and the knowledge of God!" (Rom. xi:33.)

Ver. 8. "For by grace," saith he "have ye been saved." [2]

In order then that the greatness of the benefits bestowed may not raise thee too high, observe how he brings thee down: "by grace ye have been saved," saith he,

"Through faith;"

Then, that, on the other hand, our free-will be not impaired, he adds also our part in the work, and yet again cancels it, and adds,

"And that not of ourselves."

Neither is faith,[3] he means, "of ourselves." Because had He not come, had He not called us, how had we been able to believe? for "how," saith he, "shall they believe, unless they hear?" (Rom. x: 14.) So that the work of faith itself is not our own.

"It is the gift," said he, "of God," it is "not of works."

Was faith then, you will say, enough to save us? No; but God, saith he, hath required this, lest He should save us, barren and without work at all. His expression is, that faith saveth, but it is because God so willeth, that faith saveth. Since, how, tell me, doth faith save, without works? This itself is the gift of God.

Ver. 9. "That no man should glory."

That he may excite in us proper feeling

---

[1] [This is Meyer's view. He says: "By virtue of the dynamic connection of Christ with believers as the head with its body their revivification is objectively comprehended in His." Ellicott says: "Though the simple meaning of συνήγειρεν and συνεκάθισεν seems to confine their reference to what is future and objective; still as συνεζωοποίησεν though primarily spiritual and present may have a physical and future reference, so here a present spiritual resurrection and enthronement may be alluded to."—G. A.]

[2] ["Confirmatory explanation of the truth and justice of the expression, 'the exceeding riches of His grace' by a recurrence to the statement made parenthetically in verse 5."—Ellicott.—G. A.]

[3] [Meyer objects to this interpretation saying: "How violent is this taking to pieces of the text, since οὐκ ἐξ ὑμῶν and οὐκ ἐξ ἔργων present themselves in a manner alike natural and weighty as elements belonging to one flow of the discourse! The τοῦτο refers to the salvation just designated as regards its specific mode." So substantially Ellicott.—G. A.]

touching this gift of grace. "What then?" saith a man, "Hath He Himself hindered our being justified by works?" By no means. But no one, he saith, is justified by works, in order that the grace and loving-kindness of God may be shown. He did not reject us as having works, but as abandoned of works He hath saved us by grace; so that no man henceforth may have whereof to boast. And then, lest when thou hearest that the whole work is accomplished not of works but by faith, thou shouldest become idle,[1] observe how he continues,

Ver. 10. "For we are His workmanship, created in Christ Jesus for good works, which God afore prepared that we should walk in them."

Observe the words he uses. He here alludes to the regeneration, which is in reality a second creation. We have been brought from non-existence into being. As to what we were before, that is, the old man, we are dead. What we are now become, before, we were not. Truly then is this work a creation, yea, and more noble than the first; for from that one, we have our being; but from this last, we have, over and above, our well being.

"For good works, which God afore prepared that we should walk in them."[2]

Not merely that we should begin, but that we should walk in them, for we need a virtue which shall last throughout, and be extended on to our dying day. If we had to travel a road leading to a royal city, and then when we had passed over the greater part of it, were to flag and sit down near the very close, it were of no use to us. This is the hope of our calling; for "for good works" he says. Otherwise it would profit us nothing.

MORAL. Thus here he rejoices not that we should work one work, but all; for, as we have five senses, and ought to make use of all in their proper season, so ought we also the several virtues. Now were a man to be temperate and yet unmerciful, or were he to be merciful and yet grasping, or were he to abstain indeed from other people's goods, and yet not bestow his own, it would be all in vain. For a single virtue alone is not enough to present us with boldness before the judgment-seat of Christ; no, we require it to be great, and various, and universal, and entire. Hear what Christ saith to the disciples, " Go, ye and make disciples of all the nations,—teaching them to observe all

things whatsoever I commanded you." (Matt. xxviii: 19.) And again, " Whosoever shall break one of these least commandments, shall be called least in the kingdom of Heaven," (Matt. v: 19.) that is, in the resurrection; nay, he shall not enter into the kingdom; for He is wont to call the time also of the resurrection, the kingdom. " If he break one," saith He, " he shall be called least," so that we have need of all. And observe how it is not possible to enter without works of mercy; but if even this alone be wanting, we shall depart into the fire. For, saith He, " Depart, ye cursed, into the eternal fire, which is prepared for the Devil and his angels." Why and wherefore? " For I was an hungered, and ye gave me no meat; I was thirsty, and ye gave me no drink." (Matt. xxv: 42.) Beholdest thou, how without any other charge laid against them, for this one alone they perished. And for this reason alone too were the virgins also excluded from the bride-chamber, though sobriety surely they did possess. As the Apostle saith " and the sanctification, without which no man shall see the Lord." (Heb. xii: 14.) Consider then, that without sobriety, it is impossible to see the Lord; yet it does not necessarily follow that with sobriety it is possible to see Him, because often-times something else stands in the way. Again, if we do all things ever so rightly, and yet do our neighbor no service, neither in that case shall we enter into the kingdom. Whence is this evident? From the parable of the servants entrusted with the talents. For, in that instance, the man's virtue was in every point unimpaired, and there had been nothing lacking, but forasmuch as he was slothful in his business, he was rightly cast out. Nay, it is possible, even by railing only, to fall into Hell. " For whosoever " saith Christ, " shall say to his brother, Thou fool, shall be in danger of the hell of fire." (Matt. v: 22.) And if a man be ever so right in all things, and yet be injurious, he shall not enter.

And let no one impute cruelty to God, in that he excludes those who fail in this matter, from the kingdom of Heaven. For even with men, if any one do any thing whatsoever contrary to the law, he is banished from the king's presence. And if he transgresses so much as one of the established laws, if he lays a false accusation against another, he forfeits his office. And if he commits adultery, and is detected, he is disgraced, and even though he have done ten thousand right acts, he is undone; and if he commits murder, and is convicted, this again is enough to destroy him. Now if the laws of men are so carefully guarded, how much more should those of God be. " But He is good," a man says. How long are we to be uttering this

---

[1] [This is not the object of Paul in the statement of v. 10, but as Meyer says: " Ver. 10 is the reason assigned for the immediately preceding οὐκ ἐξ ὑμῶν . . . καυχήσηται. For if we are God's handiwork our salvation cannot be of our own acquiring, and if we are created in Christ unto good works how could the merit of our works be the cause of our salvation or the subject of our boasting?"—G. A.]

[2] [God, before we were created in Christ, made ready for us, prepared a sphere of moral action or (to use the simile of Chrysostom) a road, with the intent that we should walk in it. This sphere, this road was good works, ἔργα ἀγαθά."—Ellicott.—G. A.]

foolish talk? foolish, I say, not because He is not good, but in that we keep thinking that His goodness will be available to us for these purposes, though I have again and again used ten thousand arguments on this subject. Listen to the Scripture, which saith, "Say not, His mercy is great, He will be pacified for the multitude of my sins." (Ecclus. v: 6.) He does not forbid us to say, "His mercy is great." This is not what He enjoins; rather he would have us constantly say it, and with this object Paul raises all sorts of arguments, but his object is what follows. Do not, he means, admire the loving-kindness of God with this view, with a view to sinning, and saying, "His mercy will be pacified for the multitude of my sins." For it is with this object that I too discourse so much concerning His goodness, not that we may presume upon it, and do any thing we choose, because in that way this goodness will be to the prejudice of our salvation; but that we may not despair in our sins, but may repent. For "the goodness of God leadeth thee to repentance," (Rom. ii : 4.) not to greater wickedness. And if thou become depraved, because of His goodness, thou art rather belying Him before men. I see many persons thus impugning the long-suffering of God; so that if thou use it not aright, thou shalt pay the penalty. Is God a God of loving-kindness? Yes, but He is also a righteous Judge. Is He one who maketh allowance for sins? True, yet rendereth He to every man according to his works. Doth He pass by iniquity and blot out transgressions? True, yet maketh He inquisition also. How then is it, that these things are not contradictions? Contradictions they are not, if we distinguish them by their times. He doeth away iniquity here, both by the laver of Baptism, and by penitence. There He maketh inquisition of what we have done by fire and torment. "If then," some man may say, "I am cast out, and forfeit the kingdom, whether I have wrought ten thousand evil deeds or only one, wherefore may I not do all sorts of evil deeds?" This is the argument of an ungrateful servant; still nevertheless, we will proceed to solve even this. Never do that which is evil in order to do thyself good; for we shall, all alike fall short of the kingdom, yet in Hell we shall not all undergo the same punishment, but one a severer, another a milder one. For now, if thou and another have "despised God's goodness," (Rom. ii : 4.) the one in many instances, and the other in a few, ye will alike forfeit the kingdom. But if ye have not alike despised Him, but the one in a greater, the other in a less degree, in Hell ye shall feel the difference.

Now then, why, it may be said, doth He threaten them who have not done works of mercy, that they shall depart into the fire, and not simply into the fire, but into that which is "prepared for the devil and his angels?" (Matt. xxv: 41.) Why and wherefore is this? Because nothing so provokes God to wrath. He puts this before all terrible things; for if it is our duty to love our enemies, of what punishment shall not he be worthy, who turns away even from them that love him, and is in this respect worse than the heathen? So that in this case the greatness of the sin will make such an one go away with the devil. Woe to him, it is said, who doeth not alms; and if this was the case under the Old Covenant, much more is it under the New. If, where the getting of wealth was allowed, and the enjoyment of it, and the care of it, there was such provision made for the succoring the poor, how much more in that Dispensation, where we are commanded to surrender all we have? For what did not they of old do? They gave tithes, and tithes again upon tithes for orphans, widows, and strangers; whereas some one was saying to me in astonishment at another, "Why, such an one gives tithes." What a load of disgrace does this expression imply, since what was not a matter of wonder with the Jews has come to be so in the case of the Christians? If there was danger then in omitting tithes, think how great it must be now.

Again, drunkenness shall not inherit the kingdom. Yet what is the language of most people? "Well, if both I and he are in the same case, that is no little comfort." What then? First of all, that thou and he shall not reap the same punishment; but were it otherwise, neither is that any comfort. Fellowship in sufferings has comfort in it, when the miseries have any proportion in them; but when they exceed all proportion, and carry us beyond ourselves, no longer do they allow of our receiving any comfort at all. For tell the man that is being tortured, and has entered into the flames, that such an one is undergoing the same, still he will not feel the comfort. Did not all the Israelites perish together? What manner of comfort did that afford them? Rather, did not this very thing distress them? And this was why they kept saying, We are lost, we are perished, we are wasted away. What manner of comfort then is there here? In vain do we comfort ourselves with such hopes as these. There is but one only comfort, to avoid falling into that unquenchable fire; but it is not psssible for one who has fallen into it to find comfort, where there is the gnashing of teeth, where there is the weeping, where is the worm that dieth not, and the fire that is not quenched. For shalt thou conceive any comfort at all, tell me, when thou art in so great tribulation and distress? Wilt thou then be any longer thyself? Let us not, I pray and entreat you, let us not vainly deceive ourselves and comfort ourselves with arguments like these; no, let us practise those virtues, which shall avail to save us. The object before us is to sit together with Christ, and art thou trifling about such matters as these? Why, were there no other sin at all, how great punishment ought we not to suffer for these very speeches themselves, because we are so insensate, so wretched, and so indolent, as, even with so vast a privilege before us, to talk thus? Oh! how much shalt thou have to lament, when thou shalt then consider them that have done good! When thou shalt behold slaves and base-born who have labored but a little here, there made partakers of the royal throne, will not these things be worse to thee than torment? For if even now, when thou seest any in high reputation, though

thou art suffering no evil, thou regardest this as worse than any punishment, and by this alone art consumed, and bemoanest thyself, and weepest, and judgest it to be as bad as ten thousand deaths; what shalt thou suffer then? Why, even were there no hell at all, the very thought of the kingdom, were it not enough to destroy and consume thee? And that such will be the case, we have enough in our own experience of things to teach us. Let us not then vainly flatter our own souls with speeches like these; no, let us take heed, let us have a regard for our own salvation, let us make virtue our care, let us rouse ourselves to the practice of good works, that we may be counted worthy to attain to this exceeding glory, in Jesus Christ our Lord with whom to the Father, together with the Holy Spirit be glory, might, honor, now and ever, and for ages of ages. Amen.

HOMILY V.

CHAPTER II. VERSES 11, 12.

" Wherefore remember, that aforetime ye the Gentiles in the flesh, who are called Uncircumcision by that which is called Circumcision in the flesh made by hands; that ye were at that time separate from Christ, alienated from the commonwealth of Israel, and strangers from the covenants of the promise, having no hope, and without God in the world."

THERE are many things to show the lovingkindness of God. First, the fact, that by Himself He hath saved us, and by Himself through such a method as this. Secondly, that He hath saved us, as being what we were. Thirdly, that He hath exalted us to the place where we are. For all these things both contain in themselves the greatest demonstration of His lovingkindness, and they are the very subjects which Paul is now agitating in his Epistle. He had been saying, that when we were dead through our trespasses, and children of wrath, He saved us; He is now telling us further, to whom He hath made us equal. "Wherefore," saith he, "remember;" because it is usual with us, one and all, when we are raised from a state of great meanness to corresponding, or perhaps a greater, dignity, not so much as even to retain any recollection of our former condition, being nourished in this our new glory. On this account it is that he says, "Wherefore remember." —"Wherefore." Why, "wherefore?"[1] Because

we have been created unto good works, and this were sufficient to induce us to cultivate virtue; "remember,"—for that remembrance is sufficient to make us grateful to our Benefactor, —"that ye were aforetime Gentiles." Observe how he lowers the superior advantages of the Jews and admires the disadvantages of the Gentiles; disadvantage indeed it was not, but he is arguing with each respectively from their character and manner of life.

"Who are called Uncircumcision."[2]

The honor then of the Jews is in names, their perogative then is in the flesh. For uncircumcision is nothing, and circumcision is nothing.

"By that which is called," saith he, "Circumcision in the flesh made by hands, that ye were at that time separate from Christ, alienated from the commonwealth of Israel, and strangers from the covenants of the promise, having no hope, and without God in the world.[3]

[1] ["Therefore, because such exalted and unmerited benefits have been imparted to us (vv. 4–10)," (Ellicott vv. 1–7). "These benefits should move the reader to remember his former miserable heathen state in order to appreciate by contrast the value of his present state." Meyer.—G. A.]

[2] ["They were those designated 'Foreskin' by the people who bear the name of the surgical operation performed on their flesh." —Meyer.—G. A.]

[3] ["They were without church, without promise, without hope, without God, and that in the profane wicked world (ἐν τῷ κόσμῳ being in contrast to πολιτείας τοῦ Ἰσραήλ and like it, ethical in reference.) Ἄθεοι may mean ignorant of God or forsaken by God, probably the latter."—Ellicott.—G. A.]

Ye, saith he, who were thus called by the Jews. But why when he is about to show that the benefit bestowed upon them consisted in this, in having fellowship with Israel, does he disparage the Israelitish prerogative? He does not disparage it. In essential points he enhances it, but only in these points, in which they had no fellowship, he disparages it. For further on he says, "Ye are fellow-citizens of the saints and of the household of God." Mark, how far he is from disparaging it. These points, saith he, are indifferent. Never think, saith he, that because ye happen not to be circumcised, and are now in uncircumcision, that there is any difference in this. No, the real trouble was this, the being "without Christ," the being "aliens from the commonwealth of Israel." Whereas this circumcision is not "the commonwealth." Again, the being strangers from the covenants of promise, the having no hope to come, the being without God in this world, all these were parts of their condition. He was speaking of heavenly things; he speaks also of those which are upon earth; since the Jews had a great opinion of these. Thus also Christ in comforting His disciples, after saying, "Blessed are they that have been persecuted for righteousness' sake, for theirs is the kingdom of heaven," adds the lesser point of consolation, "for so," saith He, "persecuted they the prophets which were before you." (Matt. v: 10–12.) For this, compared with the greatness of the other, is far less, yet in regard to the being nigh, and believing, it is great and sufficient, and has much force. This then was the sharing in the commonwealth. His word is not, "separated," but "alienated from the commonwealth." His word is not, "ye took no interest in," but, "ye had not so much as any part in, and were strangers." The expressions are most emphatic, and indicate the separation to be very wide. Because the Israelites themselves were without this commonwealth, not however as aliens, but as indifferent to it, and they fell from the covenants, not however as strangers, but as unworthy.

But what were "the covenants of the promise?" "To thee and to thy seed," saith He, "will I give this land," (Gen. xvii: 8.) and whatever else He promised.

"Having no hope." he adds, "and without God." Though gods indeed they worshipped, but they were no gods: "for an idol is not any thing." (1 Cor. x: 19.)

Ver. 13—15. "But now,[1] in Christ Jesus, ye that once were far off, are made nigh in the blood of Christ. For He is our peace, who made both one, and brake down the middle wall

of partition, having abolished in His flesh the enmity."

Is this then the great privilege, it may be said, that we are admitted into the commonwealth of the Jews? What art thou saying? "He hath summed up all things that are in heaven, and that are in earth," and now dost thou tell us about Israelites? Yes, he would say. Those higher privileges we must apprehend by faith; these, by the things themselves. "But now," saith he, "in Christ Jesus, ye that once were far off, are made nigh," in reference to the commonwealth. For the "far off," and the "nigh," are matters of will and choice only.

"For He[2] is our peace, Who made both one."

What is this, "both one?" He does not mean this, that He hath raised us to that high descent of theirs, but that he hath raised both us and them to a yet higher. Only that the blessing to us is greater, because to these it had been promised, and they were nearer than we; to us it had not been promised, and we were farther off than they. Therefore it is that he says, "And that the Gentiles might glorify God for His mercy." (Rom. xv: 9.) The promise indeed He gave to the Israelites, but they were unworthy; to us He gave no promise, nay, we were even strangers, we had nothing in common with them; yet hath He made us one, not by knitting us to them, but by knitting both them and us together into one. I will give you an illustration. Let us suppose there to be two statues, the one of silver, the other of lead, and then that both shall be melted down, and that the two shall come out gold. Behold, thus hath He made the two one. Or put the case again in another way. Let the two be, one a slave, the other an adopted son: and let both offend Him, the one as a disinherited child, the other as a fugitive, and one who never knew a father. Then let both be made heirs, both trueborn sons. Behold, they are exalted to one and the same dignity, the two are become one, the one coming from a longer, the other from a nearer distance, and the slave becoming more noble than he was before he offended.

"And brake down," he proceeds, "the middle wall of partition."

What the middle wall of partition is, he interprets by saying, "the enmity having abolished in His flesh, even the law of commandments contained in ordinances." Some indeed affirm that he means the wall of the Jews against the Greeks, because it did not allow the Jews to hold intercourse with the Greeks. To me, however, this does not seem to be the meaning, but

---

[1] ["This too is what they should remember, but the Apostle continues the contrast in an independent sentence."—Riddle, in *Popular Commentary.*—G. A.]

[2] ["The emphatic pronoun is used, αὐτός. But He is not put in opposition to 'ourselves' having made the peace, but as Bengel says, 'Not merely is He peacemaker, for at the cost of 'Himself' He procured peace.'"—Meyer.—G. A.]

rather that he calls "the enmity in the flesh," a middle wall, in that it is a common barrier, cutting us off alike from God.[1] As the Prophet says, "Your iniquities separate between you and Me;" (Isa. lix: 2.) for that enmity which He had both against Jews and Gentiles was, as it were, a middle wall. And this, whilst the law existed, was not only not abolished, but rather was strengthened; "for the law," saith the Apostle, "worketh wrath." (Rom. iv: 15.) Just in the same way then as when he says in that passage, "the· law worketh wrath," he does not ascribe the whole of this effect to the law itself, but it is to be understood, that it is because we have transgressed it; so also in this place he calls it a middle wall, because through being disobeyed it wrought enmity. The law was a hedge, but this it was made for the sake of security, and for this reason was called "a hedge," to the intent that it might form an inclosure. For listen again to the Prophet, where he says, "I made a trench about it." (Isa. v: 2.) And again, "Thou hast broken down her fences, so that all they which pass by the way do pluck her." (Ps. lxxx: 12.) Here therefore it means security and so again, "I will take away the hedge thereof, and it shall be trodden down." (Isa. v: 5.) And again, "He gave them the law for a defence." (Isa. viii: 20.) And again, "The Lord executeth righteous acts and made known His ways unto Israel." (Ps. ciii: 6, 7.) It became, however, a middle wall, no longer establishing them in security, but cutting them off from God. Such then is the middle wall of partition formed out of the hedge. And to explain what this is, he subjoins, "the enmity in His flesh having abolished, the law of commandments."

How so? In that He was slain and dissolved the enmity therein. And not in this way only but also by keeping it. But what then, if we are released from the former transgression, and yet are again compelled to keep it? Then were the case the same over again, whereas He hath destroyed the very law itself. For he says, "Having abolished the law of commandments contained in ordinances." Oh! amazing loving-kindness! He gave us a law that we should keep it, and when we kept it not, and ought to have been punished, He even abrogated the law itself. As if a man, who, having committed a child to a schoolmaster, if he should turn out disobedient, should set him at liberty even from the schoolmaster, and take him away. How great loving-kindness were this! What is meant by,

"Having abolished by ordinances?"[2]

For he makes a wide distinction between "commandments" and "ordinances." He either then means "faith," calling that an "ordinance," (for by faith alone He saved us,) or he means "precept," such as Christ gave, when He said, "But I say unto you, that ye are not to be angry at all." (Matt. v: 22.) That is to say, "If thou shalt believe that God raised Him from the dead, thou shalt be saved." (Rom. x: 6–9.) And again, "The word is nigh thee, in thy mouth, and in thine heart. Say not, Who shall ascend into heaven, or who shall descend into the abyss?" or, who hath "brought Him again from the dead?" Instead of a certain manner of life, He brought in faith. For that He might not save us to no purpose, He both Himself underwent the penalty, and also required of men the faith that is by doctrines.

"That he might create in Himself of the twain, one new man."

Observe thou, that it is not that the Gentile is become a Jew, but that both the one and the other are entered into another condition. It was not with a view of merely making this last other than he was, but rather, in order to create the two anew. And well does he on all occasions employ the word "create," and does not say "change," in order to point out the power of what was done, and that even though the creation be invisible, yet it is no less a creation than that is, and that we ought not henceforward start away from this, as from natural things.

"That He might in Himself of the twain."

That is, by Himself.[3] He gave not this charge to another, but Himself, by Himself, melted both the one and the other, and produced a glorious one, and one greater than the first creation; and that one, first, was Himself. For this is the meaning of "in Himself." He Himself first gave the type and example. Laying hold on the one hand of the Jew, and on the other of the Gentile, and Himself being in the midst, He blended them together, made all the estrangement which existed between them to disappear, and fashioned them anew from above by fire and by water; no longer with water and earth, but with water and fire. He became a Jew by circumcision, He became accursed, He

---

[1] ["The only mode of taking ἐχθραν in harmony with the context is not as Chrysostom, "but of the enmity which existed between Jews and Gentiles."—Meyer.

"Ἐν τῇ σαρκί, 'in the flesh,' does not belong to τὴν ἐχθραν, as Chrysostom construes it but to καταργήσας, 'having abolished.'" So Meyer and Rev. Ver.—G. A.]

[2] [The order of the Greek is as follows : τὸν νόμον τῶν ἐντολῶν ἐν δόγμασιν καταργήσας. Chrysostom has because of the order joined ἐν δόγμασιν with καταργήσας, as its modal definition. But ἐν δόγμασιν belongs to ἐντολῶν meaning ' the law of commandments consisting in ordinances,' " ἐντολῶν denoting the 'contents ' of the law and ἐν δόγμασιν the 'form' in which they were given" so Meyer.—G. A.

[3] [ἐν αὐτῷ : "This is not equivalent to δι ἑαυτοῦ, as Chrysostom, but it affirms that the unity to be brought about was to be founded in Christ Himself, was to have the basis of its existence and continuance in Him and not in any other unifying principles whatever."—Meyer.—G. A.]

became a Gentile without the law, and was over both Gentiles and Jews.

"One new man," saith he, "so making peace."

Peace for them both towards God, and towards each other. For so long as they continued still Jews and Gentiles, they could not have been reconciled. And had they not been delivered each from his own peculiar condition, they would not have arrived at another and a higher one. For the Jew is then united to the Gentile when he becomes a believer. It is like persons being in a house, with two chambers below, and one large and grand one above: they would not be able to see each other, till they had got above.

"Making peace," more especially towards God; for this the context shows, for what saith he?

Ver. 16. "And might reconcile them both in one body unto God through the Cross."

He saith, not merely "might reconcile," (καταλλάξη) but "might reconcile thoroughly" (ἀποκαταλλάξη[1]) indicating that heretofore human nature had been easily reconciled, as, e. g., in the case of the saints and before the time of the Law.

"In one body," saith he, and that His own, "unto God." How is this effected? By Himself, he means, suffering the due penalty.

"Through the cross having slain the enmity thereby."[2]

Nothing can be more decisive, nothing more expressive than these words. His death, saith the Apostle, hath "slain" the enmity. He hath "wounded" and "killed" it, not by giving charge to another, nor by what He wrought only, but also by what He suffered. He does not say "having dissolved," he does say "having cancelled," but what is stronger than all, "having slain," so that it never should rise again. How then is it that it does rise again? From our exceeding depravity. For as long as we abide in the body of Christ, as long as we are united, it rises not again, but lies dead; or rather that former enmity never rises again at all. But if we breed another, it is no longer because of Him, who hath destroyed and put to death the former one. It is thou, forsooth, that travailest with a fresh one. "For the mind of the flesh," saith he, "is enmity against God;" (Rom. viii: 6.) if we are in nothing carnally-minded, there will be no fresh enmity produced, but that "peace" shall remain.

MORAL. Think then, how vast an evil is it, when God hath employed so many methods to reconcile

us, and hath effected it, that we should again fall back into enmity! This enmity no fresh Baptism, but hell itself awaits; no fresh remission, but searching trial. The mind of the flesh is luxury and indolence, the "mind of the flesh" is covetousness and all kinds of sin. Why is it said the mind of the flesh? While yet the flesh could do nothing without the soul. He does not say this to the disparagement of the flesh, any more than when he says the "natural man," (1 Cor. ii: 14.) he uses that expression to the disparagement of the soul, for neither body nor soul in itself, if it receive not the impulse which is far above, is able to achieve any thing great or noble. Hence he calls those acts which the soul performs of herself, "natural; ψυχικά" and those which the body performs of itself "carnal." Not because these are natural, but because, inasmuch as they receive not that direction from heaven, they perish. So the eyes are good, but without light, will commit innumerable errors; this, however, is the fault of their weakness, not of nature. Were the errors natural, then should we never be able to use them aright at all. For nothing that is natural is evil. Why then does he call carnal affections sins? Because whenever the flesh exalts herself, and gets the mastery over her charioteer, she produces ten thousand mischiefs. The virtue of the flesh is, her subjection to the soul. It is her vice to govern the soul. As the horse then may be good and nimble, and yet this is not shown without a rider; so also the flesh will then show her goodness, when we cut off her prancings. But neither again is the rider shown, if he have not skill. Nay he himself will do mischief yet more fearful than that before named. So that on all hands we must have the Spirit at hand. This being at hand will impart new strength to the rider; this will give beauty both to body and soul. For just as the soul, while dwelling in the body, makes it beautiful, but when she leaves it destitute of her own native energy and departs, like a painter confounding his colors together, the greatest loathsomeness ensues, every one of the several parts hastening to corruption, and dissolution:—so is it also when the Spirit forsakes the body and the soul, the loathsomeness which ensues is worse and greater. Do not then, because the body is inferior to the soul, revile it, for neither do I endure to revile the soul because it hath no strength without the Spirit. If one need say anything at all, the soul is deserving of the greater censure than the body; for the body indeed can do no grievous harm without the soul, whereas the soul can do much without the body. Because, we know, when the one is even wasting away, and has no wantonness, the soul is busily employed. Even as those sorcerers, magicians,

---

[1] [Meyer says the ἀπό strengthens the notion of reconciliation. Ellicott that it not only strengthens but hints at a restoration to primal unity, the ἀπό meaning again.—G. A.]

[2] [" 'After he shall have slain the enmity &c.;' for it is inserted in the second half of the affirmation of 'design' and is correlative to ποιῶν εἰρήνην."—Meyer.—G. A.]

envious persons, enchanters, especially cause the body to waste away. But besides this, not even luxury is the effect of the necessity of the body, but rather of the inattentiveness of the soul; for food, not feasting, is the object of the necessity of the body. For if I have a mind to put on a strong curb, I stop the horse ; but the body is unable to check the soul in her evil courses. Wherefore then does he call it the carnal mind ? Because it comes to be wholly of the flesh, for when she has the mastery, then she goes wrong, as soon as ever she has deprived herself of reason, and of the supremacy of the soul. The virtue therefore of the body consists in this, in its submission to the soul, since of itself the flesh is neither good nor evil. For what could the body ever do of itself? It is then by its connection that the body is good, good because of its subjection, but of itself neither good nor evil, with capacity, however, both for one and for the other, and having an equal tendency either way. The body has a natural desire, not however of fornication, nor of adultery, but of pleasure ; the body has a desire not of feasting, but of food; not of drunkenness, but of drink. For in proof that it is not drunkenness that is the natural desire of the body, mark how, whenever you exceed the measure, when you go beyond the boundary-lines, it cannot hold out a moment longer. Up to this point it is of the body, but all the rest of the excesses, as e. g., when she is hurried away ento sensualities, when she becomes stupefied, these are of the soul. For though

the body be good, still it is vastly inferior to the soul, as lead is less of value than gold, and yet gold needs lead to solder it, and just so has the soul need also of the body. Or in the same way as a noble child requires a conductor, so again does the soul stand in need of the body. For, as we speak of childish things, not to the disparagement of childhood, but only of those acts which are done during childhood ; so also are we now speaking of the body.

Yet it is in our power, if we will, no longer to be in the flesh, no, nor upon the earth, but in heaven, and in the Spirit. For our being here or there, is not determined so much by our position, as by our disposition. Of many people, at least, who are in some place, we say they are not there, when we say, " Thou wast not here. And again Thou art not here." And why do I say this ? We often say, " Thou art not at (ἐν) thyself, I am not at (ἐν) myself," and yet what can be more material (a stronger instance of corporeal locality) than this, that a man is near to himself ? And yet, notwithstanding, we say that he is not at himself. Let us then be in ourselves, in heaven, in the Spirit. Let us abide in the peace and in the grace of God, that we may be set at liberty from all the things of the flesh, and may be able to attain to those good things which are promised in Jesus Christ our Lord, with whom to the Father, together with the Holy Spirit, be glory, and might, and honor, now and henceforth, and for ever and ever. Amen.

HOMILY VI.

CHAPTER II. VERSES 17–22.

" And He came and preached peace to you that were far off, and peace to them that were nigh, for through Him we both have our access in one Spirit unto the Father. So then ye are no more strangers and sojourners, but ye are fellow-citizens with the saints, and of the household of God, being built upon the foundation of the Apostles and Prophets, Christ Jesus Himself being the chief corner-stone. In whom each several building, fitly framed together, groweth into a holy temple in the Lord. In whom ye also are builded together for a habitation of God in the Spirit."

HE sent not, saith the Apostle, by the hand of another, nor did He announce these tidings to us by means of any other, but Himself did it in His own person. He sent not Angel nor

Archangel on the mission, because to repair so many and vast mischiefs and to declare what had been wrought was in the power of none other, but required His own coming.[1] The Lord then took upon Himself the rank of a servant, nay, almost of a minister, "and came, and preached peace to you," saith he, "that were far off, and to them that were nigh." To the Jews, he means, who as compared with our-

[1] [This passage does not refer to His bodily advent upon earth, as Chrysostom interprets, but following the account of his crucifixion more naturally refers to a spiritual advent, namely in the Holy Spirit, (in so far as it is Christ's spirit) Christ Himself came. He is our peace ; yes, and He came and by His spirit and the mouths of the Apostles He preached it.—Meyer and Ellicott.—G. A.]

selves were nigh. "For through Him we both have our access in one Spirit unto the Father."

"Peace," saith he, that "peace" which is towards God. He hath reconciled us. For the Lord Himself also saith, "Peace I leave with you; my peace I give unto you." (Jo. xiv: 27.) And again, "Be of good cheer, I have overcome the world." (Jo. xvi : 33.) And again, "Whatsoever ye shall ask in my name that will I do." (Jo. xiv: 14.) And again, "For the Father loveth you." (Jo. xvi : 27.) These are so many evidences of peace. But how towards the Gentiles? "Because through Him we both have our access in one Spirit unto the Father," not ye less, and they more, but all by one and the same grace. The wrath He appeased by His death, and hath made us meet for the Father's love through the Spirit. Mark again, the "in" means "by" or "through." By Himself and the Spirit that is, He hath brought us unto the Father. "So then ye are no more strangers and sojourners, but fellow-citizens with the saints."

Perceive ye that it is not with the Jews simply, no, but with those saintly and great men, such as Abraham, and Moses, and Elias? It is for the self-same city with these we are enrolled, for that we declare ourselves. "For they that say such things," saith he, "make it manifest that they are seeking after a country of their own." (Heb. xi : 14.) No longer are we strangers from the saints, nor foreigners. For they who shall not attain to heavenly blessings, are foreigners. "For the Son," saith Christ, "abideth for ever." (Jo. viii: 35.)

"And of the household," he continues, "of God."

The very thing which they at the first had, by means of so many toils and troubles, hath been for you accomplished by the grace of God. Behold the hope of your calling.

"Being built upon the foundation of the Apostles and Prophets."

Observe how he blends all together, the Gentiles, the Jews,[1] the Apostles, the Prophets, and Christ, and illustrates the union sometimes from the body, and sometimes from the building: "built," saith he, "upon the foundation of the Apostles and Prophets;" that is, the Apostles and Prophets are a foundation,[2] and he places the Apostles first, though they are in order of time last, doubtless to represent and express this, that both the one and the other are alike a

foundation, and that the whole is one building, and that there is one root. Consider, that the Gentiles have the Patriachs as a foundation. He here speaks more strongly of that point than he does when he speaks of a "grafting in." There he rather attaches them on. Then he adds, that He who binds the whole together in Christ. For the chief corner-stone binds together both the walls, and the foundations.

"In whom each several building."

Mark, how he knits it all together, and represents Him at one time, as holding down the whole body from above, and welding it together; at another time, as supporting the building from below, and being, as it were, a root, or base. And whereas he had used the expression, "He created in Himself of the twain one new man;" (Eph. ii: 15.) by this he clearly shows us, that by Himself Christ knits together the two walls: and again, that in Him it was created. And "He is the first-born,"[3] saith he, "of all creation," that is, He Himself supports all things.

"In whom each several building, fitly framed together."

Whether you speak of the roof, or of the walls, or of any other part whatsoever,[4] He it is supports the whole. Thus he elsewhere calls Him a foundation. "For other foundations," saith he, "can no man lay than that which is laid, which is Jesus Christ." (1 Cor. iii: 11.) "In whom each several building," he saith, "fitly framed together." Here he displays perfectness of it, and indicates that one cannot otherwise have place in it, unless by living with great exactness. "It groweth saith he into a holy temple in the Lord, in whom ye also," he adds, "are builded together." He is speaking continuously : "Into a holy temple, for a habitation of God in the Spirit." What then is the object of this building? It is that God may dwell in this temple. For each of you severally is a temple, and all of you together are a temple. And He dwelleth in you as in the body of Christ, and as in a spiritual temple. He does not use the word which means our coming to God, ($\pi\rho\acute{o}\sigma o\delta o\varsigma$) but which implies God's bringing us to Himself, ($\pi\rho o\sigma a\gamma\omega\gamma\acute{\eta}$) for we came not out of

---

[1] [Field's text has not the words, "the Jews;" but as there is excellent authority for them and they suit the context better, we have left them, with the Oxford translator, in our text.—G. A.]

[2] ["It is wrong to take this genitive as the genitive of apposition, as Chrysostom, for the Apostles and Prophets are not the foundation but have laid it. (1 Cor. iii: 10.) Nor are the Prophets here mentioned O. T. prophets but N. T. prophets. (cf. iii : 5 ; iv : 11).—Meyer."—G. A.]

[3] Col. i : 15. i. e. "Begotten before every creature ;" "begotten of His Father before all worlds." It is explained of our Lord's divine nature by Origen, *Periarch.* i. 2. Tertullian *in Prax.* 7. *in Marcion.* v. 19. S. Hilar. *de Trin.* viii. 50. S. Ambros. *de. Fid.* i. 14. S. Basil *in Eunom.* iv. in Col. i. 15. Others understand the expression to denote the Only-Begotten considered as becoming the origin of the new creation,—as beginning in His flesh, as being the Only-Begotten, the regenerate world. Thus S. Athanasius *Orat.* iii. 62. 63. S. Greg. Nyss. *de Perfect.* p. 722. *contra. Eunom.* i. p. 24. iii. pp. 113. 114. S. Cyril. *de Trin.* iv. p. 518. S. August. in *Rom.* 56 Theodoret interprets the word in both ways, *in loc.* and in Ps. 88, 28. S. Chrysostom too, *Hom. Son. Col.* i. 15. may be understood according .to either interpretation. Indeed they are quite consistent with each other.

[4] ["Chrysostom is wrong in holding that by $\pi\hat{a}\sigma a$ οἰκοδομή is signified every 'part' of the building (wall, roof, etc.,) since οἰκοδομή rather denotes the 'aggregate' of the single parts of the building. Πᾶσα οἰκοδομή means 'every building' and is here to be interpreted, 'every Christian community, each congregation.' "—Meyer.—G. A.]

ourselves, but we were brought nigh by Him. "No one," saith Christ, "cometh unto the Father but by Me." And again, "I am the way, and the truth, and the life." (Jo. xiv : 6.)

He joins them with the Saints and again returns to his former image, nowhere suffering them to be disunited from Christ. Doubtless then, this is a building that shall go on until His coming. Doubtlesss it was for this reason that Paul said, "As a wise master builder, I laid a foundation." (1 Cor. iii : 10, 11.) And again that Christ is the foundation. What then means all this? You observe that the comparisons have all referred to the subject-matters, and that we must not expound them to the very letter. The Apostle speaks from analogy as Christ does, where He calls the Father an husbandman, (Jo. xv : 1.) and Himself a root. (Rev. xxii : 16.)

Chap. iii. ver. 1. "For this cause I Paul, the prisoner of Christ Jesus in behalf of you Gentiles."

He has mentioned Christ's great and affectionate care; he now passes on to his own, insignificant indeed as it is, and a very nothing in comparison with that, and yet this is enough to engage them to himself. For this cause, saith he, am I also bound.[1] For if my Lord was crucified for your sakes, much more am I bound. He not only was bound Himself, but allows His servants to be bound also,—"for you Gentiles." It is full of emphasis; not only do we no longer loathe you, but we are even bound, saith he, for your sakes, and of this exceeding grace am I partaker.

Ver. 2. "If so be that ye have heard of the dispensation of that grace of God, which was given me to you-ward."

He alludes to the prediction addressed to Ananias concerning him at Damascus, when the Lord said, "Go thy way, for he is a chosen vessel unto Me, to bear My name before the Gentiles and Kings." (Acts ix : 15.)

By "dispensation of grace," he means the revelation made to him. As much as to say, "I learned it not from man. (Gal. i : 12.) He vouchsafed to reveal it even to me, though but an individual for your sakes. For Himself said unto me, saith he, "Depart, for I will send thee forth far hence unto the Gentiles." (Acts xxii : 21.) "If so be that ye have heard" for a dispensation it was, a mighty one; to call one, uninfluenced from any other quarter, immediately from above, and to say, "Saul, Saul, why persecutest thou Me?" and to strike him blind with that ineffable light! "if so be that

ye have heard,[2] saith he, "of the dispensation of that grace of God which was given me to you-ward."

Ver. 3. "How that by revelation was made known unto me the mystery, as I wrote afore in few words."

Perhaps he had informed them of it by some persons, or had not long before been writing to them.[3] Here he is pointing out that the whole is of God, that we have contributed nothing. For what? I ask, was not Paul himself, the wonderful, he that was so versed in the law, he that was brought up at the feet of Gamaliel according to the most perfect manner, was not he saved by grace? With good reason too does he call this a mystery, for a mystery it is, to raise the Gentiles in a moment to a higher rank than the Jews. "As I wrote afore," saith he, "in few words," i. e., briefly,

Ver. 4. "Whereby, when ye read, ye can perceive."

Amazing! So then he wrote not the whole, nor so much as he should have written. But here the nature of the subject prevented it. Elsewhere, as in the case of the Hebrews (Heb. v : 11.) and the Corinthians, (1 Cor. iii : 2.) the incapacity of the hearers. "Whereby, when ye read, ye can perceive," saith he, "my understanding in the mystery of Christ," i. e., how I knew, how I understood either such things as God hath spoken, or else, that Christ sitteth at the right hand of God; and then too the dignity, in that God "hath not dealt so with any nation." (Ps. cxlvii : 20.) And then to explain what nation this is with whom God hath thus dealt, he adds,

Ver. 5. "Which in other generations was not made known unto the sons of men, as it hath now been revealed unto His holy Apostles and Prophets in the Spirit."

What then, tell me, did not the Prophets[4] know it? How then doth Christ say, that Moses and the Prophets wrote "these things concerning Me?" And again, "If ye believed Moses, ye would believe Me." (John v : 46.) And again, "Ye search the Scriptures, because ye think that in them ye have eternal life, and these are they which bear witness of me." (John v : 39.) His meaning is this, either that it was not revealed unto all men, for he adds, "which in other generations was not made known unto the sons of men, as it hath now been revealed;" or else, that it was not thus made known by the very facts and realities

---

[1] [The Syraic Version followed by commentators from Chrysostom to Meyer makes ὁ δέσμιος predicate, supplying "am." "I Paul am the prisoner of Christ Jesus for you Gentiles." This is open to grave objections. 'Ο δεσμος is rather in apposition and the broken construction is resumed at ver. 14.—Riddle, Ellicott, Alford, Braune. R. V. Comp. 4 : 1.—G. A.]

[2] ["Gentle appeal, expressed in a hypothetical form and conveying the hope that his words had not been forgotten."—Ellicott. —G. A.]

[3] ["This parenthetical remark of the Apostle refers not to a lost letter but to the section last treated of concerning the Gentiles attaining salvation."—Meyer.—G. A.]

[4] [Prophets here refers, as before, to New Testament prophets, and not, as Chrysostom understands it, to O. T. phophets.—G. A.]

themselves, "as it hath now been revealed unto His holy Apostles and Prophets in the Spirit." For reflect. Peter, had he not been instructed by the Spirit, never would have gone to the Gentiles. For hear what he says, "Then hath God given unto them the Holy Ghost, as well as unto us." (Acts x: 47.) That it was by the Spirit that God chose that they should receive the grace. The Prophets then spoke, yet they knew it not thus perfectly; so far from it, that not even did the Apostles, after they had heard it. So far did it surpass all human calculation, and the common expectation.

Ver. 6. "That the Gentiles are fellow-heirs, and fellow-members of the body and fellow-partakers."[1]

What is this; "fellow-heirs, and fellow-partakers of the promise, and fellow-members of the body?" This last is the great thing, that they should be one body; this exceeding closeness of relation to Him. For that they were to be called indeed, that they knew, but that it was so great, as yet they knew not. This therefore he calls the mystery. "Of the promise." The Israelites were partakers, and the Gentiles also were fellow-partakers of the promise of God.

"In Christ Jesus through the Gospel."

That is, by His being sent unto them also, and by their believing; for it is not said they are fellow-heirs simply, but "through the Gospel." However, this indeed, is nothing so great, it is in fact a small thing, and it discloses to us another and greater thing, that not only men knew not this, but that neither Angels nor Archangels, nor any other created power, knew it. For it was a mystery, and was not revealed. "That ye can perceive," he saith, "my understanding." This alludes, perhaps, to what he said to them in the Acts, that he had some knowledge that the Gentiles also were called. This, he says, is his own knowledge, "the knowledge of the mystery," which he had mentioned, viz., "that Christ will in Himself make of the twain one new man." For by revelation he was instructed, both he and Peter, that they must not spurn the Gentiles; and this he states in his defence.

Ver. 7. "Whereof I was made a minister, according to the gift of that grace of God which was given me according to the working of His power."

He had said, "I am a prisoner;" but now again he says, that all is of God, as he says, "according to the gift of His grace;" for

---

[1] ["Fellow-heirs (συγκληρονόμα) denotes the joint possession with the believing Jews of the eternal Messianic bliss."—Meyer. "The following words (σύσσωμα καὶ συμμέτοχα), which seem to have been coined by the apostle, are well rendered by R. V., 'fellow-members of the body, and fellow-partakers,' and bring out more fully the relation of the fellow-heirs to each other."—Riddle. —G. A.]

according to the power of the gift is the dignity of this privilege. But the gift would not have been enough, had it not also implanted in him power.

MORAL. For a work indeed it was of power, of mighty power, and such as no human diligence was equal to. For he brought three qualifications to the preaching of the word, a zeal fervent and venturous, a soul ready to undergo any possible hardship, and knowledge and wisdom combined. For his love of enterprise, his blamelessness of life, had availed nothing, had he not also received the power of the Spirit. And look at it as seen first in himself, or rather hear his own words. "That our ministration be not blamed." (2 Cor. vi: 3.) And again, "For our exhortation, is not of error, nor of uncleanness, nor in guile, nor a cloke of covetousness." (1 Thes. ii: 3, 5.) Thus thou hast seen his blamelessness. And again, "For we take thought for things honorable, not only in the sight of the Lord, but also in the sight of men." (2 Cor. viii: 21.) Then again, besides these; "I protest by that glorying in you which I have in Christ Jesus our Lord, I die daily." (1 Cor. xv: 31.) And again; "Who shall separate us from the love of Christ? shall tribulation, or anguish, or persecution?" (Rom. viii: 35.) And again; "In much patience, in afflictions, in necessities, in distresses, in stripes, in imprisonments, in watchings." (2 Cor. vi: 4, 5.) Then again, his prudence and management; "To the Jews I became as a Jew, to them that are without law as without law, to them that are under the law as under the law." (1 Cor. ix: 20.) He shaves his head also, (Acts xxi: 24-26.) and does numberless things of the sort. But the crown of all is in the power of the Holy Ghost. "For I will not dare to speak," saith he, "of any things save those which Christ wrought through me." (Rom. xv: 18.) And again, "For what is there wherein you were made inferior to the rest of the Churches?" (2 Cor. xii: 13.) And again, "For in nothing was I behind the very chiefest Apostles though I am nothing." (2 Cor. xii: 11.) Without these things, the work had been impossible.

It was not then by his miracles that men were made believers; no, it was not the miracles that did this, nor was it upon the ground of these that he claimed his high pretension, but upon those other grounds. For a man must be alike irreproachable in conduct, prudent and discreet in his dealings with others, regardless of danger, and apt to teach. It was by these qualifications that the greater part of his success was achieved. Where there were these, there was no need of miracles. At least we see he was successful in numberless such cases, quite antecedently to the use of miracles. But, now-a-days, we without any of these would fain command all things. Yet if one of them be separated from the other, it henceforth becomes useless. What is the advantage of a man's being ever so regardless of danger, if his life be open to censure. "For if the light that is in thee be darkness," saith Christ, "how great is that darkness?" (Mat. vi: 23.) Again, what the advantage of a man's being of an irreproachable life, if he is sluggish and indolent? "For, he that doth not take his cross, and follow after Me," saith He, "is not worthy of Me;" (Mat. x: 38.) and so, "The good shepherd layeth down his life for the sheep." (Jo. x: 11.) Again, what is the advantage of being both these, unless a man is at the same time prudent and discreet in "knowing how he ought to answer each one?" (Col. iv: 6.) Even if miracles be not in our power, yet both these qualities are in our power. Stjll howeʋer, notwithstanding Paul contributed so much from himself, yet did he attribute all to grace. This is the act of a grateful servant. And we should never so much as have heard of his good deeds, had he not beeɴ brought to a necessity of declaring them.

And are we worthy then so much as even to mention the name of Paul? He, who had moreover grace to aid him, yet was not satisfied, but contributed to the work ten thousand perils; whilst we, who are destitute of that source of confidence, whence, tell me, do we expect either to preserve those who are committed to our charge, or to gain those who are not come to the fold;—men, as we are, who have been making a study of self-indulgence, who are searching the world over for ease, and who are unable, or rather who are unwilling, to endure even the very shadow of danger, and are as far distant from his wisdom as heaven is from earth? Hence it is too that they who are under us are at so great a distance behind the men of those days; because the disciples of those days were better than the teachers of these, isolated as they were in the midst of the populace, and of tyrants, and having all men on all sides their enemies, and yet not in the slightest degree dragged down or yielding. Hear at least what he saith to the Philippians, (Phil. i: 29.) "Because to you it hath been granted in the behalf of Christ, not only to believe on Him, but also to suffer in his behalf." And again to the Thessalonians, (1 Thes. ii: 14.) "For ye, brethren, became imitators of the churches of God which are in Judæa." And again in writing to the Hebrews (Heb. x: 34.) he said, "And ye took joyfully the spoiling of your pessessions." And to the Colossians (Col. iii: 3.) he testifies, saying, "For ye died, and your life is hid with Christ in God." And indeed to these very Ephesians he bears witness of many perils and dangers. And again

in writing to the Galatians, (Gal. iii: 4.) he says, "Did ye suffer so many things in vain? if it be indeed in vain." And you see them too, all employed in doing good. Hence it was that both grace wrought effectually in those days, hence also that they lived in good works. Hear, moreover, what he writes to the Corinthians, against whom he brings charges out of number; yet does he not bear even them record, where he says, "Yea, what zeal it wrought in you, yea, what longing!" (1 Cor. vii: 11.) And again, in how many points does he bear them record on this subject? These things one shall not see now-a-days, even in teachers. They are all gone and perished. And the cause is, that love hath waxed cold, that sinners go unpunished; (for hear what he says writing to Timothy, (1 Tim. v: 20.) "Them that sin, reprove in the sight of all;") it is that the rulers are in a sickly state; for if the head be not sound, how can the rest of the body maintain its vigor? But mark how great is the present disorder. They, who were living virtuously, and who under any circumstance might have confidence, have taken possession of the tops of the mountains,[1] and have escaped out of the world, separating themselves as from an enemy and an alien and not from a body to which they belonged.

Plagues too, teeming with untold mischiefs, have lighted upon the Churches. The chief offices have become saleable.[2] Hence numberless evils are springing, and there is no one to redress, no one to reprove them. Nay, the disorder has assumed a sort of method and consistency. Has a man done wrong, and been arraigned for it? His effort is not to prove himself guiltless, but to find if possible accomplices in his crimes. What is to become of us? since hell is our threatened portion. Believe me, had not God stored up punishment for us there, ye would see every day tragedies deeper than the disasters of the Jews. What then? however let no one take offence, for I mention no names; suppose some one were to come into this church to present you that are here at this moment, those that are now with me, and to make inquisition of them; or rather not now, but suppose on Easter day any one, endued with such a spirit, as to have a thorough knowledge of the things they had been doing, should narrowly examine all that came to Communion, and were being washed [in Baptism] after they had attended the mysteries; many things would be discovered more shocking than the Jewish

---

[1] This alludes to the Monks who lived in the mountains about Antioch, where these Homilies seem to have been written. Compare Homily xiii. p. 2. vid. *Adv. Oppugn.* i. 7. 8. Elsewhere he blames persons who retired, as hiding their talents, vid. *1 Cor. Hom. vi.* 8.

[2] The same sin is noticed among other places by S. Basil *Ep.* 53. S. Ambrose *in Luc.* lib. ix. 17—19. S. Jerome *in Mat.* xxi. 12. 13.

horrors. He would find persons who practise augury, who make use of charms, and omens, and incantations, and who have committed fornication, adulterers, drunkards, and revilers,—covetous, I am unwilling to add, lest I should hurt the feelings of any of those who are standing here. What more? Suppose any one should make scrutiny into all the communicants in the world, what kind of transgression is there which he would not detect? and what if he examined those in authority? Would he not find them eagerly bent upon gain? making traffic of high places? envious, malignant, vainglorious, gluttonous, and slaves to money?

Where then there is such impiety as this going on, what dreadful calamity must we not expect? And to be assured how sore vengeance they incur who are guilty of such sins as these, consider the examples of old. One single man, a common soldier, stole the sacred property, and all were smitten. Ye know, doubtless, the history I mean? I am speaking of Acham the son of Carmi, the man who stole the consecrated spoil. (Joshua vii: 1-26.) The time too when the Prophet spoke, was a time when their country was full of soothsayers, like that of the Philistines. (Isa. ii: 6.) Whereas now there are evils out of number at the full, and not one fears. Oh, henceforth let us take the alarm. God is accustomed to punish the righteous also with the wicked; such was the case with Daniel, and with the three holy Children, such

has been the case with ten thousand others, such is the case in the wars that are taking place even at the present day. For the one indeed, whatever burden of sins they have upon them, by this means lay aside even that; but not so the other.

On account of all these things, let us take heed to ourselves. Do ye not see these wars? Do ye not hear of these disasters? Do ye learn no lesson from these things? Nations and whole cities are swallowed up and destroyed, and myriads as many again are enslaved to the barbarians.

If hell bring us not to our senses, yet let these things. What, are these too mere threats, are they not facts that have already taken place? Great is the punishment they have suffered, yet a greater still shall we suffer, who are not brought to our senses even by their fate. Is this discourse wearing?[2] I am aware it is myself, but if we attend to it, it has its advantage; because this it has not, the quality of an address to please,—nay more, nor ever shall have, but ever those topics which may avail to humble and to chasten the soul. For these will be to us the ground-work of those blessings to come hereafter, to which God grant that we may all attain, in Jesus Christ our Lord, with whom to the Father, together with the Holy Ghost be glory and might and honor, now and henceforth, and forever and ever. Amen.

HOMILY VII.

CHAPTER III. VERSES 8—11.

" Unto me, who am less than the least of all saints, was this grace given, to preach unto the Gentiles the unsearchable riches of Christ; and to make all men see what is the dispensation of the mystery, which from all ages hath been hid in God, who created all things:[1] to the intent that now unto the principalities and the powers in the heavenly places might be made known through the Church the manifold wisdom of God, according to the eternal purpose, which He purposed in Christ Jesus our Lord."

THEY who go to the physician's have not merely to go there and nothing further; they have to learn how to treat themselves, and to

apply remedies. And so with us then who come here, we must not do this and nothing else, we must learn our lesson, the surpassing lowliness of Paul. What? when he was about to speak of the vastness of the grace of God, hear what he saith, " Unto me, who am less than the least of all saints, was this grace given." Lowliness indeed it was even to bewail his former sins, although blotted out, and to make mention of them, and to hold himself within his true measure as where he calls himself " a blasphemer, and a persecutor, and injurious; " (1 Tim. i: 13.) yet nothing was

---

[1] [The words 'through Jesus Christ' (διὰ' Ἰησοῦ Χριστοῦ) which are here found in Chrysostom's text have gotten into the *textus receptus* from the few late and mostly cursive MSS. which present the Byzantine or Constantinopolitan text and from which the *textus receptus* was made. Chrysostom is the chief witness of this Byzantine text. Schaff, *Companion to Greek Testament*, pp. 205–6. The words are omitted by Aleph A B C D, most Versions and Editors.—G. A.]

[2] S. Chrysostom complains that his rich hearers, when the choice lay between theatre or race and Church, preferred the former; alleging the heat and crowd of the latter. vid. t. 3. *Hom.* iii. xii. and xv. (Ed. Ben.) *1 Cor. Hom.* v. fin. We see his care to consult for the tastes and capacities of his hearers in his preaching, in *Ps. 41. init.* and t. 3. *Hom. vii. n. 3.* (Ed. Ben.)

equal to this: for "formerly," saith he, such was I; and again he calls himself, "one born out of due time." (1 Cor. xv: 8.) But that after so many great and good deeds and at that time he should thus humble himself, and call himself "less than the least of all," this is indeed great and surpassing moderation. "To one who am less than the least of all saints; " he saith not, "than the Apostles." So that that expression is less strong than this before us. There his words are, "I am not meet to be called an Apostle." (1 Cor. xv: 9.) Here he says that he is even "less than the least of all saints; " "to me," saith he, "who am less than the least of all saints was this grace given." What grace? "To preach unto the Gentiles the unsearchable riches of Christ, and to make all men see what is the dispensation of the mystery, which from all ages hath been hid in God, who created all things, to the intent that now unto the principalities and the powers in the heavenly places, might be made known through the Church the manifold wisdom of God." True, to man it was not revealed; and art thou enlightening Angels and Archangels and Principalities and Powers? I am, saith he. For it was " hid in God," even " in God who created all things." And dost thou venture to utter this? I do, saith he. But whence hath this been made manifest to the Angels? By the Church. Again he saith, not merely the manifold (ποικίλος) but the much-manifold (πολυποίκιλος) wisdom, that is, " the multiplied and varied." What then is this? Did not Angels know it? No, nothing of it; for if Principalities knew it not, much less could Angels ever have known it. What then? Did not even Archangels know it? No, nor even they. But whence were they going to know it? Who was to reveal it? When we were taught it, then were they also by us.[1] For hear what the Angel saith to Joseph; "Thou shalt call His Name Jesus, for it is He that shall save His people from their sins." (Matt. i: 21.)

Paul himself was sent to the Gentiles, the other Apostles to the Circumsion. So that the more marvellous and astonishing commission was given, saith he, "to me, who am less than the least." And this too was of grace, that he that was least should have the greatest things entrusted to him; that he should be made the herald of these tidings. For he that is made a herald of the greater tidings, is in this way great.

" To preach unto the Gentiles the unsearchable riches[2] of Christ."

If His "riches are unsearchahle," and that too after his appearing, much more is His essence. If it is still a mystery, much more was it before it was made known; for a mystery he calls it on this account, because neither did the Angels know it, nor was it manifest to any one else.

"And to make all men see," saith he, "what is the dispensation of the mystery which from all ages hath been hid in God, who created all things."

Angels knew only this, that "The Lord's portion was His people." (Deut. xxxii: 8, 9.) And again it is said, "The Prince of Persia withstood me." (Dan. x: 13.) So that it is nothing to be wondered at that they were ignorant of this; for if they were ignorant of the circumstances of the return from the Captivity, much more would they be of these things. For this is the gospel. "It is He that shall save," it saith, "His people." (Matt. i: 21.) Not a word about the Gentiles. But what concerns the Gentiles the Spirit revealeth. That they were called indeed, the Angels knew, but that it was to the same privileges as Israel, yea, even to sit upon the throne of God, this, who would ever have expected? who would ever have believed?

"Which hath been hid," saith he, "in God."

This "dispensation," however, he more clearly unfolds in the Epistle to the Romans. " In God," he continues, "who created all things by Jesus Christ."[3] And he does well to say " by Jesus Christ; " forasmuch as He who created all things by Him, revealeth also this by Him; for He hath made nothing without Him; for "without Him," it is said, "was not any thing made." (John i: 30.)

In speaking of " principalities " and " powers," he speaks both of those above and those beneath.

" According to the eternal purpose." It hath been now, he means, brought to pass, but not now decreed, it had been planned beforehand from the very first. " According to the eternal purpose which He purposed[4] in Christ Jesus our Lord." That is, according to the eternal foreknowledge; foreknowing the things to come, i. e., he means the ages to come; for He knew what was to be, and thus decreed it. According to the purpose of the ages, of those, perhaps, which He hath made by Christ Jesus,

---

[1] S. Chrysostom says the same, *Orat. iv. in Anom.* 2. and *Hom. i. in Joan.* 2. (ed. Ben.) vid. also Theodoret in *Ps.* 23. 7. 8. S. Greg. Nyss. *Hom. 8 in Cant.* p. 596. S. Jerome *in loc.* [Comp. 1 Pet. 1: 12, which things angels desire to look into.—G. A.]

[2] ["The whole divine fulness of salvation, of which Christ is the possessor and bestower, and which is of such a nature that the
human intellect cannot explore it so as to form an adequate conception of it. This does not hinder the proclamation which, on the contrary, is rendered possible by revelation."—Meyer.—G. A.]

[3] [See note on these words above.—G. A.]

[4] [This verb, ἐποίησεν, has been applied by many to the ' forming ' of the purpose. (So Rev. Ver.) But it seems best to refer it to the ' execution' of it, regarded as an accomplished fact. Riddle in *Popular Commentary* and in *Lange.* Braune in *Lange.* Meyer, Ellicott.—G. A.]

because it was by Christ that every thing was made.

Ver. 12. "In whom we have," saith he, "boldness, and access in confidence through our faith in him."

"Have access," not as prisoners, he says, nor yet, as persons candidates for pardon, nor as sinners ; for, saith he, we have even " boldness with confidence," that is, accompanied with cheerful trust; arising from what source ? through our faith in Him."

Ver. 13. "Wherefore[1] I ask that ye faint not at my tribulations for you, which are your glory."

How is it "for them?" How is it "their glory?" It is because God so loved them, as to give even the Son for them, and to afflict His servants for them : for it was in order that they might attain so many blessings, that Paul was in prison. Surely this was from God's exceeding love towards them : it is what God also saith concerning the Prophets, "I have slain them by the words of my mouth." (Hos. vi: 5.) But how was it that they fainted, when another was afflicted ? He means, they were troubled, were distressed. This also he says when writing to the Thessalonians, "that no man be moved by these afflictions." (1 Thes. iii: 3.) For not only ought we not to grieve, but we ought even to rejoice. If ye find consolation in the fore-warning, we tell you beforehand that here we have tribulation. And why pray? Because thus hath the Lord ordered.

Ver. 14, 15. "For this cause[2] I bow my knees unto the Father from whom every family in heaven and on earth is named."

He here shows the spirit of his prayer for them. He does not say simply, "I pray," but manifests the supplication to be heartfelt, by the "bowing of the knees."

"From whom every family."

That is, no longer, he means, reckoned, according to the number of Angels, but according to Him who hath created the tribes both in heaven above and in earth beneath, not as the Jewish.

Ver. 16, 17. "That He would grant you according to the riches of His glory that ye may be strengthened with power through His Spirit in the inward man; that Christ may dwell in your hearts through faith."

Mark with what insatiable earnestness he invokes these blessings upon them, that they may not be tossed about. But how shall this be effected? By the " Holy Spirit in your inward

man, that Christ may dwell in your hearts through faith." How again shall this be?

Ver. 18, 19. "To the end that ye being rooted and grounded in love, may be strong to apprehend with all the saints, what is the breadth, and length, and height, and depth,[3] and to know the love of Christ which passeth knowledge."

Thus is his prayer now again, the very same as when he began. For what were his words in the beginning? "That the God of our Lord Jesus Christ, the Father of glory may give unto you a Spirit of wisdom and revelation in the knowledge of Him; having the eyes of your heart enlightened, that ye may know what is the hope of His calling, what the riches of the glory of His inheritance in the saints; and what the exceeding greatness of His power to us-ward who believe." And now again he says the same. "That ye may be strong to apprehend with all the saints what is the breadth, and length, and height, and depth ; " i. e., to know perfectly the mystery which hath been providentially ordered in our behalf:[4] "and the breadth, and length, and height, and depth ; " that is, too, the immensity of the love of God, and how it extends every where. And he outlines it by the visible dimensions of solid bodies, pointing as it were to a man. He comprehends the upper and under and sides. I have thus spoken indeed, he would say, yet is it not for any words of mine to teach you these things; that must be the work of the Holy Spirit. "By His might," saith he, is it that ye must be "strengthened" against the trials that await you, and in order to remain unshaken; so that there is no other way to be strengthened but by the Holy Ghost, both on account of trials and carnal reasonings.

But how doth Christ dwell in the hearts? Hear what Christ Himself saith, "I and my Father will come unto him, and make our abode with him." (John xiv: 23.) He dwelleth in those hearts that are faithful, in those that are "rooted " in His love, those that remain firm and unshaken.

"That ye may be" thoroughly "strong," saith he ; so that there is great strength needed.

[5] "That ye may be filled unto all the fulness of God."

---

[3] [" A sensuous illustration of the idea ; 'how great in every relation.' "—Meyer. G. A.]

[4] ["Of what are these dimensions predicated ? Not of the work of redemption as Chrysostom (τὸ μυστήριον τὸ ὑπὲρ ὑμῶν οἰκονομηθέν) because after a new portion of the discourse is begun at ver. 14, the μυστήριον is not again mentioned ; nor of the love of God to us, as Chrysostom again, for the ἐν ἀγάπῃ preceding does not refer to God's love ; but of the love of Christ to men as shown in ver. 19."—Meyer. So Ellicott, Braune, Riddle.—G. A.]

[5] [This entire paragraph is omitted from Field's text. But as it is supported by several excellent authorities, as it is in Chrysostom's style and as it contains a very noble thought, we have ventured to retain it. "Field seems to rely on the probability that the shorter text is the original. One of his main authorities seems

---

[1] [Wherefore, " in view of my position as minister of such a gospel."—Riddle.—G. A.]

[2] [This τούτου χάριν is a resumption of the first verse of the chapter which was left unfinished by reason of the digression concerning his office as apostle of the Gentiles, which forms a section by itself. (ver. 2-13.)—G. A.]

What he means is this. Although the love of Christ lies above the reach of all human knowledge, yet shall ye know it, if ye shall have Christ dwelling in you, yea, not only shall know from Him this, but shall even " be filled unto all the fulness of God ; " meaning by the "fulness of God," either the knowledge how God is worshipped in the Father, the Son, and the Holy Ghost, or else urging them thus to use every effort, in order to be filled with all virtue, of which God is full.

Ver. 20. "Now unto Him that is able to do exceeding abundantly above all that we ask or think, according to the power that worketh in us."

That God hath done " abundantly above all that we ask or think," is evident from what the Apostle himself hath written. For I indeed, saith he, pray, but He of Himself, even without any prayer of mine, will do works greater than all we ask, not simply " greater," nor " abundantly greater," but " exceeding abundantly." And this is evident from " the power, that worketh in us : " for neither did we ever ask these things, nor did we expect them.

Ver. 21. "Unto Him be the glory," he concludes, " in the Church and in Christ Jesus, unto all generations forever and ever. Amen."

Well does he close the discourse with prayer and doxology ; for right were it that He, who hath bestowed upon us such vast gifts, should be glorified and blessed, so that this is even a proper part of our amazement at His mercies, to give glory for the things advanced to us at God's hands through Jesus Christ.

" The glory in the Church." Well might he say this, forasmuch as the Church alone can last on to eternity.

It seems necessary to state what are meant by "families." (πατριαί) Here on earth, indeed there are "families" that is races sprung from one parent stock ; but in heaven how can this be, where none is born of another? Surely then, by " families,"[1] he means either the assemblies

to be a Catena which would naturally abridge the portions extracted especially in a writer so given to amplifications as Chrysostom." We have in the main followed Field's text in spite of this probability, but in exceptional cases, like the present, we have ventured to demur.—G. A.]

[1] This text has various interpretations. S. Athanasius uses it to imply that God, as Father of the Son, is the only true Father, and that all created paternity is a shadow of the true. *Orat. in Arian.* i. 23. S. Jerome says, " As He who alone is good, (Luke 18, 19.) makes men good, and who is alone immortal, (1 Tim. 6, 16.) bestows immortality, and who alone is true (Rom. 3, 4.) imparts the name of truth ; so too the only Father, in that He is Creator of all, and the cause of substance to all, gives to the rest to be called Father." *in loc.* He considers that the Angels are said in the text to share His paternity in a spiritual sense, as Christ says to the sick man, "Son," and to His disciples, "Little children." Theodoret seems to say the same. *in loc.* v. also Hooker, E. P. V. liv. 2, ["The reference must be to those larger classes and communities into which, as we may also infer from other passages (1 : 21; Col. 1 : 16) the celestial hosts appear to be divided ; and to the races and tribes of men every one of which owes the very title of πατριά, by which it is defined to the great πατήρ of all the πατριαί both of angels and men."—Ellicott. " The Apostle seems regarding God as the Father of us His adopted children in Christ, to go forth into the fact that He in this relation to us is the great

and orders of heavenly beings ; as also we find it written in Scripture, " the family of Amattari : " (1 Sam. x : 21. See Septuagint.) or else that it is from Him from whom earthly fathers have their name of father.

However, he does not ask the whole of God, but demands of them also faith and love, and not simply love, but love "rooted and grounded," so that neither any blasts can shake it, nor any thing else overturn it. He had said, that " tribulations " are " glory," and if mine are so to you, he would say, much more will your own be : so that to be afflicted is no token of men being forsaken, for He who hath wrought so great things for us, never would do this.

Again, if in order to understand the love of God, it was necessary for Paul to pray, and there was need of the indwelling of the Holy Spirit, who by following mere reasonings shall understand the nature of Christ? And why is it a difficult thing to learn that God loveth us? Beloved, it is extremely difficult. For some know not even this ; wherefore, they even say, numberless evils come to be in the world ; and others know not the extent of this love. Nor, indeed, is Paul seeking to know its extent, nor with any view to measure it ; for how could he? but only to understand this, that it is transcendent, and great. And this very thing, he says, he is able to show, even from the knowledge which hath been vouchsafed to us.

However, what is higher than the being " strengthened with might," in order to have Christ within ? Vast are the things we ask, saith he, yet is He able to do above even them, so that not only doth He love us, but doth so intensely. Be it our care therefore, beloved, to understand the love of God. A great thing indeed is this ; nothing is so beneficial to us, nothing so deeply touches us : more availing this to convince our souls than the fear of hell itself. Whence then shall we understand it? Both from the sources now mentioned, and from the things which happen every day. For from what motive have these things been done for us? from what necessity on His part? None whatever. Over and over again he lays down love as the cause. But the highest degree of love is that where men receive a benefit, without any prior service on their part to call for it.

Moral. And let us then be followers of Him ; let us do good to our enemies, to them that hate us, let us draw near to those who turn their backs upon us. This renders us like unto God. " For if ye love them that love you," saith Christ, "what reward have ye ? " " Do not even the Gentiles the same." (Matt. v : 46.) But what is a sure proof of love? To love him

original and prototype of the paternal relation, wherever found." Alford in Riddle in *Pop. Com.*—G. A.]

that hates thee. I wish to give you some example, (pardon me,) and since I find it not among them that are spiritual, I shall quote an instance from them that are without. See ye not those lovers? How many insults are wreaked upon them by their mistresses, how many artifices practised, how many punishments inflicted : yet they are enchained to them, they burn for them, and love them better than their own souls, passing whole nights before their thresholds. From them let us take our example, not indeed to love such as those,—women, I mean, that are harlots; no, but thus to love our enemies. For tell me, do not harlots treat their lovers with greater insolence than all the enemies in the world, and squander away their substance, and cast insult in their face, and impose upon them more servile tasks than upon their own menials? And yet still they desist not, though no one hath so great an enemy in any one, as the lover in his mistress. Yea, this beloved one disdains, and reviles, and oftentimes maltreats him, and the more she is loved, the more she scorns him. . And what can be more brutal than a spirit like this? Yet notwithstanding he loves her still.

But possibly we shall find love like this in spiritual characters also, not in those of our day, (for it has "waxed cold,") (Matt. xxiv : 12.) but in those great and glorious men of old. Moses, the blessed Moses, surpassed even those that love with human passion. How, and in what way? First, he gave up the court, and the luxury, and the retinue, and the glory attending it, and chose rather to be with the Israelites. Yet is this not only what no one else would ever have done, but would have even been ashamed, were another to have discovered him, of being found to be a kinsman of men, who were slaves and not only slaves, but were looked upon as even execrable. Yet was he not only not ashamed of his kindred, but with all his spirit defended them, and threw himself into dangers for their sake. (Acts. vii : 24.) How? Seeing, it is said, one doing an injury to one of them, he defended him that suffered the injury, and slew him that inflicted it. But this is not as yet for the sake of enemies. Great indeed is this act of itself, but not so great as what comes afterwards. The next day, then, he saw the same thing taking place, and when he saw him whom he had defended[1] doing his neighbor wrong, he admonished him to desist from his wrong-doing. But he said, with great ingratitude, "Who made thee a ruler and a judge over us?" (Acts. vii : 27.) Who would not have taken fire at these words? Had then the

[1] [It does not appear from the account in Exodus ii : 11 ff. or from that in Acts. vii : 24 ff. that the Hebrew who did his brother wrong was the same that Moses had defended on the preceeding day, as Chrysostom here takes for granted.—G. A.]

former act been that of passion and frenzy, then would he have smitten and killed this man also; for surely he on whose behalf it was done, never would have informed against him. But because they were brethren, it is said, he spoke thus. When he [the Hebrew] was being wronged, he uttered no such word "Who made thee a ruler and a judge over us?" "Wherefore saidst thou not this yesterday?" Moses would say, "Thy injustice, and thy cruelty, these make me a ruler and a judge."

But now, mark, how that some, in fact, say as much even to God Himself. Whenever they are wronged indeed, they would have Him a God of vengeance, and complain of His long suffering; but when themselves do wrong, not for a moment.

However, what could be more bitter than words like these? And yet notwithstanding, after this, when he was sent to that ungrateful, to that thankless race, he went, and shrunk not back. Yea, and after those miracles, and after the wonders wrought by his hand, oftentimes they sought to stone him to death and he escaped out of their hands. They kept murmuring too incessantly, and yet still, notwithstanding, so passionately did he love them, as to say unto God, when they committed that heinous sin, "Yet now if Thou wilt forgive, forgive their sin ; and if not, blot even me also out of the book which Thou hast written." (Ex. xxxii : 32.) Fain would I perish, saith he, with them, rather than without them be saved. Here, verily, is love even to madness, verily, unbounded love. What sayest thou, Moses? Art thou regardless of Heaven? I am, saith he, for I love those who have wronged me. Prayest thou to be blotted out? Yea, saith he, what can I do, for it is love? And what again after these things? Hear what the Scripture saith elsewhere; "And it went ill with Moses for their sakes." (Ps. cvi : 32.) How often did they wax wanton? How often did they reject both himself and his brother? How often did they seek to return back to Egypt? and yet after all these things did he burn, yea, was beside himself with love for them, and was ready to suffer for their sakes.

Thus ought a man to love his enemies; by lamentation, by unwearied endurance, by doing everything, by showing all favor, to aim at their salvation.

And what again, tell me, did Paul? did he not ask even to be accursed in their stead ? (Rom. ix : 3.) But the great pattern we must of necessity derive from the Lord, for thus doth He also Himself, where he saith, " For He maketh His sun to rise on the evil and the good." (Matt. v : 45.) adducing the example from His Father ; but we from Christ Himself. He came unto them, in His Incarnation, I mean, He became a servant for their sakes, "He humbled Himself, He emptied Himself, He took the form of a servant." (Phil. ii: 7, 8.) And when He came unto them, He went not Himself aside "into any way of the Gentiles," (Matt. x: 5.) and gave the same charge to His disciples, and not only so, but "He went about healing all manner of disease, and all manner of sickness. (Matt. iv: 23.) And what then? All the rest indeed were astonished, and marvelled, and said, "Whence, then, hath this man all these things?" (Matt. xiii: 56.) But these, the objects of His beneficence, these said, "He hath a devil," (John x: 20.) and "blasphemeth," (John x: 36.) and "is mad," and is a "deceiver," (John vii: 12, and Matt. xxvii: 63.) Did he therefore cast them away? No, in no wise, but when He heard these sayings, He even yet more signally bestowed His benefits upon them, and went straightway to them that were about to crucify Him, to the intent that He might but only save them. And after He was crucified, what were His words? "Father, forgive them, for they know not what they do." (Luke xxiii: 34.) Both cruelly treated before this, and cruelly treated after this, even to the very latest breath, for them He did everything, in their behalf He prayed. Yea, and after the Cross itself, what did He not do for their sakes?

Did He not send Apostles? Did He not work miracles? Did He not shake the whole world?

Thus is it we ought to love our enemies, thus to imitate Christ. Thus did Paul. Stoned, suffering unnumbered cruelties, yet did he all things for their good. Hear his own words. "My heart's desire and my supplication to God is for them that they may be saved." (Rom. x: 1, 2.) And again; "For I bear them witness that they have a zeal for God." And again; "If thou, being a wild olive tree wast grafted in, how much more shall these be grafted into their own olive tree?" (Rom. xi: 24.) How tender, thinkest thou, must be the affection from which these expressions proceed, how vast the benevolence? it is impossible to express it, impossible.

Thus is it we ought to love our enemies. This is to love God, Who hath enjoined it, Who hath given it as His law. To imitate Him is to love our enemy. Consider it is not thine enemy thou art benefiting, but thyself; thou art not loving him, but art obeying God. Knowing therefore these things, let us confirm our love one to another, that we may perform this duty perfectly, and attain those good things that are promised in Christ Jesus our Lord, with Whom to the Father, together with the Holy Ghost, be glory, might, and honor, now, and for ever and ever. Amen.

HOMILY VIII.

CHAPTER iv. Verses 1, 2.

"I therefore, the prisoner in the Lord, beseech you to walk worthily of the calling wherewith ye were called, with all lowliness and meekness."

IT is the virtue of teachers to aim not at praise, nor at esteem from those under their authority, but at their salvation, and to do every thing with this object; since the man who should make the other end his aim, would not be a teacher but a tyrant. Surely it is not for this that God set thee over them, that thou shouldest enjoy greater court and service, but that thine own interests should be disregarded, and every one of theirs built up. This is a teacher's duty: such an one was the blessed Paul, a man who was free from all manner of vanity, and was contented to be one of the many, nay more, to be the very least even of them. Hence he even calls himself their servant, and so generally speaks in a tone of supplication. Observe him then even now writing

nothing dictatorial, nothing imperious, but all chastened and subdued.

"I therefore," saith he, "the prisoner in the Lord, beseech you to walk worthily of the calling wherewith ye were called." What is it, tell me, thou art beseeching? Is it that thou mayest gain any end for thyself? No, saith he, in no wise; it is that I may save others. And yet surely they who beseech, do so for things which are of importance to themselves. True; and this, saith he, is of importance to myself, according to what he says also elsewhere in his writings, "Now we live, if ye stand fast in the Lord;" (1 Thess. iii: 8.) for he ever earnestly desired the salvation of those whom he was instructing.

"I, the prisoner in the Lord." Great and mighty dignity! Greater than that of king or of consul, or of any other. Hence it is the very title he uses in writing to Philemon, "As Paul the aged, and now a prisoner also of Jesus Christ." (Philemon 9.) For nothing is so glorious as a bond for Christ's sake, as the chains that were bound around those holy hands; more glorious is it to be a prisoner for Christ's sake than to be an Apostle, than to be a Teacher, than to be an Evangelist. Is there any that loveth Christ, he will understand what I am saying. Is any transported and fired with devotion for the Lord, he knows the power of these bonds. Such an one would rather choose to be a prisoner for Christ's sake, than to have the Heavens for his dwelling. More glorious than any gold were the hands he was showing to them, yea, than any royal diadem. Yes, no jewelled tiara bound around the head invests it with such glory, as an iron chain for Christ's sake. Then was the prison more glorious than palaces, yea, than heaven itself. Why say I than palaces? Because it contained a prisoner of Christ. Is there any that loveth Christ, he knows the dignity of this title, he knows what a virtue is this, he knows how great a boon he bestowed upon mankind, even this, to be bound for His sake. More glorious this, perhaps to be bound for His sake, than " to sit at His right hand," (Matt. xx: 21.) more august this, than to "sit upon the twelve thrones." (Matt. xix: 28.)

And why speak I of human glories? I am ashamed to compare earthly riches and golden attire to these bonds. But forbearing to speak of those great and heavenly glories, even were the thing attended with no reward at all, this alone were a great reward, this an ample recompense, to suffer these hardships for the sake of the Beloved. They that love, even though it be not God, but man, they know what I am saying, since they are more delighted to suffer for, than to be honored by those they love. But to fully understand these things belongs to the holy company, the Apostles, I mean, and them alone. For hearken to what the blessed Luke saith, (Acts v: 11.) " that they departed from the presence of the council, rejoicing that they were counted worthy to suffer dishonor for the Name." To all others indeed it seems to be foolishness, that to suffer dishonor is to be counted worthy, that to suffer dishonor is to rejoice. But to them that understand the love of Christ, this is esteemed of all things the most blessed. Were any to offer me my choice, the whole Heaven or that chain, that chain I would prefer. Were any to ask whether he should place me on high with the Angels, or with Paul in his bonds, the prison I would choose. Were any about to change me into one of those powers, that are in Heaven, that are round about the throne, or into such a prisoner as this, such a prisoner I would choose to be. Nothing is more blessed than that chain.

Would that I could be at this moment in that very spot, (for the bonds are said to be still in existence,) to behold and admire those men, for their love of Christ. Would that I could behold the chains, at which the devils fear and tremble, but which Angels reverence. Nothing is more noble than to suffer any evil for Christ's sake. I count not Paul so happy, because he was "caught up into Paradise," (2 Cor. xii: 4.) as because he was cast into the dungeon; I count him not so happy, because he heard "unspeakable words," as because he endured those bonds. I count him not so happy, because he was " caught up into the third Heaven," (2 Cor. xii: 2.) as I count him happy for those bonds' sake. For that these are greater than those, hear how even he himself knew this; for he saith not, I who " heard unspeakable words," beseech you: but what? " I, the prisoner in the Lord, beseech you." Nor yet are we to wonder, though he inscribes not this in all his Epistles, for he was not always in prison, but only at certain times.

I deem it more desirable to suffer evil for Christ's sake, than to receive honor at Christ's hands. This is transcendent honor, this is glory that surpasseth all things. If He Himself who became a servant for my sake, and "emptied " (Phil. ii: 7.) His glory, yet thought not Himself so truly in glory, as when He was crucified for my sake, what ought not I to endure? For hear His own words: " Father, glorify Thou Me." (John xvii: 1.) What is this thou art saying? Thou art being led to the cross with thieves and plunderers of graves, thou endurest the death of the accursed; Thou art about to be spit upon and buffeted; and callest Thou this glory? [1]Yes, He saith, for I suffer these things for My beloved ones, and I count them altogether glory. If He who loved the miserable and wretched calleth this glory, not to be on His Father's throne, nor in His Father's glory, but in dishonor,—if this was His glory, and if this He set before the other : much more ought I to regard these things as glory. Oh ! those blessed bonds ! Oh ! those blessed hands which that chain adorned ! Not so worthy were Paul's hands when they lifted up and raised the lame man at Lystra, as when they were bound around with those chains. Had I been living in those times, how eagerly would I have embraced them, and put them to the very apple of mine eyes. Never would I have ceased kissing those hands which were counted worthy to be bound for my Lord. Marvellest thou at Paul, when the viper fastened on his hand, and did him no hurt? Marvel not. It reverenced his chain. Yea, and the whole sea reverenced it ; for then too

---

[1] [Christ referred to the glorification with His Father which was to follow his humiliation. Cf. Jo. xvii: 5. Phil. ii: 9.—G. A.]

was he bound, when he was saved from ship-wreck. Were any one to grant me power to raise the dead at this moment, I would not choose that power, but this chain. Were I free from the cares of the Church, had I my body strong and vigorous, I would not shrink from undertaking so long a journey, only for the sake of beholding those chains, for the sake of seeing the prison where he was bound. The traces indeed of his miracles are numerous in all parts of the world, yet are they not so dear as those of his scars. (Gal. vi : 17.) Nor in the Scriptures does he so delight me when he is working miracles, as when he is suffering evil, being scourged, and dragged about. Insomuch that from his body were carried away handkerchiefs or aprons. Marvellous, truly marvellous, are these things, and yet not so marvellous as those. "When they had laid many stripes upon him, they cast him into prison." (Acts xvi : 23.) And again; being in bonds, "they were singing hymns unto God." (Acts xvi: 25.) And again; "They stoned him, and dragged him out of the city, supposing that he was dead." (Acts xiv: 19.) Would ye know how mighty a thing is an iron chain for Christ's sake, bound about His servant's body? Hearken to what Christ Himself saith, "Blessed are ye." (Mat. v: 11.) Why? When ye shall raise the dead? No. But why? When ye shall heal the blind? Not at all. But why then? " When men shall reproach you, and persecute you, and say all manner of evil against you falsely for My sake." (Matt. v: 11.) Now, if to be evil spoken of renders men thus blessed, to be evil entreated, what may not that achieve? Hearken to what this blessed one himself saith elsewhere; "Henceforth there is laid up for me the crown of righteousness:" (2 Tim. iv: 8.) and yet, more glorious than this crown is the chain : of this, saith he, the Lord will count me worthy, and I am in no wise inquisitive about those things. Enough it is for me for every recompense, to suffer evil for Christ's sake. Let Him but grant me to say, that "I fill up that which is lacking of the afflictions of Christ : " (Col. i: 24.) and I ask nothing further.

Peter also was counted worthy of this chain; for he, we read, was bound, and delivered to soldiers, and was sleeping. (Acts xii : 6.) Yet he rejoiced and was not diverted from his right mind and he fell into deep sleep which could not have been, had he been in any great anxiety. However, he was sleeping, being between two soldiers : and an Angel came unto him, and smote him on the side, and raised him up. Now then, were any one to say to me, Which wouldest thou? Wouldest thou be the Angel that struck Peter, or Peter that was delivered? I would rather choose to be Peter, for whose sake even the Angel came, yea, I would that I might enjoy those chains. And how is it, say ye, that, as being released from great evils, he prays? Marvel not : he prays, because he is afraid lest he should die; and of dying he is afraid, because he would fain have his life to be still a subject for further sufferings. For hearken to what the blessed Paul himself also saith. (Phil. i :23, 24.) " To depart, and to be with Christ, is very far better ; " " Yet to abide in the flesh is more needful for your sake." This he calls even a favor where he writes, and says, " To you it hath been granted, (as a favor ἐχαρίσθη) in the behalf of Christ, not only to believe on Him, but also to suffer in His behalf." (Phil. i : 29.) So that this latter is greater than the other : for He gave it of His free grace; verily, a favor it is, exceeding great, yea greater than any one of those, greater than to make the sun and the moon stand still, than to move the world! greater this than to have power over devils, or to cast out devils. The devils grieve not so much at being cast out by the faith which we exert, as when they behold us suffering any evil, and imprisoned for Christ's sake. For this increases our boldness. Not for this is it a noble thing to be in bonds for Christ's sake that it procures for us a kingdom; it is that it is done for Christ's sake. Not for this do I bless those bonds, for that they conduct on to Heaven ; it is because they are worn for the sake of the Lord of Heaven. How great a boast to know that he was bound for Christ's sake! How great a happiness, how high an honor, how illustrious a distinction ! Fain would I ever be dwelling on these subjects. Fain would I cling to this chain. Fain would I, though in reality I have not the power, yet still in idea, bind this chain round my soul by a temper like his.

"The foundations of the prison-house, " we read, " were shaken" where Paul was bound, " and every one's bands were loosed." (Acts xvi : 26.) Beholdest thou then in bonds a nature that can dissolve bonds themselves? for as the Lord's death put death itself to death, so also did Paul's bonds loose the men in bonds, shake the house of bondage, open the doors. Yet is not this the natural effect of bonds, but the very reverse ; it is to keep him that is bound in safety, not to open for him the prison walls. No, of bonds then in general this is not the nature, but of those bonds which are for Christ's sake, it is. " The jailor fell down before Paul and Silas." (Acts xvi : 29.) And yet neither is this again the effect of chains in general, to lay the binders at the feet of the bound : no, but, on the contrary, to put these last under the hands of the former. Whereas here, the man who was free was under the feet of the man who had been bound. The binder was beseeching him whom he had bound to release him from his fear. Tell me, was it not thou that didst bind him? Didst thou not cast him into the inner prison? Didst thou not make his feet fast in the stocks? Why tremblest thou? Why art thou troubled? Why weepest thou? Why hast thou drawn thy sword? Never bound I, saith he, aught like this! I knew not that the prisoners of Christ had power so mighty as this. What sayest thou? They received power to open Heaven, and should they not be able to open a prison? They loosed them that were bound by evil spirits, and was a piece of iron likely to conquer them? Thou knowest not the men. And therefore also wert thou pardoned. That prisoner is Paul, whom all the Angels reverence. He is Paul, whose very handkerchiefs and napkins cast out devils, and chase diseases to flight. And sure the bond which is of the devil is adamantine, and far more indissoluble than iron; for this indeed binds the soul, the other only the body. He therefore that released souls that were bound, shall not he have power to release his own body? He that could burst asunder the bonds of evil spirits, shall he not unloose a rivet of iron? He that by his very garments unloosed those prisoners, and released them from the spell of devils, shall not he of himself set himself at liberty? For this was he first bound himself, and then loosed the prisoners, that thou mightest understand that Christ's servants in bonds possess a power far greater than they that are at liberty. Had one who was at liberty wrought this, then had it not been so marvellous. So then the chain was not a token of weakness, but rather of a greater power, and thus is the saint's might more illustriously displayed, when, even though in bonds, he overpowers them that are at liberty, when he that is in bonds sets not only himself at liberty, but them that are in bonds also. Where is the use of walls? What the advantage of thrusting him into the inner prison, whereas he opened the outer also? and why too was it done in the night? and why with an earthquake?

Oh, bear with me a little, and give me leave while I refrain from the Apostle's words, and revel in the Apostle's deeds, and banquet on Paul's chain; grant me still longer to dwell upon it. I have laid hold on that chain, and no one shall part me from it. More securely at this moment am I bound by affection, than was he then in the stocks. This is a bond which no one can loose, for it is formed of the love of Christ; this neither the Angels, no, nor the kingdom of Heaven, has power to unloose. We may hear Paul's own words; (Rom. viii; 38, 39.) "Neither angels, nor principalities, nor

things present, nor things to come, nor powers, nor height, nor depth, shall be able to separate us from the love of God which is in Christ Jesus our Lord."

Now then, why did the event take place at midnight? And wherefore too with an earthquake? Hearken, and marvel at the providential orderings of God. Every one's bands were loosed, and the doors were opened. And yet was this done only for the jailor's sake, not with a view to display, but with a view to his salvation: for that the prisoners knew not that they were loosed, is evident from Paul's exclamation; for what said he? "He cried with a loud voice, saying, Do thyself no harm, for we are all here." (Acts xvi: 28.) But never would they all have been within, had they seen the doors opened, and themselves set at liberty. They who were used to cut through walls, and to scale roofs and parapets, and to venture on all sorts of attempts in chains, never would have endured to remain within, with their bands loosed, and the doors opened, with the jailer himself asleep; no, but the bond of sleep was to them instead of the bonds of iron. So that the thing took place and yet no damage ensued from the miracle to the jailer who was to be saved. And besides this too, they that are bound are bound most securely in the night, not in the day; and so accordingly might we behold them bound again with all care and sleeping: but had these things been done in the day time, there would have been great stir and tumult.

Then again, wherefore was the building shaken? It was to arouse the jailer, to behold what was done, for he alone was worthy of being saved. And do thou too, behold, I pray, the exceeding greatness of the grace of Christ, for well were it in the midst of Paul's bonds to make mention also of the grace of God, nay indeed the very bonds themselves are of the gift and grace of God. Some indeed there are who complain "Why was the jailer saved?" and from those very circumstances, for which they ought to admire the loving-kindness of God they find fault with it. Nor is it anything to be wondered at. Such are those sickly persons, that find fault even with the food that nourishes them, which they ought to prize, and who affirm that honey is bitter: and those dimsighted persons who are darkened by the very thing which ought to enlighten them. Not that these effects arise from the nature of the objects themselves, but from the weakness of the persons who are unable to use them properly. What, however, was I saying? When they ought to be admiring God's loving-kindness, in that He took a man who had fallen into the most desperate wickedness, and was making him better, they find fault: "Why, how was it that he did not take the thing to be the work of witchcraft and of sorcery, and confine them the more closely, and cry out?" Many things conspired to prevent this; first, that he heard them singing praises to God. And sorcerers never would have been singing such hymns as those, for he heard them, it is said, singing praises unto God. Secondly, the fact, that they themselves did not take flight, but even withheld him from killing himself. Now had they done it for their own sake, they never would have remained still within; they would themselves have escaped first of all. Great again was their kindness also; they withheld the man from killing himself, even him who had bound them, thus all but saying unto him, "Truly, thou didst bind us with all safety, and most cruelly, that thou thyself mightest be loosed from the most cruel of all bonds." For every one is shackled with the chains of his own sins; and those bonds are accursed, whereas these for Christ's sake are blessed, and worth many an earnest prayer. For that these bonds can loose those other bonds of sin, he showed to us by things which are matters of sense. Didst thou behold them released, who had been bound with iron? Thou shalt see thyself also delivered from other galling bonds. These bonds, the prisoners' bonds, not those of Paul, I mean, are the effect of those other bonds, the bonds of sins. They who were confined within, were doubly prisoners, and the jailer himself was a prisoner. They indeed were bound both with iron and with sins, he with sins only. Them did Paul loose to assure the faith of him, for the chains which he loosed were visible. And thus too did Christ Himself; but rather in the inverse order. In that instance, there was a double palsy. What was it? There was that of the soul by sins, and also that of the body. What then did the Lord do? "Son," saith He, "be of good cheer, thy sins are forgiven." (Matt. ix: 3-6.) He first loosed the bonds of the real and true palsy, and then proceeds to the other: for when "certain of the Scribes said within themselves, This man blasphemeth; Jesus, knowing their thoughts, said, Wherefore think ye evil in your hearts? For whether is easier, to say, Thy sins are forgiven, or to say, Arise, and walk? But, that ye may know that the Son of Man hath power on earth to forgive sins, (then saith he to the sick of the palsy,) Arise, and take up thy bed, and go unto thy house." Having wrought the invisible miracle, He confirmed it by the visible, the spiritual by the bodily cure. And why did He do thus? That it might be fulfilled, which is spoken, (Luke xix: 22.) "Out of thine own mouth will I judge thee, thou wicked servant." For what said they? "None can forgive sins, but God alone" Of course, therefore, no Angel, nor Arch-

angel, nor any other created power. This ye have yourselves confessed. And what then ought to be said? If I shall be shown to have forgiven sins, it is fully evident that I am God. However, He said it not thus, but what said He? "But that ye may know that the Son of Man hath power on earth to forgive sins; then saith He to the sick of the palsy, Arise, and take up thy bed, and go unto thy house." (Matt. ix: 6.) When therefore, He would say, I work the more difficult miracle, it is plain that there is no pretext left you, no room for gainsaying about the easier one.[1] Hence it was that He wrought the invisible miracle first, because there were many gainsayers; and then He led them from the invisible to the visible itself.

Surely then the faith of the jailer was no light or hasty faith. He saw the prisoners. And he saw nothing, he heard nothing wrong; he saw that nothing was done by sorcery, for they were singing hymns unto God. He saw that every thing done proceeded from overflowing kindness, for they did not avenge themselves against him, although they had it in their power; for it was in their power to rescue both themselves and the prisoners, and escape; and if not the prisoners, at all events themselves; but they did not do this. Thus did they challenge his reverence, not only by the miracle, but also by their behavior. For how did Paul cry out? "He cried with a loud voice, saying, Do thyself no harm, for we are all here." Thou seest at once his freedom from vain-glory and arrogance, and his fellow-feeling. He said not, "It is for us these wonders have been wrought," but as though he were merely one of the prisoners, he said, "For we are all here." And yet, even though they had not before this loosed themselves, nor had done so by means of the miracle, still they might have been silent, and have set all that were bound at liberty. For had they held their peace, and had they not with their loud crying stayed his hand, he would have thrust the sword through his throat. Wherefore also Paul cried out, because he had been cast into the inner ward: as though he had said, "To thine own injury hast thou done this, that thou hast thrust in so far those that could deliver thee from the danger." However they imitated not the treatment they had received at his hands; though, had he died, all would have escaped. Thou seest that they chose rather to remain in bonds, than to suffer him to perish. Hence too might he reason within himself, "Had they been sorcerers, doubtless

---

[1] [" The one requires no less power than the other, the same divine ἐξουσία enables both to be done. But that ye may know that I was entitled to say the one, I will prove to you that I have power to say the other."—Meyer. Since neither is easier but each alike requires divine power, if I can prove to you that I have this divine power to do one, that will prove to you that I have power to do the other.—G. A.]

they would have set the others at liberty, and have released themselves from their bonds:" (for it is likely that many such had also been imprisoned.) He was the more amazed, in that having often received sorcerers in charge, he had yet witnessed nothing done like this. A sorcerer never would have shaken the foundations, so as to startle the jailer from sleep, and thus render his own escape more difficult.

Now, however, let us proceed to look at the jailor's faith. "And," saith the Scripture, " he called for lights and sprang in, and trembling for fear fell down before Paul and Silas, and brought them out, and said, Sirs, what must I do to be saved?" He grasped fire and sword, and cried, "Sirs, what must I do to be saved?" "And they said, Believe on the Lord Jesus Christ, and thou shalt be saved, thou and thy house." (Acts xvi: 29-31.) " This is not the act of sorcerers," he would say, " to deliver a doctrine like this. No mention any where here of an evil spirit." Thou seest how worthy he was to be saved: for when he beheld the miracle, and was relieved from his terror, he did not forget what most concerned him, but even in the midst of so great peril, he was solicitous about that salvation which concerned his soul: and came before them in such a manner as it was meet to come before teachers: he fell down at their feet. "And they spake," it continues, " the word of the Lord, unto him with all that were in his house. And he took them the same hour of the night, and washed their stripes; and was baptized, he and all his, immediately." (Acts xvi: 32, 33.) Observe the fervency of the man! He did not delay; he did not say, " Let day come, let us see, let us look about us;" but with great fervency, he was both himself baptized, and all his house. Yes, not like most men now-a-days, who suffer both servants and wives and children to go unbaptized [1] Be ye, I beseech you, like the jailor. I say not, in authority, but in purpose; for what is the benefit of authority, where purpose is weak? The savage one, the inhuman one, who lived in the practice of unnumbered wrongs and made this his constant study, has become all at once so humane, so tenderly attentive. " He washed," it is said, " their stripes."

And mark, on the other hand, the fervency of Paul also. Bound, scourged, thus he preached the Gospel. Oh, that blessed chain, with how great travail did it travail that night, what children did it bring forth! Yea of them too may he say, "Whom I have begotten in my bonds." (Philem. x.) Mark thou, how he glories, and will have the children thus begotten, to be on that account the more illustrious! Mark thou, how transcendant is the glory of those bonds,

[1] ἀμυήτους.

in that they give lustre not only to him that wore them, but also to them who were on that occasion begotten by him. They have some advantage, who were begotten in Paul's bonds, I say not in respect of grace, (for grace is one and the same,) nor in respect of remission, (for remission is one and the same to all,) but in that they are thus from the very outset taught to rejoice and to glory in such things. "The same hour of the night," it is said, "he took them, and washed their stripes, and was baptized."

And now then behold the fruit. He straightway recompensed them with his carnal things. "He brought them up into his house, and set meat before them, and rejoiced greatly with all his house, having believed in God." For what was he not ready to do, now that by the opening of the prison doors, heaven itself was opened to him? He washed his teacher, he set food before him, and rejoiced. Paul's chain entered into the prison, and transformed all things there into a Church; it drew in its train the body of Christ, it prepared the spiritual feast, and travailed with that birth, at which Angels rejoice. And was it without reason then that I said that the prison was more glorious than Heaven? For it became a source of joy there; yes, if " there is joy in Heaven over one sinner that repenteth," (Luke xv: 7.) if, " where two or three are gathered together in His Name, there is Christ in the midst of them;" (Matt. xviii: 20.) how much more, where Paul and Silas, and the jailor and all his house were, and faith so earnest as theirs! Observe the intense earnestness of their faith.

But this prison has reminded me of another prison. And what then is that? It is that where Peter was. Not, however, that any thing like this took place there. No. He was delivered to four quaternions of soldiers to keep him and he sang not, he watched not, but he slept; neither, again, had he been scourged. And yet was the peril greater, for in the case before us indeed the end was accomplished, and the prisoners Paul and Silas, had undergone their punishment; but in his case it was as yet to come. So that though there were no stripes to torture him, yet was there the anticipation of the future to distress him. And mark too the miracle there. " Behold, an angel of the Lord," it is related, " stood by him, and a light shined in the cell; and he smote Peter on the side, and awoke him, saying, Rise up quickly. And his chains fell off from his hands." (Acts xii: 7.) In order that he might not imagine the transaction to be the work of the light alone, he also struck Peter. Now no one saw the light, save himself only, and he thought it was a vision. So insensible are they that are asleep to the mercies of God. "And the angel," it proceeds, "said unto him, Gird thyself and bind on thy sandals; and he did so. And he saith unto him, Cast thy garment about thee, and follow me. And he went out and followed, and he wist not that it was true which was done by the angel; but thought he saw a vision. And when they were past the first and the second ward, they came unto the iron gate, that leadeth unto the city, which opened to them of his own accord; and they went out, and passed on through one street; and straightway the angel departed from him." (Acts xii: 8–10.) Why was not the same thing done here as was done in the case of Paul and Silas? Because in that case they were intending to release them. On that account God willed not that they should be released in this manner. Whereas in blessed Peter's case, they were intending to lead him forth to execution. But what then? Would it not have been far more marvellous, some one may say, had he been led forth, and delivered over into the king's hands, and then had been snatched away from the very midst of his imminent peril, and sustained no harm? For thus moreover, neither had the soldiers perished. Great is the question which has been raised upon this matter. What! did God, it is said, save His own servant with the punishment of others, with the destruction of others? Now in the first place, it was not with the destruction of others; for this did not arise from the ordering of providence, but arose from the cruelty of the judge. How so? God had so providentially ordered it, as that not only these men need not perish, but moreover that even he, the judge, should have been saved, just as in this case of the jailor. But he did not use the boon aright. "Now as soon as it was day," it continues, "there was no small stir among the soldiers, what was become of Peter." And what then? Herod makes strict inquiry into the matter, "and he examined the guards," it is related, "and commanded that they should be put to death." (Acts xii: 18–19.) Now, indeed, had he not examined them, there might have been some excuse for executing them. Whereas, as it is, he had them brought before him, he examined them, he found that Peter had been bound, that the prison had been well secured, that the keepers were before the doors. No wall had been broken through, no door had been opened, nor was there any other evidence whatever of false dealing. He ought upon this to have been awed by the power of God, which had snatched Peter from the very midst of perils, and to have adored Him who was able to do such mighty works. But, on the contrary, he ordered those men off to execution. How then in this case is God the cause? Had He indeed caused the wall to be

broken through, and thus had extricated Peter, possibly the deed might have been put to the account of their negligence. But if He so providentially ordered it, as that the matter should be shown to be the work not of the evil agency of man, but of the miraculous agency of God, why did Herod act thus? For had Peter intended to flee, he would have fled as he was, with his chains on. Had he intended to fly, in his confusion he never would have had so great forethought as to take even his sandals, but he would have left them. Whereas, as it is, the object of the Angel's saying unto him, "Bind on thy sandals," was that they might know that he had done the thing not in the act of flight, but with full leisure. For, bound as he was, and fixed between the two soldiers, he never would have found sufficient time to unbind the chains also, and especially as he too, like Paul, was in the inner ward. Thus then was the punishment of the keepers owing to the unrighteousness of the judge. For why did not the Jews[1] act in the same way? For now again I am reminded of yet another prison. The first was that at Rome, next, was this at Cæsarea, now we come to that at Jerusalem.[2] When then the chief Priests and the Pharisees heard from those whom they had sent to the prison to bring Peter out, that "they found no man within," but both doors "closed," and "the keepers standing at the doors," why was it that they not only did not put the keepers to death, but, so far from it, "they were much perplexed concerning them whereunto this would grow." Now if the Jews, murderous as they were in their designs against them, yet entertained not a thought of the kind, much more shouldest not thou, who didst every thing to please those Jews. For this unrighteous sentence vengeance quickly overtook Herod.

But now if any complain of this, then complain too about those who are killed on the highway, and about the ten thousand others who are unjustly put to death, and further, of the infants also that were slaughtered at the time of Christ's birth; for Christ also, according to what thou allegest, was the cause of their deaths. But it was not Christ, but rather the madness and tyranny of Herod's father. Dost thou ask, Why then did He not snatch Him out of Herod's hands? True, He might have done so, but there would have been nothing gained by so doing. How many times, at least, did Christ escape even from the grasp of their hands?

---

[1] [The Jews, when they imprisoned the Apostles as recorded in Acts v: 19.—G. A.]

[2] [The prison which suggested this discourse (Eph. iv: 1.) was that of Paul in Rome, but the next one mentioned and discoursed of by St. Chrysostom was the one in which Paul was at Philippi, Acts xvi. the next one was the prison where Peter was at Jerusalem, and this last one (Acts v: 19) at Jerusalem also. No mention has been made of any imprisonment at Cæsarea.—G. A.]

And yet what good did this do to that unfeeling people? Whereas here there is even much profit arising to the faithful from what was done. For as there were records made, and the enemies themselves bore testimony to the facts, the testimony was above suspicion. As therefore in that instance the mouths of the enemies were stopped in no other way whatever, but only by the persons who came acknowledging the facts, so was it also here. For why did the jailor here do nothing like what Herod did? Nay, and the things which Herod witnessed were not at all less wonderful than those which this man witnessed. So far as wonder goes, it is no less wonderful to be assured that a prisoner came out when the doors were closed, than it is to behold them set open. Indeed this last might rather have seemed to be perhaps a vision of the imagination, the other never could, when exactly and circumstantially reported. So that, had this man been as wicked as Herod, he would have slain Paul, as Herod did the soldiers; but such he was not.

If any one should ask, 'Why was it that God permitted the children also to be murdered?' I should fall, probably, into a longer discourse, than was originally intended to be addressed to you.

At this point, however, let us terminate our discourse, with many thanks to Paul's chain, for that it has been made to us the source of so many blessings, and exhorting you, should ye have to suffer any thing for Christ's sake, not only not to repine, but to rejoice, as the Apostles did, yea, and to glory; as Paul said, " Most gladly, therefore will I rather glory in my infirmities," (2 Cor. xii: 9.) for because of this it was that he heard also those words, "My grace is sufficient for thee." Paul glories in bonds; and dost thou pride thyself in riches? The Apostles rejoiced that they were counted worthy to be scourged, and dost thou seek for ease and self-indulgence? On what ground then, dost thou wish to attain the same end as they, if here on earth thou art traveling the contrary road from them? "And now," saith Paul, "I go bound in the spirit unto Jerusalem, not knowing the things that shall befall me there; save that the Holy Ghost testifieth unto me in every city, saying, that bonds and afflictions abide me." (Acts xx: 22.) And why then dost thou set out, if bonds and afflictions abide thee? For this very reason, saith he, that I may be bound for Christ's sake, that I may die for His sake. "For I am ready not to be bound only, but also to die for the name of the Lord Jesus." (Acts xxi: 13.)

MORAL. Nothing can be more blessed than that soul. In what does he glory? In bonds, in afflictions, in chains, in scars; "I bear branded on my body," saith he, "the marks of Jesus," (Gal.

vi: 17.) as though they were some great trophy. And again, " For because of the hope of Israel," saith he, "I am bound with this chain." (Acts xxviii: 20.) And again, " For which I am an ambassador in chains." (Eph. vi: 20.) What is this? Art thou not ashamed, art thou not afraid going about the world as a prisoner? Dost thou not fear lest any one should charge thy God with weakness? lest any one should on this account refuse to come near thee and to join the fold? No, saith he, not such are my bonds. They can shine brightly even in kings' palaces. "So that my bonds," saith he, "became manifest in Christ, throughout the whole prætorian guard: and most of the brethren in the Lord, being confident through my bonds, are more abundantly bold to speak the word of God without fear." (Phil. i: 13, 14.) Behold ye a force in bonds stronger than the raising of the dead. They beheld me bound, and they are the more courageous. For where bonds are, there of necessity is something great also. Where affliction is, there verily is salvation also, there verily is solace, there verily are great achievements. For when the devil kicks, then is he, doubtless, hit.[1] When he binds God's servants, then most of all does the word gain ground. And mark how this is every where the case. Paul was imprisoned; and in the prison he did these things, yea, saith he, by my very bonds themselves. He was imprisoned at Rome, and brought the more converts to the faith; for not only was he himself emboldened, but many others also because of him. He was imprisoned at Jerusalem, and preaching in his bonds he struck the king with amazement, (Acts xxvi: 28.) and made the governor tremble. (Acts xxiv: 25.) For being afraid, it is related, he let him go, and he that had bound him was not ashamed to receive instruction concerning the things to come at the hands of him whom he had bound. In bonds he sailed, and retrieved the wreck, and bound fast the tempest. It was when he was in bonds that the monster fastened on him, and fell off from his hand, having done him no hurt. He was bound at Rome, and preaching in bonds drew thousands to his cause, holding forward, in the place of every other, this very argument, I mean his chain.

It is not however our lot to be bound now-a-days. And yet there is another chain if we have a mind to wear it. And what is it? It is to restrain our hand, to be not so forward to covetousness. With this chain let us bind ourselves. Let the fear of God be unto us instead of a bond of iron. Let us loose them that are bound by poverty, by affliction. There is no

---

[1] [This reminds one of the saying of an eccentric evangelist in America who refering to those that abused and persecuted him for the severity of his preaching said, "It's always the hit dog that yelps."—G. A.]

comparison between opening the doors of a prison, and releasing an enthralled soul. There is no comparison between loosing the bonds of prisoners and "setting at liberty them that are bruised;" (Luke iv: 18.) this last is far greater than the other; for the other there is no reward in store, for this last there are ten thousand rewards.

Paul's chain has proved a long one, and has detained us a length of time. Yea, long indeed it is, and more beautiful than any cord of gold. A chain this, which draws them that are bound by it, as it were by a kind of invisible machinery, to Heaven, and, like a golden cord let down,[1] draws them up to the Heaven of heavens. And the wonderful thing is this, that, bound, as it is, below, it draws its captives upwards: and indeed this is not the nature of the things themselves. But where God orders and disposes, look not for the nature of things, nor for natural sentence, but for things above nature and natural sequence.

Let us learn not to sink under affliction, nor to repine; for look at this blessed saint. He had been scourged, and sorely scourged, for it is said, "When they had laid many stripes upon them." He had been bound too, and that again sorely, for the jailor cast him into the inner ward, and with extraordinary security. And though he was in so many perils, at midnight, when even the most wakeful are asleep with sleep, another and a stronger bond upon them, they chanted and sang praise unto the Lord. What can be more adamantine than these souls? They bethought them how that the holy Children sang even in fire and furnace. (Dan. iii: 1-30.) Perhaps they thus reasoned with themselves, "we have as yet suffered nothing like that."

But our discourse has done well, in that it has thus brought us out again to other bonds, and into another prison. What am I to do? I would fain be silent, but am not able. I have discovered another prison, far more wonderful and more astonishing than the former. But, come now, rouse yourselves, as though I were just commencing my discourse, and attend to me with your minds fresh. I would fain break off the discourse, but it will not suffer me; for just as a man in the midst of drinking cannot bear to break off his draught, whatever any one may promise him; so I too, now I have laid hold of this glorious cup of the prison of them that were bound for Christ's sake, I cannot leave off, I cannot hold my peace. For if Paul in the prison, and in the night, kept not silence, no, nor under the scourge; shall I, who am sitting[2]

here by daylight, and speaking so much at my ease, shall I hold my peace, when men in bonds, and under the scourge, and at midnight could not endure to do so? The holy Children were not silent, no, not in the furnace and in the fire, and are not we ashamed to hold our peace? Let us look then at this prison also. Here too, they were bound, but at once and from the very outset it was evident that they were not about to be burned, but only to enter as into a prison. For why do ye bind men who are about to be committed to the flames? They were bound, as Paul was, hand and foot. They were bound with as great violence as he was. For the jailor thrust him into the inner prison; and the king commanded the furnace to be intensely heated. And now let us see the issue. When Paul and Silas sang, the prison was shaken, and the doors were opened. When the three Children sang, the bonds both of their feet and hands were loosed. The prison was opened, and the doors of the furnace were opened: for a dewy breeze whistled through it.

But many thoughts crowd around me. I know not which to utter first, and which second. Wherefore, let no one, I entreat, require order of me, for the subjects are closely allied.

They who were bound together with Paul and Silas were loosed, and yet nevertheless they slept. In the case of the three Children, instead of that, something else took place. The men who had cast them in, were themselves burned to death. And then, as I was fain to tell you, the king beheld them loose, and fell down before them: he heard them singing their song of praise, and beheld four walking, and he called them. As Paul, though able to do so, came not forth, until he who had cast him in, called him, and brought him forth: so neither did the three Children come forth, until he who had cast them in commanded them to come forth. What lesson are we taught from this? Not to be over hasty in courting persecution, nor when in tribulation to be over eager for deliverance, and on the other hand when they release us not to continue in it. Further, the jailor, inasmuch as he was able to enter in where the saints were, fell down at their feet. The king came but to the door and fell down. He dared not approach into the prison which he had prepared for them in the fire. And now mark their words. The one cried, "Sirs, what must I do to be saved?" (Acts xvi: 30.) The other, though not indeed with so great humility, yet uttered a voice no less sweet, "Shadrach, Meshach, and Abednego, ye servants of the most high God, come forth, and come hither." (Dan. iii: 26.)

---

[1] [This passage reminds one of the famous golden chain of Homer, σειρὴν χρυσείην, (Iliad viii: 19-27) to which several allegorical meanings have been given.—G. A.]

[2] [The ancient custom was the reverse of ours, for the preacher commonly delivered his sermon sitting, and the people heard it standing.—Bingham *Antiquities* Bk. xiv. Ch. iv. Sec. 24.—G. A.]

Mighty dignity! "Ye servants of the most high God, come forth, and come hither." How are they to come forth, O king? Thou didst cast them into the fire bound; they have continued this long time in the fire. Why, had they been made of adamant, had they been blocks of metal, in singing that entire hymn, must they not have perished? On this account then they were saved, because they sang praises to God. The fire reverenced their readiness to suffer and afterwards it reverenced that wonderful song, and their hymns of praise. By what title dost thou call them? I said before, "Ye servants of the most high God." Yes, to the servants of God, all things are possible; for if some, who are the servants of men, have, nevertheless, power, and authority, and the disposal of their concerns, much more have the servants of God. He called them by the name most delightful to them, he knew that by this means he flattered them most: for indeed, if it was in order to continue servants of God, that they entered into the fire, there could be no sound more delightful to them than this. Had he called them kings, had he called them lords of the world, yet would he not so truly have rejoiced them as when he said, "Ye servants of the most high God." And why marvel at this? when, in writing to the mighty city, to her who was mistress of the world, and prided herself upon her high dignities, Paul set down as equivalent in dignity, nay, as far greater, yea incomparably greater than consulship, or kingly name, or than the empire of the world, this title, "Paul, a servant[1] of Jesus Christ." (Ro. i: 1.) "Ye servants of the most high God." "Yes," he would say, "if they show so great zeal as to be bond-servants, doubtless this is the title by which we shall conciliate them."

Again, observe also the piety of the Children: they showed no indignation, no anger, no gainsaying, but they came forth. Had they regarded it as an act of vengeance that they had been thrown into the furnace, they would have been grieved against the man who had cast them in; as it is, there is nothing of the kind; but, as though they were going forth from Heaven itself, so went they forth. And what the Prophet says of the Sun, that "He is as a bridegroom coming forth out of his chamber," (Ps. xix: 5.) one would not go amiss in saying also of them. But though he goes forth thus, yet came they forth there more gloriously than he, for he indeed comes forth to enlighten the world with natural light, they to enlighten the world in a different way, I mean, spiritually. For because of them the king straightway issued a decree, containing these words, "It hath seemed good

unto me to show the signs and wonders that the Most High God hath wrought toward me. How great are His signs! And how mighty are His wonders!" (Dan. iv: 2,3.) So that they went forth, shedding a yet more glorious radiance, beaming indeed in that region itself, but, what is more than all, capable, by means of the king's writings, of being diffused over the world and thus of dispelling the darkness which every where prevails. "Come forth," said he, "and come hither." He gave no commandment[2] to extinguish the flame, but hereby most especially honored them, by believing that they were able not only to walk within it, but even to come out of it while it was still burning.

But let us look again, if it seem good to you, at the words of the jailor, "Sirs, what must I do to be saved?" What language sweeter than this? This makes the very Angels leap for joy. To hear this language, even the Only-begotten Son of God Himself became a servant. This language they who believed at the beginning addressed to Peter. (Acts ii: 37.) "What shall we do?" And what said he in answer? "Repent and be baptized." To have heard this language from the Jews, gladly would Paul have been cast even in to hell, in his eagerness for their salvation and obedience. But observe, he commits the whole matter to them, he wastes no unnecessary pains. Let us however look at the next point. The king here does not say, What must I do to be saved? but the teaching is plainer in his case than any language whatever; for he straightway becomes a preacher, he needs not to be instructed like the jailor. He proclaims God, and makes confession of His power. "Of a truth your God is the God of Gods and the Lord of Kings, because He hath sent His Angel, and hath delivered you." (Dan. ii: 47; iii: 28.) And what was the sequel? Not one single jailor, but numbers are instructed by the king's writings, by the sight of the facts. For that the king would not have told a falsehood is evident enough to every one, because he never would have chosen to bear such testimony to captives, nor to overthrow his own acts; he never would have chosen to incur the imputation of such utter madness: so that had not the truth been abundantly manifest, he would not have written in such terms, and with so many persons present.

Perceive ye how great is the power of bonds? How great the force of those praises that are sung in tribulation? Their heart failed not, they were not cast down, but were then yet more vigorous, and their courage then yet greater and justly so.

While we are considering these things one

---

[1] [The word in the Greek δοῦλος which means a bond-slave, though softened in the Auth. Ver. to "servant" and in the Rev. Ver. to "bond-servant."—G. A.]

[2] [Field's text has here ἐτόλμησε, 'he did not venture;' but that gives a sense less satisfactory than the text of Savile and the Oxford translator, ἐκέλευσε, which is well attested.—G. A.]

question yet remains for us: Why was it that in the prison on the one hand, the prisoners were loosed, whilst in the furnace the executioners were burnt to death: for that indeed should have been the king's fate, because neither were they who bound them, nor they who cast them into the furnace, guilty of so great sin as the man who commanded this should be done. Why then did they perish? On this point there is not any very great need of minute examination; for they were wicked men. And therefore this was providentially ordered, that the power of the fire might be shown, and the miracle might be made more signal; for if it thus devoured them that were without, how did it show them unscathed that were within it? it was that the power of God might be made manifest. And let no one wonder that I have put the king on a level with the jailor, for he did the same thing; the one was in no wise more noble than the other, and they both had their reward.

But, as I said, the righteous, when they are in tribulations, are then especially more energetic, and when they are in bonds: for to suffer any thing for Christ's sake is the sweetest of all consolation.

Will ye that I remind you of yet another prison? It seems necessary to go on from this chain to another prison still. And which will ye? Shall it be that of Jeremiah, or of Joseph, or of John? Thanks to Paul's chain; how many prisons has it opened to our discourse? Will ye have that of John? He also was once bound for Christ's sake, and for the law of God. What then? Was he idle when he was in prison? Was it not from thence he sent, by his disciples, and said, "Art Thou He that cometh, or look we for another?"(Matt. xi: 2, 3.) Even when there, then, it seems he taught, for surely he did not disregard his duty. But again, did not Jeremiah prophesy concerning the king of Babylon, and fulfil his work even there in prison? And what of Joseph? Was he not in prison thirteen years? What then? Not even there did he forget his virtue. I have yet to mention the bonds of one and therewith will close my discourse. Our Master Himself was bound, He who loosed the world from sins. Those hands were bound, those hands that wrought ten thousand good deeds. For, "they bound Him," it saith, "and led Him away to Caiaphas;" (Matt. xxvii: 2; John. xviii: 24.) yes, He was bound who had wrought so many marvellous works.

Reflecting on these things, let us never repine; but whether we be in bonds, let us rejoice; or whether we be not in bonds, let us be as though we were bound together with Him. See how great a blessing are bonds! Knowing all these things, let us send up our thanksgiving for all things to God, through Christ Jesus our Lord with whom to the Father, together with the Holy Ghost, be glory might and honor, now and forever and ever. Amen.

HOMILY IX.

CHAPTER IV. VERSES 1—3.

"I therefore, the prisoner in the Lord, beseech you, to walk worthily of the calling wherewith ye were called, with all lowliness and meekness, with long-suffering, forbearing one another in love; giving diligence to keep the unity of the Spirit in the bond of peace."

GREAT has the power of Paul's chain been shown to be, and more glorious than miracles. It is not in vain then, as it should seem, nor without an object, that he here holds it forward, but as the means of all others most likely to touch them. And what saith he? "I therefore, the prisoner in the Lord, beseech you, to walk worthily of the calling wherewith ye were called." And how is that? "with all lowliness and meekness, with long-suffering, forbearing one another in love."

It is not the being merely a prisoner that is honorable, but the being so for Christ's sake.

Hence he saith, "in the Lord," i. e., the prisoner for Christ's sake. Nothing is equal to this. But now the chain is dragging me away still more from my subject, and pulling me back again, and I cannot bear to resist it, but am drawn along willingly,—yea, rather, with all my heart; and would that it were always my lot to be descanting on Paul's chain.

But now do not become drowsy: for I am yet desirous to solve that other question, which many raise, when they say, Why, if tribulation be a glory, how came Paul himself to say in his defence[1] to Agrippa, "I would to God that whether with little or with much not thou only,

---

[1] [Field's text has here a much shorter reading as follows: For a question now suggests itself to me ; for since Paul in his defence, etc. This reading leaves the sense incomplete. The reading of the Oxford translator, as given above, is internally more satisfactory and is attested by several excellent authorities.—G. A.]

but also all that hear me this day, might become such as I am, except these bonds?" (Acts xxvi: 29.) He said not this, God forbid! as deeming the thing a matter to be deprecated; no; for had it been such, he would not have gloried in bonds, in imprisonments, in those other tribulations; and when writing elsewhere he saith, "Most gladly will I rather glory in my weaknesses." (2 Cor. xii: 9.) But what is the case? This was itself a proof how great a thing he considered those bonds; for as in writing to the Corinthians he said, "I fed you with milk, not with meat, for ye were not yet able to bear it;" (1 Cor. iii: 2.) so also here. They before whom he spoke were not able to hear of the beauty, nor the comeliness, nor the blessing of those bonds. Hence[1] it was he added, "except these bonds." To the Hebrews however he spoke not thus, but exhorted them to "be bound with" (Heb. xiii: 3.) them that were in bonds. And hence too did he himself rejoice in his bonds, and was bound, and was led with the prisoners into the inner prison. Mighty is the power of Paul's chain! A spectacle this, which may suffice for every other, to behold Paul bound, and led forth from his prison; to behold him bound, and sitting within it, what pleasure can come up to this? What would I not give for such a sight? Do ye see the emperors, the consuls, borne along in their chariots and arrayed in gold, and their body-guard with every thing about them of gold? Their halberds of gold, their shields of gold, their raiment of gold, their horses with trappings of gold? How much more delightful than such a spectacle is his! I would rather see Paul once, going forth with the prisoners from his prison, than behold these ten thousand times over, parading along with all that retinue. When he was thus led forth, how many Angels, suppose ye, led the way before him? And to show that I speak no fiction, I will make the fact manifest to you from a certain ancient narrative.

Elisha the prophet, (perhaps ye know the man,) at the time (2 Kings vi: 8-12.) when the king of Syria was at war with the king of Israel, sitting at his own home, brought to light all the counsels which the king of Syria was taking in his chamber with them that were privy to his designs, and rendered the king's counsels of none effect, by telling beforehand his secrets, and not suffering the king of Israel to fall into the snares which he was laying. This sorely troubled the king; he was disheartened, and was reduced to greater perplexity, not knowing how to discover him who was disclosing all that passed, and plotting against him, and disappointing his schemes.

Whilst therefore he was in this perplexity, and enquiring into the cause, one of his armor-bearers told him, that there was a certain prophet, one Elisha, dwelling in Samaria, who suffered not the king's designs to stand, but disclosed all that passed. The king imagined that he had discovered the whole matter. Sure, never was any one more miserably misled than he. When he ought to have honored the man, to have reverenced him, to have been awed that he really possessed so great power, as that, seated, as he was, so many furlongs off, he should know all that passed in the king's chamber, without any one at all to tell him; this indeed he did not, but being exasperated, and wholly carried away by his passion, he equips horsemen, and soldiers, and dispatches them to bring the prophet before him.

Now Elisha had a disciple as yet only on the threshold of prophecy, (2 Kings vi: 13ff.) as yet far from being judged worthy of revelations of this kind. The king's soldiers arrived at the spot, as intending to bind the man, or rather the prophet.—Again I am falling upon bonds, so entirely is this discourse interwoven with them.—And when the disciple saw the host of soldiers, he was affrighted, and ran full of trembling to his master, and told him the calamity, as he thought, and informed him of the inevitable peril. The prophet smiled at him for fearing things not worthy to be feared, and bade him be of good cheer. The disciple, however, being as yet imperfect, did not listen to him, but being still amazed at the sight, remained in fear. Upon this, what did the prophet do? "Lord," said he, "open the eyes of this young man, and let him see that they which are with us, are more than they which are with them;" (2 Kings vi: 16, 17.) and immediately he beheld the whole mountain, where the prophet then dwelt, filled with so great a multitude of horses and chariots of fire. Now these were nothing else than ranks of Angels. But if only for an occasion like this so great a band of Angels attended Elisha what must Paul have had? This is what the prophet David tells us. "The Angel of the Lord encampeth round about them that fear Him." (Ps. xxxiv: 7.) And again; "They shall bear thee up in their hands, lest thou dash thy foot against a stone." (Ps. xci: 2.) And why do I speak of Angels? The Lord Himself was with him then as he went forth; for surely it cannot be that He was seen by Abraham, and yet was not with Paul. No, it was His own promise, "I am with you alway, even unto the end of the world." (Matt. xxviii: 20.) And again, when He appeared to him, He said, "Be not afraid, but speak, for I am with thee, and no man shall set on thee to harm thee." (Acts xviii:

---

[1] [It is very doubtful that this was Paul's design in saying "except these bonds." It is more probable he wished that others might enjoy the blessings of Christianity without sharing in those sufferings which he himself was glad to endure.—G. A.]

9, 10.) Again, He stood by him in a dream, and said, " Be of good cheer, for as thou hast testified concerning me at Jerusalem, so must thou bear witness also at Rome." (Acts xxiii : 11.)

The saints, though they are at all times a glorious sight, and are full of abundant grace, yet are so, most of all, when they are in perils for Christ's sake, when they are prisoners ; for as a brave soldier is at all times and of himself a pleasing spectacle to them that behold him, but most of all when he is standing, and in ranks at the king's side ; thus also imagine to yourselves Paul, how great a thing it was to see him teaching in his bonds.

Shall I mention, in passing, a thought, which just at this moment occurs to me ? The blessed martyr Babylas[1] was bound, and he too for the very same cause as John also was, because he reproved a king in his transgression. This man when he was dying gave charge that his bonds should be laid with his body, and that the body should be buried bound ; and to this day the fetters lie mingled with his ashes, so devoted was his affection for the bonds he had worn for Christ's sake. " He was laid in chains of iron " as the Prophet saith of Joseph. (Ps. cv : 18.) And even women have before now had trial of these bonds.

We however are not in bonds, nor am I recommending this, since now is not the time for them. But thou, bind not thine hands, but bind thy heart and mind. There are yet other bonds, and they that wear not the one, shall have to wear the other. Hear what Christ saith, " Bind him hand and foot." (Matt. xxii : 13.) But God forbid we should have trial of those bonds ! but of these may He grant us even to take our fill !

On these accounts he saith, " I, the prisoner in the Lord, beseech you to walk worthily of the calling wherewith ye were called." But what is this calling ? Ye were called as His body, it is said. Ye have Christ as your head ; and though you were " enemies," and had committed the misdeeds out of number, yet " hath He raised you up with Him and made you to sit with Him." (Eph. ii : 6.) A high calling this, and to high privileges, not only in that we have been called from that former state, but in that we are called both to such privileges, and by such a method.

But how is it possible to " walk worthily " of it ? " With all lowliness." Such an one walks worthily. This is the basis of all virtue. If thou be lowly, and bethink thee what thou art, and how thou wast saved, thou wilt take this recollection as a motive to all virtue. Thou wilt neither be elated with bonds, nor with those very privileges which I mentioned, but as knowing that all is of grace, thou wilt humble thyself. The lowly-minded man is able to be at once a generous and a grateful servant. " For what hast thou," saith he that thou didst not receive ? " (1 Cor. iv : 7.) And again, hear his words, " I labored more abundantly than they all ; yet not I, but the grace of God which was with me." (1 Cor. xv : 10.)

" With all lowliness," saith he ; not that which is in words, nor that which is in actions only, but even in one's very bearing and tone of voice : not lowly towards one, and rude towards another ; be lowly towards all men, be he friend or foe, be he great or small. This is lowliness. Even in thy good deeds be lowly ; for hear what Christ saith, " Blessed are the poor in spirit ; " (Matt. v : 3.) and He places this first in order. Wherefore also the Apostle himself saith, " With all lowliness, and meekness, and long-suffering." For it is possible for a man to be lowly, and yet quick and irritable, and thus all is to no purpose ; for oftentimes he will be possessed by his anger, and ruin all.

" Forbearing," he proceeds, " one another in love."[2]

How is it possible to forbear, if a man be passionate or censorious ? He hath told us therefore the manner : " in love," saith he. If thou, he would say, art not forbearing to thy neighbor, how shall God be forbearing to thee ? If thou bearest not with thy fellow-servant, how shall the Master bear with thee ? Wherever there is love, all things are to be borne.

" Giving diligence[3]," saith he, " to keep the unity of the Spirit in the bond of peace." Bind therefore thy hands with moderation. Again that goodly name of " bond." We had dismissed it, and it has of itself come back on us again. A goodly bond was that, and goodly is this one also, and that other is the fruit of this. Bind thyself to thy brother. They bear all things lightly who are bound together in love. Bind thyself to him and him to thee ; thou art lord of both, for whomsoever I may be desirous to make my friend, I can by means of kindliness accomplish it.

" Giving diligence," he says ; a thing not to be done easily, and not in every one's power.

" Giving diligence," he proceeds, " to keep

---

[1] S. Babylas, whom Chrysostom has commemorated in a Homily on his feast day and elsewhere, (*Hom. de Bab.* t. 2. p. 531. Ed. Ben. *Hom. in Jul. et Gent.* t. 2. p. 536.) was Bishop of Antioch about 237–250, when he was martyred in the Decian persecution, being put into prison, and dying there. The circumstance mentioned in the text is also to be found in *Gent.* p. 554.—[See Homily on Babylas, Vol. ix. p. 141, of this Series.—G. A.]

[2] [" The reciprocal forbearance in love (ethical habit) (Rom. xv : 1 ; Gal. vi : 2) is the practical expression of the 'longsuffering.' "—Meyer.—G. A.]

[3] [" Giving diligence," participial clause parallel to " forbearing one another " which is characterized by the effort by which it must be upheld."—Meyer.—G. A.]

the unity of the Spirit." What is this "unity of Spirit?" In the human body there is a spirit which holds all together, though in different members. So is it also here; for to this end was the Spirit given, that He might unite those who are separated by race and by different manners; for old and young, rich and poor, child and youth, woman and man, and every soul become in a manner one, and more entirely so than if there were one body. For this spiritual relation is far higher than the other natural one, and the perfectness of the union more entire; because the conjunction of the soul is more perfect, inasmuch as it is both simple and uniform. And how then is this unity preserved? "In the bond of peace[1]." It is not possible for this to exist in enmity and discord. "For whereas there is," saith he, "among you jealousy and strife, are ye not carnal, and walk after the manner of men?" (1 Cor. iii: 3.) For as fire when it finds dry pieces of wood works up all together into one blazing pile, but when wet, does not act at all nor unite them; so also it is here. Nothing that is of a cold nature can bring about this union, whereas any warm one for the most part can. Hence at least it is that the glow of charity is produced; by the "bond of peace," he is desirous to bind us all together. For just in the same way, he would say, as if thou wouldest attach thyself to another, thou canst do it in no other way except by attaching him to thyself; and if thou shouldest wish to make the tie double, he must needs in turn attach himself to thee; so also here he would have us tied one to another; not simply that we be at peace, not simply that we love one another, but that all should be only even one soul. A glorious bond is this; with this bond let us bind ourselves together with one another and unto God. This is a bond that bruises not, nor cramps the hands it binds, but it leaves them free, and gives them ample play, and greater courage than those which are at liberty. The strong if he be bound to the weak, will support him, and not suffer him to perish: and if again he be tied to the indolent, him he will rather rouse and animate. "Brother helped by brother," it is said, "is as a strong city[2]." This chain no distance of place can interrupt, neither heaven, nor earth, nor death, nor any thing else, but it is more powerful and strong than all things. This, though it issue from but one soul, is able to embrace numbers at once; for hear what Paul saith, ⁀Ye are not straitened in us, but ye are straitened in your own affections; be ye also enlarged." (2 Cor. vi: 12.)

Now then, what impairs this bond? Love of money, passion for power, for glory, and the like, loosens them, and severs them asunder. How then are we to see that they be not cut asunder? If these tempers be got rid of, and none of those things which destroy charity come in by the way to trouble us. For hear what Christ saith, (Matt. xxiv: 12.) "Because iniquity shall be multiplied, the love of the many shall wax cold." Nothing is so opposed to love as sin, and I mean not love towards God, but that towards our neighbor also. But how then, it may be said, are even robbers at peace? When are they, tell me? Not when they are acting in a spirit which is that of robbers; for if they fail to observe the rules of justice amongst those with whom they divide the spoil, and to render to every one his right, you will find them too in wars and broils. So that neither amongst the wicked is it possible to find peace: but where men are living in righteousness and virtue, you may find it every where. But again, are rivals ever at peace? Never. And whom then would ye have me mention? The covetous man can never possibly be at peace with the covetous. So that were there not just and good persons, even though wronged by them, to stand between them, the whole race of them would be torn to pieces. When two wild beasts are famished, if there be not something put between them to consume, they will devour one another. The same would be the case with the covetous and the vicious. So that it is not possible there should be peace where virtue is not already put in practice beforehand. Let us form, if you please, a city entirely of covetous men, give them equal privileges, and let no one bear to be wronged, but let all wrong one another. Can that city possibly hold together? It is impossible. Again, is there peace amongst adulterers? No, not any two will you find of the same mind.

So then, to return, there is no other reason for this, than that "love hath waxed cold;" and the cause again why love hath waxed cold, is that "iniquity abounds." For this leads to selfishness, and divides and severs the body, and relaxes it and rends it to pieces. But where virtue is, it does the reverse. Because the man that is virtuous is also above money; so that were there ten thousand such in poverty they would still be peaceable; whilst the covetous, where there are but two, can never be at peace. Thus then if we are virtuous, love will not perish, for virtue springs from love, and love from virtue. And how this is, I will tell you. The virtuous man does not value money above friendship, nor does he remember injuries, nor does wrong to his neighbor; he is not insolent, he endures all things nobly. Of these things

---

[1] ["While peace one towards another must be the bond which is to envelope them."—Meyer.—G. A.]
[2] [This is the rendering of the Septuagint in Prov. xviii: 19, which Chrysostom follows exactly: ἀδελφὸς ὑπὸ ἀδελφοῦ βοηθούμενος ὡς πόλις ὀχυρά. The. Rev. Ver. following the Hebrew, has "A brother offended is harder to be won than a strong city."—G. A.]

love consists. Again, he who loves submits to all these things, and thus do they reciprocally produce one another. And this indeed, that love springs from virtue, appears from hence, because our Lord when He saith, "because iniquity shall be multiplied, the love of the many shall wax cold," plainly tells us this. And that virtue springs from love, Paul tells us, saying, "He that loveth his neighbor hath fulfilled the law." (Rom. xiii: 10.) So then a man must be one of the two, either very affectionate and much beloved, or else very virtuous; for he who has the one, of necessity possesses the other; and, on the contrary, he who knows not how to love, will therefore commit many evil actions; and he who commits evil actions, knows not what it is to love.

MORAL. Let us therefore follow after charity; it is a safeguard which will not allow us to suffer any evil. Let us bind ourselves together. Let there be no deceit amongst us, no hollowness. For where friendship is, there nothing of the sort is found. This too another certain wise man tells us. "Though thou drewest a sword at thy friend, yet despair not: for there may be a returning again to favor. If thou hast opened thy mouth against thy friend, fear not; for there may be a reconciliation: except for upbraiding, or disclosing of secrets, or a treacherous wound: for for these things a friend will depart." (Ecclus. xxii: 21, 22.) For "disclosing," saith he, "of secrets." Now if we be all friends, there is no need of secrets; for as no man has any secret with himself and cannot conceal anything from himself, so neither will he from his friends. Where then no secrets exist, separation arising from this is impossible. For no other reason have we secrets, than because we have not confidence in all men. So then it is the waxing cold of love, which has produced secrets. For what secret hast thou? Dost thou desire to wrong thy neighbor? Or, art thou hindering him from sharing some benefit, and on this account concealest it? But, no, perhaps it is none of these things. What then, is it that thou art ashamed? If so, then this is a token of want of confidence. Now then if there be love, there will be no "revealing of secrets," neither any "upbraiding." For who, tell me, would ever upbraid his own

soul? And suppose even such a thing were done, it would be for some good; for we upbraid children, we know, when we desire to make them 'feel. And so Christ too on that occasion began to upbraid the cities, saying, "Woe unto thee, Chorazin! woe unto thee, Bethsaida!" (Luke x: 13.) in order that He might deliver them from upbraidings. For nothing has such power to lay hold of the mind, or can more strongly arouse it, or brace it up when relaxed. Let us then never use upbraiding to one another merely for the sake of upbraiding. For what? Wilt thou upbraid thy friend on the score of money? Surely not, if at least thou possessest what thou hast in common. Wilt thou then for his faults? No nor this, but thou wilt rather in that case correct him. Or, as it goes on, "for a treacherous wound;" who in the world will kill himself, or who wound himself? No one.

Let us then "follow after love;" he saith not simply let us love; but let us "follow after love." (1 Cor. xiv: 1.) There is need of much eagerness: she is soon out of sight, she is most rapid in her flight; so many things are there in life which injure her. If we follow her, she will not outstrip us and get away, but we shall speedily recover her. The love of God is that which united earth to Heaven. It was the love of God that seated man upon the kingly throne. It was the love of God that manifested God upon earth. It was the love of God that made the Lord a servant. It was the love of God that caused the Beloved to be delivered up for His enemies, the Son for them that hated Him, the Lord for His servants, God for men, the free for slaves. Nor did it stop here, but called us to yet greater things. Yes, not only did it release us from our former evils, but promised, moreover, to bestow upon us other much greater blessings. For these things then let us give thanks to God, and follow after every virtue; and before all things, let us with all strictness practice love, that we may be counted worthy to attain the promised blessings; through the grace and loving-kindness of our Lord Jesus Christ, with whom, to the Father together with the Holy Ghost, be glory, might, and honor, now and for ever and ever. Amen.

HOMILY X.

EPHESIANS iv. 4.

"There is one body, and one Spirit, even as ye are called in one hope of your calling."

WHEN the blessed Paul exhorts us to anything of special importance, so truly wise and spiritual as he is, he grounds his exhortation upon things in Heaven: this itself being a lesson he had learned from the Lord. Thus he saith also elsewhere, "Walk in love, even as Christ also hath loved us." (ch. v. 2.) And again, "Have this mind in you, which was also in Christ Jesus, who being in the form of God, counted it not a prize to be on an equality with God." (Phil. ii. 5, 6.) This is what he is doing here also, for whenever the examples he is setting before us are great, he is intense in his zeal and feeling. What then does he say, now he is inciting us to unity? "There is one body, and one Spirit, even as ye are called in one hope of your calling:"

Ver. 5. "One Lord, one faith, one baptism."

Now what is this one body? The faithful throughout the whole world, both which are, and which have been, and which shall be. And again, they that before Christ's coming pleased God, are "one body." How so? Because they also knew Christ. Whence does this appear? "Your father Abraham," saith He, "rejoiced to see My day, and he saw it, and was glad." (John viii. 56.) And again, "If ye had believed Moses," He saith, "ye would have believed Me, for he wrote of Me." (John v. 46.) And the prophets too would not have written of One, of whom they knew not what they said; whereas they both knew Him, and worshiped Him. Thus then were they also "one body."

The body is not disjoined from the spirit, for then would it not be a body. Thus it is customary also with us, touching things which are united, and which have any great consistency or coherence, to say, they are one body. And thus again, touching union, we take that to be a body which is under one head. If there be one head, then is there one body. The body is composed of members both honorable and dishonorable. Only the greater is not to rise up even against the meanest, nor this latter to envy the other. They do not all indeed contribute the same share, but severally according to the proportion of need. And forasmuch as all are formed for necessary and for different purposes, all are of equal honor. Some indeed there are, which are more especially principal members, others less

so: for example, the head is more a principal member than all the rest of the body, as containing within itself all the senses, and the governing principle of the soul. And to live without the head is impossible; whereas many persons have lived for a long time with their feet cut off. So that it is better than they, not only by its position, but also by its very vital energy and its function.

Now why am I saying this? There are great numbers in the Church; there are those who, like the head, are raised up to a height; who, like the eyes that are in the head, survey heavenly things, who stand far aloof from the earth, and have nothing in common with it, whilst others occupy the rank of feet, and tread upon the earth; of healthy feet indeed, for to tread upon the earth is no crime in feet, but to run to evil. "Their feet," saith the Prophet, "run to evil." (Isa. lix. 7.) Neither then let these, the head, saith he, be high-minded against the feet, nor the feet look with evil eye at them. For thus the peculiar beauty of each is destroyed, and the perfectness of its function impeded. And naturally enough; inasmuch as he who lays snares for his neighbor will be laying snares first of all for himself. And should the feet therefore not choose to convey the head anywhere upon its necessary journey, they will at the same time be injuring themselves by their inactivity and sloth. Or again, should the head not choose to take any care of the feet, itself will be the first to sustain the damage. However, those members do not rise up one against the other; it is not likely, for it has been so ordered by nature that they should not. But with man, how is it possible for him not to rise up against man? No one, we know, ever rises up against Angels; since neither do they rise against the Archangels. Nor, on the other hand, can the irrational creatures proudly exalt themselves over us; but where the nature is equal in dignity, and the gift one, and where one has no more than another, how shall this be prevented?

And yet surely these are the very reasons why thou oughtest not to rise up against thy neighbors. For if all things are common, and one has nothing more than another, whence this mad folly? We partake of the same nature, partake alike of soul and body, we breathe the same air, we use the same food. Whence this rebellious rising of one against another? And yet truly the being able by one's virtue to overcome the incorporeal powers, that were enough to lead to arrogance; or rather arrogance it would not be, for with good reason am I high-minded, and exceedingly high-minded against the evil spirit. And behold even Paul, how high-minded he was against that evil spirit. For when the evil spirit was speaking great and marvelous things concerning him, he made him hold his peace, and endured him not even in his flattery. For when that damsel, "who had the spirit of divination," cried, saying, "These men are the servants of the most high God, which show unto us the way of salvation" (Acts xvi. 16, 17), he rebuked him severely, and silenced his forward tongue. And again he elsewhere writes, and says, "God shall bruise Satan under your feet shortly." (Rom. xvi. 20.) Will the difference of nature have any effect? Perceivest thou not that the difference between natures has no effect whatever, but only the difference of purpose? Because of their principle therefore they are far worse than all. Well, a man may say, but I am not rising up against an Angel, because there is so vast a distance between my nature and his. And yet surely thou oughtest no more to rise up against a man than against an Angel, for the Angel indeed differs from thee in nature, a matter which can be neither an honor to him, nor a disgrace to thee: whereas man differs from man not at all in nature, but in principle; and there is such a thing as an Angel too even amongst men. So that if thou rise not up against Angels, much more shouldest thou not against men, against those who have become angels in this our nature; for should any one among men become as virtuous as an Angel, that man is in a far higher degree superior to thee, than an Angel is. And why so? Because what the one possesses by nature, the other has achieved of his own purpose. And again, because the Angel has his home far from thee in distance also, and dwelleth in Heaven; whereas this man is living with thee, and giving an impulse to thy emulation. And indeed he lives farther apart from thee than the Angel. For "our citizenship," saith the Apostle, "is in Heaven." (Phil. iii. 20.) And to show thee that this man hath his home still farther distant, hear where his Head is seated; upon the throne, saith he, the royal throne! And the farther distant that throne is from us, the farther is he also.

Well, but I see him, thou wilt say, in the enjoyment of honor, and I am led to jealousy. Why, this is the very thing which has turned all things upside down, which has filled not the world only, but the Church also, with countless troubles. And just as fierce blasts setting in across a calm harbor, render it more dangerous than any rock, or than any strait whatever; so

the lust of glory entering in, overturns and confounds everything.

Ye have oftentimes been present at the burning of large houses. Ye have seen how the smoke keeps rising up to Heaven; and if no one comes near to put a stop to the mischief, but every one keeps looking to himself, the flame spreads freely on, and devours everything. And oftentimes the whole city will stand around; they will stand round indeed as spectators of the evil, not to aid nor assist. And there you may see them one and all standing round, and doing nothing but each individual stretching out his hand, and pointing out to some one who may be just come to the spot, either a flaming brand that moment flying through a window, or beams hurled down, or the whole circuit of the walls forced out, and tumbling violently to the ground. Many too there are of the more daring and venturesome, who will have the hardihood even to come close to the very buildings themselves whilst they are burning, not in order to stretch forth a hand towards them, and to put a stop to the mischief, but that they may the more fully enjoy the sight, being able from the nearer place to observe closely all that which often escapes those at a distance. Then if the house happen to be large and magnificent, it appears to them a pitiable spectacle, and deserving of many tears. And truly there is a pitiable spectacle for us to behold; capitals of columns crumbled to dust, and many columns themselves shattered to pieces, some consumed by the fire, others thrown down often by the very hands which erected them, that they may not add fuel to the flame. Statues again, which stood with so much gracefulness, with the ceiling resting on them, these you may see all exposed, with the roof torn off, and themselves standing hideously disfigured in the open air. And why should one go on to describe the wealth stored up within? the tissues of gold, and the vessels of silver? And where the lord of the house and his consort scarcely entered, where was the treasurehouse of tissues and perfumes, and the caskets of the costly jewels, — all has become one blazing fire, and within now, are bath-men and street-cleaners, and runaway slaves, and everybody; and everything within is one mass of fire and water, of mud, and dust, and half-burnt beams!

Now why have I drawn out so full a picture as this? Not simply because I wish to represent to you the conflagration of a house, (for what concern is that of mine?) but because I wish to set before your eyes, as vividly as I can, the calamities of the Church. For like a conflagration indeed, or like a thunderbolt hurled from on high, have they lighted upon the roof of the Church, and yet they rouse up no one;

but whilst our Father's house is burning, we are sleeping, as it were, a deep and stupid sleep. And yet who is there whom this fire does not touch? Which of the statues that stand in the Church? for the Church is nothing else than a house built of the souls of us men. Now this house is not of equal honor throughout, but of the stones which contribute to it, some are bright and shining, whilst others are smaller and more dull than they, and yet superior again to others.[1] There we may see many who are in the place of gold also, the gold which adorns the ceiling. Others again we may see, who give the beauty and gracefulness produced by statues. Many[2] we may see, standing like pillars. For he is accustomed to call men also "pillars" (Gal. ii. 9), not only on account of their strength but also on account of their beauty, adding as they do, much grace, and having their heads overlaid with gold. We may see a multitude, forming generally the wide middle space and the whole extent of the circumference; for the body at large occupies the place of those stones of which the outer walls are built. Or rather we must go on to a more splendid picture yet. This Church, of which I speak, is not built of these stones, such as we see around us, but of gold and silver, and of precious stones, and there is abundance of gold dispersed everywhere throughout it. But, oh the bitter tears this calls forth! For all these things hath the lawless rule of vainglory consumed; that all-devouring flame, which no one has yet got under. And we stand gazing in amazement at the flames, but no longer able to quench the evil: or if we do quench it for a short time, yet after two or three days as a spark blown up from a heap of ashes overturns all, and consumes no less than it did before, so it is here also: for this is just what is wont to happen in such a conflagration. And as to the cause, it has devoured the supports of the very pillars of the Church; those of us who supported the roof, and who formerly held the whole building together it has enveloped in the flame. Hence too was a ready communication to the rest of the outer walls: for so also in the case of buildings, when the fire lays hold of the timbers, it is better armed for its attack upon the stones; but when it has brought down the pillars and leveled them with the ground, nothing more is wanted to consume all the rest in the flames. For when the props and supports of the upper parts fall down, those

parts also themselves will speedily enough follow them. Thus is it also at this moment with the Church: the fire has laid hold on every part. We seek the honors that come from man, we burn for glory, and we hearken not to Job when he saith,

"If like Adam (or after the manner of men) I covered
  my transgressions
By hiding mine iniquity in my bosom,
Because I feared the great multitude."[3]

Behold ye a virtuous spirit? I was not ashamed, he saith, to own before the whole multitude my involuntary sins: And if he was not ashamed to confess, much more were it our duty to do so. For saith the prophet, "Set thou forth thy cause, that thou mayest be justified." (Isa. xliii. 26.) Great is the violence of this evil, everything is overturned by it and annihilated. We have forsaken the Lord, and are become slaves of honor. We are no longer able to rebuke those who are under our rule, because we ourselves also are possessed with the same fever as they. We who are appointed by God to heal others, need the physician ourselves. What further hope of recovery is there left, when even the very physicians themselves need the healing hand of others?

I have not said these things without an object, nor am I making lamentations to no purpose, but with the view that one and all, with our women and children, having sprinkled ourselves with ashes, and girded ourselves about with sackcloth, may keep a long fast, may beseech God Himself to stretch forth His hand to us, and to stay the peril. For need is there indeed of His hand, that mighty, that marvelous hand. Greater things are required of us than of the Ninevites. "Yet three days," said the prophet, "and Nineveh shall be overthrown."[4] (Jonah iii. 4.) A fearful message, and burdened with tremendous threat. And how should it be otherwise? to expect that within three days, the city should become their tomb, and that all should perish in one common judgment. For if, when it happens that two children die at the same time in one house, the hardship becomes intolerable, and if to Job this of all things seemed the most intolerable, that the roof fell in upon all his children, and they were thus killed; what must it be to behold not one house, nor two children, but a nation of a hundred and twenty thousand buried beneath the ruins!

---

[1] [Field's text has here πολλῷ δὲ ἐκείνων βελτίους instead of πολλῷ δὲ ἄλλων βελτίους, which is clearly better than Field's, because it gives a better sense and is well attested. Indeed, Field, while giving ἐκείνων in his text, says it is used "durius pro ἑτέρων," and mentions Chrysostom's negligent use of pronouns.—G. A.]

[2] [In Field's text the word "many," πολλούς, is put in the preceding sentence; but it is better where it stands here, to complete the sentence and to make it correspond with the two preceding sentences.—G. A.]

[3] Job xxxi. 33, 34. The verses in the Sept. stand thus: Εἰ δὲ καὶ ἁμαρτὼν ἀκουσίως ἔκρυψα τὴν ἁμαρτίαν μου. Οὐ γὰρ διετράπην πολυοχλίαν πλήθους, τοῦ μὴ ἐξαγορεῦσαι ἐνώπιον αὐτῶν [but Chrysostom quotes only these words: εἰ καὶ ἁμαρτὼν ἀκουσίως διετράπην πολυοχλίαν. The Hebrew is quite different, as shown in rendering of Rev. Ver. (above).—G. A.]

[4] [The Septuagint has yet three days, &c., ἔτι τρεῖς ἡμέραι κ.τ.λ. So Chrysostom quotes it. The Hebrew text and the Rev. Ver., following it, have forty days.—G. A.]

Ye know how terrible a disaster is this, for lately has this very warning happened to us, not that any prophet uttered a voice, for we are not worthy to hear such a voice, but the warning crying aloud from on high more distinctly than any trumpet.[1] However, as I was saying, "Yet three days," said the prophet, "and Nineveh shall be overthrown." A terrible warning indeed, but now we have nothing even like that ; no, there are no longer "three days,"[2] nor is there a Nineveh to be overthrown, but many days are already past since the Church throughout all the world has been overthrown, and leveled with the ground, and all alike are overwhelmed in the evil ; nay more, of those that are in high places the stress is so much the greater. Wonder not therefore if I should exhort you to do greater things than the Ninevites ; and why? nay more, I do not now proclaim a fast only, but I suggest to you the remedy which raised up that city also when falling. And what was that? "God saw their works," saith the prophet, "that they turned from their evil way, and God repented of the evil which He said He would do unto them." (Jonah iii. 10.) This let us do, both we and you. Let us renounce the passion for riches, the lust for glory, beseeching God to stretch forth His hand, and to raise up our fallen members. And well may we, for our fear is not for the same objects as theirs ; for then indeed it was only stones and timbers that were to fall, and bodies that were to perish ; but now it is none of these ; no, but souls are about to be delivered over to hell fire. Let us implore, let us confess unto Him, let us give thanks unto Him for what is past, let us entreat Him for what is to come, that we may be counted worthy to be delivered from this fierce and most terrible monster, and to lift up our thanksgivings to the loving God and Father with whom, to the Son, together with the Holy Ghost, be glory, might, and honor, now, henceforth, and for ever and ever. Amen.

HOMILY XI.

EPHESIANS iv. 4–7.

"There is one body, and one Spirit, even as also ye were called in one hope of your calling; one Lord, one faith, one baptism, one God and Father of all, who is over all, and through all, and in all. But unto each one of us was the grace given according to the measure of the gift of Christ."

THE love Paul requires of us is no common love, but that which cements us together, and makes us cleave inseparably to one another, and effects as great and as perfect a union as though it were between limb and limb. For this is that love which produces great and glorious fruits. Hence he saith, there is "one body" ; one, both by sympathy, and by not opposing the good of others, and by sharing their joy, having expressed all at once by this figure. He then beautifully adds, "and one Spirit," showing[3] that from the one body there will be one Spirit : or, that it is possible that there may be indeed one body, and yet not one Spirit ; as, for instance, if any member of it should be a friend of heretics : or else he is, by this expression, shaming them into unanimity, saying, as it were, "Ye who have received one Spirit, and have been made to drink at one fountain, ought not to be divided in mind" ; or else by spirit here he means their zeal. Then he adds, "Even as ye were called in one hope of your calling," that is, God hath called you all on the same terms. He hath bestowed nothing upon one more than upon another. To all He hath freely given immortality, to all eternal life, to all immortal glory, to all brotherhood, to all inheritance. He is the common Head of all ; "He hath raised all" up, "and made them sit with Him."[2] (Eph. ii. 6.) Ye then who in the spiritual world have so great equality of privileges, whence is it that ye are high-minded? Is it that one is wealthy and another strong? How ridiculous must this be? For tell me, if the emperor some day were to take ten persons, and to array them all in purple, and seat them on the royal throne, and to bestow upon all the same honor, would any one of these, think ye, venture to reproach another, as being more wealthy or more illustrious than he? Surely never. And I have not yet said all ; for the difference is not so great in heaven as here

---

[1] Antioch was exposed to earthquakes. One happened A.D. 395, which might be about the date of these Homilies. In A.D. 458 it was almost overthrown from this cause.

[2] [See note on preceding page. — G. A.]

[3] ["The ἓν σῶμα means the totality of Christians as the *corpus (Christi) mysticum;* comp. Eph. ii. 16; Ro. xii. 5; 1 Cor. x. 17. The ἓν πνεῦμα is the Holy Spirit, the spirit of the *corpus mysticum;* comp. Eph. ii. 18; 1 Cor. xii. 13. The explanation, 'one body and one soul,' is excluded, as at variance with the context by the specifically Christian character of the other elements, and rendered impossible by the correct supplying of ἐστί (and not 'ye ought to be')." — Meyer. — G. A.]

below we differ. There is "one Lord, one faith, one baptism." [1] Behold "the hope of your calling. One God and Father of all, who is over all, and through all, and in all." For can it be, that thou art called by the name of a greater God, another, of a lesser God? That thou art saved by faith, and another by works? That thou hast received remission in baptism, whilst another has not? "There is one God and Father of all, who is over all, and through all, and in all." "Who is over all," that is, the Lord and above all; and "through all," that is, providing for, ordering all; and "in you all," that is, who dwelleth in you all. Now this they own to be an attribute of the Son; so that were it an argument of inferiority, it never would have been said of the Father.

"But [2] unto each one of us was the grace given."

What then? he saith, whence are those diverse spiritual gifts? For this subject was continually carrying away both the Ephesians themselves, and the Corinthians, and many others, some into vain arrogance, and others into despondency or envy. Hence he everywhere takes along with him this illustration of the body. Hence it is that now also he has proposed it, inasmuch as he was about to make mention of diverse gifts. He enters indeed into the subject more fully in the Epistle to the Corinthians, because it was among them that this malady most especially reigned: here however he has only alluded to it. And mark what he says: he does not say, "according to the faith of each," lest he should throw those who have no large attainments into despondency. But what saith he? "According to the measure of the gift of Christ." The chief and principal points of all, he saith, — Baptism, the being saved by faith, the having God for our Father, our all partaking of the same Spirit, — these are common to all. If then this or that man possesses any superiority in any spiritual gift, grieve not at it; since his labor also is greater. He that had received the five talents, had five required of him; whilst he that had received the two, brought only two, and yet received no less a reward than the other. And therefore the Apostle here also encourages the hearer on the same ground, showing that gifts are bestowed not for the honor of one above

another, but for the work of the church, even as he says further on:

"For the perfecting of the saints unto the work of ministering unto the building up of the body of Christ."

Hence it is that even he himself saith, "Woe is unto me, if I preach not the Gospel." (1 Cor. ix. 16.) For example: he received the grace of Apostleship, but for this very reason, "woe unto him," because he received it: whereas thou art free from the danger.

"According to the measure."

What is meant by, "according to the measure"? It means, "not according to our merit," for then would no one have received what he has received: but of the free gift we have all received. And why then one more, and another less? There is nothing to cause this, he would say, but the matter itself is indifferent; for every one contributes towards "the building." And by this too he shows, that it is not of his own intrinsic merit that one has received more and another less, but that it is for the sake of others, as God Himself hath measured it; since he saith also elsewhere, "But now hath God set the members each one of them in the body, even as it pleased Him." (1 Cor. xii. 18.) And he mentions not the reason, lest he should deject or dispirit the hearers.

Ver. 8. "Wherefore he saith, When He ascended on high, He led captivity captive, and gave gifts unto men."

As though he had said, Why art thou highminded? The whole is of God. The Prophet saith in the Psalm, "Thou hast received gifts among men" (Ps. lxviii. 18), whereas the Apostle saith, "He gave gifts unto men." The one is the same as the other. [3]

Ver. 9, 10. "Now this, He ascended, what is it, but that He also descended into the lower parts of the earth? He that descended, is the same also that ascended far above all the Heavens, that He might fill all things."

When thou hearest these words, think not of a mere removal from one place to another; for what Paul establishes in the Epistle to the Philippians (Phil. ii. 5–8), that very argument [4] is he also insisting upon here. In the same way as there, when exhorting them concerning lowliness, he brings forward Christ as an example,

---

[1] [Note the triad of trinities: —

1. The Church	{	one body.
		one spirit.
		one hope.
2. Christ	{	one Lord.
		one faith.
		one baptism.
3. God	{	over all.
		through all.
		in all.

— Meyer, substantially. — G. A.]

[2] ["But (δέ) forms the transition from the summary 'all,' 'all,' 'all' to 'each individual' among the Christians." — Meyer. — G. A.]

[3] [" He quotes Ps. lxviii. 18, with the freedom of a Messianic interpretation of the words, and his exposition of the Hebrew words yielded essentially the sense expressed by him. So he took לְקַחְתָּ in the sense: 'Thou didst take away gifts to distribute them among men,' and then translated this in an explanatory way, ἔδωκε, &c." — Meyer. — G. A.]

[4] [This view of Chrysostom is quite at variance with the context. Ellicott says: To evince still more clearly the correctness of the Messianic application of the words just cited, St. Paul urges the antithesis implied by ἀνέβη, namely, κατέβη, a predication applicable to Christ only, the tacit assumption being that He who is the subject of the citation is one whose seat was heaven. Compare John iii. 13. — G. A.]

so does he here also, saying, "He descended into the lower parts of the earth." For were not this so, this expression which he uses, "He became obedient even unto death" (Phil. ii. 8, 9), were superfluous; whereas from His ascending, he implies His descent, and by "the lower parts of the earth," he means "death," according to the notions of men; as Jacob also said, "Then shall ye bring down my gray hairs with sorrow to the grave." (Gen. xxxii. 48.) And again as it is in the Psalm, "Lest I become like them that go down into the pit" (Ps. cxliii. 7), that is like the dead. Why does he descant upon this region here? And of what captivity does he speak? Of that of the devil; for He took the tyrant captive, the devil, I mean, and death, and the curse, and sin. Behold His spoils and His trophies.

"Now this, He ascended, what is it but that He also descended?"

This strikes at Paul of Samosata and his school.[1]

"He that descended, is the same also that ascended far above all the Heavens, that He might fill all things."

He descended, saith he, into the lower parts of the earth, beyond which there are none other: and He ascended up far above all things, to that place, beyond which there is none other. This is to show His divine energy, and supreme dominion. For indeed even of old had all things been filled.

Ver. 11, 12. "And He gave some to' be apostles; and some, prophets; and some, evangelists; and some, pastors and teachers; for the perfecting of the saints, unto the work of ministering, unto the building up of the body of Christ."

What he said elsewhere, "Wherefore also God hath highly exalted Him" (Phil. ii. 9), that saith he also here. "He that descended, is the same also that ascended." It did Him no injury that He came down into the lower parts of the earth, nor was it any hindrance to His becoming far higher than the Heavens. So that the more a man is humbled, so much the more is he exalted. For as in the case of water, the more a man presses it downwards, the more he forces it up; and the further a man retires to hurl a javelin, the surer his aim; so is it also with humility. However, when we speak of ascents with reference to God, we must needs conceive a descent first; but when with reference to man, not at all so. Then he goes on to show further His providential care, and His wisdom, for He

who hath wrought such things as these, who had such might, and who refused not to go down even to those lower parts for our sakes, never would He have made these distributions of spiritual gifts without a purpose. Now elsewhere he tells us that this was the work of the Spirit, in the words, "In the which the Holy Ghost hath made you bishops to feed the Church of God."[2] And here he saith that it is the Son; and elsewhere that it is God. "And He gave to the Church some apostles, and some prophets." But in the Epistle to the Corinthians, he saith, "I planted, Apollos watered; but God gave the increase." And again, "Now he that planteth and he that watereth are one: but each shall receive his own reward according to his own labor." (1 Cor. iii. 6–8.) So is it also here; for what if thou bring in but little? Thou hast received so much. First, he says, "apostles";[3] for these had all gifts; secondarily, "prophets," for there were some who were not indeed apostles, but prophets, as Agabus; thirdly, "evangelists," who did not go about everywhere, but only preached the Gospel, as Priscilla and Aquila; "pastors and teachers," those who were entrusted with the charge of a whole nation. What then? are the pastors and the teachers inferior? Yes, surely; those who were settled and employed about one spot, as Timothy and Titus, were inferior to those who went about the world and preached the Gospel. However, it is not possible from this passage to frame the subordination and precedence, but from another Epistle. "He gave," saith he; thou must not say a word to gainsay it. Or perhaps by "evangelists" he means those who wrote the Gospel.

"For the perfecting of the saints unto the work of ministering, unto the building up of the body of Christ."[4]

Perceive ye the dignity of the office? Each one edifies, each one perfects, each one ministers.

Ver. 13. "Till we all attain," he proceeds, "unto the unity of the faith and of the knowledge of the Son of God, unto a full-grown man, unto the measure of the stature of the fullness of Christ."

By "stature" here he means perfect "knowledge"; for as a man will stand firmly, whereas

---

[1] Paul was Bishop of Antioch A.D. 260–269, when he was deposed for heresy. Very different accounts are given of his particular doctrines: St. Athanasius may be securely followed, however, who says that he denied the doctrine of our Lord's preëxistence, asserted that He was a mere man, and that the Word of God was *in* Him. vid. *Orat.* i. 25, 38; ii. 13; iii. 51. *De decret.* 24, &c., &c. [See Schaff's *History of Christian Ch.*, Vol. II., pp. 575, 576.—G. A.]

[2] [Both here and in Hom. xliv. on Acts (xx. 28) Chrysostom reads κυρίου instead of θεοῦ. The latter is, however, the reading of א B., and is adopted by W. & H. and the Rev. Ver. (as well as the *textus receptus*).—G. A.]

[3] ["The Apostles had an immediate call from Christ, a destination for all lands and a special power of miracles. Prophets: not only in the special sense, but also those who spoke under the *immediate* impulse of the Holy Spirit; Evangelists were subordinates of the Apostles who traveled about. Pastors and teachers, constituting one and the same class, were stationary, and probably included presbyters.—Ellicott.—G. A.]

[4] [The proper relation of these prepositional phrases is brought out in Meyer's translation: He has, with a view to the full furnishing of the saints, given those teachers for the work of ministering, for the edification of the body of Christ. So Ellicott.—G. A.]

children are carried about and waver in mind, so is it also with believers.

"To the unity," saith he, "of the faith."

That is, until we shall be shown to have all one faith : for this is unity of faith, when we all are one, when we shall all alike acknowledge the common bond. Till then thou must labor to this end. If for this thou hast received a gift, that thou mightest edify others, look well that thou overturn not thyself, by envying another. God hath honored thee, and ordained thee, that thou shouldest build up another. Yea, for about this was the Apostle also engaged ; and for this was the prophet prophesying and persuading, and the Evangelist preaching the Gospel, and for this was the pastor and teacher ; all had undertaken one common work. For tell me not of the difference of the spiritual gifts ; but that all had one work. Now when we shall all believe alike then shall there be unity ; for that this is what he calls "a perfect man," is plain. And yet he elsewhere calls us "babes" (1 Cor. xiii. 11), even when we are of mature age ; but he is there looking to another comparison, for there it is in comparison with our future knowledge that he there calls us babes. For having said, "We know in part" (1 Cor. xiii. 9, 12), he adds also the word "darkly," and the like : whereas here he speaks with reference to another thing, with reference to changeableness, as he saith also elsewhere, "But solid food is for full-grown men." (Heb. v. 14.) Do you see then also in what sense he there calls them full-grown ? Observe also in what sense he calls men "perfect" here, by the words next added, where he says, "that we may be no longer children." That we keep, he means to say, that little measure, which we may have received, with all diligence, with firmness and steadfastness.

Ver. 14. "That we may be no longer."—The word, "no longer," shows that they had of old been in this case, and he reckons himself moreover as a subject for correction, and corrects himself. For this cause, he would say, are there so many workmen, that the building may not be shaken, may not be "carried about," that the stones may be firmly fixed.[1] For this is the character of children, to be tossed to and fro, to be carried about and shaken. "That we may be no longer," saith he, "children, tossed to and fro, and carried about with every wind of doctrine, by the sleight of men, in craftiness, after the wiles of error." "And carried about," saith he, "with every wind." He comes to this figure of speech, to point out in how great peril doubting souls are. "With every wind," saith he,

"by the sleight of men, in craftiness, after the wiles of error." The word "sleight"[2] means the art of gamesters. Such are the "crafty," whenever they lay hold on the simpler sort. For they also change and shift about everything. He here glances also at human life.

Ver. 15, 16. "But speaking truth,"[3] saith he, "in love, may grow up in all things into Him, which is the Head, even Christ, from whom," (that is, from Christ,) "all the body fitly framed and knit together, through that which every joint supplieth, according to the working in due measure of each several part, maketh increase of the body unto the building up of itself in love."

He expresses himself with great obscurity, from his desire to utter everything at once. What he means, however, is this. In the same way as the spirit, or vital principle, which descends from the brain, communicates the sensitive faculty which is conveyed through the nerves, not simply to all the members, but according to the proportion of each member, to that which is capable of receiving more, more, to that which is capable of less, less, (for the spirit is the root or source ;) so also is Christ. For the souls of men being dependent upon Him as members, His provident care, and supply of the spiritual gifts according to a due proportion in the measure of every single member, effects their increase. But what is the meaning of this, "by the touch of the supply"?[4] that is to say, by the sensitive faculty.[5] For that spirit which is supplied to the members from the head, "touches,"[6] each single member, and thus actuates it. As though one should say, "the body receiving the supply according to the proportion of its several members, thus maketh the increase " ; or, in other words, "the members receiving the supply according to the proportion of their proper measure, thus make increase " ; or otherwise again thus, "the spirit flowing plenteously from above, and touching[7] all the members, and supplying them as each is capable of "receiving it, thus maketh increase." But wherefore doth he add, "in love "? Because in no other way is it possible for that Spirit to descend. For as, in case a hand should happen to be torn from the body, the spirit which pro-

---

[1] ["It is not the figure of a building which Paul employs here, but of a ship abandoned to the breakers, on which figurative expression of restless passive subjection to influences, compare Jas. i. 6."—Meyer.—G. A.]

[2] κυβεία κυβευταί.

[3] ["ἀληθεύοντες: The common meaning, 'To speak truth,' is clearly unsatisfactory here. It means 'holding the truth.'"—Ellicott. "Professing the truth," Thayer, Lexicon. Rev. Ver. has in margin "dealing truly." Meyer says it means here, as always, "speaking the truth," and correctly.—G. A.]

[4] ἁφῆς, "joint," Eng. Tr. Theodoret, too, in loc. interprets touch, and considers that it stands for all the senses. S. Austin translates tactus in Psalm x. 7, de Civ. D. xxii. 18, but in the received meaning. [See Meyer.—G. A.]

[5] [" Meyer still retains the interpretation of Chrysostom and Theodoret that ἁφὴ = αἴσθησις, "feeling," "perception," and connects the clause with αὔξησιν ποιεῖται: but the parallel passage, Col. ii. 19, leaves it scarcely doubtful that the meaning usually assigned is correct, and that the clause is to be connected with the participles."—Ellicott. So Thayer, Lex., Rev. Ver.—G. A.]

[6] ἁπτόμενον.   [7] ἁπτόμενον.

ceeds from the brain seeks the limb, and if it finds it not, does not leap forth from the body, and fly about and go to the hand, but if it finds it not in its place, does not touch it ; so also will it be here, if we be not bound together in love. All these expressions he uses as tending to humility. For what, he seems to say, if this or that man receives more than another? He has received the same Spirit, sent forth from the same Head, effectually working in all alike, communicating itself to all alike.

"Fitly framed and knit together."

That is, having great care bestowed upon it ; for the body must not be put together anyhow, but with exceeding art and nicety, since if it gets out of place, it is no longer. So that each must not only be united to the body, but also occupy his proper place, since if thou shalt go beyond this, thou art not united to it, neither dost thou receive the Spirit. Dost thou not see, that in those dislocations of the bones which take place in any accident, when a bone gets out of its proper place and occupies that of another, how it injures the whole body, and oftentimes will produce death? So that sometimes it will be found to be no longer worth preserving. For many in many cases will cut it off, and leave a void in its place ; because everywhere what is in excess is an evil. And so again with the elements, if they lose their proper proportion and be in excess, they impair the whole system. This is the meaning of the being "fitly framed and knit together." Consider then of how vast importance it is, that each should remain in his own proper place, and not encroach on another which in nowise appertains to him. Thou puttest the members together, He supplieth them from above. For as there are in the body such recipient organs, as we have seen, so is it also with the Spirit, the whole root or source being from above. For example, the heart is the recipient of the breath, the liver of the blood, the spleen of the bile, and the other organs, some of one thing, others of another, but all these have their source from the brain. So also hath God done, highly honoring man, and being unwilling to be far from him, He hath made Himself indeed the source of his dependence, and hath constituted them fellow-workers with Himself; and some He hath appointed to one office, and others to another. For example, the Apostle is the most vital vessel of the whole body, receiving everything from Him ; so that He maketh eternal life to run through them to all, as through veins and arteries, I mean through their discourse. The Prophet foretells things to come, whilst He alone ordereth the same ; Thou puttest the members together,[1]

but He supplies them with life, "For the perfecting of the saints, for the work of the ministry." Love builds up, and makes men cleave one to another, and be fastened and fitted together.

MORAL. If therefore we desire to have the benefit of that Spirit which is from the Head, let us cleave one to another. For there are two kinds of separation from the body of the Church ; the one, when we wax cold in love, the other, when we dare commit things unworthy of our belonging to that body ; for in either way we cut ourselves off from the "fullness of Christ." But if we are appointed to build up others also, what shall not be done to them who are first to make division? Nothing will so avail to divide the Church as love of power. Nothing so provokes God's anger as the division of the Church. Yea, though we have achieved ten thousand glorious acts, yet shall we, if we cut to pieces the fullness of the Church, suffer punishment no less sore than they who mangled His body. For that indeed was brought to pass for the benefit of the world, even though it was done with no such intention ; whereas this produces no advantage in any case, but the injury is excessive. These remarks I am addressing not to the governors only, but also to the governed. Now a certain holy man said what might seem to be a bold thing ; yet, nevertheless, he spoke it out. What then is this? He said, that not even the blood of martyrdom can wash out this sin.[2] For tell me for what dost thou suffer as a martyr? Is it not for the glory of Christ? Thou then that yieldest up thy life for Christ's sake, how dost thou lay waste the Church, for whose sake Christ yielded up His life? Hear what Paul saith, "I am not meet to be called an Apostle (1 Cor. xv. 9), because I persecuted the Church of God and made havoc of it." (Gal. i. 13.) This injury is not less than that received at the hands of enemies, nay, it is far greater. For that indeed renders her even more glorious, whereas this, when she is warred upon by her own children, disgraces her even before her enemies. Because it seems to them a great mark of hypocrisy, that those who have been born in her, and nurtured in her bosom, and have learned perfectly her secrets, that these should of a sudden change, and do her enemies' work.

I mean these remarks for those who give

---

¹ [The text fluctuates here. We have given that of Field, though neither it nor any of the other readings yields a satisfactory sense.

Field's text is, συντιθεὶς τὰ μέλη, αὐτὸς αὐτοῖς ζωὴν χορηγεῖ. Another text, attested by three MSS., has συντιθεὶς τὰ μέσα, αὐτὸς αὐτοῖς ζωὴν χορηγεῖ. Savile's text, supported by three MSS., has καὶ ἐκεῖνος μὲν συντιθεῖ τὰ ὀστᾶ, αὐτὸς δὲ ζωὴν χορηγεῖ. It will be noticed that this same expression occurs a little above, followed by a clause like that which follows here. — G. A.]

² "What sacrifice do they believe they celebrate who are rivals of the Priests?" "If such men were even killed for confession of the Christian name, not even by their blood is this stain washed out. . . . He cannot be a Martyr, who is not in the Church." — St. Cyprian, *Treat.* v. 12, p. 141.

themselves up indiscriminately to the men who are dividing the Church. For if on the one hand those men have doctrines also contrary to ours, then on that account further it is not right to mix with them: if, on the other hand, they hold the same opinions, the reason for not mixing with them is greater still. And why so? Because then the disease is from lust of authority. Know ye not what was the fate of Korah, Dathan, and Abiram? (Num. xvi. 1–35.) Of them only did I say? Was it not also of them that were with them? What wilt thou say? Shall it be said, "Their faith is the same, they are orthodox as well as we"? If so, why then are they not with us? There is "one Lord, one faith, one baptism." If their cause is right, then is ours wrong; if ours is right, then is theirs wrong. "Children," saith he, "tossed to and fro, and carried about with every wind." Tell me, dost thou think this is enough, to say that they are orthodox? Is then the ordination[1] of clergy[2] past and done away? And what is the advantage of other things,[3] if this be not strictly observed? For as we must needs contend for the faith, so must we for this also. For if it is lawful for any one, according to the phrase of them of old, "to fill his hands,"[4] and to become a priest, let all approach to minister. In vain has this altar been raised, in vain the fullness of the Church, in vain the number of the priests. Let us take them away and destroy them. "God forbid!" ye will say. You are doing these things, and do ye say, "God forbid"? How say ye, "God forbid," when the very things are taking place? I speak and testify, not looking to my own interest, but to your salvation. But if any one be indifferent, he must see to it himself: if these things are a care to no one else, yet are they a care to me. "I planted," saith he, "Apollos watered, but God gave the increase." (1 Cor. iii. 6.) How shall we bear the ridicule of the Greeks? For if they reproach us on account of our heresies, what will they not say of these things? "If they have the same doctrines, if the same mysteries, wherefore does a ruler in one Church invade another? See ye," say they, "how all things amongst the Christians are full of vainglory? And there is ambition among them, and hypocrisy. Strip

them," say they, "of their numbers, and they are nothing. Cut out the disease, the corrupt multitude." Would ye have me tell what they say of our city, how they accuse us on the score of our easy compliances? Any one, say they, that chooses may find followers, and would never be at a loss for them. Oh, what a sneer is that, what a disgrace are these things! And yet the sneer is one thing, the disgrace is another. If any amongst us are convicted of deeds the most disgraceful, and are about to meet with some penalty, great is the alarm, great is the fear on all sides, lest he should start away, people say, and join the other side. Yea, let such an one start away ten thousand times, and let him join them. And I speak not only of those who have sinned, but if there be any one free from offense, and he has a mind to depart, let him depart. I am grieved indeed at it, and bewail and lament it, and am cut to the very heart, as though I were being deprived of one of my own limbs; and yet I am not so grieved, as to be compelled to do anything wrong through such fear as this. We have "not lordship over your faith" (2 Cor. i. 24), beloved, nor command we these things as your lords and masters. We are appointed for the teaching of the word, not for power, nor for absolute authority. We hold the place of counselors to advise you. The counselor speaks his own sentiments, not forcing the hearer, but leaving him full master of his choice upon what is said; in this case alone is he blameable, if he fail to utter the things which present themselves. For this cause do we also say these things, these things do we assert, that it may not be in your power in that day to say, "No one told us, no one gave us commandment, we were ignorant, we thought it was no sin at all." Therefore I assert and protest, that to make a schism in the Church is no less an evil than to fall into heresy. Tell me, suppose a subject of some king, though he did not join himself to another king, nor give himself to any other, yet should take and keep hold of his king's royal purple, and should tear it all from its clasp, and rend it into many shreds; would he suffer less punishment than those who join themselves to the service of another? And what, if withal he were to seize the king himself by the throat and slay him, and tear his body limb from limb, what punishment could he undergo, that should be equal to his deserts? Now if in doing this toward a king, his fellow-servant, he would be committing an act too great for any punishment to reach; of what hell shall not he be worthy who slays Christ, and plucks Him limb from limb? of that one which is threatened? No, I think not, but of another far more dreadful.

Speak, ye women, that are present, — for this

---

[1] [See Bingham, Ant. Bk. iv. ch. vi. sec. 11.— G. A.]

[2] χειροτονίας. At this time there were two orthodox successions in Antioch, that of Paulinus and Evagrius, who were successively representatives of the old line which the Arians had dispossessed, and which Western Christendom supported; and that of Meletius and Flavian, to which St. Chrysostom adhered, and the Eastern Church generally, being the Arian succession conformed to orthodoxy. The schism was terminated A.D. 392, on the death of Evagrius, though his party continued for twenty years longer.

[3] [τῶν ἄλλων, wanting in the text of Field, is attested by four good authorities, and yields the only sense that suits the context. — G. A.]

[4] Exodus xxix. 9. Our translation has, "Thou shalt consecrate Aaron and his sons"; the margin gives the literal rendering, "Thou shalt fill the hands of Aaron."

generally is a failing of women,[1]—relate to them that are absent this similitude which I have made ; startle them. If any think to grieve me and thus to have their revenge, let them be well aware that they do these things in vain. For if thou wishest to revenge thyself on me, I will give thee a method by which thou mayest take vengeance without injury to thyself; or rather without injury it is not possible to revenge thyself, but at all events with less injury. Buffet me, woman, spit upon me, when thou meetest me in the public way, and aim blows at me. Dost thou shudder at hearing this? When I bid thee buffet me, dost thou shudder, and dost thou tear thy Lord and Master and not shudder? Dost thou pluck asunder the limbs of thy Lord and Master, and not tremble? The Church is our Father's house. " There is one body, and one Spirit." But dost thou wish to revenge thyself on me? Yet stop at me. Why dost thou revenge thyself on Christ in my stead? nay, rather, why kick against the nails? In no case indeed is revenge good and right, but to assault one when another has done the wrong is far worse. Is it I that wronged you? Why then inflict pain on Him who hath not wronged you? This is the very extreme of madness. I speak not in irony what I am about to say, nor without purpose, but as I really think and as I feel. I would that every one of those who with you are exasperated against me, and who by this exasperation are injuring themselves, and departing elsewhere, would direct his blows at me in my very face, would strip me and scourge me, be his charge against me just or unjust, and let loose his wrath upon me, rather than that they should dare to commit what they now dare. If this were done, it were nothing ; nothing, that a man who is a mere nothing and of no account whatever, should be so treated. And besides, I, the wronged and injured person, might call upon God, and He might forgive you your sins. Not because I have so great confidence ; but because when he who has been wronged, entreats for him who has done the wrong, he gains great confidence. " If one man sin against another," it is said, " then shall they pray for him "[2] (1 Sam. ii. 25) ; and if I were unable, I might seek for

other holy men, and entreat them, and they might do it. But now whom shall we even entreat, when God is outraged by us?

Mark the consistency; for of those who belong to this Church, some never approach to communicate at all, or but once in the year, and then without purpose, and just as it may happen ; others more regularly indeed, yet they too carelessly and without purpose, and while engaged in conversation, and trifling about nothing : whilst those who, forsooth, seem to be in earnest, these are the very persons who work this mischief. Yet surely, if it is for these things ye are in earnest, it were better that ye also were in the ranks of the indifferent ; or rather it were better still, that neither they should be indifferent, nor you such as ye are. I speak not of you that are present, but of those who are deserting from us. The act is adultery. And if ye bear not to hear these things of them, neither should ye of us. There must be breach of the law either on the one side or the other. If then thou hast these suspicions concerning me, I am ready to retire from my office, and resign it to whomsoever ye may choose. Only let the Church be one. But if I have been lawfully made and consecrated, entreat those who have contrary to the law mounted the episcopal throne to resign it.

These things I have said, not as dictating to you, but only to secure and protect you. Since every one of you is come to age, and will have to give account of the things which he has done, I entreat you not to cast the whole matter on us, and consider yourselves to be irresponsible, that ye may not go on fruitlessly deceiving yourselves, and at last bewail it. An account indeed we shall have to give of your souls ; but it will be when we have been wanting on our part, when we fail to exhort, when we fail to admonish, when we fail to protest. But after these words, allow even me to say that " I am pure from the blood of all men " (Acts xx. 26) ; and that " God will deliver my soul." (Ezek. iii. 19, 21.) Say what ye will, give a just cause why ye depart, and I will answer you. But no, ye will not state it. Wherefore I entreat you, endeavor henceforward both to resist nobly and to bring back those who have seceded, that we may with one accord lift up thanksgiving to God ; for to Him belongs the glory for ever and ever. Amen.

---

[1] St. Chrysostom was eventually banished and brought to his end by the Empress Eudoxia. Women had taken a strong part with the Arians from the first, to which perhaps he alludes. When Arius began his heresy, he was joined by seven hundred single women. Epiphan. *Hær.* 69, 3; vid. also Socr. ii. 2, *of the Court*, Greg. Naz. *Or.* 48, of Constantinople, &c., &c.

[2] [This is the reading of the Septuagint, as follows: ἂν εἰς ἄνθρωπόν τις ἁμάρτῃ, προσεύξονται περὶ αὐτοῦ. The Hebrew, however,

is different, and reads, " If one man sin against another, God shall judge him; but if a man sin against the Lord, who shall entreat for him?" So the Rev. Ver. — G. A.]

HOMILY XII.

EPHESIANS iv. 17.

"This I say therefore, and testify in the Lord, that ye no longer walk as the Gentiles also walk, in the vanity of their mind, being darkened in their understanding."

IT is the duty of the teacher to build up and restore the souls of his disciples, not only by counseling and instructing them, but also by alarming them, and delivering them up to God. For when the words spoken by men as coming from fellow-servants are not sufficient to kindle the soul, it then becomes necessary to make over the case to God. This accordingly Paul does also; for having discoursed[1] concerning lowliness, and concerning unity, and concerning our duty not to rise up one against another, hear what he says. "This I say therefore, and testify in the Lord, that ye no longer walk as the Gentiles also walk." He does not say, "That ye henceforth walk not as ye are now walking," for that expression would have struck too hard. But he plainly indicates the same thing, only he brings his example from others. And so in writing to the Thessalonians, he does this very same thing, where he says, "Not in the passion of lust, even as the Gentiles which know not God." (1 Thess. iv. 5.) Ye differ from them, he means to say, in doctrine, but that is wholly God's work: what I require on your part, is the life and the course of behavior that is after God. This is your own. And I call the Lord to witness what I have said, that I have not shrunk, but have told you how ye ought to walk.

"In the vanity," saith he, "of their mind."

What is vanity of mind? It is the being busied about vain things. And what are those vain things, but all things in the present life? Of which the Preacher saith, "Vanity of vanities, all is vanity." (Eccles. i. 2.) But a man will say, If they be vain and vanity, wherefore were they made? If they are God's works, how are they vain? And great is the dispute concerning these things. But hearken, beloved: it is not the works of God which he calls vain; God forbid! The Heaven is not vain, the earth is not vain,—God forbid! — nor the sun, nor the moon and stars, nor our own body. No, all these are "very good." (Gen. i. 31.) But what is vain? Let us hear the Preacher himself, what he saith; "I planted me vineyards, I gat me men singers and women singers, I made me pools of water, I had great possession of herds and flocks, I gathered me also silver and gold, and I saw that these are vanity." (Eccles. ii. 4–8.) And again, "Vanity of vanities, all things are vanity." (Eccles. xii. 8.) Hear also what the Prophet saith, "He heapeth up riches, and knoweth not who shall gather them." (Ps. xxxix. 6.) Such is "vanity of vanities," your splendid buildings, your vast and overflowing riches, the herds of slaves that bustle along the public square, your pomp and vainglory, your high thoughts, and your ostentation.[2] For all these are vain; they came not from the hand of God, but are of our own creating. But why then are they vain? Because they have no useful end. Riches are vain when they are spent upon luxury; but they cease to be vain when they are "dispersed and given to the needy." (Ps. cxii. 9.) But when thou hast spent them upon luxury, let us look at the end of them, what it is; — grossness of body, flatulence, pantings, fullness of belly, heaviness of head, softness of flesh, feverishness, enervation; for as a man who shall draw into a leaking vessel labors in vain, so also does the one who lives in luxury and self-indulgence draw into a leaking vessel. But again, that is called "vain," which is expected indeed to contain something, but contains it not; — that which men call empty, as when they speak of "empty hopes." And generally that is called "vain," which is bare and purposeless, which is of no use. Let us see then whether all human things are not of this sort. "Let us eat and drink, for to-morrow we die." (1 Cor. xv. 32.) What then, tell me, is the end? Corruption. Let us put on clothing and raiment. And what is the result? Nothing. Such are the lives of the Greeks. They philosophized, but in vain. They made a show of a life of hardship, but of mere hardship, not looking to any beneficial end, but to vainglory, and to honor from the many. But what is the honor of the many? It is nothing, for if they themselves which render the honor perish, much more does the honor. He that renders honor to another, ought first to render it to himself; for if he gain not honor for him-

---

[1] Modern exegesis has made more logical analysis, and indicated more carefully and correctly the transitions from one thought or branch of the subject to another, than the ancient. Comp. Meyer, Lightfoot, Schaff, and especially the paragraphing of the Rev. Ver. On this passage Meyer says: The exhortation begun at vv. 1–3, and interrupted by the digression vv. 4–16, is here resumed by the οὖν, and the "walking worthily" of v. 1 is now followed up in the form, "that ye no longer walk as the Gentiles also walk," &c.— G. A.]

[2] ["'Vanity' here is rather the subjective sphere in which the walk of the other Gentiles takes place, namely, in nothingness of their thinking and willing (νοῦς), and is to be understood of the whole intellectual and moral character of heathenism."— Meyer. — G. A.]

self, how can he ever render it to another? Whereas now we seek even honors from vile and despicable characters, themselves dishonorable, and objects of reproach. What kind of honor then is this? Perceive ye, how that all things are "vanity of vanities"? Therefore, saith he, "in the vanity of their mind."

But further, is not their religion of this sort, wood and stone? He hath made the sun to shine for a lamp to light us. Who will worship his own lamp? The sun supplies us with light, but where he cannot, a lamp can do it. Then why not worship thy lamp? "Nay," one will say, "I worship the fire." Oh, how ridiculous! So great is the absurdity, and yet look again at another absurdity. Why extinguish the object of thy worship? Why destroy, why annihilate thy god? Wherefore dost thou not suffer thy house to be filled with him? For if the fire be god, let him feed upon thy body. Put not thy god under the bottom of thy kettle, or thy cauldron.[1] Bring him into thy inner chambers, bring him within thy silken draperies. Whereas not only dost thou not bring him in, but if by any accident he has found entrance, thou drivest him out from every place, thou callest everybody together, and, as though some wild beast had entered, thou weepest and wailest, and callest the presence of thy god an overwhelming calamity. I have a God, and I do all I can to enshrine Him in my bosom, and I deem it my true bliss, not when He visits my dwelling, but when I can draw Him even to my heart. Do thou too draw the fire to thine heart. This is folly and vanity. Fire is good for use, not for adoration; good for ministration and for service, to be my slave, not to be my master. It was made for me, not I for it. If thou art a worshiper of fire, why recline upon thy couch thyself, and order thy cook to stand before thy god? Take up the art of cookery thyself, become a baker if thou wilt, or a coppersmith, for nothing can be more honorable than these arts, since these are they that thy god visits. Why deem that art a disgrace, where thy god is all in all? Why commit it to thy slaves, and not be ambitious of it thyself? Fire is good, inasmuch as it is the work of a good Creator, but it is not God. It is the work of God, it was not called God. Seest thou not how ungovernable is its nature; — how when it lays hold on a building it stops nowhere? But if it seizes anything continuous, it destroys all; and, except the hands of workmen or others quench its fury, it knows not friends nor foes, but deals with all alike. Is this then your god, and are ye not ashamed? Well indeed does he say, "in the vanity of their mind."

But the sun, they say, is God. Tell me, how and wherefore. Is it that he sheds abundance of light? Yet dost thou not see him overcome by clouds, and in bondage to the necessity of nature, and eclipsed, and hidden by the moon? And yet the cloud is weaker than the sun; but still it often gains the mastery of him. And this indeed is the work of God's wisdom. God must needs be all sufficient: but the sun needs many things; and this is not like a god. For he requires air to shine in, and that, too, thin air; since the air, when it is greatly condensed, suffers not the rays to pass through it. He requires also water, and other restraining power, to prevent him from consuming. For were it not that fountains, and lakes, and rivers, and seas, formed some moisture by the emission of their vapors, there would be nothing to prevent an universal conflagration. Dost thou see then, say ye, that he is a god? What folly, what madness! A god, say ye, because he has power to do harm. Nay, rather, for this very reason is he no god, because where he does harm he needs nothing; whereas, where he does good, he requires many things besides. Now to do harm, is foreign to God's nature; to do good, is His property. Where then the reverse is the case, how can he be God? Seest thou not that poisonous drugs injure, and need nothing; but when they are to do good, need many things? For thy sake then is he such as he is, both good, and powerless; good, that thou mayest acknowledge his Lord; and powerless, that thou mayest not say that he is lord. "But," say they, "he nourishes the plants and the seeds." What then, at that rate is not the very dung a god? for even that also nourishes. And why not at that rate the scythe as well, and the hands of the husbandman? Prove to me that the sun alone does the work of nourishing without needing the help of either earth, or water, or tillage; but let the seeds be sown, and let him shed forth his rays, and produce the ears of corn. But now if this work be not his alone, but that of the rains also, wherefore is not the water a god also? But of this I speak not yet. Why is not the earth too a god, and why not the dung, and the hoe? Shall we then, tell me, worship all? Alas, what trifling! And indeed rather might the ear of corn be produced without sun, than without earth and water; and so with plants and all other things. Were there no earth, none of these things could ever appear. And if any one, as children and women do, were to put some earth into a pot, and to fill up the pot with a quantity of dung, and to place it under the roof, plants, though they may be weak ones, will be produced from it. So that the contribution of the earth and of the dung is greater, and these therefore we ought to worship rather than the

---

sun. He requires the sky, he requires the air, he requires these waters, to prevent his doing harm, to be as bridles to curb the fierceness of his power, and to restrain him from letting loose his rays over the world, like some furious horse. And now tell me, where is he at night? Whither has your god taken his departure? For this is not like a god, to be circumscribed and limited. This is in fact the property of bodies only. But, say they, there is some sort of power residing in him, and he has motion. Is this power then, I pray you, itself God? Why then is it insufficient in itself, and why does it not restrain the fire? For again, I come to the same argument. But what is that power? Is it productive of light, or does it by the sun give light, though of itself possessing none of these qualities? If so, then is the sun superior to it. How far shall we unwind this maze?

Again, what is water? is not that too, they say, a god? This again is a matter of truly absurd disputation. Is that not a god, they say, which we make use of for so many purposes? And so again, in like manner, of the earth. Truly "they walk in the vanity of their mind, being darkened in their understanding."

But these words he is now using concerning life and conduct. The Greeks are fornicators and adulterers. Of course. They who paint to themselves such gods as these,[1] will naturally do all these things; and if they can but escape the eyes of men, there is no one to restrain them. For what will avail the argument of a resurrection, if it appear to them a mere fable? Yea, and what that of the torments of hell? — they too are but a fable. And mark the Satanic notion. When they are told of gods who are for-nicators, they deny that these are fables, but believe them. Yet whenever any shall discourse to them of punishment, "these," they say, "are poets, men who turn everything into fable, that man's happy condition may be on all sides overturned."

But the philosophers, it is said, discovered something truly grand, and far better than these. How? They who introduced fate, and who tell us that nothing is providential, and that there is no one to care for anything, but that all things consist of atoms?[2] Or, others again who say that God is a body? Or who, tell me, are they? Are they those who would turn the souls of men into the souls of dogs, and would persuade mankind that one was once a dog, and a lion, and a fish? How long will ye go on and never cease trifling, "being darkened in the understanding"? for they say and do all things as though they

were indeed in the dark, both in those things which concern doctrine, and those which concern life and conduct; for the man who is in darkness sees none of the things which lie before him, but oftentimes when he sees a rope, he will take it for a live serpent;[3] or again, if he is caught by a hedge, he will think that a man or an evil spirit has hold of him, and great is the alarm, and great the perturbation. Such as these are the things they fear. "There were they in great fear," it saith, "where no fear was" (Ps. liii. 5); but the things which they ought to fear, these they fear not. But just as children in their nurses' arms thrust their hands incautiously into the fire, and boldly into the candle also, and yet are scared at a man clothed in sackcloth; just so these Greeks, as if they were really always children, (as some one also amongst themselves has said,[4] the Greeks are always children,) fear those things that are no sins, such as filthiness of the body, the pollution of a funeral,[5] a bed, or the keeping of days, and the like: whereas those which are really sins, unnatural lust, adultery, fornication, of these they make no account at all. No, you may see a man washing himself from the pollution of a dead body, but from dead works, never; and, again, spending much zeal in the pursuit of riches, and yet supposing the whole is undone by the crowing of a single cock. "So darkened are they in their understanding." Their soul is filled with all sorts of terrors. For instance: "Such a person," one will say, "was the first who met me, as I was going out of the house"; of course ten thousand evils must certainly ensue. At another time, "the wretch of a servant in giving me my shoes,[6] held out the left shoe first," — terrible mishaps and mischiefs! "I myself in coming out set forth with the left foot foremost"; and this too is a token of misfortune. And these are the evils that occur about the house. Then, as I go out, my right eye shoots up from beneath. This is a sure sign of tears. Again the women, when the reeds strike against the standards, and ring, or when they themselves are scratched by the shuttle, turn this also into a sign. And again, when they strike the web with the shuttle, and do it with some vehemence, and then the reeds on the top from the intensity of the blow strike against the standards and ring, this again they make a sign, and ten thousand things besides, deserving of ridicule. And so if an ass should bray, or a

---

[1] [See Schaff's *History of the Christian Church*, Vol. I., pp. 72–74, with Literature there noted. — G. A.]

[2] [On Democritus and Leucippus, founders of the Atomistic philosophy, see Ueberweg's *Hist. of Philosophy* (Amer. ed.), Vol. I., pp. 67–71; on Epicurus, Vol. I., pp. 205–207. — G. A.]

[3] This was the instance in the Schools. Vid. Sextus Empiricus, *Pyrrh. Hypot.* I. 33.

[4] The Egyptian priest to Solon. Plat. Tim. p. 22, B.

[5] Vid. Theophr. *Charact.* xvi. περὶ δεισιδαιμονίας; Guther *de Jure Manium in Græv. Thes.* 12, 1175; Hes. *Opp. et D.* 765, sqq.

[6] Vid. Plin. *N. H.* 2, 7; Juv. *Sat.* 6, 579. These and like superstitions are condemned also by Clem. Alex. *Strom.* vii. 4, pp. 842–844; St. Cyril of Jerus. iv. 37, and St. Aust. *de Doctr. Christ.* ii. 20, 21. This series, Vol. II., p. 545. See also St. Chrys. *ad Illum Catech.* ii. 5. This series, Vol. IX., p. 170. — G. A.

cock should crow, or a man should sneeze, or whatever else may happen, like men bound with ten thousand chains, or, as I was saying, like men confined in the dark, they suspect everything, and are more slavish than all the slaves in the world.[1]

But let it not be so with us. But scorning all these things, as men living in the light, and having our citizenship in Heaven, and having nothing in common with earth, let us regard but one thing as terrible, that is, sin, and offending against God. And if there be not this, let us scorn all the rest, and him that brought them in, the Devil. For these things let us give thanks to God. Let us be diligent, not only that we ourselves be never caught by this slavery, but if any of those who are dear to us have been caught, let us break his bonds asunder, let us release him from this most bitter and contemptible captivity, let us make him free and unshackled for his course toward Heaven, let us raise up his flagging wings, and teach him to be wise for life and doctrine's sake. Let us give thanks to God for all things. Let us beseech Him that He will not declare us unworthy of the gifts offered to us, and let us ourselves withal endeavor to contribute our own part, that we may teach not only by speaking, but by acting also. For thus shall we be able to attain His unnumbered blessings, of which God grant we may all be counted worthy, in Christ Jesus our Lord with whom, to the Father and the Holy Ghost together, be glory, might, and honor, now, henceforth, and for ever and ever. Amen.

HOMILY XIII.

EPHESIANS iv. 17–19.

"This I say therefore, and testify in the Lord, that ye no longer walk as the Gentiles also walk, in the vanity of their mind, being darkened in their understanding, alienated from the life of God, because of the ignorance that is in them, because of the hardening of their heart: who being past feeling, gave themselves up to lasciviousness, to work all uncleanness with greediness."

These words are not addressed to the Ephesians only, but are now addressed also to you; and that, not from me, but from Paul; or rather, neither from me nor from Paul, but from the grace of the Spirit. And we then ought so to feel, as though that grace itself were uttering them. And now hear what it saith. "This I say therefore, and testify in the Lord, that ye no longer walk as the Gentiles also walk, in the vanity of their mind, being darkened in their understanding, alienated from the life of God because of the ignorance that is in them, because of the hardening of their heart." If then it is ignorance, if it is hardening, why blame it?[2] if a man is ignorant, it were just, not that he should be ill-treated for it, nor be blamed, but that he should be informed of those things of which he is ignorant. But mark how at once he cuts them off from all excuse. "Who being past feeling," saith he, "gave themselves up to lasciviousness, to work all uncleanness with greediness; but ye did not so learn Christ."

Here he shows us, that the cause of their hardening was their way of life, and that their life was the consequence of their own indolence and want of feeling.

"Who being past feeling,"[3] saith he, "gave themselves up."

Whenever then ye hear, that "God gave them up unto a reprobate mind" (Rom. i. 28), remember this expression, that "they gave themselves up." If then they gave themselves over, how did God give them over? and if again God gave them over, how did they give themselves over? Thou seest the seeming contradiction. The word, "gave them over," then, means this, He permitted[4] them to be given over. Seest thou, that the impure life is the ground for like doctrines also? "Every one," saith the Lord, "that doeth ill hateth the light, and cometh not to the light." (John iii. 20.) For how could a profligate man, one more immersed in the practice of indiscriminate lewdness than the swine[5] that wallow in the mire, and who is a lover of money, and has not so much as any desire after temperance, enter upon a life like this? They made the thing, saith he, their "work."[6] Hence their "hardening" (ver. 19), hence the "darkness of their understand-

---

[1] [Compare Chrysostom's Commentary on Gal. i. 7. — G. A.]
[2] [" The *cause* of this estrangement of the Gentiles from the life of God is the *ignorance* which is in them through *hardening* of heart, consequently due to their own fault." — Meyer. — G. A.]

[3] [" The estrangement of the Gentiles from the divine life, indicated in the preceding verse, is here proved in conformity with *experience*." — Meyer. — G. A.]
[4] [" The word implies an *active giving up*, not mere permission." — Meyer, Ellicott, Thayer. — G. A.]
[5] [The word " swine " (χοίρων), though omitted from Field's text, is clearly attested, and cannot be omitted without leaving the sense difficult and obscure. — G. A.]
[6] [Namely, " to *work* all uncleanness," &c. — G. A.]

ing." There is such a thing as being in the dark, even while the light is shining, when the eyes are weak; and weak they become, either by the influx of ill humors, or by superabundance of rheum. And so surely is it also here; when the strong current of the affairs of this life overwhelms the perceptive power of the understanding, it is thrown into a state of darkness. And in the same way as if we were placed in the depths under water, we should be unable to see the sun through the quantity of water lying, like a sort of barrier, above us, so surely, in the eyes of the understanding also a blindness of the heart takes place, that is, an insensibility, whenever there is no fear to agitate the soul. "There is no fear of God," it saith, "before his eyes" (Ps. xxxvi. 1); and again, "The fool hath said in his heart, There is no God." (Ps. xiv. 1.) Now blindness arises from no other cause than from want of feeling; this clogs the channels; for whenever the fluids are curdled and collected into one place, the limb becomes dead and void of feeling; and though thou burn it, or cut it, or do what thou wilt with it, still it feels not. So is it also with those persons, when they have once given themselves over to lasciviousness: though thou apply the word to them like fire, or steel, yet nothing touches, nothing reaches them; their limb is utterly dead. And unless thou canst remove the insensibility, so as to touch the healthy members, everything thou doest is vain.

"With greediness," saith he.

Here he has most completely taken away their excuse; for it was in their power, if at least they chose it, not to be "greedy,"[1] nor to be "lascivious," nor gluttonous, and yet to enjoy their desires. It was in their power to partake in moderation[1] of riches, and even of pleasure and of luxury; but when they indulged the thing immoderately,[1] they destroyed all.

"To work all uncleanness," saith he.

Ye see how he strips them of all excuse by speaking of "working uncleanness." They did not sin, he means, by making a false step, but they worked out these horrid deeds, and they made the thing a matter of study. "All uncleanness"; uncleanness is all adultery, fornication, unnatural lust, envy, every kind of profligacy and lasciviousness.

Ver. 20, 21. "But ye did not so learn Christ," he continues, "if so be that ye heard Him, and were taught in Him even as truth is in Jesus."

The expression, "If so be that ye heard Him," is not that of one doubting, but of one even

strongly affirming: as he also speaks elsewhere, "If so be that it is a righteous thing with God to recompense affliction to them that afflict you." (2 Thess. i. 6.) That is to say, It was not for these purposes that "ye learned Christ."

Ver. 22. "That ye put away as concerning your former manner of life, the old man."

This then surely is to learn Christ, to live rightly; for he that lives wickedly knows not God, neither is known of Him; for hear what he saith elsewhere, "They profess that they know God, but by their works they deny Him." (Tit. i. 16.)

"As truth is in Jesus; that ye put away as concerning your former manner of life, the old man."

That is to say, It was not on these terms that thou enteredst into covenant. What is found among us is not vanity, but truth. As the doctrines are true, so is the life also. Sin is vanity and falsehood; but a right life is truth. For temperance is indeed truth, for it has a great end; whereas profligacy ends in nothing.

"Which waxeth corrupt," saith he, "after the lusts of deceit." As his lusts became corrupt, so himself also. How then do his lusts become corrupt? By death all things are dissolved; for hear the Prophet, how he saith, "In that very day his thoughts perish." (Ps. cxlvi. 4.) And not by death only, but by many things besides; for instance, beauty, at the advance of either disease or old age, withdraws and dies away, and suffers corruption. Bodily vigor again is destroyed by the same means; nor does luxury itself afford the same pleasure in old age, as is evident from the case of Barzillai:[2] the history, no doubt, ye know. Or again, in another sense, lust corrupts and destroys the old man; for as wool is destroyed by the very same means by which it is produced, so likewise is the old man. For love of glory destroys him, and pleasures will often destroy him, and "lust" will utterly "deceive" him. For this is not really pleasure but bitterness and deceit, all pretense and outward show. The surface, indeed, of the things is bright, but the things themselves are only full of misery and extreme wretchedness, and loathsomeness, and utter poverty. Take off the mask, and lay bare the true face, and thou shalt see the cheat, for cheat it is, when that which is, appears not, and that which is not, is displayed. And it is thus that impositions are effected.

The Apostle delineates for us four men.[3] Of these I shall give an explanation. In this place he mentions two, speaking thus, "Putting away

---

[1] [From the word used by Chrysostom as the antithesis of πλεο-νεκτεῖν, namely, μετὰ συμμετρίας (and compare ἀμέτρως below) it is evident he understood the phrase ἐν πλεονεξίᾳ, as the Revisers of Eng. Ver. do, "with greediness." But Meyer denies that the word πλεονεξία ever means anything but "covetousness" in the New Test. So also Ellicott. — G. A.]

[2] [And David said to Barzillai, "Come and I will sustain thee in Jerusalem." And Barzillai said unto the king, "I am this day fourscore years old: can thy servant taste what I eat or what I drink? can I hear any more the voice of singing men and singing women? wherefore then should thy servant be yet a burden unto my lord the king?" — 2 Sam. xix. 31-35. — G. A.]

[3] τέσσαρας ἀνθρώπους ὑπογράφει.

the old man, be ye renewed in the spirit of your mind, and put on the new man." And in the Epistle to the Romans, two more, as where he saith, " But I see a different law in my members warring against the law of my mind, and bringing me into captivity under the law of sin which is in my members." (Rom. vii. 23.) And these latter bear affinity to those former two, the " new man" to the " inner man," and the " old man " to the " outer man." However, three of these four were subject to corruption. Or rather there are three, the new man, the old, and this, man in his substance and nature.[1]

Ver. 23. " And that ye be renewed," saith he, " in the spirit of your mind."

In order that no one may suppose that, whereas he speaks of old and new, he is introducing a different person, observe his expression, " That ye be renewed." To be renewed is, when the selfsame thing which has grown old is renewed, changed from one thing into the other. So that the subject indeed is the same, but the change is in that which is accidental. Just as the body indeed is the same, and the change in that which is accidental, so is it here. How then is the renewal to take place? " In the spirit of your mind," saith he. Whosoever therefore has the Spirit, will perform no old deed, for the Spirit will not endure old deeds. " In the spirit," saith he, " of your mind," that is, in the spirit which is in your mind.[2]

Ver. 24. " And put on the new man."

Seest thou that the subject is one, but the clothing is twofold, that which is put off, and that which is put on? " The new man," he continues, " which after God hath been created in righteousness and holiness of truth." Now wherefore does he call virtue a man? And wherefore vice, a man? Because a man cannot be shown without acting ; so that these things, no less than nature, show a man, whether he be good or evil. Now as to undress one's self and to dress one's self is easy, so may we see it is with virtue and vice. The young man is strong ; wherefore let us also become strong for the performance of good actions. The young man has no wrinkle, therefore neither should we have. The young man wavers not, nor is he easily taken with diseases, therefore neither should we be.

Observe here how he calls this realizing of virtue, this bringing of it into being from nothing, a " creation." But what? was not that other former creation after God? No, in nowise, but after the devil. He is the sole creator of sin.

How is this? For man is created henceforth, not of water, nor of earth, but " in righteousness and holiness of truth." What is this? He straightway created him, he means, to be a son : for this takes place from Baptism. This it is which is the reality, " in righteousness and holiness of truth." There was of old a righteousness, there was likewise a holiness with the Jews. Yet was that righteousness not in truth, but in figure. For the being clean in body was a type of purity, not the truth of purity ; was a type of righteousness, not the truth of righteousness. " In righteousness," saith he, " and holiness," which are " of truth."

And this expression is used with reference to falsehood ; for many there are, who to them that are without, seem to be righteous, yet are false. Now by righteousness is meant universal virtue. For hearken to Christ, how He saith, " Except your righteousness shall exceed the righteousness of the scribes and Pharisees, ye shall in nowise enter into the kingdom of heaven." (Matt. v. 20.) And again, he is called righteous, who has no charge against him ; for so even in courts of justice we say that that man is righteous, who has been unrighteously treated, and has not done unrighteously in return. If therefore we also before the terrible Tribunal shall be able to appear righteous one towards another, we may meet with some lovingkindness. Toward God indeed it is impossible we should appear so, whatever we may have to show. For everywhere He overcometh in what is righteous, as the Prophet[3] also saith, " That Thou mightest prevail when Thou comest into judgment." But if we violate not what is righteous towards each other, then shall we be righteous. If we shall be able to show that we have been treated unrighteously, then shall we be righteous.

How does he say to them who are already clothed, " put on "? He is now speaking of that clothing which is from life and good works. Before, the clothing was from Baptism, whereas now it is from the daily life and from works ; no longer " after the lusts of deceit," but " after God." But what means the word " holy "? It is that which is pure, that which is due ; hence also we use the word of the last duty in the case of the departed, as much as to say, " I owe them nothing further, I have nothing else to answer

---

[1] μᾶλλον δὲ τρεῖς εἰσι, καινὸς καὶ παλαιὸς, καὶ οὗτος ὁ οὐσιώδης καὶ φυσικός.

[2] [Meyer takes a different view, and says: The Holy Spirit is never, in the New Test., designated in such a way that man appears as the subject of the Spirit (thus never: τὸ πνεῦμα ὑμῶν, and the like, or as here: τὸ πνεῦμα τοῦ νοὸς ὑμῶν). In the second place, the Apostle is here putting forward the moral self-activity of the Christian life, and hence had no occasion to introduce the point: " Through the Holy Spirit." Hence πνεῦμα here is the " human " spirit, the spirit by which your νοῦς is governed. Otherwise Ellicott: Divine spirit united with the human; and so he understands Meyer, but incorrectly. See Ellicott and Meyer in loc.—G. A.]

[3] [This passage in the Hebrew (Ps. li. 4) reads, " And (that thou mayest) be clear when thou judgest." In the Sept. it is: καὶ νικήσῃς ἐν τῷ κρίνεσθαί σε, which is followed by Paul in Rom. iii. 4 (except νικήσεις, fut. ind., instead of aor. subj.). We have given here the rendering of the Rev. Ver. of Rom. iii. 4.—G. A.]

for." Thus it is usual for us to say, " I have acquitted myself of all obligations,"[1] and the like, meaning, " I owe nothing more."

MORAL. Our part then is, never to put off the garment of righteousness, which also the Prophet calls, "the garment of salvation" (Isa. lxi. 10), that so we may be made like unto God. For He indeed hath put on righteousness. This garment let us put on. Now the word, "put on," plainly declares nothing else, than that we should never at all put it off. For hear the Prophet, where he saith, " He clothed himself also with cursing as with his garment, and it came into his inward parts." (Ps. cix. 18.) And again, "Who coverest Thyself with light as with a garment." (Ps. civ. 2.) And again, it is usual with us to speak concerning men, such an one has " put on " such an one. So then it is not for one day, nor for two, nor for three, but he would have us ever arrayed in virtue, and never stripped of this garment. For a man is not so disfigured when he is stripped of his clothing, as when he is stripped of his virtue. In the former case his fellow-servants behold his nakedness, in the latter his Lord and the Angels. If ever thou happen to see any one going out naked through the public square, tell me, art thou not distressed? When then thou goest about stripped of this garment, what shall we say? Seest not those beggars whom we are wont to call strollers,[2] how they roam about, how we pity even them? And yet nevertheless they are without excuse. We do not excuse them when they have lost their clothes by gaming ; and how then, if we lose this garment, shall God pardon us? For whenever the devil sees a man stripped of his virtue, he straightway disguises and disfigures his face, and wounds him, and drives him to great straits.

Let us strip ourselves of our riches, that we be not stripped of righteousness. The garb of wealth mars this garment. It is a robe of thorns. Thorns are of this nature ; and the more closely they are wrapped around us, the more naked are we made. Lasciviousness strips us of this garment ; for it is a fire, and the fire will consume this garment. Wealth is a moth ; and as the moth eats through all things alike, and spares not even silken garments, so does this also. All these therefore let us put off, that we may become righteous, that we may " put on the new man." Let us keep nothing old, nothing outward, nothing that is " corrupt." Virtue is

not toilsome, she is not difficult to attain. Dost thou not see them that are in the mountains? They forsake both houses, and wives,· and children, and all preëminence, and shut themselves away from the world, and clothe themselves in sackcloth, and strew ashes beneath them ; they wear collars hung about their necks, and have pent themselves up in a narrow cell.[3] Nor do they stop here, but torture themselves with fastings and continual hunger. Did I now enjoin you to do the like, would ye not all start away? Would ye not say, it is intolerable? But no, I say not that we must needs do anything like this : — I would fain indeed that it were so, still I lay down no law. What then? Enjoy thy baths, take care of thy body, and throw thyself freely into the world, and keep a household, have thy servants to wait on thee, and make free use of thy meats and drinks ! But everywhere drive out excess, for that it is which causes sin, and the same thing, whatever it be, if it becomes excessive, becomes a sin ; so that excess is nothing else than sin. For observe, when anger is excited above what is meet, then it rushes out into insult, then it commits every sort of injury ; so does inordinate passion for beauty, for riches, for glory, or for anything else. And tell me not, that indeed, those of whom I spoke were strong ; for many far weaker and richer, and more luxurious than thou art, have taken upon them that austere and rugged life. And why speak I of men? Damsels not yet twenty years old, who have spent their whole time in inner chambers, and in a delicate and effeminate mode of life, in inner chambers full of sweet ointments and perfumes, reclining on soft couches, themselves soft in their nature, and rendered yet more tender by their over indulgence, who all the day long have had no other business than to adorn themselves, to wear jewels, and to enjoy every luxury, who never waited on themselves, but had numerous handmaids standing beside them, who wore soft raiment softer than their skin, fine linen and delicate, who reveled continually in roses and such like sweet odors, — yea, these very ones, in a moment, seized with Christ's flame, have put off all that indolence and even their very nature, have forgotten their delicateness and youth, and like so many noble wrestlers, have stripped themselves of that soft clothing, and rushed into the midst of the contest. And perhaps I shall appear to be telling things incredible, yet nevertheless are they true. These then, these very tender damsels, as I myself have heard, have brought themselves to such a degree of severe training, that they will wrap the coars-

---

[1] ἀφωσιωσάμην.

[2] λώπαγας. The word occurs also in the *Constit. Apost.* viii. 32 [along with such words as βλάξ, " dolt "; μάγος, " sorcerer "; μάντις, " soothsayer "; θηρεπῳδός, " beast-charmer "; ὀχλαγωγός, " mob-leader "; περιάμματα ποιῶν, " amulet-maker."— G. A.]. Its derivation is somewhat uncertain. [Zonaras (Constantinople, 12 cent.), in his Lexicon, gives among other definitions, αὐλητής, " flute-player "; so also Eustathius (Constantinople, d. 1198), in his famous commentary on Homer, Il. 2, 776, defines it, from the fact that λῶτος sometimes means a " flute." But this derivation is questioned.— G. A.] The persons denoted by it were wandering musicians or buffoons.

[3] [This reference to the Monks in the mountains (in the neighborhood of Antioch) is one of the indications that these Homilies on Ephesians were delivered while Chrysostom was still at Antioch, and before his elevation to the archbishopric of Constantinople. Compare also Hom. vi. on Ephesians. — G. A.]

est horsehair about their own naked bodies, and go with those tender soles unsandaled, and will lie upon a bed of leaves : nay more, that they watch the greater part of the night, and that they take no heed of perfumes nor of any other of their old delights, but will even let their head, once so carefully dressed, go without special care, with the hair just plainly and simply bound up, so as not to fall into unseemliness. And their only meal is in the evening, a meal not even of herbs nor of bread, but of flour and beans and pulse and olives and figs. They spin without intermission, and labor far harder than their handmaids at home. What more? they will take upon them to wait upon women who are sick, carrying their beds, and washing their feet. Nay, many of them even cook. So great is the power of the flame of Christ ; so far does their zeal surpass their very nature.

However, I demand nothing like this of you, seeing ye have a mind to be outstripped by women. Yet at least, if there be any tasks not too laborious, at least perform these : restrain the rude hand, and the incontinent eye. What is there, tell me, so hard, what so difficult? Do what is just and right, wrong no man, be ye poor or rich, shopkeepers or hired servants ; for unrighteousness may extend even to the poor. Or see ye not how many broils these engage in, and turn all things upside down? Marry freely, and have children. Paul also gave charge to such, to such he wrote. Is that struggle I spoke of too great, and the rock too lofty, and its top too nigh unto Heaven, and art thou unable to attain to such an height? At least then lay hold on lesser things, and aim at those which are lower. Hast thou not courage to get rid of thine own riches? At least then forbear to seize on the things of others, and to do them wrong. Art thou unable to fast? At least then give not thyself to self-indulgence. Art thou unable to lie upon a bed of leaves? Still, prepare not for yourselves couches inlaid with silver ; but use a couch and coverings formed not for display, but for refreshment ; not couches of ivory. Make thyself small. Why fill thy vessel with overwhelming cargoes? If thou be lightly equipped, thou shalt have nothing to fear, no envy, no robbers, no liers in wait. For indeed thou art not so rich in money as thou art in cares. Thou aboundest not so much in possessions, as in anxieties and in perils, "which bring in many temptations and lusts." (1 Tim. vi. 9.) These things they endure, who desire to gain great possessions. I say not, minister unto the sick ; yet, at least, bid thy servant do it. Seest thou then how that this is no toilsome task? No, for how can it be, when tender damsels surpass us by so great a distance? Let us be ashamed of ourselves, I entreat you ; for in worldly

matters, to be sure, we in no point yield to them, neither in wars, nor in games ; but in the spiritual contest they get the advantage of us, and are the first to seize the prize, and soar higher, like so many eagles :[1] whilst we, like jackdaws, are ever living in the steam and smoke ; for truly is it the business of jackdaws, and of greedy dogs, to be setting one's thoughts upon caterers and cooks. Hearken about the women of old ; they were great characters, great women and admirable ; such were Sarah, Rebekah, Rachel, Deborah, and Hannah ; and such there were also in the days of Christ. Yet did they in no case outstrip the men, but occupied the second rank. But now it is the very contrary ; women outstrip and eclipse us. How contemptible ! What a shame is this ! We hold the place of the head, and are surpassed by the body. We are ordained to rule over them ; not merely that we may rule, but that we may rule in goodness also ; for he that ruleth, ought especially to rule in this respect, by excelling in virtue ; whereas if he is surpassed, he is no longer ruler.[2] Perceive ye how great is the power of Christ's coming? how He dissolved the curse? For indeed there are more virgins than before among women, there is more modesty in those virgins, and there are more widows. No woman would lightly utter so much as an unseemly word. Wherefore then, tell me, dost thou use filthy speech? For tell me not that they were virgins in despondency or despair.

The sex is fond of ornament, and it has this failing. Yet even in this you husbands surpass them, who pride yourselves even upon them, as your own proper ornament ; for I do not think that the wife is so ostentatious of her own jewels, as the husband is of those of his wife. He is not so proud of his own golden girdle, as he is of his wife's wearing jewels of gold. So that even of this you are the causes, who light the spark and kindle up the flame. But what is more, it is not so great a sin in a woman as in a man. Thou art ordained to regulate her ; in every way thou claimest to have the preëminence. Show her then in this also, that thou takest no interest in this costliness of hers, by thine own apparel. It is more suitable for a woman to adorn herself, than for a man. If then thou escape not the temptation, how shall she escape it? They have moreover their share of vainglory, but this is common to them with men. They are in a measure passionate, and this again is common to them with men. But as to those things wherein they excel, these are

---

[1] [This passage is so like a passage in one of Pindar's Nemean odes that some have thought Chrysostom must have had that in mind. Pind. *Nem.* 3. 138: ἔστι δ' αἰετὸς ὠκὺς ἐν πετανοῖς, ὃς ἔλαβεν αἶψα, τηλόθε μεταμαιόμενος, δαφοινὸν ἄγραν ποσίν · κραγέται δὲ κολοιοὶ ταπεινὰ νέμονται. — G. A.]

[2] [Compare Carlyle's lecture on Cromwell and Napoleon in *Heroes and Hero-Worship.* — G. A.]

no longer common to them with men; their sanctity, I mean, their fervency, their devotion, their love towards Christ. Wherefore then, one may say, did Paul exclude them from the teacher's seat? And here again is a proof how great a distance they were from the men, and that the women of those days were great. For, tell me, while Paul was teaching, or Peter, or those saints of old, had it been right that a woman should intrude into the office? Whereas we have gone on till we have come so debased, that it is worthy of question, why women are not teachers. So truly have we come to the same weakness as they. These things I have said not from any desire to elate them, but to shame ourselves, to chastise, and to admonish us, that so we may resume the authority that belongs to us, not inasmuch as we are greater in size, but because of our foresight, our protection of them, and our virtue. For thus shall the body also be in the order which befits it, when it has the best head to rule. And God grant that all, both wives and husbands, may live according to His good pleasure, that we may all in that terrible day be counted worthy to enjoy the lovingkindness of our Master, and to attain those good things which are promised in Jesus Christ our Lord, with whom to the Father, together with the Holy Ghost, be glory, might, and honor, now and forever and ever. Amen.

HOMILY XIV.

Ephesians iv. 25–27.

" Wherefore, putting away falsehood, speak ye truth each one with his neighbor; for we are members one of another. Be ye angry, and sin not; let not the sun go down upon your wrath: neither give place to the devil."

Having spoken of the "old man" generally, he next draws him also in detail;[1] for this kind of teaching is more easily learned when we learn by particulars. And what saith he? "Wherefore, putting away falsehood." What sort of falsehood? Idols does he mean? Surely not; not indeed but that they are falsehood also. However, he is not now speaking of them, because these persons had nothing to do with them; but he is speaking of that which passes between one man and another, meaning that which is deceitful and false. "Speak ye truth, each one," saith he, "with his neighbor"; then what is more touching to the conscience[2] still, "because we are members one of another." Let no man deceive his neighbor. As the Psalmist says here and there; "With flattering lip and with a double heart do they speak." (Ps. xii. 2.) For there is nothing, no, nothing so productive of enmity as deceit and guile.

Observe how everywhere he shames them by this similitude of the body. Let not the eye, saith he, lie to the foot, nor the foot to the eye. For example, if there shall be a deep pit, and then by having reeds laid across upon the mouth of it upon the earth, and yet concealed under earth, it shall by its appearance furnish to the eye an expectation of solid ground, will not the eye use the foot, and discover whether it yields[3] and is hollow underneath, or whether it is firm and resists?[4] Will the foot tell a lie, and not report the truth as it is? And what again? If the eye were to spy a serpent or a wild beast, will it lie to the foot? Will it not at once inform it, and the foot thus informed by it refrain from going on? And what again, when neither the foot nor the eye shall know how to distinguish, but all shall depend upon the smelling, as, for example, whether a drug be deadly or not; will the smelling lie to the mouth? And why not? Because it will be destroying itself also. But it tells the truth as it appears to itself. And what again? Will the tongue lie to the stomach? Does it not, when a thing is bitter, reject it, and, if it is sweet, pass it on? Observe ministration, and interchange of service; observe a provident care arising from truth, and, as one might say, spontaneously from the heart. So surely should it be with us also; let us not lie, since we are "members one of another." This is a sure token of friendship; whereas the contrary is of enmity. What then, thou wilt ask, if a man shall use treachery against thee? Hearken to the truth. If he use treachery, he is not a member; whereas he saith, "lie not towards the members."

"Be ye angry, and sin not."

Observe his wisdom. He both speaks to prevent our sinning, and, if we do not listen, still

---

[1] [" And the *first* exhortation here was suggested by the immediately preceding ἀλήθεια. The figurative form of the precept also (ἀποθέμενοι, 'putting off ') is an echo from what precedes." — Meyer. — G. A.]

[2] ["'Members' one of another, and to 'lie' to one another, — how contradictory!" — Meyer. — G. A.]

[3] [εἴκει, Field's emendation for the reading εἰκῆ of the MSS. He cites the phrase τὸ εἶκον καὶ μὴ ἀντιτυποῦν from Plato, *Cratylus*, 420 D. — G. A.]

[4] ἀντιτυπεῖ.

does not forsake us; for his fatherly compassion does not desert him. For just as the physician prescribes to the sick what he must do, and if he does not submit to it, still does not treat him with contempt, but proceeding to add what advice he can by persuasion, again goes on with the cure; so also does Paul. For he indeed who does otherwise, aims only at reputation, and is annoyed at being disregarded; whereas he who on all occasions aims at the recovery of the patient, has this single object in view, how he may restore the patient, and raise him up again. This then is what Paul is doing. He has said, "Lie not." Yet if ever lying should produce anger,[1] he goes on again to cure this also. For what saith he? "Be ye angry, and sin not." It were good indeed never to be angry. Yet if ever any one should fall into passion, still let him not fall into so great a degree. "For let not the sun," saith he, "go down upon your wrath." Wouldest thou have thy fill of anger? One hour, or two, or three, is enough for thee; let not the sun depart, and leave you both at enmity. It was of God's goodness that he rose; let him not depart, having shone on unworthy men. For if the Lord of His great goodness sent him, and hath Himself forgiven thee thy sins, and yet thou forgivest not thy neighbor, look, how great an evil is this! And there is yet another besides this. The blessed Paul dreads the night,[2] lest overtaking in solitude him that was wronged, still burning with anger, it should again kindle up the fire. For as long as there are many things in the daytime to banish it, thou art free to indulge it; but as soon as ever the evening comes on, be reconciled, extinguish the evil whilst it is yet fresh; for should night overtake it, the morrow will not avail to extinguish the further evil which will have been collected in the night. Nay, even though thou shouldest cut off the greater portion, and yet not be able to cut off the whole, it will again supply from what is left for the following night, to make the blaze more violent. And just as, should the sun be unable by the heat of the day to soften and disperse that part of the air which has been during the night condensed into cloud, it affords material

for a tempest, night overtaking the remainder, and feeding it again with fresh vapors: so also is it in the case of anger.

"Neither give place to the devil."

So then to be at war with one another, is "to give place to the devil"; for, whereas we had need to be all in close array, and to make our stand against him, we have relaxed our enmity against him, and are giving the signal for turning against each other; for never has the devil such *place* as in our enmities.[3] Numberless are the evils thence produced. And as stones in a building, so long as they are closely fitted together and leave no interstice, will stand firm, while if there is but a single needle's passage through, or a crevice no broader than a hair, this destroys and ruins all; so is it with the devil. So long indeed as we are closely set and compacted together, he cannot introduce one of his wiles; but when he causes us to relax a little, he rushes in like a torrent. In every case he needs only a beginning, and this is the thing which it is difficult to accomplish; but this done, he makes room on all sides for himself. For henceforth he opens the ear to slanders, and they who speak lies are the more trusted: they have enmity which plays the advocate, not truth which judges justly. And as, where friendship[4] is, even those evils which are true appear false, so where there is enmity, even the false appear true. There is a different mind, a different tribunal, which does not hear fairly, but with great bias and partiality. As, in a balance, if lead is cast into the scale, it will drag down the whole; so is it also here, only that the weight of enmity is far heavier than any lead. Wherefore, let us, I beseech you, do all we can to extinguish our enmities before the going down of the sun. For if you fail to master it on the very first day, both on the following, and oftentimes even for a year, you will be protracting it, and the enmity will thenceforward augment itself, and require nothing to aid it. For by causing us to suspect that words spoken in one sense were meant in another, and gestures also, and everything, it infuriates and exasperates us, and makes us more distempered than madmen, not enduring either to utter a name, or to hear it, but saying everything in invective and abuse. How then are we to allay this passion? How shall we extinguish the flame? By reflecting on our own sins, and how much we have to answer for to God; by reflecting that we are wreaking vengeance, not on an enemy, but on ourselves; by reflecting that we are delighting the devil, that we are strengthening our enemy, our real

---

[1] [This seems to be a correct account of the connection, but the exact force of the first imperative it is not easy to determine. Winer (Grammar of N. T., Thayer's translation, pp. 311, 312) takes it *permissively:* Be angry (I give you leave), but do not sin. He cites in proof Jer. x. 24, which, however, can be otherwise explained, namely, as the imperative of request, used in prayer. Compare the Lord's prayer. Meyer says it does not seem logical to connect two imperatives by καὶ unless they are taken in the *same* sense. If the first imperative were *permissive*, the combination would be *exceptive*, and ἀλλά, μόνον or πλήν (Jer. x. 24) would be required. Both imperatives then are jussive, and there is an anger which a man not only may, but *ought*, to feel. So Ellicott and Riddle. — G. A.]

[2] ["There does not appear any allusion to the possible effect of *night* upon anger, as Chrysostom here, and Theophylact also." — Ellicott. The parallel Pythagorean custom is cited by Ellicott (Hammond and Wetstein): "If they were ever carried away by anger into railing, before the setting of the sun they gave the right hand to each other, embraced each other, and were reconciled." — G. A.]

[3] [This reference to church life is not implied in the context. He follows up what he said before by saying, Give not to the devil opportunity for being active by an angry state of mind. — G. A.]

[4] [Compare Goethe:
Die Freundschaft ist gerecht. Sie kann allein,
Den ganzen Umfang seines Werths erkennen. — G. A.]

enemy, and that for him we are doing wrong to our own members. Wouldest thou be revengeful and be at enmity? Be at enmity, but be so with the devil, and not with a member of thine own. For this purpose it is that God hath armed us with anger, not that we should thrust the sword against our own bodies, but that we should baptize [1] the whole blade in the devil's breast. There bury the sword up to the hilt; yea, if thou wilt, hilt and all, and never draw it out again, but add yet another and another. And this actually comes to pass when we are merciful to those of our own spiritual family and peaceably disposed one towards another. Perish money, perish glory and reputation; mine own member is dearer to me than they all. Thus let us say to ourselves; let us not do violence to our own nature to gain wealth, to obtain glory.

Ver. 28. "Let him that stole," [2] saith he, "steal no more."

Seest thou what are the members of the old man? Falsehood, revenge, theft. Why said he not, "Let him that stole" be punished, be tortured, be racked; but, "let him steal no more"? "But rather let him labor, working with his hands the thing that is good, that he may have whereof to give to him that hath need."

Where are they which are called pure; [3] they that are full of all defilement, and yet dare to give themselves a name like this? For it is possible, very possible, to put off the reproach, not only by ceasing from the sin, but by working some good thing also. Perceive ye how we ought to get quit of the sin? "They stole." This is the sin. "They steal no more." This is not to do away the sin. But how shall they? If they labor, and charitably communicate to others, thus will they do away the sin. He does not simply desire that we should work, but so "work" as to "labor," so as that we may "communicate" to others. For the thief indeed works, but it is that which is evil.

Ver. 29. "Let no corrupt speech proceed out of your mouth."

What is "corrupt speech"? That which is said elsewhere to be also "idle, backbiting, filthy communication, jesting, foolish talking." See ye how he is cutting up the very roots of anger? Lying, theft, unseasonable conversation. The words, however, "Let him steal no more," he does not say so much excusing them, as to pacify the injured parties, and to recommend them to be content, if they never suffer the like again. And well too does he give advice concerning conversation; [4] inasmuch as we shall pay the penalty, not for our deeds only, but also for our words.

"But such as is good," he proceeds, "for edifying, as the need may be, that it may give grace to them that hear."

That is to say, What edifies thy neighbor, that only speak, not a word more. For to this end God gave thee a mouth and a tongue, that thou mightest give thanks to Him, that thou mightest build up thy neighbor. So that if thou destroy that building, better were it to be silent, and never to speak at all. For indeed the hands of the workmen, if instead of raising the walls, they should learn to pull them down, would justly deserve to be cut off. For so also saith the Psalmist; "The Lord shall cut off all flattering lips." (Ps. xii. 3.) The mouth, — this is the cause of all evil; or rather not the mouth, but they that make an evil use of it. From thence proceed insults, revilings, blasphemies, incentives to lusts, murders, adulteries, thefts, all have their origin from this. And how, you will say, do murders? Because from insult thou wilt go on to anger, from anger to blows, from blows to murder. And how, again, adultery? "Such a woman," one will say, "loves thee, she said something nice about thee." This at once unstrings thy firmness, and thus are thy passions kindled within thee.

Therefore Paul said, "such as is good." Since then there is so vast a flow of words, he with good reason speaks indefinitely, charging us to use expressions of that kind, and giving us a pattern of communication. What then is this? By saying, "for edifying," either he means this, that he who hears thee may be grateful to thee: as, for instance, a brother has committed forni-

---

[1] βαπτίζωμεν τὴν μάχαιραν εἰς τὸ τοῦ διαβόλου στῆθος.

[2] ["' The stealer (ὁ κλέπτων) is to steal no more.' The present participle does not stand for the past, but is used substantively (like ὁ σπείρων, Matt. xiii. 3). As there were in the apostolic church 'fornicators' (1 Cor. v. 1), so there were also 'stealers,' and the attempts to tone down the word are arbitrary and superfluous."—Meyer.—G. A.]

[3] καθαροί. The Cathari, or pure, was the title which the Novatians indirectly assumed, by maintaining that none were in God's favor but those who had not sinned after baptism, or who were pure as baptism made them, and by separating from the Church for granting absolution to penitents. The schism originated at Rome in the middle of the third century. Accordingly St. Chrysostom in the text says, that whereas all men need pardon continually, they who affected to be clean or pure without securing it were, as being without it, of all men most unclean. [And he strongly asserts, as against the Novatians, that it is possible to put away the guilt of sins committed after baptism, by ceasing from the practice of them and working that which is good. This view, however, differs from the Protestant view, that the putting away the guilt of sin is at first and always through God's mercy and grace in Jesus Christ.—G. A.] In the sixth of eleven new Homilies edited by the Benedictines, t. xii. p. 355, he says that we may as well talk of the sea being clear of waves as any soul pure from daily sins, though not from transgressing express commandment, yet from vainglory, willfulness, impure thoughts, coveting, lying, resentment, envy, &c., and he mentions as means of washing away sins, coming to Church, grieving for them, confessing them, doing alms, praying, helping the injured, and forgiving injuries. "Let us provide ourselves with these," he proceeds, "every day, washing, wiping ourselves clean, and withal confessing ourselves unprofitable," unlike the Pharisee. "Thus ordering ourselves, we shall be able to find mercy and pardon in that fearful day, &c." This homily was delivered at Constantinople. [On the Novatians, see Schaff, *Church History*, II., pp. 196, 197.—G. A.]

[4] [The clause, "And well does he give instruction concerning our words also" (καλῶς δὲ καὶ περὶ λόγων διδάσκει), is omitted in the text of Field, but is well attested (three MSS., Sav. text), and almost indispensable to the sense of the passage. Compare note, p. 82, on Field's text in general.—G. A.]

cation ; do not make a display of the offense, nor revel in it ; thou wilt be doing no good to him that hears thee ; rather, it is likely, thou wilt hurt him, by giving him a stimulus. Whereas, advise him what to do, and thou art conferring on him a great obligation. Discipline him how to keep silence, teach him to revile no man, and thou hast taught him his best lesson, thou wilt have conferred upon him the highest obligation. Discourse with him on contrition, on piety, on almsgiving ; all these things will soften his soul, for all these things he will own his obligation. Whereas by exciting his laughter, or by filthy communication, thou wilt rather be inflaming him. Applaud the wickedness, and thou wilt overturn and ruin him.

Or else he means[1] thus, "that it may make them, the hearers, full of grace." For as sweet ointment gives grace to them that partake of it, so also does good speech. Hence it was more-over that one said, "Thy name is as ointment poured forth." (Cant. i. 3.) It caused them to exhale that sweet perfume. Thou seest that what he continually recommends, he is saying now also, charging every one according to his several ability to edify his neighbors. Thou then that givest such advice to others, how much more to thyself !

Ver. 30. "And grieve not," he adds, " the Holy Spirit of God."

A matter this more terrible and startling, as he also says in the Epistle to the Thessalonians ; for there too he uses an expression of this sort. "He that rejecteth, rejecteth not man, but God." (1 Thess. iv. 8.) So also here. If thou utter a reproachful word, if thou strike thy brother, thou art not striking him, thou art " grieving the Holy Spirit." And then is added further the benefit bestowed, in order to heighten the rebuke.

"And grieve not the Holy Spirit," saith He, "in whom ye were sealed unto the day of re-demption."

He it is who marks us as a royal flock ; He, who separates us from all former things ; He, who suffers us not to lie amongst them that are exposed to the wrath of God, — and dost thou grieve Him? Look how startling are his words there ; " For he that rejecteth," saith he, " re-jecteth not man, but God : " and how cutting they are here, " Grieve not the Holy Spirit," saith he, " in whom ye were sealed."

MORAL. Let this seal then abide upon thy mouth,[2] and never destroy the impression. A spiritual mouth never utters a thing of the kind. Say not, " It is nothing, if I do utter an unseemly word, if I do insult such an one." For this very reason is it a great evil, because it seems to be

nothing. For things which seem to be nothing are thus easily thought lightly of ; and those which are thought lightly of go on increasing ; and those which go on increasing become incurable.

Thou hast a spiritual mouth. Think what words thou didst utter immediately upon being born,[3] — what words are worthy of thy mouth. Thou callest God, " Father," and dost thou straightway revile thy brother? Think, whence is it thou callest God, " Father "? Is it from nature? No, thou couldest never say so. Is it from thy goodness? No, nor is it thus. But whence then is it? It is from pure lovingkind-ness, from tenderness, from His great mercy. Whenever then thou callest God, " Father," consider not only this, that by reviling thou art committing things unworthy of that, thy high birth, but also that it is of lovingkindness that thou hast that high birth. Disgrace it not then, after receiving it from pure lovingkindness, by showing cruelty towards thy brethren. Dost thou call God " Father," and yet revile? No, these are not the works of the Son of God. These are very far from Him. The work of the Son of God was to forgive His enemies, to pray for them that crucified Him, to shed His blood for them that hated Him. These are works worthy of the Son of God, to make His enemies, — the ungrateful, the dishonest, the reckless, the treacherous, — to make these brethren and heirs : not to treat them that are become breth-ren with ignominy like slaves.

[4] Think what words thy mouth uttered, — of what table these words are worthy. Think what thy mouth touches, what it tastes, of what man-ner of food it partakes ! Dost thou deem thyself to be doing nothing grievous in railing at thy brother? How then dost thou call him brother? And yet if he be not a brother, how sayest thou, " Our Father "? For the word " Our " is indi-cative of many persons. Think with whom thou standest at the time of the mysteries ! With the Cherubim, with the Seraphim ! The Sera-phim revile not : no, their mouth fulfills this one only duty, to sing the Hymn of praise, to glorify[5] God. And how then shalt thou be able to say with them, " Holy, Holy, Holy,"[6] if thou use thy mouth for reviling? Tell me, I pray. Suppose there were a royal vessel, and that al-ways full of royal dainties, and set apart for that

---

[1] [" It means 'that it may impart a blessing, bestow a benefit, on the hearers.' " — Meyer and Ellicott. — G. A.]

[2] [This is probably a misapplication of Paul's words here. The sealing here mentioned is quite the same as at chap. i. 13. — G. A.]

[3] [ἐννόησον τίνα εὐθέως ἐφθέγξω ῥήματα τεχθείς, κ.τ.λ. This evidently refers to baptism and the services and words used in con-nection therewith. Bingham says, " The catechumens did not learn the creed and the Lord's prayer till immediately before baptism." And Chrysostom says, " An unbaptized person cannot yet call God his Father." St. Augustine also says in one of his homilies, " Now learn the Lord's prayer, which ye must repeat eight days hence, when ye are to be baptized." So they received it (that is, the Lord's prayer) only on Saturday before Palm Sunday, in order to repeat it on Saturday before Easter, which was the day of their baptism. Antiquities, Bk. x. ch. v. sec. 9. — G. A.]

[4] [This paragraph has reference to the celebration of the Euchar-ist, concerning which, see Chrysostom's Hom. xviii. on 2 Cor. (viii. 24). — G. A.]

[5] ἁγιάζειν.

[6] ἅγιος, ἅγιος, ἅγιος.

purpose, and then that any one of the servants were to take and use it for holding dung. Would he ever venture again, after it had been filled with dung, to store it away with those other vessels, set apart for those other uses? Surely not. Now railing is like this, reviling is like this. "Our Father!" But what? is this all? Hear also the words, which follow, "which art in Heaven." The moment thou sayest, "Our Father, which art in Heaven," the word raises thee up, it gives wings to thy mind, it points out to thee that thou hast a Father in Heaven. Do then nothing, speak nothing of things upon earth. He hath set thee amongst that host above, He hath numbered thee with that heavenly choir. Why dost thou drag thyself down? Thou art standing beside the royal throne, and thou revilest? Art thou not afraid lest the king should deem it an outrage? Why, if a servant, even with us, beats his fellow-servant or assaults him, even though he do it justly, yet we at once rebuke him, and deem the act an outrage; and yet dost thou, who art standing with the Cherubim beside the king's throne, revile thy brother? Seest thou not these holy vessels? Are they not used continually for only one purpose? Does any one ever venture to use them for any other? Yet art thou holier than these vessels, yea, far holier. Why then defile, why contaminate thyself? Standest thou in Heaven, and dost thou revile? Hast thou thy citizenship with Angels, and dost thou revile? Art thou counted worthy the Lord's kiss, and dost thou revile? Hath God graced thy mouth with so many and great things, with hymns angelic, with food, not angelic, no, but more than angelic,

with His own kiss, with His own embrace, and dost thou revile? Oh, no, I implore thee. Vast are the evils of which this is the source; far be it from a Christian soul. Do I not convince thee as I am speaking, do I not shame thee? Then does it now become my duty to alarm you. For hear what Christ saith: "Whosoever shall say to his brother, Thou fool, shall be in danger of the hell of fire." (Matt. v. 22.) Now if that which is lightest of all leads to hell, of what shall not he be worthy, who utters presumptuous words? Let us discipline our mouth to silence. Great is the advantage from this, great the mischief from ill language. We must not spend our riches here. Let us put door and bolt upon them. Let us devour ourselves alive if ever a vexatious word slip out of our mouth. Let us entreat God, let us entreat him whom we have reviled. Let us not think it beneath us to do so. It is ourselves we have wounded, not him. Let us apply the remedy, prayer, and reconciliation with him whom we have reviled. If in our words we are to take such forethought, much more let us impose laws upon ourselves in our deeds. Yea, and if we have friends, whoever they may be, and they should speak evil to any man or revile him, demand of them and exact satisfaction. Let us by all means learn that such conduct is even sin; for if we learn this, we shall soon depart from it.

Now the God of peace keep both your mind and your tongue, and fence you with a sure fence, even His fear, through Jesus Christ our Lord, with whom to the Father, together with the Holy Spirit, be glory forever. Amen.

HOMILY XV.

EPHESIANS iv. 31.

"Let all bitterness, and wrath, and anger, and clamor, and railing, be put away from you, with all malice."

As bees[1] will never settle down in an unclean vessel, — and this is the reason why those who are skilled in these matters sprinkle the spot with perfumes, and scented ointments, and sweet odors; and the wicker baskets also, in which they will have to settle as soon as they come out

of the hives they sprinkle with fragrant wines, and all other sweets, that there may be no noisome smell to annoy them, and drive them away again, — so in truth is it also with the Holy Spirit. Our soul is a sort of vessel or basket, capable of receiving the swarms of spiritual gifts; but if there shall be within it gall, and "bitterness, and wrath," the swarms will fly away. Hence this blessed and wise husbandman well and thoroughly cleanses our vessels, withholding neither knife nor any other instrument of iron, and invites us to this spiritual swarm; and as he gathers it, he cleanses us with prayers, and labors, and all the rest. Mark then how he cleanses out our heart. He has banished lying, he has banished anger. Now, again, he is

[1] [Chrysostom seems to have observed everything, and he had the "homiletical habit," as Dr. Shedd calls it (Hom. p. 108), in gathering material for illustration. What has been said of a great modern preacher, may be said of Chrysostom: "He watched ships and sailors; he acquainted himself with the customs, good and bad, of commercial life; he curiously inspected a great variety of mechanical processes; he closely observed agricultural operations, and the various phases of rural life; he constantly saw and heard what occurred in his own home and other homes; and always and everywhere he asked himself, What is this like? what will this illustrate?" Dr. Broadus, in *Preparation and Delivery of Sermons.* — G. A.]

pointing out how that evil may be yet more entirely eradicated ; if we be not, saith he, "bitter" in spirit. For it is as is wont to happen with our bile, if there chance to be but little of it, there will be but little disturbance if the receptacle should burst: but if ever the strength and acridness of this quality becomes excessive, the vessel which before held it, containing it no longer, is as if it were eaten through by a scorching fire, and it is no longer able to hold it and contain it within its appointed bounds, but, rent asunder by its intense sharpness, it lets it escape and injure the whole body. And it is like some very fierce and frightful wild beast, that has been brought into a city ; as long as it is confined in the cages made for it, however it may rage, however it may roar, it will be unable to do harm to any one ; but if it is overcome by rage, and breaks through the intervening bars, and is able to leap out, it fills the city with all sorts of confusion and disturbance, and puts everybody to flight. Such indeed is the nature also of bile. As long as it is kept within its proper limits, it will do us no great mischief; but as soon as ever the membrane that incloses it bursts, and there is nothing to hinder its being at once dispersed over the whole system, then, I say, at that moment, though it be so very trifling in quantity,[1] yet by reason of the inordinate strength of its quality it taints all the other elements of our nature with its own peculiar virulence. For finding the blood, for instance, near to it, alike in place and in quality, and rendering the heat which is in that blood more acrid, and everything else in fact which is near it ; passing from its just temperature it overflows its bounds, turns all into gall, and therewith at once attacks likewise the other parts of the body ; and thus infusing into all its own poisonous quality, it renders the man speechless, and causes him to expire, expelling life. Now, why have I stated all these things with such minuteness? It is in order that, understanding from this bitterness which is of the body the intolerable evil of that bitterness which is of the soul, and how entirely it destroys first of all the very soul that engenders it, making everything bitter, we may escape experience of it. For as the one inflames the whole constitution, so does the other the thoughts, and carries away its captive to the abyss of hell. In order then that by carefully examining these matters we may escape this evil, and bridle the monster, or rather utterly root it out, let us hearken to what Paul saith, " Let all bitterness be " (not

destroyed, but) " put away " from you. For what need have I of trouble to restrain it, what necessity is there to keep watch on a monster, when it is in my power to expel him from my soul, to remove him and drive him out, as it were, into banishment? Let us hearken then to Paul when he saith, " Let all bitterness be put away from you." But, ah, the perversity that possesses us ! Though we ought to do everything to effect this, yet are there some so truly senseless as to congratulate themselves upon this evil, and to pride themselves upon it, and to glory in it, and who are envied by others. "Such a one," say they, " is a bitter man, he is a scorpion, a serpent, a viper." They look upon him as one to be feared. But wherefore, good man, dost thou fear the bitter person? " I fear," you say, " lest he injure me, lest he destroy me ; I am not proof against his malice, I am afraid lest he should take me who am a simple man, and unable to foresee any of his schemes, and throw me into his snares, and entangle us in the toils which he has set to deceive us." Now I cannot but smile. And why forsooth? Because these are the arguments of children, who fear things which are not to be feared. Surely there is nothing we ought so to despise, nothing we ought so to laugh to scorn, as a bitter and malicious man. For there is nothing so powerless[2] as bitterness. It makes men fools and senseless.

Do ye not see that malice is blind? Have ye never heard, that he that diggeth a pit for his neighbors, diggeth it for himself? How, it may be said, ought we not to fear a soul full of tumult? If indeed we are to fear the bitter in the same way as we fear evil spirits, and fools and madmen, (for they indeed do everything at random,) I grant it myself ; but if we are to fear them as men skillful in the conduct of affairs, that never. For nothing is so necessary for the proper conduct of affairs as prudence ; and there is no greater hindrance to prudence than wickedness, and malice, and hollowness. Look at bilious persons, how unsightly they are, with all their bloom withered away. How weak they are, and puny, and unfit for anything. So also are souls of this nature. What else is wickedness, but a jaundice of the soul? Wickedness then has no strength in it, indeed it has not. Have ye a mind that I again make what I am saying plain to you by an instance, by setting before you the portraits of a treacherous and a guileless man? Absalom was a treacherous man, and " stole all men's hearts." (2 Sam. xv. 6.) And observe how great was his treachery. " He went about," it saith, " and said, 'Hast thou no judgment?' "[3] wishing to

---

[1] [This seems to be in direct contradiction to what is said a few lines above, to wit, " If there chance to be but little of it, there will be but little disturbance if the receptacle should burst." The text in the former passage is in great uncertainty, however, and confusion. Field calls it a *locus conclamatus*. Perhaps, if the true text of that passage could be recovered, it would not be in conflict with the passage here. — G. A.]

[2] [Compare Prov. xxv. 28. — G. A.]

[3] [μὴ ἔστι σοι κρίσις; but Sept. (2 Sam. xv. 3) has ὁ ἀκούων οὐκ ἔστι σοι παρὰ τοῦ βασιλέως, which is well rendered by the Rev. Ver., " But there is no man deputed of the king to hear thee." — G. A.]

conciliate every one to himself. But David was guileless. What then? Look at the end of them both, look, how full of utter madness was the former! For inasmuch as he looked solely to the hurt of his father, in all other things he was blinded. But not so David. For " he that walketh uprightly, walketh surely" (Prov. x. 9); and reasonably; he is one that manages nothing over-subtilely, the man who devises no evil. Let us listen then to the blessed Paul, and let us pity, yea, let us weep for the bitter-minded, and let us practice every method, let us do everything to extirpate this vice from their souls. For how is it not absurd, that when there is bile within us, (though that indeed is a useful element, for without bile a man cannot possibly exist, that bile, I mean, which is an element of his nature,) how then, I say, is it not absurd that we should do all we can to get rid of this, though we are so highly benefited by it; and yet that we should do nothing, nor take any pains, to get rid of that which is in the soul, though it is in no case beneficial, but even in the highest degree injurious? He that thinketh that he is "wise among you," saith he, " let him become a fool, that he may become wise." (1 Cor. iii. 18.) Hearken too again to what Luke saith, "They did take their food with gladness and singleness of heart, praising God, and having favor with all the people." (Acts ii. 46, 47.) Why, do we not see even now that the simple and guileless enjoy the common esteem of all? No one envies such an one when he is in prosperity, no one tramples upon him when he is in adversity, but all rejoice with him when he does well, and grieve with him in misfortune. Whereas whenever a bitter man fares prosperously, one and all lament it, as though some evil thing happened; but if he is unfortunate, one and all rejoice. Let us then pity them, for they have common enemies all over the world. Jacob was a guileless man, yet he overcame the treacherous Esau. "For into a malicious soul wisdom shall not enter." (Wisd. i. 4.) "Let all bitterness be put away from you." Let not even a remnant remain, for it will be sure, if stirred, as if from a smouldering brand, to turn all within to an entire blaze. Let us then distinctly understand what this bitterness is. Take, for example, the hollow-hearted man, the crafty, the man who is on the watch to do mischief, the man of evil suspicion. From him then "wrath" and "anger" are ever produced; for it is not possible for a soul like this to be in tranquillity, but the very root of "anger" and "wrath" is "bitterness." The man of this character is both sullen, and never unbends his soul; he is always moody, always gloomy. For as I was saying, they themselves are the first to reap the fruit of their own evil ways.

"And clamor," he adds.

What now, and dost thou take away clamor also? Yes, for the mild man must needs be of such a character, because clamor carries anger, as a horse his rider; trip the horse, and you will throw the rider.

MORAL. This let women above all attend to, them who on every occasion cry aloud and bawl. There is but one thing in which it is useful to cry aloud, in preaching and in teaching. But in no other case whatever, no, not even in prayer. And if thou wouldest learn a practical lesson, never cry aloud at all, and then wilt thou never be angry at all. Behold a way to keep your temper; for as it is not possible that the man that does not cry out should be enraged, so is it not that the man who does cry out should be otherwise than enraged. For tell me not of a man being implacable, and revengeful, and of pure natural bitterness, and natural choler. We are now speaking of the sudden paroxysm of this passion.

It contributes then no little to this end, to discipline the soul never to raise the voice and cry aloud at all. Cut off clamor, and thou wilt clip the wings of anger, thou dost repress the first rising of the heart. For as it is impossible for a man to wrestle without lifting up his hands, so is it not possible that he should be entangled in a quarrel without lifting up his voice. Bind the hands of the boxer, and then bid him strike. He will be unable to do so. So likewise will wrath be disarmed. But clamor raises it, even where it does not exist. And hence it is especially that the female sex are so easily overtaken in it. Women, whenever they are angry with their maid-servants, fill the whole house with their own clamor. And oftentimes too, if the house happens to be built along a narrow street, then all the passers-by hear the mistress scolding, and the maid weeping and wailing. What can possibly be more disgraceful than the sound of those wailings?[1] What in the world has happened there? All the women round immediately peep in and one of them says, "Such a one is beating her own maid." Whatever can be more shameless than this? "What then, ought one not to strike at all?" No, I say not so, (for it must be done,) but then it must be neither frequently, nor immoderately, nor for any wrongs of thine own, as I am constantly saying, nor for any little failure in her service, but only if she is doing harm to her own soul. If thou chastise her for a fault of this kind, all will applaud, and there will be none to upbraid thee; but if thou do it for any reasons of thine own, all will condemn thy cruelty and harshness. And what is more base than all, there are some so fierce and so savage as to lash them to such a degree, that

---

[1] [We have here followed the text of three codices as against the emendations of Field, Savile, and the Benedictine ed. — G. A.]

the bruises will not disappear with the day. For they will strip the damsels, and call their husbands for the purpose, and oftentimes tie them to the pallets. Alas! at that moment, tell me, does no recollection of hell come over thee? What? dost thou strip thy handmaid, and expose her to thy husband? And art thou not ashamed, lest he should condemn thee for it? And then dost thou exasperate him yet more, and threaten to put her in chains, having first taunted the wretched and pitiable creature with ten thousand reproachful names, and called her "Thessalian witch,[1] runaway, and prostitute"?

For her passion allows her not to spare even her own mouth, but she looks to one single object, how she may wreak her vengeance on the other, even though she disgrace herself. And then after all these things forsooth, she will sit in state like any tyrant, and call her children, and summon her foolish husband, and treat him as a hangman. Ought these things to take place in the houses of Christians? "Aye," say ye, "but slaves are a troublesome, audacious, impudent, incorrigible race." True, I know it myself, but there are other ways to keep them in order; by terrors, by threats, by words; which may both touch her more powerfully, and save thee from disgrace. Thou who art a free woman hast uttered foul words, and dost thou not disgrace thyself more than her? Then if she shall have occasion to go out to the bath, there are bruises on her back when she is naked, and she carries about with her the marks of thy cruelty. "But," say ye, "the whole tribe of slaves is intolerable if it meet with indulgence." True, I know it myself. But then, as I was saying, correct them in some other way, not by the scourge only, and by terror, but even by flattering them, and by acts of kindness. If she is a believer, she is thy sister. Consider that thou art her mistress, and that she ministers unto thee. If she be intemperate, cut off the occasions of drunkenness; call thy husband, and admonish her. Or dost thou not feel how disgraceful a thing it is for a woman to be beaten? They at least who have enacted ten thousand punishments for men, — the stake, and the rack, — will scarcely ever hang a woman, but limit men's anger to smiting her on the cheek; and so great respect have they observed towards the sex, that not even when there is absolute necessity have they often hung a woman, if she happen to be pregnant. For it is a disgrace for a man to strike a woman; and if for a man, much more for one of her own sex. It is moreover by these things that women

become odious to their husbands. "What then," ye may say, "if she shall act the harlot?" Marry her to a husband; cut off the occasions of fornication, suffer her not to be too high fed. "What then, if she shall steal?" Take care of her, and watch her. — "Extravagant!" thou wilt say; "What, am I to be her keeper? How absurd!" And why, I pray, art thou not to be her keeper? Has she not the same kind of soul as thou? Has she not been vouchsafed the same privileges by God? Does she not partake of the same table? Does she not share with thee the same high birth? "But what then," ye will say, "if she shall be a railer, or a gossip, or a drunkard?" Yet, how many free women are such? Now, with all the failings of women God hath charged men to bear: only, He saith, let not a woman be an harlot, but every other failing besides bear with. Yea, be she drunkard, or railer, or gossip, or evil-eyed, or extravagant, and a squanderer of thy substance, thou hast her for the partner of thy life. Train and restrain her. Necessity is upon thee. It is for this thou art the head. Regulate her therefore, do thy own part. Yea, and if she remain incorrigible, yea, though she steal, take care of thy goods, and do not punish her so much. If she be a gossip, silence her. This is the very highest philosophy.

Now, however, some are come to such a height of indecency as to uncover the head, and to drag their maid-servants by the hair. — Why do ye all blush?[2] I am not addressing myself to all, but to those who are carried away into such brutal conduct. Paul saith, "Let not a woman be uncovered." (1 Cor. xi. 5–15.) And dost thou then entirely strip off her head-dress? Dost thou see how thou art doing outrage to thyself? If indeed she makes her appearance to thee with her head bare, thou callest it an insult. And dost thou say that there is nothing shocking when thou barest it thyself? Then ye will say, "What if she be not corrected?" Chasten her then with the rod and with stripes. And yet how many failings hast thou also thyself, and yet thou art not corrected! These things I am saying not for their sakes, but for the sake of you free-women, that ye do nothing so unworthy, nothing to disgrace you, that ye do yourselves no wrong.[3] If thou wilt learn this lesson in thy household in dealing with thy maid-servant, and not be harsh but gentle and forbearing, much more wilt thou be so in thy behavior to thy husband. For she who, though having authority, does nothing of the sort, will do it much less where there is a check. So that

---

[1] Vid. Aristoph. *Nub.* 749, γυναῖκα φαρμακίδ᾽ εἰ πριάμενος Θετταλήν. Schol., μέχρι καὶ νῦν φαρμακίδες αἱ Θετταλαὶ καλοῦνται. [What a fearful picture of the cruelties of the mistresses of Chrysostom's day! — G. A.]

[2] [This is direct preaching. Some would call it personal. But as Daniel Webster said of preaching, so ought we "make it a personal matter, a personal matter, a personal matter." — G. A.]

[3] [And what a graceful and conciliatory turn he gives his discourse here! — G. A.]

the discipline employed about your maid-servants, will be of the greatest service to you in gaining the goodwill of your husbands. "For with what measure ye mete," He saith, "it shall be measured unto you." (Matt. vii. 2.) Set a bridle upon thy mouth. If thou art disciplined to bear bravely with a servant when she answers back, thou wilt not be annoyed with the insolence of an equal, and in being above annoyance, wilt have attained to the highest philosophy. But some there are who add even oaths, but there is nothing more shocking than a woman so enraged. But what again, ye will say, if she dress gayly? Why then, forbid this; thou hast my consent; but check it by first beginning with thyself, not so much by fear as by example. Be in everything thyself a perfect pattern.

"And let railing," saith he, "be put away from you." Observe the progress of mischief. Bitterness produces wrath, wrath anger, anger clamor, clamor railing, that is, revilings; next from evil-speaking it goes on to blows, from blows to wounds, from wounds to death. Paul, however, did not wish to mention any of these, but only this, "let this," saith he, "be put away from you, with all malice."[1] What is "with all malice"? It ends with this. For there are some, like those dogs that bite secretly, which do not bark at all at those that come near them, nor are angry, but which fawn, and display a gentle aspect; but when they catch us off our guard, will fix their teeth in us. These are more dangerous than those that take up open enmity. Now since there are men too that are dogs, who neither cry out, nor fly in a passion, nor threaten us when they are offended, yet in secret are weaving plots, and contriving ten thousand mischiefs, and revenging themselves not in words but in deeds; he hints at these. Let those things be put away from you, saith he, "with all malice." Do not spare thy words, and then revenge thyself in acts. My purpose in chastising my tongue and curtailing its clamor, is to prevent its kindling up a more violent blaze. But if thou without any clamor art doing the same thing, and art cherishing the fire and the live coals within, where is the good of thy silence? Dost thou not know that those conflagrations are the most destructive of all which are fed within, and appear not to those that are without? And that those wounds are the deadliest which never break out to the surface; and those fevers the worst which burn up the vitals? So also is this anger the most dangerous that preys upon the soul. But let this too be put away from you, saith he, "with all malice," of every kind and degree, great and little. Let us then hearken to him, let us cast out all "bitterness and all malice," that we "grieve not the Holy Spirit." Let us destroy all bitterness; let us cut it up by the very roots. Nothing good, nothing healthful, can ever come from a bitter soul; nothing but misfortunes, nothing but tears, nothing but weeping and wailing. Do ye not see those beasts that roar or cry out, how we turn away from them; the lion, for instance, and the bear? But not so from the sheep; for there is no roaring, but a mild and gentle voice. And so again with musical instruments, those which are loud and harsh are the most unpleasant to the ear, such as the drum and trumpet; whereas those which are not so, but are soothing, these are pleasant, as the flute and lyre and pipe. Let us then prepare our soul so as never to cry aloud, and thus shall we be enabled also to gain the mastery over our anger. And when we have cut out this, we ourselves shall be the first to enjoy the calm, and we shall sail into that peaceful haven, which God grant we may all attain, in Jesus Christ our Lord, with whom, together with the Holy Ghost, be unto the Father, glory, might, and honor, now, and ever, and throughout all ages. Amen.

HOMILY XVI.

EPHESIANS iv. 31, 32.

"Let all bitterness, and wrath, and anger, and clamor, and railing be put away from you, with all malice. And be ye kind one to another, tender-hearted, forgiving each other, even as God also in Christ forgave you."

IF we are to attain to the kingdom of Heaven, it is not enough to abandon wickedness, but there must be abundant practice of that which is good also. To be delivered indeed from hell we must abstain from wickedness; but to attain to the kingdom we must cleave fast to virtue.[2] Know ye not that even in the tribunals of the heathen, when examination is made of men's deeds, and the whole city is assembled, this is the case?

---

[1] [κακία: "'Malice,' the genus to which all the above-mentioned vices belong, or rather the *active* principle to which they are all due, — *animi pravitas, humanitati et equitati opposita* (Calvin)." — Ellicott. — G. A.]

[2] [This way of putting it would imply that there is an intermediate place, neither hell nor heaven, which Chrysostom felt; and so he corrects himself a little below. This does not appear to be a trick of the orator. — G. A.]

Nay, there was an ancient custom amongst the heathen, to crown with a golden crown,[1] — not the man who had done no evil to his country, for this were in itself no more than enough to save him from punishment; — but him who had displayed great public services. It was thus that a man was to be advanced to this distinction. But what I had especial need to say, had, I know not how, well nigh escaped me. Accordingly having made some slight correction of what I have said, I retract the first portion of this division.

For as I was saying that the departure from evil is sufficient to prevent our falling into hell, whilst I was speaking, there stole upon me a certain awful sentence, which does not merely bring down vengeance on them that dare to commit evil, but which also punishes those who omit any opportunity of doing good. What sentence then is this? When the day, the dreadful day, He saith, was arrived, and the set time was come, the Judge, seated on the judgment seat, set the sheep on the right hand and the goats on the left; and to the sheep He said, "Come, ye blessed of My Father, inherit the kingdom prepared for you from the foundation of the world: for I was an hungered, and ye gave me meat." (Matt. xxv. 34.) So far, well. For it was meet that for such compassion they should receive this reward. That those, however, who did not communicate of their own possessions to them that were in need, that they should be punished, not merely by the loss of blessings, but by being also sent to hell-fire, what just reason, I say, can there be in this? Most certainly this too will have a fair show of reason, no less than the other case : for we are hence instructed, that they that have done good shall enjoy those good things that are in heaven, but they, who, though they have no evil indeed to be charged with, yet have omitted to do good, will be hurried away with them that have done evil into hell-fire. Unless one might indeed say this, that the very not doing good is a part of wickedness, inasmuch as it comes of indolence, and indolence is a part of vice, or rather, not a part, but a source and baneful root of it. For idleness is the teacher of all vice. Let us not then foolishly ask such questions as these, what place shall he occupy, who has done neither any evil nor any good? For the very not doing good, is in itself doing evil. Tell me, if thou hadst a servant, who should neither steal, nor insult, nor contradict thee, who moreover should keep from drunkenness and every other kind of vice, and yet should sit perpetually in idleness, and not doing one of those duties which a servant owes to his master,

wouldest thou not chastise him, wouldest thou not put him to the rack? Tell me. And yet forsooth he has done no evil. No, but this is in itself doing evil. But let us, if you please, apply this to other cases in life. Suppose then that of an husbandman. He does no damage to our property, he lays no plots against us, and he is not a thief, he only ties his hands behind him, and sits at home, neither sowing, nor cutting a single furrow, nor harnessing oxen to the yoke, nor looking after a vine, nor in fact discharging any one of those other labors required in husbandry. Now, I say, should we not punish such a man? And yet he has done no wrong to any one ; we have no charge to make against him. No, but by this very thing has he done wrong. He does wrong in that he does not contribute his own share to the common stock of good. And what again, tell me, if every single artisan or mechanic were only to do no harm, say to one of a different craft, — nay, were to do no harm, even to one of his own, but only were to be idle, would not our whole life at that rate be utterly at an end and perish? Do you wish that I yet further extend the discourse with reference to the body also? Let the hand then neither strike the head, nor cut out the tongue, nor pluck out the eye, nor do any evil of this sort, but only remain idle, and not render its due service to the body at large ; would it not be more fitting that it should be cut off, than that one should carry it about in idleness, and a detriment to the whole body? And what too, if the mouth, without either devouring the hand, or biting the breast, should nevertheless fail in all its proper duties ; were it not far better that it should be stopped up? If therefore both in the case of servants, and of mechanics, and of the whole body, not only the commission of evil, but also the omission of what is good, is great unrighteousness, much more will this be the case in regard to the body of Christ.

Moral. And therefore the blessed Paul also, in leading us away from sin, leads us on to virtue. For where, tell me, is the advantage of all the thorns being cut out, if the good seeds be not sown? For our labor, remaining unfinished, will come round and end in the same mischief. And therefore Paul also, in his deep and affectionate anxiety for us, does not let his admonitions stop at eradicating and destroying evil tempers, but urges us at once to evidence the implanting of good ones. For having said, "Let all bitterness, and wrath, and clamor, and railing be put away from you, with all malice," he adds, "And be[2] ye kind one to another, tenderhearted, forgiving each other." For all these

---

[1] [The Athenians, for example, bestowed a golden crown upon Demosthenes, and his celebrated oration "On the Crown" was occasioned by this custom to which Chrysostom refers.]

[2] ["Not 'be' (ἔστε), but 'become' (γίνεσθε), in keeping with the ἀρθήτω ἀφ' ὑμῶν, 'let it be put away' from you." — Meyer. — G. A.]

are habits and dispositions. And our abandonment of the one thing is not sufficient to settle us in the habitual practice of the other, but there is need again of some fresh impulse, and of an effort not less than that made in our avoidance of evil dispositions, in order to our acquiring good ones. For so in the case of the body, the black man, if he gets rid of this complexion, does not straightway become white. Or rather let us not conduct our discourse with an argument from physical subjects, but draw our example from those which concern moral choice. He who is not our enemy, is not necessarily our friend ; but there is an intermediate state, neither of enmity nor of friendship, which is perhaps that in which the greater part of mankind stand toward us. He that is not crying is not therefore necessarily also laughing, but there is a state between the two. And so, I say, is the case here. He that is not " bitter " is not necessarily " kind," neither is he that is not " wrathful " necessarily " tender-hearted " ; but there is need of a distinct effort, in order to acquire this excellence. And now look how the blessed Paul, according to the rules of the best husbandry, thoroughly cleans and works the land entrusted to him by the Husbandman. He has taken away the bad seeds ; he now exhorts us to retain the good plants. " Be ye kind," saith he, for if, when the thorns are plucked up, the field remains idle, it will again bear unprofitable weeds. And therefore there is need to preoccupy its unoccupied and fallow state by the setting of good seeds and plants. He takes away " anger," he puts in " kindness " ; he takes away " bitterness," he puts in " tender-heartedness " ; he extirpates " malice " and " railing," he plants " forgiveness " in their stead. For the expression, " forgiving one another," is this ; be disposed, he means, to forgive one another. And this forgiveness is greater than that which is shown in money-matters. For he indeed who forgives a debt of money to him that has borrowed of him, does, it is true, a noble and admirable deed, but then the kindness is confined to the body, though to himself indeed he repays a full recompense by that benefit which is spiritual and concerns the soul ; whereas he who forgives trespasses will be benefiting alike his own soul, and the soul of him who receives the forgiveness. For by this way of acting, he not only renders himself, but the other also, more charitable. Because we do not so deeply touch the souls of those who have wronged us by revenging ourselves, as by pardoning them, and thus shaming them and putting them out of countenance. For by the other course we shall be doing no good, either to ourselves or to them, but shall be doing harm to both by seeking ourselves for retaliation, like the rulers of the Jews, and by kindling up

the wrath that is in them ; but if we return injustice with gentleness, we shall disarm all his anger, and shall be setting up in his breast a tribunal which will give a verdict in our favor, and will condemn him more severely than we ourselves could. For he will convict and will pass sentence upon himself, and will look for every pretext for repaying the share of long-suffering granted him with fuller measure, knowing that, if he repay it in equal measure, he is thus at a disadvantage, in not having himself made the beginning, but received the example from us. He will strive accordingly to exceed in measure, in order to eclipse, by the excess of his recompense, the disadvantage he himself sustains in having been second in making advances towards requital ; and the disadvantage again which accrues to the other from the time, if he was the first sufferer, this he will make up by excess of kindness. For men, if they are rightminded, are not so affected by evil as by the good treatment they may receive at the hands of those whom they have injured. For it is a base sin, and it is matter of reproach and scorn for a man who is well-treated not to return it ; whilst for a man who is ill-treated, not to go about to resent it, this has the praise and applause, and the good word of all. And therefore they are more deeply touched by this conduct than any.

So that if thou hast a wish to revenge thyself, revenge thyself in this manner. Return good for evil, that thou mayest render him even thy debtor, and achieve a glorious victory. Hast thou suffered evil? Do good ; thus avenge thee of thine enemy. For if thou shalt go about to resent it, all will blame both thee and him alike. Whereas if thou shalt endure it, it will be otherwise. Thee they will applaud and admire ; but him they will reproach. And what greater punishment can there be to an enemy, than to behold his enemy admired and applauded by all men? What more bitter to an enemy, than to behold himself reproached by all before his enemy's face? If thou shalt avenge thee on him, thou wilt both be condemned perhaps thyself, and wilt be the sole avenger ; whereas, if thou shalt forgive him, all will be avengers in thy stead. And this will be far more severe than any evil he can suffer, that his enemy should have so many to avenge him. If thou openest thy mouth, they will be silent ; but if thou art silent, not with one tongue only, but with ten thousand tongues of others, thou smitest him, and art the more avenged. And on thee indeed, if thou shalt reproach him, many again will cast imputations (for they will say that thy words are those of passion) ; but when others who have suffered no wrong from him thus overwhelm him with reproaches, then is the revenge especially clear of all suspicion. For when they who have suffered no mischief, in consequence of thy excessive forbearance feel and sympathize with thee, as though they had been wronged themselves, this is a vengeance clear of all suspicion. "But what then," ye will say, "if no man should take vengeance?" It cannot be that men will be such stones, as to behold such wisdom and not admire it. And though they wreak not their vengeance on him at the time; still, afterwards, when they are in the mood, they will do so, and they will continue to scoff at him and abuse him. And if no one else admire thee, the man himself will most surely admire thee, though he may not own it. For our judgment of what is right, even though we be come to the very depth of wickedness, remains impartial and unbiased. Why, suppose ye, did our Lord Christ say, "Whosoever smiteth thee on the right cheek, turn to him the other also"? (Matt. v. 39.) Is it not because the more long-suffering a man is, the more signal the benefit he confers both on himself and on the other? For this cause He charges us to "turn the other also," to satisfy the desire of the enraged. For who is such a monster as not to be at once put to shame? The very dogs are said to feel it; for if they bark and attack a man, and he throws himself on his back and does nothing, he puts a stop to all their wrath.[1] If they then reverence the man who is ready to suffer evil from them, much more will the race of man do so, inasmuch as they are more rational.

However, it is right not to overlook what a little before came into my recollection, and was brought forward for a testimony. And what then was this? We were speaking of the Jews, and of the chief rulers amongst them, how that they were blamed, as seeking retaliation. And yet this the law permitted them; "eye for eye, and tooth for tooth." (Lev. xxiv. 20.) True, but not to the intent that men should pluck out each other's eyes, but that they should check boldness in aggression, by fear of suffering in return, and thus should neither do any evil to others, nor suffer any evil from others themselves. Therefore it was said, "eye for eye," to bind the hands of the aggressor, not to let thine loose against him; not to ward off the hurt from thine eyes only, but also to preserve his eyes safe and sound.

But, as to what I was enquiring about,—why, if retaliation was allowed, were they arraigned who practiced it? Whatever can this mean? He here speaks of vindictiveness; for on the spur of the moment he allows the sufferer to act, as I was saying, in order to check the aggressor; but to bear a grudge he permits no longer; because the act then is no longer one of passion, nor of boiling rage, but of malice premeditated. Now God forgives those who may be carried away, perhaps upon a sense of outrage, and rush out to resent it. Hence He says, "eye for eye"; and yet again, "the ways of the revengeful lead to death."[2] Now, if, where it was permitted to put out eye for eye, so great a punishment is reserved for the revengeful, how much more for those who are bidden even to expose themselves to ill-treatment. Let us not then be revengeful, but let us quench our anger, that we may be counted worthy of the lovingkindness, which comes from God ("for with what measure," saith Christ, "ye mete, it shall be measured unto you, and with what judgment ye judge, ye shall be judged") (Matt. vii. 2), and that we may both escape the snares of this present life, and in the day that is at hand, may obtain pardon at His hands, through the grace and lovingkindness of our Lord Jesus Christ, with whom, to the Father, together with the Holy Ghost, be glory, power, honor, both now and forever and ever. Amen.

HOMILY XVII.

EPHESIANS iv. 32, AND v. 1, 2.

"And be ye kind one to another, tender hearted, forgiving each other, even as God also in Christ forgave you. Be ye therefore imitators of God, as beloved children; and walk in love, even as Christ also loved you, and gave Himself up for us, an offering and a sacrifice to God for an odor of a sweet smell."

THE events which are past have greater force than those which are yet to come, and appear to be both more wonderful and more convincing. And hence accordingly Paul founds his exhortation upon the things which have already been done for us, inasmuch as they, on Christ's account, have a greater force. For to say,

---

[1] [Compare Odyssey, Bk. xiv. 33–36, where Ulysses thus quiets the dogs of Eumæus: —

"Soon as Ulysses near the enclosure drew,
With open mouths the furious mastiffs flew;
Down sat the sage, and, cautious to withstand,
Let fall the offensive truncheon from his hand."
Pope's translation. — G. A.]

[2] [Prov. xii. 28, according to Septuagint, which has ὁδοὶ δὲ μνησικάκων εἰς θάνατον. The Rev. Ver., following the Hebrew, has, "And in the pathway thereof (righteousness) there is no death." — G. A.]

"Forgive, and ye shall be forgiven" (Matt. vi. 14), and "if ye forgive not, ye shall in nowise be forgiven" (Matt. vi. 15), — this addressed to men of understanding, and men who believe in the things to come, is of great weight; but Paul appeals to the conscience not by these arguments only, but also by things already done for us. In the former way we may escape punishment, whereas in this latter we may have our share of some positive good. Thou imitatest Christ. This alone is enough to recommend virtue, that it is "to imitate God." This is a higher principle than the other, "for He maketh His sun to rise on the evil and the good, and sendeth rain on the just and the unjust." (Matt. v. 45.) Because he does not merely say that we are "imitating God," but that we do so in those things wherein we receive ourselves such benefits. He would have us cherish the tender heart of fathers towards each other. For by heart, here, is meant lovingkindness and compassion. For inasmuch as it cannot be that, being men, we shall avoid either giving pain or suffering it, he does the next thing, he devises a remedy, — that we should forgive one another. And yet there is no comparison. For if thou indeed shouldest at this moment forgive any one, he will forgive thee again in return; whereas to God thou hast neither given nor forgiven anything. And thou indeed art forgiving a fellow-servant; whereas God is forgiving a servant, and an enemy, and one that hates Him.

"Even as God," saith he, "also in Christ forgave you."

And this, moreover, contains a high allusion. Not simply, he would say, hath He forgiven us, and at no risk or cost, but at the sacrifice of His Son; for that He might forgive thee, He sacrificed the Son; whereas thou, oftentimes, even when thou seest pardon to be both without risk and without cost, yet dost not grant it.

"Be ye therefore imitators of God as beloved children; and walk in love, even as Christ also loved you, and gave Himself up for us an offering and sacrifice to God for an odor of a sweet smell."

That thou mayest not then think it an act of necessity, hear how He saith, that "He gave Himself up." As thy Master loved thee, love thou thy friend. Nay, but neither wilt thou be able so to love; yet still do so as far as thou art able. Oh, what can be more blessed than a sound like this! Tell me of royalty or whatever else thou wilt, there is no comparison. Forgive another, and thou art "imitating God," thou art made like unto God. It is more our duty to forgive trespasses than debts of money; for if thou forgive debts, thou hast not "imitated God"; whereas if thou shalt forgive trespasses,

thou art "imitating God." And yet how shalt thou be able to say, "I am poor, and am not able to forgive it," that is, a debt, when thou forgivest not that which thou art able to forgive, that is, a trespass? And surely thou dost not deem that in this case there is any loss. Yea, is it not rather wealth, is it not abundance, is it not a plentiful store?

And behold yet another and a nobler incitement:[1] — "as beloved children," saith he. Ye have yet another cogent reason to imitate Him, not only in that ye have received such good at His hands, but also in that ye are called His children. And since not all children imitate their fathers, but those which are beloved, therefore he saith, "as beloved children."

Ver. 2. "Walk in love."[2]

Behold, here, the groundwork of all! So then where this is, there is no "wrath, no anger, no clamor, no railing," but all are done away. Accordingly he puts the chief point last. Whence wast thou made a child? Because thou wast forgiven. On the same ground on which thou hast had so vast a privilege vouchsafed thee, on that selfsame ground forgive thy neighbor. Tell me, I say, if thou wert in prison, and hadst ten thousand misdeeds to answer for, and some one were to bring thee into the palace; or rather to pass over this argument, suppose thou wert in a fever and in the agonies of death, and some one were to benefit thee by some medicine, wouldest thou not value him more than all, yea and the very name of the medicine? For if we thus regard occasions and places by which we are benefited, even as our own souls, much more shall we the things themselves. Be a lover then of love; for by this art thou saved, by this hast thou been made a son. And if thou shalt have it in thy power to save another, wilt thou not use the same remedy, and give the advice to all, "Forgive, that ye may be forgiven"? Thus to incite one another, were the part of grateful, of generous, and noble spirits.

"Even as Christ also," he adds, "loved you."

Thou art only sparing friends, He enemies. So then far greater is that boon which cometh from our Master. For how in our case is the "even as" preserved. Surely it is clear that it will be, by our doing good to our enemies.

"And gave Himself up for us an offering and a sacrifice to God for an odor of a sweet smell."

Seest thou that to suffer for one's enemies is "a sweet-smelling savor," and an "acceptable

---

[1] ["Now to be God's beloved child, and not to become like the loving Father, — how contradictory were this!"— Meyer. — G. A.]

[2] ["And walk in love": "the καί annexes that wherein this imitation of God must consist, namely, that 'love' is the element in which their life-work was to take place, — love such as Christ also has displayed towards us."— Meyer. — G. A.]

sacrifice"? And if thou shalt die, then wilt thou be indeed a sacrifice. This it is to "imitate God."

Ver. 3. "But fornication, and all uncleanness, or covetousness, let it not even be named among you, as becometh saints."

He has spoken of the bitter passion, of wrath; he now comes to the lesser evil: for that lust is the lesser evil, hear how Moses also in the law says, first, "Thou shalt do no murder" (Ex. xx. 13), which is the work of wrath, and then, "Thou shalt not commit adultery" (Ex. xx. 14), which is of lust. For as "bitterness," and "clamor," and "all malice," and "railing," and the like, are the works of the passionate man, so likewise are "fornication, uncleanness, covetousness," those of the lustful; since avarice and sensuality spring from the same passion.[1] But just as in the former case he took away "clamor" as being the vehicle of "anger," so now does he "filthy talking" and "jesting" as being the vehicle of lust; for he proceeds,

Ver. 4. "Nor filthiness, nor foolish talking, or jesting, which are not befitting; but rather giving of thanks."

Have no witticisms, no obscenities, either in word or in deed, and thou wilt quench the flame — "let them not even be named," saith he, "among you," that is, let them not anywhere even make their appearance. This he says also in writing to the Corinthians. "It is actually reported that there is fornication among you" (1 Cor. v. 1); as much as to say, Be ye all pure. For words are the way to acts. Then, that he may not appear a forbidding kind of person and austere, and a destroyer of playfulness, he goes on to add the reason, by saying, "which are not befitting," which have nothing to do with us — "but rather giving of thanks." What good is there in uttering a witticism? thou only raisest a laugh. Tell me, will the shoemaker ever busy himself about anything which does not belong to or *befit* his trade? or will he purchase any tool of that kind? No, never. Because the things we do not need, are nothing to us.

MORAL. Let there not be one idle word; for from idle words we fall also into foul words. The present is no season of loose merriment, but of mourning, of tribulation, and lamentation: and dost thou play the jester? What wrestler on entering the ring neglects the struggle with his adversary, and utters witticisms? The devil stands hard at hand, "he is going about roaring" (1 Pet. v. 8) to catch thee, he is moving everything, and turning everything against thy life, and is scheming to force thee from thy retreat, he is grinding his teeth and bellowing, he is

breathing fire against thy salvation; and dost thou sit uttering witticisms, and "talking folly," and uttering things "which are not befitting." Full nobly then wilt thou be able to overcome him! We are in sport, beloved. Wouldest thou know the life of the saints? Listen to what Paul saith. "By the space of three years I ceased not to admonish every one night and day with tears." (Acts xx. 31.) And if so great was the zeal he exerted in behalf of them of Miletus and Ephesus, not making pleasant speeches, but introducing his admonition with tears, what should one say of the rest? But hearken again to what he says to the Corinthians. "Out of much affliction and anguish of heart I wrote unto you with many tears." (2 Cor. ii. 4.) And again, "Who is weak, and I am not weak?" "Who is made to stumble, and I burn not?" (2 Cor. xi. 29.) And hearken again to what he says elsewhere, desiring every day, as one might say, to depart out of the world. "For indeed we that are in this tabernacle do groan" (2 Cor. v. 4); and dost thou laugh and play? It is war-time, and art thou handling the dancers' instruments? Look at the countenances of men in battle, their dark and contracted mien, their brow terrible and full of awe. Mark the stern eye, the heart eager and beating and throbbing, their spirit collected, and trembling and intensely anxious. All is good order, all is good discipline, all is silence in the camps of those who are arrayed against each other. They speak not, I do not say, an impertinent word, but they utter not a single sound. Now if they who have visible enemies, and who are in nowise injured by words, yet observe so great silence, dost thou who hast thy warfare, and the chief of thy warfare in words, dost thou leave this part naked and exposed? Or art thou ignorant that it is here that we are most beset with snares? Art thou amusing and enjoying thyself, and uttering witticisms and raising a laugh, and regarding the matter as a mere nothing? How many perjuries, how many injuries, how many filthy speeches have arisen from witticisms! "But no," ye will say, "pleasantries are not like this." Yet hear how he excludes all kinds of jesting. It is a time now of war and fighting, of watch and guard, of arming and arraying ourselves. The time of laughter can have no place here; for that is of the world. Hear what Christ saith: "The world shall rejoice, but ye shall be sorrowful." (John xvi. 20.) Christ was crucified for thy ills, and dost thou laugh? He was buffeted, and endured so great sufferings because of thy calamity, and the tempest that had overtaken thee; and dost thou play the reveler? And how wilt thou not then rather provoke Him?

But since the matter appears to some to be one of indifference, which moreover is difficult

---

[1] ["Sensuality" and "covetousness" are the two cardinal vices of the heathen which are to be avoided by Christians."— Meyer on iv. 19.— G. A.]

to be guarded against, let us discuss this point a little, to show you how vast an evil it is. For indeed this is a work of the devil, to make us disregard things indifferent. First of all then, even if it were indifferent, not even in that case were it right to disregard it, when one knows that the greatest evils are both produced and increased by it, and that it oftentimes terminates in fornication. However, that it is not even indifferent is evident from hence. Let us see then whence it is produced. Or rather, let us see what sort of a person a saint ought to be : — gentle, meek, sorrowful, mournful, contrite. The man then who deals in jests is no saint. Nay, were he even a Greek, such an one would be scorned. These are things allowed to those only who are on the stage. Where filthiness is, there also is jesting ; where unseasonable laughter is, there also is jesting. Hearken to what the Prophet saith, "Serve the Lord in fear, and rejoice with trembling." (Ps. ii. 11.) Jesting renders the soul soft and indolent. It excites the soul unduly, and often it teems with acts of violence, and creates wars. But what more? In fine, hast thou not come to be among men? then "put away childish things." (1 Cor. xiii. 11.) Why, thou wilt not allow thine own servant in the market place to speak an impertinent word : and dost thou then, who sayest thou art a servant of God, go uttering thy witticisms in the public square? It is well if the soul that is "sober" be not stolen away ; but one that is relaxed and dissolute, who cannot carry off? It will be its own murderer, and will stand in no need of the crafts or assaults of the devil.

But, moreover, in order to understand this, look too at the very name.[1] It means the versatile man, the man of all complexions, the unstable, the pliable, the man that can be anything and everything. But far is this from those who are servants to the Rock. Such a character quickly turns and changes ; for he must needs mimic both gesture and speech, and laugh and gait, and everything, aye, and such an one is obliged to invent jokes : for he needs this also. But far be this from a Christian, to play the buffoon. Farther, the man who plays the jester must of necessity incur the signal hatred of the objects of his random ridicule, whether they be present, or being absent hear of it.

If the thing is creditable, why is it left to mountebanks? What, dost thou make thyself a mountebank, and yet art not ashamed? Why is it ye permit not your gentlewomen to do so? Is it not that ye set it down as a mark of an immodest, and not of a discreet character? Great are the evils that dwell in a soul given to jesting ;

great is the ruin and desolation. Its consistency is broken, the building is decayed, fear is banished, reverence is gone. A tongue thou hast, not that thou mayest ridicule another man, but that thou mayest give thanks unto God. Look at your merriment-makers,[2] as they are called, those buffoons. These are your jesters. Banish from your souls, I entreat you, this graceless accomplishment. It is the business of parasites, of mountebanks, of dancers, of harlots ; far be it from a generous, far be it from a highborn soul, aye, far too even from slaves. If there be any one who has lost respect, if there be any vile person, that man is also a jester. To many indeed the thing appears to be even a virtue, and this truly calls for our sorrow. Just as lust by little and little drives headlong into fornication, so also does a turn for jesting. It seems to have a grace about it, yet there is nothing more graceless than this. For hear the Scripture which says, "Before the thunder goeth lightning, and before a shamefaced man shall go favor."[3] Now there is nothing more shameless than the jester ; so that his mouth is not full of favor, but of pain. Let us banish this custom from our tables. Yet are there some who teach it even to the poor ! O monstrous ! they make men in affliction play the jester. Why, where shall not this pest be found next? Already has it been brought into the Church itself. Already has it laid hold of the very Scriptures. Need I say anything to prove the enormity of the evil? I am ashamed indeed, but still nevertheless I will speak ; for I am desirous to show to what a length the mischief has advanced, that I may not appear to be trifling, or to be discoursing to you on some trifling subject ; that even thus I may be enabled to withdraw you from this delusion. And let no one think that I am fabricating, but I will tell you what I have really heard. A certain person happened to be in company with one of those who pride themselves highly on their knowledge (now I know I shall excite a smile, but still I will say it notwithstanding) ; and when the platter was set before him, he said, "Take and eat, children, lest your belly be angry !"[4] And again, others say, "Woe unto thee, Mammon, and to him that hath thee not" ;[5] and many like enormities has jesting introduced ; as when they say, "Now is there no nativity."[6] And this I say to show the enormity of this base temper ; for these are the expressions of a soul destitute of all reverence. And are not these things enough to call down thunderbolts? And one might find many other

---

1 ["εὐτραπελία, from εὐτράπελος, which is derived from εὖ and τρέπεσθαι, 'that which easily turns,' and in this way adapts itself to the moods and conditions of those with whom at the moment it may deal."—Trench, *Synonyms of N. T.* 1 series, p. 167.—G. A.]

2 [γελωτοποιούς, literally, "laugh-makers."—G. A.]
3 [πρὸ βροντῆς κατασπεύδει ἀστραπή, καὶ πρὸ αἰσχυντηροῦ προελεύσεται χάρις. — Ecclus. xxxii. 10. — G. A.]
4 Δράξασθε, παιδία, μή ποτε ὀργισθῇ κοιλία.
5 οὐαί σοι, μαμωνᾶ, καὶ τῷ μὴ ἔχοντί σε.
6 Ἄρτι οὐκ ἔστι γένεσις. vid. Suicer, *Thesaurus*, voc. γένεσις, n. 3.

such things which have been said by these men.

Wherefore, I entreat you, let us banish the custom universally, and speak those things which become us. Let not holy mouths utter the words of dishonorable and base men. "For what fellowship have righteousness and iniquity, or what communion hath light with darkness?" (2 Cor. vi. 14.) Happy will it be for us, if, having kept ourselves aloof from all such foul things, we be thus able to attain to the promised blessings; far indeed from dragging such a train after us, and sullying the purity of our minds by so many. For the man who will play the jester will soon go on to be a railer, and the railer will go on to heap ten thousand other mischiefs on himself. When then we shall have disciplined these two faculties of the soul, anger and desire (vid. Plat. Phædr. cc. 25, 34), and have put them like well-broken horses under the yoke of reason, then let us set over them the mind as charioteer, that we may "gain the prize of our high calling" (Phil. iii. 14); which God grant that we may all attain, through Jesus Christ our Lord, with Whom, together with the Holy Ghost, be unto the Father, glory, might, and honor, now, and ever, and throughout all ages. Amen.

HOMILY XVIII.

Ephesians v. 5, 6.

"For this ye know of a surety, that no fornicator, nor unclean person, nor covetous man, which is an idolater, hath any inheritance in the kingdom of Christ and God. Let no man deceive you with empty words: for because of these things cometh the wrath of God upon the sons of disobedience."

There were, it is likely, in the time of our forefathers also, some who "weakened the hands of the people" (Jer. xxxviii. 4), and brought into practice that which is mentioned by Ezekiel, — or rather who did the works of the false prophets, who "profaned God among His people for handfuls of barley" (Ezek. xiii. 19); a thing, by the way, done methinks by some even at this day. When, for example, we say that he who calleth his brother a fool shall depart into hellfire, others say, "What? Is he that calls his brother a fool to depart into hell-fire? Impossible," say they. And again, when we say that "the covetous man is an idolater," in this too again they make abatements, and say the expression is hyperbolical. And in this manner they underrate and explain away all the commandments. It was in allusion then to these that the blessed Paul, at this time when he wrote to the Ephesians, spoke thus, "For this ye know,[1] that no fornicator, nor unclean person, nor covetous man, which is an idolater, hath any inheritance in the kingdom of Christ and God"; adding, "let no man[2] deceive you with empty words." Now "empty words" are those which for a while are gratifying, but are in nowise borne out in facts; because the whole case is a deception.

"Because of these things cometh the wrath of God upon the sons of disobedience."

Because of "fornication," he means, because of "covetousness," because of "uncleanness," or both because of these things, and because of the "deceit,"[3] inasmuch as there are deceivers. "Sons of disobedience"; he thus calls those who are utterly disobedient, those who disobey Him.

Ver. 7, 8. "Be not ye, therefore, partakers with them. For ye were[4] once darkness, but are now light in the Lord."

Observe how wisely he urges them forward; first, from the thought of Christ, that ye love one another, and do injury to no man; then, on the other hand, from the thought of punishment and hell-fire. "For ye were once darkness," says he, "but are now light in the Lord." Which is what he says also in the Epistle to the Romans; "What fruit then had ye at that time in the things whereof ye are now ashamed?" (Rom. vi. 21), and reminds them of their former wickedness. That is to say, thinking what ye once were, and what ye are now become, do not run back into your former wickedness, nor do "despite to the grace" (Heb. x. 29) of God.

"Ye were once darkness, but are now light in the Lord!"

Not, he says, by your own virtue, but through

---

[1] ["Ἴστε γινώσκοντες: 'This you are aware of from your own knowledge,' so that I need not first to instruct you with regard to it, 'that,' etc. This is not a Hebraism, since γινώσκοντες is a different verb from ἴστε, but it is like ὁρῶν καὶ ἀκούων οἶδα, Xen. Cyr. iv. 1, 14." — Meyer. — G. A.]

[2] ["In accordance with the context, this refers to unbelieving Gentiles who sought to palliate those Gentile vices, to make them out as matter of indifference, and so to entice Christians back to the Gentile life." — Meyer. — G. A.]

[3] [διὰ ταῦτα refers not "to deceiving with empty words," but to the "vices" just mentioned. Comp. parallel passage, Col. iii. 6. — G. A.]

[4] [ἦτε γάρ, &c. ἦτε prefixed with significant emphasis, has the force of a "ground": For your former state of darkness (with which those vices were in keeping) is "past." Comp. Rom. vi. 17. — Meyer and Ellicott. — G. A.]

the grace of God has this accrued to you. That is to say, ye also were sometime worthy of the same punishments, but now are so no more. "Walk" therefore "as children of light." What is meant however by "children of light," he adds afterwards.

Ver. 9, 10. "For the fruit[1] of the light is in all goodness and righteousness and truth, proving what is well-pleasing unto the Lord."

"In all goodness,"[2] he says: this is opposed to the angry, and the bitter: "and righteousness"; this to the covetous: "and truth"; this to false pleasure: not those former things, he says, which I was mentioning, but their opposites. "In all"; that is, the fruit of the Spirit ought to be evinced in everything. "Proving what is well-pleasing unto the Lord"; so that those things are tokens of a childish and imperfect mind.

Ver. 11, 12, 13. "And have no fellowship with the unfruitful works of darkness, but rather even reprove them. For the things which are done by them in secret it is a shame even to speak of. But all things when they are reproved, are made manifest by the light."

He had said, "ye are light." Now the light reproves by exposing the things which take place in the darkness. So that if ye, says he, are virtuous and conspicuous, the wicked will be unable to lie hidden. For just as when a candle is set, all are brought to light, and the thief cannot enter; so if your light shine, the wicked being discovered shall be caught. So then it is our duty to expose them. How then does our Lord say, "Judge not, that ye be not judged"? (Matt. vii. 1, 3.) Paul did not say "judge," he said "reprove," that is, correct. And the words, "Judge not, that ye be not judged," He spoke with reference to very small errors. Indeed, He added, "Why beholdest thou the mote that is in thy brother's eye, but considerest not the beam that is in thine own eye?" But what Paul is saying is of this sort. As a wound, so long as it is imbedded and concealed outwardly, and runs beneath the surface, receives no attention, so also sin, as long as it is concealed, being as it were in darkness, is daringly committed in full security; but as soon as "it is made manifest," becomes "light"; not indeed the sin itself, (for how could that be?) but the sinner. For when he has been brought out to light, when he has been admonished, when he has repented, when he has obtained pardon, hast thou not cleared away all his darkness? Hast thou not then healed his wound? Hast thou not called his

unfruitfulness into fruit? Either this is his meaning,[3] or else what I said above, that your life "being manifest, is light." For no one hides an irreproachable life; whereas things which are hidden, are hidden by darkness covering them.

Ver. 14. "Wherefore he saith, Awake thou that sleepest, and arise from the dead, and Christ shall shine upon thee."

By the "sleeper" and the "dead," he means the man that is in sin; for he both exhales noisome odors like the dead, and is inactive like one that is asleep, and like him he sees nothing, but is dreaming, and forming fancies and illusions. Some indeed read,[4] "And thou shalt touch Christ"; but others, "And Christ shall shine upon thee"; and it is rather this latter. Depart from sin, and thou shalt be able to behold Christ. "For every one that doeth ill, hateth the light, and cometh not to the light." (John iii. 20.) He therefore that doeth it not, cometh to the light.

Now he is not saying this with reference to the unbelievers only, for many of the faithful, no less than unbelievers, hold fast by wickedness; nay, some far more. Therefore to these also it is necessary to exclaim, "Awake,[5] thou that sleepest, and arise from the dead, and Christ shall shine upon thee." To these it is fitting to say this also, "God is not the God of the dead, but of the living." (Matt. xxii. 32.) If then he is not the God of the dead, let us live.

Now there are some who say that the words, "the covetous man is an idolater," are hyperbolical. However, the statement is not hyperbolical, it is true. How, and in what way? Because the covetous man apostatizes from God, just as the idolater does. And lest you should imagine this is a bare assertion, there is a declaration of Christ which saith, "Ye cannot serve God and Mammon." (Matt. vi. 24.) If then it is not possible to serve God and Mammon, they who serve Mammon have thrown themselves out of the service of God; and they who have denied His sovereignty, and serve lifeless gold, it is plain enough that they are

<hr />

1 ["'Fruit of the light' (not of the spirit, as Chrysostom's text has) denotes figuratively the aggregate of moral effects which Christian enlightenment produces."—Meyer.—G. A.]

2 ["Chrysostom's interpretation is too specific. The words mean 'good, right, true,' and embrace the *whole* of Christian morality."—Meyer.—G. A.]

3 [This difficult passage is thus translated by Ellicott: It is true these things are done in secret, but all of them, when reproved, are made manifest by the light (thus shed upon them); for everything that is made manifest is light (becomes daylight, is of the nature of light).—G. A.]

4 [ἐπιψαύσεις (instead of ἐπιφαύσει) is the reading of D* and E, and the Latin versions of these MSS. (*continges Christum*), but it *never* obtained much acceptance, and hardly appears in extant codices. See Scrivener's Introd. 632, and Westcott and Hort, Appendix, p. 125.—G. A.]

5 ["The words here quoted are not found exactly in this form in the O. T., but certainly occur in substance in Isa. lx. 1. Instead of resorting to the explanation of Meyer or De Wette (which are somewhat rationalistic), it is better to say that Paul, under the inspiration of the Holy Spirit, is expressing in a condensed form the spiritual meaning of the passage."—Ellicott. Riddle says: "It is Isa. lx. 1, partly paraphrased and partly condensed, and interpreted in the light of its fulfillment." "This call of God to the sons of disobedience to awake, confirms the necessity of the ἐλέγχειν, and the promise, 'Christ shall shine upon thee,' confirms the salutary influence of the light."—Meyer.—G. A.]

idolaters. " But I never made an idol," a man will say, " nor set up an altar, nor sacrificed sheep, nor poured libations of wine ; no, I came into the church, and lifted up my hands to the Only-begotten Son of God ; I partake of the mysteries, I communicate in prayer, and in everything else which is a Christian's duty. How then," he will say, " am I a worshiper of idols?" Yes, and this is the very thing which is the most astonishing of all, that when thou hast had experience, and hast "tasted" the lovingkindness of God, and "hast seen that the Lord is gracious" (Ps. xxxiv. 8), thou shouldest abandon Him who is gracious, and take to thyself a cruel tyrant, and shouldest pretend to be serving Him, whilst in reality thou hast submitted thyself to the hard and galling yoke of covetousness. Thou hast not yet told me of thy own duty done, but only of thy Master's gifts. For tell me, I beseech thee, whence do we judge of a soldier? Is it when he is on duty guarding the king, and is fed by him, and called the king's own, or is it when he is minding his own affairs and interests? To pretend to be with him, and to be attentive to his interests, whilst he is advancing the cause of the enemy, we declare to be worse than if he breaks away from the king's service, and joins the enemy. Now then thou art doing despite to God, just as an idolater does, not with thine own mouth singly, but with the ten thousands of those whom thou hast wronged. Yet you will say, " an idolater he is not." But surely, whenever they say, " Oh ! that Christian, that covetous fellow," then not only is he himself committing outrage by his own act, but he frequently forces those also whom he has wronged to use these words ; and if they use them not, this is to be set to the account of their reverence.

Do we not see that such is the fact? What else is an idolater? Or does not he too worship passions, oftentimes not mastering his passions? I mean, for example, when we say that the pagan idolater worships idols, he will say, " No, but it is Venus, or it is Mars." And if we say, Who is this Venus? the more modest amongst them will say, It is pleasure. Or what is this Mars? It is wrath. And in the same way dost thou worship Mammon. If we say, Who is this Mammon? It is covetousness, and this thou art worshiping. "I worship it not," thou wilt say. Why not? Because thou dost not bow thyself down? Nay, but as it is, thou art far more a worshiper in thy deeds and practices ; for this is the higher kind of worship. And that you may understand this, look in the case of God ; who more truly worship Him, they who merely stand up at the prayers, or they who do His will? Clearly enough, these latter. The same also is it with the worshipers of Mammon ;

they who do his will, they truly are his worshipers. However, they who worship the passions are oftentimes free from the passions. One may see a worshiper of Mars oftentimes governing his wrath. But this is not true of thee ; thou makest thyself a slave to thy passion.

Yes, but thou slayest no sheep? No, thou slayest men, reasonable souls, some by famine, others by blasphemies. Nothing can be more frenzied than a sacrifice like this. Who ever beheld souls sacrificed? How accursed is the altar of covetousness ! When thou passest by this idol's altar here, thou shalt see it reeking with the blood of bullocks and goats ; but when thou shalt pass by the altar of covetousness, thou shalt see it breathing the shocking odor of human blood. Stand here before it in this world, and thou shalt see, not the wings of birds burning, no vapor, no smoke exhaled, but the bodies of men perishing. For some throw themselves among precipices, others tie the halter, others thrust the dagger through their throat. Hast thou seen the cruel and inhuman sacrifices? Wouldest thou see yet more shocking ones than these? Then I will show thee no longer the bodies of men, but the souls of men slaughtered in the other world. Yes, for it is possible for a soul to be slain with the slaughter peculiar to the soul ; for as there is a death of the body,[1] so is there also of the soul. " The soul that sinneth," saith the Prophet, " it shall die." (Ezek. xviii. 4.) The death of the soul, however, is not like the death of the body ; it is far more shocking. For this bodily death, separating the soul and the body the one from the other, releases the one from many anxieties and toils, and transmits the other into a manifest abode : then when the body has been in time dissolved and crumbled away, it is again gathered together in incorruption, and receives back its own proper soul. Such we see is this bodily death. But that of the soul is awful and terrific. For this death, when dissolution takes place, does not let it pass, as the body does, but binds it down again to an imperishable body, and consigns it to the unquenchable fire. This then is the death of the soul. And as therefore there is a death of the soul, so is there also a slaughter of the soul. What is the slaughter of the body? It is the being turned into a corpse, the being stripped of the energy derived from the soul. What is the slaughter of the soul? It is its being made a corpse also. And how is the soul made a corpse? • Because as the body then becomes a corpse when the soul leaves it destitute of its own vital energy, so also does the soul then be-

---

[1] [As in other places, the text of Field is here incomplete. (ὥσπερ γάρ ἐστι ψυχῆς θάνατος, " Ψυχὴ γὰρ ἡ ἁμαρτάνουσα," etc.) It omits the clause, ὥσπερ γάρ ἐστι σώματος θάνατος, which is so necessary to the sense and which is attested by excellent manuscript authority, and adopted by Savile. — G. A.]

come a corpse, when the Holy Spirit leaves it destitute of His spiritual energy.

Such for the most part are the slaughters made at the altar of covetousness. They are not satisfied, they do not stop at men's blood; no, the altar of covetousness is not glutted, unless it sacrifice the very soul itself also, unless it receive the souls of both, the sacrificer and the sacrificed. For he who sacrifices must first be sacrificed, and then he sacrifices; and the dead sacrifices him who is yet living. For when he utters blasphemies, when he reviles, when he is irritated, are not these so many incurable wounds of the soul?

Thou hast seen that the expression is no hyperbole. Wouldest thou hear again another argument, to teach you how covetousness is idolatry, and more shocking than idolatry? Idolaters worship the creatures of God ("for they worshiped," it is said, "and served the creature rather than the Creator") (Rom. i. 25); but thou art worshiping a creature of thine own. For God made not covetousness, but thine own insatiable appetite invented it.[1] And look at the madness and folly. They that worship idols, honor also the idols they worship; and if any one speak of them with disrespect or ridicule, they stand up in their defense; whereas thou, as if in a sort of intoxication, art worshiping an object, which is so far from being free from accusation, that it is even full of impiety. So that thou, even more than they, excellest in wickedness. Thou canst never have it to say as an excuse, that it is no evil. If even they are in the highest degree without excuse, yet art thou in a far higher, who art forever censuring covetousness, and reviling those who devote themselves to it, and who yet doth serve and obey it.

We will examine, if you please, whence idolatry took its rise. A certain wise man (Wisd. xiv. 16) tells us, that a certain rich man afflicted with untimely mourning for his son, and having no consolation for his sorrow, consoled his passion in this way: having made a lifeless image of the dead, and constantly gazing at it, he seemed through the image to have his departed one still; whilst certain flatterers, "whose God was their belly" (Phil. iii. 19), treating the image with reverence in order to do him honor, carried on the custom into idolatry.[2] So then it took its rise from weakness of soul, from a senseless custom, from extravagance. But not so covetousness: from weakness of soul indeed it is, only that it is from a worse

weakness. It is not that any one has lost a son, nor that he is seeking for consolation in sorrow, nor that he is drawn on by flatterers. But how is it? I will tell you. Cain in covetousness overreached[3] God; what ought to have been given to Him, he kept to himself; what he should have kept himself, this he offered to Him; and thus the evil began even from God. For if we are God's, much more are the firstfruits of our possessions. Again, men's violent passion for women arose from covetousness.[4] "They saw the daughters of men" (Gen. vi. 2), and they rushed headlong into lust. And from hence again it went on to money; for the wish to have more than one's neighbor of this world's goods, arises from no other source, than from "love waxing cold." The wish to have more than one's share arises from no other source than recklessness, misanthropy, and arrogance toward others. Look at the earth, how wide is its extent? How far greater than we can use the expanse of the sky and the heaven? It is that He might put an end to thy covetousness, that God hath thus widely extended the bounds of the creation. And art thou then still grasping and even thus? And dost thou hear that covetousness is idolatry, and not shudder even at this? Dost thou wish to inherit the earth? Then hast thou no inheritance in heaven. Art thou eager to leave an inheritance to others, that thou mayest rob thyself of it? Tell me, if any one were to offer thee power to possess all things, wouldest thou be unwilling? It is in thy power now, if thou wilt. Some, however, say, that they are grieved when they transmit the inheritance to others, and would fain have consumed it themselves, rather than see others become its masters. Nor do I acquit thee of this weakness; for this too is characteristic of a weak soul. However, at least let as much as this be done. In thy will leave Christ thine heir. It were thy duty indeed to do so in thy lifetime, for this would show a right disposition. Still, at all events, be a little generous, though it be but by necessity. For Christ indeed charged us to give to the poor with this object, to make us wise in our lifetime, to induce us to despise money, to teach us to look down upon earthly things. It is no contempt of money, as you think, to bestow it upon this man and upon that man when one dies, and is no longer master of it. Thou art then no longer giving of thine own, but of absolute necessity: thanks to death, not to thee. This is no act of affection, it is thy loss.

However, let it be done even thus ; at least then give up thy passion.

MORAL. Consider how many acts of plunder, how many acts of covetousness, thou hast committed. Restore all fourfold. Thus plead thy cause to God. Some, however, there are who are arrived at such a pitch of madness and blindness, as not even then to comprehend their duty ; but who go on acting in all cases, just as if they were taking pains to make the judgment of God yet heavier to themselves. This is the reason why our blessed Apostle writes and says, "Walk as children of light." Now the covetous man of all others lives in darkness, and spreads great darkness over all things around.

"And have no fellowship," he adds, "with the unfruitful works of darkness, but rather even reprove them ; for the things which are done by them in secret, it is a shame even to speak of ; but all things when they are reproved are made manifest by the light." Hearken, I entreat you, all, as many of you as like not to be hated for nothing, but to be loved. "What need is there to be hated?" one says. A man commits a robbery, and dost thou not reprove him, but art afraid of his hatred? though this, however, is not being hated for nothing. But dost thou justly convict him, and yet fear the hatred? Convict thy brother, incur enmity for the love's sake which thou owest to Christ, for the love's sake which thou owest to thy brother. Arrest him as he is on his road to the pit of destruction. For to admit him to our table, to treat him with civil speeches, with salutations, and with entertainments, these are no signal proofs of friendship. No, those I have mentioned are the boons which we must bestow upon our friends, that we may rescue their souls from the wrath of God. When we see them lying prostrate in the furnace of wickedness, let us raise them up. "But," they say, "it is of no use, he is incorrigible." However, do thou thy duty, and then thou hast excused thyself to God. Hide not thy talent. It is for this that thou hast speech, it is for this thou hast a mouth and a tongue, that thou mayest correct thy neighbor.[1] It is dumb and reasonless creatures only that have no care for their neighbor, and take no account of others. But dost thou while calling God, "Father," and thy neighbor, "brother," when thou seest him committing unnumbered wickednesses, dost thou prefer his good-will to his welfare? No, do not so, I entreat you. There is no evidence of friendship so true as never to overlook the sins of

our brethren. Didst thou see them at enmity? Reconcile them. Didst thou see them guilty of covetousness? Check them. Didst thou see them wronged? Stand up in their defense. It is not on them, it is on thyself thou art conferring the chief benefit. It is for this we are friends, that we may be of use one to another. A man will listen in a different spirit to a friend, and to any other chance person. A chance person he will regard perhaps with suspicion, and so in like manner will he a teacher, but not so a friend.

"For," he says, "the things which are done by them in secret it is a shame even to speak of : but all things when they are reproved are made manifest by the light." What is it he means to say here? He means this. That some sins in this world are done in secret, and some also openly ; but in the other it shall not be so. Now there is no one who is not conscious to himself of some sin. This is why he says, "But all the things when they are reproved are made manifest by the light." What then? Is this again, it will be said, meant concerning idolatry? It is not ; the argument is about our life and our sins. "For everything that is made manifest," says he, "is light."

Wherefore, I entreat you, be ye never backward to reprove, nor displeased at being reproved.[2] For as long indeed as anything is carried on in the dark, it is carried on with greater security ; but when it has many to witness what is done, it is brought to light. By all means then let us do all we can to chase away the deadness which is in our brethren, to scatter the darkness, and to attract to us the "Sun of righteousness." For if there be many shining lights, the path of virtue will be easy to themselves, and they which are in darkness will be more easily detected, while the light is held forth and puts the darkness to flight. Whereas if it be the reverse, there is fear lest as the thick mist of darkness and of sin overpowers the light, and dispels its transparency, those shining lights themselves should be extinguished. Let us be then disposed to benefit one another, that one and all, we may offer up praise and glory to the God of lovingkindness, by the grace and lovingkindness of the only begotten Son with whom to the Father, together with the Holy Ghost, be glory, strength, honor now and forever and forever. Amen.

---

[1] [Compare John Wesley's sermon on the "Duty of Reproving our Neighbor," *Works*, Vol. II., p. 88 (New York ed.), for a thorough and fearless discussion of this difficult duty. — G. A.]

[2] [" Better is open rebuke
Than love that is hidden.
Faithful are the wounds of a friend,
But the kisses of an enemy are profuse." — Prov. xxvii. 5, 6.

" He that rebuketh a man shall afterward find more favor
Than he that flattereth with the tongue." — Prov. xxviii. 23.
Compare Chrysostom's I. Homily on Eutropius, Vol. IX., p. 249, this series. — G. A.]

HOMILY XIX.

EPHESIANS v. 15, 16, 17.

"Look then carefully how ye walk, not as unwise, but as wise; redeeming the time, because the days are evil. Wherefore be ye not foolish, but understand what the will of the Lord is."

HE is still cleansing away the root of bitterness, still cutting off the very groundwork of anger.[1] For what is he saying? "Look carefully how ye walk." "They are sheep in the midst of wolves," and he charges them to be also "as doves." For "ye shall be harmless," saith he, "as doves." (Matt. x. 16.) Forasmuch then as they were both amongst wolves, and were besides commanded not to defend themselves, but to suffer evil, they needed this admonition.[2] Not indeed but that the former was sufficient to render them stronger;[3] but now that there is besides the addition of the two, reflect how exceedingly it is heightened. Observe then here also, how carefully he secures them, by saying, "Look how ye walk." Whole cities were at war with them; yea, this war made its way also into houses. They were divided, father against son, and son against father, mother against daughter, and daughter against mother. What then? Whence these divisions? They heard Christ say, "He that loveth father or mother more than me, is not worthy of me." (Matt. x. 37.) Lest therefore they should think that he was without reason introducing wars and fightings, (since there was likely to be much anger produced, if they on their part were to retaliate,) to prevent this, he says, "See carefully how ye walk." That is to say, "Except the Gospel message,[4] give no other handle on any score whatever, for the hatred which you will incur." Let this be the only ground of hatred. Let no one have any other charge to make against you; but show all deference and obedience, whenever it does no harm to the message, whenever it does not stand in the way of godliness. For it is said, "Render to all their dues, tribute to whom tribute, custom to whom custom." (Rom. xiii. 7.) For when amongst the rest of the world they shall see us forbearing, they will be put to shame.

"Not as unwise, but as wise,[5] redeeming the time."

It is not from any wish that you should be artful, and versatile, that he gives this advice. But what he means is this. The time is not yours. At present ye are strangers, and sojourners, and foreigners, and aliens; seek not honors, seek not glory, seek not authority, nor revenge; bear all things, and in this way, "redeem the time";[6] give up many things, anything they may require. Imagine now, I say, a man had a magnificent house, and persons were to make their way in, on purpose to murder him, and he were to give a large sum, and thus to rescue himself. Then we should say, he has redeemed himself. So also hast thou a large house, and a true faith in thy keeping. They will come to take all away. Give whatever they may demand, only preserve the principal thing, I mean the faith.

"Because the days," saith he, "are evil."

What is the evil of the day? The evil of the day ought to belong to the day. What is the evil of a body? Disease. And what again the evil of the soul? Wickedness. What is the evil of water? Bitterness. And the evil of each particular thing, is with reference to that nature of it which is affected by the evil. If then there is an evil in the day, it ought to belong to the day, to the hours, to the day-light. So also Christ saith, "Sufficient unto the day is the evil thereof." (Matt. vi. 34.) And from this expression we shall understand the other. In what sense then does he call "the days evil"? In what sense the "time" evil? It is not the essence of the thing, not the things as so created, but it is the things transacted in them. In the same way as we are in the habit of saying, "I have passed a disagreeable and wretched day."[7] And yet how could it be disagreeable, except from the circumstances which took place in it? Now the events which take place in it are, good things from God, but evil things from bad men. So then of the evils which happen in the times, men are the creators, and hence it is that the times are said to be evil. And thus we also call the times evil.

Ver. 17, 18. "Wherefore,"[8] he adds, "be ye

---

[1] [The οὖν rather resumes the general directions as to how they are to walk (comp. v. 9) after the digression in ver. 11-14.—G. A.]

[2] [The text of Field omits the clause, "they needed this admonition," leaving the sense obscure and difficult. This clause is attested by five codices, and we have inserted it with Savile.—G. A.]

[3] [And with four of these codices we prefer the reading εὐσθενεστέρους, "stronger," to Field's reading ἀσθενεστέρους (which is "weaker").—G. A.]

[4] κήρυγμα.

[5] ["This is epexegetical of the preceding words, viewed nega-

tively and positively: 'presenting yourselves in your walk, not as unwise, but as wise.'"—Meyer.—G. A.]

[6] [Or rather, "buying up for yourselves the opportunity": a participial clause, which gives a modal definition to the preceding ὡς σοφοί, "as wise." "In this figurative conception the doing of that for which the point of time is fitted is thought of as the 'purchase-price by which the καιρός becomes ours.'"—Meyer.—G. A.]

[7] [Compare on Gal. i. 4. "This clause, 'because the days are evil,' supplies a motive for buying up the opportunity, namely, because moral corruption is now in vogue."—Meyer.—G. A.]

[8] ["This 'wherefore' refers to verses 15,16. For this cause, i.e. because ye ought to walk with such exactness, become not such as do not use the mind aright."—Ellicott.—G. A.]

not foolish, but understand what the will of the Lord is; and be not drunk with wine, wherein is riot."

For indeed intemperance in this renders men passionate and violent, and hot-headed, and irritable and savage. Wine has been given us for cheerfulness, not for drunkenness. Whereas now it appears to be an unmanly and contemptible thing for a man not to get drunk. And what sort of hope then is there of salvation? What? contemptible, tell me, not to get drunk, where to get drunk ought of all things in the world to be most contemptible? For it is of all things right for even a private individual to keep himself far from drunkenness; but how much more so for a soldier, a man who lives amongst swords, and bloodshed, and slaughter: much more, I say, for the soldier, when his temper is sharpened by other causes also, by power, by authority, by being constantly in the midst of stratagems and battles. Wouldest thou know where wine is good? Hear what the Scripture saith, "Give strong drink unto him that is ready to perish, and wine unto the bitter in soul." (Prov. xxxi. 6.) And justly, because it can mitigate asperity and gloominess, and drive away clouds from the brow. "Wine maketh glad the heart of man" (Ps. civ. 15), says the Psalmist. How then does wine produce drunkenness? For it cannot be that one and the same thing should work opposite effects. Drunkenness then surely does not arise from wine, but from intemperance. Wine is bestowed upon us for no other purpose than for bodily health; but this purpose also is thwarted by immoderate use. But hear moreover what our blessed Apostle writes and says to Timothy, "Use a little wine for thy stomach's sake, and thine often infirmities."[1]

This is the reason why God has formed our bodies in moderate proportions, and so as to be satisfied with a little, from thence at once instructing us that He has made us adapted to another life. And that life He would fain have bestowed upon us even from the very beginning; but since we rendered ourselves unworthy of it, He deferred it; and in the time during which He deferred it, not even in that does He allow us immoderate indulgence; for a little cup of wine and a single loaf is enough to satisfy a man's hunger. And man the lord of all the brute creation has He formed so as to require less food in proportion than they, and his body small; thereby declaring to us nothing else than this, that we are hastening onward to another life. "Be not drunk," says he, "with wine, wherein is riot"; for it does not save[2]

but it destroys; and that, not the body only, but the soul also.

Ver. 18, 19, 20, 21. "But be filled[3] with the Spirit; speaking one to another in psalms and hymns and spiritual songs, singing and making melody with your heart to the Lord; giving thanks always for all things in the name of our Lord Jesus Christ to God even the Father; subjecting yourselves one to another in the fear of Christ."

Dost thou wish, he says, to be cheerful, dost thou wish to employ the day? I give thee spiritual drink; for drunkenness even cuts off the articulate sound of our tongue; it makes us lisp and stammer, and distorts the eyes, and the whole frame together. Learn to sing psalms, and thou shalt see the delightfulness of the employment. For they who sing psalms are filled with the Holy Spirit, as they who sing satanic songs are filled with an unclean spirit.

What is meant by "with your hearts to the Lord"? It means, with close attention and understanding. For they who do not attend closely, merely sing, uttering the words, whilst their heart is roaming elsewhere.

"Always," he says, "giving thanks for all things in the name of our Lord Jesus Christ unto God even the Father, subjecting yourselves one to another in the fear of Christ."

That is, "let your requests be made known unto God, with thanksgiving" (Phil. iv. 6); for there is nothing so pleasing to God, as for a man to be thankful. But we shall be best able to give thanks unto God, by withdrawing our souls from the things before mentioned, and by thoroughly cleansing them by the means he has told us.

"But be filled," says he, "with the Spirit."

And is then this Spirit within us? Yes, indeed, within us. For when we have driven away lying, and bitterness, and fornication, and uncleanness, and covetousness, from our souls, when we are become kind, tender-hearted, forgiving one another, when there is no jesting, when we have rendered ourselves worthy of it, what is there to hinder the Holy Spirit from coming and lighting upon us? And not only will He come unto us, but He will fill our hearts; and when we have so great a light kindled within us, then will the way of virtue be no longer difficult to attain, but will be easy and simple.

"Giving thanks always,"[4] he says, "for all things."

---

[1] 1 Tim. v. 23. Cf. Vol. IX., 335.

[2] [σώζει: suggested by the word ἀσωτία ("riot") which immediately precedes, and which is derived from σώζω. Compare ἀσωτία in Thayer's *N. T. Lexicon.*—G. A.]

[3] ["The imperative *passive* finds its explanation in the possibility of resistance to the Holy Spirit. The contrast does not lie in οἶνος (wine) and πνεῦμα (spirit), otherwise these words would have stood at the beginning of their clauses, but in the two *states*,—that of intoxication and that of inspiration."—Meyer.—G. A.]

[4] ["This 'giving thanks always,' etc., is a third modal definition of the 'Be filled with the spirit,' likewise coördinate with the two preceding ones, bringing into prominence,—after the general 'singing of praise' of ver. 19, which is to take place audibly, as well as in the heart,—further and in particular, the 'thanksgiving' which the

What then? Are we to give thanks for everything that befalls us? Yes; be it even disease, be it even penury. For if a certain wise man gave this advice in the Old Testament, and said, "Whatsoever is brought upon thee take cheerfully, and be patient when thou art changed to a low estate" (Ecclus. ii. 4); much more ought this to be the case in the New. Yes, even though thou know not the word, give thanks. For this is thanksgiving. But if thou give thanks when thou art in comfort and in affluence, in success and in prosperity, there is nothing great, nothing wonderful in that. What is required is, for a man to give thanks when he is in afflictions, in anguish, in discouragements. Utter no word in preference to this, "Lord, I thank thee." And why do I speak of the afflictions of this world? It is our duty to give God thanks, even for hell[1] itself, for the torments and punishments of the next world. For surely it is a thing beneficial to those who attend to it, when the dread of hell is laid like a bridle on our hearts. Let us therefore give thanks not only for blessings which we see, but also for those which we see not, and for those which we receive against our will. For many are the blessings He bestows upon us, without our desire, without our knowledge. And if ye believe me not, I will at once proceed to make the case clear to you. For consider, I pray, do not the impious and unbelieving Gentiles ascribe everything to the sun and to their idols? But what then? Doth He not bestow blessings even upon them? Is it not the work of His providence, that they both have life, and health, and children, and the like? And again they that are called Marcionites,[2] and the Manichees, do they not even blaspheme Him? But what then? Does He not bestow blessings on them every day? Now if He bestows blessings on them that know them not, much more does he bestow them upon us. For what else is the peculiar work of God if it be not this, to do good to all mankind, alike by chastisements and by enjoyments? Let us not then give thanks only when we are in prosperity, for there is nothing great in this. And this the devil also well knows, and therefore he said, "Doth Job fear God for nought? Hast Thou not made an hedge about him and about all that he hath on every side? Touch all that he hath; no doubt, he will renounce Thee to Thy face!" (Job i. 10, 11.) However, that cursed one gained no advantage; and God forbid he should gain any advantage of us either; but whenever we are either in penury, or in sicknesses, or in disasters,

then let us increase our thanksgiving; thanksgiving, I mean, not in words, nor in tongue, but in deeds and works, in mind and in heart. Let us give thanks unto Him with all our souls. For He loves us more than our parents; and wide as is the difference between evil and goodness, so great is the difference between the love of God and that of our fathers. And these are not my words, but those of Christ Himself Who loveth us. And hear what He Himself saith, "What man is there of you, who, if his son shall ask him for a loaf, will give him a stone? If ye then, being evil, know how to give good gifts unto your children, how much more shall your Father which is in Heaven give good things to them that ask Him?" (Matt. vii. 9, 11.) And again, hear what He saith also elsewhere: "Can a woman forget her sucking child that she should not have compassion on the son of her womb? Yea, they may forget, yet will not I forget thee, saith the Lord." (Isa. xlix. 15.) For if He loveth us not, wherefore did He create us? Had He any necessity? Do we supply to Him any ministry and service? Needeth He anything that we can render? Hear what the Prophet says; "I have said unto the Lord, Thou art my Lord, I have no good beyond Thee." (Ps. xvi. 2.)

The ungrateful, however, and unfeeling say, that this were worthy of God's goodness, that there should be an equality amongst all. Tell me, ungrateful mortal, what sort of things are they which thou deniest to be of God's goodness, and what equality meanest thou? "Such an one," thou wilt say, "has been a cripple from his childhood; another is mad, and is possessed; another has arrived at extreme old age, and has spent his whole life in poverty; another in the most painful diseases: are these works of Providence? One man is deaf, another dumb, another poor, whilst another, impious, yea, utterly impious, and full of ten thousand vices, enjoys wealth, and keeps concubines, and parasites, and is owner of a splendid mansion, and lives an idle life."[3] And many instances of the sort they string together, and weave a long account of complaint against the providence of God.

What then are we to say to them? Now if they were Greeks, and were to tell us that the universe is governed by some one or other, we should in turn address. to them the self-same words, "What then, are things without a provi-

<hr/>

readers have always for all things to render to God." — Meyer. — G. A.]

[1] [Meyer says the context limits πάντων to "blessings." — G. A.]

[2] [On these heretics and their doctrines, see Vol. IX. (this series) p. 65 (notes 3 and 5), and p. 205, second column. — G. A.]

[3] This difficulty is as old as David. Chrysostom does not here suggest David's solution of the problem, — the spiritual compensations here and hereafter. And Paul could say even to a slave in his day, "Wast thou called being a slave? Care not for it. Nay, if thou art even able to be free, make use of thy having been called as a slave, rather than accept thy freedom." (1 Cor. vii. 21.) And even Epictetus said something similar. A little below, Chrysostom touches this higher Theodicy: "One thing alone is evil; that is, to sin." — G. A.]

dence? How then is it that ye reverence gods, and worship genii and heroes? For if there is a providence, some one or other superintends the whole." But if any, whether Christians or Heathen, should be impatient at this, and be wavering, what shall we say to them? "Why, could so many good things, tell me, arise of themselves? The daily light? The beautiful order and the forethought that exist in all things? The mazy dances of the stars? The equable course of nights and days? The regular gradation of nature in vegetables, and animals, and men? Who, tell me, is it that ordereth these? If there were no superintending Being, but all things combined together of themselves, who then was it that made this vault revolve, so beautiful, so vast, I mean the sky, and set it upon the earth, nay more, upon the waters? Who is it that gives the fruitful seasons? Who implanted so great power in seeds and vegetables? For that which is accidental is necessarily disorderly; whereas that which is orderly implies design. For which, tell me, of the things around us that are accidental, is not full of great disorder, and of great tumult and confusion? Nor do I speak of things accidental only, but of those also which imply some agent, but an unskillful agent. For example, let there be timber and stone, and let there be lime withal; and let a man unskilled in building take them, and begin building, and set hard to work; will he not spoil and destroy everything? Again, take a vessel without a pilot, containing everything which a vessel ought to contain, without a shipwright; I do not say that it is unequipped and unfinished, but though well equipped, it will not be able to sail. And could the vast extent of earth standing on the waters, tell me, ever stand so firmly, and so long a time, without some power to hold it together?[1] And can these views have any reason? Is it not the extreme of absurdity to conceive such a notion? And if the earth supports the heaven, behold another burden still; but if the heaven also is borne upon the waters, there arises again another question. Or rather not another question, for it is the work of providence. For things which are borne upon the water ought not to be made convex, but concave. Wherefore? Because the whole body of anything which is concave is immersed in the waters, as is the case with a ship; whereas of the convex the body is entirely above, and only the rim rests upon the surface; so that it requires a resisting body, hard, and able to sustain it, in order to bear the burden imposed. But does the atmosphere then support the heaven? Why, that is far softer, and more yielding even than water, and cannot sustain anything, no, not the very lightest things, much less so vast a bulk. In fine, if we chose to follow out the argument of providence, both generally and in detail, time itself would fail us. For I will now ask him who would start those questions above mentioned, are these things the result of providence, or of the want of providence? And if he shall say, that they are not from providence, then again I will ask, how then did they arise? But no, he will never be able to give any account at all. And dost thou not know that?

Much more then is it thy duty not to question, not to be over curious, in those things which concern man. And why not? Because man is nobler than all these, and these were made for his sake, not he for their sake. If then thou knowest not so much as the skill and contrivance that are visible in His providence, how shalt thou be able to know the reasons, where he himself is the subject? Tell me, I pray, why did God form him so small, so far below the height of heaven, as that he should even doubt of the things which appear above him? Why are the northern and southern climes uninhabitable? Tell me, I say, why is the night made longer in winter and shorter in summer? Why are the degrees of cold and heat such as they are? Why is the body mortal? And ten thousand questions besides I will ask thee, and if thou 'wilt, will never cease asking. And in one and all thou wilt surely be at a loss to answer. And thus is this of all things most providential, that the reasons of things are kept secret from us. For surely, one would have imagined man to be the cause of all things, were there not this to humble our understanding.

"But such an one," you will say, "is poor, and poverty is an evil. And what is it to be sick, and what is it to be crippled?" Oh, man, they are nothing.[2] One thing alone is evil, that is to sin; this is the only thing we ought to search to the bottom. And yet we omit to search into the causes of what are really evils, and busy ourselves about other things. Why is it that not one of us ever examines why he has sinned? To sin, — is it then in my power, or is it not in my power? And why need I go round about me for a number of reasons? I will seek for the matter within myself. Now then did I ever master my wrath? Did I ever master my anger, either through shame, or through fear of man? Then whenever

---

[1] [On Chrysostom's geography and astronomy, see Homily IX., Concerning the Statues, Vol. IX. of this series, pp. 403, 404, with notes by Rev. W. R. W. Stevens, M.A. Compare Ps. xxiv. 2. —G. A.]

[2] [Compare what is said by Epictetus concerning his own lameness: "Shall I then, because of one miserable little leg, find fault with the universe? Shall I not concede that accident to the existence of general laws, and cheerfully assent to it for the sake of him who gave it?" And again, concerning his slavery: "He is a slave whose body is free, but whose soul is bound; and on the contrary, he is free whose body is bound, but whose soul is free." —G. A.]

I discover this done, I shall discover that to sin is in my own power. No one examines these matters, no one busies himself about them. But only according to Job, " Man in a way altogether different swims upon words." [1] For why does it concern thee, if such an one is blind, or such an one poor? God hath not commanded thee to look to this, but to what thou thyself art doing. For if on the one hand thou doubtest that there is any power superintending the world, thou art of all men the most senseless; but if thou art persuaded of this, why doubt that it is our duty to please God?

" Giving thanks always," he says, " for all things to God."

Go to the physician's, and thou wilt see him, whenever a man is discovered to have a wound, using the knife and the cautery. But no, in thy case, I say not so much as this; but go to the carpenter's. And yet thou dost not examine his reasons, although thou understandest not one of the things which are done there, and many things will appear to thee to be difficulties; as, for instance, when he hollows the wood, when he alters its outward shape. Nay, I would bring thee to a more intelligible craft still, for instance, that of the painter, and there thy head will swim. For tell me, does he not seem to be doing what he does, at random? For what do his lines mean, and the turns and bends of the lines? But when he puts on the colors, then the beauty of the art will become conspicuous. Yet still, not even then wilt thou be able to attain to any accurate understanding of it. But why do I speak of carpenters, and painters, and fellow-servants? Tell me, how does the bee frame her comb, and then shalt thou speak about God also. Master the handiwork of the ant, the spider, and the swallow, and then shalt thou speak about God also. Tell me these things. But no, thou never canst. Wilt thou not cease then, O man, thy vain enquiries? For vain indeed they are. Wilt thou not cease busying thyself in vain about many things? Nothing so wise as this ignorance, where they that profess they know nothing are wisest of all, and they that spend overmuch labor on these questions, the most foolish of all. So that to profess knowledge is not everywhere a sign of wisdom, but sometimes of folly also. For tell me, suppose there were two men, and one of them should profess to stretch out his lines, and to measure the expanse that intervenes between the earth and heaven, and the other were to laugh at him, and declare that he did not understand it, tell me, I pray, which should we laugh at, him that said he knew, or him that knew not? Evidently, the man that said that he knew. He that is ignorant, there-fore, is wiser than he that professes to know.[2] And what again? If any one were to profess to tell us how many cups of water the sea contains, and another should profess his ignorance, is not the ignorance here again wiser than the knowledge?[3] Surely, vastly so. And why so? Because that knowledge itself is but intense ignorance. For he indeed who says that he is ignorant, knows something. And what is that? That it is incomprehensible to man.[4] Yes, and this is no small portion of knowledge. Whereas he that says he knows, he of all others knows not what he says he knows, and is for this very reason utterly ridiculous.

MORAL. Alas! how many things are there to teach us to bridle this unseasonable impertinence and idle curiosity; and yet we refrain not, but are curious about the lives of others; as, why one is a cripple, and why another is poor. And so by this way of reasoning we shall fall into another sort of trifling which is endless, as, why such an one is a woman? and, why all are not men? why there is such a thing as an ass? why an ox? why a dog? why a wolf? why a stone? why wood? and thus the argument will run out to an interminable length. This in truth is the reason, why God has marked out limits to our knowledge, and has laid them deep in nature. And mark, now, the excess of this busy curiosity. For though we look up to so great a height as from earth to heaven, and are not at all affected by it; yet as soon as ever we go up to the top of a lofty tower, and have a mind to stoop over a little, and look down, a sort of giddiness and dizziness immediately seizes us. Now, tell me the reason of this. No, thou couldest never find out a reason for it. Why is it that the eye possesses greater power than other senses, and is caught by more distant objects? And one might see it by comparison with the case of hearing. For no one will ever be able to shout so loudly, as to fill the air as far as the eye can reach, nor to hear at so great a distance. Why are not all the members of equal honor? Why have not all received one function and one place? Paul also searched into these questions; or rather he did not search into them, for he was wise; but where he comes by chance upon this topic, he says, " Each one of them, hath God set even as it hath pleased Him." (1 Cor. xii. 18.) He assigns the whole to His will. And so then let us only " give thanks for all things." ." Wherefore," says he, " give thanks for all things." This is the part of a well-disposed, of a wise, of an intelligent servant; the opposite is that of a tattler, and an idler, and a

---

1 [Job xi. 12, the Sept.: ἄνθρωπος δὲ ἄλλως νήχεται λόγοις; but the Rev. Ver., after the Hebrew, has: " Vain man is void of under-standing." — G. A.]

2 [A striking oxymoron. Compare the Greek, ὁ ἀγνοῶν τοῦ ὑπο-σχομένου εἰδέναι σοφώτερος. — G. A.]
3 [Compare the Greek again: οὐ πάλιν ἡ ἄγνοια τῆς εἰδήσεως ἐστι σοφωτέρα; — G. A.]
4 [Compare, Unum scio, quod nihil scio. — G. A.]

busy-body. Do we not see amongst servants, that those among them who are worthless and good for nothing, are both tattlers, and triflers, and that they pry into the concerns of their masters, which they are desirous to conceal: whereas the intelligent and well-disposed look to one thing only, how they may fulfill their service. He that says much, does nothing: as he that does much, never says a word out of season. Hence Paul said, where he wrote concerning widows, "And they learn not only to be idle, but tattlers also." (1 Tim. v. 13.) Tell me, now, which is the widest difference, between our age and that of children, or between God and men? between ourselves compared with gnats, or God compared with us? Plainly between God and us. Why then dost thou busy thyself to such an extent in all these questions? "Give thanks for all things." "But what," say you, "if a heathen should ask the question? How am I to answer him? He desires to learn from me whether there is a Providence, for he himself denies that there is any being thus exercising foresight." Turn round then, and ask him the same question thyself. He will deny therefore that there is a Providence. Yet that there is a Providence, is plain from what thou hast said; but that it is incomprehensible, is plain from those things whereof we cannot discover the reason. For if in things where men are the disposers, we oftentimes do not understand the method of the disposition, and in truth many of them appear to us inconsistent, and yet at the same time we acquiesce, how much more will this be so in the case of God? However, with God nothing either is inconsistent, or appears so to the faithful. Wherefore let us "give thanks for all things," let us give Him glory for all things.

"Subjecting[1] yourselves one to another," he says, "in the fear of Christ." For if thou submit thyself for a ruler's sake, or for money's sake, or from respectfulness, much more from the fear of Christ. Let there be an interchange of service and submission. For then will there be no such thing as slavish service. Let not one sit down in the rank of a freeman, and the other in the rank of a slave; rather it were better that both masters and slaves be servants to one another;—far better to be a slave in this way than free in any other; as will be evident from hence.

Suppose the case of a man who should have an hundred slaves, and he should in no way serve them; and suppose again a different case, of an hundred friends, all waiting upon one another. Which will lead the happier life? Which with the greater pleasure, with the more enjoyment? In the one case there is no anger, no provocation, no wrath, nor anything else of the kind whatever; in the other all is fear and apprehension. In the one case too the whole is forced, in the other is of free choice. In the one case they serve one another because they are forced to do so, in the other with mutual gratification. Thus does God will it to be; for this He washed His disciples' feet. Nay more, if thou hast a mind to examine the matter nicely, there is indeed on the part of masters a return of service. For what if pride suffer not that return of service to appear? Yet if the slave on 'the one hand render his bodily service, and thou maintain that body, and supply it with food and clothing and shoes, this is an exchange of service: because unless thou render thy service as well, neither will he render his, but will be free, and no law will compel him to do it if he is not supported. If this then is the case with servants, where is the absurdity, if it should also become the case with free men. "Subjecting yourselves in the fear," saith he, "of Christ."[2] How great then the obligation, when we shall also have a reward. But he does not choose to submit himself to thee? However do thou submit thyself; not simply yield, but submit thyself. Entertain this feeling towards all, as if all were thy masters. For thus shalt thou soon have all as thy slaves, enslaved to thee with the most abject slavery. For thou wilt then more surely make them thine, when without receiving anything of theirs, thou of thyself renderest them of thine own. This is "subjecting yourselves one to another in the fear of Christ," in order that we may subdue all the passions, be servants of God, and preserve the love we owe to one another. And then shall we be able also to be counted worthy of the lovingkindness which cometh of God, through the grace and mercies of His only-begotten Son, with whom to the Father, together with the Holy Ghost, be glory, might, honor, now and forever and ever. Amen.

---

[1] ["The words 'subjecting yourselves one to another' still belong to ver. 20 as a *fourth* modal definition of 'Be filled with the Spirit,' and are parallel to 'giving thanks for all things to God,' thus adding to this relation toward God the 'mutual' relation toward 'one another.'"—Meyer.—G. A.]

[2] [Not the fear of "God," as Chrysostom, the *textus receptus* and the Authorized Eng. Version have, but the fear of "Christ" (as Rev. Ver., Westcott and Hort, and all trustworthy authorities). That is, Christ is to be "feared" as the "Judge" (Meyer). Cornelius a Lapide (in Ellicott) says: "Because we reverence Christ and 'fear' to offend him": *quia scilicet Christum reveremur eumque timemus offendere.*—G. A.]

HOMILY XX.

EPHESIANS v. 22–24.

"Wives, be in subjection unto your own husbands, as unto the Lord. For the husband is the head of the wife, as Christ also is the head of the Church: being Himself the Saviour of the body. But as the Church is subject to Christ, so let the wives also be to their husbands in everything."

A CERTAIN wise man, setting down a number of things in the rank of blessings, set down this also in the rank of a blessing, "A wife agreeing with her husband." (Ecclus. xxv. 1.) And elsewhere again he sets it down among blessings, that a woman should dwell in harmony with her husband. (Ecclus. xl. 23.) And indeed from the beginning, God appears to have made special provision for this union; and discoursing of the twain as one, He said thus, "Male and female created He them" (Gen. i. 27); and again, "There is neither male nor female." (Gal. iii. 28.) For there is no relationship between man and man so close as that between man and wife, if they be joined together as they should be. And therefore a certain blessed man too, when he would express surpassing love, and was mourning for one that was dear to him, and of one soul with him, did not mention father, nor mother, nor child, nor brother, nor friend, but what? "Thy love to me was wonderful," saith he, "passing the love of women." (2 Sam. i. 26.) For indeed, in very deed, this love is more despotic than any despotism: for others indeed may be strong, but this passion is not only strong, but unfading. For there is a certain love deeply seated in our nature, which imperceptibly to ourselves knits together these bodies of ours. Thus even from the very beginning woman sprang from man, and afterwards from man and woman sprang both man and woman.[1] Perceivest thou the close bond and connection? And how that God suffered not a different kind of nature to enter in from without? And mark, how many providential arrangements He made. He permitted the man to marry his own sister; or rather not his sister, but his daughter; nay, nor yet his daughter, but something more than his daughter, even his own flesh.[2] And thus the whole He framed from one beginning, gathering all together, like stones in a building, into one. For neither on the one hand did He form her from without, and this was that the man might not feel towards her as

towards an alien; nor again did He confine marriage to her,[3] that she might not, by contracting herself,[4] and making all center in herself, be cut off from the rest. Thus as in the case of plants, they are of all others the best, which have but a single stem, and spread out into a number of branches; (since were all confined to the root alone, all would be to no purpose, whereas again had it a number of roots, the tree would be no longer worthy of admiration;) so, I say, is the case here also. From one, namely Adam, He made the whole race to spring, preventing them by the strongest necessity from being ever torn asunder, or separated; and afterwards, making it more restricted, He no longer allowed sisters and daughters to be wives, lest we should on the other hand contract our love to one point, and thus in another manner be cut off from one another. Hence Christ said, "He which made them from the beginning, made them male and female." (Matt. xix. 4.)

For great evils are hence produced, and great benefits, both to families and to states. For there is nothing which so welds our life together as the love of man and wife. For this many will lay aside even their arms,[5] for this they will give up life itself. And Paul would never without a reason and without an object have spent so much pains on this subject, as when he says here, "Wives, be in subjection unto your own husbands, as unto the Lord." And why so? Because when they are in harmony, the children are well brought up, and the domestics are in good order, and neighbors, and friends, and relations enjoy the fragrance. But if it be otherwise, all is turned upside down, and thrown into confusion. And just as when the generals of an army are at peace one with another, all things are in due subordination, whereas on the other hand, if they are at variance, everything is turned upside down; so, I say, is it also here. Wherefore, saith he, "Wives, be in subjection unto your own husbands, as unto the Lord."

Yet how strange! for how then is it, that it is said elsewhere, "If one bid not farewell both to wife and to husband, he cannot follow me"? (Luke xiv. 26.) For if it is their duty to be in

---

[1] [Compare what Paul says in 1 Cor. xi. 8 and 12.—G. A.]
[2] [He refers to Adam's marrying Eve.—G. A.]

[3] [That is, he did not confine marriage to woman with woman.—G. A.]
[4] [There is another reading which applies these words to the man, as follows: συστέλλων ἑαυτὸν καὶ συνάγων, "that he might not, by contracting himself and making all center in himself, be cut off from the rest," instead of συστέλλουσα, etc.—G. A.]
[5] ὅπλα.

subjection "as unto the Lord," how saith He that they must depart from them for the Lord's sake? Yet their duty indeed it is, their bounden duty. But the word "as" is not necessarily and universally expressive of exact equality. He either means this, "'as' knowing that ye are servants to the Lord"; (which, by the way, is what he says elsewhere, that, even though they do it not for the husband's sake, yet must they primarily for the Lord's sake;) or else he means, "when thou obeyest thy husband, do so as serving the Lord."[1] For if he who resisteth these external authorities, those of governments, I mean, "withstandeth the ordinance of God" (Rom. xiii. 2), much more does she who submits not herself to her husband. Such was God's will from the beginning.

Let us take as our fundamental position then, that the husband occupies the place of the "head," and the wife the place of the "body."

Ver. 23, 24. Then, he proceeds with arguments and says that "the husband is the head of the wife, as Christ also is the head of the Church, being Himself the Saviour of the body. But[2] as the Church is subject to Christ, so let the wives be to their husbands in everything."

Then after saying, "The husband is the head of the wife, as Christ also is of the Church," he further adds, "and He is the Saviour of the body." For indeed the head is the saving health of the body. He had already laid down beforehand for man and wife, the ground and provision of their love, assigning to each their proper place, to the one that of authority and forethought, to the other that of submission. As then "the Church," that is, both husbands and wives, "is subject unto Christ, so also ye wives submit yourselves to your husbands, as unto God."

Ver. 25. "Husbands, love your wives, even as Christ also loved the Church."

Thou hast heard how great the submission; thou hast extolled and marvelled at Paul, how, like an admirable and spiritual man, he welds together our whole life. Thou didst well. But now hear what he also requires at thy hands; for again he employs the same example.

"Husbands," saith he, "love your wives, even as Christ also loved the Church."

Thou hast seen the measure of obedience, hear also the measure of love.[3] Wouldest thou

have thy wife obedient unto thee, as the Church is to Christ? Take then thyself the same provident care for her, as Christ takes for the Church. Yea, even if it shall be needful for thee to give thy life for her, yea, and to be cut into pieces ten thousand times, yea, and to endure and undergo any suffering whatever, — refuse it not. Though thou shouldest undergo all this, yet wilt thou not, no, not even then, have done anything like Christ. For thou indeed art doing it for one to whom thou art already knit; but He for one who turned her back on Him and hated Him. In the same way then as He laid at His feet her who turned her back on Him, who hated, and spurned, and disdained Him, not by menaces, nor by violence, nor by terror, nor by anything else of the kind, but by his unwearied affection; so also do thou behave thyself toward thy wife. Yea, though thou see her looking down upon thee, and disdaining, and scorning thee, yet by thy great thoughtfulness for her, by affection, by kindness, thou wilt be able to lay her at thy feet. For there is nothing more powerful to sway than these bonds, and especially for husband and wife. A servant, indeed, one will be able, perhaps, to bind down by fear; nay not even him, for he will soon start away and be gone. But the partner of one's life, the mother of one's children, the foundation of one's every joy, one ought never to chain down by fear and menaces, but with love and good temper. For what sort of union is that, where the wife trembles at her husband? And what sort of pleasure will the husband himself enjoy, if he dwells with his wife as with a slave, and not as with a free-woman? Yea, though thou shouldest suffer anything on her account, do not upbraid her; for neither did Christ do this.

Ver. 26. "And gave Himself up," he says, "for it, that He might sanctify and cleanse it."

So then she was unclean! So then she had blemishes, so then she was unsightly, so then she was worthless! Whatsoever kind of wife thou shalt take, yet shalt thou never take such a bride as the Church, when Christ took her, nor one so far removed from thee as the Church was from Christ. And yet for all that, He did not abhor her, nor loathe her for her surpassing deformity. Wouldest thou hear her deformity described? Hear what Paul saith, "For ye were once darkness." (Eph. v. 8.) Didst thou see the blackness of her hue? What blacker than darkness? But look again at her boldness, "living," saith he, "in malice and envy." (Tit. iii. 3.) Look again at her impurity; "disobedient, foolish." But what am I saying? She was both foolish, and of an evil tongue; and yet notwithstanding, though so many were her blemishes, yet did He give Himself up for her in her deformity, as for one in the bloom of youth, as for one dearly be-

[1] ["ὡς expresses the mode of view in which the wives are to regard their obedience towards their husbands, namely, 'as rendered to the Lord.'"—Meyer. In Luke xiv. 26 the absolute is put for the relative, as elsewhere often, and this explains our author's difficulty.—G. A.]

[2] [This "but" is by no means easy of explanation, but probably is to be understood thus: He is the saviour of the body that man certainly is not, "but, nevertheless," as the Church is subject to Christ, so let wives be to their husbands, etc.—Ellicott, Meyer, Bengel, Calvin, and Alford.—G. A.]

[3] ["If you put all the arguments of orators together, you will not persuade husband and wife to mutual affection as Paul does in this place."—Bugenhagen, quoted by Meyer.—G. A.]

loved, as for one of wonderful beauty. And it was in admiration of this that Paul said, "For scarcely for a righteous man will one die (Rom. v. 7) ; and again, "in that while we were yet sinners, Christ died for us." (Rom. v. 8.) And though such as this, He took her, He arrayed her in beauty, and washed her, and refused not even this, to give Himself for her.

Ver. 26, 27. "That He might sanctify it having cleansed it," he proceeds, "by the washing of water with the word ; that He might present the Church to Himself a glorious Church, not having spot, or wrinkle, or any such thing, but that it should be holy and without blemish."

"By the washing or laver" He washeth her uncleanness. "By the word," saith he. What word ? "In the Name of the Father, and of the Son, and of the Holy Ghost."[1] (Matt. xxviii. 19.) And not simply hath He adorned her, but hath made her "glorious, not having spot, or wrinkle, or any such thing." Let us then also seek after this beauty ourselves, and we shall be able to create it. Seek not thou at thy wife's hand, things which she is not able to possess. Seest thou that the Church had all things at her Lord's hands? By Him was made glorious, by Him was made pure, by Him made without blemish? Turn not thy back on thy wife because of her deformity. Hear the Scripture that saith, "The bee is little among such as fly, but her fruit is the chief of sweet things."[2] (Ecclus. xi. 3.) She is of God's fashioning. Thou reproachest not her, but Him that made her ; what can the woman do? Praise her not for her beauty. Praise and hatred and love based on personal beauty belong to unchastened souls. Seek thou for beauty of soul. Imitate the Bridegroom of the Church. Outward beauty is full of conceit and great license, and throws men into jealousy, and the thing often makes thee suspect monstrous things. But has it any pleasure? For the first or second month, perhaps, or at most for the year : but then no longer ; the admiration by familiarity wastes away. Meanwhile the evils which arose from the beauty still abide, the pride, the folly, the contemptuousness. Whereas in one who is not such, there is nothing of this kind. But the love having begun on just grounds, still continues ardent, since its object is beauty of soul, and not of body. What better, tell me, than heaven? What better than the stars? Tell me of what body you will, yet is there none so fair. Tell me of what eyes you

will, yet are there none so sparkling. When these were created, the very Angels gazed with wonder, and we gaze with wonder now ; yet not in the same degree as at first. Such is familiarity ; things do not strike us in the same degree. How much more in the case of a wife ! And if moreover disease come too, all is at once fled. Let us seek in a wife affectionateness, modest-mindedness, gentleness ; these are the characteristics of beauty. But loveliness of person let us not seek, nor upbraid her upon these points, over which she has no power, nay, rather, let us not upbraid at all, (it were rudeness,) nor let us be impatient, nor sullen. Do ye not see how many, after living with beautiful wives, have ended their lives pitiably, and how many, who have lived with those of no great beauty, have run on to extreme old age with great enjoyment. Let us wipe off the "spot" that is within, let us smooth the "wrinkles" that are within, let us do away the "blemishes" that are on the soul. Such is the beauty God requires. Let us make her fair in God's sight, not in our own. Let us not look for wealth, nor for that high-birth which is outward, but for that true nobility which is in the soul. Let no one endure to get rich by a wife ; for such riches are base and disgraceful ; no, by no means let any one seek to get rich from this source. "For they that desire to be rich, fall into a temptation and a snare, and many foolish and hurtful lusts, and into destruction and perdition." (1 Tim. vi. 9.) Seek not therefore in thy wife abundance of wealth, and thou shalt find everything else go well. Who, tell me, would overlook the most important things, to attend to those which are less so? And yet, alas ! this is in every case our feeling. Yes, if we have a son, we concern ourselves not how he may be made virtuous, but how we may get him a rich wife ; not how he may be well-mannered, but well-monied :[3] if we follow a business, we enquire not how it may be clear of sin, but how it may bring us in most profit. And everything has become money ; and thus is everything corrupted and ruined, because that passion possesses us.

Ver. 28. "Even so ought husbands to love their own wives," saith he, "as their own bodies."

What, again, means this? To how much greater a similitude, and stronger example has he come ; and not only so, but also to one how much nearer and clearer, and to a fresh obligation. For that other one was of no very constraining force, for He was Christ, and was God, and gave Himself. He now manages his argument on a different ground, saying, "so ought men " ; because the thing is not a favor,

---

[1] ["'The word' (ῥῆμα) does not mean here the 'baptismal formula,' as Chrysostom holds, but 'the gospel,' and here stands without the article, because, denoting 'the word' κατ' ἐξοχήν, it could be treated as a proper noun, as νόμος, &c. All special interpretations, except that of 'gospel,' are purely invented." — Meyer. — G. A.]

[2] [Note that Chrysostom here quotes the Old Testament Apocrypha as Scripture: ἀκουε τῆς γραφῆς λεγούσης. Dr. Schaff says: "He accepts the Syrian Canon of the Peshito, which includes the Old Test. with the Apocrypha," &c. Prolegomena, p. 19.—G. A.]

[3] οὐχ ὅπως εὔτροπος ἀλλ' ὅπως εὔπορος.

but a debt. Then, "as their own bodies." And why?

Ver. 29. "For no man ever hated his own flesh, but nourisheth and cherisheth it."

That is, tends it with exceeding care. And how is she his flesh? Hearken; "This now is bone of my bones," saith Adam, "and flesh of my flesh." (Gen. ii. 23.) For she is made of matter taken from us. And not only so, but also, "they shall be," saith God, "one flesh." (Gen. ii. 24.)

"Even as Christ also the Church." Here he returns to the former example.

Ver. 30. "Because we are members of His body, of His flesh and of His bones."[1]

Ver. 31. "For this cause shall a man leave his father and mother, and shall cleave to his wife, and the twain shall become one flesh."[2]

Behold again a third ground of obligation; for he shows that a man leaving them that begat him, and from whom he was born, is knit to his wife; and that then the one flesh is, father, and mother, and the child, from the substance of the two commingled. For indeed by the commingling of their seeds is the child produced, so that the three are one flesh. Thus then are we in relation to Christ; we become one flesh by participation, and we much more than the child. And why and how so? Because so it has been from the beginning.

Tell me not that such and such things are so. Seest thou not that we have in our own flesh itself many defects? For one man, for instance, is lame, another has his feet distorted, another his hands withered, another some other member weak; and yet nevertheless he does not grieve at it, nor cut it off, but oftentimes prefers it even to the other. Naturally enough; for it is part of himself. As great love as each entertains towards himself, so great he would have us entertain towards a wife. Not because we partake of the same nature; no, this ground of duty towards a wife is far greater than that; it is that there are not two bodies but one; he the head, she the body. And how saith he elsewhere, "and the Head of Christ is God"? (1 Cor. xi. 3.) This I too say, that as we are one body, so also are Christ and the Father One. And thus then is the Father also found to be our Head. He sets down two examples, that of the natural body and that of Christ's body. And hence he further adds,

Ver. 32. "This is great mystery: but I speak in regard of Christ and of the Church."[3]

Why does he call it a great mystery? That it was something great and wonderful, the blessed Moses, or rather God, intimated. For the present, however, saith he, I speak regarding Christ, that having left the Father, He came down, and came to the Bride, and became one Spirit. "For he that is joined unto the Lord is one Spirit." (1 Cor. vi. 17.) And well saith he, "it is a great mystery." And then as though he were saying, "But still nevertheless the allegory does not destroy affection," he adds,

Ver. 33. "Nevertheless[4] do ye also severally love each one his own wife even as himself; and let the wife see that she fear her husband."

For indeed, in very deed, a mystery it is, yea, a great mystery, that a man should leave him that gave him being, him that begat him, and that brought him up, and her that travailed with him and had sorrow, those that have bestowed upon him so many and great benefits, those with whom he has been in familiar intercourse, and be joined to one who was never even seen by him and who has nothing in common with him, and should honor her before all others. A mystery it is indeed. And yet are parents not distressed when these events take place, but rather, when they do not take place; and are delighted when their wealth is spent and lavished upon it. — A great mystery indeed! and one that contains some hidden wisdom. Such Moses prophetically showed it to be from the very first; such now also Paul proclaims it, where he saith, "concerning Christ and the Church."

However not for the husband's sake alone it is thus said, but for the wife's sake also, that "he cherish her as his own flesh, as Christ also the Church," and, "that the wife fear her husband." He is no longer setting down the duties of love only, but what? "That she fear her husband." The wife is a second authority; let not her then demand equality, for she is under the head; nor let him despise her as being in subjection, for she is the body; and if the head despise the body, it will itself also perish. But let him bring in love on his part as a counterpoise to obedience on her part. For example, let the hands and the feet, and all the rest of the members be given up for service to the head, but let the head provide for the body, seeing it contains every sense in itself. Nothing can be better than this union.

And yet how can there ever be love, one may

---

[1] [The words, "of his flesh and of his bones," are omitted by א* A B, by Memphitic version, by Lach. Tish. Treg. (text) W. & H., and by the Rev. Ver. without any marginal notice whatever. — G. A.]

[2] [Meyer: "'For this reason,' namely, because we are members of Christ's body. Paul then applies what is spoken in Gen. of the union of husband and wife, by a typical interpretation, to the second coming (future, καταλείψει) of Christ, and his union with the Church, which shall take place at the Parousia." Ellicott says that Chrysostom's view is more probable, namely, that it refers to Christ's coming in the flesh. (See a little below, on ver. 32.) — G. A.]

[3] [This seems a distinct statement on the part of the Apostle, that the preceding words refer not to actual marriage of man and woman, but to the nuptial union of Christ and the Church. So Meyer. But Dr. Riddle, in the Popular Commentary, says this "mystical interpretation is unsafe." — G. A.]

[4] [Nevertheless, i.e. not to press the mystical bearings of the subject any further. — Ellicott. So substantially Meyer and Riddle. — G. A.]

say, where there is fear? It will exist there, I say, preëminently. For she that fears and reverences, loves also ; and she that loves, fears and reverences him as being the head, and loves him as being a member, since the head itself is a member of the body at large. Hence he places the one in subjection, and the other in authority, that there may be peace ; for where there is equal authority there can never be peace ; neither where a house is a democracy, nor where all are rulers ; but the ruling power must of necessity be one. And this is universally the case with matters referring to the body, inasmuch as when men are spiritual, there will be peace. There were "five thousand souls," and not one of them said, "that aught of the things which he possessed was his own" (Acts iv. 32), but they were subject one to another ; an indication this of wisdom, and of the fear of God. The principle of love, however, he explains ; that of fear he does not. And mark, how on that of love he enlarges, stating the arguments relating to Christ and those relating to one's own flesh, the words, "For this cause shall a man leave his father and mother." (Ver. 31.) Whereas upon those drawn from fear he forbears to enlarge. And why so? Because he would rather that this principle prevail, this, namely, of love ; for where this exists, everything else follows of course, but where the other exists, not necessarily. For the man who loves his wife, even though she be not a very obedient one, still will bear with everything. So difficult and impracticable is unanimity, where persons are not bound together by that love which is founded in supreme authority ; at all events, fear will not necessarily effect this. Accordingly, he dwells the more upon this, which is the strong tie. And the wife though seeming to be the loser in that she was charged to fear, is the gainer, because the principal duty, love, is charged upon the husband. "But what," one may say, "if a wife reverence me not?" Never mind, thou art to love, fulfill thine own duty. For though that which is due from others may not follow, we ought of course to do our duty. This is an example of what I mean. He says, "submitting yourselves one to another in the fear of Christ." And what then if another submit not himself? Still obey thou the law of God. Just so, I say, is it also here. Let the wife at least, though she be not loved, still reverence notwithstanding, that nothing may lie at her door ; and let the husband, though his wife reverence him not, still show her love notwithstanding, that he himself be not wanting in any point. For each has received his own.

This then is marriage when it takes place according to Christ, spiritual marriage, and spiritual birth, not of blood, nor of travail, nor of the will of the flesh. Such was the birth of Christ, not of blood, nor of travail. Such also was that of Isaac. Hear how the Scripture saith, "And it ceased to be with Sarah after the manner of women." (Gen. xviii. 11.) Yea, a marriage it is, not of passion, nor of the flesh, but wholly spiritual, the soul being united to God by a union unspeakable, and which He alone knoweth. Therefore he saith, "He that is joined unto the Lord is one spirit." (1 Cor. vi. 17.) Mark how earnestly he endeavors to unite both flesh with flesh, and spirit with spirit. And where are the heretics?[1] Never surely, if marriage were a thing to be condemned, would he have called Christ and the Church a bride and bridegroom ; never would he have brought forward by way of exhortation the words, "A man shall leave his father and his mother" ; and again have added, that it was "spoken in regard of Christ and of the Church." For of her it is that the Psalmist also saith, "Hearken, O daughter, and consider, and incline thine ear ; forget also thine own people, and thy father's house. So shall the king desire thy beauty." (Ps. xlv. 10, 11.) Therefore also Christ saith, "I came out from the Father, and am come." (John xvi. 28.) But when I say, that He left the Father, imagine not such a thing as happens among men, a change of place ; for just in the same way as the word "go forth" is used, not because He literally came forth, but because of His incarnation, so also is the expression, "He left the Father."

Now why did he not say of the wife also, She shall be joined unto her husband? Why, I say, is this? Because he was discoursing concerning love, and was discoursing to the husband. For to her indeed he discourses concerning reverence, and says, "the husband is the head of the wife" (ver. 23), and again, "Christ is the Head of the Church." Whereas to him he discourses concerning love, and commits to him this province of love, and declares to him that which pertains to love, thus binding him and cementing him to her. For the man that leaves his father for the sake of his wife, and then again, leaves this very wife herself and abandons her, what forbearance can he deserve?

Seest thou not how great a share of honor God would have her enjoy, in that he hath taken thee away from thy father, and hath linked thee to her? What then, a man may say, if our duty is done, and yet she does not follow the example? "Yet if the unbelieving departeth, let him depart ; the brother or the sister is not under bondage in such cases." (1 Cor. vii. 15.)

---

[1] The Gnostics, Encratites (Schaff, *Church Hist.* II. p. 495), and other sects forbade marriage ; vid. 1 Tim. iv. 3. Here the Marcionites seem to be intended, whom St. Chrysostom often mentions ; vid. supr. *Hom.* xix. [See Schaff's *Church Hist.*, Vol. II., p. 457. — G. A.]

However, when thou hearest of "fear," demand that fear which becomes a free woman, not as though thou wert exacting it of a slave. For she is thine own body; and if thou do this, thou reproachest thyself in dishonoring thine own body. And of what nature is this "fear"? It is the not contradicting, the not rebelling, the not being fond of the preëminence. It is enough that fear be kept within these bounds. But if thou love, as thou art commanded, thou wilt make it yet greater. Or rather it will not be any longer by fear that thou wilt be doing this, but love itself will have its effect. The sex is somehow weaker, and needs much support, much condescension.

But what will they say, who are knit together in second marriages?[1] I speak not at all in condemnation of them, God forbid; for the Apostle himself permits them, though indeed by way of condescension.

Supply her with everything. Do everything and endure trouble for her sake. Necessity is laid upon thee.

Here he does not think it right to introduce his counsel, as he in many cases does, with examples from them that are without. That of Christ, so great and forcible, were alone enough; and more especially as regards the argument of subjection. "A man shall leave," he saith, "his father and mother." Behold, this then is from without. But he does not say, and "shall dwell with," but "shall cleave unto," thus showing the closeness of the union, and the fervent love. Nay, he is not content with this, but further by what he adds, he explains the subjection in such a way as that the twain appear no longer twain. He does not say, "one spirit," he does not say, "one soul" (for that is manifest, and is possible to any one), but so as to be "one flesh." She is a second authority, possessing indeed an authority, and a considerable equality of dignity; but at the same time the husband has somewhat of superiority. In this consists most chiefly the well-being of the house. For he took that former argument, the example of Christ, to show that we ought not only to love, but also to govern; "that she may be," saith he, "holy and without blemish." But the word "flesh" has reference to love — and the word "shall cleave" has in like manner reference to love. For if thou shalt make her "holy and without blemish," everything else will follow. Seek the things which are of God, and those which are of man will follow readily enough. Govern thy wife, and thus will the whole house be in harmony. Hear what Paul saith. "And if they would learn any thing, let them ask their own husbands at home." (1 Cor. xiv. 35.) If we thus regulate our own

houses, we shall be also fit for the management of the Church. For indeed a house is a little Church. Thus it is possible for us by becoming good husbands and wives, to surpass all others.

Consider Abraham, and Sarah, and Isaac, and the three hundred and eighteen born in his house. (Gen. xiv. 14.) How the whole house was harmoniously knit together, how the whole was full of piety and fulfilled the Apostolic injunction. She also "reverenced her husband"; for hear her own words, "It hath not yet happened unto me even until now, and my lord is old also." (Gen. xviii. 12.)[2] And he again so loved her, that in all things he obeyed her commands. And the young child was virtuous, and the servants born in the house, they too were so excellent that they refused not even to hazard their lives with their master; they delayed not, nor asked the reason. Nay, one of them, the chief, was so admirable, that he was even entrusted with the marriage of the only-begotten child, and with a journey into a foreign country. (Gen. xxiv. 1–67.) For just as with a general, when his soldiery also is well organized, the enemy has no quarter to attack; so, I say, is it also here: when husband and wife and children and servants are all interested in the same things, great is the harmony of the house. Since where this is not the case, the whole is oftentimes overthrown and broken up by one bad servant; and that single one will often mar and utterly destroy the whole.

MORAL. Let us then be very thoughtful both for our wives, and children, and servants; knowing that we shall thus be establishing for ourselves an easy government, and shall have our accounts with them gentle and lenient, and say, "Behold I, and the children which God hath given me." (Isa. viii. 18.) If the husband command respect, and the head be honorable, then will the rest of the body sustain no violence. Now what is the wife's fitting behavior, and what the husband's, he states accurately, charging her to reverence him as the head, and him to love her as a wife; but how, it may be said, can these things be? That they ought indeed so to be, he has proved. But how they can be so, I will tell you. They will be so, if we will despise money, if we will look but to one thing only, excellence of soul, if we will keep the fear of God before our eyes. For what he says in his discourse to servants, "whatsoever any man doeth, whether it be good or evil, the same shall he receive of the Lord" (Eph. vi. 8); this is also the case here. Love her therefore not for her sake so much as for Christ's sake. This, at least, he as much as

---

[1] [On second marriages in the early Church, see Schaff's *History of the Christian Church*, Vol. II., p. 366. — G. A.]

[2] [This, according to the Septuagint, which has οὔπω μέν μοι γέγονεν ἕως τοῦ νῦν. ὁ δὲ κύριός μου πρεσβύτερος. The Rev. Ver., following the Hebrew, has, "After I am waxed old, shall I have pleasure, my lord being old also?" — G. A.]

intimates, in saying, "as unto the Lord." So then do everything, as in obedience to the Lord, and as doing everything for His sake. This were enough to induce and to persuade us, and not to suffer that there should be any teasing and dissension. Let none be believed when slandering the husband to his wife; no, nor let the husband believe anything at random against the wife, nor let the wife be without reason inquisitive about his goings out and his comings in. No, nor on any account let the husband ever render himself worthy of any suspicion whatever. For what, tell me, what if thou shalt devote thyself all the day to thy friends, and give the evening to thy wife, and not even thus be able to content her, and place her out of reach of suspicion? Though thy wife complain, yet be not annoyed — it is her love, not her folly — they are the complaints of fervent attachment, and burning affection, and fear. Yes, she is afraid lest any one have stolen her marriage bed, lest any one have injured her in that which is the summit of her blessings, lest any one have taken away from her him who is her head, lest any one have broken through her marriage chamber.

There is also another ground of petty jealousy. Let neither claim too much service of the servants, neither the husband from the maid-servant, nor the wife from the man-servant. For these things also are enough to beget suspicion. For consider, I say, that righteous household I spoke of. Sarah herself bade the patriarch take Hagar. She herself directed it, no one compelled her, nor did the husband[1] attempt it; no, although he had dragged on so long a period childless, yet he chose never to become a father, rather than to grieve his wife. And yet even after all this, what said Sarah? "The Lord judge between me and thee." (Gen. xvi. 5.) Now, I say, had he been any one else, would he not have been moved to anger? Would he not also have stretched forth his hand, saying as it were, "What meanest thou? I had no desire to have anything to do with the woman; it was all thine own doing; and dost thou turn again and accuse me?" — But no, he says nothing of the sort; — but what? "Behold, thy maid is in thy hand; do to her that which is good in thine eyes." (Gen. xvi. 6.) He delivered up the partner of his bed, that he might not grieve Sarah. And yet surely is there nothing greater than this for producing affection. For if partaking of the same table produces unanimity even in robbers towards their foes, (and the Psalmist[2] saith, "Who didst eat

sweet food at the same table with me") ; much more will the becoming one flesh — for such is the being the partner of the bed — be effectual to draw us together. Yet did none of these things avail to overcome him; but he delivered Hagar up to his wife, to show that nothing had been done by his own fault. Nay, and what is more, he sent her forth when with child. Who would not have pitied one that had conceived a child by himself? Yet was the just man unmoved, for he set before everything else the love he owed his wife.

Let us then imitate him ourselves. Let no one reproach his neighbor with his poverty; let no one be in love with money; and then all difficulties will be at an end.

Neither let a wife say to her husband, "Unmanly coward that thou art, full of sluggishness and dullness, and fast asleep! here is such a one, a low man, and of low parentage, who runs his risks, and makes his voyages, and has made a good fortune; and his wife wears her jewels, and goes out with her pair of milk-white mules;[3] she rides about everywhere, she has troops of slaves, and a swarm of eunuchs, but thou hast cowered down and livest to no purpose." Let not a wife say these things, nor anything like them. For she is the body, not to dictate to the head, but to submit herself and obey. "But how," some one will say, "is she to endure poverty? Where is she to look for consolation?" Let her select and put beside her those who are poorer still. Let her again consider how many noble and high-born maidens have not only received nothing of their husbands, but have even given dowries to them, and have spent their all upon them. Let her reflect on the perils which arise from such riches, and she will cling to this quiet life. In short, if she is affectionately disposed towards her husband, she will utter nothing of the sort. No, she will rather choose to have him near her, though gaining nothing, than gaining ten thousand talents of gold, accompanied with that care and anxiety which always arise to wives from those distant voyages.

Neither, however, let the husband, when he hears these things, on the score of his having the supreme authority, betake himself to revilings and to blows; but let him exhort, let him admonish her, as being less perfect, let him persuade her with arguments. Let him never once lift his hand, — far be this from a noble spirit, — no, nor give expression to insults, or taunts, or revilings; but let him regulate and direct her as being wanting in wisdom. Yet how shall this be

---

[1] [The punctuation of Field: οὐδὲ ἐπῆλθεν · ὁ ἀνὴρ, &c., is clearly not so good as that of the Oxford translator: οὐδὲ ἐπῆλθεν ὁ ἀνήρ, &c. — G. A.]

[2] [The Septuagint reads, ὃς ἐπὶ τὸ αὐτὸ ἐγλύκανας ἐδέσματα, and

this Chrysostom, not knowing Hebrew, follows. The Rev. Ver. has "We took sweet counsel together." — G. A.]

[3] So Demosthenes says of Midias, καὶ εἰς μυστήρια τὴν γυναῖκα ἄγει, κἂν ἄλλοσέ ποι βούληται, ἐπὶ τοῦ λευκοῦ ζεύγους τοῦ ἐκ Σικυῶνος. Dem. in Mid. p. 565.

done? If she be instructed in the true riches, in the heavenly philosophy, she will make no complaints like these. Let him teach her then, that poverty is no evil. Let him teach her, not by what he says only, but also by what he does. Let him teach her to despise glory; and then his wife will speak of nothing, and will desire nothing of the kind. Let him, as if he had an image given into his hands to mould, let him, from that very evening on which he first receives her into the bridal chamber, teach her temperance, gentleness, and how to live, casting down the love of money at once from the outset, and from the very threshold. Let him discipline her in wisdom, and advise her never to have bits of gold hanging at her ears, and down her cheeks, and laid round about her neck, nor laid up about the chamber, nor golden and costly garments stored up. But let her chamber be handsome, still let not what is handsome degenerate into finery. No, leave these things to the people of the stage. Adorn thine house thyself with all possible neatness, so as rather to breathe an air of soberness than much perfume. For hence will arise two or three good results. First then, the bride will not be grieved, when the apartments are opened, and the tissues, and the golden ornaments, and silver vessels, are sent back to their several owners. Next, the bridegroom will have no anxiety about the loss, nor for the security of the accumulated treasures. Thirdly again, in addition to this, which is the crown of all these benefits, by these very points he will be showing his own judgment, that indeed he has no pleasure in any of these things, and that he will moreover put an end to everything else in keeping with them, and will never so much as allow the existence either of dances, or of immodest songs. I am aware that I shall appear perhaps ridiculous to many persons, in giving such admonitions. Still nevertheless, if ye will but listen to me, as time goes on, and the benefit of the practice accrues to you, then ye will understand the advantage of it. And the laughter will pass off, and ye will laugh at the present fashion, and will see that the present practice is really that of silly children and of drunken men. Whereas what I recommend is the part of soberness, and wisdom, and of the sublimest way of life. What then do I say is our duty? Take away from marriage all those shameful, those Satanic, those immodest songs, those companies of profligate young people, and this will avail to chasten the spirit of thy bride.[1] For she will at once thus reason with herself; "Wonderful! What a philosopher this man is! he regards the present life

as nothing, he has brought me here into his house, to be a mother, to bring up his children, to manage his household affairs." "Yes, but these things are distasteful to a bride?" Just for the first or second day; — but not afterwards; nay, she will even reap from them the greatest delight, and relieve herself of all suspicion. For a man who can endure neither flute-players, nor dancers, nor broken songs,[2] and that too at the very time of his wedding, that man will scarcely endure ever to do or say anything shameful. And then after this, when thou hast stripped the marriage of all these things, then take her, and form and mould her carefully, encouraging her bashfulness to a considerable length of time, and not destroying it suddenly. For even if the damsel be very bold, yet for a time she will keep silence out of reverence for her husband, and feeling herself a novice in the circumstances. Thou then break not off this reserve too hastily, as unchaste husbands do, but encourage it for a long time. For this will be a great advantage to thee. Meanwhile she will not complain, she will not find fault with any laws thou mayest frame for her. During that time therefore, during which shame, like a sort of bridle laid upon the soul, suffers her not to make any murmur, nor to complain of what is done, lay down all thy laws. For as soon as ever she acquires boldness, she will overturn and confound everything without any sense of fear. When is there then another time so advantageous for moulding a wife, as that during which she reverences her husband, and is still timid, and still shy? Then lay down all thy laws for her, and willing or unwilling, she will certainly obey them. But how shalt thou help spoiling her modesty? By showing her that thou thyself art no less modest than she is, addressing to her but few words, and those too with great gravity and collectedness. Then entrust her with the discourses of wisdom, for her soul will receive them. And establish her in that loveliest habit, I mean modesty. If you wish me, I will also tell you by way of specimen, what sort of language should be addressed to her. For if Paul shrank not from saying, "Defraud ye not one the other" (2 Cor. vii. 5), and spoke the language of a bridesmaid, or rather not of a bridesmaid, but of a spiritual soul, much more will not we shrink from speaking. What then is the language we ought to address to her? With great delicacy then we may say to her, "I have taken thee, my child, to be partner of my life, and have brought thee in to share with me in the closest and most honorable ties, in my children, and the superintendence of my house. And what advice then shall I now recommend thee?" But rather, first talk with her of your love for her; for

---

[1] [In Hom. XII. on 1 Cor. iv. 10, Chrysostom says, "But when marriages are solemnized, dancing and cymbals and flutes and shameful words and songs and drunkenness and revelings and the Devil's great heap of trash are introduced." And much more to the same effect and in great detail. — G. A.]

[2] ἀσμάτων κεκλασμένων.

there is nothing that so contributes to persuade a hearer to admit sincerely the things that are said, as to be assured that they are said with hearty affection. How then art thou to show that affection? By saying, "when it was in my power to take many to wife, both with better fortunes, and of noble family, I did not so choose, but I was enamoured of thee, and thy beautiful life, thy modesty, thy gentleness, and soberness of mind." Then immediately from these beginnings open the way to your discourse on true wisdom, and with some circumlocution make a protest against riches. For if you direct your argument at once against riches, you will bear too heavily upon her; but if you do it by taking an occasion, you will succeed entirely. For you will appear to be doing it in the way of an apology, not as a morose sort of person, and ungracious, and over-nice about trifles. But when you take occasion from what relates to herself, she will be even pleased. You will say then, (for I must now take up the discourse again,) that "whereas I might have married a rich woman, and with good fortune, I could not endure it. And why so? Not capriciously, and without reason; but I was taught well and truly, that money is no real possession, but a most despicable thing, a thing which moreover belongs as well to thieves, and to harlots, and to grave-robbers. So I gave up these things, and went on till I fell in with the excellence of thy soul, which I value above all gold. For a young damsel who is discreet and ingenuous, and whose heart is set on piety, is worth the whole world. For these reasons then, I courted thee, and I love thee, and prefer thee to my own soul. For the present life is nothing. And I pray, and beseech, and do all I can, that we may be counted worthy so to live this present life, as that we may be able also there in the world to come to be united to one another in perfect security. For our time here is brief and fleeting. But if we shall be counted worthy by having pleased God to so exchange this life for that one, then shall we ever be both with Christ and with each other, with more abundant pleasure. I value thy affection above all things, and nothing is so bitter or so painful to me, as ever to be at variance with thee. Yes, though it should be my lot to lose my all, and to become poorer than Irus,[1] and undergo the extremest hazards, and suffer any pain whatsoever, all will be tolerable and endurable, so long as thy feelings are true towards me. And then will my children be most dear to me, whilst thou art affectionately disposed towards me.

But thou must do these duties too." Then mingle also with your discourse the Apostle's words, that "thus God would have our affections blended together; for listen to the Scripture, which saith, 'For this cause shall a man leave his father and mother, and cleave to his wife.' Let us have no pretext for narrow-minded jealousy.[2] Perish riches, and retinue of slaves, and all your outward pomps. To me this is more valuable than all." What weight of gold, what amount of treasures, are so dear to a wife as these words? Never fear that because she is beloved she will ever rave against thee, but confess that thou lovest her. For courtezans indeed, who now attach themselves to one and now to another, would naturally enough feel contempt towards their lovers, should they hear such expressions as these; but a free-born wife or a noble damsel would never be so affected with such words; no, she will be so much the more subdued. Show her too, that you set a high value on her company, and that you are more desirous to be at home for her sake, than in the market-place. And esteem her before all your friends, and above the children that are born of her, and let these very children be beloved by thee for her sake. If she does any good act, praise and admire it; if any foolish one, and such as girls may chance to do, advise her and remind her. Condemn out and out all riches and extravagance, and gently point out the ornament that there is in neatness and in modesty; and be continually teaching her the things that are profitable.

Let your prayers be common.[3] Let each go to Church; and let the husband ask his wife at home, and she again ask her husband, the account of the things which were said and read there. If any poverty should overtake you, cite the case of those holy men, Paul and Peter, who were more honored than any kings or rich men; and yet how they spent their lives, in hunger and in thirst. Teach her that there is nothing in life that is to be feared, save only offending against God. If any marry thus, with these views, he will be but little inferior to monks; the married but little below the unmarried.

If thou hast a mind to give dinners, and to make entertainments, let there be nothing immodest, nothing disorderly. If thou shouldest find any poor saint able to bless your house, able only just by setting his foot in it to bring in the whole blessing of God, invite him. And shall I say moreover another thing? Let no one of you make it his endeavor to marry a rich

---

[1] [The well-known beggar of Ithaca, the home of Ulysses. He was the messenger of the suitors of Penelope. See Odys. Bk. xviii. 1–125. Later, his name was used as an appellation, "an Irus, a beggar." Liban i. 568. — Liddell and Scott. — G. A.]

[2] μικροψυχία.

[3] [For a picture of family life drawn by Clement of Alexandria, and another drawn by Tertullian, see Schaff, *Church History*, Vol. II., p. 364. — G. A.]

woman, but much rather a poor one. When she comes in, she will not bring so great a source of pleasure from her riches, as she will annoyance from her taunts, from her demanding more than she brought, from her insolence, her extravagance, her vexatious language. For she will say perhaps, "I have not yet spent anything of thine, I am still wearing my own apparel, bought with what my parents settled upon me." What sayest thou, O woman? Still wearing thine own! And what can be more miserable than this language? Why, thou hast no longer a body of thine own, and hast thou money of thine own? After marriage ye are no longer twain, but are become one flesh, and are then your possessions twain, and not one? Oh! this love of money! Ye both are become one man, one living creature; and dost thou still say "mine own"? Cursed and abominable word that it is, it was brought in by the devil. Things far nearer and dearer to us than these hath God made all common to us, and are these then not common? We cannot say, "my own light, my own sun, my own water": all our greater blessings are common, and are riches not common? Perish the riches ten thousand times over! Or rather not the riches, but those tempers of mind which know not how to make use of riches, but esteem them above all things.

Teach her these lessons also with the rest, but with much graciousness. For since the recommendation of virtue has in itself much that is stern, and especially to a young and tender damsel, whenever discourses on true wisdom are to be made, contrive that your manner be full of grace and kindness. And above all banish this notion from her soul, of "mine and thine." If she say the word "mine," say unto her, "What things dost thou call thine? For in truth I know not; I for my part have nothing of mine own. How then speakest thou of 'mine,' when all things are thine?" Freely grant her the word. Dost thou not perceive that such is our practice with children? When, whilst we are holding anything, a child snatches it, and wishes again to get hold of some other thing, we allow it, and say, "Yes, and this is thine, and that is thine." The same also let us do with a wife; for her temper is more or less like a child's; and if she says "mine," say, "why, everything is thine, and I am thine." Nor is the expression one of flattery, but of exceeding wisdom. Thus wilt thou be able to abate her wrath, and put an end to her disappointment. For it is flattery when a man does an unworthy act with an evil object: whereas this is the highest philosophy. Say then, "Even I am thine, my child; this advice Paul gives me where he says, 'The husband hath not power over his own body, but the wife.' (1 Cor. vii. 4.) If I have no power over my body, but thou hast, much more hast thou over my possessions." By saying these things thou wilt have quieted her, thou wilt have quenched the fire, thou wilt have shamed the devil, thou wilt have made her more thy slave than one bought with money, with this language thou wilt have bound her fast. Thus then, by thine own language, teach her never to speak of "mine and thine." And again, never call her simply by her name, but with terms of endearment, with honor, with much love. Honor her, and she will not need honor from others; she will not want the glory that comes from others, if she enjoys that which comes from thee. Prefer her before all, on every account, both for her beauty and her discernment, and praise her. Thou wilt thus persuade her to give heed to none that are without, but to scorn all the world except thyself. Teach her the fear of God, and all good things will flow from this as from a fountain, and the house will be full of ten thousand blessings. If we seek the things that are incorruptible, these corruptible things will follow. "For," saith He, "seek first His kingdom, and all these things shall be added unto you." (Matt. vi. 33.) What sort of persons, think you, must the children of such parents be? What the servants of such masters? What all others who come near them? Will not they too eventually be loaded with blessings out of number? For generally the servants also have their characters formed after their master's, and are fashioned after their humors, love the same objects, which they have been taught to love, speak the same language, and engage with them in the same pursuits. If thus we regulate ourselves, and attentively study the Scriptures, in most things we shall derive instruction from them. And thus shall be able to please God, and to pass through the whole of the present life virtuously, and to attain those blessings which are promised to those that love Him, of which God grant that we may all be counted worthy, through the grace and lovingkindness of our Lord Jesus Christ, with Whom, together with the Holy Ghost, be unto the Father, glory, power, and honor, now, and ever, through all ages. Amen.

HOMILY XXI.

EPHESIANS vi. 1–3.

"Children, obey your parents in the Lord, for this is right. Honor thy father and mother (which is the first commandment with promise), that it may be well with thee, and thou mayest live long on the earth."

As a man in forming a body, places the head first, after that the neck, then the feet, so does the blessed Paul proceed in his discourse. He has spoken of the husband, he has spoken of the wife, who is second in authority, he now goes on by gradual advances to the third rank — which is that of children. For the husband has authority over the wife, and the husband and the wife over the children. Now then mark what he is saying.

"Children,[1] obey your parents in the Lord; for this is the first commandment with promise."

Here he has not a word of discourse concerning Christ, not a word on high subjects, for he is as yet addressing his discourse to tender understandings. And it is for this reason, moreover, that he makes his exhortation short, inasmuch as children cannot follow up a long argument. For this reason also he does not discourse at all about a kingdom, (because it does not belong to the tender age of childhood to understand these subjects,) but what a child's soul most especially longs to hear, that he says, namely, that it shall "live long." For if any one shall enquire why it is that he omitted to discourse concerning a kingdom, but set before them the commandment laid down in the law, he does this because he speaks to them as infantine, and because he is well aware that if the husband and the wife are thus disposed according to the law which he has laid down, there will be but little trouble in securing the submission of the children. For whenever any matter has a good and sound and orderly principle and foundation, everything will thenceforward go on with method and regularity, with much facility: the more difficult thing is to settle the foundation, to lay down a firm basis. "Children," saith he, "obey your parents in the Lord," that is, according to the Lord. This, he means to say, is what God[2] commands you. But what then if they shall command foolish things? Generally a father, however foolish he may be

himself, does not command foolish things. However, even in that case, the Apostle has guarded the matter, by saying, "in the Lord"; that is, wherever you will not be offending against God. So that if the father be a gentile or a heretic, we ought no longer to obey, because the command is not then, "in the Lord." But how is it that he says, "Which is the first commandment"? For the first is, "Thou shalt not commit adultery; — Thou shalt not kill." He does not speak of it then as first in rank,[3] but in respect of the promise. For upon those others there is no reward annexed, as being enacted with reference to evil things, and to departure from evil things. Whereas in these others, where there is the practice of good, there is further a promise held out. And observe how admirable a foundation he has laid for the path of virtue, that is, honor and reverence towards parents. When he would lead us away from wicked practices, and is just about to enter upon virtuous ones, this is the first thing he enjoins, honor towards parents; inasmuch as they before all others are, after God, the authors of our being, so that it is reasonable they should be the first to reap the fruits of our right actions; and then all the rest of mankind. For if a man have not this honor for parents he will never be gentle toward those unconnected with him.

However, having given the necessary injunctions to children, he passes to the fathers, and says,

Ver. 4. "And ye fathers, provoke not your children to wrath; but nurture them up in the chastening and admonition of the Lord."

He does not say, "love them," because to this nature draws them even against their own will, and it were superfluous to lay down a law on such subjects. But what does he say? "Provoke not your children to wrath," as many do by disinheriting them, and disowning them, and treating them overbearingly, not as free, but as slaves. This is why he says, "Provoke not your children to wrath." Then, which is the chief thing of all, he shows how they will be led to obedience, referring the whole source of it to the head and chief authority. And in the same way as he has shown the husband to be the cause of the wife's obedience, (which is the reason also why he addresses the greater part of

---

[1] [" The address to children in a letter to the Church presupposes that the Apostle regards them as belonging to the Church, present at public worship, understanding the word read to and applicable to them." — Braune in Lange. — G. A.]

[2] [" ἐν κυρίῳ. Not God, as Chrysostom, and not κατὰ κύριον, as Chrysostom, but denoting the sphere to which the action is to be limited." — Ellicott. — G. A.]

[3] τάξει. [" Paul says πρώτη, having before his mind not only the Decalogue, but also 'the entire series of divine precepts,' which begins with the Decalogue." — Meyer. — G. A.]

his arguments to him, advising him to attach her to himself by the power of love,) so, I say, here also, he refers the efficiency to him, by saying, " But bring them up in the chastening and admonition of the Lord." Thou seest that where there are spiritual ties, the natural ties will follow. Do you wish your son to be obedient? From the very first " Bring him up in the chastening and admonition of the Lord." Never deem it an unnecessary thing that he should be a diligent hearer of the divine Scriptures. For there the first thing he hears will be this, " Honor thy father and thy mother " ; so that this makes for thee. Never say, this is the business of monks. Am I making a monk of him? No. There is no need he should become a monk.[1] Why be so afraid of a thing so replete with so much advantage? Make him a Christian. For it is of all things necessary for laymen[2] to be acquainted with the lessons derived from this source ; but especially for children. For theirs is an age full of folly ; and to this folly are superadded the bad examples derived from the heathen tales, where they are made acquainted with those heroes so admired amongst them, slaves of their passions, and cowards with regard to death ; as, for example, Achilles, when he relents, when he dies for his concubine, when another gets drunk, and many other things of the sort. He requires therefore the remedies against these things. How is it not absurd to send children out to trades, and to school, and to do all you can for these objects, and yet, not to " bring them up in the chastening and admonition of the Lord"? And for this reason truly we are the first to reap the fruits, because we bring up our children to be insolent and profligate, disobedient, and mere vulgar fellows. Let us not then do this ; no, let us listen to this blessed Apostle's admonition. " Let us bring them up in the chastening and admonition of the Lord." Let us give them a pattern. Let us make them from the earliest age apply themselves to the reading of the Scriptures. Alas, that so constantly as I repeat this, I am looked upon as trifling ! Still, I shall not cease to do my duty. Why, tell me, do ye not imitate them of old? Ye women, especially, emulate those admirable women. Has a child been born to any one? Imitate Hannah's example (1 Sam. i. 24) ; look at what she did. She brought him up at once to the temple. Who amongst you would not rather that his son should become a Samuel than that he should be king of the whole world ten thousand times over? "And how," you will say, " is it possible he should become such a one?" Why is it

not possible? It is because thou dost not choose it thyself, nor committest him to the care of those who are able to make him such a one. " And who," it will be said, " is such a one as this?" God. Since she put him into the hands of God. For not even Eli himself was one of those in any great degree qualified to form him ; (how could he be, he who was not able to form even his own children?) No, it was the faith of the mother and her earnest zeal that wrought the whole. He was her first child, and her only one, and she knew not whether she should ever have others besides. Yet she did not say, " I will wait till the child is grown up, that he may have a taste of the things of this life, I will allow him to have his pastime in them a little in his childish years." No, all these thoughts the woman repudiated, she was absorbed in one object, how from the very beginning she might dedicate the spiritual image[3] to God. Well may we men be put to the blush at the wisdom of this woman. She offered him up to God, and there she left him. And therefore was her married state more glorious, in that she had made spiritual objects her first care, in that she dedicated the first-fruits to God. Therefore was her womb fruitful, and she obtained other children besides.[4] And therefore she saw him honorable even in the world. For if men when they are honored, render honor in return, will not God much more, He who does this, even without being honored? How long are we to be mere lumps of flesh? How long are we to be stooping to the earth? Let everything be secondary with us to the provident care we should take of our children, and to our " bringing them up in the chastening and admonition of the Lord." If from the very first he is taught to be a lover of true wisdom, then wealth greater than all wealth has he acquired and a more imposing name. You will effect nothing so great by teaching him an art, and giving him that outward learning by which he will gain riches, as if you teach him the art of despising riches. If you desire to make him rich, do this. For the rich man is not he who desires great riches, and is encircled with great riches ; but the man who has need of nothing.[5] Discipline your son in this, teach him this. This is the greatest riches. Seek not how to give him reputation and high character in outward learning, but consider deeply how you shall teach him to despise the glory that belongs to this present life. By this means would he become more distinguished and more truly glorious. This it is possible for the

---

[1] Fathers were very suspicious in St. Chrysostom's day of the influence of Christianity tending to make their children monks. In consequence of this prejudice against the monastic life, he wrote his *Adv. Oppugn. Mon. Vit.*

[2] τοῖς κοσμικοῖς.   [3] ἄγαλμα.

[4] [On the authority of three MSS., Savile and other editors concurring, we have departed here from the text of Field, which reverses the order of this and the following sentence, and leaves the sense less clear.   v. 1 Sam. ii. 21. — G. A.]

[5] [This reminds one of the saying of Socrates: To want nothing belongs to the gods, and to want as little as possible is to make the nearest approach to them. — G. A.]

poor man and the rich man alike to accomplish. These are lessons which a man does not learn from a master, nor by art, but by means of the divine oracles. Seek not how he shall enjoy a long life here, but how he shall enjoy a boundless and endless life hereafter. Give him the great things, not the little things. Hear what Paul saith, "Bring them up in the chastening and admonition of the Lord"; study not to make him an orator, but train him up to be a philosopher. In the want of the one there will be no harm whatever; in the absence of the other, all the rhetoric in the world will be of no advantage. Tempers are wanted, not talking; character, not cleverness; deeds, not words. These gain a man the kingdom. These confer what are benefits indeed. Whet not his tongue, but cleanse his soul. I do not say this to prevent your teaching him these things, but to prevent your attending to them exclusively. Do not imagine that the monk alone stands in need of these lessons from Scripture. Of all others, the children just about to enter into the world specially need them. For just in the same way as the man who is always at anchor in harbor, is not the man who requires his ship to be fitted out, and who needs a pilot and a crew, but he who is always out at sea; so is it with the man of the world and the monk. The one is entered as it were into a waveless harbor, and lives an untroubled life, and far removed from every storm; whilst the other is ever on the ocean, and lives out at sea in the very midst of the ocean, battling with billows without number.

And though he may not need it himself, still he ought to be so prepared as to stop the mouths of others.[1] Thus the more distinguished he is in the present life, so much the more he stands in need of this education. If he passes his life in courts, there are many Heathens, and philosophers, and persons puffed up with the glory of this life. It is like a place full of dropsical people. Such in some sort is the court. All are, as it were, puffed up, and in a state of inflammation. And they who are not so are studying to become so. Now then reflect how vast a benefit it is, that your son on entering there, should enter like an excellent physician, furnished with instruments which may allay every one's peculiar inflammation, and should go up to every one, and converse with him, and restore the diseased body to health, applying the remedies derived from the Scriptures, and pouring forth discourses of the true philosophy. For with whom is the recluse to converse? with his wall and his ceiling? yea, or again with the wilderness and the woods? or with the birds and the trees? He therefore has not so great need of this sort of discipline.

Still, however, he makes it his business to perfect this work, not so much with a view of disciplining others as himself. There is then every need of much discipline of this sort to those that are to mix in the present world, because such an one has a stronger temptation to sin than the other. And if you have a mind to understand it, he will further be a more useful person even in the world itself. For all will have a reverence for him from these words, when they see him in the fire without being burnt, and not desirous of power. But power he will then obtain, when he least desires it, and will be a still higher object of respect to the king; for it is not possible that such a character should be hid. Amongst a number of healthy persons, indeed, a healthy man will not be noticed; but when there is one healthy man amongst a number of sick, the report will quickly spread and reach the king's ears, and he will make him ruler over many nations. Knowing then these things, "bring up your children in the chastening and admonition of the Lord."

"But suppose a man is poor." Still he will be in no wise more insignificant than the man who lives in kings' courts, because he is not in kings' courts; no, he will be held in admiration, and will soon gain that authority which is yielded voluntarily, and not by any compulsion. For if a set of Greeks, men worthless as they are, and dogs,[2] by taking up that worthless philosophy of theirs, (for such the Grecian philosophy is,) or rather not itself but only its mere name, and wearing the threadbare cloak, and letting their hair grow, impress many; how much more will he who is a true philosopher? If a false appearance, if a mere shadow of philosophy at first sight so catches us, what if we should love the true and pure philosophy? Will not all court it, and entrust both houses, and wives, and children, with full confidence to such men? But there is not, no, there is not such a philosopher existing now. And therefore, it is not possible to find an example of the sort. Amongst recluses, indeed, there are such, but amongst people in the world no longer. And that amongst recluses there are such, it would be possible to adduce a number of instances. However, I will mention one out of many. Ye know, doubtless, and have heard of, and some, perhaps, have also seen, the man whom I am now about to mention. I mean, the admirable Julian. This man was a rustic, in humble life, and of humble parentage, and totally uninstructed in all outward accomplishments, but full of unadorned wisdom.[3] When he came into

---

[1] [The following part of the paragraph explains this sentence.— G. A.]

[2] τριωβολιμαῖοί τινες καὶ κύνες.

[3] St. Julian was a native of Cilicia, perhaps of Tarsus, and was martyred at Ægæ in the Dioclesian persecution. One of St. Chrysostom's orations is in his praise.

the cities, (and this was but rarely,) never did such a concourse take place, not when orators, or sophists, or any one else rode in. But what am I saying? Is not his very name more glorious than that of any king's, and celebrated even to this day? And if these things were in this world, in the world in which the Lord promised us no one good thing, in which He hath told us we are strangers, let us consider how great will be the blessings laid up for us in the heavens. If, where they were sojourners they enjoyed so great honor, how great glory shall they enjoy where their own city is! If, where He promised tribulation, they meet with such attentive care, then where He promises true honors, how great shall be their rest!

And now would ye have me exhibit examples of secular men? At present, indeed, we have none; still there are perhaps even secular men who are excellent, though not arrived at the highest philosophy. I shall therefore quote you examples from the saints of the ancient times. How many, who had wives to keep and children to bring up, were inferior in no respect, no, in no respect to those who have been mentioned? Now, however, it is no longer so, "by reason of the present distress" (1 Cor. vii. 26), as this blessed Apostle saith. Now then whom would ye have me mention? Noah, or Abraham? The son of the one or of the other? Or again, Joseph? Or would ye have me go to the Prophets? Moses I mean, or Isaiah? However, if you will, let us carry our discourse to Abraham, whom all are continually bringing forward to us above all others. Had he not a wife? Had he not children? Yes, for I too use the same language to you, as you do to me. He had a wife, but it was not because he had a wife that he was so remarkable. He had riches, but it was not because he had riches that he pleased God. He begat children, but it was not because he begat children that he was pronounced blessed. He had three hundred and eighteen servants born in his house, but it was not on this account that he was accounted wonderful. But would you know why it was? It was for his hospitality, for his contempt of riches, for his chastened conduct. For what, tell me, is the duty of a philosopher? Is it not to despise both riches and glory? Is it not to be above both envy and every other passion? Come now then, let us bring him forward and strip him, and show you what a philosopher he was. First of all, he esteemed his fatherland as nothing. God said, "Get thee out of thy country, and from thy kindred" (Gen. xii. 1), and immediately he went forth. He was not bound to his house, (or surely he would never have gone forth,) nor to his love of familiar friends, nor to anything else whatever. But what? glory and money he

despised above all others. For when he had put an end to war by turning the enemy to flight, and was requested to take the spoil, he rejected it. (Gen. xiv. 21–23.)

Again, the son of this great man was reverenced, not because of his riches, but for his hospitality: not because of his children, but for his obedience: not because of his wife, but for the barrenness inflicted on his wife. (Gen. xxv. 21.)

They looked upon the present life as nothing, they followed not after gain, they despised all things. Tell me, which sort of plants are the best? Are not those which have their strength from themselves and are injured neither by rains, nor by hailstorms, nor by gusts of wind, nor by any other vicissitude of the sort, but stand naked in defiance of them all, and needing neither wall nor fence to protect them? Such is the true philosopher, such is that wealth of which we spoke. He has nothing, and has all things: he has all things, and has nothing. For a fence is not within, but only without; a wall is not a thing of nature, but only built round from without. And what again, I ask, what sort of body is a strong one? Is it not that which is in health, and which is overcome neither by hunger nor repletion, nor by cold, nor by heat; or is it that which in view of all these things, needs both caterers, and weavers, and hunters, and physicians, to give it health? He is the rich man, the true philosopher, who needeth none of these things. For this cause it was that this blessed Apostle said, "Bring them up in the chastening and admonition of the Lord." Surround them not with outward defenses. For such is wealth, such is glory; for when these fall, and they do fall, the plant stands naked and defenseless, not only having derived no profit from them during the time past, but even injury. For those very shelters that prevented its being inured to the attacks of the winds, will now have prepared it for perishing all at once. And so wealth is injurious rather, because it renders us undisciplined for the vicissitudes of life. Let us therefore train up our children to be such, that they shall be able to bear up against every trial, and not to be surprised at what may come upon them; "let us bring them up in the chastening and admonition of the Lord." And great will be the reward which will be thus laid up in store for us. For if men for making statues and painting portraits of kings enjoy so great honor, shall not we who adorn the image of the King of kings, (for man is the image of God,) receive ten thousand blessings, if we effect a true likeness? For the likeness is in this, in the virtue of the soul, when we train our children to be good, to be meek, to be forgiving, (because all these are attributes of God,) to be beneficent, to be humane; when we train them to regard the present world as nothing. Let this then be our task, to mold and to direct both ourselves and them according to what is right. Otherwise with what sort of boldness shall we stand before the judgment-seat of Christ? If a man who has unruly children is unworthy to be a Bishop (Tit. i. 6), much more is he unworthy of the kingdom of Heaven. What sayest thou? If we have an unruly wife, or unruly children, shall we have to render account? Yes, we shall, if we do not with exactness bring in that which is due from ourselves; for our own individual virtue is not enough in order to salvation. If the man who laid aside the one talent gained nothing, but was punished even in such a manner, it is plain that one's own individual virtue is not enough in order to salvation, but there is need of that of another also. Let us therefore entertain great solicitude for our wives, and take great care of our children, and of our servants, and of ourselves. And in our government both of ourselves and of them, let us beseech God that He aid us in the work. If He shall see us interested in this work, and solicitous about it, He will aid us; but if He shall see us paying no regard to it, He will not give us His hand. For He does not vouchsafe us His assistance when we sleep, but when we labor also ourselves. For a helper, (as the name implies,) is not a helper of one that is inactive, but of one who works also himself. But the good God is able of Himself to bring the work to perfection, that we may be all counted worthy to attain to the blessings promised us, through the grace and compassions of His only begotten Son, with Whom together with the Holy Ghost be unto the Father, glory, might, and honor, now and ever, and throughout all ages. Amen.

HOMILY XXII.

EPHESIANS vi. 5–8.

"Servants, be obedient unto them that, according to the flesh, are your masters, with fear and trembling, in singleness of your heart, as unto Christ; not in the way of eye-service, as men-pleasers: but as servants of Christ, doing the will of God from the heart; with good-will doing service, as unto the Lord, and not unto men: knowing that whatsoever good thing each one doeth, the same shall he receive again from the Lord, whether he be bond or free."

THUS then it is not husband only, nor wife, nor children, but virtuous servants also that contribute to the organization and protection of a house. Therefore the blessed Paul has not overlooked this department even. He comes to it, however, in the last place, because it is last in dignity and rank. Still he addresses much discourse also to them, no longer in the same tone as to children, but in a far more advanced way, inasmuch as he does not hold out to these the promise in this world, but in that which is to come. "Knowing," saith he, "that whatsoever good or evil [1] thing each one doeth, the same shall he receive of the Lord," and thus at once instructs them to love wisdom. For though they be inferior to the children in dignity, still in mind they are superior to them.

"Servants," saith he, "be obedient to them that, according to the flesh, are your masters."

Thus at once he raises up, at once soothes the wounded soul. Be not grieved, he seems to say, that you are inferior to the wife and the children. Slavery is nothing but a name. The mastership is "according to the flesh," brief and temporary; [2] for whatever is of the flesh, is transitory.

"With fear," he adds, "and trembling." [3]

Thou seest that he does not require the same fear from slaves as from wives: for in that case he simply said, "and let the wife see that she fear her husband"; whereas in this case he heightens the expression, "with fear," he saith, "and trembling, in singleness of your heart, as unto Christ." This is what he constantly says. What meanest thou, blessed Paul? He is a brother, or rather he has become a brother, he enjoys the same privileges, he belongs to the same body. Yea, more, he is the brother, not of his own master only, but also of the Son of God, he is partaker of all the same privileges; yet sayest thou, "obey your masters according to the flesh, with fear and trembling"? Yes, for this very reason, he would say, I say it. For if I charge free men to submit themselves one to another in the fear of God, — as he said above, "submitting yourselves one to another in the fear of Christ"; — if I charge moreover the wife to fear and reverence her husband, although she is his equal; much more must I so speak to the

---

[1] [The words, "or evil," ἢ κακόν, are not in the text of this passage at all, though Chrysostom has them. Chrysostom and the Patristic writers in general often quote the New Testament without exactness. They quote often from memory, and are seldom critical. Cf. Schaff, *Companion to Greek Testament*, p. 164.—G. A.]

[2] ["Wrong. It means those who are 'your human masters,' in distinction from Christ, the 'divine' master."—Meyer.—G. A.]

[3] ["With fear and trembling, i.e. with that zeal which is ever keenly apprehensive of not doing enough."—Meyer.—G. A.]

servant. It is no sign of low birth, rather it is the truest nobility, to understand how to lower ourselves, to be modest and unassuming, and to give way to our neighbor. And the free have served the free with much fear and trembling.

"In singleness of heart," he says.

And it is well said, since it is possible to serve with fear and trembling, and yet not of good will, but in just any way that may be possible. Many servants in many instances secretly cheat their masters. And this cheating accordingly he does away, by saying, "in singleness of your heart as unto Christ, not in the way of eye-service as men-pleasers, but as servants of Christ, doing the will of God from the heart; with good-will doing service, as unto the Lord, and not unto men." Seest thou how many words he requires, in order to implant this good principle, "with good-will," I mean, and "from the heart"? That other service, "with fear and trembling" I mean, we see many rendering to their masters, and the master's threat goes far to secure that. But show, saith he, that thou servest as "the servant of Christ," not of man. Make the right action your own, not one of compulsion. Just as in the words which follow, he persuades and instructs the man who is ill-treated by another to make the right action his own, and the work of his own free choice. Because inasmuch as the man that smites the cheek, is not supposed to come to that act in consequence of any intention in the person struck, but only of his own individual malice, what saith He? "Turn to him the other also" (Matt. v. 39); to show him that in submitting to the first thou wert not unwilling. For he that is lavish in suffering wrong, makes that his own which is not his own act, by suffering himself to be smitten on the other cheek also, and not merely by enduring the first blow. For this latter will have perhaps the appearance even of cowardice; but that of a high philosophy. — Thus thou wilt show that it was for the sake of wisdom that thou didst bear the first blow also. And so in the present case, show here too, that thou bearest this slavery also willingly. The man-pleaser then is no servant of Christ. The servant of Christ is not a man-pleaser. (Gal. i. 10.) For who that is the servant of God, makes it his object to please men? And who that pleases mén, can be a servant of God?

"From the heart,"[1] saith he, "with good-will doing service." For since it is possible to do service even with singleness of heart and not wrongfully, and yet not with all one's might, but only so far as fulfilling one's bounden duty, there-

fore he says, do it with alacrity, not of necessity, upon principle, not upon constraint. If thus thou do service, thou art no slave; if thou do it upon principle, if with good-will, if from the heart, and if for Christ's sake. For this is the servitude that even Paul, the free man, serves, and exclaims, "For we preach not ourselves, but Christ Jesus, as Lord, and ourselves as your servants for Jesus' sake." (2 Cor. iv. 5.) Look how he divests thy slavery of its meanness. For just in the same way as the man who has been robbed, if he gives still more to him who has taken, is not ranked among those robbed, but rather amongst liberal givers; not amongst those who suffer evil, but amongst those who do good; and rather clothes the other with disgrace by his liberality, than is clothed with disgrace by being robbed, — so, I say, in this case, by his generosity he will appear at once more high-minded, and by showing that he does not feel the wrong,[2] will put the other to shame.

Let us then do service to our masters for Christ's sake, "knowing," he continues, "that whatsoever good thing each one doeth, the same shall he receive of the Lord, whether he be bond or free." For inasmuch as it was probable that many masters, as being unbelievers, would have no sense of shame, and would make no return to their slaves for their obedience, observe how he has given them encouragement, so that they may have no misgiving about the remuneration, but may have full confidence respecting the recompense. For as they who receive a benefit, when they make no return, make God a debtor to their benefactors; so, I say, do masters also, if, when well-treated by thee, they fail to requite thee, requite thee the more, by rendering God thy debtor.

Ver. 9. "And ye masters," he continues, "do the same things unto them."

The same things. What are these? "With good-will do service." However he does not actually say, "do service," though by saying, "the same things," he plainly shows this to be his meaning. For the master himself is a servant. "Not as men-pleasers," he means, "and with fear and trembling": that is, toward God, fearing lest He one day accuse you for your negligence toward your slaves.

"And forbear threatening;" be not irritating, he means, nor oppressive.

"Knowing that both their Master and[3] yours is in Heaven."[4]

Ah! How mighty a Master does he hint at

---

[1] ["From the heart" (ἐκ ψυχῆς) is joined by Chrysostom with what follows. (So Westcott and Hort.) But as μετ' εὐνοίας expresses the well-meaning disposition, it already includes the sense of ἐκ ψυχῆς. So that ἐκ ψυχῆς belongs to what precedes. So Meyer, Ellicott, and Rev. Ver. — G. A.]

[2] ἁρπαγῆς.

[3] [The second καὶ (καὶ αὐτῶν καὶ ὑμῶν) is omitted in Chrysostom's text of this passage, and in the textus receptus, so that it does not appear in the Authorized English Version. The Revised Version has it, however, and correctly so. — G. A.]

[4] [Meyer quotes Seneca, Thyest. 607: —
Quicquid a vobis minor extimescit
Major hoc vobis dominus minatur.
Omne sub regno graviore regnum est. — G. A.]

here ! How startling the suggestion ! It is this. "With what measure thou metest, it shall be measured unto thee again" (Matt. vii. 2) ; lest thou hear the sentence, "Thou wicked servant. I forgave thee all that debt." (Matt. xviii. 32.)

"And there is no respect of persons," he saith, "with Him."

Think not, he would say, that what is done towards a servant, He will therefore forgive, because done to a servant. Heathen laws indeed, as being the laws of men, recognize a difference between these kinds of offenses. But the law of the common Lord and Master of all, as doing good to all alike, and dispensing the same rights to all, knows no such difference.

But should any one ask, whence is slavery, and why it has found entrance into human life, (and many I know are both glad to ask such questions, and desirous to be informed of them,) I will tell you. Slavery is the fruit of covetousness, of degradation, of savagery ; since Noah, we know, had no servant, nor had Abel, nor Seth, no, nor they who came after them. The thing was the fruit of sin, of rebellion against parents. Let children hearken to this, that whenever they are undutiful to their parents, they deserve to be servants. Such a child strips himself of his nobility of birth ; for he who rebels against his father is no longer a son ; and if he who rebels against his father is not a son, how shall he be a son who rebels against our true Father? He has departed from his nobility of birth, he has done outrage to nature. Then come also wars, and battles, and take their prisoners.[1] Well, but Abraham, you will say, had servants. Yes, but he used them not as servants.

Observe how everything depends upon the head ; the wife, by telling him "to love her" ; the children, by telling him "to bring them up in the chastening and admonition of the Lord" ; the servants, by the words, "knowing that both their Master and yours is in Heaven." So, saith he, ye also in like manner, as being yourselves servants, shall be kind and indulgent. "Finally, be strong in the Lord and in the strength of His might."

But if, before considering this next, ye have a mind to hearken, I shall make the same remarks concerning servants, as I have also made before concerning children. Teach them to be religious, and everything else will follow of necessity. But now, when any one is going to the theater, or going off to the bath, he drags all his servants after him ; but when he goes to church, not for a moment ; nor does he compel them to attend and hear. Now how shall thy servant listen,

when thou his master art attending to other things? Hast thou purchased, hast thou bought thy slave? Before all things enjoin him what God would have him do, to be gentle towards his fellow-servants, and to make much account of virtue.

Every one's house is a city ; and every man is a prince in his own house. That the house of the rich is of this character, is plain enough, where there are both lands, and stewards, and rulers over rulers. But I say that the house of the poor also is a city. Because here too there are offices of authority ; for instance, the husband has authority over the wife, the wife over the servants, the servants again over their own wives ; again the wives and the husbands over the children. Does he not seem to you to be, as it were, a sort of king, having so many authorities under his own authority? and that it were meet that he should be more skilled both in domestic and general government than all the rest? For he who knows how to manage these in their several relations, will know how to select the fittest men for offices, yes, and will choose excellent ones. And thus the wife will be a second king in the house, lacking only the diadem ; and he who knows how to choose this king, will excellently regulate all the rest.

Ver. 10. "Finally," saith he, "be strong in the Lord."

Whenever the discourse is about to conclude, he always employs this turn. Said I not well from the first, that every man's house is a camp in itself? For look, having disposed of the several offices, he proceeds to arm them, and to lead them out to war.[2] If no one usurps the other's office, but every one remains at his post, all will be well ordered.

"Be strong," saith he, "in the Lord, and in the strength of His might."

That is, in the hope which we have in Him, by means of His aid. For as he had enjoined many duties, which were necessary to be done, fear not, he seems to say, cast your hope upon the Lord, and He will make all easy.

Ver. 11. "Put on the whole armor of God, that ye may be able to stand against the wiles of the devil."

He saith not, against the fightings, nor against the hostilities, but against the "wiles." For this enemy is at war with us, not simply, nor openly, but by "wiles." What is meant by wiles? To use "wiles," is to deceive and to take by artifice or contrivance ; a thing which takes place both in the case of the arts, and by words, and actions, and stratagems, in the case of those who seduce us.

---

[1] [He seems to refer slavery to three causes: 1. covetousness; 2. rebellion against parents; 3. war, where prisoners are taken and made slaves.— G. A.]

[2] [This is very beautiful, but hardly correct exegesis. "The word 'finally' introduces a general, final exhortation, winding up the whole parenetic portion of the epistle (iv. 1–vi. 9)."— Meyer.— G. A.]

I mean something like this. The Devil never proposes to us sins in their proper colors; he does not speak of idolatry, but he sets it off in another dress, using "wiles,"[1] that is, making his discourse plausible, employing disguises. Now therefore the Apostle is by this means both rousing the soldiers, and making them vigilant, by persuading and instructing them, that our conflict is with one skilled in the arts of war, and with one who wars not simply, nor directly, but with much wiliness. And first then he arouses the disciples from the consideration of the Devil's skill; but in the second place, from his nature, and the number of his forces. It is not from any desire to dispirit the soldiers that stand under him, but to arouse, and to awaken them, that he mentions these stratagems, and prepares them to be vigilant; for had he merely detailed their power, and there stopped his discourse, he must have dispirited them. But now, whereas both before and after this, he shows that it is possible to overcome such an enemy, he rather raises their courage; for the more clearly the strength of our adversaries is stated on our part to our own people, so much the more earnest will it render our soldiers.

Ver. 12. "For our wrestling is not," saith he, "against flesh and blood,[2] but against the principalities, against the powers, against the world-rulers of this darkness, against the spiritual hosts of wickedness, in the heavenly places."

Having stimulated them by the character of the conflict, he next goes on to arouse them also by the prizes set before them. For what is his argument? Having said that the enemies are fierce, he adds further, that they despoil us of vast blessings. What are these? The conflict lies "in the heavenlies";[3] the struggle is not about riches, not about glory, but about our being enslaved. And thus is the enmity irreconcilable. The strife and the conflict are fiercer when for vast interests at stake; for the expression "in the heavenlies"[3] is equivalent to, "for the heavenly things." It is not that they may gain anything by the conquest, but that they may despoil us. As if one were to say, "In what does the contract lie?" In gold. The word "in," means, "in behalf of"; the word "in," also means, "on account[4] of."[5] Observe how the power of the enemy startles us; how it makes us all circumspection, to know that the hazard is on behalf of vast interests, and the

victory for the sake of great rewards. For he is doing his best to cast us out of Heaven.

He speaks of certain "principalities, and powers, and world-rulers of this darkness." What darkness? Is it that of night? No, but of wickedness. "For ye were," saith he, "once darkness" (Eph. v. 8); so naming that wickedness which is in this present life; for beyond it, it will have no place, not in Heaven, nor in the world to come.

"World-rulers"[6] he calls them, not as having the mastery over the world, but the Scripture is wont to call wicked practices "the world," as, for example, where Christ saith, "They are not of this world, even as I am not of the world." (John xvii. 16.) What then, were they not of the world? Were they not clothed with flesh? Were they not of those who are in the world? And again; "The world hateth Me, but you it cannot hate." (John vii. 7.) Where again He calls wicked practices by this name. Thus the Apostle here by the world means wicked men, and the evil spirits have more especial power over them. "Against the spiritual hosts of wickedness," saith he, "in the heavenly places." "Principalities, and powers," he speaks of; just as in the heavenly places there are "thrones and dominions, principalities and powers." (Col. i. 16.)

Ver. 13. "Wherefore," saith he, "take up the whole armor of God, that ye may be able to withstand in the evil day, and, having done all, to stand."

By "evil day" he means the present life,[7] and calls it too "this present evil world" (Gal. i. 4), from the evils which are done in it. It is as much as to say, Always be armed. And again, "having done all," saith he; that is, both passions, and vile lusts, and all things else that trouble us. He speaks not merely of doing the deed, but of completing it,[8] so as not only to slay, but to stand also after we have slain. For many who have gained this victory, have fallen again. "Having done," saith he, "all"; not having done one, but not the other. For even after the victory, we must stand. An enemy may be struck, but things that are struck revive again if we do not stand. But if after having fallen they rise up again, so long as we stand, they are fallen. So long as we waver not, the adversary rises not again.

"Let us put on the whole armor of God." Seest thou how he banishes all fear? For if it be possible "to do all, and to stand," his de-

---

[1] μεθοδεύων.

[2] ["Flesh and blood, i.e. 'feeble men,' just as in Gal. i. 16, and Matt. xvi. 17. The word πάλη, which means nothing else than a 'wrestling,' is specially chosen by the Apostle (who elsewhere uses ἀγών or μάχη), in order to bring out the more strongly in connection with πρὸς αἶμα καὶ σάρκα the contrast between this less perilous form of contest and that which follows." — Meyer. — G. A.]

[3] ἐν τοῖς ἐπουρανίοις.

[4] ["The word ἐν does not mean 'for' or 'on account of,' and the phrase is here local (i. 3)." — Meyer. — G. A.]

[5] τὸ ἐν ὑπέρ ἐστι, καὶ τὸ ἐν, διά ἐστιν.

[6] κοσμοκράτορας.

[7] ["The use of ἡμέρᾳ, rather than αἰῶνι (Gal. i. 4) is opposed to the interpretation of Chrysostom. Still more untenable is the view of Meyer, that Paul is here specifying the day when the last great Satanic outbreak was to take place. Paul has at heart what he knew was much more present and more constantly impending, namely, the day of violent temptation." — Ellicott. — G. A.]

[8] Not ἐργασάμενοι, but κατεργασάμενοι.

scribing in detail the power of the enemy does not create cowardice and fear, but it shakes off indolence. "That ye may be able," he saith, "to withstand in the evil day." And he further gives them encouragement too from the time; the time, he seems to say, is short;[1] so that ye must needs stand; faint not when the slaughter is achieved.

MORAL. If then it is a warfare, if such are the forces arrayed against us, if "the principalities" are incorporeal, if they are "rulers of the world," if they are "the spiritual hosts of wickedness," how, tell me, canst thou live in self-indulgence? How canst thou be dissolute? How if we are unarmed, shall we be able to overcome? These words let every one repeat to himself every day, whenever he is under the influence of anger, or of lust, whenever he is aiming, and all to no profit, after this languid life. Let him hearken to the blessed Paul, saying to him, "Our wrestling is not against flesh and blood, but against the principalities, against the powers." A harder warfare this than that which is matter of sense, a fiercer conflict. Think how long time this enemy is wrestling, for what it is that he is fighting, and be more guarded than ever. "Nay," a man will say, "but as he is the devil, he ought to have been removed out of the way, and then all had been saved."[2] These are the pretenses to which some of your indolent ones in self-defense give utterance. When thou oughtest to be thankful, O man, that, if thou hast a mind, thou hast the victory over such a foe, thou art on the contrary even discontented, and givest utterance to the words of some sluggish and sleepy soldier. Thou knowest the points of attack,[3] if thou choosest. Reconnoiter on all sides, fortify thyself. Not against the devil alone is the conflict, but also against his powers. How then, you may say, are we to wrestle with the darkness? By becoming light. How with the "spiritual hosts of wickedness"? By becoming good. For wickedness is contrary to good, and light drives away darkness. But if we ourselves too be darkness, we shall inevitably be taken captive. How then shall we overcome them? If, what they are by nature, that we become by choice, free from flesh and blood, thus shall we vanquish them. For since it was probable that the disciples would have many persecutors, "imagine not," he would say, "that it is they who war with you. They that really war with you, are the spirits that work in them. Against them is our conflict." Two things he provides for by these considerations; he renders

them in themselves more courageous and he lets loose their wrath against those who war against them. And wherefore is our conflict against these? Since we have also an invincible ally, the grace of the Spirit. We have been taught an art, such as shall enable us to wrestle not against men, but against spirits. Nay, if we have a mind, neither shall we wrestle at all; for it is because we choose it, that there is a struggle, since so great is the power of Him that dwelleth in us, as that He said, "Behold, I have given you authority to tread upon serpents and scorpions, and over all the power of the enemy." (Luke x. 19.) All power hath He given us, both of wrestling and of not wrestling. It is because we are slothful, that we have to wrestle with them; for that Paul wrestled not, hear what he saith himself, "Who shall separate us from the love of Christ? shall tribulation, or anguish, or persecution, or famine, or nakedness, or peril, or sword?" (Rom. viii. 35.) And again hear his words, "God shall bruise Satan under your feet shortly." (Rom. xvi. 20.) For he had him under his subjection; whence also he said, "I charge thee in the name of Jesus Christ to come out of her." (Acts xvi. 18.) And this is not the language of one wrestling; for he that wrestles has not yet conquered, and he that has conquered no longer wrestles; he has subdued, has taken his captive. And so Peter again wrestled not with the devil, but he did that which was better than wrestling. In the case of the faithful, the obedient, the catechumens, they prevailed over him to vast advantage and over his powers. Hence too was it that the blessed Paul said, "For we are not ignorant of his devices" (2 Cor. ii. 11), which was the way moreover in which he especially overcame him; and again hear his words, "And no marvel — if his ministers also fashion themselves as ministers of righteousness." (2 Cor. xi. 14, 15.) So well knew he every part of the conflict, and nothing escaped him. Again, "For the mystery of lawlessness," saith he, "doth already work." (2 Thess. ii. 7.)

But against us is the struggle; for hearken again to him, saying, "I am persuaded, that neither angels, nor principalities, nor things present, nor things to come, nor powers, nor any other creature, shall be able to separate us from the love of Christ." (Rom. viii. 38.) He saith not simply, "from Christ," but, "from the love of Christ."[4] For many there are who are united forsooth to Christ, and who yet love Him not. Not only, saith he, shalt thou not persuade me to deny Him, but, not even to love Him less. And if the powers above had not strength to do this, who else should move him? Not,

---

[1] i.e. "but a 'day.'"

[2] [This entire sentence and the preceding one, though attested by three MSS. and read by Savile, are wanting in the text of Field, who has, in their stead, Νῦν οὖν ἦλθε, φησὶν, ἐμοὶ παλαῖσαι, "Now then," says some one, "he has come to wrestle with me," which seems to leave the sense incomplete, and does not suit the following sentence. See note on page 82. — G. A.] [3] λαβάς.

[4] [This text in Rom. has, "from the love of God which is in Christ Jesus our Lord." — G. A.]

however, that he saith this, as though they were actually attempting it, but upon the supposition; wherefore also he said, "I am persuaded." So then he did not wrestle, yet nevertheless he fears his artifices; for hear what he saith, "I fear lest by any means, as the serpent beguiled Eve in his craftiness, your minds should be corrupted from the simplicity that is toward Christ." (2 Cor. xi. 3.) True, you will say, but he uses this word touching himself also, where he saith, "For I fear[1] lest, by any means, after that I have preached to others, I myself should be rejected." How then art thou "persuaded that no one shall separate thee"? Perceivest thou that the expression is that of lowliness and of humility? For he already dwelt in Heaven. And hence also it was that he said, "For I know nothing against myself" (1 Cor. iv. 4); and again, "I have finished the course." (2 Tim. iv. 7.) So that it was not with regard to these matters that the devil placed obstacles in his way, but with reference to the interests of the disciples. And why forsooth? Because in these points he was not himself sole master, but also their own will. There the devil prevailed in some cases; nay, neither there was it over him that he prevailed, but over the indolence of persons who took no heed. If indeed, whether from slothfulness, or anything else of the sort, he had failed to fulfill his own duty, then had the devil prevailed over him; but if he himself on his part did all he could, and they obeyed not, it was not over him he prevailed, but over their disobedience; and the disease prevailed not over the physician, but over the unruliness of the patient; for, when the physician takes every precaution, and the patient undoes all, the patient is defeated, not the physician. Thus then in no instance did he prevail over Paul. But in our own case, it is matter for contentment that we should be so much as able to wrestle. For the Romans indeed this is not what he asks, but what? "He shall bruise Satan under your feet shortly." (Rom. xvi. 20.) And for these Ephesians he invokes, "Him that is able to do exceeding abundantly above all that we ask or think." (Eph. iii. 20.) He that wrestles is still held fast, but it is enough for him that he has not fallen. When we depart hence, then, and not till then, will the glorious victory be achieved. For instance, take the case of some evil lust. The extraordinary thing would be, not even to entertain it, but to stifle it. If, however, this be not possible, then though we may have to wrestle with it, and retain it to the last, yet if we depart still wrestling, we are conquerors.

For the case is not the same here as it is with wrestlers; for there if thou throw not thy antagonist, thou hast not conquered; but here if thou be not thrown, thou hast conquered; if thou art not thrown, thou hast thrown him; and with reason, because there both strive for the victory, and when the one is thrown, the other is crowned; here, however, it is not thus, but the devil is striving for our defeat; when then I strip him of that upon which he is bent, I am conqueror. For it is not to overthrow us, but to make us share his overthrow that he is eager. Already then am I conqueror, for he is already cast down, and in a state of ruin; and his victory consists not in being himself crowned, but in effecting my ruin; so that though I overthrow him not, yet if I be not overthrown, I have conquered. What then is a glorious victory? It is, over and above, to trample him underfoot, as Paul did, by regarding the things of this present world as nothing. Let us too imitate him, and strive to become above them, and nowhere to give him a hold upon us. Wealth, possessions, vain-glory, give him a hold. And oftentimes indeed this has roused him, and oftentimes exasperated him. But what need is there of wrestling? What need of engaging with him? He who is engaged in the act of wrestling has the issue in uncertainty, whether he may not be himself defeated and captured. Whereas he that tramples him under foot, has the victory certain.

Oh then, let us trample under foot the power of the devil; let us trample under foot our sins, I mean everything that pertains to this life, wrath, lust, vain-glory, every passion; that when we depart to that world, we may not be convicted of betraying that power which God hath given us; for thus shall we attain also the blessings that are to come. But if in this we are unfaithful, who will entrust us with those things which are greater? If we were not able to trample down one who had fallen, who had been disgraced, who had been despised, who was lying beneath our feet, how shall the Father give us a Father's rewards? If we subdue not one so placed in subjection to us, what confidence shall we have to enter into our Father's house? For, tell me, suppose thou hadst a son, and, that he, disregarding the well-disposed part of thy household, should associate with them that have distressed thee, with them that have been expelled his father's house, with them that spend their time at the gaming table, and that he should go on so doing to the very last; will he not be disinherited? It is plain enough he will. And so too shall we; if, disregarding the Angels who have well pleased our Father and whom He hath set over us, we have our conversation with the devil, inevitably we shall be dis-

---

[1] [The words, "I fear," φοβοῦμαι γὰρ, are not in the text of 1 Cor. ix. 27. See note 1 on page 157. — G. A.]

inherited, which God forbid; but let us engage in the war we have to wage with him.

If any one hath an enemy, if any one hath been wronged by him, if any one is exasperated, let him collect together all that wrath, all that fierceness, and pour it out upon the head of the devil. Here wrath is a good thing, here anger is profitable, here revenge is praiseworthy, for just as amongst the heathen, revenge is a vice, so truly here is revenge a virtue. So then if thou hast any failings, rid thyself of them here. And if thou art not able thyself to put them away, do it, though with thy members also.[1] Hath any one struck thee? Bear malice against the devil, and never relinquish thy hatred towards him. Or again, hath no one struck thee? Yet bear him malice still, because he insulted, because he offended thy Lord and Master, because he injures and wars against thy brethren. With him be ever at enmity, ever implacable, ever merciless. Thus shall he be humbled, thus despicable, thus shall he be an easy prey. If we are fierce towards him, he shall never be fierce towards us. If we are compliant, then he will be fierce; it is not with him as it is with our brethren. He is the foe and enemy, both of life and salvation, both ours and his own. If he loves not himself, how shall he be able to love us? Let us then put ourselves in array and wound him, having for our mighty confederate the Lord Jesus Christ, who can both render us impregnable to his snares, and worthy of the good things to come; which God grant that we may all attain, through the grace and lovingkindness of our Lord Jesus Christ, with whom, together with the Holy Ghost, be unto the Father, glory, might, and honor, now and ever, and throughout all ages. Amen.

HOMILY XXIII.

Ephesians vi. 14.

"Stand therefore, having girded your loins with truth."

Having drawn up this army, and roused their zeal, — for both these things were requisite, both that they should be drawn up in array and subject to each other, and that their spirit should be aroused, — and having inspired them with courage, for this was requisite also, he next proceeds also to arm them. For arms had been of no use, had they not been first posted each in his own place, and had not the spirit of the soldier's soul been roused; for we must first arm him within, and then without.

Now if this is the case with soldiers, much more is it with spiritual soldiers. Or rather in their case, there is no such thing as arming them without, but everything is within. He hath roused their ardor, and set it on fire, he hath added confidence. He hath set them in due array. Observe how he also puts on the armor. "Stand therefore,"[2] saith he. The very first feature in tactics is, to know how to stand well, and many things will depend upon that. Hence he discourses much concerning standing, saying else-where, "Watch ye, stand fast." (1 Cor. xvi. 13.) And again, "So stand fast in the Lord." (Phil. iv. 1.) And again, "Let him that thinketh he standeth, take heed lest he fall." (1 Cor. x. 12.) And again, "That ye may be able, having done all, to stand." (Eph. vi. 13.) Doubtless then he does not mean merely any way of standing, but a correct way, and as many as have had experience in wars know how great a point it is to know how to stand. For if in the case of boxers and wrestlers, the trainer recommends this before any-thing else, namely, to stand firm, much more will it be the first thing in warfare, and military matters.

The man who, in a true sense, stands, is up-right; he stands not in a lazy attitude, not leaning upon anything. Exact uprightness discovers itself by the way of standing, so that they who are perfectly upright, they stand. But they who do not stand, cannot be upright, but are unstrung and disjointed. The luxurious man does not stand upright, but is bent; so is the lewd man, and the lover of money. He who knows how to stand will from his very standing, as from a sort of foundation, find every part of the conflict easy to him.

"Stand therefore," saith he, "having girded your loins with truth."[3]

He is not speaking of a literal, physical gir-

---

[1] [We have here followed the text of Savile (supported by three MSS.), as follows: εἰ δὲ μὴ δύνασαι αὐτὸς ἀποθέσθαι, κἂν μετὰ τῶν μελῶν τῶν σῶν, in preference to the text of Field, which has εἰ μὴ δύνασαι αὐτὰ ἀποθέσθαι, ἢ μετὰ τῶν μελῶν τῶν σῶν. — G. A.]

[2] [" 'Stand,' here, is not, like the preceding στῆναι (in verse 13), the standing of the victor, but the 'standing forth of the man ready for the combat.'" — Meyer. — G. A.]

[3] Compare Isa. xi. 5.

dle, for all the language in this passage he employs in a spiritual sense.[1] And observe how methodically he proceeds. First he girds up his soldier.[2] What then is the meaning of this? The man that is loose in his life, and is dissolved in his lusts, and that has his thoughts trailing on the ground, him he braces up by means of this girdle, not suffering him to be impeded by the garments entangling his legs, but leaving him to run with his feet well at liberty. "Stand therefore, having girded your loins," saith he. By the "loins" here he means this; just what the keel is in ships, the same are the loins with us, the basis or groundwork of the whole body : for they are, as it were, a foundation, and upon them as the schools of the physicians tell you, the whole frame is built. So then in "girding up the loins" he compacts the foundation of our soul ; for he is not of course speaking of these loins of our body, but is discoursing spiritually : and as the loins are the foundation alike of the parts both above and below, so is it also in the case of these spiritual loins. Oftentimes, we know, when persons are fatigued, they put their hands there as if upon a sort of foundation, and in that manner support themselves ; and for this reason it is that the girdle is used in war, that it may bind and hold together this foundation, as it were, in our frame ; for this reason too it is that when we run we gird ourselves. It is this which guards our strength. Let this then, saith he, be done also with respect to the soul, and then in doing anything whatsoever we shall be strong ; and it is a thing most especially becoming to soldiers.

True, you may say, but these our natural loins we gird with a leathern band ; but we, spiritual soldiers, with what? I answer, with that which is the head and crown of all our thoughts, I mean, "with truth." "Having girded your loins," saith he, "with truth."[3] What then is the meaning of "with truth"? Let us love nothing like falsehood, all our duties let us pursue "with truth," let us not lie one to another. Whether it be an opinion, let us seek the truth, or whether it be a line of life, let us seek the true one. If we fortify ourselves with this, if we "gird ourselves with truth," then shall no one overcome us. He who seeks the doctrine of truth, shall never fall down to the earth ; for that the things which are not true are of the earth, is evident from this, that all they that are without are enslaved to the passions, following

their own reasonings ; and therefore if we are sober, we shall need no instruction in the tales of the Greeks. Seest thou how weak and frivolous they are? incapable of entertaining about God one severe thought or anything above human reasoning? Why? Because they are not "girded about with truth" ; because their loins, the receptacle of the seed of life, and the main strength of their reasonings, are ungirt ; nothing then can be weaker than these. And the Manicheans[4] again, seest thou, how all the things they have the boldness to utter, are from their own reasonings? "It was impossible," say they, "for God to create the world without matter." Whence is this so evident? These things they say, groveling, and from the earth, and from what happens amongst ourselves ; because man, they say, cannot create otherwise. Marcion again, look what he says. "God, if He took upon Him flesh, could not remain pure." Whence is this evident? "Because," says he, "neither can men." But men are able to do this. Valentinus again, with his reasonings all trailing along the ground, speaks the things of the earth ; and in like manner Paul of Samosata. And Arius, what does he say? "It was impossible for God when He begat, to beget without passion."[5] Whence, Arius, hast thou the boldness to allege this ; merely from the things which take place amongst ourselves? Seest thou how the reasonings of all these trail along on the ground? All are, as it were, let loose and unconfined, and savoring of the earth? And so much then for doctrines. With regard to life and conduct, again, whoremongers, lovers of money, and of glory, and of everything else, trail on the ground. They have not their loins themselves standing firm, so that when they are weary they may rest upon them ; but when they are weary, they do not put their hands upon them and stand upright, but flag. He, however, who "is girt about with the truth," first, never is weary ; and secondly, if he should be weary, he will rest himself upon the truth itself. What? Will poverty, tell me, render him weary? No, in nowise ; for he will repose on the true riches, and by this poverty will understand what is true poverty. Or again, will slavery make him weary? No, in nowise, for he will know what is the true slavery. Or shall disease? No, nor even that. "Let your loins," saith Christ, "be girded about, and your lamps burning" (Luke xii. 35), with that light which shall never be put out. This is what the Israelites also, when they were departing out of Egypt (Ex. xii. 11), were

---

[1] νοητῶς.
[2] ["As for the actual warrior, the whole *aptus habitus* (prepared state) for the combat would be wanting in the absence of the girdle; so also for the spiritual warrior, if he is not furnished with truth."—Meyer.—G. A.]
[3] ["It is clear that truth does not mean 'objectively the gospel,' for that is designated later, ver. 17, by ῥῆμα θεοῦ ('the word of God'), but 'subjectively,' truth as an inward property, i.e. the 'harmony of knowledge with the objective truth given in the gospel.'"—Meyer.—G. A.]

[4] The Manichees considered matter to be uncreate; vid. Note on St. Augustine's *Confessions*. i. b. The Marcionites considered matter intrinsically evil; vid. Theod. *Hær.* i. 24. Valentinus denied that our Lord was born of the substance of Mary; vid. St. Cyril, *Lect.* iv. 9. Paul of Samosata and Arius both denied His Godhead.
[5] ἀπαθῶς.

charged to do. For why did they eat the passover with their loins girded? Art thou desirous to hear the ground of it? According to the historical fact, or according to its mystical sense,[1] shall I state it? But I will state them both, and do ye retain it in mind, for I am not doing it without an object, merely that I may tell you the solution, but also that my words may become in you reality. They had, we read, their loins girded, and their staff in their hands, and their shoes on their feet, and thus they ate the Passover. Awful and terrible mysteries, and of vast depth; and if so terrible in the type, how much more in the reality? They come forth out of Egypt, they eat the Passover. Attend. "Our Passover hath been sacrificed, even Christ," it is said. Wherefore did they have their loins girded? Their guise is that of wayfarers; for their having shoes, and staves in their hands, and their eating standing, declares nothing else than this. Will ye hear the history first, or the mystery?[2] Better the history first. What then is the design of the history? The Jews were continually forgetting God's benefits to them. Accordingly then, God tied the sense of these, His benefits, not only to the time, but also to the very habit of them that were to eat. For this is why they were to eat girded and sandalled, that when they were asked the reason, they might say, "we were ready for our journey, we were just about to go forth out of Egypt to the land of promise and we were ready for our exodus." This then is the historical type. But the reality is this; we too eat a Passover, even Christ; "for," saith he, "our Passover hath been sacrificed, even Christ." (1 Cor. v. 7.) What then? We too ought to eat it, both sandalled and girded. And why? That we too may be ready for our Exodus, for our departure hence.

MORAL. Let not any one of them that eat this Passover look towards Egypt, but towards Heaven, towards "Jerusalem that is above." (Gal. iv. 26.) On this account thou eatest with thy loins girded, on this account thou eatest with shoes on thy feet, that thou mayest know, that from the moment thou first beginnest to eat the Passover, thou oughtest to set out, and to be upon thy journey. And this implies two things, both that we must depart out of Egypt, and that, whilst we stay, we must stay henceforth as in a strange country; "for our citizenship," saith he, "is in Heaven" (Phil. iii. 20); and that all our life long we should ever be prepared, so that when we are called we may not put it off, but say, "My heart is fixed." (Ps. cviii. 1.) "Yes, but this Paul indeed could say, who knew nothing against himself; but I, who require a long time for repentance, I cannot say it." Yet that to be girded is the part of a waking soul, hearken to what God says to that righteous man, "Gird up now thy loins like a man, for I will demand of thee, and declare thou unto Me." (Job xxxviii. 3.) This He says also to all the prophets, and this He says again to Moses, to be girded. And He Himself also appears to Ezekiel (Ezek. ix. 11, Sept.) girded. Nay more, and the Angels, too, appear to us girded (Rev. xv. 6), as being soldiers. From our being girded about, it comes that we also stand bravely as from our standing our being girded comes.

For we also are going to depart, and many are the difficulties that intervene. When we have crossed this plain, straightway the devil is upon us, doing everything, contriving every artifice, to the end that those who have been saved out of Egypt, those who have passed the Red Sea, those who are delivered at once from the evil demons, and from unnumbered plagues, may be taken and destroyed by him. But, if we be vigilant, we too have a pillar of fire, the grace of the Spirit. The same both enlightens and overshadows us. We have manna; yea rather not manna, but far more than manna. Spiritual drink we have, not water, that springs forth from the Rock. So have we too our encampment (Rev. xx. 9), and we dwell in the desert even now; for a desert indeed without virtue, is the earth even now, even more desolate than that wilderness. Why was that desert so terrible? Was it not because it had scorpions in it, and adders? (Deut. viii. 15.) "A land," it is said, "which none passed through." (Jer. ii. 6.) Yet is not that wilderness, no, it is not so barren of fruits, as is this human nature. At this instant, how many scorpions, how many asps are in this wilderness, how many serpents, how many "offsprings of vipers" (Matt. iii. 7) are these through whom we at this instant pass! Yet let us not be afraid; for the leader of this our Exodus is not Moses, but Jesus.

How then is it that we shall not suffer the same things? Let us not commit the same acts, and then shall we not suffer the same punishment. They murmured, they were ungrateful; let us therefore not cherish these passions. How was it that they fell all of them?

---

[1] The word ἀναγωγὴ, when used of Scripture exposition, has various senses, but always implies an interpretation not literal, grammatical, or historical. Sometimes it stands for a "moral" interpretation, i.e. one conveying a moral lesson; e.g. Chrys. *in Psalm* cxix. (120) init.; Basil. *in Esai.* v. § 152. Sometimes for an interpretation with reference simply to heavenly persons and things; vid. Mosheim, *de Reb. ante Const.* p. 644; Dionys. *Hierarch Cæl.* i. 2. Origen enumerates three senses of Scripture, literal, moral, and mystical, the last being either allegorical or anagogical; Clement four, literal, moral, mystical, and prophetical; but the more common division has into literal, tropological, allegorical, and anagogical. [Cassian, a pupil of Chrysostom, defines ἀναγωγή: *Anagoge vero de spiritalibus mysteriis ad sublimiora quaedam et sacratiora coelorum secreta conscendens,* "leading up from spiritual mysteries to higher and more sacred secrets of heaven." See also Sophocles' *Greek Lex.* sub "*voce.*"—G. A.]

[2] ἀναγωγήν.

"They despised the pleasant land." (Ps. cvi. 24.) "How 'despised' it? Surely they prized it highly." By becoming indolent and cowardly, and not choosing to undergo any labors to obtain it. Let not us then "despise" Heaven! This is what is meant by "despising." Again, among us also has fruit been brought, fruit from Heaven, not the cluster of grapes borne upon the staff (Num. xiii. 23), but the "earnest of the Spirit" (2 Cor. i. 22), "the citizenship which is in Heaven" (Phil. iii. 20), which Paul and the whole company of the Apostles, those marvelous husbandmen, have taught us. It is not Caleb the son of Jephunneh, nor Jesus the son of Nun, that hath brought these fruits; but Jesus the Son of "the Father of mercies" (2 Cor. i. 3), the Son of the Very God, hath brought every virtue, hath brought down from Heaven all the fruits that are from thence, the songs of heaven hath He brought. For the words which the Cherubim above say, these hath He charged us to say also, "Holy, Holy, Holy."[1] He hath brought to us the virtue of the Angels. "The Angels marry not, neither are given in marriage" (Matt. xxii. 30); this fair plant hath He planted here also. They love not money, nor anything like it; and this too hath He sown amongst us. They never die; and this hath He freely given us also, for death is no longer death, but sleep. For hearken to what He saith, "Our friend Lazarus is fallen asleep." (John xi. 11.)

Seest thou then the fruits of "Jerusalem that is above"? (Gal. iv. 26.) And what is indeed more stupendous than all is this, that our warfare is not decided, but all these things are given us before the attainment of the promise! For they indeed toiled even after they had entered into the land of promise; — rather, they toiled not, for had they chosen to obey God, they might have taken all the cities, without either arms or array. Jericho, we know, they overturned, more after the fashion of dancers than of warriors. We however have no warfare after we have entered into the land of promise, that is, into Heaven, but only so long as we are in the wilderness, that is, in the present life. "For he that is entered into his rest hath himself also rested from his works as God did from His." (Heb. iv. 10.) "Let us not then be weary in well-doing, for in due season we shall reap, if we faint not." (Gal. vi. 9.) Seest thou how that just as He led them, so also He leads us? In their case, touching the manna and the

wilderness, it is said, "He that gathered much had nothing over, and he that gathered little had no lack." (Ex. xvi. 18.) And we have this charge given us, "not to lay up treasure upon the earth." (Matt. vi. 19.) But if we do lay up treasure, it is no longer the earthly worm that corrupts it, as was the case with the manna, but that which dwelleth eternally with fire.[2] Let us then "subdue all things," that we furnish not food to this worm. For "he," it is said, "who gathered much had nothing over." For this too happens with ourselves also every day. We all of us have but the same capacity of hunger to satisfy. And that which is more than this, is but an addition of cares. For what He intended in after-times to deliver, saying, "Sufficient unto the day is the evil thereof" (Matt. vi. 34), this had He thus been teaching even from the very beginning,[3] and not even thus did they receive it. But as to us, let us not be insatiable, let us not be discontented, let us not be seeking out for splendid houses; for we are on our pilgrimage, not at home; so that if there be any that knows that the present life is a sort of journey, and expedition, and, as one might say, it is what they call an entrenched camp,[4] he will not be seeking for splendid buildings. For who, tell me, would he be ever so rich, would choose to build a splendid house in an encampment? No one; he would be a laughing stock, he would be building for his enemies, and would the more effectually invite them on; and so then, if we be in our senses, neither shall we. The present life is nothing else than a march and an encampment.

Wherefore, I beseech you, let us do all we can, so as to lay up no treasure here; for if the thief should come, we must in a moment arise and depart. "Watch," saith He, "for ye know not at what hour the thief cometh" (Matt. xxiv. 42, 43), thus naming death. O then, before he cometh, let us send away everything before us to our native country; but here let us be "well girded," that we may be enabled to overcome our enemies, whom God grant that we may overcome, through the grace and lovingkindness of our Lord Jesus Christ, with Whom together with the Holy Ghost, be unto the Father glory, strength, honor forever and ever. Amen.

---

[1] [For the use of these words in the church service, see Bingham, *Antiquities*, xv. 3, 10, and Hom. III. on Ephesians. — G. A.]

[2] [The text in this passage is very corrupt. Three MSS. have οὐκέτι σκώληξ ὁ αἰσθητὸς λυμαίνεται . . . ἀλλὰ ὁ τῆς δικαιοσύνης. But, as Field says, ὁ σκώληξ τῆς δικαιοσύνης ("the worm of righteousness") seems "*absurdissimum*." Three other MSS. give the reading which we have adopted: "No longer the earthly worm," &c., "but that which dwelleth eternally with fire," ἀλλ' ὁ τῷ πυρὶ συνδιαιωνίζων ἡμᾶς λυμαίνεται. Field, in his text, follows a single MS., and emends even that. — G. A.]

[3] ἄνωθεν.

[4] φωσσάτον, *fossatum*.

HOMILY XXIV.

Ephesians vi. 14–17.

"Stand therefore, having girded your loins with truth, and having on the breastplate of righteousness; and having shod your feet with the preparation of the gospel of peace; withal taking up the shield of faith, wherewith ye shall be able to quench all the fiery darts of the evil one. And take the helmet of salvation, and the sword of the Spirit, which is the word of God."

"Having girded your loins," saith he, "with truth." What can be the meaning of this? I have stated in the preceding discourse, that he ought to be lightly accoutered, in order that there should be no impediment whatever to his running.

"And having on," he continues, "the breastplate of righteousness." As the breastplate is impenetrable, so also is righteousness, and by righteousness here he means a life of universal virtue.[1] Such a life no one shall ever be able to overthrow; it is true, many wound him, but no one cuts through him, no, not the devil himself. It is as though one were to say, "having righteous deeds fixed in the breast"; of these it is that Christ saith, "Blessed are they that hunger and thirst after righteousness; for they shall be filled." (Matt. v. 6.) Thus is he firm and strong like a breastplate. Such a man will never be put out of temper.

"And having shod your feet with the preparation of the gospel of peace." It is more uncertain in what sense this was said. What then is its meaning? They are noble greaves, doubtless, with which he invests us. Either then he means this, that we should be prepared for the gospel, and should make use of our feet for this, and should prepare and make ready its way before it;[2] or if not this, at least that we ourselves should be prepared for our departure. "The preparation," then, "of the gospel of peace," is nothing else than a most virtuous life; according to what the Prophet saith. "Thou wilt prepare their heart, thou wilt cause thine ear to hear." (Ps. x. 17.) "Of the gospel," he says, "of peace," and with reason; for inasmuch as he had made mention of warfare and fighting,

he shows us that this conflict with the evil spirits we must needs have: for the gospel is "the gospel of peace"; this war which we have against them, puts an end to another war, that, namely, which is between us and God; if we are at war with the devil, we are at peace with God. Fear not therefore, beloved; it is a "gospel," that is, a word of good news; already is the victory won.

"Withal taking up the shield of faith."

By "faith" in this place, he means, not knowledge, (for that he never would have ranged last,) but that gift by which miracles are wrought.[3] And with reason does he term this "'faith' a shield"; for as the shield is put before the whole body, as if it were a sort of rampart, just so is this faith; for all things yield to it.

"Wherewith ye shall be able," saith he, "to quench all the fiery darts of the evil one."

For this shield nothing shall be able to resist; for hearken to what Christ saith to His disciples, "If ye have faith as a grain of mustard seed, ye shall say unto this mountain, Remove hence to yonder place, and it shall remove." (Matt. xvii. 20.) But how are we to have this faith? When we have rightly performed all those duties.

"By the darts of the evil one," he means, both temptations, and vile desires; and "fiery," he says, for such is the character of these desires. Yet if faith can command the evil spirits, much more can it also the passions of the soul.

"And take the helmet," he continues, "of salvation," that is, of your salvation. For he is casing them in armor.

"And the sword of the Spirit, which is the word of God." He either means the Spirit, or else, "the spiritual sword":[4] for by this[4] all things are severed, by this all things are cleft asunder, by this we cut off even the serpent's head.

Ver. 18, 19, 20. "With all prayer and supplication," saith he, "praying at all seasons in the Spirit, and watching thereunto in all perseverance and supplication for all the saints; and on my behalf that utterance may be given unto me, in opening my mouth to make known with boldness the mystery of the gospel, for which

---

[1] ["'Righteousness' here is Christian moral rectitude (Rom. vi. 13), inasmuch as, justified by faith, we are dead to sin and live in newness of life (Rom. vi. 4). As previously the 'intellectual' rectitude of the Christian was denoted by ἀλήθεια, so here his 'moral' rectitude by δικαιοσύνη."—Meyer.—G. A.]

[2] ["This means 'readiness,' the ready mind; not, however, for the proclamation of the gospel, as Chrysostom and others,—since in fact Paul is addressing fellow-Christians, and not fellow-teachers,—but the readiness for the conflict in question which the gospel bestows. And it is the gospel of peace, for the gospel proclaims peace (Rom. v. 1; Phil. i. 20), and thereby produces consecration of courageous 'readiness' for the conflict (Rom. viii. 31, 38, 39)."—Meyer.—G. A.]

[3] [This interpretation does not suit the context. "Faith is here saving faith, bringing assurance of forgiveness and future blessedness."—Meyer.—G. A.]

[4] [It simply means the sword which "is furnished by the Holy Spirit," and this sword, as the apostle himself declares, is the word of God, the gospel, which the Holy Spirit brings vividly to the consciousness of the Christian.—Meyer and Ellicott.—G. A.]

I am an ambassador in chains, that in it I may speak boldly, as I ought to speak."

As the word of God has power to do all things, so also has he who has the spiritual gift. "For the word of God," saith he, "is living, and active and sharper than any two-edged sword." (Heb. iv. 12.) Now mark the wisdom of this blessed Apostle. He hath armed them with all security. What then is necessary after that? To call upon the King, that He may stretch forth His hand. "With all prayer, and supplication, praying at all seasons in the Spirit"; for it is possible "to pray" not "in the Spirit," when one "uses vain repetitions" (Matt. vi. 7); "and watching thereunto," he adds, that is, keeping sober; for such ought the armed warrior, he that stands at the King's side, to be; wakeful and temperate : — "in all perseverance and supplication for all the saints; and on my behalf that utterance may be given unto me in opening my mouth." What sayest thou, blessed Paul? Hast thou, then, need of thy disciples? And well does he say, "in opening my mouth." He did not then study what he used to say, but according to what Christ said, "When they deliver you up, be not anxious how or what ye shall speak : for it shall be given you in that hour what ye shall speak" (Matt. x. 19) : so truly did he do everything by faith, everything by grace. "With boldness," he proceeds, "to make known the mystery of the Gospel"; that is, that I may answer for myself in its defense, as I ought. And art thou bound in thy chain, and still needest the aid of others? Yea, saith he, for so was Peter also bound in his chain, and yet nevertheless "was prayer made earnestly for him." (Acts xii. 5.) "For which I am an ambassador in chains, that in it I may speak boldly, as I ought to speak"; that is, that I may answer with confidence, with courage, with great prudence.

Ver. 21. "But that ye also[1] may know my affairs, how I do, Tychicus, the beloved brother and faithful minister in the Lord, shall make known to you all things."

As soon as he had mentioned his chains, he leaves something for Tychicus also to relate to them of his own accord. For whatever topics there were of doctrine and of exhortation, all these he explained by his letter : but what were matters of bare recital, these he entrusted to the bearer of the letter. "That ye may know my affairs," that is, may be informed of them. This manifests both the love which he entertained towards them, and their love towards him.

Ver. 22. "Whom I have sent unto you," saith he, "for this very purpose, that ye may know our state, and that he may comfort your hearts."

This language he employs, not without a purpose, but in consequence of what he had been saying previously; "having girded your loins, having on the breastplate," &c., which are a token of a constant and unceasing advance; for hear what the Prophet saith, "Let it be unto him as the raiment wherewith he covereth himself, and for the girdle wherewith he is girded continually" (Ps. cix. 19); and the Prophet Isaiah again saith, that God hath "put on righteousness as a breastplate" (Isa. lix. 17); by these expressions instructing us that these are things which we must have, not for a short time only, but continually, inasmuch as there is continual need of warfare. "For it is said the righteous are bold as a lion." (Prov. xxviii. 1.) For he that is armed with such a breastplate, it cannot be that he should fear the array that is against him, but he will leap into the midst of the enemy. And again Isaiah saith, "How beautiful are the feet of him that bringeth good tidings." (Isa. lii. 7.) Who would not run, who would not serve in such a cause; to publish the good tidings of peace, peace between God and man, peace, where men have toiled not, but where God hath wrought all?

But what is the "preparation of the Gospel"?[2] Let us hearken to what John saith, "Make ye ready the way of the Lord, make His paths straight." (Matt. iii. 3.) But again there is need also of another "preparation" after baptism, so that we may do nothing unworthy of "peace." And then, since the feet are usually a token of the way of life, hence he is constantly exhorting in this language, "Look, therefore, carefully how ye walk." (Eph. v. 15.) On this account, he would say, let us exhibit a practice and example worthy of the Gospel; that is, make our life and conduct pure. The good tidings of peace have been proclaimed to you, give to these good tidings a ready way; since if ye again become enemies, there is no more "preparation of peace." Be ready, be not backward to embrace this peace. As ye were ready and disposed for peace and faith, so also continue. The shield is that which first receives the assaults of the adversary, and preserves the armor uninjured. So long then as faith be right and the life be right, the armor remains uninjured.

He discourses, however, much concerning faith, but most especially in writing to the Hebrews, as he does also concerning hope. Believe, saith he, in the good things to come, and none of this armor shall be injured. In dangers, in toils, by holding out thy hope and thy faith to protect thee, thou wilt preserve thy armor uninjured. "He that cometh to God

---

[1] ["Ye also," as well as the Colossians (Col. iv. 8, 9). Meyer's Introd. sec. 2. The καί, on supposition of priority of Colossians, admits of an easy and natural explanation. — Ellicott. — G. A.]

[2] [After having treated this part of the chapter, our author now returns to it, and supplements what he has already said. — G. A.]

must believe that He is, and that He is a rewarder of them that seek after Him." (Heb. xi. 6.) Faith is a shield; but wherever there are quibbles, and reasonings, and scrutinizings, then is it no longer a shield, but it impedes us. Let this our faith be such as shall cover and screen the whole frame. Let it not then be scanty, so as to leave the feet or any other part exposed, but let the shield be commensurate with the whole body.

"Fiery[1] darts." For many doubtful reasonings there are, which set the soul, as it were, on fire, many difficulties, many perplexities, but all of them faith sets entirely at rest; many things does the devil dart in, to inflame our soul and bring us into uncertainty; as, for example, when some persons say, "Is there then a resurrection?" "Is there a judgment?" "Is there a retribution?" "But is there faith?" the apostle would say, "thou shalt with it quench the darts of the devil. Has any base lust assaulted thee? Hold before thee thy faith in the good things to come, and it will not even show itself, yea, it will perish." "All the darts"; not some quenched, and others not. Hearken to what Paul saith, "For I reckon that the sufferings of this present time are not worthy to be compared with the glory that shall be revealed to us-ward." (Rom. viii. 18.) Seest thou how many darts the righteous quenched in those days? Seemeth it not to thee to be "fiery darts," when the patriarch burned with inward fire, as he was offering up his son? Yea, and other righteous men also have quenched "all his darts." Whether then they be reasonings that assault us, let us hold out this; or whether they be base desires, let us use this; or whether again labors and distresses, upon this let us repose. Of all the other armor, this is the safeguard; if we have not this, they will be quickly pierced through. "Withal," saith he, "taking up the shield of faith." What is the meaning of "withal"? It means both "in truth," and "in righteousness," and "in the preparation of the gospel"; that is to say, all these have need of the aid of faith.

And therefore he adds further, "and take the helmet of salvation"; that is to say, finally by this shall ye be able to be in security. To receive the helmet of salvation is to escape the peril. For as the helmet covers the head perfectly in every part, and suffers it not to sustain any injury, but preserves it, so also does faith supply alike the place of a shield, and of a helmet[2] to preserve us. For if we quench his

darts, quickly shall we receive also those saving thoughts that suffer not our governing principle[3] to sustain any harm; for if these, the thoughts that are adverse to our salvation, are quenched, those which are not so, but which contribute to our salvation, and inspire us with good hopes, will be generated within us, and will rest upon our governing principle, as a helmet does upon the head.

And not only this, but we shall take also "the sword of the Spirit," and thus not only ward off his missiles, but smite the devil himself. For a soul that does not despair of herself, and is proof against those fiery darts, will stand with all intrepidity to face the enemy, and will cleave open his breastplate with this very sword with which Paul also burst through it, and "brought into captivity his devices" (2 Cor. x. 5); he will cut off and behead the serpent.

"Which is the word of God."

By the "word of God" in this place, he means on the one hand the ordinance of God, or the word of command; or on the other that it is in the Name of Christ. For if we keep his commandments, by these we shall kill and slay the dragon himself, "the crooked serpent." (Isa. xxvii. 1.) And as he said, "Ye shall be able to quench the fiery darts of the evil one"; that he might not puff them up, he shows them, that above all things they stand in need of God; for what does he say?

"With all prayer and supplication," he says, these things shall be done, and ye shall accomplish all by praying. But when thou drawest near, never ask for thyself only: thus shalt thou have God favorable to thee.

"With all prayer and supplication, praying at all seasons in the Spirit, and watching thereunto in all perseverance for all the saints." Limit it not, I say, to certain times of the day, for hear what he is saying; approach at all times; "pray," saith he, "without ceasing." (1 Thess. v. 17.) Hast thou never heard of that widow, how by her importunity she prevailed? (Luke xviii. 1–7.) Hast thou never heard of that friend, who at midnight shamed his friend into yielding by his perseverance? (Luke xi. 5–8.) Hast thou not heard of the Syrophœnician woman (Mark vii. 25–30), how by the constancy of her entreaty she called forth the Lord's compassion? These all of them gained their object by their importunity.

"Praying at all seasons," saith he, "in the Spirit."

That is to say, let us seek for the things which are according to God, nothing of this world, nothing pertaining to this life.

---

[1] ["The aim of this predicate is to present in strong colors the hostile and destructive character of the Satanic assaults; but more special explanations of its import are inappropriate."—Meyer.—G. A.]

[2] [Faith is not the helmet. Chrysostom's exegesis of the parts of the armor is not clear. Salvation is the helmet; for τοῦ σωτηρίου is a genitive of apposition. Receive the helmet, which is salvation.

"This salvation," says Ellicott, "is not any ideal possession, as Meyer holds. Salvation in Christ forms the subject of faith; in faith it is apprehended, and becomes in a certain sense a present possession."—G. A.]

[3] τὸ ἡγεμονικόν.

Therefore, is there need not only that we "pray without ceasing," but also, that we should do so "watching ; — and watching," saith he, "thereunto." Whether he is here speaking of vigils ;[1] or of the wakefulness of the soul, I admit both meanings. Seest thou how that Canaanitish woman watched unto prayer? and though the Lord gave her no answer, nay, even shook her off, and called her a dog, she said, "Yea, Lord : for even the dogs eat of the crumbs which fall from their masters' table" (Matt. xv. 27), and desisted not until she obtained her request. How, too, did that widow cry, and persist so long, until she was able to shame into yielding that ruler, that neither feared God, nor regarded man (Luke xviii. 1–7)? And how, again, did the friend persist, remaining before the door in the dead of night, till he shamed the other into yielding by his importunity, and made him arise. (Luke xi. 5–8.) This is to be watchful.

Wouldest thou understand what watchfulness in prayer is? Go to Hannah, hearken to her very words, "Adonai Eloi Sabaoth." (1 Sam. i. 11.) Nay, rather, hear what preceded those words ; "they all rose up," says the history, "from the table" (1 Sam. i. 9), and she, forthwith, did not betake herself to sleep, nor to repose. Whence she appears to me even when she was sitting at the table to have partaken lightly, and not to have been made heavy with viands. Otherwise never could she have shed so many tears ; for if we, when we are fasting and foodless, hardly pray thus, or rather never pray thus, much more would not she ever have prayed thus after a meal, unless even at the meal she had been as they that eat not. Let us be ashamed, us that are men, at the example of this woman ; let us be ashamed, that are suing and gasping for a kingdom, at her, praying and weeping for a little child. "And she stood," it says, "before the Lord" (1 Sam. i. 10) ; and what are her words? "Adonai, Lord, Eloi Sabaoth!" and this is, being interpreted, "O Lord, the God of Hosts." Her tears went before her tongue ; by these she hoped to prevail with God to bend to her request. Where tears are, there is always affliction also : where affliction is, there is great wisdom and heedfulness. "If thou wilt indeed," she continues, "look on the affliction of thine handmaid, and wilt give unto thine handmaid a man child, then will I give him unto the Lord all the days of his life." (1 Sam. i. 11.) She said not, "for one year," or, "for two," as we do ; — nor said she, "if thou wilt give me a child, I will give thee money" ; but, "I give back to Thee the very gift itself entire, my first-born, the son of my prayer." Truly here was a daughter of Abraham. He gave when it was demanded of him. She offers even before it is demanded.

But observe even after this her deep reverence. "Only her lips moved, but her voice," it saith, "was not heard." (1 Sam. i. 13.) And thus does he who would gain his request draw nigh unto God ; not consulting his ease, nor gaping, nor lounging, nor scratching his head, nor with utter listlessness. What, was not God able to grant, even without any prayer at all? What, did He not know the woman's desire even before she asked? And yet had He granted it before she asked, then the woman's earnestness would not have been shown, her virtue would not have been made manifest, she would not have gained so great a reward. So that the delay is not the result of envy or of witchcraft, but of providential kindness. When therefore ye hear the Scripture saying, that "the Lord had shut up her womb" (ver. 5, 6), and that, "her rival provoked her sore" ; consider that it is His intention to prove the woman's seriousness.[2] For, mark, she had a husband devoted to her, for he said (ver. 8), "Am I not better to thee than ten sons?" "And her rival," it saith, "provoked her sore," that is, reproached her, insulted over her. And yet did she never once retaliate, nor utter imprecation against her, nor say, "Avenge me, for my rival reviles me." The other had children, but this woman had her husband's love to make amends. With this at least he even consoled her, saying, "Am not I better to thee than ten sons?"

But let us look, again, at the deep wisdom of this woman. "And Eli," it says, "thought she had been drunken." (Ver. 13.) Yet observe what she says to him also, "Nay, count not thine handmaid for a daughter of Belial, for out of the abundance of my complaint and my provocation have I spoken hitherto." (Ver. 16.) Here is truly the proof of a contrite heart, when we are not angry with those that revile us, when we are not indignant against them, when we reply but in self-defense. Nothing renders the heart so wise as affliction ; nothing is there so sweet as "godly mourning." (2 Cor. vii. 10.) "Out of the abundance," saith she, "of my complaint and my provocation have I spoken hitherto." Her let us imitate, one and all. Hearken, ye that are barren, hearken, ye that desire children, hearken, both husbands and wives ; yes, for husbands, too, used oftentimes to contribute their part ; for hear what the Scripture saith, "And Isaac intreated the Lord for Rebekah his wife, because she was barren." (Gen. xxv. 21.) For prayer is able to accomplish great things.

---

[1] ταννυχίδας. St. Chrysostom often speaks of vigils, which were Church Services extending past midnight into the morning; vid. Hom. *in Esai.* i. 1, iv. 1, etc.; vid. Bingham, *Antiqu.* xiii. 9, § 4.

[2] φιλοσοφίαν.

"With all prayer and supplication," saith he, "for all the saints, and for me," placing himself last. What doest thou, O blessed Paul, in thus placing thyself last? Yea, saith he, "that utterance may be given unto me, in opening my mouth, to make known with boldness the mystery of the gospel, for which I am an ambassador in chains." And where art thou an ambassador? "To mankind," saith he. Oh! amazing lovingkindness of God! He sent from Heaven in His own Name ambassadors for peace, and lo, men took them, and bound them, and reverenced not so much as the law of nations, that an ambassador never suffers any hurt. "But, however, I am an ambassador in bonds. The chain lies like a bridle upon me, restraining my boldness, but your prayer shall open my mouth" in order that I may speak all things I was sent to speak.

"But that ye also may know my affairs, how I do, Tychicus, the beloved brother, and faithful minister in the Lord, shall make known to you all things." If "faithful," he will tell no falsehood, he will in everything speak the truth : — "whom I have sent unto you for this very purpose, that ye might know our state, and that he may comfort your hearts." Amazing, transcendent affection ! "that it may not be in the power," he means, "of them that would, to affright you." For it is probable that they were in tribulation ; for the expression, "may comfort your hearts," intimates as much ; that is, "may not suffer you to sink under it."

Ver. 23. "Peace be to the brethren, and love with faith from God the Father, and the Lord Jesus Christ."

He invokes upon them, "peace and love with faith." He saith well : for he would not that they should have regard to love by itself, and mingle themselves with those of a different faith. Either he means this, or that above described, namely, that they should have faith also, so as to have a cheerful confidence of the good things to come. The "peace" which is towards God, and the "love." And if there be peace, there will also be love ; if love, there will be peace also. "With faith," because without faith, love amounts to nothing ; or rather love could not exist at all without it.

Ver. 24. "Grace be with all them that love our Lord Jesus Christ in uncorruptness."

Why does he separate the two here, placing "peace" by itself, and "grace" by itself?

"In uncorruptness," he concludes.

What is this, "in uncorruptness"? It either means, "in purity" ; or else, "for the sake of those things which are incorruptible," as, for example, not in riches, nor in glory, but in those treasures which are incorruptible. The "in" means, "through." "Through uncorruptness,"

that is, "through virtue."[1] Because all sin is corruption. And in the same way as we say a virgin is corrupted, so also do we speak of the soul. Hence Paul says, "Lest by any means your minds should be corrupted." (2 Cor. xi. 3.) And again elsewhere, he says, "In doctrine, showing uncorruptness."[2] For what, tell me, is corruption of the body? Is it not the dissolution of the whole frame, and of its union? This then is what takes place also in the soul when sin enters. The beauty of the soul is temperance, and righteousness ; the health of the soul is courage, and prudence ; for the base man is hideous in our eyes, so is the covetous, so is the man who gives himself up to evil practices, and so the coward and unmanly man is sick, and the foolish man is out of health. Now that sins work corruption, is evident from this, that they render men base, and weak, and cause them to be sick and diseased. Nay, and when we say that a virgin is corrupted, we say so, strictly speaking, on this account also, not only because the body is defiled, but because of the transgression. For the mere act is natural ; and if in that consisted the "corruption," then were marriage corruption. Hence is it not the act that is corruption, but the sin, for it dishonors and puts her to shame. And again, what would be corruption in the case of a house? Its dissolution. And so, universally, corruption is a change which takes place for the worse, a change into another state, to the utter extinction of the former one. For hear what the Scripture saith, "All flesh had corrupted his way" (Gen. vi. 12) ; and again, "In intolerable corruption"[3] (Ex. xviii. 18) ; and again, "Men corrupted in mind." (2 Tim. iii. 8.) Our body is corruptible, but our soul is incorruptible. Oh then, let us not make that corruptible also. This, the corruption of the body, was the work of former sin ;[4] but sin which is after the Laver, has the power also to render the soul corruptible, and to make it an easy prey to "the worm that dieth not." For never had that worm touched it, had it not found the soul corruptible. The worm touches not adamant, and even if he touches it, he can do it no harm. Oh then, corrupt not the soul ; for that which is corrupted is full of foul stench ; for hearken to the Prophet who saith, "My wounds stink and are corrupt because of my foolishness." (Ps. xxxviii. 5.)

---

[1] ["ἐν here expresses the manner, and the expression means those ' who love our Lord in imperishableness,' i.e. ' so that their love does not pass away.' Comp. Tit. iii. 15." — Meyer. — G. A.]

[2] [Tit. ii. 7, where ἀφθορία is used, which, according to Meyer, does mean uncorruptedness, while ἀφθαρσία in our passage means imperishableness. — G. A.]

[3] [φθορᾷ καταφθαρήσῃ ἀνυπομονήτῳ for Hebrew נָבֹל תִּבֹּל, Rev. Ver., " Thou wilt surely wear away."— G. A.]

[4] [Comp. Rom. v. 12: "As through one man sin entered into the world, and death by sin; and so death passed unto all men." — G. A.]

However, "this corruption" of the body "shall put on incorruption" (1 Cor. xv. 53), but the other of the soul, never; for where incorruption is, there is no [1] corruption. Thus is it a corruption which is incorruptible, which hath no end, a deathless death; which would have been, had the body remained deathless. Now if we shall depart into the next world having corruption, we have that corruption incorruptible and endless; for to be ever burning, and not burnt up, ever wasted by the worm, is corruption incorruptible; like as was the case with the blessed Job. He was corrupted, and died not, and that through a lengthened period, and "wasted continually, scraping the clods of dust from his sore." [2] Some such torment as this shall it undergo, when the worms surround and devour it, not for two years nor for three, nor for ten, nor for ten thousand, but for years without end; for "their worm," saith He, "dieth not."

MORAL. Let us take the alarm then, I entreat you, let us dread the words, that we meet not with the realities. Covetousness is corruption, corruption more dangerous than any other, and leading on to idolatry. Let us shun the corruption, let us choose the incorruption. Hast thou in covetousness overreached and defrauded some one? The fruits of thy covetousness perish, but the covetousness remains; a corruption which is the foundation of incorruptible corruption. The enjoyment indeed passes away, but the sin remains imperishable. A fearful evil is it for us not to strip ourselves of everything in this present world; a great calamity to depart into the next with loads of sins about us. "For in Sheol," it is said "who shall give Thee thanks?" (Ps. vi. 5.) There is the place of judgment; then is there no longer season for repentance. How many things did the rich man bewail then? (Luke xvi. 23.) And yet it availed him nothing. How many things did they say who had neglected to feed Christ? (Matt. xxv. 41.) Yet were they led away notwithstanding into the everlasting fire. How many things had they then to say: "that had wrought iniquity"; "Lord, did we not prophesy by Thy Name, and by Thy Name cast out devils?" And yet notwithstanding, they were not owned. All these things therefore will take place then; but it will be of no avail, if they be not done now. Let us fear then, lest ever we should have to say then, "Lord, when saw we Thee an hungered, and fed Thee not?" (Matt. xxv. 44.) Let us feed Him now, not one day, nor two, nor three days. "For let not mercy and truth," saith the Wise Man, "forsake thee." (Prov. iii. 3.) He saith not "do it once, nor twice." The Virgins, we know, had oil, but not enough to last out. (Matt. xxv. 3, 8.) And thus we need much oil, and thus should we be "like a green olive tree in the house of God." (Ps. lii. 8.) Let us reflect then how many burdens of sins each of us has about him, and let us make our acts of mercy counterbalance them; nay rather, far exceed them, that not only the sins may be quenched, but that the acts of righteousness may be also accounted unto us for righteousness. For if the good deeds be not so many in number as to put aside the crimes laid against us, and out of the remainder to be counted unto us for righteousness, [3] then shall no one rescue us from that punishment, from which God grant that we may be all delivered, through the grace and lovingkindness of our Lord Jesus Christ, with whom to the Father, &c.

---

[1] [Field's text has ἔνθα γὰρ ἀφθαρσία, φθορά ἐστιν, which seems a contradiction, whereas Savile's text, with four MSS., has οὐκ ἔστιν. — G. A.]

[2] [Job vii. 5, Sept.: φύρεται δέ μου τὸ σῶμα ἐν σαπρία σκωλή-κων, τήκω δὲ βώλακας γῆς ἀπὸ ἰχῶρος ξύων: "My flesh is mingled with the filth of worms, and I pine away, scraping clods (or crusts) of earth from my sore" (discharge, matter, pus). The Rev. Ver. has: "My flesh is clothed with worms and clods of dust." So nearly Zöckler in Lange: "My flesh is clothed with worms and crusts of earth." — G. A.]

[3] [Such passages as this in the Fathers are used by Romanists and Tractarians for establishing their views, and it is no wonder the Tractarians were zealous in giving the Fathers to the English in English. But, as Jacob says (Eccl. Polity of N. T., pp. 28 and 29), "Our appeal is from the Nicene Fathers to the Apostles of Christ; from patristic literature to the New Testament; for it is not being near to the truth that makes men good and wise," but having the truth itself. — G. A.]

THE HOMILIES OF ST. JOHN CHRYSOSTOM,

ARCHBISHOP OF CONSTANTINOPLE,

ON THE

EPISTLES OF ST. PAUL THE APOSTLE

TO THE

PHILIPPIANS, COLOSSIANS, AND THESSALONIANS.

The Oxford Translation Revised, with Additional Notes, by

REV. JOHN A. BROADUS, D.D.,

PRESIDENT OF THE SOUTHERN BAPTIST THEOLOGICAL SEMINARY, LOUISVILLE, KY.

PREFACE [TO THE OXFORD ED.]

THE present Volume completes the commentaries of St. Chrysostom on the shorter Epistles of St. Paul. It consists entirely of Homilies delivered at Constantinople, and one may perhaps remark some indications of a more matured and severe character than in earlier works. He refers several times to his responsibility as presiding in the Church, and sometimes threatens discipline as in that capacity, and from this it is that the date of the Homilies is chiefly to be gathered. The end of Hom. ix. on the Philippians, is sufficient for those Homilies. The close of Hom. iii. on Colossians, is still more express for them. Hom. viii. on 1 Thessalonians, and Hom. iv. on 2 Thessalonians, are to the like purpose.

Hom. viii. on 1 Thessalonians, seems also to be that which is referred to in Hom. iii. on Ep. to Philemon, as it contains a promise to discuss at some future time the subject there taken up.

Phil. ii. 6, and Col. i. 15, &c. give rise to doctrinal discussions. The readiness in argument, which they suppose in hearers, is greater than one would expect. Hom. v. on Colossians goes farther into the system of typical interpretation than is usual with St. Chrysostom; though the system is in fact acknowledged by him frequently, as in the passage on marriage, which closes the Homilies on the Colossians, and which, though scarcely admissible in modern taste, is one of great value, and of a saintly purity. The close of Hom. iv. on Colossians is most instructive with regard to the use of the Historical Books of the Old Testament, and Hom. ix. points out one great use of the Psalms, for moral impression, and at the same time draws the necessary distinction between that and the higher aim of Hymns. In these Homilies he is particularly severe on luxury and display, by his attacks on which he is known to have incurred the displeasure of the Empress Eudoxia, and much persecution from her.

A passage on the Holy Sacraments at the end of Hom. vi. on Colossians, one on Prayers for the departed in Hom. iii. on Philippians, and one in which he urges persons at enmity to immediate reconciliation, Hom. vi. on 1 Thessalonians, as well as that in Hom. iii. in Colossians, on unworthiness of Ministers, and several hints that occur about the order of Divine service, are well worthy of remark.

Savile's text, with some comparison of others, was used for the Homilies on the Philippians, and that of the new Paris Edition, with Savile always at hand, for the rest. Collations of one MS. in British Museum (Burney 48 here marked B [called C by Field]) were also in hand, but those of MSS. at Venice and Florence came too late for part of the work. The want of them is not however very material. The Bodleian MS. referred to, as well as the Catena published by Dr. Cramer, contain only extracts. It is hoped that the Homilies on 2 Cor. will have the benefit of a well-adjusted text before the Translation is published, as they are preparing for publication by Mr. Field, whom the Editor has to thank for information on some particulars, as well as for the benefit of having his accurate edition of the Homilies on St. Matthew to refer to.

For the Translation of the Homilies on the Philippians, the Editors are indebted to the Rev. W. C. COTTON, M.A. of Ch. Ch. Chaplain to the Bishop of New Zealand; for that of the Homilies on the Colossians, to the Rev. J. ASHWORTH, M.A. Fellow of Brasenose College; and for the rest of the volume, to the Rev. JAMES TWEED, M.A. of Corpus Christi College, Cambridge, the Translator of the Homilies on the Pastoral Epistles of St. Paul. The Index to the two former is by the Rev. F. BOWLES, M.A. of Exeter College, and to the latter by the Editor, which is noticed in order that the reader may find the less difficulty from any difference in the heads under which similar matter may be placed, as the two were made simultaneously to save time.

A few points on which the Editor was not informed until the sheets were printed are noticed in the Addenda and Corrigenda. [In the Amer. ed. these are inserted in their proper places. For the text followed in Amer. ed., see Preface at the beginning of the volume.]

C. M.

CONTENTS.

HOMILIES ON PHILIPPIANS.

EPISTLE TO THE COLOSSIANS.

FIRST EPISTLE TO THE THESSALONIANS.

HOMILIES OF ST. JOHN CHRYSOSTOM,

ARCHBISHOP OF CONSTANTINOPLE,

ON THE

EPISTLE OF ST. PAUL THE APOSTLE

TO THE

PHILIPPIANS

INTRODUCTORY DISCOURSE.

THE Philippians are of a city in Macedonia, a city that is a colony, as Luke saith. Here that seller of purple was converted, a woman of uncommon piety and heedfulness. Here the ruler of the synagogue[1] believed. Here was Paul scourged with Silas. Here the magistrates requested them to depart, and were afraid of them, and the preaching had an illustrious commencement. And he bears them many and high testimonies himself, calling them his own crown, and saying they had suffered much. For, "To you," he saith, "it hath been granted of God,[2] not only to believe on Him, but also to suffer in His behalf." (Phil. i. 29.) But when he wrote to them, it happened that he was in bonds. Therefore he says, "So that my bonds became manifest in Christ in the whole prætorium," calling the palace of Nero the prætorium.[3] But he was bound and let go again,[4] and this he showed to Timothy by saying, "At my first defence no one took my part, but all forsook me : may it not be laid to their account.

But the Lord stood by me and strengthened me." (2 Tim. iv. 16.) He speaks of the bonds then in which he was before that defence. For that Timothy was not present then, is evident : for, "At my first defence," he says, "no man took my part"; and this, by writing, he was making known to him. He would not then, had he already known it, have written thus to him. But when he wrote this epistle, Timothy was with him. And he shows it by what he says : "But I hope in the Lord Jesus to send Timothy shortly unto you." (Phil. ii. 19.) And again, "Him I hope to send forthwith so soon as I shall see how it will go with me." For he was loosed from his bonds and again bound after he had been to them. But if he saith, "Yea, and I am[5] offered upon the sacrifice and service of your faith," it is not as though this were now come to pass, but as much as to say, "and whenever this takes place I am glad," raising them from their dejection at his bonds. For that he was not about to die at that time is plain from what he saith : "But I hope[6] in the Lord that I myself also shall come shortly unto you." (Phil. ii. 24.) And again, "And having this confidence, I know that I shall abide, yea, and abide with you all."

2. But the Philippians had sent to him Epaphroditus, to carry him money, and to know the things concerning him, for they were most lovingly disposed toward him. For that they sent, hear himself, saying, "I have all things, and

---

[1] [This reading contains an obvious error, and would be readily altered by students or copyists; and one manuscript gives "keeper of the prison." Chrysostom not unfrequently makes slips in quoting from memory, as do most preachers. He is here doubtless thinking of Crispus. (Acts xviii. 8.) Below, in paragraph 3, he has it right. — J. A. B.]
[2] [All documents for New Testament give "in behalf of Christ." Chrysostom was quoting from memory. — J. A. B.]
[3] [Scholars now generally understand the prætorian camp or the prætorian guard. See Lightfoot here. — J. A. B.]
[4] His statement amounts to this, that the present epistle was written in St. Paul's first imprisonment, when Timothy was with him, for that the second to Timothy was written in a second imprisonment, from which he was only released by martyrdom. The "first defence" belongs to the second imprisonment. Between the two, it is probable that he visited the Philippians, according to his intention.

[5] The *if* is omitted, perhaps in order to put the objection in a strong light.
[6] [Correct New Testament text, "trust." — J. A. B.]

abound ; I am filled, having received from Epaphroditus the things that came from you." At the same time they sent to know this. For that they sent also to know this he shows at once in the beginning of the epistle, writing of his own matters, and saying, "But I would have you know that the things which happened unto me have fallen out rather unto the progress of the Gospel." (Phil. i. 12.) And again, "I hope to send Timothy shortly unto you, that I also may be of good comfort when I know your state." This, "that I also," is as if he meant, "as you for full assurance sent to know the things concerning me, so 'I also,' that I may be of good comfort when I know the things concerning you." Since then they had also been a long time without sending[1] (for this he proves by saying, "Now at length you have revived your thought for me") (Phil. iv. 10), and then they heard that he was in bonds (Phil. ii. 26) ; for if they heard about Epaphroditus, that he was sick, he being no such very remarkable person as Paul was, much more did they hear about Paul, and it was reasonable that they should be disturbed ; therefore, in the opening of the epistle he offers them much consolation about his bonds, showing that they should not merely not be disturbed, but even rejoice. Then he gives them counsel about unanimity and humility, teaching them that this was their greatest safety, and that so they could easily overcome their enemies. For it is not being in bonds that is painful to your teachers, but their disciples not being of one mind. For the former brings even furtherance to the Gospel, but the latter distracts.

3. So then after admonishing them to be of one mind, and showing that unanimity comes of humility, and then aiming a shaft at those Jews who were everywhere corrupting the doctrine under a show of Christianity, and calling them "dogs" and "evil workers" (Phil. iii. 2), and giving admonition to keep away from them, and teaching to whom it is right to attend, and discoursing at length on moral points, and bringing them to order, and recalling them to themselves, by saying, "The Lord is at hand" (Phil. iv. 5), he makes mention also, with his usual wisdom, of what had been sent, and then offers them abundant consolation. But he appears in writing to be doing them special honor, and never in any place writes any thing of reproof, which is a proof of their virtue, in that they gave no occasion to their teacher, and that he has written to them not in the way of rebuke, but throughout in the way of encouragement. And as I said also at first, this city showed great readiness for the faith ; inasmuch as the very jailor, (and you know it is a business full of all wickedness,)

at once, upon one miracle, both ran to them, and was baptized with all his house. For the miracle that took place he saw alone, but the gain he reaped not alone, but jointly with his wife and all his house. Nay, even the magistrates who scourged him seem to have done this rather of sudden impulse than out of wickedness, both from their sending at once to let him go, and from their being afterwards afraid. And he bears testimony to them not only in faith, or in perils, but also in well-doing, where he says, "That even in the beginning of the Gospel, ye sent once and again unto my need" (Phil. iv. 15, 16), when no one else did so ; for he says, "no Church had fellowship with me in the matter of giving and receiving" ; and that their intermission had been rather from lack of opportunity than from choice, saying, "Not that ye took no thought for me, but ye lacked opportunity." (Phil. iv. 10.) Let us also, knowing these things, and having so many patterns, and the love that he bore them — for that he loved them greatly appears in his saying, "For I have no man like minded, who will care truly for your state" (Phil. ii. 20) ; and again, "Because I have you in my heart, and in my bonds," —

4. let us also, knowing these things, show ourselves worthy of such examples, by being ready to suffer for Christ.[2] But now the persecution is no more. So then, if there is nothing else, let us imitate their earnestness in well doing, and not think, if we have given once or twice, that we have fulfilled all. For we must do this through our whole life. For it is not once that we have to please God, but constantly. The racer, if, after running even ten heats, he leave the remaining one undone, has lost all ; and we, if we begin with good works, and afterward faint, have lost all, have spoiled all. Listen to that profitable admonition that saith, "Let not mercy[3] and truth forsake thee." (Prov. iii. 3.) He saith not do so once, nor the second time, nor the third, nor the tenth, nor the hundredth, but continually : "let them not forsake thee." And he did not say, Do not forsake them, but, "Let them not forsake thee," showing that we are in need of them, and not they of us ; and teaching us that we ought to make every effort to keep them with us. And "bind them," saith he, "about thy neck." For as the children of the wealthy have an ornament of gold about their neck, and never put it off, because it exhibits a token of their high birth, so should we too wear mercy ever about us, showing that we are children of the compassionate one, "who

---

[1] [The altered text and most editions add " but had then done it," through misunderstanding of the rather obscure connection.—J.A.B.]

[2] [Such a digressive and awkward sentence is of course smoothed out in the altered text, but is perfectly natural in a freely spoken discourse. — J. A. B.]

[3] The same word is here used for " mercy " and " alms." [And it is quoted from the Sept. in the plural, " mercies," or " almsgivings." — J. A. B.]

makes the sun to rise upon the evil and the good " (Matt. v. 45). " But the unbelievers," you say, " do not believe it." I say then, hereby shall they believe, if we do these works. If they see that we take pity on all, and are enrolled under Him for our Teacher, they will know that it is in imitation of Him that we so act. For, " mercy," it says, " and true faith." [1] He well said " true." For He willeth it not to be of rapine or fraud. For this were not " faith " ; this were not " truth." For he that plundereth must lie and forswear himself. So do not thou, saith he, but have faith with thy mercy.

Let us put on this ornament. Let us make a golden chain for our soul, of mercy I mean, while we are here. For if this age [2] pass, we can use it no longer. And why? THERE there are no poor, THERE there are no riches, no more want THERE. While we are children, let us not rob ourselves of this ornament. For as with children, if they become men, these are taken away, and they are advanced to other adornment ; so too is it with us. There will be no more alms by money, but other and far nobler.[3] Let us not then deprive ourselves of this ! Let us make our soul appear beautiful ! Great is alms, beautiful, and honorable, great is that gift, but greater is goodness. If we learn to despise riches, we shall learn other things besides. For behold how many good things spring from hence ! He that giveth alms, as he ought to give, learns to despise wealth. He that has learned to despise wealth has cut up the root of evils. So that he does not do a greater good than he receives, not merely in that there is a due recompense and a requital for alms, but also in that his soul becomes philosophic, and elevated, and rich. He that gives alms is instructed not to admire riches or gold. And this lesson once fixed in his mind, he has gotten a great step toward mounting to Heaven, and has cut away ten thousand occasions of strife, and contention, and envy, and dejection. For ye know, ye too know, that all things are done for riches, and unnumbered wars are made for riches. But he that has learned to despise them, has placed himself in a quiet harbor, he no longer fears damage. For this hath alms taught him. He no longer desires what is his neighbor's ; for how should he, that parts with his own, and gives? He no longer envies the rich man ; for how should he, that is willing to become poor? He clears the eye of his soul. And these are but here. But hereafter it is not to be told what blessings he shall win. He shall not abide without with the foolish virgins, but shall enter in with those that were wise, together with the Bridegroom, having his lamps bright. And though they have endured hardship in virginity, he that hath not so much as tasted these hardships shall be better than they. Such is the power of Mercy.[4] She brings in her nurslings with much boldness. For she is known to the porters in Heaven, that keep the gates of the Bride-Chamber, and not known only, but reverenced ; and those whom she knows to have honored her, she will bring in with much boldness, and none will gainsay, but all make room. For if she brought God down to earth, and persuaded him to become man, much more shall she be able to raise a man to Heaven ; for great is her might. If then [5] from mercy and lovingkindness God became man, and He persuaded Himself to become a servant, much rather will He bring His servants into His own house. Her let us love, on her let us set our affection, not one day, nor two, but all our life long, that she may acknowledge us. If she acknowledge us, the Lord will acknowledge us too. If she disown us, the Lord too will disown us, and will say, " I know you not." But may it not be ours to hear this voice, but that happy one instead, " Come, ye blessed of my Father, inherit the kingdom prepared for you from the foundation of the world." (Matt. xxv. 34.) Which may we all obtain, by His grace and lovingkindness, in Christ Jesus our Lord, with whom to the Father and the Holy Ghost, be glory, strength, honor, now and for ever, and world without end. Amen.

---

[1] The LXX. have "faith," probably in the sense of "truth," which Aquila has, and the Hebrew requires; "true" is added by St. Chrys. to mark this.

[2] ἡλικία, which carries on the simile. [He means the age of childhood, when ornaments are a pleasure. — J. A. B.]

[3] He probably refers to the benefits conferred by the Saints on those on earth.

[4] [The same Greek word that above is translated "alms." — J. A. B.]

[5] Such a repetition is common with Chrysostom, sometimes perhaps from his own excitement. Here it seems rather meant to temper the warmth of his eloquence, and fix a sober thought.

HOMILY I.

"Paul and Timothy, servants of Christ Jesus, to all the saints in Christ Jesus which are at Philippi, fellow-Bishops[1] and Deacons: Grace to you, and peace, from God our Father, and the Lord Jesus Christ."

HERE, as writing to those of equal honor, he does not set down his rank of Teacher, but another, and that a great one. And what is that? He calls himself a "servant," and not an Apostle. For great truly is this rank too, and the sum of all good things, to be a servant of Christ, and not merely to be called so. "The servant of Christ," this is truly a free man in respect to sin, and being a genuine servant, he is not a servant to any other, since he would not be Christ's servant, but by halves. And in again writing to the Romans also, he says, "Paul, a servant of Jesus Christ." (Rom. i. 1.) But writing to the Corinthians and to Timothy he calls himself an "Apostle." On what account then is this? Not because they were superior to Timothy. Far from it. But rather he honors them, and shows them attention, beyond all others to whom he wrote. For he also bears witness to great virtue in them. For besides, there indeed he was about to order many things, and therefore assumed his rank as an Apostle. But here he gives them no injunctions but such as they could perceive of themselves.

"To the saints in Christ Jesus which are at Philippi." Since it was likely that the Jews too would call themselves "saints" from the first oracle, when[2] they were called a "holy people, a people for God's own possession" (Ex. xix. 6; Deut. vii. 6, etc.); for this reason he added, "to the saints in Christ Jesus." For these alone are holy, and those henceforward profane. "To the fellow-Bishops[3] and Deacons." What is this? were there several Bishops of one city? Certainly not; but he called the Presbyters so. For then they still interchanged the titles, and the Bishop was called a Deacon.[4] For this cause in writing to Timothy, he said, "Fulfil thy ministry," when he was a Bishop. For that he was a Bishop appears by his saying to him, "Lay hands hastily on no man." (1 Tim. v. 22.) And again, "Which was given thee with the laying on of the hands of the Presbytery." (1 Tim. iv. 14.) Yet Presbyters would not have laid hands on a Bishop. And again, in writing to Titus, he says, "For this cause I left thee in Crete, that thou shouldest appoint elders[5] in every city, as I gave thee charge. If any man is blameless, the husband of one wife" (Tit. i. 5, 6); which he says of the Bishop.[6] And after saying this, he adds immediately, "For the Bishop must be blameless, as God's steward, not self willed." (Tit. i. 7.) So then, as I said, both the Presbyters were of old called Bishops and Deacons of Christ, and the Bishops Presbyters; and hence even now many Bishops write, "To my fellow-Presbyter," and, "To my fellow-Deacon." But otherwise the specific name is distinctly appropriated to each, the Bishop and the Presbyter. "To the fellow-Bishops," he says, "and Deacons,

Ver. 2. "Grace to you and peace from God our Father and the Lord Jesus Christ."

How is it that though he nowhere else writes to the Clergy, not in Rome, nor in Corinth, nor in Ephesus, nor anywhere, but in general, to "all the saints, the believers, the beloved," yet here he writes to the Clergy? Because it was they that sent, and bare fruit, and it was they that dispatched Epaphroditus to him.

Ver. 3. "I thank my God," he says, "upon all my remembrance of you."

He said in another of his writings, "Obey them that have the rule over you, and submit to them: for they watch in behalf of your souls, as they that shall give account; that they may do this with joy, and not with grief." (Heb. xiii. 17.) If then the "grief" be due to the wickedness of the disciples, the doing it "with joy" would be due to their advancement. As often as I remember you, I glorify God. But this he does from his being conscious of many good things in them. I both glorify, he says, and pray. I do not, be-

---

[1] E. V. "with the bishops," reading the preposition separately. [See below.]
[2] [Viz. in the times of "the first oracle," i.e. the Old Test.— J. A. B.]
[3] [A good many late manuscripts of N. T., and several late Fathers, read with Chrys. συνεπισκόποις, "to the co-bishops"; but the early documents and modern critics give σὺν ἐπισκόποις, "with the bishops," as in the Eng. versions.— J. A. B.]
[4] Διάκονος, usually [translated] in E. V. "Minister," when thus used.

[5] Gr. Presbyters.
[6] See 1 Tim. iii. 2, but Chrys.'s reason for taking it thus is rather that κατὰ πόλιν seems to imply one for each city.

cause ye have advanced unto virtue, cease praying for you. But " I thank my God," he says, " upon all my remembrance of you,"

Ver. 4. " Always in every prayer of mine for you all making request also with joy."

" Always," [1] not only while I am praying. " With joy." For it is possible to do this with grief too, as when he says elsewhere, " For out of much affliction and anguish of heart I wrote unto you with many tears." (2 Cor. ii. 4.)

Ver. 5. " For your fellowship in furtherance of the Gospel from the first day even until now."

Great is that he here witnesseth of them, and very great, and what one might have witnessed of Apostles and Evangelists. Ye did not, because ye were entrusted with one city, he saith, care for that only, but ye leave nothing undone to be sharers of my labors, being everywhere at hand, and working with me, and taking part in my preaching. It is not once, or the second, or third time, but always, from the time ye believed until now, ye have assumed the readiness of Apostles. Behold how those indeed that were in Rome turned away from him; [2] for hear him saying, " This thou knowest, that all that are in Asia turned away from me." (2 Tim. i. 15.) And again, " Demas forsook me " : and " at my first defence no one took my part." (2 Tim. iv. 10, 16.) But these, although absent, shared in his tribulations, both sending men to him, and ministering to him according to their ability, and leaving out nothing at all. And this ye do not now only, saith he, but always, in every way assisting me. So then it is a " fellowship in furtherance of the Gospel." For when one preacheth, and thou waitest on the preacher, thou sharest his crowns. Since even in the contests that are without, the crown is not only for him that striveth, but for the trainer, and the attendant, and all that help to prepare the athlete. For they that strengthen him, and recover him, may fairly participate in his victory. And in wars too, not only he that wins the prize of valor, but all they too that attend him, may fairly claim a share in the trophies, and partake of the glory, as having shared in his conflict by their attendance on him. For it availeth not a little to wait on saints, but very much. For it makes us sharers in the rewards that are laid up for them. Thus; suppose some one hath given up great possessions for God, continually devotes himself to God, practices great virtue, and even to words, and even to thoughts, and even in everything observes extreme strictness. It is open to thee too, even without showing such strictness, to

have a share in the rewards that are laid up for him for these things. How? If thou aid him both in word and deed. If thou encourage him both by supplying his needs, and by doing him every possible service. For then the smoother of that rugged path will be thyself. So then if ye admire those in the deserts that have adopted the angelic life, those in the churches that practice the same virtues with them; if ye admire, and are grieved that ye are far behind them; ye may, in another way, share with them, by waiting on them, and aiding them. For indeed this too is of God's lovingkindness, to bring those that are less zealous,[3] and are not able to undertake the hard and rugged and strict life, to bring, I say, even those, by another way, into the same rank with the others. And this Paul means by " fellowship." They give a share to us, he means, in carnal things, and we give a share to them in spiritual things. For if God for little and worthless things granteth the kingdom, His servants too, for little and material things, give a share in spiritual things : or rather it is He that giveth both the one and the other by means of them. Thou canst not fast, nor be alone, nor lie on the ground, nor watch all night? Yet mayest thou gain the reward of all these things, if thou go about the matter another way, by attending on him that laboreth in them, and refreshing and anointing him constantly, and lightening the pains of these works. He, for his part, stands fighting and taking blows. Do thou wait on him when he returns from the combat, receive him in thy arms, wipe off the sweat, and refresh him ; comfort, soothe, restore his wearied soul. If we will but minister to the saints with such readiness, we shall be partakers of their rewards. This Christ also tells us. " Make to yourselves friends by means of the mammon of unrighteousness, that they may receive you into their eternal tabernacles." (Luke xvi. 9.) Seest thou that they are become sharers ? " From the first day," he says, " even until now." And " I rejoice " not only for what is past, but also for the future ; for from the past I guess that too.

Ver. 6. " Being confident of this very thing, that He which began a good work in you will perfect it until the day of Jesus Christ."

See how he also teaches them to be unassuming. For since he had witnessed a great thing of them, that they may not feel as men are apt to do, he presently teaches them to refer both the past and the future to Christ. How? By saying, not, " Being confident that as ye will finish," but what? " He which began a good work in you will perfect it." He did not rob them of the achievement, (for he said, " I

---

[3] ῥᾳθυμοτέρους. The words " are not able " seem to show that this is here used of natural character.

rejoice for your fellowship," clearly as if making it their act,) nor did he call their good deeds solely their own, but primarily of God. "For I am confident," saith he, "that He which began a good work in you will perfect it until the day of Jesus Christ." That is, God will. And it is not about yourselves, he implies, but about those descending from you that I feel thus. And indeed it is no small praise, that God should work in one. For if He is "no respecter of persons," as indeed He is none, but is looking to our purpose[1] when He aids us in good deeds, it is evident that we are agents in drawing Him to us; so that even in this view he did not rob them of their praise. Since if His inworking were indiscriminate, there would have been nothing to hinder but that even Heathens and all men might have Him working in them, that is, if He moved us like logs and stones, and required not our part. So that in saying "God will perfect it," this also again is made their praise, who have drawn to them the grace of God, so that He aids them in going beyond human nature. And in another way also a praise, as that "such are your good deeds that they cannot be of man, but require the divine impulse." But if God will perfect, then neither shall there be much labor, but it is right to be of good courage, for that they shall easily accomplish all, as being assisted by Him.

Ver. 7. "Even as it is right for me to be thus minded on behalf of you all, because I have you in my heart, inasmuch as both in my bonds, and in the defence and confirmation of the Gospel, ye all are partakers with me of grace."

Greatly still does he show here his longing desire, in that he had them in his heart; and in the very prison, and though bound, he remembered the Philippians. And it is not a little to the praise of these men, since it is not of prejudice that this Saint conceived his love, but of judgment, and right reasons. So that to be loved of Paul so earnestly is a proof of one's being something great and admirable. "And in the defense,"[2] he says, "and confirmation of the Gospel." And what wonder if he had them when in prison, since not even at the moment of going before the tribunal to make my defense, he says, did ye slip from my memory. For so imperial a thing is spiritual love, that it gives way to no season, but ever keeps hold of the soul of him who loves, and allows no trouble or pain to overcome that soul. For as in the case of the Babylonian furnace, when so vast a flame was raised, it was a dew to those blessed Children. So too does friendship occupying the soul of one who loves, and who pleases God, shake off every flame, and produce a marvelous dew.

"And in the confirmation of the Gospel," he says. So then his bonds were a confirmation of the Gospel, and a defense. And most truly so. How? For if he had shunned bonds, he might have been thought a deceiver; but he that endures every thing, both bonds and affliction, shows that he suffers this for no human reason, but for God, who rewards. For no one would have been willing to die, or to incur such great risks, no one would have chosen to come into collision with such a king,[3] I mean Nero, unless he looked to another far greater King. Truly a "confirmation of the Gospel" were his bonds. See how he more than succeeded in turning all things to their opposite. For what they supposed to be a weakness and a detraction, that he calls a confirmation; and had this not taken place, there had been a weakness. Then he shows that his love was not of prejudice, but of judgment. Why? I have you (in my heart), he says, in my bonds, and in my defense, because of your being "partakers of my grace." What is this? Was this the "grace" of the Apostle, to be bound, to be driven about, to suffer ten thousand evils? Yes. For He says, "My grace is sufficient for thee, for my power is made perfect in weakness." (2 Cor. xii. 9.) "Wherefore," saith he, "I take pleasure in weaknesses, in injuries." Since then I see you in your actions giving proof of your virtue, and being partakers of this grace, and that with readiness, I reasonably suppose thus much. For I that have had trial of you, and more than any have known you, and your good deeds; how that even when so distant from us, ye strive not to be wanting to us in our troubles, but to partake in our trials for the Gospel's sake, and to take no less share than myself, who am engaged in the combat, far off as ye are; am doing but justice in witnessing to these things.

And why did he not say "partakers," but "partakers with me"[4]? I myself too, he means, share with another, that I may be a partaker of the Gospel; that is, that I may share in the good things laid up for the Gospel.[5] And the wonder indeed is, that they were all so minded; for he says that "ye all are fellow-partakers of grace." From these beginnings, then, I am confident that such ye will be even to the end. For it cannot be that so bright a commencement should be quenched, and fail, but it points to[6] great results.

[1] So he explains Rom. viii. 28, where "His" is not in the Greek, though rightly (as it seems) understood by St. Augustine and others. See on Rom. Hom. xv. Tr. p. 453.
[2] ἀπολογία.
[3] [The Greek word for "king" was often applied to the Roman emperor (1 Tim. ii. 2; 1 Pet. ii. 13).—J. A. B.]
[4] "Or fellow-partakers," συγκοινωνούς, see marginal version [and Rev. Ver.—J. A. B.].
[5] The word may be here used, as often, for the "preaching" of the Gospel.
[6] al. and end without producing.

Since then it is possible also in other ways[1] to partake of grace, and of trials, and of tribulations, let us also, I beseech you, be partakers. How many of those who stand here, yea, rather all, would fain share with Paul in the good things to come ! It is in your power if ye are willing, on behalf of those who have succeeded to his ministry, when they suffer any hardship for Christ's sake, to take their part and succor them. Hast thou seen thy brother in trial ? Hold out a hand ! Hast thou seen thy teacher in conflict ? Stand by him ! But, says one, there is no one like Paul ! now for disdain ! now for criticism ! So there is no one like Paul ? Well, I grant it. But, " He that receiveth," saith He, " a prophet in the name of a prophet, shall receive a prophet's reward." (Matt. x. 41.) For was it for this that these were honored, that they coöperated with *Paul?* Not for this, but because they coöperated with one who had undertaken the preaching. Paul was honorable for this, that he suffered these things for Christ's sake.

There is indeed no one like Paul. No, not even but a little approaching to that blessed one. But the preaching is the same as it was then.

And not only in his bonds did they have fellowship with him, but also from the beginning. For hear him saying, " And ye yourselves also know, ye Philippians, that in the beginning of the Gospel, no Church had fellowship with me in the matter of giving and receiving, but ye only." (Phil. iv. 15.) And even apart from trials, the teacher has much labor, watching, toiling in the word, teaching, complaints, accusations, imputations, envyings. Is this a little matter, to bear ten thousand tongues, when one might have but one's own anxieties ? Alas ! what shall I do ? for I am in a strait between two things. I long to urge you on and encourage you to the alliance and succor of the saints of God ; but I fear lest some one should suspect another thing, that I say this not for your sakes, but for theirs. But know that it is not for their sakes I say these things, but for your own. And if ye are willing to attend, I convince you by my very words ; the gain is not equal to you and to them. For ye, if ye give, will give those things from which, willing or unwilling, ye must soon after part, and give place to others ; but what thou receivest is great and far more abundant. Or, are ye not so disposed, that in giving ye will receive ? For if ye are not so disposed, I do not even wish you to give. So far am I from making a speech for them ! Except one have first so disposed himself, as receiving rather than giving, as gaining ten thousand fold, as benefited

rather than a benefactor, let him not give. If as one granting a favor to the receiver, let him not give. For this is not so much my care, that the saints may be supported. For even if thou give not, another will give. So that what I want is this, that you may have a relief from your own sins. But he that gives not so will have no relief. For it is not giving that is doing alms, but the doing it with readiness ; the rejoicing, the feeling grateful to him that receives. For, " not grudgingly," saith he, " or of necessity ; for God loveth a cheerful giver." (2 Cor. ix. 7.) Except then one so give, let him not give : for that is loss, not alms. If then ye know that ye will gain, not they, know that your gain becomes greater.[2] For as for them the body is fed, but your soul is approved ; for them, not one of their sins is forgiven when they receive, but for you, the more part of your offenses is removed. Let us then share with them in their great prizes.[3] When men adopt kings they do not think they give more than they receive! Adopt thou Christ, and thou shalt have great security. Wilt thou also share with Paul ? Why do I say Paul when it is Christ that receiveth ?

But that ye may know that all is for your sakes that I say and do, and not of care for the comfort of others, if there is any of the rulers of the church that lives in abundance and wants nothing, though he be a saint, give not, but prefer to him one that is in want, though he be not so admirable. And wherefore ? Because Christ too so willeth, as when He saith, " If thou make a supper or a dinner, call not thy friends, neither thy kinsmen, but the maimed, the lame, the blind, that cannot recompense thee." (Luke xiv. 12.) For it is not indiscriminately that one should pay such attentions, but to the hungry, but to the thirsty, but to those who need clothing, but to strangers, but to those who from riches have been reduced to poverty.[4] For He said not simply, " I was fed," but ' I was an hungered," for, " Ye saw me an hungered," He says, " and fed me." (Matt. xxv. 35.) Twofold is the claim, both that he is a saint and that he is hungry. For if he that is simply hungry ought to be fed, much more when he is a saint too that is hungry. If then he is a saint, but not in need, give not ; for this were no gain. For neither did Christ enjoin it ; or rather, neither is he a saint[5] that is in abundance and receiveth. Seest thou that it is not for filthy lucre that these things have been said to you, but for your profit ? Feed the hungry, that thou mayest not

---

[1] ἑτέρως, in other ways than by actually undergoing the trials; but Savile conjectures ἑτέροις, " with others."

[2] i.e. than if ye did not acknowledge this.
[3] al. " in their toils in order that we may share also in their great prizes."
[4] [This last clause was wanting in the text of the printed editions earlier than the Benedictine. It is found in a good group of MSS. — J. A. B.]
[5] There is a MS. discourse of St. Macarius on the danger of monastic life in a town, from the multitude of presents.

feed the fire of hell. He, eating of what is thine, sanctifies also what remains. (Luke xi. 41.) Think how the widow maintained Elias; and she did not more feed than she was fed: she did not more give than receive. This now also takes place in a much greater thing. For it is not a "barrel of meal," nor "a cruse of oil" (1 Kings xvii. 14), but what? "An hundred fold, and eternal life" (Matt. xix. 21, 29), is the recompense for such — the mercy of God thou becomest; the spiritual food; a pure leaven. She was a widow, famine was pressing, and none of these things hindered her. Children too she had, and not even so was she withheld. (1 Kings xvii. 12.) This woman is become equal to her that cast in the two mites. She said not to herself, "What shall I receive from this man? He stands in need of me. If he had any power he had not hungered, he had broken the drought, he had not been subject to like sufferings. Perchance he too offends God." None of these things did she think of. Seest thou how great a good it is to do well with simplicity, and not to be over curious about the person benefited? If she had chosen to be curious she would have doubted; she would not have believed. So, too, Abraham, if he had chosen to be curious, would not have received angels. For it cannot, indeed it cannot be, that one who is exceeding nice in these matters, should ever meet with them. No, such an one usually lights on impostors; and how that is, I will tell you. The pious man is not desirous to appear pious, and does not clothe himself in show, and is likely to be rejected. But the impostor, as he makes a business of it, puts on a deal of piety that is hard to see through. So that while he who does good, even to those who seem not pious, will fall in with those who are so, he who seeks out those who are thought to be pious, will often fall in with those who are not so. Wherefore, I beseech you, let us do all things in simplicity. For let us even suppose that he is an impostor that comes; you are not bidden to be curious about this. For, "Give," saith he, "to every one that asketh thee" (Luke vi. 30); and, "Forbear not to redeem him that is to be slain." (Prov. xxiv. 11.) Yet most of those that are slain suffer this for some evil they are convicted of; still he saith, "Forbear not." For in this shall we be like God, thus shall we be admired, and shall obtain those immortal blessings, which may we all be thought worthy of, through the grace and lovingkindness of Jesus Christ our Lord, with whom, to the Father, together with the Holy Spirit, be glory, power, honor, now and forever, and world without end. Amen.

HOMILY II.

PHILIPPIANS i. 8–11.

"For God is my witness, how I long after you all in the tender mercies of Jesus Christ. And this I pray, that your love may abound yet more and more in knowledge and all discernment; that ye may approve the things that are excellent; that ye may be sincere and void of offense unto the day of Christ; being filled with the fruits of righteousness, which are through Jesus Christ, unto the glory and praise of God."

He calls not God to witness as though he should be doubted, but does this from his great affection, and his exceeding persuasion and confidence; for after saying that they had fellowship with him, he adds this also, "in the tender mercies of Christ," lest they should think that his longing for them was for this cause, and not simply for their own sake. And what mean these words, "in the tender mercies of Christ"? They stand for "according to Christ." Because ye are believers, because ye love Christ, because of the love that is according to Christ. He does not say "love," but uses a still warmer expression, "the tender mercies of Christ," as though he had said, "having become as a father to you through the relationship which is in Christ." For this imparts to us bowels[1] warm and glowing. For He gives such bowels to His true servants. "In these bowels," saith He, as though one should say, "I love you with no natural bowels, but with warmer ones, namely, those of Christ." "How I long after you all." I long after all, since ye are all of this nature; I am unable in words to represent to you my longing; it is therefore impossible to tell. For this cause I leave it to God, whose range is in the heart, to know this. Now had he been flattering them, he would not have called God to witness, for this cannot be done without peril.

Ver. 9. "And this," saith he, "I pray, that your love may abound yet more and more." For this is a good of which there is no satiety;

---

[1] [Above translated "tender mercies."—J. A. B.]

for see, being so loved he wished to be loved still more, for he who loves the object of his love, is willing to stay at no point of love, for it is impossible there should be a measure of so noble a thing. Paul desires that the debt of love should always be owing; "Owe no man any thing, save to love one another." (Rom. xiii. 8.) The measure of love is, to stop nowhere; "that your love," says he, "may abound yet more and more." Consider the character of the expression, "that it may abound yet more and more," he says, "in knowledge and all discernment." He does not extol friendship merely, nor love merely, but such as comes of knowledge; that is, Ye should not apply the same love to all: for this comes not of love, but from want of feeling. What means he by "in knowledge"? He means, with judgment, with reason, with discrimination. There are who love without reason, simply and any how, whence it comes that such friendships are weak. He says, "in knowledge and all discernment, that ye may approve the things that are excellent," that is, the things that are profitable. This I say not for my own sake, says he, but for yours, for there is danger lest any one be spoiled by the love of the heretics; for all this he hints at, and see how he brings it in. Not for my own sake, says he, do I say this, but that ye may be sincere, that is, that ye receive no spurious doctrine under the pretence of love. How then, says he, "If it be possible, live peaceably with all men"? "Live peaceably" (Rom. xii. 18), he says, not, Love so as to be harmed by that friendship; for he says, "if thy right eye causeth thee to stumble, pluck it out, and cast it from thee; that ye may be sincere" (Matt. v. 29), that is, before God, "and without offence," that is, before men, for many men's friendships are often a hurt to them. Even though it hurts thee not, says he, still another may stumble thereat. "Unto the day of Christ"; i.e. that ye may then be found pure, having caused no one to stumble.

Ver. 11. "Being filled with the fruits of righteousness which are through Jesus Christ unto the glory and praise of God;" i.e. holding, together with true doctrine, an upright life.

And not merely upright, but "filled with the fruits of righteousness." For there is indeed a righteousness not according to Christ, as, for example, a moral life. "Which are through Jesus Christ to the glory and praise of God." Seest thou[1] that I speak not of mine own glory, but the righteousness of God; and oftentimes he calls mercy itself too righteousness; let not your love, he says, indirectly injure you, by hindering your perception of things profitable, and take heed lest you fall through your love to any one. For I would indeed that your love should be increased, but not so that ye should be injured by it. And I would not that it should be simply of prejudice, but upon proof whether I speak well or no. He says not, that ye may take up my opinion, but that ye may "prove" it. He does not say outright, join not yourself to this or that man, but, I would that your love should have respect to what is profitable, not that ye should be void of understanding. For it is a foolish thing if ye work not righteousness for Christ's sake and through Him. Mark the words, "through Him." Does he then use God as a mere assistant? Away with the thought. Not that I may receive praise, says he, but that God may be glorified.

Ver. 12, 13. "Now I would have you know, brethren, that the things which happened unto me have fallen out rather unto the progress of the Gospel, so that my bonds became manifest in Christ throughout the whole prætorian guard, and to all the rest."

It was likely they would grieve when they heard he was in bonds, and imagine that the preaching was at a stand. What then? He straightway destroys this suspicion. And this also shows his affection, that he declares the things which had happened to him, because they were anxious. What say you? you are in bonds! you are hindered! how then does the Gospel advance? He answers, "so that my bonds in Christ became manifest in all the prætorium." This thing not only did not silence the rest, nor affright them, but contrariwise rather encouraged them. If then they who were near the dangers were not only nothing hurt, but even received greater confidence, much more should you. Had he when in bonds taken it hardly, and held his peace, it were probable that they would be affected in like sort. But as he spoke more boldly when in bonds, he gave them more confidence than if he had not been bound. And how have his bonds "turned to the progress of the Gospel"? So God in His dispensation ordered, he means, that my bonds were not hid, my bonds which were "in" Christ, which were "for" Christ.

"In the whole prætorium." For up to that time they so called the palace.[2] And in the whole city,[3] says he.

Ver. 14. "And that most of the brethren in the Lord, being confident through my bonds,

---

[1] This is still in the person of St. Paul. Of this use of the word Righteousness, see on Rom. iii. 22.

[2] βασίλεια. This is the eastern and despotic name; the other was a remnant of the republic. [The Rev. Ver. understands the word prætorium here to mean the prætorian guard. See Lightfoot on Phil. Others, the prætorian barracks, or the great prætorian camp; but without distinct warrant of usage. — J. A. B.]

[3] [This seems to be Chrys.'s interpretation, or recollection, of the Apostle's phrase, "and to all the rest." — J. A. B.]

are more abundantly bold to speak the word without fear."

This shows that they were of good courage even before, and spoke with boldness, but much more now. If others then, says he, are of good courage through my bonds, much more am I; if I am the cause of confidence to others, much more to myself. "And most of the brethren in the Lord." As it was a great thing to say, My bonds gave confidence to them, he therefore adds beforehand, "in the Lord." Do you see how, even when he sees himself constrained to speak great things, he departs not from moderation? "Are more abundantly bold," he says, "to speak the word without fear"; the words "more abundantly" show that they had already begun.

Ver. 15. "Some indeed preach Christ even of envy and strife, and some also of good will."

And what this means is worth enquiry. Since Paul was under restraint, many of the unbelievers, willing to stir up more vehemently the persecution from the Emperor, themselves also preached Christ, in order that the Emperor's wrath might be increased at the spread of the Gospel, and all his anger might fall on the head of Paul. From my bonds then two lines of action have sprung. One party took great courage thereat; the other, from hope to work my destruction, set themselves to preach Christ; "some of them through envy," that is, envying my reputation and constancy, and from desire of my destruction, and the spirit of strife, work with me; or that they themselves may be esteemed, and from the expectation that they will draw to themselves somewhat of my glory. "And some also of good will," that is, without hypocrisy, with all earnestness.

Ver. 16. "The one proclaim Christ of faction, not sincerely." [1]

That is, not with pure motives, nor from regard to the matter itself; but why? "thinking to add affliction to my bonds." [2] As they think that I shall thus fall into greater peril, they add affliction to affliction. O cruelty! O devilish instigation! They saw him in bonds, and cast into prison, and still they envied him. They would increase his calamities, and render him subject to greater anger: well said he, "thinking," for it did not so turn out. They thought indeed to grieve me by this; but I rejoiced that the Gospel was furthered.

Ver. 17. "But the other of love, knowing that I am set for the defense of the Gospel."

What means, "that I am set for the defense

of the Gospel"? [3] It is, They are preparing for [4] the account which I must give to God, and assisting me.

What is meant by "for the defense"? I have been appointed to preach, I must give account, and answer for the work to which I have been appointed; they assist me, that my defense may be easy; for if there be found many who have been instructed and have believed, my defense will be easy. So it is possible to do a good work, from a motive which is not good. And not only is there no reward in store for such an action, but punishment. For as they preached Christ from a desire to involve the preacher of Christ in greater perils, not only shall they receive no reward, but shall be subject to vengeance and punishment. [5] "And some of love." That is, they know that I must give account for the Gospel.

Ver. 18. "What then? only that every way, whether in pretense, or in truth, Christ is proclaimed."

But see the wisdom of the Man. He did not vehemently accuse them, but mentioned the result; what difference does it make to me, says he, whether it be done in this or that way? only that every way, "whether in pretense or in truth, Christ is proclaimed." He did not say, "Let him be proclaimed," as some suppose, stating that he opens the way for the heresies, but, "He is proclaimed." [6] For in the first place he did not lay down the law and say, as if laying down the law, "Let Him be proclaimed," but he reported what was taking place; secondly, if he even spoke as laying down the law, not even thus would he be opening the way for the heresies.

For let us examine the matter. For even if he gave permission to preach as they preached, not even thus was he opening the way for the heresies. How so? In that they preached healthfully; though the aim and purpose on which they acted was corrupted, still the preaching itself was not changed, and they were forced so to preach. And why? Because, had they preached otherwise than as Paul preached, had they taught otherwise than as he taught, they would not have increased the wrath of the Emperor. But now by furthering his preaching, by teaching in the same way, and making disciples as he did, they had power to exasperate the Emperor, when he saw the multitude of the disciples

---

[3] He takes "the Gospel" here in the sense of St. Paul's preaching of the Gospel. Theodoret takes it of his being a champion of the Gospel among men.

[4] [The altered text has "cutting down," "lessening."—J. A. B.]

[5] [The altered text puts these three last sentences under ver. 16. —J. A. B.]

[6] [This sentence, wanting in all known MSS. of Chrys., is supplied by Field from a Catena. It evidently fell out, as often happened in copying, through similarity to the following sentence. The amplifying repetition is quite in Chrys.'s manner.—J. A. B.]

[1] [The order of vers. 16 and 17 is transposed in Rev. Ver., upon the authority of nearly all the uncial MSS., nearly all the ancient versions, and other documents. It is best here to leave Chrys.'s order, which is that of the Common Ver., but the translation of Rev. Ver. is given as elsewhere.—J. A. B.]

[2] [So Chrys.'s text. The true text is (as Rev. Ver.) "thinking to raise up affliction for me in my bonds."—J. A. B.]

numerous. But then some wicked and senseless man, taking hold of this passage, says, Verily they would have done the contrary, they would have driven off those who had already believed, instead of making believers to abound, had they wished to annoy him. What shall we answer? That they looked to this thing only, how they might involve him in present danger, and leave him no escape; and thus they thought to grieve him, and to quench the Gospel, rather than in the other way.

By that other course they would have extinguished the wrath of the Emperor, they would have let him go at large and preach again; but by this course they thought that because of him all would be ruined, could they but destroy him. The many however could not have this intention, but certain bitter men alone.

Then, "and therein," says he, "I rejoice, yea, and will rejoice." What means, "yea, I will rejoice"? Even if this be done still more, he means. For they coöperate with me even against their will; and will receive punishment for their toil, whilst I, who contributed nothing thereto, shall receive reward. Is there anything beyond this villainy of the Devil, to contrive the punishment of the preaching, and vengeance for the toils? Seest thou with how many evils he pierces through his own! How else would a hater and an enemy of their salvation have arranged all this? Seest thou how he who wages war against the truth has no power, but rather wounds himself, as one who kicks against the goads?

Ver. 19. "For I know," says he, "that this shall turn to my salvation through your supplication, and the supply of the Spirit of Jesus Christ."

Nothing is more villainous than the Devil. So does he everywhere involve his own in unprofitable toils, and rends them. Not only does he not suffer them to obtain the prizes, but he even subjects them to punishment.

For not only does he command them the preaching of the Gospel, but likewise fasting and virginity, in such sort as will not only deprive them of their reward, but will bring down heavy evil on those who pursue that course. Concerning whom he says elsewhere, also, "Branded in their own conscience as with a hot iron." (1 Tim. iv. 2.)

Wherefore, I beseech you, let us give thanks to God for all things, since he hath both lightened our toil, and increased our reward. For such as among them live in virginity enjoy not the rewards, which they do who among us live chastely in wedlock; but they who live as virgins among the heretics are subject to the condemnation of the fornicators. All this springs from their not acting with a right aim,

but as accusing God's creatures,[1] and His unspeakable Wisdom.

Let us not then be sluggish. God hath placed before us contests within measure, having no toil. Yet let us not despise them for this. For if the heretics put themselves to the stretch in unprofitable toils, what excuse shall we have if we will not endure those which are less, and which have a greater reward? For which of Christ's ordinances is burdensome? which is grievous? Art thou unable to live a virgin life? Thou art permitted to marry. Art thou unable to strip thyself of all thou hast? Thou art permitted to supply the needs of others from what thou hast. Let "your abundance be a supply for their want." (2 Cor. viii. 14.) These things indeed appear burdensome. What things? I mean to despise money, and to overcome the desires of the body. But His other commands require no cost, no violence. For tell me, what violence is there in speaking no ill, in simply abstaining from slander?[2] What violence is there in envying not another man's goods? What violence in not being led away by vain-glory? To be tortured, and endure it, is the part of strength. The exercise of philosophy is the part of strength. To bear poverty through life is the part of strength. It is the part of strength to wrestle with hunger and thirst. Where none of these things are, but where you may enjoy your own, as becomes a Christian, without envying others, what violence is there?

From this source springs envy; nay, rather all evils spring from no other source than this, that we cleave to things present. For did you hold money and the glory of this world to be nought, you would not cast an evil eye on its possessors. But since you gape at these things, and idolize them, and are flattered by them, for this reason envy troubles you, and vain-glory; it all springs from idolizing the things of the present life. Art thou envious because another man is rich? Nay, such an one is an object for pity and for tears. But you laugh and answer straight, I am the object for tears, not he! Thou also art an object for tears, not because thou art poor, but because thou thinkest thyself wretched. For we weep for those who have nothing the matter, and are discontented, not because they have anything the matter, but because, without having, they think they have. For example: if any one, cured of a fever, still is restless and rolls about, lying in health on his bed, is he not more to be wept for than those in fever, not that he has a fever, for he has none, but because having no sickness he still thinks he has? And thou art an object for tears just

---

[1] See on 1 Tim. iv. Hom. xii. and article Manichees in indices.
[2] Or "in keeping from needless evil speaking."

because thou thinkest thyself wretched, not for thy poverty. For thy poverty thou art to be thought happy.

Why enviest thou the rich man? Is it because he has subjected himself to many cares? to a harder slavery? because he is bound like a dog, with ten thousand chains — namely, his riches? Evening overtakes him, night overtakes him, but the season of rest is to him a time of trouble, of anguish, of pain, of anxiety. There is a noise: he straightway jumps up. Has his neighbor been plundered? He who has lost nothing cares more for it than the loser. For that man has lost once, but having endured the pain he lays aside his care; but the other has it always with him. Night comes on, the haven of our ills, the solace of our woes, the medicine of our wounds. For they who are weighed down by excess of grief, often give no ear to their friends, to their relations, to their intimates, — ofttimes not even to a father when he would give comfort, but take their very words amiss; but when sleep bids them rest, none has the power to look him in the face. For worse than any burning does the bitterness of grief afflict our souls. And as the body, when parched and worn down by struggling against the violence of the sunbeams, is brought to a caravansary with many fountains, and the soothing of a gentle breeze, so does night hand over our soul to sleep. Yea, rather, I should say, not night nor sleep does this, but God, who knoweth our toil-worn race, has wrought this, while we have no compassion on ourselves, but, as though at enmity with ourselves, have devised a tyranny more powerful than natural want of rest — the sleeplessness which comes of wealth. For it is said, "The anxieties of wealth drive away sleep." (Ecclus. xxxi. 1.) See how great is the care of God. But He hath not committed rest to our will, nor our need of sleep to choice, but hath bound it up in the necessities of nature, that good may be done to us even against our wills. For to sleep is of nature. But we, as mighty haters of ourselves, like enemies and persecutors of others, have devised a tyranny greater than this necessity of nature, that, namely, which comes of money. Has day dawned? Then such an one is in dread of the informers. Hath night overtaken him? He trembles at robbers. Is death at hand? The thought that he must leave his goods to others preys upon him worse than death. Hath he a son? His desires are increased; and then he fancies himself poor. Has he none? His pains are greater. Deemest thou him blessed who is unable to receive pleasure from any quarter? Can you envy him thus tempest-tossed, while you yourself are placed in the quiet haven of poverty? Of a truth this is the imperfection of

human nature; that it bears not its good nobly, but casts insults on its very prosperity.

And all this on earth; but when we depart thither, listen what the rich man, who was lord of innumerable goods, as you say (since for my part I call not these things good, but indifferent), listen to what this lord of innumerable goods says, and of what he stands in need: "Father Abraham," he exclaims, "send Lazarus, that with the tip of his finger he may drop water on my tongue, for I am scorched in this flame." For even if that rich man had endured none of the things I have mentioned, if he had passed his whole life without dread and care — why say I his whole life? rather that one moment (for it is a moment, our whole life is but one moment, compared with that eternity which has no end) — if all things had turned out according to his desire; must he not be pitied for these words, yea, rather, for this state of things? Was not your table once deluged with wine? Now you are not master even of a drop of water, and that, too, in your greatest need. Did not you neglect that poor man full of sores? But now you ask a sight of him, and no one gives leave. He lay at your gate; but now in Abraham's bosom. You then lay under your lofty ceiling; but now in the fire of hell.

These things let the rich men hear. Yea, rather not the rich, but the pitiless. For not in that he was rich was he punished, but because he showed no pity; for it is possible that a man who is at the same time rich and pitiful, should meet with every good. And for this cause the rich man's eyes were fixed on no one else, but on him alone, who then begged his alms; that he might learn from memory of his former actions, that his punishment was just. Were there not ten thousand poor men who were righteous? But he, who then lay at his gate, alone is seen by him, to instruct him and us, how great a good it is to put no trust in riches. His poverty hindered not the one in obtaining the kingdom; his riches helped not the other to avoid hell. Where is the point at which a man is poor? where is the point at which he is reduced to beggary?[1] He is not, he is not poor, who has nought, but he who desires many things! He is not rich who has large possessions, but he who stands in need of nothing. For what profit is there to possess the whole world, and yet live in greater despondency than he who has nothing? Their dispositions make men rich and poor, not the abundance or the want of money. Would you, who are a poor man, become rich? You may have your will, and no one can hinder you. Despise the world's

---

[1] Or " Till when (lasts) poverty? Till when beggary?"

wealth, think it nought, as it is nought. Cast out the desire of wealth, and you are straightway rich. He is rich who does not desire to become rich; he who is unwilling to be poor, is the poor man. As he is the diseased man,[1] who even in health bemoans his case, and not the man who bears his disease more lightly than perfect health, so also he is poor who cannot endure poverty, but in the midst of wealth thinks himself poorer than the poor; not he who bears his poverty more lightly than they their riches, for he is a richer man.

For tell me, wherefore fearest thou poverty? wherefore tremblest thou? is it not by reason of hunger? is it not for thirst? is it not for cold? Is it not indeed for these things? There is not, there is not any one who is ever destitute in these things! "For look at the generations of old, and see, did ever any one trust in the Lord, and was forsaken? or did any one hope in Him, and was made ashamed?" (Ecclus. ii. 11.)

And again, "Behold the birds of the heaven, that they sow not, neither do they reap, nor gather into barns; and your heavenly Father feedeth them." (Matt. vi. 26.) No one can readily point us out any one who has perished by hunger and cold. Wherefore then dost thou tremble at poverty? Thou canst not say. For if thou hast necessaries enough, wherefore dost thou tremble at it? Because thou hast not a multitude of servants? This truly is to be quit of masters; this is continual happiness, this is freedom from care. Is it because your vessels, your couches, your furniture are not formed of silver? And what greater enjoyment than thine has he who possesses these things? None at all. The use is the same, whether they are of this or that material. Is it because thou art not an object of fear to the many? May you never become so! For what pleasure is it that any should stand in dread and fear of thee? Is it

because thou art afraid of others? But thou canst not be alarmed. For "wouldest thou have no fear of the power? do that which is good, and thou shalt have praise from the same." (Rom. xiii. 3.) Does any say, It is because we are subject to contempt, and apt to suffer ill? It is not poverty but wickedness which causes this; for many poor men have quietly passed through life, whilst rulers, and the rich, and powerful, have ended their days more wretchedly than all evil doers, than bandits, than grave-robbers. For what poverty brings in thy case, that doth wealth in theirs. For that which they who would ill-treat thee do through thy contemptible estate, they do to him from envy and the evil eye they cast upon him, and the latter still more than the former, for this is the stronger craving to ill-treat another. He who envies does everything with all his might and main, while the despiser ofttimes has even pity on the despised; and his very poverty, and utter want of power, has often been the cause of his deliverance.

And sometimes by saying to him,[2] "A great deed it will be if you make away with such an one! If you slay one poor man, what vast advantage will you reap?" we may thus soften down his anger. But envy sets itself against the rich, and ceases not until it has wrought its will, and has poured forth its venom. See you, neither poverty nor wealth is good in itself, but our own disposition. Let us bring it to a good tone, let us discipline it in true wisdom. If this be well affected, riches cannot cast us out of the kingdom, poverty will not make us come short. But we shall meekly bear our poverty, and receive no loss in respect to the enjoyment of future goods, nor even here on earth. But we shall both enjoy what is good on earth, and obtain the good things in heaven, which may we all obtain, through the grace and lovingkindness, &c.

HOMILY III.

PHILIPPIANS i. 18–20.

"And therein I rejoice, yea, and will rejoice. For I know that this shall turn to my salvation through your supplication, and the supply of the Spirit of Jesus Christ, according to my earnest expectation and hope, that in nothing shall I be put to shame, but that with all boldness, as always, so now also Christ shall be magnified in my body, whether by life, or by death."

NONE of the grievous things which are in this present life can fix their fangs upon that lofty

soul, which is truly philosophic, neither enmity, nor accusations, nor slanders, nor dangers, nor plots. It flies for refuge as it were to a mighty fortress, securely defended there against all that attack it from this lower earth. Such was the soul of Paul; it had taken possession of a place higher than any fortress, the seat of spiritual wisdom, that is, true philosophy. For that of those without, i.e. the heathen, is mere words,

---

[1] νοσῶν. Perhaps alluding to the sense "insane."

[2] The reading is doubtful, but the sense clear.

and childish toys. But it is not of these we now speak, but at present concerning the things of Paul. That blessed one had both the Emperor for his enemy, and in addition, many other foes many ways afflicting him, even with bitter slander. And what says he? Not only do I not grieve nor sink beneath these things, but " I even rejoice, yea, and will rejoice," not for a season, but always will I rejoice for these things. " For I know that this shall turn out to my salvation," that which is to come, when even their enmity and jealousy towards me further the Gospel. " Through your supplication," he adds, " and the supply of the Spirit of Jesus Christ, according to my earnest expectation and hope." Behold the humble-mindedness of this blessed one ; he was striving in the contest, he was now close to his crown, he had done ten thousand exploits, for he was Paul, and what can one add to this? still he writes to the Philippians, I may be saved " through your supplication," I who have gained salvation through countless achievements. " And the supply," saith he, " of the Spirit of Jesus Christ." It is as though he said, if I am thought worthy of your prayers, I shall also be thought worthy of more grace. For the meaning of " supply " is this, if the Spirit be supplied to me, be given to me more abundantly. Or he is speaking of deliverance, " unto salvation " ; that is, I shall also escape the present as I did the former danger. Of this same matter he says, " At my first defense no one took my part, but all forsook me ; may it not be laid to their account. But the Lord stood by me, and strengthened me." (2 Tim. iv 16.) This then he now predicts : " Through your supplication and the supply of the Spirit of Jesus Christ, according to my earnest expectation and hope," for thus do I hope. For that he may persuade us not to leave the whole matter to the prayers made for us,[1] and contribute nothing ourselves, behold how he lays down his own part, which is Hope, the source of all good, as the Prophet says. " Let thy mercy, O Lord, be upon us, according as we have hoped in Thee." (Ps. xxxiii. 22.) And as it is written in another place, " Look to the generations of old and see, did any one hope in the Lord, and was made ashamed?" (Ecclus. ii. 10.) And again, this same blessed one says, " Hope putteth not to shame." (Rom. v. 5.) This is Paul's hope, the hoping that I shall nowhere be put to shame.

" According to my earnest expectation and hope," says he, " that in nothing shall I be put to shame." Do you see how great a thing it is to hope in God? Whatever happens, he says,

I shall not be put to shame, i.e. they will not obtain the mastery over me, " but with all boldness, as always, so now also, Christ shall be magnified in my body." They forsooth expected to catch Paul in this snare, and to quench the preaching of the Gospel, as though their craftiness were of any power. This then, he says, shall not be so, I shall not now die, but " as always, so now also, Christ shall be magnified in my body." How so? Ofttimes have I fallen into dangers, when all men gave us up, and what is more, when I myself did. For " we had the answer of death within ourselves " (2 Cor. i. 9), but from all the Lord delivered me, so now too he shall be magnified in my body. What then? Lest any one should suppose and say, If you die, will He not then be magnified? Yes, he answers, I know He will ; for this cause I did not say that my life alone shall magnify him, but my death too. At present he means " by life " ; they will not destroy me ; even did they so, Christ will even thus be magnified. How so? Through life, because He delivered me, but through my death, because even death itself could not persuade me to deny Him, since He gave me such readiness, and made me stronger than death. On the one hand because He freed me from peril ; on the other, because He suffered me not to fear the tyranny of death : thus shall he be magnified through life and death. And this he says, not as though he were about to die, but lest on his death they should be affected as men are apt to be.

But that you may know these his words did not point to immediate death, the thought that pained them most, see how he relieves it by almost saying, These things I say, not as one about to die ; wherefore he soon after adds, " And having this confidence I know that I shall abide, yea and abide with you all." " In nothing," says he, " shall I be put to shame " ; that is, death brings no shame to me, but rather great gain. Why so? Because I am not immortal, but I shall shine more brightly than if I were so, for it is not the same thing for one immortal, and for one who is mortal, to despise death ; so that not even instant death is shame to me, yet shall I not die ; " in nothing shall I be put to shame," neither in life nor death. For I will bear either nobly, whether life or death. Well says he! This is the part of a Christian soul ! but he adds, " with all boldness." Seest thou how entirely I am freed from shame? For if the fear of death had cut short my boldness, death would have been worthy of shame, but if death at its approach cast no terror on me, no shame is here ; but whether it be through life I shall not be put to shame, for I still preach the Preaching, or whether it be through death I shall not be put

---

[1] This may possibly refer especially to departed Saints. See Hom. vi. on Stat. fin. [But does it not manifestly mean the prayers which others now living make for us, as the Philippians then did for Paul? — J. A. B.]

to shame ; fear does not hold me back, since I still exhibit the same boldness. Do not, when I mention my bonds, think shame of the matter ; so manifold good hath it caused to me, that it hath even given confidence to others. For that we should be bound for Christ, is no shame, but for fear of bonds to betray aught that is Christ's, this is shame. When there is no such thing, bonds are even a cause of boldness. But since I have ofttimes escaped dangers, and have this to boast of to the unbelievers, do not straightway think I am put to shame, if now it should turn out otherwise. The one event no less than the other gives you boldness. Note how he brings this forward in his own person, which he does in many places, as in the Epistle to the Romans ; " For I am not ashamed of the Gospel." (Rom. i. 16.) And again in that to the Corinthians ; "And these things I have in a figure transferred to myself and Apollos." (1 Cor. iv. 6.) — "Whether by life or by death " : this he says not as in ignorance, (for he knew that he was not then to die, but some time after) ; yet even now does he prepare their soul.

Ver. 21. "For to me," he says, "to live is Christ, and to die is gain."

For even in dying, he means, I shall not have died, for I have my life in myself : then would they truly have slain me, had they had power through this fear to cast faith out of my soul. But as long as Christ is with me, even though death overtake me, still I live, and in this present life, not this, but Christ is my life. Since, then, not even in the present life is it so, " but that life which I now live in the flesh I live in faith ; " so I say in that state also, " I live, yet not I, but Christ liveth in me." (Gal. ii. 20.) Such ought a Christian to be ! I live not, he says, the common life. How livest thou then, O blessed Paul? Dost thou not see the sun, dost thou not breathe the common air? art thou not nourished with the same food as others? dost thou not tread the earth as we? needest thou not sleep, nor clothing, nor shoes? what meanest thou by, " I live not "? how dost thou not live? Why boastest thou thyself? No boasting is here. For if indeed the fact did not witness to him, a man might with some show have called it boasting ; but if facts do witness, how is boasting here? Let us then learn how he lives not, for he himself says in another place, " I have been crucified to the world, and the world to me." (Gal. vi. 14.) Hear then how he says, " I no longer live." And how he says, " to me to live is Christ." The word " life " is much significant, beloved, as also the word " death." There is this life of the body, there is the life of sin, as he himself elsewhere says, " But if we died to sin, how shall we any longer live therein?" (Rom. vi. 2.) It is

then possible to live the life of sin. Attend diligently, I entreat you, lest my labor be vain. There is the life everlasting and immortal ; with eternal life the heavenly ; " for our citizenship," says he, " is in heaven." (Phil. iii. 20.) There is the life of the body whereof he speaks, " through him we live and move and have our being." (Acts xvii. 28.) He does not then deny that he lives the natural life, but that of sin, which all men live. He who desires not the present life, how does he live it? He who is hastening to another, how does he live this life? He who despiseth death, how does he live this life? He who desires nothing, how does he live it? For as one made of adamant, though he were struck a thousand blows, would never attend to it, no more would Paul. And " I live," says he, " but no longer I," that is, no longer the old man ; as again elsewhere, " Wretched man that I am, who shall deliver me out of the body of this death !" (Rom. vii. 24.) How too does he live who does nought for the sake of food, nought for the sake of clothing, nought for any of these present things? Such an one does not even live the natural life : he who takes thought for none of the things which sustain life, lives not. We live this life, whose every action regards it. But he lived not ; he busied himself about nought of the things here. How then lived he? Just as we are accustomed to say, in common matters, such an one is not with me, when he does nothing that pertains to me. Again, in like sort, such a man lives not for me. Elsewhere he shows that he rejects not the natural life : " The life which I now live in the flesh, I live in the faith of the Son of God, who loved me, and gave himself for me " (Gal. ii. 20) ; i.e. a certain new life I live, an altered one. And truly all these things he said to comfort the Philippians. Think not, says he, that I shall be deprived of this life, for neither whilst alive did I live this life, but that which Christ willed. For tell me? He who despises money, luxury, hunger, thirst, dangers, health, safety, does he live this life? He who has nothing here, and is ofttimes willing to cast life away, if need be, and clings not to it, does he live this life? By no means. This I must make clear to you by a kind of example. Let us imagine some one in great wealth, with many servants, and much gold, and who makes no use of all these things ; is such an one rich for all his wealth? By no means. Let him see his children dissipating his property, strolling idly about ; let him feel no concern for them ; when beaten let him not even be pained ; shall we call him a man of wealth? By no means ; although his wealth is his own. "To me," he says, " to live is Christ ; " if you will enquire of my life, it is He. " And to die is gain." Wherefore? Because I shall more clearly be present with Him; so that my death is rather a coming to life; they who kill me will work on me no dreadful thing, they will only send me onward to my proper life, and free me from that which is not mine. What then, while thou wert here, wert thou not Christ's? Yes, and in a high degree.

Ver. 22. "But if to live in the flesh, — if this is the fruit of my work, then what I shall choose I wot not."

Lest any should say, If what you say is life, wherefore hath Christ left you here? "It is," he says, "the fruit of my work;" so that it is possible to use to good purpose the present life, while not living it. Lest you should think that reproach is cast upon life. For if we gain no advantage here, wherefore do we not make away with ourselves, nor slay ourselves? By no means, he answers. It is open to us to profit even here, if we live not this, but another life. But perchance one will say, does this bear thee fruit? Yes! he answers. Where are now the heretics? Behold now; "to live in the flesh," this is "the fruit of his work." "That which I now live in the flesh, I live in faith;" therefore it is "the fruit of my work."

"And what I shall choose I know not." Marvelous! How great was his philosophy! How hath he both cast out the desire of the present life, and yet thrown no reproach upon it! For in that he saith, "to die is gain," by this he hath cast out the desire, but in that he saith, "to live in the flesh is the fruit of my work," here he shows that the present life also is needful, if we use it as need is, if we bear fruit; since if it be unfruitful, it is no longer life. For we despise those trees which bear no fruit, as though they were dry, and give them up to the fire. Life itself belongs to that middle class of indifferent things, whilst to live well or ill is in ourselves. We do not then hate life, for we may live well too. So even if we use it ill, we do not even then cast the blame on it. And wherefore? Because not itself, but the free choice of those who use it ill is to blame. For God hath made thee live, that thou mayest live to Him. But thou, by living through corruption unto sin, makest thyself accountable for all blame. What sayest thou, tell me. Thou knowest not what to choose? Here hath he revealed a great mystery, in that his departure was in his own power; for where choice is, there have we power. "What I shall choose," says he, "I know not." Is it in thine own power? Yes, he answers, if I would ask this grace of God.

Ver. 23. "I am in a strait betwixt the two, having the desire."

See the affection of this blessed one; in this way too he comforts them, when they see that he is master of his own choice, and that this is

done not by man's sin, but by the dispensation of God. Why mourn ye, says he, at my death? It had been far better to have passed away long since. "For to depart," he says, "and to be with Christ, is very far better."

Ver. 24. "Yet to abide in the flesh is more needful for your sake."

These words were to prepare them for his death when it came, that they might bear it nobly: this was to teach true wisdom. "It is good for me to depart and be with Christ," for even death is a thing indifferent; since death itself is no ill, but to be punished after death is an ill. Nor is death a good, but it is good after our departure "to be with Christ." What follows death is either good or ill.

Let us then not simply grieve for the dead, nor joy for the living simply. But how? Let us grieve for sinners, not only when dying, but also while living. Let us joy for the just, not only while living, but also when dead. For those though living are dead, while these although dead, yet live: those even while living are to be pitied of all, because they are at enmity with God; the other even when they have departed Thither, are blessed, because they are gone to Christ. Sinners, wherever they are, are far from the King. Therefore they are subjects for tears; while the just, be they here, or be they there, are with the King; and there, in a higher and nearer degree, not through an entrance,[1] or by faith, but "face to face." (1 Cor. xiii. 12.)

Let us then not make wailings for the dead simply, but for those who have died in sins. They deserve wailing; they deserve beating of the breast and tears. For tell me what hope is there, when our sins accompany us Thither, where there is no putting off sins? As long as they were here, perchance there was great expectation that they would change, that they would become better; but when they are gone to Hades, where nought can be gained from repentance (for it is written, "In Sheol who shall give thee thanks?") (Ps. vi. 5), are they not worthy of our lamentation? Let us wail for those who depart hence in such sort; let us wail, I hinder you not; yet in no unseemly way, not in tearing our hair, or baring our arms, or lacerating our face, or wearing black apparel, but only in soul, shedding in quiet the bitter tear. For we may weep bitterly without all that display. And not as in sport only. For the laments which many make differ not from sport. Those public mournings do not proceed from sympathy, but from display, from emulation and vainglory. Many women do this as of their craft. Weep bitterly; moan at home, when no one sees you; this is the part of true sym-

---

[1] διὰ εἰσόδου Ben. διὰ εἰδους, "through a figure," but it should probably be δι' ἐσόπτρου, "in a mirror," as in the text (1 Cor. xiii. 12).

pathy; by this you profit yourself too. For he who laments another in such sort, will be much the more earnest never to fall into the same sins. Sin henceforth will be an object of dread to thee. Weep for the unbelievers; weep for those who differ in nowise from them, those who depart hence without the illumination,[1] without the seal! they indeed deserve our wailing, they deserve our groans; they are outside the Palace, with the culprits, with the condemned: for, "Verily I say unto you, Except a man be born of water and the Spirit, he shall not enter into the kingdom of Heaven." Mourn for those who have died in wealth, and did not from their wealth think of any solace for their soul, who had power to wash away their sins and would not. Let us all weep for these in private and in public, but with propriety, with gravity, not so as to make exhibitions of ourselves; let us weep for these, not one day, or two, but all our life. Such tears spring not from senseless passion, but from true affection. The other sort are of senseless passion. For this cause they are quickly quenched, whereas if they spring from the fear of God, they always abide with us. Let us weep for these; let us assist them according to our power; let us think of some assistance for them, small though it be, yet still let us assist them. How and in what way? By praying and entreating others to make prayers for them, by continually giving to the poor on their behalf. This deed hath some consolation; for hear the words of God Himself, when He says, "I will defend this city for Mine own sake, and for My servant David's sake." (2 Kings xx. 6.) If the remembrance only of a just man had so great power when deeds are done for one, how great power will it not have? Not in vain did the Apostles order[2] that remembrance should be made of the dead in the dreadful Mysteries. They know that great gain resulteth to them, great benefit; for when the whole people stands with uplifted hands, a priestly assembly, and that awful Sacrifice lies displayed, how shall we not prevail with God by our entreaties for them? And this we do for those who have departed in faith,[3] whilst

the catechumens are not thought worthy even of this consolation, but are deprived of all means of help save one. And what is this? We may give to the poor on their behalf. This deed in a certain way refreshes them. For God wills that we should be mutually assisted; else why hath He ordered us to pray for peace and the good estate of the world? why on behalf of all men? since in this number are included robbers, violaters of tombs, thieves, men laden with untold crimes; and yet we pray on behalf of all; perchance they may turn. As then we pray for those living, who differ not from the dead, so too we may pray for them. Job offered sacrifice for his children, and freed them from their sins. "It may be," said he, "that they have renounced God in their hearts." (Job i. 5.) Thus does one provide for one's children! He said not, as many do nowadays, I will leave them property; he said not, I will procure them honor; he said not, I will purchase an office; he said not, I will buy them land; but, "it may be that they have renounced God in their hearts." For what profit is there in those things? None at all, in those that remain here. I will make the King of all things favorable to them, and then they will no more want any thing. "The Lord," saith one, "is my Shepherd, I shall not want." (Ps. xxiii. 4.) This is great wealth, this is treasure. If we have the fear of God, we want nothing; if we have not this, though we have royalty itself, we are the poorest of all men. Nothing is like the man that feareth the Lord. For "the fear of the Lord," it is said, "surpasseth all things." (Ecclus. xxv. 11.) This let us procure; let us do all things for its sake. If need be that we lay down our lives, if our body must be mangled, let us not spare them; let us do all, to obtain this fear. For thus shall we abound above all men; and shall obtain those good things to come in Christ Jesus our Lord, to whom, &c.

---

xv. 46. Hom. xli. [8]. On Stat. xxi. 15 Tr. p. 487. St. Chrys. makes Flavian speak to Theodosius of the prayers for him after death, that might be won by an act of mercy. Comp. S. Ambr. de ob. Theod. § 37. Tert. de Corona, c. iii. speaks of oblations for the deceased as a general tradition in his time. St. Cyprian, Ep. 66, forbids Eucharistic prayer for one who makes a clergyman his executor. Euseb. Vit. Const. iv. 71, speaks of Constantine sharing in the prayers of the Faithful in connection with his burial near the relics of the Apostles. He does not directly mention this as depending on his "Baptism," but the terms of the Eucharistic prayer seem to have marked this, and it is implied in the rule given by St. Cyprian, and the whole principle of that commemoration stated in the passage cited of St. Chrys. on 1 Cor. xv.

---

[1] [A common expression among the Fathers for baptism.— J. A. B.]

[2] [The reference doubtless is to the so-called "Apostolical Constitutions," which direct the observance of the Eucharist in commemoration of the departed. See Smith's Dict. Chr. Antiq., pp. 1436 f.— J. A. B.]

[3] See Hom. vi. on the Statues, Tr. p. 387, note 6; also on 1 Cor.

HOMILY IV.

PHILIPPIANS i. 22–26.

" Then what I shall choose I wot not. But I am in a strait betwixt the two, having the desire to depart and be with Christ; which is very far better: yet to abide in the flesh is more needful for your sake. And having this confidence, I know that I shall abide, yea and abide with you all, for your progress and joy in the faith; that your glorying may abound in Jesus Christ in me, through my presence with you again."

NOTHING can be more blessed than the spirit of Paul, for the reason that nothing is more noble. We all shudder at death, I am wont to say, some by reason of our many sins, of whom I too am one, others from love of life, and cowardice, of whom may I never be one ; for they who are subject to this fear are mere animals. This then, which we all shudder at, he prayed for, and hasted toward Him ; saying, " To depart is very far better." What sayest thou ? when thou art about to change from earth to heaven, and to be with Christ, dost thou not know what to choose? Nay, far is this from the spirit of Paul ; for if such an offer were made to any one on sure grounds, would he not straightway seize it? Yes, for as it is not ours " to depart and be with Christ," neither, if we were able to attain to this, were it ours to remain here. Both are of Paul, and of his spirit. He was confidently persuaded. What? Art thou about to be with Christ? and dost thou say, " What I shall choose I wot not "? and not this only, but dost thou choose that which is here, " to abide in the flesh "? What in the world? didst thou not live an exceeding bitter life, in " watchings," in shipwrecks, in " hunger and thirst," and " nakedness," in cares and anxiety? " with the weak " thou wert " weak," and for those who " were made to stumble " thou dost " burn." (2 Cor. xi. 23, 29.) " In much patience, in afflictions, in necessities, in distresses, in stripes, in imprisonments, in tumults, in fastings, in pureness." (2 Cor. vi. 5, 6.) " Five times " didst thou " receive forty stripes save one," " thrice " wast thou " beaten with rods, once " wast thou " stoned," " a night and a day " thou hast " been in the deep, in perils of waters, in perils of robbers, in perils in the city, in perils in the wilderness, in perils among false brethren." (2 Cor. xi. 24–26.) Didst thou not, when the whole nation of the Galatians returned to the observance of the law, didst thou not cry aloud, and say, " Whosoever of you would be justified by the law, ye are fallen away from grace "? (Gal. v. 4.) How great was then

thy grief, and still dost thou desire this perishing life? Had none of these things befallen thee, but had thy success, wherever success attended thee, been without fear, and full of delight, yet shouldest not thou hasten to some harbor, from fear of the uncertain future? For tell me, what trader, whose vessel is full of untold wealth, when he may run into port, and be at rest, would prefer to be still at sea? what wrestler, when he might be crowned, would prefer to contend? what boxer, when he might put on his crown, would choose to enter afresh into the contest, and offer his head to wounds? what general is there, who when he might be quit of war with good report, and trophies, and might with the king refresh himself in the palace, would choose still to toil, and to stand in battle array? How then dost thou, who livest a life so exceeding bitter, wish to remain still here? Didst thou not say, I am in dread, " lest by any means, after that I have preached to others, I myself should be rejected?" (1 Cor. ix. 27.) If for no other cause, yet surely for this, thou oughtest to desire thy release ; were the present full of innumerable goods, yet for the sake of Christ thy Desire.[1]

Oh that spirit of Paul ! nothing was ever like it, nor ever will be ! Thou fearest the future, thou art compassed by innumerable dreadful things, and wilt thou not be with Christ? No, he answers, and this for Christ's sake, that I may render more loving unto Him those whom I have made his servants, that I may make the plot[2] which I have planted bear much fruit. (1 Cor. iii. 9). Didst thou not hear me, when I declared that I sought not " that which profited myself" (1 Cor. x. 33), but my neighbor? Heardest thou not these words, " I could wish that I myself were anathema from Christ " (Rom. ix. 3), that many might come unto Him? I, who chose that part, shall I not much rather choose this, shall I not with pleasure harm myself by this delay and postponement, that they may be saved?

" Who shall utter Thy mighty acts, O Lord " (Psa. cvi. 2), because Thou sufferedst not Paul to be hidden, because Thou madest manifest to the world such a man ? All the Angels of God

---

[1] [The editions in Greek, and the Latin translations, without support from any known Greek MS., here repeat, " thou oughtest to desire thy release from these things." Field retains it as if necessary. Yet it is not necessary, and is in character quite similar to the additions which are so common in the altered text. — J. A. B.]

[2] γεώργιον.

praised Thee with one accord, when Thou madest the stars (Job xxxviii. 7), and so too surely when Thou madest the sun, but not so much as when Thou didst manifest Paul to the whole world. By this, the earth was made more brilliant than the heaven, for he is brighter than the solar light, he hath shot forth more brilliant rays, he hath shed abroad more joyous beams. What fruit hath this man borne for us! not by making fat our corn, not by nurturing our pomegranates, but by producing and perfecting the fruit of holiness, and when falling to pieces, continually recovering them. For the sun itself can nothing profit fruits that are once decayed, but Paul has called out of their sins those who had manifold decays. And it gives place to the night, but he had mastery over the Devil. Nothing ever subdued him, nothing mastered him. The sun, when it mounts the heavens, darts down its rays, but he, as he rose from beneath, filled not the mid space of heaven and earth with light, but as soon as he opened his mouth, filled the Angels with exceeding joy. For if "there is joy in heaven over one sinner that repenteth" (Luke xv. 7), while he at his first address caught multitudes, does he not fill with joy the Powers above? What say I? It sufficeth that Paul should only be named, and the heavens leap for joy. For if when the Israelites "went forth out of Egypt, the mountains skipped like rams" (Psa. cxiv. 4), how great, thinkest thou, was the joy, when men ascended from earth to heaven!

Ver. 24. For this cause "to abide in the flesh is more needful for your sake."

And what excuse is left to us? ofttimes it happens that a man who possesses a little and poor city, chooses not to depart to another place, preferring his own rest. Paul might depart to Christ, and would not, (Christ whom he so desired, as for his sake to choose even hell,[1]) but still remained in the contest on behalf of man. What excuse shall we have? May we then even make mention of Paul? Look to his deeds. He showed that to depart was better, persuading himself not to grieve: he showed them, that if he remained, he remained for their sake, that it proceeded not from wickedness of those who plotted against him. He subjoined also the reason, that he might secure their belief. For if this is necessary, that is, I shall by all means remain, and I will not "remain" simply, but "will remain with you." For this is the meaning of the word, "and I shall abide with," i.e. I shall see you. For what cause? "For your progress and joy in the faith." Here too he rouses them, to take heed unto themselves. If, says he, for your sakes I abide, see that ye shame

not my abiding. "For your progress," I have chosen to remain, when I was about to see Christ. I have chosen to remain, because my presence advances both your faith and your joy. What then? Did he remain for the sake of the Philippians only? He stayed not for their sake only; but this he says, that he may show regard to them. And how were they to "progress" in "the faith"? That you may be more strengthened, like young fowl, who need their mother until their feathers are set. This is a proof of his great love. In like sort, we also rouse some of you, when we say, for your sake have I remained, that I may make you good.

Ver. 26. "That your glorying may abound in Christ Jesus in me, through my presence with you again."

You see that this explains the word "abide with you." Behold his humility. Having said, "for your progress," he shows that it was for his own profit too. This also he does, when he writes to the Romans, and says, "That is, that we may be comforted together in you." (Rom. i. 11, 12.) Having previously said, "That I may impart unto you some spiritual gift." And what means, "That your glorying may abound"? This glorying was, their establishment in the faith. For an upright life is glorying in Christ. And sayest thou, "Your glorying in me, through my presence with you again"? Yes, he answers; "For what is our hope, or crown of glorying? Are not even ye?" (1 Thess. ii. 19.) Because "you are our glorying, even as we also are yours" (2 Cor. i. 14), i.e. that I may be able to rejoice in you greatly. How sayest thou, "That your glorying may abound"? I may glory the more when you make progress.[2]

"Through my presence with you again." What then! Did he come to them? Search ye whether he came.

Ver. 27. "Only let your manner of life be worthy of the Gospel of Christ."

Do you see, how all that he has said, tends to turn them to this one thing, advancement in virtue? "Only let your manner of life be worthy of the Gospel of Christ." What means this word "only," but that this, and nought else, is the only thing we should seek? If we have this, nothing grievous will befall us. "That whether I come and see you, or be absent, I may hear of your state." This he says not as if he had changed his purpose, and no longer meant to visit them. But if this come to pass, he says, even though absent, I am able to rejoice. "If," that is, "I hear that ye stand fast in one spirit, with one soul." This is what above all things unites believers, and maintains love unbroken,

---

[1] [Chrys. frequently refers to Rom. ix. 3, according to his mistaken interpretation. — J. A. B.]

[2] St. Chrys. seems to take "your glorying" as "the glorying which I Paul have in you." The passage quoted from 2 Cor. i. 14 shows that the two senses are connected. Compare 2 Cor. v. 12.

"that they may be one." (John xvii. 11.) For a "kingdom divided against itself shall not stand." (Mark iii. 24.) For this cause he everywhere counsels his disciples much to be of one mind. And Christ says, " By this shall all men know that ye are My disciples, if ye love one another." (John xiii. 35.) That is, do not look with expectation toward me, and therefore slumber, as waiting for my coming, and then, when ye see me not coming faint. For even from report I can receive pleasure likewise.

What means, " In one spirit "? By the same gift of grace, viz. that of concord, and zeal; for the Spirit[1] is one, and he shows it; for then are we able to stand in " one soul," also, when we all have " one Spirit." See how the word " one " is used for concord. See how their souls being many are called one. Thus was it of old. " For they were all," it is written, " of one heart and of one soul. Striving together for the faith of the Gospel." (Acts iv. 32.) Does he say, striving together for each other,[2] as though the faith did strive? For did they wrestle against each other? But help each other, he says, in your striving for the faith of the Gospel.

Ver. 28. " And in nothing affrighted by the adversaries; which is for them an evident token of perdition, but to you of salvation."

Well said he, " affrighted," this is what befalls us from our enemies, they only frighten. " In nothing " therefore, he says, whatever happens, whether dangers — whether plots. For this is the part of those who stand upright; the enemy can do nought but frighten only. Since it was likely that they should be greatly troubled, when Paul suffered such numberless ills, he says, I exhort you not only not to be shaken, but not to be affrighted, yea rather to despise them heartily; for if ye are thus affected, ye will straightway, by this means, make evident at once their destruction, and your salvation. For when they see, that with their innumerable plots they are unable to frighten you, they will take it as a proof of their own destruction. For when the persecutors prevail not over the persecuted, the plotters over the objects of their plots, the powerful over those subject to their power, will it not be self-evident, that their perdition is at hand, that their power is nought, that their part is false, that their[3] part is weak? " And this," he says, " comes from God."

Ver. 29. " For unto you it is given in the behalf of Christ, not only to believe on Him, but also to suffer in his behalf."

Again does he teach them moderation of spirit by referring all to God, and saying that sufferings in behalf of Christ are of grace, the gift of grace, a free gift. Be not then ashamed of the gift of grace, for it is more wonderful than the power of raising the dead, or working miracles; for there I am a debtor, but here I have Christ for my debtor. Wherefore ought we not only not to be ashamed, but even to rejoice, in that we have this gift. Virtues he calls gifts, yet not in like sort as other things, for those are entirely of God, but in these we have a share. But since even here the greatest part is of God, he ascribes it entirely to Him, not to overturn our free will, but to make us humble and rightly disposed.

Ver. 30. " Having the same conflict which ye saw in me "; i.e. ye have also an example. Here again he raises them up, by showing them that everywhere their conflicts were the same with his, their struggles were the same with his, both severally, and in that they united with him in bearing trials. He said not, ye have heard, but " ye saw," for he strove too at Philippi. Truly this is an exceeding virtue. Wherefore writing to the Galatians, also he said, " Did ye suffer so many things in vain, if it be indeed in vain." (Gal. iii. 4.) And again, writing to the Hebrews, he said, " But call to remembrance the former days, in which, after ye were enlightened, ye endured a great conflict of suffering; partly, being made a gazing-stock both by reproaches and afflictions." (Heb. x. 32, 33.) And writing again to Macedonians, that is, to the Thessalonians, he said, " For they themselves report concerning us, what manner of entering in we had unto you." (1 Thess. i. 9.) And again, " For yourselves, brethren, know our entering in unto you, that it hath not been found vain." (1 Thess. ii. 1.) And in like sort does he witness the same things of them all, labors and strivings. But such things ye will not now find among us; now it is much if one suffer a little in goods alone. And in respect of their goods also he witnesses great things of them. For to some he says, " For ye took joyfully the spoiling of your possessions" (Heb. x. 34); and to others, " For it hath been the good pleasure of Macedonia and Achaia to make a certain contribution for the poor " (Rom. xv. 26); and " your zeal hath stirred up very many of them." (2 Cor. ix. 2.)

Seest thou the praises of the men of that time? But we endure not so much as buffetings or blows, neither insult nor loss of our possessions: they were straightway zealous, and all of them strove as martyrs, whilst we have grown cold in love toward Christ. Again I am constrained to accuse things present; and what shall I do? It is against my will, yet am I constrained. Were

---

[1] The punctuation is altered. He seems to be proving, not the unity of the Spirit, but the relation of that doctrine to practice.
[2] [i.e. you and the faith. — J. A. B.]
[3] Chrys. seems to make a false opposition between ἐκείνων and αὐτῶν; but if the reading is correct, this is really one of his rapid changes of the " point of view," though not amounting to a change of person. Dounæus suggests ὅτι τὰ ἐκείνων ἀληθῆ; (for ἀσθενῆ;) ' That the others' (principles) ' are true.' Compare the letter of Antoninus [Hadrian] quoted by Justin Martyr. Apol. i. 70.

I able by my silence of things which are done, by holding my peace, and not mentioning aught, to remove them, it would behoove me to be silent. But if the contrary comes to pass ; if not only are these things not removed by our silence, but even become worse, we are forced to speak. For he who rebukes sinners, if he does nought else, suffers them not to go farther. For there is no such shameless and rash soul, as not to turn, and remit the extravagance of its evil deeds, on hearing any one continually rebuking it. There is, there is indeed, even in the shameless, a small portion of shame. For God hath sown in our nature the seeds of shame ; for since fear was insufficient to bring us to a right tone, He hath also prepared many other ways for avoiding sin. For example, that a man should be accused, fear of the enacted laws,[1] love of reputation, the desire of forming friendships ; for all these are paths to avoid sin. Ofttimes that which was not done for God's sake, was done through shame ; that which was not done for God's sake, was done for fear of men. That which we seek for is, in the first place not to sin, and we shall afterwards succeed in doing this for God's sake. Else why did Paul exhort those, who were about to overcome[2] their enemies, not by the fear of God, but on the score of waiting for the vengeance ?[3] "For by so doing," he says, "thou shalt heap coals of fire upon his head." (Rom. xii. 20.) For this is his first wish, that our virtue should be established. As I said then, there is in us a sense of shame. We have many good natural affections, which lead to virtue ; as, for example, all of us men are naturally moved to pity, and no other good thing so inheres in our nature, but this alone. Whence any one might reasonably enquire, wherefore these seeds have above all others been sown in our nature, by which we melt[4] at tears, by which we are turned to compassion, and are ready to pity. No one is naturally idle,[5] no one is naturally regardless of his reputation, no one is naturally above emulation, but pity lies deep in every one's nature, however fierce and ungentle he be. And what wonder ? we pity beasts, such a superabundance of pity lies deep in us. If we see a lion's whelp, we are somewhat affected ; much more in the case of one of our race. See, how many maimed are there ! and this is sufficient to lead us to pity. Nothing so much pleases God as mercy.[6] Wherefore with this the priests were anointed, and the kings, and the prophets, for they had, in oil, a type of God's love to man ;

and they further learnt, that rulers should have a greater share of mercy.[7] It showed that the Spirit is to come to men through mercy, since God pities and is kind to man. For, "Thou hast mercy upon all," it is written, "for Thou canst do all things." (Wisd. xi. 23.) For this cause they were anointed with oil : and indeed it was from mercy He appointed the priesthood. And kings were anointed with oil ; and would one praise a ruler, he can make mention of nothing so becoming him as mercy. For pity is peculiar to power. Consider that the world was established by pity,[8] and then imitate thy Lord. "The mercy of man is toward his neighbor, but the mercy of the Lord is upon all flesh." (Ecclus. xviii. 13.) How "upon all flesh"? Whether you mean sinners, or just men, we all need the mercy of God ; we all enjoy it, be it Paul, be it Peter, or be it John. And listen to their own words ; there is no need of mine. For what says this blessed one? "But I obtained mercy, because I did it ignorantly." (1 Tim. i. 13.) What then, was there afterwards no need of mercy? Hear what he says ; "But I labored more abundantly than they all ; yet not I, but the grace of God which was with me." (1 Cor. xv. 10.) And of Epaphroditus he says, "For indeed he was sick, nigh unto death ; but God had mercy on him ; and not on him only, but on me also, that I might not have sorrow upon sorrow." (Phil. ii. 27.) And again he says, "We were weighed down exceedingly, beyond our power, insomuch that we despaired even of life. Yea, we ourselves have had the answer of death within ourselves, that we should not trust in ourselves, but in God, who delivered us out of so great a death, and will deliver." (2 Cor. i. 8, 9, 10.) And again, "And I was delivered out of the mouth of the lion ; and the Lord will deliver me." (2 Tim. iv. 17, 18.) And everywhere we shall find him glorying in this, that by mercy he was saved. Peter, too, became so great, because mercy was shown him. For hear Christ saying to him, "Satan hath desired to sift you as wheat ; and I made supplication for thee, that thy faith fail not." (Luke xxii. 31, 32.) John, too, became so great through mercy, and in short all of them. For listen to Christ when He says, "Ye did not choose Me, but I chose you." (John xv. 16.) For we all have need of the mercy of God, as it is written, "The mercy of God is upon all flesh."[9] But if these men needed the mercy of God, what should one say of the rest? For why, tell me, doth He "make the sun to rise on the evil and the good"? Did He withhold the rain for one year, would He not destroy all? And what if He caused

---

[1] See on Stat. Hom. vi.
[2] κρατεῖν. He seems to mean "to have them in their power."
[3] See on the passage, Hom. xxii., Tr. p. 508.
[4] κατακλᾶσθαι. See on Stat. Hom. xiii. § 9, Tr. p. 429. In that and Hom. xii. the law of nature is discussed at some length.
[5] [This is obscure, and the Oxford editor follows the suggestion of Downes that for ἀργός, "idle," we should read ἄοργος, "without anger," but, as Field points out, there is no such word. — J. A. B.]
[6] ἐλεημοσύνη.

[7] ἐλέου.
[8] Comp. Wisd. i. 14, xi. 24.
[9] Ecclus. xviii. 13, as above. Compare Ps. cxlv. 9 and Job iv. 18.

overwhelming rain? what if He rained down fire? what if He sent flies? But what do I say? if He were so to do [1] as He once did, would not all perish? If He were to shake the earth, would not all perish? It is now seasonable to say, "What is man, that Thou art mindful of him?" (Ps. viii. 4.) Were He only to threaten the earth, all men would become one tomb. "As a drop of water from the bucket," it is written, "so are the nations in His sight, they shall be counted as very small dust, as the turning of the balance." (Isa. xl. 15.) It were as easy for Him to destroy all things, and to make them again, as for us to turn the balance. He then who has such power over us, and sees us sinning every day, and yet punishes us not, how is it but by mercy He bears with us? Since beasts too exist by mercy: "Thou, Lord, wilt preserve both men and beasts." (Ps. xxxvi. 7.) He looked upon the earth, and filled it with living things. And wherefore? For thy sake! And wherefore did He make thee? Through His goodness.

There is nothing better than oil. It is the cause of light, and there also it is the cause of light.[2] "Then shall thy light break forth as the morning" (Isa. lviii. 8), saith the Prophet, if thou showest pity upon thy neighbour. And as natural oil contains light, so then doth mercy [alms] grant us a great, a marvelous light. Much mention doth Paul, too, make of this mercy. In one place, hear him say, "Only that we should remember the poor." (Gal. ii. 10.) And in another, "If it be meet for me to go also." (1 Cor. xvi. 4.) And in every place, turn where you will, ye see him anxious about this very thing. And again, "And let our people also learn to maintain good works." (Tit. iii. 14.) And again, "These things are good and profitable unto men." (Tit. iii. 8.) Listen to a certain other one who saith, "Alms [3] do deliver from death" (Tob. xii. 9); If Thou takest away pity, "Lord, Lord, who shall stand" (Ps. cxxx. 3); and it is said, If Thou enterest "into judgment with thy servant" (Ps. cxliii. 2); "A great thing

is man"; why? "and an honorable thing is a merciful man." (Prov. xx. 6, LXX.) For this is the true character of man, to be merciful, yea rather the character of God, to show mercy. Dost thou see, how strong is the mercy of God? This made all things, this formed the world, this made the angels, it was through mere goodness. For this cause, too, He threatened hell, that we may attain unto the kingdom, and through mercy we do attain unto the kingdom. For wherefore did God, being alone, create so many beings? was it not through goodness? was it not through love to men? If you ask why such and such things are, you will always find your answer in Goodness. Let us show mercy to our neighbors, that mercy may be shown to us. These acts of mercy [4] we show not so much to them, as lay up for ourselves against That Day. When the flame of the fire is great, this oil (mercy) is that which quenches the fire, and this brings light to us. Thus by this means shall we be freed from the fire of hell. For whence will He be compassionate and show mercy? Mercy comes of love! Nothing incenses God so much as to be pitiless. "A man was brought to him who owed him ten thousand talents, and he was moved with compassion, and forgave him. And there were owing to that man from his fellow-servant a hundred pence, and he caught him by the throat. Therefore the Lord delivered him to the tormentors, till he should pay what was due." Let us on hearing this be merciful to those who are our debtors in money or in sins. Let no one remember evils, if at least he does not wish to injure himself; for he does not so much aggrieve the other (as he injures himself). For he [5] either will follow him with vengeance, or he has not done so; but dost thou thyself, while not forgiving thy neighbor his sins, seek for a kingdom? Lest this should happen to us, let us forgive all, (for it is ourselves that we pardon,) that God may forgive us our sins, and so we may obtain the good things which are in store, through the grace and lovingkindness, &c.

---

[1] [So the best group of MSS., though Field retains the reading of the other group, " if he were to make darkness." The vague expression, " so to do as He once did," probably refers to the universal destruction at the Deluge.— J. A. B.]

[2] [There is a queer play upon the words ἐλαίου, "oil," and ἐλέου, "mercy," which in Chrys.'s day (as in Mod. Greek) were pronounced alike. As oil in the natural, so mercy in the spiritual sphere, he says, is the cause of light. — J. A. B.]

[3] [The Greek word which we borrow and contract into "alms" is derived from the word here rendered pity and mercy.— J. A. B.]

[4] al. This oil; see note 2; and on Rom. xiv. 13, Hom. xxv., Tr. p. 425, note g; and on Matt. xxv., Hom. lxxviii. init., also Hom. on Stat. vi., Tr. p. 130, note c. He may mean here to distinguish the fire of Hell, from which we may be freed, from that which is to rage, but to be quenched.

[5] [This probably means God, as suggested by the altered text, which of course tinkered so obscure a passage. — J. A. B.]

HOMILY V.

PHILIPPIANS ii. 1–4.

"If there is therefore any comfort in Christ, if any consolation of love, if any fellowship of the Spirit, if any tender mercies and compassions, fulfil ye my joy, that ye be of the same mind, having the same love, being of one accord, of one mind; doing nothing through faction or through vainglory; but in lowliness of mind, each counting other better than himself; not looking each of you to his own things, but each of you also to the things of others."

THERE is nothing better, there is nothing more affectionate, than a spiritual teacher; such an one surpasses the kindness of any natural father. Do but consider, how this blessed one entreats the Philippians concerning the things which were to their own advantage. What says he, in exhorting them concerning concord, that cause of all good things? See how earnestly, how vehemently, with how much sympathy he speaks, "If there be therefore any comfort in Christ," that is, if ye have any comfort in Christ, as if he had said, If thou makest any account of me, if thou hast any care of me, if thou hast ever received good at my hands, do this. This mode of earnestness we use when we claim a matter which we prefer to everything else. For if we did not prefer it to everything, we should not wish to receive in it our recompense for all things, nor say that through it all is represented. We indeed remind men of our carnal claims; for example, if a father were to say, If thou hast any reverence for thy father, if any remembrance of my care in nourishing thee, if any affection towards me, if any memory of the honor thou hast received of me, if any of my kindness, be not at enmity with thy brother; that is, for all those things, this is what I ask in return.

But Paul does not so; he calls to our remembrance no carnal, but all of them spiritual benefits. That is, if ye wish to give me any comfort in my temptations, and encouragement in Christ, if any consolation of love, if ye wish to show any communion in the Spirit, if ye have any tender mercies and compassions, fulfil ye my joy. "If any tender mercies and compassions." Paul speaks of the concord of his disciples as compassion towards himself, thus showing that the danger was extreme, if they were not of one mind. If I can obtain comfort from you, if I can obtain any consolation from your love, if I can communicate with you in the Spirit, if I can have fellowship with you in the Lord, if I can find mercy and compassion at your hands,

show by your love the return of all this. All this have I gained, if ye love one another.

Ver. 2. "Fulfil ye my joy."

That the exhortation might not seem to be made to people who were still deficient, see how he says not, "do me joy," but "fulfil my joy"; that is, Ye have begun to plant it in me, ye have already given me some portion of peacefulness, but I desire to arrive at its fulness? Say, what wouldest thou? that we deliver thee from dangers? that we supply somewhat to thy need? Not so, but "that ye be of the same mind, having the same love," in which ye have begun, "being of one accord, of one mind." Just see, how often he repeats the same thing by reason of his great affection! "That ye be of the same mind," or rather, "that ye be of one mind." For this is more than "the same."

"Having the same love." That is, let it not be simply about faith alone, but also in all other things; for there is such a thing as to be of the same mind, and yet not to have love. "Having the same love," that is, love and be loved alike; do not thou enjoy much love, and show less love, so as to be covetous even in this matter; but do not suffer it in thyself. "Of one accord," he adds, that is, appropriating with one soul, the bodies of all, not in substance, for that is impossible, but in purpose and intention. Let all things proceed as from one soul. What means "of one accord"? He shows when he says "of one mind." Let your mind be one, as if from one soul.

Ver. 3. "Doing nothing through faction."

He finally demands this of them, and tells[1] them the way how this may be. "Doing nothing through faction or vainglory." This, as I always say, is the cause of all evil. Hence come fightings and contentions. Hence come envyings and strifes. Hence it is that love waxes cold, when we love the praise of men, when we are slaves to the honor which is paid by the many, for it is not possible for a man to be the slave of praise, and also a true servant of God. How then shall we flee vainglory? for thou hast not yet told us the way. Listen then to what follows.

"But in lowliness of mind, each counting other better than himself." Oh how full of true wisdom, how universal a gathering-word[2] of our

---

[1] [Field here makes a conjectural alteration which is little better, and we follow the documents. — J. A. B.]   [2] συγκρότημα.

salvation is the lesson he has put forth ! If thou deemest, he means, that another is greater than thyself, and persuadest thyself so, yea more, if thou not only sayest it, but art fully assured of it, then thou assignest him the honor, and if thou assignest him the honor, thou wilt not be displeased at seeing him honored by another. Do not then think him simply greater than thyself, but " better," which is a very great superiority, and thou dost not think it strange nor be pained thereby, if thou seest him honored. Yea, though he treat thee with scorn, thou dost bear it nobly, for thou hast esteemed him greater than thyself. Though he revile thee, thou dost submit. Though he treat thee ill, thou bearest it in silence. For when once the soul is fully assured that he is greater, it falls not into anger when it is ill-treated by him, nor yet into envy, for no one would envy those who are very far above himself, for all things belong to his superiority.

Here then he instructs the one party to be thus minded. But when he too, who enjoys such honor from thee, is thus affected toward thee, consider what a double wall there is erected of gentle forbearance [comp. Phil. iv. 5] ; for when thou esteemest him thus worthy of honor, and he thee likewise, no painful thing can possibly arise ; for if this conduct when shown by one is sufficient to destroy all strife, who shall break down the safeguard, when it is shown by both? Not even the Devil himself. The defense is threefold, and fourfold, yea manifold, for humanity is the cause of all good ; and that you may learn this, listen to the prophet, saying, " Hadst thou desired sacrifice, I would have given it : Thou wilt not delight in burnt offerings. The sacrifice for God is a broken spirit, a broken and a contrite heart God will not despise." [1] (Ps. li. 16, 17.) Not simply humility, but intense humility. As in the case of bodily substances, that which is " broken " will not rise against that which is " solid," but, how many ills soever it may suffer, will perish itself rather than attack the other, so too the soul, even if constantly suffering ill, will choose rather to die, than to avenge itself by attack.

How long shall we be puffed up thus ridiculously? For as we laugh, when we see children drawing themselves up, and looking haughty, or when we see them picking up stones and throwing them, thus too the haughtiness [2] of men belongs to a puerile intellect, and an unformed mind. " Why are earth and ashes proud? " (Ecclus. x. 9.) Art thou highminded, O man? and why? tell me what is the gain? Whence art thou highminded against those of thine own kind? Dost not thou share the same nature?

the same life? Hast not thou received like honor from God? But thou art wise? Thou oughtest to be thankful, not to be puffed up. Haughtiness is the first act of ingratitude, for it denies [3] the gift of grace. He that is puffed up, is puffed up as if he had excelled by his own strength, and he who thinks he has thus excelled is ungrateful toward Him who bestowed that honor. Hast thou any good? Be thankful to Him who gave it. Listen to what Joseph said, and what Daniel. For when the king of Egypt sent for him, and in the presence of all his host asked him concerning that matter in which the Egyptians, who were most learned in these things, had forsaken the field, when he was on the point of carrying off everything from them, and of appearing wiser than the astrologers, the enchanters, the magicians, and all the wise men of those times, and that from captivity and servitude, and he but a youth (and his glory was thus greater, for it is not the same thing to shine when known, and contrary to expectation, so that its being unlooked for rendered him the more admirable) ; what then, when he came before Pharaoh? Was it " Yea, I know "? But what? When no one urged it on him, he said from his own excellent spirit, " Do not interpretations belong to God? " [4] Behold he straightway glorified his Master, therefore he was glorified. And this also is no small thing. For that God had revealed it to him was a far greater thing than if he had himself excelled. For he showed that his words were worthy of credit, and it was a very great proof of his intimacy with God. There is no one thing so good as to be the intimate friend of God. " For if," says the Scripture, " he [Abraham] was justified by works, he hath whereof to glory, but not toward God." (Rom. iv. 2.) For if he who has been vouchsafed grace maketh his boast in God, that he is loved of Him, because his sins are forgiven, he too that worketh hath whereof to boast, but not before God, as the other (for it [5] is a proof of our excessive weakness) ; he who has received wisdom of God, how much more admirable is he? He glorifies God and is glorified of Him, for He says, " Them that honor Me, I will honor." (1 Sam. ii. 30.)

Again, listen to him who descended from Joseph, than whom no one was wiser. " Art thou wiser," [6] says he, " than Daniel? " (Ezek. xxviii. 3.) This Daniel then, when all the wise men that were in Babylon, and the astrologers moreover, the prophets, the magicians, the en-

---

[1] [Quoted, of course, from the Sept., which here differs considerably from the Hebrew. — J. A. B.]
[2] ἀπόνοια.

[3] Lit. " takes away," i.e. takes the credit from the Giver.
[4] Gen. xl. 8. This he said to the baker and cupbearer in prison, but he also said to Pharaoh, " It is not in me: God shall give Pharaoh an answer of pence," c. xli. 16.
[5] He may mean our " boasting " of " such " things as we do, or the fact that our goodness extends not to God.
[6] E. V. " Thou art," but [Chrys. quotes the Sept. — J. A. B.]

chanters, yea when the whole of their wisdom was not only coming to be convicted, but to be wholly destroyed (for their being destroyed was a clear proof that they had deceived before), this Daniel coming forward, and preparing to solve the king's question, does not take the honor to himself, but first ascribes the whole to God, and says, " But as for me, O king, it is not revealed to me for any wisdom that I have beyond all men." (Dan. ii. 30,) And " the king worshiped him, and commanded that they should offer an oblation." (Dan. ii. 46.) Seest thou his humility? seest thou his excellent spirit? seest thou this habit of lowliness? Listen also to the Apostles, saying at one time, " Why fasten ye your eyes on us, as though by our own power or godliness we had made this man to walk? (Acts iii. 12.) And again, " We are men of like passions with you." (Acts xiv. 15.) Now if they thus refused the honors paid them, men who by reason of the humility and power of Christ wrought greater deeds than Christ (for He says, " He that believeth in Me shall do greater works than those that I do " (John xiv. 12, abr.)), shall not we wretched and miserable men do so, who cannot even beat away gnats,[1] much less devils? who have not power to benefit a single man, much less the whole world, and yet think so much of ourselves that the Devil himself is not like us?

There is nothing so foreign to a Christian soul as haughtiness. Haughtiness, I say, not boldness nor courage, for these are congenial. But these are one thing, and that another; so too humility is one thing, and meanness, flattery, and adulation another.

I will now, if you wish, give you examples of all these qualities. For these things which are contraries, seem in some way to be placed near together, as the tares to the wheat, and the thorns to the rose. But while babes might easily be deceived, they who are men in truth, and are skilled in spiritual husbandry, know how to separate what is really good from the bad. Let me then lay before you examples of these qualities from the Scriptures. What is flattery, and meanness, and adulation? Ziba flattered[2] David out of season, and falsely slandered his master. (2 Sam. xvi. 1–3.) Much more did Ahitophel flatter Absalom. (2 Sam. xvii. 1–4.) But David was not so, but he was humble. For the deceitful are flatterers, as when they say, " O king, live for ever." (Dan. ii. 4.) Again, what flatterers the magicians are.

We shall find much to exemplify this in the case of Paul in the Acts. When he disputed with the Jews he did not flatter them, but was humble-minded (for he knew how to speak boldly), as when he says, " I, brethren, though I had done nothing against the people, or the customs of our fathers, yet was delivered prisoner from Jerusalem." (Acts xxviii. 17.)

That these were the words of humility, listen how he rebukes them in what follows, " Well spake the Holy Ghost, By hearing ye shall hear, and shall in nowise understand, and seeing ye shall see, and in nowise perceive." (Acts xxviii. 25 ; ib. 26.)

Seest thou his courage? Behold also the courage of John the Baptist, which he used before Herod ; when he said, " It is not lawful for thee to have thy brother Philip's wife." (Mark vi. 18.) This was boldness, this was courage. Not so the words of Shimei, when he said, " Begone, thou man of blood " (2 Sam. xvi. 7), and yet he too spake with boldness; but this is not courage, but audacity, and insolence, and an unbridled tongue. Jezebel too reproached Jehu, when she said, " The slayer of his master " (2 Kings ix. 31), but this was audacity, not boldness. Elias too reproached, but this was boldness and courage ; " I do not trouble Israel, but thou and thy father's house." (1 Kings xviii. 18.) Again, Elias spake with boldness to the whole people, saying, " How long will ye go lame on both your thighs?" (1 Kings xviii. 21, LXX.) Thus to rebuke was boldness and courage. This too the prophets did, but that other was audacity.

Would you see words both of humility and not of flattery,[3] listen to Paul, saying, " But with me it is a very small thing that I should be judged of you, or of man's judgment; yea, I judge not mine own self. For I know nothing against myself, yet am I not hereby justified." (1 Cor. iv. 3, 4.) This is of a spirit that becomes a Christian ; and again, " Dare any of you, having a matter against his neighbor, go to law before the unrighteous, and not before the saints "? (1 Cor. vi. 1.)

Would you see the flattery of the foolish Jews? listen to them, saying, " We have no king but Cæsar." (John xix. 15.) Would you see humility? listen to Paul again, when he says, " For we preach not ourselves, but Christ Jesus as Lord, and ourselves as your servants for Jesus' sake." (2 Cor. iv. 5.) Would you see both flattery and audacity? " Audacity " (1 Sam. xxv. 10) in the case of Nabal, and " flattery " (1 Sam. xxiii. 20) in that of the Ziphites? For in their purpose they betrayed David. Would you see " wisdom " (1 Sam. xxvi. 5–12) and not flattery,

---

[1] This hyperbolical expression may have a moral meaning with respect to petty annoyances, and in allusion to the fan used in the Holy Eucharist. Bingham xv. c. 3, § 6.

[2] Compare 2 Sam. xix. 26. He means that Ziba had recourse to unworthy means of winning David's favor. And that Ahitophel was ready to serve Absalom from selfish motives.

[3] [All of Field's MSS. give " flattery " (instead of " freedom." as the text of most editions), and he has inserted " not " by conjecture, as it is said below in the case of David. — J. A. B.]

that of David, how he gat Saul into his power, and yet spared him? Would you see the flattery of those who murdered Mephibosheth,[1] whom also David slew? In fine, and as it were in outline, to sum up all, audacity is shown when one is enraged, and insults another for no just cause, either to avenge himself, or in some unjust way is audacious; but boldness and courage are when we dare to face perils and deaths, and despise friendships and enmities for the sake of what is pleasing to God. Again, flattery and meanness are when one courts another not for any right end, but hunting after some of the things of this life; but humility, when one does this for the sake of things pleasing to God, and descends from his own proper station that he may perform something great and admirable. If we know these things, happy are we if we do them. For to know them is not enough. For Scripture says, "Not the hearers of a law, but the doers of a law shall be justified." (Rom. ii. 13.) Yea, knowledge itself condemneth, when it is without action and deeds of virtue. Wherefore that we may escape the condemnation, let us follow after the practice, that we may obtain those good things that are promised to us, by the grace and love of our Lord Jesus Christ.

HOMILY VI.

PHILIPPIANS ii. 5–8.

"Have this mind in you, which was also in Christ Jesus: who, being in the form of God, counted it not a prize to be on an equality with God, but emptied Himself, taking the form of a servant, being made in the likeness of men; and being found in fashion as a man, He humbled Himself, becoming obedient *even* unto death, yea, the death of the cross."

OUR Lord Jesus Christ, when exhorting His disciples to great actions, places before them Himself, and the Father, and the Prophets, as examples; as when He says, "For thus they did unto the Prophets which were before you" (Matt. v. 12; Luke vi. 23); and again, "If they persecute Me, they will also persecute you" (John xv. 20); and, "Learn of me, for I am meek" (Matt. xi. 29); and again, "Be ye merciful, as your Father which is in heaven is merciful." (Luke vi. 36.) This too the blessed Paul did; in exhorting them to humility, he brought forward Christ. And he does so not here only, but also when he discourses of love towards the poor, he speaks in this wise. "For ye know the grace of our Lord Jesus Christ, that though He was rich, yet for your sakes He became poor." (2 Cor. viii. 9.) Nothing rouses a great and philosophic soul to the performance of good works, so much as learning that in this it is likened to God. What encouragement is equal to this? None. This Paul well knowing, when he would exhort them to humility, first beseeches and supplicates them, then to awe[2] them he says, "That ye stand fast in one Spirit"; he says also, that it "is for them an evident token of perdition, but your salvation." (Phil. i. 27, 28.) And last of all he says this, "Have this mind in you, which was also in Christ Jesus, who, being in the form of God, counted it not a prize to be on an equality with God, but emptied Himself, taking upon Him the form of a servant." (Phil. ii. 5–7.) Attend, I entreat you, and rouse yourselves. For as a sharp two-edged sword, wheresoever it falls, though it be among ten thousand phalanxes, easily cuts through and destroys, because it is sharp on every side, and nought can bear its edge; so are the words of the Spirit. (Heb. iv. 12; Rev. i. 16.) For by these words he has laid low the followers of Arius of Alexandria, of Paul of Samosata, of Marcellus the Galatian, of Sabellius the Libyan, of Marcion that was of Pontus, of Valentinus, of Manes, of Apollinarius of Laodicea, of Photinus, of Sophronius, and, in one word, all the heresies. Rouse yourselves then to behold so great a spectacle, so many armies falling by one stroke, lest the pleasure of such a sight should escape you. For if when chariots contend in the horse race there is nothing so pleasing as when one of them dashes against and overthrows whole chariots with their drivers, and after throwing down many with the charioteers that stood thereon, drives by alone towards the goal, and the end of the course, and amid the applause and clamor which rises on all sides to heaven, with coursers winged as it were by that joy and that applause, sweeps over the whole ground; how much greater will the pleasure be here, when by the grace of God we overthrow at once and in a body the combinations and devilish machinations of all these heresies together with their charioteers?

And if it seem good to you, we will first

---

[1] 2 Sam. iv. 8. So some copies of LXX., for Ishbosheth.
[2] ἐντρπτικῶς, usually to "shame," here rather to "make serious," i.e. by representing to them the presence of the Holy Spirit. See Phil. ii. 12, 13.

arrange the heresies themselves in order. Would you have them in the order of their impiety, or of their dates? In the order of time, for it is difficult to judge of the order of their impiety. First then let Sabellius[1] the Libyan come forward. What does he assert? that the Father, Son, and Holy Spirit, are mere names given to one Person. Marcion[2] of Pontus says, that God the Creator of all things is not good, nor the Father of the good Christ, but another righteous one,[3] and that he did not take flesh for us. Marcellus,[4] and Photinus,[5] and Sophronius assert, that the Word is an energy, and that it was this energy that dwelt in Him who was of the seed of David, and not a personal substance.

Arius confesses indeed the Son, but only in word; he says that He is a creature, and much inferior to the Father. And others say that He has not a soul. Seest thou the chariots standing? See then their fall, how he overthrows them all together, and with a single stroke. How? " Have the same mind in· you," he says, " which was in Christ Jesus, who being in the form of God, counted it not a prize to be on an equality with God." And Paul[6] of Samosata has fallen, and Marcellus, and Sabellius. For he says, " Being in the form of God." If " in the form " how sayest thou, O wicked one, that He took His origin from Mary, and was· not before? and how dost thou say that He was an energy? For it is written, " The form of God took the form of a servant." " The form of a servant," is it the energy of a servant, or the nature of a servant? By all means, I fancy, the nature of a servant. Thus too the form of God, is the nature of God, and therefore not an energy. Behold also Marcellus of Galatia, Sophronius and Photinus have fallen.

Behold Sabellius too. It is written, " He counted it not a prize to be on an equality with God." Now equality is not predicated, where there is but one person, for that which is equal hath somewhat to which it is equal. Seest thou not the substance of two Persons, and not empty names without things? Hearest thou not the eternal pre-existence of the Only-begotten?

Lastly, What shall we say against Arius,[7] who asserts the Son is of a different substance? Tell me now, what means, " He took the form of a servant "? It means, He became man. Wherefore " being in the form of God," He was God. For one " form " and another " form " is named;

if the one be true, the other is also. "The form of a servant " means, Man by nature, wherefore "the form of God" means, God by nature. And he not only bears record of this, but of His equality too, as John also doth, that he is no way inferior to the Father, for he saith, " He thought it not a thing to seize,[8] to be equal with God." Now what is their wise reasoning? Nay, say they, he proves the very contrary; for he says, that, " being in the form of God, He seized not equality with God." How if He were God, how was He able " to seize upon it "? and is not this without meaning? Who would say that one, being a man, seized not on being a man? for how would any one seize on that which he is? No, say they, but he means that being a little God, He seized not upon being equal to the great God, Who was greater than He. Is there a great and a little God? And do ye bring in the doctrines of the Greeks upon those of the Church? With them there is a great and a little God. If it be so with you, I know not. For you will find it nowhere in the Scriptures: there you will find a great God throughout, a little one nowhere. If He were little, how would he also be God? If man is not little and great, but one nature, and if that which is not of this one nature is not man, how can there be a little God and a great one?

He who is not of that nature is not God. For He is everywhere called great in Scripture; " Great is the Lord, and highly to be praised." (Ps. xlviii. 1.) This is said of the Son also, for it always calls Him Lord. " Thou art great, and doest wondrous things. Thou art God alone." (Ps. lxxxvi. 10.) And again, " Great is our Lord, and great is His power, and of His greatness there is no end." (Ps. cxlv. 3.)

But the Son, he says, is little. But it is thou that sayest this, for the Scripture says the contrary: as of the Father, so it speaks of the Son; for listen to Paul, saying, " Looking for the blessed hope, and appearing of the glory of our great God." (Tit. ii. 13.) But can he have said " appearing " of the Father? Nay, that he may the more convince you, he has added with reference to the appearing of " of the great God." Is it then not said of the Father? By no means. For the sequel suffers it not which says, "The appearing of our great God and Saviour Jesus Christ."[9] See, the Son is great also. How then speakest thou of small and great?

Listen to the Prophet too, calling him " The Messenger[10] of great counsel." (Isa. ix. 6.) " The Messenger of great counsel," is He not great

---

[1] See Euseb. vii. 6. His heresy had been held before by Praxeas; he was himself later than Marcion.

[2] Euseb. iv. 11. Tertullian wrote a treatise against him.

[3] Tert. adv. Marc. i. 6.

[4] Theod. ii. 6, 8. Socr. ii. 19, 20.

[5] Theodoret. v. 11.

[6] Euseb. vii. 27-30.

[7] See St. Ath. Disc. i. c. xi. § 4. [For the various heretics here mentioned, see in Smith's Dict. Christian Biog., or in the Schaff-Herzog Encyc. of Religious Knowledge. — J. A. B.]

[8] [Rev. Ver. " a prize," a thing seized, or a thing to be seized. — J. A. B.]

[9] [Chrys.'s whole argument shows that he understands this passage as here translated, after Rev. Ver. Comp. Ellicott on Titus. — J. A. B.]

[10] See also Jer. xxxii. 18. Some copies of LXX. omit the latter part of Isa. ix. 6, probably because it was not understood.

Himself? "The mighty God," is He small and not great? What mean then these shameless and reckless men when they say, that being little He is a God? I repeat ofttimes what they say, that ye may the more avoid them. He being a lesser God seized not for Himself to be like the greater God! Tell me now (but think not that these words are mine), if he were little, as they say, and far inferior to the Father in power, how could He possibly have seized to Himself equality with God? For an inferior nature could not seize for himself admission into that which is great; for example, a man could not seize on becoming equal to an angel in nature; a horse could not, though he wished it, seize on being equal to a man in nature. But besides all that, I will say this too. What does Paul wish to establish by this example? Surely, to lead the Philippians to humility. To what purpose then did he bring forward this example? For no one who would exhort to humility speaks thus; "Be thou humble, and think less of thyself than of thine equals in honor, for such an one who is a slave has not risen against his master; do thou imitate him." This, any one would say, is not humility, but arrogance.[1] Learn ye what humility is, ye who have a devilish pride! What then is humility? To be lowly minded. And he is lowly minded who humbles himself, not he who is lowly by necessity. To explain what I say; and do ye attend; he who is lowly minded, when he has it in his power to be high minded, is humble, but he who is so because he is not able to be high minded, is no longer humble. For instance, If a King subjects himself to his own officer, he is humble, for he descends from his high estate; but if an officer does so, he will not be lowly minded; for how? he has not humbled himself from any high estate. It is not possible to show humble-mindedness except it be in our power to do otherwise. For if it is necessary for us to be humble even against our will, that excellency comes not from the spirit or the will, but from necessity. This virtue is called humble-mindedness, because it is the humbling of the mind.

If he who has it not in his power to snatch at another's goods, continues in the possession of his own; should we praise him, think you, for his justice? I trow not, and why? The praise of free choice is taken away by the necessity. If he, who has it not in his power to usurp and be a king, remains a private citizen, should we praise him for his quietness? I trow not. The same rule applies here. For praise, O ye most senseless ones, is not given for abstaining from these things, but for the performance of good deeds; for the former is free indeed from blame,

but partakes not yet of praise, while eulogy of the other is meet. Observe accordingly that Christ gives praise on this principle, when He says, "Come, ye blessed of My Father, inherit the kingdom prepared for you from the foundation of the world. For I was an hungered, and ye gave Me meat; I was thirsty, and ye gave Me drink." (Matt. xxv. 34, 35.) He did not say, Because ye have not been covetous, because ye have not robbed; these are slight things; but because "ye saw Me an hungered, and fed Me." Who ever praised either his friends or his enemies in this sort? No one ever praised even Paul. Why say Paul? no one ever praised even a common man, as thou dost praise Christ, because he did not take that rule which was not his due. To admire for such things as this, is to give evidence of much evil. And why? because with evil men this is a matter of praise, as of one that stealeth, if he steal no more; but it is otherwise among good men. (Eph. iv. 28.) Because a man has not seized on a rule and an honor which was not his due, is he praiseworthy? What folly is this?

Attend, I entreat you, for the reasoning is long. Again, who would ever exhort to humility from such grounds as this? Examples ought to be much greater than the subject, to which we are exhorting, for no one will be moved by what is foreign to the subject. For instance, when Christ would lead us to do good to our enemies, He brought a great example, even that of His Father, "For He maketh His sun to rise on the evil and the good, and sendeth rain on the just and the unjust." (Matt. v. 45.) When He would lead to endurance of wrong He brought an example, "Learn of Me, for I am meek and lowly in heart." (Matt. xi. 29.) And again, "If I your Lord and Master do these things, how much more should ye"? (John xiii. 14.) Seest thou how these examples are not distant,[2] for there is no need they should be so distant, for indeed we also do these things, especially as in this case the example is not even near. And how? If He be a servant, He is inferior, and subject to Him that is greater; but this is not lowliness of mind. It was requisite to show the contrary, namely, that the greater person subjected himself to the lesser. But since he found not this distinction in the case of God, between greater and lesser, he made at least an equality. Now if the Son were inferior, this were not a sufficient example to lead us to humility. And why? because it is not humility, for the lesser not to rise against the greater, not to snatch at rule, and to be "obedient unto death."

---

[1] ἀπονοίας. He means either that calling it humility were arrogance, or "this is not a question of humility, but of presumption."

[2] This sentence is difficult, but it seems to mean that the example of our Lord as Man is less evidently "distant" than that given just before, but is still above the lesson; whereas this passage explained as by Arians would be far short of its purpose.

Again, consider what he says after the example, "In lowliness of mind, each counting other better than themselves." (Phil. ii. 3.) He says, "counting," for as ye are one in substance, and in the honor which cometh of God, it follows that the matter is one of estimation. Now in the case of those who are greater and lesser, he would not have said "counting," but honor them that are better than yourselves, as he says in another place, "Obey them that have the rule over you, and submit to them." (Heb. xiii. 17.) In that instance subjection is the result of the nature of the case, in this of our own judgment. "In lowliness of mind," he says, "each counting other better than themselves," as Christ also did.

Thus are their explanations overthrown. It remains that I speak of our own after I have first spoken of theirs summarily. When exhorting to lowliness of mind, Paul would never have brought forward a lesser one, as obedient to a greater. If he were exhorting servants to obey their masters, he might have done so with propriety, but when exhorting the free to obey the free, to what purpose could he bring forward the subjection of a servant to a master? of a lesser to a greater? He says not, "Let the lesser be subject to the greater," but ye who are of equal honor with each other be ye subject, "each counting other better than themselves." Why then did he not bring forward even the obedience of the wife, and say, As the wife obeys her husband, so do ye also obey. Now if he did not bring forward that state in which there is equality and liberty, since in that the subjection is but slight, how much less would he have brought forward the subjection of a slave? I said above, that no one so praises a man for abstaining from evil, nor even mentions him at all ; no one who desires to praise a man for continence would say, he has not committed adultery, but, he has abstained from his own wife ; for we do not consider abstinence from evil as a matter of praise at all, it would be ridiculous.

I said that the "form of a servant" was a true form, and nothing less. Therefore "the form of God" also is perfect, and no less. Why says he not, "being made in the form of God," but "being in the form of God"? This is the same as the saying, "I am that I am." (Ex. iii. 14.) "Form" implies unchangeableness, so far as it is form. It is not possible that things of one substance should have the form of another, as no man has the form of an angel, neither has a beast the form of a man. How then should the Son?

Now in our own case, since we men are of a compound nature, form pertains to the body, but in the case of a simple and altogether uncompounded nature it is of the substance. But if thou contendest that he speaks not of the Father, because the word is used without the article, in many places this is meant, though the word be used without the article. Why say I, in many places? for in this very place he says, "He counted it not a prize to be on an equality with God," using the word without the article, though speaking of God the Father.

I would add our own explanation, but I fear that I shall overwhelm your minds. Meanwhile remember what has been said for their refutation ; meanwhile let us root out the thorns, and then we will scatter the good seed after that the thorns have been rooted out, and a little rest has been given to the land ; that when rid of all the evil thence contracted, it may receive the divine seed with full virtue.

Let us give thanks to God for what has been spoken ; let us entreat Him to grant us the guarding and safe keeping thereof, that both we and ye may rejoice, and the heretics may be put to shame. Let us beseech Him to open our mouth for what follows, that we may with the same earnestness lay down our own views. Let us supplicate Him to vouchsafe us a life worthy of the faith, that we may live to His glory, and that His name may not be blasphemed through us. For, "woe unto you," it is written, "through whom the name of God is blasphemed." (Isa. lii. 5, LXX. nearly.) For if, when we have a son, (and what is there more our own than a son,) if therefore when we have a son, and are blasphemed through him, we publicly renounce him, turn away from him, and will not receive him ; how much more will God, when He has ungrateful servants who blaspheme and insult Him, turn away from them and hate them? And who will take up him whom God hates and turns away from, but the Devil and the demons? And whomsoever the demons take, what hope of salvation is left for him? what consolation in life?

As long as we are in the hand of God, "no one is able to pluck us out" (John x. 28), for that hand is strong ; but when we fall away from that hand and that help, then are we lost, then are we exposed, ready to be snatched away, as a "bowing wall, and a tottering fence" (Ps. lxii. 3) ; when the wall is weak, it will be easy for all to surmount. Think not this which I am about to say refers to Jerusalem alone, but to all men. And what was spoken of Jerusalem? "Now will I sing to my well-beloved a song of my beloved touching His vineyard. My well-beloved hath a vineyard in a very fruitful hill, and I made a fence about it, and surrounded it with a dike, and planted it with the vine of Sorech, and built a tower in the midst of it, and also dug a wine press in it, and I looked that it should bring forth grapes, and it brought forth thorns. And now, O men of Judah and inhabitants of Jerusalem, judge between Me and My vineyard. What should have been done to My vineyard, that I have not done to it? Wherefore, when I looked that it should bring forth grapes, brought it forth thorns? Now therefore I will tell you what I will do to My vineyard: I will take away the hedge thereof, and it shall be for a prey, and I will break down the wall thereof, and it shall be trodden down. And I will leave My vineyard, and it shall not be pruned or digged, but thorns shall come up upon it, as upon a desert land. I will also command the clouds, that they rain no rain upon it. For the vineyard of the Lord of Sabaoth is the house of Israel, and the men of Judah His pleasant plant. I looked that it should do judgment, but it did iniquity, and a cry instead of righteousness." (Isa. v. 1–7, LXX.) This is spoken also of every soul. For when God who loveth man hath done all that is needful, and man then bringeth forth thorns instead of grapes, He will take away the fence, and break down the wall, and we shall be for a prey. For hear what another prophet speaks in his lamentations: "Why hast thou broken down her fences, so that all they which pass by the way do pluck her? The boar out of the wood doth ravage it, and the wild beasts of the field feed on it." (Ps. lxxx. 12, 13.) In the former place He speaks of the Mede and the Babylonian, here nought is said of them, but "the boar," and "the solitary beast" is the Devil and all his host, because of the ferocity and impurity of his disposition. For when it would show us his rapacity, it saith, "As a roaring lion he walketh about, seeking whom he may devour" (1 Pet. v. 8): when his poisonous, his deadly, his destructive nature, it calleth him a snake, and a scorpion; "For tread," saith He, "upon serpents and scorpions, and upon all the power of the enemy" (Luke x. 19): when it would represent his strength as well as his venom, it calleth him a dragon; as when it says, This dragon "whom thou hast formed to take his pastime therein." (Ps. civ. 26.) Scripture everywhere calleth him a dragon, and a crooked serpent, and an adder (Ps. lxxiv. 13, 14); he is a beast of many folds, and varied in his devices, and his strength is great, he moves all things, he disturbs all things, he turns all things up and down. (Isa. xxvii. 1; li. 9; Ezek. xxix. 3; xxxii. 2.) But fear not, neither be afraid; watch only, and he will be as a sparrow; "for," saith He, "tread upon serpents and scorpions." If we will, He causes him to be trodden down under our feet.

See now what scorn is it, yea, what misery, to see him standing over our heads, who has been given to us to tread down. And whence is this?

it is of ourselves. If we choose, he becomes great; and if we choose, he becomes of small power. If we take heed to ourselves, and take up our stand with Him who is our King, he draws himself in, and will be no better than a little child in his warfare against us. Whensoever we stand apart from Him, he puffeth himself up greatly, he uttereth terrible sounds, he grindeth his teeth, because he finds us without our greatest help. For he will not approach to us, except God permit him; for if he dared not to enter into the herd of swine, except by God's permission, how much less into men's souls. But God does permit him, either chastening or punishing us, or making us more approved, as in the case of Job. Seest thou that he came not to him, neither dared to be near him, but trembled and quaked? Why speak I of Job? When he leaped upon Judas, he dared not to seize on him wholly, and to enter into him, until Christ had severed him from the sacred band. He attacked him indeed from without, but he dared not enter in, but when he saw him cut off from that holy flock, he leaped upon him with more than wolfish vehemence, and left him not till he had slain him with a double death.

These things are written for our admonition. What gain have we from knowing that one of the twelve was a traitor? what profit? what advantage? Much. For, when we know whence it was that he arrived at this deadly counsel, we are on our guard that we too suffer not the like. Whence came he to this? From the love of money. He was a thief. For thirty pieces of silver he betrayed his Lord. So drunken was he with the passion, he betrayed the Lord of the world for thirty pieces of silver. What can be worse than this madness? Him to whom nothing is equivalent, nothing is equal, "before whom the nations are as nothing" (Isa. xl. 15), Him did he betray for thirty pieces of silver. A grievous tyrant indeed is the love of gold, and terrible in putting the soul beside itself. A man is not so beside himself through drunkenness[1] as through love of money, not so much from madness and insanity as from love of money.

For tell me, why didst thou betray Him? He called thee, when a man unmarked and unknown. He made thee one of the twelve, He gave thee a share in His teaching, He promised thee ten thousand good things, He caused thee to work wonders, thou wert sharer of the same table, the same journeys, the same company, the same intercourse, as the rest. And were not these things sufficient to restrain thee? For what reason didst thou betray Him? What hadst thou to charge Him with, O wicked one? Rather, what good didst thou not receive at His hands? He knew thy mind, and ceased

---

[1] See on Rom. vii. 11, Hom. xiii., Tr. p. 438.

not to do His part. He often said, "One of you shall betray Me." (Matt. xxvi. 21.) He often marked thee, and yet spared thee, and though He knew thee to be such an one, yet cast thee not out of the band. He still bore with thee, He still honored thee, and loved thee, as a true disciple, and as one of the twelve, and last of all (oh, for thy vileness!), He took a towel, and with His own unsullied hands He washed thy polluted feet, and even this did not keep thee back. Thou didst steal the things of the poor, and that thou mightest not go on to greater sin, He bore this too. Nothing persuaded thee. Hadst thou been a beast, or a stone, wouldest thou not have been changed by these kindnesses towards thee, by these wonders, by these teachings? Though thou wast thus brutalized, yet still He called thee, and by wondrous works He drew thee, thou wast more senseless than a stone, to Himself. Yet for none of these things didst thou become better.

Ye wonder perhaps at such folly of the traitor; dread therefore that which wounded him. He became such from avarice, from the love of money. Cut out this passion, for to these diseases does it give birth; it makes us impious, and causes[1] us to be ignorant of God, though we have received ten thousand benefits at His hands. Cut it out, I entreat you, it is no common disease, it knoweth how to give birth to a thousand destructive deaths. We have seen his tragedy. Let us fear lest we too fall into the same snares. For this is it written, that we too should not suffer the same things. Hence did all the Evangelists relate it, that they might restrain us. Flee then far from it. Covetousness consisteth not alone in the love of much money, but in loving money at all. It is grievous avarice to desire more than we need. Was it talents of gold that persuaded the traitor? For thirty pieces of silver he betrayed his Lord. Do ye not remember what I said before, that covetousness is not shown in receiving much, but rather in receiving little things? See how great a crime he committed for a little gold, rather not for gold, but for pieces of silver.

It cannot, it cannot be that an avaricious man should ever see the face of Christ! This is one of the things which are impossible. It is a root of evils, and if he that possesses one evil thing, falls from that glory, where shall he stand who bears with him the root? He who is the servant of money cannot be a true servant of Christ. Christ Himself hath declared that the thing is impossible. "Ye cannot," He says, "serve God and Mammon," and, "No man can serve two masters" (Matt. vi. 24), for they lay upon us contrary orders. Christ says, "Spare the poor";

Mammon says, "Even from the naked[2] strip off the things they have." Christ says, "Empty thyself of what thou hast"; Mammon says, "Take also what thou hast not." Seest thou the opposition, seest thou the strife? How is it that a man cannot easily obey both, but must despise one? Nay, does it need proof? How so? Do we not see in very deed, that Christ is despised, and Mammon honored? Perceive ye not how that the very words are painful? How much more then the thing itself? But it does not appear so painful in reality, because we are possessed with the disease. Now if the soul be but a little cleansed of the disease, as long as it remains here, it can judge right; but when it departs elsewhere, and is seized by the fever, and is engaged in the pleasure of the thing, it hath not its perception clear, it hath not its tribunal uncorrupt. Christ says, "Whosoever he be of you that renounceth not all that he hath, he cannot be My disciple" (Luke xiv. 33); Mammon says, "Take bread from the hungry." Christ says, "Cover the naked" (Isa. lviii. 7); the other says, "Strip the naked." Christ says, "Thou shalt not hide thyself from thine own flesh," (Isa. lviii. 7) and those of thine own house;[3] Mammon says,[4] "Thou shalt not pity those of thine own seed; though thou seest thy mother or thy father in want, despise them." Why say I father or mother? "Even thine own soul," he says, "destroy it also." And he is obeyed! Alas! he who commands us cruel, and mad, and brutal things, is listened to rather than He who bids us gentle and healthful things! For this is hell appointed; for this, fire; for this, a river of fire; for this, a worm that dieth not.

I know that many hear me say these things with pain, and indeed it is not without pain I say them. But why need I say these things? I could wish the things concerning the kingdom to be ever my discourse, of the rest, of the waters of rest, of the green pastures, as the Scripture says, "He maketh me to lie down in green pastures, He leadeth me beside the still waters" (Ps. xxiii. 2), there He maketh me to dwell. I could wish to speak of the place, whence "sorrow and sighing shall flee away." (Isa. li. 11.)

I could wish to discourse of the pleasures of being with Christ, though they pass all expression and all understanding. Yet would I speak of these things according to my power. But what shall I do? it is not possible to speak concerning a kingdom[5] to one that is diseased and in fever; then we must needs speak of health.

[1] παρασκευάζει, which, when used without a preposition, is more immediate than "prepares."

[2] [So the best group of MSS. Field retains from the editions the feebler phrase of the altered text, "Mammon says, Strip off even the things they have." To strip even the naked is a phrase quite in Chrys.'s vein. — J. A. B.]
[3] See 1 Tim. v. 8, and Gal. vi. 10.   [4] See Mark vii. 11.
[5] He means an earthly kingdom in the first instance.

It is not possible to speak of honor to one that is brought to trial, for at that time his desire is that he be freed from judgment, and penalty, and punishment. If this be not effected, how shall the other be? It is for this cause that I am continually speaking of these things, that we may the sooner pass over to those other. For this cause does God threaten hell, that none may fall into hell, that we all may obtain the kingdom; for this cause we too make mention continually of hell, that we may thrust you onward towards the kingdom, that when we have softened your minds by fear, we may bring you to act worthily of the kingdom. Be not then displeased at the heaviness of our words, for the heaviness of these words lightens our souls from sin.[1] Iron is heavy, and the hammer is heavy, but it forms vessels fit for use, both of gold and silver, and straightens things which are crooked; and if it were not heavy, it would have no power to straighten the distorted substance. Thus too our heavy speech has power to bring the soul into its proper tone. Let us not then flee from heaviness of speech, nor the strokes it gives; the stroke is not given that it may break in pieces or tear the soul, but to straighten it. We know how we strike, how by the grace of God we inflict the stroke, so as not to crush the vessel, but to polish it, to render it straight, and meet for the Master's use, to offer it glittering in soundness, skillfully wrought against that Day of the river of fire, to offer it having no need of that burning pile. For if we expose not ourselves to fire here, we must needs be burned there, it cannot be otherwise; "For the day of the Lord is revealed by fire." (1 Cor. iii. 13.) Better is it that ye be burned for a little space by our words, than for ever in that flame. That this will indeed be so, is plain, and I have ofttimes given you reasons[3] which cannot be gainsaid. We ought truly to be persuaded from the Scriptures, but forasmuch as some are contentious, we have also brought forward many arguments from reason. Nothing hinders that I now mention them, and what were they? God is just. We all acknowledge this, both Greeks and Jews, and Heretics, and Christians. But many sinners have had their departure without punishment, many righteous men have had their departure after suffering ten thousand grievous things. If then God be just, where will He reward their good to the one, and their punishment to the other, if there be no hell, if there be no resurrection? This reason then do ye constantly repeat[4] to them and to yourselves, and it will not suffer you to disbelieve the resurrection, and whoso disbelieves not the resurrection will take care to live with all heed so as to obtain eternal happiness, of which may we all be counted worthy, by the grace and lovingkindness of our Lord Jesus Christ, with whom, &c.

HOMILY VII.

PHILIPPIANS ii. 5–11.

"Have this mind in you which was also in Christ Jesus: who, being in the form of God, counted it not a prize to be on an equality with God; but emptied Himself, taking upon Him the form of a servant, being made in the likeness of men: and being found in fashion as a man, He humbled Himself, becoming obedient unto death, yea, the death of the cross. Wherefore also God highly exalted Him, and gave Him the Name which is above every name: that in the Name of Jesus every knee should bow, of things in heaven, and things on earth, and things under the earth; and that every tongue should confess that Jesus Christ is Lord, to the glory of God the Father."

I HAVE stated the views of[2] the heretics. It is befitting that I now speak of what is our own. They say that the words, "He counted it not a prize," are of wrongfully seizing.[5] We have proved, that this is altogether vapid and impertinent, for no man would exhort another to humility on such grounds, nor in this sort does he praise God, or even man. What is it then, beloved? Give heed to what I now say. Since many men think, that, when they are lowly, they are deprived of their proper right, and debased, Paul, to take away this fear, and to show that we must not be affected thus, says that God, the only begotten, who was in the form of God, who was no whit inferior to the Father, who was equal to Him, "counted it not a prize to be on an equality with God."

Now learn what this meaneth. Whatsoever a man robs, and takes contrary to his right, he

---

[1] Al. "is the very thing that gives occasion to our souls to fly from sins."
[2] [So Field, after the Catena alone, instead of "I have said all that pertains to the heretics" (παρὰ, περὶ). The text of Field looks strange at first, but well suits what follows, and so is probably correct. —J. A. B.]

[3] See on Rom. xvi. 16, Hom. xxxi., Tr. p. 556.
[4] κατεπᾴδετε, sing as a charm.
[5] Meaning, "He thought it not a robbery for himself to commit." The phrase being always used in the sense of "a gain." Our language does not seem capable of expressing it exactly.

dares not lay aside, from fear lest it perish, and fall from his possession, but he keeps hold of it continually.   He who possesses some dignity which is natural to him, fears not to descend from that dignity, being assured that nothing of this sort will happen to him.   As for example, Absalom usurped the government, and dared not afterwards to lay it aside.   We will go to another example, but if example cannot present the whole matter to you, take it not amiss, for this is the nature of examples, they leave the greater part for the imagination to reason out. A man rebels against his sovereign, and usurps the kingdom : he dares not lay aside and hide the matter, for if he once hide it, straightway it is gone.   Let us also take another example ; if a man takes anything violently, he keeps firm hold of it continually, for if he lay it down, he straightway loses it.   And generally speaking, they who have aught by rapine are afraid to lay it by, or hide it, or not to keep constantly in that state which they have assumed.   Not so they, who have possessions not procured by rapine, as Man, who possesses the dignity of being a reasonable being.   But here examples fail me, for there is no natural preëminence amongst us, for no good thing is naturally our own ; but they are inherent in the nature of God.   What does one say then?   That the Son of God feared not to descend from His right, for He thought not Deity a prize seized.   He was not afraid that any would strip Him of that nature or that right, Wherefore He laid it[1] aside, being confident that He should take it up again. He hid it, knowing that He was not made inferior by so doing.   For this cause, Paul says not, " He seized not," but, " He counted it not a prize " ; He possessed not that estate by seizure, but it was natural, not conferred,[2] it was enduring and safe.   Wherefore he refused not to take the form of an inferior.[3]   The tyrant fears to lay aside the purple robe in war, while the king does it with much safety.   Why so? because he holds his power not as a matter of seizure. He did not refuse to lay it aside, as one who had usurped it, but since He had it as His own by nature, since it could never be parted from Him, He hid it.

This equality with God He had not by seizure, but as his own by nature.   Wherefore " He emptied Himself."   Where be they who affirm, that He underwent constraint, that He was subjected?   Scripture says, " He emptied Himself, He humbled Himself, and became obedient unto death."   How did He empty Himself?   By taking " the form of a servant, being made in the

likeness of men, and being found in fashion as a man."   It is written, " He emptied Himself" in reference to the text, " each counting other better than himself."   Since had He been subjected, had He not chosen it of His own accord, and of His own free will, it would not have been an act of humility.   For if He knew not that so it must be, He would have been imperfect.   If, not knowing it, He had waited for the time of action, then would He not have known the season.   But if He both knew that so it must be, and when it must be, wherefore should He submit to be subjected?   To show, they say, the superiority of the Father.   But this shows not the superiority of the Father, but His own inferiority.   For is not the name of the Father sufficient to show the priority of the Father?   For apart from Him, the son has all the same things. For this honor is not capable of passing from the Father to the Son.

What then say the heretics?   See, say they, He did not become man.   The Marcionites, I mean.[4]   But why?   He was " made in the likeness of man."   But how can one be " made in the likeness of men "?   by putting on a shadow? But this is a phantom, and no longer the likeness of a man, for the likeness of a man is another man.   And what wilt thou answer to John, when he says, " The Word became flesh "?   (John i. 14.)   But this same blessed one himself also says in another place, " in the likeness of sinful flesh."   (Rom. viii. 3.)

" And being found in fashion as a man."   See, they say, both " in fashion," and " as a man."   To be as a man, and to be a man in fashion, is not to be a man indeed.   To be a man in fashion is not to be a man by nature.   See with what ingenuousness I lay down what our enemies say, for that is a brilliant victory, and amply gained, when we do not conceal what seem to be their strong points.   For this is deceit rather than victory.   What then do they say? let me repeat their argument.   To be a man in fashion is not to be a man by nature ; and to be as a man, and in the fashion of a man, this is not to be a man. So then to take the form of a servant, is not to take the form[5] of a servant.   Here then is an inconsistency ; and wherefore do you not first of all solve this difficulty?   For as you think that this contradicts us, so do we say that the other contradicts you.   He says not, " as the form of a servant," nor " in the likeness of the form of a servant," nor " in the fashion of the form of a servant," but " He took the form of a servant." What then is this? for there is a contradiction. There is no contradiction.   God forbid ! it is a cold and ridiculous argument of theirs.   He

---

[1] The word is neuter, and refers only to " right " (ἀξίωμα). Some copies omit " nature."

[2] δεδομένην, which would imply an " act " of giving.

[3] ὑπασπιστῶν, a soldier of the ranks, who attended on an officer. Herod. v. 111.   Xen. Anab. iv. 2, 21.

[4] [These dramatic and characteristic utterances are smoothed down in the altered text. — J. A. B.]

[5] Old Lat. " nature."

took, say they, the form of a servant, when He girded Himself with a towel, and washed the feet of His disciples. Is this the form of a servant? Nay, this is not the form, but the work of a servant. It is one thing that there should be the work of a servant, and another to take the form of a servant. Why did he not say, He did the work of a servant, which were clearer? But nowhere in Scripture is "form" put for "work," for the difference is great: the one is the result of nature, the other of action. In common speaking, too, we never use "form" for "work." Besides, according to them, He did not even take the work of a servant, nor even gird Himself. For if all was a mere shadow,[1] there was no reality. 'If He had not real hands, how did He wash their feet? If He had not real loins, how did He gird Himself with a towel? and what kind of garments did he take? for Scripture says, "He took His garments." (John xiii. 12.) So then not even the work is found to have really taken place, but it was all a deception, nor did He even wash the disciples. For if that incorporeal nature did not appear, it[2] was not in a body. Who then washed the disciples' feet?

Again, what in opposition to Paul of Samosata? for what did he affirm? The very same. But it is no emptying of Himself, that one who is of human nature, and a mere man, should wash his fellow-servants. For what we said against the Arians, we must repeat against these too, for they differ not from one another, save by a little space of time; both the one and the other affirm the Son of God to be a creature. What then shall we say to them? If He being a man washed man, He emptied not, He humbled not Himself. If He being a man seized not on being equal with God, He is not deserving of praise. That God should become man, is great, unspeakable, inexpressible humility; but what humility is there in that one, who was a man, should do the works of men? And where is the work of God ever called "the form of God"? for if he were a mere man, and was called the form of God by reason of His works, why do we not do the same of Peter, for he wrought greater deeds than Christ Himself? Why say you not of Paul, that he had the form of God? Why did not Paul give an example of himself, for he wrought a thousand servile works, and did not even refuse to say, "For we preach not ourselves, but Christ Jesus as Lord, and ourselves as your servants for Jesus' sake." (2 Cor. iv. 5.) These are absurdities and trifles! Scripture

says, He "emptied Himself." How did He empty Himself? tell me. What was His emptying? what His humiliation? was it because He wrought wonders? This both Paul and Peter did, so that this was not peculiar to the Son. What then means, "Being made in the likeness of men"? He had many things belonging to us, and many He had not; for instance, He was not born of wedlock. He did no sin. These things had He which no man has. He was not what he seemed only, but He was God also; He seemed to be a man, but He was not like the mass of men. For He was like them in flesh. He means then, that He was not a mere man. Wherefore he says, "in the likeness of men." For we indeed are soul and body, but He was God, and soul and body, wherefore he says, "in the likeness." For lest when you hear that He emptied Himself, you should think that some change, and degeneracy, and loss is here; he says, whilst He remained what He was, He took that which He was not, and being made flesh He remained God, in that He was the Word. (John i. 14.)

In this then He was like man, and for this cause Paul says, "and in fashion." Not that His nature degenerated, nor that any confusion arose, but He became man in fashion. For when He had said that "He took the form of a servant," he made bold[3] to say this also, seeing that the first would silence all objectors; since when he says, "In the likeness of sinful flesh," he says not that He had not flesh, but that that flesh sinned not, but was like to sinful flesh. Like in what? in nature, not in sin, therefore was His like a sinful soul. As then in the former case the term similarity was used, because He was not equal in everything, so here also there is similarity, because He is not equal in everything, as His not being born of wedlock, His being without sin, His being not a mere man. •And he well said "as a man," for He was not one of the many, but "as" one of the many. The Word who was God did not degenerate into man, nor was His substance changed, but appeared as a man; not to delude us with a phantom, but to instruct us in humility. When therefore he says, "as a man," this is what He means; since he calls Him a man elsewhere also, when he says, "there is one God, one Mediator also between God and men, Himself man, Christ Jesus." (1 Tim. ii. 5.)

Thus much against these heretics. I must now speak against such as deny that He took a soul.[4] If "the form of God" is "perfect God," then the "form of a servant" is "a perfect servant." Again, against the Arians. Here concerning His

---

[1] [He refers to the various Docetic theories, that the body of Christ was only an appearance. — J. A. B.]

[2] Or He. The sense is difficult. Old Lat. "For if He was an incorporeal being, He was not seen, He was not in a body." Ben. Lat. omits the first "not," and has "and was not," but without Greek authority.

[3] i.e. without fear of giving countenance to the Docetæ or Marcionites, as he had used so strong an expression of reality; or as on the next page.

[4] The Apollinarian heresy.

divinity, we no longer find "He became," "He took," but "He emptied Himself, taking the form of a servant, being made in the likeness of men"; here concerning his humanity we find "He took, He became." He became the latter, He took the latter; He was the former. Let us not then confound nor divide the natures. There is one God, there is one Christ, the Son of God; when I say "One," I mean a union, not a confusion; the one Nature did not degenerate into the other, but was united with it.

"He humbled Himself, becoming obedient unto death, yea, the death of the cross." See, says one, He voluntarily became obedient; he was not equal to Him whom He obeyed. O ye obstinate ones and unwise! This doth not at all lower Him. For we too become obedient to our friends, yet this has no effect. He became obedient as a Son to His Father; He fell not thus into a servile state, but by this very act above all others guarded his wondrous Sonship, by thus greatly honoring the Father. He honored the Father, not that thou shouldest dishonor Him, but that thou shouldest the rather admire Him, and learn from this act, that He is a true Son, in honoring His Father more than all besides. No one hath thus honored God. As was His height, such was the correspondent humiliation which He underwent. As He is greater than all, and no one is equal to Him, so in honoring His Father, He surpassed all, not by necessity, nor unwillingly, but this too is part of His excellence; yea, words fail me. Truly it is a great and unspeakable thing, that He became a servant; that He underwent death, is far greater; but there is something still greater, and more strange; why? All deaths are not alike; His death seemed to be the most ignominious of all, to be full of shame, to be accursed; for it is written, "Cursed is every one that hangeth on a tree." (Deut. xxi. 23; Gal. iii. 13.) For this cause the Jews also eagerly desired to slay Him in this manner, to make Him a reproach, that if no one fell away from Him by reason of His death, yet they might from the manner of His death. For this cause two robbers were crucified with Him, and He in the midst, that He might share their ill repute, and that the Scripture might be fulfilled, "And he was numbered with the transgressors." (Isa. liii. 12.) Yet so much the more doth truth shine forth, so much the more doth it become bright; for when His enemies plot such things against His glory, and it yet shines forth, so much the greater does the matter seem. Not by slaying Him, but by slaying Him in such sort did they think to make Him abominable, to prove Him more abominable than all men, but they availed nothing. And both the robbers also were such impious ones, (for it was afterward that the one repented,)

that, even when on the cross, they reviled Him; neither the consciousness of their own sins, nor their present punishment, nor their suffering the same things themselves, restrained their madness. Wherefore the one spake to the other, and silenced him by saying, "Dost thou not even fear God, seeing thou art in the same condemnation?" (Luke xxiii. 40.) So great was their wickedness. Wherefore it is written, "God also highly exalted Him, and gave Him the Name which is above every name." When the blessed Paul hath made mention of the flesh, he fearlessly speaks of all His humiliation. For until he had mentioned that He took the form of a servant, and while he was speaking of His Divinity, behold how loftily he doth it, (loftily, I say, according to his power; for he speaks not according to His own worthiness, seeing that he is not able). "Being in the form of God, He counted it not a prize to be equal with God." But when he had said, that He became Man, henceforth he fearlessly discourseth of His low estate, being confident that the mention of His low estate would not harm His Divinity, since His flesh admitted this.

Ver. 9–11. "Wherefore also God highly exalted Him, and gave Him the Name which is above every name: that in the Name of Jesus every knee should bow, of things in heaven, and things in earth, and things under the earth; and that every tongue should confess that Jesus Christ is Lord, to the glory of God the Father." Let us say against the heretics, If this is spoken of one who was not incarnate, if of God the Word, how did He highly exalt Him? Was it as if He gave Him something more than He had before? He would then have been imperfect in this point, and would have been made perfect for our sakes. For if He had not done good deeds to us, He would not have obtained that honor! "And gave Him the Name." See, He had not even a name, as you say! But how, if He received it as His due, is He found here to have received it by grace, and as a gift? And that "the Name which is above every name": and of what kind, let us see, is the Name? "That at the Name of Jesus," saith He, "every knee should bow." They (the heretics) explain name by glory. This glory then is above all glory, and this glory is in short that all worship Him! But ye hold yourselves far off from the greatness of God, who think that ye know God, as He knoweth Himself, and from this it is plain, how far off ye are from right thoughts of God. And this is plain from hence. Is this, tell me, glory? Therefore before men were created, before the angels or the archangels, He was not in glory. If this be the glory which is above every glory, (for this is the name that is "above every name,") though He were in glory before, yet was He in glory inferior to this. It was for this then that He made the things that are, that He might be raised to glory, not from His own goodness, but because He required glory from us ! See ye not their folly? see ye not their impiety?

Now if they had said this of Him that was incarnate, there had been reason, for God the Word allows that this be said of His flesh. It touches not His divine nature, but has to do altogether with the dispensation. What means " of things in heaven, and things in the earth, and things under the earth "? It means the whole world, and angels, and men, and demons ; or that both the just and the living and sinners,

"And every tongue," should "confess that Jesus Christ is Lord, to the glory of God the Father." That is, that all should say so ; and this is glory to the Father. Seest thou how wherever the Son is glorified, the Father is also glorified? Thus too when the Son is dishonored, the Father is dishonored also. If this be so with us, where the difference is great between fathers and sons, much more in respect of God, where there is no difference, doth honor and insult pass on to Him. If the world be subjected to the Son, this is glory to the Father. And so when we say that He is perfect, wanting nothing, and not inferior to the Father, this is glory to the Father, that he begat such a one. This is a great proof of His power also, and goodness, and wisdom, that He begat one no whit inferior, neither in wisdom nor in goodness. When I say that He is wise as the Father, and no whit inferior, this is a proof of the great wisdom of the Father ; when I say that He is powerful as the Father, this is a proof of the Father's power. When I say that He is good as the Father,· this is the greatest evidence of His goodness, that He begat such (a Son), in no whit less or inferior to Himself. When I say that He begat Him not inferior in substance but equal, and not of another substance, in this I again wonder at God, His power, and goodness, and wisdom, that He hath manifested to us another, of Himself, such as Himself, except in His not being the Father. Thus whatsoever great things I say of the Son, pass on to the Father. Now if this small and light matter (for it is but a light thing to God's glory that the world should worship Him) is to the glory of God, how much more so are all those other things?

Let us then believe to His glory, let us live to His glory, for one is no use without the other ; when we glorify Him rightly, but live not rightly, then do we especially insult Him, because we are enrolled under Him as a Master and Teacher, and yet despise Him, and stand in no dread of that fearful judgment seat. It is no wonder that the heathen live impurely ; this merits not such condemnation. But that Christians, who

partake in such great mysteries, who enjoy so great glory, that they should live thus impurely, this is worst of all, and unbearable. For tell me ; He was obedient to the uttermost, wherefore He received the honor which is on high. He became a servant, wherefore He is Lord of all, both of Angels, and of all other. Let us too not suppose then that we descend from what is our due, when we humble ourselves. For thus may we be more highly exalted ; and with reason ; then do we especially become admirable. For that the lofty man is really low, and that the lowly man is exalted, the sentence of Christ sufficiently declares. Let us however examine the matter itself. What is it to be humbled? Is it not to be blamed, to be accused, and calumniated? What is it to be exalted? It is to be honored, to be praised, to be glorified. Well. Let us see how the matter is. Satan was an angel, he exalted himself. What then? was he not humbled beyond all other? has he not the earth as his place? is he not condemned and accused by all? Paul was a man, and humbled himself. What then? is he not admired? is he not praised? is he not lauded? is he not the friend of Christ? Wrought he not greater things than Christ? did he not ofttimes command the devil as a captive slave? did he not carry him about as an executioner?[1] did he not hold him up to scorn? held he not his head bruised under his feet? did he not with much boldness beg of God that others too might do the same? Why am I saying? Absalom exalted himself, David humbled himself ; which of the twain was raised up, which became glorious? For what could be a more evident proof of humility than these words which that blessed Prophet spoke of Shimei, " Let him curse, for the Lord hath bidden him." (2 Sam. xvi. 11.) And if you please, we will examine the very cases themselves.[2] The Publican humbled himself, although the case can hardly be called humility ; but how? He answered in a right-minded manner. The Pharisee exalted himself. What then? let us also examine the matters. Let there be two men, both rich, and highly honored, and elevated by wisdom and power, and other worldly advantages ; then let one of them seek honor from all, let him be angry if he receive it not, let him require more than is due and exalt himself ; let the other despise the whole matter, bear himself unkindly towards no one on this account, and evade honor when offered to him. For it is not possible to obtain

---

[1] See on 1 Tim. i. 20, Hom. v. (2), where he says that Satan seems to have been " forced " to execute judgment.

[2] [This somewhat obscure sentence is omitted in the Oxford tr., on the authority of one MS., with brackets in Savile's edition. The tr. was much influenced by this MS., which is in the British Museum. and had been collated for him ; but Field's digest shows that it belongs to an inferior group, though its individual readings sometimes commend themselves, and especially its readings when supported by the Catena. The tr. calls it B, Field calls it C. — J. A. B.]

glory any other way than by fleeing from glory, for as long as we pursue it, it flies from us, but when we flee from it, then it pursues us. If thou wouldest be glorious, do not desire glory. If thou wouldest be lofty, do not make thyself lofty. And further, all honor him who does not grasp at honor, but spurn him who seeks it. For the human race somehow or other is fond of contention, and leans to contrary feeling. Let us therefore despise glory, for thus we shall be enabled to become lowly, or rather to become exalted. Exalt not thyself, that thou mayest be exalted by another; he that is exalted by himself is not exalted by others, he who is humbled by himself is not humbled by others. Haughtiness is a great evil, it is better to be a fool than haughty; for in the one case, the folly is only a perversion of intellect, but in the other case it is still worse, and is folly joined with madness : the fool is an evil to himself; but the haughty man is a plague to others too. This misery comes of senselessness. One cannot be haughty-minded without being a fool; and he that is brimfull of folly is haughty.

Listen to the Wise Man, who says, "I saw a man wise in his own conceit; there is more hope of a fool than of him." (Prov. xxvi. 12.) Seest thou how it was not without reason I said, that the evil of which I am speaking is worse than that of folly, for it is written, "There is more hope of a fool than of him"? Wherefore, Paul too said, "Be not wise in your own conceits." (Rom. xii. 16.) Tell me what description of bodies do we say are in good health, those which are much inflated, and are inwardly full of much air and water, or those which are kept low, and have their surface such as marks restraint? It is manifest that we should choose the latter. So, too with the soul, that which is puffed up has a worse disease than dropsy, whilst that which is under restraint is freed from all evil. How great then are the good things which lowliness of mind bringeth to us ! What wouldest thou have? For-bearance? freedom from anger? love to our fel-low-men? soberness? attentiveness? All these good things spring from lowly-mindedness, and their contraries from haughtiness : the haughty man must needs be also insolent, a brawler, wrathful, bitter, sullen, a beast rather than a man. Art thou strong, and proud thereat? Thou shouldest rather be humble on this ac-count. Why art thou proud for a thing of nought? For even a lion is bolder than thou, a wild boar is stronger, and thou art not even as a fly in comparison with them. Robbers too, and violaters of tombs, and gladiators, and even thine own slaves, and those perchance who are more stupid still, are stronger than thou. Is this then a fit subject for praise? Art thou proud of such a matter? Bury thyself for shame !

But art thou handsome and beautiful? This is the boast of crows ! Thou art not fairer than the peacock, as regards either its color or its plumage ; the bird beats thee in plumage, it far surpasseth thee in its feathers and in its color. The swan too is passing fair, and many other birds, with whom if thou art compared thou wilt see that thou art nought. Often too worth-less boys, and unmarried girls, and harlots, and effeminate men have had this boast ; is this then a cause for haughtiness? But art thou rich? Whence so? what hast thou? Gold, silver, precious stones ! This is the boast of robbers also, of man-slayers, of those who work in the mines. That which is the labor of criminals becomes to thee a boast ! But dost thou adorn and deck thyself out? Well, we may see horses also decked out, and among the Persians camels too, and as for men, all those who are about the stage. Art thou not ashamed to boast thyself of these things, if unreasoning animals, and slaves, and man-slayers, and effeminate, and robbers, and violaters of tombs, share with thee? Dost thou build splendid palaces? and what of this? Many jackdaws dwell in more splendid houses, and have more noble retreats. Dost thou not see how many, who were mad after money, have built houses in fields and desert places, that are retreats for jackdaws? But art thou proud on account of thy voice. Thou canst by no means sing with clearer and sweeter tones than the swan or the nightingale. Is it for thy varied knowledge of arts? But what is wiser than the bee in this ; what embroiderer, what painter, what geometrician, can imitate her works? Is it for the fineness of thy apparel? But here the spiders beat thee. Is it for the swiftness of thy feet? Again the first prize is with unreasoning animals, the hare, and the gazelle, and all the beasts[1] which are not want-ing in swiftness of foot. Hast thou traveled much? Not more than the birds; their transit is more easily made, they have no need of pro-visions for the way, nor beasts of burden, for their wings are all-sufficient for them ; this is their vessel, this their beast of burden, this their car, this is even their wind, in short, all that a man can name. But art thou clear sighted? Not as the gazelle ; not as the eagle. Art thou quick of hearing? the ass is more so. Of scent? the hound suffers thee not to surpass him. Art thou a good provider? yet thou art inferior to the ant. Dost thou gather gold? Yet not as the Indian ants. Art thou proud because of thy health? Unreasoning creatures are far better than we both in habit of body, and in indepen-dence ; they fear no poverty. "Behold the

---

[1] ἀπολείπεται is better with a word after it, read perhaps πτηνῶν, "and the beasts that are not left behind by the birds for swiftness of foot."

birds of the heaven, that they sow not, neither do they reap, nor gather into barns." (Matt. vi. 26.) "And surely," He means, "God has not created the irrational animals superior to ourselves." Dost thou mark what want of consideration is here? Dost thou observe the lack of all investigation? Dost thou observe the great advantage which we derive from an investigation of the points? He, whose mind is lifted up above all men, is found to be even lower than the irrational creatures.

But we will have pity upon him, and not follow his example; nor because the limits of our mortal nature are too narrow for his conceit of himself, will we proceed to lower him to the level of the beasts that are without reason, but will lift him up from thence, not for his own sake, for he deserves no better fate, but that we may set forth the lovingkindness of God, and the honor which He has vouchsafed us. For there are things, yes, there are things wherein the irrational animals have no participation with us. And of what sort are these? Piety, and a life based on virtue. Here thou canst never speak of fornicators, nor of effeminate persons, nor of murderers, for from them we have been severed. And what then is this which is found here? We know God, His Providence we acknowledge, and are embued with true philosophy concerning immortality. Here let the irrational animals give place. They cannot contend with us in these points. We live in self-command.[1] Here the irrational animals have nothing in common with us. For, while coming behind all of them, we exercise dominion over them; for herein lies the superiority of our dominion, that, while coming behind them, we yet reign over them : that thou mightest be instructed that the cause of these things is, not thyself, but God who made thee, and gave thee reason. We set nets and toils for them, we drive them in, and they are at our mercy.

Self-command, a compliant temper, mildness, contempt of money, are prerogatives of our

race; but since thou who art one o those blinded by presumption hast none of these, thou doest well in entertaining notions either above the level of mankind, or beneath the very irrational creatures. For this is the nature of folly and of audacity; it is either unduly elevated, or on the other hand it is equally depressed, never observing a proper proportion. We are equal to angels in this respect, that we have a Kingdom pledged to us, the choir,[2] unto which Christ is joined. He that is a man may be scourged, yet does he not succumb. A man laughs at death, is a stranger to fear and trembling, he does not covet more than he has. So that they all who are not like this are beneath the irrational animals. For when in the things of the body thou wouldest have the advantage, but hast no advantage in the things that concern the soul, how art thou aught else than inferior to the irrational animals? For bring forward one of the vicious and unthinking, of those that are living in excess and to self. The horse surpasses him in warlike spirit, the boar in strength, the hare in swiftness, the peacock in grace, the swan in fineness of voice, the elephant in size, the eagle in keenness of sight, all birds in wealth. Whence then dost thou derive thy title to rule the irrational creatures? from reason? But thou hast it not? For whosoever ceases to make a due use of it, is again inferior to them; for when though possessing reason he is more irrational than they, it had been better if he had never from the first become capable of exercising reason. For it is not the same thing after having received dominion to betray the trust, as to let pass the season to receive it. That sovereign, who is below the level of his guards, had better never have had on the purple. And it is the very self-same thing in this case. Knowing then that without virtue we are inferior to the very irrational animals, let us exercise ourselves therein, that we may become men, yea rather angels, and that we may enjoy the promised blessings, through the grace and lovingkindness of our Lord Jesus Christ, with whom, &c.

---

[1] σωφρονοῦμεν. The word may be used of sobriety, chastity, or moderation.

[2] ἡ μετὰ Χ χορεία, see Rev. xiv. 4.

HOMILY VIII.

PHILIPPIANS ii. 12–16.

"So then, my beloved, even as ye have always obeyed, not as in my presence only, but now much more in my absence, work out your own salvation with fear and trembling; for it is God which worketh in you both to will and to work for His good pleasure. Do all things without murmurings and disputings: that ye may be blameless and harmless, children of God without blemish in the midst of a crooked and perverse generation, among whom ye are seen as lights in the world, holding forth the word of life; that I may have whereof to glory in the day of Christ."

THE admonitions which we give ought to be accompanied with commendations; for thus they become even welcome, when we refer those whom we admonish to that measure of zeal which they have themselves exhibited; as Paul, for instance, did here; and observe with what singular discretion; "So then, my beloved," he says; he did not say simply "be obedient," not until he had first commended them in these words, "even as ye have always obeyed"; i.e. "it is not other men, but your own selves, whom I bid you take example by." "Not as in my presence only, but much more in my absence." And why, "much more in my absence"? "Ye seemed perhaps at that time to be doing everything out of respect to me, and from a principle of shame, but that is no longer so; if then ye make it evident that ye now strive more earnestly, it is also made evident that neither then was it done out of consideration to me, but for God's sake." Tell me, what wouldest thou? "not that ye give heed to me, but that ye 'work out your own salvation with fear and trembling'"; for it is impossible for one, who lives devoid of fear, to set forth any high or commanding example; and he said not merely "with fear," but "and with trembling," which is an excessive degree of fear. Such fear had Paul: and therefore he said, I fear "lest having preached to others, I myself should be rejected." (1 Cor. ix. 27.) For if without the aid of fear temporal things can never be achieved, how much less spiritual matters; for I desire to know, who ever learnt his letters without fear? who has become a proficient in any art, without fear? But if, when the devil does not lie in the way, where indolence is the only obstacle, so much of fear is necessary merely in order that we may master that indolence which is natural to us; where there is so fierce a war, so great hindrances, how can we by any possibility be saved without fear?

And how may this fear be produced? If we but consider that God is everywhere present, heareth all things, seeth all things, not only whatsoever is done and said, but also all that is in the heart, and in the depth of the soul, for He is "quick to discern the thoughts and intents of the heart" (Heb. iv. 12), if we so dispose ourselves, we shall not do or say or imagine aught that is evil. Tell me, if thou hadst to stand constantly near the person of a ruler, wouldest not thou stand there with fear? and how standing in God's presence, dost thou laugh and throw thyself back, and not conceive fear and dread? Let it never be that thou despisest His patient endurance, for it is to bring thee to repentance that He is longsuffering. Whenever thou eatest, consider that God is present, for He *is* present; whenever thou art preparing to sleep, or giving way to passion, if thou art robbing another, or indulging in luxury, or whatever thou art about, thou wilt never fall into laughter, never be inflamed with rage. If this be thy thought continually, thou wilt continually be in "fear and trembling," forasmuch as thou art standing beside the King. The architect, though he be experienced, though he be perfectly master of his art, yet stands with "fear and trembling," lest he fall down from the building. Thou too hast believed, thou hast performed many good deeds, thou hast mounted high: secure thyself, be in fear as thou standest, and keep a wary eye, lest thou fall thence. For manifold are the spiritual sorts of wickedness which aim to cast thee down. (Eph. vi. 12.) "Serve the Lord with fear," he says, "and rejoice unto Him with trembling." (Ps. ii. 11.) And how is rejoicing compatible with "trembling"? Yet this, be assured, is the only rejoicing; for when we perform some good work, and such as beseemeth those who do anything "with trembling," then only do we rejoice. "Work out your own salvation with fear and trembling": he says not "work," but "work out," i.e. with much earnestness, with much diligence; but as he had said, "with fear and trembling," see how he relieves their anxiety: for what does he say? "It is God that worketh in you." Fear not because I said, "with fear and trembling." I said it not with this view, that thou shouldest give up in despair, that thou shouldest suppose virtue to be somewhat difficult to be attained, but that thou mightest be led to follow after it, and not spend thyself in vain pursuits; if this be the case, God will work all things. Do thou be bold; "for it is God that worketh in you." If then He worketh, it is our part to bring a mind ever resolute, clenched and unrelaxed. "For it is God that worketh in you both to will and to work." "If He does Himself work in us to will, how dost thou exhort us? for if He works Himself even the will, the words, which you speak to us, have no meaning, 'that ye have obeyed'; for we have not 'obeyed'; it is without meaning that thou sayest, 'with fear and trembling'; for the whole is of God." It was not for this that I said to you, "for it is He that worketh in you both to will and to work," but my object was to relieve your anxiety. If thou wilt, in that case He will "work in thee to will." Be not affrighted, thou art not·worsted; both the hearty desire and the accomplishment are a gift from Him: for where we have the will, thenceforward He will increase our will. For instance, I desire to do some good work: He has wrought the good work itself, and by means of it He has wrought also the will. Or he says this in the excess of his piety, as when he declares that our well-doings are gifts of grace.

As then, when he calls these gifts, he does not put us out of the pale of free will, but accords to us free will, so when he says, "to work in us to will," he does not deprive us of free will, but he shows that by actually doing right we greatly increase our heartiness in willing. For as doing comes of doing, so of not doing comes not doing. Hast thou given an alms? thou art the more incited to give. Hast thou refused to give? thou art become so much the more disinclined. Hast thou practiced temperance for one day? Thou hast an incitement for the next likewise. Hast thou indulged to excess? Thou hast increased the inclination to self-indulgence. "When a wicked man cometh into the depth of vice, then he despises." (Prov. xviii. 3.) As, then, when a man cometh into the depth of iniquity, he turns a despiser; so·when he cometh into the depth of goodness, he quickens his exertions. For as the one runs riot in despair, so the second, under a sense of the multitude of good things, exerts himself the more, fearing lest he should lose the whole. "For His good pleasure," he says, that is, "for love's sake," for the sake of pleasing Him; to the end that what is acceptable to Him may take place; that things may take place according to His will. Here he shows, and makes it a ground of confidence, that He is sure to work in us, for it is His will that we live as He desires we should, and if He desires it, He Himself both worketh in us to this end,[1] and will certainly accomplish

it; for it is His will that we live aright. Seest thou, how he does not deprive us of free will?

"Do all things without murmurings and disputings." The devil, when he finds that he has no power to withdraw us from doing right, wishes to spoil our reward by other means. For he has taken occasion to insinuate pride or vainglory, or if none of these things, then murmuring, or, if not this, misgivings. Now then see how Paul sweeps away all these. He said on the subject of humility all that he did say, to overthrow pride; he spoke of vainglory, that is, "not as in my presence only"; he here speaks of "murmuring and disputing." But why, I want to know, when in the case of the Corinthians he was engaged in uprooting this evil tendency, did he remind them of the Israelites, but here has said nothing of the sort, but simply charged them? Because in that case the mischief was already done, for which reason there was need of a more severe stroke and a sharper rebuke; but here he is giving admonitions to prevent its being done. Severe measures then were not called for in order to secure those that had not yet been guilty; as in leading them to humility he did not subjoin the instance in the Gospel, wherein the proud were punished, but laid the charge as from God's lips (Luke xvi. 23? xviii. 14?) ; and he addresses them as free, as children of pure birth, not as servants; for in the practice of virtue a rightminded and generous person is influenced by those who do well, but one of bad principles by those who do not do well; the one by the consideration of honor, the other of punishment. Wherefore also writing to the Hebrews, he said, bringing forward the example of Esau, "Who for one mess of meat sold his own birthright" (Heb. xii. 16) ; and again, "if he shrink back, my soul hath no pleasure in him." (Heb. x. 38.) And among the Corinthians were many who had been guilty of fornication. Therefore he said, "Lest when I come again my God should humble me before you, and I should mourn for many that have sinned heretofore, and repented not of the uncleanness, and fornication, and lasciviousness which they committed. (2 Cor. xii. 21.) That ye may be blameless," says he, "and harmless"; i.e. irreproachable, unsullied; for murmuring occasions no slight stain. And what means "without disputing"? Is it good, or not good? Do not dispute, he says, though it be trouble, or labor, or any thing else whatever. He did not say, "that ye be not punished," for punishment is reserved for the thing; and this he made evident in the Epistle to the Corinthians; but here he said nothing of the sort; but he says, "That ye may be blameless and harmless, children of God without blemish, in the midst of a crooked and perverse generation,

---

[1] This clause, πρὸς δὲ τοῦτο αὐτὸς ἐνεργεῖ, is difficult. Old Lat. seems to have used ἐνάγει, making the sense, "and thus far Himself instructs us."

among whom ye are seen as lights in the world, holding forth the word of life, that I may have whereof to glory in the day of Christ." Observest thou that he is instructing these not to murmur? So that murmuring is left for unprincipled and graceless slaves. For tell me, what manner of son is that, who murmurs at the very time that he is employed in the affairs of his father, and is working for his own benefit? Consider, he says, that you are laboring for yourself, that it is for yourself that you are laying up; it is for those to murmur, when others profit by their labors, others reap the fruit, while they bear the burden; but he that is gathering for himself, why should he murmur? Because his wealth does not increase? But it is not so. Why does he murmur who acts of free-will, and not by constraint? It is better to do nothing than to do it with murmuring, for even the very thing itself is spoilt. And do you not remark that in our own families we are continually saying this; "it were better for these things never to be done, than to have them done with murmuring"? and we had often rather be deprived of the services some one owes us, than submit to the inconvenience of his murmuring. For murmuring is intolerable, most intolerable; it borders upon blasphemy. Otherwise why had those men to pay a penalty so severe? It is a proof of ingratitude; the murmurer is ungrateful to God, but whoso is ungrateful to God does thereby become a blasphemer. Now there were at that time, if ever, uninterrupted troubles, and dangers without cessation: there was no pause, no remission: innumerable were the horrors, which pressed upon them from all quarters; but now we have profound peace, a perfect calm.

Wherefore then murmur? Because thou art poor? Yet think of Job. Or because sickness is thy lot? What then if, with the consciousness of as many excellencies and as high attainments as that holy man, thou hadst been so afflicted? Again reflect on him, how that for a long time he never ceased to breed worms, sitting upon a dunghill and scraping his sores; for the account says that "(after a long time had passed,) then said his wife unto him, How long wilt thou persist, saying, Yet a little while I bide in expectation? Speak some word against the Lord, and die."[1] (Job ii. 9, LXX.) But your child is dead? What then if thou hadst lost all thy children, and that by an evil fate, as he did? For ye know, ye know well, that it is no slight alleviation to take our place beside the sick man, to close the mouth, to shut the eyes, to stroke the beard, to hear the last accents; but that just man was vouchsafed none of these consolations, they all being overwhelmed

at once. And what do I say? Hadst thou, thine own self, been bidden to slay and offer up thine own son, and to see the body consumed, like that blessed Patriarch, what then wouldst thou have felt whilst erecting the altar, laying on the wood, binding the child? But there are some who revile thee? What then would be thy feelings did thy friends, come to administer consolation to thee, speak like Job's? For, as it is, innumerable are our sins, and we deserve to be reproached; but in that case he who was true, just, godly, who kept himself from every evil deed, heard the contrary of those laid to his charge by his friends. What then, tell me, if thou hadst heard thy wife exclaiming in accents of reproach; "I am a vagabond and a servant, wandering from place to place, and from house to house, waiting until the sun goes down, that I may rest from the woes that encompass me." (Job ii. 9, LXX.) Why dost thou speak so, O foolish woman? for is thine husband to blame for these things? Nay, but the devil. "Speak a word against God," she says, "and die"; — and if thereupon the stricken man had cursed and died, how wouldest thou be the better? — No disease you can name is worse than that of his, though you name ten thousand. It was so grievous, that he could no longer be in the house and under cover; such, that all men gave him up. For if he had not been irrecoverably gone, he would never have taken his seat without the city, a more pitiable object than those afflicted with leprosy; for these are both admitted into houses, and they do herd together; but he passing the night in the open air, was naked upon a dunghill, and could not even bear a garment upon his body. How so? Perhaps there would only have been an addition to his pangs. For "I melt the clods of the earth," he says, "while I scrape off my sore."[2] (Job vii. 5, LXX.) His flesh bred sores and worms in him, and that continually. Seest thou how each one of us sickens at the hearing of these things? but if they are intolerable to hear, is the sight of them more tolerable? and if the sight of them is intolerable, how much more intolerable to undergo them? And yet that righteous man did undergo them, not for two or three days, but for a long while, and he did not sin, not even with his lips. What disease can you describe to me like this, so exquisitely painful? for was not this worse than blindness? "I look on my food," he says, "as a fetid mass." (Job vi. 7.) And not only this, but that which affords cessation to others, night and sleep, brought no alleviation to him, nay, were worse than any torture. Hear his words: "Why dost thou scare me with dreams, and terrify me through

---

[1] [The Sept. uses this vague euphemism in place of "curse God." The Oxford tr. omits the clause. — J. A. B.]

[2] Eng. Vers. "My flesh is clothed with worms and clods of dust."

visions? If it be morning, I say, When will it be evening?" (Job vii. 14, 4), and he murmured not. And there was not only this; but reputation in the eyes of the world was added; for they forthwith concluded him to be guilty of endless crimes, judging from all that he suffered. And accordingly this is the consideration, which his friends urged upon him; "Know therefore that God exacteth less of thee than thine iniquities deserve." (Job xi. 6.) Wherefore he himself said, "But now they that are younger than I have me in derision, whose fathers I disdained to set with the dogs of my flock." (Job xxx. 1.) And was not this worse than many deaths? Yet though assaulted on all sides by a flood like this, when there raged around him a fearful storm, clouds, rain, lightnings, whirling winds, and waterspouts, he remained himself unmoved, seated as it were in the midst of this surge, thus awful and overwhelming, as in a perfect calm, and no murmur escaped him; and this before the gift of grace, before that aught was declared concerning a resurrection, before aught concerning hell and punishment and vengeance. Yet we, who hear both Prophets and Apostles and Evangelists speaking to us, and have innumerable examples set before us, and have been taught the tidings of a Resurrection, yet harbor discontent, though no man can say that such a fate as this has been his own. For if one has lost money, yet not all that great number of sons and daughters, or if he has, perchance it was that he had sinned; but for him, he lost them suddenly, in the midst of his sacrifices, in the midst of the service which he was rendering to God. And if any man has at one blow lost property to the same amount, which can never be, yet he has not had the further affliction of a sore all over his body, he has not scraped the humors that covered him; or if this likewise has been his fate, yet he has not had men to upbraid and reproach him, which is above all things calculated to wound the feelings, more than the calamities we suffer. For if when we have persons to cheer and console us in our misfortunes, and to hold out to us fair prospects, we yet despond, consider what it was to have men upbraiding him. If the words, " I looked for some to have pity, but there was no man, and for comforters, but I found none" (Ps. lxix. 20), describe intolerable misery, how great an aggravation to find revilers instead of comforters! " Miserable comforters are ye all" (Job xvi. 2), he says. If we did but revolve these subjects continually in our minds, if we well weighed them, no ills of this present time could ever have force to disturb our peace, when we turned our eyes to that athlete, that soul of adamant, that spirit impenetrable as brass. For as though he had borne about him

a body of brass or stone, he met all events with a noble and constant spirit.

Taking these things to heart, let us do everything " without murmuring and disputing." Is it some good work that thou hast before thee, and dost thou murmur? wherefore? art thou then forced? for that there are many about you who force you to murmur, I know well, says he. This he intimated by saying, " in the midst of a crooked and perverse generation"; but it is this that deserves admiration, that we admit no such feeling when under galling provocation. For the stars too give light in the night, they shine in the dark, and receive no blemish to their own beauty, yea they even shine the brighter; but when light returns, they no longer shine so. Thus thou too dost appear with the greater lustre, whilst thou holdest straight in the midst of the crooked. This it is which deserves our admiration, the being " blameless"; for that they might not urge this plea,[1] he himself set it down by anticipation. What means "holding fast the word of life"? i.e. " being destined to live, being of those that are gaining salvation."[2] Observe how immediately he subjoins the rewards, which are in reserve. Lights [i.e. luminaries], he says, retain the principle of light; so do ye the principle[3] of life. What means "the word of life"? Having the seed of life, i.e. having pledges of life, holding life itself, i.e. " having in yourselves the seed of life," this is what he calls " the word of life." Consequently the rest are all dead, for by these words he signified as much; for otherwise those others likewise would have held " the word of life." "That I may have whereof to glory," he says; what is this? I too participate in your good deeds, he says. So great is your virtue, as not only to save yourselves, but to render me illustrious. Strange kind of " boasting," thou blessed Paul! Thou art scourged, driven about, reviled for our sakes: therefore he adds, " in the day of Christ, that I did not run," he says, " in vain, nor labored in vain," but I always have a right to glory, he means, that I did not run in vain.

"Yea, and if I am offered." He said not, " and if I die even," nor did he when writing to Timothy, for there, too, he has made use of the same expression, "For I am already being offered." (2 Tim. iv. 6.) He is both consoling them about his own death, and instructing them to bear gladly the death that is for Christ's sake. I am become, he says, as it were a libation and a sacrifice. O blessed soul! His bringing them to God he calls a sacrifice. It is much better to present a soul than to present oxen. " If, then,

---

[1] Viz. that they were forced.   [2] σωζομένων.
[3] [The term λόγος, "word," Chrys. here fancifully takes in the sense of ground, reason, principle, and so quite misinterprets the clause. See Meyer.— J. A. B.]

over and above this offering," he says, " I add myself, my death as a libation, I rejoice." For this he implies, when he says, " Yea, and if I am offered upon the sacrifice and service, I joy and rejoice with you all ; and in the same manner do ye also joy and rejoice with me." Why dost thou rejoice with them? Seest thou that he shows that it is their duty to rejoice? On the one hand then, I rejoice in being made a libation ; on the other, I rejoice with you, in having presented a sacrifice ; " and in the same manner do ye also joy and rejoice with me," that I am offered up ; " rejoice with me," " who rejoice in myself." So that the death of the just is no subject for tears, but for joy. If they rejoice, we should rejoice with them. For it is misplaced for us to weep, while they rejoice. " But," it is urged, " we long for our wonted intercourse." This is a mere pretext and excuse ; and that it is so, mark what he enjoins : " Rejoice with me, and joy." Dost thou miss thy wonted intercourse? If thou wert thyself destined to remain here, there would be reason in what thou sayest ; but if after a brief space thou wilt overtake him who has departed, what is that intercourse which thou dost seek? for it is only when he is forever severed from him that a man misses the society of another, but if he will go the same way that thou wilt go, what is the intercourse which thou

longest for? Why do we not bewail all that are upon foreign travel? Do we not just a little, and cease after the first or the second day? If thou longest for thy wonted intercourse with him, weep so far only. " It is no evil that I suffer," says he, " but I even rejoice in going to Christ, and do ye not rejoice." " Rejoice with me." Let us too rejoice when we see a righteous man dying, and yet more even when any of the desperately wicked ; for the first is going to receive the reward of his labors, but the other has abated somewhat from the score of his sins.[1] But it is said, perhaps he might have altered, had he lived. Yet God would never have taken him away, if there had been really a prospect of an alteration. For why should not He who orders all events for our salvation, allow him the opportunity, who gave promise of pleasing Him? If He leaves those, who never alter, much more those that do. Let then the sharpness of our sorrow be everywhere cut away, let the voice of lamentation cease. Let us thank God under all events : let us do all things without murmuring ; let us be cheerful, and let us become pleasing to Him in all things, that we may also attain the good things to come, by the grace and lovingkindness of our Lord Jesus Christ, with whom, &c.

HOMILY IX.

PHILIPPIANS ii. 19–21.

" But I hope in the Lord Jesus to send Timothy shortly unto you, that I also may be of good comfort, when I know your state. For I have no man likeminded, who will care truly for your state. For they all seek their own, not the things of Jesus Christ."

HE had said, " have fallen out unto the progress of the Gospel ; so that my bonds became manifest in Christ throughout the whole prætorian guard." (Phil. i. 12, 13.) Again, " Yea, and if I am offered upon the sacrifice and service of your faith." (Phil. ii. 17.) By these words he strengthened them. Perchance they might suspect that his former words were spoken just to comfort them. What then? " I send Timothy unto you," says he ; for they desired to hear all things that concerned him. And wherefore said he not, " that ye may know my state," but, " that I may know yours "? Because Epaphroditus would have reported his state before the arrival of Timothy. Wherefore further on he says, " But I counted it necessary to send to

you Epaphroditus, my brother (Phil. ii. 25) ; but I wish to learn of your affairs. For it is likely that he had remained long time with Paul through his bodily weakness. So that he says, I wish to " know your state." See then how he refers everything to Christ, even the mission of Timothy, saying, " I hope in the Lord Jesus," that is, I am confident that God will facilitate this for me, that I too may be of good courage, when I know your state. As I refreshed you when ye heard the very things of me which ye had prayed for, that the Gospel had advanced, that its enemies were put to shame, that the means by which they thought to injure, rather made me rejoice ; thus too do I wish to learn of your affairs, that I too may be of good courage

---

[1] ἐνέκοψε. See on Stat. Hom. v. (4), Tr. p. 372. Here, however, he rather means sins that might have been committed. He certainly rather strains the principle of trying to view things as they are, seeing that, to us at least, while there is life there is hope. Still a more thorough feeling of God's mercy, and of our own ignorance, would make us better understand the general use of thanksgiving in our funeral service.

when I know your state. Here he shows that they ought to rejoice for his bonds, and to be conformed to them, for they begat in him great pleasure ; for the words, " that I too may be of good comfort," imply, just as you are.

Oh, what longing had he toward Macedonia ! He testifies the same to the Thessalonians, as when he says, " But we, brethren, being bereaved of[1] you for a short season," &c. (1 Thess. ii. 17.) And here he says, " I hope to send Timothy " that I may " know your state," which is a proof of excessive care : for when he could not himself be with them, he sent his disciples, as he could not endure to remain, even for a little time, in ignorance of their state. For he did not learn all things by revelation of the Spirit, and for this we can see some reason ; for if the disciples had believed that it were so, they would have lost all sense of shame,[2] but now from expectation of concealment, they were more easily corrected. In a high degree did he call their attention by saying, " that I too may be of good comfort," and rendered them more zealous, so that, when Timothy came he might not find any other state of things, and report it to him. He seems to have acted in like sort in his own person, when he delayed his coming to the Corinthians, that they might repent ; wherefore he wrote, " to spare you I forbare to come to Corinth." (2 Cor. i. 23.) For his love was manifested not simply in reporting his own state, but in his desire to learn of theirs ; for this is the part of a soul which has a care of others, which takes thought for them, which is always wrestling for them.

At the same time too, he honors them by sending Timothy. " What sayest thou ? dost thou send Timothy ? and wherefore ? " Because " I have no one likeminded " ; that is, none of those whose care is like mine, none who " will care truly for you." (Phil. ii. 20.) Had he then no one of those who were with him ? No one likeminded, that is, who has yearnings and takes thought for you as I do. No one would lightly choose, he means, to make so long a journey for this purpose. Timothy is the one with me who loves you.[3] For I might have sent others, but there was none like him. This then is that likemindedness, to love the disciples as the master loves them. " Who," says he, " will truly care for you," that is, as a father. " For they all seek their own, not the things of Jesus Christ " (Phil. ii. 21), their own comfort, their own safety. This too he writes to Timothy. But why doth he lament such things as

these ? To teach us his hearers not to fall in like sort, to teach his hearers not to seek for remission from toil ; for he who seeks remission from toil, seeks not the things that are Christ's, but his own. We ought to be prepared against every toil, against every distress.

Ver. 22. " Ye know the proof of him, that as a child serveth a father, so he served with me in furtherance of the Gospel."

And that I speak not at random, " ye yourselves," he says, " know, that as a child serveth a father, so he served with me in furtherance of the Gospel." He presents then Timothy to them, and with reason, that he might enjoy much honor from them. This too he does when he writes to the Corinthians, and he says, " Let no man therefore despise him, for he worketh the work of the Lord as I also do." (1 Cor. xvi. 10.) This he said not as caring for him, but for those who receive him, that they might receive a great reward.

Ver. 23. " Him therefore," he says, " I hope to send forthwith, so soon as I shall see how it will go with me," that is, when I see where I stand, and what end my affairs will have.

Ver. 24. " But I trust in the Lord that I also myself shall come to you shortly."

I am not therefore sending him, as though I myself would not come, but that I may be of good courage when I know your state, that even in the mean time I may not be ignorant of it. " But I trust in the Lord," says he. See how he makes all things depend on God, and speaks nothing of his own mind. That is, God willing.[4]

Ver. 25. " But I counted it necessary to send to you Epaphroditus, my brother, and fellow-worker, and fellow-soldier."

And him too he sends with the same praises as Timothy, for he commended him on these two points ; first, in that he loved them, when he says, " who will care truly for you " ; and secondly, in that he had approved himself in the Gospel. And for the same reason, and in the same terms, he praises this man also : and how ? By calling him a brother, and a fellow-worker, and not stopping at this point, but also " fellow-soldier," he showed how he shared in his dangers, and testifies of him the same things which he testifies of himself. For " fellow-soldier " is more than " fellow-worker " ; for perchance he gave aid in quiet matters, yet not so in wars and dangers ; but in saying " fellow-soldier," he showed this too.

Ver. 25. " To send to you your messenger, and minister to my needs " ; that is, I give you your own, since I send to you him that is your

---

[1] ἀπορφανισθέντες.
[2] He means that if they thought he knew their exact condition by revelation, they would lose a motive for improvement, in the hope of standing well in his eyes. Such motives are of course still a part of our moral education.
[3] Or, " the one who loves you with me," i.e. " as I."

[4] [This has the appearance of rough notes taken in shorthand. The usual editions place this brief sentence before " see," and thus make a somewhat better connection, but without known MS. authority. — J. A. B.]

own, or, perhaps, that is your Teacher.[1] Again he adds many things concerning his love, in saying,

Ver. 26, 27. " Since he longed after you all, and was sore troubled, because ye had heard that he was sick. For indeed he was sick nigh unto death : but God had mercy on him ; and not on him only, but on me also, that I might not have sorrow upon sorrow."

Here he aims at a farther point, making it manifest, that Epaphroditus too was well aware, how he was beloved of them. And this is no light thing toward loving. You know how he was sick, he says ; and he grieved that on his recovery he did not see you, and free you from the grief ye had by reason of his sickness. Here too he gives another reason for sending so late to them, not from any remissness, but he kept Timothy because he had no one else, (for, as he had written, he had " no one likeminded,") and Epaphroditus because of his sickness. He then shows that this was a long sickness, and had consumed much time, by adding, " for he was sick nigh unto death." You see how anxious Paul is to cut off from his disciples all occasion of slighting or contempt, and every suspicion that his not coming was because he despised them. For nothing will have such power to draw a disciple toward one, as the persuasion that his superior cares for him, and that he is full of heaviness on his account, for this is the part of exceeding love. Because " ye have heard," he says, " that he was sick ; for he was sick nigh unto death." And that I am not making an excuse, hear what follows. " But God had mercy on him." What sayest thou, O heretic? Here it is written, that God's mercy retained and brought back again him who was on the point of departure. And yet if the world is evil, it is no mercy to leave a man in the evil. Our answer to the heretic is easy, but what shall we say to the Christian? for he perchance will question, and say, " if to depart and to be with Christ is far better," how saith he that he hath obtained mercy? I would ask why the same Apostle says, that "it is more needful to abide with you "?[2] For as it was needful for him, so too for this man, who would hereafter depart to God with more exceeding riches, and greater boldness. Hereafter that would take place, even if it did not now, but the winning souls is at an end for those who have once departed thither. In many places too, Paul speaks according to the common habits of his hearers, and not every where in accordance with his own heavenly wis-

dom : for he had to speak to men of the world who still feared death. Then he shows how he esteemed Epaphroditus, and thence he gets for him respect, by saying, that his preservation was so useful to himself, that the mercy which had been shown to Epaphroditus reached him also. Moreover, without this the present life is a good ; were it not so, why does Paul rank with punishment untimely deaths? as when he says, " For this cause many are weak and sickly among you, and not a few sleep " (1 Cor. xi. 30) ; for the future life is not (merely) better than an evil state, since (then) it were not good, but better than a good state.

" Lest I should have," he says, " sorrow upon sorrow " ; sorrow from his death in addition to that which sprung from his sickness. By this he shows how much he prized Epaphroditus.

Ver. 28. " I have sent him therefore the more diligently." What means " more diligently "? It is, without procrastination, without delay, with much speed, having bidden him lay all aside, and to go to you, that he might be freed from heaviness ; for we rejoice not on hearing of the health of those we love, so much as when we see them, and chiefly so when this happens contrary to hope, as it was in the case of Epaphroditus.

" I have sent him therefore the more diligently, that when ye see him again, ye may rejoice, and that I may be the less sorrowful." How " less sorrowful "? Because if ye rejoice, I too rejoice, and he too joys at a pleasure of such sort, and I shall be " less sorrowful." He said not sorrowless, but " less sorrowful," to show that his soul never was free from sorrow : for he who said, " Who is weak, and I am not weak? who is made to stumble, and I burn not? " (2 Cor. xi. 29), when could such an one be free from sorrow? That is, this despondency I now cast off.

Ver. 29. " Receive him therefore in the Lord with all joy."

" In the Lord " either means spiritually and with much zeal, or rather " in the Lord " means God willing. Receive him in a manner worthy of saints, as saints should be received with all joy.

All this he does for their sakes, not for that of his messengers, for greater gain has the doer than the receiver of a good deed. " And such hold in honor," that is, receive him in a manner worthy of saints.

Ver. 30. " Because for the work of Christ he came nigh unto death, hazarding his life, to supply that which was lacking in your service towards me."

This man had been publicly sent by the city of the Philippians, who had come as minister to Paul, and perchance bringing him some contri-

---

[1] Referring to the word translated " Messenger," which is "Apostle," and may mean " Bishop," as Theodoret clearly takes it here. In 2 Cor. viii. 23, St. Chrys. understands it " messengers " or " deputies."

[2] [So Field, with most documents. The altered text has " for you," " on your account," as in Phil. i. 24.—J. A. B.]

bution, for toward the end of the Epistle he shows that he also brought him money, when he says, "Having received of Epaphroditus the things that came from you." (Phil. iv. 18.)

It is probable then, that on his arrival at the city of Rome, he found Paul in great and urgent peril, so that those who were accustomed to resort to him were unable safely to do so, but were themselves in peril by their very attendance; which is wont to happen chiefly in very great dangers, and the exceeding wrath of kings, (for when any one has offended the king, and is cast into prison, and is strictly guarded, then even his servants are debarred from access, which probably then befell Paul,) and that Epaphroditus, being of a noble nature, despised all danger, that he might go in unto him, and minister unto him, and do everything which need required. He therefore sets forth two facts, by which he gains for him their respect; the one, that he was in jeopardy well nigh unto death, he says, for my sake; the other, that in so suffering he was representing their city, so that the recompense for that his peril would be accounted to those who sent him, as if the city had sent him as their ambassador, so that a kind reception of him and approval of what he had done may rather be called a participation in the things that he had dared. And he said not, "for my sake," but obtains the more credit for his words, by saying, "because for the work of God," since he acted not for my sake, but for God's sake "he was nigh unto death." What then? though by the providence of God he died not, yet he himself regarded not his life, and gave himself up to any suffering that might befall him, so as not to remit his attendance on me. And if he gave himself up to death to attend on Paul, much more would he have endured this for the Gospel's sake. Or rather, this also had been for the Gospel's sake, even to have died for Paul. For we may bind about our brows the crown of martyrdom, not only by refusing to sacrifice, but such causes as these also make death martyrdom, and if I may say something startling, these latter do so far more than the former. For he who dares to face death for the lesser cause, will much rather for the greater. Let us therefore, when we see the Saints in danger, regard not our life, for it is impossible without daring ever to perform any noble act, but need is that he who takes thought beforehand for his safety here, should fall from that which is to come.

"To supply," he says, "your lack of service toward me." What is this? the city was not present, but by sending him, it fulfilled through him all service toward me. He therefore supplied your lack of service, so that for this reason too he deserves to enjoy much honor, since,

what ye all should have done, this hath he performed on your behalf. Here he shows that there is also a foregoing service rendered by those in safety to those in danger, for so he speaks of the lack,[1] and the lack of service. Seest thou the spirit of the Apostle? These words spring not from arrogance, but from his great care towards them; for he calls the matter a "service" and a "lack," that they may not be puffed up, but be moderate, nor think that they have rendered some great thing, but rather be humble-minded.

For we owe the saints a debt, and are not doing them a favor. For as supplies are due by those who are in peace and not engaged in war to such as stand in the army and fight (for these stand on their behoof), thus too is it here. For if Paul had not taught, who would have cast him into prison? Wherefore we ought to minister to the Saints. For is it not absurd to contribute to an earthly king, when engaged in war, all that he wants, as clothing and food, not according to his need alone, but abundantly, whilst to the King of Heaven, when engaged in war, and contending against far more bitter foes (for it is written, "our wrestling is not against flesh and blood") (Eph. vi. 12), we will not supply urgent necessity? What folly is this! What ingratitude! What base love of gain! But, as it seems, the fear of man has greater force with us than hell, and the future torments. For this cause, in truth, all things are turned upside down; for political affairs are daily accomplished with much earnestness, and one must not be left behind, whilst of spiritual things there is no account taken at all; but the things which are demanded of us of necessity, and with compulsion, as though we were slaves, and against our wills, are laid down by us with much readiness, while such as are asked from willing minds, and as if from free men, are again deficient. I speak not against all, but against those who are behindhand with these supplies. For might not God have made these contributions compulsory? Yet He would not, for He has more care of you than of those whom you support. Wherefore He would not that you should contribute of necessity, since there is no recompense. And yet many of those who stand here are lower minded[2] than the Jews. Consider how great things the Jews gave, tithes,[3] first-fruits, tithes again, and again other tithes, and besides this thirteenths, and the shekel, and no one said, how much they devour; for the more they receive, the greater is the reward.

---

[1] [The word means "a falling behind," in contrast with something foregoing. — J. A. B.]
[2] ταπεινότεροι, in a bad sense.
[3] Lev. xxvii. 30-32. Deut. xiv. 22, 28; xxvi. 12. Of the shekel, see on St. Matt. Hom. lviii. init., where he says it was paid by all the first-born. He is probably mistaken, as St. Peter paid it, though he was a younger brother.

They say not, They receive much, they are gluttons; which words I hear now from some. They for their part, while they are building houses, and buying estates, still think they have nothing; but if any priest is clothed in dress more bright than usual, and enjoys more than what is necessary for his sustenance, or has an attendant, that he may not be forced himself to act unbecomingly, they set the matter down for riches. And in truth we are rich even at this rate, and they admit it against their will; for we, though we have but little, are rich, whilst they, though they get everything about them, are poor.

How far shall our folly extend? does it not suffice to our punishment that we do no good deed, but must we add to it the punishment of evil speaking? For if what he has were your gifts, you lose your reward by upbraiding him for what you gave. In a word, if thou didst give it, why dost thou upbraid him? You have already borne witness to his poverty, by saying that what he has are your gifts. Why then dost thou upbraid? Thou shouldest not have given, didst thou intend so to do. But dost thou speak thus, when another gives? It is then more grievous, in that when thou thyself hast not given, thou upbraidest for another man's good deeds. How great reward thinkest thou those who are thus spoken of will receive? It is for God's sake they thus suffer. How and wherefore? Had they so willed, they might have taken up a trader's life, even though they received it not from their ancestors. For I hear many speaking thus at random, when we say that a certain man is poor. Had he willed, they say, he might have been rich, and then tauntingly add, His father, his grandfather, and I know not who was so; but now see what a robe he wears! But what? tell me, ought he to go about naked? You then start nice questionings on these points, but see lest thou thus speakest against thyself. Listen to that exhortation of Christ, which says, "Judge not that ye be not judged." (Matt. vii. 1.) He might, it is true, if he had willed, have led a trader's or a merchant's life, and would surely not have lacked. But he would not. What then, says one, is he here profited? Tell me, what is he profited? Does he wear silken robes? Does he proudly clear his way through the forum with a troop of followers? Is he borne along on horseback? Does he build houses, having where to dwell? If he act so, I too accuse him, and spare him not, but declare that he is unworthy of the priesthood. For how can he exhort others not to spend their time on these superfluities, who cannot advise himself? But if he has sufficient for support, is he therefore doing wrong? Would you have him lead a vagabond life, and beg? Wouldest not thou too, his disciple, be put to shame? But

if thy father in the flesh did this, thou wouldest think shame of the thing. If thy spiritual father be compelled so to do, wilt thou not veil thy head, and even think thou art sinking into the earth? It is written, "A father's dishonor is a reproach to the children." (Ecclus. iii. 11.) But what? Should he perish with famine? This were not like a pious man; for God willeth it not. But what do they straightway philosophize? It is written, say they, "Get you no gold, nor silver, nor brass in your purses, neither two coats, nor yet staves" (Matt. x. 9, 10), whilst these men have three or four garments, and beds well spread. I am forced now to heave a bitter sigh, and, but that it had been indecorous, I had wept too! How so? Because we are such curious searchers into the motes of others, while we feel not the beams in our own eyes. Tell me, why sayest thou not this to thyself? The answer is, Because the command is laid only on our Teachers. When then Paul says, "having food and covering we shall be therewith content" (1 Tim. vi. 8), says he this only to Teachers? By no means, but to all men; and this is clear, if we will begin farther back. For what does he say? "Godliness with contentment is great gain (1 Tim. vi. 6); for we brought nothing into this world, and it is certain that neither can we carry anything out" (1 Tim. vi. 7); he then straightway adds, "And having food and covering, we shall be therewith content; but they that desire to be rich, fall into a temptation and a snare, and many foolish and hurtful lusts." (1 Tim. vi. 8, 9.) You see that this is spoken to all; and how is it when he says again, "Make not provision for the flesh to fulfill the lusts thereof" (Rom. xiii. 14), is not this said absolutely to all? and what when he says, "Meats for the belly, and the belly for meats, but God shall bring to nought both it and them" (1 Cor. vi. 13); or what when he says, "But she that giveth herself to pleasure, is dead while she liveth" (1 Tim. v. 6), speaking of a widow. Is then the widow a Teacher? Has not he said himself, "But I permit not a woman to teach, nor to have dominion over a man"? (1 Tim. ii. 12.) But if a widow, in old age, (and age has need of great attendance,) and a woman's nature too, (for the woman's sex, being weak, has need of more refreshment,) if then, where there is both the age and the nature, he suffers her not to live in luxury, but even says that she is dead, (for he did not simply forbid a life of luxury, but said, "she who giveth herself to luxury is dead while she liveth,") and thus hath cut her off, (for she that is dead is cut off,) what indulgence then will any man have, who does those things, for which a woman and an aged one too is punished?

Yet no one gives a thought to these things,

no one searches them out. And this I have been compelled to say, not from any wish to free the priests from these charges, but to spare you. They indeed suffer no harm at your hands, even if it is with cause and justice that they are thus charged of being greedy of gain; for, whether ye speak, or whether ye forbear, they must there give an account to the Judge, so that your words hurt them not at all; but if your words are false besides, they for their part gain by these false accusations, whilst ye hurt yourselves by these means. But it is not so with you; for be the things true, which ye bring against them, or be they false, ye speak ill of them to your hurt. And how so? If they be true, in that ye judge your Teachers, and subvert order, ye do it to your hurt. For if we must not judge a brother, much less a Teacher. But if they be false, the punishment and retribution is intolerable; for of "every idle word ye shall give account." (Matt. xii. 36.) For your sake then I thus act and labor.

But as I said, no one searches out these things, no one busies himself about these things, no one communes with himself on any of these things. Would ye that I should add still more? "Whosoever forsaketh not all that he hath, saith the Christ, is not worthy of Me." (Luke xiv. 33; Matt. x. 37.) What when he says, "It is hard for a rich man to enter into the kingdom of heaven"? (Matt. xix. 23; Mark x. 24.) What when he says again, "Woe unto you that are rich, for ye have received your consolation"? (Luke vi. 24.) No one searches this out, no one bears it in mind, no one reasons with himself, but all sit as severe inquisitors on other men's cases. Yet this is to make themselves sharers in the charges. But listen, that for your own sake I may free the priests from the charges, which ye say lie against them, for the persuasion that they transgress the law of God, inclines you not a little towards evil. Come then, let us examine this matter. Christ said, "Provide neither gold nor silver, neither two coats, neither shoes, nor girdle, nor yet staves." (Matt. x. 9, 10.) What then? tell me, did Peter transgress this command? Surely he did so, in having a girdle and a garment, and shoes, for listen to the words of the Angel, "Gird thyself, and bind on thy sandals." (Acts xii. 8.) And yet he had no such great need of sandals, for at that season a man may go even unshod; their great use is in the winter, and yet he had them. What shall we say of Paul, when he writes thus to Timothy, "Do thy diligence to come before winter"? (2 Tim. iv. 21.) He gives him orders too and says, "The cloak that I left at Troas with Carpus bring when thou comest, and the books, especially the parchments." (2 Tim. iv. 13.) See he speaks of a cloak, and no one can say that he had not another which he wore; for

if he did not wear one at all, it were superfluous to order this one to be brought, and if he could not be without one to wear, it is clear he had a second.

What shall we say of his remaining "two whole years in his own hired dwelling"? (Acts xxviii. 30.) Did then this chosen vessel disobey Christ? this man who said, "Yet I live; and yet no longer I, but Christ liveth in me" (Gal. ii. 20), concerning whom Christ testified, saying, "He is a chosen vessel unto Me"? (Acts ix. 15.) I ought to leave this difficulty with you, without supplying any solution to the question. I ought to exact of you this penalty for your negligence in the Scriptures, for this is the origin of all such difficulties. For we know not the Scriptures, we are not trained in the law of God, and so we become sharp inquirers into the faults of others, whilst we take no account of our own. I ought then to have exacted from you this penalty. But what shall I do? Fathers freely give to their sons many things beyond what is fitting: when their fatherly compassion is kindled, on seeing their child with downcast look, and wasted with grief, they themselves also feel sharper pangs than he, and rest not until they have removed the ground of his dejection.

So be it at least here, be ye at least dejected at not receiving, that ye may receive well. What then is it? They opposed not, far be it; but diligently followed the commands of Christ, for those commands were but for a season, and not enduring; and this I say not from conjecture, but from the divine Scriptures. And how? Luke relates that Christ said to His disciples, "When I sent you forth without purse, and wallet, and girdle, and shoes, lacked ye anything? And they said nothing. (Luke xxii. 35.) But for the future provide them." But tell me, what could he do? could he have but one coat? How then? If need was that this be washed, should he, because without it, stay at home? should he without it go abroad in an unbecoming manner, when need called? Consider what a thing it would have been that Paul, who made the circuit of the world with such great success, should remain at home for want of raiment, and thus hinder his noble work. And what if violent cold had set in, or rain had drenched it, or perhaps frozen in, how could he dry his raiment? must he again remain without it? And what if cold had deprived his body of strength? must he waste away with disease, and be unable to speak? For hear what he says to Timothy, to prove that they were not furnished with adamantine bodies, "Use a little wine for thy stomach's sake, and thine often infirmities." (1 Tim. v. 23.) And again, when he speaks of another, "I counted it necessary to send to you your messenger, and minister to my needs." (Phil. ii. 25.) "For indeed he was sick, nigh unto death; but God had mercy on him, and not on him only, but on me also." (Phil. ii. 27.) So that they were subject to every sort of sickness. What then? must they die? By no means. For what cause then did Christ at that time give them that comman'd? To show His own power, and to prove that in after times He was able to do it, though He did it not. But wherefore did He not do it? They were much more admirable than the Israelites, whose shoes did not wax old, neither their garments, and that too whilst they were journeying through that desert where the glowing rays of the sun strike so hot, that they are capable of consuming even stones. (Ref. to Deut. xxix. 5.) Why then did he do this? For thy sake. For since thou wouldest not remain in health, but be full of wounds, He gave you that which might serve for medicine. And this is hence manifest; could He not Himself have fed them? He that gave to thee, who wast an enemy with Him, would He not much more have given to Paul? He who gave to the Israelites, those murmurers, those fornicators, those idolaters, would He not much more have given to Peter, who spent all for His sake? He who suffered wicked men to possess aught, would He not much more have freely given to John, who for Him forsook even his father? Yet he would not: through your hands he feeds them, that you may be sanctified. And see the excess of His lovingkindness. He chose that His disciples should be in want, that thou mightest be a little refreshed.

For if He had freed them from all want, they would have been much more admirable, far more glorious. But then that which is to thee salvation would have been cut off. God willed not then that they should be admirable, that thou mightest be saved, but that they should rather be lowered. He hath suffered them to be less accounted of, that thou mightest be able to be saved. The Teacher who receiveth is not equally reverenced, but he who receives not is chiefly honored. But then in the latter case the disciple is not benefited, he is hindered of his fruit. Seest thou the wisdom of God who thus loveth man? For as He Himself sought not His own glory, nor had respect to Himself, but when He was in glory, chose to be dishonored for thy sake, thus too is it in the case of your Teachers. When they might have been highly reverenced, He preferred that they should be subject to contempt for thy sake, that thou mightest be able to profit, that thou mightest be able to be rich. For he is in want of the things of this life, that you may abound in things spiritual. If then He might have made them above all want, He showed that for thy sake He suffers them to be in want. Knowing then these things, let us turn ourselves to well doing, not to accusations. Let us not be overcurious about the failings of others, but take account of our own; let us reckon up the excellences of other men, while we bear in mind our faults; and thus shall we be well pleasing to God. For he who looks at the faults of others, and at his own excellences, is injured in two ways; by the latter he is carried up to arrogance, through the former he falls into listlessness. For when he perceives that such an one hath sinned, very easily will he sin himself; when he perceives that he hath in aught excelled, very easily becometh he arrogant. He who consigns to oblivion his own excellences, and looks at his failings only, whilst he is a curious enquirer of the excellences, not the sins, of others, is profited in many ways. And how? When he sees that such an one hath done excellently, he is raised to emulate the same; when he sees that he himself hath sinned, he is rendered humble and modest. If we act thus, if we thus regulate ourselves, we shall be able to obtain the good things which are promised, through the grace and lovingkindness of our Lord Jesus Christ, with whom, &c.

HOMILY X.

PHILIPPIANS iii. 1–3.

"Finally, my brethren, rejoice in the Lord. To write the same things to you, to me indeed is not irksome, but for you it is safe. Beware of the dogs, beware of the evil workers, beware of the concision. For we are the circumcision, who worship God in the spirit, and glory in Christ Jesus, and have no confidence in the flesh."

DEJECTION and care, whenever they strain the soul beyond due measure, bereave it of its native force. And therefore Paul relieves the Philippians, who were in great despondency, and they were in despondency because they did not know how matters were with Paul; they were in despondency because they thought that it was already over with him, because of the preaching, because of Epaphroditus. It is in giving them assurance on all these points that he introduces the words, "Finally, my brethren, rejoice." "You no longer have," he says, "cause for despondency. You have Epaphroditus, for whose sake you were grieved; you have Timothy; I am myself coming to you; the Gospel is gaining ground. What is henceforth wanting to you? Rejoice!"

Now he calls the Galatians indeed "children" (Gal. iv. 19), but these "brethren." For when he aims either to correct anything or to show his fondness, he calls them "children"; but when he addresses them with greater honor, "brethren" is the title. "Finally, my brethren," he says, "rejoice in the Lord." He said rightly "in the Lord," not "after the world," for this is no rejoicing. These tribulations, he says, which are according to Christ bring joy. "To write the same things to you, to me indeed is not irksome, but for you it is safe. Beware of the dogs." Dost thou mark how he forbears to bring in the exhortation at the beginning? But after he had given them much commendation, after he had shown his admiration of them, then he does this, and again repeats his commendation. For this mode of speech seems to bear somewhat hard upon them. Wherefore he overshadows it on every side. But whom does he style "dogs"? There were at this place some of those, whom he hints at in all his Epistles, base and contemptible Jews, greedy of vile lucre and fond of power, who, desiring to draw aside many of the faithful, preached both Christianity and Judaism at the same time, corrupting the Gospel. As then they were not easily discernible, therefore he says, "beware of the dogs": the Jews are no longer children; once the Gentiles were called dogs, but now the Jews. Wherefore? because as the Gentiles were strangers both to God and to Christ, even so are these become this now. And he shows forth their shamelessness and violence, and their infinite distance from the relation of children, for that the Gentiles were once called "dogs," hear what the Canaanitish woman says, "Yea, Lord: for even the dogs eat of the crumbs which fall from their masters' table." (Matt. xv. 27.) But that they might not have this advantage, since even dogs are at the table, he adds that, whereby he makes them aliens also, saying, "Beware of the evil workers"; he admirably expressed himself, "beware of the evil workers"; they work, he means, but for a bad end, and a work that is much worse than idleness, plucking up what is laid in goodly order.

"Beware," he says, "of the concision." The rite of circumcision was venerable in the Jews' account, forasmuch as the Law itself gave way thereto, and the Sabbath was less esteemed than circumcision. For that circumcision might be performed the Sabbath was broken; but that the Sabbath might be kept, circumcision was never broken; and mark, I pray, the dispensation of God. This is found to be even more solemn than the Sabbath, as not being omitted at certain times.[1] When then it is done away, much more is the Sabbath. Wherefore Paul makes a concision of the name, and says, "Beware of the concision"; and he did not say "that circumcision is evil, that it is superfluous," lest he should strike the men with dismay, but he manages it more wisely, withdrawing them from the thing, but gratifying them with the word, nay, rather with the thing too, in a more serious way. But not so in the case of the Galatians, for since in that case the disease was great, he forthwith adopts the remedy of amputation with open front and with all boldness; but in this case, as they had done nothing of the sort, he vouchsafes them the gratification of the title, he casts out the others, and says, "Beware of the concision; for we are the circumcision" — how? — "who worship God in spirit,[2] and have no confidence in the flesh." He said not that "we test the one circumcision and the other, which is the better of the two"; but he would not even allow it a share in the name; but what does he say? That that circumcision is "concision." Why? Because they do nothing but cut the flesh up. For when what is done is not of the law, it is nothing else than a concision and cutting up of the flesh; it was then either for this reason that he called it so, or because they were trying to cut the Church in twain; and we call the thing "cutting up" in those who do this at random, without aim and without skill. Now if you must seek circumcision, he says, you will find it among us, "who worship God in spirit," i.e. who worship spiritually.

For answer me, which is superior, the soul or the body? Evidently the former. Therefore that circumcision is also superior, or rather, no longer superior, but this is the only circumcision; for while the type stood, He rightly brought it forward in conjunction, writing, "For ye shall circumcise the foreskins of your hearts." (Jerem. iv. 4.) In the same way in the Epistle to the Romans he does away with it, saying, "for he is not a Jew which is one outwardly, neither is that circumcision which is outward in the flesh; but he is a Jew which is one inwardly, and circumcision is that of the heart, in the spirit, not in the letter." (Rom. ii. 28, 29.) And lastly, he takes from it the very name,

---

[1] [The text is very obscure. Field, by altering two words without documentary evidence, makes it "even that of the Sabbath, which is more to be reverenced, is found not to be adopted at certain times"; or possibly, "even that which is more to be reverenced than the Sabbath, is found not to be adopted," etc.— J. A. B.]

[2] [Field here reads (with all his MSS.) as in Rev. Ver. πνεύματι θεοῦ, "worship by the Spirit of God." But Chrys.'s explanation (below) indicates that he read θεῷ, "worship God in spirit," as in the common printed text of Chrys. and the Textus Rec. of the N. T.— J. A. B.]

" neither is it circumcision," he maintains; for the type while the reality is yet to come, is called this, but when the reality has come, it no longer retains the title. As in delineation, a man has drawn a king in outline ; so long as the colors are not put on we say, Lo, there is the king, but when they are added, the type is lost in the reality, and ceases to show. And he said not, " for the circumcision is in us," but " we are the circumcision," and justly ; for this is the Man, the circumcision in virtue, this is really the Man. And he did not say, " For among them is the concision " ; for they themselves are henceforth in a condition of ruin and of wickedness. But no longer, says he, is circumcision performed in the body, but in the heart. " And have no confidence," says he, " in the flesh ; though I myself might have confidence even in the flesh." (v. 4.) What does he call " confidence " here, and " in the flesh " ? Boasting, boldness, a high tone. And he did well to add this ; for if he had been of the Gentiles, and had condemned circumcision, and not only circumcision, but all those that adopted it out of place, it would have seemed that he was running it down, because he lacked the high ancestry of Judaism, as being a stranger to its solemn rites, and having no part therein. But as it is, he, who, though a sharer, yet blames them, will not therefore blame them as having no share in them, but as disowning them ; not from ignorance, but most especially from acquaintance with them. Accordingly observe what he says in his Epistle to the Galatians also ; having been brought into a necessity of saying great things about himself, how even in these circumstances does he manifest nought but humility. " For ye have heard of my manner of life in time past," he says, " in the Jews' religion " (Gal. i. 13) ; and again here ; " if any other man thinketh to have confidence in the flesh, I more." (v. 4.) And he immediately added, " a Hebrew of Hebrews." But " if any other man," says he, showing the necessity, showing that it was on their account that he spoke. " If ye have confidence," he says, I also say so, since I am silent.[1] And observe the absence of all ungraciousness in the reproofs ; by forbearing to do it by name, he gave even them the opportunity of retracing their steps. " If any one thinketh to have confidence " ; and it was well to say " thinketh," either inasmuch as they really had no such confidence, or as that confidence was no real confidence, for all was by necessity, and not of choice. " Circumcised on the eighth day " ; and he sets down the first that wherein they chiefly boasted, viz. the ordinance of circumcision. " Of the stock of Israel." He pointed out both these circumstances, that he was neither a proselyte, nor born of proselytes ;

for from his being circumcised on the eighth day, it follows that he was not a proselyte, and from his being of the stock of Israel, that he was not of proselyte parents. But that you may not imagine that he was of the stock of Israel as coming of the. ten tribes, he says, " of the tribe of Benjamin." So that he was of the more approved portion, for the place of the priests was in the lot of this tribe. " An Hebrew of Hebrews." Because he was not a proselyte, but from of old, of distinguished Jews ; for he might have been of Israel, and yet not " an Hebrew of Hebrews," for many were already corrupting the matter,[2] and were strangers to the language, being encircled by other nations ; it is either this then, or the great superiority of his birth, that he shows. " According to the law a Pharisee." He is coming now to the circumstances dependent on his own will ; for all those things were apart from the will, for his being circumcised was not of himself, nor that he was of the stock of Israel, nor that he was of the tribe of Benjamin. So that, even among these he has a larger share, even though there were really many who partook with him. Where then are we to place the " rather"? Particularly herein that he was not a proselyte ; for to be of the most distinguished tribe and sect, and this from his ancestors of old, was a thing which belonged not to many. But he comes to the things which are matters of choice, wherein we have the " rather." " As touching the law, a Pharisee ; as touching zeal, persecuting the Church." But this is not sufficient ; for it is possible to be a Pharisee even, and yet not very zealous. But this also he adds ; behold the " rather." " According to righteousness." It is possible, however, to be adventurous, or to act thus[3] from ambition, and not out of zeal for the law, as the chief priests did. Yet neither was this the case, but, " according to the righteousness which is in the law, found blameless." If then both for purity of descent, and earnestness, and habits, and mode of life, I surpassed all, why have I renounced all those dignities, he asks, but because I found that the things of Christ are better, and better far ? Wherefore he added ; " howbeit what things were gain to me, these have I counted loss for Christ." (v. 7.)

Such a course of life, so strictly regulated, and entered upon from earliest childhood, such unblemished extraction, such dangers, plots, labors, forwardness, did Paul renounce, " counting them but loss," which before were "; gain," that he might " win Christ." But we do not even contemn money, that we may " win Christ," but prefer to fail of the life to come rather than of the good things of the present life. And yet

---

[1] [This is very obscure. The altered text does not help. —J. A. B.]

[2] i.e. the purity of their descent.
[3] i.e. to show zeal, as he had done in persecuting.

this is nothing else than loss; for tell me now, let us examine in detail the conditions of riches, and see whether it be not loss accompanied with trouble, and without any gain. For tell me, what is the advantage of those stores of costly garments, what good do we gain when we are arrayed in them? None, nay, we are only losers. How so? Because even the poor man, in his cheap and threadbare clothing, does not bear the scorching in time of heat any wise worse than yourself; nay, rather he bears it better, for clothes that are threadbare and worn single allow more ease to the body, but not so with those which are new made, though they be finer than the spider's web. Besides, you, from your excessive self-importance, wear even two and often three inner garments, and a cloak and girdle, and breeches too, but no one blames him if he wears but a single inner garment; so that he is the man that endures most easily. It is owing to this that we see rich men sweating, but the poor subject to nothing of the sort. Since then his cheap clothing, which is sold for a trifle, answers the same or even a better purpose to him, and those clothes, which oblige a man to pay down much gold, do only the same thing, is not this great superabundance so much loss? For it has added nothing in respect of its use and service, but your purse is emptied of so much the more gold, and the same use and service. You who have riches have purchased for a hundred pieces of gold, or even more, but the poor man for a trifling sum of silver. Do you perceive the loss? No, for your pride will not let you see it. Would you have us make out this account in the case of the gold ornaments too, which men put alike about their horses and their wives? For besides the other evils, the possession of money makes fools of men; they account their wives and horses to be worthy of the same honor, and the ornamentation of both is the same; and they would make themselves finer by the same means as the very beasts that carry them, or as the very skins of the awnings, wherein they are borne. What now is the use of decking out a mule or a horse with gold? or the lady, that has such a weight of gold and jewels about her person, what does she gain? "But the golden ornaments are never worn out," he answers. Assuredly this also is said that in the baths and many places both precious stones and gold ornaments lose much of their value. But be it so, and grant that they are not injured, tell me, what is the gain? And how is it when they drop out, and are lost? is there no loss sustained? And how when they draw down upon you envy and intrigues? is there no loss then? For when they do the wearer no good, but rather inflame the eyes of the envious, and act as an incitement to the robber, do they not

become loss? And again, say, when a man may use them for a serviceable purpose, but is unable on account of the extravagance of his wife, and is obliged to starve and to stint himself, that he may see her arrayed in gold, is it not a matter of loss? For it was on this account that goods have their name from use,[1] not that we should use them thus like goldsmiths' samples, but that we should do some good therewith; so then when love of gold does not allow this, is not the whole thing loss? for he that dares not use them forbears the use as if they were another's property, and there is no use of them in any way.

Again, how is it when we erect splendid and spacious mansions, decorated with columns, marbles, porticos, arcades, and in every possible way, setting images and statues everywhere? Many indeed even call demons out of these, i.e. the images, but let us omit the examination of those points. What too is the meaning of the gilded ceiling? Does it not supply the same need as to him, whose house is on a moderate scale? "But there is great delight in it," he says. Yes, for the first or second day, and afterwards, none at all, but it stands merely for nothing. For if the sun does not strike us with wonder, from its being customary, much more do works of art fail, and we only look at them like things of clay. For tell me, what does a range of pillars contribute to make your dwelling superior to others, or the finest statues, or the gilding spread over the wall? Nothing; rather, these come of luxury and insolence, and overweening pride and folly; for everything there ought to be necessary and useful, not superfluous things. Do you see that the thing is loss? Do you see that it is superfluous and unprofitable? for if it supplies no further use or delight, (and it "does," in the course of time, bring satiety,) it is nothing else than loss, and vainglory is the hindrance, which will not let us see this.

Did Paul then forsake those things which he "counted gain," and shall not we even quit our loss, for Christ's sake? How long shall we be riveted to the earth? How long till we shall look up to heaven? Do ye not mark the aged, what little perception they have of the past? Do ye not mark those that are finishing their course, both men in age, and men in youth? Do ye not see persons in the midst of life bereft of them? Why are we so wedded to unstable objects? Why are we linked to things that are shifting? How long before we lay hold of the things that last? What would not the old give, were it granted them to divest themselves of their old age? How irrational then to wish to return to our former youth, and gladly to give everything for the sake of this, that we might become younger, and yet when it is ours to re-

---

[1] i.e. χρήματα, from χρᾶσθαι "to use."

ceive a youth that knows no old age, a youth too, which, joined with great riches, hath far more of spirit, to be unwilling to give up a little trifle, but to hold fast things that contribute not a whit to the present life. They can never rescue you from death, they have no power to drive away disease, to stay old age, or any one of those events, which happen by necessity and according to the law of nature. And do you still hold to them? Tell me, what do you gain? Drunkenness, gluttony, pleasures contrary to nature and various in kind, which are far worse torturers than the hardest masters.

These are the advantages which we gain from riches, nor is there one besides, since we are not so minded, for if we had had the mind, we might have won heaven itself for our inheritance by our riches. "So then riches are good," he says. It is not riches, but the will of the possessor that effects this, for because it is the will that does this, it is in the power even of a poor man to win heaven. For, as I have often said, God does not regard the amount of the gifts, but the will of the givers; it is possible even for one in poverty, who has given but little, to bear off all, for God requires a measure proportioned to our ability, neither will riches secure heaven to us, nor poverty, hell; but a good or a bad will, either one or the other. This then let us correct, this let us repossess, this let us regulate, and all will then be easy to us.

For as the artificer works the wood the same, whether his axe be of iron or of gold, or rather he does it the better with an implement of iron, so here too, the straight path of virtue is more easily kept in a state of poverty. For touching riches we read, "It is easier for a camel to go through a needle's eye, than for a rich man to enter into the kingdom of Heaven." (Matt. xix. 24.) But He has made no such declarations about poverty; nay, the very reverse. "Sell thy goods, and give to the poor, and come follow Me" (v. 21); as if the act of following were to spring from the selling.

Never then let us flee from poverty as an evil, for it is the procurer of heaven. Again, let us never follow riches as a good; for they are the ruin of such as walk unwarily, but in everything directing our eyes to God, let us, as occasion requires, use those gifts which He has vouchsafed us, both strength of body, and abundance of money, and every other gift; for it is unnatural that we, who have our being for Him, should make these things serviceable to others, yet not to Him who has made us. He formed thine eye: make it serviceable to Him, not to the devil. But how serviceable to Him? By contemplating His creatures and praising and glorifying Him, and by withdrawing it from all gaze at women. Did He make thy hands? Preserve

them for His use, not for the devil, not putting them out for robbery and rapine, but for His commandments and for good deeds, for earnest prayers, for holding out help to the fallen. Hath He made thine ears? Give these to Him, and not to effeminate[1] strains nor to disgraceful tales; but "let all thy communication be in the law of the Most High." (Ecclus. ix. 15.) For "stand," he says, "in the multitude of the elders, and whoever is wise, cleave unto him." (Ecclus. vi. 34.) Did he make thy mouth? Let it do nought that is displeasing to Him, but sing psalms, hymns, and spiritual songs. "Let no corrupt speech proceed out of your mouth," says the Apostle, "but such as is good for edifying for the need may be, that it may give grace to them that hear" (Eph. iv. 29); for edification and not for subversion, for fair words and not for evil speaking and plotting against other, but the very opposite. He hath made thy feet, not that thou shouldest run to do evil, but to do good. He made thy belly, not that thou shouldest cram it to bursting, but to practice lessons of wisdom. For the production of children, He implanted desire in thy mind, not for fornication, nor for adultery. He gave thee understanding, not to make of thee a blasphemer or a reviler, but that thou mightest be without falsehood. He gave us both money to be used on fitting occasion, and strength likewise to be used on fitting occasion. He instituted arts, that our present state of existence might be held together by them, not that we should separate ourselves from spiritual things, not that we should devote ourselves to the base arts but to the necessary ones, that we might minister to one another's good, and not that we should plot one against another. He gave us a roof, that it might afford shelter from the rain, and no more, not that it should be decked out with gold, while the poor man perishes with hunger. He gave clothing to cover us, not to make a display withal, not that things like these should have much gold lavished upon them, and that Christ should perish naked. He gave you a place of shelter, not that you should keep it to yourself, but to offer it to others also. He gave thee land, not that, cutting off the chief portion of it, you should spend the good gifts of God upon harlots, and dancers, and actors, and flute players, and harp players, but upon those that hunger and are in want. He gave you the sea to sail on, that you might not be wearied with journeying, not that you should pry into its depths, and bring up thence precious stones and all the other things of the same kind, nor that you should make this your business.

"Why then are there precious stones?" he

---

[1] διακεκλασμέναις, "broken," so called from using the chromatic scale to excess.

says. Nay, do you tell me why these stones are such, and why one class are regarded as of great value, while the others are more useful? For these may be conducive to building, but those to no purpose; and these are stronger than those. "But they," he says, "produce a beautiful effect." How so? it is a matter of fancy. Are they whiter? No, they are not whiter than pure white marble, nor nearly equal to it. But are they stronger? Not even this can be said for them.[1] Well then, are they more useful? are they larger? Not even this. Whence then are they so admired, save from fancy? For if they are neither more beautiful, (for we shall find others more shining and more white,) nor useful, nor stronger, whence came they to be so admired? Was it not from mere fancy? Why then did God give them? They were not His gift, but it is your own imagination that they are anything great. "How is it, then," he answers, "that even the Scripture shows admiration of them?" So far it addresses itself to your fancy. As a master too in talking to a child often admires the same object as it does, when he desires to attract and engage it.

Why do you aim at finery in your clothing? He clothed thee with a garment and with sandals. But where is there any reason for these things? "The judgments of God," he says, "are more to be desired than gold, yea than much fine gold." (Ps. xix. 10.) These, beloved, are of no use. Had they been of use, he would not have bidden us despise them. And for Holy Scripture, it speaks with reference to our notion, and this too is an instance of God's lovingkindness. "Why then," he asks, "did He give purple and the like?" These things are products of God's gift. For He has willed by other things also to show forth His own riches. And He gave you corn too by itself; but from this you make many things, cakes and sweetmeats, of every sort and variety, having much enjoyment. Pleasure and vainglory give rise to all these inventions. It pleased you to set them before everything. For if a foreigner or a rustic, who was ignorant of the land, should put the question, and, seeing your admiration, were to say, "Why do you admire these?" What have you to say? that they are fair to look at? But not so. Let us then give up such notions; let us lay hold of the things that are truly real. These are not, but simply pass away, only flowing past like a river. Wherefore I charge you, let us take our stand upon the rock, that we both escape being easily turned about, and that we may obtain the good things to come, by the grace and lovingkindness of our Lord Jesus Christ, with whom, &c.

HOMILY XI.

Philippians iii. 7-10.

"Howbeit what things were gain to me, these have I counted loss for Christ. Yea verily, and I counted all things to be loss for the excellency of the knowledge of Christ Jesus my Lord: for whom I suffered the loss of all things, and do count them but dung, that I may gain Christ, and be found in Him, not having a righteousness of mine own, even that which is of the law, but that which is through faith in Christ, the righteousness which is of God."

In our contests with heretics, we must make the attack with minds in vigor, that they may be able to give exact attention. I will therefore begin my present discourse where the last ended. And what was that? Having enumerated every Jewish boast, both those from his birth, and those that were from choice, he added, "Howbeit, what things were gain to me, these have I counted to be loss for the excellency of the knowledge of Christ Jesus my Lord; for whom I suffered the loss of all things, and do count them but dung, that I may gain Christ." Here

the heretics spring to their attack: for even this comes of the wisdom of the Spirit, to suggest to them hopes of victory, that they may undertake the fight.

For if it had been spoken plainly, they would have acted here as they have done in other places, they would have blotted out the words, they would have denied the Scripture, when they were unable at all to look it in the face. But as in the case of fishes, that which can take them is concealed so that they may swim up, and does not lie open to view; this in truth hath come to pass here too. The Law, they say, is called "dung" by Paul, it is called "loss." He says, it was not possible to gain Christ except I "suffered" this "loss." All these things induced the heretics to accept this passage, thinking it to be favorable to them: but when they had taken it, then did he enclose them on all sides with his nets. For what do they themselves say? Lo! the Law is "loss," is "dung"; how then do ye say that it is of God?

---

[1] He refers to pearls.

But these very words are favorable to the Law, and how they are so, shall be hence manifest. Let us attend accurately to his very words. He said not, The Law is loss: but "I counted it loss." But when he spake of gain, he said not, I counted them, but "they were gain." But when he spake of loss he said, "I counted": and this rightly; for the former was naturally so, but the latter became so, from my opinion. "What then? Is it not so?" says he. It is loss for Christ.

And how has the law become gain? And it was not *counted* gain, but *was* so. For consider how great a thing it was, to bring men, brutalized in their nature, to the shape of men. If the law had not been, grace would not have been given. Wherefore? Because it became a sort of bridge; for when it was impossible to mount on high from a state of great abasement, a ladder was formed. But he who has ascended has no longer need of the ladder; yet he does not despise it, but is even grateful to it. For it has placed him in such a position, as no longer to require it. And yet for this very reason, that he doth not require it, it is just that he should acknowledge his obligation, for he could not fly up. And thus is it with the Law, it hath led us up on high; wherefore it was gain, but for the future we esteem it loss. How? Not because it is loss, but because grace is far greater. For as a poor man, that was in hunger, as long as he has silver, escapes hunger, but when he finds gold, and it is not allowable to keep both, considers it loss to retain the former, and having thrown it away, takes the gold coin; so also here; not because the silver is loss, for it is not; but because it is impossible to take both at once, but it is necessary to leave one. Not the Law then is loss, but for a man to cleave to the Law, and desert Christ. Wherefore it is then loss when it leads us away from Christ. But if it sends us on to Him, it is no longer so. For this cause he saith "loss for Christ"; if for Christ, it is not so naturally. But why doth not the Law suffer us to come to Christ? For this very cause, he tells us, was it given. And Christ is the fulfilling of the Law, and Christ is the end of the Law. It doth suffer us if we will. "For Christ is the end of the Law." He who obeyeth the Law, leaves the Law itself. It suffers, if we take heed to it, but if we do not take heed, it suffers not. "Yea verily, and I have counted all things but loss." Why, he means, do I say this of the Law? Is not the world good? Is not the present life good? but if they draw me away from Christ, I count these things loss. Why? "for the excellency of the knowledge of Jesus Christ my Lord." For when the sun hath appeared, it is loss to sit by a candle: so that the loss comes by comparison, by the superiority

of the other. You see that Paul makes a comparison from superiority, not from diversity of kind; for that which is superior, is superior to somewhat of like nature to itself. So that he shows the connection of that knowledge by the same means, by which he draws the superiority from the comparison. "For whom I suffered the loss of all things, and do count them dung, that I may gain Christ." It is not yet manifest, whether he speaks of the Law, for it is likely that he applies it to the things of this world. For when he says, "the things which were gain to me, those I have counted loss for Christ; yea verily," he adds, "I count all things loss." Although he said all things, yet it is things present; and if you wish it to be the Law too, not even so is it insulted. For dung comes from wheat, and the strength of the wheat is the dung, I mean, the chaff. But as the dung was useful in its former state, so that we gather it together with the wheat, and had there been no dung, there would have been no wheat, thus too is it with the Law.

Seest thou, how everywhere he calls it "loss," not in itself, but for Christ. "Yea verily, and I count all things but loss." Wherefore again? "For the excellency of the knowledge (of Him), for whom I suffered the loss of all things." Again, "wherefore too I count all things to be loss, that I may gain Christ."

See how, from every point, he lays hold of Christ as his foundation, and suffers not the Law to be anywhere exposed, or receive a blow, but guards it on every side. "And that I may be found in Him, not having a righteousness of mine own, even that which is of the Law." If he who had righteousness, ran to this other righteousness because his own was nothing, how much rather ought they, who have it not, to run to Him? And he well said, "a righteousness of mine own," not that which I gained by labor and toil, but that which I found from grace. If then he who was so excellent is saved by grace, much more are you. For since it was likely they would say that the righteousness which comes from toil is the greater, he shows that it is dung in comparison with the other. For otherwise I, who was so excellent in it, would not have cast it away, and run to the other. But what is that other? That which is from the faith of God, i.e. it too is given by God. This is the righteousness of God; this is altogether a gift. And the gifts of God far exceed those worthless good deeds, which are due to our own diligence.

But what is "By faith that I may know Him"?[1] So then knowledge is through faith,

---

[1] [The words "by faith," literally, "upon faith," are usually understood as connected with "righteousness"; but in strictness of Greek syntax this cannot be, and they are better connected with

and without faith it is impossible to know Him. Why how? Through it we must "know the power of His resurrection." For what reason can demonstrate to us the Resurrection? None, but faith only. For if the resurrection of Christ, who was according to the flesh, is known by faith, how can the generation of the Word of God be comprehended by reasoning? For the resurrection is less than the generation. Why? Because of that there have been many examples, but of this none ever; for many dead arose before Christ, though after their resurrection they died, but no one was ever born of a virgin. If then we must comprehend by faith that which is inferior to the generation according to the flesh, how can that which is far greater, immeasurably and incomparably greater, be comprehended by reason? These things make the righteousness; this must we believe that He was able to do, but how He was able we cannot prove. For from faith is the fellowship of His sufferings. But how? Had we not believed, neither should we have suffered: had we not believed, that "if we endure with Him, we shall also reign with Him" (2 Tim. ii. 12), we should not have endured the sufferings. Both the generation and the resurrection is comprehended by faith. Seest thou, that faith must not be absolutely, but through good works; for he especially believes that Christ hath risen, who in like sort gives himself up to dangers, who hath fellowship with Him in His sufferings. For he hath fellowship with Him who rose again, with Him who liveth; wherefore he saith, "And may be found in Him, not having a righteousness of mine own, even that which is of the law, but that which is through faith in Christ, the righteousness which is of God by faith: that I may know Him, and the power of His resurrection, and the fellowship of His sufferings, becoming conformed unto His death; if by any means I may attain unto the resurrection from the dead." He saith, being made conformable unto His death, i.e. having fellowship; whereas He suffered from men, thus I too; wherefore he said, "becoming conformed" and again in another place, "and fill up on my part that which is lacking of the afflictions of Christ in my flesh." (Col. i. 24.) That is, these persecutions and sufferings work the image of His death, for He sought not His own, but the good of many.

Therefore persecutions, and afflictions, and straits, ought not to disturb you, but ought even to make you glad, because through them we are "conformed to His death." As if he had said, We are molded to His likeness; as he says in

another place, where he writeth, "bearing about in the body the dying of the Lord Jesus." (2 Cor. iv. 10.) And this too comes from great faith. For we not only believe that He arose, but that after His resurrection also He hath great power: wherefore we travel the same road which He travelled, i.e. we become brethren to Him in this respect also. As if he had said, We become Christs in this respect. O how great is the dignity of sufferings! We believe that we become "conformed to His death" through sufferings! For as in baptism, we were "buried with the likeness of His death," so here, with His death. There did he rightly say, "The likeness of His death" (Rom. vi. 4, 5), for there we died not entirely, we died not in the flesh, to the body, but to sin. Since then a death is spoken of, and a death; but He indeed died in the body, whilst we died to sin, and there the Man died which He assumed, who was in our flesh, but here the man of sin; for this cause he saith, "the likeness of His death," but here, no longer the likeness of His death, but His death itself. For Paul, in his persecutions, no longer died to sin, but in[1] his very body. Wherefore, he endured the same death. "If by any means," saith he, "I may attain unto the resurrection from the dead." What sayest thou? All men will have a share in that. "For we shall not all sleep, but we shall all be changed" (1 Cor. xv. 51), and shall all share not only in the Resurrection, but in incorruption. Some indeed to honor, but others as a means of punishment. If therefore all have a share in the Resurrection, and not in the Resurrection only, but also in incorruption, how said he, "If by any means I may attain," as if about to share in some especial thing? "For this cause," saith he, "I endure these things, if by any means I may attain unto the resurrection from the dead." For if thou hadst not died, thou wouldest not arise. What is it then? Some great thing seems here to be hinted at. So great was it, that he dared not openly assert it, but saith, "If by any means." I have believed in Him and His resurrection, nay, moreover, I suffer for Him, yet I am unable to be confident concerning the Resurrection. What resurrection doth he here mention? That which leads to Christ Himself. I said, that I believed in "Him, and in the power of His resurrection," and that I "have fellowship with His sufferings," and that I "become conformed to His death." Yet after all these things I am by no means confident; as he said elsewhere, "Let him that thinketh he standeth, take heed lest he fall." (1 Cor. x. 12.) And again, "I fear lest by any means, after that I have preached to others, I myself should be rejected." (1 Cor. ix. 27.)

"having" as repeated before "that which" (comp. Meyer). Not seeing this, and feeling the grammatical difficulty of the other connection, Chrys. quite fancifully joins them with the words that follow, and proceeds to say some very striking things. — J. A. B.]

[1] or to.

Ver. 12. "Not that I have already obtained, or am already made perfect: but I press on, if so be that I may apprehend that for which also I was apprehended by Christ Jesus."

"Not that I have already obtained." What means "already obtained"? He speaks of the prize, but if he who had endured such sufferings, he who was persecuted, he "who had in him the dying of the Lord Jesus," was not yet confident about that resurrection, what can we say? What meaneth, "if I may apprehend"? What he before said, "If I may attain to the resurrection of the dead." (2 Cor. iv. 10.) If I may apprehend, he saith, His resurrection; i.e. if I may be able to endure so great things, if I may be able to imitate Him, if I may be able to become conformed to Him. For example, Christ suffered many things, He was spit upon, He was stricken, was scourged, at last He suffered what things he suffered.[1] This is the entire course. Through all these things it is needful that men should endure the whole contest, and so come to His resurrection. Or he means this, if I am thought worthy to attain the glorious resurrection, which is a matter of confidence, in order to His resurrection. For if I am able to endure all the contests, I shall be able also to have His resurrection, and to rise with glory. For not as yet, saith he, am I worthy, but "I press on, if so be that I may apprehend." My life is still one of contest, I am still far from the end, I am still distant from the prize, still I run, still I pursue. And He said not, I run, but "I pursue." For you know with what eagerness a man pursues. He sees no one, he thrusts aside with great violence all who would interrupt his pursuit. He collects together his mind, and sight, and strength, and soul, and body, looking to nothing else than the prize. But if Paul, who so pursued, who had suffered so many things, yet saith, "if I may attain," what should we say, who have relaxed our efforts? Then to show that the thing is of debt, he saith, "For which also I was apprehended by Christ Jesus." I was, he saith, of the number of the lost, I gasped for breath, I was nigh dead, God apprehended me. For He pursued us, when we fled from Him, with all speed. So that he points out all those things; for the words, "I was apprehended," show the earnestness of Him who wishes to apprehend us, and our great aversion to Him, our wandering, our flight from Him.

So that we are liable for a vast debt, and no one grieves, no one weeps, no one groans, all having returned to their former state. For as before the appearance of Christ we fled from God, so now also. For we can flee from God, not in place, for He is everywhere; and hear the Prophet, when he says, "Whither shall I go from Thy Spirit, or whither shall I flee from Thy presence"? (Ps. cxxxix. 7.) How then can we flee from God? Even as we can become distant from God, even as we can be removed afar off. "They that are far from Thee," it says, "shall perish." (Ps. lxxiii. 27.) And again, "Have not your iniquities separated between Me and you?" (Isa. lix. 2.) How then comes this removal, how comes this separation? In purpose and soul: for it cannot be in place. For how could one fly from Him who is everywhere present? The sinner then flies. This is what the Scripture saith, "The wicked fleeth when no man pursueth him." (Prov. xxviii. 1.) We eagerly fly from God, although He always pursueth us. The Apostle hasted, that he might be near Him. We haste, that we may be far off.

Are not these things then worthy of lamentation? Are they not worthy of tears? Whither fliest thou, wretched and miserable man? Whither fliest thou from thy Life and thy Salvation? If thou fly from God, with whom wilt thou take refuge? If thou fly from the Light, whither wilt thou cast thine eyes? If thou fly from thy Life, whence wilt thou henceforth live? Let us fly from the enemy of our Salvation! Whensoever we sin we fly from God, we are as runaways, we depart to a foreign land, as he who consumed his paternal goods and departed into a foreign land, who wasted all his father's substance, and lived in want. We too have substance from our Father; and what is this? He hath freed us from our sins; He hath freely given to us power, strength for works of virtue; He hath freely given to us readiness, patience; He hath freely given to us the Holy Ghost in our baptism; if we waste these things we shall henceforth be in want. For as the sick, as long as they are troubled with fevers, and badness of their juices, are unable to arise or work, or do anything, but if any one sets them free, and brings them to health, if they then work not, this comes from their own sloth; thus too is it with us. For the disease was heavy and the fever excessive. And we lay not upon a bed, but upon wickedness itself, cast away in crime, as on a dunghill, full of sores, and evil odors, squalid, wasting away, more like ghosts than men. Evil spirits encompassed us about, the Prince of this world deriding and assaulting us; the Only-Begotten Son of God came, sent forth the rays of His Presence, and straightway dispelled the darkness. The King, who is on His Father's throne, came to us, having left His Father's throne. And when I say having left, think not of any removal, for He filleth the heavens and the earth, but I speak of the economy; He came to an enemy, who hated Him, who turned himself away, who could not endure

---

[1] [i.e. the well-known sufferings, the Passion. — J. A. B.]

to behold Him, who blasphemed Him every day. He saw him lying on a dunghill, eaten with worms, afflicted with fever and hunger, having every sort of disease; for both fever vexed him, which is evil desire; and inflammation lay heavy on him, this is pride; and gnawing hunger had hold of him, which is covetousness; and putrefying sores on every side, for this is fornication; and blindness of eyes, which is idolatry; and dumbness, and madness, which is to worship stocks and stones, and address them; and great deformity, for wickedness is this, foul to behold, and a most heavy disease. And he saw us speaking more foolishly than the mad, and calling stocks our God, and stones likewise; He saw us in such great guilt, he did not reject us; was not wroth, turned not away, hated us not, for He was a Master, and could not hate His own creation. But what does he do? As a most excellent physician, He prepareth medicines of great price, and Himself tastes them first. For He Himself first followed after virtue, and thus gave it to us. And He first gave us the washing,[1] like some antidote, and thus we vomited up all our guilt, and all things took their flight at once, and our inflammation ceased, and our fever was quenched, and our sores were dried up. For all the evils which are from covetousness, and anger, and all the rest, were dissipated by the Spirit. Our eyes were opened, our ears were opened, our tongue spake holy words: our soul received strength, our body received such beauty and bloom, as it is like that he who is born a son of God should have from the grace of the Spirit; such glory as it is like that the new-born son of a king should have, nurtured in

purple. Alas! How great nobility did He confer on us!

We were born, we were nurtured, why do we again fly from our Benefactor? He then, who hath done all these things, giveth us strength too, for it was not possible, for a soul bowed down by the disease to endure it, did not He Himself give us the strength. He gave us remission of our sins. We devoured all things. He gave us strength, we wasted it. He gave us grace, we quenched it; and how? we consumed it upon nought that was fitting, we used it for no useful end. These things have destroyed us, and what is more dreadful than all, when we are in a foreign country, and feeding on husks, we say not, Let us return to our Father, and say, "We have sinned against Heaven, and against Thee." (Luke xv. 18.) And that too, when we have so loving a Father, who eagerly desires our return. If we will only return to Him, He does not even bear to call in question our former deeds, only let us quit them. It is sufficient apology with Him, that we have returned. Not only He Himself calls not in question, but if another does so, He stops his mouth, though the accuser be one of good repute. Let us return! How long do we stand afar off? Let us perceive our dishonor, let us be sensible of our vileness. Sin makes us swine, sin brings famine to the soul; let us regain ourselves, and be sober again, and return to our former high birth, that we may obtain the good things which are to come, in Christ Jesus our Lord, with whom to the Father together with the Holy Spirit be glory, might, honor, now and ever and world without end.

HOMILY XII.

PHILIPPIANS iii. 13, 14.

"Brethren, I count not myself yet to have apprehended: but one thing I do, forgetting the things which are behind, and stretching forward to the things which are before, I press on toward the goal unto the prize of the high calling of God in Christ Jesus."

NOTHING so renders our real excellences vain and puffs them away, as to be remembering the good deeds we have done; for this produces two evils, it both renders us remiss, and raises us to haughtiness. Wherefore see how Paul, since he knew our nature to be easily inclined to remissness, though he had given great praise to

the Philippians, now subdues their mind by many other things above, but chiefly by his present words. And what are they? "Brethren, I count not myself[2] to have apprehended." But if Paul had not as yet apprehended, and is not confident about the Resurrection and things to come, hardly should they be so, who have not attained the smallest proportion of his excellence. That is, I consider that I have not as

---

[1] [Or "bath," "laver." He refers to Tit. iii. 5.— J. A. B.]

[2] [Nearly all documents of Chrys. here read simply "not," as in Textus Receptus. Yet the connection following seems to show that Chrys. really read "not yet," as in the Rev. Eng. Bible. Early copyists made the quotation conform to the text of Scripture with which they were familiar, but left the comment unaltered,—a frequent occurrence in the Fathers.— J. A. B.]

yet apprehended all virtue, as if one were speaking of a runner. Not as yet, saith he, have I completed all. And if in another place he saith, "I have fought the good fight" (2 Tim. iv. 7), but here, "I count myself not as yet to have apprehended"; any one who reads carefully will well know the reason both of those, and of the present words; (for it is not necessary to dwell continually on the same point;) and that he spoke these words at a much earlier date, but the others near his death. But I am solely engaged on "one thing," says he, "in stretching forward to the things which are before." But "one thing," says he, "forgetting the things which are behind, and stretching forward to the things which are before, I press on toward the goal unto the prize of the high calling of God in Christ Jesus." For what made him reach forward unto the things which are before, was his forgetting the things that are behind. He then, who thinks that all is accomplished, and that nothing is wanting to him for the perfecting of virtue, may cease running, as having apprehended all. But he who thinks that he is still distant from the goal, will never cease running. This then we should always consider, even though we have wrought ten thousand good deeds; for if Paul, after ten thousand deaths, after so many dangers, considered this, how much more should we? For I fainted not, saith he, although I availed not, after running so much; nor did I despair, but I still run, I still strive. This thing only I consider, that I may in truth advance. Thus too we should act, we should forget our successes, and throw them behind us. For the runner reckons not up how many circuits he hath finished, but how many are left. We too should reckon up, not how far we are advanced in virtue, but how much remains for us. For what doth that which is finished profit us, when that which is deficient is not added? Moreover he did not say, I do not reckon up, but I do not even remember. For we thus become eager, when we apply all diligence to what is left, when we give to oblivion everything else. "Stretching forward," saith he; before we arrive, we strive to obtain. For he that stretches forward is one who, though his feet are running, endeavors to outstrip them with the rest of his body, stretching himself towards the front, and reaching out his hands, that he may accomplish somewhat more of the course. And this comes from great eagerness, from much warmth; thus the runner should run with great earnestness, with so great eagerness, without relaxation. As far as one who so runs differs from him who lies supine, so far doth Paul differ from us. He died daily, he was approved daily, there was no season, there was no time in which his course advanced not. He wished not to take,

but to snatch the prize; for in this way we may take it. He who giveth the prize standeth on high, the prize is laid up on high.

See how great a distance this is that must be run over! See how great an ascent! Thither we must fly up with the wings of the Spirit, otherwise it is impossible to surmount this height. Thither must we go with the body, for it is allowed. "For our citizenship is in heaven" (Phil. iii. 20), there is the prize; seest thou the runners, how they live by rule, how they touch nothing that relaxes their strength, how they exercise themselves every day in the palæstra, under a master, and by rule? Imitate them, or rather exhibit even greater eagerness, for the prizes are not equal: many are those who would hinder you; live by rule: many are the things which relax your strength; make its feet[1] agile: for it is possible so to do, it comes not naturally, but by our will. Let us bring it to lightness, lest our swiftness of foot be hindered by the weight of other things. Teach thy feet to be sure, for there are many slippery places, and if thou fallest, straightway thou losest much. But yet if thou fall, rise up again. Even thus mayst thou obtain the victory. Never attempt slippery things, and thou wilt not fall; walk upon firm ground, up with thy head, up with thine eyes; these commands the trainers give to those who run. Thus thy strength is supported; but if thou stoopest downward, thou fallest, thou art relaxed. Look upward, where the prize is; the sight of the prize increaseth the determination of our will. The hope of taking it suffereth not to perceive the toils, it maketh the distance appear short. And what is this prize? No palm branch; but what? The kingdom of heaven, everlasting rest, glory together with Christ, the inheritance, brotherhood, ten thousand good things, which it is impossible to name. It is impossible to describe the beauty of that prize; he who hath it alone knoweth it, and he who is about to receive it. It is not of gold, it is not set with jewels, it is far more precious. Gold is mire, in comparison with that prize, precious stones are mere bricks in comparison with its beauty. If thou hast this, and takest thy departure to heaven, thou wilt be able to walk there with great honor; the angels will reverence thee, when thou bearest this prize, with much confidence wilt thou approach them all. "In Christ Jesus." See the humility of his mind; this I do, saith he, "in Christ Jesus," for it is impossible without an impulse from Him to pass over so vast an interval: we have need of much aid, of a mighty alliance; He hath willed that thou shouldest struggle below, on high He crowns thee. Not as in this world; the crown is not

---

[1] [i.e. the feet of your strength. — J. A. B.]

here, where the contest is; but the crown is in that bright place. See ye not, even here, that the most honored of the wrestlers and charioteers are not crowned in the course below, but the king calls them up, and crowns them there? Thus too is it here, in heaven thou receivest the prize.

Ver. 15. "Let us, therefore, as many as be perfect, be thus minded," saith he. "And if in anything ye are otherwise minded, even this shall God reveal unto you." What sort of thing? That we should "forget the things which are behind." Wherefore it belongs to him who is perfect not to consider himself perfect. How therefore sayest thou, "as many as are perfect"? For tell me, are we minded as thou art? For if thou hast not attained nor art perfected, how dost thou command those that are perfect to be so minded as thou art, who art not yet perfect? Yea, for this, saith he, is perfection. And "if ye are in anything otherwise minded, even this shall God reveal unto you." That is, if any one considers that he has attained all excellence. He puts them on their guard, not by speaking directly, but what saith he? "If in anything ye are otherwise minded, even this shall God reveal unto you." See how humbly he saith this! God shall teach you, i.e. God shall persuade you,[1] not teach you; for Paul was teaching, but God shall lead them on. And he said not, shall lead you on, but "shall reveal," that this may rather seem to spring from ignorance. These words were spoken not concerning doctrines, but concerning perfection of life, and our not considering ourselves to be perfect, for he who considers that he hath apprehended all, hath nothing.

Ver. 16. "Only, whereunto we have already attained, by that same rule let us walk, let us mind the same thing."

"Only, whereunto we have attained." What means this? Let us hold fast, he saith, that in which we have succeeded; love, concord, and peace: for in this we have succeeded.[2] "Whereto we have attained: to walk by the same rule, to mind the same thing." "Whereunto we have attained," i.e. in this we have already succeeded. Seest thou, that he wills that his precepts should be a rule to us? And a rule admits neither addition, nor subtraction, since that destroys its being a rule. "By the same rule," i.e. by the same faith, within the same limits.

Ver. 17. "Brethren, be ye imitators of me, and mark them which so walk even as ye have us for an ensample."

He had said above, "beware of dogs," from such he had led them away; he brings them near to these whom they ought to imitate. If any one, saith he, wishes to imitate me, if any one wishes to walk the same road, let him take heed to them; though I am not present, ye know the manner of my walk, that is, my conduct in life. For not by words only did he teach, but by deeds too; as in the chorus, and the army, the rest must imitate the leader of the chorus or the army, and thus advance in good order. For it is possible that the order may be dissolved by sedition.

The Apostles therefore were a type, and kept throughout a certain archetypal model. Consider how entirely accurate their life was, so that they are proposed as an archetype and example, and as living laws. For what was said in their writings, they manifested to all in their actions. This is the best teaching; thus he will be able to carry on his disciple. But if he indeed speaks as a philosopher, yet in his actions doth the contrary, he is no longer a teacher. For mere verbal philosophy is easy even for the disciple: but there is need of that teaching and leading which comes of deeds. For this both makes the teacher to be reverenced, and prepares the disciple to yield obedience. How so? When one sees him delivering philosophy in words, he will say he commands impossibilities; that they are impossibilities, he himself is the first to show, who does not practice them. But if he sees his virtue fully carried out in action, he will no longer be able to speak thus. Yet although the life of our teacher be careless, let us take heed to ourselves, and let us listen to the words of the prophet; "They shall be all taught of God." (Isa. liv. 13.) "And they shall teach no more every man his brother, saying, Know the Lord, for they shall all know me from the least of them to the greatest of them." (Jer. xxxi. 34.) Hast thou a teacher who is not virtuous? Still thou hast Him who is truly a Teacher, whom alone thou shouldest call a Teacher. Learn from Him: He hath said, "Learn of Me, for I am meek." (Matt. xi. 29.) Take not heed, then, to thy teacher, but to Him and to His lessons. Take thence thy examples, thou hast a most excellent model, to it conform thyself. There are innumerable models laid before thee in the Scriptures of virtuous lives; whichsoever thou wilt, come, and after the Master find it in the disciples. One hath shown forth through poverty, another through riches; for example, Elijah through poverty, Abraham through riches. Go to that example, which thou esteemest most easy, most befitting thyself to practice. Again, one by marriage, the other by virginity; Abraham by marriage, the other by virginity. Follow whichever thou wilt: for both lead to heaven. One shone forth by fasting, as John, another without fasting, as Job. Again, this latter had a

---

[1] i.e. succeed in persuading.
[2] He applies this to walking by the same rule "with each other," &c.

care for his wife, his children, his daughters, his family, and possessed great wealth; the other possessed nothing but the garment of hair. And why do I make mention of family, or wealth, or money, when it is possible that even one in a kingdom should lay hold on virtue, for the house of a king would be found more full of trouble than any private family. David then shone forth in his kingdom; the purple and the diadem rendered him not at all remiss. To another it was entrusted to preside over a whole people, I mean Moses, which was a more difficult task, for there the power was greater, whence the difficulty too became greater. Thou hast seen men approved in wealth, thou hast seen them in poverty also, thou hast seen them in marriage, thou hast seen them in virginity too; on the contrary, behold some lost in marriage and in virginity, in wealth and in poverty. For example, many men have perished in marriage, as Samson,[1] yet not from marriage, but from their own deliberate choice. Likewise in virginity, as the five virgins. In wealth, as the rich man, who disregarded Lazarus: in poverty, innumerable poor men even now are lost. In a kingdom, I can point to many who have perished, and in ruling the people. Wouldest thou see men saved in the rank of a soldier? there is Cornelius; and in the government of a household? there is the eunuch of the Ethiopian Queen. Thus is it universally. If we use our wealth as is fit, nothing will destroy us; but if not, all things will destroy us, whether a kingdom, or poverty, or wealth. But nothing will have power to hurt the man, who keeps well awake.

For tell me, was captivity any harm? None at all. For consider, I pray thee, Joseph, who became a slave, and preserved his virtue. Consider Daniel, and the Three Children, who became captives, and how much the more they shone forth, for virtue shineth everywhere, is invincible, and nothing can put hindrances in its way. But why make I mention of poverty, and captivity, and slavery; and hunger, and sores, and grievous disease? For disease is more hard to endure than slavery. Such was Lazarus, such was Job, such was also Timothy, straitened by "often infirmities." (1 Tim. v. 23.) Thou seest that nothing can obtain the mastery over virtue; neither wealth, nor poverty, nor dominion, nor subjection, nor the preëminence in affairs, nor disease, nor contempt, nor abandonment. But having left all these things below, and upon the earth, it hastens towards Heaven. Only let the soul be noble, and nought can hinder it from being virtuous. For when he who

works is in vigor, nothing external can hinder him; for as in the arts, when the artificer is experienced and persevering, and thoroughly acquainted with his art, if disease overtakes him, he still hath it; if he became poor, he still hath it; whether he hath his tools in his hand or hath them not, whether he works or worketh not, he loseth not at all his art: for the science of it is contained within him. Thus too the virtuous man, who is devoted to God, manifests his art, if you cast him into wealth, or if into poverty, if into disease, if into health, if into dishonor, if into great honor. Did not the Apostles work in every state, "By glory and dishonor, by good report and evil report"? (2 Cor. vi. 8.) This is an athlete, to be prepared for everything; for such is also the nature of virtue.

If thou sayest, I am not able to preside over many, I ought to lead a solitary life; thou offerest an insult to virtue, for it can make use of every state, and shine through all: only let it be in the soul. Is there a famine? or is there abundance? It shows forth its own strength, as Paul saith, "I know how to abound, and how to be in want." (Phil. iv. 12; Acts xxviii. 30.) Was he required to work? He was not ashamed, but wrought two years. Was hunger to be undergone? He sank not under it, nor wavered. Was death to be borne? He became not dejected, through all he exhibited his noble mind and art. Him therefore let us imitate, and we shall have no cause of grief: for tell me, what will have power to grieve such an one? Nothing. As long as no one deprives us of this art, this will be the most blessed of all men, even in this life as well as in that to come. For suppose the good man hath a wife and children, and riches, and great honor, with all these things he remaineth alike virtuous. Take them away, and again in like sort he will be virtuous, neither overwhelmed by his misfortunes, nor puffed up by prosperity, but as a rock standeth equally unmoved in the raging sea and in calm, neither broken by the waves nor influenced at all by the calm, thus too the solid mind stands firm both in calm and in storm. And as little children, when sailing in a ship, are tossed about, whilst the pilot sits by, laughing and undisturbed, and delighted to see their confusion; thus too the soul which is truly wise, when all others are in confusion, or else are inopportunely smiling at any change of circumstance, sits unmoved, as it were, at the tiller and helm of piety. For tell me, what can disturb the pious soul? Can death? This is the beginning of a better life. Can poverty? This helps her on toward virtue. Can disease? She regards not its presence. She regards neither ease, nor affliction; for being beforehand with it, she hath afflicted herself. Can dishonor? The world hath been crucified to her. Can the loss of children? She fears it not, when she is fully persuaded of the Resurrection. What then can surprise her? None of all these things. Doth wealth elevate her? By no means, she knoweth that money is nothing. Doth glory? She hath been taught that "all the glory of man is as the flower of grass." (Isa. xl. 6.) Doth luxury? She hath heard Paul say, "She that giveth herself to pleasure is dead while she liveth." (1 Tim. v. 6.) Since then she is neither inflamed nor cramped, what can equal such health as this?

Other souls, meanwhile, are not such, but change more frequently than the sea, or the cameleon, so that thou hast great cause to smile, when thou seest the same man at one time laughing, at another weeping, at one time full of care, at another beyond measure relaxed and languid. For this cause Paul saith, " Be not fashioned according to this world." (Rom. xii. 2.) For we are citizens of heaven, where there is no turning. Prizes which change not are held out to us. Let us make manifest this our citizenship, let us thence already receive our good things. But why do we cast ourselves into the Euripus; into tempest, into storm, into foam? Let us be in calm. It all depends not on wealth, nor on poverty, nor honor, nor dishonor, nor on sickness, nor on health, nor on weakness, but on our own soul. If it is solid, and well-instructed in the science of virtue, all things will be easy to it. Even hence it will already behold its rest, and that quiet harbor, and, on its departure, will there attain innumerable good things, the which may we all attain, by the grace and love of our Lord Jesus Christ, with whom, to the Father, together with the Holy Spirit, be glory, dominion, honor, now and ever, and world without end. Amen.

HOMILY XIII.

PHILIPPIANS iii. 18–21.

" For many walk, of whom I told you often, and now tell you even weeping, that they are the enemies of the cross of Christ: whose end is perdition, whose god is the belly, and whose glory is in their shame, who mind earthly things. For our citizenship is in heaven; from whence also we wait for a Saviour, the Lord Jesus Christ: who shall fashion anew the body of our humiliation, that it may be conformed to the body of his glory, according to the working whereby He is able even to subject all things unto Himself."

NOTHING is so incongruous in a Christian, and foreign to his character, as to seek ease and rest; and to be engrossed with the present life is foreign to our profession and enlistment. Thy Master was crucified, and dost thou seek ease? Thy Master was pierced with nails, and dost thou live delicately? Do these things become a noble soldier? Wherefore Paul saith, " Many walk, of whom I told you often, and now tell you even weeping, that they are the enemies of the cross of Christ." Since there were some who made a pretense of Christianity, yet lived in ease and luxury, and this is contrary to the Cross: therefore he thus spoke. For the cross belongs to a soul at its post for the fight, longing to die, seeking nothing like ease, whilst their conduct is of the contrary sort. So that even if they say, they are Christ's, still they are as it were enemies of the Cross. For did they love the Cross, they would strive to live the crucified life. Was not thy Master hung upon the tree? Do thou otherwise imitate Him. Crucify thyself, though no one crucify thee. Crucify thyself, not that thou mayest slay thyself, God forbid, for that is a wicked thing, but as Paul said, " The world hath been crucified unto me and I unto the world." (Gal. vi. 14.) If thou lovest thy Master, die His death. Learn how great is the power of the Cross; how many good things it hath achieved, and doth still: how it is the safety of our life. Through it all things are done. Baptism is through the Cross, for we must receive that seal. The laying on of hands is through the Cross. If we are on journeys, if we are at home, wherever we are, the Cross is a great good, the armor of salvation, a shield which cannot be beaten down, a weapon to oppose the devil; thou bearest the Cross when thou art at enmity with him, not simply when thou sealest thyself by it, but when thou sufferest the things belonging to the Cross. Christ thought fit to call our sufferings by the name of the Cross. As when he saith, " Except a man take up his cross and follow Me " (Matt. xvi. 24), i.e. except he be prepared to die.

But these being base, and lovers of life, and lovers of their bodies, are enemies of the Cross. And every one, who is a friend of luxury, and of present safety, is an enemy of that Cross in which Paul makes his boast: which he embraces, with which he desires to be incorporated. As when he saith, "I am crucified unto the world, and the world unto me." But here he saith, "I now tell you weeping." Wherefore? Because the evil was urgent, because such deserve tears. Of a truth the luxurious are worthy of tears, who make fat that which is thrown about them, I mean the body, and take no thought of that soul which must give account. Behold thou livest delicately, behold thou art drunken, to-day and to-morrow, ten years, twenty, thirty, fifty, a hundred, which is impossible ; but if thou wilt, let us suppose it. What is the end? What is the gain? Nought at all. Doth it not then deserve tears, and lamentations, to lead such a life ; God hath brought us into this course, that He may crown us, and we take our departure without doing any noble action. Wherefore Paul weepeth, where others laugh, and live in pleasure. So sympathetic is he : such thought taketh he for all men. "Whose god," saith he, " is the belly." For this have they a God !¹ That is, "let us eat and drink !" Dost thou see, how great an evil luxury is? to some their wealth, and to others their belly is a god. Are not these too idolaters, and worse than the common? And their "glory is in their shame." (1 Cor. xv. 32.) Some say it is circumcision. I think not so, but this is its meaning, they make a boast of those things, of which they ought to be ashamed. It is a fearful thing to do shameful actions ; yet to do them, and be ashamed, is only half so dreadful. But where a man even boasts himself of them, it is excessive senselessness.

Do these words apply to them alone? And do those who are here present escape the charge? And will no one have account to render of these things? Does no one make a god of his belly, or glory in his shame? I wish, earnestly I wish, that none of these charges lay against us, and that I did not know any one involved in what I have said. But I fear lest the words have more reference to us than to the men of those times. For when one consumes his whole life in drinking and reveling, and expends some small trifle on the poor, whilst he consumes the larger portion on his belly, will not these words with justice apply to him? No words are more apt to call attention, or more cutting in reproof, than these : "Whose god is the belly, whose glory is in their shame." And who are these? They, he says, who mind earthly things. "Let us build houses." Where, I ask? On the earth, they answer. Let us purchase farms ; on the earth again : let us obtain power ; again on the earth : let us gain glory ; again on the earth : let us enrich ourselves ; all these things are on the earth. These are they, whose god is their belly ; for if they have no spiritual thoughts, but have all their possessions here, and mind these things, with

reason have they their belly for their god, in saying, " Let us eat and drink, for to-morrow we die." And about thy body, thou grievest, tell me, that it is of earth, though thus thou art not at all injured. But thy soul thou draggest down to the earth, when thou oughtest to render even thy body spiritual ; for thou mayest, if thou wilt. Thou hast received a belly, that thou mayest feed, not distend it, that thou mayest have the mastery over it, not have it as mistress over thee : that it may minister to thee for the nourishment of the other parts, not that thou mayest minister to it, not that thou mayest exceed limits. The sea, when it passes its bounds, doth not work so many evils, as the belly doth to our body, together with our soul. The former overfloweth all the earth, the latter all the body. Put moderation for a boundary to it, as God hath put the sand for the sea. Then if its waves arise, and rage furiously, rebuke it, with the power which is in thee. See how God hath honored thee, that thou mightest imitate Him, and thou wilt not ; but thou seest the belly overflowing, destroying. and overwhelming thy whole nature, and darest not to restrain or moderate it.

"Whose God," he saith, " is their belly." Let us see how Paul served God : let us see how gluttons serve their belly. Do not they undergo ten thousand such deaths? do not they fear to disobey whatever it orders? do not they minister impossibilities to it? Are not they worse than slaves? "But our citizenship," says he, " is in Heaven." Let us not then seek for ease here ; there do we shine, where also our citizenship is. "From whence also," saith he, " we wait for a Saviour," the Lord Jesus Christ : "who shall fashion anew the body of our humiliation, that it may be conformed to the body of his glory." By little and little he hath carried us up. He saith, " From Heaven " and " Our Saviour," showing, from the place and from the Person, the dignity of the subject. "Who shall fashion anew the body of our humiliation," saith he. The body now suffereth many things : it is bound with chains, it is scourged, it suffereth innumerable evils ; but the body of Christ suffered the same. This, then, he hinted at when he said, " That it may be conformed to the body of his glory." Wherefore the body is the same, but putteth on incorruption. " Shall fashion anew." Wherefore the fashion is different ; or perchance he has spoken figuratively of the change.

He saith, " the body of our humiliation," because it is now humbled, subject to destruction, to pain, because it seemeth to be worthless, and to have nothing beyond that of other animals. "That it may be conformed to the body of his glory." What? shall this our body be fashioned like unto Him, who sitteth at the right

---

¹ There is some false reading here. Old Lat. has " What is their God? This, ' Let us eat and drink!' "

hand of the Father, to Him who is worshiped by the Angels, before whom do stand the incorporeal Powers, to Him who is above all rule, and power, and might? If then the whole world were to take up weeping and lament for those who have fallen from this hope, could it worthily lament? because, when a promise is given us of our body being made like to Him, it still departs with the demons. I care not for hell henceforth; whatever can be said, having fallen from so great glory, now and henceforth consider hell to be nothing to this falling away. What sayest thou, O Paul? To be made like unto Him? Yes, he answereth; then, lest you should disbelieve, he addeth a reason; "According to the working whereby He is able even to subject all things unto Himself." He hath power, saith he, to subject all things unto Himself, wherefore also destruction and death. Or rather, He doth this also with the same power. For tell me, which requireth the greater power, to subject demons, and Angels, and Archangels, and Cherubim, and Seraphim, or to make the body incorruptible and immortal? .The latter certainly much more than the former; he showed forth the greater works of His power, that you might believe these too. Wherefore, though ye see these men rejoicing, and honored, yet stand firm, be not offended at them, be not moved. These our hopes are sufficient to raise up even the most sluggish and indolent.

Chap. iv. ver. 1. "Wherefore," saith he, "my brethren, beloved and longed for, my joy and crown, so stand fast in the Lord, my beloved."

"So." How? Unmoved. See how he addeth praise after exhortation, "my joy and my crown," not simply joy but glory too, not simply glory but my crown too. Which glory nought can equal, since it is the crown of Paul. "So stand fast in the Lord, my beloved," i.e. in the hope of God.[1]

Ver. 2, 3. "I exhort Euodia, and exhort Syntyche, to be of the same mind in the Lord. Yea, I beseech thee also, true yokefellow, help these women."

Some say Paul here exhorts his own wife; but it is not so, but some other woman, or the husband of one of them. "Help these women, for they labored with me in the Gospel, with Clement also, and the rest of my fellow-workers whose names are in the book of life." Seest thou how great a testimony he beareth to their virtue? For as Christ saith to his Apostles, "Rejoice not that the spirits are subject to you, but rejoice that your names are written in the

book of life" (Luke x. 20); so Paul testifieth to them, saying, "whose names are in the book of life." These women seem to me to be the chief of the Church which was there, and he commendeth them to some notable man whom he calls his "yokefellow," to whom perchance he was wont to commend them, as to a fellow-worker, and fellow-soldier, and brother, and companion, as he doth in the Epistle to the Romans, when he saith, "I commend unto you Phebe our sister, who is a servant of the Church that is at Cenchrea." (Rom. xvi. 1.) "Yokefellow;" either some brother of theirs, or a husband of hers; as if he had said, Now thou art a true brother, now a true husband, because thou hast become a Member. "For they labored with me in the Gospel." This protection[2] came from home, not from friendship, but for good deeds. "Labored with me." What sayest thou? Did women labor with thee? Yes, he answereth, they too contributed no small portion. Although many were they who wrought together with him, yet these women also acted with him amongst the many. The Churches then were no little edified, for many good ends are gained where they who are approved, be they men, or be they women, enjoy from the rest such honor. For in the first place the rest were led on to a like zeal; in the second place, they also gained[3] by the respect shown; and thirdly, they made those very persons more zealous and earnest. Wherefore thou seest that Paul hath everywhere a care for this, and commendeth such men for consideration. As he saith in the Epistle to the Corinthians: "Who are the first-fruits of Achaia." (1 Cor. xvi. 15.) Some say that the word "yokefellow," (Syzygus,) is a proper name. Well, what? Whether it be so, or no, we need not accurately enquire,[4] but observe that he gives his orders, that these women should enjoy much protection.

All we have, saith he, is in the heavens, our Saviour, our city, whatever a man can name: "whence," saith he, "we wait for a Saviour, the Lord Jesus Christ." And this is an act of His kindness and love toward man. He Himself again cometh to us, he doth not drag us thither, but takes us, and so departs with us. And this is a mark of great honor; for if He came to us when we were enemies, much rather doth He now when we are become friends. He doth not commit this to the Angels, nor to servants, but Himself cometh to call us to His royal man-

---

[1] [Chrys. strangely overlooks the fact that in the Epistle "the Lord" usually means Christ. Standing in the Lord may be readily understood if we contrast it with efforts to stand outside of Christ, apart from him. Compare (Meyer) 1 Thess. iii. 8, and often in Paul's writings. — J. A. B.]

[2] προστασία, he means the recommendation to protection.
[3] i.e. a reward, see on 1 Tim. v. 6, Hom. xv.
[4] [Upon this whole passage, ver. 2, 3, nothing is really known to this day beyond what Chrys. here says. The view that Syzygus is a proper name is preferred by Meyer and Grimm (Thayer), and Westcott and Hort so print in the margin. A complete discussion may be found in Lightfoot. — J. A. B.]

sion. See, we also " shall be caught up in the clouds " (1 Thess. iv. 17), doing him honor.

Who then is to be found " the faithful and wise servant "? Who are they that are deemed worthy of such good things? How miserable are those who fail! For if we were forever to weep, should we do aught worthy of the occasion? For were you to make mention of hells innumerable, you would name nothing equal to that pain which the soul sustaineth, when all the world is in confusion, when the trumpets are sounding, when the Angels are rushing forward, the first, then the second, then the third, then ten thousand ranks, are pouring forth upon the earth; then the Cherubim, (and many are these and infinite;) the Seraphim; when He Himself is coming, with His ineffable glory; when those meet Him, who had gone to gather the elect into the midst; when Paul and his companions, and all who in his time had been approved, are crowned, are proclaimed aloud, are honored by the King, before all His heavenly host. For if hell did not exist, how fearful a thing it is, that the one part should be honored, and the other dishonored! Hell, I confess, is intolerable, yea, very intolerable, but more intolerable than it is the loss of the Kingdom. Consider; if any king, or the son of a king, having taken his departure, and been successful in innumerable wars, and become the object of admiration, should with his army entire, return to any city, in his chariot, with his trophies, with his innumerable ranks of golden shields, with his spearmen, his body-guard all about him, whilst the whole city was adorned with crowns, whilst all the rulers of the world accompanied him, and all the soldiery of foreign nations followed him as captives, then præfects, satraps, and in the presence of all the rulers, and all that splendor, he should receive the citizens who meet him, and kiss them, and stretch forth his hand, and give them freedom of access, and converse with them, all standing around, as with friends, and tell them that all that journey was undertaken for their sake, and should lead them into his palace, and give them a share of it, even if the rest should not be punished, to how great punishment would not this be equal? But if in the case of men it were a bitter thing to fall away from this glory, much more is it so with God, when all the heavenly Powers are present with the King, when the demons, bound, and bowing down their heads, and the devil himself is led along in chains, and all military force that opposeth itself, when the Powers of the heavens, when He Himself, cometh upon the clouds.

Believe me, I am not even able to finish my words, from the grief which lays hold of my soul at this relation. Consider of how great glory we shall be deprived, when it is in our power not to be deprived of it. For this is the misery, that we suffer these things, when it is in our power not to suffer them. When he receiveth the one part and leadeth them to His Father in heaven, and rejecteth the other, whom Angels take and drag against their will, weeping, and hanging down their heads, to the fire of hell, when they have first been made a spectacle to the whole world, what grief, think you, is there? Let us then make haste, while there is time, and take great thought of our own salvation. How many things have we to say like the rich man? If any one would now suffer us, we would take counsel of the things that are profitable! But no one doth suffer us. And that we shall so say, is clear, not from him alone,) but from many others. And that you may learn this, how many men have been in fevers, and said, if we recover, we shall never again fall into the same state. Many such words we shall then say, but we shall be answered as the rich man was, that there is a gulf, that we have received our good things here. (Luke xvi. 25, 26.) Let us groan then, I entreat you, bitterly, rather let us not only groan, but pursue virtue too; let us lament now, for salvation, that we may not then lament in vain. Let us weep now, and not weep then, at our evil lot. This weeping is of virtue, that of unprofitable repentance; let us afflict ourselves now, that we may not then; for it is not the same thing to be afflicted here and there. Here, thou art afflicted for a little time, or rather thou dost not perceive thy affliction, knowing that thou art afflicted for thy good. But there, the affliction is more bitter, because it is not in hope,[1] nor for any escape, but without limit, and throughout.

But may we all be freed from this, and obtain remission. But let us pray and be diligent, that we may obtain the remission. Let us be diligent, I entreat; for if we are diligent, we prevail even through our prayer: if we pray earnestly, God grants our request; but if we neither ask Him, nor do earnestly aught of this sort, nor work, how is it possible that we should ever succeed? By sleeping? Not at all. For it is much if even by running, and stretching forth, and being conformed to His death, as Paul said, we shall be able to succeed, not to say sleeping. " If by any means I may attain," saith he. But if Paul said, " If by any means I may attain," what shall we say? For it is not possible by sleeping to accomplish even worldly business, not to say spiritual. By sleeping, not even from friends can anything be received, far less from God. Not even fathers honor them who sleep, far less doth God. Let us labor

---

[1] It is worth observing, that, although he has referred to the rich man in *Hades*, he is here speaking of *Gehenna*, and of present self-denial as a means of escaping *eternal* punishment after Judgment.

for a little time, that we may have rest for ever. We must at all events be afflicted. If we are not afflicted here, it awaits us there. Why choose we not to be afflicted here, that there we may have rest, and obtain the unspeakable

blessings, in Christ Jesus, with whom, to the Father together with the Holy Spirit, be glory, power, and honor, now and ever, world without end. Amen.

HOMILY XIV.

PHILIPPIANS iv. 4–7.

" Rejoice in the Lord alway: again I will say, Rejoice. Let your forbearance be known unto all men." The Lord is at hand. In nothing be anxious; but in everything by prayer and supplication with thanksgiving let your requests be made known unto God. And the peace of God, which passeth all understanding, shall guard your hearts and your thoughts through Christ Jesus."

" BLESSED[1] are they that mourn," and " woe unto them that laugh" (Matt. v. 4 ; Luke vi. 25), saith Christ. How then saith Paul, " Rejoice in the Lord alway"? " Woe to them that laugh," said Christ, the laughter of this world, which ariseth from the things which are present. He blessed also those that mourn, not simply for the loss of relatives, but those who are pricked at heart, who mourn their own faults, and take count of their own sins, or even those of others. This joy is not contrary to that grief, but from that grief it too is born. For he who grieveth for his own faults, and confesseth them, rejoiceth. Moreover, it is possible to grieve for our own sins, and yet to rejoice in Christ. Since then they were afflicted by their sufferings, " for to you it is given not only to believe in him, but also to suffer for him " (Phil. i. 29), therefore he saith, " Rejoice in the Lord." For this can but mean, If you exhibit such a life that you may rejoice. Or when your communion with God is not hindered, rejoice. Or else the word " in " may stand for " with " :[2] as if he had said, with the Lord. " Alway; again I will say, Rejoice." These are the words of one who brings comfort ; as, for example, he who is in God rejoiceth alway. Yea though he be afflicted, yea whatever he may suffer, such a man alway rejoiceth. Hear what Luke saith, that " they returned from the presence of the Council, rejoicing that they were counted worthy to be scourged for His name." (Acts v. 41.) If scourging and bonds, which

seem to be the most grievous of all things, bring forth joy, what else will be able to produce grief in us?

" Again I will say, Rejoice." Well hath he repeated. For since the nature of the things brought forth grief, he shows by repeating, that they should by all means rejoice.

" Let your forbearance be known unto all men." He said above, " Whose god is the belly, and whose glory is in their shame," and that they " mind earthly things." (Phil. iii. 19.) It was probable that they would be at enmity with the wicked ; he therefore exhorted them to have nothing in common with them, but to use them with all forbearance, and that not only their brethren, but also their enemies and opposers. " The Lord is at hand,[3] in nothing be anxious." For why, tell me? do they ever rise in opposition? And if ye see them living in luxury, why are ye in affliction? Already the judgment is nigh ; shortly will they give account of their actions. Are ye in affliction, and they in luxury? But these things shall shortly receive their end. Do they plot against you, and threaten you? " In nothing be anxious." The judgment is already at hand, when these things shall be reversed. " In nothing be anxious." If ye are kindly affected toward those who prepare evil against you, yet it shall not at last turn out to their profit. Already the recompense is at hand, if poverty, if death, if aught else that is terrible be upon you. " But in everything, by prayer and supplication, with thanksgiving, let your requests be made known unto God." There is this for one consolation, " the Lord is at hand." And again, " I will be with you alway, even unto the end of the world." (Matt. xxviii. 20.) Behold another consolation, a medicine which healeth grief, and distress, and all that is painful. And what is this? Prayer, thanksgiving in all things. And so He wills that our prayers should not simply

---

[1] [" Happy " would be more exact, but " blessed " has a fixed association with the passage quoted from the Sermon on the Mount. — J. A. B.]

[2] [Chrys. had little notion of scientific precision in the use or interpretation of language. The word ἐν, " in," sometimes introduces the instrument, where we in English say " with " ; but it would be hard to find any passage in which it is clearly equivalent to σύν, " with," i.e. in company with, in connection with. — J. A. B.]

[3] [It is evident from the connection that Chrys. connects " the Lord is at hand " with what follows, and not (as Meyer wrongly states) with what precedes. Yet recent commentators generally connect it with what precedes, and are pretty certainly right. — J. A. B.]

be requests, but thanksgivings too for what we have. For how should he ask for future things, who is not thankful for the past? "But in everything by prayer and supplication." Wherefore we ought to give thanks for all things, even for those which seem to be grievous, for this is the part of the truly thankful man. In the other case the nature of the things demands it; but this springs from a grateful soul, and one earnestly affected toward God. God acknowledgeth these prayers, but others He knoweth not. Offer up such prayers as may be acknowledged; for He disposeth all things for our profit, though we know it not. And this is a proof that it greatly profiteth, namely, that we know it not. "And the peace of God which passeth all understanding shall guard your hearts and your thoughts in Christ Jesus." What meaneth this? "The peace of God" which He hath wrought toward men, surpasseth all understanding. For who could have expected, who could have hoped, that such good things would have come? They exceed all man's understanding, not his speech alone. For His enemies, for those who hated Him, for those who determined to turn themselves away, for these, he refused not to deliver up His Only Begotten Son, that He might make peace with us. This peace then, i.e. the reconciliation, the love of God, shall guard your hearts and your thoughts.

For this is the part of a teacher, not only to exhort, but also to pray, and to assist by supplication, that they may neither be overwhelmed by temptations, nor carried about by deceit. As if he had said, May He who hath delivered you in such sort as mind cannot comprehend, may He Himself guard you, and secure you, so that you suffer no ill. Either he means this, or that that peace of which Christ saith, "Peace I leave with you, My peace I give unto you" (John xiv. 27): this shall guard you, for this peace exceedeth all man's understanding. How? When he tells us to be at peace with our enemies, with those who treat us unjustly, with those who are at war and enmity toward us; is it not beyond man's understanding? But rather let us look to the former. If the peace surpasseth all understanding, much more doth God Himself, who giveth peace, pass all understanding, not ours only, but also that of Angels, and the Powers above. What meaneth "in Christ Jesus"? Shall guard us in Him, so that ye may remain firm, and not fall from His faith.

Ver. 8. "Finally, brethren, whatsoever things are honorable, whatsoever things are true, whatsoever things are just." What is "Finally"? It stands for, "I have said all." It is the word of one that is in haste, and has nothing to do with present things.

"Finally, brethren, whatsoever things are honorable, whatsoever things are true, whatsoever things are just, whatsoever things are pure, whatsoever things are lovely, whatsoever things are of good report, if there be any virtue, and if there be any praise, think on these things."

Ver. 9. "The things which ye both learned and received, and heard and saw in me."

What meaneth, "whatsoever things are lovely"? Lovely to the faithful, lovely to God. "Whatsoever things are true." Virtue is really true, vice is falsehood. For the pleasure of it is a falsehood, and its glory is falsehood, and all things of the world are falsehood. "Whatsoever things are pure." This is opposed to the words "who mind earthly things." "Whatsoever things are honorable." This is opposed to the words "whose god is their belly." "Whatsoever things are just," i.e. saith he,[1] "whatsoever things are of good report." "If there be any virtue, if there be any praise." Here he willeth them to take thought of those things too which regard men. "Think on these things," saith he. Seest thou, that he desires to banish every evil thought from our souls; for evil actions spring from thoughts. "The things which ye both learned and received." This is teaching, in all his exhortations to propose himself for a model: as he saith in another place, "even as ye have us for an ensample." (Phil. iii. 17.) And again here, "What things ye learned and received," i.e. have been taught by word of mouth, "and heard and saw in me": both in respect of my words and actions and conduct. Seest thou, how about everything he lays these commands on us? For since it was not possible to make an accurate enumeration of all things, of our coming in, and going out, and speech, and carriage, and intercourse (for of all these things it is needful that a Christian should have thought), he said shortly, and as it were in a summary, "ye heard and saw in me." I have led you forward both by deeds and by words.[2] "These things do," not only in words, but do them also. "And the God of peace shall be with you," i.e. ye shall be in a calm, in great safety, ye shall suffer nothing painful, nor contrary to your will. For when we are at peace with Him, and we are so through virtue, much more will He be at peace with us. For He who so loved us, as to show favor to us even against our will, will He not, if He sees us

---

[1] [These are hasty jottings by Chrys. or a reporter, and might easily be altered in copying. He can hardly have meant to define "just" by "of good report," yet so the Greek stands; or else (as in some documents) he defines "of good report" by "if there be any virtue," etc. The abridgment in the Catena may have caught the real meaning. It omits "whatsoever things are just," and puts together the three remaining clauses as the occasion of the remark which follows. Or perhaps "i.e. saith he" is a corrupt addition, and all four clauses should be simply taken together; for the remark applies to them all. — J. A. B.]

[2] [All of Field's MSS. here insert "For nothing is such an enemy of our nature as vice," which, however, seems here out of place, and fits well below, where it is placed by the altered text. — J. A. B.]

hastening toward Him, Himself yet much more exhibit His love toward us?

Nothing is such an enemy of our nature as vice. And from many things it is evident, how vice is at enmity with us, and virtue friendly toward us. What will ye? That I should speak of fornication? It makes men subject to reproach, poor, objects of ridicule, despicable to all, just as enemies treat them. Ofttimes it hath involved men in disease and danger; many men have perished or been wounded in behalf of their mistresses. And if fornication produces these things, much rather doth adultery. But doth almsgiving so? By no means. But as a loving mother setteth her son in great propriety, in good order, in good report, and gives him leisure to engage in necessary work, thus almsgiving doth not release us nor lead us away from our necessary work, but even renders the soul more wise. For nothing is more foolish than a mistress.

But what willest thou? To look upon covetousness? It too treats us like an enemy. And how? It makes us hated by all. It prepareth all men to vaunt themselves against us; both those who have been treated unjustly by us, and those who have not, who share the grief of the former, and are in fear for themselves. All men look upon us as their common foes, as wild beasts, as demons. Everywhere are there innumerable accusations, plots against us, envyings, all which are the acts of enemies. But justice, on the contrary, makes all men friends, all men sociable, all men well disposed towards us, by all men prayers are made in our behalf; our affairs are in perfect safety, there is no danger, there is no suspicion. But sleep also fearlessly comes over us with perfect safety, no care is there, no lamenting.

How much better this sort of life is! And what? Is it best to envy, or to rejoice with one another? Let us search out all these things, and we shall find that virtue, like a truly kind mother, places us in safety, while vice is a treacherous thing, and full of danger. For hear the prophet, who saith, "The Lord is a stronghold of them that fear Him, and His covenant is to show them." (Ps. xxv. 14, Sept.) He feareth no one, who is not conscious to himself of any wickedness; on the contrary, he who liveth in crime is never confident, but trembles at his domestics, and looks at them with suspicion. Why say, his domestics? He cannot bear the tribunal of his own conscience. Not only those who are without, but his inward thoughts affect him likewise, and suffer him not to be in quiet. What then, saith Paul? Ought we to live dependent on praise? He said not, look to praise, but do praiseworthy actions, yet not for the sake of praise.

"Whatsoever things are true," for the things we have been speaking of are false. "Whatsoever things are honorable." That which is "honorable" belongs to external virtue, that which is "pure" to the soul. Give no cause of stumbling, saith he, nor handle of accusation. Because he had said, "Whatsoever things are of good report," lest you should think that he means only those things which are so in the sight of men, he proceeds, "if there be any virtue, and if there be any praise, think on these things" — do these things. He wills us ever to be in these things, to care for these things, to think on these things. For if we will be at peace with each other, God too will be with us, but if we raise up war, the God of peace will not be with us. For nothing is so hostile to the soul as vice. That is, peace and virtue place it in safety. Wherefore we must make a beginning on our part, and then we shall draw God toward us.

God is not a God of war and fighting. Make war and fighting to cease, both that which is against Him, and that which is against thy neighbor. Be at peace with all men, consider with what character God saveth thee. "Blessed are the peacemakers, for they shall be called sons of God." (Matt. v. 9.) Such always imitate the Son of God: do thou imitate Him too. Be at peace. The more thy brother warreth against thee, by so much the greater will be thy reward. For hear the prophet who saith, "With the haters of peace I was peaceful." (Ps. cxx. 7, Sept.) This is virtue, this is above man's understanding, this maketh us near God; nothing so much delighteth God as to remember no evil. This sets thee free from thy sins, this looseth the charges against thee: but if we are fighting and buffeting, we become far off from God: for enmities are produced by conflict, and from enmity springs remembrance of evil.

Cut out the root, and there will be no fruit. Thus shall we learn to despise the things of this life, for there is no conflict, none, in spiritual things, but whatever thou seest, either conflicts or envy, or whatever a man can mention, all these spring from the things of this life. Every conflict hath its beginning either in covetousness, or envy, or vainglory. If therefore we are at peace, we shall learn to despise the things of the earth. Hath a man stolen our money? He hath not injured us, only let him not steal our treasure which is above. Hath he hindered thy glory? Yet not that which is from God, but that which is of no account. For this is no glory, but a mere name of glory, or rather a shame. Hath he stolen thy honor? Rather not thine but his own. For as he who committeth injustice doth not so much inflict as receive injustice, thus too he who plots against his neighbor, first destroyeth himself.

For "he who diggeth a pit for his neighbor, falleth into it." (Prov. xxvi. 27.) Let us then not plot against others, lest we injure ourselves. When we supplant the reputation of others, let us consider that we injure ourselves, it is against ourselves we plot. For perchance with men we do him harm, if we have power, but we injure ourselves in the sight of God, by provoking Him against us. Let us not then harm ourselves. For as we injure ourselves when we injure our neighbors, so by benefiting them we benefit ourselves. If then thy enemy harm thee, he hath benefited thee if thou art wise, and so requite him not with the same things, but even do him good. But the blow, you say, remains severe. Consider then that thou dost not benefit, but punishest him, and benefitest thyself, and quickly you will come to do him good. What then? Shall we act from this motive? We ought not to act on this motive, but if thy heart will not hear other reason, induce it, saith he,[1] even by this, and thou wilt quickly persuade it to dismiss its enmity, and wilt for the future do good to thine enemy as to a friend, and wilt obtain the good things which are to come, to which God grant that we may all attain in Christ Jesus. Amen.

HOMILY XV.

PHILIPPIANS iv. 10–14.

"But I rejoice in the Lord greatly, that now at length ye have revived your thought for me; wherein ye did indeed take thought, but ye lacked opportunity. Not that I speak in respect of want: for I have learned, in whatsoever state I am, therein to be content. I know how to be abased, and I know also how to abound: in everything and in all things have I learned the secret both to be filled and to be hungry, both to abound and to be in want. I can do all things in him that strengtheneth me. Howbeit, ye did well, that ye had fellowship with my affliction."

I HAVE ofttimes said, that almsgiving hath been introduced not for the sake of the receivers, but of the givers, for the latter are they which make the greatest gain. And this Paul shows here also. In what way? The Philippians had sent him somewhat, after a long time, and had committed the same to Epaphroditus. See then, how when he is about to send Epaphroditus as the bearer of this Epistle, he praises them, and shows that this action was for the need, not of the receiver, but of the givers. This he doth, both that they who benefited him may not be lifted up with arrogance, and that they may become more zealous in well-doing, since they rather benefit themselves; and that they who receive may not fearlessly rush forward to receive, lest they meet with condemnation. For "it is more blessed," He saith, "to give than to receive." (Acts xx. 35.) Why then does he say, "I rejoice in the Lord greatly"? Not with worldly rejoicing, saith he, nor with the joy of this life, but in the Lord. Not because I had refreshment, but because ye advanced; for this is my refreshment. Wherefore he also saith "greatly"; since this joy was not corporeal, nor on account of his own refreshment, but because of their advancement.

And see how, when he had gently rebuked them on account of the times that were passed, he quickly throweth a shadow over this, and teacheth them constantly and always to remain in well doing. "Because at length," saith he. The words, "at length," show long time to have elapsed. "Ye have revived," as fruits which have shot forth, dried up, and afterwards shot forth. Here he showeth, that being at first blooming, then having faded, they again budded forth. So that the word "flourished again," has both rebuke and praise. For it is no small thing, that he who hath withered should flourish again. He showeth also, that it was from indolence all this had happened to them. But here he signifies, that even in former time they were wont to be zealous in these things. Wherefore he addeth, "your thought for me, wherein ye did indeed take thought." And lest you should think, that in other things too they had been more zealous, and had then withered, but in this thing alone, behold how he has added, "your thought for me." I apply the words, "now at length," only to this; for in other things it is not so.

Here some one may enquire, how when he had said, "It is more blessed to give than to receive" (Acts xx. 25, 34); and, "These hands ministered to my necessities, and to them that were with me"; and again when writing to the Corinthians, "For it were good for me rather to

---

[1] i.e. St. Paul, Rom. xii. 20, on which passage see St. Chrys., who there fully states this view, perhaps the only one that fully explains the difficulty.

die, than that any man should make my glory-ing void " (1 Cor. ix. 15) ; he suffereth his glory-ing to be made void? And how? By receiving. For if his glorying was, that he received not, how doth he now endure so to do? What is it then? Probably, he then did not receive on account of the false Apostles, "that wherein they glory" (2 Cor. xi. 12), saith he, "they may be found even as we." And he said not "are," but "glory"; for they received but secretly. Wherefore he said, "wherein they glory." Wherefore he also said, "No man shall stop me of this glorying." (2 Cor. xi. 10.) And he said not simply, shall not stop me, but what? "in the regions of Achaia." And again, "I robbed other Churches, taking wages of them that I might minister unto you." (2 Cor. xi. 8.) Here he showed that he did receive. But Paul indeed received rightly, having so great a work; if in truth he did receive. But they who work not, how can they receive? "Yet I pray," saith one. But there is no work. For this may be done together with work. "But I fast." Neither is this work. For see this blessed one, preach-ing in many places, and working too. "But ye lacked opportunity." What meaneth lacked opportunity? It came not, saith he, of indo-lence, but of necessity.[1] Ye had it not in your hands, nor were in abundance. This is the meaning of, "Ye lacked opportunity." Thus most men speak, when the things of this life do not flow in to them abundantly, and are in short supply.

"Not that I speak in respect of want." I said, saith he, "now at length," and I rebuked you, not seeking mine own, nor censuring you on this account, as if I were in want: for I sought it not on this account. Whence is this, O Paul, that thou makest no vain boasting? To the Corinthians he saith, "For we write none other things unto you, than what ye read or even ac-knowledge." (2 Cor. i. 13.) And in this case he would not have spoken to them so as to be convicted, he would not, had he been making boasts, have spoken thus. He was speaking to those who knew the facts, with whom detection would have been a greater disgrace. "For I have learnt," saith he, "in whatsoever state I am, therein to be content." Wherefore, this is an object of discipline, and exercise, and care, for it is not easy of attainment, but very difficult, and a new thing. "In whatsoever state I am," saith he, "therein to be content. I know how to be abased, and I know also how to abound. In everything and in all things have I learned the secret." That is, I know how to use little, to bear hunger and want. "Both to abound, and to suffer need." "But, says one, there is no

need of wisdom or of virtue in order to abound." There is great need of virtue, not less than in the other case. For as want inclines us to do many evil things, so too doth plenty. For many ofttimes, coming into plenty, have become indo-lent, and have not known how to bear their good fortune. Many men have taken it as an occa-sion of no longer working. But Paul did not so, for what he received he consumed on others, and emptied himself for them. This is to know. He was in nowise relaxed, nor did he exult at his abundance; but was the same in want and in plenty, he was neither oppressed on the one hand, nor rendered a boaster on the other. "Both to be filled," saith he, "and to be hun-gry, both to abound, and to be in want." Many know not how to be full, as for example, the Israelites, "ate, and kicked" (Deut. xxxii. 15), but I am equally well ordered in all. He showeth that he neither is now elated, nor was before grieved : or if he grieved, it was on their account, not on his own, for he himself was sim-ilarly affected.

"In everything," saith he, "and in all things I have learned the secret," i.e. I have had ex-perience of all things in this long time, and these things have all succeeded with me. But since boasting might seem to have a place here, see how quickly he checks up, and says, "I can do all things in Christ[2] that strengtheneth me." The success is not mine own, but His who has given me strength. But since they who confer benefits, when they see the receiver not well af-fected toward them, but despising the gifts, are themselves rendered more remiss, (for they con-sidered themselves as conferring a benefit and refreshment,) if therefore Paul despises the re-freshment, they must necessarily become remiss, in order then that this may not happen, see how he healeth it again. By what he hath said above, he hath brought down their proud thoughts, by what followeth he maketh their readiness revive, by saying, "Howbeit ye did well, that ye had fellowship with my affliction." Seest thou, how he removed himself, and again united himself to them. This is the part of true and spiritual friendship. Think not, saith he, because I was not in want, that I had no need of this act of yours. I have need of it for your sake. How then, did they share his afflictions? By this means. As he said when in bonds, "Ye all are partakers with me of grace." (Phil. i. 7.) For it is grace to suffer for Christ, as he himself saith in another place, "For to you it is given from God not only to believe on Him, but also to suffer for Him." (Phil. i. 29.) For since those former words by themselves might have made them regardless,

---

[1] St. Chrys. understands him to be "partially" excusing them.

[2] [Chrys. here reads "Christ," the "Syrian" text; but the true text is simply "in him that," as in Rev. Ver. — J. A. B.]

for this cause he consoleth them, and receiveth them, and praiseth them again. And this in measured words. For he said not, "gave," but "had fellowship," to show that they too were profited by becoming partakers of his labors. He said not, ye did lighten, but ye did communicate with my affliction, which was something more elevated. Seest thou the humility of Paul? seest thou his noble nature? When he has shown that he had no need of their gifts on his own account, he afterward uses freely such lowly words as they do who make a request; "since thou art wont to give." For he refuseth neither to do, nor say anything. That is, "Think not that my words show want of shame, wherein I accuse you, and say, 'Now at length ye have revived,' or are those of one in necessity; I speak not thus because I am in need, but why? From my exceeding confidence in you, and of this also ye yourselves are the authors."

Seest thou how he sootheth them? How are ye the authors? In that ye hasted to the work before all the others; and have given me confidence to remind you of these things. And observe his elevation; he accuseth them not while they did not send, lest he should seem to regard his own benefit, but when they had sent, then he rebuked them for the time past, and they received it, for he could not seem after that to regard his own benefit.

Ver. 15. "Ye yourselves also know, ye Philippians, that in the beginning of the Gospel, when I departed from Macedonia, no Church had fellowship with me, in the matter of giving and receiving, but ye only."

Lo, how great is his commendation! For the Corinthians and Romans are stirred up by hearing these things from him, whilst the Philippians did it without any other Church having made a beginning. For "in the beginning of the Gospel," saith he, they manifested such zeal towards the holy Apostle, as themselves first to begin, without having any example, to bear this fruit. And no one can say that they did these things because he abode with them, or for their own benefit; for he saith, "When I departed from Macedonia, no Church had fellowship with me, in the matter of giving and receiving, but ye only." What meaneth "receiving," and what "had fellowship"? Wherefore said he not, "no Church gave to me," but "had fellowship with me, in the matter of giving and receiving"? Because it is a case of communication. He saith, "If we sowed unto you spiritual things, is it a great matter if we shall reap your carnal things." (1 Cor. ix. 11.) And again, "That your abundance may be a supply to their want." (2 Cor. viii. 14.) How did they communicate? In the matter of giving carnal things, and receiving spiritual. For as they who sell and buy communicate with each other, by mutually giving what they have, (and this is communication,) so too is it here. For there is not anything more profitable than this trade and traffic. It is performed on the earth, but is completed in heaven. They who buy are on the earth, but they buy and agree about heavenly things, whilst they lay down an earthly price.

But despond not; heavenly things are not to be bought with money, riches cannot purchase these things, but the purpose of him who giveth the money, his true wisdom, his superiority to earthly things, his love toward man, his mercifulness. For if money could purchase it, she who threw in the two mites would have gained nothing great. But since it was not the money, but the purpose that availed, she received everything, who exhibited a full purpose of mind. Let us not then say, that the Kingdom can be bought with money; it is not by money, but by purpose of mind which is exhibited by the money. Therefore, will one answer, there is no need of money? There is no need of money, but of the disposition; if thou hast this, thou wilt be able even by two mites to purchase Heaven; where this is not, not even ten thousand talents of gold will be able to do that, which the two mites could. Wherefore? Because if thou who hast much throwest in but a small portion, thou gavest an alms indeed, but not so great as the widow did; for thou didst not throw it in with the same readiness as she. For she deprived herself of all she had, or rather she deprived not, but gave it all as a free gift to herself. Not for a cup of cold water hath God promised the kingdom, but for readiness of heart; not for death, but for purpose of mind. For indeed it is no great thing. For what is it to give one life? that is giving one man; but one man is not of worth enough.

Ver. 16. "For even in Thessalonica, ye sent once and again unto my need."

Here again is great praise, that he, when dwelling in the metropolis,[1] should be nourished by a little city. And lest, by always withdrawing himself from the supposition of want, he should, as I said at first, render them amiss, having previously shown by so many proofs that he is not in want, he here does it by one word only, by saying "needs." And he said not "my,"[2] but absolutely, — having a care of dignity. And not this only, but what followeth too, for since he was conscious that it was a very lowly thing, he again secures it, by adding as a correction,

Ver. 17. "Not that I seek for the gift."

As he said above, "Not that I speak in re-

---

[1] The difference was probably less marked in St. Paul's time than in St. Chrysostom's.
[2] The Greek is, "Ye sent to me unto the needs."

spect of want"; that is stronger than this. For it is one thing, that he who is in want, should not seek, and another that he who is in want should not even consider himself to be in want. "Not that I seek for the gift," he says, "but I seek for the fruit, that increaseth to your account." Not mine own. Seest thou, that the fruit is produced for them? This say I for your sake, says he, not for my own, for your salvation. For I gain nothing when I receive, but the grace belongeth to the givers, for the recompense is yonder in store for givers, but the gifts are here consumed by them who receive. Again even his desire is combined with praise and sympathy.

When he had said, I do not seek, lest he should again render them remiss, he adds,

Ver. 18. "But I have all things and abound," i.e. through this gift ye have filled up what was wanting, which would make them more eager. For benefactors, the wiser they are, the more do they seek gratitude from the benefited. That is, ye have not only filled up what was deficient in former time, but ye have gone beyond. For lest by these words he should seem to accuse them, see how he seals up all. After he had said, "Not that I seek for the gift," and "Now at length"; and had shown that their deed was a debt, for this is meant by, "I have all," then again he showeth, that they had acted above what was due, and saith, "I have all things and abound, I am filled." I say not this at hazard, or only from the feeling of my mind, but why? "Having received of Epaphroditus the things that came from you, an odor of a sweet smell; a sacrifice acceptable, well pleasing to God." Lo, whither he hath raised their gift; not I, he saith, received, but God through me. Wherefore though I be not in need, regard it not, for God had no need, and He received at their hands in such sort, that the Holy Scriptures shrunk not from saying, "God smelled a sweet savor" (Gen. viii. 21), which denotes one who was pleased. For ye know, indeed ye know, how our soul is affected by sweet savors, how it is pleased, how it is delighted. The Scriptures therefore shrunk not from applying to God a word so human, and so lowly, that it might show to men that their gifts are become acceptable. For not the fat, not the smoke, made them acceptable, but the purpose of mind which offered them. Had it been otherwise, Cain's offering too had been received. It saith then, that He is even pleased, and how He is pleased. For men could not without this have learned. He then, who hath no need, saith that He is thus pleased, that they may not become remiss by the absence of need. And afterward, when they had no care for other virtues, and trusted to their offerings alone, behold, how again he

setteth them right by saying, "Will I eat the flesh of bulls, or drink the blood of goats?" (Ps. l. 13.) This Paul also saith. "Not that I seek," saith he, "for the gift."

Ver. 19. "And may[1] my God fulfill every need of yours, according to His riches in glory, in Christ Jesus."

Behold how he invokes blessings upon them, as poor men do. But if even Paul blesseth those who give, much more let us not be ashamed to do this when we receive. Let us not receive as though we ourselves had need, let us not rejoice on our own account, but on that of the givers. Thus we too who receive shall have a reward, if we rejoice for their sake. Thus we shall not take it hardly, when men do not give, but rather shall grieve for their sake. So shall we render them more zealous, if we teach them, that not for our own sake do we so act; "but may my God" fulfill every need of yours, or every grace, or every joy.[2] If the second be true, "every grace," he meaneth not only the alms, which are of earth, but every excellency. If the first, "your every need," which I think too should rather be read, this is what he means to show. As he had said, "ye lacked opportunity," he here maketh an addition, as he doth in the Epistle to the Corinthians, saying, "And He that supplieth seed to the sower, may He supply bread for food, and multiply your seed for sowing, and increase the fruits of your righteousness." (2 Cor. ix. 10.) He invokes blessings upon them, that they may abound, and have wherewith to sow. He blesseth them too, not simply that they might abound, but "according to His riches," so that this too is done in measured terms. For had they been as he was, so truly wise, so crucified, he would not have done this; but since they were men that were handicraftsmen, poor, having wives, bringing up children, ruling their families, and who had given these very gifts out of small possessions, and had certain desires of the things of this world, he blesseth them appropriately. For it is not unseemly to invoke sufficiency and plenty upon those who thus use them. See too what he said. He said not, May He make you rich, and to abound greatly; but what said he? "May He fulfill every need of yours," so that ye may not be in want, but have things for your necessities. Since Christ too, when He gave us a form of prayer, inserted also this in the prayer, when He taught us to say, "Give us this day our daily bread." (Matt. vi. 11.)

"According to His riches." That is, accord-

1 [This is the reading for the N.T. text of a good many documents, but both the best and the majority there read, "And my God shall fulfill," as do also several documents for Chrys. here. — J. A. B.]
2 [The words χρείαν, "need," χάριν, "grace," and χαρὰν, "joy," are similar, and Chrys. indulges in some conjectures. Tisch. gives no evidence of any question as to the reading. — J. A. B.]

ing to His free gift, i.e. it is easy to Him, and possible, and quickly. And since I have spoken of need, do not think that he will drive you into straits. Wherefore he added, "according to his riches in glory in Christ Jesus." So shall all things abound to you, that you may have them to His glory. Or, ye are wanting in nothing; (for it is written, "great grace was upon them all, neither was there any that lacked.") (Acts iv. 33.) Or, so as to do all things for His glory, as if he had said, that ye may use your abundance to His glory.

Ver. 20. "Now unto our God and Father be the glory for ever and ever. Amen." For the glory of which he speaks belongs not only to the Son, but to the Father too, for when the Son is glorified, then is the Father also. For when he said, This is done to the glory of Christ, lest any one should suppose that it is to His glory alone, he continued, "Unto our God and Father be the glory," that glory which is paid to the Son.

Ver. 21. "Salute every saint in Christ Jesus."

This also is no small thing. For it is a proof of great good will, to salute them through letters. "The brethren which are with me salute you." And yet thou saidst that thou hast "no one like-minded, who will care truly for your state." How then sayest thou now, "The brethren which are with me"? He either saith, "The brethren which are with me," because he hath no one like-minded of those who are with him, (where he doth not speak of those in the city, for how were they constrained to undertake the affairs of the Apostles?) or that he did not refuse to call even those brethren.

Ver. 22, 23. "All the saints salute you, especially they that are of Cæsar's household. The grace of the Lord Jesus Christ be with your spirit."

He elevated them and strengthened them, by showing that his preaching had reached even to the king's[1] household. For if those who were in the king's palace despised all things for the sake of the King of Heaven, far more ought they to do this. And this too was a proof of the love of Paul, and that he had told many things of them, and said great things of them, whence he had even led those who were in the palace to a longing for them, so that those who had never seen them saluted them. Especially because the faithful were then in affliction, his love was great. And those who were absent from each other were closely conjoined together as if real limbs. And the poor man was similarly disposed toward the rich, and the rich toward the poor, and there was no preëminence, in that they were all equally hated and cast out, and

[1] [It must be remembered that "king" was the regular Greek term for the Roman imperator (emperor).— J. A. B.]

that for the same cause. For as, if captives taken from divers cities should arise and come to the same towns, they eagerly embrace each other, their common calamity binding them together; thus too at that time they had great love one toward another, the communion of their afflictions and persecutions uniting them.

Moral. For affliction is an unbroken bond, the increase of love, the occasion of compunction and piety. Hear the words of David, "It is good for me that I have been afflicted, that I might learn Thy statutes." (Ps. cxix. 71.) And again another prophet, who saith, "It is good for a man that he bear the yoke in his youth." (Lam. iii. 27.) And again, "Blessed is the man whom Thou chastenest, O Lord." (Ps. xciv. 12.) And another who saith, "Despise not the chastening of the Lord." (Prov. iii. 11.) And "if thou come near to serve the Lord, prepare thy soul for temptation." (Ecclus. xi. 1.) And Christ also said to His disciples, "In the world ye shall have tribulation, but be of good cheer." (John xvi. 33.) And again, "Ye shall weep and lament, but the world shall rejoice." (John xvi. 20.) And again, "Narrow and straitened is the way." (Matt. vii. 14.) Dost thou see how tribulation is everywhere lauded, everywhere assumed as needful for us? For if in the contests of the world, no one without this receiveth the crown, unless he fortify himself by toil, by abstinence from delicacies, by living according to rule, by watchings, and innumerable other things, much more so here. For whom wilt thou name as an instance? The king? Not even he liveth a life free from care, but one burdened with much tribulation and anxiety. For look not to his diadem, but to his sea of cares, by which the crown is produced for him. Nor look to his purple robe, but to his soul, which is darker than that purple. His crown doth not so closely bind his brow, as care doth his soul. Nor look to the multitude of his spearmen, but to the multitude of his disquietudes. For it is not possible to find a private house laden with so many cares as a king's palace. Violent deaths are each day expected, and a vision of blood is seen as they sit down to eat and drink. Nor can we say how oft he is disturbed in the night season, and leaps up, haunted with visions. And all this in peace; but if war should overtake him, what could be more piteous than such a life as this! What evils has he from those that are his own, I mean, those who are under his dominion. Nay, and of a truth the pavement of a king's house is always full of blood, the blood of his own relations. And if ye will, I will also relate some instances, and ye will presently know; chiefly old occurrences — but also some things that have happened in our own times — yet still preserved in memory. One,[1] it is said, having suspected his wife of adultery, bound her naked upon mules, and exposed her to wild beasts, though she had already been the mother to him of many princes. What sort of life, think ye, could that man have lived? For he would not have broken out into such vengeance, had he not been deeply affected with that distress. Moreover, this same man slew his own son,[2] or rather his brother did so. Of his sons, the one indeed slew himself, when seized by a tyrant,[3] and another put to death his cousin, his colleague in the kingdom, to which he had appointed him; and[4] saw his wife destroyed by pessaries, for when she bore not, a certain wretched and miserable woman (for such indeed she was who thought to supply the gift of God by her own wisdom) gave her pessaries, and destroyed the queen, and herself perished with her. And this man is said to have also killed his own brother.[5] Another again, his successor, was destroyed by noxious drugs, and his cup was to him no longer drink, but death. And his son had an eye put out, from fear of what was to follow, though he had done no wrong.

---

[1] After these words the Greek text is disarranged, and irreconcilable with itself and with the real history. Chrysostom seems, however, to intend to say what follows; that the brother of Crispus, i.e. Constantius Augustus, caused his father's brother, Julius Constantius, and his sons, Dalmatius and Annibalianus, to be put to death. They were in fact slain by the soldiery, and as some thought, at the instigation of Constantius Augustus, son of Constantine. He adds afterwards, that his brother was taken by an usurper, and killed himself. Now Constans Augustus, the brother of Constantius, was taken by the usurper Magnentius, or rather by his generals, and slain, but no writer except Chrysostom says that he killed himself. He adds that Constantius slew his cousin. This was Gallus, who was made his colleague in the Empire by Constantius, and put to death by his order, A.D. 345.—*Montf.*

(Tillemont understands this otherwise, and more according to the Greek, which is not difficult to construe as it stands; viz. that *Constans* killed himself and his children [if he had any, which does not otherwise appear] when taken by Magnentius, and that he [*Constans*] caused the death of his brother Constantine the younger.)

[2] Here Chrysostom relates the violent deaths that had occurred within memory in the imperial palace; he goes, however, by common report, which usually varies from the real fact. He mentions the events without the names. There is no doubt, however, that the first example brought forward is Constantine the Great, who caused his son Crispus to be put to death, and afterwards his wife Fausta. Chrysostom says he exposed her to wild beasts; others, however, relate that she was suffocated by his order in a hot bath. Tillemont gives the most accurate of all the accounts of this affair.—*Montf.*

[3] [There is no known warrant for translating τύραννος by "rebel," as the Oxford tr. does. It probably means some local usurping despot. In the Hom. on the return of Bishop Flavian, Chrysostom makes the emperor speak of the Antiochene mob who insulted his statues as "tyrants," just as we say, "the tyranny of a mob."—J. A. B.]

[4] As for what Chrysostom adds (as usual, without names) of the wife of one of the Augusti who used drugs to cure barrenness, and perished together with the woman who supplied the drugs, also of another Augustus who was poisoned, and whose son had an eye put out, and another who perished in some horrible manner, I have not yet been able to find out to whom it applies. But what follows, of one burnt among beams and horses and all sorts of things, relates to Valens, who after his defeat at Hadrianople retired to a house, and was burnt to ashes with it. The reigning emperor was Arcadius, with respect to whom the history of that age attests the truth of his words.—*Montf.*

Tillemont understands the one poisoned to be Jovian, and says that his son Varronianus was treated as here mentioned, and afterwards put to death; and so Montf., in his Introduction to St. Chrys., "ad Viduam Juniorem," t. i. p. 337.

[5] [The older text, as here given after Field, may afford some help in these inquiries. The altered text, to which the notes refer, makes the brother of the first-mentioned baby slay himself and his children. He whose wife was destroyed is there different from the one just preceding; and he who killed his brother is there the suicide. These differences are stated for the sake of those who are curious about such matters.—J. A. B.]

It is not befitting to mention how another ended his life miserably. And after them, one was burnt, like some miserable wretch, amongst horses, and beams, and all sorts of things, and left his wife in widowhood. For it is not possible to relate the woes which he was compelled to undergo in his lifetime, when he rose up in revolt. And hath not he who now rules, from the time he received the crown, been in toil, in danger, in grief, in dejection, in misfortune, exposed to conspiracies? Such is not the kingdom of heaven, but after it is received, there is peace, life, joy, delight. But as I said, life cannot be without pain. For if in the affairs of this world even he who is accounted most happy, if the king is burdened with so many misfortunes, what thinkest thou must be true of private life? I cannot say how many other evils there are! How many stories have ofttimes been woven on these subjects! For nearly all the tragedies of the stage, as well as the mythical stories, have kings for their subjects. For most of these stories are formed from true incidents, for it is thus they please. As for example, Thyestes' banquet, and the destruction of all that family by their misfortunes.

These things we know from the writers[6] that are without: but if ye will, I will adduce instances from the Scripture too. Saul was the first king, and ye knew how he perished, after experiencing numberless ills. After him, David, Solomon, Abia, Hezekiah, Josiah, in like sort. For it is not possible, without affliction and toil, and without dejection of mind, to pass through the present life. But let us be cast down in mind, not for such things as these, for which kings grieve, but for those things, whence we (thus) have great gain. "For godly sorrow worketh repentance unto salvation, a repentance which bringeth no regret." (2 Cor. vii. 10.) On account of these things we should be grieved, for these things we should be pained, for these things we should be pricked at heart; thus was Paul grieved for sinners, thus did he weep. "For out of much affliction and anguish of heart I wrote unto you in many tears." (2 Cor. ii. 4.) For when he had no cause of grief on his own account, he did so on account of others, or rather he accounted these things too to be his own, at least as far as grief went. Others were offended, and he burned; others were weak, and he was weak; such grief as this is good, is superior to all worldly joy. Him who so grieves I prefer to all men, or rather the Lord Himself pronounces them blessed, who so grieve, who are sympathizing. I do not so much admire him in dangers, or rather I do not admire him less for the dangers by which he died daily, yet this still more captivates me. For it came of a soul

---

[6] *The civil historians.*

devoted to God, and full of affection : from the love which Christ Himself seeketh : from a brotherly and a fatherly sympathy, or rather, of one greater than both these. Thus we should be affected, thus weep ; such tears as these are full of great delight ; such grief as this is the ground of joy.

And say not to me : What do they for whom I grieve gain by my so doing? Though we no way profit them for whom we grieve, at all events we shall profit ourselves. For he who grieveth thus on account of others, much more will so do for himself ; he who thus weepeth for the sins of others will not pass by his own transgressions unwept, or rather, he will not quickly sin. But this is dreadful, that when we are ordered so to grieve for them that sin, we do not even exhibit any repentance for our own sins, but when sinning remain without feeling, and have care for and take account of anything, rather than our own sins. For this cause we rejoice with a worthless joy, which is the joy of the world, and straightway quenched, and which brings forth griefs innumerable. Let us then grieve with grief which is the mother of joy, and let us not rejoice with joy which brings forth grief. Let us shed tears which are the seeds of great joy, and not laugh with that laughter, which brings forth the gnashing of teeth for us.

Let us be afflicted with affliction, from which springs up ease, and let us not seek luxury, whence great affliction and pain is born. Let us labor a little time upon the earth, that we may have continual enjoyment in heaven. Let us afflict ourselves in this transitory life, that we may attain rest in that which is endless. Let us not be remiss in this short life, lest we groan in that which is endless.

See ye not how many are here in affliction for the sake of worldly things? Consider that thou also art one of them, and bear thy affliction and thy pain, feeding on the hope of things to come. Thou art not better than Paul or Peter, who never obtained rest, who passed all their life in hunger and thirst and nakedness. If thou wouldest attain the same things with them, why journeyest thou along a contrary road? If thou wouldest arrive at that City, of which they have been deemed worthy, walk along the path which leadeth thither. The way of ease leadeth not thither, but that of affliction. The former is broad, the latter is narrow ; along this let us walk, that we may attain eternal life in Christ Jesus our Lord, with whom, to the Father, together with the Holy Ghost, be honor, might, power, now and ever, and world without end. Amen.

HOMILIES OF ST. JOHN CHRYSOSTOM,

ARCHBISHOP OF CONSTANTINOPLE,

ON THE

EPISTLE OF ST. PAUL THE APOSTLE

TO THE

COLOSSIANS.

HOMILY I

COLOSSIANS i. 1, 2.

" Paul, an Apostle of Christ Jesus through the will of God, and Timothy our brother, to the saints and faithful brethren in Christ which are at Colossæ: Grace to you, and peace, from God our Father."

HOLY indeed are all the Epistles of Paul: but some advantage have those which he sent after he was in bonds: those, for instance, to the Ephesians and Philemon: that to Timothy, that to the Philippians, and the one before us: for this also was sent when he was a prisoner, since he writes in it thus: "for which I am also in bonds: that I may make it manifest as I ought to speak." (Col. iv. 3, 4.) But this Epistle appears to have been written after that to the Romans. For the one to the Romans he wrote before he had seen them, but this Epistle, after; and near upon the close of his preaching.[1] And it is evident from hence; that in the Epistle to Philemon he says, "Being such an one as Paul the aged" (ver. 9), and makes request for Onesimus; but in this he sends Onesimus himself, as he says, "With Onesimus the faithful and beloved brother" (Col. iv. 9): calling him faithful, and beloved, and brother. Wherefore also he boldly says in this Epistle, "from the hope of the Gospel which ye heard, which was preached in all creation under heaven." (Col. i. 23.) For it had now been preached for a long time. I think then that the Epistle to Timothy was written after this; and when he was now come to the very end of his life, for there he says, "for I am already being offered " (2 Tim. iv. 6) ; this is later[2] however than that to the Philippians, for in that Epistle he was just entering upon his imprisonment at Rome.

But why do I say that these Epistles have some advantage over the rest in this respect, because he writes while in bonds? As if a champion were to write in the midst of carnage and victory;[3] so also in truth did he. For himself too was aware that this was a great thing, for writing to Philemon he saith, "Whom I have begotten in my bonds." (Ver. 10.) And this he said, that we should not be dispirited when in adversity, but even rejoice. At this place was Philemon with these (Colossians). For in the Epistle to him he saith, "And to Archippus our fellow-soldier " (ver. 2); and in this, "Say to Archippus." (Col. iv. 17.) This man seems to me to have been charged with some office in the Church.

But he had not seen either these people, or the Romans, or the Hebrews, when he wrote to them. That this is true of the others, he shows in many places; with regard to the Colossians, hear him saying, "And as many as have

---

[1] Ed. Par. suspects that a sentence is lost here, but without reason, as he had just mentioned the Epistle to Philemon as written in imprisonment, and consequently later than that to the Romans.

[2] πρεσβυτέρα. Lit. "older." The argument allows no other sense. It may mean "written at a greater age," or "of higher honor" (because written after longer imprisonment).

[3] Lit. "while raising trophies."

not seen my face in the flesh" (Col. ii. 1. 5) : and again, "Though I am absent in the flesh, yet am I with you in the spirit." So great a thing did he know his presence everywhere to be. And always, even though he be absent, he makes himself present. So, when he punishes the fornicator, look how he places himself on the tribunal ; "for," he saith, "I verily being absent in body, but present in spirit, have judged already as though I were present" (1 Cor. v. 3) : and again, "I will come to you, and will know not the word of them which are puffed up, but the power" (1 Cor. iv. 19) : and again, "Not only when I am present with you, but much more when I am absent." (Phil. ii. 12 ; Gal. iv. 18.)

"Paul an Apostle of Jesus Christ through the will of God."

It were well also to say, what from considering this Epistle we have found to be its occasion and subject. What then is it? They used to approach [1] God through angels ; they held many Jewish and Grecian observances. These things then he is correcting. Wherefore in the very outset he says, "Through the will of God." So here again he hath used the expression "through."[2] "And Timothy the brother," he saith ; of course then he too was an Apostle,[3] and probably also known to them. "To the saints which are at Colossæ." This was a city of Phrygia, as is plain from Laodicea's being near to it. "And faithful brethren in Christ." (Col. iv. 16.) Whence, saith he, art thou made a saint? Tell me. Whence art thou called faithful? Is it not because thou wert sanctified through death? Is it not because thou hast faith in Christ? Whence art thou made a brother? for neither in deed, nor in word, nor in achievement didst thou show thyself faithful. Tell me, whence is it that thou hast been entrusted with so great mysteries? Is it not because of Christ?

"Grace to you and peace from God our Father." Whence cometh grace to you? Whence peace? "From God," saith he, "our Father." Although he useth not in this place the name of Christ.

I will ask those who speak disparagingly of the Spirit, Whence is God the Father of servants? Who wrought these mighty achievements? Who made thee a saint? Who faithful? Who a son of God? He who made thee worthy to be trusted, the same is also the cause of thy being entrusted with all.

For we are called faithful, not only because we have faith, but also because we are entrusted of God with mysteries which not even angels knew before us. However, to Paul it was indifferent whether or not to put it thus.

Ver. 3. "We give thanks to God,[4] the Father of our Lord Jesus Christ."

He seems to me to refer everything to the Father, that what he has to say may not at once offend them.[5]

"Praying always for you."

He shows his love, not by giving thanks only, but also by continual prayer, in that those whom he did not see, he had continually within himself.

Ver. 4. ["Having heard of your faith in Christ Jesus."

A little above he said, "our Lord." "He," saith he, "is Lord, not the servants." "Of Jesus Christ." These names also are symbols of His benefit to us, for "He," it means, "shall save His people from their sins."[6] (Matt. i. 21.)]

Ver. 4. "Having heard of your faith in Christ Jesus, and of the love which ye have toward all the saints."

Already he conciliates them. It was Epaphroditus[7] who brought him this account. But he sends the Epistle by Tychicus, retaining Epaphroditus with himself. "And of the love," he saith, "which ye have toward all the saints," not toward this one and that : of course then toward us also.

Ver. 5. "Because of the hope which is laid up for you in the heavens."

He speaks of the good things to come. This is with a view to their temptations, that they should not seek their rest here. For lest any should say, "And where is the good of their love toward the saints, if they themselves are in affliction?" he says, "We rejoice that ye are securing for yourselves a noble reception in heaven." "Because of the hope," he saith, "which is laid up." He shows its secureness. "Whereof ye heard before in the word of the truth." Here the expression is as if he would chide them, as having changed from it when they had long held it.

"Whereof," saith he, "ye heard before in the word of the truth of the Gospel." And he bears witness to its truth. With good reason, for in it there is nothing false.

"Of the Gospel." He doth not say, "of the preaching," but he calleth it the "Gospel," con-

---

[1] Προσήγοντο, v. Hom. ii. § i.
[2] τὸ διὰ, here used with the genitive. He mentions it as applied to the will of the Father, and consequently not, as some supposed, proving an inferiority in the Son.
[3] [Even in the New Test. the term "apostle" is sometimes applied to others than the twelve and Paul: as in Acts xiv. 14, probably in Gal. i. 19, and as implied in the phrase "false apostle." Compare Lightfoot on Gal., ed. 2, pp. 95 ff. — J. A. B.]

[4] Rec. text inserts "and" (καὶ for τῷ), but with the same sense.
[5] [The reading προσστῆναι (Field, after one MSS.) accounts for the others, προσστῆναι and προτιθέναι, the latter followed here by the Oxford ed.; but see its Addenda. — J. A. B.]
[6] Savile includes this paragraph in brackets, and so Ed. Par., as it is not in some MSS. and Versions, and is thought not to fit in well; but they have missed the sense.
[7] Called Epaphras in the text, c. i. 7, and c. iv. 12. [A familiar contraction of such names. — J A. B.]

tinually reminding them of God's benefits.[1] And having first praised them, he next reminds them of these.

Ver. 6. "Which is come unto you, even as it is also in all the world."

He now gives them credit. "Is come," he said metaphorically. He means, it did not come and go away, but that it remained, and was there. Then because to the many the strongest confirmation of doctrines is that they hold them in common with many, he therefore added, "As also it is in all the world."

It is present everywhere, everywhere victo-rious, everywhere established.

"And is bearing fruit, and increasing,[2] as it doth in you also."

"Bearing fruit." In works. "Increasing." By the accession of many, by becoming firmer; for plants then begin to thicken when they have become firm.

"As also among you," says he.

He first gains the hearer by his praises, so that even though disinclined, he may not refuse to hear him.

"Since the day ye heard it."

Marvelous! that ye quickly came unto it and believed; and straightway, from the very first, showed forth its fruits.

"Since the day ye heard, and knew the grace of God in truth."

Not in word, saith he, nor in deceit, but in very deeds. Either then this is what he means by "bearing fruit," or else, the signs and won-ders. Because as soon as ye received it, so soon ye knew the grace of God. What then forthwith gave proofs of its inherent virtue, is it not a hard thing that that should now be dis-believed?

Ver. 7. "Even as ye learned of Epaphras our beloved fellow-servant."

He, it is probable, had preached there. "Ye learned" the Gospel. Then to show the trust-worthiness of the man, he says, "our fellow servant."

"Who is a faithful minister of Christ on your[3] behalf; who also declared unto us your love in the Spirit."

Doubt not, he saith, of the hope which is to come: ye see that the world is being converted. And what need to allege the cases of others? what happened in your own is even indepen-dently a sufficient ground for belief, for, "ye knew the grace of God in truth:" that is, in works. So that these two things, viz. the belief of all, and your own too, confirm the things that are to come. Nor was the fact one thing, and what Epaphras said, another. "Who is," saith he, "faithful," that is, true. How, "a minister on your behalf"? In that he had gone to him. "Who also declared to us," saith he, "your love in the Spirit," that is, the spiritual love ye bear us. If this man be the minister of Christ; how say ye, that you approach God by angels? "Who also declared unto us," saith he, "your love in the Spirit." For this love is wonderful and steadfast; all other has but the name. And there are some persons who are not of this kind, but such is not friendship, wherefore also it is easily dissolved.

There are many causes which produce friend-ship; and we will pass over those which are in-famous, (for none will take an objection against us in our favor, seeing they are evil.) But let us, if you will, review those which are natural, and those which arise out of the relations of life. Now of the social sort are these, for instance; one receives a kindness, or inherits a friend from forefathers, or has been a companion at table or in travel: or is neighbor to another (and these are virtuous); or is of the same trade, which last however is not sincere; for it is attended by a certain emulation and envy. But the natural are such as that of father to son, son to father, brother to brother, grandfather to descendant, mother to children, and if you like let us add also that of wife to husband; for all matrimonial attachments are also of this life, and earthly. Now these latter appear stronger than the for-mer: appear, I said, because often they are sur-passed by them. For friends have at times shown a more genuinely kind disposition than brothers, or than sons toward fathers; and when he whom a man hath begotten would not succor him, one who knew him not has stood by him, and succored him. But the spiritual love is higher than all, as it were some queen ruling her subjects; and in her form is bright: for not as the other, hath she aught of earth for her parent; neither habitual intercourse, nor benefits, nor nature, nor time; but she descendeth from above, out of heaven. And why wonderest thou that she needeth no benefits in order that she should subsist, seeing that neither by injuries is she overthrown?

Now that this love is greater than the other, hear Paul saying; "For I could wish that I my-self were anathema from Christ for my brethren." (Rom. ix. 3.) What father would have thus wished himself in misery? And again, "To de-part, and to be with Christ" is "very far better; yet to abide in the flesh" is "more needful for your sake." (Phil. i. 23, 24.) What mother would have chosen so to speak, regardless of herself? And again hear him saying, "For be-ing bereaved of you for a short season, in pres-

---

[1] The passage just above in brackets may have been for the sake of this.

[2] Rec. text omits "and increasing" (καὶ αὐξανόμενον), but it is in some of the oldest MSS.

[3] ["On our behalf" is the correct N. T. text. Chrys. here, as commonly, has what Westcott and Hort call the "Syrian" type of N. T. text. — J. A. B.]

ence, not in heart." (1 Thess. ii. 17.) And here indeed [in the world], when a father hath been insulted, he withdraws his love; not so however there, but he went to those who stoned him, seeking to do them good. For nothing, nothing is so strong as the bond of the Spirit. For he who became a friend from receiving benefits, will, should these be discontinued, become an enemy; he whom habitual intercourse made inseparable, will, when the habit is broken through, let his friendship become extinct. A wife again, should a broil have taken place, will leave her husband, and withdraw affection; the son, when he sees his father living to a great age, is dissatisfied. But in case of spiritual love there is nothing of this. For by none of these things can it be dissolved; seeing it is not composed out of them. Neither time, nor length of journey, nor ill usage, nor being evil spoken of, nor anger, nor insult, nor any other thing, make inroads upon it, nor have the power of dissolving it. And that thou mayest know this; Moses was stoned, and yet he made entreaty for them. (Ex. xvii. 4.) What father would have done this for one that stoned him, and would not rather have stoned him too to death?

Let us then follow after these friendships which are of the Spirit, for they are strong, and hard to be dissolved, and not those which arise from the table, for these we are forbidden to carry in Thither. For hear Christ saying in the Gospel, Call not thy friends nor thy neighbors, if thou makest a feast, but the lame, the maimed. (Luke xiv. 12.) With reason: for great is the recompense for these. But thou canst not, nor endurest to feast with lame and blind, but thinkest it grievous and offensive, and refusest. Now it were indeed best that thou shouldest not refuse, however it is not necessary to do it. If thou seatest them not with thee, send to them of the dishes on thy own table. And he that inviteth his friends, hath done no great thing: for he hath received his recompense here. But he that called the maimed, and poor, hath God for his Debtor. Let us then not repine when we receive not a reward here, but when we do receive; for we shall have nothing more to receive There. In like manner, if man recompense, God recompenseth not; if man recompense not, then God will recompense. Let us then not seek those out for our benefits, who have it in their power to requite us again, nor bestow our favors on them with such an expectation: this were a cold thought. If thou invite a friend, the gratitude lasts till evening; and therefore the friendship for the nonce is spent more quickly than the expenses are paid. But if thou call the poor and the maimed, never shall the gratitude perish, for God, who remembereth ever, and never forgetteth, thou hast even Him for

thy Debtor. What squeamishness is this, pray, that thou canst not sit down in company with the poor? What sayest thou? He is unclean and filthy? Then wash him, and lead him up to thy table. But he hath filthy garments? Then change them, and give him clean apparel. Seest thou not how great the gain is? Christ cometh unto thee through him, and dost thou make petty calculations of such things? When thou art inviting the King to thy table, dost thou fear because of such things as these?

Let us suppose two tables, and let one be filled with those, and have the blind, the halt, the maimed in hand or leg, the barefoot, those clad with but one scanty garment, and that worn out: but let the other have grandees, generals, governors, great officers, arrayed in costly robes, and fine lawn, belted with golden girdles. Again, here at the table of the poor let there be neither silver, nor store of wine, but just enough to refresh and gladden, and let the drinking cups and the rest of the vessels be made from glass only; but there, at the table of the rich, let all the vessels be of silver and gold, and the semicircular table,[1] not such as one person can lift, but as two young men can with difficulty move, and the wine-jars lie in order, glittering far beyond the silver with gold, and let the semicircle[2] be smoothly laid all over with soft drapery. Here, again, let there be many servants, in garments not less ornamented than those of the guests, and bravely appareled, and wearing loose trowsers, men beauteous to look upon, in the very flower of life, plump, and well conditioned; but there let there be only two servants disdaining all that proud vanity. And let those have costly meats, but these only enough to appease hunger and inspire cheerfulness. Have I said enough? and are both tables laid out with sufficient minuteness? Is anything wanting? I think not. For I have gone over the guests, and the costliness both of the vessels, and of the linen,[3] and the meats.[4] However, if we should have omitted aught, we shall discover it as we proceed with the discourse.

---

1 [So Field, after several MSS. But " the semicircular " (no substantive, see a few lines below) was an obscure word in such a connection, and the idea of one man lifting a table seemed strange. So, as the preceding and following portions treat of vessels, several other MSS. *substitute* for this whole statement (down to "move") the following: " and let there be a gilded bowl of half a talent weight, so that two young men can with difficulty move it," the last clause being the same as in the other text. Montfaucon admitted both into his edition, thus making a *conflate* reading.— J. A. B.] Montfaucon in a note mentions William the Conqueror being represented sitting at such a table, sometimes called a sigma, from the form C. He refers to his *Antiquité Expliquée*, T. iii. p. 111. [That the three tables arranged as a hollow square (triclinium) should be sometimes converted into a semicircle would be a natural piece of luxury, but not likely to become common, because really less convenient.— J. A. B.]
2 Here, the couch which belongs to the table. Such is the stibadium described in the accounts of Pompeii.
3 στρωμάτων, carpets, cushions, coverings for the tables, &c., &c.
4 [This labored exuberance of descriptive detail is a grave fault of Chrysostom's style, but was highly acceptable to his contemporaries. — J. A. B.]

Come then, now that we have correctly drawn each table in its proper outline, let us see at which ye will seat yourselves. For I for my part am going to that of the blind, and the lame, but probably the more part of you will choose the other, that of the generals, that is so gay and splendid. Let us then see which of them doth more abound in pleasure; for as yet let us not examine into the things of hereafter, seeing that in those at least this of mine hath the superiority. Wherefore? Because this one hath Christ sitting down at it, the other men, this hath the Master, that the servants. But say we nothing of these things as yet; but let us see which hath the more of present pleasure. And even in this respect, then, this pleasure is greater, for it is more pleasure to sit down with a King than with his servants. But let us withdraw this consideration also; let us examine the matter simply by itself. I, then, and those who choose the table I do, shall with much freedom and ease of mind both say and hear everything: but you trembling and fearing, and ashamed before those you sit down with, will not even have the heart to reach out your hands, just as though you had got to a school, and not a dinner, just as though you were trembling before dreadful masters. But not so they. But, saith one, the honor is great. Nay, I further am in more honor; for your mean estate appears grander, when even whilst sharing the same table, the words ye utter are those of slaves.

For the servant then most of all shows as such, when he sits down with his master; for he is in a place where he ought not to be; nor hath he from such familiarity so much dignity as he hath abasement, for he is then abased exceedingly. And one may see a servant by himself make a brave appearance, and the poor man seem splendid by himself, rather than when he is walking with a rich one; for the low when near the lofty, then appears low, and the juxtaposition makes the low seem lower, not loftier. So too your sitting down with them makes you seem as of yet meaner condition. But not so, us. In these two things, then, we have the advantage, in freedom, and in honor; which have nothing equal to them in regard of pleasure. For I at least would prefer a crust with freedom, to thousands of dainties with slavery. For, saith one, "Better is an entertainment of herbs with love and kindness, than an ox from the stall with hatred." (Prov. xv. 17.) For whatsoever those may say, they who are present must needs praise it, or give offense; assuming thus the rank of parasites, or rather, being worse than they. For parasites indeed, even though it be with shame and insult, have yet liberty of speech: but ye have not even this. But your meanness is indeed as great, (for ye fear and crouch,) but

not so your honor. Surely then that table is deprived of every pleasure, but this is replete with all delight of soul.

But let us examine the nature even of the meats themselves. For there indeed it is necessary to burst one's self with the large quantity of wine, even against one's will, but here none who is disinclined need eat or drink. So that there indeed the pleasure arising from the quality of the food is cancelled by the dishonor which precedes, and the discomfort which follows the surfeit. For not less than hunger doth surfeiting destroy and rack our bodies; but even far more grievously; and whomsoever you like to give me, I shall more easily destroy by bursting him with surfeit than by hunger. For thus the latter is easier to be borne than the other, for one might indeed endure hunger for twenty days, but surfeiting not for as many as two only. And the country people who are perpetually struggling with the one, are healthy, and need no physicians; but the other, surfeiting I mean, none can endure without perpetually calling in physicians; yea, rather, its tyranny hath often baffled even their attempt to rescue.

So far then as pleasure is concerned, this [table of mine] hath the advantage. For if honor hath more pleasure than dishonor, if authority than subjection, and if manly confidence than trembling and fear, and if enjoyment of what is enough, than to be plunged out of depth in the tide of luxury; on the score of pleasure this table is better than the other. It is besides better in regard of expense; for the other is expensive, but this, not so.

But what? is it then to the guests alone that this table is the more pleasurable, or bringeth it more pleasure than the other to him who inviteth them, as well? for this is what we are enquiring after rather. Now he who invites those makes preparation many days before, and is forced to have trouble and anxious thoughts and cares, neither sleeping by night, nor resting by day; but forming with himself many plans, conversing with cooks, confectioners, deckers of tables. Then when the very day is come, one may see him in greater fear than those who are going to fight a boxing match, lest aught should turn out other than was expected, lest he be shot with the glance of envy, lest he thereby procure himself a multitude of accusers. But the other escapeth all this anxious thought and trouble by extemporizing his table, and not being careful about it for many days before. And then, truly, after this, the former indeed hath straightway lost the grateful return; but the other hath God for his Debtor; and is nourished with good hopes, being every day feasted from off that table. For the meats indeed are spent, but the grateful thought is never spent, but every day he rejoices and exults more than they that are gorged with their excess of wine. For nothing doth so nourish the soul as a virtuous hope, and the expectation of good things.

But now let us consider what follows. There indeed are flutes, and harps, and pipes; but here is no music of sounds unsuitable; but what? hymns, singing of psalms. There indeed the Demons are hymned; but here, the Lord of all, God. Seest thou with what gratitude this one aboundeth, with what ingratitude and insensibility that? For, tell me, when God hath nourished thee with His good things, and when thou oughtest to give Him thanks after being fed, dost thou even introduce the Demons? For these songs to the lyre, are none other than songs to Demons. When thou oughtest to say, "Blessed art Thou, O Lord, that Thou hast nourished me with Thy good things," dost thou like a worthless dog not even so much as remember Him, but, over and above, introducest the Demons? Nay rather, dogs, whether they receive anything or not, fawn upon those they know, but thou dost not even this. The dog, although he receives nothing, fawns upon his master; but thou, even when thou hast received, barkest at Him. Again, the dog, even though he be well treated by a stranger, not even so will be reconciled of his hatred of him, nor be enticed on to be friends with him: but thou, even though suffering mischief incalculable from the Demons, introducest them at thy feasts. So that, in two ways, thou art worse than the dog. And the mention I have now made of dogs is happy, in regard of those who give thanks then only when they receive a benefit. Take shame, I pray you, at the dogs, which when famishing still fawn upon their masters. But thou, if thou hast haply heard that the Demon has cured any-one, straightway forsakest thy Master; O more unreasoning than the dogs!

But, saith one, the harlots are a pleasure to look upon. What sort of pleasure are they? yea rather what infamy are they not? Thy house has become a brothel, madness, and fury; and art thou not ashamed to call this pleasure? If then it be allowed to use them,[1] greater than all pleasure is the shame, and the discomfort which arises from the shame, to make one's house a brothel, like hogs in wallowing in the mire? But if so far only be allowed as to see them, lo! again the pain is greater. For to see is no pleasure, where to use is not allowed, but the lust becomes only the greater, and the flame the fiercer.

But wouldest thou learn the end? Those, indeed, when they rise up from the table, are like the madmen and those that have lost their wits; foolhardy, quarrelsome, laughing-stocks for the very slaves; and the servants indeed retire sober, but these, drunk. O the shame! But with the other is nothing of this sort; but closing the table with thanksgiving, they so retire to their homes, with pleasure sleeping, with pleasure waking, free from all shame and accusation.

If thou wilt consider also the guests themselves, thou wilt see that the one are within just what the others are without; blind, maimed, lame; and as are the bodies of these, such are the souls of those, laboring under dropsy and inflammation. For of such sort is pride; for after the luxurious gratification a maiming takes place; of such sort is surfeiting and drunkenness, making men lame and maimed. And thou wilt see too that these have souls like the bodies of the others, brilliant, ornamented. For they who live in giving of thanks, who seek nothing beyond a sufficiency, they whose philosophy is of this sort are in all brightness.

But let us see the end both here and there. There, indeed, is unchaste pleasure, loose laughter, drunkenness, buffoonery, filthy language; (for since they in their own persons are ashamed to talk filthily, this is brought about by means of the harlots;) but here is love of mankind, gentleness. Near to him who invites those stands vainglory arming him, but near the other, love of man, and gentleness. For the one table, love of man prepareth, but the other, vainglory, and cruelty, out of injustice and grasping. And that one ends in what I have said, in loss of wits, in delirium, in madness; (for such are the offshoots of vainglory;) but this one in thanksgiving and the glory of God. And the praise too, which cometh of men, attendeth more abundantly upon this; for that man is even regarded with an envious eye, but this all men regard as their common father, even they who have received no benefit at his hands. And as with the injured even they who have not been injured sympathize, and all become in common enemies (to the injurer): so too, when some receive kindness, they also who have not received any, not less than they who have, praise and admire him that conferred it. And there indeed is much envy, but here much tender solicitude, many prayers from all.

And so much indeed here; but There, when Christ is come, this one indeed shall stand with much boldness, and shall hear before the whole world, "Thou sawest Me an hungered, and didst feed Me; naked, and didst clothe Me; a stranger, and didst take Me in" (Matt. xxv. 35); and all the like words: but the other shall hear the contrary; "Wicked and slothful servant" (Matt. xxv. 26); and again, "Woe unto them that luxuriate upon their couches, and sleep upon beds of ivory, and drink the refined wine,

---

[1] [The text is confused, but the reading adopted by Field, and here given, accounts for the others. — J. A. B.]

and anoint themselves with the chief ointments; they counted upon these things as staying, and not as fleeting." (Amos vi. 4, 5, 6, Sept.)

I have not said this without purpose, but with the view of changing your minds; and that you should do nothing that is fruitless. What then, saith one, of the fact that I do both the one and the other? This argument is much resorted to by all. And what need, tell me, when everything might be done usefully, to make a division, and to expend part on what is not wanted, but even without any purpose at all, and part usefully? Tell me, hadst thou, when sowing, cast some upon a rock, and some upon very good ground; is it likely that thou wouldest have been contented so, and have said, Where is the harm, if we cast some to no purpose, and some upon very good ground? For why not all into the very good ground? Why lessen the gain? And if thou have occasion to be getting money together, thou wilt not talk in that way, but wilt get it together from every quarter; but in the other case thou dost not so. And if to lend on usury; thou wilt not say, "Wherefore shall we give some to the poor, and some to the rich," but all is given to the former:[1] yet in the case before us, where the gain is so great, thou dost not thus calculate, and will not at length desist from expending without purpose, and laying out without return?

"But," saith one, "this also hath a gain." Of what kind, tell me? "It increaseth friendships." Nothing is colder than men who are made friends by these things, by the table, and surfeiting. The friendships of parasites are born only from that source.

Insult not a thing so marvelous as love,[2] nor say that this is its root. As if one were to say, that a tree which bore gold and precious stones had not its root of the same, but that it was gendered of rottenness; so doest even thou: for even though friendship should be born from that source, nothing could possibly be colder. But those other tables produce friendship, not with man, but with God: and that an intense[3] one, so thou be intent on preparing them. For he that expendeth part in this way and part in that, even should he have bestowed much, hath done no great thing: but he that expendeth all in this way, even though he should have given little, hath done the whole. For what is required is that we give, not much or little, but not less than is in our power. Think we on him with the five talents, and on him with the two. (Matt. xxv. 15.) Think we on her who cast in those two mites. (Mark xii. 41.) Think we on the widow in Elijah's days. She who threw in those two mites said not, What harm if I keep the one mite for myself, and give the other? but gave her whole living. (1 Kings xvii.) But thou, in the midst of so great plenty, art more penurious than she. Let us then not be careless of our own salvation, but apply ourselves to almsgiving. For nothing is better than this, as the time to come shall show; meanwhile the present shows it also. Live we then to the glory of God, and do those things that please Him, that we may be counted worthy of the good things of promise; which may all we obtain, through the grace and love toward man of our Lord Jesus Christ, to whom be the glory and the power and honor, now and ever, and world without end. Amen.

---

[1] Because their distress would make them willing to give a higher interest. This place may bear the sense here given, but it seems corrupt. The sense requires, "shall we not give?" or else, "wilt thou not say?" interrogatively, or the expulsion of διὰ τί.

[2] Compare St. Clem. Al. Pædag. l. ii. c. 1.
[3] ἐπιτεταμένην.

HOMILY II.

COLOSSIANS i. 9, 10.

" For this cause we also, since the day we heard it, do not cease to pray and make request for you, that ye may be filled with the knowledge of His will in all spiritual wisdom and understanding; to walk worthily of the Lord unto all pleasing, bearing fruit in every good work, and increasing in the knowledge of God."

" FOR this cause." What cause? Because we heard of your faith and love, because we have good hopes, we are hopeful to ask for future blessings also. For as in the games we cheer on those most who are near upon gaining the victory, just so doth Paul also most exhort those who have achieved the greater part.

" Since the day we heard it," saith he, " we do not cease to pray for you." Not for one day do we pray for you, nor yet for two, nor three. Herein he both shows his love, and gives them a gentle hint that they had not yet arrived at the end. For the words, " that ye may be filled," are of this significancy. And observe, I pray, the prudence of this blessed one. He nowhere says that they are destitute of everything, but that they are deficient; everywhere the words, " that ye may be filled," show this. And again, " unto all pleasing, in every good work " (ver. 11), and again, " strengthened with all power," and again, " unto all patience and long-suffering "; for the constant addition of " all " bears witness to their doing well in part, though, it might be, not in all. And, " that ye may be filled," he saith ; not, " that ye may receive," for they had received ; but " that ye may be filled " with what as yet was lacking. Thus both the rebuke was given without offense, and the praise did not suffer them to sink down, and become supine, as if it had been complete. But what is, " that ye may be filled with the knowledge of His will "? That through the Son we should be brought unto Him, and no more through Angels. Now that ye must be brought unto Him, ye have learnt, but it remains for you to learn this, and why He sent the Son. For had it been that we were to have been saved by Angels,[1] He would not have sent Him, would not have given Him up. · " In all spiritual wisdom," he saith, " and understanding." For since the philosophers deceived them ; I wish you, he

saith, to be in spiritual wisdom, not after the wisdom of men. But if in order to know the will of God, there needs spiritual wisdom ; to know His Essence what it is, there is need of continual prayers.

And Paul shows here, that since that time he has been praying, and has not yet prevailed, and yet has not desisted ; for the words, " from the day we heard it," show this. But it implies condemnation to them, if, from that time, even assisted by prayers, they had not amended themselves. " And making request," he says, with much earnestness, for this the expression " ye knew "[2] shows. But it is necessary still to know somewhat besides. " To walk worthily," he says, " of the Lord." Here he speaks of life and its works, for so he doth also everywhere : with faith he always couples conduct. " Unto all pleasing." And how, " all pleasing "? " Bearing fruit in every good work, and increasing in the knowledge of God." Seeing, saith he, He hath fully revealed Himself unto you, and seeing ye have received knowledge so great ; do ye then show forth a conduct worthy of the faith ; for this needeth elevated conduct, greater far than the old dispensation. For, he that hath known God, and been counted worthy to be God's servant, yea, rather, even His Son, see how great virtue he needeth. " Strengthened with all power." He is here speaking of trials and persecutions. We pray that ye might be filled with strength, that ye faint not for sorrow, nor despair. " According to the might of His glory." But that ye may take up again such forwardness as it becometh the power of His glory to give. " Unto all patience and long-suffering." What he saith is of this sort. Summarily, he saith, we pray that ye may lead a life of virtue, and worthy of your citizenship, and may stand firmly, being strengthened as it is reasonable to be strengthened by God. For this cause he doth not as yet touch upon doctrines, but dwells upon life, wherein he had nothing to charge them with, and having praised them where praise was due, he then comes down to accusation. And this he does everywhere : when he is about writing to any with somewhat to blame them for, and somewhat to praise, he first praises them, and then comes down to his charges. For he first conciliates the hearer, and frees his accusation from all suspicion, and

---

[1] It may be asked how St. Chrysostom could use this argument, and yet speak as he does of the intercession of Saints (see the end of Hom. vi. on the Statues, and note). The reason is, that he viewed the Saints as in the Kingdom of Christ, and subordinate; but the error here referred to seems to have made the Angels independent of Him, and the means of an approach to God without reference to His Atonement. St. Augustine refers to such systems, *De Civ. Dei*, lib. ix. 15, 21; x. 1, &c.

[2] ἔγνωτε. This is implied in his wishing them " more " knowledge.

shows that for his own part he could have been glad to praise them throughout; but by the necessity of the case is forced into saying what he does. And so he doth in the first[1] Epistle to the Corinthians. For after having exceedingly praised them as loving him, even from the case of the fornicator, he comes down to accuse them. But in that to the Galatians not so, but the reverse. Yea, rather, if one should look close into it, even there the accusation follows upon praise. For seeing he had no good deeds of theirs then to speak of, and the charge was an exceeding grave one, and they were every one of them corrupted; and were able to bear it because they were strong, he begins with accusation, saying, " I marvel."[2] (Gal. i. 6.) So that this also is praise. But afterwards he praises them, not for what they were, but what they had been, saying, " If possible, ye would have plucked out your eyes, and given them to me." (Gal. v. 15).

" Bearing fruit," he saith : this hath reference to works. " Strengthened " : this to trials. " Unto all patience and longsuffering " : longsuffering towards one another, patience towards those without. For longsuffering is toward those whom we can requite, but patience toward those whom we cannot. For this reason the term patient is never applied to God, but longsuffering frequently; as this same blessed one saith otherwhere in his writings, " Or despisest thou the riches of His goodness, and forbearance, and longsuffering?" " Unto all pleasing." Not, one while, and afterwards not so. " In all spiritual wisdom," he saith, " and understanding." For otherwise it is not possible to know His will. Although indeed they thought they had His will ; but that wisdom was not spiritual. " To walk," saith he, " worthily of the Lord." For this is the way of the best life. For he that hath understood God's love to man, (and he doth understand it if he have seen the Son delivered up,) will have greater forwardness. And besides, we pray not for this alone that ye may know, but that ye may show forth your knowledge in works ; for he that knows without doing, is even in the way to punishment. " To walk," he saith, that is, always, not once, but continually. As to walk is necessary for us, so also is to live rightly. And when on this subject he constantly uses the term " walk," and with reason, showing that such is the life set before us. But not of this sort is that of the world. And great too is the praise. " To walk," he saith, " worthily of the Lord," and " in every good work," so as to be always advancing, and nowhere standing still, and, with a metaphor,

" bearing fruit and increasing in the knowledge of God," that ye might be in such measure " strengthened," according to the might of God, as is possible for man to be. " Through His power," great is the consolation. — He said not strength, but " power," which is greater : " through the power," he saith, " of His glory," because that everywhere His glory hath the power. He thus comforts him that is under reproach : and again, " To walk worthily of the Lord." He saith of the Son, that He hath the power everywhere both in heaven and in earth, because His glory reigneth everywhere. He saith not " strengthened " simply, but so, as they might be expected to be who are in the service of so strong a Master. " In the knowledge of God." And at the same time he touches in passing upon the methods of knowledge ; for this is to be in error, not to know God as one ought ; or he means, so as to increase in the knowledge of God. For if he that hath not known the Son, knoweth not the Father either ; justly is there need of increased[3] knowledge : for there is no use in life without this. " Unto all patience and longsuffering," he saith, " with joy, giving thanks " (ver. 12) unto God. Then being about to exhort them, he makes no mention of what by and by shall be laid up for them ; he did hint at this however in the beginning of the Epistle, saying, " Because of the hope which is laid up for you in the heavens " (ver. 5) : but in this place he mentions the things which were already theirs, for these are the causes of the other. And he doth the same in many places. For that which hath already come to pass gains belief, and more carries the hearer along with it. " With joy," he saith, " giving thanks " to God. The connection is this. We cease not praying for you, and giving thanks for the benefits already received.

Seest thou how he bears himself along into speaking of the Son? For if " we give thanks with much joy," it is a great thing that is spoken of. For it is possible to give thanks only from fear, it is possible to give thanks even when in sorrow. For instance ; Job gave thanks indeed, but in anguish ; and he said, " The Lord gave, the Lord hath taken away." (Job i. 21.) For, let not any say that what had come to pass pained him not, nor clothed him with dejection of soul ; nor let his great praise be taken away from that righteous one. But when it is thus, it is not for fear, nor because of His being Lord alone, but for the very nature of the things themselves, that we give thanks. " To Him who made us meet to be partakers of the inheritance of the saints in light." He hath said a great thing. What

---

[1] Perhaps it should be " second." [All documents read " first," and there is really no occasion for the conjectural alteration, for the statement applies to the first, as well as the second, Epistle. — J. A. B.]

[2] Vid. St. Chrys. in loc.

[3] [The apostle's word rendered " knowledge " is ἐπίγνωσις, which etymologically signifies additional or full knowledge, and often has distinctively that sense. — J. A. B.]

has been given, he saith, is of this nature ; He hath not only given, but also made us strong to receive. Now by saying, "Who made us meet," he showed that the thing was one of great weight. For example, were some low person to have become a king, he hath it in his power to give a governorship to whom he will ; and this is the extent of his power, to give the dignity : he cannot also make the person fit for the office, and oftentimes the honor makes one so preferred even ridiculous. If however he have both conferred on one the dignity, and also made him fit for the honor, and equal to the administration, then indeed the thing is an honor. This then is what he also saith here ; that He hath not only given us the honor, but hath also made us strong enough to receive it.

For the honor here is twofold, the giving, and the making fit for the gift. He said not, gave, simply ; but, "made us meet to be partakers of the inheritance of the saints in light," that is, who hath appointed us a place with the saints. But he did not say simply placed us, but hath given us to enjoy even the very same things, for "the portion"[1] is that which each one receives. For it is possible to be in the same city, and yet not enjoy the same things ; but to have the same "portion," and yet not enjoy the same, is impossible. It is possible to be in the same inheritance, and yet not to have the same portion ; for instance, all we (clergy) are in the inheritance,[2] but we have not all the same portion.[3] But here he doth not say this, but with the inheritance adds the portion also. But why doth he call it inheritance (or lot) ? To show that by his own achievements no one obtains the kingdom, but as a lot[4] is rather the result of good luck,[5] so in truth is it here also. For a life so good as to be counted worthy of the kingdom doth no one show forth, but the whole is of His free gift. Therefore He saith, "When ye have done all, say, We are unprofitable servants, for we have done that which was our duty to do." (Luke xvii. 10.) "To be partakers of the inheritance of the saints in light," — he means, both the future and the present light,[6] — that is, in knowledge. He seems to me to be speaking at once of both the present and the future. Then he shows of what things we have been counted worthy. For this is not the only mar-

vel, that we are counted worthy of the kingdom ; but it should also be added who we are that are so counted ; for it is not unimportant. And he doth this in the Epistle to the Romans, saying, "For scarcely for a righteous[7] man will one die, but peradventure for the good man some one would even dare to die." (Rom. v. 7.)

Ver. 13. "Who delivered us," he saith, "from the power of darkness."

The whole is of Him, the giving both of these things and those ; for nowhere is any achievement of ours. "From the power of darkness," he saith, that is, of error, the dominion of the devil. He said not "darkness," but "power" ; for it had great power over us, and held us fast. For it is grievous indeed even to be under the devil at all, but to be so "with power," this is far more grievous. "And translated us," he saith, "into the kingdom of the Son of His love." Not then so as to deliver man from darkness only, did He show His love toward him. A great thing indeed is it to have delivered from darkness even ; but to have brought into a kingdom too, is a far greater. See then how manifold the gift, that he hath delivered us who lay in the pit ; in the second place, that He hath not only delivered us, but also hath translated us into a kingdom. "Who delivered us." He said not, hath sent us forth, but "delivered" : showing our great misery, and their[8] capture of us. Then to show also the ease with which the power of God works, he saith, "And translated us," just as if one were to lead over a soldier from one position to another. And he said not, "hath led over" ; nor yet "hath transposed," for so the whole would be of him who transposed, nothing of him who went over ; but he said, "translated"[9] ; so that it is both of us and of Him. "Into the kingdom of the Son of His love." He said not simply, "the kingdom of heaven," but gave a grandeur to his discourse by saying, "The kingdom of the Son," for no praise can be greater than this, as he saith elsewhere also : "If we endure, we shall also reign with Him." (2 Tim. ii. 12.) He hath counted us worthy of the same things with the Son ; and not only so, but what gives it greater force, with His Beloved Son.[10] Those that were enemies, those that were in darkness, as it were on a sudden he had translated to where the Son is, to the same honor with Him. Nor was he content with only this, in order to show the greatness of the gift ; he was not content with saying, "kingdom," but he also added, "of the Son" ; nor yet with this, but he added also "beloved" ;

---

[1] [" To be partakers " is, literally, " for the portion."— J. A. B.]
[2] κλήρῳ.   [3] μερίδα.
[4] [κλῆρος signifies " lot," " inheritance," &c. From the notion that Christian ministers were the Lord's heritage (like the tribe of Levi) came the application to them of the terms *clerus, clerici*, whence clergy, clerk, &c.— J. A. B.]
[5] The whole passage shows that he uses this word *merely* to imply man's insufficiency, and not at all to introduce the notion of chance as opposed to Divine agency. He constantly uses the word at the end of his Homilies, as well as ἀξιωθῆναι, " to be thought worthy," to show at once the necessity of good works, and our unworthiness after all.
[6] [This clause Field restores from several MSS. and the Catena. The substantial repetition of it just after is characteristic. — J. A. B.]

[7] ἀδίκου, 2 [4] MSS. and Sav. marg. St. Chrys. does not, however, read so on the passage. Hom. ix. on Ep. to Romans.
[8] i.e. the devils', αἰχμαλωσίαν.
[9] μετέστησε. The word in Heb. xi. 3, is μετετέθη, which agrees with this criticism.
[10] [" The Son of His love " really means greatly more than " His Beloved Son." See Lightfoot on Col. — J. A. B.]

nor yet with this, but he added yet, the dignity of His nature. For what saith he? "Who is the Image of the invisible God." But he proceeded not to say this immediately, but meanwhile inserted the benefit which He bestowed upon us. For lest, when thou hearest that the whole is of the Father, thou shouldest suppose the Son excluded, he ascribes the whole to the Son, and the whole to the Father. For He indeed translated us, but the Son furnished the cause. For what saith he? "Who delivered us out of the power of darkness." But the same is, "In whom we have the full redemption, even the forgiveness of sins." For had we not been forgiven our sins, we should not have been "translated." So here again the words, "In whom." And he said not "redemption," but "full redemption," so that we shall not fall any more, nor become liable to death.

Ver. 15. "Who is the image of the invisible God, the First-born of all creation."

We light here upon a question of heresy. So it were well we should put it off to-day and proceed with it to-morrow, addressing it to your ears when they are fresh.

But if one ought to say anything more: the work of the Son is the greater. How? Because it were a thing impossible to give the kingdom to men whilst continuing in their sins; but thus it is an easier thing, so that He prepared the way for the gift. What sayest thou? He Himself loosed thee from thy sins: surely then He Himself also hath brought thee nigh; already he has laid by anticipation the foundation of his doctrine.

But we must put a close to this discourse, when first we have made one remark. And what is this? Seeing we have come to enjoy so great a benefit, we ought to be ever mindful of it, and continually to turn in our minds the free gift of God, and to reflect upon what we have been delivered from, what we have obtained; and so we shall be thankful; so we shall heighten our love toward Him. What sayest thou, O man? Thou art called to a kingdom, to the kingdom of the Son of God — and art thou full of yawning, and scratching, and dozing? If need were that thou shouldest leap into ten thousand deaths every day, oughtest thou not to endure all? For the sake of office thou doest all manner of things; when then thou art going to share the kingdom of the Only-Begotten, wilt thou not spring down upon ten thousand swords? wouldest thou not leap into fire? And this is not all that is strange, but that when about to depart even, thou bewailest, and wouldest gladly dwell amongst the things which are here, being a lover of the body. What fancy is this? Dost thou regard even death as a thing of terror? The cause of this is luxury,

ease: for he at least that should live an embittered life would wish even for wings, and to be loosed from hence. But now it is the same with us as with the spoiled nestlings, which would willingly remain for ever in the nest. But the longer they remain, the feebler they become. For the present life is a nest cemented together with sticks and mire. Yea, shouldest thou show me even the great mansions, yea the royal palace itself glittering with all its gold and precious stones; I shall think them no better than the nests of swallows, for when the winter is come they will all fall of themselves. By winter I mean That Day, not that it will be a winter to all. For God also calleth it both night and day; the first in regard of sinners, the latter of the just. So do I also now call it winter. If in the summer we have not been well brought up, so as to be able to fly when winter is come, our mothers will not take us, but will leave us to die of hunger, or to perish when the nest falls; for easily as it were a nest, or rather more easily, will God in that day remove all things, undoing and new molding all. But they which are unfledged, and not able to meet Him in the air, but have been so grossly brought up that they have no lightness of wing, will suffer those things which reason is such characters should suffer. Now the brood of swallows, when they are fallen, perish quickly; but we shall not perish, but be punished for ever. That season will be winter; or rather, more severe than winter. For, not winter torrents of water roll down, but rivers of fire; not darkness that riseth from clouds is there, but darkness that cannot be dispelled, and without a ray of light, so that they cannot see either the heaven, or the air, but are more straitened than those who have been buried in the earth.

Oftentimes do we say these things, but there are whom we cannot bring to believe. But it is nothing wonderful if we, men of small account, are thus treated, when we discourse of such things, since the same happened to the Prophets also; when they spoke not of such matters only, but also of war and captivity. (Jer. xxi. 11; xxvii. 12, &c.) And Zedekiah was rebuked by Jeremiah, and was not ashamed. Therefore the Prophets said, "Woe unto them that say, Let God hasten with speed His work, that we may see it, and let the counsel of the Holy One of Israel come, that we may know it." (Isa. v. 18, 19.) Let us not wonder at this. For neither did those believe who were in the days of the ark; they believed, however, when their belief was of no gain to them; neither did they of Sodom expect [their fate], howbeit they too believed, when they gained nothing by believing. And why do I speak of the future? Who would have expected these things which are now happening in divers places; these earthquakes, these overthrows of cities? And yet were these things easier to believe than those; those, I mean, which happened in the days of the ark.

Whence is this evident? Because that the men of those times had no other example to look at, neither had they heard the Scriptures, but with us, on the other hand, are countless instances that have happened both in our own, and in former years. But whence arose the unbelief of these persons? From a softened soul; they drank and ate, and therefore they believed not. For, what a man wishes, he thinks, and expects; and they that gainsay him are a jest.

But let it not be so with us; for hereafter it will not be a flood; nor the punishment till death only; but death will be the beginning of punishment for persons who believe not that there is a Judgment. And doth any ask, who has come from thence, and said so? If now thou speakest thus in jest, not even so is it well; for one ought not to jest in such matters; and we jest, not where jesting is in place, but with peril; but if what thou really feelest, and thou art of opinion that there is nothing hereafter, how is it that thou callest thyself a Christian? For I take not into account those who are without. Why receivest thou the Laver? Why dost thou set foot within the Church? Is it that we promise thee magistracies? All our hope is in the things to come. Why then comest thou, if thou believest not the Scriptures? If thou dost not believe Christ, I cannot call such an one a Christian; God forbid! but worse than even Greeks. In what respect? In this; that when thou thinkest Christ is God, thou believest Him not as God. For in that other impiety there is at least consistency; for he who thinks not that Christ is God, necessarily will also not believe Him; but this impiety has not even consistency; to confess Him to be God, and yet not to think Him worthy of belief in what He has said; these are the words of drunkenness, of luxury, of riot. "Let us eat and drink, for to-morrow we die." (1 Cor. xv. 32.) Not to-morrow; but now ye are dead, when ye thus speak. Shall we then be in nothing different from swine and asses? tell me. For if there be neither a judgment, nor a retribution, nor a tribunal, wherefore have we been honored with such a gift as reason, and have all things put under us? Why do we rule, and are they ruled? See how the devil is on every side urgent to persuade us to be ignorant of the Gift of God. He mixes together the slaves with their masters, like some man-stealer[1] and ungrateful servant; he strives to degrade

the free to the level of the criminal. And he seems indeed to be overthrowing the Judgment, but he is overthrowing the being of God.

For such is ever the devil's way; he puts forward everything in a wily, and not in a straightforward manner, to put us on our guard. If there is no Judgment, God is not just (I speak as a man): if God is not just, then there is no God at all: if there is no God, all things go on at haphazard, virtue is nought, vice nought. But he says nothing of this openly. Seest thou the drift of this satanical argument? how, instead of men, he wishes to make us brutes, or rather, wild beasts, or rather, demons? Let us then not be persuaded by him. For there is a Judgment, O wretched and miserable man! I know whence thou comest to use such words. Thou hast committed many sins, thou hast offended, thou hast no confidence, thou thinkest that the nature of things will even follow thy arguments. Meanwhile, saith he, I will not torment my soul with the expectation of hell, and, if there be a hell, I will persuade it that there is none; meanwhile I will live here in luxury! Why dost thou add sin to sin? If when thou hast sinned thou believest that there is a hell, thou wilt depart with the penalty of thy sins only to pay; but if thou add this further impiety, thou wilt also for thine impiety, and for this thy thought, suffer the uttermost punishment; and what was a cold and shortlived comfort to thee, will be a ground for thy being punished for ever. Thou hast sinned: be it so: why dost thou encourage others also to sin, by saying that there is no hell? Why didst thou mislead the simpler sort? Why unnerve the hands of the people? So far as thou art concerned, everything is turned upside down; neither will the good become better, but listless; nor the wicked desist from their wickedness. For, if we corrupt others, do we get allowance for our sins? Seest thou not the devil, how he attempted to bring down Adam? And has there then been allowance for him? Nay, surely it will be the occasion of a greater punishment, that he may be punished not for his own sins only, but also for those of others. Let us not then suppose that to bring down others into the same destruction with ourselves will make the Judgment-seat more lenient to us. Surely this will make it more severe. Why thrust we ourselves on destruction? The whole of this cometh of Satan.

O man, hast thou sinned? Thou hast for thy Master One that loveth man. Entreat, implore, weep, groan; and terrify others, and pray them that they fall not into the same. If in a house some servant, of those that had offended their master, says to his son, "My child, I have offended the master, do thou be careful to please him, that thou be not as I": tell me, will he

---

[1] ἀνδραποδιστὴς, one who steals freemen for slaves. [Literally, "enslaver" (1 Tim. i. 10).— J. A. B.]

not have some forgiveness? will he not bend and soften his master? But if, leaving so to speak, he shall say such words as these, that he[1] will not requite every one according to his deserts; that all things are jumbled together indiscriminately, both good and bad; that there is no thanks in this house; what thinkest thou will be the master's mind concerning him? will he not suffer a severer punishment for his own misdoings? Justly so; for in the former case his feeling will plead for him, though it be but weakly; but in this, nobody. If no other then, yet imitate at least that rich man in hell,[2] who said, "Father Abraham, send to my kinsmen, lest they come into this place," since he could not go himself, so that they might not fall into the same condemnation. Let us have done with such Satanical words.

What then, saith he, when the Greeks put questions to us; wouldest thou not that we should try to cure[3] them? But by casting the Christian into perplexity, under pretense of curing the Greek, thou aimest at establishing thy Satanical doctrine. For since, when communing with thy soul alone of these things, thou persuadest her not; thou desirest to bring forward others as witnesses. But if one must reason with a Greek, the discussion should not begin with this; but whether Christ be God, and the Son of God; whether those gods of theirs be demons. If these points be established, all the others follow; but, before making good the beginning, it is vain to dispute about the end; before learning the first elements, it is superfluous and unprofitable to come to the conclusion. The Greek disbelieves the Judgment, and he is in the same case with thyself, seeing that he too hath many who have treated these things in their philosophy; and albeit when they so spoke they held the soul as separated from the body, still they set up a seat of judgment. And the thing is so very clear, that no one scarcely is ignorant of it, but both poets and all are agreed among themselves that there is both a Tribunal and a Judgment. So that the Greek also disbelieves[4] his own authorities; and the Jew doth not doubt about these things, nor in a word doth any man.

Why then deceive we ourselves? See, thou sayest these things to me. What wilt thou say to God, "that fashioned our hearts one by one"[5] (Ps. xxxiii. 15); that knoweth everything that is in the mind; "that is living and active,

and sharper than any two-edged sword"? (Heb. iv. 12.) For tell me with truth; Dost thou not condemn thyself? And how should wisdom so great, as that one who sins should condemn himself, come by chance, for this is a work of mighty wisdom. Thou condemnest thyself. And will he who giveth thee such thoughts leave everything to go on at hazard? The following rule then will hold universally and strictly. Not one of those who live in virtue wholly disbelieves the doctrine of the Judgment, even though he be Greek or heretic. None, save a few, of those who live in great wickedness, receives the doctrine of the Resurrection. And this is what the Psalmist says, "Thy judgments are taken away from before his face." (Ps. x. 5.) Wherefore? Because "his ways are always profane"; for he saith, "Let us eat and drink, for to-morrow we die."

. Seest thou that thus to speak is the mark of the grovelling? Of eating and drinking come these sayings which are subversive of the Resurrection. For the soul endures not, I say, it endures not the tribunal which the conscience supplieth, and so it is with it, as with a murderer, who firsts suggests to himself that he shall not be detected, and so goes on to slay; for had his conscience been his judge, he would not hastily have come to that daring wickedness. And still he knows, and pretends not to know, lest he should be tortured by conscience and fear, for, certainly, in that case, he would have been less resolute for the daring deed. So too, assuredly, they who sin, and day by day wallow in the same wickedness, are unwilling to know it, although their consciences pluck at them.

But let us give no heed to such persons, for there will be, there will assuredly be, a Judgment and a Resurrection, and God will not leave so great works without direction. Wherefore, I beseech you, let us leave off wickedness, and lay fast hold on virtue, that we may receive the true doctrine in Christ Jesus our Lord. And yet, which is easier to receive? the doctrine of the Resurrection, or that of Fate? The latter is full of injustice, of absurdity, of cruelty, of inhumanity; the other of righteousness, awarding according to desert; and still men do not receive it. But the fault is, indolence, for no one that hath understanding receives the other. For amongst the Greeks even, they who did receive that doctrine, were those who in their definition of pleasure affirmed it to be the "end," but they who loved virtue, would not receive it, but they cast it out as absurd. But if among the Greeks this were so, much more will it hold good with the doctrine of the Resurrection. And observe, I pray you, how the devil hath established two contrary things: for in order that we may neglect virtue; and pay honor to demons,

---

[1] The master.   [2] γεέννη.
[3] θεραπεύειν. As we say, familiarly, "doctor them." The term was commonly used. Theodoret has a treatise called, "The Remedy of Greekish affections." Here it is "humor them" by palatable doctrine.
[4] [Various documents have "does not disbelieve," through failing to observe that it means the Greek above mentioned, and that the expression changes with the next clause as to the Jew.—J. A. B.]
[5] καταμόνας, Sept. E. V. "alike."

he brought in this Necessity, and by means of each he procured the belief of both. What reason then will he be able to give, who obstinately disbelieves a thing so admirable, and is persuaded by those who talk so idly? Do not then support thyself with the consolation, that thou wilt meet with forgiveness; but let us, collecting all our strength, stir ourselves up to virtue, and let us live truly to God, in Christ Jesus our Lord, &c.

HOMILY III.

COLOSSIANS i. 15–18.

" Who is the Image of the invisible God, the Firstborn of all creation: for in Him were all things created, in the heavens, and upon the earth, things visible and things invisible, whether thrones or dominions or principalities or powers: all things have been created through Him, and unto Him; and He is before all things, and in Him all things consist. And He is the head of the body, the Church."

TO-DAY it is necessary for me to pay the debt, which yesterday[1] I deferred, in order that I might address it to your minds when in full force. Paul, discoursing as we showed of the dignity of the Son, says these words: " Who is the Image of the invisible God." Whose image then wilt thou have Him be? God's? Then he is exactly like the one to whom you assign Him. For if as a man's image, say so, and I will have done with you as a madman. But if as God and God's Son, God's image, he shows the exact likeness. Wherefore hath no Angel anywhere been called either " image " or " son," but man both? Wherefore? Because in the former case indeed the exaltedness of their nature might presently have thrust the many into this impiety[2]; but in the other case the mean and low nature is a pledge of security against this, and will not allow any, even should they desire it, to suspect anything of the kind, nor to bring down the Word so low. For this cause, where the meanness is great, the Scripture boldly asserts the honor, but where the nature is higher, it forbears. " The Image of the Invisible " is itself also invisible, and invisible in like manner, for otherwise it would not be an image. For an image, so far as it is an image, even amongst us, ought to be exactly similar, as, for example, in respect of the features and the likeness.[3] But here indeed amongst us, this is by no means

possible; for human art fails in many respects, or rather fails in all, if you examine with accuracy. But where God is, there is no error, no failure.

But if a creature: how is He the Image of the Creator? For neither is a horse the image of a man. If " the Image " mean not exact likeness to the Invisible, what hinders the Angels also from being His Image? for they too are invisible; but not to one another: but the soul is invisible: but because it is invisible, it is simply on that account an image, and not in such sort as he and angels are images.[4]

" The Firstborn of all creation." " What then," saith one, " Lo, He is a creature." Whence? tell me. " Because he said ' firstborn.' " However, he said not " first created," but " firstborn." Then it is reasonable that he should be called many things. For he must also be called a brother " in all things." (Heb. ii. 17.) And we must take from Him His being Creator; and insist that neither in dignity nor in any other thing is He superior to us? And who that hath understanding would say this? For the word " firstborn " is not expressive of dignity and honor, nor of anything else, but of time only. What does " the firstborn " signify? That he is created, is the answer. Well. If then this be so, it has also kindred expressions. But otherwise the firstborn is of the same essence with those of whom he is firstborn. Therefore he will be the firstborn son of all things — for it said " of every creature "; therefore of stones also, and of me, is God the Word firstborn. But again, of what, tell me, are the words " firstborn from the dead " (Col. i. 18; Rom. viii. 29) declaratory? Not that He first rose; for he said not simply, " of the dead," but " firstborn from the dead," nor yet, " that He died first," but that He rose the firstborn from the dead. So that they declare nothing else

---

[1] See Hom. ii. § 3 fin.   [2] Viz. Arianism.

[3] χαρακτῆρων καὶ ὁμοιώσεως. The argument is, that invisibleness being mentioned, the image must have it, as if one should say, " the picture of a venerable man," one would understand a venerable expression in the features. Compare St. Athanasius against Arianism, Disc. 1, c. vi. § 20, Tr. and note d. [The argument is fine spun, and not convincing. The image must be of the same essence, or substance in this case; but an image cannot be invisible, otherwise it were not an image. Compare Meyer, and especially Lightfoot. — J. A. B.]

[4] [The words, " and angels are images " are omitted by the common text, with several MSS., but manifestly to escape an apparent difficulty, because it has been noticed above that angels are never called images. — J. A. B.]

than this, that He is the Firstfruits of the Resurrection. Surely then neither in the placé before us.[1] Next he proceeds to the doctrine itself. For that they may not think Him to be of more recent existence, because that in former times the approach was through Angels, but now through Him; he shows first, that they had no power (for else it had not been "out of darkness" (ver. 13) that he brought), next, that He is also before them. And he uses as a proof of His being before them, this; that they were created by him. "For in Him," he saith, "were all things created." What say here the followers of Paul of Samosata?[2] "The things in the heavens." What was in question, he has placed first;[3] "and the things upon the earth." Then he says, "the visible and the invisible things"; invisible, such as soul, and all that has come to exist in heaven; visible, such as men, sun, sky. "Whether thrones." And what is granted, he lets alone, but what is doubted he asserts. "Whether thrones, or dominions, or principalities, or powers." The words "whether," "or," comprehend the whole of things; but by means of the greater things show it of the less also. But the Spirit is not amongst the "powers." "All things," he saith, "have been created through Him, and unto Him." Lo, "in Him," is[4] "through Him," for having said "in Him," he added, "through Him." But what "unto Him"? It is this; the subsistence of all things depends on Him. Not only did He Himself bring them out of nothing into being, but Himself sustains them now, so that were they dissevered from His Providence, they were at once undone and destroyed. But He said not, "He continues them," which had been a grosser way of speaking, but what is more subtle, that "on" Him they depend. To have only a bearing on Him is enough to continue anything and bind it fast. So also the word "firstborn," in the sense of a foundation. But this doth not show the creatures to be consubstantial with Him; but that all things are through Him, and in Him are upheld. Since Paul also when he says elsewhere, "I have laid a foundation" (1 Cor. iii. 10), is speaking not concerning substance, but operation. For, that thou mayest not think Him to be a minister, he says that He continues them,

which is not less than making them. Certainly, with us it is greater even: for to the former, art conducts us; but to the latter, not so, it does not even stay a thing in decay.

"And He is before all things," he saith. This is befitting God. Where is Paul of Samosata? "And in Him all things consist," that is, they are created into[5] Him. He repeats these expressions in close sequence; with their close succession, as it were with rapid strokes, tearing up the deadly doctrine by the roots. For, if even when such great things had been declared, still after so long a time Paul of Samosata sprung up, how much more [would such have been the case], had not these things been said before? "And in Him," he saith, "all things consist." How "consist" in one who was not? So that the things also done through Angels are of Him.

"And He is the head of the body, the Church."

Then having spoken of His dignity, he afterwards speaks of His love to man also. "He is," saith he, "the Head of the body, the Church." And he said not "of the fullness,"[6] (although this too is signified,) out of a wish to show His great friendliness to us, in that He who is thus above, and above all, connected Himself with those below. For everywhere He is first; above first; in the Church first, for He is the Head; in the Resurrection first. That is,

Ver. 18. "That He might have the preëminence." So that in generation also He is first. And this is what Paul is chiefly endeavoring to show. For if this be made good, that He was before all the Angels; then there is brought in along with it this also as a consequence, that He did their works by commanding them. And what is indeed wonderful, he makes a point to show that He is first in the later generation. Although elsewhere he calls Adam first (1 Cor. xv. 45), as in truth he is; but here he takes the Church for the whole race of mankind. For He is first of the Church; and first of men after the flesh, like as of the Creation.[7] And therefore he here uses the word "firstborn."

What is in this place the meaning of "the Firstborn"? Who was created first, or rose before all; as in the former place it means, Who was before all things. And here indeed he uses the word "firstfruits," saying, "Who is the[8]

---

[1] i.e. is anything else meant by the word πρωτότοκος, than that He is the Firstfruits of the Creation. This may be his meaning, or "that he, the Only-begotten, is the Beginning of the Creation." See note on St. Athanasius against Arianism, Disc. 1, Oxf. Tr.

[2] P. of Samosata held the Divine Word, or Reason, to be a mere Attribute, and not a Person. The Person of our Lord would thus be simply Human, only with a Divine influence. See St. Ath. Def. of Nic. Def. c. v. § 11, Tr. This text of St. Paul is quoted against P. of Samosata, Conc. Ant. i. Labbe, t. 1, p. 846, by the orthodox Bishops. See also Epiph. Hær. 45. The heretics might allow what is said here of the Word as an Attribute; the refutation follows presently.

[3] One MS. has, "first the things in heaven," &c., which agrees with the sense.

[4] i.e. "In Him," in the beginning of the verse, is said in such a sense as to agree with "through Him."

[5] [Chrys. here seems to insist on the local sense of εἰς, "into," which above, and in Rev. Ver., is translated "unto." All things in Him consist, being created into Him. But the fancy is of doubtful value.—J. A. B.]

[6] τοῦ πληρώματος. Here used of the universe, somewhat as 1 Cor. x. 26, only in a more extended sense.

[7] Cat. "and first of men even as he that was first of Creation after the flesh," then one Par. adds, "For this cause both here and there the word 'Firstborn' is used. But what is 'Firstborn of all creation'? It is for 'First Created,' as 'Firstborn from the dead' is for 'Who rose again before all.' And as there he puts 'Who is before all,' so here also he has put 'Firstfruits.'" [A Paris MS. has the same reading, except that for "First Created" it has "First Creator."—J. A. B.]

[8] Rec. text ἀρχή, St. Chrys. has ἀπαρχή [and so six cursives.

Firstfruits, the Firstborn from the dead, that in all things He might have the preëminence," showing that the rest also are such as He; but in the former place it is not the "Firstfruits" of creation.[1] And it is there, "The Image of the invisible God," and then, "Firstborn."

Ver. 19, 20. "For it was the good pleasure of the Father, that in Him should all the fullness dwell. And having made peace through the Blood of His Cross, through Him to reconcile all things unto Himself, whether things upon the earth, or things in the heavens."

Whatsoever things are of the Father, these he saith are of the Son also, and that with more of intensity, because that He both became "dead"[2] for, and united Himself to us. He said, "Firstfruits," as of fruits. He said not "Resurrection," but "Firstfruits," showing that He hath sanctified us all, and offered us, as it were, a sacrifice. The term "fullness" some use of the Godhead, like as John said, "Of His fullness have all we received." That is, whatever was the Son, the whole Son dwelt there, not a sort of energy, but a Substance.

He hath no cause to assign but the will of God: for this is the import of, "it was the good pleasure . . . in Him. And . . . through Him to reconcile all things unto Himself." Lest thou shouldest think that He undertook the office of a minister only, he saith, "unto Himself."[3] (2 Cor. v. 18.) And yet he elsewhere says, that He reconciled us to God, as in the Epistle he wrote to the Corinthians. And he well said, "Through Him to make an end of reconciling";[4] for they were already reconciled; but completely, he says, and in such sort, as no more to be at enmity with Him. How? For not only the reconciliation was set forth, but also the manner of the reconciliation. "Having made peace through the Blood of His Cross." The word "reconcile," shows the enmity; the words "having made peace," the war. "Through the Blood of His Cross, through Himself, whether things upon the earth, or things in the heavens." A great thing indeed it is to reconcile; but that this should be through Himself too, is a greater thing; and a greater still,—how through Himself? Through His Blood. Through His Blood; and he said not simply His Blood, but what is yet greater, through the Cross. So that the marvels are five: He reconciled us; to God; through Himself; through Death;

through the Cross. Admirable again! How he has mixed them up! For lest thou shouldest think that it is one thing merely, or that the Cross is anything of itself,[5] he saith "through Himself." How well he knows that this was a great thing. Because not by speaking words, but by giving Himself up for the reconciliation, He so wrought everything.

But what is "things in the heavens"? For with reason indeed is it said, "the things upon the earth," for those were filled with enmity, and manifoldly divided, and each one of us was utterly at variance with himself, and with the many; but how made He peace amongst "the things in the heavens"? Was war and battle there also? How then do we pray, saying, "Thy will be done, as in heaven, so on earth"? (Matt. vi. 10.) What is it then? The earth was divided from heaven, the Angels were become enemies to men, through seeing the Lord insulted. "To sum up," he saith, "all things in Christ, the things in the heavens, and the things upon the earth." (Eph. i. 10.) How? The things in heaven indeed in this way: He translated Man thither, He brought up to them the enemy, the hated one. Not only made He the things on earth[6] to be at peace, but He brought up to them him that was their enemy and foe. Here was peace profound. ·Angels again appeared on the earth thereafter, because that Man too had appeared in heaven. And it seems to me that Paul was caught up on this account (2 Cor. xii. 2), and to show that the Son also had been received up thither. For in the earth indeed, the peace was twofold; with the things of heaven, and with themselves; but in heaven it was simple. For if the Angels rejoice over one sinner that repenteth, much more will they over so many.

All this God's power hath wrought. Why then place ye confidence in Angels?[7] saith he. For so far are they from bringing you near, that they were ever your enemies, except God Himself had reconciled you with them. Why then run ye to them? Wouldest thou know the hatred which the Angels had against us, how great it was; and how averse to us they always were? They were sent to take vengeance in the cases of the Israelites, of David, of the Sodomites, of the Valley of weeping.[8] (Ex. xxiii. 20.) Not so however now, but, on the contrary, they sang upon the earth[9] (2 Sam. xxiv. 16) with exceed-

---

But this reading is clearly wrong, and vitiates the following statements of Chrys. For the meaning of "beginning" here, see Lightfoot. — J. A. B.]

[1] The same MSS. add, "but only *the Firstborn*, and not even this in the first place, but after saying, 'Who is the Image,'" &c.

[2] νεκρὸς γέγονε, alluding to the expression, πρωτότοκος ἐκ νεκρῶν.

[3] ["The reconciliation is always represented as made to the Father. The reconciler is sometimes the Father Himself, sometimes the Son." — Lightfoot. — J. A. B.]

[4] ἀποκαταλλάξαι as ἀπολύτρωσις, above? [The compound verb may mean to reconcile completely or finally. — J. A. B.]

[5] Or "by itself" (ἑαυτὸ), i.e. separate from the Divine Person, as it would be if there had been a several Human Personality. (Cat. and Bodl. ἑαυτὸν.)

[6] Bodl. Extr. [Catena], "He made not him staying on earth," &c.

[7] [Chrys. shows no suspicion of that combination of the Jewish (Essene) doctrine of angels with the Gnostic doctrine of æons, which we now know to have prevailed at Colossæ (see Lightfoot on Col., Int. II.). — J. A. B.]

[8] Judg. ii. 5; see Ps. lxxxiv. 6 (2 Sam. v. seems hardly applicable).

[9] Downes conjectures, "Peace on earth." Luke ii. 13.

ing joy. And He led these down to men [1] (Gen. xix. 13), and led men up to them.

And observe, I pray you, the marvel in this: He brought these first down hither, and then he took up man to them; earth became heaven, because that heaven was about to receive the things of earth. Therefore when we give thanks, we say, "Glory to God in the highest, and on earth peace, good will to men." Behold, he saith, even men appeared well-pleasing to Him thereafter. What is "good will"? (Eph. ii. 14; Deut. xxxii. 8, Sept.) Reconciliation. No longer is the heaven a wall of partition. At first the Angels were according to the number of the nations; but now, not according to the number of the nations, but that of the believers. Whence is this evident? Hear Christ saying, "See that ye despise not one of these little ones, for their Angels do always behold the face of My Father which is in heaven." (Matt. xviii. 10.) For each believer hath an Angel; since even from the beginning, every one of those that were approved had his Angel, as Jacob says, "The Angel that feedeth me, and delivereth me from my youth." [2] (Gen. xlviii. 15, 16, nearly.) If then we have Angels, let us be sober, as though we were in the presence of tutors; for there is a demon present also. [3] Therefore we pray, asking [4] for the Angel of peace, and everywhere we ask for peace [5] (for there is nothing equal to this); peace, in the Churches, in the prayers, in the supplications, in the salutations; and once, and twice, and thrice, and many times, does he that is over the Church give it, " Peace be unto you." Wherefore? Because this is the Mother of all good things; this is the foundation of joy. Therefore Christ also commanded the Apostles on entering into the houses straightway to say this, as being a sort of symbol of the good things; for He saith, "When ye come into the houses, say, Peace be unto you·;" [6] for where this is wanting, everything is useless. And to His disciples Christ said, "Peace I leave with you, My peace I give unto you." (John xiv. 27.) This prepareth the way for love. And he that is over the Church, says not, "Peace be unto you," simply, but "Peace be unto all." For what if

with this man we have peace, but with another, war and fighting? what is the gain? For neither in the body, should some of its elements be at rest and others in a state of variance, is it possible that health should ever be upheld; but only when the whole of them are in good order, and harmony, and peace, and except the whole are at rest, and continue within their proper limits, all will be overturned. And, further, in our minds, except all our thoughts are at rest, peace will not exist. So great a good is peace, as that the makers and producers of it are called the sons of God (Matt. v. 9, 45), with reason; because the Son of God for this cause came upon the earth, to set at peace the things in the earth, and those in the heavens. But if the peacemakers are the sons of God, the makers of disturbance are sons of the devil.

What sayest thou? Dost thou excite contentions and fightings? And doth any ask who is so unhappy? Many there are who rejoice at evil, and who do rather rend in pieces the Body of Christ, than did the soldiers pierce it with the spear, or the Jews who struck it through with the nails. A less evil was that than this; those Members, so cut through, again united, but these when torn off, if they be not united here, will never be united, but remain apart from the Fullness. When thou art minded to war against thy brother, bethink thee that thou warrest against the members of Christ, and cease from thy madness. For what if he be an outcast? What if he be vile? What if he be open to contempt? So saith He, "It is not the will of My Father that one of these little ones should perish." (Matt. xviii. 14.) And again, "Their Angels do always behold the face of My Father which is in heaven." (Ib. ver. 10.) God for his sake and thine even became a servant, and was slain; and dost thou consider him to be nothing? Surely in this respect also thou fightest against God, in that thou deliverest a judgment contrary to His. When he that is over the Church cometh in, he straightway says, "Peace unto all"; when he preacheth, "Peace unto all"; when he blesseth, "Peace unto all"; when he biddeth to salute, "Peace unto all"; when the Sacrifice is finished, "Peace unto all": and again, in the middle, "Grace to you and peace." How then is it not monstrous, if, while hearing so many times that we are to have peace, we are in a state of feud with each other; and receiving peace, and giving it back, are at war with him [7] that giveth it to us? Thou sayest, "And to thy spirit." And dost thou traduce him abroad? Woe is me! that the majestic usages [8] of the Church are become

---

[1] Gr. αὐτοὺς, one suspects ἄνους (ἀνθρώπους), which has been conjectured.

[2] "Feedeth" is said of God in the text. On the passage, St. Chrys. does not notice the mention of the Angel. He quotes it, however, in his first Homily de laudibus B. Pauli. He also infers the doctrine from Acts xii. 15; Hom. xxvi. St. Jerome, on Isa. lxvi. 20, quotes all these passages. Bp. Bull, Ser. xii. adds, Eccl. v. 6.

[3] See St. Hermas, Past. 1, ii. pr. 6, § 1, and Cotelerius, note 14, t. 1, p. 93; who cites Origen, Hom. xii. in Luc. S. Greg. Nyss. de Vita Mosis, p. 194; Petavius, Theol. Dog. de Ang. l. ii. c. 8, cites St. Basil. contr. Eunom. p. 70, and on Ps. xxxiii. p. 220, &c.

[4] [There was among the forms of prayer in Chrys.'s day this, "Ask for the angel of peace." See Field's Annotations. — J. A. B.]

[5] In Hom. xxxii. on St. Matt. he mentions a prayer for Peace. See also Const. Ap. 1. viii. c. 37 fin.

[6] St. Matt. x. 12, St. Luke x. 5, but neither accurately. [That is, neither Gospel is here accurately quoted. Chrys. often makes slight mistakes in quoting, as we do. — J. A. B.]

[7] i.e. the Bishop. [This is the person several times above called "he that is over," ὁ προεστὼς, the same word that is employed by Justin Martyr, I. Apol. c. 65, for the person presiding in an assembly for worship. — J. A. B.]   [8] τὰ σεμνὰ.

forms of things merely, not a truth. Woe is me! that the watchwords of this army proceed no farther than to be only words. Whence also ye are ignorant wherefore is said, "Peace unto all." But hear what follows, what Christ saith; "And into whatsoever city or village ye shall enter . . . as ye enter into the house, salute it; and if the house be worthy, let your peace come upon it, but if it be not worthy, let your peace return to you." (Matt. x. 11, 13.) We are therefore ignorant; because we look upon this merely as a figure of words; and we assent not to them in our minds. For do I[1] give the Peace? It is Christ who deigneth to speak by us. Even if at all other times we are void of grace, yet are we not now, for your sakes. For if the Grace of God wrought in an ass and a diviner, for the sake of an economy, and the advantage of the Israelites (Num. 22), it is quite clear that it will not refuse to operate even in us, but for your[2] sakes will endure even this.

Let none say then that I am mean, and low, and worthy of no consideration, and in such a frame of mind attend to me.[3] For such I am; but God's way always is, to be present even with such for the sake of the many. And, that ye may know this, with Cain He vouchsafed to talk for Abel's sake (Gen. iv.), with the devil for Job's (Job i.), with Pharaoh for Joseph's (Gen. xli.), with Nebuchadnezzar for Daniel's (Dan. ii., iv.), with Belshazzar, for the same (Dan. v.). And Magi moreover obtained a revelation (Matt. ii.); and Caiaphas prophesied, though a slayer of Christ, and an unworthy man, because of the worthiness of the priesthood. (John xi. 49.) And it is said to have been for this reason that Aaron was not smitten with leprosy. For why, tell me, when both had spoken against Moses did she[4] alone suffer the punishment? (Num. xii.) Marvel not: for if in worldly dignities, even though ten thousand charges be laid against a man, yet is he not brought to trial before he has laid down his office, in order that it may not be dishonored along with him; much more in the case of spiritual office, be he whosoever he may, the grace of God works in him, for otherwise everything is lost: but when he hath laid it down, either after he is departed or even here, then indeed, then he will suffer a sorer punishment.

Do not, I pray you, think that these things are spoken from us; it is the Grace of God which worketh in the unworthy, not for our sakes, but for yours. Hear ye then what Christ saith. "If the house be worthy, let your peace come upon it." (Matt. x. 13–15.) And how becometh it worthy? If "they receive you" (Luke x. 8), He saith. "But if they receive you not, nor hear your words, . . . verily I say unto you, it shall be more tolerable for the land of Sodom and Gomorrah in the day of judgment, than for that city." What boots it then, that ye receive us, and hear not the things we say? What gain is it that ye wait upon[5] us, and give no heed to the things which are spoken to you? This will be honor to us, this the admirable service, which is profitable both to you and to us, if ye hear us. Hear also Paul saying, "I wist not, brethren, that he was High Priest." (Acts xxiii. 5.) Hear also Christ saying, "All whatsoever they bid you observe" (Matt. xxiii. 3), that "observe and do." Thou despisest not me, but the Priesthood; when thou seest me stripped of this, then despise me; then no more will I endure to impose commands. But so long as we sit upon this throne,[6] so long as we have the first place, we have both the dignity and the power, even though we are unworthy. If the throne of Moses was of such reverence, that for its sake they were to be heard, much more the throne of Christ. It, we have received by succession; from it we speak; since the time that Christ hath vested in us the ministry of reconciliation.

Ambassadors, whatever be their sort, because of the dignity of an embassy, enjoy much honor. For observe; they go alone into the heart of the land of barbarians, through the midst of so many enemies; and because the law of embassy is of mighty power, all honor them; all look towards them with respect, all send them forth with safety. And we now have received a word of embassy, and we are come from God, for this is the dignity of the Episcopate. We are come to you on an embassy, requesting you to put an end to the war, and we say on what terms; not promising to give cities, nor so and so many measures of corn, nor slaves, nor gold; but the kingdom of heaven, eternal life, society with Christ, the other good things, which neither are we able to tell you, so long as we are in this flesh, and the present life. Ambassadors then we are, and we wish to enjoy honor, not for our own sakes, far be it, for we know its worthlessness, but for yours; that ye may hear with earnestness the things we say; that ye may be profited, that not with listlessness or indifference ye may attend to what is spoken. See ye not ambassadors, how all pay court to them? We are God's ambassadors to men; but, if this of-

---

[1] This implies that he was Bishop, and consequently that these Homilies were delivered at Constantinople. [Below he distinctly declares himself to be the Bishop. — J. A. B.]

[2] So Sav. Ben. "our."

[3] Or "even so, let him attend to me."

[4] Miriam.

[5] θεραπεύετε.

[6] [This would seem clearly to indicate that these homilies were delivered at Constantinople. The passage below, on ch. iii. 2–4, does not necessarily show the contrary. — J. A. B.]

fend you,[1] not we, but the Episcopate itself, not this man or that, but the Bishop. Let no one hear me, but the dignity. Let us then do everything according to the will of God, that we may live to the glory of God, and be counted worthy of the good things promised to those that love Him, through the grace and lovingkindness, &c. &c.

HOMILY IV.

Colossians i. 21, 22.

"And you, being in time past, enemies and alienated[2] in your mind, in your evil works, yet now hath He reconciled in the body of His flesh through death, to present you holy and without blemish and unreprovable before Him."

Here he goes to show that He reconciled those even who were unworthy of reconciliation. For by the saying that they were under the power of darkness, he shows the calamity in which they were. (v. 13.) But lest, on hearing of "the power of darkness," thou shouldest consider it Necessity, he adds, "And you that were alienated," so that though it appear to be the same thing that he says, yet it is not so; for it is not the same thing to deliver out of the evils him that through necessity came to suffer, and him that of his own will endures. For the former indeed is worthy to be pitied, but the latter hated. But nevertheless, he saith, you that are not against your wills, nor from compulsion, but with your wills, and wishes, sprang away from Him, and are unworthy of it, He hath reconciled.[3] And seeing he had made mention of the "things in the heavens," he shows, that all the enmity had its origin from hence, not thence. For they indeed were long ago desirous, and God also, but ye were not willing.

And throughout he is showing that the Angels had no power in the successive times,[4] forasmuch as men continued enemies; they could neither persuade them, nor, if persuaded, could they deliver them from the devil. For neither would persuading them be any gain, except he that held them were bound; nor would binding him have been of any service, except they whom he detained were willing to return. But both of these were needed, and they could do neither of them, but Christ did both. So that even more marvelous than loosing death, is the persuading them. For the former was wholly of Himself, and the power lay wholly in Himself, but of the latter, not in Himself alone, but in us also; but we accomplish those things more easily of which the power lies in ourselves. Therefore, as being the greater, he puts it last. And he said not simply "were at enmity,"[5] but "were alienated," which denotes great enmity, nor yet "alienated"[6] [only], but without any expectation even of returning. "And enemies in your mind," he says; then the alienation had not proceeded so far as purpose only—but what? "in your wicked works" also. Ye were both enemies, he saith, and ye did the works of enemies.

"Yet now hath He reconciled in the body of His flesh through death to present you holy and without blemish and unreprovable before Him." Again he lays down also the manner of the reconciliation, that it was "in the Body," not by being merely beaten, nor scourged, nor sold, but even by dying a death the most shameful. Again he makes mention of the Cross, and again lays down another benefit. For He did not only "deliver," but, as he says above, "Who made us meet" (ver. 12), to the same he alludes here also. "Through" His "death," he says, "to present you holy and without blemish and unreprovable before Him." For truly, He hath not only delivered from sins, but hath also placed amongst the approved. For, not that He might deliver us from evils only, did He suffer so great things, but that also we might obtain the first rewards; as if one should not only free a condemned criminal from his punishment, but also advance him to honor. And he hath ranked you with those who have not sinned, yea rather not with those who have done no sin only, but even with those who have wrought the greatest righteousness; and, what is truly a great thing, hath given the holiness which is before Him, and the being unreprovable. Now an advance upon unblamable is unreprovable, when we have done nothing either to be condemned for, or charged with. But, since he

---

[1] πρόσαντες. "Up hill," "against the grain."
[2] The order of words, "enemies" and "alienated," is here inverted as compared with the Rec. text, and the Commentary that follows here requires the common order.
[3] Edd. have ἀπήλλαξε, but the Translator conjectures ἀποκατήλλαξε, which is confirmed by a MS. in Brit. M.
[4] τοῖς κάτω χρόνοις, usually "latter times"; here it seems to be "down the stream of time." One suspects ἄνω, but it may be reckoned from the Fall.

[5] ἐχθραίνοντας, which is less than ἐχθρούς.
[6] Here ἠλλοτριωμένους, not ἀπηλλοτριωμένους, as above.

ascribed the whole to Him, because through His death He achieved these things; "what then, says one, is it to us? we need nothing." Therefore he added,

Ver. 23. "If so be that ye continue in the faith grounded and steadfast, and not moved away from the hope of the Gospel."

Here he strikes a blow at their listlessness. And he said not simply "continue," for it is possible to continue wavering, and vacillating; it is possible to stand, and continue, though turned this way and that. "If so be that ye continue," he saith, "grounded and steadfast, and not moved away." Wonderful! What a forcible metaphor he uses; he says not only not tossed to and fro, but not even moved. And observe, he lays down so far nothing burdensome, nor toilsome, but faith and hope; that is, if ye continue believing, that the hope of the things to come is true. For this indeed is possible; but, as regards virtuous living, it is not possible to avoid being shaken about, though it be but a little; so (what he enjoins) is not grievous.

"From the hope," he saith, "of the Gospel, which ye heard, which was preached in all creation under heaven." But what is the hope of the Gospel, except Christ? For He Himself is our peace, that hath wrought all these things: so that he who ascribes them to others is "moved away": for he has lost all, unless he believe in Christ. "Which ye heard," he saith. And again he brings themselves as witnesses, then the whole world. He saith not, "which is being preached," but hath already been believed and preached. As he did also at the outset (ver. 6), being desirous by the witness of the many to establish these also. "Whereof I Paul was made a minister." This also contributes to make it credible; "I," saith he, "Paul a minister." For great was his authority, as being now everywhere celebrated, and the teacher of the world.

Ver. 24. "Now I rejoice in my sufferings for your sake, and fill up on my part that which is lacking of the afflictions of Christ in my flesh for His Body's sake, which is the Church."

And what is the connection of this? It seems indeed not to be connected, but it is even closely so. And "minister," he says, that is, bringing in nothing from myself, but announcing what is from another. I so believe, that I suffer even for His sake, and not suffer only, but even rejoice in suffering, looking unto the hope which is to come, and I suffer not for myself, but for you. "And fill up," he saith, "that which is lacking of the afflictions of Christ in my flesh." It seems indeed to be a great thing he has said; but it is not of arrogancy, far be it, but even of much tender love towards Christ; for he will not have the sufferings to be his own, but His,

through desire of conciliating these persons to Him. And what things I suffer, I suffer, he saith, on His account: not to me, therefore, express your gratitude, but to him, for it is He Himself who suffers. Just as if one, when sent to a person, should make request to another, saying, I beseech thee, go for me to this person, then the other should say, "it is on his account I am doing it." So that He is not ashamed to call these sufferings also his own.[1] For He did not only die for us, but even after His death He is ready to be afflicted for your sakes. He is eagerly and vehemently set upon showing that He is even now exposed to peril in His own Body for the Church's sake, and he aims at this point, namely, ye are not brought unto God by us, but by Him, even though we do these things, for we have not undertaken a work of our own, but His. And it is the same as if there were a band which had its allotted leader to protect it, and it should stand in battle, and then when he was gone, his lieutenant should succeed to his wounds until the battle were brought to a close.

Next, that for His sake also he doeth these things, hearken: "For His Body's sake," he saith, assuredly meaning to say this: "I pleasure not you, but Christ: for what things He should have suffered, I suffer instead of Him." See how many things he establishes. Great, he shows, is the claim upon their love. As in his second Epistle to the Corinthians, he wrote, saying, "he committed unto us the ministry of reconciliation" (2 Cor. v. 20); and again, "We are ambassadors on behalf of Christ; as though God were entreating by us." So also here he saith, "For his sake I suffer," that he may the more draw them to Him. That is, though He who is your debtor is gone away, yet I repay. For, on this account he also said, "that which is lacking," to show that not even yet does he consider Him to have suffered all. "For your sake," he saith, and even after His death He suffers; seeing that still there remains a deficiency. The same thing he doeth in another way in the Epistle to the Romans, saying, "Who also maketh intercession for us" (Rom. viii. 34), showing that He was not satisfied with His death alone, but even afterwards He doeth countless things.

He does not then say this to exalt himself, but through a desire to show that Christ is even yet caring for them. And he shows what he says to be credible, by adding, "for His Body's sake." For that so it is, and that there is no unlikelihood in it, is plain from these things being done for His body's sake. Look how He hath knitted us unto Himself. Why then introduce Angels between? "Whereof I was made," he saith, "a minister." Why introduce Angels

---

[1] As Acts ix. 5.

besides? " I am a minister." Then he shows that he had himself done nothing, albeit he is a minister. " Of which I was made," saith he, " a minister, according to the dispensation of God which is given me to youward, to fulfill the word of God." " The dispensation." Either he means, He so willed that after His own departure we should succeed to the dispensation, in order that ye might not feel as deserted, (for it is Himself that suffers, Himself that is ambassador;) or he means this, namely, me who was more than all a persecutor, for this end He permitted to persecute, that in my preaching I might gain belief; or by " dispensation " he means, that He required not deeds, nor actions, nor good works, but faith and baptism. For ye would not otherwise have received the word. " For you," he saith, " to fulfill the word of God." He speaks of the Gentiles, showing that they were yet wavering, by the expression, " fulfill." For that the cast-away Gentiles should have been able to receive such lofty doctrines was not of Paul, but of the dispensation of God; " for I never could have had the power," he saith. Having shown that which is greater, that his sufferings are Christ's, he next subjoins what is more evident, that this also is of God, " to fulfill His word in you." And he shows here covertly, that this too is of dispensation, that it is spoken to you now, when ye are able to hear it, and cometh not of neglect, but to the end ye may receive it. For God doeth not all things on a sudden, but useth condescension because of His plenteous love toward man. And this is the reason why Christ came at this time, and not of old. And He shows in the Gospel, that for this reason He sent the servants first, that they might not proceed to kill the Son. For if they did not reverence the Son, even when He came after the servants, much less would they had He come sooner; if they gave no heed to the lesser commandments, how would they to the greater? What then, doth one object? Are there not Jews even now, and Greeks who are in a very imperfect condition? This, however, is an excess of listlessness. For after so long a time, after such great instructions, still to continue imperfect, is a proof of great stupidity.

When then the Greeks say, why did Christ come at this time? let us not allow them so to speak, but let us ask them, whether He did not succeed? For as, if He had come at the very first, and had not succeeded, the time would not have been for us a sufficient excusation, so, seeing He hath succeeded, we cannot with justice be brought to account on the score of " the time." For neither does any one demand of a physician, who has removed the disease, and restored one to health, to give an account of

his treatment, nor yet does any examine closely a general who has gained a victory, why at this time, and why in this place. For these things it were in place to ask, had he not been successful; but when he has been successful, they must even be taken for granted. For, tell me, whether is more worthy of credit, thy reasoning and calumny, or the 'perfection of the thing? Conquered He, or conquered He not? show this. Prevailed He, or prevailed He not? Accomplished He what He said, or no? These are the articles of enquiry. Tell me, I pray. Thou fully grantest that God is, even though not Christ? I ask thee then; Is God without beginning? Thou wilt say, Certainly. Tell me then, why made He not men myriads of years before? For they would have lived through a longer time. They were now losers by that time during which they were not. Nay, they were not losers; but how, He who made them alone knows. Again, I ask thee, why did He not make all men at once? But his soul, whoever was first made, hath so many years of existence, of which that one is deprived which is not yet created. Wherefore made He the one to be brought first into this world, and the other afterwards?

Although these things are really fit subjects for enquiry: yet not for a meddling curiosity: for this is not for enquiry at all. For I will tell you the reason I spoke of. For suppose human nature as being some one continued life, and that in the first times our race was in the position of boyhood; in those that succeeded, of manhood; and in these that are near extreme age, of an old man. Now when the soul is at its perfection, when the limbs of the body are unstrung, and our war is over, we are then brought to philosophy. On the contrary, one may say, we teach boys whilst young. Yes, but not the great doctrines, but rhetoric, and expertness with language; and the other when they are come to ripeness of age. See God also doing the same with the Jews. For just as though the Jews had been little children, he placed Moses over them as a schoolmaster, and like little children he managed these things for them through shadowy representations, as we teach letters. " For the law had a shadow of the good things to come, and not the very image of the things." (Heb. x. 1.) As we both buy cakes for children and give them pieces of money, requiring of them one thing only, that for the present they would go to school; so also God at that time gave them both wealth and luxury, purchasing from them by this His great indulgence one only thing, that they would listen to Moses. Therefore He delivered them over to a schoolmaster, that they might not despise Himself as a tender, loving Father. See then that they feared him only; for they said not, Where is God? but, Where is Moses? and his very presence was fearful. So when they did amiss, observe how he punished them. For God indeed was desirous of casting them off; but he would not permit Him. Or rather the whole was of God; just as when a Father threatens whilst a schoolmaster entreats Him, and says, "Forgive them, I pray, on my account, and henceforward I undertake for them." In this way was the wilderness a school. And as children who have been a long while at school are desirous of quitting it, so also were they at that time continually desiring Egypt, and weeping, saying, "We are lost, we are wholly consumed, we are utterly undone." (Ex. xvi. 3.) And Moses broke their tablet, having written for them, as it were, certain words (Ex. xxxii. 19); just as a schoolmaster would do, who having taken up the writing tablet, and found it badly written, throws away the tablet itself, desiring to show great anger; and if he have broken it, the father is not angry. For he indeed was busy writing, but they not attending to him, but turning themselves other ways, were committing disorder. And as in school, they strike each other, so also, on that occasion, he bade them strike and slay each other. And again, having given them as it were lessons to learn, then asking for them, and finding they had not learnt them, he would punish them. For instance. What writings were those that denoted the power of God? The events in Egypt? Yes, saith one, but these writings represented the plagues, that He punishes His enemies. And to them it was a school. For what else was the punishment of your enemies but your benefit? And in other respects too, He benefited you. And it was the same as if one should say he knew his letters, but when asked up and down, should be at fault, and be beaten. So they also said indeed that they knew the power of God, but when asked their knowledge up and down, they could not give it, and therefore were beaten. Hast thou seen water? Thou oughtest to be reminded of the water in Egypt. For He that of water made blood, will be also of power to do this.[1] As we also say often to the children, "when in a book thou seest the letter A, remember that thou hadst it in thy tablet." Hast thou seen famine? Remember that it was He that destroyed the crops! Hast thou seen wars? Remember the drowning! Hast thou seen that they are mighty who inhabit the land? But not mightier than the Egyptians. He who took thee out of the midst of them, will He not much more save thee when out? But they knew not how to answer their letters out of order, and therefore they were beaten. "They ate," and drank, "and kicked."

(Deut. xxxii. 15.) When fed with their manna they ought not to have asked for luxury, seeing they had known the evils which proceed from it. And they acted precisely as if a free child, when sent to school, should ask to be reckoned with the slaves, and to wait on them, — so did these also in seeking Egypt — and when receiving all needful sustenance, and such as becomes a free person, and sitting at his father's table, should have a longing for the ill-savored and noisy one of the servants. And they said to Moses, "Yea, Lord, all that thou hast spoken will we do, and be obedient." (Ex. xxiv. 7.) And as it happens in the case of desperately bad children, that when the father would put them to death,[2] the schoolmaster perseveringly entreats for them, the same was the case at that time also.

Why have we said these things? Because we differ in nothing from children. Wilt thou hear their doctrines also, that they are those of children? "Eye for eye," it is said, "and tooth for tooth." (Lev. xxiv. 20.) For nothing is so eager to revenge as a childish mind. For seeing it is a passion of irrationality, and there is much irrationality, and great lack of consideration in that age, no wonder the child is tyrannized over by anger; and so great is the tyranny, that ofttimes after stumbling and getting up again, they will smite their knee for passion, or overturn the footstool, and so will allay their pain, and quench their rage. In some such way as this did God also deal with them, when He allowed them to strike out "Eye for eye, and tooth for tooth," and destroyed the Egyptians and the Amalekites that had grieved them. And He promised such things; as if to one who said, "Father, such and such an one has beaten me," the father should then reply, "Such and such an one is a bad man, and let us hate him." So also doth God say, "I will be their enemy that are thine enemies, and I will hate them that hate thee." (Ex. xxiii. 22.) And again, when Balaam prayed, the condescension which was used towards them was childish. For as with children, when having been frightened at anything not frightful, such as either a lock of wool, or any other thing of like sort, they are suddenly alarmed; that their fear may not continue in them, we bring the thing up to their hands, and make their nurses show it them: so also did God; seeing that the Prophet was a terror to them, he turned the terror of him into confidence. And as children who are under weaning have all manner of things in little baskets, so also did He give them everything, and dainties in abundance. Still the child longs for the breast; so did these also for Egypt and the flesh that was there.

---

[1] Or, "to produce this," if he refers to the *want* of water.

[2] ἀνελεῖν. Perhaps he means no more than to renounce or disinherit, as he said above.

So that one would not be wrong in calling Moses both a teacher, and a nursing-father, and a conductor (Ex. xvi. 3; Num. xi. 4, 5); the man's wisdom was great. Howbeit it is not the same thing to guide men who are already philosophers, and to rule unreasoning children. And, if you are inclined to hear yet another particular; as the nurse says to the child, When thou easest thyself, take up thy garments, and for as long as thou sittest, so also did Moses. (Deut. xxiii. 13.) For all the passions are tyrannous in children (for as yet they have not that which is to bridle them), vainglory, desire, irrationality, anger, envy; just as in children, so they prevailed; they spat upon, they beat, Moses. And as a child takes up a stone, and we all exclaim, O do not throw it; so did they also take up stones against their father; and he fled from them. And as, if a father have any ornament, the child, being fond of ornament, asks him for it, in like manner, truly, did the party of Dathan and Abiram act, when they rebelled for the priesthood. (Num. xvi.) And besides, they were of all people the most envious, and little-minded, and in all respects imperfect.

Ought then Christ, tell me, to have appeared at that time, at that time to have given them these teachings of true wisdom, when they were raging with lust, when they were as horses mad for the mare, when they were the slaves of money, of the belly? Nay, He would but have wasted his lessons of wisdom in discoursing with those of no understanding; and they would have neither learnt one thing nor the other. And as he who teaches to read before he has taught the alphabet, will never teach even so much as the alphabet; so indeed would it then have been also. But not so now, for by the grace of God much forbearance, much virtue, hath been planted everywhere. Let us give thanks then for all things, and not be over curious. For it is not we that know the due time, but He, The Maker of the time, and The Creator of the ages.

In everything then yield we to Him: for this is to glorify God, not to demand of Him an account of what He doeth. In this way too did Abraham give glory to God; "And being fully persuaded," we read, "that what He had promised, He was able to perform." (Rom. iv. 21.) He did not ask about the future even; but we scrutinize the account even of the past. See how great folly, how great ingratitude, is here. But let us for the future have done, for no gain comes of it, but much harm even; and let our minds be gratefully disposed towards our Master, and let us send up glory to God, that making for all things an offering of thanksgiving, we may be counted worthy of His lovingkindness, through the grace and love toward man of His Only-begotten, with whom, &c.

HOMILY V.

Colossians i. 26–28.

"Even the mystery which hath been hid from all ages and generations: but now hath it been manifested to His saints, to whom God was pleased to make known what is the riches of the glory of this mystery among the Gentiles, which is Christ in you, the hope of glory: whom we proclaim, admonishing every man, and teaching every man in all wisdom, that we may present every man perfect in Christ."

Having said what we have come to, and showed the lovingkindness of God and the honor, by the greatness of the things given, he introduces yet another consideration that heightens them, namely, that neither before us did any one know Him.[1] As he doth also in the Epistle to the Ephesians, saying, neither Angels, nor principalities, nor any other created power, but only the Son of God knew. (Eph. iii. 5, 9,

10.) And he said, not simply hid, but "quite hid," and that even if it hath but now come to pass, yet it is of old, and from the beginning God willed these things, and they were so planned out; but why, he saith not yet. "From the ages," from the beginning, as one might say. And with reason he calleth that a mystery, which none knew, save God. And where hid? In Christ; as he saith in the Epistle to the Ephesians (Eph. iii. 9), or as when the Prophet saith, "From everlasting even to everlasting Thou art." (Ps. xc. 2.) But now hath been manifested, he saith, "to His saints." So that it is altogether of the dispensation of God. "But now hath been manifested," he saith. He saith not, "is come to pass," but, "hath been manifested to His saints." So that it is even now still hid, since it hath been manifested to His saints alone.

---

[1] [Or, "know it," a reading having some support, and adopted by Field. — J. A. B.]

Let not others therefore deceive you, for they know not. Why to them alone? "To whom He was pleased," he saith. See how everywhere He stops the mouth of their questions. "To whom God was pleased to make known," he saith. Yet His will is not without reason. By way of making them accountable for grace, rather than allowing them to have high thoughts, as though it were of their own achieving, he said, "To whom he was pleased to make known." "What is the riches of the glory of this mystery among the Gentiles." He hath spoken loftily, and accumulated emphasis, seeking, out of his great earnestness, for amplification upon amplification. For this also is an amplification, the saying indefinitely, "The riches of the glory of this mystery among the Gentiles." For it is most of all apparent among the Gentiles, as he also says elsewhere, "And that the Gentiles might glorify God for His mercy." (Rom. xv. 9.) For the great glory of this mystery is apparent among others also, but much more among these. For, on a sudden, to have brought men more senseless than stones to the dignity of Angels, simply through bare words, and faith alone, without any laboriousness, is indeed glory and riches of mystery: just as if one were to take a dog, quite consumed with hunger and the mange, foul, and loathsome to see, and not so much as able to move, but lying cast out, and make him all at once into a man, and to display him upon the royal throne. They were wont to worship stones and the earth; but they learned that themselves are better both than the heaven and the sun, and that the whole world serveth them; they were captives and prisoners of the devil: on a sudden they are placed above his head, and lay commands on him and scourge him: from being captives and slaves to demons, they are become the body of The Master of the Angels and the Archangels; from not knowing even what God is, they are become all at once sharers even in God's throne. Wouldest thou see the countless steps they overleaped? First, they had to learn that stones are not gods; secondly, that they not only are not gods, but inferior even to men; thirdly, to brutes even; fourthly, to plants even; fifthly, they brought together the extremes:[1] that not only stones but not earth even, nor animals, nor plants, nor man, nor heaven; or, to begin again, that not stones, not animals, not plants, not elements, not things above, not things below, not man, not demons, not Angels, not Archangels, not any of those Powers above, ought to be worshiped by the nature of man. Being drawn up,[2] as it were, from some deep, they had to

learn that the Lord of all, He is God, that Him alone is it right to worship; that the virtuous life[3] is a good thing; that this present death is not death, nor this life, life; that the body is raised, that it becomes incorruptible, that it will ascend into heaven, that it obtains even immortality, that it standeth with Angels, that it is removed thither. But Him who was there below, having cleared at a bound all these steps, He has placed on high upon the throne, having made Him that was lower than the stones, higher in dominion than the Angels, and the Archangels, and the thrones, and the dominions. Truly "What is the riches of the glory of this mystery?" Just as if one should show a fool to be all at once made a philosopher; yea rather, whatsoever one should say, it would be as nothing: for even the words of Paul are undefined. "What is the riches," he saith, "of the glory of this mystery among the Gentiles, which is Christ in you?" Again, they had to learn that He who is above, and who ruleth Angels and dominions, and all the other Powers, came down below, and was made Man, and suffered countless things, and rose again, and was received up.

All these things were of the mystery; and he sets them down together with lofty praise, saying, "Which is Christ in you?" But if He be in you, why seek ye Angels? "Of this mystery." For there are other mysteries besides. But this is really a mystery, which no one knew, which is marvelous, which is beside the common expectation, which was hid. "Which is Christ in you," he saith, "the hope of glory, whom we proclaim," bringing Him from above. "Whom we," not Angels: "teaching" and "admonishing": not imperiously nor using constraint, for this too is of God's lovingkindness to men, not to bring them to Him after the manner of a tyrant. Seeing it was a great thing he had said, "teaching," he added, "admonishing," which is rather like a father than an instructor. "Whom," saith he, "we proclaim, admonishing every man, and teaching every man in all wisdom." So that all wisdom is needed. That is, saying all things in wisdom. For the ability to learn such things exists not in every one. "That we may present every man perfect in Christ Jesus." What sayest thou, "every man"? Yea; this is what we are earnestly desirous of doing, he saith. For what, if this do not come to pass? the blessed Paul endeavored. "Perfect." This then is perfection, the other is imperfect: so that if one have not even the whole of wisdom, he is imperfect. "Perfect in Christ Jesus," not in the Law, nor in Angels, for that is not per-

---

[1] ὅτι τὰ ἄκρα συνήγαγον εἰς ταὐτόν. There is no authority for thus omitting ὅτι. It may mean, "That I (i.e. God) have brought together the extremes into one, and not," &c.

[2] ἀνιμωμένος. Compare Plato, Rep. lib. vii. init.

[3] καλὸν ἡ θαυμαστὴ πολιτεία. Lit. "the admirable conversation [course of life]." He seems to mean a life of Virginity, which he says is peculiar to the Gospel; lib. cont. Judæos, § 7; Ben. t. i. p. 568 a; and elsewhere, as on Rom. viii. 7, Hom. xiii.

fection. "In Christ," that is, in the knowledge of Christ. For he that knows what Christ has done, will have higher thoughts than to be satisfied with Angels.

"In Christ Jesus"; Ver. 29. "Whereunto I labor also, striving." And he said not, "I am desirous" merely, nor in any indifferent way, but, "I labor, striving," with great earnestness, with much watching. If I, for your good, thus watch, much more 'ought ye. Then again, showing that it is of God, he saith, "according to His working which worketh in me mightily." He shows that this is the work of God. He, now, that makes me strong for this, evidently wills it. Wherefore also when beginning he saith, "Through the will of God." (Ver. 1.) So that it is not only out of modesty he so expresses himself, but insisting on the truth of the Word as well. "And striving." In saying this, he shows that many are fighting against him. Then great is his tender affection.

Chap. ii. v. 1. "For I would have you know how greatly I strive for you, and for them at Laodicea."

Then lest this should seem owing to their peculiar weakness, he joined others also with them, and as yet condemned them not. But why does he say, "And as many as have not seen my face in the flesh"? He shows here after a divine manner, that they saw him constantly in the Spirit. And he bears witness to their great love.

Ver. 2, 3. "That their hearts may be comforted, they being knit together in love, and unto all riches of the full assurance of understanding, that they may know the mystery of God the Father,[1] and of Christ: in whom are all the treasures of wisdom and knowledge hidden."

Now henceforward he is hastening and in pangs to enter upon the doctrine, neither accusing them, nor clearing them of accusation. "I strive," he saith. To what end? That they may be knit together. What he means is something like this; that they may stand firm in the faith. He doth not however so express himself; but extenuates the matter of accusation. That is, that they may be united with love, not with necessity nor with force. For as I have said, he always avoids offending, by leaving it to themselves;[2] and therefore "striving," because I wish it to be with love, and willingly. For I do not wish it to be with the lips merely, nor merely that they shall be brought together, but "that their hearts may be comforted."

"Being knit together in love unto all riches of the full assurance of understanding." That

is, that they may doubt about nothing, that they may be fully assured in all things. But I meant full assurance which is by faith, for there is a full assurance which cometh by arguments, but that is worthy of no consideration. I know, he saith, that ye believe, but I would have you fully assured: not "unto riches" only, but "unto all riches"; that your full assurance may be intense, as well as in all things. And observe the wisdom of this blessed one. He said not, "Ye do ill that ye are not fully assured," nor accused them; but, ye know not how desirous I am that ye may be fully assured, and not merely so, but with understanding. For seeing he spoke of faith; suppose not, he saith, that I meant barely and unprofitably, but with understanding and love. "That they may know the mystery of God the Father and of Christ." So that this is the mystery of God, the being brought unto Him by the Son. "And of Christ, in whom are hid all the treasures of wisdom and knowledge." But if they are in Him, then wisely also no doubt He came at this time. Wherefore then do some foolish persons object to Him, "See how He discourseth with the simpler sort." "In whom are all the treasures." He himself knows all things. "Hid," for think not in truth that ye already have all; they are hidden also even from Angels, not from you only; so that you ought to ask all things from Him. He himself giveth wisdom and knowledge. Now by saying, "treasures," he shows their largeness, by "All," that He is ignorant of nothing, by "hid," that He alone knoweth.

Ver. 4. "This I say, that no one may delude you with persuasiveness of speech."

Seest thou that he saith, I have therefore said this, that ye may not seek it from men. "Delude you," he saith, "with persuasiveness of speech." For what if any doth speak, and speak persuasively?

Ver. 5. "For though I am absent in the flesh, yet am I with you in the spirit."

The direct thing to have said here was, "even though I be absent in the flesh, yet, nevertheless, I know the deceivers"; but instead he has ended with praise, "Joying and beholding your order, and the steadfastness of your faith in Christ." "Your order," he means, your good order. "And the steadfastness of your faith in Christ." This is still more in the way of encomium. And he said not "faith," but steadfastness, as to soldiers standing in good order and firmly. Now that which is steadfast, neither deceit nor trial can shake asunder. Not only, he saith, have ye not fallen, but no one hath so much as thrown you into disorder. He hath set himself over them, that they may fear him as though present; for thus is order preserved. From solidity follows compactedness, for you

---

[1] Rec. text καὶ πατρὸς, E. V. "of God, and of the Father"; but the sense in either case is, of Him Who is God and Father.

[2] ἐπιτρέπων, i.e. to draw such inferences as would be harsh if stated by himself.

will then produce solidity, when having brought many things together, you shall cement them compactedly and inseparably; thus a solidity is produced, as in the case of a wall. But this is the peculiar work of love; for those who were by themselves, when it hath closely cemented and knit them together, it renders solid. And faith, again, doeth the same thing; when it allows not reasonings to intrude themselves. For as reasonings divide, and shake loose, so faith causes solidity and compactness.

For seeing God hath bestowed upon us benefits surpassing man's reasoning, suitably enough He hath brought in faith. It is not possible to be steadfast, when demanding reasons. For behold all our lofty doctrines, how destitute they are of reasonings, and dependent upon faith alone. God is not anywhere, and is everywhere. What hath less reason in it than this? Each by itself is full of difficulty. For, indeed, He is not in place; nor is there any place in which He is. He was not made, He made not Himself, He never began to be. What reasoning will receive this, if there be not faith? Does it not seem to be utterly ridiculous, and more endless than a riddle?

Now that He hath no beginning, and is uncreate, and uncircumscribed, and infinite, is, as we have said, a manifest difficulty; but let us consider His incorporealness, whether we can search out this by reasoning. God is incorporeal. What is incorporeal? A bare word, and no more, for the apprehension has received nothing, has impressed nothing upon itself; for if it does so impress, it comes to nature, and what constitutes body. So that the mouth speaks indeed, but the understanding knows not what it speaks, save one thing only, that it is not body, this is all it knows. And why do I speak of God? In the case of the soul, which is created, inclosed, circumscribed, what is incorporealness? say! show! Thou canst not. Is it air? But air is body, even though it be not compact, and it is plain from many proofs that it is a yielding body. Fire is body, whilst the energy of the soul is bodiless. Wherefore? Since it penetrateth everywhere. If it is not[1] itself body, then that which is incorporeal exists in place, therefore it is circumscribed; and that which is circumscribed has figure; and figures are linear, and lines belong to bodies. Again, that which is without figure, what conception does it admit? It has no figure, no form, no outline. Seest thou how the understanding becomes dizzy?

Again, That Nature [viz. God's] is not susceptible of evil. But He is also good of His own will; it is therefore susceptible. But one

may not so say, far be it! Again, was He brought into being, willing it, or not willing it? But neither may one say this. Again, circumscribes He the world, or no? If He circumscribes it not, He is Himself circumscribed, but if He circumscribes it, He is infinite in His nature. Again, circumscribes He Himself? If He circumscribes Himself, then He is not without beginning to Himself, but to us; therefore He is not in His nature without beginning. Everywhere one must grant contradictories.

Seest thou how great the darkness is; and how everywhere there is need of faith. This it is, that is solid. But, if you will, let us come to things which are less than these. That Substance hath an operation. And what in His case is operation? Is it a certain motion? Then He is not immutable: for that which is moved, is not immutable: for, from being motionless it becomes in motion. But nevertheless He is in motion, and never stands still. But what kind of motion, tell me; for amongst us there are seven kinds; down, up, in, out, right, left, circular, or, if not this, increase, decrease, generation, destruction, alteration. But is His motion none of these, but such as the mind is moved with? No, nor this either. Far be it! for in many things the mind is even absurdly moved. Is to will, to operate, or not? If to will is to operate, and He wills all men to be good, and to be saved (1 Tim. ii. 4), how comes it not to pass? But to will is one thing, to operate, another. To will then is not sufficient for operation. How then saith the Scripture, "He hath done whatsoever He willed"? (Ps. cxv. 3.) And again, the leper saith unto Christ, "If Thou wilt, Thou canst make me clean." (Matt. viii. 2.) For if this follows in company with the will, what is to be said? Will ye that I mention yet another thing? How were the things that are, made out of things that are not? How will they be resolved into nothing? What is above the heaven? And again, what above that? and what above that? and beyond that? and so on to infinity. What is below the earth? Sea, and beyond this, what? and beyond that again? Nay; to the right, and to the left, is there not the same difficulty?

But these indeed are things unseen. Will ye that I lead the discourse to those which are seen; those which have already happened? Tell me, how did the beast contain Jonah in its belly, without his perishing? Is it not void of reason, and its motions without control? How spared it the righteous man? How was it that the heat did not suffocate him? How was it that it putrefied him not? For if to be in the deep only, is past contriving, to be both in the creature's bowels, and in that heat, is very far

---

[1] Savile conjectures that "not" should be inserted, and the sense seems absolutely to require it.

more unaccountable. If from within we breathe[1] the air, how did the respiration suffice for two animals? And how did it also vomit him forth unharmed? And how too did he speak? And how too was he self-possessed, and prayed? Are not these things incredible? If we test them by reasonings, they are incredible, if by faith, they are exceeding credible.

Shall I say something more than this? The wheat in the earth's bosom decays, and rises again. Behold marvels, opposite, and each surpassing the other; marvelous is the not becoming corrupted, marvelous, after becoming so, is the rising again. Where are they that make sport of such things, and disbelieve the Resurrection and say, This bone how shall it be cemented to that? and introduce such like silly tales. Tell me, how did Elias ascend in a chariot of fire? Fire is wont to burn, not to carry aloft. How lives he so long a time? In what place is he? Why was this done? Whither was Enoch translated? Lives he on like food with us? and what is it hinders him from being here? Nay, but does he not eat? And wherefore was he translated? Behold how God schooleth us by little and little. He translated Enoch; no very great thing that. This instructed us for the taking up of Elias. He shut in Noe into the ark (Gen. vii. 7); nor is this either any very great thing. This instructed us for the shutting up of the prophet within the whale. Thus even the things of old stood in need of forerunners and types. For as in a ladder the first step sends on to the second, and from the first it is not possible to step to the fourth, and this sends one on to that, that that may be the way to the next; and as it is not possible either to get to the second before the first; so also is it here.

And observe the signs of signs, and thou wilt discern this in the ladder which Jacob saw. "Above," it is said, "the Lord stood fast, and underneath Angels were ascending and descending." (Gen. xxviii. 13.) It was prophesied that the Father hath a Son; it was necessary this should be believed. Whence wouldest thou that I show thee the signs of this? From above, downward? From beneath, upward? Because He begetteth without passion,[2] for this reason did she that was barren first bear. Let us rather go higher. It was necessary to be believed, that He begat of Himself. What then? The thing happens obscurely indeed, as in type and shadow, but still it doth happen, and as it goes on it becomes somehow clearer. A woman is formed out of man alone, and he remains whole and entire. Again, it was necessary there should be some sure sign of the Conception of a Virgin. So the barren beareth, not once only, but a second time and a third, and many times. Of His birth then of a Virgin, the barren is a type, and she sends the mind forward to faith. Again, this was a type of God being able to beget alone. For if man is the chief agent,[3] and birth takes place without him, in a more excellent way, much rather, is One begotten of the Chiefest Agent. There is still another generation, which is a type of the Truth. I mean, ours by the Spirit. Of this again the barren is a type, the fact that it is not of blood (John i. 13); this pertains to the generation above. The one — as also the types — shows that the generation is to be without passion; the other, that it could proceed from one above.

Christ is above, ruling over all things: it was necessary this should be believed. The same takes place in the earth with respect to man. "Let Us make man after Our image and likeness" (Gen. i. 26), for dominion of all the brutes. Thus He instructed us, not by words, but by actions. Paradise showed the separateness of his nature, and that man was the best thing of all. Christ was to rise again; see now how many sure signs there were; Enoch, Elias, Jonas, the fiery furnace, the case of Noah, baptism, the seeds, the plants, our own generation, that of all animals. For since on this everything was at stake, it, more than any other, had abundance of types.

That the Universe[4] is not without a Providence we may conjecture from things amongst ourselves, for nothing will continue to exist, if not provided for; but even herds, and all other things stand in need of governance. And that the Universe was not made by chance, Hell is a proof, and so was the deluge in Noah's day, the fire,[5] the overwhelming of the Egyptians in the sea, the things which happened in the wilderness.

It was necessary too that many things should prepare the way for Baptism; yea, thousands of things; those, for instance, in the Old Testament, those in the Pool,[6] the cleansing of him that was not sound in health, the deluge itself, and all the things that have been done in water, the baptism of John.

It was necessary to be believed that God giveth up His Son; a man did this by anticipation, Abraham the Patriarch. Types then of all these things, if we are so inclined, we shall

---

[1] [This is obscure, and was altered by the simplifying text into "For how breathed he the air in that place? How," &c.— J. A. B.]
[2] ἀπαθῶς, i.e. without being changed. This refers to the Eternal Generation, as the sequel shows. Compare St. Athanasius against Arianism, Disc. I. c. 8.

[3] κυριώτερον ἄνθρωπος. One would have expected ἀνήρ, but ἄνθρωπος has just been opposed to γυνή.
[4] τὰ πάντα.   [5] i.e. of Sodom.
[6] Hales suggests that this may be the Laver in the Temple, but it is not called κολυμβήθρα in LXX. The pool of Bethesda is meant, as is evident from the like mention of types increasing in clearness on John v. 2, Hom. xxxvi. init., where this is classed with those of the Old Testament. The following instance refers to the cleansing in Lev. xv. 13.

find by searching in the Scriptures. But let us not be weary, but attune ourselves by these things. Let us hold the faith steadfastly, and show forth strictness of life : that having through all things returned thanks to God, we may be counted worthy of the good things promised to them that love Him, through the grace and lovingkindness of our Lord Jesus Christ, with whom, &c.

HOMILY VI.

COLOSSIANS ii. 6, 7.

" As therefore ye received Christ Jesus the Lord, so walk in Him, rooted and built up in Him, and stablished in your faith, even as ye were taught, abounding in thanksgiving."

AGAIN, he takes hold on them beforehand with their own testimony, saying, " As therefore ye received." We introduce no strange addition, he saith, neither do ye. " Walk ye in Him," for He is the Way that leadeth to the Father : not in the Angels ; this way leadeth not thither. " Rooted," that is, fixed ; not one while going this way, another that, but "rooted " : now that which is rooted, never can remove. Observe how appropriate are the expressions he employs. " And built up," that is, in thought attaining unto Him. " And stablished " in Him, that is, holding Him, built as on a foundation. He shows that they had fallen down, for the word " built "[1] has this force. For the faith is in truth a building ; and needs both a strong foundation, and secure construction. For both if any one build not upon a secure foundation it will shake ; and even though he do, if it be not firm, it will not stand. " As ye were taught." Again, the word " As." " Abounding," he saith, " in thanksgiving " ; for this is the part of well-disposed persons, I say not simply to give thanks, but with great abundance, more than ye learned, if possible, with much ambition.

Ver. 8. " Take heed lest there shall be any one that maketh spoil of you."

Seest thou how he shows him to be a thief, and an alien, and one that enters in softly ? For he has already represented him to be entering in. " Beware." And he well said " maketh spoil." As one digging away a mound from underneath, may give no perceptible sign, yet it gradually settles, so do you also beware ; for this is his main point, not even to let himself be perceived. As if some one were robbing every day, and he (the owner of the house) were told, " Beware lest there be some one " ; and he shows the way — through this way — as if we were to say, through this chamber ;[2] so, " through philosophy," says he.

Then because the term " philosophy " has an appearance of dignity, he added, " and vain deceit." For there is also a good deceit ; such as many have been deceived by, which one ought not even to call a deceit at all. Whereof Jeremiah speaks ; " O Lord, Thou hast deceived me, and I was deceived "[3] (Jer. xx. 7) ; for such as this one ought not to call a deceit at all ; for Jacob also deceived his father, but that was not a deceit, but an economy. " Through his philosophy," he saith, " and vain deceit, after the tradition of men, after the rudiments[4] of the world, and not after Christ." Now he sets about to reprove their observance of particular[5] days, meaning by elements of the world the sun and moon ;[6] as he also said in the Epistle to the Galatians, " How turn ye back again to the weak and beggarly elements?" (Gal. iv. 9.) And he said not observances of days, but in general of the present world, to show its worthlessness : for if the present world be nothing, much more then its elements. Having first shown how great benefits and kindnesses they had received, he afterwards brings ·on his accusation, thereby to show its greater seriousness, and to convict his hearers. Thus too the Prophets do. They always first point out the benefits, and then they magnify their accusation ; as Esaias saith, " I have begotten children, and exalted them, but they have rejected me " (Isa. i. 2, Sept.) ; and

---

[1] Present participle.

[2] [This comparison, wanting in all previous editions of the Greek, given by the Oxford tr. in a footnote, is found in all the MSS. collated for Field. It is somewhat obscure (and probably on that account omitted from some copies), but the general meaning is not hard to find.—J. A. B.]

[3] [Some documents (followed by Field) here insert, " But I am not persuaded," probably an addition to rescue Chrys. from the position of defending deceit. But he has done this elaborately in his beautiful treatise on the Priesthood, employing the same arguments and expressions as here. It is an error not surprising in an Asiatic Greek.—J. A. B.]

[4] στοιχεῖα, elements.

[5] τῶν ἡμερῶν. Montfaucon refers to his Suppl. de l'Ant. Expl. l. iii. vol. 1, p. 112, where he shows that the observance of heathen customs about lucky and unlucky days, and the like, was common in France in the thirteenth century. Such were the Dies Ægyptiaci, &c.

[6] [This misinterpretation is found in many Fathers. See Lightfoot here, and on Gal. iv. 9.—J. A. B.]

again, "O my people, what have I done unto thee, or wherein have I grieved thee, or wherein have I wearied thee"? (Mic. vi. 3) and David; as when he says, "I heard thee in the secret place of the tempest" (Ps. lxxxi. 7, Sept.); and again, "Open thy mouth, and I will fill it." (Ps. lxxxi. 10.) And everywhere you will find it the same.

That indeed were most one's duty, not to be persuaded by them, even did they say aught to the purpose; as it is, however, obligations apart even, it would be our duty to shun those things. "And not after Christ," he saith. For were it in such sort a matter done by halves, that ye were able to serve both the one and the other, not even so ought ye to do it; as it is, however, he suffers you not to be "after Christ." Those things withdraw you from Him. Having first shaken to pieces the Grecian observances, he next overthrows the Jewish ones also. For both Greeks and Jews practiced many observances, but the former from philosophy, the latter from the Law. First then, he makes at those against whom lay the heavier accusation. How, "not after Christ"?

Ver. 9, 10. "For in Him dwelleth all the fullness of the Godhead bodily: and in Him ye are made full, who is the head of all principality and power."

Observe how in his accusing of the one he thrusts through the other, by first giving the solution, and then the objection. For such a solution is not suspected, and the hearer accepts it the rather, that the speaker is not making it his aim. For in that case indeed he would make a point of not coming off worsted, but in this, not so. "For in Him dwelleth," that is, for God dwelleth in Him. But that thou mayest not think Him enclosed, as in a body, he saith, "All the fullness of the Godhead bodily: and ye are made full in Him." Others say that he intends the Church filled by His Godhead, as he elsewhere saith, "of Him that filleth all in all" (Eph. i. 23), and that the term "bodily" is here, as the body in the head. How is it then that he did not add, "which is the Church"? Some again say it is with reference to The Father, that he says that the fullness of the Godhead dwells in Him, but wrongly.[1] First, because "to dwell," cannot strictly be said of God: next, because the "fullness" is not that which receives, for "the earth is the Lord's, and the fullness thereof" (Ps. xxiv. 1); and again the Apostle, "until the fullness of the Gentiles be come in." (Rom. xi. 25.) By "fullness" is meant "the whole." Then the word "bodily," what did it intend? "As in a head." But why does he say the

same thing over again? "And ye are made full in Him." What then does it mean? That ye have nothing less than He. As it dwelt in Him, so also in you. For Paul is ever straining to bring us near to Christ; as when he says, "Hath raised us up with Him, and made us to sit with Him" (Eph. ii. 6): and, "If we endure, we shall also reign with Him" (2 Tim. ii. 12): and, "How shall He not also with Him freely give us all things" (Rom. viii. 32): and calling us "fellow-heirs." Then as for His dignity. And He "is the head of all principality and power." (Eph. iii. 6.) He that is above all, The Cause, is He not Consubstantial? Then he has added the benefit in a marvelous way; and far more marvelous than in the Epistle to the Romans. For there indeed he saith, "circumcision of the heart in the spirit, not in the letter" (Rom. ii. 29), but here, in Christ.

Ver. 11. "In whom ye were also circumcised with a circumcision not made with hands, in the putting off of the body of the flesh in the circumcision of Christ."

See how near he is come to the thing. He saith, "In the putting" quite away,[2] not putting off merely. "The body of sins." He means, "the old life." He is continually adverting to this in different ways, as he said above, "Who delivered us out of the power of darkness, and reconciled us who were alienated," that we should be "holy and without blemish." (Col. i. 13, 21.) No longer, he saith, is the circumcision with[3] the knife, but in Christ Himself; for no hand imparts this circumcision, as is the case there, but the Spirit. It circumciseth not a part, but the whole man. It is the body both in the one and the other case, but in the one it is carnally, in the other it is spiritually circumcised; but not as the Jews, for ye have not put off flesh, but sins. When and where? In Baptism. And what he calls circumcision, he again calls burial. Observe how he again passes on to the subject of righteous doings; "of the sins," he saith, "of the flesh," the things they had done in the flesh. He speaks of a greater thing than circumcision, for they did not merely cast away that of which they were circumcised, but they destroyed it, they annihilated it.

Ver. 12. "Buried with him," he saith, "in Baptism, wherein ye were also raised with Him, through faith in the working of God, who raised Him from the dead."

But it is not burial only: for behold what he says, "Wherein ye were also raised with Him, through faith in the working of God, who raised Him from the dead." He hath well said, "of faith,"[4] for it is all of faith. Ye believed that

---

1 ["But wrongly" seems a necessary addition, though omitted by Field, doubtless because supported chiefly by the group of MSS. found to make so many unwarrantable additions and other alterations.— J. A. B.]

2 ἀπεκδύσει, putting off for good, once for all.   3 ἐν, "in."
4 [The repetition of πίστεως, "of faith," which Field had previously conjectured as required by the sense, is found in the Catena;

God is able to raise, and so ye were raised. Then note also His worthiness of belief, "Who raised Him," he saith, "from the dead."

He now shows the Resurrection. "And you who sometime were dead through your trespasses and the uncircumcision of your flesh, you, I say, did He quicken together with Him." For ye lay under judgment of death. But even though ye died, it was a profitable death. Observe how *again* he shows what they deserved in the words he subjoins:

Ver. 13, 14, 15. "Having forgiven us all our trespasses; having blotted out the bond written in ordinances that was against us, which was contrary to us: and he hath taken it out of the way, nailing it to the Cross; having put off from himself the principalities and the powers, He made a show of them openly,[1] triumphing over them in it."

"Having forgiven us," he saith, "all our trespasses," those which produced that deadness. What then? Did He allow them to remain? No, He even wiped them out; He did not scratch them out merely; so that they could not be seen. "In doctrines"[2] [ordinances], he saith. What doctrines? The Faith. It is enough to believe. He hath not set works against works, but works against faith. And what next? Blotting out is an advance upon remission; again he saith, "And hath taken it out of the way." Nor yet even so did He preserve it, but rent it even in sunder, "by nailing it to His Cross." "Having put off from himself the principalities and the powers, He made a show of them openly, triumphing over them in it." Nowhere has he spoken in so lofty a strain.

Seest thou how great His earnestness that the bond should be done away? To wit, we all were under sin and punishment. He Himself, through suffering punishment, did away with both the sin and the punishment, and He was punished on the Cross. To the Cross then He affixed it; as having power, He tore it asunder. What bond? He means either that which they said to Moses, namely, "All that God hath said will we do, and be obedient" (Ex. xxiv. 3), or, if not that, this, that we owe to God obedience; or if not this, he means that the devil held possession of it, the bond which God made for Adam, saying, "In the day thou eatest of the tree, thou shalt die." (Gen. ii. 17.) This bond then the devil held in his possession. And Christ did not give it *to* us, but Himself tore it in two, the action of one who remits joyfully.

"Having put off from himself the principalities and the powers." He means the diabolical powers; because human nature had arrayed itself in these, or because they had,[3] as it were, a hold, when He became Man He put away from Himself that hold. What is the meaning of "He made a show of them"? And well said he so; never yet was the devil in so shameful a plight. For whilst expecting to have Him, he lost even those he had; and when That Body was nailed to the Cross, the dead arose. There death received his wound, having met his death-stroke from a dead body. And as an athlete, when he thinks he has hit his adversary, himself is caught in a fatal grasp; so truly doth Christ also show, that to die with confidence[4] is the devil's shame.

For he would have done everything to persuade men that He did not die, had he had the power. For seeing that of His Resurrection indeed all succeeding time was proof demonstrative; whilst of His death, no other time save that whereat it happened could ever furnish proof; therefore it was, that He died publicly in the sight of all men, but He arose not publicly, knowing that the aftertime would bear witness to the truth. For, that whilst the world was looking on, the serpent should be slain on high upon the Cross, herein is the marvel. For what did not the devil do, that He might die in secret? Hear Pilate saying, "Take ye Him away, and crucify Him, for I find no fault in Him" (John xix. 6), and withstanding them in a thousand ways. And again the Jews said unto Him, "If Thou art the Son of God, come down from the Cross." (Matt. xxvii. 40.) Then further, when He had received a mortal wound, and He came not down, for this reason He was also committed to burial; for it was in His power to have risen immediately: but He did not, that the fact might be believed. And yet in cases of private death indeed, it is possible to impute them to a swoon, but here, it is not possible to do this either. For even the soldiers brake not His legs, like those of the others, that it might be made manifest that He was dead. And those who buried The Body are known; and therefore too the Jews themselves seal the stone along with the soldiers. For, what was most of all attended to, was this very thing, that it should not be in obscurity. And the witnesses to it are from enemies, from the Jews. Hear them saying to Pilate, "That deceiver said, while he was yet alive, After three days I rise again. Command therefore that the sep-

---

and the simplifying group of documents changed it into "He hath well said so, for," &c. — J. A. B.]

[1] ἐδειγμάτισεν ἐν παρρησίᾳ, so commented on below as seemingly to require to be thus translated, "He inflicted disgrace on them through His confidence in dying."

[2] τοῖς δόγμασιν. Theodoret also takes it so, but the use of δογματίζεσθε, in ver. 20, agrees better with E. V. "The handwriting [bond] in ordinances," and the Vulgate, *Chirographum decreti*.

[3] All copies of St. Chrys. read "had them as a hold," which makes no sense. The Catena omits "them," which has been adopted, though the authority is slight. Compare John xiv. 30.

[4] μετὰ παρρησίας, referring to ἐδειγμάτισεν ἐν παρρησίᾳ. "Confidence" sometimes has the meaning of "standing without fear before God." Here he refers also to publicity.

ulchre" (Matt. xxvi. 63, 64) be guarded by the soldiers. This was accordingly done, themselves also sealing it. Hear them further saying even afterwards to the Apostles, "Ye intend to bring this Man's blood upon us." (Acts v. 28.) He suffered not the very fashion of His Cross to be put to shame. For since the Angels have suffered nothing like it, He therefore doth everything for this, showing that His death achieved a mighty work. There was, as it were, a single combat. Death wounded Christ: but Christ, being wounded, did afterwards kill death. He that seemed to be immortal, was destroyed by a mortal body; and this the whole world saw. And what is truly wonderful is, that He committed not this thing to another. But there was made again a second bond of another kind than the former.

Beware then lest we be condemned by this, after saying, I renounce Satan, and array myself with Thee, O Christ. Rather however this should not be called " a bond," but a covenant. For that is " a bond," whereby one is held accountable for debts: but this is a covenant. It hath no penalty, nor saith it, If this be done, or if this be not done: what Moses said when he sprinkled the blood of the covenant, This God also promised everlasting life. All this is a covenant. There, it was slave with master, here, it is friend with friend: there, it is said, "In the day that thou eatest thereof thou shalt die" (Gen. ii. 17); an immediate threatening; but here is nothing of the kind. God arrives, and here is nakedness, and there was nakedness; there, however, one that had sinned was made naked, because he sinned, but here, one is made naked, that he may be set free. Then, man put off the glory which he had; now, he puts off the old man; and before going up (to the contest), puts him off as easily, as it were his garments.[1] He is anointed,[2] as wrestlers about to enter the lists. For he is born at once; and as that first man was, not by little and little, but immediately. (He is anointed,) not as the priests of old time, on the head alone, but rather in more abundant measure. For he indeed was anointed on the head, the right ear, the hand (Lev. viii. 23, 24); to excite him to obedience, and to good works; but this one, all over. For he cometh not to be instructed merely; but to wrestle, and to be exercised; he is advanced to another creation. For when one confesses (his belief) in the life everlasting,[3] he has confessed a second creation. He took dust from the earth, and formed man (Gen. ii. 7): but now, dust no longer, but the Holy Spirit; with This he is formed, with this harmonized, even as Himself

was in the womb of the Virgin. He said not in Paradise, but "in Heaven." For deem not that, because the subject is earth, it is done on earth; he is[4] removed thither, to Heaven, there these things are transacted, in the midst of Angels: God taketh up thy soul above, above He harmonizeth it anew, He placeth thee near to the Kingly Throne. He is formed in the water, he receiveth spirit instead of a soul.[5] And after he is formed, He bringeth to him, not beasts, but demons, and their prince, and saith, "Tread upon serpents and scorpions." (Luke x. 19.) He saith not, "Let Us make man in our image, and after our likeness" (Gen. i. 26), but what? "He giveth them to become the sons of God; but of God," he saith, "they were born." (John i. 12, 13.) Then that thou give no ear to the serpent, straightway he teaches thee to say, "I renounce thee," that is, "whatsoever thou sayest, I will not hear thee." Then, that he destroy thee not by means of others, it is said,[6] "and thy pomp, and thy service, and thy angels." He hath set him no more to keep Paradise, but to have his citizenship in heaven. For straightway when he cometh up he pronounceth these words, "Our Father, Which art in Heaven, . . . Thy will be done, as in Heaven, so on earth." The plain falleth not on thy sight,[7] thou seest not tree, nor fountain, but straightway thou takest into thee the Lord Himself, thou art mingled with His Body, thou art intermixed with that Body that lieth above, whither the devil cannot approach. No woman is there, for him to approach, and deceive as the weaker; for it is said, "There is neither female, nor male." (Gal. iii. 28.) If thou go not down to him, he will not have power to come up where thou art; for thou art in Heaven, and Heaven is unapproachable by the devil. It hath no tree with knowledge of good and evil, but the Tree of Life only. No more shall woman be formed from thy side, but we all are one from the side of Christ. For if they who have been anointed of men take no harm by serpents, neither wilt thou take any harm at all, so long as thou art anointed; that thou mayst be able to grasp the Serpent and choke him, " to tread upon serpents and scorpions." (Luke x. 19.) But as the gifts are great, so is the punishment great also. It is not possible for him that hath fallen from Para-

---

[1] See St. Cyril, Catech. XX.
[2] See St. Cyril, Catech. XXI.
[3] In the Apostles' Creed, recited at Baptism.

[4] Old Lat. "thou art." The former clause may be, "think not, because the earth is under thee, that thou art in earth."
[5] ἀντίψυχον πνεῦμα, i.e. as Adam received a soul. The Spirit becoming, as it were, the life of the new man. See on Rom. viii. 11.
[6] φησὶ, the person who directs the catechumen.
[7] No meaning appears in this, οὐκ ἐπ᾽ ὄψιν πίπτει τὸ παιδίον, though old Lat. also has, "The child falleth not on his face"; but we have only to read πεδίον, as in a doubtful passage of Hom. xvi. on Rom. Tr. p. 467, note. This has been done in the text, not to spoil so beautiful a passage. [There may be a fanciful notion of the person newly baptized and thereby regenerated ("formed in the water") as a child. Upon coming up and pronouncing the Lord's Prayer, "the child does not fall on his face." The meaning will still be obscure, but the whole passage is highly fanciful, and there is thus at least a possible sense. — J. A. B.]

dise, to dwell " in front of Paradise "¹ (Gen. iii. 24), nor to reascend thither from whence we have fallen. But what after this? Hell, and the worm undying. But far be it that any of us should become amenable to this punishment ! but living virtuously, let us earnestly strive to do

throughout His will. Let us become well-pleasing to God, that we may be able both to escape the punishment, and to obtain the good things eternal, of which may we all be counted worthy, through the grace and love toward man, &c.

HOMILY VII.

COLOSSIANS ii. 16–19.

" Let no man therefore judge you in meat, or in drink, or in respect of a feast day, or a new moon, or a sabbath day: which are a shadow of the things to come; but the body is Christ's. Let no man rob you of your prize by a voluntary humility and worshiping of the Angels, dwelling in the things which he hath not seen, vainly puffed up by his fleshly mind, and not holding fast the Head, from whom all the body being supplied and knit together, through the joints and bands, increaseth with the increase of God."

HAVING first said darkly, " Take heed lest there shall be any one that maketh spoil of you after the tradition of men " (ver. 8) ; and again, further back, " This, I say, that no one may delude you with persuasiveness of speech " (ver. 4) ; thus preoccupying their soul, and working in it anxious thoughts ; next, having inserted those benefits, and increased this effect, he then brings in his reproof last, and says, " Let no man therefore judge you in meat, or in drink, or in respect of a feast day, or a new moon, or a sabbath day." Seest thou how he depreciates them? If ye have obtained such things, he saith, why make yourselves accountable for these petty matters? And he makes light of them, saying, " or in the part² of a feast day," for in truth they did not retain the whole of the former rule, " or a new moon, or a sabbath day." He said not, " Do not then observe them," but, " let no man judge you." He showed that they were transgressing, and undoing, but he brought his charge against others. Endure not those that judge you, he saith, nay, not so much as this either, but he argues with those persons, almost stopping their mouths, and saying, Ye ought not to judge. But he would not have reflected on these. He said not " in clean and unclean," nor yet " in feasts of Tabernacles, and unleavened

bread, and Pentecost," but " in part of a feast " : for they ventured not to keep the whole ; and if they did observe it, yet not so as to celebrate the feast. " In part," he saith, showing that the greater part is done away. For even if they did keep sabbath, they did not do so with precision. " Which are a shadow of the things to come " ; he means, of the New Covenant ; " but the body " is " Christ's." Some persons here punctuate thus, " but the body " is " of Christ," i.e. the truth is come in with Christ : others thus ; " The Body of Christ let no man adjudge away from you," that is, thwart you of it. The term καταβραβευθῆναι, is employed when the victory is with one party, and the prize with another, when though a victor thou art thwarted. Thou standest above the devil and sin ; why dost thou again subject thyself to sin? Therefore he said that " he is a debtor to fulfill the whole law " (Gal. v. 3) ; and again, " Is Christ " found to be " the minister of sin " (Gal. ii. 17)? which he said when writing to the Galatians. When he had filled them with anger through saying, " adjudge away from you," then he begins ; " being a voluntary,"³ he saith, " in humility and worshiping of Angels, intruding into things he hath not seen, vainly puffed up by his fleshly mind." How " in humility," or how " puffed up "? He shows that the whole arose out of vainglory. But what is on the whole the drift of what is said? There are some who maintain that we must be brought near by Angels, not by Christ, that were too great a thing for us. Therefore it is that he turns over and over again what has been done by Christ, " through the Blood of His Cross " (c. i. 20) ; on this account he says that " He suffered for us " ; that " He loved us." (1 Pet. ii. 21.) And besides in this very same thing, moreover, they were elevated afresh. And he said not " introduction by," but " worshiping of " Angels. " Intruding into things he hath not⁴

---

¹ LXX. has κατῴκισεν αὐτὸν ἀπέναντι τοῦ παραδείσου, " He placed him opposite Paradise." And it is generally thought that Adam approached the gate of Paradise to worship.
² [The word here rendered " respect " means primarily " part." But it is exegetically wrong to insist on this sense as Chrys. does, for the *phrase* designates the category or class of things. See Meyer or Lightfoot. — J. A. B.]

³ E. V. marg.
⁴ [" Not " is wanting in the best documents for N. T. text, and

seen." (Eph. ii. 4.) For he hath not seen Angels, and yet is affected as though he had. Therefore he saith, "Puffed up by his fleshly mind vainly," not about any true fact. About this doctrine, he is puffed up, and puts forward a show of humility. By his carnal mind, not spiritual; his reasoning is of man. "And not holding fast the Head," he saith, "from whom all the body." All the body thence hath its being, and its well-being. Why, letting go the Head, dost thou cling to the members? If thou art fallen off from it, thou art lost. "From whom all the body." Every one, be he who he may, thence has not life only, but also even connection. All the Church, so long as she holds The Head, increaseth; because here is no more passion of pride and vainglory, nor invention of human fancy.

Mark that "from [1] whom," meaning the Son. "Through the joints and bands," he says, "being supplied, and knit together, increases with the increase of God"; he means, that which is according to God, that of the best life.

Ver. 20. "If ye died with Christ."

He puts that in the middle, and on either side, expressions of greater vehemence. "If ye died with Christ from the elements of the world," he saith, "why as though living in the world do ye subject yourselves to ordinances?" This is not the consequence, for what ought to have been said is, "how as though living are ye subject to those elements?" But letting this pass, what saith he?

Ver. 21, 22. "Handle not, nor taste, nor touch; all which things are to perish with the using; after the precepts and doctrines of men."

Ye are not in the world, he saith, how is it ye are subject to its elements? how to its observances? And mark how he makes sport of them, "touch not, handle not, taste not," as though they were cowards and keeping themselves clear of some great matters, "all which things are to perish with the using." He has taken down the swollenness of the many, and added, "after the precepts and doctrines of men." What sayest thou? Dost thou speak even of the Law? Henceforth it is but a doctrine of men, after the time is come.[2] Or, because they adulterated it, or else, he alludes to the Gentile institutions. The doctrine, he says, is altogether of man.

Ver. 23. "Which things have indeed a show of wisdom in will worship, and humility, and severity to the body; but are not of any value against the indulgence of the flesh."

"Show," he saith; not power, not truth. So that even though they have a show of wisdom, let us turn away from them. For he may seem to be a religious person, and modest, and to have a contempt for the body.

"Not of any value against the indulgence of the flesh." For God hath given it honor, but they use it not with honor. Thus, when it is a doctrine, he knows how to call it honor. They dishonor the flesh, he says, depriving it, and stripping it of its liberty, not giving leave to rule it with its will. God hath honored the flesh.

Chap. iii. ver. 1. "If then ye were raised together with Christ."

He brings them together, having above established that He died. Therefore he saith, "If then ye were raised together with Christ, seek the things that are above." No observances are there. "Where Christ is seated on the right hand of God." Wonderful! Whither hath he led our minds aloft! How hath he filled them with mighty aspiration! It was not enough to say, "the things that are above," nor yet, "where Christ is," but what? "seated on the right hand of God." From that point he was preparing them henceforward to see the earth.

Ver. 2, 3, 4. "Set your mind on the things that are above, not on the things that are upon the earth. For ye died, and your life is hid with Christ in God. When Christ who is your life shall be manifested, then shall ye also with Him be manifested in glory."

This is not your life, he saith, it is some other one. He is now urgent to remove them, and insists upon showing that they are seated above, and are dead; from both considerations establishing the position, that they are not to seek the things which are here. For whether ye be dead, ye ought not to seek them; or whether ye be above, ye ought not to seek them. Doth Christ appear? Neither doth your life. It is in God, above. What then? When shall we live? When Christ shall be manifested, who is your life; then seek ye glory, then life, then enjoyment.

This is to prepare the way for drawing them off from pleasure and ease. Such is his wont: when establishing one position, he darts off to another; as, for instance, when discoursing of those who at supper were beforehand with one another, he all at once falls upon the observance of the Mysteries.[3] For he hath a great rebuke when it is administered unsuspected. "It is hid," he saith, from you. "Then shall ye also with Him be manifested." So that, now, ye do not appear. See how he hath removed them into the very heaven. For, as I said, he is always bent upon showing that they have the

---

so is rightly omitted in Rev. Ver. The participle must then take a different sense, such as dwelling in the things which he hath seen, poring over and confining himself to these. The expression is obscure, and was simplified by inserting "not." Comp. Meyer. — J. A. B.]
[1] ἐξ, which makes Him a source of action in Himself.
[2] καιρὸν, i.e. *the* time of Christ's Advent, or "after its time."

[3] See his Comment on 1 Cor. xi. 17-21. Hom. xxvii. on 1 Cor., where he says that the supper referred to was "when the solemn service was *completed, after* the Communion of the Mysteries."

very same things which Christ hath; and through all his Epistles, the tenor is this, to show that in all things they are partakers with Him. Therefore he uses the terms, Head, and Body, and does everything to convey this to them.

If therefore we shall then be manifested, let us not grieve, when we enjoy not honor: if this life be not life, but it be hidden, we ought to live this life as though dead. "Then shall ye also," he saith, "with Him be manifested in glory." "In glory," he said, not merely "manifested." For the pearl too is hidden so long as it is within the oyster. If then we be treated with insult, let us not grieve; or whatever it be we suffer; for this life is not our life, we are strangers and sojourners. "For ye died," he saith. Who is so witless, as for a corpse, dead and buried, either to buy servants, or build houses, or prepare costly raiment? None. Neither then do ye; but as we seek one thing only, namely, that we be not in a naked state, so here too let us seek one thing and no more. Our first man is buried: buried not in earth, but in water; not death-destroyed, but buried by death's destroyer, not by the law of nature, but by the governing command that is stronger than nature. For what has been done by nature, may perchance be undone; but what has been done by His command, never. Nothing is more blessed than this burial, whereat all are rejoicing, both Angels, and men, and the Lord of Angels. At this burial, no need is there of vestments, nor of coffin, nor of anything else of that kind. Wouldest thou see the symbol of this? I will show thee a pool wherein the one was buried, the other raised; in the Red Sea the Egyptians were sunk beneath it, but the Israelites went up from out of it; in the same act he buries the one, generates the other.

Marvel not that generation and destruction take place in Baptism; for, tell me, dissolving and cementing, are they not opposite? It is evident to all. Such is the effect of fire; for fire dissolves and destroys wax, but it cements together metallic earth, and works it into gold. So in truth here also, the force of the fire, having obliterated the statue of wax, has displayed a golden one in its stead; for in truth before the Bath we were of clay, but after it of gold. Whence is this evident? Hear him saying, "The first man is of the earth, earthy, the second man is the Lord from heaven." (1 Cor. xv. 47.) I spoke of a difference as great as that between clay and gold; but greater still do I find the difference between heavenly and earthy; not so widely do clay and gold differ, as do things earthy and heavenly. Waxen we were, and clay-formed. For the flame of lust did much more melt us, than fire doth wax, and any chance temptation did far rather shatter us

than a stone doth things of clay. And, if ye will, let us give an outline of the former life, and see whether all was not earth and water, and full of fluctuation and dust, and instability, and flowing away.

And if ye will, let us scrutinize not the former things, but the present, and see whether we shall not find everything that is, mere dust and water. For what wilt thou tell me of? authority and power? for nothing in this present life is thought to be more enviable than these. But sooner may one find the dust when on the air stationary, than these things; especially now. For to whom are they not under subjection? To those who are lovers of them; to eunuchs; to those who will do anything for the sake of money; to the passions of the populace; to the wrath of the more powerful. He who was yesterday up high on his tribunal,[1] who had his heralds shouting with thrilling voice, and many to run before, and haughtily clear the way for him through the forum, is to-day mean and low, and of all those things bereft and bare, like dust blast-driven, like a stream that hath passed by. And like as the dust is raised by our feet, so truly are magistracies also produced by those who are engaged about money, and in the whole of life have the rank and condition of feet; and like as the dust when it is raised occupies a large portion of the air, though itself be but a small body, so too doth power; and like as the dust blindeth the eyes, so too doth the pride of power bedim the eyes of the understanding.

But what? Wilt thou that we examine that object of many prayers, wealth? Come, let us examine it in its several parts. It hath luxury, it hath honors, it hath power. First then, if thou wilt, let us examine luxury. Is it not dust? yea, rather, it goeth by swifter than dust, for the pleasure of luxurious living reacheth only to the tongue, and when the belly is filled, not to the tongue even. But, saith one, honors are of themselves pleasant things. Yet what can be less pleasant than that same honor, when it is rendered with a view to money? When it is not from free choice and with a readiness of mind, it is not thou that reapest the honor, but thy wealth. So that this very thing makes the man of wealth, most of all men, dishonored. For, tell me; suppose all men honored thee, who hadst a friend; the while confessing that thou, to be sure, wert good for nothing, but that they were compelled to honor thee on his account; could they possibly in any other way have so dishonored thee? So that our wealth is the cause of dishonor to us, seeing it is more honored than are its very possessors, and a

---

[1] Montfaucon thinks this refers to Eutropius, whose disgrace occasioned two Homilies of St. Chrys. Ben. t. iii. This is questioned in the recent Paris Edition.

proof rather of weakness than of power. How then is it not absurd that we are not counted of as much value as earth and ashes, (for such is gold,) but that we are honored for its sake? With reason. But not so he that despiseth wealth; for it were better not to be honored at all, than so honored. For tell me, were one to say to thee, I think thee worthy of no honor at all, but for thy servants' sakes I honor thee, could now anything be worse than this dishonor? But if to be honored for the sake of servants, who are partakers of the same soul and nature with ourselves, be a disgrace, much more then is it such, to be honored for the sake of meaner things, such as the walls and courts of houses, and vessels of gold, and garments. A scorn indeed were this, and shame; better die than be so honored. For, tell me, if thou wert in peril in this thy pride, and some low and disgusting person were to be willing to extricate thee from thy peril, what could be worse than this? What ye say one to another about the city, I wish to say to you. Once on a time our[1] city gave offense to the Emperor,[2] and he gave orders that the whole of it should utterly be destroyed, men, children, houses, and all. (For such is the wrath of kings, they indulge their power as much as ever they choose, so great an evil is power.) It was then in the extremest of perils. The neighboring city, however, this one on the sea-coast, went and besought the king in our behalf: upon which the inhabitants of our city said that this was worse than if the city had been razed to the ground. So, to be thus honored is worse than being dishonored. For see whence honor hath its root. The hands of cooks procure us to be honored, so that to them we ought to feel gratitude; and swineherds supplying us with a rich table, and weavers, and spinners, and workers in metal, and confectioners, and table furnishers.

Were it not then better not to be honored at all, than to be beholden to these for the honor? And besides this, moreover, I will endeavor to prove clearly that opulence is a condition full of dishonor; it embases the soul; and what is more dishonorable than this? For tell me, suppose one had a comely person, and passing all in beauty, and wealth were to go to him and promise to make it ugly, and instead of healthy, diseased, instead of cool, inflamed; and having filled every limb with dropsy, were to make the

countenance bloated, and distend it all over; and were to swell out the feet, and make them heavier than logs, and to puff up the belly, and make it larger than any tun; and after this, it should promise not even to grant permission to cure him, to those who should be desirous of doing so, (for such is the way with power,) but would give him so much liberty as to punish any one that should approach him to withdraw him from what was harming him; well then, tell me, when wealth works these effects in the soul, how can it be honorable?

But this power is a more grievous thing than the disease itself; as for one in disease not to be obedient to the physician's injunctions is a more serious evil than the being diseased; and this is the case with wealth, seeing it creates inflammation in every part of the soul, and forbids the physicians to come near it. So let us not felicitate these on the score of their power, but pity them; for neither were I to see a dropsical patient lying, and nobody forbidding him to take his fill of whatever drinks he pleased and of meats that are harmful, would I felicitate him because of his power. For not in all cases is power a good thing, nor are honors either, for these too fill one with much arrogance. But if thou wouldest not choose that the body should along with wealth contract such a disease, how comest thou to overlook the soul, and when contracting not this scourge alone, but another also? For it is on fire all over with burning fevers and inflammations, and that burning fever none can quench, for wealth will not allow of this, having persuaded it that those things are gains, which are really losses, such as not enduring any one and doing everything at will. For no other soul will one find so replete with lusts so great and so extravagant, as theirs who are desirous of being rich. For what silly trifles do they not picture to themselves! One may see these devising more extravagant things than limners of hippocentaurs, and chimæras, and dragon-footed things, and Scyllas, and monsters. And if one should choose to give a picture of one lust of theirs, neither Scylla, nor chimæra, nor · hippocentaur will appear anything at all by the side of such a prodigy; but you will find it to contain every wild beast at once.

And perchance some one will suppose that I have been myself possessed of much wealth, seeing I am so true to what really comes of it. It is reported of one (for I will first confirm what I have said from the legends of the Greeks) — it is reported amongst them of a certain king, that he became so insolent in luxury, as to make a plane tree of gold,[3] and

---

[1] i.e. his native Antioch.
[2] τῷ κρατοῦντι, the Emperor Theodosius. This was preached under his successor Arcadius. For an account of the events referred to, see Pref. to Homilies on the Statues. The "neighboring city," however, is not named there, though the sympathy of neighboring cities is mentioned in Hom. ii. It is supposed to be Seleucia. ["Our city" might be naturally used to denote what *was*, at the time of which he is speaking, the city of himself and his fellow-citizens. See above, Hom. iii., near the end, the clear proof that these homilies on Colossians were delivered in Constantinople. — J. A. B.]

[3] Ed. Par. refers to Herod. vii. 27, where such a tree is men-

a sky above it, and there sate, and this too when invading a people skilled in warfare. Now was not this lust hippocentaurean, was it not Scyllæan? Another, again, used[1] to cast men into a wooden bull. Was not this a very Scylla? And even him,[2] the king I just mentioned, the warrior,[3] wealth made, from a man, a woman, from a woman, what shall I say? a brute beast, and yet more degraded than this; for the beasts, if they lodge under a tree, take up with nature, and seek for nothing further; but the man in question overshot the nature even of beasts.

What then can be more senseless than are the wealthy? And this arises from the greediness of their desires. But, are there not many that admire him? Therefore truly do they share in the laughter he incurs. That displayed not his wealth but his folly. How much better than that golden plane tree is that which the earth produceth! For the natural is more grateful than the unnatural. But what meant that thy golden heaven, O senseless one? Seest thou how wealth that is abundant maketh men mad? How it inflamed them? I suppose he knows not the sea even, and perchance will presently have a mind to walk upon it.[4] Now is not this a chimæra? is it not a hippocentaur? But there are, at this time also, some who fall not short even of him, but are actually much more senseless. For in point of senselessness, wherein do they differ, tell me, from that golden plane tree, who make silver jars, pitchers, and scent bottles? And wherein do those women differ, (ashamed indeed I am, but it is necessary to speak it,) who make chamber utensils of silver?[5] It is ye should be ashamed, that are the makers of these things. When Christ is famishing, dost thou so revel in luxury? yea rather, so play the fool! What punishment shall these not suffer? And inquirest thou still, why there are robbers? why murderers? why such evils? when the devil has thus made you ridiculous. For the mere having of silver dishes indeed, this even is not in keeping with a soul devoted to wisdom, but is altogether a piece of luxury; but the making unclean vessels also of silver, is this then luxury? nay, I will not call it luxury, but senselessness; nay, nor yet this, but madness; nay rather, worse than even madness.

I know that many persons make jokes at me

for this; but I heed them not, only let some good result from it. In truth, to be wealthy does make people senseless and mad. Did their power reach to such an excess, they would have the earth too of gold, and walls of gold, perchance the heaven too, and the air of gold. What a madness is this, what an iniquity, what a burning fever! Another, made after the image of God, is perishing of cold; and dost thou furnish thyself with such things as these? O the senseless pride! What more would a madman have done? Dost thou pay such honor to thine excrements, as to receive them in silver? I know that ye are shocked at hearing this; but those women that make such things ought to be shocked, and the husbands that minister to such distempers. For this is wantonness, and savageness, and inhumanity, and brutishness, and lasciviousness. What Scylla, what chimæra, what dragon, yea rather what demon, what devil would have acted on this wise? What is the benefit of Christ? what of the Faith? when one has to put up with men being heathens, yea rather, not heathens, but demons? If to adorn the head with gold and pearls be not right; one that useth silver for a service so unclean, how shall he obtain pardon? Is not the rest enough, although even it is not bearable, chairs and footstools all of silver? although even these come of senselessness. But everywhere is excessive pride; everywhere is vainglory. Nowhere is it use, but everywhere excess.

I am afraid lest, under the impulse of this madness, the race of woman should go on to assume some portentous form: for it is likely that they will wish to have even their hair of gold. Else declare that ye were not[6] at all affected by what was said, nor were excited greatly, and fell a longing, and had not shame withheld you, would not have refused. For if they dare to do what is even more absurd than this, much more, I think, will they long for their hair, and lips, and eyebrows, and every part to be overlaid with molten gold.

But if ye are incredulous, and think I am speaking in jest, I will relate what I have heard, or rather what is now existing. The king of the Persians wears his beard golden; those who are adepts at such work winding leaf of gold about his hairs as about the woof, and it is laid up as a prodigy.

Glory to Thee, O Christ; with how many good things hast Thou filled us! How hast Thou provided for our health! From how great monstrousness, from how great unreasonable-

---

tioned as given to Darius; also to Diod. Sic. xix. 49, and Brisson de Regn. Pers. l. i. c. 77.

[1] Sav. ἐνέβαλλε. He must mean the brazen bull of Phalaris.

[2] τέως δὲ τῶν πρότερον. And besides among them of earlier times, wealth made that king, the warrior, from a man, a woman; from a woman, what shall I say? Savile τὸν, which is better, and neglected by Ed. Par. The sequel shows that the same king is meant.

[3] [The syntax is obscure, and the passage probably corrupt; but the general meaning is plain. — J. A. B.]

[4] Alluding to Xerxes, see Herod. vii. 35.

[5] ἀμίδας. St. Clem. Al. mentions the like absurdity, Pædag. ii. 3.

[6] [The "not," though found in all documents, seems (Field) quite out of place. Without it, the meaning is, "Now confess that you were somewhat attracted towards the idea expressed, and started up, and fell a longing," &c. Copyists probably understood "the thing said" to be the rebuke just given, and hence felt the "not" to be necessary. — J. A. B.]

ness, hast Thou set us free ! Mark ! I forewarn you, I advise no longer ; but I command and charge ; let him that wills, obey, and him that wills not, be disobedient ; that if ye women do continue thus to act, I will not suffer it, nor receive you, nor permit you to pass across this threshold. For what need have I of a crowd of distempered people ? And what if, in my training of you, I do not forbid what is not[1] excessive ? And yet Paul forbade both gold and pearls. (1 Tim. ii. 9.) We are laughed at by the Greeks, our religion appears a fable.

And to the men I give this advice : Art thou come to school to be instructed in spiritual philosophy ? Divest thyself of that pride ! This is my advice both to men and women ; and if any act otherwise, henceforward I will not suffer it. The disciples were but twelve, and hear what Christ saith unto them, "Would ye also go away ?" (John vi. 67.) For if we go on for ever flattering you, when shall we reclaim you ? when shall we do you service ? "But," saith one, "there are other sects, and people go over." This is a cold argument, "Better is one that doeth the will of the Lord, than ten thousand transgressors." (Ecclus. xvi. 3.) For, what wouldest thou choose thyself, tell me ; to have ten thousand servants that were runaways and thieves, or a single one that loved thee ? Lo ! I admonish and command you to break up both those gay deckings for the face, and such vessels as I have described, and give to the poor, and not to be so mad.

Let him that likes quit me at once ; let him that likes accuse me, I will not suffer it in any one. When I am about to be judged at the Tribunal of Christ, ye stand afar off, and your favor, while I am giving in my account. "Those words have ruined all ! he says,[3] 'let him not[4] go and transfer himself to another sect !' Nay ! he is weak ! condescend to him !" To what point ? Till when ? Once, and twice, and thrice, but not perpetually.

Lo ! I charge you again, and protest after the pattern of the blessed Paul, "that if I come again I will not spare." (2 Cor. xiii. 2.) But when ye have done as ye ought, then ye will know how great the gain is, how great the advantage. Yes ! I entreat and beseech you, and would not refuse to clasp your knees and supplicate you[5] in this behalf. What softness is it ! What luxury, what wantonness ! This is not luxury, but wantonness. What senselessness is it ! What madness ! So many poor stand around the Church ; and though the Church has so many children, and so wealthy, she is unable to give relief to even one poor person ; "but one is hungry, and another is drunken" (1 Cor. xi. 21) ; one voideth his excrement even into silver, another has not so much as bread ! What madness ! what brutishness so great as this ? May we never come to the proof, whether we will prosecute the disobedient, nor to the indignation which allowing[6] these practices would cause us ; but that willingly and with patience we may avoid all this, that we may live to God's glory, and be delivered from. the punishment in the other world, and may obtain the good things promised to those who love Him, through the grace and love toward man, &c.

HOMILY VIII.

COLOSSIANS iii. 5-7.

"Mortify your members which are upon the earth; fornication, uncleanness, passion, evil desire, and covetousness, which is idolatry; for which things' sake, cometh the wrath of God upon the sons of disobedience; in the which ye also walked aforetime, when ye lived in these things."

I KNOW that many are offended by the foregoing discourse, but what can I do? ye heard what the Master enjoined. Am I to blame? what shall I do? See ye not the creditors, when debtors are obstinate, how they wear[2] collars? Heard ye what Paul proclaimed today? "Mortify," he saith, "your members which are upon the earth ; fornication, uncleanness, passion, evil desire, and covetousness, which is idolatry." What is worse than such a covetousness? This is worse than any desire. This is still more grievous than what I was speaking of, the madness, and the silly weakness about silver. "And covetousness," he

---

[1] [Here again the "not" seems unsuitable, if not destructive of the sense, and is omitted by Field. — J. A. B.]

[2] [This very natural inadvertence in free speaking is duly changed, by the group of MSS. which make so many changes, into "how they put collars on them." These wooden collars were a disgrace, like the stocks. — J. A. B.]

[3] i.e. the Preacher says.

[4] [Field inserts "not" upon the authority of one MS. The sentence is intelligible without it. — J. A. B.]

[5] ἱκετηρίαν θεῖναι. He alludes to the ancient custom of formally supplicating for defense or relief, as by sitting on the hearth. Sophocl. Œd. Tyr. 1, &c.

[6] ἐπιτρέψαι. Perhaps ἐπιτρῖψαι, "aggravating," as Ben. t. i. p. 24. B, and p. 225. A.

saith, "which is idolatry." See in what the evil ends. Do not, I pray, take what I said amiss, for not by my own good-will, nor without reason, would I have enemies; but I was wishful ye should attain to such virtue, as that I might hear of you the things I ought.[1] So that I said it not for authority's sake, nor of imperiousness,[2] but out of pain and of sorrow. Forgive me, forgive! I have no wish to violate decency by discoursing upon such subjects, but I am compelled to it.

Not for the sake of the sorrows of the poor do I say these things, but for your salvation; for they will perish, will perish, that have not fed Christ. For what, if thou dost feed some poor man? still so long as thou livest so voluptuously and luxuriously, all is to no purpose. For what is required is, not the giving much, but not too little for the property thou hast; for this is but playing at it.

" Mortify therefore your members," he saith, " which are upon the earth." What sayest thou? Was it not thou that saidst, " Ye are buried; ye are buried together with Him; ye are circumcised: we have put off the body of the sins of the flesh " (c. ii. 11, 12 ; Rom. vi. 4) ; how then again sayest thou, " Mortify"?[3] Art thou sporting? Dost thou thus discourse, as though those things were in us? There is no contradiction; but like as if one, who has clean scoured a statue that was filthy, or rather who has recast it, and displayed it bright afresh,[4] should say that the rust was eaten off and destroyed, and yet should again recommend diligence in clearing away the rust, he doth not contradict himself, for it is not that rust which he scoured off that he recommends should be cleared away, but that which grew afterwards; so it is not that former putting to death he speaks of, nor those fornications, but those which do afterwards grow.

He said that this is not our life, but another, that which is in heaven. Tell me now. When he said, Mortify your members that are upon the earth, is then the earth also accused? or does he speak of the things upon the earth as themselves sins?[5]

" Fornication, uncleanness," he saith. He has passed over the actions which it is not becoming even to mention, and by " uncleanness " has expressed all together.

" Passion," he said, " evil desire."

Lo! he has expressed the whole in the class. For envy, anger, sorrow, all are " evil desire."

" And covetousness," he saith, " which is idolatry. For which things' sake cometh the wrath of God upon the sons of disobedience."

By many things he had been withdrawing them; by the benefits which are already given, by the evils to come from which we had been delivered, being who, and wherefore; and all those considerations, as, for instance, who we were, and in what circumstances, and that we were delivered therefrom, how, and in what manner, and on what terms. These were enough to turn one away, but this one is of greater force than all; unpleasant indeed to speak of, not however to disservice, but even serviceable. " For which things' sake cometh," he saith, " the wrath of God upon the sons of disobedience." He said not, " upon you," but, " upon the sons of disobedience."

" In the which ye also walked aforetime, when ye lived in them." In order to shame them, he saith, " when ye lived in them," and implying praise, as now no more so living: at that time they might.

Ver. 8. " But now put ye also away all these."

He speaks always both universally and particularly; but this is from earnestness.

Ver. 8, 9. " Anger, wrath, malice, railing, shameful speaking out of your mouth. Lie not one to another."

" Shameful speaking," he saith, " out of your mouth," clearly intimating that it pollutes it.

Ver. 9, 10. " Seeing that ye have put off the old man with his doings, and have put on the new man, which is being renewed unto knowledge after the image of Him that created him."

It is worth enquiring here, what can be the reason why he calls the corrupt life, " members," and " man," and " body," and again the virtuous life, the same. And if " the man " means " sins," how is it that he saith, " with his doings "? For once he said, " the old man," showing that this is not man, but the other. The moral choice doth rather determine one than the substance, and is rather " man " than the other. For his substance casteth him not into hell, nor leadeth him into the kingdom, but men themselves : and we neither love nor hate any one so far as he is man, but so far as he is such or such a man. If then the substance be the body, and in either sort cannot be accountable, how doth he say that it is evil?[6] But what is that he saith, " with

---

[1] Or perhaps, " I could wish . . . that I might hear from you what is right." Gr. παρ᾽ ὑμῶν.

[2] ἀξιώματος, wish to maintain dignity.

[3] i.e. put to death.

[4] [The word is ἄνωθεν, as in John iii. 3, 7, and here necessarily means anew or afresh, — a sense so rare as to justify calling attention to it. — J. A. B.]

[5] [This is a passing allusion to the Manichæans, who held that matter is necessarily the seat of evil, and might try to interpret the apostle as here accusing the earth of being evil. The passage has been expanded in the often above mentioned group of documents, and so in the editions before Field, so as to be fuller and more perspicuous, thus: " But lo! say the heretics, Paul accuseth the creation; for he said before, ' Set your mind on the things that are above, not on the things that are upon the earth'; again he saith, ' Mortify your members which are upon the earth.' But the words ' upon earth' are here expressive of sin, not an accusing of creation. For it is thus he calls sins themselves, things upon earth, either from their being wrought by earthly thoughts and upon earth, or from their showing sinners to be earthly." — J. A. B.]

[6] As the Manichees interpreted his words.

his doings"? He means the choice, with the acts. And he calleth him "old," on purpose to show his deformity, and hideousness, and imbecility; and "new," as if to say, Do not expect that it will be with this one even as with the other, but the reverse: for ever as he farther advances, he hasteneth not on to old age, but to a youthfulness greater than the preceding. For when he hath received a fuller knowledge, he is both counted worthy of greater things, and is in more perfect maturity, in higher vigor; and this, not from youthfulness alone, but from that "likeness" also, "after" which he is. Lo! the best life is styled a creation, after the image of Christ: for this is the meaning of, "after the image of Him that created him," for Christ too came not finally to[1] old age, but was so beautiful as it is not possible to tell.

Ver. 11. "Where there cannot be Greek and Jew, circumcision and uncircumcision, Barbarian, Scythian, bondman, freeman: but Christ is all, and in all."

Lo! here is a third encomium of this "man." With him, there is no difference admitted either of nation, or of rank, or of ancestry, seeing he hath nothing of externals, nor needeth them; for all external things are such as these, "circumcision, and uncircumcision, bondman, freeman, Greek," that is, proselyte, "and Jew," from his ancestors. If thou have only this "man," thou wilt obtain the same things with the others that have him.

"But Christ," he saith, "is all, and in all": Christ will be all things to you, both rank, and descent, "and" Himself "in you all." Or he says another thing, to wit, that ye all are become one Christ, being His body.

Ver. 12. "Put on, therefore, as the elect of God, holy and beloved."

He shows the easiness of virtue, so that they might both possess it continually, and use it as the greatest ornament. The exhortation is accompanied also with praise, for then its force is greatest. For they had been before[2] holy, but not elect; but now both "elect, and holy, and beloved."

"A heart of compassion." He said not "mercy," but with greater emphasis used the two words. And he said not, that it should be as towards brethren, but, as fathers towards children. For tell me not that he sinned, therefore he said "a heart." And he said not "compassion,"[3] lest he should place them[3] in light estimation, but "a heart of compassion, kindness, humility, meekness, longsuffering; forbearing

one another, and forgiving each other, if any man have a complaint against any: even as Christ forgave you, so also do ye."

Again, he speaks after the class,[4] and he always does it; for from kindness comes humbleness of mind, and from this, longsuffering. "Forbearing," he saith, "one another," that is, passing things over.[5] And see, how he has shown it to be nothing, by calling it a "complaint," and saying, "even as Christ forgave you." Great is the example! and thus he always does; he exhorts them after Christ. "Complaint," he calls it. In these words indeed he showed it to be a petty matter; but when he has set before us the example, he has persuaded us that even if we had serious charges to bring, we ought to forgive. For the expression, "Even as Christ," signifies this, and not this only, but also with all the heart; and not this alone, but that they ought even to love. For Christ being brought into the midst, bringeth in all these things, both that even if the matters be great, and even if we have not been the first to injure, even if we be of great, they of small account, even if they are sure to insult us afterwards, we ought to lay down our lives for them, (for the words, "even as," demand this;) and that not even at death only ought one to stop, but if possible, to go on even after death.

Ver. 14. "And above all these things put on love, which is the bond of perfectness."

Dost thou see that he saith this? For since it is possible for one who forgives, not to love; yea, he saith, thou must love him too, and he points out a way whereby it becomes possible to forgive. For it is possible for one to be kind, and meek, and humbleminded, and longsuffering, and yet not affectionate. And therefore, he said at the first, "A heart of compassion," both love and pity. "And above all these things, love, which is the bond of perfectness." Now what he wishes to say is this; that there is no profit in those things, for all those things fall asunder, except they be done with love; this it is which clenches them all together; whatsoever good thing it be thou mentionest, if love be away, it is nothing, it melts away. And it is as in a ship, even though her rigging be large, yet if there be no girding ropes, it is of no service; and in an house, if there be no tie beams, it is the same; and in a body, though the bones be large, if there be no ligaments, they are of no service. For whatsoever good deeds any may have, all do vanish away, if love be not there. He said not that it is the summit, but what is greater, "the bond"; this is more necessary than the other. For "summit" indeed is an intensity of perfectness, but "bond" is the holding fast

---

[1] οὐ πρὸς γῆρας ἐτελεύτησεν, Lat. "Nec senex mortuus est" (died not old). But the other sense seems more suitable. In either sense it is opposed to the view ascribed to Byzantine artists. See Rio's Poésie Chrétienne.

[2] ἐγένοντο, i.e. he had before called them holy, c. l. v. 2.

[3] ἐκείνους, "the objects."

[4] κατ᾽ εἶδος, from genus to species, as remarked above, on v. 7.

[5] παραπεμπόμενοι, al. παραδεχόμενοι, "receiving one another."

together of those things which produce the perfectness; it is, as it were, the root.

Ver. 15. "And let the peace of God rule in your hearts, to the which also ye were called in one body; and be ye thankful."

"The peace of God." This is that which is fixed and steadfast. If on man's account indeed thou hast peace, it quickly comes to dissolution, but if on God's account, never. Although he had spoken of love universally, yet again he comes to the particular. For there is a love too which is immoderate; for instance, when out of much love one makes accusations without reason, and is engaged in contentions, and contracts aversions. Not this, saith he, not this do I desire; not overdoing things,[1] but as God made peace with you, so do ye also make it. How made He peace? Of His own will, not having received anything of you. What is this? "Let the peace of God rule[2] in your hearts." If two thoughts are fighting together, set not anger, set not spitefulness to hold the prize, but peace; for instance, suppose one to have been insulted unjustly; of the insult are born two thoughts, the one bidding him to revenge, the other to endure; and these wrestle with one another: if the Peace of God stand forward as umpire, it bestows the prize on that which bids endure, and puts the other to shame. How? by persuading him that God is Peace, that He hath made peace with us. Not without reason he shows the great struggle there is in the matter. Let not anger, he saith, act as umpire, let not contentiousness, let not human peace, for human peace cometh of avenging, of suffering no dreadful ill. But not this do I intend, he saith, but that which He Himself left.

He hath represented an arena within, in the thoughts, and a contest, and a wrestling, and an umpire. Then again, exhortation, "to the which ye were called," he saith, that is, for the which ye were called. He has reminded them of how many good things peace is the cause; on account of this He called thee, for this He called thee, so as to receive a worthy[3] prize. For wherefore made He us "one body"? Was it not that she might rule? Was it not that we might have occasion of being at peace? Wherefore are we all one body? and now are we one body? Because of peace we are one body, and because we are one body, we are at peace. But why said he not, "Let the peace of God be victorious," but "be umpire"? He made her the more honorable. He would not have the evil thought to come to wrestle with her, but to stand

below. And the very name "prize" cheered the hearer. For if she have given the prize to the good thought, however impudently the other behave, it is thereafter of no use. And besides, the other being aware that, perform what feats he might, he should not receive the prize; however he might puff, and attempt still more vehement onsets, would desist as laboring without profit. And he well added, "And be ye thankful." For this is to be thankful, and very effectively,[4] to deal with his fellow-servants as God doth with himself, to submit himself to the Master, to obey; to express his gratitude for all things,[5] even though one insult him, or beat him.

For in truth he that confesses thanks due to God for what he suffers, will not revenge himself on him that has done him wrong, since he at least that takes revenge, acknowledges no gratitude. But let not us follow him (that exacted)[6] the hundred pence, lest we hear, "Thou wicked servant," for nothing is worse than this ingratitude. So that they who revenge are ungrateful.

But why did he begin his list with fornication? For having said, "Mortify your members which are upon the earth" (c. iii. 5), he immediately says, "fornication"; and so he does almost everywhere. Because this passion hath the greatest sway. For even when writing his Epistle to the Thessalonians he did the same. (1 Thess. iv. 3.) And what wonder? since to Timothy even he saith, "Keep thyself pure" (1 Tim. v. 22); and again elsewhere, "Follow after peace with all men, and the sanctification," without which "no man shall see the Lord." (Heb. xii. 14.) "Put to death," he says, "your members." Ye know of what sort that is which is dead, namely, hated, loathed, dropping to decay. If thou put anything to death, it doth not when dead continue dead, but presently is corrupted, like the body. Extinguish then the heat; and nothing that is dead will continue. He shows one having the same thing in hand, which Christ wrought in the Laver; therefore also he calleth them "members," as though introducing some champion, thus advancing his discourse to greater emphasis. And he well said, "Which are upon the earth," for here they continue, and here they are corrupted, far rather than these our members. So that not so truly is the body of the earth, as sin is earthly, for the former indeed appears even beautiful at times, but those members never. And those members lust after all things that are

---

[1] [Literally, "not superperfectly," a singular expression, omitted in all editions before Field, but found in all the MSS. he cites. — J. A. B.]

[2] [Literally, act as umpire, or as judge in the games. — J. A. B.]

[3] ἀξιόπιστον. Usually "worthy of credit," but sometimes rather in a secondary sense, "worthy of honor."

[4] This must mean "in a way that has power of prevailing with God," so to speak, "putting Him to shame, if he do not grant the favor." Comp. Hebrew vi. 10.

[5] [Compare Chrys.'s famous motto, "Glory to God for all things." — J. A. B.]

[6] Sav. [and one MS.] has ὀφείλοντα, "that owed," which makes no sense; MSS. Par. only τὸν τὰ ἑκατὸν; Downes conj. ἀπαιτοῦντα τά.

upon the earth. If the eye be such, it seeth not the things in the heavens; if the ear, if the hand, if thou mention any other member whatsoever. The eye seeth bodies, and beauties, and riches; these are the things of earth, with these it is delighted: the ear with soft strains, and harp, and pipe, and filthy talking; these are things which are concerned with earth.

When therefore he has placed his hearers above, near the throne, he then says, "Mortify your members which are upon the earth." For it is not possible to stand above with these members; for there is nothing there for them to work upon. And this clay is worse than that, for that clay indeed becometh gold, "for this corruptible," he saith, "must put on incorruption" (1 Cor. xv. 53), but this clay can never be retempered more. So that these members are rather "upon the earth" than those. Therefore he said not, "of the earth," but, "which are upon the earth," for it is possible that these should not be upon the earth. For it is necessary that these[1] should be "upon the earth," but that those[2] should, is not necessary. For when the ear hears nothing of what is here uttered, but only in the heavens, when the eye sees nothing of what is here, but only what is above, it is not "upon the earth"; when the mouth speaketh nothing of the things here, it is not "upon the earth"; when the hand doeth no evil thing — these are not of things "upon the earth," but of those in the heavens.

So Christ also saith, "If thy right eye causeth thee to stumble," that is, if thou lookest unchastely, "cut it out" (Matt. v. 29), that is, thine evil thought. And he (Paul) seems to me to speak of "fornication, uncleanness, passion, desire," as the same, namely fornication: by means of all these expressions drawing us away from that thing. For in truth this is "a passion"; and like as the body is subject to any affection, either to fever or to wounds, so also is it with this. And he said not Restrain, but "Mortify" (put to death), so that they never rise up more, and "put them away." That which is dead, we put away; for instance, if there be callosities in the body, their body is dead, and we put it away. Now, if thou cut into that which is quick, it produces pain, but if into that which is dead, we are not even sensible of it. So, in truth, is it with the passions; they make the soul unclean; they make the soul, which is immortal, passible.

How covetousness is said to be idolatry, we have oftentimes explained. For the things which do most of all lord it over the human race, are these, covetousness, and unchasteness, and evil desire. "For which things' sake cometh," he

saith, "the wrath of God upon the sons of disobedience." Sons of disobedience, he calls them, to deprive them of excuse, and to show that it was because they would not be obedient, that they were in that condition. "In the which ye also," he saith, "walked aforetime," and (afterward) became obedient. He points them out as still in them, and praises them, saying, "But now do ye also put away all these, anger, wrath, malice, railing, shameful speaking." But against others he advanceth his discourse. Under the head of "passion and railing" he means revilings, just as under "wrath" he means wickedness.[3] And in another place, to shame them, he says, "for we are members one of another." (Eph. iv. 25.) He makes them out to be as it were manufacturers of men; casting away this one, and receiving that. He spoke of a man's "members" (v. 5); here he saith, "all." He spoke of his heart, wrath, mouth, blasphemy, eyes, fornication, covetousness, hands and feet, lying, the understanding itself, and the old mind. One royal form it hath, that, namely, of Christ. They whom he has in view, appear to me rather to be of the Gentiles. For like as earth, being but sand, even though one part be greater, another less, losing its own previous form, doth afterwards become gold; and like as wool, of whatever kind it be, receiveth another aspect, and hides its former one: so truly is it also with the faithful. "Forbearing," he saith, "one another"; he showeth what is just. Thou forbearest him, and he thee; and so he says in the Epistle to the Galatians, "Bear ye one another's burdens." (Gal. vi. 2.) "And be ye thankful," he saith. For this is what he everywhere especially seeks; the chiefest of good things.

Give we thanks then in all things; whatever may have happened; for this is thankfulness. For to do so in prosperity indeed, is no great thing, for the nature of the circumstances of itself impels one thereto; but when being in extremities we give thanks, then it is admirable. For when, in circumstances under which others blaspheme, and exclaim discontentedly, we give thanks, see how great philosophy is here. First, thou hast rejoiced God; next, thou hast shamed the devil; thirdly, thou hast even made that which hath happened to be nothing; for all at once, thou both givest thanks, and God cuts short the pain, and the devil departs. For if thou have exclaimed discontentedly, he, as having succeeded to his wish, standeth close by thee, and God, as being blasphemed, leaveth thee, and thy calamity is heightened; but if thou have given thanks, he, as gaining nought, departs; and God, as being honored, requites

---

[1] The sinful passions.　　　[2] The bodily organs.

[3] He means that the word used expresses a natural emotion or act, but the abuse of this is intended; and so it may be necessary to speak evil of one.

thee with greater honor. And it is not possible, that a man, who giveth thanks for his evils, should be sensible of them. For his soul rejoiceth, as doing what is right; forthwith his conscience is bright, it exults in its own commendation; and that soul which is bright, cannot possibly be sad of countenance. But in the other case, along with the misfortune, conscience also assails him with her lash; whilst in this, she crowns, and proclaims him.

Nothing is holier than that tongue, which in evils giveth thanks to God; truly in no respect doth it fall short of that of martyrs; both are alike crowned, both this, and they. For over this one also stands the executioner to force it to deny God, by blasphemy; the devil stands over it, torturing it with executioner thoughts, darkening it with despondencies. If then one bear his griefs, and give thanks, he hath gained a crown of martyrdom. For instance, is her little child sick, and doth she give God thanks? this is a crown to her. What torture so bad that despondency is not worse? still it doth not force her to vent forth a bitter word. It dies: again she hath given thanks. She hath become the daughter of Abraham. For if she sacrificed not with her own hand, yet was she pleased with the sacrifice, which is the same; she felt no indignation when the gift was taken away.

Again, is her child sick? She hath made no amulets.[1] It is counted to her as martyrdom, for she sacrificed her son in her resolve. For what, even though those things are unavailing, and a mere cheat and mockery, still there were nevertheless those who persuaded her that they do avail: and she chose rather to see her child dead, than to put up with idolatry. As then she is a martyr, whether it be in her own case, or in her son's, that she hath thus acted; or in her husband's, or in any other's of her dearest; so is that other one an idolatress. For it is evident that she would have done sacrifice, had it been allowed her to do sacrifice; yea, rather, she hath even now performed the act of sacrifice. For these amulets, though they who make money by them are forever rationalizing about them, and saying, "we call upon God, and do nothing extraordinary," and the like; and "the old woman is a Christian," says he, "and one of the faithful"; the thing is idolatry. Art thou one of the faithful? sign the Cross; say, this I have for my only weapon; this for my remedy; and other I know none. Tell me, if a physician should come to one, and, neglecting the remedies belonging to his art, should use incantation, should we call that man a physician? By no means: for we see not the medi-

cines of the healing art; so neither, in this case, do we see those of Christianity.

Other women again tie about them[2] the names of rivers, and venture numberless things of like nature. Lo, I say, and forewarn you all, that if any be detected, I will not spare them again, whether they have made amulet, or incantation, or any other thing of such an art as this. What then, saith one, is the child to die? If he have lived through this means, he did then die, but if he have died without this, he then lived. But now, if thou seest him attaching himself to harlots, thou wishest him buried, and sayest, "why, what good is it for him to live?" but when thou seest him in peril of his salvation, dost thou wish to see him live? Heardest thou not Christ saying, "He that loseth his life, shall find it; and he that findeth it, shall lose it"? (Matt. xvi. 25.) Believest thou these sayings, or do they seem to thee fables? Tell me now, should one say, "Take him away to an idol temple, and he will live"; wouldest thou endure it? No! she replies. Why? "Because," she saith, "he urges me to commit idolatry; but here, there is no idolatry, but simple incantation:" this is the device of Satan, this is that wiliness of the devil to cloak over the deceit, and to give the deleterious drug in honey. After he found that he could not prevail with thee in the other way,[3] he hath gone this way about, to stitched charms, and old wives' fables; and the Cross indeed is dishonored, and these charms preferred before it. Christ is cast out, and a drunken and silly old woman is brought in. That mystery of ours is trodden under foot, and the imposture of the devil dances.

Wherefore then, saith one, doth not God reprove the aid from such sources? He hath many times reproved, and yet hath not persuaded thee; He now leaveth thee to thine error, for It saith, "God gave them up unto a reprobate mind." (Rom. i. 28.) These things, moreover, not even a Greek who hath understanding could endure. A certain demagogue in Athens is reported once to have hung these things about him: when a philosopher who was his instructor, on beholding them, rebuked him, expostulated, satirized, made sport of him. For in so wretched a plight are we, as even to believe in these things!

Why, saith one, are there not now those who raise the dead, and perform cures? Yes, then, why, I say: why are there not now those who have a contempt for this present life? Do we serve God for hire? When man's nature was weaker, when the Faith had to be planted, there were even many such; but now he would

---

[1] περίαπτα. See on Stat. Hom. xix. p. 470 and note 4. Perhaps it should be ἐπέδησε, "she hath tied on."

[2] i.e. their children, περιάπτουσι. In what he says presently after, he must be referring to the temporal ill effects of immorality.
[3] i.e. of direct idolatry.

not have us to hang upon these signs, but to be ready for death. Why then clingest thou to the present life? why lookest thou not on the future? and for the sake of this indeed canst bear even to commit idolatry, but for the other not so much as to restrain sadness? For this cause it is that there are none such now; because that (future) life hath seemed to us honorless, seeing that for its sake we do nothing, whilst for this, there is nothing we refuse to undergo. And why too that other farce, ashes, and soot, and salt? and the old woman again brought in? A farce truly, and a shame! And then, "an eye," say they, "hath caught the child."

Where will these satanical doings end? How will not the Greeks laugh? how will they not gibe when we say unto them, "Great is the virtue of the Cross"; how will they be won, when they see us having recourse to those things, which themselves laugh to scorn? Was it for this that God gave physicians and medicines? What then? Suppose they do not cure him, but the child depart? Whither will he depart? tell me, miserable and wretched one! Will he depart to the demons? Will he depart to some tyrant? Will he not depart to heaven? Will he not depart to his own Lord? Why then grievest thou? why weepest thou? why mournest thou? why lovest thou thine infant more than thy Lord? Is it not through Him that thou hast this also? Why art thou ungrateful? Dost thou love the gift more than the Giver? "But I am weak," she replies, "and cannot bear the fear of God." Well, if in bodily evils the greater covers the less, much rather in the soul, fear destroyed fear, and sorrow, sorrow. Was the child beautiful? But be it what it may, not more beauteous is he than Isaac: and he too was an only one. Was it born in thine old age? So too was he. But is it fair? Well: however fair it may be, it is not lovelier than Moses (Acts vii. 20), who drew even barbarian eyes unto a tender love of him, and this too at a time of life when beauty is not yet disclosed; and yet this beloved thing did the parents cast into the river. Thou indeed both seest it laid out, and deliverest it to the burying, and goest to its monument; but they did not so much as know whether it would be food for fishes, or for dogs, or for other beasts that prey in the sea; and this they did, knowing as yet nothing of the Kingdom, nor of the Resurrection.

But suppose it is not an only child; but that after thou hast lost many, this also hath departed. But not so sudden is thy calamity as was Job's, and (his was) of sadder aspect?[1] It is not when a roof has fallen in, it is not as they are

feasting the while, it is not following on the tidings of other calamities.

But was it beloved by thee? But not more so than Joseph, the devoured of wild beasts; but still the father bore the calamity, and that which followed it, and the next to that. He wept; but acted not with impiety; he mourned, but he uttered not discontent, but stayed at those words, saying, "Joseph is not, Simeon is not, and will ye take Benjamin away? all these things are against me."[2] (Gen. xlii. 36.) Seest thou how the constraint of famine prevailed with him to be regardless of his children? and doth not the fear of God prevail with thee as much as famine?

Weep: I do not forbid thee: but aught blasphemous neither say nor do. Be thy child what he may, he is not like Abel; and yet nought of this kind did Adam say; although that calamity was a sore one, that his brother should have killed him. But I am reminded of others also that have killed their brothers; when, for instance, Absalom killed Amnon the eldest born (2 Sam. 13), and King David loved his child,[3] and sat indeed in sackcloth and ashes, but he neither brought soothsayers, nor enchanters, (although there were such then, as Saul shows,) but he made supplication to God. So do thou likewise: as that just man did, so do thou also; the same words say thou, when thy child is dead, "I shall go to him, but he will not come to me." (2 Sam. xii. 23.) This is true wisdom, this is affection. However much thou mayst love thy child, thou wilt not love so much as he did then. For even though his child were born of adultery, yet that blessed man's love of the mother was at its height,[4] and ye know that the offspring shares the love of the parents. And so great was his love toward it, that he even wished it to live, though it would be his own accuser, but still he gave thanks to God. What, thinkest thou, did Rebecca suffer, when his brother threatened Jacob, and she grieved not her husband, but bade him send her son away? (Gen. xxvii. 46; xxviii. 1.) When thou hast suffered any calamity, think on what is worse than it; and thou wilt have a sufficient consolation; and consider with thyself, what if he had died in battle? what if in fire? And whatsoever our sufferings may be, let us think upon things yet more fearful, and we shall have comfort sufficient, and let us ever look around us on those who have undergone more terrible things, and if we ourselves have ever suffered heavier calamities. So doth Paul also exhort us; as when he saith, "Ye have not

---

[1] [This abrupt sentence was expanded as usual, in what came to be the common printed text. — J. A. B.]

[2] Or (Gr.), "are come upon me."

[3] He passes on to the child of Bathsheba.

[4] ἤκμαζεν. 2 Sam. xii. 24 gives the impression that David laid the crime to his own charge, and regarded her as wronged.

yet resisted unto blood, striving against sin"
(Heb. xii. 4) : and again, "There hath no
temptation taken you but such as man can
bear." (1 Cor. x. 13.) Be then our sufferings
what they may, let us look round on what is
worse ; (for we shall find such,) and thus shall

we be thankful. And above all, let us give
thanks for all things continually ; for so, both
these things will be eased, and we shall live to
the glory of God, and obtain the promised good
things, whereunto may all we attain, through the
grace and love toward man, &c.

HOMILY IX.

COLOSSIANS iii. 16, 17.

"Let the word of Christ dwell in you richly in all wis-
    dom; teaching and admonishing one another with
    psalms and hymns and spiritual songs, singing with
    grace in your hearts to God.[1] And whatsoever ye
    do in word or in deed, do all in the name of the Lord
    Jesus, giving thanks to God the Father through
    Him."

HAVING exhorted them to be thankful, he
shows also the way, that, of which I have lately
discoursed to you. And what saith he? "Let
the word of Christ dwell in you richly" ; or
rather not this way alone, but another also. For
I indeed said that we ought to reckon up those
who have suffered things more terrible, and
those who have undergone sufferings more grievous than ours, and to give thanks that such have
not fallen to our lot ; but what saith he? "Let
the word of Christ dwell in you" ; that is, the
teaching, the doctrines, the exhortation, wherein
He says, that the present life is nothing, nor yet
its good things. If we know this, we shall yield
to no hardships whatever. (Matt. vi. 25, &c.)
"Let it dwell in you," he saith, "richly," not
simply dwell, but with great abundance. Hearken
ye, as many as are worldly,[2] and have the charge
of wife and children ; how to you too he commits especially the reading of the Scriptures ;
and that not to be done lightly, nor in any sort
of way, but with much earnestness. For as the
rich in money can bear fine and damages, so he
that is rich in the doctrines of philosophy will
bear not poverty only, but all calamities also
easily, yea, more easily than that one. For as
for him, by discharging the fine, the man who
is rich must needs be impoverished, and found
wanting,[3] and if he should often suffer in that
way, will no longer be able to bear it, but in this
case it is not so ; for we do not even expend
our wholesome thoughts when it is necessary for
us to bear aught we would not choose, but they
abide with us continually. And mark the wis-

dom of this blessed man. He said not, "Let
the word of Christ" be in you, simply, but what?
"dwell in you," and "richly."

"In all wisdom, teaching and admonishing one
another." "In all," says he. Virtue he calls
wisdom, and lowliness of mind is wisdom, and
almsgiving, and other such like things, are wisdom ; just as the contraries are folly, for cruelty
too cometh of folly. Whence in many places
it calleth the whole of sin folly. "The fool,"
saith one, "hath said in his heart, There is no
God" (Ps. xiv. 1) ; and again, "My wounds
stink and are corrupt from the face of my foolishness." (Ps. xxxviii. 5, Sept.) For what is
more foolish, tell me, than one who indeed
wrappeth himself about in his own garments, but
regardeth not his brethren that are naked ; who
feedeth dogs, and careth not that the image of
God is famishing ; who is merely persuaded that
human things are nought, and yet clings tó them
as if immortal. As then nothing is more foolish
than such an one, so is nothing wiser than one
that achieveth virtue. For mark ; how wise he
is, says one. He imparteth of his substance, he
is pitiful, he is loving to men, he hath well considered that he beareth a common nature with
them ; he hath well considered the use of wealth,
that it is worthy of no estimation ; that one
ought to be sparing of bodies that are of kin to
one, rather than of wealth. He that is a despiser of glory is wholly wise, for he knoweth
human affairs ; the knowledge of things divine
and human, is philosophy. So then he knoweth
what things are divine, and what are human, and
from the one he keeps himself, on the other he
bestoweth his pains. And he knows how to give
thanks also to God in all things, he considers
the present life as nothing ; therefore he is neither delighted with prosperity, nor grieved with
the opposite condition.

Tarry not, I entreat, for another to teach thee ;
thou hast the oracles of God. No man teacheth
thee as they ; for he indeed oft grudgeth much
for vainglory's sake and envy. Hearken, I entreat you, all ye that are careful for this life, and

---

[1] ["God" is the correct N. T. text (as in Rev. Ver.), and is
here given by several MSS. of Chrys. — J. A. B.]
[2] Not in a bad sense.
[3] ἐλέγχεσθαι, not in money to pay, but in power to prevent loss.
Or it may be, "must be in process of being found wanting."

procure books that will be medicines for the soul. If ye will not any other, yet get you at least the New Testament, the Apostolic Epistles, the Acts, the Gospels, for your constant teachers. If grief befall thee, dive into them as into a chest of medicines ; take thence comfort of thy trouble, be it loss, or death, or bereavement of relations ; or rather dive not into them merely, but take them wholly to thee ; keep them in thy mind.

This is the cause of all evils, the not knowing the Scriptures. We go into battle without arms, and how ought we to come off safe? Well contented should we be if we can be safe with them, let alone without them. Throw not the whole upon us ! Sheep ye are, still not without reason, but rational ; Paul committeth much to you also. They that are under instruction, are not for ever learning ; for then they are not taught. If thou art for ever learning, thou wilt never learn. Do not so come as meaning to be always learning ; (for so thou wilt never know ;) but so as to finish learning, and to teach others. In the arts, do not all persons continue for set times, in the sciences, and in a word, in all the arts? Thus we all fix definitely a certain known time ; but if ye are ever learning, it is a certain proof that ye have learned nothing.

This reproach God spake against the Jews. "Borne from the belly, and instructed even to old age." (Isa. xlvi. 3, 4, Sept.) If ye had not always been expecting this, all things would not have gone backward in this way. Had it been so, that some had finished learning, and others were about to have finished, our work would have been forward ; ye would both have given place to others, and would have helped us as well. Tell me, were some to go to a grammarian and continue always learning their letters, would they not give their teacher much trouble? How long shall I have to discourse to you concerning life? In the Apostles' times it was not thus, but they continually leaped from place to place, appointing those who first learned to be the teachers of any others that were under instruction. Thus they were enabled to circle the world, through not being bound to one place. How much instruction, think ye, do your brethren in the country stand in need of, [they] and their teachers? But ye hold me riveted fast here. For, before the head is set right, it is superfluous to proceed to the rest of the body. Ye throw everything upon us. Ye alone ought to learn from us, and your wives from you, your children from you ; but ye leave all to us. Therefore our toil is excessive.

"Teaching," he saith, "and admonishing one another with psalms and hymns and spiritual songs." Mark also the considerateness of Paul. Seeing that reading is toilsome, and its irksome-

ness great, he led them not to histories, but to psalms, that thou mightest at once delight thy soul with singing, and gently beguile thy labors. "Hymns," he saith, "and spiritual songs." But now your children will utter songs and dances of Satan, like cooks, and caterers, and musicians ; no one knoweth any psalm, but it seems a thing to be ashamed of even, and a mockery, and a joke. There is the treasury house of all these evils. For whatsoever soil the plant stands in, such is the fruit it bears ; if in a sandy and salty soil, of like nature is its fruit ; if in a sweet and rich one, it is again similar. So the matter of instruction is a sort of fountain. Teach him to sing those psalms which are so full of the love of wisdom ; as at once concerning chastity, or rather, before all, of not companying with the wicked, immediately with the very beginning of the book ; (for therefore also it was that the prophet began on this wise, "Blessed is the man that hath not walked in the counsel of the ungodly" ; Ps. i. 1, and again, "I have not sat in the council of vanity" ; Ps. xxvi. 4, Sept., and again, "in his sight a wicked doer is contemned, but he honoreth those that fear the Lord," Ps. xv. 4, Sept.,) of companying with the good, (and these subjects thou wilt find there in abundance,) of restraining the belly, of restraining the hand, of refraining from excess, of not overreaching ; that money is nothing, nor glory, and other things such like.

When in these thou hast led him on from childhood, by little and little thou wilt lead him forward even to the higher things. The Psalms contain all things, but the Hymns again have nothing human.[1] When he has been instructed out of the Psalms, he will then know hymns also, as a diviner thing. For the Powers above chant hymns, not psalms. For "a hymn," saith one, "is not comely in the mouth of a sinner" (Ecclus. xv. 9) ; and again, "Mine eyes shall be upon the faithful of the land, that they sit together with me" (Ps. ci. 6, 7, Sept.) ; and again, "he that worketh haughtiness hath not dwelt in the midst of my house" ; and again, "He that walketh in a blameless way, he ministered unto me." (Ps. ci. 6, Sept.)

So that ye should safely guard them from intermixing themselves, not only with friends, but even with servants. For the harm done to the free is incalculable, when we place over them corrupt slaves. For if when enjoying all the benefit of a father's affection and wisdom, they can with difficulty be preserved safe throughout ; when we hand them over to the unscrupulous-

---

[1] [This distinction is unfounded. It is likely that by "psalms" the Apostle meant especially the Psalms of the Old Test., and by "hymns" those which were already being written among the Christians ; while "spiritual songs" might include both the others, as being contrasted with secular songs. But the distinction cannot be confidently made. Compare Lightfoot here. — J. A. B.]

ness of servants, they use them like enemies, thinking that they will prove milder masters to them, when they have made them perfect fools, and weak, and worthy of no respect.

More then than all other things together, let us attend seriously to this. "I have loved," saith he, "those that love thy law." (Ps. cxix. 165, not exact.) This man then let us too emulate, and such let us love. And that the young may further be taught chastity, let them hear the Prophet, saying, "My loins are filled with illusions"[1] (Ps. xxxviii. 7, Sept.) ; and again let them hear him saying, "Thou wilt utterly destroy every one that goeth a whoring from Thee." (Ps. lxxiii. 27, Sept.) And, that one ought to restrain the belly, let them hear again, "And slew," he saith, "the more part of them[2] while the meat was yet in their mouths." (Ps. lxxviii. 30, Sept.) And that they ought to be above bribes, "If riches become abundant, set [not][3] your heart upon them" (Ps. lxii. 10) ; and that they ought to keep glory in subjection, "Nor shall his glory descend together after him." (Ps. xlix. 17.) And not to envy the wicked, "Be not envious against them that work unrighteousness." (Ps. xxxvii. 1.) And to count power as nothing, "I saw the ungodly in exceeding high place, and lifting himself up as the cedars of Libanus, and I passed by, and lo ! he was not." (Ps. xxxvii. 35.) And to count these present things as nothing, "They counted the people happy, that are in such a case ; happy are the people, whose helper is the Lord their God." (Ps. cxliv. 15, Sept.) That we do not sin without notice, but that there is a retribution, "for," he saith, "Thou shalt render to every man according to his works." (Ps. lxii. 12, Sept.) But why doth he not so requite them day by day? "God is a judge," he says; "righteous, and strong, and longsuffering." (Ps. vii. 11.) That lowliness of mind is good, "Lord," he saith, "my heart is not lifted up" (Ps. cxxxi. 1) : that pride is evil, "Therefore," he said, "pride took hold on them wholly" (Ps. lxxiii. 6, Sept.) ; and again, "The Lord resisteth the proud"; and again, "Their injustice shall come out as of fatness." That almsgiving is good, "He hath dispersed, he hath given to the needy, his righteousness endureth for ever." (Prov. iii. 34.) And that to pity is praiseworthy, "He is a good man that pitieth, and lendeth." (Ps. lxxiii. 7, Sept.) And thou wilt find there many more doctrines than these, full of true philosophy ; such as, that one ought not to speak evil, "Him that privily slandereth

his neighbor, him did I chase from me." (Ps. cxii. 9.)

What is the hymn of those above? The Faithful know. What say the cherubim above? What say the Angels? "Glory to God in the highest." (Ps. cxii. 5.) Therefore after the psalmody come the hymns, as a thing of more perfection. "With psalms," he saith, "with hymns, with spiritual songs, with grace singing in your hearts to God." (Ps. ci. 5, Sept.) He means either this, that God because of grace hath given us these things ; or, with the songs in grace ; or, admonishing and teaching one another in grace ; or, that they had these gifts in grace ; or, it is an epexegesis[4] and he means, from the grace of the Spirit. "Singing in your hearts to God." Not simply with the mouth, he means, but with heedfulness. For this is to "sing to God," but that to the air, for the voice is scattered without result. Not for display, he means. And even if thou be in the market-place, thou canst collect thyself, and sing unto God, no one hearing thee. For Moses also in this way prayed, and was heard, for He saith, "Why criest thou unto Me?" (Ex. xiv. 15) albeit he said nothing, but cried in thought — wherefore also God alone heard him — with a contrite heart. For it is not forbidden one even when walking to pray in his heart, and to dwell above.

Ver. 17. "And whatsoever ye do," he saith, "in word or in deed, do all in the name of the Lord Jesus, giving thanks to God the Father through Him."

For if we thus do, there will be nothing polluted, nothing unclean, wherever Christ is called on. If thou eat, if thou drink, if thou marry, if thou travel, do all in the Name of God, that is, calling Him to aid thee : in everything first praying to Him, so take hold of thy business. Wouldest thou speak somewhat? Set this in front. For this cause we also place in front of our epistles the Name of the Lord. Wheresoever the Name of God is, all is auspicious. For if the names of Consuls make writings sure, much more doth the Name of Christ. Or he means this ; after God say ye and do everything, do not introduce the Angels besides. Dost thou eat? Give thanks to God both before and afterwards. Dost thou sleep? Give thanks to God both before and afterwards. Launchest thou into the forum? Do the same — nothing worldly, nothing of this life. Do all in the Name of the Lord, and all shall be prospered to thee. Whereonsoever the Name is placed, there all things are auspicious. If it casts out devils, if it drives away diseases, much more does it render business easy.

And what is to "do in word or in deed"?

---

[1] ἐμπαιγμάτων. Evil spirits being supposed to "make sport of" the soul by means of the body.

[2] πίοσιν, Savile, marg. and 1 MS. and so Sept. and E. V. "fattest," Edd. πλείοσιν. [So Chrys. on that Psalm. — Field. — J. A. B.]

[3] The MSS. omit the negative, which would easily be lost in the preceding word. One might take it, "Beware of them." [Field inserts the negative without remark. — J. A. B.]

[4] i.e. an additional explanation, viz. of "singing in your hearts."

Either requesting or performing anything whatever. Hear how in the Name of God Abraham sent his servant; David in the Name of God slew Goliath. Marvelous is His Name and great. Again, Jacob sending his sons sáith, " My God give you favor in the sight of the man." (Gen. xliii. 14.) For he that doeth this hath for his ally, God, without whom he durst do nothing. As honored then by being called upon, He will in turn honor by making their business easy. Invoke the Son, give thanks to the Father. For when the Son is invoked, the Father is invoked, and when He is thanked, the Son has been thanked.

These things let us learn, not as far as words only, but to fulfill them also by works. Nothing is equal to this Name, marvelous is it everywhere. " Thy Name," he saith, " is ointment poured forth." (Cant. i. 3.) He that hath uttered it is straightway filled with fragrance. " No man," it is said, " can call Jesus Lord, but by the Holy Ghost." (1 Cor. xii. 3.) So great things doth this Name work. If thou have said, In [1] the Name of Father, and Son, and Holy Ghost, with faith, thou hast accomplished everything. See, how great things thou hast done ! Thou hast created a man, and wrought all the rest (that cometh) of Baptism ! So, when used

in commanding diseases, terrible is The Name. Therefore the devil introduced those [3] of the Angels, envying us the honor. Such incantations are for the demons. Even if it be Angel, even if it be Archangel, even if it be Cherubim, allow it not ; for neither will these Powers accept such addresses, but will even toss them away from them, when they have beheld their Master dishonored. " I have honored thee," He saith, " and have said, Call upon Me " ; and dost thou dishonor Him ? If thou chant this incantation with faith, thou wilt drive away both diseases and demons, [4] and even if thou have failed to drive away the disease, this is not from lack of power, but because it is expedient it should be so. " According to Thy greatness," he saith, " so also is Thy praise." (Ps. xlviii. 10.) By this Name hath the world been converted, the tyranny dissolved, the devil trampled on, the heavens opened. We have been regenerated by this Name. This if we have, we beam forth ; This maketh both martyrs and confessors ; This let us hold fast as a great gift, that we may live in glory, and be well-pleasing to God, and be counted worthy of the good things promised to them that love Him, through the grace and lovingkindness, &c.

HOMILY X.

COLOSSIANS iii. 18–25.

" Wives, be in subjection to. your husbands, as is fitting in the Lord. Husbands, love your wives, and be not bitter against them. Children, obey your parents in all things, for this is well-pleasing in [2] the Lord. Fathers, provoke not your children, that they be not discouraged. Servants, obey in all things them that are your masters according to the flesh; not with eyeservice, as menpleasers, but in singleness of heart, fearing the Lord : whatsoever ye do, work heartily, as unto the Lord, and not unto men; knowing that from the Lord ye shall receive the recompense of the inheritance : ye serve the Lord Christ. For he that doeth wrong shall receive again for the wrong that he hath done : and there is no respect of persons with God. (Chap. iv. 1.) Masters, render unto your servants that which is just and equal; knowing that ye also have a Master in heaven."

WHY does he not give these commands everywhere, and in all the Epistles, but only here, and in that to the Ephesians, and that to Timothy, and that to Titus ? Because probably there were dissensions in these cities ; or probably they

were correct in other respects, so that it was expedient they should hear about these things. Rather, however, what he saith to these, he saith to all. Now in these things also this Epistle bears great resemblance to that to the Ephesians, either [5] because it was not fitting to write about these things to men now [6] at peace, who needed

---

[1] [He uses ἐν τῷ ὀνόματι, which in this connection amounts to substantially the same as the Evangelist's εἰς τὸ ὄνομα (Matt. xxviii. 19). . Compare Acts viii. 16 with x. 48. — J. A. B.]

[2] R. t. and E. V. " unto."

[3] Or, " the matters of the Angels " (τὰ τῶν ἀγγέλων).

[4] Gretser de S. Cruce, l. iv. c. 3, quotes the Emperor Leo as speaking of curing a demoniac " by the Sign of the Cross, and the invocation of the Holy and life-giving Trinity." This agrees with what he has said before, Hom. viii. p. 298, on the use of the Holy Sign. G. also quotes Tertullian de Bapt. 6, who alludes to this form of using it. " The Faith *sealed* (obsignata) in the Father and the Son and the Holy Ghost." There were, however, other forms, as " In the Name of our Lord Jesus Christ." " Deus in adjutorium meum intende," &c. Gretser also refers to St. Chrys. Catech. ii. fin., where he bids every one on leaving his house cross himself, saying, " I renounce thee, Satan, and thy pomp, and thy angels, and I place myself with thee, O Christ." St. Cyr. Cat. iv. 10 also connects the Invocation of His Name with the Sign. St. Cyprian, Test. ii. 21, quotes Rev. xiv. 1, so as to imply this connection.

[5] [In these apparently hasty notes, perhaps composed by dictation, or more probably taken down in shorthand, we are not surprised to find a frequent lack of clear connection. Here, as often elsewhere, the altered text followed in most editions has inserted clauses to bring out the supposed meaning. — J. A. B.]

[6] He seems to class the Romans, Hebrews, Corinthians, and Galatians together, as needing doctrinal instruction before these particulars, and to consider the Thessalonians and Philippians as needing them less from their state of suffering.

to be instructed in high doctrines as yet lacking to them, or because that for persons who had been comforted under trials, it were superfluous to hear on these subjects. So that I conjecture, that in this place the Church was now well-grounded, and that these things are said as in finishing.

Ver. 18. "Wives, be in subjection to your husbands, as is fitting in the Lord."

That is, be subject for God's sake, because this adorneth you, he saith, not them. For I mean not that subjection which is due to a master, nor yet that alone which is of nature, but that for God's sake.

Ver. 19. "Husbands, love your wives, and be not bitter against them."

See how again he has exhorted to reciprocity. As in the other case he enjoineth fear and love, so also doth he here. For it is possible for one who loves even, to be bitter. What he saith then is this. Fight not; for nothing is more bitter than this fighting, when it takes place on the part of the husband toward the wife. For the fightings which happen between beloved persons, these are bitter; and he shows that it ariseth from great bitterness, when, saith he, any one is at variance with his own member. To love therefore is the husband's part, to yield pertains to the other side. If then each one contributes his own part, all stands firm. From being loved, the wife too becomes loving; and from her being submissive, the husband becomes yielding. And see how in nature also it hath been so ordered, that the one should love, the other obey. For when the party governing loves the governed, then everything stands fast. Love from the governed is not so requisite, as from the governing towards the governed; for from the other obedience is due. For that the woman hath beauty, and the man desire, shows nothing else than that for the sake of love it hath been made so. Do not therefore, because thy wife is subject to thee, act the despot; nor because thy husband loveth thee, be thou puffed up. Let neither the husband's love elate the wife, nor the wife's subjection puff up the husband. For this cause hath He subjected her to thee, that she may be loved the more. For this cause He hath made thee to be loved, O wife, that thou mayest easily bear thy subjection. Fear not in being a subject; for subjection to one that loveth thee hath no hardship. Fear not in loving, for thou hast her yielding. In no other way then could a bond have been. Thou hast then thine authority of necessity, proceeding from nature; maintain also the bond that proceedeth from love, for this alloweth the weaker to be endurable.[1]

Ver. 20. "Children, obey your parents in all things, for this is well-pleasing in the Lord."

Again he has put that, "in the Lord," at once laying down the laws of obedience, and shaming them, and casting them down. For this, saith he, is well-pleasing to the Lord. See how he would have us do all not from nature only, but, prior to this, from what is pleasing to God, that we may also have reward.

Ver. 21. "Fathers, provoke not your children, that they be not discouraged."

Lo! again here also is subjection and love. And he said not, "Love your children," for it had been superfluous, seeing that nature itself constraineth to this; but what needed correction he corrected; that the love should in this case also be the more vehement, because that the obedience is greater. For it nowhere lays down as an exemplification the relation of husband and wife; but what? hear the prophet saying, "Like as a father pitieth his children, so the Lord pitied them that fear Him" (Ps. ciii. 13, Sept.) And again Christ saith, "What man is there of you, whom if his son ask bread, will he give him a stone? or if he ask a fish, will he give him a serpent?" (Matt. vii. 9.)

"Fathers, provoke not your children, that they be not discouraged."

He hath set down what he knew had the greatest power to seize upon them; and whilst commanding them he has spoken more like a friend; and nowhere does he mention God, for he would overcome parents, and bow their tender affections. That is, "Make them not more contentious, there are occasions when you ought even to give way."

Next he comes to the third kind of authority. There is here also a certain love, but that no more proceeding from nature, as above, but from habit, and from the authority itself, and the works done. Seeing then that in this case the sphere of love is narrowed, whilst that of obedience is amplified, he dwelleth upon this, wishing to give to these from their obedience, what the first have from nature. So that what he discourseth with the servants alone[2] is not for their masters' sakes, but for their own also, that they may make themselves the objects of tender affection to their masters. But he sets not this forth openly; for so he would doubtless have made them supine.

Ver. 22. "Servants," he saith, "obey in all things your masters according to the flesh."

And see how always he sets down the names, "wives, children, servants," being at once a just

---

[1] ἀνεκτὴν. He seems to mean, "to be in an endurable position." [Downes suggested, and Field inclines to approve, that the reading should be ἄνετον, "unrestrained," which in another passage is confused in a MS. with ἀνεκτόν. — J. A. B.]

[2] μόνοις. One would expect μόνον, as he speaks to the masters afterwards. But he may either mean that they were chiefly addressed, or that this is the object even of what is addressed to them separately.

claim upon their obedience. But that none might be pained, he added, "to your masters according to the flesh." Thy better part, the soul, is free, he saith; thy service is for a season. It therefore do thou subject, that thy service be no more of constraint. "Not with eye-service, as men-pleasers." Make, he saith, thy service which is by the law, to be from the fear of Christ. For if when thy master seeth thee not, thou doest thy duty and what is for his honor, it is manifest that thou doest it because of the sleepless Eye. "Not with eye-service," he saith, "as men-pleasers"; thus implying, "it is you who will have to sustain the damage." For hear the prophet saying, "God hath scattered the bones of the men-pleasers." (Ps. liii. 6, Sept.) See then how he spares them, and brings them to order. "But in singleness of heart," he saith, "fearing God."[1] For that is not singleness, but hypocrisy, to hold one thing, and act another; to appear one when the master is present, another when he is absent. Therefore he said not simply, "in singleness of heart," but, "fearing God." For this is to fear God, when, though none be seeing, we do not aught that is evil; but if we do, we fear not God, but men. Seest thou how he bringeth them to order?

Ver. 23. "Whatsoever ye do, work heartily, as unto the Lord, and not unto men."

He desires to have them freed not only from hypocrisy, but also from slothfulness. He hath made them instead of slaves free, when they need not the superintendence of their master; for the expression "heartily" means this, "with good will," not with a slavish necessity, but with freedom, and of choice. And what is the reward?

Ver. 24. "Knowing," he saith, "that from the Lord ye shall receive the recompense of your[2] inheritance : for ye serve the Lord Christ."

For from Him also it is evident that ye shall receive the reward. And that ye serve the Lord is plain from this.

Ver. 25. "For he that doeth wrong," he saith, "shall receive again for the wrong that he hath done."

Here he confirmeth his former statements. For that his words may not appear to be those of flattery, "he shall receive," he saith, "the wrong he hath done," that is, he shall suffer punishment also, "for there is no respect of persons."[3] For what if thou art a servant? it is no shame to thee. And truly he might have said this to the masters, as he did in the Epistle

to the Ephesians. (Eph. vi. 9.) But here he seems to me to be alluding to the Grecian masters. For, what if he is a Greek and thou a Christian? Not the persons but the actions are examined, so that even in this case thou oughtest to serve with good will, and heartily.

Chap. iv. 1. "Masters, render unto your servants that which is just and equal."

What is "just"? What is "equal"? To place them in plenty of everything, and not allow them to stand in need of others, but to recompense them for their labors. For, because I have said that they have their reward from God, do not thou therefore deprive them of it. And in another place he saith, "forbearing threatening" (Eph. vi. 9), wishing to make them more gentle; for those were perfect men; that is, "with what measure ye mete, it shall be measured unto you." (Matt. vii. 2.) And the words, "there is no respect of persons," are spoken with a view to these,[4] but they are assigned to the others, in order that these may receive them. For when we have said to one person what is applicable to another, we have not corrected him so much, as the one who is in fault. "Ye also," along with them, he saith. He has here made the service common, for he saith, "knowing that ye also have a Master in heaven."

Ver. 2. "Continue in prayer, watching therein with thanksgiving."

For, since continuing in prayers frequently makes persons listless, therefore he saith, "watching," that is, sober, not wandering. For the devil knoweth, how great a good prayer is; therefore he presseth heavily. And Paul also knoweth how careless[5] many are when they pray, wherefore he saith, "continue"[6] in prayer, as of somewhat laborious, "watching therein with thanksgiving." For let this, he saith, be your work, to give thanks in your prayers both for the seen and the unseen, and for His benefits to the willing and unwilling, and for the kingdom, and for hell, and for tribulation, and for refreshment. For thus is the custom of the Saints to pray, and to give thanks for the common benefits of all.

I know a certain holy man who prayeth thus. He used to say nothing before these words, but thus, "We give Thee thanks for all Thy benefits bestowed upon us the unworthy, from the first day until the present, for what we know, and what we know not, for the seen, for the unseen, for those in deed, those in word, those with our wills, those against our wills, for all that have been bestowed upon the unworthy, even us; for

---

[1] [The correct text, as in Rev. Ver., is "fearing the Lord." Chrys. very often has an erroneous type of N. T. text, which spread from Constantinople, and became the so-called Textus Receptus. — J. A. B.]

[2] [Some documents for N. T. also give "your," but the correct N. T. text has simply "the," and omits "for." — J. A. B.]

[3] [Some documents for Chrys., and some for N. T., add "with God." — J. A. B.]

[4] The masters.

[5] ἀκηδιῶσι, generally used of giving up caring for anything in despair. But the name "acedia" amongst the seven deadly sins is of this origin.

[6] προσκαρτερεῖτε, "persevere."

tribulations, for refreshments, for hell, for punishment, for the kingdom of heaven. We beseech Thee to keep our soul holy, having a pure
conscience; an end worthy of thy lovingkindness. Thou that lovedst us so as to give Thy
Only-Begotten for us, grant us to become worthy
of Thy love; give us wisdom in Thy word, and
in Thy fear. Only-Begotten Christ, inspire the
strength that is from Thee. Thou that gavest
The Only-Begotten for us, and hast sent Thy
Holy Spirit for the remission of our sins, if in
aught we have wilfully or unwillingly transgressed,
pardon, and impute it not. Remember all that
call upon Thy Name in truth; remember all
that wish us well, or the contrary, for we are all
men." Then having added the Prayer [1] of the
Faithful, he there ended; having made that
prayer, as a certain crowning part, and a binding
together for all. For many benefits doth God
bestow upon us even against our wills; many
also, yea more, without our knowledge even.
For when we pray for one thing, and He doeth
to us the reverse, it is plain that He doeth us
good even when we know it not.

Ver. 3. "Withal praying for us also." See his
lowlymindedness; he sets himself after them.

"That God may open to us a door for the
word, to speak the mystery of Christ." He
means an entrance, and boldness in speaking.
Wonderful! The great athlete said not "that I
may be freed from my bonds," but being in
bonds he exhorted others; and exhorted them
for a great object, that himself might get boldness in speaking. Both the two are great, both
the quality of the person, and of the thing.
Wonderful! how great is the dignity! "The
mystery," he saith, "of Christ." He shows that
nothing was more dearly desired by him than
this, to speak. "For which I am also in bonds;
that I may make it manifest, as I ought to speak."
(Ver. 4.) He means with much boldness of
speech, and withholding nothing. His bonds
display, not obscure him. With much boldness,
he means. Tell me, art thou in bonds, and dost
thou exhort others? Yea, my bonds give me
the greater boldness; but I pray for God's furtherance, for I have heard the voice of Christ
saying, "When they deliver you up, be not anxious how or what ye shall speak." (Matt. x. 19.)
And see, how he has expressed himself in metaphor, "that God may open to us a door for the
word"; (see, how unassuming he is; even in his
bonds, how he expresses himself;) that is, that
He would soften their hearts. Still he said not
so; but, "that He would give us boldness"; out
of lowlymindedness he thus spoke, and that
which he had, he asks to receive.

He shows in this Epistle, why Christ came not
in those times, in that he calleth the former

things "shadow, but the body," saith he, "is of
Christ." So that it was necessary they should be
formed to habits under the shadow. At the
same time also he exhibits the greatest proof of
the love he bears to them; "in order that ye,"
he saith, "may hear, for that reason, 'I am in
bonds.'" Again he sets before us those bonds of
his; which I so greatly love, which rouse up my
heart, and always draw me into longing to see
Paul bound, and in his bonds writing, and preaching, and baptizing, and catechizing. In his
bonds he was referred to on behalf of the
Churches everywhere; in his bonds he builded
up incalculably. Then was he rather at large.
For hear him saying, "So that most of the
brethren being confident through my bonds are
more abundantly bold to speak the word without
fear." (Phil. i. 14.) And again he makes the
same avowal of himself, saying, "For when I am
weak, then am I strong." (2 Cor. xii. 10.)
Wherefore he said also, "But the word of God
is not bound." (2 Tim. ii. 9.) He was bound
with malefactors, with prisoners, with murderers;
he, the teacher of the world, he that had ascended into the third heaven, that had heard the
unspeakable words, was bound. (2 Cor. xii. 4.)
But then was his course the swifter. He that
was bound, was now loosed; he that was un-
bound, was bound. For he indeed was doing
what he would; whilst the other prevented him
not, nor accomplished his own purpose.

What art thou about, O senseless one? Thinkest thou he is a fleshly runner? Doth he strive
in our race-course? His course of life is in
heaven; him that runneth in heaven, things on
earth cannot bind nor hold. Seest thou not this
sun? Enclose his beams with fetters! stay him
from his course! Thou canst not. Then neither
canst thou Paul! Yea, much less this one than
that, for this enjoyeth more of Providence than
that, seeing he beareth to us light, not such as
that is, but the true.

Where now are they who are unwilling to suffer
aught for Christ? But why do I say "suffer,"
seeing that they are unwilling even to give up
their wealth? In time past Paul also used to bind,
and cast into prison; but since he is become
Christ's servant, he glorieth no more of doing,
but of suffering. And this, moreover, is marvelous in the Preaching, when it is thus raised up
and increased by the sufferers themselves, and
not by the persecutors. Where hath any seen
such contests as this? He that suffereth ill,
conquers; he that doeth ill, is worsted. Brighter
is this man than the other. Through bonds the
Preaching entered. "I am not ashamed" (Rom.
i. 16), yea, I glory even, he saith, in preaching The Crucified. For consider, I pray: the
whole world left those who were at large, and
went over to those that are bound; turning away

from the imprisoners, it honoreth those laden with chains; hating the crucifiers, it worships the Crucified.

Not the only marvel is it that the preachers were fishermen, that they were ignorant; but that there were also other hindrances, hindrances too by nature; still the increase was all the more abundant. Not only were their ignorance no hindrance; but even it itself caused the Preaching to be manifested. For hear Luke saying, "And perceiving that they were unlearned and ignorant men, they marveled." (Acts iv. 13.) Not only were bonds no hindrance, but even of itself this made them more confident. Not so bold were the disciples when Paul was at large, as when he was bound. For he saith, they "are more abundantly bold to speak the word" of God "without fear." (Phil. i. 14.) Where are they that will gainsay the divinity of the Preaching? Was not their ignorance enough to procure them to be condemned? Would it not then in this case too, affright them? For ye know that by these two passions the many are possessed, vainglory and cowardice. Suppose their ignorance suffered them not to feel ashamed, still the dangers must have put them in fear.

But, saith one, they wrought miracles. Ye do believe then that they wrought miracles. But did they not work miracles? This is a greater miracle than to work them, if men were drawn to them without miracles. Socrates too amongst the Greeks was put in bonds. What then? Did not his disciples straightway flee to Megara? Assuredly, why not? They admitted[1] his arguments about immortality. But see here. Paul was put in bonds, and his disciples waxed the more confident, with reason, for they saw that the Preaching was not hindered. For, canst thou put the tongue in bonds? hereby chiefly it runneth. For as, except thou have bound the feet of a runner, thou hast not prevented him from running; so, except thou have bound the tongue of an evangelist, thou hast not hindered him from running. And as the former, if thou have bound his loins, runneth on the rather, and is supported, so too the latter preacheth the rather, and with greater boldness.

A prisoner is in fear, when there is nothing beyond bonds: but one that despiseth death, how should he be bound? They did the same as if they had put in bonds the shadow of Paul, and had gagged its mouth. For it was a fighting with shadows; for he was both more tenderly regretted by his friends, and more reverenced by his enemies, as bearing the prize for courage in his bonds. And a crown binds the head; but it disgraces it not, yea rather, it makes it brilliant. Against their wills they crowned him

with his chain. For, tell me, was it possible he could fear iron, who braved the adamantine gates of death? Come we, beloved, to emulate these bonds. As many of you women as deck yourselves with trinkets of gold, long ye for the bonds of Paul. Not so glitters the collar round your necks, as the grace of these iron bonds gleamed about his soul! If any longs for those, let him hate these. For what communion hath softness with courage; tricking out of the body with philosophy? Those bonds Angels reverence, these they even make a mock of; those bonds are wont to draw up from earth to heaven; these bonds draw down to earth from heaven. For in truth these are bonds, not those; those are ornament, these are bonds; these, along with the body, afflict the soul also; those, along with the body, adorn as well the soul.

Wouldest thou be convinced that those are ornament? Tell me which would more have won the notice of the spectators? thou or Paul? And why do I say, "thou"? the queen[2] herself who is all bedecked with gold would not have attracted the spectators so much; but if it had chanced that both Paul in his bonds and the queen had entered the Church at the same time, all would have removed their eyes from her to him; and with good reason. For to see a man of a nature greater than human, and having nought of man, but an angel upon earth, is more admirable than to see a woman decked with finery. For such indeed one may see both in theaters, and in pageants, and at baths, and many places; but whoso seeth a man with bonds upon him, and deeming himself to have the greatest of ornaments, and not giving way under his bonds, doth not behold a spectacle of earth, but one worthy of the heavens. The soul that is in that way attired looks about,— who hath seen? who not seen?—is filled with pride, is possessed with anxious thoughts, is bound with countless other passions: but he that hath these bonds on him, is without pride: his soul exulteth, is freed from every anxious care, is joyous, hath its gaze on heaven, is clad with wings. If any one were to give me the choice of seeing Paul either stooping out of heaven, and uttering his voice, or out of the prison, I would choose the prison. For they of heaven visit him when he is in the prison. The bonds of Paul were the bond of the Preaching, that chain of his was its foundation. Long we for those bonds!

And how, some one says, may this be? If we break up and dash in pieces these. No good results to us from these bonds, but even harm. These will show us as prisoners There; but the bonds of Paul will loose those bonds; she that is bound with these here, with those

---

[1] [Ironical.—J. A. B.]

[2] [Meaning the Empress, as king meant the Emperor.—J. A. B.]

deathless bonds shall she also be bound There, both hands and feet; she that has been bound with Paul's, shall have them in that day as it were an ornament about her. Free both thyself from thy bonds, and the poor man from his hunger. Why rivetest thou fast the chains of thy sins? Some one saith, How? When thou wearest gold whilst another is perishing, when thou, to get thee vainglory, takest so much gold, whilst another hast not even what to eat, hast thou not wedged fast thy sins? Put Christ about thee, and not gold; where Mammon is, there Christ is not, where Christ is, there Mammon is not. Wouldest not thou put on the King of all Himself? If one had offered thee the purple, and the diadem, wouldest thou not have taken them before all the gold in the world? I give thee not the regal ornaments, but I offer thee to put on the King Himself. And how can one put Christ on, doth any say? Hear Paul saying, "As many of you as were baptized into Christ, did put on Christ." (Gal. iii. 27.) Hear the Apostolical precept, "Make not provision for the flesh to fulfill the lusts thereof." (Rom. xiii. 14.) Thus doth one put on Christ, if one provide not for the flesh unto its lusts. If thou have put on Christ, even the demons will fear thee; but if gold, even men will laugh thee to scorn: if thou have put on Christ, men also will reverence thee.

Wouldest thou appear fair and comely? Be content with the Creator's fashioning. Why dost thou overlay these bits of gold, as if about to put to rights God's creation? Wouldest thou appear comely? Clothe thee in alms; clothe thee in benevolence; clothe thee in modesty, humbleness. These are all more precious than gold; these make even the beautiful yet more comely; these make even the ill formed to be well formed. For when any one looks upon a countenance with good will, he gives his judgment from love; but an evil woman, even though she be beautiful, none can call beautiful; for the mind being confounded pronounceth not its sentence aright.

That Egyptian woman of old was adorned; Joseph too was adorned; which of them was the more beautiful? I say not when she was in the palace, and he in the prison.[1] He was naked, but clothed in the garments of chastity; she was clothed, but more unseemly than if she had been naked; for she had not modesty. When thou hast excessively adorned thee, O woman, then thou art become more unseemly than a naked one; for thou hast stripped thee of thy fair adorning. Eve also was naked; but when she had clothed herself, then was she more

unseemly, for when she was naked indeed, she was adorned with the glory of God; but when she had clothed herself with the garment of sin, then was she unseemly. And thou, when arraying thyself in the garment of studied finery, dost then appear more unseemly. For that costliness availeth not to make any appear beautiful, but that it is possible even for one dressed out to be even more unseemly than if naked, tell me now; if thou hadst ever put on the dresses of a piper or a flute-player, would it not have been unseemliness? And yet those dresses are of gold; but for this very reason it were unseemliness, because they are of gold. For the costliness suits well with people on the stage, tragedians, players, mimes, dancers, fighters with wild beasts; but to a woman that is a believer, there are given other robes from God, the Only-Begotten Son of God Himself. "For," he saith, "as many as were baptized into Christ, did put on Christ." (Gal. iii. 27.) Tell me, if one had given thee kingly apparel, and thou hadst taken a beggar's[2] dress, and put this on above it, wouldest thou not, besides the unseemliness, have also been punished for it? Thou hast put on the Lord of Heaven, and of the Angels, and art thou still busied about earth?

I have spoken thus, because love of ornament is of itself a great evil, even were no other gendered by it, and it were not possible to hold it without peril, (for it inciteth to vainglory and to pride,) but now many other evils are gendered by finery, evil suspicions, unseasonable expenses, evil speakings, occasions of rapacity. For why dost thou adorn thyself? Tell me. Is it that thou mayest please thy husband? Then do it at home. But here the reverse is the case. For if thou wouldest please thine own husband, please not others; but if thou please others, thou wilt not be able to please thine own. So that thou shouldest put away all thine ornaments, when thou goest to the forum or proceedest to the church. Besides, please not thy husband by those means which harlots use, but by those rather which wives that are free employ. For wherein, tell me, doth a wife differ from a harlot? In that the one regardeth one thing only, namely, that by the beauty of her person she may attract to herself him whom she loves; whilst the other both ruleth the house, and shareth in the children, and in all other things.

Hast thou a little daughter? look to it lest she inherit the mischief, for they are wont to form their manners according to their nurture, and to imitate their mothers' behavior. Be a pattern to thy daughter of modesty, deck thy-

---

[1] Downes would remove the negative; but the meaning is "not only when," &c., but "even when he was exposed by the loss of his garment."

[2] [The Greek has a word, λωτός, not elsewhere found in this sense, but explained (Field's Annotations) by a similar word, λωτάξ, employed and interpreted in another passage by Chrys. The correctors changed λωτοῦ into the familiar εἴλωτος, a Helot.— J. A. B.]

self with that adorning, and see that thou despise the other ; for that is in truth an ornament, the other a disfigurement. Enough has been said. Now God that made the world, and hath given to us the ornament[1] of the soul, adorn us, and clothe us with His own glory, that all shining brightly in good works, and living unto His glory, we may send up glory to the Father, and to the Son, and to the Holy Spirit, now and always, &c.

HOMILY XI.

COLOSSIANS iv. 5, 6.

"Walk in wisdom toward them that are without, redeeming the time. Let your speech be always with grace, seasoned with salt, that ye may know how ye ought to answer each one."

WHAT Christ said to His disciples, that doth Paul also now advise. And what did Christ say? "Behold, I send you forth as sheep in the midst of wolves : be ye therefore wise as serpents, and harmless as doves." (Matt. x. 16.) That is, be upon your guard, giving them no handle against you. For therefore it is added, "towards them that are without," in order that we may know that against our own members we have no need of so much caution as against those without. For where brethren are, there are both many allowances and kindnesses. There is indeed need of caution even here ; but much more without, for it is not the same to be amongst enemies and foes, and amongst friends.

Then because he had alarmed them, see how again he encourages them ; "Redeeming," he saith, "the time" : that is, the present time is short. Now this he said, not wishing them to be crafty, nor hypocrites, (for this is not a part of wisdom, but of senselessness,) but what? In matters wherein they harm you not, he means, give them no handle ; as he says also, when writing to the Romans, "Render to all their dues : tribute to whom tribute is due, custom to whom custom, honor to whom honor." (Rom. xiii. 7.) On account of the Preaching alone have thou war, he saith, let this war have none other origin. For though they were to become our foes for other causes besides, yet neither shall we have a reward, and they will become worse, and will seem to have just complaints against us. For instance, if we pay not the tribute, if we render not the honors that are due, if we be not lowly. Seest thou not Paul, how submissive he is, where he was not likely to harm the Preaching. For hear him saying to Agrippa, "I think myself happy, because I shall answer for myself this day before thee, especially because I know thee to be expert in all customs and questions which are among the Jews." (Acts xxvi. 2, 3.) But had he thought it his duty to insult the ruler, he would have spoiled everything. And hear too those of blessed Peter's company, how gently they answer the Jews, saying, "we must obey God rather than men." (Acts v. 29.) And yet men who had renounced their own lives, might both have insulted, and have done anything whatever ; but for this object they had renounced their lives, not that they might win vainglory, (for that way had been vainglorious,) but that they might preach and speak all things with boldness. That other course marks want of moderation.

"Let your speech be always with grace, seasoned with salt" ; that is, that this graciousness may not lapse into indifferentism. For it is possible to be simply agreeable, it is possible also to be so with due seemliness. "That ye may know how ye ought to answer each one." So that one ought not to discourse alike to all, Greeks, I mean, and Brethren. By no means, for this were the very extreme of senselessness.

Ver. 7. "All my affairs shall Tychicus make known unto you, the beloved brother and faithful minister and fellow-servant in the Lord."

Admirable ! how great is the wisdom of Paul ! Observe, he doth not put everything into his Epistles, but only things necessary and urgent. In the first place, being desirous of not drawing them out to a length ; and secondly, to make his messenger more respected, by his having also somewhat to relate ; thirdly, showing his own affection towards him ; for he would not else have entrusted these communications to him. Then, there were things which ought not to be declared in writing. "The beloved brother," he saith. If beloved, he knew all, and he concealed nothing from him. "And faithful minister and fellow-servant in the Lord." If "faithful," he will speak no falsehood ; if "a fellow-servant," he hath shared his trials, so

---

[1] [The word κόσμος denotes order and ornament, and so the world, as being orderly and beautiful. — J. A. B.]

that he has brought together from all sides the grounds of trustworthiness.

Ver. 8. "Whom I have sent unto you for this very purpose."

Here he shows his great love, seeing that for this purpose he sent him, and this was the cause of his journey; and so when writing to the Thessalonians, he said, "Wherefore when we could no longer forbear, we thought it good to be left behind at Athens alone, and sent Timothy our brother." (1 Thess. iii. 1, 2.) And to the Ephesians he sends this very same person, and for the very same cause, "That he might know your estate, and comfort your hearts." (Eph. vi. 21, 22.) See what he saith, not "that ye might know my estate," but "that I might know yours." So in no place doth he mention what is his own. He shows that they were in trials too, by the expression, "comfort your hearts."

Ver. 9. "With Onesimus, the beloved and faithful brother, who is one of you. They shall make known unto you all things that are done here."

Onesimus is the one about whom, writing to Philemon, he said, "Whom I would fain have kept with me, that in thy behalf he might minister unto me in the bonds of the Gospel: but without thy mind I would do nothing." (Philem. 13, 14.) And he adds too the praise of their city, that they might not only not[1] be ashamed, but even pride themselves on him. "Who is one of you," he saith. "They shall make known unto you all things that are done here."

Ver. 10. "Aristarchus my fellow-prisoner saluteth you."

Nothing can surpass this praise. This is he that was brought up from Jerusalem with him. This man hath said a greater thing than the prophets; for they call themselves "strangers and foreigners," but this one calleth himself even a prisoner. Just like a prisoner of war he was dragged up and down,[2] and lay at every one's will to suffer evil of them, yea rather worse even than prisoners. For those indeed their enemies, after taking them, treat with much attention, having a care for them as their own property: but Paul, as though an enemy and a foe, all men dragged up and down, beating him, scourging, insulting, and maligning. This was a consolation to those also (to whom he wrote), when their master even is in such circumstances.

"And Mark, the cousin of Barnabas"; even this man he hath praised still from his relationship, for Barnabas was a great man; "touching whom ye received commandments; if he come unto you, receive him." Why? would they not

have received him? Yes, but he means, with much attention; and this shows the man to be great. Whence they received these commandments, he does not say.

Ver. 11. "And Jesus which is called Justus."

This man was probably a Corinthian. Next, he bestows a common praise on all, having already spoken that of each one in particular; "who are of the circumcision: these only are my fellow-workers unto the kingdom of God, men that have been a comfort unto me." After having said, "fellow-prisoner"; in order that he may not therewith depress the soul of his hearers, see how by this expression he rouseth them up. "Fellow-workers," he saith, "unto the kingdom of God." So that being partakers of the trials, they become partakers of the kingdom. "Who have been a comfort to me." He shows them to be great persons, seeing that to Paul they have been a comfort.

But[3] let us see the wisdom of Paul. "Walk in wisdom" he saith, "towards them that are without, redeeming the time." (Ver. 5.) That is, the time is not yours, but theirs. Do not then wish to have your own way,[4] but redeem time. And he said not simply, "Buy," but "redeem," making it yours after another manner. For it were the part of excessive madness, to invent occasions of war and enmity. For over and above the undergoing of superfluous and profitless dangers, there is this additional harm, that the Greeks will not come over to us. For when thou art amongst the brethren, reason is thou shouldest be bold; but when without, thou oughtest not to be so.

Seest thou how everywhere he speaks of those without, the Greeks? Wherefore also when writing to Timothy, he said, "Moreover, he must have good testimony from them that are without." (1 Tim. iii. 7.) And again, "For what have I to do with judging them that are without." (1 Cor. v. 12.) "Walk in wisdom," he saith, "toward them that are without." For "without," they are, even though they live in the same world with us, seeing they are without the kingdom, and the paternal mansion. And he comforts them withal, by calling the others "without," as he said above, "Your life is hid with Christ in God." (Col. iii. 3.)

Then, he saith, seek ye glory, then honors, then all those other things, but not so now, but give them up to those without. Next, lest thou think that he is speaking of money, he adds,

---

[1] Sav. adds οὐκ, but without necessity.

[2] ἤγετο καὶ ἐφέρετο, which is most properly said of property plundered in war.

[3] The transition here is so sudden, that one suspects the text; but it may be only that he is catching himself up, to make a longer comment on the last few verses. [There may be two sets of rough notes, prepared for different occasions, with the same general discussion used in both cases, and the two combined by an editor. But the suggestion of the Oxford tr. is supported by a similar practice in several of the Homilies on Acts. Comp. below, on Hom. xii.—J. A. B.]

[4] αὐθεντεῖν, i.e. in the world, as men of the world.

" Let your speech be always with grace, seasoned with salt, that ye may know how ye ought to answer each one." That it may not be full of hypocrisy, for this is not " grace," nor " a seasoning with salt." For instance, if it be needful to pay court to any one without incurring danger, refuse not [to do so] ; if the occasion require that thou discourse civilly, think not the doing so flattery, do everything that pertaineth to honor, so that piety be not injured. Seest thou not how Daniel payeth court to an impious man? Seest thou not the three children, how wisely they bore themselves, showing both courage, and boldness in speaking, and yet nothing rash nor galling, for so it had not been boldness, but vainglory. " That ye may know," he saith, " how ye ought to answer every man." For the ruler ought to be answered in one way, the ruled in another, the rich in one way, the poor in another. Wherefore? Because the souls of those who are rich, and in authority, are weaker, more inflammable, more fluctuating, so that towards them, one should use condescension ; those of the poor, and the ruled, firmer and more intelligent, so that to these one should use greater boldness of speech ; looking to one thing, their edification. Not that because one is rich, another poor, the former is to be honored more, the latter less, but because of his weakness, let the former be supported, the latter not so : for instance, when there is no cause for it, do not call the Greek " polluted," nor be insulting ; but if thou be asked concerning his doctrine, answer that it is polluted, and impious ; but when none asketh thee, nor forceth thee to speak, it becomes thee not causelessly to challenge to thee his enmity. For what need is there to prepare for thyself gratuitous hostilities? Again, if thou art instructing any one ; speak on the subject at present before thee, otherwise be silent.[1] If the speech be " seasoned with salt," should it fall into a soul that is of loose texture, it will brace up its slackness ; into one that is harsh, it will smooth its ruggedness. Let it be gracious, and so neither hard, nor yet weak, but let it have both sternness and pleasantness therewith. For if one be immoderately stern, he doth more harm than good ; and if he be immoderately complaisant, he giveth more pain than pleasure, so that everywhere there ought to be moderation. Be not downcast, and sour visaged, for this is offensive ; nor yet be wholly relaxed, for this is open to contempt and treading under foot ; but, like the bee, culling the virtue of each, of the one its cheerfulness, of the other its gravity, keep clear of the fault. For if a physician dealeth not with all bodies alike, much more ought not a teacher. And yet better will the body bear unsuitable medicines, than the

soul language ; for instance, a Greek cometh to thee, and becomes thy friend ; discourse not at all with him on this subject, until he have become a close friend, and after he hath become so, do it gradually.

See, when Paul also had come to Athens, how he discoursed with them. He said not, " O polluted, and all-polluted " ; but what? " Ye men of Athens, in all things I perceive that ye are somewhat superstitious."[2] (Acts xvii. 22.) Again, when to insult was needful, he refused not ; but with great vehemency he said to Elymas, " O full of all guile and all villainy, son of the devil, enemy of all righteousness." For as to have insulted those had been senselessness, so not to have insulted this one had been softness. Again, art thou brought unto a ruler on a matter of business, see that thou render him the honors that are his due.

Ver. 9. " They shall make known unto you," he saith, " all things that are done here." Why didst thou not come with them, says one? But what is, " They shall make known unto you all things " ? My bonds, that is, and all the other things that detain me. I then, who pray to see them, who also send others, should not myself have remained behind, had not some great necessity detained me. And yet this is not the language of accusation — yes, of vehement accusation. For the assuring them that he had both fallen into trials, and was bearing them nobly, is the part of one who was confirming the fact, and lifting up again their souls.

Ver. 9. " With Onesimus," he saith, " the beloved, and faithful brother."

Paul calleth a slave, brother : with reason ; seeing that he styleth himself the servant of the faithful. (2 Cor. iv. 5.) Bring we down all of us our pride, tread we under foot our boastfulness. Paul nameth himself a slave, he that is worth the world, and ten thousands of heavens ; and dost thou entertain high thoughts? He that seizeth all things for spoil as he will, he that hath the first place in the kingdom of heaven, he that was crowned, he that ascended into the third heaven, calleth servants, " brethren," and " fellow-servants." Where is your madness? where is your arrogance?

So trustworthy was Onesimus become, as to be entrusted even with such things as these.

Ver. 10. " And Mark," he saith, " the cousin of Barnabas, touching whom ye received commandments, receive him." Perhaps they had received commandments from Barnabas.

---

[1] ἐπεὶ σίγα, i.e. since (if it be not so) be silent.

[2] δεισιδαιμονεστέρους. The word does not convey quite the reproach which the E. V. does. It may be rendered, " I see that ye are rather given to the fear of divinities." [Or more probably, " very religious," as in American App. to Rev. Ver. The adjective may have either the good or the bad sense; and the comparative may mean more than a little, " somewhat," or more than common, " quite," " remarkably," or more than enough, " too." Only the connection can in such cases decide, and that is not here conclusive. — J. A. B.]

Ver. 11. "Who are of the circumcision." He represseth the swelling pride of the Jews, and inspiriteth the souls of these, [the Colossians,] because few of them were of the circumcision, the greater number of the Gentiles.

"Men that have been," he saith, "a comfort unto me." He shows himself to be set in the midst of great trials. So that neither is this a small thing. When we comfort the Saints by presence, by words, by assiduous attendance, when we suffer adversity together with them, (for he saith, "as bound with those in bonds"; [Heb. xiii. 3]) when we make their sufferings ours, we shall also be partakers in their crowns. Hast thou not been dragged to the stadium? Hast thou not entered into the lists? It is another that strips himself, another that wrestles; but if thou be so minded, thou too shalt be a sharer. Anoint him, become his favorer and partisan, from without the lists shout loudly for him, stir up his strength, refresh his spirit. It follows that the same things should be done in all other cases. For Paul stood not in need, but in order to stimulate them he said these things. Thou therefore in the case of all others, stop the mouths of those who would abuse such an one, procure favorers for him, receive him as he cometh forth with great attention, so shalt thou be a sharer in his crowns, so, in his glory; and if thou do no other thing, but only hast pleasure in what is done, even thus thou sharest in no common degree, for thou hast contributed love, the sum of all good things.

For if they that weep seem to share in the grief of those in sorrow, and gratify them mightily, and remove the excess of their woe, much more do they also that rejoice with others, make their pleasure greater. For how great an evil it is not to have companions in sorrow, hear the Prophet saying, "And I looked for one to lament with me, but there was none."[1] Wherefore Paul also saith, "Rejoice with them that rejoice; and weep with them that weep." (Rom. xii. 15.) Increase their pleasure. If thou see thy brother in good esteem, say not, "the esteem is his, why should I rejoice." These words are not those of a brother, but of an enemy. If thou be so minded, it is not his, but thine. Thou hast the power of making it greater, if thou be not downcast, but pleased, if thou be cheerful, if joyous. And that it is so, is evident from this; the envious envy not those only who are in good esteem, but those as well who rejoice at their good esteem, so conscious are they that these also are interested in that good esteem; and these are they who do glory most in it. For the other even blushes when praised exceedingly; but these with great pleasure pride themselves upon it. See ye not in the case of

athletes, how the one is crowned, the other is not crowned; but the grief and the joy is amongst the favorers and disfavorers,[2] these are they that leap, they that caper?

See how great a thing is the not envying. The toil is another's, the pleasure is thine; another wears the crown, and thou caperest, thou art gay. For tell me, seeing it is another that hath conquered, why dost thou leap? But they also know well, that what hath been done is common. Therefore they do not accuse this man[3] indeed, but they try to beat down the victory; and you hear them saying such words as these, "(There) I expunged thee," and, "I beat thee down." Although the deed was another's, still the praise is thine. But if in things without, not to envy, but to make another's good one's own, is so great a good, much more in the victory of the devil over us he breathes the more furiously, evidently because we are more pleased.[4] Wicked though he is, and bitter, he well knows that this pleasure is great. Wouldest thou pain him? Be glad and rejoice. Wouldest thou gladden him? Be sad-visaged. The pain he has from thy brother's victory, thou soothest by thy sadness; thou standest with him, severed from thy brother, thou workest greater mischief than he. For it is not the same for one that is an enemy to do the deeds of an enemy, and for a friend to stand with an enemy; such an one is more detestable than an enemy. If thy brother have gained good reputation[5] either by speaking, or by brilliant[6] or successful achievement, become thou a sharer in his reputation, show that he is a member of thine.

"And how?" saith one, "for the reputation is not mine." Never speak so. Compress thy lips. If thou hadst been near me, thou that speakest on that wise, I would have even put my hand over thy lips: lest the enemy should hear thee. Oftentimes we have enmities with one another, and we discover them not to our enemies; dost thou then discover thine to the devil? Say not so, think not so; but the very reverse: "he is one of my members, the glory passes on to the body." "How then is it," saith one, "that those without are not so minded?" Because of thy fault: when they see thee counting his pleasure not thine own, they too count it not thine: were they to see thee appropriating it, they durst not do so, but thou

---

[2] See Tac. An. xiii. 25. The spectators at theaters and at the games were so eager in their favor toward one or another as sometimes to cause serious breaches of the peace. The factions of the Circus in the time of Justinian are described by Gibbon, c. xl.; see also the massacre of A.D. 501. Tillemont, Hist. des Emp. t. vi.; Anastasius, art. x.

[3] τουτῳ, the partisan of the victor.

[4] [The persons designated as "we" seem to be conceived as divided into two parts. The altered text has smoothed down the difficulty: "much more in the victory over the devil. For he then breathes the more furiously against us, evidently," &c.—J. A. B.]

[5] [Above rendered "good esteem."—J. A. B.]

[6] ἐπιδεικνύμενος, al. ἐπαινόμενος, "by being praised."

wouldest become equally illustrious with him. Thou hast not gained reputation by speaking; but by sharing in his joy thou hast gained more renown than he. For if love be a great thing, and the sum of all, thou hast received the crown this gives; he, that for oratory, thou, that for exceeding love; he displayed force of words, but thou by deeds hast cast down envy, hast trodden under foot the evil eye. So that in reason thou oughtest rather to be crowned than he, thy contest is the more brilliant; thou hast not only trodden under foot envy, but thou hast even done somewhat else. He hath one crown only, but thou two, and those both brighter than his one. What are these? One, that which thou wonnest against envy, another, which thou art encircled with by love. For the sharing in his joy is a proof not only of thy being free from envy, but also of being rooted in love. Him ofttimes some human passion sorely disquieteth, vainglory for instance; but thou art free from every passion, for it is not of vainglory that thou rejoicest at another's good. Hath he righted up the Church, tell me? hath he increased the congregation? Praise him; again thou hast a twofold crown; thou hast struck down envy; thou hast enwreathed thee with love. Yea, I implore and beseech thee. Wilt thou hear of a third crown even? Him, men below applaud, thee, the Angels above. For it is not the same thing, to make a display of eloquence, and to rule the passions. This praise is for a season, that for ever; this, of men, that, of God; this man is crowned openly; but thou art crowned in secret, where thy Father seeth. If it were possible to have peeled off the body and seen the soul of each, I would have shown thee that this is more dignified than the other, more resplendent.

Tread we under foot the goads of envy, we advantage ourselves, beloved, ourselves shall we enwreath with the crown. He that envieth another fighteth with God, not with him; for when he seeth him to have grace, and is grieved, and wisheth the Church pulled down, he fighteth not with him, but with God. For tell me, if one should adorn a king's daughter, and by his adorning and gracing her, gain for himself renown; and another person should wish her to be ill attired, and him to be unable to adorn her; against whom would he have been plotting mischief? Against the other? or against her and her father? So too now, thou that enviest, fightest with the Church, thou warrest with God. For, since with the good repute of thy brother is interwoven also the Church's profit, need is, that if the one be undone, the other shall be undone also. So that, in this regard also, thou doest a deed of Satan, seeing thou plottest mis-

chief against the body of Christ. Art thou pained at this man? Wrongly, when he hath in nothing wronged thee; yea, much rather, thou art pained at Christ. Wherein hath He wronged thee, that thou wilt not suffer His body to be decked with beauty? that thou wilt not suffer His bride to be adorned? Consider, I pray thee, the punishment, how sore. Thou gladdenest thine enemies; and him too himself, the man in good esteem, whom through thy envy thou wishest to grieve, thou dost the rather gladden; thou dost by thine envy the rather show that he is in good esteem, for otherwise thou wouldest not have envied him. Thou showest the rather that thou art in punishment.

I am ashamed indeed to exhort you from such motives, but seeing our weakness is so great, let us be instructed even from these, and free ourselves from this destructive passion. Grievest thou that he is in good esteem? then why swellest thou that esteem by envying? Wishest thou to punish him? Why then showest thou that thou art pained? Why punish thyself before him, whom thou wouldest not have well esteemed? Thereafter double will be his pleasure, and thy punishment; not only because thou provest him to be great; but because thou begettest in him yet another pleasure, by punishing thyself; and again, at what thou art pained, he is pleased, whilst thou enviest. See how we deal ourselves heavy blows without perceiving it! He is an enemy. And yet, why an enemy? What wrong hath he done? Still, however, by this we make our enemy the more illustrious, and thereby punish ourselves the more. And herein again we punish ourselves, if we have discovered that he knows it. For perhaps he is not pleased,[1] but we thinking him to be so, are again pained on that account. Cease then your envying. Why inflictest thou wounds upon thyself?

Think we of these things, beloved; of those two crowns for them that envy not; of those praises from men, of those from God; of the evils that come of envying; and so shall we be able to quell the brute, and to be in good esteem before God, and to obtain the same things with those who are of good esteem. For perhaps we shall obtain them, and if we obtain them not, it will be for our advantage; still, even so, we shall be able, if we have lived to the glory of God, to obtain the good things promised to them that love Him, through the grace and love toward man of our Lord Jesus Christ, with whom, &c.

---

[1] The Empress Eudoxia is thought to have been reflected on in some of the passages against extravagance. This whole passage probably alludes to the enmity which prevailed at court in consequence, and these words were probably meant to hint at the real love of St. Chrysostom for his bitterest enemies.

HOMILY XII.

COLOSSIANS iv. 12, 13.

" Epaphras, who is one of you, a servant of Christ Jesus,
saluteth you, always striving for you in his prayers,
that ye may stand perfect and fully assured in all the
will of God. For I bear him witness, that he hath
much zeal[1] for you, and for them in Laodicea, and
for them in Hierapolis."

IN the commencement of this Epistle also, he
commended this man for his love ; for even to
praise is a sign of love ; thus in the beginning
he said, "Who also declared unto us your love
in the Spirit." (Col. i. 8.) To pray for one is
also a sign of love, and causeth love again. He
commends him moreover in order to open a door
to his teachings, for reverendness in the teacher
is the disciples' advantage ; and so again is his
saying,[2] " one of you," in order that they might
pride themselves upon the man, as producing
such men. And he saith, "always striving for
you in prayers." He said not simply "praying,"
but "striving," trembling and fearing. "For I
bear him witness," he saith, "that he hath much
zeal for you." A trustworthy witness. "That
he hath," he saith, "much zeal for you," that is,
that he loveth you exceedingly ; and burneth with
passionate affection for you. "And them in Laodicea, and them in Hierapolis." He commendeth him to those also. But whence were they to
know this? They would assuredly have heard ;
however, they would also learn it when the Epistle
was read. For he said, "Cause that it be read
also in the church of the Laodiceans." "That
ye may stand perfect," he saith. At once he both
accuseth them, and without offensiveness gives
them advice and counsel. For it is possible both
to be perfect, and withal not to stand, as if one
were to know all, and still be wavering ; it is
possible also not to be perfect, and yet to stand,
as if one were to know a part, and stand [not[3]]
firmly. But this man prayeth for both : "That
ye may stand perfect," he saith. See how again
he has reminded them of what he said about
the Angels, and about life. "And fully assured,"
he saith, "in all the will of God." It is not
enough, simply to do His will. He that is
"filled," suffereth not any other will to be within
him, for if so, he is not wholly filled. "For I
bear him witness," he saith, "that he hath much
zeal." Both "zeal," and "great" ; both are
intensive. As he saith himself, when writing

to the Corinthians, "For I am jealous[4] over you
with a godly jealousy." (2 Cor. xi. 2.)

Ver. 14. "Luke, the beloved physician, saluteth you." This is the Evangelist. It is not
to lower this man that he placeth him after, but
to raise the other, viz. Epaphroditus. It is
probable that there were others called by this
name.[5] "And Demas," he says. After saying,
"Luke, the physician, saluteth you," he added,
"the beloved." And no small praise is this, but
even great exceedingly, to be beloved of Paul.

Ver. 15. "Salute the brethren that are in
Laodicea, and Nymphas, and the Church that
is in their house."

See how he cements, and knits them together
with one another, not by salutation only, but
also by interchanging his Epistles. Then again
he pays a compliment by addressing him indi-
vidually. And this he doth not without a reason,
but in order to lead the others also to emulate
his zeal. For it is not a small thing not to be
numbered with the rest. Mark further how he
shows the man to be great, seeing his house was
a church.

Ver. 14. "And when this Epistle hath been
read among you, cause that it be read also in
the church of the Laodiceans." I suppose there
are some of the things therein written, which
it was needful that those also should hear. And
they would have the greater advantage of recog-
nizing their own errors in the charges brought
against others.

"And that ye also read the Epistle from
Laodicea." Some say that this is not Paul's to
them, but theirs to Paul, for he said not that
to the Laodiceans, but that written "from
Laodicea."

Ver. 17. "And say to Archippus, Take heed
to the ministry which thou hast received in the
Lord, that thou fulfill it." Wherefore doth he
not write to him? Perhaps he needed it not,
but only a bare reminding, so as to be more
diligent.

Ver. 18. "The salutation of me, Paul, with
mine own hand." This is a proof of their sincerity and affection ; that they both looked at
his handwriting, and that with emotion. "Remember my bonds." Wonderful ! How great
the consolation ! For this is enough to cheer
them on to all things, and make them bear them-

---

[1] [Correct text of N. T., as in Rev. Ver., "much labor."—
J. A. B.]

[2] Ed. Par. [and Field] conj. τῷ for τὸ, " again (he commends
him) by saying."

[3] Hales seems right in expunging this word; otherwise the sense
is " though not." [Omitted in one MS. and in Field.— J. A. B.]

[4] [The Greek word means both zealous and jealous. In fact, the
English word "jealous" is only a corrupt form of "zealous."—
J. A. B.]

[5] i.e. Luke. Perhaps " and Demas " should come after the next
clause. [It is evident that we have here only rough notes, dictated,
or, more likely, taken in shorthand.—J. A. B.]

selves more nobly in their trials; but he made them not only the braver, but also the more nearly interested. "Grace be with you. Amen."

It is great praise, and greater than all the rest, his saying of Epaphras, "who is [one] of you, a servant of Christ."[1] And he calleth him a minister for them, like as he termeth himself also a minister of the Church, as when he saith, "Whereof I Paul was made a minister." (Col. i. 23.) To the same dignity he advances this man; and above he calleth him a "fellow-servant" (Col. i. 7), and here, "a servant." "Who is of you," he saith, as if speaking to a mother, and saying, "who is of thy womb." But this praise might have gendered envy; therefore he commendeth him not from these things only, but also from what had regard to themselves; and so he does away with envy, both in the former place, and here. "Always," he saith, "striving for you," not now only, whilst with us, to make a display; nor yet only whilst with you, to make a display before you. By saying, "striving," he hath showed his great earnestness. Then, that he might not seem to be flattering them, he added, "that he hath much zeal for you, and for them in Laodicea, and for them in Hierapolis." And the words, "that ye may stand perfect," are not words of flattery, but of a reverend teacher. Both "fully assured" he saith, "and perfect." The one he granted them, the other he said was lacking. And he said not, "that ye be not shaken," but, "that ye may stand." Their being saluted, however, by many, is refreshing to them, seeing that not only their friends from among themselves, but others also, remember them.

"And say to Archippus, Take heed to the ministry which thou hast received in the Lord." His chief aim is to subject them to him[2] entirely. For they could no more have complaint against him for rebuking them, when they themselves had taken it all upon them; for it is not reasonable to talk to the disciples about the teacher. But to stop their mouths, he writes thus to them; "Say to Archippus," he saith, "Take heed." This word is everywhere used to alarm; as when he saith, "Take heed of dogs." (Phil. iii. 2.) "Take heed lest there shall be any one that maketh spoil of you." (Col. ii. 8.) "Take heed lest by any means this liberty of yours become a stumblingblock to the weak." (1 Cor. viii. 9.) And he always so expresses himself when he would terrify. "Take heed," he saith, "to the ministry which thou hast received in the Lord, that thou fulfill it." He doth not even

allow him the power of choosing, as he saith himself, "For if I do this of mine own will, I have a reward: but if not of mine own will, I have a stewardship entrusted to me." (1 Cor. ix. 17.) "That thou fulfill it," continually using diligence. "Which thou hast received in the Lord, that thou fulfill it." Again, the word "in" means "through the Lord." He gave it thee, says he, not we. He subjects them also to him,[3] when he shows that they had been committed to his hands by God.

"Remember my bonds. Grace be with you. Amen." He hath released their terror. For although their teacher be in bonds, yet "grace" releaseth him. This too is of grace, the granting him to be put in bonds. For hear Luke saying, The Apostles returned "from the presence of the council, rejoicing that they were counted worthy to suffer dishonor for the Name." (Acts v. 41.) For both to suffer shame, and to be put in bonds, is indeed to be "counted worthy." For, if he that hath one whom he loveth, deemeth it gain to suffer aught for his sake, much rather then is it so to suffer for the sake of Christ. Repine we not then at our tribulations for Christ's sake, but let us also remember Paul's bonds, and be this our incitement. For instance: dost thou exhort any to give to the poor for Christ's sake? Remind them of Paul's bonds, and bemoan thy misery and theirs, seeing that he indeed gave up even his body to bonds for His sake, but thou wilt not give a portion even of thy food. Art thou lifted up because of thy good deeds? Remember Paul's bonds, that thou hast suffered nought of that kind, and thou wilt be lifted up no more. Covetest thou any of the things that are thy neighbor's? Remember Paul's bonds, and thou wilt see how unreasonable it is, that whilst he was in perils, thou shouldest be in delights. Again, is thine heart set upon self-indulgence? Picture to thy mind Paul's prison-house; thou art his disciple, his fellow-soldier. How is it reasonable, that thy fellow-soldier should be in bonds, and thou in luxury? Art thou in affliction? Dost thou deem thyself forsaken? Hear Paul's bonds,[4] and thou wilt see, that to be in affliction is no proof of being forsaken. Wouldest thou wear silken robes? Remember Paul's bonds; and these things will appear to thee more worthless than the filth-bespattered rags of her that sitteth apart.[5] Wouldest thou array thee with golden trinkets? Picture to thy mind Paul's bonds, and these things will seem to thee no better than a withered bulrush. Wouldest thou tire thine hair, and be beautiful to see? Think

---

[1] [The two following paragraphs go again over the ground of the preceding. Are they notes taken by two hearers, or notes made by the preacher for two occasions? Or does he return and run over the passage again, to see what further remarks it will suggest? The latter seems to be the case in a good many of the Homilies on Acts. Comp. above, on Hom. xi. — J. A. B.]

[2] i.e. Archippus.

[3] i.e. Archippus.

[4] [So in all the MSS. known to Field. Notice how jejune is the correction, "words," which went into the printed editions. — J. A. B.]

[5] [This also is wanting in the editions, but found in the MSS., and indeed quite in Chrys.'s manner. See Isa. lxiv. 6. — J. A. B.]

of Paul's squalidness within that prison-house, and thou wilt burn for that beauty, and deem this the extreme of ugliness, and wilt groan bitterly through longing for those bonds. Wouldest thou daub thee with pastes and pigments, and such like things? Think of his tears: a three-years space, night and day, he ceased not to weep. (Acts xx. 31.) With this adorning deck thy cheek; these tears do make it bright. I say not, that thou weep for others, (I wish indeed it could be even so, but this is too high for thee,) but for thine own sins I advise thee to do this. Hast thou ordered thy slave to be put in bonds, and wast thou angry, and exasperated? Remember Paul's bonds, and thou wilt straightway stay thine anger; remember that we are of the bound, not the binders, of the bruised in heart, not the bruisers. Hast thou lost self-control, and shouted loud in laughter? Think of his lamentations, and thou wilt groan; such tears will show thee brighter far. Seest thou any persons rioting and dancing? Remember his tears. What fountain has gushed forth so great streams as those eyes did tears? "Remember my tears" (Acts xx. 31), he saith, as here "bonds." And with reason he spoke thus to them, when he sent for them from Ephesus to Miletus. For he was then speaking to teachers. He demands of those therefore, that they should sympathize[1] also, but of these that they should only encounter dangers.

What fountain wilt thou compare to these tears? That in Paradise, which watereth the whole earth? But thou wilt have mentioned nothing like it. For this fount of tears watered souls, not earth. If one were to show us Paul bathed in tears, and groaning, would not this be better far to see, than countless choirs gayly crowned? I am not now speaking of you; but, if one, having pulled away from the theater and the stage some wanton fellow, burning and drunken with carnal love, were to show him a young virgin in the very flower of her age, surpassing her fellows, both in other respects, and in her face more than the rest of her person, having an eye, tender and soft, that gently resteth, and gently rolleth, moist, mild, calmly smiling, and arrayed in much modesty and much grace, fringed with dark lashes both under and over, having an eyeball, so to speak, alive, a forehead radiant; underneath, again, a cheek shaded to exact redness, lying smooth as marble, and even; and then any one should show me Paul weeping; leaving that maiden, I would have eagerly sprung away to the sight of him; for from his eyes there

beamed spiritual beauty. For that other transporteth the souls of youths, it scorcheth and inflameth them; but this, on the contrary, subdueth them. This maketh the eyes of the soul more beauteous, it curbeth the belly: it filleth with the love of wisdom, with much sympathy: and it is able to soften even a soul of adamant. With these tears the Church is watered, with these souls are planted; yea, though there be fire sensible and substantial, yet can these tears quench it; these tears quench the fiery darts of the wicked one.

Remember we then these tears of his, and we shall laugh to scorn all present things. These tears did Christ pronounce blessed, saying, "Blessed are they that mourn, and blessed are they that weep, for they shall laugh." (Matt. v. 4; Luke vi. 21.) Such tears did Isaiah too, and Jeremiah weep; and the former said, "Leave me alone, I will weep bitterly" (Isa. xxii. 4, Sept.): and the latter, "Who will give my head water, and mine eyes fountains of tears?" (Jer. ix. 1); as though the natural fount were not enough.

Nothing is sweeter than these tears; sweeter are they than any laughter. They that mourn, know how great consolation it possesseth. Let us not think this a thing to be deprecated, but one to be even exceedingly prayed for; not that others may sin, but that, when they sin, we may be heart-broken for them. Remember we these tears, these bonds. Surely too upon those bonds tears descended; but the death of the perishing, of those that had bound him in them, suffered him not to taste the pleasure of the bonds. For in their behalf he grieved, being a disciple of Him that bewept the priests of the Jews; not because they were going to crucify Him, but because they were themselves perishing. And He doeth not this Himself alone, but He thus exhorteth others also, saying, "Daughters of Jerusalem, weep not for Me." (Luke xxiii. 28.) These eyes saw Paradise, saw the third heaven: but I count not them so blessed because of this sight, as because of those tears, through which they saw Christ. Blessed, indeed, was that sight; for he himself even glories in it, saying, "Have I not seen Jesus Christ our Lord?" (1 Cor. ix. 1); but more blessed so to weep.

In that sight many have been partakers, and those who have not so been, Christ the rather calls blessed, saying, "Blessed are they that have not seen, and yet have believed" (John xx. 29); but unto this not many have attained. For if to stay here for Christ's sake were more needful than to depart to Him (Phil. i. 23, 24), for the sake of the salvation of others; surely then to groan for others' sakes, is more needful even than to see Him. For if for His sake to be in

---

[1] [This συναλγεῖν was changed in most MSS. and the editions into συνάγειν, "gather together." Hales conjectured συναλγεῖν. Field finds it in a MS. The other is indeed the more difficult reading, and likely to have been altered into an easy one, but the difficulty in this case becomes practically unintelligible. — J. A. B.]

hell,[1] is rather to be desired, than to be with Him; and to be separated from Him for His sake more to be desired than to be with Him, (for this is what he said, "For I could wish that I myself were anathema from Christ" (Rom. ix. 3)), much more is weeping for His sake. "I ceased not," he saith, "to admonish every-one with tears." (Acts xx. 31.) Wherefore? Not fearing the dangers; no; but as if one sit-ting by a sick man's side, and not knowing what would be the end, should weep for affec-tion, fearing lest he should lose his life; so too did he; when he saw any one diseased, and could not prevail by rebuke, he thenceforward wept. So did Christ also, that happily they might reverence His tears: thus, one sinned, He rebuked him; the rebuked spat upon Him, and sprang aloof; He wept, that haply He might win him even so.

Remember we these tears: thus let us bring up our daughters, thus our sons; weeping when we see them in evil. As many women as wish to be loved, let them remember Paul's tears, and groan: as many of you as are counted blest, as many as are in bridal chambers, as many as are in pleasure, remember these; as many as are in mourning, exchange tears for tears. He mourned not for the dead; but for those that were per-ishing whilst alive. Shall I tell of other tears? Timothy also wept; for he was this man's dis-ciple; wherefore also when writing to him he said, "Remembering thy tears, that I may be filled with joy." (2 Tim. i. 4.) Many weep even from pleasure. So it is also a matter of pleasure, and that of the utmost intensity. So the tears are not painful: yea, the tears that flow from such sorrow are even better far than those due to worldly pleasure. Hear the Prophet saying, "The Lord hath heard the voice of my weep-ing, he hath heard the voice of my supplica-tion." (Ps. vi. 8.) For where is the tear not useful? in prayers? in exhortations? We get them an ill name, by using them not to what they are given us for. When we entreat a sin-ning brother, we ought to weep, grieving and groaning; when we exhort any one, and he giveth us no heed, but goeth on perishing, we ought to weep. These are the tears of heavenly wisdom. When however one is in poverty, or bodily disease, or dead, not so; for these are not things worthy of tears.

As then we gain an ill name for laughter also, when we use it out of season; so too do we for tears, by having recourse to them unseasonably. For the virtue of each thing then discovers it-self when it is brought to its own fitting work, but when to one that is alien, it doth no longer so. For instance, wine is given for cheerfulness,

not drunkenness, bread for nourishment, sexual intercourse for the procreation of children. As then these things have gained an ill name, so also have tears. Be there a law laid down, that they be used in prayers and exhortations only, and see how desirable a thing they will become. Nothing doth so wipe out sins, as tears. Tears show even this bodily countenance beautiful; for they win the spectator to pity, they make it respected in our eyes. Nothing is sweeter than tearful eyes. For this is the noblest member we have, and the most beautiful, and the soul's own. And therefore we are so bowed there-with, as though we saw the soul itself lamenting.

I have not spoken these things without a reason; but in order that ye may cease your attendance at weddings, at dancings, at Satanical performances. For see what the devil hath invented. Since nature itself hath withheld women from the stage, and the disgraceful things enacted there, he hath introduced into the women's apartment the furniture of the theater, I mean, wanton men and harlots. This pestilence the custom of marriages hath intro-duced, or rather, not of marriages, far be it, but of our own silliness. What is it thou doest, O man? Dost thou not know what thou art at? Thou marriest a wife for chastity, and pro-creation of children; what then mean these harlots? That there may be, one answereth, greater gladness. And yet is not this rather mad-ness? Thou insultest thy bride, thou insultest the women that are invited. For if they are delighted with such proceedings, the thing is an insult. If to see harlots acting indecorously conferreth any honor, wherefore dost thou not drag thy bride also thither, that she too may see? It is quite indecent and disgraceful to introduce into one's house lewd fellows and dancers, and all that Satanic pomp.

"Remember," he saith, "my bonds." Mar-riage is a bond, a bond ordained of God, a harlot is a severing and a dissolving. It is per-mitted you to embellish marriage with other things, such as full tables, and apparel. I do not cut off these things, lest I should seem to be clownish to an extreme; and yet Rebecca was content with her veil[2] only (Gen. xxiv. 65); still I do not cut them off. It is permitted you to embellish and set off marriage with apparel, with the presence of reverend men and reverend women. Why introducest thou those mock-eries?[3] why those monsters? Tell us what it is thou hearest from them? What? dost thou blush to tell? Dost thou blush, and yet force them to do it? If it is honorable, wherefore dost thou not do it thyself as well? but if dis-graceful, wherefore dost thou compel another?

---

[1] See St. Chrysostom on Rom. ix. 3, where he says the wish was "to be separated from His presence, not from His love."

[2] θέριστρον, "summer robe."

[3] ἐπιχάρματα, subjects of rejoicing for the enemy.

Everything should be full of chasteness, of gravity, of orderliness; but I see the reverse, people frisking like camels and mules. For the virgin, her chamber[1] is the only befitting place. "But," saith one, "she is poor." Because she is poor, she ought to be modest also; let her have her character in the place of a fortune. Has she no dowry to give with herself? Then why dost thou make her otherwise contemptible through her life and manners? I praise the custom, that virgins attend to do honor to their fellow; matrons attend to do honor to her who is made one of their order. Rightly hath this been ordered. For these are two companies, one of virgins, the other of the married; the one are giving her up, the other receiving her. The bride is between them, neither virgin, nor wife, for she is coming forth from those, and entering into the fellowship of these. But those harlots, what mean they? They ought to hide their faces when marriage is celebrated; they ought to be dug into the earth, (for harlotry is the corruption of marriage,) but we introduce them at our marriages. And, when ye are engaged in any work, ye count it ill-omened to speak even a syllable of what is adverse to it; for instance, when thou sowest, when thou drawest off the wine from thy vats, thou wouldest not, even if asked, utter a syllable about vinegar; but here, where the object is chasteness, introduce ye the vinegar? for such is an harlot. When ye are preparing sweet ointment, ye suffer nought ill-scented to be near. Marriage is a sweet ointment. Why then introducest thou the foul stench of the dunghill into the preparation of thy ointment? What sayest thou? Shall the virgin dance, and yet feel no shame before her fellow? For she ought to have more gravity than the other; she hath at least come forth from the [nurse's] arm, and not from the palæstra. For the virgin ought to not appear publicly at all at a marriage.

Seest thou not how in kings' houses, the honored are within, about the king, the unhonored without? Do thou too be within about the bride. But remain in the house in chasteness, expose not thy virginity. Either company is standing by, the one to show of what sort she is whom they are giving up, the other in order that they may guard her. Why disgracest thou the virgin estate? For if thou art such as this, the same will the bridegroom suspect her to be. If thou wishest to have men in love with thee, this is the part of saleswomen, green-grocers, and handicrafts-people. Is not this a shame? To act unseemly is a shame even though it be a king's daughter.[2] For doth her poverty stand in the way? or her course of life? Even if a

virgin be a slave, let her abide in modesty. "For in Christ Jesus there can be neither bond nor free." (Gal. iii. 28.)

What? is marriage a theater? It is a mystery and a type of a mighty thing; and even if thou reverence not it, reverence that whose type it is. "This mystery," saith he, "is great, but I speak in regard of Christ and of the Church." (Eph. v. 32.) It is a type of the Church, and of Christ, and dost thou introduce harlots at it? If then, saith one, neither virgins dance, nor the married, who is to dance? No one, for what need is there of dancing? In the Grecian mysteries there are dancings, but in ours, silence and decency, modesty, and bashfulness. A great mystery is being celebrated: forth with the harlots! forth with the profane! How is it a mystery? They come together, and the two make one. Wherefore is it that at his entrance indeed, there was no dancing, no cymbals, but great silence, great stillness; but when they come together, making not a lifeless image, nor yet the image of anything upon earth, but of God Himself, and after his likeness, thou introducest so great an uproar, and disturbest those that are there,[3] and puttest the soul to shame, and confoundest it? They come, about to be made one body. See again a mystery of love! If the two become not one, so long as they continue two, they make not many, but when· they are come into oneness, they then make many. What do we learn from this? That great is the power of union. The wise counsel of God at the beginning divided the one into two; and being desirous of showing that even after division it remaineth still one, He suffered not that the one should be of itself enough for procreation. For he is not one who is not yet [united,[4]] but the half of one; and it is evident from this, that he begetteth no offspring, as was the case also beforetime.[5] Seest thou the mystery of marriage? He made of one, one[6]; and again, having made these two, one, He so maketh one, so that now also man is produced of·one. For man and wife are not two men, but one Man. And this may be confirmed from many sources; for instance, from James,[7] from Mary the Mother of Christ, from the words, "He made them male and female." (Gen. i. 27.) If he

---

[1] θάλαμος, which is used for any retired chamber.
[2] i.e. at whose wedding it is done.

[3] τοὺς ὄντας. Possibly "those that are [that image]." Downes proposes συνόντας, with some probability.
[4] ὁ οὐδέπω. The word ἠνωμένος, which Ed. Par. would supply, may be understood.
[5] καθάπερ καὶ πρότερον. Downes and others give up this passage as corrupt. The Translator suggests, "as was the case with Adam before Eve was formed." There is still a difficulty, though this has a meaning, in that God withheld the power then from the undivided Man, as he does now from the not yet reunited.
[6] i.e. "one other." Savile needlessly conjectures "two."
[7] The word is declined, and so would not mean Jacob. One MS. has Joseph, which is no plainer. [Three MSS. have Joseph, but they are the group of three that are so often palpably altering.— J. A. B.] One would expect a solution from the end of Hom. v., but none seems to occur there, unless Jacob's birth after Rebecca's long barrenness be deemed sufficient.

be the head, and she the body, how are they two? Therefore the one holdeth the rank of a disciple, the other of a teacher, the one of a ruler, the other of a subject. Moreover, from the very fashioning of her body, one may see that they are one, for she was made from his side, and they are, as it were, two halves.

For this cause He also calleth her a help, to show that they are one (Gen. ii. 18); for this cause He honoreth their cohabitation beyond both father and mother, to show that they are one. (Gen. ii. 24.) And in like manner a father rejoiceth both when son and daughter marry, as though the body were hastening to join a member of its own; and though so great a charge and expenditure of money is incurred, still he cannot bear with indifference to see her[1] unmarried. For as though her own flesh itself were severed from her, each one separately is imperfect for the procreation of children, each one is imperfect as regards the constitution of this present life. Wherefore also the Prophet saith, "the residue of thy spirit." (Mal. ii. 15, Sept.) And how become they one flesh? As if thou shouldest take away the purest part of gold, and mingle it with other gold; so in truth here also the woman as it were receiving the richest part fused by pleasure, nourisheth it and cherisheth it, and withal contributing her own share, restoreth it back a Man. And the child is a sort of bridge, so that the three become one flesh, the child connecting, on either side, each to other. For like as two cities, which a river divides throughout, become one, if a bridge connect them on both sides, so is it in this case; and yet more, when the very bridge in this case is formed of the substance of each. As the body and the head are one body; for they are divided by the neck; but not divided more than connected, for it, lying between them, brings together each with the other. And it is the same as if a chorus that had been severed should, by taking one part of itself from this quarter, and the other again from the right, make one; or as these when come into close rank, and extending hands, become one; for the hands extended admit not of their being two. Therefore to wit He said with accuracy of expression, not "they shall be one flesh" but joined together "into one flesh" (Gen. ii. 2, Sept.), namely, that of the child. What then? when there is no child, will they not be two? Nay, for their coming together hath this effect, it diffuses and commingles the bodies of both. And as one who hath cast ointment into oil, hath made the whole one; so in truth is it also here.

I know that many are ashamed at what is said,

and the cause of this is what I spoke of, your own lasciviousness, and unchasteness. The fact of marriages being thus performed, thus depraved, hath gained the thing an ill name : for "marriage is honorable, and the bed undefiled." (Heb. xiii. 4.) Why art thou ashamed of the honorable, why blushest thou at the undefiled? This is for heretics,[2] this is for such as introduce harlots thither. For this cause I am desirous of having it thoroughly purified, so as to bring it back again to its proper nobleness, so as to stop the mouths of the heretics. The gift of God is insulted, the root of our generation; for about that root there is much dung and filth. This then let us cleanse away by our discourse. Endure then a little while, for he that holdeth filth must endure the stench. I wish to show you that ye ought not to be ashamed at these things, but at those which ye do; but thou, passing by all shame at those, art ashamed at these; surely then thou condemnest God who hath thus decreed.

Shall I tell how marriage is also a mystery of the Church? As Christ came into the Church, and she was made of him,[3] and he united with her in a spiritual intercourse, "for," saith one, "I have espoused you to one husband, a pure virgin." (2 Cor. xi. 2.) And that we are of Him, he saith, of His members, "and of His flesh." Thinking then on all these things, let us not cast shame upon so great a mystery. Marriage is a type of the presence of Christ, and art thou drunken at it? Tell me; if thou sawest an image of the king, wouldest thou dishonor it? By no means.

Now the practices at marriages seem to be a matter of indifference, but they are the causes of great mischiefs. All is full of lawlessness. "Filthiness, and foolish talking, and jesting, let it not proceed," saith he, "out of your mouth." (Eph. v. 4; iv. 29.) Now all these things are filthiness, foolish talking, and jesting; and not these simply, but with aggravation, for the thing has become an art, and there are great praises for those that pursue it. Sins have become an art! We pursue them not in any chance way, but with earnestness, with science, and thenceforth the devil takes the command of his own array. For where drunkenness is, there is unchasteness: where filthy talking, there the devil is at hand bringing in his own contributions; with such an entertainment, tell me, dost thou celebrate the mystery of Christ? and invitest thou the devil?

I dare say you consider me offensive. For

---

[1] Implied in αὐτῇ below. The word is of common gender.

[2] On 1 Tim. iv. 3 he mentions the Manichees, Marcionites, and Encratites.

[3] [The three MSS. which so often alter have made an important alteration here, from "she was made of him" into "he was made of her," and this became the common printed text. Were the critics thinking of a typical relation between the Virgin Mary and the Church, or of transubstantiation?—J. A. B.]

this too is a property of extreme pervertedness, that even one that rebuketh you incurs your ridicule as one that is austere. Hear ye not Paul, saying, "Whatsoever ye do, whether ye eat or drink or whatsoever ye do, do all to the glory of God"? (1 Cor. x. 31.) But ye do all to ill report and dishonor. Hear ye not the Prophet, saying, "Serve the Lord with fear, and rejoice unto Him with trembling?" (Ps. ii. 11.) But ye are wholly without restraint.[1] Is it not possible both to enjoy pleasure, and to do so with safety? Art thou desirous of hearing beautiful songs? Best of all indeed, thou oughtest not; nevertheless, I condescend if thou wilt have it so: do not hear those Satanic ones, but the spiritual. Art thou desirous of seeing choirs of dancers? Behold the choir of Angels. And how is it possible, saith one, to see them? If thou drive away all these things, even Christ will come to such a marriage, and Christ being present, the choir of Angels is present also. If thou wilt, He will even now work miracles as He did then; He will make even now the water, wine (John ii.); and what is much more wonderful, He will convert this unstable and dissolving pleasure, this cold desire, and change it into the spiritual. This is to make of water, wine. Where pipers are, by no means there is Christ; but even if He should have entered, He first casts these forth,[2] and then He works His wonders. What can be more disagreeable than this Satanic pomp? where everything is inarticulate, everything without significancy; and if there be anything articulate, again all is shameful, all is noisome.

Nothing is more pleasurable than virtue, nothing sweeter than orderliness, nothing more amiable than gravity. Let any celebrate such a marriage as I speak of; and he shall find the pleasure; but what sort of marriages these are, take heed. First seek a husband for the virgin, who will be truly a husband, and a protector; as though thou wert intending to place a head upon a body; as though about to give not a slave, but a daughter into his hands. Seek not money, nor splendor of family, nor greatness of country; all these things are superfluous; but piety of soul, gentleness, the true understanding, the fear of God, if thou wishest thy darling to live with pleasure. For if thou seek a wealthier husband, not only wilt thou not benefit her, but thou wilt even harm her, by making her a slave instead of free. For the pleasure she will reap from her golden trinkets will not be so great as will be the annoyance that comes of her slavery. I pray thee, seek not these things, but most of all, one of equal condition; if however this cannot be, rather one poorer than in better circumstances; if at least thou be desirous not of selling thy daughter to a master, but of giving her to a husband. When thou hast thoroughly investigated the virtue of the man, and art about to give her to him, beseech Christ to be present: for He will not be ashamed to be so; it is the mystery of His presence. Yea rather beseech Him even in the first instance, to grant her such a suitor. Be not worse than the servant of Abraham, who, when sent on a pilgrimage so important, saw whither he ought to have recourse; wherefore also he obtained everything. When thou art taking anxious pains, and seeking a husband for her, pray; say unto God, "whomsoever Thou wilt do Thou provide:" into His hands commit the matter; and He, honored in this way by thee, will requite thee with honor.

Two things indeed it is necessary to do; to commit the thing into His hands, and to seek such an orderly person as He Himself approves.

When[3] then thou makest a marriage, go not round from house to house borrowing mirrors and dresses; for the matter is not one of display, nor dost thou lead thy daughter to a pageant; but decking out thine house with what is in it, invite thy neighbors, and friends, and kindred. As many as thou knowest to be of a good character, those invite, and bid them be content with what there is. Let no one from the orchestra be present, for such expense is superfluous, and unbecoming. Before all the rest, invite Christ. Knowest thou whereby thou wilt invite Him? Whosoever, saith He, "hath done it to one of these least, hath done it to Me." (Matt. xxv. 40.) And think it not an annoying thing to invite the poor for Christ's sake; to invite harlots is an annoyance. For to invite the poor is a means of wealth, the other of ruin. Adorn the bride not with these ornaments that are made of gold, but with gentleness and modesty, and the customary robes; in place of all golden ornament and braiding, arraying her in blushes, and shamefacedness, and the not desiring such things. Let there be no uproar, no confusion; let the bridegroom be called, let him receive the virgin. The dinners and suppers, let them not be full of drunkenness, but of abundance and pleasure. See how many good things will result, whenever we see such marriages as those; but from the marriages that are now celebrated, (if at least one ought to call them marriages and not pageants,) how many are the evils! The banquet hall is no sooner broken up, than straightway comes care and fear, lest aught that is borrowed should have been lost, and there succeeds to the pleasure melancholy intolerable. But this distress belongs to the mother-in-law,—

---

[1] διαχεῖσθε, are dissolute: lit. "poured abroad."
[2] As when He would raise Jairus's daughter, Matt. ix. 25.
[3] Here he addresses the mother, all the participles being feminine.

nay, rather not even is the bride herself free; all that follows at least belongs to the bride herself. For to see all broken up, is a ground for sadness, to see the house desolate.

There is Christ, here is Satan; there is cheerfulness, here anxious care; there pleasure, here pain; there expense, here nothing of the kind; there indecency, here modesty; there envy, here no envy; there drunkenness, here soberness, here health, here temperance. Bearing in mind all these things, let us stay the evil at this point, that we may please God, and be counted worthy to obtain the good things promised to them that love Him, through the grace and love toward man of our Lord Jesus Christ, with whom, to the Father, together with the Holy Ghost, be glory, power, honor, now and for ever, and world without end. Amen.

HOMILIES OF ST. JOHN CHRYSOSTOM,

ARCHBISHOP OF CONSTANTINOPLE,

ON THE

FIRST EPISTLE OF ST. PAUL THE APOSTLE

TO THE

THESSALONIANS.

HOMILY I

1 THESSALONIANS i. 1–3.

" Paul, and Silvanus, and Timothy, unto the Church of the Thessalonians in God the Father and the Lord Jesus Christ: Grace to you, and peace.[1] We give thanks to God always for you all, making mention of you in our prayers; remembering without ceasing your work of faith and labor of love and patience of hope in our Lord Jesus Christ, before our God and Father."

WHEREFORE then, when writing to the Ephesians,[2] and having Timothy with him, did he not include him with himself (in his salutation), known as he was to them and admired, for he says, " Ye know the proof of him, that as a child serveth the father, so he served with me in the Gospel " (Phil. ii. 22) ; and again, " I have no man like-minded who will care truly for your state " (ver. 20) ; but here he does associate him with himself? It seems to me, that he was about to send him immediately, and it was superfluous for him to write, who would overtake the letter. For he says, " Him therefore I hope to send forthwith." (Phil. ii. 23.) But here it was not so ; but he had just returned to him, so that he naturally joined in the letter. For he says, " Now when Timothy came from you unto us." (1 Thess. iii. 6.) But why does he place Silvanus before him,[3] though he testifies to his numberless good qualities, and prefers him above all? Perhaps Timothy wished and requested him to do so from his great humility ; for when he saw his teacher so humble-minded, as to associate his disciple with himself, he would much the more have desired this, and eagerly sought it. For he says,

" Paul, and Silvanus, and Timothy, unto the Church of the Thessalonians." Here he gives himself no title — not " an Apostle," not " a Servant " ; I suppose, because the men were newly instructed, and had not yet had any experience of him,[4] he does not apply the title ; and it was as yet the beginning of his preaching to them.

" To the Church of the Thessalonians," he says. And well. For it is probable there were few, and they not yet formed into a body ; on this account he consoles them with the name of the Church. For where much time had passed, and the congregation of the Church was large, he does not apply this term. But because the name of the Church is for the most part a name

---

[1] [Some MSS. and editions add, " from God our Father, and the Lord Jesus Christ," as it is added in Text. Rec. of the N. T. — J. A. B.]
[2] This mistake cannot be charged on the transcribers, as Timothy is mentioned in Phil. i. 1 [and it is Philippians that he proceeds to quote from. — J. A. B.].

[3] [The natural explanation is that Silas was an older man, Timothy being at the time of writing 1 Thess. (prob. A.D. 52) quite young, and indeed still noticeably young a dozen years later (1 Tim. iv. 12). Chrys. seems to have made no systematic study of the chronology of the Epistles. — J. A. B.]
[4] αὐτοῦ, perhaps " of the thing."

of multitude, and of a system [1] now compacted, on this account he calls them by that name.

"In God the Father," he says, "and the Lord Jesus Christ." "Unto the Church of the Thessalonians," he says, "which is in God." Behold again the expression, "in," [2] applied both to the Father and to the Son. For there were many assemblies, [3] both Jewish and Grecian; but he says, "to the (Church) that is in God." It is a great dignity, and to which there is nothing equal, that it is "in God." God grant therefore that this Church may be so addressed! But I fear that it is far from that appellation. For if any one were the servant of sin, he cannot be said to be "in God." If any one walks not according to God, he cannot be said to be "in God." [4]

"Grace be unto you, and peace." [5] Do you perceive that the very commencement of his Epistle is with encomiums? "We give thanks to God always for you all, making mention of you in our prayers." For to give thanks to God for them is the act of one testifying to their great advancement, when they are not only praised themselves, but God also is thanked for them, as Himself having done it all. He teaches them also to be moderate, all but saying, that it is all of the power of God. That he gives thanks for them, therefore, is on account of their good conduct, but that he remembers them in his prayers, proceeds from his love towards them. Then as he often does, he says that he not only remembers them in his prayers, but apart from his prayers. "Remembering without ceasing," he says, "your work of faith and labor of love and patience of hope in our Lord Jesus Christ, before our God and Father." What is remembering without ceasing? Either remembering before God and the Father, or remembering your labor of love that is before God and the Father, or simply, "Remembering you without ceasing." Then again, that you may not think that this "remembering you without ceasing" is said simply, he has added, "before our God and Father." And because no one amongst men was praising their actions, no one giving them any reward, he says this, "You labor before God." What is "the work of faith"? That nothing has turned aside your steadfastness. For this is the work of faith. If thou believest, suffer all things; if thou dost not suffer, thou dost not believe. For are not the things promised such, that he who believes would choose to suffer even ten thousand deaths? The kingdom of heaven is set before him, and immortality, and eternal life. He therefore who believes will suffer all things. Faith then is shown through his works. Justly might one have said, not merely did you believe, but through your works you manifested it, through your steadfastness, through your zeal.

And your labor "of love." Why? what labor is it to love? Merely to love is no labor at all. But to love genuinely is great labor. For tell me, when a thousand things are stirred up that would draw us from love, and we hold out against them all, is it not labor? For what did not these men suffer, that they might not revolt from their love? Did not they that warred against the Preaching go to Paul's host, and not having found him, drag Jason before the rulers of the city? (Acts xvii. 5, 6.) Tell me, is this a slight labor, when the seed had not yet taken root, to endure so great a storm, so many trials? And they demanded security of him. And having given security, he says, Jason sent away Paul. [6] Is this a small thing, tell me? Did not Jason expose himself to danger for him? and this he calls a labor of love, because they were thus bound to him.

And observe: first he mentions their good actions, then his own, that he may not seem to boast, nor yet to love them by anticipation. [7] "And patience," he says. For that persecution was not confined to one time, but was continual, and they warred not only with Paul, the teacher, but with his disciples also. For if they were thus affected towards those who wrought miracles, those venerable men; what think you were their feelings towards those who dwelt among them, their fellow-citizens, who had all of a sudden revolted from them? Wherefore this also he testifies of them, saying, "For ye became imitators of the Churches of God which are in Judæa."

"And of hope," he says, "in our Lord Jesus Christ, before our God and Father." For all these things proceed from faith and hope, so that what happened to them showed not their fortitude only, but that they believed with full assurance in the rewards laid up for them. For on this account God permitted that persecutions should arise immediately, that no one might say, that the Preaching was established lightly or by flattery, and that their fervor might be shown, and that it was not human persuasion, but the power of God, that persuaded the souls of the believers, so that they were prepared even for ten thousand deaths, which would not have been the case, if the Preaching had not immediately been deeply fixed and remained unshaken.

---

[1] [Here the same Greek word (*systema*) is translated "body," "congregation," and "system." — J. A. B.]

[2] [Most editions have "the word God," and one MS. has "in God," both obviously alterations, and really unsuitable to the connection. — J. A. B.]

[3] ἐκκλησίαι. Churches, or assemblies. New converts would be more familiar with the word in its secular sense.

[4] [Most editions omit this sentence, but it is found in several MSS., and the amplification is quite after the manner of Chrys. — J. A. B.]

[5] [This seems to belong (as Hales suggested) after the next sentence, which is a remark upon the foregoing. — J. A. B.]

[6] See Acts xvii. 9.

[7] προλήψει. Assuming good of them before trial.

Ver. 4, 5. "Knowing, brethren beloved of God, your election, how that our Gospel came not unto you in word only, but also in power, and in the Holy Ghost, and in much assurance; even as ye know what manner of men we showed ourselves among[1] you for your sake."

Knowing what? How "we showed ourselves among you"? Here he also touches upon his own good actions, but covertly. For he wishes first to enlarge upon their praises, and what he says is something of this sort. I knew that you were men of great and noble sort, that you were of the Elect. For this reason we also endure all things for your sake. For this, "what manner of men we showed ourselves among you," is the expression of one showing that with much zeal and much vehemence we were ready to give up our lives for your sake; and for this thanks are due not to us, but to you, because ye were elect. On this account also he says elsewhere, "And these things I endure for the Elect's sake." (2 Tim. ii. 10.) For what would not one endure for the sake of God's beloved ones? And having spoken of his own part, he all but says, For if you were both beloved and elect, we suffer all things with reason. For not only did his praise of them confirm them, but his reminding them that they too themselves had displayed a fortitude corresponding to their zeal: he says,

Ver. 6. "And ye became imitators of us, and of the Lord, having received the word in much affliction, with joy of the Holy Ghost."

Strange! what an encomium is here! The disciples have suddenly become teachers! They not only heard the word, but they quickly arrived at the same height with Paul. But this is nothing; for see how he exalts them, saying, "Ye became imitators of the Lord." How? "Having received the word in much affliction, with joy of the Holy Ghost." Not merely with affliction, but with much affliction. And this we may learn from the Acts of the Apostles, how they raised a persecution against them. (Acts xvii. 5–8.) And they troubled all the rulers of the city, and they instigated the city against them. And it is not enough to say, ye were afflicted indeed, and believed, and that grieving, but even rejoicing. Which also the Apostles did: "Rejoicing," it is said, "that they were counted worthy to suffer dishonor for the Name." (Acts v. 41.) For it is this that is admirable. Although neither is that a slight matter, in any way to bear afflictions. But this now was the part of men surpassing human nature, and having, as it were, a body incapable of suffering.

But how were they imitators of the Lord?

Because He also endured many sufferings, but rejoiced. For He came to this willingly. For our sakes He emptied Himself. He was about to be spit upon, to be beaten and crucified, and He so rejoiced in suffering these things, that He said to the Father, "Glorify Me." (John xvii. 1–5.)

"With joy of the Holy Ghost," he says. That no one may say, how speakest thou of "affliction"? how "of joy"? how can both meet in one? he has added, "with joy of the Holy Ghost." The affliction is in things bodily, and the joy in things spiritual. How? The things which happened to them were grievous, but not so the things which sprang out of them, for the Spirit does not allow it.[2] So that it is possible both for him who suffers, not to rejoice, when one suffers for his sins; and being beaten to take pleasure, when one suffers for Christ's sake. For such is the joy of the Spirit. In return for the things which appear to be grievous, it brings out delight. They have afflicted you, he says, and persecuted you, but the Spirit did not forsake you, even in those circumstances. As the Three Children in the fire were refreshed with dew,[3] so also were you refreshed in afflictions. But as there it was not of the nature of the fire to sprinkle dew, but of the "whistling wind,"[4] so also here it was not of the nature of affliction to produce joy, but of the suffering for Christ's sake, and of the Spirit bedewing them, and in the furnace of temptation setting them at ease. Not merely with joy, he says, but "with much joy." For this is of the Holy Spirit.

Ver. 7. "So that ye became ensamples[5] to all that believe in Macedonia and Achaia."

And yet it was later that he went to them. But ye so shone, he says, that ye became teachers of those who received (the word) before you. And this is like the Apostle. For he did not say, so that ye became ensamples in regard to believing, but ye became an ensample to those who already believed; how one ought to believe in God, ye taught, who from the very beginning entered into your conflict.

"And in Achaia," he says; that is, in Greece.

Do you see how great a thing is zeal? that it does not require time, nor delay, nor procrastination, but it is sufficient only to venture one's self, and all is fulfilled. Thus then though coming in later to the Preaching, they became teachers of those who were before them.

MORAL. Let no one therefore despair, even though he has lost much time, and has done nothing. It is possible for him even in a little

---

[1] [It is very doubtful whether Rev. Ver. of N. T. is here right in omitting ἐν (as in ii. 10), and so translating "towards." Chrys. has the ἐν, and so must be tr. "among."—J. A. B.]

[2] οὐκ ἀφίησι. Perhaps, "does not forsake us," as just below.
[3] Song, ver. 27.
[4] διασυρίζοντος, as Sept. Dan. iii. 28.
[5] [Rev. Ver. right for N. T., "an ensample"; but Chrys. has the plural, employing (as he commonly does) that which spread from Constantinople, and became the prevalent text.—J. A. B.]

while to do so much, as he never has done in all his former time. For if he who before did not believe, shone so much at the beginning, how much more those who have already believed! Let no one, again, upon this consideration be remiss, because he perceives that it is possible in a short time to recover everything. For the future is uncertain, and the Day of the Lord is a thief, setting upon us suddenly when we are sleeping. But if we do not sleep, it will not set upon us as a thief, nor carry us off unprepared. For if we watch and be sober, it will not set upon us as a thief, but as a royal messenger, summoning us to the good things prepared for us. But if we sleep, it comes upon us as a thief. Let no one therefore sleep, nor be inactive in virtue, for that is sleep. Do you not know how, when we sleep, our goods are not in safety, how easy they are to be plotted against? But when we are awake, there needs not so much guarding. When we sleep, even with much guarding we often perish. There are doors, and bolts, and guards, and outer guards, and the thief has come upon us.

Why then do I say this? Because, if we wake we shall not need the help of others; but if we sleep, the help of others will profit us nothing, but even with this we perish. It is a good thing to enjoy the prayer of the Saints, but it is when we ourselves also are on the alert. And what need, you say, have I of another's prayer, if I am on the alert myself. And in sooth, do not place yourself in a situation to need it; I do not wish that you should; but we are always in need of it, if we think rightly. Paul did not say, what need have I of prayer? and yet those who prayed were not worthy of him,[1] or rather not equal to him; and you say, what need have I of prayer? Peter did not say, What need have I of prayer, for " prayer," it says, " was made earnestly of the Church unto God for him." (Acts xii. 5.) And thou sayest, What need have I of prayer? On this account thou needest it, because thou thinkest that thou hast no need. Yea, though thou become as Paul, thou hast need of prayer. Do not exalt thyself, lest thou be humbled.

But, as I said, if we be active also ourselves, the prayers for us avail too. Hear Paul saying, " For I know that this shall turn to my salvation, through your supplication, and the supply of the Spirit of Jesus Christ." (Phil. i. 19.) And again, " That for the gift bestowed upon us by means of many, thanks may be given by many persons on our behalf." (2 Cor. i. 11.) And thou sayest, what need have I of prayer? But if we be idle, no one will be able to profit us. What did Jeremiah profit the Jews? Did he not thrice draw nigh to God, and the third time

hear, " Pray not thou for this people, neither lift up cry nor prayer, for I will not hear thee"? (Jer. vii. 16.) What did Samuel profit Saul? Did he not mourn for him even to his last day, and not merely pray for him only? What did he profit the Israelites? Did he not say, " God forbid that I should sin in ceasing to pray for you"? (1 Sam. xii. 23.) Did they not all perish? Do prayers then, you say, profit nothing? They profit even greatly: but it is when we also do something. For prayers indeed coöperate and assist, but a man coöperates with one[2] that is operating, and assists one that is himself also working. But if thou remainest idle, thou wilt receive no great benefit.

For if prayers had power to bring us to the kingdom while we do nothing, why do not all the Greeks become Christians? Do we not pray for all the world? Did not Paul also do this? Do we not intreat that all may be converted? Why do not the wicked become good without contributing anything of themselves? Prayers, then, profit greatly, when we also contribute our own parts.

Would you learn how much prayers have profited? consider, I pray, Cornelius, Tabitha. (Acts x. 3 and ix. 36.) Hear also Jacob saying to Laban, " Except the Fear of my father had been with me, surely thou hadst now sent me away empty." (Gen. xxxi. 42.) Hear also God again, saying, " I will defend this city for Mine own sake, and for My servant David's sake." (2 Kings ix. 34.) But when? In the time of Hezekiah, who was righteous. Since if prayers availed even for the extremely wicked, why did not God say this also when Nebuchadnezzar came, and why did He give up the city? Because wickedness availed more. Again, Samuel himself also prayed for the Israelites, and prevailed. But when? When they also pleased God, then they put their enemies to flight. And what need, you say, of prayer from another, when I myself please God? Never, O man, say this. There is need, aye, and need of much prayer. For hear God saying concerning the friends of Job; " And he shall pray for you, and your sin shall be forgiven you."[3] (Job xlii. 8.) Because they had sinned indeed, but not a great sin. But this just man, who then saved his friends by prayer, in the season of the Jews was not able to save the Jews who were perishing. And that you may learn this, hear God saying through the prophet; " If Noah, Daniel, and Job stood, they shall not deliver their sons and their daughters." (Ezek. xiv. 14, 16.) Because wickedness prevailed. And again, " Though Moses and Samuel stood." (Jer. xv. 1.)

And see how this is said to the two Prophets,

---

[1] i.e. worthy to pray for him.

[2] So B. Edd. om. one, &c.

[3] [Quoting from memory. So below.— J. A. B.]

because both prayed for them, and did not prevail. For Ezekiel says, "Ah Lord, dost thou blot out the residue of Israel?" (Ezek. ix. 8.) Then showing that He does this justly, He shows him their sins; and showing that not through despising him does He refuse to accept his supplication for them, he says, Even these things are enough even to persuade thee, that not despising thee, but on account of their many sins, I do not accept thy supplication. Nevertheless He adds, "Though Noah, Job, and Daniel stood." (From Ezek. xiv.) And with good reason does He the rather say this to him, because it is he who suffered so many things. Thou badest me, he says, eat upon dung, and I ate upon it.[1] Thou badest me, and I shaved my head. Thou badest me, and I lay upon one side. Thou badest me go out through a hole in the wall, bearing a burden, and I went out. Thou tookest away my wife, and badest me not mourn, and I did not mourn, but bore it with fortitude. (Ezek. xxiv. 18.) Ten thousand other things have I wrought for their sake: I entreat for them, and dost Thou not comply? Not from despising thee, says he, do I do this, but though Noah, Job, and Daniel were there, and were entreating for sons and daughters, I would not comply.

And again to Jeremiah, who suffered less from the commandments of God, but more from their wickedness, what does He say? "Seest thou not what these do?" (Jer. vii. 17.) "Yea," he says, "they do so — but do Thou do it for my sake." On this account He says to him, "Though Moses and Samuel stood." Their first lawgiver, who often delivered them from dangers, who had said, "If now thou forgivest their sins, forgive it; but if not, blot me out also." (Ex. xxxii. 32, Sept.) If therefore he were now alive, and spoke thus, he would not have prevailed, — nor would Samuel, again, who himself also delivered them, and who from his earliest youth was admired. For to the former indeed I said, that I conversed with him as a friend with a friend, and not by dark sayings. And of the latter I said, that in his first youth I was revealed to him, and that on his account, being prevailed upon, I opened the prophecy that had been shut up. For "the word of the Lord," it is said, "was precious in those days; there was no open vision." (1 Sam. iii. 1.) If these men, therefore, stood before Me, they would profit nothing. And of Noah He says, "Noah was a righteous man, and perfect in his generations." (Gen. vi. 9.) And concerning Job, He was "blameless, just, true, fearing God." (Job i. 1, Sept.) And concerning Daniel, whom they even thought a God; and they will not deliver, says he, their sons and daughters. Knowing these things, therefore, let us neither despise the prayers of the Saints, nor throw everything upon them: that we may not, on the one hand, be indolent and live carelessly; nor on the other deprive ourselves of a great advantage. But let us both beseech them to pray and lift up the hand for us, and let us adhere to virtue; that we may be able to obtain the blessings promised to those who love Him by the grace and lovingkindness of our Lord Jesus Christ, with whom, &c.

HOMILY II.

1 THESSALONIANS i. 8–10.

" For from you hath sounded forth the word of the Lord, not only in Macedonia and Achaia, but also in every place your faith to God-ward is gone forth; so that we need not to speak anything. For they themselves report concerning us what manner of entering in we had unto you; and how ye turned unto God from idols, to serve a living and true God, and to wait for His Son from Heaven, whom He raised from the dead, even Jesus, which delivereth us from the wrath to come."

As a sweet-smelling ointment keeps not its fragrance shut up in itself, but diffuses it afar, and scenting the air with its perfume, so conveys it also to the senses of the neighbors; so too illustrious and admirable men do not shut up their virtue within themselves, but by their good report benefit many, and render them better. Which also then happened. Wherefore he said, "So that ye became ensamples to all that believe in Macedonia and Achaia." "For from you," he says, "hath sounded forth the word of the Lord, not only in Macedonia and Achaia, but also in every place your faith to God-ward is gone forth." Ye have filled, therefore, all your neighbors with instruction, and the world with wonder. For this is meant by the expression, "in every place." And he has not said, your faith is noised abroad, but "has sounded out"; as every place near is filled with the sound of a loud trumpet, so the report

---

[1] i.e. food baked on it. Ezek. iv. 12, 15.

of your manfulness is loud, and sounding even like that, is sufficient to fill the world, and to fall with equal sound upon all that are round about. For great actions are more loudly celebrated there, where they have taken place; afar off indeed they are celebrated, but not so much.

But in your case it was not so, but the sound of good report was spread abroad in every part of the earth. And whence know we, says one, that the words were not hyperbolical? For this nation of the Macedonians, before the coming of Christ, was renowned, and celebrated everywhere more than the Romans. And the Romans were admired on this account, that they took them captive. For the actions of the Macedonian king exceeded all report, who, setting out from a little city indeed, yet subdued the world. Wherefore also the Prophet saw him, a winged leopard, showing his swiftness, his vehemence, his fiery nature, his suddenly in a manner flying over the whole world with the trophies of his victory. And they say, that hearing from a certain philosopher, that there were infinite worlds, he groaned bitterly, that when they were numberless, he had not conquered even one. So high-minded was he, and high-souled, and celebrated everywhere. And with the fame of the king the glory of the nation also kept pace. For he was called "Alexander, the Macedonian." So that what took place there was also naturally much talked of. For nothing can be concealed that relates to the illustrious. The Macedonians then were not inferior to the Romans.

And this has also arisen from their vehemence. For as if he were speaking of something living, he introduces the word "gone forth"; so vehement and energetic was their faith. "So that we need not to speak anything," says he, "for they themselves report concerning us what entering in we had unto you." They do not wait to hear from us,[1] but those who were not present, and have not seen, anticipate those who were present, and have seen your good deeds. So manifest were they everywhere made by report. We shall not therefore need, by relating your actions, to bring them to equal zeal. For the things which they ought to have heard from us, these they themselves talk of, anticipating us. And yet in the case of such there is frequently envy, but the exceeding greatness of the thing conquered even this, and they are the heralds of your conflicts. And though left behind, not even so are they silenced, but they are beforehand with us. And being such, it is not possible for them to disbelieve our report. What means, "What manner of entering in we had unto you"? That it was full of dangers,

and numberless deaths, but that none of these things troubled you. But as if nothing had happened, so you adhered to us; as if ye had suffered no evil, but had enjoyed infinite good, so you received us after these things. For this was the second entering.[2] They went to Berœa, they were persecuted, and when they came after this they so received them, as though they had been honored by these also, so that they even laid down their lives for them. The expression, "What manner of entering in we had," is complicated, and contains an encomium both of them and of themselves. But he himself has turned this to their advantage. "And how," he says, "ye turned to God from idols, to serve a living and true God"; that is, that ye did it readily, that ye did it with much eagerness, that it did not require much labor to make you. "In order to serve," says he, "a living and true God."

Here also he introduced an exhortation, which is the part of one who would make his discourse less offensive. "And to wait," he says, "for His Son from heaven, whom He raised from the dead, even Jesus, which delivereth us from the wrath to come." "And to wait," he says, "for His Son from heaven"; Him that was crucified, Him that was buried; to wait for Him from heaven. And how "from heaven"? "Whom He raised from the dead." You see all things at the same time; both the Resurrection, and the Ascension, and the second Coming, the Judgment, the retribution of the just, the punishment of the wicked. "Jesus," he says, "which delivereth us from the wrath to come." This is at once comfort, and exhortation, and encouragement. For if He raised Him from the dead, and He is in heaven, and thence will come, (and ye believed in Him; for if ye had not believed in Him, ye would not have suffered so much), this of itself is sufficient comfort. These shall suffer punishment, which he says in his second epistle, and you will have no small consolation.

And to "wait," he says, "for His Son from heaven." The terrible things are in hand, but the good things are in the future, when Christ shall come from heaven. See how much hope is required, in that He who was crucified has been raised, that He has been taken up into heaven, that He will come to judge the quick and the dead.

Chap. ii. 1, 2. "For yourselves, brethren, know our entering in unto you, that it hath not been found vain: but having suffered before, and been shamefully entreated, as ye know, at Philippi, we waxed bold in our God to speak

---

[1] [This παρ' ἡμῶν, "from us" (see below), was easily changed into περὶ ὑμῶν, "concerning us," the text of most editions. — J. A. B.]

[2] This is not quite clear from Acts xvii., though "those that conducted Paul," ver. 15, may have been Thessalonians. The ill-treatment presently mentioned by St. Paul was at Philippi previously.

unto you the Gospel of God in much conflict."

Great indeed were your actions also, but yet neither did we have recourse to human speech. But what he says above, that also he repeats here, that from both sides is shown what was the nature of the Preaching, from the miracles, and from the resolution of the preachers, and from the zeal and fervor of those who received it. "For yourselves," he says, "know our entering in unto you, that it hath not been found vain," that is, that it was not according to man, nor of any common kind. For being fresh from great dangers, and deaths, and stripes, we immediately fell into dangers. "But," he says, "having suffered before, and been shamefully entreated, as ye know, at Philippi, we waxed bold in our God." Do you see how again he refers the whole to God? "To speak unto you," says he, "the Gospel of God in much conflict."[1] It is not possible to say, that there indeed we were in danger, but here we are not; yourselves also know, how great was the danger, with how much contention we were among you. Which also he says in his Epistle to the Corinthians; "And I was with you in weakness," and in labor, "and in fear, and in much trembling." (1 Cor. ii. 3.)

Ver. 3, 4. "For our exhortation is not of error nor of uncleanness, nor in guile : but even as we have been approved of God to be entrusted with the Gospel, so we speak; not as pleasing men, but God which proveth our hearts."

Do you see that, as I said, from their perseverance he makes a proof that the Preaching is divine? For, if it were not so, if it were a deceit, we should not have endured so many dangers, which allowed us not even to take breath. You were in tribulation, we were in tribulation. What then was it? Unless somewhat of things future had excited us, unless we had been persuaded that there is a good hope, we should not have been filled with the more alacrity by suffering. For who would have chosen for the sake of what we have here to endure so many sufferings, and to live a life of anxiety, and full of dangers? For whom would they persuade? For are not these things of themselves enough to trouble the disciples, when they see their teachers in dangers? But this was not your case.

"For our exhortation," that is, our teaching, "is not of error." The matter, he says, is not guile nor deceit, that we should give it up. It is not for things abominable, as the tricks of jugglers and sorcerers. "And of uncleanness," says he, "nor in guile," nor for any insurrection, like what Theudas did. "But even as we have

been approved of God to be entrusted with the Gospel, so we speak, not as pleasing men, but God." Do you see, that it is not vainglory? "But God," he says, "which proveth our hearts." We do nothing for the sake of pleasing men, he says. For on whose account should we do these things? Then having praised them, he says, Not as wishing to please men, nor seeking the honors that are from men, he adds, "But as we have been approved of God to be entrusted with the Gospel." Unless He had seen that we were free from every worldly consideration, He would not have chosen us. As therefore He approved us, such we remain, as having been "approved of God." Whence did he approve us, and entrust us with the Gospel? We appeared to God approved, so we remain. It is a proof of our virtue, that we are entrusted with the Gospel; if there had been anything bad in us, God would not have approved us. But the expression that He approved us, does not here imply search. But what we do upon proving, that he does without proving. That is, as he found us proof, and trusted us, so we speak; as it is reasonable that those should, who are approved and entrusted to be worthy of the Gospel, so we speak, "not as pleasing men," that is, not on your account do we do all these things.[2] Because previously he had praised them, that he might not bring his speech under suspicion, he says,

Ver. 5, 6. "For neither at any time were we found using words of flattery, as ye know, nor a cloak of covetousness, God is witness; nor seeking glory of men, neither from you, nor from others, when we might have been burdensome, as Apostles of Christ."

For "neither at any time," he says, "were we found using words of flattery"; that is, we did not flatter, which is the part of deceivers, who wish to get possession and to domineer. No one can say that we flattered in order to rule, nor that we had recourse to it for the sake of wealth. Of this, which was manifest, he afterwards calls them to be witnesses. "Whether we flattered," he says, "ye know." But as to what was uncertain, namely, whether it were in the way of covetousness, he calls God to witness. "Nor seeking glory of men, neither from you, nor from others, when we might have been burdensome, as Apostles of Christ;" that is, not seeking after honors either, nor boasting ourselves, nor requiring attendance of guards. And yet even if we had done this, we should have done nothing out of character. For if persons sent forth by kings are nevertheless[3] in

---

[1] ἀγῶνι.

[2] [This sentence, after Field's text, is awkward; but the manifest alterations introduced into the text followed in most editions do not really mend matters. — J. A. B.]

[3] i.e. though sent by mere earthly kings. The Catena omits the word.

honor, much more might we be. And he has not said, that "we were dishonored," nor that "we did not enjoy honors," which would have been to reproach them, but "we did not seek them." We therefore, who, when we might have sought them, sought them not, even when the preaching required it, how should we do anything for the sake of glory? And yet even if we had sought them, not even in that case would there have been any blame. For it is fit that those men who are sent forth from God, as ambassadors now coming from heaven, should enjoy great honor.

But with an excess of forbearance we do none of these things, that we may stop the mouths of the adversaries. And it cannot be said, that to you we act thus, but not so others. For thus also he said in his Epistle to the Corinthians: "For ye bear with a man if he bringeth you into bondage, if he devoureth you, if he taketh you captive, if he exalteth himself, if he smiteth you on the face." (2 Cor. xi. 20.) And again, "His bodily presence is weak, and his speech of no account." (2 Cor. x. 10.) And again, "Forgive me this wrong." (2 Cor. xii. 13.) He shows there also that he was exceeding humble from his suffering so many things. But here he also says concerning money, "when we might have been burdensome, as Apostles of Christ."

Ver. 7, 8. "But we were gentle in the midst of you, as when a nurse cherisheth her own children: even so, being affectionately desirous of you, we were well pleased to impart unto you, not the Gospel of God only, but also our own souls, because ye were become very dear to us."

"But we were gentle," he says; we exhibited nothing that was offensive or troublesome, nothing displeasing, or boastful. And the expression, "in the midst of you," is as if one should say, we were as one of you, not taking the higher lot. "As when a nurse cherisheth her own children." So ought the teacher to be. Does the nurse flatter that she may obtain glory? Does she ask money of her little children? Is she offensive or burdensome to them? Are they not more indulgent to them than mothers? Here he shows his affection. "Even so, being affectionately desirous of you," he says, we are so bound to you, he says, and we not only take nothing of you, but if it be necessary even to impart to you our souls, we should not have refused. Tell me, then, is this of a human view? and who is so foolish as to say this? "We were well pleased to impart to you," he says, "not the Gospel of God only, but also our own souls." So that this is greater than the other. And what is the gain? For from the Gospel is gain, but to give our souls, is with respect to

difficulty a greater thing than that. For merely to preach is not the same thing as to give the soul. For that indeed is more precious, but the latter is a matter of more difficulty. We were willing, he says, if it were possible, even to spend our souls upon you. And this we should have been willing to do; for if we had not been willing, we should not have endured the necessity. Since then he praised, and does praise, on this account he says, that, not seeking money, nor flattering you, nor desiring glory, do we do this. For observe; they had contended much, and so ought to be praised and admired even extraordinarily, that they might be more firm; the praise was suspicious. On this account he says all these things, by way of repelling the suspicion. And he also mentions the dangers. And again, that he may not be thought to speak of the dangers on this account, as if laboring for them, and claiming to be honored by them, therefore again, as he had to mention the dangers, he added, "Because ye were become very dear to us"; we would willingly have given our souls for you, because we were vehemently attached to you. The Gospel indeed we proclaim, because God commanded it; but so much do we love you, that, if it were possible, we would have given even our souls.

He who loves, ought so to love, that if he were asked even for his soul,[1] and it were possible, he would not refuse it. I do not say "if he were asked," but so that he would even run to present him with the gift. For nothing, nothing can be sweeter than such love; nothing will fall out there that is grievous. Truly "a faithful friend is the medicine of life." (Ecclus. vi. 16.) Truly "a faithful friend is a strong defense." (Ib. 14.) For what will not a genuine friend perform? What pleasure will he not afford? what benefit? what security? Though you should name infinite treasures, none of them is comparable to a genuine friend. And first let us speak of the great delight of friendship itself. A friend rejoices at seeing his friend, and expands with joy. He is knit to him with an union of soul that affords unspeakable pleasure. And if he only calls him to remembrance, he is roused in mind, and transported.

I speak of genuine friends, men of one soul, who would even die for each other, who love fervently. Do not, thinking of those who barely love, who are table-companions, mere nominal friends, suppose that my discourse is refuted. If any one has a friend such as I speak of, he will acknowledge the truth of my words. He, though he sees his friend every day, is not satiated. For him he prays for the same things as for himself. I know one, who calling upon holy men in behalf of his friend, besought them to

---

[1] ψυχήν, both "soul" and "life."

pray first for him, and then for himself. So dear a thing is a good friend, that times and places are loved on his account. For as bodies that are luminous spread their radiance to the neighboring places, so also friends leave a grace of their own in the places to which they have come. And oftentimes in the absence of friends, as we have stood on those places, we have wept, and remembering the days which we passed together, have sighed. It is not possible to represent by speech, how great a pleasure the intercourse with friends affords. But those only know, who have experience. From a friend we may both ask a favor, and receive one without suspicion. When they enjoin anything upon us, then we feel indebted to them; but when they are slow to do this, then we are sorrowful. We have nothing which is not theirs. Often despising all things here, on their account we are not willing to depart hence; and they are more longed for by us than the light.

For, in good truth, a friend is more to be longed for than the light; I speak of a genuine one. And wonder not: for it were better for us that the sun should be extinguished, than that we should be deprived of friends; better to live in darkness, than to be without friends. And I will tell you why. Because many who see the sun are in darkness, but they can never be even in tribulation, who abound in friends. I speak of spiritual friends, who prefer nothing to friendship. Such was Paul, who would willingly have given his own soul, even though not asked, nay would have plunged into hell[1] for them. With so ardent a disposition ought we to love.

I wish to give you an example of friendship. Friends, that is, friends according to Christ, surpass fathers and sons. For tell me not of friends of the present day, since this good thing also has past away with others. But consider, in the time of the Apostles, I speak not of the chief men, but of the believers themselves generally; "all," he says, "were of one heart and soul: and not one of them said that aught of the things which he possessed was his own . . . and distribution was made unto each, according as any one had need." (Acts iv. 32, 35.) There were then no such words as "mine" and "thine." This is friendship, that a man should not consider his goods his own, but his neighbor's, that his possessions belong to another; that he should be as careful of his friend's soul,[2] as of his own; and the friend likewise.

And where is it possible, somebody says, that such an one should be found? Because we have not the will; for it is possible. If it were not

possible, neither would Christ have commanded it; he would not have discoursed so much concerning love. A great thing is friendship, and how great, no one can learn, and no discourse represent, but experience itself. It is this[3] that has caused the heresies. This makes the Greeks to be Greeks. He who loves does not wish to command, nor to rule, but is rather obliged when he is ruled and commanded. He wishes rather to bestow a favor than to receive one, for he loves, and is so affected, as not having satisfied his desire. He is not so much gratified when good is done to him, as when he is doing good. For he wishes to oblige, rather than to be indebted to him; or rather he wishes both to be beholden to him, and to have him his debtor. And he wishes both to bestow favors, and not to seem to bestow them, but himself to be the debtor. I think that perhaps many of you do not understand what has been said. He wishes to be the first in bestowing benefits, and not to seem to be the first, but to be returning a kindness. Which God also has done in the case of men. He purposed to give His own Son for us; but that He might not seem to bestow a favor, but to be indebted to us, He commanded Abraham to offer his son,[4] that whilst doing a great kindness, He might seem to do nothing great.

For when indeed there is no love, we both upbraid men with our kindnesses and we exaggerate little ones; but when there is love, we both conceal them and wish to make the great appear small, that we may not seem to have our friend for a debtor, but ourselves to be debtors to him, in having him our debtor. I know that the greater part do not understand what is said, and the cause is, that I am speaking of a thing which now dwells in heaven. As therefore if I were speaking of any plant growing in India, of which no one had ever had any experience, no speech would avail to represent it, though I should utter ten thousand words: so also now whatever things I say, I say in vain, for no one will be able to understand me. This is a plant that is planted in heaven, having for its branches not heavy-clustered pearls, but a virtuous life, much more acceptable than they. What pleasure would you speak of, of the foul and the honorable? But that of friendship excelleth them all, though you should speak of the sweetness of honey. For that satiates, but a friend never does, so long as he is a friend; nay, the desire of him rather increases, and such pleasure never admits of satiety. And a friend is sweeter than the present life. Many therefore after the death of their friends have not wished to live any longer. With a friend one would bear even banishment; but without a friend would not choose to inhabit even his own country. With a friend even pov-

---

[1] [The reference is to Chrys.'s (erroneous) interpretation of Rom. ix. 3. See his Homily on that passage, and above, on Col. iv. 18.— J. A. B.]
[2] Or "life." The double meaning of the word should be kept in sight throughout.
[3] i.e. the want of love.   [4] See Gen. xxii. 16, 18.

erty is tolerable, but without him both health and riches are intolerable. He has another self: I am straitened, because I cannot instance by an example. For I should in that case make it appear that what has been said is much less than it ought to be.

And these things indeed are so here. But from God the reward of friendship is so great, that it cannot be expressed. He gives a reward, that we may love one another, the thing for which we owe a reward. "Pray," He says, "and receive a reward," for that for which we owe a reward, because we ask for good things. "For that which you ask," He says, "receive a reward. Fast, and receive a reward. Be virtuous, and receive a reward," though you rather owe a reward. But as fathers, when they have made their children virtuous, then further give them a reward; for they are debtors, because they have afforded them a pleasure; so also God acts. "Receive a reward," He says, "if thou be virtuous, for thou delightest thy Father, and for this I owe thee a reward. But if thou be evil, not so: for thou provokest Him that begot thee." Let us not then provoke God, but let us delight Him, that we may obtain the kingdom of Heaven, in Christ Jesus our Lord, to whom be the glory and the strength, world without end. Amen.

HOMILY III.

1 THESSALONIANS ii. 9–12.

" For ye remember, brethren, our labor and travail: for working night and day, that we might not burden any of you, we preached unto you the Gospel of God. Ye are witnesses, and God also, how holily and righteously and unblamably we behaved ourselves toward you that believe: as ye know how we dealt with each one of you, as a father with his own children, exhorting you, and encouraging you, and testifying, to the end that ye should walk worthily of God, who calleth you into His own kingdom and glory."

THE teacher ought to do nothing with a feeling of being burdened, that tends to the salvation of his disciples. For if the blessed Jacob was buffeted night and day in keeping his flocks, much more ought he, to whom the care of souls is entrusted, to endure all toils, though the work be laborious and mean, looking only to one thing, the salvation of his disciples, and the glory thence arising to God. See then, Paul, a man that was a Preacher, an Apostle of the world, and raised to so great honor, worked with his hands that he might not be burdensome to his disciples.

" For ye remember," he says, " my brethren, our labor and travail." He had said previously, " we might have been burdensome as the Apostles of Christ," as he also says in the Epistle to the Corinthians, " Know ye not that they which minister about sacred things eat of the things of the Temple? Even so also did Christ ordain that they which proclaim the Gospel should live of the Gospel." (1 Cor. ix. 13, 14.) But I, he says, would not, but I labored; and he did not merely work, but with much diligence. Observe then what he says; " For ye remember," he has not said, the benefits received from me, but, " our labor and travail: for working night and day, that we might not burden any of you, we preached unto you the Gospel of God." And to the Corinthians he said a different thing, " I robbed other Churches, taking wages of them that I might minister unto you." (2 Cor. xi. 8.) And yet even there he worked, but of this he made no mention, but urged what was more striking,[1] as if he had said, I was maintained by others when ministering to you. But here it is not so. But what? " Working night and day." And there indeed he says, " And when I was present with you, and was in want, I was not a burden on any man," and, " I took wages that I might minister unto you." (2 Cor. xi. 8, 9.) And here he shows that the men were in poverty, but there it was not so.

On this account he frequently addresses them as witnesses. For " ye are witnesses," he says, " and God also"; God was worthy to be believed, but this other was that which most fully assured them. For that indeed was uncertain to those who were ignorant of it; but this was without doubt to all. For do not enquire whether it was Paul who said these things. Much beyond what was necessary he gives them assurance. Wherefore he says, " Ye are witnesses, and God also, how holily and righteously and unblamably we behaved ourselves toward you that believe." It was proper to praise them again. On this account he sets these things before them, which were sufficient to persuade them. For he that stood there in want, and did not receive anything, would much more not receive anything

---

[1] Or " wounding"; πληκτικώτερον.

now. "How holily," says he, "and righteously and unblamably we behaved ourselves toward you that believe."

"As ye know how we exhorted and comforted each one of you, as a father doth his own children." Above having spoken of his behavior, here he speaks of his love, which was more than what belonged to his rule over them. And what is said marks his freedom from pride. "As a father his own children, exhorting you, and encouraging you, and testifying, to the end that ye should walk worthily of God, who calleth you into His own kingdom and glory." When he says, "and testifying," then he makes mention of "fathers"; although we testified, it was not violently, but like fathers. "Each one of you." Strange! in so great a multitude to omit no one, neither small nor great, neither rich nor poor. "Exhorting" you, he says; to bear. "And comforting and testifying." "Exhorting,"[1] therefore they did not seek glory; and "testifying," therefore they did not flatter. "That ye should walk worthily of God, who calleth you into His own kingdom and glory." Observe again, how, in relating, he both teaches and comforts. For if He hath called them unto His kingdom, if He called them unto glory, they ought to endure all things. We "entreat"[2] you, not that you should grant us any favor, but that you should gain the kingdom of heaven.

Ver. 13. "And for this cause we also thank God without ceasing, that when ye received from us the word of the message, even the word of God, ye accepted it not as the word of men, but as it is in truth, the word of God, which also worketh in you that believe."

It cannot be said, he says, that we indeed do all things unblamably, but you on the other hand have done things unworthy of our course of life. For in hearing us, you gave such heed, as if not hearing men, but as if God Himself were exhorting you. Whence is this manifest? Because as he shows from his own temptations and their testimony, and the way in which he acted, that he did not preach with flattery or vainglory; so from their trials, he shows also that they rightly received the word. For whence, he says, unless ye had heard as if God were speaking, did ye endure such perils? And observe his dignity.

Ver. 14, 15, 16. "For ye, brethren, became imitators of the Churches of God, which are in Judæa in Christ Jesus: for ye also suffered the same things of your own countrymen, even as they did of the Jews; who both killed the Lord Jesus and their own prophets, and drave out us, and please not God, and are contrary to all men; forbidding us to speak to the Gentiles

that they may be saved; to fill up their sins alway: but the wrath is come upon them to the uttermost."

"For ye," he says, "became imitators of the Churches of God which are in Judæa." This is a great consolation. It is no wonder, he says, that they should do these things to you, inasmuch as they have done it also to their own countrymen. And this too is no little proof that the Preaching is true, that even Jews were able to endure all things. "For ye also," he says, "have suffered the same things of your own countrymen, even as they did of the Jews." There is something more in his saying, "as they also did in Judæa"; it shows that everywhere they rejoiced, as having nobly contended. He says therefore, "that ye also suffered the same things." And again, what wonder is it, if to you also, when even to the Lord they dared do such things?

Do you see how he introduces this as containing great consolation? And constantly he adverts to it; and upon a close examination one may find it in nearly all his Epistles, how variously,[3] upon all occasions of temptation, he brings foward Christ. Observe accordingly, that here also, when accusing the Jews, he puts them in mind of the Lord, and of the sufferings of the Lord; so well does he know that this is a matter of the greatest consolation.

"Who both killed the Lord," he says — but, perhaps, they did not know Him, — assuredly they did know Him. What then? Did they not slay and stone their own prophets, whose books even they carry about with them? And they did not do this for the sake of truth. There is therefore not only a consolation under the temptations, but they are reminded not to think that (the Jews) did it for the truth's sake, and be troubled on that account. "And drave out us,"[4] he says. And we also, he says, have suffered numberless evils. "And please not God, and are contrary to all men; forbidding us to speak to the Gentiles, that they may be saved." "Contrary to all men," he says. How? Because if we ought to speak to the world, and they forbid us, they are the common enemies of the world. They have slain Christ and the prophets, they insult God, they are the common enemies of the world, they banish us, when coming for their salvation. What wonder if they have done such things also to you, when they have done them even in Judæa? "Forbidding us to speak to the Gentiles, that they might be saved." It is a mark of envy therefore to hinder the salvation of all. "To fill up their sins alway. But the wrath is come upon them to the uttermost."

---

[1] Or "entreating," and so he takes it below.
[2] E. V. "exhorting."

[3] Or "especially"; διαφόρως.
[4] ἐκδιωξάντων, "drove us out," see Acts xvii. 5, 14; or "persecuted us to the utmost."

What is "to the uttermost"? These things are no longer like the former. There is here no return back, no limit. But the wrath is nigh at hand. Whence is this manifest? From that which Christ foretold. For not only is it a consolation to have partakers in our afflictions, but to hear also that our persecutors are to be punished. And if the delay is a grievance, let it be a consolation that they will never lift up their heads again; or rather he hath cut short the delay, by saying, "THE wrath," showing that it was long ago due, and predetermined, and predicted.

Ver. 17. "But we, being taken from you[1] for a short time in presence, not in heart, endeavored the more abundantly to see your face with great desire."

He has not said "separated," but what was much more.[2] He had spoken above of flattery, showing that he did not flatter, that he did not seek glory. He speaks here concerning love. Because he had said above, "as a father his children," "as a nurse," here he uses another expression, "being made orphans," which is said of children who have lost their fathers. And yet they[3] were made orphans. "No"—he says—"but we. For if any one should examine our longing, even as little children without a protector, having sustained an untimely bereavement, long for their parents, not only from the feelings of nature itself, but also on account of their deserted state, so truly do we too feel." From this also he shows his own despondency on account of their separation. And this we cannot say, he says, that we have waited a long period, but "for a short time," and that "in presence, not in heart." For we always have you in our mind. See how great is his love! Although having them always in his heart, he sought also their presence face to face. Tell me not of your superlative[4] philosophy! This is truly fervent love; both to see, and to hear, and speak; and this may be of much advantage. "We endeavored the more exceedingly." What is "more exceedingly"? He either means to say, "we are vehemently attached to you," or, "as was likely, being bereaved for a season, we endeavored to see your face." Observe the blessed Paul. When of himself he cannot satisfy his longing, he does it through others, as when he sends Timothy to the Philippians, and the same person again to the Corinthians, holding intercourse with them through others, when he cannot of himself. For in loving them, he was like some mad person, not

to be restrained, nor to command himself in his affection.

Ver. 18. "Wherefore we would fain have come unto you."

Which is the part of love; yet here he mentions no other necessity but "that we might see you." "I Paul once and again, and Satan hindered us."

What sayest thou? does Satan hinder? Yes, truly, for this was not the work of God. For in the Epistle to the Romans, he says this, that God hindered him (from Rom. xv. 22); and elsewhere Luke says, that "the Spirit" hindered them from going into Asia. (Acts xvi. 7.) And in the Epistle to the Corinthians he says, that it is the work of the Spirit, but here only of Satan. But what hindrance of Satan is he speaking of? Some unexpected and violent temptations:[5] for a plot, it says, being formed against him by the Jews, he was detained three months in Greece. But it is another thing to remain for the sake of the dispensation, and willingly. For there he says, "Wherefore having no more place in these parts" (Rom. xv. 23), and, "To spare you I forbare to come unto Corinth." (2 Cor. i. 23.) But here nothing of this sort. But what? That "Satan hindered" him. "Even I Paul," he says, "both once and again." Observe, how ambitious he is, and what a display he makes, in his willingness to show that he loved them most of all. "I Paul," he says, instead of Although no others. For they indeed were only willing, but I even attempted it.

Ver. 19. "For what is our hope, or joy, or crown of glorying? Are not even ye before our Lord Jesus at His coming?"

Are the Macedonians, tell me, thy hope, O blessed Paul? Not these alone, he says. Therefore he has added, "Are not ye also?" For "what," he says, "is our hope, or joy, or crown of glorying"? Observe then the words, which are those of women, inflamed with tenderness, talking to their little children. "And crown of glorying," he says. For the name of "crown" was not sufficient to express the splendor, but also "of glorying." Of what fiery warmth is this! Never could either mother, or father, yea if they even met together, and commingled their love, have shown their own affection to be equivalent to that of Paul. "My joy and crown," he says, that is, I rejoice in you more than in a crown. For consider how great a thing it is, that an entire Church should be present, planted and rooted by Paul. Who would not rejoice in such a multitude of children, and in the goodness of those children? So that this also is not

---

[1] ἀπορφανισθέντες, "bereaved," "made orphans."

[2] [This last clause is interpolated by some documents, but may be retained because it makes the meaning clearer to the English reader. — J. A. B.]

[3] The Thessalonians.

[4] Gr. superfluous. He means such as would make friendship quite independent of such helps.

[5] [We are not told how Satan hindered, though we have distinctly brought before us the personal devil as acting. It is not necessary to confine his agency to temptation to sin; he may have hindered by the continuance of that spirit of persecution which he prompted at Thessalonica. Acts xvii. 5. — J. A. B.]

flattery. For he has not said "ye," but "ye also "[1] together with the others.

Ver. 20. "For ye are our glory and our joy."

Chap. iii. 1, 2. "Wherefore, when we could no longer forbear, we thought it good to be left behind at Athens alone." Instead of saying, "we chose." "And sent Timothy, our brother and God's minister and our fellow-worker in the Gospel of Christ."

And this he says, not as extolling Timothy, but honoring them, that he sent them the fellow-worker, and minister of the Gospel. As if he had said, Having withdrawn him from his labors, we have sent to you the minister of God, and our fellow-laborer in the Gospel of Christ.

"To establish you, and to comfort you concerning your faith."

Ver. 3. "That no man be moved by these afflictions."

What then does he say here? Because the temptations of the teachers trouble their disciples, and he had then fallen into many temptations, as also he himself says, that "Satan hindered us," always saying this; "both once," he says, "and again I would have come to you," and was not able, which was a proof of great violence. And it was reasonable that this should trouble them, for they are not so much troubled at their own temptations, as at those of their teachers; as neither is the soldier so much troubled at his own trials,[2] as when he sees his general wounded. "To establish you," he says; not that they were at all deficient in faith, nor that they required to learn anything.

"And to comfort you concerning your faith; that no man be moved by these afflictions; for yourselves know that hereunto we are appointed."

Ver. 4. "For verily, when we were with you, we told you beforehand that we are to suffer affliction; even as it came to pass, and ye know."

Ye ought not, he says, to be troubled, for nothing strange, nothing contrary to expectation is happening; which was sufficient to raise them up. For do you see that on this account also Christ foretold to His disciples? For hear Him saying, "Now I have told you before it came to pass, that, when it is come to pass ye may believe." (John xiv. 29.) For greatly indeed, greatly does it tend to the comfort of others, to have heard from their teachers what is to happen. For as he that is sick, if he hear from his physician that this or that is taking place, is not much troubled; but if anything happen unexpectedly, as if he too were at a loss, and the

disorder was beyond his art, he is afflicted and troubled; so also is it here. Which Paul foreknowing, foretold to them, "we are about to be afflicted," "as it came to pass, and ye know." He not only says that this came to pass, but that he foretold many things, and they happened. "Hereunto we are appointed." So that not only ye ought not to be troubled and disturbed about the past, but not even about the future, if any such thing should happen, "for hereunto we are appointed."

MORAL. Let us hear, who have ears to hear. The Christian is appointed hereunto. For concerning all the faithful is this said, "Hereunto we are appointed." And we, as if we were appointed[3] for ease, think it strange if we suffer anything; and yet what reason have we for thinking anything strange? For no season of affliction or temptation has overtaken us, but what is common to man. It is a fit season for us to say to you, "Ye have not yet resisted unto blood, striving against sin" (Heb. xii. 4). Or rather, this is not seasonable for us to say to you — but what? Ye have not yet despised riches. For to them indeed these words were said with reason, when they had lost all their own possessions,[4] but this is said to those who retain theirs. Who has been robbed of his riches for Christ's sake? Who has been beaten? Who has been insulted? even in words, I mean. What have you to boast of? What confidence have you to say anything? So many things Christ suffered for us when we were enemies. What can we show that we have suffered for Him? Nothing that we have suffered indeed, but infinite good things that we have received from Him. Whence shall we have confidence in that Day? Know ye not, that the soldier too, when he can show numberless wounds and scars, will then be able to shine in the presence of the king? But if he has no good action to show, though he may have done no harm, he will take rank among the least.

But, you say, it is not the season of war. But if it was, tell me, who would contend? Who would attack? Who would break through[5] the phalanx? Perhaps no one. For when I see that you do not despise riches for the sake of Christ, how shall I believe that you will despise blows? Tell me, do you bear manfully those who insult you, and do you bless them? You do not — but you disobey. What is attended with no danger, you do not; and will you endure blows, in which there is much pain and suffering? Know ye not that it is proper in peace to keep up the exercises of war?[6] Do you not

---

[1] [καὶ ὑμεῖς signifies "ye also," or "even ye," according to the connection. Ellicott thinks Chrys. here displays his "accurate observation of language,"—"ye, as well as my other converts."— J. A. B.]

[2] [The Greek word is equivalent to both "temptations" and "trials." "Temptations" formerly had a like breadth of meaning, but has been restricted to the bad sense. — J. A. B.]

[3] κείμενοι. He alludes to the sense "laid," as if it were "laid down to repose."   [4] See Heb. x. 34.

[5] διεξῶσε, "push through"; thus we read of ὠθισμὸς, Angl. "shoving" in hard-fought battles.

[6] In pace, ut sapiens, aptârit idonea bello. — Hor.

see these[1] soldiers, who though no war disturbs them, but it is profound peace, brightening up their arms, and going forth with the teachers who teach them tactics, into the broad and level plains, I may say, every day, keep up with the greatest strictness the exercises of war? Of our spiritual soldiers, who has done this? No one. For this reason we become in war weak and ignoble, and easily led captive by any.

But what stupidity is this, not to think the present a season of war, when Paul is crying out, " Yea, and all that would live godly in Christ Jesus shall suffer persecution " (2 Tim. iii. 12); and Christ says, " In the world ye shall have tribulation." (John xvi. 33.) And again the blessed Paul with a loud voice cries out, saying, " Our wrestling is not against flesh and blood," and again, " Stand therefore, having girded your loins with truth." (Eph. vi. 12 and 14.) Why dost thou arm us, tell me, when it is not war? Why dost thou give us trouble to no purpose? Thou puttest breast-plates on the soldiers, when it is allowed them to rest and revive. But he would have said, Certainly, however, though it were not war, it would be right to attend to the concerns of war. For he who in peace considers the business of battle, will be formidable in the season of battle ; but he who is without experience in the things of war, will be more troubled even in peace. Why so? Because he will weep for the things which he possesses, and not being able to fight for them, will be in anguish. For the possessions of the cowardly and inexperienced and ignoble in war, are the property of all who are brave and warlike. So that on this account first I arm you. But then also the whole time of our life is the season of war. How and in what respect? The devil is ever at hand. Hear what it says, " As a roaring lion, he walketh about, seeking whom he may devour." (1 Pet. v. 8.) Numberless bodily affections assail us, which it is necessary to enumerate, that we may not vainly deceive ourselves. For tell me, what does not war against us? Riches, beauty, pleasure, power, authority, envy, glory, pride? For not only does our own glory war against us, forbidding us to descend to humility ; but the glory of others also, leading us to envy and ill-nature. But what do their opposites, poverty, dishonor, the being despised, rejected, the having no power? These things indeed are in us. But from men proceed wickedness, plots, deceits, slanders, assaults innumerable. In like manner on the part of the demons, " principalities, powers, the world-rulers of this darkness, spiritual hosts of wickedness." Some of us are rejoicing, others grieving, both are deviations from the right course. But health and sickness (war

against us). From what quarter will not man be falling into sin? Would you that I should tell you from the beginning, commencing even immediately from Adam? What took captive the first created? Pleasure, and eating, and the love of dominion. What the son who came next after him? Grudging and envy. What those in the time of Noah? Fleshly pleasures, and the evils issuing from them. What his son? Insolence and irreverence. What the Sodomites? Insolence, wantonness; and fullness of bread. But often even poverty has this effect. On this account a certain wise man said, " Give me neither poverty nor riches." (Prov. xxx. 8.) However it is neither poverty nor riches, but the will that cannot use either of them. " Acknowledge," he says, " that thou passest through the midst of snares." (Ecclus. ix. 13.)

The blessed Paul has admirably said, " Hereunto we are appointed." He has not said merely, that we are tempted, but that " hereunto we are appointed," as if he had said, For this were we born. This is our business, this our life, and dost thou seek rest? The executioner does not stand over us, lacerating our sides, and compelling us to sacrifice ; but the desire of riches, and of possessing more, is instant, tearing out our eyes. No soldier has kindled a pile, nor placed us on a gridiron,[2] but more than this, the flames of the flesh set fire on our souls. No king is present promising numberless bounties, and putting us out of countenance. But there is present a rage for glory, tickling us worse than he. A great war, truly, exceedingly great, if we would watch.

And the present season too has its crowns. Hear Paul saying, " Henceforth there is laid up for me the crown of righteousness, which the righteous Judge shall give me . . . and not only to me, but also to all them that have loved His appearing." (2 Tim. iv. 8.) When thou hast lost a beloved and only son, whom thou wert bringing up in much wealth, displaying good hopes, himself being the only one to succeed to thine inheritance ; do not complain, but give thanks to God, and glorify Him who has taken him, and in this respect thou wilt not be worse than Abraham. For as he gave him to God, when he commanded it, so thou hast not complained, when He has taken him. Hast thou fallen into a severe sickness, and do many come, constraining thee, some with charms, some with amulets, and others with other things, to remedy the evil? and hast thou borne it firmly and unflinchingly from the fear of God, and wouldst thou have chosen to suffer all things rather than submit to do any of those idolatrous practices?

[1] i.e. earthly.

[2] ἐπὶ κρατίκλης. From the Latin " Craticula." Such was the " Catasta " in the martyrdom of St. Laurence. Prud. Peristeph. H. ii. 399. An iron seat is mentioned as thus used at Vienne. Euseb. v. 1.

This brings to thee the crown of martyrdom. Doubt it not. And how and by what means, I will tell thee. For as such an one bears firmly the pains of torture, so as not to worship the image, so thou also bearest the sufferings of thy disease, so as to want nothing of those remedies which the other offers, nor to do the things which he prescribes. "But those pains are more violent"—yes, but these are of longer duration, so that it is the same in the end; nay often these are more violent too. For tell me, when fever is raging and burning within, and thou rejectest the charm that others recommend to thee, hast thou not bound on thee the crown of martyrdom?

Again, has any one lost money? many advise thee to have recourse to diviners; but thou, from fear of God, because it is forbidden, choosest rather not to receive thy money than to disobey God — thou hast a reward equal to him who has given it to the poor, if having lost, thou givest thanks, and when able to have recourse to diviners, thou bearest not to receive, rather than so to receive it. For as he from the fear of God has given all to the needy, so thou also from fear of God, when they have plundered thee, hast not recovered it.

We are the masters of injuring or not injuring ourselves. And if you will, let us make the whole matter plain in the case of theft itself. The thief has cut through the wall, he has rushed into the chamber, he has carried off costly golden vessels, and precious stones, in short, he has cleared thy whole treasure, and has not been taken. The fact is grievous, and it seems to be a loss; still as yet it is not so, but it depends on thee to make it either a loss or a gain. And how, sayest thou, can this be a gain? I will endeavor to show thee how, if thou art willing, it will be a great gain, but if unwilling, the loss will be severer than that which has taken place. For as in the case of artificers, when material is before them, he who is skilled in his art uses it to good purpose, but he that is unskillful spoils it, and makes it a loss to him, so also in these matters. How then will it be a gain? If thou givest thanks to God, if thou dost not wail bitterly, if thou utterest the words of Job, "The Lord gave and the Lord hath taken away. Naked came I out of my mother's womb, naked shall I also go away." (Job i. 21, Sept.)

"What?" sayest thou, "the Lord hath taken away? The thief hath taken away, and how canst thou say, the Lord hath taken away?" Wonder not, for even Job, of things which the devil took away, said, These the Lord hath taken away? And shalt not thou say of what the thief took, The Lord hath taken away? Tell me, whom dost thou admire? him who has

bestowed all his goods upon the poor, or Job for these words? Is he, who did not then give, inferior to him, who has given alms? For say not, "I feel no thankfulness. The matter was not done with my consent, or knowledge, or will. The robber took it. What will be my reward?" Neither did these things happen with Job's knowledge or will. For how could it be? Nevertheless, he wrestled.[1]

And it is in thy power to receive as great a reward, as if thou hadst cast it away willingly. And perhaps we admire this man more, who thankfully suffers wrongs, than him who gives spontaneously. And why? Because the latter indeed is fed with praises, and supported by conscience, and has good hopes; and having before[2] borne manfully the privation of his goods, he then cast them away; but the former, whilst yet bound to them, was forcibly deprived of them. And it is not the same thing, having first been induced to part with riches, in that way to bestow them, as it is while yet longing to be deprived of them. If thou wilt say these words, thou wilt receive many times as much, and even more than Job. For he received twice as much here, but to thee Christ has promised a hundred fold. From the fear of God, thou hast not blasphemed? thou hast not had recourse to diviners? suffering wrong, thou hast been thankful? Thou art like one who despises wealth, for thou couldest not do this, hadst thou not first despised it. And is it not the same thing in a long time to practice the contempt of riches, and all at once to bear a loss that has happened. Thus the loss becomes gain, and thou wilt not be injured, but even benefited by the devil.

But how does the loss also become grievous? When thou losest thy soul! Tell me, the thief has deprived thee of thy possessions: wilt thou deprive thyself of salvation? Wherefore, grieving at the evils which thou hast suffered from others, dost thou plunge thyself into more evils? He perhaps has involved thee in poverty: but thou perversely injurest thyself in things that are fatal. He hath deprived thee of things that are without thee, and that hereafter would spring away from thee even against thy will. But thou deprivest thyself of the eternal riches. The devil hath grieved thee by taking away thy wealth; do thou also grieve him, and do not delight him. If thou hast recourse to diviners, thou delightest him. If thou renderest thanks to God, thou givest him his death-blow.

And see what happens. Thou wilt not still find it, if thou goest to the diviners, for it is not in their power to know; and even if by any chance they have told thee, thou both losest thy

---

[1] i.e. with the temptation. See on Stat. Hom. i.
[2] i.e. in preparation.

own soul besides, and thou wilt be derided by thy brethren, and again wilt lose it wretchedly. For the demon, knowing that thou canst not bear thy loss, but for the sake of these things deniest even thy God, again gives thee wealth, that he may have an opportunity of deceiving thee again, and making thee fall away. And if the diviners should tell thee, wonder not. The demon is without body: he is everywhere going about. It is he who arms the robbers themselves. For these things do not take place without the demon. If therefore he arms them, he knows also where it is deposited. He is not ignorant of his own ministers. And this is not wonderful. If he sees thee grieving at the loss, he adds yet another to it. If he sees thee laughing at it, and despising it, he will desist from this course. For as we deal to our enemies those things by which we grieve them, but if we see that they do not grieve, we henceforth desist, as being unable to plague them; so does the devil also.

What sayest thou? Dost thou not see those who sail on the sea, how, when a storm arises, they regard not their wealth, but even throw overboard their substance? "O man, what dost thou say? Art thou coöperating with the storm and the shipwreck? Before the wave has taken away thy wealth, dost thou do it with thine own hands? Why, before the shipwreck, dost thou wreck thyself?" But indeed a rustic inexperienced in the trials of the sea might say this. But the naval man, and one who truly knows what are the causes of calm, and what of storm, will even laugh at him who talks thus. For I throw it overboard, he says, that there may be no whelming sea.[1] So he who is experienced in the events and trials of life, when he sees the storm impending, and the spirits of evil wishing to cause shipwreck, throws overboard even the remainder of his wealth. Hast thou been plundered? Do alms, and thou lightenest the ship. Have robbers ravaged thee? Give what remains to Christ. So thou wilt console thy poverty from thy former loss. Lighten

the ship, do not hold fast what remains, lest the vessel fill with water. They, to preserve their bodies, throw their goods overboard, and wait not for the assailing wave to overturn the vessel. And wilt thou not stay the shipwreck, that thou mayest save souls?

Make the trial, I beseech you — if you disbelieve, make the trial, and you will see the glory of God. When anything grievous has happened, immediately give alms; render thanks that it has happened, and thou wilt see how much joy will come upon thee. For spiritual gain, though it be small, is so great as to throw into the shade all bodily loss. As long as thou hast to give to Christ, thou art rich. Tell me, if when thou wast robbed, the king coming to thee held out his hand, begging to receive something from thee, wouldest thou not then think thyself richer than all, if the king not even after so great poverty was ashamed of thee? Be not carried away with thy wealth, only overcome thyself, and thou wilt overcome the assault of the devil. It is in thy power to acquire great gain.

Let us despise wealth, that we may not despise the soul. But how can any one despise it? Dost thou not see in the case of beautiful bodies, and the lovers of them, how as long as they are in their sight the fire is kindled, the flame rises bright; but when any one has removed them afar off, all is extinguished, all is lulled to sleep; so also in the case of wealth, let no one provide gold, nor precious stones, nor necklaces; when seen, they ensnare the eyes. But if thou wouldest be rich like the ancients, be rich not in gold, but in necessary things, that thou mayest bestow on others from that which thou hast ready. Be not fond of ornament. Such wealth is both easy to be plotted against by robbers, and a thing that brings us cares. Not vessels of gold and silver, but let there be stores of bread and wine and oil, not that being sold again they may procure money, but that they may be supplied to those who need. If we withdraw ourselves from those superfluities, we shall obtain the heavenly goods; which God grant that we may all obtain, in Jesus Christ our Lord, with whom, &c.

---

[1] Calm, storm, &c., seem to be used here in a relative sense: what is a storm to a deep-laden vessel being less to a light one.

HOMILY IV.

1 THESSALONIANS iii. 5–8.

"For this cause I also, when I could no longer forbear, sent that I might know your faith, lest by any means the tempter had tempted you, and our labor should be in vain. But when Timothy came even now unto us from you, and brought us glad tidings of your faith and love, and that ye have good remembrance of us always, longing to see us, even as we also to see you; for this cause, brethren, we were comforted over you in all our distress and affliction through your faith: for now we live, if ye stand fast in the Lord."

A QUESTION lies before us to-day, which is much disputed, and which is gathered from many sources. But what is this question? "For this cause," he says, "when I could no longer forbear, I sent Timothy that I might know your faith." What sayest thou? He, who knew so many things, who heard unutterable words, who ascended even to the third heaven, doth not he know, even when he is in Athens? And yet the distance is not great, nor has he been long parted from them. For he says, "Being bereaved of you for a short season." He does not know the affairs of the Thessalonians, but is compelled to send Timothy to know their faith, "lest," he says, "the tempter had tempted you, and our labors should be in vain."

What then is one to say? That the Saints knew not all things. And this one might learn from many instances, both of the early ones, and of those who came after them, as Elisha knew not concerning the woman (2 Kings iv. 27); as Elijah said to God, "I only am left, and they seek my life." Wherefore he heard from God, "I have left me seven thousand men." (1 Kings xix. 10 and 18.) Samuel again, when he was sent to anoint David; "The Lord said to him, Look not on his countenance, nor on the height of his stature; because I have rejected him: for God seeth not as man seeth; for man looketh on the outward appearance, but God looketh on the heart." (1 Sam. xvi. 7.)

And this comes to pass out of great care on God's part. How, and in what way? For the sake both of the Saints themselves, and of those who believe in them. For as He permits that there should be persecutions, so He permits that they should also be ignorant of many things, that they may be kept humble. On this account also Paul said, "There was given to me a thorn in the flesh, a messenger of Satan to buffet me, that I should not be exalted over much." (2 Cor. xii. 7.) And again, lest others also should have great imaginations concerning them. For if they thought they were gods from their miracles, much more if they had continued always knowing all things. And this again he also says: "Lest any man should account of me above that which he seeth me to be, or heareth from me." (2 Cor. xii. 6.) And again hear Peter, when he healed the lame man, saying, "Why fasten ye your eyes on us, as though by our own power or godliness we had made him to walk." (Acts iii. 12.) And if even when they were saying and doing these things, and from these few and small miracles, evil imaginations were thus engendered, much more would they have been from great ones.

But for another reason too these things were allowed. For that no one might be able to say it was as being other than men that they performed those excellent actions, and so all should become supine, he shows their infirmity, that from their folly he might cut off every pretext of shamelessness. For this reason he is ignorant, for this reason also, after having purposed, he frequently does not come, that they might perceive there were many things he knew not. Great advantage then came of this. For if there were some yet saying, "This man is that power of God which is called Great" (Acts viii. 10), and some, that it is this person, or that; unless these things had been so, what would they not have thought?

But here, however, there seems to be a censure on them. But quite otherwise, it even shows their admirable conduct, and proves the excess of their temptations. How? Attend. For if thou first sayest "that we are appointed thereunto," and "let no man be moved," why again dost thou send Timothy, fearing that something might happen which thou wouldest not wish. This indeed he does from his great love. For those who love suspect even what is safe, from their exceeding warmth. But this is caused by their great temptations. For I said indeed that we are appointed thereunto, but the excess of the temptations alarmed me. Wherefore he has not said, I send him as condemning you, but "when I could no longer forbear," which is rather an expression of love.

What means, "Lest by any means the tempter had tempted you"? Dost thou see that to be shaken in afflictions proceeds from the devil, and from his seduction? For when he cannot shake us ourselves, he takes another way,[1] and shakes the weaker sort through our means, which argues exceeding infirmity, and such as admits of no excuse; as he did in the case of Job, having stirred up his wife, "Speak some word against the Lord," she says, "and die." (Job ii. 9, Sept.) See how he tempted her.

But wherefore has he not said, "shaken," but "tempted"? Because, he says, I only suspected so much, as that you had been tempted. For he does not call his temptation a wavering. For he who admits his attack is shaken. Strange! how great is the affection of Paul! He did not regard afflictions, nor plots against him. For I think that he then remained there, as Luke says, that "he abode in Greece three months, when[2] the Jews laid a plot against him." (Acts xx. 3.)

His concern therefore was not for his own dangers, but for his disciples. Seest thou how he surpassed every natural parent? For we in our afflictions and dangers lose the remembrance of all. But he so feared and trembled for his children, that he sent to them Timothy, whom alone he had for his consolation, his companion and fellow-laborer, and him too in the very midst of dangers.

"And our labor," he says, "should be in vain." Wherefore! for even if they were turned aside, it was not through thy fault, not through thy negligence. But nevertheless, though this were the case, I think, from my great love of the brethren, that my labor had been rendered vain.

"Lest by any means the tempter had tempted you." But he tempts, not knowing whether he shall overthrow. Does he then, even though he knows not, yet assail us, and do we, who know that we shall completely overcome him, not watch? But that he does attack us, though he knows not, he showed in the case of Job. For that evil demon said to God, "Hast Thou not made a hedge about his things within, and his things without? Take away his goods, and surely he will bless[3] Thee to Thy face." (Job i. 10, 11, Sept.) He makes trial; if he sees anything weak, he makes an attack, if strong, he desists. "And our labor," he says, "be in vain." Let us all hear, how Paul labored. He does not say work, but "labor"; he does not say, and you be lost, but "our labor."[4] So

that even if anything had happened, it would be happening with some reason. But that it did not happen was a great wonder. These things indeed we expected, he says, but the contrary happened. For not only did we receive from you no addition to our affliction but even consolation.

"But when Timothy came even now unto us, and brought us glad tidings of your faith and love." "Brought us glad tidings," he says. Do you see the excessive joy of Paul? he does not say, brought us word, but "brought us glad tidings." So great a good did he think their steadfastness and love. For it was necessary, the one remaining firm, that the other also must be steadfast. And he rejoiced in their love, because it was a sign of their faith. "And that ye have," he says, "good remembrance of us always, longing to see us, even as we also to see you." That is, with praises. Not when we were present, nor when we were working miracles, but even now, when we are far off, and are scourged, and are suffering numberless evils, "ye have good remembrance of us." Hear how disciples are admired, who have good remembrance of their teachers, how they are called blessed. Let us imitate these. For we benefit ourselves, not those who are loved by us. "Longing to see us," he says, "as we also to see you." And this too cheered them; for to him who loves, to perceive that the beloved person knows that he is beloved, is a great comfort and consolation.

"For this cause, brethren, we were comforted over you in all our distress and affliction through your faith. For now we live if ye stand fast in the Lord." What is comparable to Paul, who thought the salvation of his neighbors was his own, being so affected towards all, as really towards members? Who now would be able to break forth into such speech? Or rather, who will ever be able to have such a thought? He did not require them to be thankful to him for the trials which he suffered for them, but he was thankful to them that they were not moved on account of his trials. As if he had said, that to you rather than to us was injury done by those trials; you were tempted rather than we, you who suffered nothing, rather than we who suffered. Because, he says, Timothy brought us these good tidings, we feel nothing of our sorrows, but were comforted in all our affliction; not in this affliction only. For nothing besides can touch a good teacher, as long as the affairs of his disciples go on to his mind. Through you, he says, we were comforted; you confirmed us. And yet the reverse was the case. For

---

[1] ἑτέρως might be taken thus, "when he cannot shake us otherwise," the other being a last resource *against us.*

[2] The Greek will read thus, but will hardly bear the construction. [The plot was at the end of the three months, and caused him to change his course. — J. A. B.]

[3] [The Hebrew word denotes both bless and curse (perhaps both derived from the idea of supplicating God). The Septuagint translates "bless" in i. 11 and ii. 5, and evades by paraphrases in i. 5, "devised evil against God," and ii. 9, "say some word unto the Lord." — J. A. B.]

[4] [Three Greek words are employed. The Apostle's term would be better translated "toil"; and so Chrys. remarks, "He does not say work, but toil." The same distinction is to be observed in Rev.

xiv. 13, " in that they shall rest from their toils, for their works follow with them." The verb here employed by Chrys., " how Paul labored," signifies weary or suffering labor. — J. A. B.]

that when suffering they did not yield, but stood manfully, was sufficient to confirm the disciples. But he reverses the whole matter, and turns the encomium over to them. You have anointed us, he says, you have caused us to breathe again; you have not suffered us to feel our trials. And he has not said, we breathe again, nor we are comforted, but what? "Now we live," showing that he thinks nothing is either trial or death, but their stumbling, whereas their advancement was even life. How else could any one have set forth either the sorrow for the weakness of one's disciples, or the joy? He has not said we rejoice, but "we live," the life to come.

So that without this we do not even think it life to live. So ought teachers to be affected, so disciples; and there will be nothing at any time amiss.[1] Then further softening the expression, see what he says,

Ver. 9, 10. "For what thanksgiving can we render again unto God for you, for all the joy wherewith we joy for your sakes before our God; night and day praying exceedingly that we may see your face, and may perfect that which is lacking in your faith?"

Not only, he says, are ye the causes of life to us, but also of much joy, and so much that we cannot worthily give thanks to God. Your[2] good behavior, he says, we consider to be the gift of God. Such kindnesses have you shown to us, that we think it to be of God; yea, rather, and it is of God. For such a disposition of mind comes not of a human soul or carefulness. "Night and day," he says, "praying exceedingly." This too is a sign of joy. For as any husbandman, hearing concerning his land that has been tilled by himself, that it is burdened with ears of grain, longs with his own eyes to see so pleasant a sight, so Paul to see Macedonia. "Praying exceedingly." Observe the excess; "that we may see your face, and may perfect that which is lacking in your faith."

Here there is a great question. For if now thou livest, because they stand fast, and Timothy brought thee "glad tidings of their faith and love," and thou art full of so much joy as not to be able worthily to give thanks to God, how sayest thou here that there are deficiencies in their faith? Were those then the words of flattery? By no means, far be it. For previously he testified that they endured many conflicts, and were no worse affected than the Churches in Judæa. What then is it? They had not enjoyed the full benefit of his teaching, nor learned all that it behoved them to learn. And

this he shows toward the end. Perhaps there had been questionings among them concerning the Resurrection, and there were many who troubled them, not by temptations, nor by dangers, but by acting the part of teachers. This is what he says is lacking in their faith, and for this reason, he has so explained himself, and has not said, that you should be confirmed, where indeed he feared concerning the faith itself, "I have sent," he says, "Timothy 'to confirm you,'" but here, "to perfect that which is lacking," which is rather a matter of teaching than of confirming. As also he says elsewhere, "that ye may be perfected unto every good work." (From 1 Cor. i. 10, or 2 Tim. iii. 17.) Now the perfected thing is one in which there is some little deficiency: for it is that which is brought to perfection.

Ver. 11, 12. "Now may our God and Father Himself, and our Lord Jesus Christ direct our way unto you: and the Lord make you to increase and abound in love one toward another, and toward all men, even as we also do toward you."

This is a proof of excessive love, that he not only prays for them by himself, but even in his Epistles inserts his prayer. This argues a fervent soul, and one truly not to be restrained. This is a proof of the prayers made there also, and at the same time also an excuse, as showing that it was not voluntarily, nor from indolence, that they[3] did not go to them. As if he had said, May God Himself cut short the temptations that everywhere distract us, so that we may come directly to you. "And the Lord make you to increase and abound." Do you see the unrestrainable madness of love that is shown by his words? "Make you to increase and abound,"[4] instead of cause you to grow. As if one should say, that with a kind of superabundance he desires to be loved by them. "Even as we do also toward you," he says. Our part is already done, we pray that yours may be done. Do you see how he wishes love to be extended, not only toward one another, but everywhere? For this truly is the nature of godly love, that it embraces all. If you love indeed such an one, but do not love such an one, it is human love. But such is not ours. "Even as we do also toward you."

Ver. 13. "To the end He may establish your hearts unblamable in holiness before our God and Father, at the coming of our Lord Jesus Christ with all His saints."

He shows that love produces advantage to themselves, not to those who are loved. I wish, he says, that this love may abound, that there may be no blemish. He does not say to stablish

---

[1] ἄτοπον.
[2] So Musculus, who may have had MS. authority. All Greek copies except Catena read "our," which requires κατόρθωμα to be rendered "achievement" in a less proper sense. [Three MSS. give "our," and although two of them form a group that abounds in wrong alterations, yet the present reading is probably correct. — J. A. B.]

[3] St. Paul and Silvanus.
[4] The words are strong, "make you to exceed and overflow."

you, but your hearts. "For out of the heart come forth evil thoughts." (Matt. xv. 19.) For it is possible, without doing anything, to be a bad man; as for example, to have envy, unbelief, deceit, to rejoice at evils, not to be loving, to hold perverted doctrines, all these things are of the heart; and to be pure of these things is holiness. For indeed chastity is properly by preëminence called holiness, since fornication and adultery is also uncleanness.[1] But universally all sin is uncleanness, and every virtue is purity. For, "Blessed," it is said, "are the pure in heart." (Matt. v. 8.) By "the pure" He means those who are in every way pure.

For other things also know how to pollute the soul, and no less. For that wickedness defiles the soul, hear the prophet, saying, "O Jerusalem, wash thine heart from wickedness." (Jer. iv. 14.) And again, "Wash you, make you clean, put away the wickednesses from your souls." (Isa. i. 16, Sept.) He did not say "fornications," so that not only fornication, but other things also defile the soul.

"To establish your hearts," he says, "unblamable in holiness before our God and Father, at the coming of our Lord Jesus Christ with all His saints." Therefore Christ will then be a Judge, but not before Him (only), but also before the Father we shall stand to be judged. Or does he mean this, to be unblamable before God, as he always says, "in the sight of God," for this is sincere virtue — not in the sight of men?

It is love then that makes them unblamable. For it does make men really unblamable. And once when I was discoursing of this to a certain one, and saying, that love makes men unblamable, and that love to our neighbor does not suffer any entrance of transgression, and in my discourse going over, and pursuing all the rest — some one of my acquaintance interposing himself said, What then of fornication, is it not possible both to love, and to commit fornication? And it is indeed from love that this springs. Covetousness indeed, and adultery, and envy, and hostile designs, and everything of this sort can, from love of one's neighbor, be stopped; but how fornication? he said. I therefore told him, that even this can love stop. For if a man should love a woman that commits fornication, he will endeavor both to draw her off from other men, and not himself also to add to her sin. So that to commit fornication with a woman is the part of one exceedingly hating her with whom he commits the fornication, but one who truly loved her would withdraw her from that abominable practice. And there is not, there is not any sin, which the power of love, like fire, cannot consume. For it is easier for a

vile faggot to resist a great pile of fire, than for the nature of sin to resist the power of love.

This then let us plant in our own souls, that we may stand with all the Saints. For they all pleased God by their love to their neighbor. Whence was Abel slain, and did not slay? From his vehement love to his brother, he could not even admit such a thought. Whence was the destructive pest of envy received by Cain? For I will no longer call him the brother of Abel! Because the foundations of love had not been firmly fixed in him. Whence did the sons of Noah obtain a good report? was it not because they vehemently loved their father, and did not endure to see his exposure? And whence was the other cursed? was it not from not loving him? And whence did Abraham obtain a good report? was it not from love in doing what he did concerning his nephew? what he did as to his supplication for the Sodomites? For strongly, strongly, were the Saints affected with love and with sympathy.

For consider, I pray; Paul, he that was bold in the face of fire, hard as adamant, firm and unshaken, on every side compact, riveted in the fear of God, and inflexible; for, "who (said he) shall separate us from the love of Christ? Shall tribulation, or anguish, or persecution, or famine, or nakedness, or peril, or sword "? (Rom. viii. 35) he that was bold in the face of all these things, and of earth and sea, he that laughed to scorn the adamantine gates of death,[2] whom nothing ever withstood, — he, when he saw the tears of some whom he loved, was so broken and crushed, — the adamantine man, — that he did not even conceal his feelings, but said straightway, "What do ye, weeping and breaking my heart?" (Acts xxi. 13.) What sayest thou, tell me? Had a tear the power to crush that soul of adamant? Yea, he says, for I hold out against all things except love. This prevails over me, and subdues me. This is the mind of God. An abyss of water[3] did not crush him, and a few tears crushed him. "What do ye, weeping and crushing my heart?" For great is the force of love. Dost thou not see him again weeping? Why weepest thou? Tell me. "By the space of three years," he says, "I ceased not to admonish every one night and day with tears." (Acts xx. 31.) From his great love he feared, lest some plague should be introduced among them. And again, "For out of much affliction and anguish of heart I wrote unto you with many tears." (2 Cor. ii. 4.)

And what did Joseph? tell me, that firm one, who stood up against so great a tyranny, who appears so noble against so great a flame of love,

---

[1] This is legally opposed to holiness.

[2] [Field's MSS. all give "death"; the previous editions all had "Hades," a natural alteration. Cases are not very rare in which the editions were without known MS. support. — J. A. B.]

[3] Perhaps alluding to 2 Cor. xi. 25.

who so out-battled and overcame the madness of his mistress. For what was there not then to charm him? A beautiful person, the pride of rank, the costliness of garments, the fragrance of perfumes, (for all these things know how to soften the soul,) words more soft than all the rest! For ye know that she who loves, and so vehemently, nothing so humble but she will bring herself to say it, taking upon her the attitude of a supplicant. For so broken was this woman, though wearing gold, and being of royal dignity, that she threw herself at the knees perhaps of the captive boy, and perhaps even intreated him weeping and clasping his knees, and had recourse to this not once, and a second time, but oftentimes. Then he might see her eye shining most brilliantly. For it is probable that she not simply but with excessive nicety would set off her beauty; as wishing by many nets to catch the lamb of Christ. Add here I pray also many magic charms. Yet nevertheless this inflexible, this firm man, of rocky hardness, when he saw his brothers who had bartered him away, who had thrown him into a pit, who had sold him, who had even wished to murder him, who were the causes both of the prison and the honor, when he heard from them how they had worked upon their father, (for, we said, it says, that one was devoured by a wild beast [Gen. xxxvii. 20, and lxiv. 28,]) he was broken, softened, crushed, "And he wept," it says, and not being able to bear his feelings, he went in, and composed himself (Gen. xliii. 30), that is, wiped away his tears.

What is this? dost thou weep, O Joseph? and yet the present circumstances are deserving not of tears, but of anger, and wrath, and indignation, and great revenge and retribution. Thou hast thine enemies in thy hands, those fratricides; thou canst satiate thy wrath. And yet neither would this be injustice. For thou dost not thyself begin the unjust acts, but defendest thyself against those who have done the wrong. For look not to thy dignity. This was not of their contrivance, but of God, who shed His favor upon thee. Why dost thou weep? But he would have said, far be it that I, who in all things have obtained a good report, should by this remembrance of wrongs overturn them all. It is truly a season for tears. I am not more brutish than beasts. They pour out a libation to nature, whatever harm they suffer. I weep, he says, that they ever treated me thus.

This man let us also imitate. Let us mourn and weep for those who have injured us. Let us not be angry with them. For truly they are worthy of tears, for the punishment and condemnation to which they make themselves liable.

I know, how you now weep, how you rejoice, both admiring Paul, and amazed at Joseph, and pronouncing them blessed. But if any one has an enemy, let him now take him into recollection, let him bring him to his mind, that whilst his heart is yet warm with the remembrance of the Saints, he may be enabled to dissolve the stubbornness of wrath, and to soften what is harsh and callous. I know, that after your departure hence, after that I have ceased speaking, if anything of warmth and fervor should remain, it will not be so great, as it now is whilst you are hearing me. If therefore any one, if any one has become cold, let him dissolve the frost. For the remembrance of injuries is truly frost and ice. But let us invoke the Sun of Righteousness, let us entreat Him to send His beams upon us, and there will no longer be thick ice, but water to drink.

If the fire of the Sun of Righteousness has touched our souls, it will leave nothing frozen, nothing hard, nothing burning,[1] nothing unfruitful. It will bring out all things ripe, all things sweet, all things abounding with much pleasure. If we love one another, that beam also will come. Allow me, I beseech you, to say these things with earnestness. Cause me to hear, that by these words we have produced some effect; that some one has gone and thrown both his arms about his enemy, has embraced him, has twined himself around him, has warmly kissed him, has wept. And though the other be a wild beast, a stone, or whatever he be, he will be made gentle by such affectionate kindness. For on what account is he thine enemy? Hath he insulted thee? yet he has not injured thee at all. But dost thou for the sake of money suffer thy brother to be at enmity with thee? Do not so, I beseech you. Let us do away all. It is our season. Let us use it to good purpose. Let us cut asunder the cords of our sins. Before we go away to judgment, let us not ourselves judge one another. "Let not the sun" (it is said) "go down upon your wrath." (Eph. iv. 26.) Let no one put it off. These puttings off produce delays. If you have deferred it to-day, you blush the more, and if you add to-morrow, the shame is greater, and if a third day, yet worse. Let us not then put ourselves to shame, but let us forgive, that we may be forgiven. And if we be forgiven, we shall obtain all blessings, through Jesus Christ our Lord, with whom, &c.

---

[1] The translator suggests Milton's sense:—

　　　　"The parching air
　Burns frore, and cold performs th' effects of fire."

The extreme harshness of some fruits without the sun may be meant. In Hom. xvi. on St. Matt. Ben. p. 215 A, τὰ καυστικὰ is used for "combustibles," but there is a various reading, ὑπαναπτικὰ in one MS.; see Ed. Field, p. 229.

HOMILY V.

1 THESSALONIANS iv. 1–3.

"Finally then, brethren, we beseech and exhort you in the Lord Jesus, that, as ye received of us how ye ought to walk and to please God, so ye abound more and more. For ye know what charge we gave you through the Lord Jesus Christ. For this is the will of God, even your sanctification."

WHEN he has met what was pressing, and what was upon his hands, and is about henceforth to enter upon things that are perpetual, and which they ought continually to hear, he adds this expression, "finally," that is, always and forever. "We beseech and exhort you in the Lord." Strange! He does not even speak of himself as of sufficient credit to exhort. And yet who was so worthy of credit? But he takes Christ along with him. We exhort you, he says, by God. Which also he said to the Corinthians, "God entreats (exhorts) you through us." (2 Cor. v. 20.) "That as ye received of us." This "received" is not of words only, but of actions also, viz. "how ye ought to walk," and he means thereby the whole conduct of life. "And to please God, that ye abound more and more. That is, that by more abounding ye do not stop at the limit of the commandments, but that you even go beyond them. For this it is, that "ye abound more and more." In what preceded he accepts the marvel of their firm faith, but here he regulates their life. For this is proficiency, even to go beyond the commandments and the statutes. For no longer from the constraint of a teacher, but from their own voluntary choice, is all this performed. For as the earth ought not to bear only what is thrown upon it, so too ought the soul not to stop at those things which have been inculcated, but to go beyond them. Do you see that he has properly said "to go beyond"? For virtue is divided into these two things, to decline from evil, and to do good. For the withdrawal from evil is not sufficient for the arrival at virtue, but it is a kind of path, and a beginning leading thereto; still we have need of great alacrity. The things therefore to be avoided he tells them in the order of commandment. And justly. For these things indeed being done bring punishment, but not being done, yet bring no praise. The acts of virtue however, such as to give away our goods, and such like, are not of the order of commandment, he says. But what? "He that is able to receive, let him receive." (Matt. xix. 12.) It is profitable, therefore, that as he with much fear and trembling had given these commandments

to them, he also by these letters reminds them of that his care. Wherefore he does not repeat them, but reminds them of them.

"For ye know," he says, "what charge we gave you through our Lord Jesus Christ. For this is the will of God, even your sanctification." And observe how he nowhere so vehemently glances at any other thing, as at this. As elsewhere also he writes to this effect; "Follow after peace with all men, and the sanctification without which no man shall see the Lord." (Heb. xii. 14.) And why dost thou wonder, if he everywhere writes to his disciples upon this subject, when even in his Epistle to Timothy he has said, "Keep thyself pure." (1 Tim. v. 22.) Also in his second Epistle to the Corinthians he has said, "In much patience, in fastings, by pureness." (2 Cor. vi. 5, 6.) And one may find this in many places, both in this Epistle to the Romans, and everywhere, and in all his Epistles. For in truth this is an evil pernicious to all. And as a swine full charged with mire, wherever he enters, fills all places with his ill odor, and chokes the senses with dung, so too does fornication; it is an evil not easy to be washed away. But when some even who have wives practice this, how excessive is the outrage! "For this," he says, "is the will of God, even your sanctification, that ye abstain from all fornication." For there are many forms of disorderly conduct. The pleasures of wantonness are of many kinds and various, it were not tolerable to mention them. But having said "from all fornication," he leaves it to those who know them.

Ver. 4, 5. "That each one of you know how to possess himself of his own vessel in sanctification and honor, not in the passion of lust, even as the Gentiles which know not God."

He says, "That each one of you know how to possess himself of his own vessel." It is, then, a matter to be learnt, and that diligently, not to be wanton. But we possess our vessel, when it is pure; when it is impure, sin possesses it. And reasonably. For it does not do the things which we wish, but what sin commands. "Not in the passion of lust," he says. Here he shows also the manner, according to which one ought to be temperate; that we should cut off the passions of lust. For luxury, and wealth, and idleness, and sloth, and ease, and all such things, lead us on to irregular lust. "Even as the Gentiles," he says, "which know not God." For such are they who do not expect that they shall suffer punishment.

Ver. 6. "That no man transgress, and wrong his brother in the matter."

He has well said, "that no man transgress." To each man God has assigned a wife, he has set bounds to nature, that intercourse with one only : therefore intercourse with another is transgression, and the taking of more than belongs to one,[1] and robbery ; or rather it is more cruel than any robbery ; for we grieve not so much, when our riches are carried off, as when marriage is invaded. Dost thou call him brother, and wrongest him, and that in things which are unlawful? Here he speaks concerning adultery, but above also concerning "all fornication." For since he was about to say, "That no man transgress and wrong his brother," Do not think, he says, that I say this only in the case of brethren ; you must not have the wives of others at all, nor even women that have no husbands, and that are common. You must abstain from "all fornication" ; "Because," he says, "the Lord is an avenger in all these things." He exhorted them first, he shamed them, saying, "even as the Gentiles." Then from reasonings he showed the impropriety of defrauding a brother. Afterwards he adds the principal thing ; "Because," he says, "the Lord is an avenger in all these things, as also we forewarned you and testified." For we do not these things without being punished, neither do we enjoy so much pleasure, as we undergo punishment.

Ver. 7. "For God called us not for uncleanness, but in sanctification."

Because he had said "his brother," and had also added, that God is the avenger, showing that even if an unbeliever has suffered this, he who has done it shall suffer punishment, he says, it is not as avenging him that He punishes thee, but because thou hast insulted Himself. He Himself called thee, thou hast insulted Him who called thee. On this account, he has added,

Ver. 8. "Therefore he that rejecteth, rejecteth not man, but God, who giveth His Holy Spirit unto you."

So that even if thou shouldest defile the Empress, he says, or even thine own handmaid, that hath a husband, the crime is the same. Why? Because He avenges not the persons that are injured, but Himself. For thou art equally defiled, thou hast equally insulted God ; for both the one and the other is adultery, as both the one and the other is marriage. And though thou shouldest not commit adultery, but fornication, though the harlot has no husband, yet nevertheless God avenges, for He avenges Him-

self. For thou dost this act, not despising the man,[2] so much as God. And it is manifest from this, that thou doest it concealing it from man, but thou pretendest that God doth not see thee. For tell me, if one who was thought worthy of the purple, and of infinite honor from the king (Emperor), and was commanded to live suitably to the honor, should go and defile himself with any woman ; whom has he insulted? her, or the king who gave him all? She indeed is insulted too,.but not equally.

Wherefore, I beseech you, let us guard against this sin. For as we punish women, when, being married to us, they give themselves to others, so also are we punished, though not by the Roman laws, yet by God. For this also is adultery. For not only is adultery committed in doing so by her who is married to another, but by him also, who is yoked to a wife. Attend carefully to what I say. For although what is said is offensive to many, it is necessary to be said, to set the matter right for the future. Not only is this adultery, when we defile a woman who is married to a man ; but if we ourselves being married to a woman defile one who is free and disengaged, the matter is adultery. For what, if she with whom the adultery is committed is not bound? Yet art thou bound. Thou hast transgressed the law. Thou hast injured thine own flesh. For tell me, wherefore dost thou punish thy wife, if she commit fornication with a man who is loosed, and has not a wife? Because it is adultery. Why? Yet he who defiled her has not a wife, but she is bound to a husband. Well then, thou also art bound to a wife ; so that in like manner thy offence also is adultery. For it is said, "Every one that putteth away his wife, saving for the cause of fornication, maketh her an adulteress : and whosoever shall marry her when she is put away, committeth adultery." (Matt. v. 32.) If he who marries her who is divorced commits adultery, he who, with a wife of his own, defiles himself also with that other — it is manifest to every one. But perhaps to you who are men, enough has been said on this subject. For concerning them that are such, Christ says, "Their worm will not die and the fire will not be quenched." (Mark ix. 44.) But for the sake of the young it is necessary to speak to you, not to the young themselves so much, but to you. For these things are suitable not to them only, but also to you. And how? I will now tell you. He who has not learnt to commit fornication, will neither know how to commit adultery. But he who walloweth among harlots, will quickly also arrive at the other, and will defile himself, if not with the married, yet with those who are disengaged.

---

[1] πλεονεξία, E. V. "covetousness." [The corresponding verb is here inadequately translated "wrong." It designates a man who is not content with his own wife, but takes possession of his brother's. — J. A. B.]

[2] ἐκεῖνον, i.e. the husband.

What then do I advise, so as to extirpate the roots? So many of you as have young sons, and are bringing them up to a worldly life,[1] quickly draw them under the yoke of marriage. For since whilst he is yet young desires trouble him, for the time before marriage, by admonitions, threats, fears, promises, and numberless other methods restrain them. But at the season of marriage, let no one defer it. Behold, I speak the words of a match-maker, that you should let your sons marry. But I am not ashamed to speak thus, since not even Paul was ashamed to say, "Defraud ye not one the other" (1 Cor. vii. 5), which seems more shameful than what I have said; yet he was not ashamed. For he did not pay heed to words, but to the acts that were set right by words. When thy son is grown up, before he enters upon warfare, or any other course of life, consider of his marriage. And if he sees that thou wilt soon take a bride for him, and that the time intervening will be short, he will be able to endure the flame patiently. But if he perceives that thou art remiss and slow, and waitest until he shall acquire a large income, and then thou wilt contract a marriage for him, despairing at the length of the time, he will readily fall into fornication. But alas! the root of evils here also is the love of money. For since no one cares how far his son shall be sober and modest, but all are mad for gold, for this reason no one makes this a matter of concern. Wherefore I exhort you first to regulate well their souls. If he find his bride chaste, and know that body alone, then will both his desire be vehement, and his fear of God the greater, and the marriage truly honorable, receiving bodies pure and undefiled; and the offspring will be full-charged with blessing, and the bride and bridegroom will comply with one another, for both being inexperienced in the manners of others, they will submit to one another. But one that begins when younger to wax wanton, and to have experience of the ways of harlots, for the first and second evening will praise his own wife; but after that he will soon fall back into that wantonness, seeking that dissolute and disorderly laughter, the words that are full of base import, the dissolute deportment,[2] and all the other indecency, which it is not tolerable that we should mention. But a woman of free estate would not endure to make such exhibitions, nor to tarnish herself. For she was espoused to her husband to be his partner in life, and for the procreation of children, not for the purposes of indecency and laughter; that she might keep the house, and instruct him

also to be grave, not that she might supply to him the fuel of fornication.

But the gestures[3] of a harlot seem to you agreeable. I know it. For the Scripture says, "The lips of a strange woman drop honey." (Prov. v. 3.) For on this account I take all this trouble, that ye may have no experience of that honey, for it straightway turns into gall. And this also the Scripture says, "Who for a season is smooth to thy throat, but afterwards thou shalt find her more bitter than gall, and sharper than a two-edged sword." (Prov. v. 3, 4, Sept.) What sayest thou? Bear with me speaking somewhat impure, if I may say so — and expressing myself as one shameless and unblushing. For I do not submit to this willingly, but on account of those who are shameless in their actions, I am compelled to speak this sort of words. And many such we see even in the Scriptures. For even Ezekiel, reproaching Jerusalem, utters many such things, and is not ashamed. And justly. For he did not say them from his own inclination, but from his concern. For although the words seem to be indecent, yet his aim is not indecent, but even highly becoming one who wishes to banish uncleanness from the soul. For if the shameless soul does not hear the very words, it is not affected. For a physician wishing to remove a putrid sore, first thrusts his fingers into the wound, and if he does not first defile his healing hands, he will not be able to cure it. So it is with me. Unless I first defile my mouth, that heals your passions, I shall not be able to heal you. But rather neither is my mouth defiled, nor his hands. Why then? Because the uncleanness is not that of nature, nor from our own body,[4] as neither in that case from his hands, but from what is another's. But if where the body is another's, he does not refuse to dip his own hands, tell me, shall we refuse, where it is our own body? For you are our body, sickly indeed and impure, but ours nevertheless.

What then is this which I say, and for which I have made so long a digression? A garment indeed which your slave wears, you would not choose ever to wear, being disgusted on account of its filth, but you would rather go naked than make use of it. But a body that is unclean and filthy, and which is used not only by your slave, but by numberless others, that will you abuse, and not be disgusted? Are you ashamed at hearing this? But be ashamed of the actions, not of the words. And I pass over all other things, the rudeness, and the corruption of their manners, the servility and illiberality of the

---

[1] [i.e. not designing them to religious celibacy. — J. A. B.]
[2] σχήματα διακεκλασμένα. See on 1 Tim. i. 17, Hom. iv., where he advises the wife to please her husband by modesty and simplicity.

[3] [One MS. has "words," which seems to suit the connection better. — J. A. B.]
[4] Downes would read στόματος, "mouth."

rest of their life. Tell me, should you and your servant go to the same woman? and I wish it were only your servant, and not, it may be, the executioner! And yet you could not bear to take the executioner by the hand; but her who has been made one body with him you kiss and embrace, and do not shudder, nor fear! Are you not ashamed? are you not abashed? are you not pierced with anguish?

I said indeed to your fathers, that they ought early to lead you to marriage: but nevertheless neither are you without liability to punishment. For if there were not other young men also, more numerous than you, living in chastity, both formerly, and now, there would perhaps be some excuse for you. But if there are, how can you say, that we were not able to restrain the flame of lust? For they, who have been able, are your accusers, in that they are partakers of the same nature. Hear Paul saying, " Follow after peace . . . and the sanctification, without which no man shall see the Lord." (Heb. xii. 14.) Is not this threat sufficient to terrify you? Do you see others continuing altogether in chastity, and in gravity passing their lives; and cannot you command yourself even so long as the period of youth? Do you see others ten thousand times overcoming pleasure, and cannot you once refrain? With your leave, I will tell you the cause. For youth is not the cause, since then all young men would be dissolute. But we thrust ourselves into the fire. For when you go up to the theater, and sit feasting your eyes with the naked limbs of women, for the time indeed you are delighted, but afterwards, you have nourished thence a mighty fever. When you see women exhibited as it were in the form of their bodies, and spectacles and songs containing nothing else but irregular loves: such a woman, it is said, loved such a man, and not obtaining him, hanged herself; and unlawful loves having mothers for their object; when you receive these things by hearing also, and through women, and through figures, yea, and even through old men, (for many there put masks upon their faces, and play the parts of women,) tell me, how will you be able to continue chaste afterwards, these narratives, these spectacles, these songs occupying

your soul, and dreams of this sort henceforth succeeding. For it is the nature of the soul for the most part to raise visions of such things, as it wishes for and desires in the daytime. Therefore when you there both see base actions, and hear baser words, and receive indeed the wounds but do not apply the remedies, how will not the sore naturally be increased? how will not the disease become more intense; and in a much greater degree than in our bodies? For if we were willing, our will admits of correction more easily than our bodies. For there indeed drugs, and physicians, and time are required, but here it is sufficient having but the will, to become both good and bad. So that you have rather admitted the disorder. When therefore we gather to us indeed the things that injure, but pay no regard to the things that benefit, how can there ever be any health?

On this account Paul said, " even as the Gentiles who knew not God." Let us be ashamed, let us be afraid, if the Gentiles, that know not God, are often chaste. Let us turn for shame, when we are worse than they. It is easy to achieve chastity, if we will, if we withdraw ourselves from those things that are injurious, since it is not even easy to avoid fornication, if we will not. For what is more easy than to walk in the market-place? but from the excess of laziness it is become difficult, not only in the case of women, but sometimes even in that of men. What is more easy than to sleep? but we have made even this difficult. Many however of the rich toss themselves through a whole night, from their not waiting for the need of sleep, and then sleeping. And in short nothing is difficult, when men are willing; as nothing is easy, when they are unwilling; for we are masters of all these things. On this account the Scripture says, " If ye be willing and hear me." (Isa. i. 19, Sept.) And again, " If ye be unwilling, and hear not." (Ver. 20.) So that all depends upon being willing or unwilling. On this account we both are punished and are praised. But may it be ours, being of those who are praised, to obtain the promised blessings, by the grace and lovingkindness, &c.

HOMILY VI.

1 THESSALONIANS iv. 9, 10.

"But concerning love of the brethren we[1] have no need to write unto you: for ye yourselves are taught of God to love one another; for indeed ye do it toward all the brethren, and those which are in all Macedonia."

WHY then having discoursed with them earnestly concerning chastity, and being about to discourse about the duty of working, and about the not sorrowing for the departed, does he introduce that which was the principal of all good things, love, as if he were passing it over, saying, "We have no need to write to you"? This also is from his great wisdom, and belongs to spiritual instruction. For here he shows two things. First, that the thing is so necessary, as not to require instruction. For things that are very important are manifest to all. And secondly, by saying this he makes them more ashamed than if he had admonished them. For he who thinks that they have behaved aright, and therefore does not admonish them, even if they had not behaved aright, would the sooner lead them to it. And observe, he does not speak of love towards all,[2] but of that towards the brethren. "We have no need to write unto you." He ought then to have been silent, and to say nothing, if there was no need. But now by saying there is no need, he has done a greater thing, than if he had said it.

"For ye yourselves are taught of God." And see with how high a praise he has made God their Teacher in this matter. Ye need not, he says, to learn from man. Which also the prophet says, "and they shall all be taught of God." (Isa. liv. 13.) "For ye yourselves," he says, "are taught of God to love one another. For indeed ye do it toward all the brethren, and those which are in all Macedonia"; and toward all the others, he means. These words are very encouraging to make them do so. And I do not merely say, that ye are taught of God, but I know it from the things which you do. And in this respect he bore many testimonies to them.

"But we exhort you, brethren, that ye abound more and more, and study;" that is, increase and study.

Ver. 11, 12. "To be quiet, and to do your own business, and to work with your hands, even as we charged you: that ye may walk honestly[3] toward them that are without, and may have need of nothing."

He shows of how many evils idleness is the cause, and of how many benefits industry. And this he makes manifest from things which happen among us, as he often does, and that wisely. For by these things the majority are led on more than by spiritual things. For it is a mark of love to our neighbors not to receive from them, but to impart to them. And observe. Being about to exhort and admonish, he places in the middle their good conduct, both that they may recover even from the preceding admonition, and from the threat, when he said, "He therefore that rejecteth, rejecteth not man, but God," and that they may not be restive at this. And this is the effect of working, that one does not receive of others, nor live idly, but by working imparts to others. For it is said, "It is more blessed to give than to receive." (Acts xx. 35.) "And to work," he says, "with your hands." Where are those, who look out for work that is spiritual? Seest thou how he takes from them every excuse, saying, "with your hands"? But does one practice fasting with his hands? or watchings all night? or lyings on the ground? This no one can say. But he is speaking of spiritual work. For it is truly spiritual, that one should by working impart to others, and there is nothing equal to this. "That ye may walk," he says, "becomingly." Seest thou whence he touches them? He has not said, that ye may not be shamed by begging. But he has indeed insinuated the same, yet he puts it in a milder way, so as both to strike and not to do this severely. For if those who are among us are offended at these things, much more those who are without, finding numberless accusations and handles, when they see a man who is in good health and able to support himself, begging and asking help of others. Wherefore also they call us Christ-mongers. On this account, he means, "the name of God is blasphemed." (Rom. ii. 24.) But none of these things has he stated; but that which was able to touch them most nearly, the disgracefulness of the thing.

Ver. 13. "But we would not have you ignorant, brethren, concerning them that are asleep;

---

[1] [Chrys. reads "we," as do many N. T. documents; yet "ye" is pretty certainly right, having been altered because "ye have no need to write to you" is a harsh construction. The "and" after "brethren" is quite certainly genuine for Chrys., but has very slight authority for the N. T. text. — J. A. B.]

[2] φιλαδελφία is strictly "lovingness *toward* brethren," not merely "as of brethren."

[3] [This ought to be now rendered "becomingly," the English word "honestly" having ceased to carry that meaning. — J. A. B.]

that ye sorrow not, even as the rest, which have no hope."

These two things, poverty and despondency, distressed them most, which also pertain to all men. See therefore how he remedies them. But their poverty arose from their goods being taken from them. But if he commands those, whose goods had been taken from them for Christ's sake, to support themselves by working, much more then others. For that they were taken away is manifest from his saying, Ye became partakers[1] with the churches of God. How partakers with them? "And ye took joyfully the spoiling of your possessions." (Heb. x. 34.)

Here he proceeds now to start his discourse concerning the Resurrection. And why? Had he not discoursed with them upon that point?[2] Yes, but here he glances at some further mystery. What then is this? "That we that are alive," he says, "that are left unto the coming of the Lord, shall in nowise precede them that are fallen asleep." The discourse then of the Resurrection was sufficient to comfort him that was grieving. But that which is now said is sufficient also to make the Resurrection eminently worthy of credit. But first let us speak of what precedes, "But we would not have you ignorant, brethren, concerning them that are asleep; that ye sorrow not, even as the rest, which have no hope." See how here also he treats them mildly. He does not say, "Are ye so without understanding?" as he said to the Corinthians, "foolish"? that, knowing there is a resurrection, ye so sorrow, as those who do not believe; but he speaks very mildly, showing respect to their other virtues. And he has not said "concerning the dead," but "them that are asleep,"[3] even at the beginning suggesting consolation to them. "That ye sorrow not," he says, "even as the rest, which have no hope." Therefore to afflict yourselves for the departed is to act like those who have no hope. And they justly. For a soul that knows nothing of the Resurrection, but thinks that *this* death is death, naturally afflicts itself, and bewails and mourns intolerably as for lost ones. But thou, who expectest a resurrection, on what account dost thou lament? To lament then is the part of those who have no hope.

Hear this, ye women, as many of you as are fond of wailing, as many as at times of mourning take the sorrow impatiently, that ye act the part of heathens. But if to grieve for the departed is the part of heathens, then tell me whose part it is to beat one's self, and tear the cheeks? On what account do you lament, if you believe that he will rise again, that he has not perished, that the matter is but a slumber and a sleep? You say, On account of his society, his protection, his care of our affairs, and all his other services. When therefore you lose a child at an untimely age, who is not yet able to do anything, on what account do you lament? Why do you seek to recall him? He was displaying, you say, good hopes, and I was expecting that he would be my supporter. On this account I miss my husband, on this account my son, on this account I wail and lament, not disbelieving the Resurrection, but being left destitute of support, and having lost my protector, my companion, who shared with me in all things — my comforter. On this account I mourn. I know that he will rise again, but I cannot bear the intermediate separation. A multitude of troubles rushes in upon me. I am exposed to all who are willing to injure me. Those of my servants who formerly feared me now despise me, and trample upon me. If any one has been benefited, he has forgotten the benefit he received from him; if any one was ill-treated by the departed, to return the grudge against him, he lets loose his anger upon me. These things do not suffer me to bear my widowhood. It is for these things that I afflict myself, for these things I bewail.

How then shall we comfort such? What shall we say? How shall we banish their sorrow?[4] In the first place I shall endeavor to convict them, that their wailing proceeds not from these things they say, but from an unreasonable passion. For if you mourn for these things, you ought always to mourn the departed. But if when a year has passed away, you forget him as if he had never been, you do not bewail the departed nor his protection. But you cannot endure the separation, nor the breaking off of your society? And what can they say, who even enter into second marriages? Sure enough! It is the former husbands that they long for. But let us not direct our discourse to them, but to those who preserve a kind affection towards the departed. Wherefore dost thou lament thy child? Wherefore thine husband? The former, because I had not enjoyed him, you say; the latter, because I expected that I should have enjoyed him longer. And this very thing, what

---

[1] [Chrys. is aiming to quote (ii. 14), "Ye became imitators of the churches of God which are in Judæa"; and he then explains the situation in Judæa by quoting from the Epistle to the Hebrews. The chronology of the Epistles is seldom very real to his mind. The inaccurate and abridged quotation is natural, but of course the amended text filled it out, as seen in the earlier editions. — J. A. B.]

[2] [Chrys. thinks of 1 Cor. xv. as preceding Thess. in time, and he had himself previously discoursed thereon. — J. A. B.]

[3] [Chrys. has, as so often, the reading which became the Textus Receptus, viz. here the perfect participle, "them that are asleep." The Rev. Ver. properly adopts the other reading, the present participle, "them that fall asleep," in the successive instances. In ver. 14 and 15 (Hom. vii.) both Chrys. and N. T. have the aorist participle, "them that fell asleep," loosely translated, "them that are fallen asleep." — J. A. B.]

[4] [See this subject copiously and admirably treated in one of Chrys.'s seven sermons on the Rich Man and Lazarus, entitled "Excessive Grief at the Death of Friends," and translated in Fish's "Masterpieces of Pulpit Eloquence" (New York), Vol. I., pp. 83 ff. — J. A. B.]

want of faith does it argue, to suppose that thy husband or thy son constitutes thy safety, and not God! How dost thou not think to provoke Him? For often on this account He takes them away, that thou mayest not be so bound to them, so that it may withdraw thy hopes from them. For God is jealous, and wills to be loved by us most of all things: and that, because He loves us exceedingly. For ye know that this is the custom of those who love to distraction. They are excessively jealous, and would choose rather to throw away their life, than to be surpassed in esteem by any of their rival lovers. On this account also God hath taken him, because of these words.[1]

For, tell me, on what account were there not in old times widowhoods, and untimely orphanhoods? Wherefore did He permit Abraham and Isaac to live a long time? Because even when he was living he preferred God before him. He said indeed, slay; and he slew him. Why did he bring Sarah to so great an age? Because, even whilst she was living, he listened to God rather than to her. For this reason God said to him, "Hear Sarah thy wife." (From Gen. xxi. 12.) No one then either from love to husband or wife, or on account of the protection of a child, provoked God to anger. But now because we are declining downwards, and have exceedingly fallen off, we men love our wives more than God, and we women honor our husbands more than God. It is on this account that He draws us even against our will to the love of Himself. Love not thy husband more than God, and thou shalt not ever experience widowhood. Or rather, even if it should happen, thou shalt not have the feeling of it. Why? Because thou hast an immortal Protector who loves thee better. If thou lovest God more, mourn not: for He who is more beloved is immortal, and does not suffer thee to feel the loss of him who is less beloved. This I will make manifest to thee by an example. Tell me, if thou hast a husband, complying with thee in all things, one that is respected, and that makes thee honorable everywhere, and not to be despised, one respected amongst all, intelligent and wise, and loving thee, thou being esteemed happy on his account, and in conjunction with him shouldest thou also bring forth a child, and then before it has arrived at the age of maturity, that child should depart; wilt thou then feel the affliction? By no means. For he that is more beloved makes it disappear. And now if thou love God more than thy husband, assuredly He will not soon take him away. But even if He should take him, thou wilt not be sensible of the affliction. For this reason the blessed Job felt no severe suffering, when

he heard of the death of his children all at once, because he loved God more than them. And whilst He whom he loved was living, those things would not be able to afflict him.

What sayest thou, O woman? Thy husband or thy son was thy protector? But does not thy God spare thee? Who gave thee thy very husband? Was it not He? And who made thee? Was it not He? He surely who brought thee out of nothing into being, and breathed into thee a soul, and put in thee a mind, and vouchsafed to favor thee with the knowledge of Himself, and for thy sake spared not His only-begotten Son, does not He spare thee? And does thy fellow-servant spare thee? What wrath is due to these words! What of this kind hast thou had from thy husband? Thou canst not say anything. For if he has even done thee any kindness, it was after he had received kindness, you having previously begun. But in the case of God no one can say any such thing. For it is not as having received any favors from us that God benefits us, but being incapable of want, from His goodness alone He does good to mankind. He has promised thee a kingdom, He has given immortal life, glory, brotherhood, adoption. He has made thee fellow-heir with His Only-Begotten. And dost thou after so great benefits remember thy husband? What has he bestowed of this kind? He has made His sun to shine, He has given rain, He sustains thee with yearly nourishment. Woe to us for our great ingratitude!

For this reason He takes thy husband, that thou mayest not seek him. But dost thou still cling to him though departed, and forsakest God, when it was thy duty to give thanks, to cast it all upon Him? For what is it that thou hast received from thy husband? The pains of childbirth, and labors, and insults and reproaches often, and chidings, and bursts of anger. Are not these the things that come from husbands? But there are, you say, other things too that are good. Of what sort then are these? Did he set off thy beauty with costly garments? Did he put gold ornaments about thy face? Did he make thee respected by all? But if thou wilt, thou shalt adorn thyself with a much better ornament than the departed. For gravity makes its possessor much more admirable than golden ornaments. This King also has garments, not of this sort, but much better. With those, if thou wilt, invest thyself. Of what sort then are they? There is a clothing which has fringes of gold; if thou wilt, array the soul. But did he make thee not to be despised by men? And what is there great in that? Thy widowhood suffers thee not to be despised by the demons. Then thou ruledst over thy servants, if at least thou didst at all

---

[1] i.e. "because you say such things about him."

rule over them. But now, instead of thy servants, thou hast mastery over unbodied powers, principalities, authorities, the ruler of this world. And thou dost not mention the troubles, in which thou sharedst with him, sometimes the fear of magistrates, sometimes the preference given to neighbors. From all these things thou art now delivered, from dread and fear. But art thou solicitous who will support the children that are left thee? The "Father of the fatherless." For tell me, who gave them? Dost thou not hear Christ in the Gospels saying, "Is not the life more than the food, and the body than the raiment?" (Matt. vi. 25.)

Seest thou, that thy lamentation is not from loss of his society, but from want of faith. But the children of a father that is dead are not equally illustrious. Wherefore? They have God for their Father, and are they not illustrious? How many can I show you brought up by widows, who have become famous, how many who have been under their fathers, and have been undone! For if thou bringest them up from their first youth, as they ought to be brought up, they will enjoy an advantage much greater than a father's protection. For that it is the business of widows — I speak of the bringing up of children — hear Paul saying, "If she hath brought up children" (1 Tim. v. 10); and again, "She shall be saved through the child-bearing," (he has not said through her husband,) ´ if they continue in faith and love and sanctification with sobriety." (1 Tim. ii. 15.) Instill into them the fear of God from their first youth, and He will protect them better than any father; this will be a wall not to be broken. For when there is a guard seated within, we have no need of contrivances without: but where he is not, all our outward contrivances are vain.

This will be to them wealth and glory too and ornament. This will make them illustrious, not upon earth, but even in heaven. For do not look to those who are begirt with the golden girdles, nor those who are borne on horses, nor those who shine in kings' palaces on account of their fathers, nor those who have footmen and tutors. For these things perhaps cause widows to bewail over their orphans, thinking that this my son also, if his father at least were living, would have enjoyed so much happiness; but now he is in a state of depression and dishonor, and worthy of no consideration. Think not of these things, O woman, but open to thee in thought the gates of heaven, consider the palace there, behold the King who is there seated. Consider if those who are upon the earth can be more illustrious than thy son there — and then groan. But if some are of good repute on earth, this is not worth any consideration. It is allowed him, if thou wilt, to be a soldier in heaven, to enlist him in the ranks of that army. For those who are enlisted there are not borne on horses, but in the clouds. They walk not upon earth, but are caught up into heaven. They have not slaves to go before them, but the Angels themselves. They stand not in the presence of a mortal king, but of Him who is immortal, the King of kings and Lord of lords. They have not a leathern girdle about their loins, but that glory which is unspeakable, and they are more splendid than kings, or whoever have been most illustrious. For in those royal courts not wealth is required, nor noble birth, nothing else than virtue alone; and where that is present, nothing is wanting to their obtaining the chief place.

Nothing is painful to us, if we are willing to cultivate wisdom. Look up to heaven, and see how much more splendid it is than the roofs of palaces. And if the pavement of the palaces above is so much more grand than those below, that the one may be considered as dirt in comparison with the other; if any one should be thought worthy to see those palaces perfectly, what blessedness will not be his!

"But she," he says, "that is a widow indeed, and desolate, hath her hope set on God." (1 Tim. v. 5.) To whom is this said? To those who have no[1] children, because they are more highly approved, and have a greater opportunity of pleasing God, because all their chains are loosened to them. There is no one to hold them fast, no one to compel them to drag their chains after them. Thou art separated from thy husband, but art united to God. Thou hast not a fellow-servant for thy associate, but thou hast thy Lord. When thou prayest, tell me, dost thou not converse with God? When thou readest, hear Him conversing with thee. And what does He say to thee? Much kinder words than thy husband. For though indeed thy husband should flatter thee, the honor is not great, for he is thy fellow-servant. But when the Lord flatters the slave, then is the courtship great. How then does He court us? Hear by what means he does it. "Come," He says, "unto Me, all ye that labor and are heavy laden, and I will give you rest." (Matt. xi. 28.) And again through the Prophet He calls, saying, "Will a woman forget to have compassion on the offspring of her womb? But even if a woman should forget, yet will I not forget thee, saith the Lord." (Isa. xlix. 15, Sept.) Of how great a love are these words? And again, "Turn unto Me"

---

[1] [Two MSS., which generally present good readings, give the negative. Other MSS. and two editions have no negative, and that is the harder reading, likely to be altered. It may possibly be explained (Field) by understanding the foregoing question thus: "With reference to whom is this said?" i.e. in comparison with whom? Then the thought is that, in comparison with those who have children, a widow that is really such has better opportunities of usefulness. Comp. 1 Cor. vii. 32. — J. A. B.]

(Isa. xlv. 22) ; and again elsewhere, "Turn unto Me, and thou shalt be saved." (Isa. xliv. 22.) And if one was willing to select too from the Canticles, taking them in the more mystical way, he will hear Him conversing and saying to every soul that is fitted for Him, "My fair one, my dove." (Cant. ii. 10.) What is sweeter than these words? Seest thou the conversation of God with men? But what? tell me, seest thou not how many children of those blessed women are gone, and are in their tombs ; how many have suffered more severely, and with their husbands have lost also their children? To these things let us attend ; let us be anxious about these things, and nothing will be grievous to us, but we shall continue passing all our time in spiritual joy ; and we shall enjoy the eternal blessings, of which may we all be partakers, by the grace and lovingkindness, &c.

HOMILY VII.

1 THESSALONIANS iv. 13.

"But we would not have you ignorant, brethren, concerning them that are asleep; that ye sorrow not, even as the rest, which have no hope."

THERE are many things which from ignorance alone cause us sorrow, so that if we come to understand them well, we banish our grief. This therefore Paul also showing, says, "I would not have you ignorant, that ye sorrow not, even as the rest, which have no hope." Is it on this account thou wouldest not have them ignorant? But wherefore dost thou not speak of the punishment that is laid up? Ignorant, says he, of the doctrine of the Resurrection. But why? This is manifest from the other, and is admitted. But meanwhile, together with that, there will also be this not inconsiderable gain. For since they did not disbelieve the Resurrection, but nevertheless bewailed, on this account he speaks. And he discourses indeed with those who disbelieve the Resurrection in one way, but with these in another. For it is manifest that they knew, who were enquiring about the "times and seasons." (1 Thess. v. 1.)

Ver. 14. "For if we believe," he says, "that Jesus died and rose again," and lived,[1] "even so them also that are fallen asleep in Jesus will God bring with Him."

Where are they who deny the Flesh?[2] For if He did not assume Flesh, neither did He die. If He did not die, neither did He rise again. How then does he exhort us from these things to faith? Was he not then according to them a trifler and a deceiver? For if to die proceeds from sin, and Christ did not sin, how does he now encourage us? And now, concerning whom does he say, O men, for whom do ye mourn? For whom do ye sorrow? for sinners, or simply for those who die? And why does he say, "Even as the rest, which have no hope"? For whom do the rest mourn? so that to them all these things are vapid.[3] "The firstborn from the dead" (Col. i. 18), he says, the first-fruits. Therefore there must also be others left. And see how here he introduces nothing from reasonings, because they were docile. For in writing to the Corinthians, he started many things also from reasonings, and then he added, "Thou fool, that which thou sowest is not quickened." (1 Cor. xv. 36.) For this is more authoritative, but it is when he converses with the believer. But with him who is without, what authority would this have? "Even so," he says, "them also that are fallen asleep in Jesus will God bring with Him." Again, "fallen asleep": he nowhere says, the dead. But with respect to Christ, his words are, "He died," because there followed mention of the Resurrection, but here "them that are fallen asleep." How "through Jesus"?[4] Either that they fell asleep through Jesus, or that through Jesus will He bring them. The phrase "that fell asleep through Jesus" means the faithful. Here the heretics say, that he is speaking of the baptized. What place then is there for "even so"? For Jesus did not fall asleep through Baptism. But on what account does he say, "them that are fallen asleep"? So that he is discoursing not of a general Resurrection, but of a partial one. Them that are fallen asleep through Jesus, he says, and thus he speaks in many places.

Ver. 15. "For this we say unto you by the word of the Lord, that we that are alive, that are

---

[1] [This passage is here enlarged from Rom. xiv. 9, even as in many documents and Textus Receptus of N. T. that passage is enlarged from this. — J. A. B.]

[2] i.e. the Incarnation, as the Docetæ, and in a manner the Marcionites and the Manichees. St. Aug. Conf.

[3] ἕωλα. He means to those who deny the Incarnation.

[4] [The Greek rendered "in Jesus" is properly "through Jesus," and stands between "them that fell asleep" and "will bring," so that it may be understood as connected with either. Modern commentators usually prefer to connect with the participle, and then the natural meaning is that through Jesus death became to them a falling asleep. Comp. Ellicott. The amenders of Chrys.'s text made it "them that fell asleep by faith in Jesus." — J. A. B.]

left unto the coming of the Lord, shall in nowise precede them that are fallen asleep."

Speaking concerning the faithful, and them "which are fallen asleep in[1] Christ" (1 Cor. xv. 18); and again, "the dead shall rise in Christ." Since his discourse is not concerning the Resurrection only, but both concerning the Resurrection and concerning the honor in glory; all then shall partake of a Resurrection, he says, but not all shall be in glory, only those in Christ. Since therefore he wishes to comfort them, he comforts them not with this only, but also with the abundant honor, and with its speedy arrival, since they knew that. For in proof that he wishes to comfort them with the honor, as he goes on, he says, "And we shall be ever with the Lord": and "we shall be caught up in the clouds."

But how do the faithful fall asleep in Jesus? It means having Christ within themselves. But the expression, "He shall bring with Him," shows that they are brought from many places. "This." Something strange he was about to tell them. On this account he also adds what makes it worthy of credit; "From the word of the Lord," he says, that is, we speak not of ourselves, but having learnt from Christ, "That we that are alive, that are left unto the coming of the Lord, shall in nowise precede them that are fallen asleep." Which also he says in his Epistle to the Corinthians; "In a moment, in the twinkling of an eye." (1 Cor. xv. 52.) Here he gives a credibility to the Resurrection by the manner also [in which it will occur].

For because the matter seems to be difficult, he says that as it is easy for the living to be taken up, so also for the departed. But in saying "we," he does not speak of himself, for he was not about to remain until the Resurrection, but he speaks of the faithful. On this account he has added, "We that are left unto the coming of the Lord shall in nowise precede them that are fallen asleep." As if he had said, Think not that there is any difficulty. It is God that does it. They who are then alive shall not anticipate those who are dissolved, who are rotted, who have been dead ten thousand years. But as it is easy to bring those who are entire, so is it also those who are dissolved.

But there are some who disbelieve the matter, because they know not God. For, tell me, which is the more easy, to bring one into being out of nothing, or to raise up again him that was dissolved? But what say they? A certain one suffered shipwreck and was drowned in the sea, and having fallen many fishes caught him, and

each of the fish devoured some member. Then of these very fishes, one was caught in this gulf, and one in that, and this was eaten by one man, and that by another, while having in it the devoured pieces of flesh. And again, those who ate the fishes, that had eaten up the man, died in different places, and were themselves perhaps devoured by wild beasts. And — when there has been so great a confusion and dispersion — how shall the man rise again? Who shall gather up the dust? But wherefore dost thou say this, O man, and weavest strings of trifles, and makest it a matter of perplexity? For tell me, if the man had not fallen into the sea, if the fish had not eaten him, nor the fish again been devoured by numberless men — but he had been preserved with care in a coffin, and neither worms nor anything else had disturbed him, how shall that which is dissolved rise again? How shall the dust and ashes be again conglutinated?[2] Whence shall there be any more its bloom for the body? But is not this a difficulty?

If indeed they be Greeks who raise these doubts, we shall have numberless things to say to them. What then? For there are among them those who convey souls into plants, and shrubs, and dogs. Tell me, which is more easy, to resume one's own body, or that of another? Others again say that they are consumed by fire, and that there is a resurrection of garments and of shoes, and they are not ridiculed. Others say atoms. With them, however, we have no argument at all; but to the faithful, (if we ought to call them faithful who raise questions,) we will still say what the Apostle has said, that all life springs from corruption, all plants, all seeds.[3] Seest thou not the fig tree, what a trunk it has, what stems, how many leaves, and branches, stalks, and roots, occupying so much ground and embosomed therein. This then, such and so great as it is, springs from the grain which was thrown into the ground and itself first corrupted. And if it be not rotted and dissolved, there will be none of these things. Tell me, whence does this happen? And the vine too, which is so fair both to see and to partake of, springs from that which is vile in appearance. And what, tell me, is not the water that descends from above one thing? how is it changed into so many things? For this is more wonderful than the Resurrection. For there indeed the same seed and the same plant is the subject, and there is a great affinity. But here tell me how, having one quality and one nature, it turns into so many things? In the vine it becomes wine, and not only wine, but leaves and sap. For not only is the cluster of grapes, but the rest of the vine nourished by

---

[1] [Here Chrys. first quotes accurately from 1 Cor. xv. 18, and then adds from iv. 15 below, there taking "in Christ" with the verb, when the connection requires us to understand, "the dead in Christ shall rise." Comp. Ellicott on iv. 15, and notice below, at the beginning of Hom. viii., that Chrys. connects as here. — J. A. B.]

[2] This word is used by Bp. Pearson in this very argument, which he may have borrowed from St. Chrys.; see his work on the Creed, art. Resurrection.

[3] See 1 Cor. xv. 36.

it. Again, in the olive (it becomes) oil, and the other so numerous things. And what is wonderful, here it is moist, there dry, here sweet, there sour, here astringent, elsewhere bitter. Tell me how it turns into so many things? Show me the reason! But you cannot.

And in the case of thyself, tell me, for this comes nearer, this seed, that is deposited, how is it fashioned and molded into so many things? how into eyes? how into ears? how into hands? how into heart? Are there not in the body ten thousand differences of figures, of sizes, of qualities, of positions, of powers, of proportions? Nerves and veins and flesh and bones and membranes, and arteries and joints and cartilages, and as many more things beside these, as the sons of the physicians precisely specify, which compose our nature — and these come from that one seed! Does not this then seem to you much more difficult than those things? How is the moist and soft congealed into the dry and cold, that is, bone? How into the warm and moist, which are united in the blood? How into the cold and soft, the nerve? How into the cold and moist, the artery?[1] Tell me, whence are these things? Art thou not quite at a loss about these things? Dost thou not see every day a resurrection and a death taking place in the periods of our life? Whither is our youth gone? whence is our age come? how is it that he who is grown old cannot indeed make himself young, but begets another, a very young child, and what he cannot give to himself, that he bestows upon another?

This also we may see in trees and in animals. And yet that which gives to another ought first to bestow upon itself. But this is what human reasoning demands. But when God creates, let all things give way. If these things are so difficult, nay, so excessively difficult, I am reminded of those mad persons, who are curious about the incorporeal Generation of the Son. Things that take place every day, that are within the grasp of our hands, and that have been enquired into ten thousand times, no one has yet been able to discover; tell me, then, how is it they are curious about that secret and ineffable Generation? Is not the mind of such men wearied in treading that void? Has it not been whirled into ten thousand giddinesses? Is it not dumfounded? And yet not even so are they instructed. When they are able to say nothing about grapes and figs, they are curious about God! For tell me, how is that grape-stone resolved into leaves and stems? How before this were they not in it, nor seen in it? But it is not the grape-stone, you say, but all is from the earth. Then how is it that without this the earth bears nothing of itself? But let us not be

void of understanding. What takes place is neither from the earth, nor from the grape-stone, but from Him who is Lord both of the earth and of its seeds. For this reason He has caused the same thing to be made both without them, and with them. In the first place, showing His own power, when he said, "Let the earth bring forth the herb of grass." (From Gen. i. 11.) And secondly, besides showing His power, instructing us also to be laborious and industrious.

Why then have these things been said by us? Not idly, but that we may believe also in the Resurrection, and that, when we again wish to apprehend something by our reasonings, but do not find it, we may not be angry and take offense, but discreetly withdrawing and checking our reasoning, we may take refuge in the power and skillfulness of God. Knowing these things therefore, let us put a curb upon our reasonings. Let us not transgress our bounds, nor the measures that have been assigned to our knowledge. For, "If any man," he says, "thinketh that he knoweth anything, he knoweth nothing yet as he ought to know." (1 Cor. viii. 2.)

I speak not concerning God, he says, but concerning everything. For what? wouldest thou learn about the earth? What dost thou know? Tell me. How great is its measure? What is its size? What is its manner of position? What is its essence? What is its place? Where does it stand, and upon what? None of these things can you tell? But that it is cold, and dry, and black, this you can tell — and nothing farther. Again, concerning the sea? But there you will be reduced to the same uncertainty, not knowing where it begins, and where it ends, and upon what it is borne, what supports the bottom of it, and what sort of place there is for it, and whether after it there is a continent, or it ends in water and air. And what dost thou know of the things that are in it? But what? Let me pass over the elements. Would you have us select the smallest of plants? The unfruitful grass, a thing which we all know, tell me, how it is brought forth? Is not the material of it water, and earth, and dung? What is it that makes it appear so beautiful, and have such an admirable color? Whence does that beauty so fade away? This is not the work of water, or of earth. Seest thou that there is everywhere need of faith? How does the earth bring forth, how does it travail? Tell me. But you can tell me none of these things.

Be instructed, O man, in things that are here below, and be not curious nor overmeddling about heaven. And would it were heaven, and not the Lord of heaven! Dost thou not know the earth from which thou wast brought forth, in which thou wast nourished, which thou in-

---

[1] The arteries were then thought to convey air through the body.

habitest, on which thou walkest, without which thou canst not even breathe ; and art thou curious about things so far removed? Truly "man is vanity." (Ps. xxxix. 5, and cxliv. 5.) And if any one should bid thee descend into the deep, and trace out things at the bottom of the sea, thou wouldest not tolerate the command. But, when no one compels thee, thou art willing of thyself to fathom the unsearchable abyss? Do not so, I beseech you. But let us sail upwards, not floating, for we shall soon be weary, and sink ; but using the divine Scriptures, as some vessel, let us unfurl the sails of faith. If we sail in them, then the Word of God will be present with us as our Pilot. But if we float upon human reasonings, it will not be so. For

to whom of those who float, is a Pilot present? So that the danger is twofold, in that there is no vessel, and that the Pilot is absent. For if even the boat without a pilot is unsafe, when both are wanting, what hope is there of safety? Let us not then throw ourselves into manifest danger, but let us go upon a safe vessel, having fastened ourselves by the sacred anchor. For thus we shall sail into the tranquil haven, with much merchandise,[2] and at the same time with great safety, and we shall obtain the blessings laid up for them that love Him, in Christ Jesus our Lord, with whom, to the Father, together with the Holy Spirit, be glory, power, honor, now and always and world without end. Amen.

HOMILY VIII.

1 Thessalonians iv. 15–17.

" For this we say unto you by the word of the Lord, that we that are alive, that are left unto the coming of the Lord, shall in nowise precede them that are fallen asleep. For the Lord Himself shall descend from heaven, with a shout, with the voice of the Archangel, and with the trump of God: and the dead in Christ shall rise first: then we that are alive, that are left, shall together with them be caught up in the clouds, to meet the Lord in the air: and so shall we ever be with the Lord."

THE Prophets indeed, wishing to show the credibility of the things said by them, before all other things say this, " The vision which Isaiah saw " (Isa. i. 1) ; and again, " The word of the Lord which came to Jeremiah " (Jer. i. 1, Sept.) ; and again, " Thus saith the Lord " ; with many such expressions. And many of them even saw God sitting, as far as it was possible for them to see Him. But Paul not having seen Him sitting, but having Christ speaking in himself, instead of Thus saith the Lord, said, " Do ye seek a proof of Christ speaking in me ? " (2 Cor. xiii. 3.) And again, " Paul, an Apostle of Jesus Christ." For the "Apostle" speaks the things of Him who sent him ; showing that nothing is of himself. And again, " I think that I also have the Spirit of God." (1 Cor. vii. 40.) All those things therefore he spake by the Spirit, but this, which he now says, he heard even expressly from God. As also that which he had said discoursing to the Elders of Ephesus, " It is more blessed to give than to receive," he heard among things not recorded.[1] (Acts xx. 35.)

Let us then see what he now also says. " For this we say unto you by the word of the Lord, that we that are alive, that are left unto the coming of the Lord, shall in nowise precede them that are fallen asleep. For the Lord Himself shall descend from heaven, with a shout, with the voice of the Archangel, and with the last trump." For then, he saith, " The powers of the heavens shall be shaken." (Matt. xxiv. 29.) But wherefore with the trumpet? For we see this on Mount Sinai too, and Angels there also. But what means the voice of the Archangel? As he said in the parable of the Virgins, Arise ! " The Bridegroom cometh." (From Matt. xxv. 6.) Either it means this, or that as in the case of a king, so also shall it then be, Angels ministering at the Resurrection. For He says, let the dead rise, and the work is done, the Angels not having power to do this, but His word. As if upon a king's commanding and saying it, those who were shut up should go forth, and the servants should lead them out, yet they do this not from their own power, but from that Voice. This also Christ says in another place : " He shall send forth his Angels with a great trumpet, and they shall gather together his Elect from the four winds, from one end of heaven to the other." (Matt. xxiv. 31.) And everywhere you see the Angels running to and fro. The Archangel therefore I think is he, who is set over those who are sent forth, and who shouts thus : " Make all men ready, for the Judge

1 [The saying was probably in circulation among the Christians, for Paul bids the elders " remember the words."—J. A. B.]

2 ἐμπορίας, al. εὐπορίας, facility.

is at hand." And what is "at the last trumpet"?[1] Here he implies that there are many trumpets, and that at the last the Judge descends. "And the dead," he says, "in Christ shall rise first. Then we that are alive, that are left, shall together with them be caught up in the clouds, to meet the Lord in the air : and so shall we ever be with the Lord."

Ver. 18. "Wherefore comfort one another with these words."

If He is about to descend, on what account shall we be caught up? For the sake of honor. For when a king drives into a city, those who are in honor go out to meet him ; but the condemned await the judge within. And upon the coming of an affectionate father, his children indeed, and those who are worthy to be his children, are taken out in a chariot, that they may see and kiss him ; but those of the domestics who have offended remain within. We are carried upon the chariot of our Father. For He received Him up in the clouds, and "we shall be caught up in the clouds." (Acts i. 9.) Seest thou how great is the honor? and as He descends, we go forth to meet Him, and, what is more blessed than all, so we shall be with Him.

"Who shall speak of the mightinesses of the Lord, and make all His praises to be heard?" (Ps. cvi. 2, Sept.) How many blessings has He vouchsafed to the human race ! Those who are dead are raised first, and thus the meeting takes place together. Abel who died before all shall then meet Him together with those who are alive. So that they in this respect will have no advantage, but he who is corrupted, and has been so many years in the earth, shall meet Him with them, and so all the others. For if they awaited us, that we might be crowned, as elsewhere he says in an Epistle, "God having provided some better thing concerning us, that apart from us they should not be made perfect" (Heb. xi. 40), much more shall we also await them ; or rather, they indeed awaited, but we not at all. For the Resurrection takes place "in a moment, in the twinkling of an eye."

But as to the saying, that they are gathered together ; they arise indeed everywhere, but are gathered together by the Angels. The former therefore is the work of the power of God commanding the earth to give up its deposit, and there is no one who ministers in it, as He then called Lazarus, "Lazarus, come forth" (John xi. 43) ; but the gathering is the work of ministers. But if Angels gather them together, and run to and fro, how are they[2] caught up here?

They are caught up after the descent,[3] after that they are gathered together.

For this is also done without any one being aware.[4] For when they see the earth agitated, the dust mingling, the bodies rising perchance[5] on every side, no one ministering to this, but the "shout" being sufficient, the whole earth filled (for consider how great a thing it is that all the men from Adam unto His coming shall then stand with wives and children), — when they see so great a tumult upon the earth, — then they shall know. As therefore in the Dispensation that was in the Flesh, they had foreseen nothing of it, so also will it then be.

When these things then are done, then also will be the voice of the Archangel shouting and commanding the Angels, and the trumpets, or rather the sound of the trumpet. What trembling then, what fear will possess those that remain upon the earth. For one woman is caught up and another is left behind, and one man is taken, and another is passed over. (Matt. xxiv. 40, 41 ; Luke xvii. 34, 35.) What will be the state of their souls, when they see some indeed taken up, but themselves left behind? Will not these things be able to shake their souls more terribly than any hell? Let us represent then in word that this is now present. For if sudden death, or earthquakes in cities, and threatenings thus terrify our souls ; when we see the earth breaking up, and crowded with all these, when we hear the trumpets, and the voice of the Archangel louder than any trumpet, when we perceive the heaven shriveled up, and God the King of all himself coming nigh — what then will be our souls? Let us shudder, I beseech you, and be frightened as if these things were now taking place. Let us not comfort ourselves by the delay. For when it must certainly happen, the delay profits us nothing.

How great will then be the fear and trembling ! Have you ever seen men led away to death? What do you think is the state of their souls, as they are going on the way to the gate? is it not worse than many deaths? What would they not choose both to do and to suffer, so that they might be delivered from that cloud of darkness? I have heard many say, who have been recalled by the mercy of the king (Emperor), after having been led away, that they did not even see men as men, their souls being so troubled, so horror-struck, and beside themselves. If then the death of the body thus frightens us, when eternal death approaches, what will be our feelings? And why do I speak of those who are

---

[1] [The N. T. text is, without variation, "with the trump of God." Chrys. mingles in his recollection this and the kindred passage in 1 Cor. xv. 53. The quotation at the head of the Homily is correct. — J. A. B.]

[2] i.e. How are those, whom the Angels have already taken and

gathered, still " here," that they should be caught up? L. places ἐνταῦθα before αὐτοί, which gives that sense more decidedly. Or " here " may only mean " in this passage."

[3] Musculus takes it of our Lord's descent, Hervetus otherwise.

[4] He seems to allude to Matt. xxiv. 36.

[5] ἴσως, which has been translated " equally."

led away? A crowd then stands around, the greater part not even knowing them. If any one looked into their souls, no one is so cruel, no one so hard-hearted, no one so firm, as not to have his soul dejected, and relaxed with fear and despair. And if when others are taken off by this death, which differs nothing from sleep, those who are not concerned in it are thus affected; when we ourselves fall into greater evils, what then will be our state? It is not, believe me, it is not possible to represent the suffering by words.

Nay, you say, but God is full of love to man, and none of these things will happen! Then it is written in vain! No, you say, but only as a threat, that we may become wise! If then we are not wise, but continue evil, will He not, tell me, inflict the punishment? Will He not then recompense the good either with rewards? Yes, you say, for that is becoming to Him, to do good even beyond desert. So that those things indeed are true and will certainly be, while the punishments will not be at all, but are only for the purpose of a threat, and of terror! By what means I shall persuade you, I know not. If I say, that "the worm will not die, and the fire will not be quenched" (Mark ix. 44); if I say, that "they shall go away into everlasting fire" (Matt. xxv. 41, 46); if I set before you the rich man already suffering punishment, you will say that it is all a matter of threatening. Whence then shall I persuade you? For this is a Satanic reasoning, indulging you with a favor that will not profit, and causing you to be slothful.

How then can we banish it? Whatever things we say from Scripture, you will say, are for the purpose of threatening. But with respect to future things this indeed might be said, but not so concerning things that have happened, and have had an end. You have heard of the deluge. And were those things also said by way of threat? Did they not actually happen? Those men too said many such things, and for a hundred years while the ark was building, and the wood was being wrought, and the righteous man was calling aloud, there was no one who believed. But because they did not believe the threat in words, they suffered the punishment in very deed. And this will be our fate too, if we shall not have believed. On this account it is that He compares His coming with the days of Noah, because as some disbelieved in that deluge, so will they in the deluge of hell. Were these things a threat? were they not a fact? Then will not He, who then brought punishment upon them so suddenly, much more inflict it now also? For the things that are committed now are not less than the offenses of that time. How? — because then, it says, "the sons of God went in unto the daughters of men" (Gen.

vi. 4), and those mixtures were the great offense. But now there is no form of wickedness, which is unattempted. Do you then believe that the deluge took place? Or does it seem to you a fable? And yet even the mountains where the ark rested, bear witness; I speak of those in Armenia.

But, even superabundantly, I will turn my discourse to another thing more evident than that. Has any one of you ever traveled in Palestine? For I will no longer mention report, but facts, and yet the other were clearer than facts. For whatever things the Scripture says, are more to be trusted than things we see. Has any one of you then ever traveled in Palestine? I suppose so. What then? Bear witness then for me, ye who have seen the places, to those who have not been there. For above Ascalon and Gaza up to the very end of the river Jordan there is a country wide and fruitful — or rather there was — for it is not now. This then is that which was as a garden. For it is said, "Lot beheld all the plain[1] of Jordan — and it was well watered everywhere, like the garden of the Lord." (Gen. xiii. 10.) This, therefore, that was so flourishing, and that rivaled all countries, which for thrivingness exceeded the Paradise of God, is now more desolate than any wilderness. And there stand trees, indeed, and they bear fruit. But the fruit is a monument of the wrath of God. For there stand pomegranates, I speak both of the tree and the fruit, having a very fine appearance, and to the ignorant man holding out great hopes. But if they are taken into the hand, being broken open they display no fruit indeed, but much dust and ashes stored up within. Such also is the whole land. If you find a stone, you will find it full of ashes. And why do I speak of stone and wood and earth, where the air and water partake of the calamity? For as when a body is burnt and consumed, the shape remains, and the outline in the appearance of the fire, and the bulk and the proportion, but the power is no more, so truly there you may see earth, which yet has nothing of earth about it, but all ashes; trees and fruit, but nothing of trees and fruit about them; air and water, but nothing of water nor of air about them, for even these are turned to ashes. And yet how could air ever have been burnt, or water, whilst it remained water? For wood and stones indeed it is possible to burn, but air and water it is altogether impossible. Impossible to us, but possible to Him who did these things. Therefore the air is nothing else than a furnace, the water is a furnace. All things are unfruitful,

---

[1] [Properly "the region around Jordan," and denoting the deep and rather wide valley through which it flows. Chrys. makes it include all of central Judea, and applies to that whole district what he had heard of the desolate country between Jerusalem and the Dead Sea, the N. T. "wilderness of Judea."— J. A. B.]

all unproductive, all for vengeance; images of wrath that has gone before, and proofs of that which is to come.

Are these too but threatening words? Are these but the sound of words? For to me indeed the former things were not incredible, but things not seen were equally credible with things that were seen. But even to the unbeliever these are sufficient to produce faith. If any one disbelieves hell, let him consider Sodom, let him reflect upon Gomorrah, the vengeance that has been inflicted, and which yet remains. This is a proof of the eternity of punishment. Are these things grievous? And is it not grievous, when you say that there is no hell, but that God has merely threatened it? when you slack the hands of the people?[1] It is thou who disbelievest that compellest me to say these things; it is thou that hast drawn me out into these words. If thou believedst the words of Christ, I should not be compelled to bring forward facts to induce belief. But since you have evaded them, you shall be persuaded henceforth, whether willing or unwilling. For what have you to say concerning Sodom? Would you wish also to know the cause, for which these things were then done? It was one sin, a grievous and accursed one certainly, yet but one. The men of that time had a passion for boys, and on that account they suffered this punishment. But now ten thousand sins equal and even more grievous than these are committed. Then He who for one sin poured forth so much anger, and neither regarded the supplication of Abraham, nor yet Lot who dwelt among them, the man who from honor to His servants offered his own daughters to insult, will He spare, when there are so many sins? These things truly are ridiculous, trifling, delusion, and diabolical deceit!

Do you wish that I should also bring forward another? You have certainly heard of Pharaoh, king of the Egyptians; you know therefore the punishment also which he suffered, how even with his whole host, chariots and horses and all, he was engulfed in the Erythræan sea. Would you hear also other examples? he perhaps was an impious man, or rather not perhaps, but certainly he was an impious man. Would you see those also punished, who were of the number of believers, and who held fast to God, but were not of upright life? Hear Paul saying, "Neither let us commit fornication, as some of them committed, and fell in one day three and twenty thousand. Neither let us murmur, as some of them murmured, and perished by the destroyer. Neither let us tempt Christ, as some of them tempted, and perished by the serpents." (1 Cor. x. 8–10.) And if fornication, and if mur-

muring had such power, what will not be the effect of our sins?

And if thou dost not now pay the penalty, do not wonder. For they knew not of a hell, therefore they were visited with punishments following close at their heels. But thou, whatever sins thou commit, though thou shouldest escape present penalty, wilt pay for it all There. Did he so punish those who were nearly in the state of children, and who did not sin so greatly — and will He spare us? It would not be reasonable. For if we commit the same sins with them, we shall deserve a greater punishment than they did. Wherefore? Because we have enjoyed more grace. But when our offenses are numerous, and more heinous than theirs, what vengeance shall we not undergo? They — and let no one think I say it as admiring them, or excusing them; far be it: for when God punishes, he who passes a contrary sentence, does it at the suggestion of the devil; I say this therefore, not praising them nor excusing them, but showing our wickedness — they therefore, although they murmured, were, however, traveling a wilderness road: but we murmur though we have a country, and are in our own houses. They, although they committed fornication, yet it was just after they came out of the evils of Egypt, and had hardly heard of such a law. But we do it, having previously received from our forefathers the doctrine of salvation, so that we are deserving of greater punishment.

Would you hear also of other things? what were their sufferings in Palestine, famines, pestilences, wars, captivities, under the Babylonians, and under the Assyrians, and their miseries from the Macedonians, and those under Hadrian and Vespasian? I have something that I wish, beloved, to relate to thee; nay, do not run away![2] Or rather I will tell thee another thing before it. There was once a famine, it says, and the king was walking upon the wall; then a woman came to him and uttered these words: "O king, this woman said to me, Let us roast thy son to-day, and eat him — to-morrow mine. And we roasted and ate, and now she does not give me hers." (From 2 Kings vi. 28.) What can be more dreadful than this calamity? Again, in another place the Prophet says, "The hands of the pitiful women have sodden their own children." (Lam. iv. 10.) The Jews then suffered such punishment, and shall we not much rather suffer?

Would you also hear other calamities of theirs? Read over Josephus, and you will learn that whole tragedy, if perchance we may persuade you from these things, that there is a hell. For consider, if they were punished, why are we not punished? or how is it reasonable that we are not now punished, who sin more grievously than

---

[1] See Heb. xii. 12; Jer. xxxviii. 4.

[2] μὴ ἀποπηδήσῃς, perhaps only "turn away."

they? Is it not manifest that it is, because the punishment is kept in store for us? And, if you please, I will tell you in the person of every individual how they were punished. Cain murdered his brother. A horrible sin indeed, who can deny it? But he suffered punishment; and a heavy one, equivalent to ten thousand deaths, for he would rather have died ten thousand times. For hear him saying, "If Thou castest me out from the land, and I shall be hidden from Thy face, then it will happen that every one who findeth me will slay me." (Gen iv. 14, Sept.) Tell me then, do not many even now do the same things that he did? For when thou slayest not thy brother according to the flesh, but thy spiritual brother, dost thou not do the same? For what, though not by the sword? yet by some other means; when being able to relieve his hunger, thou neglectest him. What then? Has no one now envied his brother? has no one plunged him into dangers? But here they have not suffered punishment, yet they will suffer it. Then he, who never heard the written laws, nor the prophets, nor saw great miracles, suffered such great vengeance; and shall he, who has done the same things in another way, and was not rendered wise by so many examples, shall he go unpunished? Where then is the justice of God, and where His goodness?

Again, a certain one for having gathered sticks on the Sabbath was stoned, and yet this was a small commandment, and less weighty than circumcision. He then who gathered sticks on the Sabbath was stoned; but those who often commit ten thousand things contrary to the Law have gone off unpunished! If then there be not a hell, where is His justice, where His impartiality, that respects not persons? And yet He lays to their charge many such things, that they did not observe the Sabbath. Again, another, Charmi,[1] having stolen a devoted thing, was stoned with all his family. What then? Has no one from that time committed sacrilege? Saul, again, having spared contrary to the command of God, suffered so great punishment. Has no one from that time spared? Would indeed that it were so! Have we not, worse than wild beasts, devoured one another contrary to the command of God, and yet no one has fallen in war?[2] Again, the sons of Eli, because they ate before the incense was offered, suffered the most severe punishment together with their father. Has no father then been neglectful with respect to his children? and are there no wicked sons? But no one has

suffered punishment. Where will they suffer it then, if there be no hell?

Again, numberless instances one might enumerate. What? Ananias and Sapphira were immediately punished, because they stole part of what they had offered. Has no one then since that time been guilty of this? How was it then that they did not suffer the same punishment?

Do we then persuade you that there is a hell, or do you need more examples? Therefore we will proceed also to things that are unwritten, such as now take place in life. For it is necessary that this idea should be gathered by us from every quarter, that we may not, by vainly gratifying ourselves, do ourselves harm. Do you not see many visited by calamities, maimed in their bodies, suffering infinite troubles, but others in good repute? For what reason do some suffer punishment for murders, and others not? Hear Paul saying, "Some men's sins are evident, . . . and some men they follow after." (1 Tim. v. 24.) How many murderers have escaped! how many violators of the tombs! But let these things pass. How many do you not see visited with the severest punishment? Some have been delivered to a long disease, others to continued tortures, and others to numberless other ills. When therefore you see one who has been guilty of the same things as they, or even much worse —and yet not suffering punishment, will you not suspect, even against your will, that there is a hell? Reckon those here who before you have been severely punished, consider that God is no respecter of persons, and that though you have done numberless wickednesses, you have suffered no such thing, and you will have the idea of hell. For God has so implanted that idea within us, that no one can ever be ignorant of it. For poets and philosophers and fabulists, and in short all men, have philosophized concerning the retribution that is there, and have said that the greater number are punished in Hades. And if those things are fables, yet what we have received are not so.

I say not these things as wishing to frighten you, nor to lay a burden on your souls, but to make them wise, and render them easier. I could wish also myself that there were no punishment—yes, myself most of all men. And why so? Because whilst each of you fears for his own soul, I have to answer for this office also in which I preside over you. So that most of all it is impossible for me to escape. But it cannot be that there is not punishment and a hell. What can I do? Where then, they say, is the kindness of God to men? In many places. But on this subject I will rather discourse at some other season, that we may not confuse the discourses concerning hell. In the meantime let not that slip, which we have gained. For

---

[1] [This is an error in the documents, or a slip of memory in the preacher, for he means Achan the son of Carmi, Josh. vii. 1.—J. A. B.]

[2] [No one of us has been punished for it, as Saul was, by falling in battle.—J. A. B.]

it is no small advantage to be persuaded concerning hell. For the recollection of such discourses, like some bitter medicine, will be able to clear off every vice, if it be constantly settled in your mind. Let us therefore use it, that having a pure heart, we may so be thought worthy to see those things, which eye hath not seen, nor ear heard, nor have entered into the heart of man. Which may we all obtain by the grace and mercy of our Lord Jesus Christ, with whom, &c.

HOMILY IX.

1 THESSALONIANS v. 1, 2.

"But concerning the times and the seasons, brethren, ye have no need that aught be written unto you. For yourselves know perfectly that the day of the Lord so cometh as a thief in the night."

NOTHING, as it seems, is so curious, and so fondly prone to pry into things obscure and concealed, as the nature of men. And this is wont to happen to it, when the mind is unsettled and in an imperfect state. For the simpler sort of children never cease teasing their nurses, and tutors, and parents, with their frequent questions, in which there is nothing else but "when will this be?" and "when that?" And this comes to pass also from living in indulgence, and having nothing to do. Many things therefore our mind is in haste to learn already and to comprehend, but especially concerning the period of the consummation; and what wonder if we are thus affected, for those holy men, themselves, were most of all affected in the same way? And before the Passion, the Apostles come and say to Christ, "Tell us, when shall these things be, and what shall be the sign of Thy coming, and of the end of the world?" (Matt. xxiv. 23.) And after the Passion and the Resurrection from the dead, they said to Him, Tell us, "dost Thou at this time restore again the kingdom to Israel?" (From Acts i. 6.) And they asked Him nothing sooner than this.

But it was not so afterwards, when they had been vouchsafed the Holy Ghost. Not only do they not themselves inquire, nor complain of this ignorance, but they repress those who labor under this unseasonable curiosity. Hear for instance what the blessed Paul now says, "But concerning the times and the seasons, brethren, ye have no need that aught be written unto you." Why has he not said that no one knows? why has he not said, that it is not revealed, instead of saying, "Ye have no need that aught be written unto you"? Because in that case he would have grieved them more, but by speaking thus he comforted them. For by the expression, "Ye have no need," as if it were both superfluous, and inexpedient, he suffers them not to enquire.

For tell me, what would be the advantage? Let us suppose that the end would be after twenty or thirty or a hundred years, what is this to us? Is not the end of his own life the consummation to every individual? Why art thou curious, and travailest about the general end? But the case is the same with us in this, as in other things. For as in other things, leaving our own private concerns, we are anxious about things in general, saying, Such an one is a fornicator, such an one an adulterer, that man has robbed, another has been injurious; but no one takes account of what is his own, but each thinks of anything rather than his own private concerns; so here also, each omitting to take thought about his own end, we are anxious to hear about the general dissolution. Now what concern is that of yours? for if you make your own a good end, you will suffer no harm from the other; be it far off, or be it near. This is nothing to us.

For this reason Christ did not tell it, because it was not expedient. How, you say, was it not expedient? He who also concealed it knows wherefore it was not expedient. For hear Him saying to His Apostles, "It is not for you to know times, or seasons, which the Father hath set within His own authority." (Acts i. 7.) Why are you curious? Peter, the chief of the Apostles, and his fellows, heard this said, as if they were seeking things too great for them to know. True, you say; but it were possible to stop the mouths of the Greeks in this way. How? tell me. Because they say, that this world is a god; if we knew the period of its dissolution, we should have stopped their mouths. Why, is this what will stop their mouths, to know when it will be destroyed, or to know that it will be destroyed? Tell them this, that it will have an end. If they do not believe this, neither will they believe the other.

Hear Paul saying, "For yourselves know perfectly that the day of the Lord so cometh as a thief in the night." Not the general day only, but that of every individual. For the one resembles the other, is also akin to it. For what the one does collectively, that the other does partially. For the period of consummation took its beginning from Adam, and then is the end of the consummation;[1] since even now one would not err in calling it a consummation. For when ten thousand die every day, and all await That Day, and no one is raised before it, is it not the work[2] of That Day? And if you would know on what account it is concealed, and why it so cometh as a thief in the night, I will tell you how I think I can well account for it. No one would have ever cultivated virtue during his whole life; but knowing his last day, and, after having committed numberless sins, then having come to the Laver, he would so have departed. For if now, when the fear arising from its uncertainty shakes the souls of all, still all,[3] having spent their whole former life in wickedness, at their last breath give themselves up to Baptism, — if they had fully persuaded themselves concerning this matter, who would ever have cultivated virtue? If many have departed without Illumination, and not even this fear has taught them, whilst living, to cultivate the things that are pleasing to God; if this fear also had been removed, who would ever have been sober, or who gentle? There is not one! And another thing again. The fear of death and the love of life restrain many. But if each one knew that to-morrow he would certainly die, there is nothing he would refuse to attempt before that day, but he would murder whomsoever he wished, and would retrieve himself by taking vengeance on his enemies, and would perpetrate ten thousand crimes.

For a wicked man, who despairs of his life here, pays no regard even to him who is invested with the purple. He therefore who was persuaded that he must at all events die would both be revenged upon his enemy, and after having first satisfied his own soul, so would meet his end. Let me mention also a third thing. Those who are fond of life, and vehemently attached to the things of this world, would[4] be ruined by despair and grief. For if any of the young knew that before he reached old age, he should meet his end, as the most sluggish of wild beasts, when they are taken, become still more sluggish from expecting their end, so would he also be affected. Besides, not even the men that are courageous would have had their reward. For if they knew that after three years they must certainly die, and before that time it was not possible, what reward would they have gained for daring in the face of dangers? For any one might say to them,

Because you are confident of the three years of life, for this reason you throw yourselves into dangers, knowing that it is not possible for you to pass away. For he, that expects from each danger that he may come by his death, and knows that he shall live indeed, if he does not expose himself to peril, but shall die if he attempts such and such actions, he gives the greatest proof of his zeal, and of his contempt for the present life. And this I will make plain to you by an example. Tell me, if the patriarch Abraham, foreknowing that he should not have to sacrifice his son, had brought him to the place, would he then have had any reward? And what if Paul, foreknowing that he should not die, had despised dangers, in what respect would he have been admirable? For so even the most sluggish would rush into the fire, if he could find any one he could trust to ensure his safety. But not such were the Three Children. For hear them saying, "O king, there is a God in heaven, who will deliver us out of thine hands, and out of this furnace; and if not, be it known to thee that we do not serve thy gods, nor worship the golden image which thou hast set up." (Dan. iii. 17, Sept.)

Ye see how many advantages there are, and yet there are more than these that arise from not knowing the time of our end. Meanwhile it is sufficient to learn these. On this account He so cometh as a thief in the night; that we may not abandon ourselves to wickedness, nor to sloth; that He may not take from us our reward. "For yourselves know perfectly," he says. Why then are you curious, if you are persuaded? But that the future is uncertain, learn from what Christ has said. For that on this account He said it, hear what he says, "Watch therefore: for ye know not at what hour" the thief[5] "cometh." (Matt. xxiv. 42.) On this account also Paul said,

Ver. 3. "When they are saying peace and safety, then sudden destruction cometh upon them, as travail upon a woman with child; and they shall in nowise escape."

Here he has glanced at something which he has also said in his second Epistle. For since[6] they indeed were in affliction, but they that warred on them at ease and in luxury, and then while he comforted them in their present sufferings by this mention of the Resurrection, the others insulted them with arguments taken from their forefathers, and said, When will it happen?

---

[1] [This is obscure as to the exact purport. Does "then" mean the end of the individual life, or the time of Christ's coming? The expanded text understood it in the former sense. — J. A. B.]

[2] τὸ ἔργον, i.e. is not what is now doing part of That Day's work? Or it might be rendered "reality."

[3] i.e. as we say loosely, "every one." St. Greg. Naz. complains of this practice, Or. XL., preached at Constantinople, A.D. 381.

[4] διεφθάρησαν.

[5] [This may be considered a mere slip of memory, or Chrys. may have inserted "the thief" as representing our Lord. The Rev. Ver. properly reads "on what day," in ver. 42, "at what hour" having been drawn from ver. 44, where all documents have it. Chrys. has, as so often, the reading which passed into the Textus Receptus. — J. A. B.]

[6] [To this "since" answers "see then," below. He digresses to quote the Prophets, and then returns in a way very natural to free speaking. — J. A. B.]

— which the Prophets also said, "Woe unto them that say, Let him make speed, let God hasten his work, that we may see it: and let the counsel of the Holy One of Israel come, that we may know it!" (Isa. v. 19); and again "Woe unto them that desire the day of the Lord." (Amos v. 18.) He means this day; for he does not speak simply of persons who desire it, but of those who desire it because they disbelieve it: and "the day of the Lord," he says, "is darkness, and not light"—see then how Paul consoles them, as if he had said, Let them not account their being in a prosperous state, a proof that the Judgment is not coming. For so it is that it will come.

But it may be worth while to ask, If Antichrist comes, and Elias comes, how is it "when they say Peace and safety," that then a sudden destruction comes upon them? For these things do not permit the day to come upon them unawares, being signs of its coming. But he does not mean this to be the time of Antichrist, and the whole day, because that will be a sign of the coming of Christ, but Himself will not have a sign, but will come suddenly and unexpectedly. For travail, indeed, you say, does not come upon the pregnant woman unexpectedly: for she knows that after nine months the birth will take place. And yet it is very uncertain. For some bring forth at the seventh month, and others at the ninth. And at any rate the day and the hour is uncertain. With respect to this therefore, Paul speaks thus. And the image is exact. For there are not many sure signs of travail; many indeed have brought forth in the high roads, or when out of their houses and abroad, not foreseeing it. And he has not only glanced here at the uncertainty, but also at the bitterness of the pain. For as she while sporting, laughing, not looking for anything at all, being suddenly seized with unspeakable pains, is pierced through with the pangs of labor—so will it be with those souls, when the Day comes upon them.

"And they shall in nowise escape." As he was saying just now.

Ver. 4. "But ye, brethren, are not in darkness, that that day should overtake you as a thief."

Here he speaks of a life that is dark and impure. For it is just as corrupt and wicked men do all things as in the night, escaping the notice of all, and inclosing themselves in darkness. For tell me, does not the adulterer watch for the evening, and the thief for the night? Does not the violator of the tombs carry on all his trade in the night? What then? Does it not overtake them as a thief? Does it not come upon them also uncertainly, but do they know it beforehand? How then does he say, "Ye have no need that aught be written unto you"?

He speaks here not with respect to the uncertainty, but with respect to the calamity, that is, it will not come as an evil to them. For it will come uncertainly indeed even to them, but it will involve them in no trouble. "That that Day," he says, "may not overtake you as a thief." For in the case of those who are watching and who are in the light, if there should be any entry of a robber, it can do them no harm: so also it is with those who live well. But those who are sleeping he will strip of everything, and go off; that is, those who are trusting in the things of this life.

Ver. 5. "For ye are all," he says, "sons of light, and sons of the day."

And how is it possible to be "sons of the day"? Just as it is said, "sons of destruction" and "sons of hell." Wherefore Christ also said to the Pharisees, "Woe unto you—for ye compass sea and land to make one proselyte, and when he is become so, ye make him a son of hell." (Matt. xxiii. 15.) And again Paul said, "For which things' sake cometh the wrath of God upon the sons of disobedience." (Col. iii. 6.) That is, those who do the works of hell and the works of disobedience. So also sons of God are those who do things pleasing to God; so also sons of day and sons of light, those who do the works of light.

"And we are not of the night nor of darkness."

Ver. 6, 7, 8. "So then let us not sleep, as do also the rest, but let us watch and be sober. For they that sleep sleep in the night; and they that be drunken are drunken in the night. But let us, since we are of the day, be sober."

Here he shows, that to be in the day depends on ourselves. For here indeed, in the case of the present day and night, it does not depend on ourselves. But night comes even against our will, and sleep overtakes us when we do not wish it. But with respect to that night and that sleep, it is not so, but it is in our power always to have it day, it is in our power always to watch. For to shut the eyes of the soul, and to bring on the sleep of wickedness, is not of nature, but of our own choice. "But let us watch," he says, "and be sober." For it is possible to sleep while awake, by doing nothing good. Wherefore he has added, "and be sober." For even by day, if any one watches, but is not sober, he will fall into numberless dangers, so that sobriety is the intensity of watchfulness. "They that sleep," he says, "sleep in the night, and they that be drunken are drunken in the night." The drunkenness he here speaks of is not that from wine only, but that also which comes of all vices. For riches and the desire of wealth is a drunkenness of the soul, and so carnal lust; and every sin you can name is a drunkenness of the soul. On what account then has he called vice sleep?

Because in the first place the vicious man is inactive with respect to virtue : again, because he sees everything as a vision, he views nothing in its true light, but is full of dreams, and often-times of unreasonable actions : and if he sees anything good, he[1] has no firmness, no fixed-ness. Such is the present life. It is full of dreams, and of phantasy. Riches are a dream, and glory, and everything of that sort. He who sleeps sees not things that are and have a real subsistence, but things that are not he fancies as things that are. Such is vice, and the life that is passed in vice. It sees not things that are, that is, spiritual, heavenly, abiding things, but things that are fleeting and fly away, and that soon recede from us.

But it is not sufficient to watch and be sober, we must also be armed. For if a man watch and is sober, but has not arms, the robbers soon dispatch him. When therefore we ought both to watch, and to be sober, and to be armed, and we are unarmed and naked and asleep, who will hinder him from thrusting home his sword? Wherefore showing this also, that we have need of arms, he has added :

Ver. 8. "Putting on the breastplate of faith and love : and for a helmet the hope of sal-vation."

"Of faith and love," he says. Here he glances at life and doctrine. He has shown what it is to watch and be sober, to have "the breastplate of faith and love." Not a common faith, he says, but as nothing can soon pierce through a breastplate, but it is a safe wall to the breast ; — so do thou also, he says, surround thy soul with faith and love, and none of the fiery darts of the devil can ever be fixed in it. For where the power of the soul is preoccupied with the armor of love, all the devices of those who plot against it are vain and ineffectual. For neither wick-edness, nor hatred, nor envy, nor flattery, nor hypocrisy, nor any other thing will be able to penetrate such a soul. He has not simply said "love," but he has bid them put it on as a strong breastplate. "And for a helmet the hope of salvation." For as the helmet guards the vital part in us, surrounding the head and cover-ing it on every side, so also this hope does not suffer the reason to falter, but sets it upright as the head, not permitting anything from without to fall upon it. And whilst nothing falls on it, neither does it slip of itself. For it is not pos-sible that one who is fortified with such arms as these, should ever fall. For "now abideth faith, hope, love." (1 Cor. xiii. 13.) Then having said, Put on, and array yourselves, he himself provides the armor, whence faith, hope, and love may be produced, and may become strong.

Ver. 9. "For God appointed us not unto

wrath, but unto the obtaining of salvation through our Lord Jesus Christ, who died for us."

Thus God has not inclined to this,[2] that He might destroy us, but that He might save us. And whence is it manifest that this is His will? He has given His own Son for us. So does He desire that we should be saved, that He has given His Son, and not merely given, but given Him to death. From these considerations hope is produced. For do not despair of thyself, O man, in going to God, who has not spared even His Son for thee. Faint not at present evils. He who gave His Only-Begotten, that He might save thee and deliver thee from hell, what will He spare henceforth for thy salvation? So that thou oughtest to hope for all things kind. For neither should we fear, if we were going to a judge who was about to judge us, and who had shown so much love for us, as to have sacrificed his son. Let us hope therefore for kind and great things, for we have received the principal thing ; let us believe, for we have seen an example ; let us love, for it is the extreme of madness for one not to love who has been so treated.

Ver. 10, 11. "That, whether we wake or sleep," he says, "we should live together with Him. Wherefore exhort one another, and build each other up, even as also ye do."

And again, "whether we wake or sleep"; by sleep there he means one thing, and here another. For here, "whether we sleep" signi-fies the death of the body ; that is, fear not dan-gers ; though we should die, we shall live. Do not despair because thou art in danger. Thou hast a strong security. He would not have given His Son if He had not been inflamed by vehement love for us. So that, though thou shouldest die, thou wilt live ; for He Himself also died. Therefore whether we die, or whether we live, we shall live with Him. This is a matter of indifference : it is no concern of mine, whether I live or die ; for we shall live with Him. Let us therefore do everything for that life : looking to that, let us do all our works. Vice, O beloved, is darkness, it is death, it is night ; we see nothing that we ought, we do nothing that becomes us. As the dead are un-sightly and of evil odor, so also the souls of those who are vicious are full of much impurity. Their eyes are closed, their mouth is stopped, they remain without motion in the bed of vice ; or rather more wretched than those who are naturally dead. For they truly are dead to both, but these are insensible indeed to virtue, but alive to vice. If one should strike a dead man, he perceives it not, he revenges it not, but is like a dry stick. So also his soul is truly dry, having lost its life ; it receives daily num-

---

[1] Or "it."

berless wounds, and has no feeling of any, but lies insensible to everything.

One would not err in comparing such men to those who are mad, or drunk, or delirious. All these things belong to vice, and it is worse than all these. He that is mad is much allowed for by those who see him, for his disease is not from choice, but from nature alone ; but how shall he be pardoned, who lives in vice? Whence then is vice? whence are the majority bad? Tell me, whence have diseases their evil nature? whence is frenzy? whence is lethargy? Is it not from carelessness? If physical disorders have their origin in choice, much more those which are voluntary. Whence is drunkenness? Is it not from intemperance of soul? Is not frenzy from excess of fever? And is not fever from the elements too abundant in us? And is not this superabundance of elements from our carelessness? For when either from deficiency or excess we carry any of the things within us beyond the bounds of moderation, we kindle that fire. Again, if when the fire is kindled, we continue to neglect it, we make a conflagration for ourselves, which we are not able to extinguish. So is it also with vice. When we do not restrain it at its beginning, nor cut it off, we cannot afterwards reach to the end of it, but it becomes too great for our power. Wherefore, I beseech you, let us do everything that we may never become drowsy. Do you not see that when sentinels have only given way a little to sleep, they derive no advantage from their long watch, for by that little they have ruined the whole, having given perfect security to him who is prepared to steal. For as we do not see thieves in the same way that they see us, so also the devil most of all is ever instant, and lying in wait, and grinding his teeth. Let us not then slumber. Let us not say, on this side there is nothing, on that side nothing ; we are often plundered from a quarter whence we did not expect it. So it is with vice ; we perish from a quarter whence we did not expect it. Let us look carefully round upon all things, let us not be drunken, and we shall not sleep. Let us not be luxurious, and we shall not slumber. Let us not be mad for external things, and we shall continue in sobriety. Let us discipline ourselves on every side. And as men who walk upon a tight rope cannot be off their guard ever so little, for that little causes great mischief: for the man losing his balance is at once precipitated down and perishes ; so neither is it possible for us to be off our guard. We walk upon a narrow road intercepted by precipices on either side, not admitting of two feet at the same time. Seest thou not how much carefulness is necessary? Seest thou not how those who travel on such roads guard not only their

feet, but their eyes also? For if he should choose to gaze on one side, though his foot stand firm, his eye becoming dizzy from the depth, plunges the whole body down. But he must take heed to himself and to his steps ; wherefore he says, "neither to the right hand, nor to the left." (Prov. iv. 27.) Great is the depth of vice, high the precipices, much darkness below. Let us take heed to the narrow way, let us walk with fear and trembling. No one, who is traveling such a road, is dissolved in laughter nor heavy with drunkenness, but travels such a road with sobriety and fasting. No one traveling such a road carries with him any superfluities ; for he would be contented even lightly equipped to be able to escape. No one entangles his own feet, but leaves them disengaged, and free to move.

But we, chaining ourselves down with numberless cares, and carrying with us the numberless burdens of this life, staring about, and loosely rambling, how do we expect to travel in that narrow road? He has not merely said that "narrow is the way" (Matt. vii. 14), but with wonder, "how [1] narrow is the way," that is, exceedingly narrow. And this we also do in things that are quite objects of wonder. And "straitened," he says, "is the way which leadeth unto life." And he has well said it. For when we are bound to give an account of our thoughts, and words, and actions, and all things, truly it is narrow. But we ourselves make it more narrow, spreading out and widening ourselves, and shuffling out our feet. For the narrow way is difficult to every one, but especially to him who is incumbered with fat, as he who makes himself lean will not perceive its narrowness. So that he who has practiced himself in being pinched, will not be discouraged at its pressure.

Let not any one therefore expect that he shall see heaven with ease. For it cannot be. Let no one hope to travel the narrow road with luxury, for it is impossible. Let no one traveling in the broad way hope for life. When therefore thou seest such and such an one luxuriating in baths, in a sumptuous table, or in other matters having troops of attendants ; think not thyself unhappy, as not partaking of these things, but lament for him, that he is traveling the way to destruction. For what is the advantage of this way, when it ends in tribulation? And what is the injury of that straitness, when it leads to rest? Tell me, if any one invited to a palace should walk through narrow ways painful

---

[1] [All the MSS. examined for Field give not ὅτι, "because," but τί, "what," "to what extent," "how." This more difficult reading of Matt. vii. 14 is quite probably correct. See Margin of Rev. Ver. Observe also that Chrys. seems to omit "the gate," connecting "narrow and straitened" with the way, as do several other Fathers (see Tisch.). Many now speak of the "strait and narrow way," and often imagine that it means "straight." Chrys. has a different text of this passage in his Homilies on Matthew, though some MSS. there also give τί. See Amer. ed. of Tr. p. 162. — J. A. B.]

and precipitous, and another led to death should be dragged through the midst of the market-place, which shall we call happy? which shall we commiserate? Him, shall we not, who walks through the broad road? So also now, let us think happy, not those who are luxurious, but those who are not luxurious. These are hastening to heaven, those to hell.

And perhaps indeed many of them will even laugh at the things that are said by us. But I most of all lament and bewail them on this account, that they do not even know what they ought to laugh at, and for what they ought especially to mourn, but they confound and disturb and disorder everything. On this account I bewail them. What sayest thou, O man, when thou art to rise again, and to give an account of thy actions, and to undergo the last sentence, dost thou pay no regard indeed to these, but give thought to gratifying thy belly, and being drunken? And dost thou laugh at these things? But I bewail thee, knowing the evils that await thee, the punishment that is about to overtake thee. And this I most especially bewail, that thou dost laugh! Mourn with me, bewail with me thine own evils. Tell me, if one of thy friends perishes, dost thou not turn from those who laugh at his end, and think them enemies, but love those who weep and sympathize with thee? Then indeed if the dead body of thy wife were laid out, thou turnest from him that laughs: but when thy soul is done to death, dost thou turn from him that weeps, and laugh thyself? Seest thou how the devil has disposed us to be enemies and adversaries to ourselves? For once let us be sober, let us open our eyes, let us watch, let us lay hold on eternal life, let us shake off this long sleep. There is a Judgment, there is a Punishment, there is a Resurrection, there is an Inquisition into what we have done! The Lord cometh in the clouds. "Before Him," he says, "a fire will be kindled, and round about Him a mighty tempest." (Ps. l. 3, Sept.) A river of fire rolls before him, the undying worm, unquenchable fire, outer darkness, gnashing of teeth. Although you should be angry with me ten thousand times for mentioning these things, I shall not cease from mentioning them. For if the prophets, though stoned, did not keep silence, much more ought we to bear with enmities, and not to discourse to you with a view to please, that we may not, for having deceived you, be ourselves cut in sunder. There is punishment, deathless, unallayed, and no one to stand up for us. "Who will pity," he says, "the charmer that is bitten by a serpent?" (Ecclus. xii. 13.) When we pity not our own selves, tell me, who will pity us? If you see a man piercing himself with a sword, will you be able to spare his life? By no means. Much more, when having it in our power to do well we do not do well, who will spare us? No one! Let us pity ourselves. When we pray to God, saying, "Lord, have mercy[1] upon me," let us say it to ourselves, and have mercy upon ourselves. We are the arbiters[2] of God's having mercy upon us. This grace He has bestowed upon us. If we do things worthy of mercy, worthy of His loving-kindness towards us, God will have mercy upon us. But if we have not mercy on ourselves, who will spare us? Have mercy on thy neighbor, and thou shalt find mercy of God Himself. How many every day come to thee, saying, "Have pity on me," and thou dost not turn towards them; how many naked, how many maimed, and we do not bend toward them, but dismiss their supplications. How then dost thou claim[3] to obtain mercy, when thou thyself dost nothing worthy of mercy? Let us become compassionate, let us become pitiful, that so we may be well-pleasing to God, and obtain the good things promised to those that love Him, by the grace and lovingkindness of our Lord Jesus Christ, with whom, &c.

---

[1] [It is the word above rendered "pity," but the other rendering is made familiar in this phrase by the Litany. "Have pity," just below, is still the same word. — J. A. B.]

[2] Gr. "We are lords," but the phrase is more familiar in Greek.

[3] [The verb translated "claim" is based on the adjective meaning "worthy." Chrys. is somewhat fond of the play upon words. — J. A. B.]

HOMILY X.

I THESSALONIANS V. 12, 13.

" But we beseech you, brethren, to know them that labor among you, and are over you in the Lord, and admonish you; and to esteem them exceeding highly in love for their work's sake. Be at peace among yourselves."

IT must needs happen that a ruler should have many occasions of enmities.[1] As physicians[2] are compelled to give much trouble to the sick, preparing for them both diet and medicines, that are not pleasant indeed, but attended with benefit; and as fathers are often annoying to their children: so also are teachers, and much more. For the physician, though he be odious to the sick man, yet has the relations and friends on good terms with him,[3] nay, and often the sick man himself. And a father also, both from the force of nature and from external laws, exercises his dominion over his son with great ease; and if he should chastise and chide his son against his will, there is no one to prevent him, nor will the son himself be able to raise a look against him. But in the case of the Priest there is a great difficulty. For in the first place, he ought to be ruling people willing to obey, and thankful to him for his rule; but it is not possible that this should soon come to pass. For he who is convicted and reproved, be he what he may, is sure to cease from being thankful, and to become an enemy. In like manner he will act who is advised, and he who is admonished and he who is exhorted. If therefore I should say, empty out wealth on the needy, I say what is offensive and burdensome. If I say, chastise thine anger, quench thy wrath, check thine inordinate desire, cut off a small portion of thy luxury, all is burdensome and offensive. And if I should punish one who is slothful, or should remove him from the Church, or exclude him from the public prayers, he grieves, not because he is deprived of these things, but because of the public disgrace. For this is an aggravation of the evil, that, being interdicted from spiritual things, we grieve not on account of our deprivation of these great blessings, but because of our disgrace in the sight of others. We do not shudder at, do not dread, the thing itself.

For this reason Paul from one end to the other discourses largely concerning these persons. And Christ indeed has subjected them with so strict a necessity, that He says, " The Scribes and the Pharisees sit on Moses' seat. All things therefore whatsoever they bid you, these do and observe: but do not ye after their works." (Matt. xxiii. 2, 3.) And again, when He healed the leper, He said, " Go thy way, show thyself to the priest, and offer the gift that Moses commanded for a testimony unto them." (Matt. viii. 4.) And yet Thou sayest, " Ye make him twofold more a son of hell than yourselves." (Matt. xxiii. 15.) For this reason I said, answers He, " Do not the things which they do." Therefore he hath shut out all excuse from him that is under rule. In his Epistle to Timothy also this Apostle said, " Let the elders that rule well be counted worthy of double honor." (1 Tim. v. 17.) And in his Epistle to the Hebrews also he said, " Obey them that have the rule over you, and submit to them." (Heb. xiii. 17.) And here again, " But we beseech you, brethren, to know them that labor among you, and are over you in the Lord." For since he had said, " build each other up," lest they should think that he raised them to the rank of teachers, he has added, See, however, that I gave leave to you also to edify one another, for it is not possible for a teacher to say everything. " Them that labor among you," he says, " and are over you in the Lord, and admonish you." And how, he says, is it not absurd? If a man stand up for thee before a man, thou doest anything, thou confessest thyself much indebted; but he stands up for thee before God, and thou dost not own the favor. And how does he stand up for me? thou sayest. Because he prays for thee, because he ministers to thee the spiritual gift that is by Baptism, he visits, he advises and admonishes thee, he comes at midnight if thou callest for him; he is nothing else than the constant subject of thy mouth, and he bears thy injurious speeches. What necessity had he? Has he done well or ill? Thou indeed hast a wife, and livest luxuriously, and choosest a life of commerce. But from this the Priest has hindered himself by his occupation; his life is no other than to be employed about the Church. " And to esteem them," he says, " exceeding highly in love for their work's sake; be at peace with them."[4] Seest thou how well he is aware

---

[1] Μικροψυχίων, Montf. here remarks that this word has often led to mistranslations, being used for any *result* of littlemindedness.

[2] [Literally, " physicians' boys," apparently a familiar phrase for physicians, employed also by Lucian. It perhaps originally denoted medical students,—a sense possible here also, and in Lucian (On Writing History, ch. vii.).—J. A. B.]

[3] B. and L. ἔχει πρὸς αὐτὸν ἡδέως ἔχοντας.

[4] ἐν αὑτοῖς, and so several MSS.; Rec. t. ἐν ἑαυτοῖς, " among yourselves," and so L. [I. Cat.] here, but the comment hardly bears it.

that unpleasant feelings arise? He does not merely say "love," but "very highly," as children love their fathers. For through them ye were begotten by that eternal generation: through them you have obtained the kingdom: through their hands all things are done, through them the gates of heaven are opened to you. Let no one raise divisions, let no one be contentious. He who loves Christ, whatever the Priest may be, will love him, because through him he has obtained the awful Mysteries. Tell me, if wishing to see a palace resplendent with much gold, and radiant with the brightness of precious stones, thou couldest find him who had the key, and he being called upon immediately opened it, and admitted thee within, wouldest thou not prefer him above all men? Wouldest thou not love him as dearly as thine eyes? Wouldest thou not kiss him? This man hath opened heaven to thee, and thou dost not kiss him, nor pay him court. If thou hast a wife, dost thou not love him above all, who procured her for thee? So if thou lovest Christ, if thou lovest the kingdom of heaven, acknowledge through whom thou obtainedst it. On this account he says, "for their work's sake, be at peace with them."

Ver. 14. "And we exhort you, brethren, admonish the disorderly, encourage the fainthearted, support the weak, be longsuffering toward all."

Here he addresses those who have rule. Admonish, he says, "the disorderly," not of imperiousness, he says, nor of self-will rebuke them, but with admonition. "Encourage the fainthearted, support the weak, be longsuffering toward all." For he who is rebuked with harshness, despairing of himself, becomes more bold in contempt.[1] On this account it is necessary by admonition to render the medicine sweet. But who are the disorderly? All those who do what is contrary to the will of God. For this order of the Church is more harmonious than the order of an army; so that the reviler is disorderly, the drunkard is disorderly, and the covetous, and all who sin; for they walk not orderly in their rank, but out of the line, wherefore also they are overthrown.[2] But there is also another kind of evils, not such as this indeed, but itself also a vice, littlemindedness. For this is destructive equally with sloth. He who cannot bear an insult is feeble-minded. He who cannot endure trial is feeble-minded. This is he who is sown upon the rock. There is also another sort, that of weakness. "Support the weak," he

says; now weakness occurs in regard to faith. But observe how he does not permit them to be despised. And elsewhere also in his Epistles he says, "Them that are weak in the faith receive ye." (Rom. xiv. 1.) For in our bodies too we do not suffer the weak member to perish. "Be longsuffering toward all," he says. Even toward the disorderly? Yes, certainly. For there is no medicine equal to this, especially for the teacher, none so suitable to those who are under rule. It can quite shame and put out of countenance him that is fiercer and more shameless than all men.

Ver. 15. "See that none render unto any one evil for evil."

If we ought not to render evil for evil, much less evil for good; much less, when evil has not been previously done, to render evil. Such an one, you say, is a bad man, and has aggrieved me, and done me much injury. Do you wish to revenge yourself upon him? Do not retaliate. Leave him unpunished. Well, is this the stopping-place? By no means;

"But alway follow after that which is good, one toward another, and toward all."

This is the higher philosophy, not only not to requite evil with evil, but to render good for evil. For this is truly revenge that brings harm to him and advantage to thyself, or rather great advantage even to him, if he will. And that thou mayest not think that this is said with respect to the faithful, therefore he has said, "both one toward another and toward all."

Ver. 16. "Rejoice alway."

This is said with respect to the temptations that bring in affliction. Hear ye, as many as have fallen into poverty, or into distressing circumstances. For from these joy is engendered. For when we possess such a soul that we take revenge on no one, but do good to all, whence, tell me, will the sting of grief be able to enter into us? For he who so rejoices in suffering evil, as to requite even with benefits him that has done him evil, whence can he afterwards suffer grief? And how, you say, is this possible? It is possible, if we will. Then also he shows the way.

Ver. 17, 18. "Pray without ceasing; In every thing giving thanks: for this is the will of God."

Always to give thanks, this is a mark of a philosophic soul. Hast thou suffered any evil? But if thou wilt, it is no evil. Give thanks to God, and the evil is changed into good. Say thou also as Job said, "Blessed be the name of the Lord for ever."[3] (Job i. 21.) For tell me, what such great thing hast thou suffered? Has disease befallen thee? Yet it is nothing strange. For our body is mortal, and liable to

---

[1] [Field here retains the common text, though supported only by B K, the group found to be in its peculiar readings almost uniformly wrong. This reading seems required by the next sentence, but that of the better MSS. is perhaps possible, viz., "For he who is harsh and rebukes, growing desperate, becomes more bold in despising and rebuking."—J. A. B.]

[2] [Or, by another reading, "turned aside," perhaps meaning that they abandon the army.—J. A. B.]

[3] ["For ever" is not in the common Vatican text of the Septuagint, but is in the Codex Alexandrinus.—J. A. B.]

suffer. Has a want of possessions overtaken thee? But these also are things to be acquired, and again to be lost, and that abide here. But is it plots and false accusations of enemies? But it is not we that are injured by these, but they who are the authors of them. "For the soul," he says, "that sinneth, itself shall also die." (Ezek. xviii. 4.) And he has not sinned who suffers the evil, but he who has done the evil.

Upon him therefore that is dead you ought not to take revenge, but to pray for him that you may deliver him from death. Do you not see how the bee dies upon the sting? By that animal God instructs us not to grieve our neighbors. For we ourselves receive death first. For by striking them perhaps we have pained them for a little time, but we ourselves shall not live any longer, even as that animal will not. And yet the Scripture commends it, saying that it is a worker, whose work kings and private men make use of for their health. (Ecclus. xi. 3.) But this does not preserve it from dying, but it must needs perish. And if its other excellence does not deliver it when it does injury, much less will it us.

For indeed it is the part of the fiercest beasts, when no one has injured thee, to begin the injury, or rather not even of beasts. For they, if thou permittest them to feed in the wilderness, and dost not by straitening them reduce them to necessity, will never harm thee, nor come near thee, nor bite thee, but will go their own way.

But you being a rational man, honored with so much rule and honor and glory, do not [1] even imitate the beasts in your conduct to your fellow-creature, but you injure your brother, and devour him. And how will you be able to excuse yourself? Do you not hear Paul saying, "Why not rather take wrong? Why not rather be defrauded? Nay, but ye yourselves do wrong, and defraud, and that your brethren." (1 Cor. vi. 7, 8.) Do you see that suffering wrong consists in doing wrong, but that to suffer wrongfully is to receive a benefit? For tell me, if any one were to revile his rulers, if he were to insult those in power, whom does he injure? Himself, or them? Clearly himself. Then he who insults a ruler insults not him, but himself —and he that insults a Christian does he not through him insult Christ? By no means, thou sayest. What sayest thou? He that casts a stone at the images of the king (Emperor), at whom does he cast a stone? is it not at himself? Then does he who casts a stone at the image of an earthly king, cast a stone at himself, and does not he who insults the image of God (for man is the image of God) injure himself?

How long shall we love riches? For I shall not cease exclaiming against them: for they are the cause of everything. How long do we not get our fill of this insatiable desire? What is the good of gold? I am astonished at the thing! There is some enchantment in the business, that gold and silver should be so highly valued among us. For our own souls indeed we have no regard, but those lifeless images engross much attention. Whence is it that this disease has invaded the world? Who shall be able to effect its destruction? What reason can cut off this evil beast, and destroy it with utter destruction? The desire is deep sown in the minds of men, even of those who seem to be religious. Let us be put to shame by the commands of the Gospel. Words only lie there in Scripture, they are nowhere shown by works.

And what is the specious plea of the many? I have children, one says, and I am afraid lest I myself be reduced to the extremity of hunger and want, lest I should stand in need of others. I am ashamed to beg. For that reason therefore do you cause others to beg? I cannot, you say, endure hunger. For that reason do you expose others to hunger? Do you know what a dreadful thing it is to beg, how dreadful to be perishing by hunger? Spare also your brethren! Are you ashamed, tell me, to be hungry, and are you not ashamed to rob? Are you afraid to perish by hunger, and not afraid to destroy others? And yet to be hungry is neither a disgrace nor a crime; but to cast others into such a state brings not only disgrace, but extreme punishment.

All these are pretenses, words, trifles. For that it is not on account of your children that you act thus, they testify who indeed have no children, nor will have, but who yet toil and harass themselves, and are busy in acquiring wealth, as much as if they had innumerable children to leave it to. It is not the care for his children that makes a man covetous, but a disease of the soul. On this account many even who have not children are mad about riches, and others living with a great number of children even despise what they have. They will accuse thee in that Day. For if the necessities of children compelled men to accumulate riches, they also must necessarily have the same longing, the same lust. And if they have not, it is not from the number of children that we are thus mad, but from the love of money. And who are they, you say, who having children, yet despise riches? Many, and in many places. And if you will allow me, I will speak also of instances among the ancients.

Had not Jacob twelve children? Did he not lead the life of a hireling? Was he not wronged by his kinsman? and did he not often disap-

---

[1] [This negative, given in the printed editions, though wanting in the known MSS., seems a necessity to the sense. — J. A. B.]

point him? And did his number of children ever compel him to have recourse to any dishonest counsel? What was the case with Abraham? With Isaac, had he not also many other children? What then? Did he not possess all he had for the benefit of strangers? Do you see, how he not only did not do wrong, but even gave up his possessions, not only doing good, but choosing to be wronged by his nephew? For to endure being robbed for the sake of God is a much greater thing than to do good. Why? Because the one is the fruit of the soul and of free choice, whence also it is easily performed: but the other is injurious treatment and violence. And a man will more easily throw away ten thousand talents voluntarily, and will not think that he has suffered any harm, than he will bear meekly being robbed of three pence against his will. So that this rather is philosophy of soul. And this, we see, happened in the case of Abraham. "For Lot," it is said, "beheld all the plain; and it was well watered as the garden of God, and he chose it." (Gen. xiii. 10, 11.) And Abraham said nothing against it. Seest thou, that he not only did not wrong him, but he was even wronged by him? Why, O man, dost thou accuse thine own children? God did not give us children for this end, that we should seize the possessions of others. Take care, lest in saying this thou provoke God. For if thou sayest that thy children are the causes of thy grasping and thine avarice, I fear lest thou be deprived of them, as injuring and ensnaring thee. God hath given thee children that they may support thine old age, that they may learn virtue from thee.

For God on this account hath willed that mankind should thus be held together, providing for two most important objects: on the one hand, appointing fathers to be teachers, and on the other, implanting great love. For if men were merely to come into being, no one would have any relation towards any other. For if now, when there are the relations of fathers, and children, and grandchildren, many do not regard many, much more would it then be the case. On this account God hath given thee children. Do not therefore accuse the children.

But if they who have children have no excuse, what can they say for themselves, who having no children wear themselves out about the acquisition of riches? But they have a saying for themselves, which is destitute of all excuse. And what is this? That, instead of children we may have, they say, may have[1] our riches as a memorial. This is truly ridiculous. Instead of children, one says, my house becomes the im-

mortal memorial of my glory. Not of thy glory, O man, will it be the memorial, but of thy covetousness. Dost thou not see how many now as they pass the magnificent houses say one to another, What frauds, what robberies such an one committed, that he might build this house, and now he is become dust and ashes, and his house has passed into the inheritance of others! It is not of thy glory then that thou leavest a memorial, but of thy covetousness. And thy body indeed is concealed in the earth, but thou dost not permit the memorial of thy covetousness to be concealed, as it might have been[2] by length of time, but causest it to be turned up and disinterred through thy house. For as long as this stands, bearing thy name, and called such an one's, certainly the mouths of all too must needs be opened against thee. Dost thou see that it is better to have nothing than to sustain such an accusation?

And these things indeed here. But what shall we do There? tell me, having so much at our disposal here, if we have imparted to no one of our possessions, or at least very little; how shall we put off our dishonest gains? For he that wishes to put off covetous gain, does not give a little out of a great deal, but many times more than he has robbed, and he ceases from robbing. Hear what Zacchæus says, "And for as many things as I have taken wrongfully, I restore fourfold." (Luke xix. 8.) But thou, taking wrongfully ten thousand talents, if thou give a few drachmas, thinkest thou hast restored the whole, and art affected as if thou hadst given more. And even this grudgingly. Why? Because thou oughtest both to have restored these, and to have added other out of thine own private possessions. For as the thief is not excused when he gives back only what he has stolen, but often he has added even his life; and often he compounds upon restoring many times as much: so also should the covetous man. For the covetous man also is a thief and a robber, far worse than the other, by how much he is also more tyrannical. He indeed by being concealed, and by making his attack in the night, cuts off much of the audacity of the attempt, as if he were ashamed, and feared to sin. But the other having no sense of shame, with open face in the middle of the market-place steals the property of all, being at once a thief and a tyrant. He does not break through walls, nor extinguish the lamp, nor open a chest, nor tear off seals. But what? He does things more insolent than these, in the sight of those who are injured he carries things out by the door, he with confidence opens everything, he compels them to expose all their possessions themselves.

---

[1] [The repetition is supported by a good group of documents, and accords with Chrys.'s rhetorical manner. The reading is therefore adopted here, though not by Field. — J. A. B.]

[2] δυναμένην.

Such is the excess of his violence. This man is more wicked than those, inasmuch as he is more shameless and tyrannical. For he that has suffered by fraud is indeed grieved, but he has no small consolation, that he who injured him was afraid of him. But he who together with the injury he suffers is also despised, will not be able to endure the violence. For the ridicule is greater. Tell me, if one committed adultery with a woman in secret, and another committed it in the sight of her husband, who grieved him the most, and was most apt to wound him. For he indeed, together with the wrong he has done, treated him also with contempt. But the former, if he did nothing else, showed at least that he feared him whom he injured. So also in the case of money. He that takes it secretly, does him honor in this respect, that he does it secretly; but he who robs publicly and openly, together with the loss adds also the shame.

Let us therefore, both poor and rich, cease from taking the property of others. For my present discourse is not only to the rich, but to the poor also. For they too rob those who are poorer than themselves. And artisans who are better off, and more powerful, outsell the poorer and more distressed, tradesmen outsell tradesmen, and so all who are engaged in the market-place. So that I wish from every side to take away injustice. For the injury consists not in the measure of the things plundered and stolen, but in the purpose of him that steals. And that these are more thieves and defrauders, who do not despise little gains, I know and remember that I have before told you, if you also remember it. But let us not be over exact. Let them be equally bad with the rich. Let us instruct our mind not to covet greater things, not to aim at more than we have. And in heavenly things let our desire of more never be satiated, but let each be ever coveting more. But upon earth let every one be for what is needful and sufficient, and seek nothing more, that so he may be able to obtain the real goods, by the grace and lovingkindness of our Lord Jesus Christ, with whom to the Father, together with the Holy Spirit, be glory, strength, honor, now and always, and world without end. Amen.

HOMILY XI.

1 THESSALONIANS v. 19–22.

" Quench not the Spirit. Despise not prophesyings. But prove all things; hold fast that which is good. Abstain from every form of evil."

A THICK mist, a darkness and cloud is spread over all the earth. And, showing this, the Apostle said, " For we[1] were once darkness." (Eph. v. 8.) And again, " Ye, brethren, are not in darkness, that that day should overtake you as a thief." Since therefore there is, so to speak, a moonless night, and we walk in that night, God hath given us a bright lamp, having kindled in our souls the grace of the Holy Spirit. But some who have received this light have rendered it more bright and shining, as, for instance, Paul and Peter, and all those Saints; while others have even extinguished it, as the five virgins, as those who have " made shipwreck concerning the faith," as the fornicator of Corinth, as the Galatians who were perverted.

On this account Paul says, " Quench not the Spirit," that is, the gift of grace, for it is his custom so to call the gift of the Spirit. But this an impure life extinguishes. For as any one, who has sprinkled both water and dust upon the light of our[2] lamp, extinguishes it, and if he does not this, but only takes out the oil — so it is also with the gift of grace. For if you have cast over it earthly things, and the cares of fluctuating matters,[3] you have quenched the Spirit. And if you have done none of these things, but a temptation coming from some other quarter has vehemently assailed it, as some wind, and if the light be not strong, and it has not much oil, or you have not closed the opening, or have not shut the door, all is undone. But what is the opening? As in the lamp, so is it also in us: it is the eye and the ear. Suffer not a violent blast of wickedness to fall upon these, since it would extinguish the lamp, but close them up with the fear of God. The mouth is the door. Shut it, and fasten it, that it may both give light, and repel the attack from without. For instance,

---

[1] [A slip of memory. N. T. text, without variation, "ye were," &c.— J. A. B.]

[2] τούτου, "this," often used for the natural as opposed to the spiritual.

[3] Alluding to " water."

has any one insulted and reviled you? Do you shut the mouth; for if you open it, you add force to the wind. Do you not see in houses, when two doors stand directly opposite, and there is a strong wind, if you shut one, and there is no opposite draught, the wind has no power, but the greater part of its force is abated? So also now, there are two doors, thy mouth, and his who insults and affronts thee; if thou shuttest thy mouth, and dost not allow a draught on the other side, thou hast quenched the whole blast; but if thou openest it, it will not be restrained. Let us not therefore quench it.

And the flame is often liable to be extinguished even when no temptation assails it. When the oil fails, when we do not alms,[1] the Spirit is quenched. For it came to thee as an alms from God. Then He sees this fruit not existing in thee, and he abides not with an unmerciful soul. But the Spirit being quenched, ye know what follows, as many of you as have walked on a road in a moonless night. And if it is difficult to walk by night in a road from land to land, how is it safe in the road that leads from earth to heaven? Know ye not how many demons there are in the intervening space, how many wild beasts, how many spirits of wickedness? If indeed we have that light, they will be able to do us no hurt; but if we extinguish it, they soon take us captive, they soon rob us of everything. Since even robbers first extinguish the lamp, and so plunder us. For they indeed see in this darkness, since they do the works of darkness: but we are unaccustomed to that light.[2] Let us not then extinguish it. All evil doing extinguishes that light, whether reviling, or insolence, or whatever you can mention. For as in the case of fire, everything that is foreign to its nature is destructive of it, but that kindles it which is congenial to it; whatever is dry, whatever is warm, whatever is fiery, kindles the flame of the Spirit. Let us not therefore overlay it with anything cold or damp; for these things are destructive of it.

But there is also another explanation. There were among them many indeed who prophesied truly, but some prophesied falsely. This also he says in the Epistle to the Corinthians, that on this account He gave "the discernings of spirits." (1 Cor. xii. 10.) For the devil, of his vile craft, wished through this gift of grace to subvert everything pertaining to the Church. For since both the demon and the Spirit prophesied concerning the future, the one indeed uttering falsehood, and the other truth, and it was not possible from any quarter to receive a proof of one or the other, but each spoke without being called to account, as Jeremiah and Ezekiel had done, but when the time came they were convicted, He

gave also the "discernings of spirits."[3] Since therefore then also among the Thessalonians many were prophesying, glancing at whom he says, "Neither by word, nor by epistle, as from us, as that the day of the Lord is now present" (2 Thess. ii. 2), he says this here. That is, do not, because there are false prophets among you, on their account prohibit also these, and turn away from them; "quench" them "not," that is, "despise not prophesyings."

Seest thou that this is what he means by, "Prove all things"? Because he had said, "Despise not prophesyings," lest they should think that he opened the pulpit to all, he says, "Prove all things," that is, such as are really prophecies; "and hold fast that which is good. Abstain from every form of evil"; not from this or that, but from all; that you may by proof distinguish both the true things and the false, and abstain from the latter, and hold fast the former. For thus both the hatred of the one will be vehement and the love of the other arises, when we do all things not carelessly, nor without examination, but with careful investigation.

Ver. 23. "And the God of peace Himself sanctify you wholly; and may your spirit and soul and body be preserved entire, without blame at the coming of our Lord Jesus Christ."

Observe the affection of the Teacher. After the admonition he adds a prayer; not only that, but even introduces it in his letter.[4] For we need both counsel and prayer. For this reason we also first giving you counsel, then offer prayers for you. And this the Initiated know. But Paul indeed did this with good reason, having great confidence towards God, whereas we are confounded with shame, and have no freedom of speech. But because we were appointed to this we do it, being unworthy even to stand in His presence, and to hold the place of the lowest disciples. But because grace works even through the unworthy, not for our own sakes but for theirs who are about to be benefited, we contribute our parts.

"Sanctify you wholly," he says, and may "your spirit and soul and body be preserved entire, without blame at the coming of our Lord Jesus Christ." What does he here call the spirit? The gift of grace.[5] For if we depart hence

---

[1] Of this play upon the word, see Hom. iv. on Philip., near the end.

[2] One MS., "that space," i.e. between earth and heaven.

[3] [When the time of fulfillment or the contrary came, the prophets were convicted, and it was shown which were from the devil. But the power of discerning between good and evil spirits in their predictions would make it unnecessary to wait for the time of fulfillment. —J. A. B.]

[4] The same omits "but even," &c., and proceeds, For the Teacher needs, &c.

[5] [See his remarks above, on ver. 19. To understand so here is a groundless fancy. The Scripture writers sometimes speak of soul and body, sometimes of spirit and body, and occasionally of spirit and soul and body. Some able writers (as Ellicott here) understand this form of expression as teaching an essential psychological distinction between spirit and soul; but it is probable that we have only the Pauline accumulation of terms to make a complete and emphatic statement. —J. A. B.]

having our lamps bright, we shall enter into the bridechamber. But if they are quenched, it will not be so. For this reason he says "your spirit." For if that remains pure, the other remains also. "And soul and body," he says. For neither the one nor the other then admits anything evil.

Ver. 24. "Faithful is He that calleth you, who will also do it."

Observe his humility. For, because he had prayed, Think not, he says, that this happens from my prayers, but from the purpose, with which He called you. For if He called you to salvation, and He is true, He will certainly save you, in that He wills it.

Ver. 25. "Brethren, pray for us also."[1]

Strange! what humility is here! But he indeed said this for the sake of humility, but we,[2] not from humility, but for the sake of great benefit, and wishing to gain some great profit from you, say, "Pray for us also." For although you do not receive any great or wonderful benefit from us, do it nevertheless for the sake of the honor and the title itself. Some one has had children, and even if they had not been benefited by him, nevertheless, because he has been their father, he perhaps sets this before them, saying, "For one day I have not been called father by thee."[3] On this account we too say, "Pray for us also." I am not merely saying this, but really desiring your prayers. For if I have become responsible for this presidency over you all, and shall have to render an account, much more ought I to have the benefit of your prayers. On your account my responsibilities are greater, therefore the help also from you should be greater.

Ver. 26. "Salute all the brethren with a holy kiss."

Oh! what fervor! Oh! what mad passion is here! Because being absent he could not greet them with the kiss, he greets them through others, as when we say, Kiss him for me. So also do ye yourselves retain the fire of love. For it does not admit of distances, but even through long intervening ways it extends itself, and is everywhere present.

Ver. 27. "I adjure you by the Lord that this Epistle be read unto all the holy[4] brethren."

And this command is rather from love, and not so much in the way of teaching; that with them also, he means, I may be conversing.

Ver. 28. "The grace of our Lord Jesus Christ be with you. Amen."[5]

And he does not merely command, but adjures them, and this from a fervent mind, that even though they should despise him, for the sake of the adjuration they may practice what is commanded. For men had a great dread of that appeal, but now that too is trampled under foot. And often when a slave is scourged, and adjures by God and His Christ, and says, "So may you die a Christian," yet no one gives heed, no one regards it; but if he adjures him by his own son, immediately, though unwilling, and grinding his teeth, he gives up his anger. Again, another being dragged and led away through the middle of the market-place,[6] in the presence both of Jews and Greeks, adjures him that leads him away with the most fearful adjurations, and no one regards it. What will not the Greeks say, when one of the faithful adjures a faithful man and a Christian, and no regard is paid to it, but we even despise him.

Will you allow me to tell you a certain story which I myself have heard? For I do not say it of my own invention, but having heard it from a person worthy of credit. There was a certain maid-servant united to a wicked man, a vile run-away slave; she, when her husband having committed many faults was about to be sold by her mistress; (for the offenses were too great for pardon, and the woman was a widow, and was not able to punish him who was the plague of her house, and therefore resolved to sell him; then considering that it was an unholy thing to separate the husband from the wife, the mistress, although the girl was useful, to avoid separating her from him, made up her mind to sell her also with him;) then the girl seeing herself in these straits, came to a venerable person who was intimate with her mistress, and who also told it to me, and clasping her knees, and with a thousand lamentations, besought her to entreat her mistress in her behalf; and having wasted many words, at last she added this also, as thereby especially to persuade her, laying on her a most awful adjuration, and the adjuration was this, "So mayest thou see Christ at the Day of Judgment, as thou neglectest not my petition." And having so said, she departed. And she who had been entreated, upon the intrusion of some worldly care, such as happens in families, forgot the matter. Then suddenly late in the afternoon, the most awful adjuration came into her mind, and she felt great compunction, and she went and with great earnestness asked, and obtained her request. And that very night she suddenly saw the heavens opened, and Christ Himself.

---

[1] [Some leading documents for N. T. give this "also." See margin Rev. Ver. — J. A. B.]

[2] [i.e. Chrys. himself. Below, with heightened earnestness, he says "I." By the "honor" and the "title" he means those pertaining to himself. — J. A. B.]

[3] Downes would read, "for one day, however, I was called your father." There is most likely some unknown allusion in the words.

[4] [Textus Rec. of N. T. has "holy"; Rev. Ver. properly omits it. — J. A. B.]

[5] [Ver. 28 seems inserted out of place. What follows refers to "adjure," in ver. 27. — J. A. B.]

[6] i.e. for debt, to which he probably refers also in speaking against covetousness, Hom. x., near the end.

But she saw Him, as far as it was possible for a woman to see Him. Because she at all regarded the adjuration, because she was afraid, she was thought worthy of this vision.

And these things I have said, that we may not despise adjurations, especially when any entreat us for things that are good, as for alms, and for works of mercy. But now poor men, who have lost their feet, sit and see thee hastening by, and when they cannot follow thee with their feet, they expect to detain thee, as with a kind of hook, by the fear of an adjuration, and stretching out their hands, they adjure thee to give them only one or two pennies. But thou hastenest by, though adjured by thy Lord. And if he adjure thee by the eyes either of thy husband, who is gone abroad, or of thy son, or thy daughter, immediately thou yieldest, thy mind is transported, thou art warmed ; but if he adjure thee by thy Lord, thou hastenest by. And I have known many women who, hearing indeed the name of Christ, have hastened by ; but being commended for their beauty by those who came to them, have been melted and softened, and have stretched out their hand.

Yea thus they have reduced suffering and wretched beggars to this, even to deal in making sport ! For when they do not touch their souls by uttering vehement and bitter words, they have recourse to this way by which they delight them exceedingly. And our great wickedness compels him that is in calamity or is straitened by hunger, to utter encomiums upon the beauty of those who pity him. And I wish this were all. But there is even another form worse than this. It compels the poor to be jugglers, and buffoons, and filthy jesters. For when he fastens on his fingers cups and bowls and cans, and plays on them as cymbals, and having a pipe, whistles on it those base and amorous melodies, and sings them at the top of his voice ; and then many stand round, and some give him a piece of bread, some a penny, and others something else, and they detain him long, and both men and women are delighted ; what is more grievous than this ? Are not these things deserving of much groaning ? They are indeed trifling, and are considered trifling, but they engender great sins in our character. For when any obscene and sweet melody is uttered, it softens the mind, and corrupts the very soul itself. And the poor man indeed who calls upon God, and invokes a thousand blessings upon us, is not vouchsafed a word from you ; but he who instead of these things introduces sportive sallies, is admired.

And what has now come into my mind to say to you, that I will utter. And what is this ? When you are involved in poverty and sickness, if from no other quarter, at least from those who beg, who wander through the narrow streets, learn to give thanks to the Lord. For they, spending their whole life in begging, do not blaspheme, are not angry, nor impatient, but make the whole narrative of their beggary in thanksgiving, magnifying God, and calling Him merciful. He indeed that is perishing with hunger, calls Him merciful, but you who are living in plenty, if you cannot get the possessions of all, call Him cruel. How much better is he ! how will he condemn us ! God has sent the poor through the world, as common teachers in our calamities, and consolation under them. Hast thou suffered anything contrary to thy wishes ? yet nothing like what that poor man suffers. Thou hast lost an eye, but he both his. Thou hast long labored under disease, but he has one that is incurable. Thou hast lost thy children, but he even the health of his own body. Thou hast suffered a great loss, but thou art not yet reduced to supplicate from others. Give thanks to God. Thou seest them in the furnace of poverty, and begging indeed from all, but receiving from few. When thou art weary of praying, and dost not receive, consider how often thou hast heard a poor man calling upon thee, and hast not listened to him, and he has not been angry nor insulted thee. And yet thou indeed actest thus from cruelty ; but God from mercy even declines to hear. If therefore thou, thyself from cruelty not hearing thy fellow-servant, expectest not to be found fault with, dost thou find fault with the Lord, who out of mercy does not hear His servant ? Seest thou how great the inequality, how great the injustice ?

Let us consider these things constantly, those who are below us, those who are under greater calamities, and so we shall be able to be thankful to God. Life abounds with many such instances. And he who is sober, and willing to attend, gains no small instruction from the houses of prayer. For on this account the poor sit before the vestibule both in the churches and in the chapels of the Martyrs,[1] that we may receive great benefit from the spectacle of these things. For consider, that when we enter into earthly palaces, we can see nothing of this kind ; but men that are dignified and famous, and wealthy and intelligent, are everywhere hastening to and fro. But into the real palaces, I mean the Church, and the oratories[2] of the Martyrs, enter the demoniacs, the maimed, the poor, the aged, the blind, and those whose limbs are distorted. And wherefore ? That thou mayest be instructed by the spectacle of these things ; in the first place that if thou hast entered

---

[1] μαρτυρίοις. Of these, see Bingham, viii. 8, who quotes Eusebius Vit. Const. iii. 48, saying that Constantine built several in Constantinople. See also on Stat. Hom. i.
[2] [i.e. houses of prayer, as just above. This was an adaptation of a Jewish custom, as in Acts xvi. 13 (Rev. Ver.) and 16. —J. A. B.]

drawing after thee any pride from without, having looked upon these, and laid aside thy arrogance, and become contrite in heart, so thou mayest go in, and hear the things that are said ; for it is not possible that he who prays with an arrogant mind should be heard.　That when thou seest an aged man, thou mayest not be elated at thy youth, for these old men were once young.　That when thou boastest highly of thy warfare, or thy kingly power, thou mayest consider that from these are sprung those who are become illustrious in kings' courts.　That, when thou presumest upon thy bodily health, taking heed to these, thou mayest abate thy lofty spirit. For the healthy man who continually enters here, will not be highminded on account of his bodily health ; and the sick man will receive no slight consolation.

But they do not sit here only on this account, but that they may also make thee compassionate, and thou mayest be inclined to pity ; that thou mayest admire the lovingkindness of God ; for if God is not ashamed of them, but has set them in His vestibules, much less be thou ashamed ; that thou mayest not be highminded on account of palaces upon earth.　Be not ashamed, when called upon by a poor man ; and if he should draw near, if he should catch thy knees, shake him not off.　For these are certain admirable dogs of the Royal Courts.　For I do not call them dogs as dishonoring them — far be it — but even highly commending them.　They guard the King's court.　Therefore feed them.　For the honor passes on to the King.　There all is pride, — I speak of the palaces on earth — here all is humility.　You learn especially from the very vestibules that human beings are nothing. From the very persons who sit before them, you are taught that God delights not in riches.　For their sitting and assembling there is all but an admonition, sending forth a clear voice regarding the nature of all men, and saying that human things are nothing, that they are shadow and smoke.　If riches were a good, God would not have seated the poor before His own vestibule. And if He admits rich people also, wonder not, for He admits them not on this account, that they may continue rich, but that they may be delivered from their encumbrance.　For hear what Christ says to them, " Ye cannot serve God and Mammon " (Matt. vi. 24.) ; and again, " It is hard for a rich man to enter into the kingdom of heaven " ; and again, " It is easier for a camel to go through a needle's eye, than for a rich man to enter into the kingdom of heaven."　·(Matt. xix. 23, 24.)　On this account He receives the rich, that they may hear these words, that they may long for the eternal riches, that they may covet things in heaven.　And why dost thou wonder that He does not disdain to seat such

at His vestibules ? for He does not disdain to call them to His spiritual Table, and make them partakers of that Feast.　But the maimed and the lame, the old man that is clothed in rags and filth, and has catarrh, comes to partake of that Table with the young and the beautiful, and with him even who is clothed in purple, and whose head is encircled with a diadem — and is thought worthy of the spiritual Feast, and both enjoy the same benefits, and there is no difference.

Does then Christ not disdain to call them to His Table with the king (Emperor) — for both are called together — and thou perhaps disdainest even to be seen giving to the poor, or even conversing with them ?　Fie upon thy haughtiness and pride !　See that we suffer not the same with the rich man formerly.　He disdained even to look upon Lazarus, and did not allow him to share his roof or shelter, but he was without, cast away at his gate, nor was he even vouchsafed a word from him.　But see how, when fallen into straits, and in want of his help, he failed to obtain it.　For if we are ashamed of those of whom Christ is not ashamed, we are ashamed of Christ, being ashamed of His friends.　Let thy table be filled with the maimed and the lame.　Through them Christ comes, not through the rich.　Perhaps thou laughest at hearing this ; therefore, that thou mayest not think it is my word, hear Christ Himself speaking, that thou mayest not laugh, but shudder : " When thou makest a dinner or a supper, call not thy friends nor thy brethren, nor thy kinsmen, nor rich neighbors ; lest haply they also bid thee again, and a recompense be made thee. But when thou makest a feast, bid the poor, the maimed, the halt, the blind ; and thou shalt be blessed ; because they have not wherewith to recompense thee : for thou shalt be recompensed in the Resurrection of the just."　(Luke xiv. 12–14.)　And greater is thy glory even here, if thou lovest that.　For from the former class of guests arise envy, and malice, and slanders, and revilings, and much fear lest anything unbecoming should occur.　And thou standest like a servant before his master, if those who are invited are thy superiors, fearing their criticism and their lips.　But in the case of these there is nothing of this sort, but whatever you bring them, they receive all with pleasure ; and ample is the applause, brighter the glory, higher the admiration.　All they that hear do not so much applaud the former, as the latter.　But if thou disbelievest, thou who art rich, make the trial, thou who invitest generals and governors.　Invite the poor, and fill thy table from them, and see if thou art not applauded by all, if thou art not loved by all, if all do not hold thee as a father. For of those feasts there is no advantage, but for these heaven is in store, and the good things of heaven — of which may we all be partakers, by the grace and lovingkindness of our Lord Jesus Christ, with whom to the Father, together with the Holy Spirit, be glory, power, honor, now and ever, and world without end.   Amen.

HOMILIES OF ST. JOHN CHRYSOSTOM,

ARCHBISHOP OF CONSTANTINOPLE,

ON THE

SECOND EPISTLE OF ST. PAUL THE APOSTLE

TO THE

THESSALONIANS.

HOMILY I

ARGUMENT.

HAVING said in his former Epistle that " we pray night and day to see you, and that we could not forbear, but were left in Athens alone," and that " I sent Timothy " (from 1 Thess. iii. 1, 2, 10), by all these expressions he shows the desire which he had to come amongst them. When therefore he had perhaps not had time to go, and to perfect what was lacking in their faith, on this account he adds a second Epistle, filling up by his writings what was wanting of his presence. For that he did not depart, we may conjecture from hence : for he says in this Epistle, " We beseech you by the coming of our Lord Jesus Christ." (2 Thess. ii. 1.) For in his first Epistle he said, " Concerning the times and the seasons ye have no need that aught be written unto you." (1 Thess. v. 1.) So that if he had gone, there would have been no need of his writing. But since the question was deferred, on this account he adds this Epistle, as in his Epistle to Timothy he says, " They subvert the faith of some, saying that the Resurrection is already past " (from 2 Tim. ii. 18) ; that the faithful henceforth hoping for nothing great or splendid, might faint under their sufferings.

For since that hope supported them, and did not allow them to yield to the present evils, the devil wishing to cut it off, as being a kind of anchor, when he was not able to persuade them that the things to come were false, went to work another way, and having suborned certain pestilential men, endeavored to deceive those who believed into a persuasion that those great and splendid things had received their fulfillment. Accordingly these men then said that the Resurrection was already past. But now they said that the Judgment and the coming of Christ were at hand, that they might involve even Christ in a falsehood, and having pointed out to them that there is hereafter no retribution, nor judgment-seat, nor punishment and vengeance for those who had done them evil, they might both render these more bold, and those more dispirited. And, what was worse than all, some attempted merely to report words as if they were said by Paul, but others even to forge Epistles as written by him. On this account, cutting off all access for them, he says, " Be not quickly shaken from your mind, nor yet be troubled, either by spirit, or by word, or by epistle as from us." (2 Thess. ii. 2.) "Neither by spirit " he says, glancing at the false prophets. Whence then shall we know them, he says ? For this very reason, he added, " The salutation of me Paul with mine own hand, which is the token in every Epistle : so I write. The grace of our Lord Jesus Christ be with you all." (2 Thess. iii. 17, 18.) He does not here mean, that this is the token, — for it is probable that others also imitated this,—but that I write the salutation with mine own hand, as is the custom also now among us. For by the subscription the writings of those who send letters are made known. But he comforts them, as being excessively pinched[1] by their troubles; both praising them from their present state, and encouraging them from a prospect of the futurity, and from the punishment, and from the recompense of good things prepared for them; and he more clearly enlarges upon the topic, not indeed revealing the time itself, but showing the sign of the time, namely, Antichrist. For a weak soul is then most fully assured, not when it merely hears, but when it learns something more particular.

And Christ too bestowed great care upon this point, and being seated on the Mount, He with great particularity discoursed to His disciples upon the Consummation. And wherefore? that there might be no room for those who introduce Antichrists and false Christs. And He Himself also gives many signs, one indeed, and that the most important, saying, when "the Gospel shall be preached to all nations" (from Matt. xxiv. 14), and another also, that they should not be deceived with respect to His coming. "As the lightning" (ver. 27), He says, shall He come; not concealed in any corner, but shining everywhere. It requires no one to point it out, so splendid will it be, even as the lightning needs no one to point it out. And He has spoken in a certain place also concerning Antichrist, when He said, "I am come in My Father's name, and ye receive Me not: if another shall come in His own name, Him ye will receive." (John v. 43.) And He said that those unspeakable calamities one after another were a sign of it, and that Elias must come.

The Thessalonians indeed were then perplexed, but their perplexity has been profitable to us. For not to them only, but to us also are these things useful, that we may be delivered from childish fables and from old women's fooleries. And have you not often heard, when you were children, persons talking much even about the name of Antichrist, and about his bending the knee? For the devil scatters these things in our minds, whilst yet tender, that the doctrine may grow up with us, and that he may be able to deceive us. Paul therefore, in speaking of Antichrist, would not have passed over these things if they had been profitable. Let us not therefore enquire into these things. For he will not come so bending his knees, but "exalting himself against all that is called God, or that is worshiped; so that he sitteth in the temple of God, setting himself forth as God." (2 Thess. ii. 4.) For as the

devil fell by pride, so he who is wrought upon by him is anointed unto pride.

Wherefore, I beseech you, let us all be earnest to be far removed from this affection, that we may not fall into his condemnation, that we may not subject ourselves to the same punishment, that we may not partake of the vengeance. "Not a novice," he says, "lest being puffed up he fall into the condemnation of the devil." (1 Tim. iii. 6.) He who is puffed up therefore, suffers the same punishment with the devil. "For the beginning of pride is not to know the Lord." (Ecclus. x. 12, 13.) Pride is the beginning of sin, the first impulse and movement toward evil. Perhaps indeed it is both the root and the foundation. For "the beginning" means either the first impulse towards evil, or the grounding. As if one should say, the beginning of chastity is to abstain from the sight of an improper object, that is the first impulse. But if we should say, the beginning of chastity is fasting, that is the foundation and establishment. So also pride is the beginning of sin. For every sin begins from it, and is maintained by it. For that, whatever good things we do, this vice suffers them not to remain and not fall away, but is as a certain root not letting them abide unshaken, is manifest from hence: see what things the Pharisee did, but they profited him nothing. For he did not extirpate the root, but it corrupted all his performances, because the root remained. From pride springs contempt of the poor, desire of riches, the love of power, the longing for much glory. Such an one is prompt to revenge an insult. For he who is proud cannot bear to be insulted even by his superiors, much less by his inferiors. But he who cannot bear to be insulted cannot bear either to suffer any ill. See how pride is the beginning of sin.

But how is it the beginning of pride, not to know the Lord? Justly. For he who knows God as he ought to know Him, he who knows that the Son of God humbled Himself so much, is not lifted up. But he who knows not these things, is lifted up. For pride anoints him unto arrogance. For tell me, whence is it that they who make war upon the Church say that they know God? Is it not from arrogance? See into what a precipice it plunges them, not to know the Lord! For if God loveth a contrite spirit (Ps. li. 17, etc.), He on the other hand "resisteth the proud, and giveth grace to the humble." (1 Pet. v. 5.) There is therefore no evil like pride. It renders a man a demon, insolent, blasphemous, perjured, and makes him desirous of deaths and murders. The proud man always lives in troubles, is always angry, always unhappy. There is nothing which can satiate his passion. If he should see the king

---

[1] τεταριχευμένους, see on Stat. Hom. vi. Tr. p. 388, note 6.

stooping down to him, and prostrating himself, he is not satisfied, but is the more inflamed. For as the lovers of money, the more they receive, want so much the more, so also the proud, the more honor they enjoy, the more they desire. For their passion is increased; for a passion it is, and a passion knows not limit, but then stops when it has slain its possessor. Do you not see that drunkards are always thirsty? for it is a passion, not the desire of nature, but some perverted disease. Do you not see how those who are affected with bulimy, as it is called, are always hungry? For it is a passion, as the children of the physicians say, already exceeding the bounds of nature. The busy-bodies, and the over-curious, whatever they have learnt, do not stop. For it is a passion, and has no limit. (Ecclus. xxiii. 17.) Again, they who delight in fornication, they too cannot desist. "To a fornicator," it is said, "all bread is sweet." He will not cease, till he is devoured. For it is a passion.

But they are indeed passions, not however incurable, but admitting of cure, and much more than bodily affections. For if we will, we can extinguish them. How then can a man extinguish pride? By knowing God. For if it arises from not knowing God, if we know Him, all pride is banished. Think of Hell. Think of those who are much better than yourself. Think of your sins. Think for how many things you deserve punishment from God. If you think of these, you will soon bring down your proud mind, you will soon bend it. But can you not do these things? are you too weak? Consider things present, human nature itself, the nothingness of man! When thou seest a dead body carried through the market-place, orphan children following it, a widow beating her breast, servants bewailing, friends looking dejected, reflect upon the nothingness of things present, and that they differ not from a shadow, or a dream.

Does this not suit you? Think of those who are very rich, who perish anyhow in war; look round on the houses, that belonged to the great and illustrious, and are now leveled to the ground. Consider how mighty they were, and now not even a memorial of them is left. For, if you will, every day you may find examples of these things — the successions of rulers, — the confiscations of rich men's goods. "Many tyrants have sat upon the ground — and he who was never thought on, has worn a diadem." (Ecclus. xi. 15.) Do not these things happen every day? Do not our affairs resemble a kind of wheel? Read, if you will, both our own (books), and those without:[1] for they also abound in such examples. If you despise ours, and this from pride; if you admire the works of philosophers, go even to them. They will instruct thee, relating ancient calamities, as will poets, and orators, and sophists, and all historians. From every side, if you will, you may find examples.

But if you will none of these things, reflect upon our very nature, of what it consists, and wherein it ends. Consider, when you sleep, of what worth are you? Will not even a little beast be able to destroy thee? For often a little animal falling from the roof has deprived many persons of sight, or has been the cause of some other danger. But what? art thou not less than all beasts? But what sayest thou? that thou excellest in reason? But behold, thou hast not reason: for pride is a sign of the want of reason. And for what, tell me, art thou high-minded after all? Is it upon the good constitution of thy body? But the prize of victory here is with the irrational creatures; this is possessed also by robbers and murderers, and violators of the tombs. But art thou proud of thine understanding? It is no proof of understanding to be proud. By this then first thou deprivest thyself of becoming intelligent. Let us bring down our high thoughts. Let us be moderate, and lowly, and gentle. For such even Christ has pronounced blessed above all, saying, "Blessed are the poor in spirit." (Matt. v. 3.) And again, He cried, saying, "Learn of Me, for I am meek and lowly in heart." (Matt. xi. 29.) For this reason He washed the feet of His disciples, affording us an example of humility. From all these things let us gain profit, that we may be able to obtain the blessings promised to those who love Him, by the grace and lovingkindness, &c.

---

[1] The sequel clearly shows that he means Christian and Heathen books, and so the words themselves mean, rather than domestic and foreign history.

HOMILY II.

2 THESSALONIANS i. 1, 2.

" Paul, and Silvanus, and Timothy, unto the Church of the Thessalonians in God our Father and the Lord Jesus Christ: Grace to you and peace from God the Father and the Lord Jesus Christ."

THE greater part of men do and devise all things with a view to ingratiate themselves with rulers, and with those who are greater than themselves; and they account it a great thing, and think themselves happy, if they can obtain that object. But if to obtain favor with men is so great an advantage, how great must it be to find favor with God? On this account he always thus prefaces his Epistle, and invokes this upon them, knowing that if this be granted, there will be nothing afterwards grievous, but whatever troubles there may be, all will be done away. And that you may learn this, Joseph was a slave, a young man, inexperienced, unformed, and suddenly the direction of a house was committed to his hands, and he had to render an account to an Egyptian master. And you know how prone to anger and unforgiving that people is, and when authority and power is added, their rage is greater, being inflamed by power. And this too is manifest from what he did afterwards. For when the mistress made accusation, he bore with it. And yet it was not the part of those who held the garment, but of him who was stripped, to have suffered violence. For he ought to have said, If he had heard that thou didst raise thy voice, as thou sayest, he would have fled, and if he had been guilty, he would not have waited for the coming of his master. But nevertheless he took nothing of this sort into consideration, but unreasonably giving way altogether to anger, he cast him into prison. So thoughtless a person was he. And yet even from other things he might have conjectured the good disposition and the intelligence of the man. But nevertheless, because he was very unreasonable, he never considered any such thing. He therefore who had to do with such a harsh master, and who was intrusted with the administration of his whole house, being a stranger, and solitary, and inexperienced; when God shed abundant grace upon him, passed through all, as if his temptations had not even existed, both the false accusation of his mistress, and the danger of death, and the prison, and at last came to the royal throne.

This blessed man therefore saw how great is the grace of God, and on this account he invokes it upon them. And another thing also

he effects, wishing to render them well-disposed to the remaining part of the Epistle; that, though he should reprove and rebuke them, they might not break away from him. For this reason he reminds them before all things of the grace of God, mollifying their hearts, that, even if there be affliction, being reminded of the grace by which they were saved·from the greater evil, they may not despair at the less, but may thence derive consolation. As also elsewhere in an Epistle he has said, " For if, while we were enemies, we were reconciled to God through the death of His Son, much more, being reconciled, shall we be saved by His life." (Rom. v. 10.)

" Grace to you and peace," he says, " from God the Father and the Lord Jesus Christ."

Ver. 3. " We are bound to give thanks to God alway for you, brethren, even as it is meet."

Again a sign of great humility. For he led them to reflect and consider, that if for our good actions others do not admire us first, but God, much more also ought we. And in other respects too he raises up their spirits, because they suffer such things as are not worthy of tears and lamentations, but of thanksgiving to God. But if Paul is thankful for the good of others, what will they suffer, who not only are not thankful, but even pine at it.

" For that your faith groweth exceedingly, and the love of each one of you all toward one another aboundeth."

And how, you say, can faith increase? That is when we suffer something dreadful for it. It is a great thing for it to be established, and not to be carried away by reasonings. But when the winds assail us, when the rains burst upon us, when a violent storm is raised on every side, and the waves succeed each other — then that we are not shaken, is a proof of no less than this, that it grows, and grows exceedingly, and becomes loftier. For as in the case of the flood all the stony and lower parts are soon hidden, but as many things as are above, it reaches not them, so also the faith that is become lofty, is not drawn downwards. For this reason he does not say " your faith groweth," but " groweth exceedingly, and the love of each one of you all toward one another aboundeth." Seest thou how this contributes for the ease of affliction, to be in close guard together, and to adhere to one another? From this also arose much consolation. The love and faith, therefore, that is weak, afflictions shake, but that which is strong they render stronger. For a soul that is in grief, when it is weak, can add nothing to itself; but that which is strong doth it then most. And observe their love. They did not love one indeed, and not love another, but it was equal on the part of all. For this he has intimated, by saying, " of each one of you all toward one another." For it was equally poised, as that of one body. Since even now we find love existing among many, but this love becoming the cause of division. For when we are knit together in parties of two or three, and the two indeed, or three or four, are closely bound to one another, but draw themselves off from the rest, because they can have recourse to these, and in all things confide in these ; this is the division of love — not love. For tell me, if the eye should bestow upon the hand the foresight which it has for the whole body, and withdrawing itself from the other members, should attend to that alone, would it not injure the whole? Assuredly. So also if we confine to one or two the love which ought to be extended to the whole Church of God, we injure both ourselves and them, and the whole. For these things are not of love, but of division ; schisms, and distracting rents. Since even if I separate and take a member from the whole man, the part separated indeed is united in itself, is continuous, all compacted together, yet even so it is a separation, since it is not united to the rest of the body.

For what advantage is it, that thou lovest a certain person exceedingly? It is a human love. But if it is not a human love, but thou lovest for God's sake, then love all. For so God hath commanded to love even our enemies. And if He hath commanded to love our enemies, how much more those who have never aggrieved us? But, sayest thou, I love, but not in that way. Rather, thou dost not love at all. For when thou accusest, when thou enviest, when thou layest snares, how dost thou love? " But," sayest thou, " I do none of these things." But when a man is ill spoken of, and thou dost not shut the mouth of the speaker, dost not disbelieve his sayings, dost not check him, of what love is this the sign? " And the love," he says, " of each one of you all toward one another aboundeth."

Ver. 4. " So that we ourselves glory in you in the Churches of God."

Indeed in the first Epistle he says, that all the Churches of Macedonia and Achaia resounded, having heard of their faith. " So that we need not," he says, " to speak anything. For they themselves report concerning us what manner of entering in we had unto you." (1 Thess. i. 8.) But here he says, " so that

we glory." What then is it that is said? There he says that they need not instruction from him, but here he has not said that we teach them, but "we glory," and are proud of you. If therefore we both give thanks to God for you, and glory among men, much more ought you to do so for your own good deeds. For if your good actions are worthy of boasting from others, how are they worthy of lamentation from you? It is impossible to say. "So that we ourselves," he says, "glory in you in the Churches of God, for your patience and faith."

Here he shows that much time had elapsed. For patience is shown by much time, not in two or three days. And he does not merely say patience. It is the part of patience indeed properly not yet to enjoy the promised blessings. But here he speaks of a greater patience. And of what sort is that? That which is shown in persecutions. "For your patience," he says, "and faith in all your persecutions and in the afflictions which ye endure." For they were living with enemies who were continually endeavoring on every side to injure them, and they were manifesting a patience firm and immovable. Let all those blush who for the sake of the patronage of men pass over to other doctrines. For whilst it was yet the beginning of the preaching, poor men who lived by their daily earnings took upon themselves enmities from rulers and the first men of the state, when there was nowhere king or governor who was a believer ; and submitted to irreconcilable war, and not even so were unsettled.

Ver. 5. "Which is a manifest token of the righteous judgment of God."

See how he gathers comfort for them. He had said, We give thanks to God, he had said, We glory among men : these things indeed are honorable. But that which he most seeks for, who is in suffering, is, deliverance from evils, and vengeance upon those who are evil entreating them. For when the soul is weak, it most seeks for these things, for the philosophic soul does not even seek these things. Why then does he say, "a token of the righteous Judgment of God"? Here he has glanced at the retribution on either side, both of those who do the ill, and of those who suffer it, as if he had said, that the justice of God may be shown when He crowns you indeed, but punishes them. At the same time also he comforts them, showing that from their own labors and toils they are crowned, and according to the proportion of righteousness. But he puts their part first. For although a person even vehemently desires revenge, yet he first longs for reward. For this reason he says,

"That ye may be counted worthy of the kingdom of God, for which ye also suffer."

This then does not come to pass from the circumstance that those who injure them are more powerful than they, but because it is so that they must enter into the kingdom. " For through many tribulations," he says, " we must enter into the kingdom of God." (Acts xiv. 22.)

Ver. 6, 7. " If so be that it is a righteous thing with God to recompense affliction to them that afflict you, and to you that are afflicted rest with us at the revelation of the Lord Jesus from heaven with the Angels of His power."

The phrase " If so be that " here is put for " because," which we also use, in speaking of things that are quite evident and not to be denied ; instead of saying, " Because it is exceedingly righteous." " If so be," he says, " that it is a righteous thing " with God to punish these, he will certainly punish them. As if he had said, " If God cares for human affairs," " If God takes thought." And he does not put it of his own opinion, but among things confessedly true ; as if one said, " If God hates the wicked," that he may compel them to grant that He does hate them. For such sentences are above all indisputable, inasmuch as they also themselves know that it is just. For if this is just with men, much more with God.

" To recompense," he says, " affliction to them that afflict you, and to you that are afflicted rest." What then ? Is the retribution equal ?[1] By no means, but see by what follows how he shows that it is more severe, and the " rest " much greater. Behold also another consolation, in that they have their partners in the afflictions, as partners also in the retribution. He joins them in their crowns with those who had performed infinitely more and greater works. Then he adds also the period, and by the description leads their minds upward, all but opening heaven already by his word, and setting it before their eyes ; and he places around Him the angelic host, both from the place and from the attendants amplifying the image, so that they may be refreshed a little. " And to you that are afflicted rest with us," he says, " at the revelation of the Lord Jesus from heaven with the Angels of his power."

Ver. 8. " In flaming fire rendering vengeance to them that know not God, and to them that obey not the Gospel of our Lord Jesus."

If they that have not obeyed the Gospel suffer vengeance, what will not they suffer who besides their disobedience also afflict you? And see his intelligence ; he says not here those who afflict you, but those " who obey not." So that although not on your account, yet on His own it is necessary to punish them. This then is said in order to full assurance, that it is altogether necessary for them to be punished : but

what was said before, was said that they also might be honored, because they suffer these things on your account. The one causes them to believe concerning the punishment ; the other to be pleased, because for the sake of what has been done to them they suffer these things.

All this was said to them, but it applies also to us. When therefore we are in affliction, let us consider these things. Let us not rejoice at the punishment of others as being avenged, but as ourselves escaping from such punishment and vengeance. For what advantage is it to us when others are punished? Let us not, I beseech you, have such souls. Let us be invited to virtue by the prospect of the kingdom. For he indeed who is exceedingly virtuous is induced neither by fear nor by the prospect of the kingdom, but for Christ's sake alone, as was the case with Paul. Let us, however, even thus consider the blessings of the kingdom, the miseries of hell, and thus regulate and school ourselves ; let us in this way bring ourselves to the things that are to be practiced. When you see anything good and great in the present life, think of the kingdom, and you will consider it as nothing. When you see anything terrible, think of hell, and you will deride it. When you are possessed by carnal desire, think of the fire, think also of the pleasure of sin itself, that it is nothing worth, it has not even pleasure in it. For if the fear of the laws that are enacted here has so great power as to withdraw us from wicked actions, how much more should the remembrance of things future, the vengeance that is immortal, the punishment that is everlasting? If the fear of an earthly king withdraws us from so many evils, how much more the fear of the King Eternal?

Whence then can we constantly have this fear? If we continually hearken to the Scriptures. For if the sight only of a dead body so depresses the mind, how much more must hell and the fire unquenchable, how much more the worm that never dieth. If we always think of hell, we shall not soon fall into it. For this reason God has threatened punishment ; if it was not attended with great advantage to think of it, God would not have threatened it. But because the remembrance of it is able to work great good, for this reason He has put into our souls the terror of it, as a wholesome medicine. Let us not then overlook the great advantage arising from it, but let us continually advert to it, at our dinners, at our suppers. For conversation about pleasant things profits the soul nothing, but renders it more languid, while that about things painful and melancholy cuts off all that is relaxed and dissolute in it, and converts it, and braces it when unnerved. He who converses of theaters and actors does not benefit

---

[1] i.e. to the works.

the soul, but inflames it more, and renders it more careless. He who concerns himself and is busy in other men's matters, often even involves it in dangers by this curiosity. But he who converses about hell incurs no dangers, and renders it more sober.

But dost thou fear the offensiveness of such words? Hast thou then, if thou art silent, extinguished hell? or if thou speakest of it, hast thou kindled it? Whether thou speakest of it or not, the fire boils forth. Let it be continually spoken of, that thou mayest never fall into it. It is not possible that a soul anxious about hell should readily sin. For hear the most excellent advice, " Remember," it says, " thy latter end " (Ecclus. xxviii. 6), and thou wilt not sin for ever. A soul that is fearful of giving account cannot but be slow to transgression. For fear being vigorous in the soul does not permit anything worldly to exist in it. For if discourse raised concerning hell so humbles and brings it low, does not the reflection constantly dwelling upon the soul purify it more than any fire?

Let us not remember the kingdom so much as hell. For fear has more power than the promise. And I know that many would despise ten thousand blessings, if they were rid of the punishment, inasmuch as it is even now sufficient for me to escape vengeance, and not to be punished. No one of those who have hell before their eyes will fall into hell. No one of those who despise hell will escape hell. For as among us those who fear the judgment-seats will not be apprehended by them, but those who despise them are chiefly those who fall under them, so it is also in this case. If the Ninevites had not feared destruction, they would have been overthrown, but because they feared, they were not overthrown. If in the time of Noah they had feared the deluge, they would not have been drowned. And if the Sodomites had feared, they would not have been consumed by fire. It is a great evil to despise a threat. He who despises threatening will soon experience its reality in the execution of it. Nothing is so profitable as to converse concerning hell. It renders our souls purer than any silver. For hear the prophet saying, " Thy judgments are always before me." (From Ps. xvii. 22, Sept.) For although it pains the hearer, it benefits him very much.

For such indeed are all things that profit. For medicines too, and food, at first annoy the sick, and then do him good. And if we cannot bear the severity of words, it is manifest that we shall not be able to bear affliction in very deed. If no one endures a discourse concerning hell, it is evident, that if persecution came on, no one would ever stand firm against fire, against sword. Let us exercise our ears not to be over

soft and tender : for from this we shall come to endure even the things themselves. If we be habituated to hear of dreadful things, we shall be habituated also to endure dreadful things. But if we be so relaxed as not to endure even words, when shall we stand against things? Do you see how the blessed Paul despises all things here, and dangers one after another, as not even temptations? Wherefore? Because he had been in the practice of despising hell, for the sake of what was God's will. He thought even the experience of hell to be nothing for the sake of the love of Christ ; while we do not even endure a discourse concerning it for our own advantage. Now therefore having heard a little, go your ways ; but I beseech you if there is any love in you, constantly to revert to discourses concerning these things. They can do you no harm, even if they should not benefit, but assuredly they will benefit you too. For according to our discourses, the soul is qualified. For evil communications, he says, " corrupt good manners." Therefore also good communications improve it ; therefore also fearful discourses make it sober. For the soul is a sort of wax. For if you apply cold discourses, you harden and make it callous ; but if fiery ones, you melt it ; and having melted it, you form it to what you will, and engrave the royal image upon it. Let us therefore stop up our ears to discourses that are vain. It is no little evil ; for from it arise all evils.

If our mind had been practiced to apply to divine discourses, it would not apply to others ; and not applying to others, neither would it betake itself to evil actions. For words are the road to works. First we think, then we speak, then we act. Many men, even when before sober, have often from disgraceful words gone on to disgraceful actions. For our soul is neither good nor evil by nature, but becomes both the one and the other from choice. As therefore the sail carries the ship wherever the wind may blow, or rather as the rudder moves the ship, if the wind be favorable, so also thought will sail without danger, if good words from a favorable quarter waft it. But if the contrary, often they will even overwhelm the reason. For what winds are to ships, that discourses are to souls. Wherever you will, you may move and turn it. For this reason one exhorting says, " Let thy whole discourse be in the law of the Most High." (Ecclus. xx. 20.) Wherefore, I exhort you, when we receive children from the nurse, let us not accustom them to old wives' stories, but let them learn from their first youth that there is a Judgment, that there is a punishment ; let it be infixed in their minds. This fear being rooted in them produces great good effects. For a soul that has learnt from its first youth to be subdued by this expectation, will not soon shake off this fear. But like a horse obedient to the bridle, having the thought of hell seated upon it, walking orderly, it will both speak and utter things profitable ; and neither youth nor riches, nor an orphan state, nor any other thing, will be able to injure it, having its reason so firm and able to hold out against everything.

By these discourses let us regulate as well ourselves as our wives too, our servants, our children, our friends, and, if possible, our enemies. For with these discourses we are able to cut off the greater part of our sins, and it is better to dwell upon things grievous than upon things agreeable, and it is manifest from hence. For, tell me, if you should go into a house where a marriage is celebrated, for a season you are delighted at the spectacle, but afterwards having gone away, you pine with grief that you have not so much. But if you enter the house of mourners, even though they are very rich, when you go away you will be rather refreshed. For there you have not conceived envy, but comfort and consolation in your poverty. You have seen by facts, that riches are no good, poverty no evil, but they are things indifferent. So also now, if you talk about luxury, you the more vex your soul, that is not able perhaps to be luxurious. But if you are speaking against luxury, and introduce discourse concerning hell, the thing will cheer you, and beget much pleasure. For when you consider that luxury will not be able to defend us at all against that fire, you will not seek after it ; but if you reflect that it is wont to kindle it even more, you will not only not seek, but will turn from it and reject it.

Let us not avoid discourses concerning hell, that we may avoid hell. Let us not banish the remembrance of punishment, that we may escape punishment. If the rich man had reflected upon that fire, he would not have sinned ; but because he never was mindful of it, therefore he fell into it. Tell me, O man, being about to stand before the Judgment-seat of Christ, dost thou speak of all things rather than of that? And when you have a matter before a judge, often only relating to words, neither day nor night, at no time or season dost thou talk of anything else, but always of that business, and when thou art about to give an account of thy whole life, and to submit to a trial, canst thou not bear even with others reminding thee of that Judgment? For this reason therefore all things are ruined and undone, because when we are about to stand before a human tribunal concerning matters of this life, we move everything, we solicit all men, we are constantly anxious about it, we do everything for the sake of it : but when we are about, after no long time, to come before the Judgment-seat of Christ, we do nothing either by ourselves, or by others ; we do not entreat the Judge. And yet He grants to us a long season of forbearance, and does not snatch us away in the midst of our sins, but permits us to put them off, and that Goodness and Lovingkindness leaves nothing undone of all that belongs to Himself. But all is of no avail ; on this account the punishment will be the heavier. But God forbid it should be so ! Wherefore, I beseech you, let us even if but now become watchful. Let us keep hell before our eyes. Let us consider that inexorable Account, that, thinking of those things, we may both avoid vice, and choose virtue, and may be able to obtain the blessings promised to those who love Him, by the grace and lovingkindness, &c.

HOMILY III.

2 THESSALONIANS i. 9, 10.

"Who shall suffer punishment, even eternal destruction from the face of the Lord, and from the glory of His might, when He shall come to be glorified in His Saints, and to be marveled at in all them that believed."

THERE are many men, who form good hopes not by abstaining from their sins, but by thinking that hell is not so terrible as it is said to be, but milder than what is threatened, and temporary, not eternal ; and about this they philosophize much. But I could show from many reasons, and conclude from the very expressions concerning hell, that it is not only not milder, but much more terrible than is threatened. But I do not now intend to discourse concerning these things. For the fear even from bare words is sufficient, though we do not fully unfold their meaning. But that it is not temporary, hear Paul now saying, concerning those who know not God, and who do not believe in the Gospel, that "they shall suffer punishment, even eternal destruction." How then is that temporary which is everlasting? "From the face of the Lord," he says. What is this? He here wishes to say how easily it might be. For since they were then much puffed up, there is no need, he says, of much trouble; it is enough that God comes and is seen, and all are involved in punishment and vengeance. His coming only to some indeed will be Light, but to others vengeance.

"And from the glory of His might," he says, "when He shall come to be glorified in His Saints, and to be marveled at in all them that believed."

Is God glorified? Yea, he says, in all the Saints. How? For when they that puff so greatly see those who were scourged by them, who were despised, who were derided, even those now near to Him, it is His glory, or rather it is their glory, both theirs and His; His indeed, because He did not forsake them; theirs, because they were thought worthy of so great honor. For as it is His riches, that there are faithful men, so also it is His glory that there are those who are to enjoy His blessings. It is the glory of Him that is good, to have those to whom He may impart His beneficence. "And to be marveled at," he says, "in all them that believed," that is, "through them that believed." See here again, "in" is used for "through." For through them He is shown to be admirable, when He brings to so much splendor those who were pitiable and wretched, and who had suffered unnumbered ills, and had believed. His power is shown then; because although they seem to be deserted here, yet nevertheless they there enjoy great glory; then especially is shown all the glory and the power of God. How?

"Because our testimony unto you was believed in that day."

Ver. 11. "To which end also we pray always for you."

That is, when those are brought into public view, who have suffered unnumbered ills, designed to make them apostatize from the faith, and yet have not yielded, but have believed, God is glorified. Then is shown the glory of these men also. "Judge none blessed," it says, "before his death." (Ecclus. xi. 28.) On this account he says, in that day will be shown those who believed. "To which end also we pray," he says, "always for you, that our God may count you worthy of your calling, and fulfill every desire of goodness and work of faith, with power."

"That He may count you," he says, "worthy of calling"; for they were not called. Therefore he has added, "and fulfill every desire of goodness." Since he also who was clothed in filthy garments, was called, but did not abide in his calling, but for this reason was the more rejected. "Of the calling," namely, that to the bridechamber. Since the five virgins also were called. "Arise," it says, "the bridegroom cometh."

(From Matt. xxv. 6.) And they prepared themselves, but did not enter in. But he speaks of that other calling. Showing therefore what calling he is speaking of, he has added, "And fulfill every desire of goodness and every work of faith, with power." This is the calling, he says, that we seek. See how gently he takes them down. For that they may not be rendered vain by the excess of commendation, as if they had done great deeds, and may not become slothful, he shows that something still is wanting to them, so long as they are in this life. Which also he said in his Epistle to the Hebrews. "Ye have not yet resisted unto blood, striving against sin." (Heb. xii. 4.) "Unto all wellpleasing," he says, that is, His gratification, persuasion, full assurance. That is, that the persuasion [1] of God may be fulfilled, that nothing may be wanting to you, that you may be so, as He wills. "And every work of faith," he says, "with power." What is this? The patient endurance of persecutions, that we may not faint, he says.

Ver. 12. "That the name of our Lord Jesus Christ may be glorified in you, and ye in Him, according to the grace of our God and the Lord Jesus Christ."

He spoke there of glory, he speaks of it also here. He said, that they are glorified, so that they might even boast. He said, what was much more, that they also glorify God. He said, that they will receive that glory. But here too he means; For the Master being glorified, the servants also are glorified. For those who glorify their Master, are much more glorified themselves, both by that very thing, and apart from it. For tribulation for the sake of Christ is glory, and that thing he everywhere calls glory. And by how much the more we suffer anything dishonorable, so much the more illustrious we become. Then again showing that this also itself is of God, he says, "according to the grace of our God and the Lord Jesus Christ"; that is, this grace He Himself has given us, that He may be glorified in us, and that He may glorify us in Him. How is He glorified in us? Because we prefer nothing before Him. How are we glorified in Him? Because we have received power from Him, so that we do not at all yield to the evils that are brought upon us. For when temptation happens, at the same time God is glorified, and we too. For they glorify Him, because He has so nerved us; they admire us, because we have rendered ourselves worthy. And all these things are done by the grace of God.

Chap. ii. 1, 2. "Now we beseech you, brethren, touching the coming of our Lord Jesus Christ, and our gathering together unto

---

[1] Downes explains this, "that which will persuade, i.e. satisfy God." The word is usually put for "determination."

Him ; to the end that ye be not quickly shaken from your mind."

When the Resurrection will be, he has not said, but that it will not be now, he has said. "And our gathering together unto Him." This also is no little matter. See how the exhortation also is again accompanied with commendation and encouragement, in that He and all the Saints will certainly appear with us. Here he is discoursing concerning the resurrection and our gathering together. For these things will happen at the same time. He raises up their minds. "That ye be not quickly shaken," he says, "nor yet be troubled, either by spirit, or by word, or by epistle as from us, as that the day of the Lord is now present."

Here he seems to me to intimate that certain persons went about having forged an Epistle, as if from Paul, and showing this, said that the Day of the Lord is at hand, that thence they might lead many into error. Therefore that they might not be deceived, Paul gives security by the things he writes, and says, " be not troubled, either by spirit, or by word": and this is the meaning of what he says: Though any one having the spirit of prophecy should say this, believe it not. For when I was with you I told you these things, so that you ought not to change your persuasion from the things which you were taught. Or thus, " by spirit ": so he calls the false prophets, speaking what they spoke by an unclean spirit. For these men, willing the more to be believed, not only endeavored to deceive by persuasive words, (for this he shows, saying, " or by word,") but they also showed a forged letter, as from Paul, declaring the same thing. Wherefore pointing out this also, he has added, " or by letter as from us." Having therefore secured them on every side, he thus sets forth his own doctrine, and says :[1]

Ver. 3, 4. " Let no man beguile you in any wise : for it will not be, except the falling away come first, and the man of sin be revealed, the son of perdition, he that opposeth and exalteth himself against all that is called God or that is worshiped ; so that he sitteth in the temple of God, setting himself forth as God."

Here he discourses concerning the Antichrist, and reveals great mysteries. What is " the falling away "?[2] He calls him Apostasy, as being about to destroy many, and make them fall away. So that if it were possible, He says, the very Elect should be offended. (From Matt. xxiv. 24.) And he calls him " the man of sin." For he shall do numberless mischiefs, and shall

cause others to do them. But he calls him " the son of perdition," because he is also to be destroyed. But who is he? Is it then Satan? By no means ; but some man, that admits his fully working in him. For he is a man. " And exalteth himself against all that is called God or is worshiped." For he will not introduce idolatry, but will be a kind of opponent to God ; he will abolish all the gods, and will order men to worship him instead of God, and he will be seated in the temple of God, not that in Jerusalem only, but also in every Church. " Setting himself forth," he says ; he does not say, saying it, but endeavoring to show it. For he will perform great works, and will show wonderful signs.

Ver. 5. " Remember ye not, that when I was yet with you, I told you these things?"

Seest thou that it is necessary continually to say the same things, and to enlarge upon them in the same words? For behold, they heard him saying these things when present, and again they had need to be reminded of them. For as when they had heard concerning afflictions, " For verily," he says, " when we were with you, we told you beforehand that we are to suffer affliction " (1 Thess. iii. 4) ; they nevertheless forgot it, and he confirms them again by letters ; so also having heard concerning the Coming of Christ, they again needed letters to compose them. He therefore reminds them, showing that he speaks of nothing strange, but what he had always said.

For as in the case of husbandmen, the seeds are indeed cast into the earth once for all, yet do not constantly remain, but require much preparation withal, and if they do not break up the earth, and cover over the seeds sown, they sow for the birds that gather grain ; so we also, unless by constant remembrance we cover over what has been sown, have but cast it all into the air. For both the devil carries it away, and our sloth destroys it, and the sun dries it up, and the rain washes it away, and the thorns choke it : so that it is not sufficient after once sowing it to depart, but there is need of much assidulity, driving off the birds, rooting up the thorns, filling up the stony ground with much earth, checking, and fencing off, and taking away everything injurious. But in the case of the earth all depends upon the husbandman, for it is a lifeless subject, and prepared only to be passive. But in the spiritual soil it is quite otherwise. All is not the teachers' part, but half at least, if not more, that of the disciples. It is our part indeed to cast the seed, but yours to do the things spoken for your recollection, by your works to show the fruits, to pull up the thorns by the roots.

For wealth truly is a thorn, bearing no fruit, both uncomely to the sight, and unpleasant for

---

[1] [The paragraph that here ends is wanting in a group of documents which for this epistle is very generally correct. The contents of this paragraph give no decisive indication as to genuineness. — J. A. B.]

[2] [The Greek word translated " falling away " is that which we borrow as apostasy. — J. A. B.]

use, injuring those that meddle with it, not only not itself bearing fruit, but even hindering that which was shooting forth. Such is wealth. It not only does not bear eternal fruit, but it even hinders those who wish to gain it. Thorns are the food of irrational camels; they are devoured and consumed by fire, being useful for nothing. Such also is wealth, useful for nothing, but to kindle the furnace, to light up The Day that burns as an oven, to nourish passions void of reason, revenge and anger. For such is also the camel that feeds on thorns. For it is said by those who are acquainted with such things, that there is no animal so implacable, so sulky and revengeful, as a camel. Such is wealth. It nourishes the unreasonable passions of the soul, but it pierces and wounds the rational, as is the case with thorns. This plant is hard and rough, and grows up of itself.

Let us see how it grows up, that we may root it out. It grows in places that are precipitous, stony and dry, where there is no moisture. When therefore any one is rough and precipitous, that is unmerciful, the thorn grows in him. But when the sons of husbandmen wish to root them up, they do it not with iron. How then? Having set fire to it, they in that way extract all the bad quality of the land. For since it is not enough to cut away the upper part, whilst the root remains below, nor even to extirpate the root, (for it remains in the earth from its bad quality, and, as when some pestilence has assailed the body, there are still left the remains of it,) the fire from above, drawing up all that moisture of the thorns,[1] like some poison, extracts it by means of the heat from the bowels of the earth. For as the cupping glass placed upon the part draws all the disorder to itself, so also the fire draws off all the base quality that was in the thorns, and makes the land pure.

On what account then do I say these things? Because it behoves you to purge off all affection for riches. With us also there is a fire that draws this bad quality from the soul; I mean that of the Spirit. This if we let work on them, we shall be able not only to dry up the thorns, but also the humor from them, since if they be deeply fixed, all is rendered vain. For mark, Has a rich man entered here, or also a rich woman? She does not regard how she shall hear the oracles of God, but how she shall make a show, how she shall sit with pomp, how with much glory, how she shall surpass all other women in the costliness of her garments, and render herself more dignified both by her dress, and look, and gait. And all her care and concern is, Did such a woman see

me? did she admire me? Is my beauty handsomely set off? so that her garments may not rot, nor be rent; and about this is all her care. In like manner also the rich man enters, meaning to exhibit himself to the poor man, and to strike him with awe by the garments which are about him, and by the number of his slaves, who also stand round, driving off the crowd. But he from his great pride does not condescend even to do this, but considers it a work so unworthy of a gentleman, that although excessively puffed up, he cannot bear to do it, but commits it to his slaves. For to do this requires truly servile and impudent manners. Then when he is seated, the cares of his house immediately intrude themselves, distracting him on every side. The pride that possesses his soul overflows. He thinks that he does a favor both to us, and to the people, and perhaps even to God, because he has entered into the house of God. But he who is thus inflamed, how shall he ever be cured?

Tell me then, if any one should go to the shop of a physician, and not ask a favor of the physician, but think that he was doing him a favor, and declining to request a medicine for his wound, should concern himself about his garments; would he go away having received any benefit? I think not indeed. But, with your leave, I will tell you the cause of all these things. They think when they enter in here, that they enter into our presence, they think that what they hear they hear from us. They do not lay to heart, they do not consider, that they are entering into the presence of God, that it is He who addresses them. For when the Reader standing up says, "Thus saith the Lord," and the Deacon stands and imposes silence on all, he does not say this as doing honor to the Reader, but to Him who speaks to all through him. If they knew that it was God who through His prophet speaks these things, they would cast away all their pride. For if when rulers are addressing them, they do not allow their minds to wander, much less should they, when God is speaking. We are ministers, beloved. We speak not our own things, but the things of God, letters coming from heaven are every day read.

Tell me then, I beseech you, if now, when we are all present, some one entered, having a golden girdle, and drawing himself up, and with an air of consequence said that he was sent by the king that is on the earth, and that he brought letters to the whole city concerning matters of importance; would you not then be all turned towards him? Would you not, without any command from a deacon, observe a profound silence? Truly I think so. For I have often heard letters from kings read here. Then if any one comes from a king, you all attend; and does a Prophet come from God, and speak from heaven, and

---

[1] So Virgil: —
　　　　" Sive illis omne per ignem
Excoquitur vitium atque exudat inutilis humor."—Georg. i. 87, 88.

no one attend? Or do you not believe that these things are messages from God? These are letters sent from God; therefore let us enter with becoming reverence into the Churches, and let us hearken with fear to the things here said.

What do I come in for, you say, if I do not hear some one discoursing? This is the ruin and destruction of all. For what need of a person to discourse? This necessity arises from our sloth. Wherefore any necessity for a homily? All things are clear and open that are in the divine Scriptures; the necessary things are all plain. But because ye are hearers for pleasure's sake, for that reason also you seek these things. For tell me, with what pomp of words did Paul speak? and yet he converted the world. Or with what the unlettered Peter? But I know not, you say, the things that are contained in the Scriptures. Why? For are they spoken in Hebrew? Are they in Latin, or in foreign tongues? Are they not in Greek? But they are expressed obscurely, you say: What is it that is obscure? Tell me. Are there not histories? For (of course) you know the plain parts, in that you enquire about the obscure. There are numberless histories in the Scriptures. Tell me one of these. But you cannot. These things are an excuse, and mere words. Every day, you say, one hears the same things. Tell me, then, do you not hear the same things in the theaters? Do you not see the same things in the race-course? Are not all things the same? Is it not always the same sun that rises? Is it not the same food that we use? I should like to ask you, since you say that you every day hear the same things; tell me, from what Prophet was the passage that was read? from what Apostle, or what Epistle? But you cannot tell me — you seem to hear strange things. When therefore you wish to be slothful, you say that they are the same things. But when you are questioned, you are in the case of one who never heard them. If they are the same, you ought to know them. But you are ignorant of them.

This state of things is worthy of lamentation — of lamentation and complaint: for the coiner coineth but in vain.[1] For this you ought more especially to attend, because they are the same things, because we give you no labor, nor speak things that are strange or variable. What then, since you say, that those are the same things, but our discourses are not the same things, but we always speak things that are new to you, do you pay heed to these? By no means. But if we say, Why do you not retain even these? "We hear them but once," you say, "and how can we retain them?" If we say, Why do ye not attend to those other things? "The same things," you say, "are always said" — and every way these are words of sloth and excuse. But they will not always serve, but there will be a time when we shall lament in vain and without effect. Which may God forbid, and grant that having repented here, and attending with understanding and godly fear to the things spoken, we may both be urged on to the due performance of good works, and may amend our own lives with all diligence, that we may be able to obtain the blessings promised to those who love Him, by the grace and lovingkindness, &c.

HOMILY IV.

2 THESSALONIANS ii. 6–9.

"And now ye know that which restraineth, to the end that he may be revealed in his own season. For the mystery of lawlessness doth already work: only there is one that restraineth now, until he be taken out of the way. And then shall be revealed the lawless one, whom the Lord Jesus shall slay with the breath of His mouth, and bring to nought by the manifestation of His coming: even he whose coming is according to the working of Satan."

ONE may naturally enquire, what is that which withholdeth, and after that would know, why Paul expresses it so obscurely. What then is it that withholdeth, that is, hindereth him from being revealed? Some indeed say, the grace of the Spirit, but others the Roman empire, to whom I most of all accede. Wherefore? Because if he meant to say the Spirit, he would not have spoken obscurely, but plainly, that even now the grace of the Spirit, that is the gifts, withhold him. And otherwise he ought now to have come, if he was about to come when the gifts ceased; for they have long since ceased. But because he said this of the Roman empire, he naturally glanced at it, and speaks covertly and darkly. For he did not wish to bring upon himself superfluous enmities, and useless dangers. For if he had said that after a little while

---

[1] ὅτι εἰς κενὸν ἀργυροκόπος ἀργυροκοπεῖ. [Perhaps, rather, "the hammerer (of silver) hammereth upon nothing." — J. A. B.]

the Roman empire would be dissolved, they would immediately have even overwhelmed him, as a pestilent person, and all the faithful, as living and warring to this end. And he did not say that it will be quickly, although he is always saying it — but what? "that he may be revealed in his own season," he says,

"For the mystery of lawlessness doth already work." He speaks here of Nero, as if he were the type of Antichrist. For he too wished to be thought a god. And he has well said, "the mystery"; that is, it worketh not openly, as the other, nor without shame. For if there was found a man before that time, he means, who was not much behind Antichrist in wickedness, what wonder, if there shall now be one? But he did not also wish to point him out plainly: and this not from cowardice, but instructing us not to bring upon ourselves unnecessary enmities, when there is nothing to call for it. So indeed he also says here. "Only there is one that restraineth now, until he be taken out of the way," that is, when the Roman empire is taken out of the way, then he shall come. And naturally. For as long as the fear of this empire lasts, no one will willingly exalt himself, but when that is dissolved, he will attack the anarchy, and endeavor to seize upon the government both of man and of God. For as the kingdoms before this were destroyed, for example, that of the Medes by the Babylonians, that of the Babylonians by the Persians, that of the Persians by the Macedonians, that of the Macedonians by the Romans: so will this also be by the Antichrist, and he by Christ, and it will no longer withhold. And these things Daniel delivered to us with great clearness.

"And then," he says, "shall be revealed the lawless one." And what after this? The consolation is at hand. "Whom the Lord Jesus shall slay with the breath of His mouth, and bring to nought by the manifestation of His coming, even he whose coming is according to the working of Satan."

For as fire merely coming on even before its arrival makes torpid and consumes the little animals that are afar off; so also Christ, by His commandment only, and Coming. It is enough for Him to be present, and all these things are destroyed. He will put a stop to the deceit, by only appearing. Then who is this, whose coming is after the working of Satan, "With all power," he says, "and signs and lying wonders." These things he foretold, that the men of that time might not be deceived. That is, he will display all power, but nothing true, but for deceit. "And lying wonders," he says, that is, false, or leading to falsehood.

Ver. 10. "And with all deceit of unrighteousness for them that are perishing."

Why then, you say, did God permit this to be? and what dispensation is this? And what is the advantage of his coming, if it takes place for the ruin of our race? Fear not, beloved, but hear Him saying, "In them that are perishing," he hath strength, who, even if he had not come, would not have believed. What then is the advantage? That these very men who are perishing will be put to silence. How? Because both if he had come, and if he had not come, they would not have believed in Christ; He comes therefore to convict them. For that they may not have occasion to say, that since Christ said that He was God, — although He nowhere said this openly, — but since those who came after proclaimed it, we have not believed. Because we have heard that there is One God from whom are all things, therefore we have not believed. This their pretext then Antichrist will take away. For when he comes, and comes commanding nothing good, but all things unlawful, and is yet believed from false signs alone, he will stop their mouths. For if thou believest not in Christ, much more oughtest thou not to believe in Antichrist. For the former said that He was sent from the Father, but the latter the contrary. For this reason Christ said, "I am come in My Father's name, and ye receive Me not: if another shall come in his own name, him ye will receive." (John v. 43.) But we have seen signs, you say. But many and great signs were also wrought in the case of Christ; much more therefore ought ye to have believed in Him. And yet many things were predicted concerning this one, that he is the lawless one, that he is the son of perdition, that his coming is after the working of Satan. But the contrary concerning the other, that He is the Saviour, that He brings with Him unnumbered blessings.

Ver. 10, 11, 12. "For because they received not the love of the truth, that they might be saved; for this cause God will send them a working of error, that they should believe a lie: that they all might be judged who believed not the truth, but had pleasure in unrighteousness."

"That they might be judged." He does not say, that they might be punished; for even before this they were about to be punished; but "that they might be condemned," that is, at the dreadful Seat of Judgment, in order that they might be without excuse. "Who believed not the truth, but had pleasure in unrighteousness." He calls Christ, "the Love of the Truth." "For because," says he, "they received not the love of the truth." For He was both, and came for the sake of both, both as loving men, and on behalf of things that were true.[1]

"But had pleasure," he says, "in unrighteous-

---

[1] Compare John xviii. 37.

ness." For he came to the destruction of men, and to injure them. For what will he not then work? He will change and confound all things, both by his commandments, and by the fear of him. He will be terrible in every way, from his power, from his cruelty, from his unlawful commandments.

But fear not. "In those that perish" he will have his strength.[1] For Elijah too will then come to give confidence to the faithful, and this Christ says; "Elijah cometh, and shall restore all things." (Matt. xvii. 11.) Therefore it is said, "In the spirit and power of Elijah." (Luke i. 17.) For he neither wrought signs nor wonders, as Elijah did. For "John," it is said, "did no miracle, but all things which John spake of this Man were true." How then was it "in the spirit and power of Elijah"? That is, he will take upon him the same ministry. As the one was the forerunner of His first Coming, so will the other be of His second and glorious Coming, and for this he is reserved. Let us not therefore fear. He has calmed the minds of the hearers. He causes them no longer to think present things dreadful, but worthy of thankfulness. Wherefore he has added,

Ver. 13. "But we are bound to give thanks alway to God for you, brethren beloved of the Lord, for that God chose you from the beginning unto salvation, in sanctification of the Spirit and belief of the truth."

How unto salvation? By sanctifying you through the Spirit. For these are the things that are the efficient causes[2] of our salvation. It is nowhere of works, nowhere of righteous deeds, but through belief of the truth. Here again, "in" is used for "through." "And through sanctification of the Spirit," he says,

Ver. 14. "Whereunto He called you through our Gospel, to the obtaining of the glory of our Lord Jesus Christ."

This too is no little thing, if Christ considers our salvation His glory. For it is the glory of the Friend of man that they that are saved should be many. Great then is our Lord, if the Holy Spirit so desires our salvation. Why did he not say faith first? Because even after sanctification we have yet need of much faith, that we may not be shaken. Seest thou how He shows that nothing is of themselves, but all of God?

Ver. 15. "So then, brethren, stand fast, and hold the traditions which ye were taught, whether by word, or by Epistle of ours."

Hence it is manifest, that they did not deliver all things by Epistle, but many things also unwritten, and in like manner both the one and the other are worthy of credit. Therefore let us think the tradition of the Church also worthy of credit. It is a tradition, seek no farther. Here he shows that there were many who were shaken.

Ver. 16, 17. "Now our Lord Jesus Christ Himself, and God our Father, which loved us, and gave us eternal comfort and good hope through grace, comfort your hearts, and stablish them in every good work and word."

Again a prayer after an admonition. For this is truly to benefit. "Which loved us," he says, "and gave us eternal comfort and good hope through grace." Where now are those who lessen the Son, because He is named in the grace of the Laver after the Father? For, lo, here it is the contrary. "Which loved us," he says, "and gave us eternal comfort." Of what sort then is this? Even the hope of things future. Seest thou how by the method of prayer he stirs up their mind, giving them the unspeakable care of God for pledges and signs. "Comfort your heart," he says, "in every good work and word," that is, through every good work and word. For this is the comfort of Christians, to do something good and pleasing to God. See how he brings down their spirit. "Which gave us comfort," he says, "and good hope through grace." At the same time he makes them also full of good hopes with respect to future things. For if He has given so many things by grace, much more things future. I indeed, he says, have spoken, but the whole is of God. "Stablish"; confirm you, that you be not shaken, nor turned aside. For this is both His work and ours, so that it is in the way both of doctrines, and of actions. For this is comfort, to be stablished. For when any one is not turned aside, he bears all things, whatever may happen to him, with much longsuffering; whereas if his mind be shaken, he will no longer perform any good or noble action, but like one whose hands are paralyzed, so also his soul is shaken, when it is not fully persuaded that it is advancing to some good end.

Chap. iii. 1. "Finally, brethren, pray for us, that the word of the Lord may run and be glorified, even as also it is with you."

He indeed had prayed for them, that they might be stablished; and now he asks of them, entreating them to pray for him, not that he may not incur danger, for to this he was appointed, but that "the word of the Lord may run and be glorified, even as also it is with you." And the request is accompanied with commendation. "Even as also it is with you."

Ver. 2. "And that we may be delivered from unreasonable and evil men; for all have not faith."

This is the manner of one showing also his dangers; as to which especially he besought

---

[1] He seems only to refer to the words of ver. 10, with the general sense of the context.
[2] τὰ συνεκτικὰ; lit. "the things that keep together."

them. "From unreasonable and evil men," he says, "for all have not faith." Thus he is speaking of those who contradict the Preaching, who oppose and contend against the doctrines. For this he has intimated by saying, "For all men have not faith." And here he seems to me not to glance at dangers, but at the men who contradicted and hindered his word, as did Alexander the copper-smith. For he says, "he greatly withstood our words." (2 Tim. iv. 15.) That is, there are some to whom it is given. As if he were speaking of a paternal inheritance, that "it is not for all to serve in the Palace." And at the same time he also excites them, as already having such ground of confidence as to be able both to deliver their Teacher from dangers, and to facilitate his preaching.

Therefore we also say the same things. Let no one condemn us of arrogance, nor from an excessive humility deprive us of so great an assistance. For neither do we speak from the same motive from which Paul spoke. For he indeed said these things from a wish to comfort his disciples; but we to reap some great and good fruit. And we are very confident, if ye all be willing with one mind to stretch forth your hands to God in behalf of our littleness, that you will succeed in all things. Thus let us make war with our enemies with prayers and supplications. For if thus the ancients made war with men in arms, much more ought we so to make war with men without arms. So Hezekiah triumphed over the Assyrian king, so Moses over Amalek, so Samuel over the men of Ascalon, so Israel[1] over the thirty-two kings. If where there was need of arms, and of battle array, and of fighting, they, leaving their arms, had recourse to prayer; here where the matter has to be accomplished by prayers alone, does it not much more behove us to pray?

But there, you say, the rulers entreated for the people, but you request the people to entreat for the ruler. I also know it. For those under rule at that time were wretched and mean persons. Wherefore they were saved by the claims and the virtue of their commander alone; but now, when the grace of God has prevailed, and we shall find among those who are ruled many or rather the greater part excelling their ruler in a great degree; do not deprive us of this succor, raise up our hands that they may not be faint, open our mouth for us, that it may not be closed. Entreat God — for this cause entreat Him. It is in our behalf indeed that it is done, but it is wholly for your sakes. For we are appointed for your advantage, and for your interests we are concerned. Entreat every one of you, both privately and publicly. Mark

Paul saying, "That for the gift bestowed upon us by means of many, thanks may be given by many persons on our behalf" (2 Cor. i. 11); that is, that He may give grace to many. If in the case of men, the people coming forward ask a pardon for persons condemned and led away to execution, and the king from regard to the multitude revokes the sentence, much more will God be influenced by regard to you, not by your multitude, but your virtue.

For violent is the enemy we have. For each of you indeed anxiously thinks of his own interests, but we the concerns of all together. We stand in the part of the battle that is pressed on. The devil is more violently armed against us. For in wars too, he that is on the opposite side endeavors before all others to overthrow the general. For this reason all his fellow-combatants hasten there. For this reason there is much tumult, every one endeavoring to rescue him; they surround him with their shields, wishing to preserve his person. Hear what all the people say to David. (I say not this, as comparing myself to David, I am not so mad, but because I wish to show the affection of the people for their ruler.) "Thou shalt go no more out with us to battle," they say, "that thou quench not the lamp of Israel." (2 Sam. xxi. 17.) See how anxious they were to spare the old man. I am greatly in need of your prayers. Let no one, as I have said, from an excessive humility deprive me of this alliance and succor. If our part be well approved, your own also will be more honorable. If our teaching flow abundantly, the riches will redound to you. Hear the prophet saying, "Do the shepherds feed themselves?" (From Ezek. xxxiv. 2, Sept.)

Do you observe Paul constantly seeking these prayers? Do you hear that thus Peter was delivered from prison, when fervent prayer was made for him? (Acts xii. 5.) I verily believe that your prayer will have great effect, offered with so great unanimity. Do you not think that it is a matter much too great for my littleness to draw nigh to God, and entreat Him for so numerous a people? For if I have not confidence to pray for myself, much less for others. For it belongs to men of high estimation, to beseech God to be merciful to others; it is for those who have rendered Him favorable to themselves. But he who is himself an offender, how shall he entreat for another? But nevertheless, because I embrace you with a father's heart, because love dares everything, not only in the Church, but in the house also, I make my prayer above all other things for your health both in soul and in body. For there is no other prayer so becoming to a Priest, as to draw nigh to God and entreat Him for the good of the people, before his own. For if Job rising up

---

[1] [Field reads "Joshua," after one MS., but the correction is too obvious. — J. A. B.]

immediately made so many offerings for his children in the flesh, how much more ought we to do this for our spiritual children?

Why do I say these things? Because if we, who are so far removed from the greatness of the work, offer supplications and prayers for you, much more is it just that you should do it. For that one should entreat for many, is exceedingly bold, and requires much confidence: but that many having met together should offer supplication for one, is nothing burdensome. For every one does this not trusting to his own virtue, but to the multitude, and to their unanimity, to which God everywhere has much respect. For He says, "where two or three are gathered together in My Name, there am I in the midst of them." (Matt. xx. 18.) If where two or three are gathered together, He is in the midst, much more is He among you. For that which a man praying by himself is not able to receive, that he shall receive praying with a multitude. Why? Because although his own virtue has not, yet the common consent has much power.

"Where two or three," it is said, "are gathered together." Why didst thou say, "Two"? For if there be one in Thy Name, why art Thou not there? Because I wish all to be together, and not to be separated. Let us therefore close up together; let us bind one another together in love, let no one separate us. If any one accuses, or is offended, let him not retain it in his mind, whether against his neighbor, or against us. This favor I ask of you, to come to us, and bring the accusation, and receive our defense. "Reprove him," it says, "lest haply he hath not said it. Reprove him, lest haply he hath not done it" (Ecclus. xix. 14, 15); and if he hath done it, that he add not thereto. For we have either defended ourselves, or being condemned have asked pardon, and henceforth endeavor not to fall into the same faults. This is expedient both for you and for us. For you indeed having accused us perhaps without reason, when you have learned the truth of the matter, will stand corrected, and we have offended unawares and are corrected. For you indeed it is not expedient.[1] For punishment is appointed for those who utter any idle word. But we put off accusations, whether false or true. The false, by showing that they are false; the true, by not again doing the same things. For it must needs happen that he who has the care of so many things should be ignorant, and through ignorance commit errors. For if every one of you having a house, and presiding over wife and children, and slaves, one more and another

fewer, among souls that are so easily numbered, is nevertheless compelled to commit many errors involuntarily, or from ignorance, or when wishing to set something right; much more must it be so with us who preside over so many people.

And may God still multiply you and bless you, the little with the great! For although the care becomes greater from the increase of numbers, we do not cease praying that this our care may be increased, and that this number may be added to, and be many times as great and without limit. For fathers, although often harassed by the number of their children, nevertheless do not wish to lose any one. All things are equal between us and you, even the very chief of our blessings. I do not partake of the holy Table with greater abundance, and you with less, but both equally participate of the same. And if I take it first, it is no great privilege, since even among children, the elder first extends his hand to the feast, but nevertheless no advantage is gained thereby. But with us all things are equal. The saving life that sustains our souls is given with equal honor to both. I do not indeed partake of one Lamb[2] and you of another, but we partake of the same. We both have the same Baptism. We have been vouchsafed the same Spirit. We are both hastening to the same kingdom. We are alike brethren of Christ, we have all things in common.

Where then is my advantage? In cares, in labors, in anxieties, in grieving for you. But nothing is sweeter than this grief, since even a mother grieving for her child is delighted with her grief, she thinks carefully of those whom she has brought forth, she is delighted at her cares. And yet care in itself is bitter, but when it is for children, at least it has in it much pleasure. Many of you have I begotten, but after this are my pangs. For in the case of mothers in the flesh the pangs are first, and then the birth. But here the pangs last till the latest breath, lest there should be anywhere some abortion even after the birth. And I indeed have a further longing; for although perchance another has begotten you, yet I nevertheless am harassed with cares. For we do not of ourselves beget you, but it is all of the grace of God. But if we both through the Spirit beget, he will not err who calls those begotten by me, his children, and those begotten by him, mine. All these things then consider, and stretch forth your hand, that you may be our boast and we yours, in the day of our Lord Jesus Christ, which God grant that we may all see with confidence, through Jesus Christ our Lord, with whom, &c.

---

[1] [Something must be supplied, most probably "to accuse without reason," as suggested by the foregoing. — J. A. B.]

[2] προβάτου, sheep in general, but he seems to have the Passover in mind.

HOMILY V.

2 Thessalonians iii. 3–5.

"But the Lord is faithful, who shall stablish you, and guard you from the evil one. And we have confidence in the Lord touching you, that ye both do and will do the things which we command you. And the Lord direct your hearts into the love of God, and into the patience of Christ."

NEITHER ought we, having committed everything to the prayers of the Saints, to be idle ourselves, and run into wickedness, and to lay hold of nothing; nor again when working good to despise that succor. For great indeed are the things which prayer for us can effect, but it is when we ourselves also work. For this reason Paul also, praying for them, and again giving them assurance from the promise, says, "But the Lord is faithful, who shall stablish you, and guard you from the evil one." For if He has chosen you to salvation, He does not deceive you, nor suffer you utterly to perish. But that he may not by these means lead them to sloth, and lest they thinking the whole to be of God should themselves sleep, see how he also demands coöperation from them, saying, "And we have confidence in the Lord touching you, that ye both do and will do the things which we command you." "The Lord" indeed, he says, "is faithful," and having promised to save will certainly save; but as He promised. And how did He promise? If we be willing, and hear Him; not simply (hearing), nor like stocks and stones, being inactive.

And he has well introduced the words, "We have confidence in the Lord," that is, we trust to His lovingkindness. Again he brings them down, making everything depend thereupon. For if he had said, We have confidence in you, the commendation indeed was great, but it would not have taught them to make all things dependent upon God. And if he had said, We have confidence in the Lord, that He will preserve you, and had not added "as touching you," and, "that ye do and will do the things which we command you," he would have made them more slothful, by casting everything upon the power of God. For it becomes us indeed to cast everything upon Him, yet working also ourselves, embarked in the labors and the conflicts. And he shows that even if our virtue alone were sufficient to save, yet nevertheless it ought to be persevering, and to abide with us until we come to our latest breath.

"But the Lord," he says, "direct your hearts into the love of God, and the patience of Christ."

Again he commends them, and prays, showing his concern for them. For when he is about to enter upon reproof, he previously smooths down their minds, by saying, "I am confident that ye will hear," and by requesting prayers from them, and by again invoking upon them infinite blessings.

"But the Lord," he says, "direct your hearts into the love of God." For there are many things that turn us aside from love, and there are many paths that draw us away from thence. In the first place the path of Mammon, laying, as it were, certain shameless hands upon our soul, and tenaciously holding it in its grasp, draws and drags us thence even against our will. Then vainglory, and often afflictions and temptations, turn us aside. For this reason we need, as a certain wind, the assistance of God, that our sail may be impelled, as by some strong wind, to the love of God. For tell me not, "I love Him, even more than myself." These are words. Show it to me by thy works, if thou lovest Him more than thyself. Love Him more than money, and then I shall believe that thou lovest Him even more than thyself. But thou who despisest not riches for the sake of God, how wilt thou despise thyself? But why do I say riches? Thou who despisest not covetousness, which thou oughtest to do even without the commandments of God, how wilt thou despise thyself?

"And into the patience of Christ," he says. What is "into the patience"? That we should endure even as He endured, or that we should do those things, or that with patience also we should wait for Him, that is, that we should be prepared. For since He has promised many things, and Himself is coming to judge the quick and the dead, let us wait for Him, and let us be patient. But wherever he speaks of patience, he of course implies affliction. For this is to love God; to endure, and not to be troubled.

Ver. 6. "Now we command you, brethren, in the name of our Lord Jesus Christ, that ye withdraw yourselves from every brother that walketh disorderly, and not after the tradition which they received of us."

That is, it is not we that say these things, but Christ, for that is the meaning of "in the name of our Lord Jesus Christ"; equivalent to "through Christ." Showing the fearfulness of the message, he says, through Christ. Christ therefore commanded us in no case to be idle. "That ye withdraw yourselves," he says, "from every brother." Tell me not of the rich, tell me not of the poor, tell me not of the holy. This is disorder. "That walketh," he says, that is, liveth. "And not after the tradition which they received from me." Tradition, he says, which is through works. And this he always calls properly[1] tradition.

Ver. 7, 8. "For yourselves know how ye ought to imitate us: for we behaved not ourselves disorderly among you; neither did we eat bread for nought at any man's hand."

And yet even if they had eaten, it would not have been for nought. "For the laborer," he says, "is worthy of his hire." (Luke x. 7.) "But in labor and travail, working night and day, that we might not burden any of you. Not because we have not the right, but to make ourselves an ensample unto you that ye should imitate us. For even when we were with you, this we commanded you, If any will not work, neither let him eat."

See how in the former Epistle indeed he discourses somewhat more mildly concerning these things; as when he says, "We beseech you, brethren, — that ye would abound more and more — and that ye study" (1 Thess. iv. 1–11) — and nowhere does he say, "we command," nor "in the Name of our Lord Jesus Christ," which was fearful and implied danger, but that "ye abound," he says, and "study," which are the words of one exhorting to virtue; "that ye may walk honestly" (becomingly), he says. (1 Thess. iv. 12.) But here is nothing of this kind, but "if any one will not work," says he, "neither let him eat." For if Paul, not being under a necessity, and having a right to be idle, and having undertaken so great a work, did nevertheless work, and not merely work, but "night and day," so that he was able even to assist others, — much more ought others to do this.

Ver. 11. "For we hear of some that walk among you disorderly, that work not at all, but are busybodies."

This indeed he says here; but there, in the first Epistle, he says, "that ye may walk honestly towards them that are without." On what account? Perhaps there was as yet no such thing. For upon another occasion also admonishing, he says, "It is more blessed to give than to receive." (Acts xx. 35.) But the expression, "walk honestly," has no reference to disorder; wherefore he added, "that ye may have need of nothing." (1 Thess. iv. 12.) And here he sets down another necessity, for thus doing what was honorable and good towards all. (For

as he proceeds, he says, "be not weary in well doing.") For certainly he that is idle and yet able to work must needs be a busybody. But alms are given to those only who are not able to support themselves by the work of their own hands, or who teach, and are wholly occupied in the business of teaching. "For thou shalt not muzzle the ox," he says, "when he treadeth out the corn." (Deut. xxv. 4.) "And the laborer is worthy of his hire." (1 Tim. v. 18, and Luke x. 7.) So that neither is he idle, but receives the reward of work, and great work too. But to pray and fast, being idle,[2] is not the work of the hands. For the work that he is here speaking of is the work of the hands. And that you may not suspect any such thing, he has added,

"That work not at all, but are busybodies. Now them that are such we command and exhort through our Lord Jesus Christ."

Because he had touched them severely, wishing to render his discourse more mild, he adds, "through the Lord," again what is authoritative and fearful.

"That with quietness," he says, "they work, and eat their own bread."

For why has he not said, But if they are not disorderly, let them be maintained by you; but requires both, that they be quiet, and that they work? "That they may eat their own bread," says he, not that of another.

Ver. 13. "But ye, brethren, be not weary in well doing."

See how immediately the fatherly heart was overcome. He was not able to carry out his reproof farther, but again pitied them. And see with what discretion! He has not said, But pardon them, until they are amended; but what? "But ye, be not weary in well doing." Withdraw yourselves, he says, from them, and reprove them; do not, however, suffer them to perish with hunger. What then, he says, if having abundance from us, he should remain idle? In that case, he says, I have spoken of a mild remedy, that you withdraw yourselves from him, that is, do not partake with him in free conversation; show that you are angry. This is no little matter. For such is the reproof that is given to a brother, if we wish really to amend him. We are not ignorant of the methods of reproof. For tell me, if you had a brother in the flesh, would you then overlook him pining with hunger? Truly I think not; but perhaps you would even correct him.

Ver. 14. "And if any man obeyeth not our word by this Epistle."

He has not said, He that disobeys, disobeys

---

[1] Or "especially" (κυρίως).

[2] See on 1 Thess. iv. 12, where he says nearly the same. On 1 Tim. v. 10 he praises the Monks near Antioch, but it appears that they were industrious.

me, but "note that man." This is no slight chastisement. "Have no company with him." Then again he says, "that he may be ashamed." And he does not permit them to proceed farther. For as he had said, "if any does not work neither let him eat," fearing lest they should perish by hunger, he has added, "But in doing good, be not ye weary." Thus having said, "Withdraw yourselves, and have no company with him," then fearing lest this very thing might cut him off from the brotherhood — for he who gives himself up to despair, will quickly be lost if he is not admitted to freedom of conversation — he has added,

Ver. 15. "Yet count him not as an enemy, but admonish him as a brother."

By this he shows that he has assigned a heavy punishment against him, in depriving him of freedom of conversation.

For if to be a receiver even with many others is worthy of disgrace, when they even reprove whilst they offer it, and withdraw themselves, how great is the reproach, quite sufficient to sting the soul. For if only giving rather tardily, and with murmuring, they inflame the receivers — for tell me not of impudent beggars, but of the faithful — if they were to reprove whilst they give, what would they not do? to what punishment would it not be equal? We do not do so, but as if we had been greatly injured, we so insult and turn away from those who beg of us. Thou dost not give, but why dost thou also grieve him? "Admonish them," he says, "as brethren," do not insult them as enemies. He who admonishes his brother, does it not publicly. He does not make an open show of the insult, but he does it privately and with much address, and grieving, as hurt, and weeping and lamenting. Let us bestow therefore with the disposition of a brother, let us admonish with the good will of a brother, not as if we grieved at giving, but as if we grieved for his transgressing the commandment. Since what is the advantage? For if, even after giving, you insult, you destroy the pleasure of giving. But when you do not give and yet insult, what wrong do you not do to that wretched and unfortunate man? He came to you, to receive pity from you, but he goes away having received a deadly blow, and weeps the more. For when by reason of his poverty he is compelled to beg, and is insulted on account of his begging, think how great will be the punishment of those who insult him. "He that dishonoreth the poor," it says, "provoketh his Maker." (Prov. xiv. 12, 31, Sept.) For tell me, did He suffer him to be poor for thy sake, that thou mightest be able to heal thyself — and dost thou insult him who for thy sake is poor? What obstinacy is this! what an act of ingratitude is it! "Admonish him as a

brother," he says, and after having given, he orders you to admonish him. But if even without giving we insult him, what excuse shall we have?

Ver. 16. "Now the Lord of peace Himself give you peace at all times in all ways."

See how, when he mentions the things that are to be done, he sets his mark upon them by prayer, adding prayer and supplication, like certain marks set upon things that are laid up. "Give you peace," he says, "at all times, in all ways." For since it was likely that contentions would arise from these things, those men becoming exasperated, and the others not supplying such persons so readily as formerly, he with good reason now offered this prayer for them, saying, "Give you peace at all times." For this is what is sought, that they may ever have it. "In every way," says he. What is, "in every"? So that they may have no occasion of contention from any quarter. For everywhere peace is a good thing, even towards those who are without. For hear him elsewhere saying, "If it be possible, as much as in you lieth, be at peace with all men." (Rom. xii. 18.) For nothing is so conducive to the right performance of the things which we wish, as to be peaceable and undisturbed, and to be free from all hatred, and to have no enemy.

"The Lord be with you all."

Ver. 17, 18. "The salutation of me Paul with mine own hand, which is the token in every Epistle: so I write. The grace of our Lord Jesus Christ be with you all."

This he says that he writes in every Epistle, that no one may be able to counterfeit them, his subscription being subjoined as a great token. And he calls the prayer a salutation, showing that everything they then did was spiritual; even when it was proper to offer salutation, the thing was attended with advantage; and it was prayer, not merely a symbol of friendship. With this he began, and with it he ended, guarding with strong walls what he had said elsewhere, and laying safe foundations, he brought it also to a safe end. "Grace be unto you and peace," he says; and again, "The grace of our Lord Jesus Christ be with you all. Amen." This the Lord also promised, saying to His disciples, "Lo, I am with you alway, even unto the end of the world." (Matt. xxviii. 20.) But this takes place when we are willing. For He will not be altogether with us, if we place ourselves at a distance. "I will be with you," He says, "always." Let us not therefore drive away grace. He tells us to withdraw from every brother that walketh disorderly. This was then a great evil, to be separated from the whole body of the brethren. By this indeed he punishes all, as elsewhere in his Epistle to the

Corinthians he said, "With such a one no, not to eat." (1 Cor. v. 11.) But now the majority do not think this a great evil. But all things are confounded and corrupted. With adulterers, with fornicators, with covetous persons, we mix freely, and as a matter of course. If we ought to withdraw ourselves from one who was only supported in idleness, how much more from the others. And that you may know how fearful a thing it was to be separated from the company of the brethren, and what advantage it produces to those who receive reproof with a right mind, hear how that man, who was puffed up with sin, who had proceeded to the extreme of wickedness, who had committed such fornication as is not named even among the heathens, who was insensible of his wound — for this is the excess of perversion — he after all, though such an one, was so bent down and humbled, that Paul said, "Sufficient to such a one is this punishment which was inflicted by the many. Wherefore confirm your love toward him." (2 Cor. ii. 6, 8.) For as a member separated from the rest of the body, so was he at that time.

But the cause, and that from which this was then so terrible, was, because even the being with them was thought by them a great blessing. For like men who inhabit one house, and are under one father, and partake of one table, so did they then dwell in every Church. How great an evil therefore was it to fall from so great love! But now it is not even thought to be a great evil, because neither is it considered any great thing when we are united with one another. What was then in the order of punishment, this, on account of the great coldness of love, now takes place even apart from punishment, and we withdraw from one another causelessly, and from coldness. For it is the cause of all evils that there is no love. This has dissolved all ties, and has disfigured all that was venerable and splendid in the Church, in which we ought to have gloried.

Great is the confidence of the Teacher, when from his own good actions he is entitled to reprove his disciples. Wherefore also Paul said, "For yourselves know how ye ought to imitate us." (2 Thess. iii. 7.) And he ought to be a Teacher more of life than of the word. And let no one think that this is said from a spirit of boasting. For it was as reduced to necessity that he spoke it, and with a view to general advantage. "For we behaved not ourselves," he says, "disorderly among you." From this do you not see his humility, in that he calls it, "for nought," and "disorderly behavior"? "We did not behave ourselves disorderly among you," he says, "neither did we eat any man's bread for nought." Here he shows that perhaps also they were poor; and tell me not, that they

were poor. For he is discoursing concerning the poor, and those who obtained their necessary subsistence from no other source than from the work of their hands. For he has not said, that they may have it from their fathers, but that by working they should eat their own bread. For if I, he says, a herald of the word of doctrine, was afraid to burden you, much more he who does you no service. For this is truly a burden. And it is a burden too, when one does not give with much alacrity; but this is not what he hints at, but as if they were not able to do it easily. For why dost thou not work? For God hath given thee hands for this purpose, not that thou shouldest receive of others, but that thou shouldest impart to others.

But "the Lord," he says, "be with you." This prayer also we may offer for ourselves, if we do the things of the Lord. For hear Christ saying to His disciples, "Go ye and make disciples of all the nations, baptizing them into the Name of the Father, and of the Son, and of the Holy Ghost: teaching them to observe all things whatsoever I commanded you: and, lo, I am with you alway, even unto the end of the world." (Matt. xxviii. 19, 20.) If ye do these things, assuredly. For that the promise is not made to them only, but to those also who walk in their steps, is manifest from His saying "to the end of the world."

What then does He say to those who are not teachers? Each of you, if he will, is a teacher, although not of another, yet of himself. Teach thyself first. If thou teachest to observe all things whatsoever He commanded, even by this means thou wilt have many emulating thee. For as a lamp, when it is shining, is able to light ten thousand others, but being extinguished will not give light even to itself, nor can it lighten other lamps; so also in the case of a pure life, if the light that is in us be shining, we shall make both disciples and teachers numberless, being set before them as a pattern to copy. For neither will the words proceeding from me be able so to benefit the hearers, as your life. For let a man, tell me, be dear to God, and shining in virtue, and having a wife; (for it is possible for a man having a wife and children and servants and friends to please God;) will he not be able much more than I to benefit them all? For me they will hear once or twice in a month, or not even once, and even though they have kept what they have heard as far as the threshold of the Church, they presently let it drop away from them: but seeing the life of that man constantly, they receive great advantage. For when being insulted he insults not again, does he not almost infix and engrave upon the soul of the insulter the reverence of his meekness? And though he does not immediately confess the benefit, being ashamed from anger, or put to confusion, yet nevertheless he immediately is made sensible of it. And it is impossible for a man that is insolent, though he be a very beast, to associate with one who is patient of evil, without going away much benefited. For although we do not what is good, we however all praise it and admire it. Again, the wife, if she see her husband gentle, being always with him, receives great advantage, and the child also. It is therefore in the power of every one to be a teacher. For he says, "Build each other up, even as also ye do." (1 Thess. v. 11.) For tell me, has any loss befallen the family? The wife is disturbed, as being weaker, and more extravagant, and fond of ornament; the man if he be a philosopher, and a derider of loss, both consoles her, and persuades her to bear it with fortitude. Tell me, then, will he not benefit her much more than our words? For it is easy to talk, but to act, when we are reduced to the necessity, is in every way difficult. On this account human nature is wont rather to be regulated by deeds. And such is the superiority of virtue, that even a slave often benefits a whole family together with the master.

For not in vain, nor without reason, does Paul constantly command them to practice virtue, and to be obedient to their masters, not so much regarding the service of their masters, as that the word of God and the doctrine be not blasphemed. But when it is not blasphemed, it will soon also be admired. And I know of many families, that they have greatly benefited by the virtue of their slaves. But if a servant placed under authority can improve his master, much more can the master his servants. Divide then with me, I beseech you, this ministry. I address all generally, do you each individual privately, and let each charge himself with the salvation of his neighbors. For that it becomes one to preside over those of his household in these matters, hear where Paul sends women for instruction; "And if they would learn anything, let them ask their own husbands at home " (1 Cor. xiv. 35) ; and he does not lead them to the Teacher. For as in the schools of learning, there are teachers even among the disciples, so also in the Church. For he wishes the Teacher not to be troubled by all. Wherefore? Because then there will be great advantages, not only that the labor will be light to the Teacher, but that each of the disciples also, having taken pains, is soon able to become a teacher, making this his concern.

For see how great a service the wife contributes. She keeps the house, and takes care of all things in the house, she presides over her handmaids, she clothes them with her own hands, she causes thee to be called the father of chil-

dren, she delivers thee from brothels, she aids thee to live chastely, she puts a stop to the strong desire of nature. And do thou also benefit her. How? In spiritual things stretch forth thy hand. Whatever useful things thou hast heard, these, like the swallows, bearing off in thy mouth, carry away and place them in the mouth of the mother and the young ones. For how is it not absurd, in other things to think thyself worthy of the pre-eminence, and to occupy the place of the head, but in teaching to quit thy station. The ruler ought not to excel the ruled in honors, so much as in virtues. For this is the duty of a ruler, for the other is the part of the ruled, but this is the achievement of the ruler himself. If thou enjoyest much honor, it is nothing to thee, for thou receivedst it from others. If thou shinest in much virtue, this is all thine own.

Thou art the head of the woman, let then the head regulate the rest of the body. Dost thou not see that it is not so much above the rest of the body in situation, as in forethought, directing like a steersman the whole of it? For in the head are the eyes both of the body, and of the soul. Hence flows to them both the faculty of seeing, and the power of directing. And the rest of the body is appointed for service, but this is set to command. All the senses have thence their origin and their source. Thence are sent forth the organs of speech, the power of seeing, and of smelling, and all touch. For thence is derived the root of the nerves and of the bones. Seest thou not that it is superior in forethought more than in honor? So let us rule the women ; let us surpass them, not by seeking greater honor from them, but by their being more benefited by us.

I have shown that they afford us no little benefits, but if we are willing to make them a return in spiritual things, we surpass them. For it is not possible in bodily things to offer an equivalent. For what? dost thou contribute much wealth? but it is she who preserves it, and this care of hers is an equivalent, and thus there is need of her, because many, who had great possessions, have lost all because they had not one to take care of them. But as for the children, you both communicate, and the benefit from each is equal. She indeed in these things rather has the more laborious service, always bearing the offspring, and being afflicted with the pains of childbirth ; so that in spiritual things only wilt thou be able to surpass her.

Let us not therefore regard how we shall have wealth, but how we shall present with confidence to God the souls with which we are entrusted. For by regulating them we shall also most highly benefit ourselves. For he who teaches another, although he does nothing else, yet in speaking is affected with compunction, when he sees himself responsible for those things, on account of which he reproves others. Since therefore we benefit both ourselves and them, and through them the household, and this is preëminently pleasing to God ; let us not be weary of taking care both of our own souls, and of those who minister to us, that for all we may receive a recompense, and with much riches may arrive at the holy City our mother, the Jerusalem that is above, from which God grant that we may never fall, but that having shone in the most excellent course of life, we may be thought worthy with much confidence to see our Lord Jesus Christ ; with whom to the Father, together with the Holy Ghost, be glory, power, and honor, now and ever, and world without end. Amen.

THE HOMILIES OF ST. JOHN CHRYSOSTOM,

ARCHBISHOP OF CONSTANTINOPLE,

ON THE

EPISTLES OF ST. PAUL THE APOSTLE

TO

TIMOTHY, TITUS, AND PHILEMON.

The Oxford Translation Edited, with Additional Notes, by

REV. PHILIP SCHAFF, D.D., LL.D.

PREFACE.

THE remark of Photius, that St. Chrysostom's more finished works were those which he composed at Antioch, does not seem to afford a sufficient criterion for assigning a date to each set of Homilies. Tillemont appears to have been misled by it in the instance of those on the Epistles to Timothy, which he has on such grounds supposed to have been delivered at Constantinople. Montfaucon, however, alleges two reasons for placing them at Antioch.

1. That he speaks much of the Monks, as he used to do there, owing to the neighborhood of a large number of them, who lived in strict discipline and exemplary devotion. 2. That in speaking of Timothy's office as Bishop, he never says a word of being one himself. A third reason may be added, which is perhaps more conclusive than either of these. In Hom. viii. on 2 Tim. iii. he seems pretty evidently to allude to the burning of the Temple of Apollo at Daphne. One can hardly doubt the allusion, in reading the full account in the Homily on St. Babylas ; nor can it well be supposed that he would thus refer to it as a thing well known at any other place than Antioch.

The Homilies on the Epistle to Titus are fixed at Antioch by the mention of Daphne and the cave of Matrona in Hom. iii. (2). A passage in Hom. i. (4) seems to place him in a paternal relation to the people, as the plural *we* is constantly used by him for the singular. But the whole context seems rather to allude to another as Bishop, and he must be understood to speak as one of a body of clergy, in which in fact he held the second place.

Those on the Epistle to Philemon cannot easily be assigned to any particular date. The promise he mentions in the last Homily does not seem to afford a clue to it, but may possibly do so. The composition of these Homilies has been remarked on as negligent by Hemsterhusius, so that he takes them to have been extemporaneous effusions taken down by others. There may be some ground for this in the style, and in the paraphrastic character of the various readings, but as a commentary they are unusually close and exact, and point out much of what regards the persuasive character of the Epistle that is not generally noticed.

For the Translation and some illustrative notes, the Editors are indebted to the Rev. JAMES TWEED, M.A., of Corpus Christi College, Cambridge. The text of the New Paris edition has been chiefly used, as it is improved from the Benedictine. Savile's has been compared with it in many parts, and in every difficulty, and where both failed, a better reading has been sometimes found in the MS. marked B, which is in the British Museum marked Burney 48. The differences are, however, slight, and affect the Greek more than the Translation. A Venice MS. which usually agrees with this has been collated for the Homilies on the Epistle to Philemon. An old Latin version published at Basle has been noticed in some places, where its variations appear to be derived from Greek copies.

C. M[ARRIOT].

OXFORD, 1843.

CONTENTS.

HOMILIES ON FIRST EPISTLE TO TIMOTHY.

SECOND EPISTLE TO TIMOTHY.

EPISTLE TO TITUS.

EPISTLE TO PHILEMON.

HOMILIES OF ST. JOHN CHRYSOSTOM,

ARCHBISHOP OF CONSTANTINOPLE,

ON THE

FIRST EPISTLE OF ST. PAUL THE APOSTLE

TO

TIMOTHY

ARGUMENT.

1. TIMOTHY too[1] was one of the disciples of the Apostle Paul. To the extraordinary qualities of this youth testimony is borne by Luke, who informs us, that he was "well reported of by the brethren that were at Lystra and Iconium." (Acts xvi. 2.) He became at once a disciple and a teacher, and gave this singular instance of his prudence, that hearing Paul preach without insisting upon circumcision, and understanding that he had formerly withstood Peter upon that point, he chose not only not to preach against it, but to submit to that rite. For Paul, it is said, "took and circumcised him" (Acts xvi. 3), though he was of adult age, and so trusted him with his whole economy.[2]

The affection of Paul for him is a sufficient evidence of his character. For he elsewhere says of him, "Ye know the proof of him, that as a son with a father, he hath served with me in the Gospel." (Phil. ii. 22.) And to the Corinthians again he writes: "I have sent unto you Timothy, who is my beloved son, and faithful in the Lord." (1 Cor. iv. 17.) And again: "Let no man despise him, for he worketh the work of the Lord, as I also do." (1 Cor. xvi. 10, 11.) And to the Hebrews he writes, "Know that our brother Timothy is set at liberty." (Heb. xiii. 23.) Indeed his love for him is everywhere apparent, and the miracles[3] that are now wrought still attest his claims.[4]

2. If it should be asked why he addresses Epistles to Titus and Timothy alone, though Silas was approved, as also was Luke, for he writes, "Only Luke is with me" (2 Tim. iv. 11), and Clement was one of his associates, of whom he says, "with Clement and other my fellow-laborers" (Phil. iv. 3), for what reason then does he write only to Titus and Timothy? It is because he had already committed the care of churches to these, and certain marked[5] places had been assigned to them, but the others were in attendance upon him. For so preëminent in virtue was Timothy, that his youth was no impediment to his promotion; therefore he writes, "Let no man despise thy youth" (1 Tim. iv. 12, and v. 2); and again, "The younger women as sisters."[6] For where there is virtue, all other things are superfluous, and there can be no impediment. Therefore when the Apostle discourses of Bishops, among the many things he requires of them, he makes no particular mention of age. And if he speaks of a Bishop "being the husband of one wife," and "having his children in subjection" (1 Tim. iii. 2, 4), this is not said, as if it were necessary he should have a wife and children; but that if any should

---

[1] καί. The reference is not clear. It may possibly be to Titus, whom he presently names before Timothy; but the explanations that follow would be hardly needed in that case.
[2] i.e. his plan of meeting Jewish prejudices.

[3] Of miracles said to be wrought by the bones of Timothy, see Hom. on Stat. 1, § 2, Ben.
[4] παρρησίαν. His freedom of speech in the court of Heaven. See Hom. i. on Stat. § 2, and note at the end of Hom. vi. on Stat. Hom. i. on Stat. enlarges on the character of Timothy, from 1 Tim. v. 23.
[5] Or conspicuous φανεροῖς.
[6] Some copies omit the latter quotation.

happen from a secular life to be advanced to that office, they might be such as knew how to preside over their household and children, and all others committed to them. For if a man were both secular and deficient in these points, how should he be[1] intrusted with the care of the Church?

3. But why, you will say, does he address an Epistle to a disciple already appointed to the office of a Teacher? Ought he not to have been made perfect for his office, before he was sent? Yes; but the instruction which he needed was not that which was suited to a disciple, but that which was proper for a Teacher. You will perceive him therefore through the whole Epistle adapting his instructions to a Teacher. Thus at the very beginning he does not say, "Do not attend to those who teach otherwise," but, "Charge them that they teach no other doctrine." (1 Tim. i. 3.)

HOMILY I.

1 TIMOTHY i. 1, 2.

"Paul, an Apostle of Jesus Christ by the commandment of God our Saviour, and Lord Jesus Christ, which is our hope; unto Timothy, my own son in the faith: Grace, mercy, and peace, from God our Father and Jesus Christ our Lord." [The R. V. omits κυρίου and translates: Christ Jesus our hope, τῆς ἐλπίδος ἡμῶν.]

1. GREAT and admirable is the dignity of an Apostle, and we find Paul constantly setting forth the causes of it, not as if he took the honor to himself, but as intrusted with it, and being under the necessity of so doing. For when he speaks of himself as "called," and that "by the will of God," and again elsewhere, "a necessity is laid upon me" (1 Cor. ix. 16), and when he says, "for this I was separated," by these expressions all idea of arrogance and ambition is removed. For as he deserves the severest blame, who intrudes into an office which is not given him of God, so he who refuses, and shrinks from it when offered to him, incurs blame of another kind, that of rebellion and disobedience. Therefore Paul, in the beginning of this Epistle, thus expresses himself, "Paul, an Apostle of Jesus Christ by the commandment of God." He does not say here, "Paul called," but "by commandment." He begins in this manner, that Timothy may not feel any human infirmity from supposing that Paul addresses him on the same terms as his disciples. But where is this commandment given? We read in the Acts of the Apostles: "The Spirit said, Separate me Paul and Barnabas." (Acts xiii. 2.) And everywhere in his writings Paul adds the name of Apostle, to instruct his hearers not to consider the doctrines he delivered as proceeding from man. For an Apostle[2] can say nothing of his own, and by calling himself an Apostle, he at once refers his hearers to Him that sent him. In all his Epistles therefore he begins by assuming this title, thus giving authority to his words, as here he says, "Paul, an Apostle of Jesus Christ according to the commandment of God our Saviour." Now it does not appear that the Father anywhere commanded him. It is everywhere Christ who addresses him. Thus, "He said unto me, Depart, for I will send thee far hence unto the Gentiles" (Acts xxii. 21); and again, "Thou must be brought before Cæsar." (Acts xxvii. 24.) But whatever the Son commands, this he considers to be the commandment of the Father, as those of the Spirit are commandments of the Son. For he was sent by the Spirit, he was separated by the Spirit, and this he says was the commandment of God. What then? does it derogate from the power of the Son, that His Apostle was sent forth by the commandment of the Father? By no means. For observe, how he represents the power as common to both. For having said, "according to the commandment of God our Saviour"; he adds, "and Lord Jesus Christ, our hope." And observe, with what propriety he applies the titles.[3] And indeed, the Psalmist applies this to the Father, saying, "The hope of all the ends of the earth." (Ps. lxiv. 5.) And again, the blessed Paul in another place writes, "For therefore we both labor, and suffer reproach, because we have hope in the living God." The teacher must suffer dangers even more than the disciple. "For I will smite the shepherd, (he says,) "and the sheep shall be scattered abroad." (Zech. xiii. 7.) Therefore the devil rages with greater violence against teachers, because by their destruction the flock also is scattered. For by slaying the sheep, he has lessened the flock, but when he has made away with the shepherd, he has ruined the whole flock, so that he the

---

[1] So. Sav. Ben. have been.
[2] He refers to the sense of the term in Greek, which is, "One who is sent." See Heb. iii. 1; John viii. 28; xiv. 10.

[3] ἐπώνυμα, viz. "Saviour" and "Hope."

rather assaults him, as working greater mischief by a less effort; and in one soul effecting the ruin of all. For this reason Paul, at the beginning, elevates and encourages the soul of Timothy, by saying, We have God for our Saviour and Christ for our hope. We suffer much, but our hopes are great; we are exposed to snares and perils, but to save us we have not man but God. Our Saviour is not weak, for He is God, and whatever be our dangers they will not overcome us; nor is our hope made ashamed, for it is Christ.[1] For in two ways we are enabled to bear up against dangers, when we are either speedily delivered from them, or supported by good hopes under them.

But Paul never calls himself the Apostle of the Father, but always of Christ. Because he makes everything common to both. The Gospel itself he calls "the Gospel of God."[2] And whatever we suffer here, he implies, things present are as nothing.

"Unto Timothy, my own son in the faith."

This too is encouraging. For if he evinced such faith as to be called peculiarly Paul's "own" son, he might be confident also with respect to the future. For it is the part of faith not to be cast down or disturbed, though circumstances occur that seem contrary to the promises. But observe, he says, "my son," and even "mine own son," and yet he is not of the same substance. But what? was he of irrational kind? "Well," says one, "he was not of Paul, so this does not imply 'being of' another." What then? was he of another substance? neither was it so, for after saying "mine own son," he adds, "in the faith," to show that he was really "his own son," and truly from him. There was no difference. The likeness he bore to him was in respect to his faith, as in human births there is a likeness in respect of substance. The son is like the father in human beings, but with respect to God the proximity is greater.[3] For here a father and a son, though of the same substance, differ in many particulars, as in color, figure, understanding, age, bent of mind, endowments of soul and body, and in many other things they may be like or unlike, but there is no such dissimilarity in the divine Essence.

"By commandment." This is a stronger expression than "called," as we learn from other passages. As he here calls Timothy "mine own son," in like manner he says to the Corinthians, "in Christ Jesus I have begotten you," i.e. in faith; but he adds the word "own,"[4] to show his particular likeness to himself, as well as his own love and great affection for him. Notice again the "in" applied to the faith. "My own son," he says, "in the faith." See what an honorable distinction, in that he calls him not only his "son," but his "own" son.

Ver. 2. "Grace, mercy, and peace from God our Father and Jesus Christ our Lord."

Why is mercy mentioned here, and not in the other Epistles? This is a further mark of his affection. Upon his son he invokes greater blessings, with the anxious apprehension of a parent. For such was his anxiety, that he gives directions to Timothy, which he has done in no other case, to attend to his bodily health; where he says, "Use a little wine for thy stomach's sake, and thine often infirmities." (1 Tim. v. 23.) Teachers indeed stand more in need of mercy.

"From God our Father," he says, "and Jesus Christ our Lord."

Here too is consolation. For if God is our Father, He cares for us as sons, as Christ says, "What man is there of you, whom if his son ask bread, will he give him a stone?" (Matt. vii. 9.)

Ver. 3. "As I besought thee to abide still at Ephesus, when I went into Macedonia."

Observe the gentleness of the expression, more like that of a servant than of a master. For he does not say "I commanded," or "bade" or even "exhorted," but "I besought thee." But this tone is not for all: only meek and virtuous disciples are to be treated thus. The corrupt and insincere are to be dealt with in a different manner, as Paul himself elsewhere directs, "Rebuke them with all authority" (Tit. ii. 15); and here he says "charge," not "beseech," but "charge some that they teach no other doctrine." What means this? That Paul's Epistle which he sent them was not sufficient? Nay, it was sufficient; but men are apt sometimes to slight Epistles, or perhaps this may have been before the Epistles were written. He had himself passed some time in that city. There was the temple of Diana, and there he had been exposed to those great sufferings. For after the assembly in the Theater had been dissolved, and he had called to him and exhorted the disciples, he found it necessary to sail away, though afterwards he returned to them. It were worth enquiry, whether he stationed Timothy there at that time.[5] For he says, that "thou

---

[1] Montfaucon adopts Savile's conjecture. MSS. Christ's. The mistake would be easily made by a transcriber who did not follow the sense entirely.

[2] Ver. 11. 1 Thess. ii. 4.

[3] He supposes an Arian objector to argue that St. Paul here calls one a "son," and his "own son," who was not of his substance, and so our Lord may be called the Son of God, and yet not be of His substance. St. Chrysostom replies (1) that even so St. Paul does not leave room to suppose a different *kind* of substance, as though he had called a brute his son. The objector rejoins, that still he calls one a son who was not of "his own" substance. He answers (2) that even this does not follow, since he adds, "in the faith," and the faith of Timothy was both exactly similar to his own, and derived from it. Thus the passage affords no countenance even to the doctrine of "like," as opposed to "one substance." See Epistle of St. Athanasius in def. of Nicene Def. c. v. § 8, Oxf. Tr. p. 39, and Disc. I, c. v. p. 203.

[4] γνήσιον.

[5] He must mean to suggest that this is a reference to former

mightest charge some that they teach no other doctrine " : he does not mention the persons by name, that he might not, by the openness of his rebuke, render them more shameless. There were in that city certain false Apostles of the Jews, who wished to oblige the faithful to observe the Jewish law, a fault he is everywhere noticing in his Epistles ; and this they did not from motives of conscience, so much as from vainglory, and a wish to have disciples, from jealousy of the blessed Paul, and a spirit of opposition to him. This is meant by " teaching another doctrine."

Ver. 4. " Neither give heed to fables and endless genealogies."

By " fables " he does not mean the law ; far from it ; but inventions and forgeries and counterfeit doctrines. For, it seems, the Jews wasted their whole discourse on these unprofitable points. They numbered up their fathers and grandfathers, that they might have the reputation of historical knowledge and research. " That thou mightest charge some," he says, " that they teach no other doctrine, neither give heed to fables and endless genealogies." Why does he call them " endless "? It is because they had no end, or none of any use, or none easy for us to apprehend. Mark how he disapproves of questioning. For where faith exists, there is no need of question. Where there is no room 'for curiosity, questions are superfluous. Questioning is the subversion of faith.[1] For he that seeks has not yet found. He who questions cannot believe. Therefore it is his advice that we should not be occupied with questions, since if we question, it is not faith ; for faith sets reasoning at rest. But why then does Christ say, " Seek and ye shall find, knock and it shall be opened unto you " (Matt. vii. 7) ; and, " Search the Scriptures, for in them ye think ye have eternal life "? (John v. 39.) The seeking there is meant of prayer and vehement desire, and He bids " search the Scriptures," not to introduce the labors of questioning, but to end them, that we may ascertain and settle their true meaning, not that we may be ever questioning, but that we may have done with it. And he justly said, " Charge some that they teach no other doctrine, neither give heed to fables, and endless genealogies, which minister questions ⟨rather than the dispensation of God in faith."[2] Justly has he said, " the dispensation of God." For great are the blessings which God is willing to dispense ; but the greatness of them is not conceived by reasoning. This must then be the work of faith,

which is the best medicine of our souls. This questioning therefore is opposed to the dispensation of God. For what is dispensed by faith? To receive His mercies and become better men ; to doubt and dispute of nothing ; but to repose in confidence. For what " ministers questions " displaces faith and that which faith hath wrought and builded. Christ has said that we must be saved by faith ; this these teachers questioned and even denied. For since the announcement was present, but the issue of it future, faith was required. But they being preoccupied by legal observances threw impediments in the way of faith. He seems also here to glance at the Greeks, where he speaks of " fables and genealogies," for they enumerated their Gods.

MORAL. Let us not then give heed to questions. For we were called Faithful, that we might unhesitatingly believe what is delivered to us, and entertain no doubt. For if the things asserted were human, we ought to examine them ; but since they are of God, they are only to be revered and believed. If we believe not, how shall we be persuaded of the existence of a God ? For how knowest thou that there is a God, when thou callest Him to account ? The knowledge of God is best shown by believing in Him without proofs and demonstrations. Even the Greeks know this ; for they believed their Gods, telling them, saith one, even without proof ; and what ? — That[3] they were the offspring of the Gods. But why do I speak of the Gods ? In the case of a man, a deceiver and sorcerer,[4] (I speak of Pythagoras,) they acted in like manner, for of him it was said,[5] He said it.[6] And over their temples was an image of Silence, and her finger on her mouth, compressing her lips, and significantly exhorting all that passed by to be silent. And were their doctrines so sacred, and are ours less so ? and even to be ridiculed ? What extreme madness is this ! The tenets of the Greeks indeed are rightly questioned. For they were of that nature, being but disputes, conflicts of reasonings, and doubts, and conclusions. But ours are far from all these. For human wisdom invented theirs, but ours were taught by the grace of the Spirit. Their doctrines are madness and folly, ours are true wisdom. In their case there is neither teacher nor scholar ; but all alike are disputants. Here whether teacher or scholar, each is to learn[7] of him from whom he ought to learn, and not to doubt, but obey ; not to dispute, but be-

times, for he knew the history too well to suppose that this Epistle was written then.
[1] Or " incompatible with " ἀναιρετική.
[2] The English version is " godly edifying," from the reading οἰκοδομίαν. Οἰκονομίαν, as here, is the reading of MSS. nearly all Greek. [Adopted in the R. V.]

[3] Or " and wherefore," " because," &c. See Acts xvii. 28.
[4] γόητος καὶ μάγου.
[5] αὐτὸς ἔφα.
[6] So Sav. mar. and MS. Colb. and afterwards, " And his was the five years' silence, he closed his mouth with his finger, and compressing his lips," &c.
[7] This seems the only way in which the Greek can be construed. The word vult, in the Latin, may come from another reading, but the sense is plain.

lieve. For all the 'ancients obtained a good report through faith, and without this everything is subverted. And why do I speak of it in heavenly things? We shall find upon examination that earthly things depend upon it no less. For without this there would be no trade nor contracts, nor anything of the sort. And if it be so necessary here in things that are false, how much more in those.[1]

This then let us pursue, to this let us adhere, so shall we banish from our souls all destructive doctrines, such, for instance, as relate to nativity[2] and fate.[3] If you believe that there is a resurrection and a judgment, you will be able to expel from your mind all those false opinions. Believe that there is a just God, and you will not believe that there can be an unjust nativity. Believe that there is a God, and a Providence,[4] and you will not believe that there can be a nativity, that holds all things together.[5] Believe that there is a place of punishment, and a Kingdom, and you will not believe in a nativity that takes away our free agency, and subjects us to necessity and force. Neither sow, nor plant, nor go to war, nor engage in any work whatever! For whether you will or not, things will proceed according to the course of nativity! What need have we more of Prayer? And why should you deserve to be a Christian, if there be this nativity? for you will not then be responsible. And whence proceed the arts of life? are these too from nativity? Yes, you say, and it is fated to one to become wise with labor. But can you show me one who has learnt an art without labor? You cannot. It is not then from nativity but from labor that he derives his skill.

But why does a man who is corrupt and wicked become rich, without inheriting it from his father, while another, amidst infinite labors, remains poor? For such are the questions they raise, always arguing upon wealth and poverty, and never taking the case of vice and virtue. Now in this question talk not of that, but show me a man who has become bad, whilst he was striving to be good; or one that, without striving, has become good. For if Fate has any power, its power should be shown in the most important things; in vice and virtue, not in poverty and riches. Again you ask, why is one man sickly and another healthy? why is one honored, another disgraced? Why does every thing succeed well with this man, whilst another meets with nothing but failure and impediments? Lay aside the notion of nativity, and you will

know. Believe firmly that there is a God and a Providence, and all these things will be cleared up. " But I cannot," you say, " conceive that there is a Providence, when there is such disorder. Can I believe that the good God gives wealth to the fornicator, the corrupt and dishonest man, and not to the virtuous? How can I believe this? for there must be facts to ground belief." Well then, do these cases proceed from a nativity that was just, or unjust? "Unjust," you say. Who then made it? "Not God," you say, " it was unbegotten." But how can the unbegotten produce these things? for they are contradictions. "These things are not then in any wise the works of God." Shall we then enquire who made the earth, the sea, the heavens, the seasons? "Nativity," you answer. Did nativity then produce in things inanimate such order and harmony, but in us, for whom these things were made, so much disorder? As if one, in building a house, should be careful to make it magnificent, but bestow not a thought upon his household. But who preserves the succession of the seasons? Who established the regular laws of nature? Who appointed the courses of day and night? These things are superior to any such nativity. " But these," you say, " came to be of themselves." And yet, how can such a well-ordered system spring up of itself?

" But whence," you say, " come the rich, the healthy, the renowned, and how are some made rich by covetousness, some by inheritance, some by violence? and why does God suffer the wicked to be prosperous?" We answer, Because the retribution, according to the desert of each, does not take place here, but is reserved for hereafter. Show me any such thing taking place Then! "Well," say you, " give me here, and I do not look for hereafter."[6] But it is because you seek here, that you receive not. For if when earthly enjoyment is not within your reach, you seek present things so eagerly as to prefer them to future, what would you do if you were in possession of unmixed pleasure? God therefore shows you that these things are nothing, and indifferent; for if they were not indifferent, He would not bestow them on such men. You will own that it is a matter of indifference whether one be tall or short, black or white; so is it whether one be rich or poor. For, tell me, are not things necessary bestowed on all equally, as the capacity for virtue, the distribution of spiritual gifts? If you understood aright the mercies of God, you would not complain of wanting worldly things, whilst you enjoyed these best gifts equally with others; and knowing that equal distribution, you would not desire superi-

---

[1] ἐκείναις. Sav. conj. ἐκείνοις, which seems necessary, unless the fault be elsewhere; he must mean " heavenly things." Comp. Luke xvi. 11.
[2] Γένεσις. The same word is kept throughout the passage, though it sounds ill in places, for the sake of fidelity.
[3] Εἱμαρμένη.
[4] Θεὸς προνοῶν, " a God providing."
[5] συνέχουσα.

[6] Compare Jas. iv. 3.

ority in the rest. As if a servant enjoying from his master's bounty food, clothing, and lodging, and all other necessaries equally with his fellow-servants, should pride himself upon having longer nails, or more hair upon his head ; so it is for a Christian to be elated on account of those things, which he enjoys only for a time. For this reason it is, that God withdraws those things from us, to extinguish this madness, and transfer our affections from them to heaven. But nevertheless we do not learn wisdom. As if a child possessing a toy, should prefer it to things necessary, and his father, to lead him against his will to what was better for him, should deprive him of his toy ; so God takes these things from us, that He may lead us to heaven. If you ask then why He permits the wicked to be rich, it is because they are not high in His esteem. And if the righteous too are rich, it is rather that He allows it to be, than that He makes them so.

Now these things we say superficially, as to men not knowing the Scriptures. But our discourses would be unnecessary if you would believe and take heed to the divine word, for that would teach you all things. And that you may understand that neither riches, nor health, nor glory, are anything, I can show you many, who, when they might gain wealth, do not seek wealth ; when they might enjoy health, mortify their bodies ; when they might rise to glory, make it their aim to be despised. But there is no good man, who ever studied to be bad. Let us therefore desist from seeking things below, and let us seek heavenly things ; for so we shall be able to attain them, and we shall enjoy eternal delights,[2] by the grace and lovingkindness of our Lord Jesus Christ. To Whom with the Father and the Holy Ghost be glory, power, and honor, now, and ever, and world without end. Amen.

HOMILY II.

1 TIMOTHY i. 5–7.

" Now the end of the commandment is charity out of a pure heart, and of a good conscience, and of faith unfeigned: From which some having swerved have turned aside unto vain jangling ; Desiring to be teachers of the law ; understanding neither what they say, nor whereof they affirm."

NOTHING is so injurious to mankind as to undervalue friendship[1] ; and not to cultivate it with the greatest care ; as nothing, on the other hand, is so beneficial, as to pursue it to the utmost of our power. This Christ has shown, where He says, " If two of you shall agree on earth, as touching anything that they shall ask, it shall be done for them of My Father " (Matt. xviii. 19) ; and again, " Because iniquity shall abound, love shall wax cold." (Matt. xxiv. 12.) It is this that has been the occasion of all heresies. For men, because they loved not their brethren, have envied those who were in high repute, and from envying, they have become eager for power, and from a love of power have introduced heresies. On this account Paul having said, " that thou mightest charge some that they teach no other doctrine," now shows that the manner in which this may be effected is by charity. As therefore when he says, " Christ is the end of the Law " (Rom. x. 4), that is, its fulfillment, and this is connected with the former,

so this[3] commandment is implied in love. The end of medicine is health, but where there is health, there is no need to make much ado ; so where there is love, there is no need of much commanding. But what sort of love does he speak of? That which is sincere, which is not merely in words, but which flows from the disposition, from sentiment, and sympathy. " From a pure heart," he says, either with respect to a right conversation, or sincere affection. For an impure life too produces divisions. " For every one that doeth evil, hateth the light." (John iii. 20.) There is indeed a friendship even among the wicked. Robbers and murderers may love one another, but this is not " from a good conscience," not " from a pure " but from an impure " heart," not from " faith unfeigned," but from that which is false and hypocritical. For faith points out the truth, and a sincere faith produces love, which he who truly believes in God cannot endure to lay aside.

Ver. 6. " From which some having swerved have turned aside to vain jangling."

He has well said, " swerved," for it requires skill,[4] to shoot straight and not beside the mark,

---

[1] φιλίας. He uses a term common to the Heathen in speaking of all mankind.

[2] Ed. τροφῆς, " food." St. Chrys. undoubtedly wrote τρυφῆς.

[3] Rather, perhaps, " the commandment itself," reading αὐτὴ for αυτη. The sense is, " as the law conducts to love, and love supersedes the law, so," &c., we might also read καὶ τοῦτο ἐκείνῳ ἐνέχεται for κ. τ. ἐκείνων ἔχεται, which does away with all difficulty.

[4] τέχνης.

to have [1] the direction of the Spirit. For there are many things to turn us aside from the right course, and we should look but to one object.

Ver. 7. "Desiring to be teachers of the law."

Here we see another cause of evil, the love of power. Wherefore Christ said, "Be not ye called Rabbi" (Matt. xxiii. 8) ; and the Apostle again, "For neither do they keep the law, but that they may glory in your flesh." (Gal. vi. 13.) They desire preëminence, he means, and on that account disregard truth.

"Understanding neither what they say, nor whereof they affirm."

Here he censures them, because they know not the end and aim of the Law, nor the period for which it was to have authority. But if it was from ignorance, why is it called a sin? Because it was incurred not only from their desiring to be teachers of the law,[2] but from their not retaining love. Nay, and their very ignorance arose from these causes. For when the soul abandons itself to carnal things, the clearness of its vision is dimmed, and falling from love, it drops into contentiousness, and the eye of the mind is blinded. For he that is possessed by any desire for these temporal things, intoxicated, as he is, with passion, cannot be an impartial judge of truth.[3]

"Not knowing whereof they affirm."

For it is probable that they spoke of the law, and enlarged on its purifications and other bodily rites. The Apostle then forbearing to censure these, as either nothing, or at best a shadow and figure of spiritual things, proceeds in a more engaging way to praise the law, calling the Decalogue here the law, and by means of it discarding the rest. For if even these precepts punish transgressors, and become useless to us, much more the others.

Ver. 8, 9. "But we know that the law is good, if a man use it lawfully. Knowing this, that the law is not made for a righteous man."

The law, he seems to say, is good, and again, not good. What then? if one use it not lawfully, is it not good? Nay, even so it is good. But what he means is this ; if any one fulfills it in his actions ; for that is to "use it lawfully," as here intended. But when they expound it in their words, and neglect it in their deeds, that is using it unlawfully. For such an one uses it, but not to his own profit. And another way may be named besides. What is it? that the law, if thou use it aright, sends thee to Christ. For since its aim is to justify man, and it fails

to effect this, it remits us to Him who can do so. Another way again of using the law lawfully, is when we keep it, but as a thing superfluous. And how as a thing superfluous? As the bridle is properly used, not by the prancing horse that champs it, but by that which wears it only for the sake of appearance, so he uses the law lawfully, who governs himself, though not as constrained by the letter of it. He uses the law lawfully who is conscious that he does not need it, for he who is already so virtuous that he fulfills it not from fear of it, but from a principle of virtue,[4] uses it lawfully and safely : that is, if one so use it, not as being in fear of it, but having before his eyes rather the condemnation of conscience than the punishment hereafter. Moreover he calls him a righteous man, who has attained unto virtue. He therefore uses the law lawfully, who does not require to be instructed by it. For as points in reading are set before children ; but he who does what they direct, without their aid, from other knowledge, shows more skill, and is a better reader ; so he who is above the law, is not under the schooling of the law. For he keeps it in a much higher degree, who fulfills it not from fear, but from a virtuous inclination ; since he that fears punishment does not fulfill it in the same manner as he that aims at reward. He that is under the law doth it not as he that is above the law. For to live above the law is to use it lawfully. He uses it lawfully, and keeps it, who achieves things beyond the law, and who does not need its instructions. For the law, for the most part, is prohibition of evil ; now this alone does not make a man righteous, but the performance of good actions besides. Hence those, who abstain from evil like slaves, do not come up to the mark of the law. For it was appointed for the punishment of transgression. Such men indeed use it, but it is to dread its punishment. It is said, "Wilt thou not be afraid of the power? do that which is good " (Rom. xiii. 3) : which implies, that the law threatens punishment only to the wicked. But of what use is the law to him whose actions deserve a crown? as the surgeon is of use only to him who hath some hurt, and not to the sound and healthy man. "But for the lawless and disobedient, for the ungodly and for sinners." He calls the Jews "lawless and disobedient" too. "The law (he says) worketh wrath," that is, to the evil doers. But what to him who is deserving of reward? "By the law is the knowledge of sin." (Rom. iii. 20.) What then with respect to the righteous? "the law is not made," he says, "for a righteous man." Wherefore? Because he is exempted from its punishment, and

---

[1] Montf. would insert δεῖ, "so that we have need of the direction," and so old Lat.

[2] i.e. as being attached to *it*.

[3] So Horace : —

　　Male verum examinat omnis,
　　Corruptus judex.
　　Ill holds that judge the balances of truth,
　　Who takes a bribe. — 1 Ep. xvi. 52.

Oderunt peccare boni virtutis amore.
'Tis love of virtue makes good men hate vice. — Hor.

he waits not to learn from it what is his duty, since he has the grace of the Spirit within to direct him. For the law was given that men might be chastened by fear of its threatenings. But the tractable horse needs not the curb, nor the man that can dispense with instruction the schoolmaster.

"But for the lawless and disobedient, for the ungodly and for sinners, for the unholy and profane, for murderers of fathers and murderers of mothers." Thus he does not stop at the mention of sins in general, nor of these only, but goes over the several kinds of sin, to shame men, as it were, of being under the direction of the law; and having thus particularized some, he adds a reference to those omitted, though what he had enumerated were sufficient to withdraw men. Of whom then does he say these things? Of the Jews, for they were "murderers of fathers and murderers of mothers": they were "profane and unholy," for these too he means when he says, "ungodly and sinners," and being such, the law was necessarily given to them. For did they not repeatedly worship idols? did they not stone Moses? were not their hands imbrued in the blood of their kindred? Do not the prophets constantly accuse them of these things? But to those who are instructed by a heavenly philosophy, these commandments are superfluous. "For murderers of fathers and murderers of mothers, for manslayers, for whoremongers, for them that defile themselves with mankind, for menstealers, for liers, for perjured persons, and if there be any other thing that is contrary to sound doctrine"; for all the things which he had mentioned were the passions of a corrupted soul, and contrary, therefore, to sound doctrine.

Ver. 11. "According to the glorious Gospel of the blessed God, which was committed to my trust."

Thus the Law is still necessary for the confirmation of the Gospel, yet to those who obey it is unnecessary. And he calls the Gospel "glorious." There were some who were ashamed of its persecutions, and of the sufferings of Christ, and so for the sake of these, as well as for others, he has called it "the glorious Gospel," thus showing that the sufferings of Christ are our glory. And perhaps he glances too at the future. For if our present state is exposed to shame and reproach, it will not be so hereafter; and it is to things future, and not to things present, that the Gospel belongs. Why then did the Angel say, "Behold, I bring you good tidings of great joy, for unto you is born a Saviour"? (Luke ii. 10.) Because He was born to be their Saviour, though His miracles did not commence from His birth. "According to the Gospel," he saith, "of the blessed God." The

glory[1] he means is either that of the service of God, or, in that if present things are filled with its glory, yet much more will things future be so; when "His enemies shall be put under His feet" (1 Cor. xv. 25), when there shall be nothing opposed, when the just shall behold all those blessed things, which "eye hath not seen, nor ear heard, and which hath not entered into the heart of man." (1 Cor. ii. 9.) "For I will," says our Saviour, "that they also may be with Me, where I am, that they may behold My glory, which Thou hast given Me." (John xvii. 24.)

Moral. Let us then learn who these are, and let us esteem them blessed, considering what felicities they will then enjoy, of what light and glory they will then participate. The glory of this world is worthless and not enduring, or if it abides, it abides but till death, and after that is wholly extinguished. For "his glory," it says, "shall not descend after him." (Ps. xlix. 17.) And with many it lasts not even to the end of life. But no such thing is to be thought of in that glory; it abides, and will have no end. For such are the things of God, enduring, and above all change or end. For the glory of that state is not from without, but from within. I mean, it consists not in a multitude of servants, or of chariots, nor in costly garments. Independently of these things, the man himself is clothed with glory. Here, without these things, the man appears naked. In the baths, we see the illustrious, the undistinguished, and the base, alike bare. Often have the great been exposed to danger in public, being left on some occasion by their servants. But in that world men carry their glory about with them, and the Saints, like the Angels, wherever they appear, have their glory in themselves. Yea rather as the sun needs no vestures, and requires no foreign aid, but wherever he appears, his glory at once shines forth; so shall it then be.

Let us then pursue that glory, than which nothing is more venerable; and leave the glory of the world, as beyond anything worthless. "Boast not of thy clothing and raiment." (Ecclus. xi. 4.) This was the advice given of old to the simple. Indeed the dancer, the harlot, the player, are arrayed in a gayer and more costly robe than thou. And besides, this boasting were of that, which if but moths attack, they can rob thee of its enjoyment. Dost thou see what an unstable thing it is, this glory of the present life? Thou pridest thyself upon that which insects make and destroy. For Indian insects, it is said, spin those fine threads of which your robes are made. But rather seek a clothing woven from things above, an admirable and radiant vesture, raiment of real gold; of gold not dug

---

[1] It is literally, "The Gospel of the glory of the Blessed God." Comp. Rom. ix. 4, and viii. 30; 2 Cor. iii. 7, seqq.; Heb. ix. 1, 14.

by malefactors' hands out of the mine, but the produce of virtue. Let us clothe ourselves with a robe not the manufacture of poor men or slaves, but wrought by our Lord Himself. But your garments, you say, are in-wrought with gold! And what is that to thee? He that wrought it, not he that wears it, is the object of admiration, for there it is really due. It is not the frame on which the garment is stretched at the fuller's, but the maker of it, that is admired. Yet the block wears it, and has it bound on itself. And as that wears it, but not for use, even so do some of these women, for the benefit of the garment, to air it, they say, that it may not be moth-eaten! Is it not then the extreme of folly to be solicitous about a thing so worthless, to do anything whatever, to risk your salvation for it, to make a mock at Hell, to set God at defiance, to overlook Christ hungering? Talk not of the precious spices of India, Arabia, and Persia, the moist and the dry, the perfumes and unguents, so costly and so useless. Why, O woman, dost thou lavish perfumes upon a body full of impurity within? why spend on what is offensive, as if one should waste perfumes upon dirt, or distill balms upon a brick. There is, if you desire it, a precious ointment and a fragrance, with which you might anoint your soul; not brought from Arabia, or Ethiopia, nor from Persia, but from heaven itself; purchased not by gold, but by a virtuous will, and by faith unfeigned. Buy this perfume, the odor of which is able to fill the world. It was of this the Apostles savored. "For we are (he says) a sweet savor, to some of death, to others of life." (2 Cor. ii. 15, 16.) And what means this? That it is as they say, that the swine is suffocated by perfumes! But this spiritual fragrance scented not only the bodies but the garments of the Apostles; and Paul's garments were so impregnated with it, that they cast out devils. What balmy leaf, what cassia, what myrrh so sweet or so efficacious as this perfume? For if it put devils to flight, what could it not effect? With this ointment let us furnish ourselves. And the grace of the Spirit will provide it through almsgiving. Of these we shall savor, when we go into the other world. And as here, he[1] that is perfumed with sweet odors draws upon himself the notice of all, and whether at the bath, or the assembly, or any other concourse of men, all follow him, and observe him; so, in that world, when souls come in that are fragrant with this spiritual savor, all arise and make room. And even here devils and all vices are afraid to approach it, and cannot endure it, for it chokes them. Let us then not bear about us that perfume which is a mark of effeminacy, but this, which is a mark of man-

hood, which is truly admirable, which fills us with a holy confidence. This is a spice which is not the produce of the earth, but springs from virtue, which withers not, but blooms for ever. This is it that renders those who possess it honorable. With this we are anointed at our Baptism, then we savor sweetly of it; but it must be by our care afterwards that we retain the savor. Of old the Priests were anointed with ointment, as an emblem of the virtue, the fragrance of which a Priest should diffuse around him.

But nothing is more offensive than the savor of sin, which made the Psalmist say, "My wounds stink and are corrupt." (Ps. xxxviii. 5.) For sin is more foul than putrefaction itself. What, for instance, is more offensive than fornication? And if this is not perceived at the time of its commission, yet, after it is committed, its offensive nature, the impurity contracted in it, and the curse,[2] and the abomination of it is perceived. So it is with all sin. Before it is committed it has something of pleasure, but after its commission, the pleasure ceases and fades away, and pain and shame succeed. But with righteousness it is the reverse. At the beginning it is attended with toil, but in the end with pleasure and repose. But even here, as in the one case the pleasure of sin is no pleasure, because of the expectation of disgrace and punishment, so in the other the toil is not felt as toil, by reason of the hope of reward. And what is the pleasure of drunkenness? The poor gratification of drinking, and hardly that. For when insensibility follows, and the man sees nothing that is before him, and is in a worse state than a madman, what enjoyment remains? Nay, one might well say there is no pleasure in fornication itself. For when passion has deprived the soul of its judgment, can there be any real delights? As well might we say that the itch is a pleasure! I should call that true pleasure, when the soul is not affected by passion, not agitated nor overpowered by the body. For what pleasure can it be to grind the teeth, to distort the eyes, to be irritated and inflamed beyond decency? But so far is it from being pleasant, that men hasten to escape from it, and when it is over are in pain. But if it were pleasure, they would wish not to escape from it, but to continue it. It has therefore only the name of pleasure.

But not such are the pleasures enjoyed by us; they are truly delightful, they do not agitate nor inflame. They leave the soul free, and cheer and expand it. Such was the pleasure of Paul when he said, "In this I rejoice, yea, and I will rejoice"; and again, "Rejoice in the Lord always." (Phil. i. 18, and iv. 4.) For sinful

---

[1] al. she, &c.

[2] Sav. ἄγος, Ben. ἅλγος.

pleasure is attended with shame and condemnation; it is indulged in secret, and is attended with infinite uneasiness. But from all these the true pleasure is exempt. This then let us pursue, that we may attain those good things to come, through the grace and mercy of our Lord Jesus Christ, to whom, &c.

HOMILY III.

1 TIMOTHY i. 12–14.

"And I thank Christ Jesus our Lord, who hath enabled me, for that he counted me faithful, putting me into the ministry [R. V.: to his service, εἰς διακονίαν]; who was before a blasphemer, and a persecutor, and injurious: but I obtained mercy, because I did it ignorantly in unbelief. And the grace of our Lord was exceeding abundant, with faith and love which is in Christ Jesus."

THE advantages arising from humility are generally acknowledged, and yet it is a thing not easily to be met with. There is affectation of humble talking enough and to spare, but humbleness of mind is nowhere to be found. This quality was so cultivated by the blessed Paul, that he is ever looking out for inducements to be humble. They who are conscious to themselves of great merits must struggle much with themselves if they would be humble. And he too was one likely to be under violent temptations, his own good conscience swelling him up like a gathering humor. Observe therefore his method in this place. "I was intrusted," he had said, "with the glorious Gospel of God, of which they who still adhere to the law have no right to partake; for it is now opposed to the Gospel, and their difference is such, that those who are actuated by the one, are as yet unworthy to partake of the other; as we should say, that those who require punishments, and chains, have no right to be admitted into the train of philosophers." Being filled therefore with high thoughts, and having used magnificent expressions, he at once depresses himself, and engages others also to do the like. Having said therefore that "the Gospel was committed to his trust"; lest this should seem to be said from pride, he checks himself at once, adding by way of correction, "I thank Christ Jesus our Lord, who hath enabled me, for that He counted me faithful, putting me into the ministry." Thus everywhere, we see, he conceals his own merit, and ascribes everything to God, yet so far only, as not to take away free will. For the unbeliever might perhaps say, If everything is of God, and we contribute nothing of ourselves, while He turns us, as if we were mere wood and stone, from wickedness to the love of wisdom, why then did He make Paul such as he was, and not Judas? To remove this objection, mark the prudence of his expression, "Which was committed," he says, "to my trust." This was his own excellence and merit, but not wholly his own; for he says, "I thank Christ Jesus, who enabled me." This is God's part: then his own again, "Because He counted me faithful." Surely because he would be serviceable of his own part.

Ver. 13. "Putting me into his service, who was before a blasphemer, and a persecutor, and injurious; but I obtained mercy, because I did it ignorantly in unbelief."

Thus we see him acknowledge both his own part and that of God, and whilst he ascribes the greater part to the providence of God, he extenuates his own, yet so far only, as we said before, as was consistent with free will. And what is this, "Who enabled me"? I will tell you. He had so heavy a burden to sustain, that he needed much aid from above. For think what it was to be exposed to daily insults, and mockeries, and snares, and dangers, scoffs, and reproaches, and deaths; and not to faint, or slip, or turn backward, but though assaulted every day with darts innumerable, to bear up manfully, and remain firm and imperturbable. This was the effect of no human power, and yet not of Divine influence alone, but of his own resolution also. For that Christ chose him with a foreknowledge of what he would be, is plain from the testimony He bore to him before the commencement of his preaching. "He is a chosen vessel unto me, to bear my name before the Gentiles and kings." (Acts ix. 15.) For as those who bear the royal standard in war[1] require both strength and address, that they may not let it fall into the hands of the enemy; so those who sustain the name of Christ, not only in war but in peace, need a mighty strength, to preserve it uninjured from the attacks of accusers. Great indeed is

---

[1] One copy has, "which is usually called Laburum," perhaps a mistake for Labarum, but Socrates has Laborum. The first standard known to have been so called was that of Constantine, which bore the Christian symbol. [See Schaff, Church Hist. III. 27.]

the strength required to bear the name of Christ, and to sustain it well, and bear the Cross. For he who in action, or word, or thought, does anything unworthy of Christ, does not sustain His name, and has not Christ dwelling in him. For he that sustains that name bears it in triumph, not in the concourse of men, but through the very heavens, while all angels stand in awe, and attend upon him, and admire him.

"I thank the Lord, who hath enabled me." Observe how he thanks God even for that which was his own part. For he acknowledges it as a favor from Him that he was "a chosen vessel." For this, O blessed Paul, was thy own part. "For God is no respecter of persons."[1] But I thank Him that he "thought me worthy of this ministry." For this is a proof that He esteemed me faithful. The steward in a house is not only thankful to his master that he is trusted, but considers it as a sign that he holds him more faithful than others: so it is here. Then observe how he magnifies the mercy and lovingkindness of God, in describing his former life, "who was formerly," he says, "a blasphemer, and a persecutor, and injurious." And when he speaks of the still unbelieving Jews, he rather extenuates their guilt. "For I bear them record that they have a zeal for God, but not according to knowledge." (Rom. x. 2.) But of himself he says, "Who was a blasphemer and a persecutor." Observe his lowering of himself! So free was he from self-love, so full of humility, that he is not satisfied to call himself a persecutor and a blasphemer, but he aggravates his guilt, showing that it did not stop with himself, that it was not enough that he was a blasphemer, but in the madness of his blasphemy he persecuted those who were willing to be godly.[2]

"But I obtained mercy because I did it ignorantly in unbelief."

Why then did other Jews not obtain mercy? Because what they did, they did not ignorantly, but willfully, well knowing what they did. For this we have the testimony of the Evangelist. "Many of the Jews believed on Him, but because of the Pharisees they did not confess Him. For they loved the praise of men more than the praise of God." (John xii. 42, 43.) And Christ again said to them, "How can ye believe, who receive honor one of another" (John v. 44)? and the parents of the blind man "said these things for fear of the Jews, lest they should be put out of the synagogue." (John ix. 22.) Nay the Jews themselves said, "Perceive ye how we avail nothing? behold, the world is gone after Him." (John xii. 19.) Thus their love of

power was everywhere in their way. When they admitted that no one can forgive sins but God only, and Christ immediately did that very thing,[3] which they had confessed to be a sign of divinity, this could not be a case of ignorance. But where was Paul then? Perhaps one should say he was sitting at the feet of Gamaliel, and took no part with the multitude who conspired against Jesus: for Gamaliel does not appear to have been an ambitious man. Then how is it that afterwards Paul was found joining with the multitude? He saw the doctrine growing, and on the point of prevailing, and being generally embraced. For in the lifetime of Christ, the disciples consorted with Him, and afterwards with their teachers,[4] but when they were completely separated, Paul did not act as the other Jews did, from the love of power, but from zeal. For what was the motive of his journey to Damascus? He thought the doctrine pernicious, and was afraid that the preaching of it would spread everywhere. But with the Jews it was no concern for the multitude, but the love of power, that influenced their actions. Hence they say, "The Romans will come and take away both our place and nation." (John xi. 48.) What fear was this that agitated them, but that of man? But it is worthy of enquiry, how one so skillful in the law as Paul could be ignorant? For it is he who says, "which He had promised before by His holy prophets." (Rom. iv. 2.) How is it then that thou knowest not, thou who art zealous of the law of their fathers, who wert brought up at the feet of Gamaliel? Yet they who spent their days on lakes and rivers, and the very publicans, have embraced the Gospel, whilst thou that studiest the law art persecuting it! It is for this he condemns himself, saying, "I am not meet to be called an Apostle." (1 Cor. ix. 9.) It is for this he confesses his ignorance, which was produced by unbelief. For this cause, he says, that he obtained "mercy." What then does he mean when he says, "He counted me faithful"? He would give up no right of his Master's: even his own part he ascribed to Him, and assumed nothing to himself, nor claimed for his own the glory which was due to God. Hence in another place we find him exclaiming, "Sirs, why do ye these things to us? we also are men of like passions with you." (Acts xiv. 15.) So again, "He counted me faithful." And again, "I labored more abundantly than they all, yet not I, but the grace of God which was with me." (1 Cor. xv. 10.) And again, "It is He that worketh in us both to will and to do." (Phil. ii. 13.) Thus in acknowledging that he "obtained mercy," he owns that he deserved pun-

---

[1] He would be a respecter of persons who, without regard to a man's qualities, should arbitrarily (or on external grounds, such as birth, wealth, &c.) prefer him to others; God therefore does not do this. Rom. ii. 11; Col. iii. 25; Acts x. 34.

[2] εὐσεβεῖν, "to worship aright."

[3] i.e. proved that He had done it, by a direct appeal to God.

[4] i.e. Jewish teachers.

ishment, since mercy is for such. And again in another place he says of the Jews, "Blindness in part is happened to Israel." (Rom. xi. 25.)

Ver. 14. "And the grace of our Lord was exceeding abundant with faith and love which is in Christ Jesus."

This is added, lest hearing that he obtained mercy, we should understand by it only, that being deserving of punishment, as a persecutor and blasphemer, nevertheless he was not punished. But mercy was not confined to this, that punishment was not inflicted; many other great favors are implied by it. For not only has God released us from the impending punishment, but He has made us "righteous" too, and "sons," and "brethren," and "heirs," and "joint-heirs." Therefore it is he says, that "grace was exceeding abundant." For the gifts bestowed were beyond mercy, since they are not such as would come of mercy only, but of affection and excessive love. Having thus enlarged upon the love of God which, not content with showing mercy to a blasphemer and persecutor, conferred upon him other blessings in abundance, he has guarded against that error of the unbelievers which takes away free will, by adding, "with faith and love which is in Christ Jesus." Thus much only, he says, did we contribute. We have believed that He is able to save us.

Moral. Let us then love God through Christ. What means "through Christ"? That it is He, and not the Law, who has enabled us to do this. Observe what blessings we owe to Christ, and what to the Law. And he says not merely that grace has abounded, but "abounded exceedingly," in bringing at once to the adoption those who deserved infinite punishment.

And observe again that "in"[1] is used for "through."[1] For not only faith is necessary, but love. Since there are many still who believe that Christ is God, who yet love Him not, nor act like those who love Him. For how is it when they prefer everything to Him, money, nativity, fate, augury, divinations, omens? When we live in defiance of Him, pray, where is our love? Has any one a warm and affectionate friend? Let him love Christ but equally. So, if no more, let him love Him who gave His Son for us His enemies, who had no merits of our own. Merits did I say? who had committed numberless sins, who had dared Him beyond all daring, and without cause! yet He, after numberless instances of goodness and care, did not even then cast us off. At the very time when we did Him the greatest wrong, then did He give His Son for us. And still we, after so great benefits, after being made His friends, and counted worthy through Him of all blessings,

have not loved Him as our friend![2] What hope then can be ours? You shudder perhaps at the word, but I would that you shuddered at the fact! What? How shall it appear that we do not love God even as our friends, you say? I will endeavor to show you — and would that my words were groundless, and to no purpose! but I am afraid they are borne out by facts. For consider: friends, that are truly friends, will often suffer loss for those they love. But for Christ, no one will suffer loss, or even be content with his present state. For a friend we can readily submit to insults, and undertake quarrels; but for Christ, no one can endure enmity: and the saying is, "Be loved for nothing — but be not hated for nothing."

None of us would fail to relieve a friend who was hungering, but when Christ comes to us from day to day, and asks no great matter, but only bread, we do not even regard him, yea though we are nauseously over full, and swollen with gluttony: though our breath betrays the wine of yesterday, and we live in luxury, and waste our substance on harlots and parasites and flatterers, and even on monsters, idiots, and dwarfs; for men convert the natural defects of such into matter for amusement. Again, friends, that are truly such, we do not envy, nor are mortified at their success, yet we feel this toward (the minister of)[3] Christ, and our friendship for men is seen to be more powerful than the fear of God, for the envious and the insincere plainly respect men more than God. And how is this? God sees the heart, yet man does not forbear to practice deceit in His sight; yet if the same man were detected in deceit by men, he thinks himself undone, and blushes for shame. And why speak of this? If a friend be in distress, we visit him, and should fear to be condemned, if we deferred it for a little time. But we do not visit Christ, though He die again and again in prison; nay, if we have friends among the faithful, we visit them, not because they are Christians, but because they are our friends. Thus we do nothing from the fear or the love of God, but some things from friendship, some from custom. When we see a friend depart on travel, we weep and are troubled, and if we see his death, we bewail him, though we know that we shall not be long separated, that he will be restored to us at the Resurrection. But though Christ departs from us, or rather we reject Him daily, we do not grieve, nor think it strange, to injure, to offend, to provoke Him by doing what is displeasing to Him; and the fearful thing is not that we do not treat Him as a friend; for I will show that we even treat Him as

---

[1] ἐν — διά — see Hom. i.

[2] See next paragraph, and Hom. on Stat. XX. and Herbert's Poems, No. LXVIII.
[3] See on Rom. Hom.

an enemy. How, do you ask? because "the carnal mind is enmity against God," as Paul has said, and this we always carry about us. And we persecute Christ, when He advances toward us, and comes to our very doors.[1] For wicked actions in effect do this, and every day we subject him to insults by our covetousness and our rapacity. And does any one by preaching His word, and benefiting His Church, obtain a good reputation? Then he is the object of envy, because he does the work of God. And we think that we envy him, but our envy passes on to Christ. We affect to wish the benefit to come not from others, but from ourselves. But this cannot be for Christ's sake, but for our own: otherwise, it would be a matter of indifference, whether the good were done by others or ourselves. If a physician found himself unable to cure his son, who was threatened with blindness, would he reject the aid of another, who was able to effect the cure? Far from it! "Let my son be restored," he would almost say to him, "whether it is to be by you or by me." And why? Because he would not consider himself, but what was beneficial to his son. So, were our regard "to Christ," it would lead us to say, "Let good be done, whether by ourselves or by any other." As Paul said, "Whether in pretense or in truth, Christ is preached." (Phil. i. 18). In the same spirit Moses answered, when some would have excited his displeasure against Eldad and Modad, be-

cause they prophesied, "Enviest thou for my sake? Would God that all the Lord's people were prophets!" (Num. xi. 29.) These jealous feelings proceed from vainglory; and are they not those of opponents and enemies? Doth any one speak ill of you? Love him! It is impossible, you say. Nay, if you will, it is quite possible. For if you love him only who speaks well of you, what thanks have you? It is not for the Lord's sake, but for the sake of the man's kind speech that you do it. Has any one injured you? Do him good! For in benefiting him who has benefited you there is little merit. Have you been deeply wronged and suffered loss? Make a point of requiting it with the contrary. Yes, I entreat you. Let this be the way we do our own part. Let us cease from hating and injuring our enemies. He commands us "to love our enemies" (Matt. v. 44): but we persecute Him while He loves us. God forbid! we all say in words, but not so in deeds. So darkened are our minds by sin, that we tolerate in our actions what in words we think intolerable. Let us desist then from things that are injurious and ruinous to our salvation, that we may obtain those blessings which as His friends we may obtain. For Christ says, "I will that where I am, there My disciples may be also, that they may behold My glory" (John xvii. 24), which may we all attain, through the grace and love of Jesus Christ.

HOMILY IV.

1 Timothy i. 15, 16.

"This is a faithful saying, and worthy of all acceptation, that Christ Jesus came into the world to save sinners; of whom I am chief. Howbeit for this cause I obtained mercy, that in me first Jesus Christ might show forth all longsuffering, for a pattern to them which should hereafter believe on Him to life everlasting."

The favors of God so far exceed human hope and expectation, that often they are not believed. For God has bestowed upon us such things as the mind of man never looked for, never thought of. It is for this reason that the Apostles spend much discourse in securing a belief of the gifts that are granted us of God. For as men, upon receiving some great good, ask themselves if it is not a dream, as not believing it; so it is with respect to the gifts of God. What then was it

that was thought incredible? That those who were enemies, and sinners, neither justified by the law, nor by works, should immediately through faith alone be advanced to the highest favor. Upon this head accordingly Paul has discoursed at length in his Epistle to the Romans, and here again at length. "This is a faithful saying," he says, "and worthy of all acceptation, that Christ Jesus came into the world to save sinners."

As the Jews were chiefly attracted by this, he persuades them not[2] to give heed to the law, since they could not attain salvation by it without faith. Against this he contends; for it seemed to them incredible, that a man who had mis-spent all his former life in vain and wicked actions, should afterwards be saved by his faith

---

[1] This idea is beautifully illustrated by the *Christuskopf* of Overbeck.

[2] Sav. omits "not"; so the sense will be, that a due consideration of the Law would prove that men could not be saved by it.

alone. On this account he says, "It is a saying to be believed." But some not only disbelieved, but even objected, as the Greeks do now. "Let us then do evil, that good may come." This was the consequence they drew in derision of our faith, from his words, "Where sin abounded, grace did much more abound." (Rom. iii. 8, and v. 20.) So when we discourse to them of Hell, they say, How can this be worthy of God? When man has found his servant offending, he forgives it, and thinks him worthy of pardon; and does God punish eternally? And when we speak of the Laver, and of the remission of sins through it, this too they say is unworthy of God, that he who has committed offenses without number should have his sins remitted. What perverseness of mind is this, what a spirit of contention does it manifest! Surely if forgiveness is an evil, punishment is a good; but if punishment is an evil, remission of it is a good. I speak according to their notions, for according to ours, both are good. This I shall show at another time, for the present would not suffice for a matter so deep, and which requires to be elaborately argued. I must lay it before your Charity at a fitting season. At present let us proceed with our proposed subject. "This is a faithful saying," he says. But why is it to be believed?

This appears both from what precedes and from what follows. Observe how he prepares us[1] for this assertion, and how he then dwells upon it. For he hath previously declared that He showed mercy to me "a blasphemer and a persecutor"; this was in the way of preparation. And not only did He show mercy, but "He accounted me faithful." So far should we be, he means, from disbelieving that He showed mercy. For no one, who should see a prisoner admitted into a palace, could doubt whether he obtained mercy. And this was visibly the situation of Paul, for he makes himself the example. Nor is he ashamed to call himself a sinner, but rather delights in it, as he thus can best demonstrate the miracle of God's regard for him, and that He had thought him worthy of such extraordinary kindness.

But how is it, that he here calls himself a sinner, nay, the chief of sinners, whereas he elsewhere asserts that he was "touching the righteousness which is in the law blameless"? (Phil. iii. 6.) Because with respect to the righteousness which God has wrought, the justification which is really sought, even those who are righteous[2] in the law are sinners, "for all have sinned, and come short of the glory of God." (Rom. iii. 23.) Therefore he does not say righteousness simply, but "the righteousness which is in the law." As a man that has acquired wealth, with respect to himself appears rich, but upon a comparison with the treasures of kings is very poor and the chief of the poor; so it is in this case. Compared with Angels, even righteous men are sinners; and if Paul, who wrought the righteousness that is in the law, was the chief of sinners, what other man can be called righteous? For he says not this to condemn his own life as impure, let not this be imagined; but comparing his own legal righteousness with the righteousness of God, he shows it to be nothing worth, and not only so, but he proves those who possess it to be sinners.

Ver. 16. "Howbeit for this cause I obtained mercy, that in me first Jesus Christ might show forth all longsuffering, for a pattern to them which should hereafter believe on Him to life everlasting."

See how he further humbles and depreciates himself, by naming a fresh and less creditable reason. For that he obtained mercy on account of his ignorance, does not so much imply that he who obtained mercy was a sinner, or under deep condemnation; but to say that he obtained mercy in order that no sinner hereafter might despair of finding mercy, but that each might feel sure of obtaining the like favor, this is an excess of humiliation, such that even in calling himself the chief of sinners, "a blasphemer and a persecutor, and one not meet to be called an Apostle," he had said nothing like it. This will appear by an example. Suppose a populous city, all whose inhabitants were wicked, some more so, and some less, but all deserving of condemnation; and let one among that multitude be more deserving of punishment than all the rest, and guilty of every kind of wickedness. If it were declared that the king was willing to pardon all, it would not be so readily believed, as if they were to see this most wicked wretch actually pardoned. There could then be no longer any doubt. This is what Paul says, that God, willing to give men full assurance that He pardons all their transgressions, chose, as the object of His mercy, him who was more a sinner than any; for when I obtained mercy, he argues, there could be no doubt of others: as familiarly speaking we might say, "If God pardons such an one, he will never punish anybody"; and thus he shows that he himself, though unworthy of pardon, for the sake of others' salvation, first obtained that pardon. Therefore, he says, since I am saved, let no one doubt of salvation. And observe the humility of this blessed man; he says not, "that in me he might show forth" His "longsuffering," but "all longsuffering"; as if he had said, greater longsuffering He could not

---

[1] Or, "gives proof beforehand."
[2] The word "righteous" seems to be understood in "righteousness," just before.

show in any case than in mine, nor find a sinner that so required all His pardon, all His longsuffering; not a part only, like those who are only partially sinners, but " all " His longsuffering.

" For a pattern to those who should hereafter believe." This is said for comfort, for encouragement.[1] But because he had spoken highly of the Son, and of the great love which He hath manifested, lest he should be thought to exclude the Father from this, he ascribes the glory to Him also.

Ver. 17. " Now unto the King eternal, immortal, invisible, the only wise God, be honor and glory for ever and ever. Amen."

For these things, then, we glorify not the Son only, but the Father. Here let us argue with the heretics. Speaking of the Father, he says, " To the only God." Is the Son then not God? " The only immortal."[2] Is the Son then not immortal? Or does He not possess that Himself, which hereafter He will give to us? Yes, they say, He is God and immortal, but not such as the Father. What then? is He of inferior essence, and therefore of inferior immortality? What then is a greater and a less immortality? For immortality is nothing else than the not being subject to destruction. For there is a greater and a less glory; but immortality does not admit of being greater or less: as neither is there a greater and a less health. For a thing must either be destructible, or altogether indestructible. Are we men then immortal even as He? God forbid! Surely not! Why? because He has it by nature, but we adventitiously. Why then do you make the difference? Because the Father, he says, is made such as He is by no other: but the Son is what He is, from the Father. This we also confess, not denying that the Son is generated from the Father incorruptibly.[3] And we glorify the Father, he means, for having generated the Son, such as He is. Thus you see the Father is most glorified, when the Son hath done great things. For the glory of the Son is referred again to Him. And since He generated Him omnipotent and such as He is in Himself, it is not[4] more the glory of the Son than of the Father, that He is self-sufficient, and self-maintained, and free from infirmity. It has been said of the Son, " By whom He made the worlds." (Heb. i. 2.) Now there is a distinction observed among us between creation and workmanship.[5] For one works and toils and executes, another rules ; and why ? because he that executes is the inferior. But it is not so

there ; nor is the sovereignty with One, the workmanship with the Other. For when we hear, " By whom He made the worlds,"[6] we do not exclude the Father from creation. Nor when we say, " To the King immortal,"[7] do we deny dominion to the Son. For these are common to the One and the Other, and each belongs to Both. The Father created, in that He begat the creating Son ; the Son rules, as being Lord of all things created. For He does not work for hire, nor in obedience to others, as workmen do among us, but from His own goodness and love for mankind. But has the Son[8] ever been seen? No one can affirm this. What means then, " To the King immortal, invisible, the only wise[9] God "? Or when it is said, " There is no other name whereby we must be saved " : and again, " There is salvation in no other "? (Acts iv. 12.)

" To Him be honor and glory forever. Amen."

Now honor and glory are not mere words ; and since He has honored us not by words only, but by what He has done for us, so let us honor Him by works and deeds. Yet this honor touches us, while that reaches not Him, for He needs not the honor that comes from us, we do need that which is from Him.

In honoring Him, therefore, we do honor to ourselves. He who opens his eyes to gaze on the light of the sun, receives delight himself, as he admires the beauty of the star, but does no favor to that luminary, nor increases its splendor, for it continues what it was ; much more is this true with respect to God. He who admires and honors God does so to his own salvation, and highest benefit ; and how? Because he follows after virtue, and is honored by Him. For " them that honor Me," He says, " I will honor." (1 Sam. iv. 30.) How then is He honored, if He enjoys no advantage from our honor? Just as He is said to hunger and thirst. For He assumes everything that is ours, that He may in anywise attract us to Him. He is said to receive honors, and even insults, that we may be afraid. But with all this we are not attracted towards Him !

MORAL. Let us then " glorify God," and bear God[10] both " in our body and in our spirit." (1 Cor. vi. 20.) And how is one to glorify Him in the body? saith one, and how in the spirit? The soul is here called the spirit to distinguish it from the body. But how may we glorify Him

---

[1] προτροπήν, al. ἐπιστρόφην, " bringing about conversion."
[2] Lit. " incorruptible."
[3] al. " out of time."
[4] It is necessary here to insert a negative, or to read οὐκοῦν for οὐκοῦν.
[5] κτίσις. Hales conjectures κτῆσις, possession. But this may be doubted, as κτίζειν means " to found," as a king founds a city. The workmen *build*, but do not *found*.

[6] Or " the ages." Heb. i. 2.
[7] Or " King of Ages " (αἰώνων, for which we have no word but " worlds," taken in an extended sense).
[8] i.e. in His Divine Nature.
[9] B. omits " wise " throughout, and then " only " applies to the words before, and the argument here is complete; viz., that there is One God, of whom all this is said, that is, the Ever Blessed Trinity. Some good MSS. favor this reading in the text.
[10] ἀρωμεν. St. Chrys. is almost the only Greek authority for the reading of the Vulgate, well known as the Capitulum of the 9th hour, " glorificate *et portate* Deum in corpore vestro." On the passage his reading so seems not quite decided. See Scholz, and Hom. xviii. on 1 Cor. vi. 20.

in the body and in the spirit? He glorifies Him in the body, who does not commit adultery or fornication, who avoids gluttony and drunkenness, who does not affect a showy exterior, who makes such provision for himself as is sufficient for health only: and so the woman, who does not perfume nor paint her person, but is satisfied to be such as God made her, and adds no device of her own. For why dost thou add thy own embellishments to the work which God made? Is not His workmanship sufficient for thee? or dost thou endeavor to add grace to it, as if forsooth thou wert the better artist?[1] It is not for thyself, but to attract crowds of lovers, that thou thus adornest thy person, and insultest thy Creator. And do not say, "What can I do? It is no wish of my own, but I must do it for my husband. I cannot win his love except I consent to this." God made thee beautiful, that He might be admired even in thy beauty, and not that He might be insulted. Do not therefore make Him so ill a return, but requite Him with modesty and chastity. God made thee beautiful, that He might increase the trials of thy modesty. For it is much harder for one that is lovely to be modest, than for one who has no such attractions, for which to be courted. Why does the Scripture tell us, that "Joseph was a goodly person, and well favored" (Gen. xxxix. 6), but that we might the more admire his modesty coupled with beauty? Has God made thee beautiful? Why dost thou make thyself otherwise? For as though one should overlay a golden statue with a daubing of mire, so it is with those women that use paints. Thou besmearest thyself with red and white earth! But the homely, you say, may fairly have recourse to this. And why? To hide their ugliness? It is a vain attempt. For when was the natural appearance improved upon by that which is studied and artificial? And why shouldest thou be troubled at thy want of beauty, since it is no reproach? For hear the saying of the Wise Man, "Commend not a man for his beauty, neither abhor a man for his outward appearance." (Ecclus. xi. 2.) Let God be rather admired, the best Artificer, and not man, who has no merit in being made such as he is. What are the advantages, tell me, of beauty? None. It exposes its possessor to greater trials, mishaps, perils, and suspicions. She that wants it escapes suspicion; she that possesses it, except she practice a great and extraordinary reserve, incurs an evil report, and what is worse than all, the suspicion of her husband, who takes less pleasure in beholding her beauty, than he suffers pain from jealousy. And her beauty fades in his sight from familiarity, whilst she suffers in her character from the imputation of weakness, dis-

sipation, and wantonness, and her very soul[2] becomes degraded and full of haughtiness. To these evils personal beauty is exposed. But she who has not this attraction, escapes unmolested. The dogs do not assail her; she is like a lamb, reposing in a secure pasture, where no wolf intrudes to harass her, because the shepherd is at hand to protect her.

The real superiority[3] is, not that one is fair, and the other homely, but it is a superiority that one, even if she is not fair, is unchaste, and the other is not wicked. Tell me wherein is the perfection of eyes? Is it in their being soft, and rolling, and round, and dark, or in their clearness and quicksightedness. Is it the perfection of a lamp to be elegantly formed, and finely turned, or to shine brightly, and to enlighten the whole house? We cannot say it is not this, for the other is indifferent, and this the real object. Accordingly we often say to the maid whose charge it is, "You have made a bad lamp of it." So entirely is it the use of a lamp to give light. So it matters not what is the appearance of the eye, whilst it performs its office with full efficiency. We call the eye bad, which is dim or disordered, and which, when open, does not see. For that is bad, which does not perform its proper office — and this is the fault of eyes. And for a nose, tell me, when is it a good one? When it is straight, and polished on either side, and finely proportioned? or when it is quick to receive odors, and transmit them to the brain? Any one can answer this.

Come now, let us illustrate this by an example — as of gripers, I mean the instruments so called; we say those are well-made, which are able to take up and hold things, not those which are only handsomely and elegantly shaped. So those are good teeth which are fit for the service of dividing and chewing our food, not those which are beautifully set. And applying the same reasoning to other parts of the body, we shall call those members beautiful, which are sound, and perform their proper functions aright. So we think any instrument, or plant, or animal good, not because of its form or color, but because it answers its purpose. And he is thought a good[4] servant, who is useful and ready for our service, not one who is comely but dissolute. I trust ye now understand how it is in your power to be beautiful.

And since the greatest and most important benefits are equally enjoyed by all, we are under no disadvantage. Whether we are beautiful or not, we alike behold this universe, the sun, the

---

[1] "God never made his work for man to mend." — Dryden.

[2] Stopping the passage thus, the present reading may stand.
[3] πλεονεξία seems here to be used for "superiority," if the reading of B. (*not* wicked) is correct; and this makes the best sense. Otherwise, it must stand for "excess."
[4] καλός.

moon, and the stars; we breathe the same air, we partake alike of water, and the fruits of the earth. And if we may say what will sound strange, the homely are more healthy than the beautiful. For these, to preserve their beauty, engage in no labor, but give themselves up to indolence and delicate living, by which their bodily energies are impaired; whilst the others, having no such care, spend all their attention simply and entirely on active pursuits.

Let us then "glorify God, and take and bear Him in our body." (1 Cor. vi. 20.) Let us not affect a beautiful appearance; that care is vain and unprofitable. Let us not teach our husbands to admire the mere outward form; for if such be thy adornment, his very habit of viewing thy face will make him easy to be captivated by a harlot. But if thou teachest him to love good manners, and modesty, he will not be ready to wander, for he will see no attractions in a harlot, in whom those qualities are not found, but the reverse. Neither teach him to be captivated by laughter, nor by a loose dress, lest thou prepare a poison against thyself. Accustom him to delight in modesty, and this thou wilt do, if thy attire be modest. But if thou hast a flaunting air, an unsteady manner, how canst thou address[1] him in a serious strain? and who will not hold thee in contempt and derision?

But how is it possible to glorify God in our spirit?[2] By practicing virtue, by adorning the soul. For such embellishment is not forbidden. Thus we glorify God, when we are good in every respect, and we shall be glorified by Him in a much higher degree in that great day. For "I reckon that the sufferings of this present time are not worthy to be compared with the glory that shall be revealed in us." (Rom. viii. 18.) Of which that we may all be partakers, God grant, by the grace and lovingkindness of our Lord Jesus Christ.

HOMILY V.

1 TIMOTHY i. 18, 19.

"This charge I commit unto thee, son [my child, τέκνον] Timothy, according to the prophecies which went before on thee, that thou by them mightest [mayest] war a good warfare; holding faith, and a good conscience; which some having put away have made shipwreck concerning the faith."

THE office of a Teacher and that of a Priest is of great dignity, and to bring forward one that is worthy requires a divine election. So it was of old, and so it is now, when we make a choice without human passion, not looking to any temporal consideration, swayed neither by friendship, nor enmity. For though we be not partakers of so great a measure of the Spirit as they, yet a good purpose is sufficient to draw unto us the election of God. For the Apostles, when they elected Matthias, had not yet received the Holy Spirit, but having committed the matter to prayer, they chose him into the number of the Apostles. For they looked not to human friendships. And so now too it ought to be with us. But we have advanced to the extreme of negligence; and even what is clearly evident, we let pass. Now when we overlook what is manifest, how will God reveal to us what is unseen? as it is said, "If ye have not been faithful in that which is little, who will commit to you that which is great and true?" (Luke xvi. 11.) But then, when nothing human was done, the appointment of Priests too was by prophecy. What is "by prophecy"? By the Holy Spirit. For prophecy is not only the telling of things future, but also of the present. It was by prophecy that Saul was discovered "hidden among the stuff." (1 Sam. x. 22.) For God reveals things to the righteous. So it was said by prophecy, "Separate me Barnabas and Saul." (Acts xiii. 2.) In this way Timothy also was chosen, concerning whom he speaks of prophecies in the plural; that, perhaps, upon which[3] he "took and circumcised him," and when he ordained him, as he himself says in his Epistle to him, "Neglect not the gift that is in thee." (1 Tim. iv. 14.) Therefore to elevate him, and prepare him to be sober and watchful, he reminds him by whom he was chosen and ordained, as if he had said, "God hath chosen thee. He gave thee thy commission, thou wast not made by human vote. Do not therefore abuse or bring into disgrace the appointment of God." When again he speaks of a charge, which implies something burdensome,[4] he adds, "This charge I commit to thee, son Timothy." He charges him as

---

[1] Ben. προσενεγκεῖν, Sav. προεν.
[2] Ben. "to bear God in our body." But this seems rather the subject that has been already discussed. See the beginning of the Moral.
[3] μεθ' ἧς.
[4] Or "galling"; the word "charge" is in the sense of "injunction."

his son, his own son, not so much with arbitrary or despotic authority as like a father, he says, " my son Timothy." The "committing," however, implies that it is to be diligently kept, and that it is not our own. For we did not obtain it for ourselves, but God conferred it upon us ; and not it only, but also "faith and a good conscience." What He hath given us then, let us keep. For if He had not come, the faith had not been to be found, nor that pure life which we learn by education. As if he had said, " It is not I that charge thee, but He who chose thee," and this is meant by "the prophecies" that went before on thee." Listen to them, obey them.

And say; what chargest thou? "That by them thou shouldest war a good warfare." They chose thee, that then for which they chose thee do thou, "war a good warfare." He named " a good warfare," since there is a bad warfare, of which he says, "As ye have yielded your members instruments[1] to uncleanness and to iniquity." (Rom. vi. 19.) Those men serve under a tyrant, but thou servest under a King. And why calls he it a warfare? To show how mighty a contest is to be maintained by all, but especially by a Teacher ; that we require strong arms, and sobriety, and awakenedness, and continual vigilance : that we must prepare ourselves for blood and conflicts, must be in battle array, and have nothing relaxed. "That thou shouldest war in them," he says. For as in an army all do not serve in the same capacity, but in their different stations ; so also in the Church one has the office of a Teacher, another that of a disciple, another that of a private man. But thou art in this. And, because this is not sufficient, he adds,

Ver. 19. " Holding faith, and a good conscience."

For he that would be a Teacher must first teach himself. For as he who has not first been a good soldier, will never be a general, so it is with the Teacher ; wherefore he says elsewhere, " Lest when I have preached to others, I myself should be a cast-away." (1 Cor. ix. 27.) " Holding faith," he says, "and a good conscience," that so thou mayest preside over others. When we hear this, let us not disdain the exhortations of our superiors, though we be Teachers. For if Timothy, to whom all of us together are not worthy to be compared, receives commands and is instructed, and that being himself in the Teacher's office, much more should we. " Which some having put away, have made shipwreck concerning the faith."[2] And this follows naturally. For when the life is corrupt, it engenders a doctrine congenial to it, and from this circumstance many are seen to fall into a gulf of evil, and to turn aside into Heathenism. For that they may not be tormented with the fear of futurity, they endeavor to persuade their souls, that what we preach is false. And some turn aside from the faith, who seek out everything by reasoning ; for reasoning produces shipwreck, while faith is as a safe ship.

They then who turn aside from the faith must suffer shipwreck ; and this he shows by an example.

Ver. 20. " Of whom are Hymenæus and Alexander."

And from them he would instruct us. You see how even from those times there have been seducing Teachers, curious enquirers, and men holding off from the faith, and searching out[3] by their own reasonings. As the shipwrecked man is naked and destitute of all things, so is he that falls away from the faith without resource, he knows not where to stand or where to stay himself, nor has he the advantage of a good life so as to gain anything from that quarter. For when the head is disordered, what avails the rest of the body? and if faith without a good life is unavailing, much more is the converse true. If God despises His own for our sakes, much more ought we to despise our own for His sake.[4] For so it is, where any one falls away from the faith, he has no steadiness, he swims this way and that, till at last he is lost in the deep.

" Whom I delivered to Satan, that they might be taught not to blaspheme ! " Thus it is blasphemy to search into divine things by our own reasonings. For what have human reasonings in common with them? But how does Satan instruct them not to blaspheme? can he instruct others, who has not yet taught himself, but is a blasphemer still? It is not that "he should instruct," but *that they should be instructed*. It is not he that does it, though such is the result. As elsewhere he says in the case of the fornicator : "To deliver such an one to Satan for the destruction of the flesh." Not that he may save the body, but " that the spirit may be saved." (1 Cor. v. 5.) Therefore it is spoken impersonally. How then is this effected? As executioners, though themselves laden with numberless crimes, are made the correctors of others ; so it is here with the evil spirit. But why didst thou not punish them thyself, as thou didst that Bar-Jesus, and as Peter did Ananias, instead of delivering them to Satan? It was not that they might be punished, but that they might

---

[1] The word used, Rom. vi. 13, which may mean " arms " (ὅπλα).
[2] [This is the order of the R. V.]

[3] al. " searching into divine Mysteries by."
[4] i.e. if God regards not our *faith*, which is most towards Him of all we do, unless we perform the duties of life, much more ought we not to pride ourselves on any such duties, while we neglect that duty to Him. See St. Chrys. on Rom. iv. 1, 2, Hom. viii.

be instructed. For that he had the power appears from other passages, "What will ye? Shall I come unto you with a rod?" (1 Cor. iv. 21.) And again, "Lest I should use sharpness, according to the power which the Lord hath given me to edification, and not to destruction." (2 Cor. xiii. 10.) Why did he then call upon Satan to punish them? That the disgrace might be greater, as the severity and the punishment was more striking. Or rather, they themselves chastised those who did not yet believe, but those who turned aside, they delivered to Satan. Why then did Peter punish Ananias? Because whilst he was tempting the Holy Ghost, he was still an unbeliever. That the unbelieving therefore might learn that they could not escape, they themselves inflicted punishment upon them ; but those who had learnt this, yet afterwards turned aside, they delivered to Satan ; showing that they were sustained not by their own power, but by their care for them ; and as many as were lifted up into arrogance were delivered to him. For as kings with their own hands slay their enemies, but deliver their subjects to executioners for punishment, so it is in this case. And these acts were done to show the authority committed to the Apostles. Nor was it a slight power, to be able thus to subject the devil to their commands. For this shows that he served and obeyed them even against his will, and this was no little proof of the power of grace. And listen how he delivered them : "When ye are gathered together, and my spirit, with the power of our Lord Jesus Christ, to deliver such an one unto Satan." (1 Cor. v. 4.) He was then immediately expelled from the common assembly, he was separated from the fold, he became deserted and destitute ; he was delivered to the wolf. For as the cloud designated the camp of the Hebrews, so the Spirit distinguished the Church. If any one therefore was without, he was consumed,[1] and it was by the judgment of the Apostles that he was cast out of the pale. So also the Lord delivered Judas to Satan. For immediately "after the sop Satan entered into him." (John xiii. 27.) Or this may be said ; that those whom they wished to amend, they did not themselves punish, but reserved their punishments for those who were incorrigible. Or otherwise, that they were the more dreaded for delivering them up to others. Job also was delivered to Satan, but not for his sins, but for fuller proof of his worth.

Many such instances still occur. For since the Priests cannot know who are sinners, and unworthy partakers of the holy Mysteries, God often in this way delivers them to Satan. For

when diseases, and attacks,[2] and sorrows, and calamities, and the like occur, it is on this account that they are inflicted. This is shown by Paul. "For this cause many are weak and sickly among you, and many sleep." (1 Cor. xi. 30.) But how? saith one, when we approach but once a year ! But this is indeed the evil, that you determine the worthiness of your approach, not by the purity of your minds, but by the interval of time. You think it a proper caution not to communicate often ; not considering that you are seared by partaking unworthily, though only once, but to receive worthily, though often, is salutary. It is not presumptuous to receive often, but to receive unworthily, though but once in a whole life. But we are so miserably foolish, that, though we commit numberless offenses in the course of a year, we are not anxious to be absolved from them, but are satisfied, that we do not often make bold impudently to insult the Body of Christ, not remembering that those who crucified Christ, crucified Him but once. Is the offense then the less, because committed but once? Judas betrayed his Master but once. What then, did that exempt him from punishment? Why indeed is time to be considered in this matter? let our time of coming be when our conscience is pure. The Mystery at Easter is not of more efficacy than that which is now celebrated. It is one and the same. There is the same grace of the Spirit, it is always a Passover.[3] You who are initiated know this. On the Preparation,[4] on the Sabbath, on the Lord's day, and on the day of Martyrs, it is the same Sacrifice that is performed. "For as often," he saith, "as ye eat this bread and drink this cup, ye do show the Lord's death." (1 Cor. xi. 26.) No time is limited for the performance of this Sacrifice, why then is it then called the Paschal feast?[5] Because Christ suffered for us then. Let not the time, therefore, make any difference in your approach. There is at all times the same power, the same dignity, the same grace, one and the same body ; nor is one celebration of it more or less holy than another. And this you know, who see upon these occasions nothing new, save these worldly veils, and a more splendid attendance. The only thing that these days have more is that from them commenced the day of our salvation when Christ was sacrificed. But with respect to these mysteries, those days have no further preëminence.

---

[1] See Ex. xiv. 20. The converse is not stated here, but is implied of the Christian Church in Zech. ii. 5.

[2] ἐπιβουλαί. He seems to mean those of Satan. Of affliction as a warning against sin, see on Stat. Hom. iii. and Hom. iv.
[3] See Hom. iii. of St. Chrys. against the Jews, § 4. Ben. t. i. p. 611.
[4] παρασκευῇ, Friday [preparation day for the Jewish Sabbath, Sabbath-eve].
[5] πάσχα. He seems to allude to the Greek word for "suffering," though the reason will hold otherwise. [πάσχα is not from the Greek πάσχω, to suffer, but from the Hebrew חֶסַּפ, a passing over, a sparing.]

When you approach to take bodily food, you wash your hands and your mouth, but when you draw nigh to this spiritual food, you do not cleanse your soul, but approach full of uncleanness. But you say, Are not the forty days' fastings sufficient to cleanse the huge heap of our sins? But of what use is it, tell me? If wishing to store up some precious unguent, you should make clean a place to receive it, and a little after having laid it up, should throw dung upon it, would not the fine odor vanish? This takes place with us too. We make ourselves to the best of our power worthy to approach; then we defile ourselves again! What then is the good of it? This we say even of those who are able in those forty days to wash themselves clean.

Let us then, I beseech you, not neglect our salvation, that our labor may not be in vain. For he who turns from his sins, and goes and commits the same again, is "like a dog that returneth to his vomit." (Prov. xxvi. 11.) But if we act as we ought, and take heed to our ways, we shall be thought worthy of those high rewards, which that we may all obtain, God grant through the grace and lovingkindness of our Lord Jesus Christ, with whom, &c.

HOMILY VI.

1 TIMOTHY ii. 1–4.

" I exhort therefore that, first of all, supplications, prayers, intercessions, and giving of thanks be made for all men; for kings, and for all that are in authority; that we may lead a quiet and peaceable life in all godliness and honesty. For this is good and acceptable in the sight of God our Saviour; who will have all men to be saved, and to come unto the knowledge of the truth." [R. V.: who willeth that all men should be saved, &c.]

THE Priest is the common father, as it were, of all the world ; it is proper therefore that he should care for all, even as God, Whom he serves.[1] For this reason he says, " I exhort therefore that, first of all, supplications, prayers, intercessions, and giving of thanks be made for all men." From this, two advantages result. First, hatred towards those who are without is done away ; for no one can feel hatred towards those for whom he prays : and they again are made better by the prayers that are offered for them, and by losing their ferocious disposition towards us. For nothing is so apt to draw men under teaching, as to love, and be loved. Think what it was for those who persecuted, scourged, banished, and slaughtered the Christians, to hear that those whom they treated so barbarously offered fervent prayers to God for them.[2] Observe how he wishes a Christian to be superior to all ill-treatment. As a father who was struck on the face by a little child which he was carrying, would not lose anything of his affection for it ; so we ought not to abate in our good will towards those who are without, even when we are stricken by them. What is " first of all "? It means in the daily Service ; and the initiated know how this is done every day both in the evening and the morning, how we offer prayers for the whole world, for kings and all that are in authority. But some one perhaps will say, he meant not for all men, but for all the faithful. How then does he speak of kings? for kings were not then worshipers of God, for there was a long succession of ungodly princes. And that he might not seem to flatter them, he says first, " for all men," then " for kings " ; for if he had only mentioned kings, that might have been suspected. And then since the soul of some Christians ·might be· slow[3] at hearing this, and reject the exhortation, if at the celebration of the holy Mysteries it was necessary to offer prayers for a heathen king, he shows them the advantage of it, thus at least to reconcile them to the advice, " that we may lead a quiet and peaceable life " ; as much as to say, Their safety is a security to us ;[4] as also in his Epistle to the Romans, he exhorts them to obey their rulers, " not for wrath but for conscience' sake." (Rom. xiii. 5.) For God has appointed government for the public good. When therefore they make war for this end, and stand on guard for our security, were it not unreasonable that we should not offer prayers for their safety in wars and dangers? It is not therefore flattery, but agreeable to the rules of justice. For if they were not preserved, and prospered in their wars, our affairs must necessarily be involved in confusion and trouble ; and if they were cut off, we must either serve ourselves, or be scattered up and down as fugitives. For they are a sort of bul-

---

[1] ὡ ἱερᾱται.
[2] This is urged by Tertullian, Apol. i. § 30, and Address to Scapula, § 2. See also St. Justin, M. Apol. i. § 23.
[3] ναρκᾳν.
[4] See on Rom. xiii. 6, Hom. xxiii.

warks thrown up before us, within which those who are inclosed are in peace and safety.

He says, " supplications, prayers, intercessions, and giving of thanks." For we must give thanks to God for the good that befalls others, as that He maketh the sun to shine upon the evil and the good, and sendeth His rain both upon the just and the unjust. Observe how he would unite and bind us together, not only by prayer but by thanksgiving. For he who is urged to thank God for his neighbor's good, is also bound to love him, and be kindly disposed towards him. And if we must give thanks for our neighbor's good, much more for what happens to ourselves, and for what is unknown, and even for things against our will, and such as appear grievous to us, since God dispenses all things for our good.

MORAL. Let every prayer of ours, then, be accompanied with thanksgiving. And if we are commanded to pray for our neighbors, not only for the faithful, but for the unbelieving also, consider how wrong it is to pray against your brethren. What? Has He commanded you to pray for your enemies, and do you pray against your brother? But your prayer is not against him, but against yourself. For you provoke God by uttering those 'impious words, " Show him the same ! " " So do to him ! " " Smite him ! " " Recompense him ! " Far be such words from the disciple of Christ, who should be meek and mild. From the mouth that has been vouchsafed such holy Mysteries, let nothing bitter proceed.[1] Let not the tongue that has touched the Lord's Body utter anything offensive, let it be kept pure, let not curses be borne upon it. For if " revilers shall not inherit the kingdom of God " (1 Cor. vi. 10), much less those who curse. For he that curses must be injurious ; and injuriousness and prayer are at variance with each other, cursing and praying are far apart, accusation and prayer are wide asunder. Do you propitiate God with prayer, and then utter imprecations? If you forgive not, you will not be forgiven. (Matt. vi. 15.) But instead of forgiving, you beseech God not to forgive ; what excessive wickedness in this ! If the unforgiving is not forgiven, he that prays his Lord not to forgive, how shall he be forgiven? The harm is to yourself, not him. For though your prayers were on the point of being heard for yourself, they would never be accepted in such a case, as offered with a polluted mouth. For surely the mouth that curses is polluted with all that is offensive and unclean.

When you ought to tremble for your own sins, to wrestle earnestly for the pardon of them, you come to move God against your brother — do you not fear, nor think of what concerns yourself? do you not see what you are doing? Imitate even the conduct of children at school. If they see their own class within giving account of their lessons, and all beaten for their idleness, and one by one severely examined and chastised with blows, they are frightened to death, and if one of their companions strikes them, and that severely, they cannot have while to be angry, nor complain to their master ; so is their soul possessed with fear. They only look to one thing, that they may go in and come out without stripes, and their thoughts are on that time. And when they come out, whether beaten or not, the blows they have received from their playfellows never enter their minds for the delight. And you, when you stand anxiously concerned for your own sins, how can you but shudder at making mention of others' faults?[2] How can you implore pardon of God? For your own case is made worse on the terms of your imprecations against another, and you forbid Him to make allowance for your own faults. Might He not say, " If thou wouldest have Me so severe in exacting offenses against thee, how canst thou expect Me to pardon thy offenses against Me ? " Let us learn at last to be Christians ! If we know not how to pray, which is a very simple and easy thing, what else shall we know? Let us learn to pray like Christians. Those are the prayers of Gentiles, the supplications of Jews. The Christian's are the reverse, for the forgiveness and forgetting of offenses against us. " Being reviled," it is said, " we bless ; being persecuted, we suffer it ; being defamed, we entreat." (1 Cor. iv. 12, 13.) Hear Stephen saying, " Lord, lay not this sin to their charge." (Acts vi. 60.) Instead of praying against them, he prayed for them. You, instead of praying for them, utter imprecations against them. You then are wicked in the degree that he was excellent. Whom do we admire, tell me ; those for whom he prayed, or him who prayed for them? Him certainly ! and if we, much more then God. Would you have your enemy stricken? pray for him : yet not with such intention, not to strike him. That will indeed be the effect, but let it not be your object. That blessed martyr suffered all unjustly, yet he prayed for them : we suffer many things justly from our enemies. And if he who suffered unjustly durst not forbear to pray for his enemies, what punishment do we deserve, who suffer justly, and yet do not pray for them, nay, pray against them? Thou thinkest indeed that thou art inflicting a blow upon another, but in truth thou art thrust-

---

[1] See Jas. iii. 11.

[2] In the Apostolical Constitutions, b. viii. c. 12, the Deacon says, just before the Offertory Prayer, " No man against another ! no man in hypocrisy ! Upright before the Lord with fear and trembling let us stand to offer ! " The first sentence shows that the like abuse was apprehended.

ing the sword against thyself. Thou sufferest not the Judge to be lenient to thy own offenses, by this way of urging Him to anger against others. For, "with what measure ye mete," He saith, "it shall be measured to you again; and with what judgment ye judge, ye shall be judged." (Matt. vii. 2.) Let us therefore be disposed to pardon, that God may be so disposed towards us.

These things I wish you not only to hear, but to observe. For now the memory retains only the words, and perhaps hardly those. And after we are separated, if any one who was not present were to ask you, what had been our discourse, some could not tell: others would know merely the subject we had spoken of, and answer that there had been a Homily upon the subject of forgiving injuries, and praying for our enemies, but would omit all that had been said, as they could not remember: others remember a little, but still somewhat. If therefore you gain nothing by what you hear, I entreat you not even to attend at the discourse. For of what use is it? The condemnation is greater, the punishment more severe, if after so many exhortations, we continue in the same course. For this reason God has given us a definite form of prayer, that we might ask for nothing human, nothing worldly. And you that are faithful know what you ought to pray for, how the whole Prayer is common. But one says, "It is not commanded there to pray for unbelievers." This you would not say, if you understood the force, the depth, the hidden treasure of that [1] Prayer. Only unfold it, and you find this also comprised within it. For it is implied, when one says in prayer, "Thy will be done on earth, as it is in Heaven." Now, because in heaven there is no unbeliever, nor offender; if therefore it was for the faithful alone, there would be no reason in that expression. If the faithful were to do the will of God, and the unbelievers not to do it, His will were not done in earth as it is in heaven. But it means; As there is none wicked in heaven, so let there be none on earth; but draw all men to the fear of Thee, make all men angels, even those who hate us, and are our enemies. Dost thou not see how God is daily blasphemed and mocked by believers and unbelievers, both in word and in deed? What then? Has He for this extinguished the sun? or stayed the course of the moon? Has He crushed the heavens and uprooted the earth? Has He dried up the sea? Has He shut up the fountains of waters? or confounded the air? Nay, on the contrary, He makes His sun to rise, His rain to descend, gives the fruits of the earth in their seasons, and thus supplies yearly nourishment to the blas-

phemers, to the insensible, to the polluted, to persecutors; not for one day or two, but for their whole life. Imitate Him then, emulate Him as far as human powers admit. Canst thou not make the sun arise? Abstain from evil speaking. Canst thou not send rain? Forbear reviling. Canst thou not give food? Refrain from insolence. Such gifts from thee are sufficient. The goodness of God to His enemies is shown by His works. Do thou so at least by words: pray for thine enemies, so wilt thou be like thy Father who is in heaven. How many times have we discoursed upon this subject! nor shall we cease to discourse; only let something come of it. It is not that we are drowsy, and weary of speaking; only do not you that hear be annoyed. Now a person seems to be annoyed, when he will not do what one says. For he who practices, loves often to hear the same thing, and is not annoyed by it; for it is his own commendation. But annoyance arises simply from not doing what is prescribed. Hence the speaker is troublesome. If a man practices almsgiving, and hears another speak of almsgiving, he is not wearied,[2] but pleased, for he hears his own good actions recommended and proclaimed. So that when we are displeased at hearing a discourse upon the forgiveness of injuries, it is because we have no interest in forbearance, it is not practiced by us; for if we had the reality, we should not be pained at its being named. If therefore you would not have us wearisome or annoying, practice as we preach, exhibit in your actions the subject of our discourses. For we shall never cease discoursing upon these things till your conduct is agreeable to them. And this we do more especially from our concern and affection for you. For the trumpeter must sound his trumpet, though no one should go out to war; he must fulfill his part. We do it, not as wishing to bring heavier condemnation upon you, but to avert it from ourselves. And besides this, love for you constrains us, for it would tear and torture our hearts if that should befall you, which God avert! It is not any costly process that we recommend to you: it does not require the spoiling of goods, nor a long and toilsome journey. It is only to will. It is a word, it is a purpose of the mind. Let us only set a guard on our tongues, a door and a bar upon our lips, that we may utter nothing offensive to God. It is for our own advantage, not for theirs for whom we pray, to act thus. For let us ever consider, that he who blesses his enemy, blesses himself, he who curses his enemy, curses himself, and he who prays for his enemy, prays not for him, but

---

[1] Gr. "the."

for himself. If we thus act, we shall be able to reduce to practice this excellent virtue,[1] and so to obtain the promised blessings, through the grace and lovingkindness of our Lord Jesus Christ.

HOMILY VII.

1 TIMOTHY ii. 2–4.

"That we may lead a quiet and peaceable life in all god-liness and honesty. For this is good and acceptable in the sight of God our Saviour; who willeth that all men should be saved, and come unto the knowl-edge of the truth."

If in order to put an end to public wars, and tumults, and battles, the Priest is exhorted to offer prayers for kings and governors, much more ought private individuals to do it. For there are three very grievous kinds of war. The one is public, when our soldiers are attacked by foreign armies: The second is, when even in time of peace, we are at war with one another: The third is, when the individual is at war with himself, which is the worst of all. For foreign war will not be able to hurt us greatly. What, I pray, though it slaughters and cuts us off? It injures not the soul. Neither will the second have power to harm us against our will; for though others be at war with us, we may be peaceable ourselves. For so says the Prophet, "For my love they are my adversaries, but I give myself unto prayer" (Ps. cix. 4); and again, "I was at peace with them that hate peace"; and, "I am for peace; but when I speak, they are for war." (Ps. cxx. 6, 7, Sept.) But from the third, we cannot escape without danger. For when the body is at variance with the soul, and raises up evil desires, and arms against it sensual pleasures, or the bad passions of anger, and envy; we cannot attain the promised blessings, till this war is brought to an end; who-ever does not still this tumult, must fall pierced by wounds that will bring that death that is in hell. We have daily need therefore of care and great anxiety, that this war may not be stirred up within us, or that, if stirred up, it may not last, but be quelled and laid asleep. For what advantage is it, that the world enjoys profound peace, if thou art at war with thyself? This then is the peace we should keep. If we have it, nothing from without will be able to harm us. And to this end the public peace contributes no little: whence it is said, "That we may lead a quiet and peaceable life." But if any one is dis-turbed when there is quiet, he is a miserable creature. Seest thou that He speaks of this peace which I call the third kind? Therefore when he has said, "that we may lead a quiet and peaceable life," he does not stop there, but adds, "in all godliness and honesty." But we cannot live in godliness and honesty, unless that peace be established. For when curious reasonings disturb our faith, what peace is there? or when spirits of uncleanness, what peace is there?

For that we may not suppose that he speaks of that sort of life which all men live, when he says, "that we may lead a quiet and peaceable life," he adds, "in all godliness and honesty," since a quiet and peaceable life may be led by heathens, and profligates, and voluptuous and wanton persons may be found living such a life. That this cannot be meant, is plain, from what he adds, "in all godliness and honesty." Such a life is exposed to snares, and conflicts, and the soul is daily wounded by the tumults of its own thoughts. But what sort of life he really means is plain from the sequel, and plain too, in that he speaks not simply of godliness, but adds, of "all godliness." For in saying this he seems to insist on a godliness not only of doc-trine, but such as is supported by life, for in both surely must godliness be required. For of what advantage is it to be godly as to doc-trine, but ungodly in life? and that it is very possible to be ungodly in life, hear this same blessed Apostle saying elsewhere, "They pro-fess that they know God, but in works they deny Him." (Tit. i. 16.) And again, "He hath denied the faith, and is worse than an in-fidel." (1 Tim. v. 8.) And, "If any man that is called a brother be a fornicator, or covetous, or an idolater" (1 Cor. v. 11), such a man honors not God. And, "He that hateth his brother, knoweth not God." (1 John ii. 9.) Such are the various ways of ungodliness. There-fore he says, "All godliness and good order."[2] For not only is the fornicator not honest, but

---

[1] He evidently hints at a higher degree of Christian feeling, in which a man would simply wish well to his enemies, and *therefore* pray for them. See on Phil. i. 30, Hom. iv., and on Rom. xii. 20, Hom. xxii.

[2] σεμνότητι. This word expresses the highest kind of "sobriety." "Honesty," when used for it, has the Latin meaning.

the covetous man may be called disorderly and intemperate. For avarice is a lust no less than the bodily appetites, which he who does not chastise, is called dissolute.[1] For men are called dissolute from not restraining their desires, so that the passionate, the envious, the covetous, the deceitful, and every one that lives in sin, may be called dissolute, disorderly, and licentious.

Ver. 3. "For this is good and acceptable in the sight of God our Saviour."

What is said to be "acceptable"? The praying for all men. This God accepts, this He wills.

Ver. 4. "Who willeth that all men should be saved, and come to the knowledge of the truth."

Imitate God! if He willeth that all men should be saved, there is reason why one should pray for all, if He hath willed that all should be saved, be thou willing also; and if thou wishest it, pray for it, for wishes lead to prayers. Observe how from every quarter He urges this upon the soul, to pray for the Heathen, showing how great advantage springs from it; "that we may lead a quiet and peaceable life"; and what is much more than this, that it is pleasing to God, and thus men become like Him, in that they will the same that He does. This is enough to shame a very brute. Fear not therefore to pray for the Gentiles, for God Himself wills it; but fear only to pray against any, for that He wills not. And if you pray for the Heathens, you ought of course to pray for Heretics also, for we are to pray for all men, and not to persecute.[2] And this is good also for another reason, as we are partakers of the same nature, and God commands and accepts benevolence and affection towards one another.

But if the Lord Himself wills to give, you say, what need of my prayer? It is of great benefit both to them and to thyself. It draws them to love, and it inclines thee to humanity. It has the power of attracting others to the faith; (for many men have fallen away from God, from contentiousness towards one another;) and this[3] is what he now calls the salvation of God, "who will have all men to be saved"; without this all other is nothing great, a mere nominal salvation,[4] and only in words. "And to come to the knowledge of the truth." The truth: what truth? Faith in Him. And indeed he had previously said, "Charge some that they teach no other doctrine." But that no one may consider such as enemies, and on that account raise troubles[5] against them; he says that "He willeth that all men should be saved, and come to the knowledge of the truth"; and having said this, he adds,

Ver. 5. "For there is one God, and one Mediator between God and men."

He had before said, "to come to the knowledge of the truth," implying that the world is not in the truth. Now he says, "that there is one God," that is, not as some say, many, and that He has sent His Son as Mediator, thus giving proof that He will have all men to be saved. But is not the Son God? Most truly He is; why then does he say, "One God"? In contradistinction to the idols; not to the Son. For he is discoursing about truth and error. Now a mediator ought to have communion with both parties, between whom he is to mediate. For this is the property of a mediator, to be in close communion with each of those whose mediator he is. For he would be no longer a mediator, if he were connected with one but separated from the other.[6] If therefore He partakes not of the nature of the Father, He is not a Mediator, but is separated. For as He is partaker of the nature of men, because He came to men, so is He partaker of the nature of God, because He came from God. Because He was to mediate between two natures, He must approximate to the two natures; for as the place situated between two others is joined to each place, so must that between natures be joined to either nature. As therefore He became Man, so was He also God. A man could not have become a mediator, because he must also plead with God. God could not have been mediator, since those could not receive Him, toward whom He should have mediated. And as elsewhere he says, "There is one God the Father, . . . and one Lord Jesus Christ" (1 Cor. viii. 6); so also here "One" God, and "One" Mediator; he does not say two; for he would not have that number wrested to Polytheism, of which he was speaking. So he wrote "One" and "One." You see how accurate are the expressions of Scripture! For though one and one are two, we are not to say this, though reason suggests it. And here thou sayest not one and one are two, and yet thou sayest what reason does not suggest. "If He begat He also suffered."[7] "For there is one God," he says, "and one Mediator between God and men, the Man Christ Jesus."

[1] ἀκόλαστος.
[2] This of course does not imply that Heretics might not be prevented from usurping churches, nor their persons shunned, Hom. de Incompr. ii. fin. Ben. t. i. p. 462, nor their doctrines anathematized. Hom. de Anathemat. fin. t. i. p. 696. On the Church's disapproval of putting them to death, see the case of Priscillian, in the vol. of Fleury's Eccl. History [Schaff, Ch. Hist. III. 143].
[3] i.e. the coming to the Faith. Sav. mar. has "and this is what he now calls salvation" (this fem.). See Ps. xcviii. 3.
[4] The Greek word is applicable to bodily safety.

[5] μάχας.
[6] See St. Athanasius, Ep. on Nicene Decrees, § 24, Tr. p. 41.
[7] ἔπαθεν. Not in the sense implied in Sabellianism. He refers to an Arian argument against the proper Divinity of the Son, which he means is less plausible than one which this passage of St. Paul shows not to be legitimate. See St. Ath. against Arians, Disc. 1, Ben. § 16, t. i. p. 421 a, Tr. c. v. § 6, p. 204.

Ver. 6. "Who gave Himself a ransom for all, to be testified [1] in due time."

Was Christ then a ransom for the Heathen? Undoubtedly Christ died even for Heathen; and you cannot bear to pray for them. Why then, you ask, did they not believe? Because they would not: but His part was done. His suffering was a "Testimony," he says; for He came, it is meant, "to bear witness to the truth" of the Father, and was slain.[2] Thus not only the Father bore witness to Him, but He to the Father. "For I came," He saith, "in my Father's name." (John v. 43.) And again, "No man hath seen God at any time." (John i. 18.) And again, "That they might know Thee, the only true God." (John xvii. 3.) And, "God is a Spirit." (John iv. 24.) And He bore witness even to the death. But this, "in due time," means, In the fittest time.

Ver. 7. "Whereunto I am ordained a preacher and an Apostle, (I speak the truth in Christ, and lie not:) a teacher of the Gentiles in faith and verity."

Since therefore Christ suffered for the Gentiles, and I was separated to be a "teacher of the Gentiles," why dost thou refuse to pray for them? He fully shows his own credibility, by saying that he was "ordained" (Acts xiii. 2), that is, separated, for this purpose, the other Apostles being backward [3] in teaching the Gentiles; he adds, "in faith and verity," to show that in that faith there was no deceit. Here is observable the extension of grace. For the Jews had no prayers for the Gentiles; but now grace is extended to them: and when he says that he was separated to be a Teacher of the Gentiles, he intimates that grace was now shed over every part of the world.

"He gave himself a ransom," he saith, how then was He delivered up by the Father? Because it was of His goodness. And what means "ransom"? God was about to punish them, but He forbore to do it. They were about to perish, but in their stead He gave His own Son, and sent us as heralds to proclaim the Cross. These things are sufficient to attract all, and to demonstrate the love of Christ. MORAL. So truly, so inexpressibly great are the benefits which God has bestowed upon us. He sacrificed Himself for His enemies, who hated and rejected Him. What no one would do for friends, for brethren, for children, that the Lord hath done for His servants; a Lord not Himself such an one as His servants, but God for men; for men not deserving. For had they been deserving, had they done His pleasure, it would

have been less wonderful; but that He died for such ungrateful, such obstinate creatures, this it is which strikes every mind with amazement. For what men would not do for their fellow-men, that has God done for us! Yet after such a display of love towards us, we hold back,[4] and are not in earnest in our love of Christ. He has sacrificed Himself for us; for Him we make no sacrifice. We neglect Him when He wants necessary food; sick and naked we visit Him not. What do we not deserve, what wrath, what punishment, what hell? Were there no other inducement, it should be sufficient to prevail with every one that He condescended to make human sufferings His own, to say I hunger, I thirst.

O the tyranny of wealth! or rather the wickedness of those who are its willing slaves! for it has no great power of itself, but through our weakness and servility:[5] it is we that are mean and groveling, that are carnal and without understanding. For what power has money? It is mute and insensible. If the devil, that wicked spirit, that crafty confounder of all things, has no power,[6] what power has money? When you look upon silver, fancy it is tin! Cannot you? Then hold it for what it really is; for earth it is. But if you cannot reason thus, consider that we too shall perish, that many of those who have possessed it have gained scarce any advantage by it, that thousands who gloried in it are now dust and ashes. That they are suffering extreme punishment, and far more beggarly than they that fed from glass and earthenware; that those who once reclined on ivory couches, are poorer now than those who are lying on the dunghill. But it delights the eyes! How many other things delight them more! The flowers, the pure sky, the firmament, the bright sun, are far more grateful to the eye. For it hath much of rust, whence some have asserted that it was black, which appears from the images that turn black. But there is no blackness in the sun, the heaven, the stars. Much greater delight is there in these brilliants[7] than in its color. It is not therefore its brilliancy[8] that makes it please, but covetousness and iniquity; these, and not money, give the pleasure. Cast these from thy soul, and what appeared so precious will seem to thee more worthless than clay. Those who are in a fever long for mud when they see it, as if it were spring water; but those in sound health seldom wish even for water. Cast off this morbid longing, and thou wilt see things as they are. And to prove that I do not speak falsely, know, that I can point out many who

---

[1] Lit. "the Testimony."
[2] He seems to mean, "was slain for that purpose."
[3] ἐνάρκων. Montf. observes that all copies agree, and that this may be true of the countries mentioned in the Acts of the Apostles, but not universally.

[4] ἀκκιζόμεθα.
[5] One MS. and old Lat. "dissoluteness."
[6] i.e. over those who resist him.
[7] Lit. "flowers." See on Stat. Hom. ix. 3.
[8] Lit. "flower."

have done so. Quench this flame, and thou wilt see that these things are of less worth than flowers.

Is gold good? Yes, it is good for almsgiving, for the relief of the poor ; it is good, not for unprofitable use, to be hoarded up or buried in the earth, to be worn on the hands or the feet or the head. It was discovered for this end, that with it we should loose the captives, not form it into a chain for the image of God. Use thy gold for this, to loose him that is bound, not to chain her that is free. Tell me, why dost thou value above all things what is of so little worth? Is it the less a chain, because it is of gold? does the material make any difference?[1] whether it be gold or iron, it is still a chain ; nay the gold is the heavier. What then makes it light, but vainglory, and the pleasure of being seen to wear a chain, of which you ought rather to be ashamed? To make this evident, fasten it, and place the wearer in a wilderness or where there is no one to see, and the chain will at once be felt heavy, and thought burdensome.

Beloved, let us fear, lest we be doomed to hear those terrible words, " Bind him hand and foot." (Matt. xxii. 13.) And why, O woman, dost thou now do so to thyself? No prisoner has both his hands and his feet bound. Why bindest thou thy head too? For thou art not content with hands and feet, but bindest thy head and thy neck with many chains. I pass over the care that comes of these things, the fear, the alarm, the strife occasioned by them with thy husband if ever he wants them, the death it is to people when they lose any of them. Canst thou call this a pleasure? To gratify the eyes of others, dost thou subject thyself to chains, and cares, and perils, and uneasiness, and daily quarrels? This is deserving of every censure and condemnation. Nay, I entreat you, let us not do thus, let us burst every " bond of iniquity " (Acts viii. 23) ; let us break our bread to the hungry, and let us do all other things, which may ensure to us confidence before God, that we may obtain the blessings promised through Jesus Christ our Lord, with whom, &c.

HOMILY VIII.

1 TIMOTHY ii. 8–10.

" I will therefore that men pray everywhere, lifting up holy hands, without wrath and doubting. In like manner also, that women adorn themselves in modest apparel, with shamefacedness and sobriety; not with broidered hair, or gold, or pearls, or costly array; but (which becometh women professing godliness) with good works."

" WHEN thou prayest," saith Christ, " thou shalt not be as the hypocrites are ; for they love to pray standing in the synagogues and in the corners of the streets, that they may be seen of men. Verily I say unto you, they have their reward. But thou, when thou prayest, enter into thy closet, and when thou hast shut thy door, pray to thy Father, which is in secret ; and thy Father, which seeth in secret, shall reward thee openly." (Matt. vi. 5, 6.) What then says Paul? " I will therefore that men pray everywhere, lifting up holy hands, without wrath and doubting." This is not contrary to the other, God forbid, but quite in harmony with it. But how, and in what way? We must first consider what means, " enter into thy closet," and why Christ commands this, if we are to pray in every place? or whether we may not pray in the church, nor in any other part of the house, but the closet? What then means that saying? Christ is recommending us to avoid ostentation, when He bids us offer our prayers not only privately, but secretly. For, when He says, " Let not thy left hand know what thy right hand doeth " (Matt. vi. 3), it is not the hands that He considers, but He is bidding them use the utmost caution against ostentation : and He is doing the like here ; He did not limit prayer to one place, but required one thing alone, the absence of vainglory. The object of Paul is to distinguish the Christian from the Jewish prayers, therefore observe what he says : " In every place lifting up holy hands," which was not permitted the Jews, for they were not allowed to approach God, to sacrifice and perform their services, elsewhere, but assembling from all parts of the world in one place, they were bound to perform all their worship[2] in the temple. In opposition to this he introduces his precept, and freeing them from this necessity, he says in effect, Our ways are not like the Jewish ; for as Christ commanded us to pray for all men because He died for all men, and I preach these things for all men, so it is good to " pray everywhere." Henceforth the consider-

---

[1] Lit. " Is it the material that makes (an iron chain) a chain? "

[2] τὰ τῆς ἁγιστείας.

ation is not of the place but of the manner of the prayer; "pray everywhere," but "everywhere lift up holy hands." That is 'the thing required. And what is "holy"?[1] Pure. And what is pure? Not washed with water, but free from covetousness, murder, rapacity, violence, "without wrath and doubting." What means this? Who is angry when he prays? It means, without bearing malice. Let the mind of him that prays be pure, freed from all passion. Let no one approach God in enmity, or in an unamiable temper, or with "doubting." What is "without doubting"? Let us hear. It implies that we should have no misgiving but that we shall be heard. For it is said, "whatever ye ask believing ye shall receive." (Matt. xxi. 22.) And again, "when ye stand praying forgive, if ye have aught against any one." (Mark xi. 25.) This is to pray without wrath and doubting. But how can I believe that I shall obtain my request? By asking nothing opposed to that which He is ready to grant, nothing unworthy of the great King, nothing worldly, but all spiritual blessings; if you approach Him "without wrath," having pure hands, "holy hands": hands employed in almsgiving are holy. Approach Him thus, and you will certainly obtain your request. "For if ye being evil know how to give good gifts to your children, how much more shall your Father which is in Heaven give good things to them that ask Him?" (Matt. vii. 11.) By doubting he means misgiving. In like manner he says, I will that women approach God without wrath and doubting, lifting up holy hands: that they should not follow their own desires, nor be covetous or rapacious. For what if a woman does not rob or steal herself, but does it through means of her husband? Paul however requires something more of women, that they adorn themselves "in modest apparel, with shamefacedness and sobriety; not with broidered hair or gold or pearls or costly array; but (which becometh women professing godliness) with good works." But what is this "modest apparel"? Such attire as covers them completely, and decently, not with superfluous ornaments, for the one is becoming, the other is not.

Moral. What? Dost thou approach God to pray, with broidered hair and ornaments of gold? Art thou come to a dance? to a marriage? to a gay procession? There such a broidery, such costly garments, had been seasonable, here not one of them is wanted. Thou art come to pray, to supplicate for pardon of thy sins, to plead for thine offenses, beseeching the Lord, and hoping to render Him propitious to thee. Why dost thou adorn thyself? This is

not the dress of a suppliant. How canst thou groan? How canst thou weep? How pray with fervency, when thus attired? Shouldest thou weep, thy tears will be the ridicule of the beholders. She that weeps ought not to be wearing gold. It were but acting, and hypocrisy. For is it not acting to pour forth tears from a soul so overgrown with extravagance and ambition? Away with such hypocrisy! God is not mocked! This is the attire of actors and dancers, that live upon the stage. Nothing of this sort becomes a modest woman, who should be adorned "with shamefacedness and sobriety."

Imitate not therefore the courtesans. For by such a dress they allure their many lovers; and hence many have incurred a disgraceful suspicion, and, instead of gaining any advantage from their ornaments, have injured many[2] by bearing this character. For as the adulteress, though she may have a character for modesty, derives no benefit from that character, in the Day, when He who judges the secrets of men shall make all things manifest; so the modest woman, if she contrive by this dress to pass for an adulteress, will lose the advantage of her chastity. For many have suffered harm by this opinion. "What can I do," thou sayest, "if another suspects me?" But thou givest the occasion by thy dress, thy looks, thy gestures. It is for this reason that Paul discourses much of dress and much of modesty. And if he would remove those things which are only the indications of wealth, as gold, and pearls, and costly array; how much more those things which imply studied ornament, as painting, coloring the eyes, a mincing gait, the affected voice, a languishing and wanton look; the exquisite care in putting on the cloak and bodice, the nicely wrought girdle, and the closely-fitted shoes? For he glances at all these things, in speaking of "modest apparel" and "shamefacedness." For such things are shameless and indecent.

Bear with me, I beseech you, for it is not my aim by this plain reproof to wound or pain you, but to remove from my flock all that is unbecoming to them. But if these prohibitions are addressed to those who have husbands, who are rich, and live luxuriously; much more to those who have professed virginity. But what virgin, you say, wears gold, or broidered hair? Yet there may be such a studied nicety in a simple dress, as that these are nothing to it. You may study appearance in a common garment more than those who wear gold. For when a very dark colored robe is drawn closely round the breast with the girdle (as dancers on the stage are attired), with such nicety that it may neither

---

[1] ὁσίους.

[2] He means either by jealousy or temptation.

spread into breadth nor shrink into scantiness, but be between both; and when the bosom is set off with many folds, is not this more alluring than any silken robes? and when the shoe, shining through its blackness, ends in a sharp point, and imitates the elegance of painting, so that even the breadth of the sole is scarce visible — or when, though you do not indeed paint the face, you spend much time and pains on washing it, and spread a veil across the forehead,[1] whiter than the face itself — and above that put on a hood,[2] of which the blackness may set off the white by contrast — is there not in all this the vanity of dress? What can one say to the perpetual rolling of the eyes? to the putting on of the stomacher, so artfully as sometimes to conceal, sometimes to disclose, the fastening? For this too they sometimes expose, so as to show the exquisiteness of the cincture, winding the hood entirely round the head. Then like the players, they wear gloves so closely fitted, that they seem to grow upon the hands: and we might speak of their walk, and other artifices more alluring than any ornament of gold. Let us fear, beloved, lest we also hear what the Prophet said to the Hebrew women who were so studious of outward ornament; "Instead of a girdle, thou shalt be girded with a halter, instead of well-set hair, baldness." (Isa. iii. 24, Sept.) These things and many others, invented only to be seen and to attract beholders, are more alluring than golden ornaments. These are no trifling faults, but displeasing to God, and enough to mar all the self-denial of virginity.

Thou hast Christ for thy Bridegroom, O virgin, why dost thou seek to attract human lovers? He will judge thee as an adulteress. Why dost thou not wear the ornament that is pleasing to Him; modesty, chastity, orderliness, and sober apparel? This is meretricious, and disgraceful. We can no longer distinguish harlots and virgins, to such indecency have they advanced. A virgin's dress should not be studied, but plain, and without labor; but now they have many artifices to make their dress conspicuous. O woman, cease from this folly. Transfer this care to thy soul, to the inward adorning. For the outward ornament that invests thee, suffers not that within to become beautiful. He that is concerned for that which is without, despises that which is within, even as he that is unconcerned about the exterior, bestows all his care upon the interior. Say not, "Alas! I wear a threadbare garment, mean shoes, a worthless veil; what is there of ornament in these?" Do not deceive thyself. It is impossible, as I said, to study appearance more by these than by costlier dresses; especially when they are close-fitted to the body, fashioned to an immodest show, and of shining neatness.[3] Thou excusest thyself to me, but what canst thou say to God, who knows the heart and the spirit with which thou doest these things? "It is not done for fornication!" Perhaps not, but for admiration; and dost thou not blush for shame to be admired for such things? But thou sayest, "It is but chance I am so dressed, and for no motive of this kind." God knoweth what thou sayest to me: is it to me thou must give account? Nay, it is to Him who is present at thy actions, and will one day inquire into them, to whom all things are naked and open. It is on this account that we now urge these things, that we may not let you be amenable to those severe judgments. Let us fear, therefore, lest He reprove you in the words of the Prophet to the Jewish women. "They come to be seen of me wantoning and mincing as they go, and making a tinkling with their feet." (Isa. iii. 16.)

Ye have taken upon you a great contest, where wrestling, not ornament is required; where the battle awaits you, not sloth and ease. Observe the combatants and wrestlers in the games. Do they concern themselves about their walk or their dress? No, but scorning all these, and throwing about them a garment[4] dripping with oil, they look only to one thing, to wound, and not be wounded. The devil stands grinding his teeth, watching to destroy thee every way, and thou remainest unconcerned, or concerned only about this satanic ornament. I say nothing about the voice, though much affectation is shown in this also, nor about perfumes, and other such luxuries. It is for these things we are ridiculed by the women of the world. The respect for virginity is lost. No one honors a virgin as she ought to be honored. They have given occasion to their own dishonor. Ought not they to be looked up to in the Church of God, as women coming from heaven? but now they are despised, and deservedly, though not those among them who are discreet. But when one who has a husband and children, and presides over a household, sees thee, who ought to be crucified to the world, more devoted to the world than herself, will she not ridicule and despise thee? See what care! what pains! In thy humble dress, thou exceedest her who wears the costliest ornament, and art more studious of appearance than she who is arrayed in gold. What is becoming to thee thou seekest not; that which misbecomes thee thou pursuest, when thou oughtest to be occupied in good works. On this account virgins are less honored than women of the world. For they do not perform

---

[1] μετὰ τοῦ μετώπου. The reading is suspected, but it seems to mean, "so as to make one effect with the forehead."
[2] φάρος.

[3] So B. (doubtful reading).
[4] See on Stat. Hom. i. 16.

works worthy of their virgin profession. This is not said to all; or rather it is said to all; to those who are in fault, that they may learn modesty; to those who are free from blame, that they may teach modesty to others. But beware lest this rebuke be verified in deed. For we have not said these things that we may grieve, but that we may correct you, that we may glory in you. And may we all do those things which are acceptable to God, and live to His glory, that we may obtain the blessings promised by the grace and lovingkindness of our Lord Jesus Christ, with whom, &c.

HOMILY IX.

1 TIMOTHY ii. 11–15.

" Let the women learn in silence with all subjection. But I suffer not a woman to teach, nor to usurp authority over the man, but to be in silence. For Adam was first formed, then Eve. And Adam was not deceived, but the woman being deceived was in the transgression. Notwithstanding she shall be saved in [through the] child-bearing, if they continue in faith and charity and holiness with sobriety."

GREAT modesty and great propriety does the blessed Paul require of women, and that not only with respect to their dress and appearance: he proceeds even to regulate their speech. And what says he? " Let the woman learn in silence "; that is, let her not speak at all in the church; which rule he has also given in his Epistle to the Corinthians, where he says, " It is a shame for women to speak in the church " (1 Cor. xiv. 35); and the reason is, that the law has made them subject to men. And again elsewhere, " And if they will learn anything, let them ask their husbands at home." (Ibid.) Then indeed the women, from such teaching, kept silence; but now there is apt to be great noise among them, much clamor and talking, and nowhere so much as in this place. They may all be seen here talking more than in the market, or at the bath. For, as if they came hither for recreation, they are all engaged in conversing upon unprofitable subjects. Thus all is confusion, and they seem not to understand, that unless they are quiet, they cannot learn anything that is useful. For when our discourse strains against the talking, and no one minds what is said, what good can it do to them? To such a degree should women be silent, that they are not allowed to speak not only about worldly matters, but not even about spiritual things, in the church. This is order, this is modesty, this will adorn her more than any garments. Thus clothed, she will be able to offer her prayers in the manner most becoming.

" But I suffer not a woman to teach." " I do not suffer," he says. What place has this command here? The fittest. He was speaking of quietness, of propriety, of modesty, so having said that he wished them not to speak in the church, to cut off all occasion of conversation, he says, let them not teach, but occupy the station of learners. For thus they will show submission by their silence. For the sex is naturally somewhat talkative: and for this reason he restrains them on all sides. " For Adam," says he, " was first formed, then Eve. And Adam was not deceived, but the woman being deceived was in the transgression."

If it be asked, what has this to do with women of the present day? it shows that the male sex enjoyed the higher honor. Man was first formed; and elsewhere he shows their superiority. " Neither was the man created for the woman, but the woman for the man." (1 Cor. xi. 9.) Why then does he say this? He wishes the man to have the preëminence in every way; both for the reason given above, he means, let him have precedence, and on account of what occurred afterwards. For the woman taught the man once, and made him guilty of disobedience, and wrought our ruin. Therefore because she made a bad use of her power over the man, or rather her equality with him, God made her subject to her husband. " Thy desire shall be to thy husband." (Gen. iii. 16.) This had not been said to her before.

But how was Adam not deceived? If he was not deceived, he did not then transgress? Attend carefully. The woman said, " The serpent beguiled me." But the man did not say, The woman deceived me, but, " she gave me of the tree, and I did eat." Now it is not the same thing to be deceived by a fellow-creature, one of the same kind, as by an inferior and subordinate animal. This is truly to be deceived. Compared therefore with the woman, he is spoken of as " not deceived." For she was beguiled by an inferior and subject, he by an equal. Again, it is not said of the man, that he " saw the tree was good for food," but of the woman, and that she " did eat, and gave it to her husband " : so that he transgressed, not captivated by appetite, but merely from the persuasion of his wife. The woman taught once, and ruined all. On this account therefore he saith, let her not teach. But what is it to other women, that she suffered this? It certainly concerns them ; for the sex is weak and fickle, and he is speaking of the sex collectively. For he says not Eve, but "the woman," which is the common name of the whole sex, not her proper name. Was then the whole sex included in the transgression for her fault? As he said of Adam, "After the similitude of Adam's transgression, who is the figure of Him that was to come" (Rom. v. 14) ; so here the female sex transgressed, and not the male. Shall not women then be saved? Yes, by means of children. For it is not of Eve that he says, " If they continue in faith and charity and holiness with sobriety." What faith? what charity? what holiness with sobriety? It is as if he had said, "Ye women, be not cast down, because your sex has incurred blame. God has granted you another opportunity of salvation, by the bringing up of children, so that you are saved, not only by yourselves, but by others." See how many questions are involved in this matter. "The woman," he says, "being deceived was in the transgression." What woman? Eve. Shall she then be saved by child-bearing? He does not say that, but, the race of women shall be saved. Was not it then involved in transgression? Yes, it was, still Eve transgressed, but the whole sex shall be saved, notwithstanding, " by childbearing." And why not by their own personal virtue? For has she excluded others from this salvation? And what will be the case with virgins, with the barren, with widows who have lost their husbands, before they had children? will they perish? is there no hope for them? yet virgins are held in the highest estimation. What then does he mean to say?

Some interpret his meaning thus. As what happened to the first woman occasioned the subjection of the whole sex, (for since Eve was formed second and made subject, he says, let the rest of the sex be in subjection,) so because she transgressed, the rest of the sex are also in transgression. But this is not fair reasoning ; for at the creation all was the gift of God, but in this case, it is the consequence of the woman's sin. But this is the amount of what he says. As all men died through one, because that one sinned, so the whole female race transgressed, because the woman was in the transgression. Let her not however grieve. God hath given her no small consolation, that of childbearing. And if it be said that this is of nature, so is that [1]

also of nature ; for not only that which is of nature has been granted, but also the bringing up of children. " If they continue in faith and charity and holiness with sobriety" ; that is, if after childbearing, they keep them [2] in charity and purity. By these means they will have no small reward on their account, because they have trained up wrestlers for the service of Christ. By holiness he means good life, modesty, and sobriety.

Chap. iii. ver. 1. " This is a faithful saying."

This relates to the present subject, not to what follows, respecting the office of a Bishop. For as it was doubted, he affirms it to be a true saying, that fathers may be benefited by the virtue of their children, and mothers also, when they have brought them up well. But what if she be herself addicted to wickedness and vice? Will she then be benefited by the bringing up of children? Is it not probable that she will bring them up to be like herself? It is not therefore of any woman, but of the virtuous woman, that it is said she shall receive a great recompense for this also.

Moral. Hear this, ye fathers and mothers, that your bringing up of children shall not lose its reward. This also he says, as he proceeds, " Well reported of for good works; if she have brought up children." (1 Tim. v. 10.) Among other commendations he reckons this one, for it is no light praise to devote to God those children which are given them of God. For if the basis, the foundation which they lay be good, great will be their reward ; as great, if they neglect it, will be their punishment. It was on account of his children that Eli perished. For he ought to have admonished them, and indeed he did admonish them, but not as he ought ; but from his unwillingness to give them pain he destroyed both himself and them. Hear this, ye fathers, bring your children up with great care " in the nurture and admonition of the Lord." (Eph. vi. 4.) Youth is wild, and requires many governors, teachers, directors, attendants, and tutors ; and after all these, it is a happiness if it be restrained. For as for a horse not broken in, or a wild beast untamed, such is youth. But if from the beginning, from the earliest age, we fix it in good rules, much pains will not be required afterwards ; for good habits formed will be to them as a law. Let us not suffer them to do anything which is agreeable, but injurious ; nor let us indulge them, as forsooth but children. Especially let us train them in chastity, for there is the very bane of youth. For this many struggles, much attention will be necessary. Let us take wives for them early, so that their brides

---

[1] The sense is obscure, but he seems to mean, " the ordinary way of salvation," and by " consolation," a way of obtaining relief from the consequences of sin. See on Stat. Hom. ii. 19, and παραμυθία elsewhere.

[2] i.e. their children. Colb. ἑαυτοὺς, which cannot be right.

may receive their bodies pure and unpolluted, so their loves will be more ardent. He that is chaste before marriage, much more will he be chaste after it; and he that practiced fornication before, will practice it after marriage. "All bread," it is said, "is sweet to the fornicator." (Ecclus. xxiii. 17.) Garlands are wont to be worn on the heads of bridegrooms, as a symbol of victory, betokening that they approach the marriage bed unconquered by pleasure. But if captivated by pleasure he has given himself up to harlots, why does he wear the garland, since he has been subdued?

Let us admonish them of these things. Let us employ sometimes advice, sometimes warnings, sometimes threatening. In children we have a great charge committed to us. Let us bestow great care upon them, and do everything that the Evil One may not rob us of them. But now our practice is the very reverse of this. We take all care indeed to have our farm in good order, and to commit it to a faithful manager, we look out for it an ass-driver, and muleteer, and bailiff, and a clever accomptant. But we do not look out for what is much more important, for a person to whom we may commit our son as the guardian of his morals, though this is a possession much more valuable than all others. It is for him indeed that we take such care of our estate. We take care of our possessions for our children, but of the children themselves we take no care at all. What an absurdity is this! Form the soul of thy son aright, and all the rest will be added hereafter. If that is not good, he will derive no advantage from his wealth, and if it is formed to goodness he will suffer no harm from poverty. Wouldest thou leave him rich? teach him to be good: for so he will be able to acquire wealth, or if not, he will not fare worse than they who possess it. But

if he be wicked, though you leave him boundless wealth, you leave him no one to take care of it, and you render him worse than those who are reduced to extreme poverty. For poverty is better than riches for those children who are not well-disposed. For it retains them in some degree of virtue even against their will. Whereas money does not suffer those who would be sober to continue so, it leads them away, ruins them, and plunges them into infinite dangers.

Mothers, be specially careful to regulate your daughters well; for the management of them is easy. Be watchful over them, that they may be keepers at home. Above all, instruct them to be pious, modest, despisers of wealth, indifferent to ornament. In this way dispose of them in marriage. For if you form them in this way, you will save not only them, but the husband who is destined to marry them, and not the husband only, but the children, not the children only, but the grandchildren. For the root being made good, good branches will shoot forth, and still become better, and for all these you will receive a reward. Let us do all things therefore, as benefiting not only one soul, but many through that one. For they ought to go from their father's house to marriage, as combatants from the school of exercise, furnished with all necessary knowledge, and to be as leaven able to transform the whole lump to its own virtue. And let your sons be so modest, as to be distinguished for their steadiness and sobriety, that they may receive great praise both from God and men. Let them learn to govern their appetites, to avoid extravagance, to be good economists, affectionate, and submissive to rule. For so they will be able to secure a good reward to their parents, so all things will be done to the glory of God, and to our salvation, through Christ Jesus our Lord, with whom, &c.

HOMILY X.

1 Timothy iii. 1–4.

"If a man desire the office of a Bishop, he desireth a good work. A Bishop then must be blameless, the husband of one wife, vigilant, sober, of good behavior, given to hospitality, apt to teach; not given to wine, no striker, not greedy of filthy lucre; but patient, not a brawler, not covetous; one that ruleth well his own house, having his children in subjection with all gravity."

As now proceeding to discourse of the Episcopal office, he sets out with showing what sort

of a person a Bishop ought to be. And here he does not do it as in the course of his exhortation to Timothy, but addresses all, and instructs others through him. And what says he? "If a man desire the office of a Bishop," I do not blame him, for it is a work of protection. If any one has this desire, so that he does not covet the dominion and authority, but wishes to protect the Church, I blame him not. "For he desireth a good work." Even Moses desired the office, though not the power, and his desire exposed him to that taunt, "Who made thee a ruler and a judge over us?" (Acts vii. 27; Ex. ii. 14.) If any one, then, desire it in this way, let him desire it. For the Episcopate is so called from having the oversight of all.

"A Bishop then," he says, "must be blameless, the husband of one wife." This he does not lay down as a rule, as if he must be without one, but as prohibiting his having more than one.[1] For even the Jews were allowed to contract second marriages, and even to have two wives at one time. For "marriage is honorable." (Heb. xiii. 4.) Some however say, that this is said that he should be the husband of one wife.[2] "Blameless." Every virtue is implied in this word; so that if any one be conscious to himself of any sins, he doth not well to desire an office for which his own actions have disqualified him. For such an one ought to be ruled, and not to rule others. For he who bears rule should be brighter than any luminary; his life should be unspotted, so that all should look up to him, and make his life the model of their own. But in employing this exhortation, he had no common object in view. For he too[3] was about to appoint Bishops, (which also he exhorts Titus to do in his Epistle to him,) and as it was probable that many would desire that office, therefore he urges these admonitions. "Vigilant," he says, that is, circumspect, having a thousand eyes about him, quicksighted, not having the eyes of his mind dimmed. For many things occur which permit not a man to see clearly, to see things as they are. For care and troubles, and a load of business on all sides, press upon him. He must therefore be vigilant, not only over his own concerns, but over those of others. He must be well awake, he must be fervent in spirit, and, as it were, breathe fire; he must labor and attend upon his duty by day and by night, even more than a general upon his army; he must be careful and concerned for all. "Sober, of good behavior, given to hospitality." Because these qualities are possessed by most of those who are under their rule, (for in these respects they ought to be equal to those who rule over them,) he, to show what is peculiar to the Bishops, adds, "apt to teach." For this is not required of him that is ruled, but is most essential to him who has this rule committed to him.[4]

"Not given to wine": here he does not so much mean intemperate, as insolent and impudent. "No striker": this too does not mean a striker with the hands. What means then "no striker"? Because there are some who unseasonably smite the consciences of their brethren, it seems to be said with reference to them. "Not greedy of filthy lucre, but patient: not a brawler, not covetous; one that ruleth well his own house, having his children in subjection with all gravity." If then "he who is married cares for the things of the world" (1 Cor. vii. 33), and a Bishop ought not to care for the things of the world, why does he say the husband of one wife? Some indeed think that he says this with reference to one who remains free[5] from a wife. But if otherwise, he that hath a wife may be as though he had none. (1 Cor. vii. 29.) For that liberty was then properly granted, as suited to the nature of the circumstances then existing. And it is very possible, if a man will, so to regulate his conduct. For as riches make it difficult to enter into the kingdom of Heaven, yet rich men have often entered in, so it is with marriage. But why does he say, speaking of a Bishop, that he should be "not given to wine, hospitable," when he should name greater things? Why said he not that he should be an Angel, not subject to human passions? Where are those great qualities of which Christ speaks, which even those under their rule ought to possess? To be crucified to the world, to be always ready to lay down their lives, as Christ said. "The good Shepherd giveth his life for the sheep" (John x. 11); and again, "He that taketh not his cross and followeth after me, is not worthy of me." (Matt. x. 38.) But "not given to wine," he says; a good prospect indeed, if such are the things of which a Bishop is to be admonished! Why has he not said that he ought to be already raised above the world? But dost thou demand less of the Bishop, than even of those in the world? For to these he saith, "Mortify your members which are upon the earth" (Col. iii. 5), and "He that is dead, is freed from sin." (Rom. vi. 7.) "They that are Christ's have crucified the flesh"; and Christ again says, "Whosoever forsaketh not all that he hath, he is not worthy of Me." (Luke xv. 33.) Why are not these things required by Paul? Plainly because few could be found of such a character, and there was need of many Bishops, that one might preside in every city.

But because the Churches were to be exposed to attacks,[6] he requires not that superior and

---

[1] ἀμετρίαν.
[2] This is literal from the Greek, but the sense is difficult to make out from the seeming tautology, unless he means that some supposed marriage *enjoined*. The Greek will bear, "and some say, 'Let him be the husband of one wife,' was said with a view to this." See below. (Œcumenius says that some take it of one. See Comp. Ezek. xliv. 22.
[3] i.e. Timothy.
[4] παροινον. A word often used as he here explains it; and παροινία is used even for contumely apart from insolence. Theodoret, Eccl. Hist. v. 17.

[5] He seems to mean without a second marriage. See 1 Cor. vii. 27. An old Latin translation has this expressly. The reading is not quite certain.
[6] i.e. and therefore to want many guardians.

highly exalted virtue, but a moderate degree of it; for to be sober, of good behavior, and temperate, were qualities common to many. "Having his children in subjection with all gravity." This is necessary, that an example might be exhibited in his own house. For who would believe that he who had not his own son in subjection, would keep a stranger under command? "One that ruleth well his own house." Even those who are without say this, that he who is a good manager of a house will be a good statesman. For the Church is, as it were, a small[1] household, and as in a house there are children and wife and domestics, and the man has rule over them all; just so in the Church there are women, children, servants. And if he that presides in the Church has partners in his power, so hath the man a partner, that is, his wife. Ought the Church to provide for her widows and virgins? so there are in a family servants, and daughters, to be provided for. And, in fact, it is easier to rule the house; therefore he asks, "if a man know not how to rule his own house, how shall he take care of the Church of God?"

Ver. 6. "Not a novice."[2] He does not say, not a young man, but not a new convert. For he had said, "I have planted, Apollos watered, but God gave the increase." (1 Cor. iii. 6.) Wishing them to point out such an one, he used this word. For, otherwise, what hindered him from saying, "Not a young man"? For if youth only was an objection, why did he himself appoint Timothy, a young man? (and this he proves by saying to him, "Let no man despise thy youth.") (1 Tim. iv. 12.) Because[3] he was aware of his great virtue, and his great strictness of life. Knowing which he writes, "From a child thou hast learned the holy Scriptures." (2 Tim. iii. 15.) And that he practiced intense fasting is proved by the words, "Use a little wine for thine often infirmities"; which he wrote to him amongst other things, as, if he had not known of such good works of his, he would not have written, nor given any such charge to his disciple. But as there were many then who came over from the Heathen, and were baptized, he says, "Do not immediately advance to a station of dignity a novice, that is, one of these new converts." For, if before he had well been a disciple, he should at once be made a Teacher, he would be lifted up into insolence. If before he had learnt to be under rule, he should be appointed one of the rulers, he would be puffed up: therefore he adds, "Lest being lifted up with pride, he fall

into the condemnation of the devil," that is, into the same condemnation which Satan incurred by his pride.

Ver. 7. "Moreover he must have a good report of them which are without; lest he fall into reproach and the snare of the devil."

This is rightly said, as he was certain to be reproached by them, and for the same reason perhaps he said, "the husband of one wife," though elsewhere he says, "I would that all men were even as I myself!" (1 Cor. vii. 7), that is, practicing continency. That he may not therefore confine them within too narrow a limit, by requiring an over-strict conversation, he is satisfied to prescribe moderate virtue. For it was necessary to appoint one to preside in every city, as he writes to Titus, "That thou shouldest ordain elders in every city, as I had appointed thee." (Tit. i. 5.) But what if he should have a good report, and fair reputation, and not be worthy of it? In the first place this would not easily happen. It is much for good men to obtain a good report among their enemies. But, in fact, he has not left this to stand by itself; a good report "also," he says, that is, besides other qualities. What then, if they should speak evil of him without a cause from envy, especially as they were Heathens? This was not to be expected. For even they will reverence a man of blameless life. Why then does he say, speaking of himself, "Through evil report and good report"? (2 Cor. vi. 6.) Because it was not his life that they assailed, but his preaching. Therefore he says, "through evil report." They were slandered as deceivers and impostors, on account of their preaching, and this because they could not attack their moral characters and lives. For why did no one say of the Apostles, that they were fornicators, unclean, or covetous persons, but that they were deceivers, which relates to their preaching only? Must it not be that their lives were irreproachable? It is manifest.

Therefore so let us too live, and no enemy, no unbeliever, will be able to speak evil of us. For he whose life is virtuous, is revered even by them. For truth stops the mouths even of enemies.

But how does he "fall into a snare"? By falling often into the same sins, as those who are without. For if he be such a character, the evil one soon lays another snare for him, and they soon effect his destruction. But if he should have a good report from his enemies, much more will he have it from his friends. For that it is not likely that he, whose life is blameless, should be ill-reported of, we may infer from the words of Christ; "Let your light so shine before men, that they may see your good works, and glorify your Father which is in Heaven." (Matt.

---

[1] Doun. conj. "great."
[2] νεόφυτον, one newly "planted."
[3] These words, down to "disciple," are not in Sav.; they are supplied from a Colb. MS. in the last Paris ed.

v. 16.)   But what if one be falsely accused, and from peculiar circumstances be slandered? Well, this is a possible case; but even such an one ought not to be promoted. For the result is much to be feared. Therefore it is said he should have "a good report," for your good works are to shine. As therefore no one will say that the sun is dark, not even the blind, (for he will be ashamed to oppose the opinion of all,) so him that is of remarkable goodness no one will blame. And though, on account of his doctrines, the Heathen will often slander him, yet they will not attack his virtuous life, but will join with others in admiring and revering it.

Moral.   Let us then so live, that the name of God be not blasphemed. Let us not, on the one hand, look to human reputation; nor on the other, subject ourselves to an evil report, but on both sides let us observe moderation; as he saith, "Among whom ye shine as lights in the world." (Phil. ii. 15.) For on this account He left us here, that we may be as luminaries, that we may be appointed Teachers of others, that we may be as leaven; that we may converse as angels among men, as men with children, as spiritual with natural men, that they may profit by us, that we may be as seed, and may bring forth much fruit. There were no need of words, if we so shone forth in our lives, there were no need of Teachers, did we but exhibit works. There would be no Heathen, if we were such Christians as we ought to be. If we kept the commandments of Christ, if we suffered injury, if we allowed advantage to be taken of us, if being reviled we blessed, if being ill-treated we did good (1 Cor. iv. 12); if this were the general practice among us, no one would be so brutal as not to become a convert to godliness. And to show this; Paul was but one man, yet how many did he draw after him? If we were all such as he, how many worlds might we not have drawn to us? Behold, Christians are more numerous than Heathens. And in other arts, one man can teach a hundred boys together; but here, where there are many more teachers, and many more than the learners, no one is brought over. For those who are taught, look to the virtue of their teachers: and when they see us manifesting the same desires, pursuing the same objects, power and honor, how can they admire Christianity? They see our lives open to reproach, our souls worldly. We admire wealth equally with them, and even more. We have the same horror of death, the same dread of poverty, the same impatience of disease, we are equally fond of glory and of rule. We harass ourselves to death from our love of money, and serve the time. How then can they believe? From miracles? But these are no longer wrought. From our conversation? It has be-

come corrupt. From charity? Not a trace of it is anywhere to be seen. Therefore we shall have to give an account not only of our own sins, but of the injury done by them to others.

Let us then return to a sound mind; let us watch, and show forth a heavenly conversation upon earth. Let us say, "Our conversation is in heaven" (Phil. iii. 20), and let us upon earth maintain the contest. There have been great men, it may be said, amongst us, but "how," says the Greek, "shall I believe it? for I do not see anything like it in your conduct. If this is to be said, we too have had our philosophers, men admirable for their lives." "But show me another Paul, or a John: you cannot." Would he not then laugh at us for reasoning in this manner? Would he not continue to sit still in ignorance, seeing that the wisdom we profess is in words, not in works? For now for a single halfpenny ye are ready to slay or be slain! For a handful of earth thou raisest lawsuit after lawsuit! For the death of a child thou turnest all upside down! I omit other things that might make us weep; your auguries, your omens, your superstitious observances, your casting of nativities, your signs, your amulets, your divinations, your incantations, your magic arts. These are crying sins, enough to provoke the anger of God; that after He has sent His own Son, you should venture on such things as these.

What then can we do but weep? For hardly is a small portion of the world in the way of salvation, and they who are perishing hear it, and rejoice that they are not destined to suffer alone, but in company with numbers. But what cause is this for joy? That very joy will subject them to punishment. For do not think that it is there as here, that to have companions in suffering affords consolation. And whence is this manifest? I will make it clear. Suppose that a man were commanded to be burnt, and that he saw his own son burning with him, and that the smell of his scorched flesh rose to his nostrils; would it not be of itself death to him? No doubt. And I will tell you how it is. If those who are not suffering, yet seeing those things are benumbed and faint with terror, much more will they be so affected, who are themselves sufferers. Wonder not at this. Hear a certain wise one saying, "Art thou become weak as we? art thou become like unto us?" (Isa. xiv. 10.) For human nature is disposed to sympathy, and the affections of others move us to pity. Will then a father seeing his son in the same condemnation, or a husband his wife, or a man his fellow-man, receive consolation, and not rather an aggravation of his sufferings? Are not we in such case the more overcome? But there, you say, there are no such feelings. I know there are not; but there are others much more wretched.

For there will be wailing inconsolable, all witnessing each other's torments. Do they who are famishing derive comfort in their distress from the participation of others? It is no consolation surely to see a son, a father, a wife, or grandchildren, suffering the same punishment. If one sees friends in such a case, is it any comfort? None! None! It rather adds to the intensity of our own sufferings! Besides, there are evils, which by reason of their severity cannot be mitigated by being common. If two men were together thrown into the fire, would they comfort one another? Tell me; if we have ever been attacked by a violent fever, have we not found that all consolation has failed us? for there are calamities, so overwhelming as to leave no room for comfort in the soul. When a wife has lost her husband, is it a lessening of her grief to number up the many who have suffered the like loss? Let us not therefore be supported by any such hope, rather let us find our sole consolation in repenting of our sins, in pursuing the good path that leads to Heaven, that we may obtain the kingdom of Heaven, by the grace and lovingkindness of Jesus Christ our Lord, with whom, &c.

HOMILY XI.

1 TIMOTHY iii. 8-10.

"Likewise must the Deacons be grave, not doubletongued, not given much to wine, not greedy of filthy lucre; holding the mystery of the faith in a pure conscience. And let these also first be proved: then let them use the office of a Deacon, being found blameless."

DISCOURSING of Bishops, and having described their character, and the qualities which they ought to possess, and having passed over the order of Presbyters, he proceeds to that of Deacons. The reason of this omission was, that between Presbyters and Bishops there was no great difference. Both had undertaken the office of Teachers and Presidents in the Church, and what he has said concerning Bishops is applicable to Presbyters. For they are only superior in having the power of ordination, and seem to have no other advantage over Presbyters. "Likewise the Deacons." That is, they should have the same qualities as Bishops. And what are these same? To be blameless, sober, hospitable, patient, not brawlers, not covetous. And that he means this when he says "likewise," is evident from what he says in addition, "grave, not doubletongued"; that is, not hollow or deceitful. For nothing so debases a man as deceit, nothing is so pernicious in the Church as insincerity. "Not given to much wine, not greedy of filthy lucre; holding the mystery of the faith in a pure conscience." Thus he explains what he means by "blameless." And here he requires, though in other words, that he be "not a novice," where he says, "Let these also first be proved," where the conjunction "also" is added, as connecting this with what had been said before of Bishops, for nothing intervenes between. And there is the same reason[1] for the "not a novice" in that case.

For would it not be absurd, that when a newly purchased slave is not entrusted with anything in a house, till he has by long trial given proofs of his character, yet that one should enter into the Church of God from a state of heathenism, and be at once placed in a station of preëminence?

Ver. 11. "Even so must the women[2] be grave, not slanderers, sober, faithful in all things."

Some have thought that this is said of women generally, but it is not so, for why should he introduce anything about women to interfere with his subject? He is speaking of those who hold the rank of Deaconesses.

Ver. 12. "Let the Deacons be husbands of one wife."

This[3] must be understood therefore to relate to Deaconesses. For that order is necessary and useful and honorable in the Church. Observe how he requires the same virtue from the Deacons, as from the Bishops, for though they were not of equal rank, they must equally be blameless; equally pure.

"Ruling their children and their own houses well."

Ver. 13. "For they that have used the office of a Deacon well purchase to themselves a good degree, and much boldness in the faith which is in Christ Jesus."

Everywhere they are required to rule their children well, that others may not be scandalized by their misconduct.

"They that use the office of a Deacon well, purchase to themselves a good degree," that is, advancement, "and much boldness in the faith of Jesus Christ"; as if he would say, that those

---

[1] He had not noticed this reason on the passage, probably because he considered that St. Paul purposely deferred it to this place.

[2] E. V.: "Their wives." The other is literal. [R. V.: "Women."]

[3] i.e. the verse before.

who have been found vigilant in the lower degree [1] will soon ascend to the higher.

Ver. 14, 15. "These things write I unto thee, hoping to come unto thee shortly. But if I tarry long, that thou mayest know how thou oughtest to behave thyself in the house of God, which is the Church of the living God, the pillar and ground of the truth."

That he may not plunge Timothy into dejection by giving him orders about such matters, he says, I write thus not as though I were not coming, but I will indeed come, still in case I should be delayed, that thou mayest not be distressed. And this he writes to him to prevent his being dejected, but to others in order to rouse them to greater earnestness. For his presence, though only promised, would have great effect. Nor let it seem strange that, though foreseeing everything through the Spirit, he was yet ignorant of this, and only says, I hope to come, but if I tarry, which implies uncertainty. For since he was led by the Spirit, and did not act from his own inclination, he was naturally uncertain about this matter.

"That thou mayest know," he says, "how thou oughtest to behave thyself in the house of God, which is the Church of the living God, the pillar and ground of the truth." Not like that Jewish house. For it is this that maintains the faith and the preaching of the Word. For the truth is the pillar and the ground of the Church.[2]

Ver. 16. "And without controversy great is the mystery of godliness; God [He who][3] was manifest in the flesh, justified in the Spirit."

Here he speaks of the Dispensation in our behalf. Tell me not of the bells, nor of the holy of holies, nor of the high priest. The Church is the pillar of the world. Consider this mystery, and thou mayest be struck with awe: for it is indeed "a great mystery," and "a mystery of godliness," and that "without controversy" or question, for it is beyond all doubt. Since in his directions to the Priests he had required nothing like what is found in Leviticus, he refers the whole matter to Another, saying, "God was manifest in the flesh." The Creator was seen incarnate. "He was justified in the Spirit." As it is said, "Wisdom is justified of her children," or because He practiced no guile, as the Prophet says, "Because he had done no violence, neither was guile found in his mouth." (Isa. liii. 9; 1 Pet. ii. 22.) "Seen of Angels." So that Angels together with us saw the Son of God, not having before seen Him. Great, truly great, was this mystery! "Preached unto the

Gentiles, believed on in the world." He was heard of and believed in through all parts of the world, as the Prophet foreshowed, saying, "Their sound is gone out into all the world." (Ps. xix. 4.) Think not that these things are mere words, for they are not, but full of hidden realities. "Received up into glory." He ascended upon clouds. "This Jesus," it is said, "Who is taken up from you, shall so come in like manner as ye have seen Him go into heaven." (Acts i. 11.)

The discretion of the blessed Paul is observable. When he would exhort the Deacons to avoid excess in wine, he does not say, "Be not drunken," but "not" even "given to much wine." A proper caution; for if those who served in the Temple did not taste wine at all, much more should not these. For wine produces disorder of mind, and where it does not cause drunkenness, it destroys the energies and relaxes the firmness of the soul.

The dispensation in our behalf he calls a "mystery," and well may it be so called, since it is not manifest to all, nay, it was not manifest to the Angels, for how could it, when it was "made known by the Church"? (Eph. iii. 10.) Therefore he says, "without controversy great is the mystery." Great indeed was it. For God became Man, and Man became God. A Man was seen without sin! A Man was received up, was preached in the world! Together with us the Angels saw Him. This is indeed a mystery! Let us not then expose [4] this mystery. Let us not lay it forth everywhere, but let us live in a manner worthy of the mystery. They to whom a mystery is intrusted are great persons. We account it a mark of favor, if a king intrusts a secret to us. But God has committed His mystery to us, yet are we ungrateful to our Benefactor, as if we had not received the greatest benefits. Our insensibility to such a kindness should strike us with horror. And how is that a mystery which all know? In the first place all do not know it, and before then too they knew it not, but now it is made manifest.[5]

MORAL. In keeping this mystery, then, let us be faithful to our trust. So great a mystery has He intrusted to us, and we do not trust Him even with our money, though He has bid us lay up our wealth with Him, where none can take it away, neither can moth nor thief waste it. And He promises to pay us a hundred-fold, yet we obey Him not. Yet here if we intrust any with a deposit, we receive nothing back in addition, but are thankful if that is restored which we deposited. If a thief steals it there, He saith, set that to My account; I say not to thee, a thief

---

[1] Or, "in things below." He may refer to the Deacon's temporal ministry.

[2] i.e. the truth in itself supports the Church, the Church through it supports the world.

[3] [ὅς is better attested than θεός, and has been adopted in the R. V.—P. S.]

[4] The word ἐκπομπεύωμεν seems to be used in a bad sense, as of disgracing, or irreverently handling, the sacred doctrine.

[5] So B. Sav. mar. and Old Lat. The printed text is, "It is a mystery which all know, yea, rather, which all knew not before, but which is now made manifest to all."

has taken it, or moth devoured it. He repays a hundred-fold here, and eternal life is superadded hereafter, yet do we not lay up our treasure there ! " But," you say, " He repays slowly." Well this too is a proof of the greatness of His gift, that He does not repay here in this mortal life ; or rather He does repay even here a hundred-fold. For did not Paul leave here his tools,[1] Peter his rod and hook, and Matthew his seat of custom? and was not the whole world opened to them more than to kings? Were not all things laid at their feet? Were they not appointed rulers,[2] and lords? Did not men commit their lives into their hands? suspend themselves wholly upon their counsel, and enlist in their service? And do we not see many similar occurrences even now? Many men of poor and humble means, who did but handle the spade, and had hardly a sufficiency of necessary food, having but the character of monks, have been celebrated above all men, and honored of kings.

Are these things inconsiderable? Well, consider that these are but additions, the principal sum is stored up for the life to come. Despise riches, if thou wouldest have riches. If thou wouldest be truly rich, become poor. For such are the paradoxes of God. He would not have thee rich from thy own care, but from His grace. Leave these things to Me, He says ; make spiritual things thy concern, that thou mayest know My power. Flee from that yoke of slavery, which riches impose. As long as thou cleavest to them, thou art poor. When thou despisest them, thou art doubly rich, in that such things shall flow in upon thee from every side, and in that thou shalt want none of those things, which the multitude want. For not to possess much, but to need little, is to be rich indeed. The king, so long as he wants aught, differs not from the poor man. For this is poverty, to stand in need of others ; and by this argument the king is poor, in so far as he stands in need of his subjects. But he that is crucified to the world is not so ; he wants for nothing ; for his hands are sufficient for his subsistence, as Paul said, " These hands have ministered to my necessities, and to them that were with me." (Acts xx. 34.) These are his words who says, " As having nothing, yet possessing all things." (2 Cor. vi. 20.) This is he who was thought a God by the inhabitants of Lystra. If thou wouldest obtain worldly things, seek Heaven ; if you wouldest enjoy things here, despise them. For, " Seek ye first the kingdom of God," He saith, " and all these things shall be added unto you." (Matt. vi. 33.)

Why dost thou admire these trifles ? Why long for things of no real worth? How long is one poor?[3] how long a beggar? Raise thine eyes to heaven, think of the riches there, and smile at gold ; think of how little use it is ; that the enjoyment of it lasts but for the present life, and that compared with eternity, the present life is as a grain of sand, or as a drop of water to the boundless ocean. This wealth is not a possession, it is not property, it is a loan for use. For when thou diest, willingly or unwillingly, all that thou hast goes to others, and they again give it up to others, and they again to others. For we are all sojourners ; and the tenant of the house is more truly perchance the owner of it, for the owner dies, and the tenant lives, and still enjoys the house. And if the latter hires it, the other might be said to hire it too : for he built it, and was at pains with it, and fitted it up. Property, in fact, is but a word : we are all owners in fact but of other men's possessions. Those things only are our own, which we have sent before us to the other world. Our goods here are not our own ; we have only a life interest in them ; or rather they fail us during our lives. Only the virtues of the soul are properly our own, as almsgiving and charity. Worldly goods, even by those without, were called external things, because they are without us. But let us make them internal. For we cannot take our wealth with us, when we depart hence, but we can take our charities. But let us rather send them before us, that they may prepare for us an abode in the eternal mansions. (Luke xvi. 9.)

Goods[4] are named from use,[5] not from lordship, and are not our own, and possessions are not a property but a loan. For how many masters has every estate had, and how many will it have ! There is a sensible proverb, (and popular proverbs, when they contain any wisdom, are not to be despised,) " O field, how many men's hast thou been, and how many men's wilt thou be?" This we should say to our houses and all our goods. Virtue alone is able to depart with us, and to accompany us to the world above. Let us then give up and extinguish that love of wealth, that we may kindle in us an affection for heavenly things. These two affections cannot possess one soul. For it is said, " Either he will hate the one, and love the other ; or else he will hold to the one, and despise the other." (Matt. vi. 24.) Seest thou a man with a long train of attendants, clearing a way[6] along the streets, clothed in silken garments, riding aloft, and stiffening his neck? Be not overawed, but smile. As we laugh when we see children playing at kings, so laugh at his state, for it is no better than theirs, nor indeed so pleasant, for there is not the same innocence

---

[1] σμίλην.　　　[2] διοικητὰς.　　　[3] See on Phil. i. 19, Hom. ii.
[4] χρήματα.　　　[5] κεχρῆσθαι.　　　[6] σοβοῦντα.

and simplicity as with children. With them it is laughter and pleasure, here is a man made ridiculous and contemptible.

Glorify God, Who has kept thee free from this theatrical ostentation. For, if thou wilt, humble as thy station is, thou mayest be higher than he who is exalted in his chariot. And why? because, though his body is a little raised from the earth, his soul is fixed upon it, for "My strength," he saith, "cleaveth to my flesh" (Ps. cii. 6), but thou in thy spirit walkest in heaven. What though he has many attendants clearing his way? is he more honored by this than his horse? and what an absurdity is it, to drive men before one to clear the way for a beast to pass! Then what sort of honor is it to bestride a horse? an honor shared by his slaves! Yet some are so vain of this, that they have it led after them even though they do not want it. What greater folly can there be? To wish to be distinguished by their horses, by the costliness of their garments, by their retinue! What can be more contemptible than glory which consists in horses, and servants? Art thou vir-

tuous? use not such distinctions. Have ornaments in thyself. Be not indebted for thy glory to the presence of others. To such honor the most wicked, corrupt, and base of men may attain; all indeed who are rich. Actors and dancers may ride on horseback with a servant running before them, yet are they but actors and dancers still. Their horses and attendants procure them no respect. For when the graces of the soul are wanting to such persons, the addition of these external things is superfluous and vain. And as when a wall is weak, or a body disordered, whatever you put upon it, it still remains unsound and decayed; so in this case; the soul continues the same, and receives no advantage from things without, not though the man wear a thousand ornaments of gold. Let us not therefore be anxious for such things. Let us withdraw ourselves from temporal things, and pursue greater, even spiritual distinctions, which will render us truly objects of veneration, that we also may obtain the blessings of futurity, through the grace and lovingkindness of our Lord Jesus Christ, with whom, &c.

HOMILY XII.

1 TIMOTHY iv. 1–3.

"Now the Spirit speaketh expressly, that in the latter times some shall depart from the faith, giving heed to seducing spirits, and doctrines of demons; speaking lies in hypocrisy; having their conscience seared with a hot iron; forbidding to marry, and commanding to abstain from meats, which God hath created to be received with thanksgiving of them which believe and know the truth."

As those who adhere to the faith are fixed on a safe anchor, so those who fall from the faith can nowhere rest; but after many wanderings to and fro, they are borne at last into the very gulf of perdition. And this he had shown before, saying, that some had "already made shipwreck concerning the faith," and now he says, "Now the Spirit speaketh expressly, that in the latter times some shall depart from the faith, giving heed to seducing spirits." This is said of the Manichæans, the Encratites,[1] and the Marcionites, and the whole of their tribe,[2] that

they should hereafter depart from the faith. Seest thou that this departure from the faith is the cause of all the evils that follow!

But what is "expressly"? Plainly, clearly, and beyond doubt. Marvel not, he says, if some having departed from the faith still adhere to Judaism. There will be a time, when even those who have partaken of the faith will fall into a worse error, not only with respect to meats, but to marriages, and other such things, introducing the most pernicious notions. This refers not to the Jews, (for "the latter times," and a "departure from the faith," is not applicable to them;) but to the Manichees, and the founders of these sects. And he calls them very justly, "seducing spirits," since it was by these they were actuated in speaking such things. "Speaking lies in hypocrisy." This implies that they utter not these falsehoods through ignorance and unknowingly, but as acting a part, knowing the truth, but "having their conscience seared," that is, being men of evil lives.

But why does he speak only of these heretics? Christ had before said, "Offenses must need come" (Matt. xviii. 7), and he had predicted the same in his parable of the sower, and of the

---

[1] St. Chrys. often speaks of the Manichees and Marcionites, but rarely of the Encratites. They are mentioned more than once by Clem. Al., who says (Strom. 7) that they are named from "Temperance" (ἐγκράτεια). Origen (cont. Cel. v. 65, p. 628) says they did not acknowledge St. Paul's Epistles. Eusebius, iv. 28, 29, that Tatian was the author of this heresy, and so Epiphanius, who treats of its several points at length. Her. 26 (Montf.).

[2] Literally, "shop."

springing up of the tares. But here admire with me the prophetic gift of Paul, who, before the times in which they were to appear, specifies the time itself. As if he had said, Do not wonder, if, at the commencement of the faith, some endeavor to bring in these pernicious doctrines; since, after it has been established for a length of time, many shall depart from the faith. "Forbidding to marry, and commanding to abstain from meats." Why then has he mentioned no other heresies? Though not particularized, they are implied by the expressions of "seducing spirits and doctrines of demons." But he did not wish to instill these things into the minds of men before the time; but that which had already commenced, the case of meats, he specifies. "Which God hath created to be received with thanksgiving of them which believe and know the truth." Why did he not say, by the unbelievers too? How by the unbelievers, when they exclude themselves from them by their own rules? But is not luxury forbidden? Certainly it is. But why? if good things are created to be received. Because He created bread, and yet too much is forbidden; and wine also, and yet excess is forbidden; and we are not commanded to avoid dainties as if they were unclean in themselves, but as they corrupt the soul by excess.

Ver. 4. "For every creature of God is good, and nothing to be refused, if it be received with thanksgiving."

If it be the creature of God, it is good. For "all things," it is said, "were very good." (Gen. i. 31.) By speaking thus of things eatable, he by anticipation impugns the heresy of those who introduce an uncreated matter, and assert that these things proceed from it. But if it is good, why is it "sanctified by the word of God and prayers"? For it must be unclean, if it is to be sanctified? Not so, here he is speaking to those who thought that some of these things were common; therefore he lays down two positions: first, that no creature of God is unclean: secondly, that if it were become so, you have a remedy, seal it,[1] give thanks, and glorify God, and all the uncleanness passes away. Can we then so cleanse that which is offered to an idol? If you know not that it was so offered. But if, knowing this, you partake of it, you will be unclean; not because it was offered to an idol, but because contrary to an express command, you thereby communicate with devils. So that it is not unclean by nature, but becomes so through your wilful disobedience. What then, is not swine's flesh unclean? By no means, when it is received with thanksgiving, and with the seal; nor is anything else. It is your unthankful disposition to God that is unclean.

[1] i.e. with the sign of the cross, σφράγισον.

Ver. 6. "If thou put the brethren in remembrance of these things, thou shalt be a good minister of Jesus Christ, nourished up in the words of faith and of good doctrine, whereunto thou hast attained."

What are the things here meant? The same which he had before mentioned, that "great is the mystery"; that to abstain from meats is the doctrine of devils, that they are "cleansed by the word of God and prayer."

Ver. 7. "But refuse profane and old wives' fables, and exercise thyself rather unto godliness."

"Putting them in remembrance," he says; here you observe no authority; but all is condescension: he does not say "commanding" or "enjoining," but reminding them: that is, suggest these things as matter of advice, and so enter into discourses with them concerning the faith, "being nourished up," he says, meaning to imply constancy in application to these things.

For as we set before us day by day this bodily nourishment, so he means, let us be continually receiving discourses concerning the faith, and ever be nourished with them. What is this, "being nourished up"? Ruminating upon them; attending ever to the same things, and practicing ever the same, for it is no common nourishment that they supply.

"But refuse profane and old wives' fables." By these are meant Jewish traditions, and he calls them "fables," either because of their falsehood or their unseasonableness. For what is seasonable is useful, but what is unseasonable is not only useless but injurious. Suppose a man of adult age to be suckled by a nurse, would he not be ridiculous, because it is unseasonable? "Profane and old wives' fables," he calls them, partly because of their obsoleteness, and partly because they are impediments to faith. For to bring souls under fear, that are raised above these things, is an impious commandment. "Exercise thyself unto godliness." That is, unto a pure faith and a moral life; for this is godliness. So then we need "exercise."

Ver. 8. "For bodily exercise[2] profiteth little."

This has by some been referred to fasting; but away with such a notion! for that is not a bodily but a spiritual exercise. If it were bodily it would nourish the body, whereas it wastes and makes it lean, so that it is not bodily. Hence he is not speaking of the discipline[3] of the body. What we need, therefore, is the exercise[4] of the soul. For the exercise of the body hath no profit, but may benefit the body a little, but the exercise[5] of godliness yields fruit and advantage both here and hereafter.

[2] γυμνασία.   [3] ἀσκήσεως.   [4] γυμνασία.
[5] ἄσκησις, the proper word for spiritual exercise. St. Paul uses the other, because bodily exercise for bodily purposes was familiar to all Greeks.

"This is a faithful saying," that is, it is true that godliness is profitable both here and hereafter. Observe how everywhere he brings in this, he needs no demonstration, but simply declares it, for he was addressing Timothy.

So then even here, we have good hopes? For he who is conscious to himself of no evil, and who has been fruitful in good, rejoices even here: as the wicked man on the other hand is punished here as well as hereafter. He lives in perpetual fear, he can look no one in the face with confidence, he is pale, trembling, and full of anxiety. Is it not so with the fraudulent, and with thieves, who have no satisfaction even in what they possess? Is not the life of murderers and adulterers most wretched, who look upon the sun itself with suspicion? Is this to be called life? No; rather a horrid death!

Ver. 10. "For therefore we both labor and suffer reproach, because we trust in the living God, who is the Saviour of all men, specially of them that believe."

This in effect is to say, wherefore do we mortify ourselves, unless we expect future blessings? Have we endured so many evils, submitted to so many reproaches, suffered such insults and calumnies, and such numerous calamities in vain? For if we did not trust in the living God, on what account did we submit to these things? But if God is here the Saviour [1] of the unbelieving, much more is He of the faithful hereafter. What salvation does he speak of? That to come? [2] "Who is the Saviour," he says, "of all men, specially of them that believe." At present he is speaking of that which is here. But how is He the Saviour of the faithful? Had he not been so, they must long since have been destroyed, for all men have made war upon them. He calls him here to endure perils, that having God for his Saviour he may not faint, nor need any aid from others, but willingly and with fortitude endure all things. Even those who eagerly grasp at worldly advantages, supported by the hope of gain, cheerfully undertake laborious enterprises.

It is then the last time. For "in the latter times," he says, "some shall depart from the faith." "Forbidding to marry." And do not we forbid to marry? God forbid. We do not forbid those who wish to marry, but those who do not wish to marry, we exhort to virginity. It is one thing to forbid, and another to leave one to his own free choice. He that forbids, does it once for all, but he who recommends virginity as a higher state, does not forbid marriage, because he prefers virginity.

"Forbidding to marry," he says, "and commanding to abstain from meats, which God hath created to be received with thanksgiving of them which believe and know the truth." It is well said, "who know the truth." The former things then were a type. For nothing is unclean by nature, but it becomes so through the conscience of him that partakes of it. And what was the object of the prohibition of so many meats? To restrain excessive luxury. But had it been said, "eat not for the sake of luxury," it would not have been borne. They were therefore shut up under the necessity of the law, that they might abstain from the stronger principle of fear. The fish was not forbidden, though it was manifestly more unclean than the swine. But they might have learned how pernicious luxury was from that saying of Moses, "Jeshurun waxed fat, and kicked." (Deut. xxxii. 15.) Another cause of these prohibitions might be, that being straitened for other food, they might be reduced to slaughter sheep and oxen; he therefore restrained them from other things, on account of Apis and the calf, which was an abomination, ungrateful, polluted, and profane.[3]

"Put them in remembrance of these things, meditate upon[4] these things," for by the expression, "nourished up in the words of faith and sound doctrine," is implied that he should not only recommend these things to others, but himself practice them. For he says, "Nourished up in the words of faith, and of good doctrine, whereunto thou hast attained. But refuse profane and old wives' fables." Why does he not say, abstain from them, but "refuse"? He thus intimates that they should be utterly rejected. His meaning is, that he should not enter into any disputation with the teachers of them, but recommend to his own people the things prescribed above. For nothing is to be gained by contending with perverse men, unless where it might have an injurious effect, if we were supposed from weakness to decline arguing with them.

"But exercise thyself unto godliness," that is, unto a pure life, and the most virtuous conversation. He that exerciseth himself, even when it is not the season of contest, acts always as if he were contending, practices abstinence, endures all toils, is always anxious, endures much labor. "Exercise thyself," he saith, "unto godliness; for bodily exercise profiteth little, but godliness is profitable for all things, having the promise of the life that now is, and of that which is to come." And why, says one, does he mention this bodily exercise? To show by comparison the superiority of the other, in that the former

---

[1] Or Preserver.
[2] The Editor ventures to mark this as a question, though not so printed, or so taken in the old Translation. B. once had εὖ, which gives this sense with or without a question.

[3] This is scarcely intelligible. B. has, "for he is unclean, who is unthankful, wicked, and profane."
[4] Or practice, v. 15.

is of no solid advantage, though it is attended with many toils, whilst the latter has a lasting and abundant good. As when he bids women "adorn themselves, not with broidered hair, or gold, or costly array : but which becometh women possessing godliness ; with good works." (1 Tim. ii. 9, 10.)

MORAL. "This is a faithful saying, and worthy of all acceptation. For therefore we both labor and suffer reproach." Did Paul then suffer reproach, and art thou impatient? Did Paul labor, and wouldest thou live luxuriously? But had he lived luxuriously, he would never have attained such great blessings. For if worldly goods, which are uncertain and perishable, are never gained by men without labor and pains, much less are spiritual. Well, saith one, but some inherit them. Yet even when inherited they are not guarded and preserved without labor, and care, and trouble, no less than those have that have gained them. And I need not say that many who have toiled and endured hardships have been disappointed at the very entrance of the harbor, and an adverse wind has caused the wreck of their hopes, when they were upon the point of possession. But with us there is nothing like this. For it is God who promised, and that "hope maketh not ashamed." (Rom. v. 5.) Ye who are conversant with worldly affairs, know ye not how many men, after infinite toils, have not enjoyed the fruit of their labors, either being previously cut off by death, or overtaken by misfortune, or assailed by disease, or ruined by false accusers, or some other cause, which amidst the variety of human casualties, has forced them to go with empty hands?

But do you not see the lucky men, says one, who with little labor acquire the good things of life? What good things? Money, houses, so many acres of land, trains of servants, heaps of gold and silver? Can you call these good things, and not hide your head for shame? A man called to the pursuit of heavenly wisdom, and gaping after worldly things, and calling them "goods," which are of no value ! If these things are good, then the possessors of them must be called good. For is not he good, who is the possessor of what is good? But when the possessors of these things are guilty of fraud and rapine, shall we call them good? For if wealth is a good, but is increased by grasping, the more it is increased, the more will its possessor be considered to be good. Is the grasping man then good? But if wealth is good, and increases by grasping, the more a man grasps, the better he must be. Is not this plainly a contradiction? But suppose the wealth is not gained wrongfully. And how is this possible? So destructive a passion is avarice, that to grow rich without injustice is impossible. This Christ declared, saying, "Make to yourselves friends of the Mammon of unrighteousness." (Luke xvi. 19.) But what if he succeeded to his father's inheritance? Then he received what had been gathered by injustice. For it was not from Adam that his ancestor inherited riches, but, of the many that were before him, some one must probably have unjustly taken and enjoyed the goods of others. What then? he says, did Abraham hold unrighteous wealth; and Job, that blameless, righteous, and faithful man, who "feared God and eschewed evil"? Theirs was a wealth that consisted not in gold and silver, nor in houses, but in cattle. Besides this, he was enriched by God.[1] And the author of that book, relating what happened to that blessed man, mentions the loss of his camels, his mares and asses, but does not speak of treasures of gold or silver being taken away. The riches of Abraham too were his domestics. What then? Did he not buy them? No, for to this very point the Scripture says, that the three hundred and eighteen were born in his house. (Gen. xix. 14.) He had also sheep and oxen. Whence then did he send gold to Rebekah? (Gen. xxiv. 22 ; xii. 16.) From the gifts which he received from Egypt without violence or wrong.

Tell me, then, whence art thou rich? From whom didst thou receive it, and from whom he who transmitted it to thee? From his father and his grandfather. But canst thou, ascending through many generations, show the acquisition just? It cannot be. The root and origin of it must have been injustice. Why? Because God in the beginning made not one man rich, and another poor. Nor did He afterwards take and show to one treasures of gold, and deny to the other the right of searching for it : but He left the earth free to all alike. Why then, if it is common, have you so many acres of land, while your neighbor has not a portion of it? It was transmitted to me by my father. And by whom to him? By his forefathers. But you must go back and find the original owner. Jacob had wealth, but it was earned as the hire of his labors.

But I will not urge this argument too closely. Let your riches be justly gained, and without rapine. For you are not responsible for the covetous acts of your father. Your wealth may be derived from rapine ; but you were not the plunderer. Or granting that he did not obtain it by robbery, that his gold was cast up somewhere out of the earth. What then? Is wealth therefore good? By no means. At the same time it is not bad, he says, if its possessor be not covetous ; it is not bad, if it be distributed

---

[1] θεόπλουτος.

to the poor, otherwise it is bad, it is ensnaring. "But if he does not evil, though he does no good, it is not bad," he argues. True. But is not this an evil, that you alone should have the Lord's property, that you alone should enjoy what is common? Is not "the earth God's, and the fullness thereof"? If then our possessions belong to one common Lord, they belong also to our fellow-servants. The possessions of one Lord are all common. Do we not see this the settled rule˙in great houses? To all is given an equal portion of provisions, for it proceeds from the treasures of their Lord. And the house of the master is opened to all. The king's possessions are all common, as cities, market-places, and public walks. We all share them equally.

Mark the wise dispensation of God. That He might put mankind to shame, He hath made certain things common, as the sun, air, earth, and water, the heaven, the sea, the light, the stars; whose benefits are dispensed equally to all as brethren. We are all formed with the same eyes, the same body, the same soul, the same structure in all respects,[1] all things from the earth, all men from one man, and all in the same habitation. But these are not enough to shame us. Other things then (as we have said) He hath made common, as baths, cities, market-places, walks. And observe, that concerning things that are common there is no contention, but all is peaceable. But when one attempts to possess himself of anything, to make it his own, then contention is introduced, as if nature herself were indignant, that when God brings us together in every way, we are eager to divide and separate ourselves by appropriating things, and by using those cold words "mine and thine." Then there is contention and uneasiness. But where this is not, no strife or contention is bred. This state therefore is rather our inheritance, and more agreeable to nature. Why is it, that there is never a dispute about a market-place? Is it not because it is common to all? But about a house, and˙about property, men are always disputing. Things necessary are set before us in common; but even in the least things we do not observe a community. Yet those greater things He hath opened freely to all, that we might thence be instructed to have these inferior things in common. Yet for all this, we are not instructed.

But as I said, how can he, who is rich, be a good man? When he distributes his riches, he is good, so that he is good when he has ceased to have it, when he gives it to others; but whilst he keeps it himself, he is not good. How then is that a good which being retained renders men evil, being parted with makes them good? Not therefore to have wealth, but to have it not, makes one appear to be good. Wealth therefore is not a good. But if, when you can receive it, you receive it not, again you are good.

If then we are good, when having it, we distribute it to others; or when offered to us we refuse it, and if we are not good, when we receive or gain it, how can it be a good thing in itself? Call it not therefore a good. You possess it not, because you think it a good, because you are anxious to possess it. Cleanse thy mind, and rectify thy judgment, and then thou wilt be good. Learn what are really goods. What are they? Virtue and benevolence. These and not that, are truly good. According to this rule, the more charitable thou art, the more good thou wilt be considered. But if thou art rich, thou art no longer good. Let us therefore become thus good, that we may be really good, and may obtain the good things to come in Jesus Christ, with whom, &c.

---

[1] "Hath not a Jew the same organs, the same dimensions?" — Shakespeare, Merchant of Venice.

HOMILY XIII.

1 Timothy iv. 11-14.

"These things command and teach. Let no man despise thy youth; but be thou an example of the believers, in word, in conversation, in charity, in spirit, in faith, in purity. Till I come, give attendance to reading, to exhortation, to doctrine. Neglect not the gift that is in thee, which was given thee by prophecy, with the laying on of the hands of the presbytery."

In some cases it is necessary to command, in others to teach; if therefore you command in those cases where teaching is required, you will become ridiculous. Again, if you teach where you ought to command, you are exposed to the same reproach. For instance, it is not proper to teach a man not to be wicked, but to command; to forbid it with all authority. Not to profess Judaism, should be a command, but teaching is required, when you would lead men to part with their possessions, to profess virginity, or when you would discourse of faith. Therefore Paul mentions both: "Command and teach." When a man uses amulets, or does anything of that kind, knowing it to be wrong, he requires only a command; but he who does it ignorantly, is to be taught his error.

"Let no one despise thy youth."

Observe that it becomes a priest to command and to speak authoritatively, and not always to teach. But because, from a common prejudice, youth is apt to be despised, therefore he says, "Let no man despise thy youth." For a teacher ought not to be exposed to contempt. But if he is not to be despised, what room is there for meekness and moderation? Indeed the contempt that he falls into personally he ought to bear; for teaching is commended by longsuffering. But not so, where others are concerned; for this is not meekness, but coldness. If a man revenge insults, and ill language, and injuries offered to himself, you justly blame him. But where the salvation of others is concerned, command, and interpose with authority. This is not a case for moderation, but for authority, lest the public good suffer. He enjoins one or the other as the case may require. Let no one despise thee on account of thy youth. For as long as thy life is a counterpoise, thou wilt not be despised for thy youth, but even the more admired: therefore he proceeds to say,

"But be thou an example of the believers in word, in conversation, in charity, in faith, in purity." In all things showing thyself an example of good works: that is, be thyself a pattern

of a Christian life, as a model set before others, as a living law, as a rule and standard of good living, for such ought a teacher to be. "In word," that he may speak with facility, "in conversation, in charity, in faith, in "true "purity, in temperance."

"Till I come give attendance to reading, to exhortation, to doctrine."

Even Timothy is commanded to apply to reading. Let us then be instructed not to neglect the study of the sacred writings. Again, observe, he says, "Till I come." Mark how he consoles him, for being as it were an orphan, when separated from him, it was natural that he should require such comfort. "Till I come," he says, give attendance to reading the divine writings, to exhortation of one another, to teaching of all.

"Neglect not the gift that is in thee, which was given thee by prophecy."

Here he calls teaching prophecy.[1]

"With the laying on of the hands of the presbytery." He speaks not here of Presbyters, but of Bishops. For Presbyters cannot be supposed to have ordained a Bishop.

Ver. 15. "Meditate upon these things; give thyself wholly to them."

Observe how often he gives him counsel concerning the same things, thus showing that a teacher ought above all things to be attentive to these points.

Ver. 16. "Take heed," he says, "unto thyself, and unto the doctrine: continue in them." That is, take heed to thyself, and teach others also.

"For in so doing thou shalt both save thyself and them that hear thee."

It is well said, "Thou shalt save thyself." For he that is "nourished up in the words of sound doctrine," first receives the benefit of it himself. From admonishing others, he is touched with compunction himself. For these things are not said to Timothy only, but to all. And if such advice is addressed to him, who raised the dead, what shall be said to us? Christ also shows the duty of teachers, when He says, "The kingdom of heaven is like unto an householder, who bringeth forth out of his treasure things new and old." (Matt. xiii. 52.) And the blessed Paul gives the same advice, that "we through patience and comfort of the Scriptures might have hope."

---

[1] He means that it was a gift of Prophecy, which the Greek διὰ may bear.

(Rom. xv. 4.) This he practiced above all men, being brought up in the law of his fathers, at the feet of Gamaliel, whence he would afterwards naturally apply to reading: for he who exhorted others would himself first follow the advice he gave. Hence we find him continually appealing to the testimony of the prophets, and searching into their writings. Paul then applies to reading, for it is no slight advantage that is to be reaped from the Scriptures. But we are indolent, and we hear with carelessness and indifference. What punishment do we not deserve !

"That thy profiting may appear," he says, "to all."

Thus he would have him appear great and admirable in this respect also, showing that this was still necessary for him, for he wished that his "profiting should appear" not only in his life, but in the word of doctrine.

Chap. v. ver. 1. "Rebuke not an elder."

Is he now speaking of the order? I think not, but of any elderly man. What then if he should need correction? Do not rebuke him, but address him as you would a father offending.

Ver. 1. "The elder women as mothers, the younger men as brethren; the younger women as sisters, with all purity."

Rebuke is in its own nature offensive, particularly when it is addressed to an old man, and when it proceeds from a young man too, there is a threefold show of forwardness. By the manner and the mildness of it, therefore, he would soften it. For it is possible to reprove without offense, if one will only make a point of this: it requires great discretion, but it may be done.

"The younger men as brethren." Why does he recommend this too here? With a view to the high spirit natural to young men, whence it is proper to soften reproof to them also with moderation.

"The younger women as sisters"; he adds, "with all purity." Tell me not, he means, of merely avoiding sinful intercourse with them. There should not be even a suspicion. For since intimacy with young women is always suspicious, and yet a Bishop cannot always avoid it, he shows by adding these words, that "all purity" is required in such intimacy. But does Paul give this advice to Timothy? Yes, he says, for I am speaking to the world through him. But if Timothy was thus advised, let others consider what sort of conduct is required of them, that they should give no ground for suspicion, no shadow of pretext, to those who wish to calumniate.

Ver. 3. "Honor widows, that are widows indeed."

Why does he say nothing of virginity, nor command us to honor virgins? Perhaps there were not yet any professing that state, or they might have fallen from it. "For some," he says, "are already turned aside after Satan." (1 Tim. v. 15.) For a woman may have lost her husband, and yet not be truly a widow. As in order to be a virgin, it is not enough to be a stranger to marriage, but many other things are necessary, as blamelessness and perseverance; so the loss of a husband does not constitute a widow, but patience, with chastity and separation from all men. Such widows he justly bids us honor, or rather support. For they need support, being left desolate, and having no husband to stand up for them. Their state appears to the multitude despicable and inauspicious. Therefore he wishes them to receive the greater honor from the Priest, and the more so, because they are worthy of it.

Ver. 4. "But if any widow have children or grandchildren, let them learn first to show piety at home, and to requite their parents."

Observe the discretion of Paul; how often he urges men from human considerations. For he does not here lay down any great and lofty motive, but one that is easy to be understood: "to requite their parents." How? For bringing them up and educating them. As if he should say, Thou has received from them great care. They are departed. Thou canst not requite them. For thou didst not bring them forth, nor nourish them. Requite them [1] in their descendants, repay the debt through the children. "Let them learn first to show piety at home." Here he more simply exhorts them to acts of kindness; then to excite them the more, he adds,

"For that is good and acceptable before God." And as he had spoken of those "who are widows indeed," he declares who is indeed a widow.

Ver. 5. "Now she that is a widow indeed, and desolate, trusteth in God, and continueth in supplications and prayers night and day. But she that liveth in pleasure is dead while she liveth."

She who being a widow has not made choice of a worldly life, is a widow indeed; she who trusts in God as she ought, and continues instant in prayer night and day, is a widow indeed. Not that she, who has children, is not a widow indeed. For he commends her who brings up children as she ought. But if any one has not children, he means, she is desolate, and her he consoles, saying, that she is most truly a widow, who has lost not only the consolation of a husband, but that arising from children, yet she has

---

[1] αὐτοῦ seems unintelligible, read αὐτούς. B. has ἐκείνου, which would be, " in his (her husband's) grandchildren." It is not easy to see why St. Chrys. takes this as a direction to the widow herself, except it be from a grateful remembrance of his own mother's devoting herself to him as she did. Theodoret follows him, but says more of the corresponding duty of the children.

God in the place of all. She is not the worse for not having children, but He fills up her need with consolation, in that she is without children. What he says amounts to this. Grieve not, when it is said that a widow ought to bring up children, as if, because thou hast no children, thy worth were on that account inferior. Thou art a widow indeed, whereas she who liveth in pleasure is dead while she liveth.

But since many who have children choose[1] the state of widowhood, not to cut off the occasions of a worldly life, but rather to enhance them, that they may do what they will with the greater license, and indulge the more freely in worldly lusts : therefore he says, " She that liveth in pleasure is dead while she liveth." Ought not a widow then to live in pleasure? Surely not. If then when nature and age is weak, a life of pleasure is not allowable, but leads to death, eternal death ; what have men to say, who live a life of pleasure? But he says with reason, " She that liveth in pleasure is dead while she liveth." But that thou mayest see this, let us now see what is the state of the dead, and what of the living, and in which shall we place such an one? The living perform the works of life, of that future life, which is truly life. And Christ has declared what are the works of that future life, with which we ought always to be occupied. " Come, inherit the kingdom prepared for you from the foundation of the world. For I was an hungered, and ye gave me meat. I was thirsty, and ye gave me drink." (Matt. xxv. 34, 35.) The living differ from the dead, not only in that they behold the sun, and breathe the air, but in that they are doing some good. For if this be wanting, the living are not better than the dead. That you may learn this, hear how it is possible that even the dead should live. For it is said, " God is not the God of the dead, but of the living." (Matt. xxii. 32.) But this again you say is a riddle. Let us therefore solve them both. A man who liveth in pleasure, is dead whilst he liveth. For he liveth only to his belly. In his other senses he lives not. He sees not what he ought to see, he hears not what he ought to hear, he speaks not what he ought to speak. Nor does he perform the actions of the living. But as he who is stretched upon a bed, with his eyes closed, and his eyelids fast, perceives nothing that is passing ; so it is with this man, or rather not so, but worse. For the one is equally insensible to things good and evil, but the latter is sensible to things evil only, but as insensible as the former to things good. Thus he is dead. For nothing relating to the life to come moves or affects him. For intemperance, taking him into her own bosom, as into some

dark and dismal cavern, full of all uncleanness, causes him to dwell altogether in darkness, like the dead. For when all his time is spent between feasting and drunkenness, is he not dead, and buried in darkness? Even in the morning when he seems to be sober, he is not sober in reality, since he has not yet rid and cleansed himself of yesterday's excess and is still longing for a repetition, and in that his evening and noon he passes in revels, and all the night, and most of the morning in deep sleep.

Is he then to be numbered with the living? Who can describe that storm that comes of luxury, that assails his soul and body? For as a sky continually clouded admits not the sunbeams to shine through it, so the fumes of luxury and wine enveloping his brain, as if it were some rock, and casting over it a thick mist, suffer not reason to exert itself, but overspread the drunken man with profound darkness. With him who is thus affected, how great must be the storm within, how violent the tumult. As when a flood of water has risen, and has surmounted the entrances of the workshops,[2] we see all the inmates in confusion, and using tubs and pitchers and sponges, and many other contrivances to bale it out, that it may not both undermine the building, and spoil all that is contained in it : so it is when luxury overwhelms the soul ; its reasonings within are disturbed. What is already collected, cannot be discharged, and by the introduction of more, a violent storm is raised. For look not at the cheerful and merry countenance, but examine the interior, and you will see it full of deep dejection. If it were possible to bring the soul into view, and to behold it with our bodily eyes, that of the luxurious would seem depressed, mournful, miserable, and wasted with leanness ; for the more the body grows sleek and gross, the more lean and weakly is the soul ; and the more one is pampered,[3] the more is the other hampered.[4] As, when the pupil of the eye has the external coats over it too thick, it cannot put forth the power of vision,[5] and look out, because the light is excluded by the thick covering, and darkness often ensues ; so when the body is constantly full fed, the soul must be invested with grossness. But the dead rot, and are corrupted, you say ; and an unwholesome moisture distills from them. So in her " that liveth in pleasure," may be seen rheums, and phlegm, catarrh, hiccough, vomitings, eructations, and the like, which, as too unseemly, I forbear to name. For such is the dominion of luxury, that it makes one endure things, which we do not even think proper to mention.

---

² ἐργαστηρίων, probably cellars.
³ θάλπεται.
⁴ θάπτεται, buried.
⁵ It was commonly thought that a certain effluence from the eye was required to meet the light.

But you still ask, how is the body dissolved whilst it yet eats and drinks? Surely this is no sign of human life, since creatures without reason too eat and drink. Where the soul lies dead, what do eating and drinking avail? The dead body, that is invested with a flowery garment, is not benefited by it, and when a blooming body invests a dead soul, the soul is not benefited. For when its whole discourse is of cooks, and caterers, and confectioners, and it utters nothing pious,[1] is it not dead? For let us consider what is man? The Heathens say that he is a rational animal, mortal, capable of intelligence and knowledge. But let us not take our definition from them, but whence? From the sacred writings. Where then has the Scripture given a definition of man? Hear its words. "There was a man perfect and upright, one that feared God, and eschewed evil." (Job i. 2.) This was indeed a man! Again, another says, "Man is great, and the merciful man is precious." (Prov. xx. 6, Sept.) Those who answer not to this description, though they partake of mind, and are never so capable of knowledge, the Scripture refuses to acknowledge them as men, but calls them dogs, and horses, and serpents, and foxes, and wolves, and if there be any animals more contemptible. If such then is man, he that liveth in pleasure is not a man; for how can he be, who never thinks of anything that he ought? Luxury and sobriety cannot exist together: they are destructive of one another. Even the Heathens say,

"A heavy paunch bears not a subtle mind."[2]

Such as these the Scripture calls men without souls. "My Spirit (it is said) shall not always abide in these men, because they are flesh." (Gen. vi. 3, Sept.) Yet they had a soul, but because it was dead in them, He calls them flesh. For as in the case of the virtuous, though they have a body, we say, "he is all soul, he is all spirit," so the reverse is said of those who are otherwise. So Paul also said of those, who did not fulfill the works of the flesh, "Ye are not in the flesh." (Rom. viii. 9.) Thus those who live in luxury are not in the soul or in the spirit.

MORAL. "She that liveth in pleasure is dead while she liveth." Hear this, ye women, that pass your time in revels and intemperance, and who neglect the poor, pining and perishing with hunger, whilst you are destroying yourself with continual luxury. Thus you are the causes of two deaths, of those who are dying of want, and of your own, both through ill measure. But if out of your fullness you tempered their want, you would save two lives. Why do you thus gorge your own body with excess, and waste that of the

poor with want; why pamper this above measure, and stint that too beyond measure? Consider what comes of food, into what it is changed. Are you not disgusted at its being named? Why then be eager for such accumulations? The increase of luxury is but the multiplication of dung! For nature has her limits, and what is beyond these is not nourishment, but injury, and the increase of ordure. Nourish the body, but do not destroy it. Food is called nourishment, to show that its design is not to injure the body, but to nourish it. For this reason perhaps food passes into excrement, that we may not be lovers of luxury. For if it were not so, if it were not useless and injurious to the body, we should not cease from devouring one another. If the belly received as much as it pleased, digested it, and conveyed it to the body, we should see wars and battles innumerable. Even now when part of our food passes into ordure, part into blood, part into spurious and useless phlegm, we are nevertheless so addicted to luxury, that we spend perhaps whole estates on a meal. What should we not do, if this were not the end of luxury? The more luxuriously we live, the more noisome are the odors with which we are filled. The body is like a swollen bottle, running out every way. The eructations are such as to pain the head of a bystander. From the heat of fermentation within, vapors are sent forth, as from a furnace, if bystanders are pained, what, think you, is the brain within continually suffering, assailed by these fumes? to say nothing of the channels of the heated and obstructed blood, of those reservoirs, the liver and the spleen, and of the canals by which the fæces are discharged. The drains in our streets we take care to keep unobstructed. We cleanse our sewers with poles and drags, that they may not be stopped, or overflow, but the canals of our bodies we do not keep clear, but obstruct and choke them up, and when the filth rises to the very throne of the king, I mean the brain, we do not regard it, treating it not like a worthy king, but like an unclean brute. God hath purposely removed to a distance those unclean members, that we might not receive offense from them. But we suffer it not to be so, and spoil all by our excess. And other evils might be mentioned. To obstruct the sewers is to breed a pestilence; but if a stench from without is pestilential, that which is pent up within the body, and cannot find a vent, what disorders must it not produce both to body and soul? Some have strangely complained, wondering why God has ordained that we should bear a load of ordure with us. But they themselves increase the load. God designed thus to detach us from luxury, and to persuade us not to attach ourselves to worldly

---

[1] μηδὲν εὐσεβὲς, perhaps an euphemism for loose and profane talking.
[2] The English proverb is, "Fat paunches make lean pates."

things. But thou art not thus to be persuaded to cease from gluttony, but though it is but as far as the throat, and as long as the hour of eating, nay not even so long, that the pleasure abides, thou continuest in thine indulgence. Is it not true that as soon as it has passed the palate and the throat, the pleasure ceases? For the sense of it is in the taste, and after that is gratified, a nausea succeeds, the stomach not digesting the food, or not without much difficulty. Justly then is it said, that "she that liveth in pleasure is dead while she liveth." For the luxurious soul is unable to hear or to see anything. It becomes weak, ignoble, unmanly, illiberal, cowardly, full of impudence, servility, ignorance, rage, violence, and all kinds of evil, and destitute of the opposite virtues. Therefore he says,

Ver. 7. "These things give in charge, that they may be blameless."

He does not leave it to their choice. Command them, he says, not to be luxurious, assuming it to be confessedly an evil, as not holding it lawful or admissible for the luxurious to partake of the Holy Mysteries. "These things command," he says, "that they may be blameless." Thus you see it is reckoned among sins. For if it were a matter of choice, though it were left undone, we might still be blameless. Therefore in obedience to Paul, let us command the luxurious widow not to have place in the list of widows.[1] For if a soldier, who frequents the bath, the theater, the busy scenes of life, is judged to desert his duty, much more the widows. Let us then not seek our rest here, that we may find it hereafter. Let us not live in pleasure here, that we may hereafter enjoy true pleasure, true delight, which brings no evil with it, but infinite good. Of which God grant that we may all be partakers, in Jesus Christ, with whom, &c.

HOMILY XIV.

1 Timothy v. 8.

"But if any provide not for his own, and especially for those of his own house, he hath denied the faith, and is worse than an infidel."

Many consider that their own virtue is sufficient for their salvation, and if they duly regulate their own life, that nothing further is wanting to save them. But in this they greatly err, which is proved by the example of him who buried his one talent, for he brought it back not diminished but entire, and just as it had been delivered to him. It is shown also by the blessed Paul, who says here, "If any one provide not for his own." The provision of which he speaks is universal, and relates to the soul as well as the body, since both are to be provided for.

"If any provide not for his own, and especially for those of his own house," that is, those who are nearly related to him, "he is worse than an infidel." And so says Isaiah, the chief of the Prophets, "Thou shalt not overlook thy kinsmen of thy own seed." (Isa. lviii. 7, Sept.) For if a man deserts those who are united by ties of kindred and affinity, how shall he be affectionate towards others? Will it not have the appearance of vainglory, when benefiting others he slights his own relations, and does not provide for them? And what will be said, if instructing others, he neglects his own, though he has greater facilities, and a higher obligation to benefit them? Will it not be said, These Christians are affectionate indeed, who neglect their own relatives?[2] "He is worse than an infidel." Wherefore? Because the latter, if he benefits not aliens, does not neglect his near kindred. What is meant is this: The law of God and of nature is violated by him who provides not for his own family. But if he who provides not for them has denied the faith, and is worse than an infidel, where shall he be ranked who has injured his relatives? With whom shall he be placed? But how has he denied the faith? Even as it is said, "They profess that they know God, but in works they deny Him." (Tit. i. 16.) What has God, in whom they believe, commanded? "Hide not thyself from thine own flesh." (Isa. lviii. 7.) How does he then believe who thus denies God? Let those consider this, who to spare their wealth neglect their kindred. It was the design of God, in uniting us by the ties of kindred, to afford us many opportunities of doing good to one another. When therefore thou neglectest a duty which infidels perform, hast thou not denied the faith? For it is not faith merely to profess belief, but to do works worthy of faith. And it is possible in each particular to believe and not to believe.[3] For since he had spoken

---

[1] Of the "list of widows" relieved by the Church, see St. Chrys. on the Priesthood, book iii. c. 16, Ben. p. 396, A.
[2] Colb., "For the heathen will presently say, Well! these Christians are affectionate indeed, to neglect their own relatives! And he well said," &c.　　　[3] Colb. omits this sentence.

of luxury and self-indulgence, he says that it is not for this only that such a woman is punished, because she is luxurious, but because her luxury compels her to neglect her household. This he says with reason ; for she that liveth to the belly, perishes hereby also, as "having denied the faith." But how is she worse than an infidel? Because it is not the same thing to neglect our kindred, as to neglect a stranger. How should it be? But the fault is greater here, to desert one known than one who is unknown to us, a friend than one who is not a friend.

Ver. 9, 10. "Let not a widow be taken into the number under threescore years old, having been the wife of one man. Well reported of for good works."

He had said, "Let them learn first to show piety at home, and to requite their parents." He had also said, "She that liveth in pleasure is dead whilst she liveth." He had said, "If 'she[1] provides not for her own she is worse than an infidel." Having mentioned the qualities which not to have would render a woman unworthy to be reckoned among the widows, he now mentions what she ought to have besides. What then? are we to receive her for her years? What merit is there in that? It is not her own doing that she is threescore years old. Therefore he does not speak of her age merely, as, if she has even reached those years, she may not yet, he says, without good works, be reckoned among the number. But why then is he particular about the age? He afterwards assigns a cause not originating with himself, but with the widows themselves. Meanwhile let us hear what follows. "Well reported of for good works, if she have brought up children." Truly, it is no unimportant work to bring up children ; but bringing them up is not merely taking care of them ; they must be brought up well ; as he said before, "If they continue in faith, and charity, and holiness." (1 Tim. ii. 15.) Observe how constantly he sets kindnesses to our own relatives before those to strangers. First, he says, "If she have brought up children," then, "If she have lodged strangers, if she have washed the Saints' feet, if she have relieved the afflicted, if she have diligently followed every good work." But what if she be poor? Not even in that case is she debarred from bringing up children, lodging strangers, relieving the afflicted. She is not more destitute than the widow who gave the two mites. Poor though she be, she has an house, she does not lodge in the open air. "If," he says, "she have washed the Saints' feet." This is not a costly work. "If she have diligently followed every good work." What precept does he give here? He

exhorts them to contribute bodily service, for women are peculiarly fitted for such attendance, for making the bed of the sick, and composing them to rest.

Strange ! what strictness does he require of widows ; almost as much as of the Bishop himself. For he says, "If she have diligently followed every good work." This is as though he meant that, if she could not of herself perform it, she shared and coöperated in it. When he cuts off luxury, he would have her provident, a good economist, and at the same time continually persevering in prayer. Such was Anna. Such strictness does he require of widows. Greater even than of virgins, from whom he yet requires much strictness, and eminent virtue. For when he speaks of "that which is comely," and "that she may attend upon the Lord without distraction" (1 Cor. vii. 35), he gives, in a manner, a summary of all virtue. You see that it is not merely the not contracting a second marriage that is enough to make a widow, many other things are necessary. But why does he discourage second marriages? Is the thing condemned? By no means. That is heretical. Only he would have her henceforth occupied in spiritual things, transferring all her care to virtue. For marriage is not an impure state, but one of much occupation. He speaks of their having leisure, not of their being more pure by remaining unmarried. For marriage certainly implies much secular engagement. If you abstain from marriage that you may have leisure for the service of God, and yet do not so employ that leisure, it is of no advantage to you, (if you do not use your leisure,) to perform all services to strangers, and to the Saints.[2] If you do not thus, you abstain from marriage not for any good end, but as though you condemned the state. So the virgin, who is not truly crucified to the world, by declining marriage, appears to condemn it as accursed and impure.

Observe, the hospitality here spoken of is not merely a friendly reception, but one given with zeal and alacrity, with readiness, and going about it as if one were receiving Christ Himself. The widows should perform these services themselves, not commit them to their handmaids. For Christ said, "If I your Master and Lord have washed your feet, ye ought also to wash one another's feet." (John xiii. 14.) And though a woman may be very rich, and of the highest rank, vain of her birth and noble family, there is not the same distance between her and others, as between God and the disciples. If thou receivest the stranger as Christ, be not ashamed, but rather glory : but if you receive

---

[1] The feminine is not marked, but implied by his comment; see p. 450.

[2] The sense is clear, but the Greek admits of no grammatical construction. Downes, as usual, alters it boldly. This translation supposes an abrupt construction, reading ἐπιδεικνύῃ.

him not as Christ, receive him not at all. "He that receiveth you," He said, "receiveth Me." (Matt. x. 40.) If you do not so receive him, you have no reward. Abraham was receiving men that passed as travelers, as he thought, and he did not leave to his servants to make the preparations for their entertainment, but took the greater part of the service upon himself, and commanded his wife to mix the flour, though he had three hundred and eighteen servants born in his house, of whom there must have been many[1] maidservants; but he wished that himself and his wife should have the reward, not of the cost only, but of the service. Thus ought we ever to exercise hospitality by our own personal exertions, that we may be sanctified, and our hands be blessed. And if thou givest to the poor, disdain not thyself to give it, for it is not to the poor that it is given, but to Christ; and who is so wretched, as to disdain to stretch out his own hand to Christ?

This is hospitality, this is truly to do it for God's sake. But if you give orders with pride, though you bid him take the first place, it is not hospitality, it is not done for God's sake. The stranger requires much attendance, much encouragement, and with all this it is difficult for him not to feel abashed; for so delicate is his position, that whilst he receives the favor, he is ashamed. That shame we ought to remove by the most attentive service, and to show by words and actions, that we do not think we are conferring a favor, but receiving one, that we are obliging less than we are obliged. So much does good will multiply the kindness. For as he who considers himself a loser, and thinks that he is doing a favor, destroys all the merit of it; so he who looks upon himself as receiving a kindness, increases the reward. "For God loveth a cheerful giver." (2 Cor. ix. 7.) So that you are rather indebted to the poor man for receiving your kindness. For if there were no poor, the greater part of your sins would not be removed. They are the healers of your wounds, their hands are medicinal to you. The physician, extending his hand to apply a remedy, does not exercise the healing art more than the poor man, who stretches out his hand to receive your alms, and thus becomes a cure[2] for your ills. You give your money, and with it your sins pass away. Such were the Priests of old, of whom it was said, "They eat up the sin of My people." (Hosea iv. 8.) Thus thou receivest more than thou givest, thou art benefited more than thou benefitest. Thou lendest to God, not to men. Thou increasest thy wealth, rather than dimin-

ishest it. But if thou dost not lessen it by giving, then it is indeed diminished!

"If she have received strangers, if she have washed the Saints' feet." But who are these? The distressed saints, not any saints whatever. For there may be saints, who are much waited on by every one. Do not visit these, who are in the enjoyment of plenty, but those who are in tribulation, who are unknown, or known to few. He who hath "done it unto the least of these," He saith, "hath done it unto Me." (Matt. xxv. 40.)

MORAL. Give not thy alms to those who preside in the Church to distribute. Bestow it thyself, that thou mayest have the reward not of giving merely, but of kind service. Give with thine own hands. Cast into the furrow thyself. Here it is not required to handle the plow, to yoke the ox, to wait the season, nor to break up the earth, or to contend with the frost. No such trouble is required here, where thou sowest for heaven, where there is no frost nor winter nor any such thing. Thou sowest in souls, where no one taketh away what is sown, but it is firmly retained with all care and diligence. Cast the seed thyself, why deprive thyself of thy reward. There is great reward in dispensing[3] even what belongs to others. There is a reward not only for giving, but for dispensing well the things that are given. Why wilt thou not have this reward? For that there is a reward for this, hear how we read that the Apostles appointed Stephen to the ministry of the widows. (Acts vi. 5-7.)

Be thou the dispenser of thine own gifts. Thine own benevolence and the fear of God appoint thee to that ministry. Thus vainglory is excluded. This refreshes the soul, this sanctifies the hands, this pulls down pride. This teaches thee philosophy, this inflames thy zeal, this makes thee to receive blessings. Thy head, as thou departest, receives all the blessings of the widows.

Be more earnest in thy prayers. Inquire diligently for holy men, men that are truly such, who, in the retirement of the desert, cannot beg, but are wholly devoted to God. Take a long journey to visit them, and give with thine own hand. For thou mayest profit much in thine own person, if thou givest. Dost thou see their tents, their lodging? dost thou see the desert? dost thou see the solitude? Often when thou hast gone to bestow money, thou givest thine whole soul. Thou art detained, and hast become his fellow-captive, and hast been alike estranged from the world.

It is of great benefit even to see the poor. "It is better," he saith, "to go to the house of mourning, than to the house of feasting."

---

[1] Old Lat., "Many wives that were." "Of whom" may also be taken collectively of the household.
[2] ἐκμαγεῖον, as if wiping a sore clean.

[3] Gr. "being able to dispense."

(Eccles. vii. 2.) By the latter the soul is inflamed. For if thou canst imitate the luxury, then thou art encouraged to self-indulgence, and if thou canst not, thou art grieved. In the house of mourning there is nothing of this kind. If thou canst not afford to be luxurious, thou art not pained; and if thou canst, thou art restrained. Monasteries are indeed houses of mourning. There is sackcloth and ashes, there is solitude, there is no laughter, no pressure of worldly business. There is fasting, and lying upon the ground; there is no impure savor of rich food, no blood shed,[1] no tumult, no disturbance, or crowding. There is a serene harbor. They are as lights shining from a lofty place to mariners afar off. They are stationed at the port, drawing all men to their own calm, and preserving from shipwreck those who gaze on them, and not letting those walk in darkness who look thither. Go to them, and make friends with them, embrace their holy feet, more honorable to touch than the heads of others. If some clasp the feet of statues, because they bear but a likeness of the king, wilt thou not clasp his feet who has Christ within him, and be saved? The Saints' feet are holy, though they are poor men, but not even the head of the profane is honorable. Such efficacy is there in the feet of the Saints, that when they shake off the dust of their feet, they inflict punishment. When a saint is among us, let us not be ashamed of anything that belongs to him.[2] And all are saints, who unite a holy life with a right faith: and though they do not work miracles nor cast out devils, still they are saints.

Go then to their tabernacles. To go to the monastery of a holy man[3] is to pass, as it were, from earth to heaven. Thou seest not there what is seen in a private house. That company is free from all impurity. There is silence and profound quiet. The words "mine and thine" are not in use among them. And if thou remainest there a whole day or even two, the more pleasure thou wilt enjoy. There, as soon as it is day, or rather before day, the cock crows, and you see it not as you may see it[4] in a house, the servants snoring, the doors shut, all sleeping like the dead, whilst the muleteer without is ringing his bells. There is nothing of all this. All, immediately shaking off sleep, reverently rise when their President calls them, and forming themselves into a holy choir, they stand, and lifting up their hands all at once sing the sacred hymns. For they are not like us, who require many hours to shake off sleep from our heavy heads. We indeed, as soon as we are waked, sit some time stretching our limbs, go as nature calls, then proceed to wash our face and our hands; afterwards we take our shoes and clothes, and a deal of time is spent.

It is not so there. No one calls for his servant, for each waits upon himself: neither does he require many clothes, nor need to shake off sleep. For as soon as he opens his eyes, he is like one who has been long awake in collectedness.[5] For when the heart is not stifled within by excess of food, it soon recovers itself, and is immediately wakeful. The hands are always pure; for his sleep is composed and regular. No one among them is found snoring or breathing hard, or tossing about in sleep, or with his body exposed; but they lie in sleep as decently as those who are awake, and all this is the effect of the orderly state of their souls. These are truly saints and angels among men. And marvel not when you hear these things. For their great fear of God suffers them not to go down into the depths of sleep, and to drown their minds, but it falls lightly upon them, merely affording them rest. And as their sleep is, such are their dreams, not full of wild fancies and monstrous visions.

But, as I said, at the crowing of the cock their President comes, and gently touching the[6] sleeper with his foot, rouses them all. For there are none sleeping naked. Then as soon as they have arisen they stand up, and sing the prophetic hymns with much harmony, and well composed tunes. And neither harp nor pipe nor other musical instrument utters such sweet melodies, as you hear from the singing of these saints in their deep and quiet solitudes. And the songs themselves too are suitable, and full of the love of God. "In the night," they say, "lift up your hands unto God. With my soul have I desired Thee in the night, yea with my spirit within me will I seek Thee early." (Isa. xxvi. 9.) And the Psalms of David, that cause fountains of tears to flow. For when he sings, "I am weary with my groaning, all the night make I my bed to swim; I water my couch with my tears" (Ps. vi. 6): and, again, "I have eaten ashes like bread." (Ps. cii. 9.) "What is man that thou art mindful of him?" (Ps. viii. 4.) "Man is like to vanity, his days are as a shadow that passeth away." (Ps. cxliv. 4.) "Be not afraid when one is made rich, when the glory of his house is increased" (Ps. xlix. 16); and, "Who maketh men to be of one mind in a house" (Ps. lxviii. 6): and, "Seven times a day do I praise Thee, because of Thy righteous judgments" (Ps. cxix. 164): and, "At midnight will I rise to give thanks unto Thee,

---

[1] They commonly abstained from all animal food; see p. 457.
[2] Sav. mar. τῶν αὐτοῦ. The other reading is scarcely intelligible.
[3] μοναστήριον. The monasteries of that date were formed by those who gathered round some holy man. For instances, see Theodoret, Hist. Relig.
[4] Some words added from Colb.

[5] τῆς νήψεως ἕνεκεν.　　　　　[6] al. each.

because of Thy righteous judgments " (Ps. cxix. 62) : and, " God will redeem my soul from the power of the grave " (Ps. xlix. 15) : and, " Though I walk through the valley of the shadow of death, I will fear no evil, for Thou art with me " (Ps. xxiii. 4) : and, " I will not be afraid for the terror by night, nor for the arrow that flieth by day, nor for the pestilence that walketh in darkness, nor for the destruction that wasteth at noonday " (Ps. xci. 5, 6) : and, " We are counted as sheep for the slaughter " (Ps. xliv. 22) : he expresses their ardent love to God. And again, when they sing with the Angels, (for Angels too are singing then,) " Praise ye the Lord from the Heavens." (Ps. cxlviii. 1.) And we meanwhile are snoring, or scratching our heads, or lying supine meditating endless deceits.[1] Think what it was for them to spend the whole night in this employment.

And when the day is coming on, they take rest again ; for when we begin our works, they have a season of rest.[2] But each of us, when it is day, calls upon his neighbor, takes account of his outgoings, then[3] goes into the forum ; trembling he appears before the magistrate, and dreads a reckoning. Another visits the stage, another goes about his own business. But these holy men, having performed their morning prayers and hymns, proceed to the reading of the Scriptures. There are some too that have learned to write out books, each having his own apartment assigned to him, where he lives in perpetual quiet ; no one is trifling, not one speaks a word. Then at the third, sixth, and ninth hours, and in the evening, they perform their devotions, having divided the day into four parts, and at the conclusion of each they honor God with psalms and hymns, and whilst others are dining, laughing, and sporting, and bursting with gluttony, they are occupied with their hymns. For they have no time for the table, nor for these things of sense. After their meal[4] they again pursue the same course, having previously given themselves a while to sleep. The men of the world sleep during the day : but these watch during the night. Truly children of light are they ! And while the former, having slept away the greater part of the day, go forth oppressed with heaviness, these are still collected,[5] remaining without food[6] till the evening, and occupied in hymns. Other men, when evening overtakes them, hasten to the baths, and different recreations, but these, being relieved from their labors, then betake themselves to their table, not calling up a multitude of servants, nor throwing the house into bustle and confusion, nor setting before them high-seasoned dishes, and rich-steaming viands, but some only partaking of bread and salt, to which others add oil, whilst the weakly have also herbs and pulse. Then after sitting a short time, or rather after concluding all with hymns, they each go to rest upon a bed made for repose only and not for luxury. There is no dread of magistrates, no lordly arrogance, no terror of slaves, no disturbance of women or children, no multitudes of chests, or superfluous laying by of garments, no gold or silver, no guards and sentinels, no storehouse. Nothing of all these, but all there is full of prayer, of hymns, and of a spiritual savor. Nothing carnal is there. They fear no attacks of robbers, having nothing of which they can be deprived, no wealth, but a soul and body, of which if they are robbed, it is not a loss but a gain. For it is said, " To me to live is Christ, and to die is gain." (Phil. i. 21.) They have freed themselves from all bonds. Truly, " The voice of gladness is in the tabernacles of the righteous." (Ps. cxviii. 15.)

There is no such thing to be heard there as wailing and lamentation. Their roof is free from that melancholy and those cries. Deaths happen there indeed, for their bodies are not immortal, but they know not death, as death. The departed are accompanied to the grave with hymns. This they call a procession,[7] not a burial ;[8] and when it is reported that any one is dead, great is their cheerfulness, great their pleasure ; or rather not one of them can bear to say that one is dead, but that he is perfected. Then there is thanksgiving, and great glory, and joy, every one praying that such may be his own end, that so his own combat may terminate, and he may rest from his labor and struggles, and may see Christ. And if any is sick, instead of tears and lamentations they have recourse to prayers. Often not the care of physicians, but faith alone relieves the sick. And if a physician be necessary, then too there is the greatest firmness and philosophy. There is no wife tearing her hair, nor children bewailing their orphan state before the time, nor slaves entreating the dying man to give them an assurance that they shall be committed to good hands. Escaping from all these, the soul looks but to one thing at its last breath, that it may depart in favor with God. And if disease occurs, the causes of it are matter of glory rather than of reproach, as in other cases. For it proceeds not from gluttony nor fullness of the head,

---

[1] He means not self-deceits, but actual frauds, for he is now as it were on a sally, among the enemy's works.
[2] Not their principal rest, but an interval.
[3] So Old Lat. (prob. from εἶτα εἰς) Edd. εἰ εἰς, " if he goes." Colb. om. εἰ.
[4] ἄριστον. See on Stat. Hom. ix. 1, note e, and x. 1, note a.
[5] νήφουσιν.
[6] This seems to contradict what was said just before, but it need not be taken quite strictly, as the former meal was not at table, and extremely light.
[7] προπομπήν.   [8] ἐκφοράν.

but from intense watchfulness and fasting, or the like causes; and hence it is easily removed, for it is sufficient for its removal to abate the severity of these exercises.

Tell me then, you will say, whether any one could wash the Saints' feet in the Church? Whether such are to be found among us? Yes: undoubtedly they are such. Let us not, however, when the life of these saints is described, despise those that are in the Churches. There are many such often among us, though they are in secret. Nor let us despise them, because they go from house to house, or go into the forum, or stand forth in public.[1] God hath even commanded such services, saying, " Judge the fatherless, plead for the widow." (Isa. i. 17.) Many are the ways of being virtuous, as there are many varieties of jewels,[2] though all are called jewels; one is bright and round on all sides, another has some different beauty. And how is this? As coral has, by a kind of art, its line extended, and its angles shaped off, and another color more delicious than white, and the prasius above every green, another has the rich color of blood, another an azure surpassing the sea, another is more brilliant than the purple, and thus rivaling in their varieties all the colors of flowers or of the sun. Yet all are called jewels. So it is with the Saints. Some discipline[3] themselves, some the Churches. Paul therefore has well said, " If she have washed the Saints' feet, if she have relieved the afflicted." For he speaks thus, that he may excite us all to imitation. Let us hasten then to perform such actions, that we may be able hereafter to boast that we have washed the Saints' feet. For if we ought to wash their feet, much more ought we to give them our money with our own hands, and at the same time study to be concealed. " Let not thy left hand know," He says, " what thy right hand doeth." (Matt. vi. 3.)

Why takest thou so many witnesses? Let not thy servant know it, nor, if possible, thy wife. Many are the impediments of the deceitful one.

Often she who never before interfered, will impede such works, either from vainglory, or some other motive. Even Abraham, who had an admirable wife, when he was about to offer up his son, concealed it from her, though he knew not what was to happen, but was fully persuaded that he must slaughter his son. What then, would any one that was but an ordinary man have said? Would it not be, " Who is this that perpetrates such acts?" Would he not have accused him of cruelty and brutality? His wife was not even allowed to see her son, to receive his last words, to witness his dying struggles. But he led him away like a captive. That just man though not of any such thing, inebriated as he was with zeal,[4] so that he looked only how to fulfill that which was commanded. No servant, no wife was present, nay, he himself knew not what would be the issue. But intent upon offering up a pure victim, he would not defile it with tears, or with any opposition. Mark too with what gentleness Isaac asks, " Behold the fire and the wood, but where is the lamb for a burnt offering?": and what was the father's answer? " My son, God will provide Himself a lamb for a burnt offering." (Gen. xxii. 7, 8.) In this he uttered a prophecy that God would provide Himself a burnt offering in His Son, and it also came true at the time. But why did he conceal it from him who was to be sacrificed? Because he feared lest he should be astounded,[5] lest he should prove unworthy. With such care and prudence did he act throughout this affair ! Well then hath the Scripture said, " Let not thy left hand know what thy right hand doeth." If we have one dear to us as one of our own members, let us not be anxious to show to him our charitable works, unless it be necessary. For many evils may arise from it. A man is excited to vainglory, and impediments are often raised. For this reason let us conceal it, if possible, from our own selves, that we may attain the blessings promised, through the grace and lovingkindness of Jesus Christ our Lord, with whom, &c.

---

[1] προΐστανται. " Stand forth in behalf of another."
[2] μαργαριτῶν, pearls.
[3] ἀσκοῦσιν.

[4] πόθῳ. Love of God, or desire to do His will.
[5] ναρκήσῃ.

HOMILY XV.

1 Timothy v. 11–15.

"But the younger widows refuse: for when they have begun to wax wanton against Christ, they will marry; having condemnation, because they have cast off their first faith. And withal they learn to be idle, wandering about from house to house; and not only idle, but tattlers also and busybodies, speaking things which they ought not. I will therefore that the younger widows marry, bear children, guide the house, give none occasion to the adversary to speak reproachfully. For some are already turned aside after Satan."

Paul having discoursed much concerning widows, and having settled the age at which they were to be admitted, saying, "Let not a widow be taken into the number under threescore years old," and having described the qualifications of a widow, "If she have brought up children, if she have lodged strangers, if she have washed the Saints' feet," proceeds now to say, "But the younger widows refuse." But concerning virgins, though the case of their falling is a much more gross one, he has said nothing of this kind, and rightly. For they had enrolled themselves on higher views, and the work with them proceeded from a greater elevation of mind. Therefore the receiving of strangers, and the washing of the Saints' feet, he has represented by "attending upon the Lord without distraction"[1] (1 Cor. vii. 34, 35), and by saying, "The unmarried careth for the things that belong to the Lord." (1 Cor. vii. 34, 35.) And if he has not limited a particular age for them, it is most likely because that point is settled by what he has said in this case. But indeed, as I said, the choice of virginity proceeded from a higher purpose. Besides, in this case there had been falls, and thus they had given occasion for his rule, but nothing of that kind had occurred among the virgins. For that some had already fallen away is plain, in that he says, "When they have begun to wax wanton against Christ, they will[2] marry"; and again, "For some have already turned aside after Satan."

"The younger widows refuse, for when they have begun to wax wanton against Christ, they will marry"; that is, when they have become scornful[3] and luxurious. For as in the case of a just man, we might say, "Let her depart, for she has become another's."[4] He shows there-fore that though they chose widowhood, it was not the choice of their judgment. So then a widow, by the state of widowhood, is espoused to Christ. For He has said, "I am the defender of the widows and the father of the orphans." (Ps. lxviii. 5.) He shows that they do not choose widowhood as they ought, but wax wanton: however he bears with them. Elsewhere indeed he says, "I have espoused you to one husband, that I may present you as a chaste virgin to Christ." (2 Cor. xi. 2.) After having given their names to Him,[5] "they will marry," he says, "having condemnation, because they have cast off their first faith." By faith he means, fidelity to their covenant. As if he had said, They have been false to Christ, they have dishonored Him, and transgressed His covenant. "And withal they learn to be idle."

Thus he commands not only men, but women also, to work. For idleness is the teacher of every sin. And not only are they exposed to this condemnation, but to other sins. If therefore it is unbecoming for a married woman "to go from house to house," much more is it for a virgin. "And not only idle, but tattlers also and busybodies, speaking things which they ought not. I will therefore that the younger widows marry, bear children, guide the house."

What then happens, when the care for the husband is withdrawn, and the care to please God does not constrain them? They naturally become idlers, tattlers, and busybodies. For he who does not attend to his own concerns will be meddling with those of others, even as he who minds his own business will take no account of and have no care about the affairs of another. And nothing is so unbecoming to a woman, as to busy herself in the concerns of others, and it is no less unbecoming to a man. This is a great sign of impudence and forwardness.

"I will therefore," he says, (since they themselves wish it,) "that the younger widows marry, bear children, guide the house."

This course is at least preferable to the other. They ought indeed to be concerned for the things of God, they ought to preserve their faith. But since they do not this, it is better to avoid a worse course. God is not dishonored by their marrying again, and they do not fall into those practices, which have been censured. From such a widowhood, no good could arise, but good may come out of this marriage. Hence

---

[1] εὐπροσέδρον.

[2] θέλουσι.

[3] ἀκκίσθωσιν.

[4] He seems to mean that a professed widow, giving up her profession, is like a woman betrothed to a man, and then disliking him, and giving her affections to another.

[5] i.e. by the profession of a devout widowhood.

the women will be able to correct that indolence and vanity of mind.

But why, since some have fallen away, does he not say that much care is to be taken of them, that they may not fall into the error he has mentioned? Why has he commanded them to marry? Because marriage is not forbidden, and it is a safeguard to them. Wherefore he adds, that they "give none occasion," or handle, "to the adversary to speak reproachfully. For some are already turned aside after Satan." Such widows as these then he would have refused, not meaning that there should be no younger widows, but that there should be no adulteresses, that none should be idle, busybodies, speaking things that they ought not, that no occasion should be given to the adversary. Had nothing of this kind taken place, he would not have forbidden them.

Ver. 16. "If any man or woman that believeth have widows, let them relieve them, and let not the Church be charged, that it may relieve them that are widows indeed."

Observe how again he speaks of those as "widows indeed," who are left destitute, and have no resource from any other quarter. It was better to have it so. For thus two great objects were attained. Those [1] had an opportunity of doing good, whilst these were honorably maintained, and the Church not burdened. And he has well said, "If any believer." For it is not fit that believing women should be maintained by unbelievers, lest they should seem to stand in need of them. And observe how persuasively he speaks; he has not said, "let them maintain them expensively," but "let them relieve them." "That the Church," he says, "may relieve them that are widows indeed." She therefore has the reward of this help also, for she that helps the Church, helps not her only, but those widows too whom the Church is thus enabled to maintain more bountifully. "I will therefore that the younger widows" — do what? live in luxury and pleasure? By no means; but — "marry, bear children, guide the house." That he may not be supposed to encourage them to live luxuriously, he adds, that they give no occasion to the adversary to speak reproachfully. They ought indeed to have been superior to the things of this world, but since they are not, let them abide in them at least upright.

Ver. 17, 18. "Let the elders that rule well be counted worthy of double honor, especially they who labor in the word and doctrine. For the Scripture saith, Thou shalt not muzzle the

ox that treadeth out the corn. And, The laborer is worthy of his reward."

The "honor" of which he here speaks is attention to them, and the supply of their necessities, as is shown by his adding, "Thou shalt not muzzle the ox that treadeth out the corn" (Deut. xxv. 4); and, "The laborer is worthy of his reward." (Luke x. 7.) So when he says, "Honor widows," he means, "support" them in all that is necessary. Thus he says, "That it may relieve those that are widows indeed"; and again, "Honor widows that are widows indeed," that is, who are in poverty, for the greater their poverty, the more truly are they widows. He alleges the Law, he alleges the words of Christ, both agreeing herein. For the Law says, "Thou shalt not muzzle the ox that treadeth out the corn." See how he would have the teacher labor! For there is not, indeed there is not, any other labor such as his. But this is from the Law. But how does he quote from Christ? "The laborer is worthy of his reward." Let us not then look only to the reward, but to the terms of the commandment. "The laborer," he says, "is worthy of his reward." So that if any one lives in sloth and luxury, he is unworthy of it. Unless he is as the ox treading out the corn, and bearing the yoke, in spite of heat and thorns, and ceases not till he has carried the corn into the granary, he is not worthy. Therefore to teachers should be granted a supply of their necessities without grudging, that they may not faint nor be discouraged, nor by attention to inferior things deprive themselves of greater; that they may labor for spiritual things, paying no regard to worldly things. It was thus with the Levites; they had no worldly concerns, because the laity took care to provide for them, and their revenues were appointed by the law, as tythes, offerings of gold,[2] first-fruits, vows, and many other things. And the law properly assigned these things to them, as seeking things present. But I shall say no more than that those who preside ought to have food and raiment, that they may not be distracted by care for these things. But what is double support? Double that of the widows, or of the deacons, or simply, liberal support. Let us not then think only of the double maintenance granted them, but of what is added, "Those who rule well." And what is it to rule well? Let us hear Christ, Who says, "The good shepherd giveth his life for his sheep." (John x. 11.) Thus to rule well is, from our concern for them, never to spare ourselves.

"Especially those who labor in the word and doctrine." Where then are those who say that there is no occasion for the word and doctrine?

---

[1] Gr. fem. referring to the widows kept by their relations, see Hom. xiii. and xiv., or perhaps to *women* relieving them. See below, l. 9 of this page. Downes, missing the sense, guesses it should be ἐκεῖνοι.

[2] Colb. omits this clause; it is perhaps too bold to guess τὰ ἀπὸ τῶν θυσιῶν, for χρυσίων, making it, "the share of the sacrifices."

Whereas he says to Timothy, "Meditate upon these things; give thyself wholly to them"; and, "Give attendance to reading, to exhortation, to doctrine; for in doing this thou shalt save both thyself, and them that hear thee." (1 Tim. iv. 15, 16.) These are the men whom he wishes to be honored most of all, and he adds the reason, for they sustain great labor. For when one is neither watchful, nor diligent, but merely sits in his stall easy and unconcerned,[1] whilst another wears himself out with anxiety and exertion,[2] especially if he is ignorant of profane literature, ought not the latter to be honored above all others, who more than others gives himself up to such labors? For he is exposed to numberless tongues. One censures him, another praises him, a third mocks him, another finds fault with his memory and his composition, and it requires great strength of mind to endure all this. It is an important point, and contributes much to the edification of the Church, that the rulers of it should be apt to teach. If this be wanting, many things in the Church go to ruin. Therefore in addition to the qualifications of hospitality, moderation, and a blameless life, he enumerates this also, saying, "Apt to teach." For why else indeed is he called a teacher? Some say that he may teach philosophy by the example of his life, so that all else is superfluous, and there is no need of verbal instruction in order to proficiency. But why then does Paul say, "especially they who labor in the word and doctrine"? For when doctrines are concerned, what life will answer the purpose? And of what word is he speaking? Not of pompous language, nor of discourse set off with external[3] decorations, but that which possesses the mighty power of the Spirit, and abounds with wisdom and understanding. It needs not set phrases, but thoughts to give it utterance, not skill in composition, but power of mind.

Ver. 19. "Against an elder receive not an accusation, but before two or three witnesses."

May we then receive an accusation against a younger man, or against any one at all without witnesses? Ought we not in all cases to come to our judgments with the greatest exactness? What then does he mean? Do not so, he means, with any, but especially in the case of an elder. For he speaks of an elder not with respect to office, but to age, since the young more easily fall into sin than their elders. And it is manifest from hence that the Church, and even the whole people of Asia, had been now intrusted to Timothy, which is the reason why he discourses with him concerning elders.

Ver. 20. "Them that sin rebuke before all, that others also may fear."

Do not, he says, hastily cut them off, but carefully enquire into all the circumstances, and when thou hast thoroughly informed thyself, then proceed against the offender with rigor, that others may take warning. For as it is wrong to condemn hastily and rashly, so not to punish manifest offenses is to open the way to others, and embolden them to offend.

"Rebuke," he says, to show that it is not to be done lightly, but with severity. For thus others will be deterred. How is it then that Christ says, "Go and tell him his fault between him and thee alone, if one sin against thee." (Matt. xviii. 15.) But Christ Himself permits him to be censured in the Church. What then? is it not a greater scandal, that one should be rebuked before all? How so? For it is a much greater scandal, that the offense should be known, and not the punishment. For as when sinners go unpunished, many commit crimes; so when they are punished, many are made better. God Himself acted in this manner. He brought forth Pharaoh, and punished him openly. And Nebuchadnezzar too, and many others, both cities and individuals, we see visited with punishment. Paul therefore would have all stand in awe of their Bishop, and sets him over all.

And because many judgments are formed upon suspicion, there ought, he says, to be witnesses, and men to convict the offender according to the ancient law. "At the mouth of two or three witnesses shall every matter be established. Against an elder receive not an accusation." (Deut. xix. 15.) He does not say, "do not condemn," but "receive not an accusation," bring him not to judgment at all. But what if the two witnesses are false? This rarely happens, and it may be discovered upon examination on the trial. For since offenses are committed in secret, we ought to be satisfied with two witnesses, and this is sufficient proof of investigation.

But what if the offenses be notorious, and yet there are no witnesses, only a strong suspicion? It has been said above that he ought "to have a good report of them which are without." (1 Tim. iii. 7.)

Let us therefore love God with fear. The law indeed is not made for a righteous man; but since the greater part are virtuous from constraint rather than from choice, the principle of fear is of great advantage to them in eradicating their desires. Let us therefore listen to the threatenings of hell fire, that we may be benefited by the wholesome fear of it. For if God, intending to cast sinners into it, had not previously threatened them with it, many would have plunged into it. For, if with this terror agitat-

---

[1] συνεδρεύῃ.
[2] μελετῶν. He seems to mean in preparing his discourses.
[3] Or perhaps "heathenish."

ing our souls, some sin as readily as if there were no such thing in existence, what enormities should we not have committed, if it had not been declared and threatened? So that, as I have ever said, the threatenings of hell show the care of God for us no less than the promises of heaven. For the threat coöperates with the promise, and drives men into the kingdom by means of terror. Let us not think it a matter of cruelty, but of pity and mercy; of God's concern and love for us. If in the days of Jonah the destruction of Nineveh had not been threatened, that destruction had not been averted. Nineveh would not havé stood but for the threat, "Nineveh shall be overthrown." (Jonah iii. 4.) And if hell had not been threatened, we should all have fallen into hell. If the fire had not been denounced, no one would have escaped the fire. God declares that He will do that which He desires not to do, that He may do that which He desires to do. He willeth not the death of a sinner, and therefore He threatens the sinner with death, that He may not have to inflict death. Ahd not only has He spoken the word, but He has exhibited the thing itself, that we may escape it. And lest it should be supposed to be a mere threat, He has manifested the reality of it by what He has already done on earth. Dost thou not see in the flood a symbol of hell, in that rain of all-destroying water an image of the all-devouring fire?[1] "For as it was in the days of Noah," He says, "they were marrying and giving in marriage" (Matt. xxiv. 38), so is it even now. It was then predicted[2] long before it took place, and it is now predicted four hundred years or more beforehand:[3] but no one heeds it. It is looked upon as a mere fable, as a matter of derision; no one fears it, no one weeps or beats his breast at the thought of it. The stream of fire is boiling up, the flame is kindled, and we are laughing, taking our pleasure, and sinning without fear. No one even bears in mind That Day. No one considers that present things are passing away, and that they are but temporal, though events are every day crying out and uttering a fearful voice. The untimely deaths, the changes that take place in our lives, our own infirmities and diseases, fail to instruct us. And not only in our own bodies are these changes visible, but in the elements themselves. Every day in our different ages we experience a kind of death, and in every case instability is the characteristic of things we see. Neither winter, nor summer, nor spring, nor autumn, is permanent; all are run-

ning, flying, and flowing past. Why should I speak of fading flowers, of dignities, of kings that are to-day, and to-morrow cease to be, of rich men, of magnificent houses, of night and day, of the sun and the moon? for the moon wanes, and the sun is sometimes eclipsed, and often darkened with clouds? Of things visible, in short, is there anything that endures for ever? Nothing! No, nor anything in us but the soul, and that we neglect. Of things subject to change we take abundant care, as if they were permanent: but that which is to endure for ever we neglect, as if it were soon to pass away. Some one is enabled to perform mighty actions, but they shall last till to-morrow, and then he perishes, as we see in the instances of those who have had yet greater power, and are now to be seen no more. Life is a dream, and a scene; and as on the stage when the scene is shifted the various pageants disappear, and as dreams flit away when the sunbeams rise, so here when the end comes, whether the universal or thát of each one, all is dissolved and vanishes away. The tree that you have planted remains, and the house that you have built, it too stands on. But the planter and the builder go away, and perish. Yet these things happen without our regarding it, and we live on in luxury and pleasure, and are ever furnishing ourselves with such things, as if we were immortal.

Hear what Solomon says, who knew the present world by actual experience. "I builded me houses, I planted me vineyards, I made me gardens, and orchards and pools of water. I gathered me also silver and gold. I gat myself men-singers, and women-singers, and flocks, and herds." (Eccles. ii. 4, 5.) There was no one who lived in greater luxury, or higher glory. There was no one so wise or so powerful, no one who saw all things so succeeding to his heart's desire. What then? He had no enjoyment from all these things. What after all does he say of it himself? "Vanity of vanities, all is vanity." (Eccles. xii. 8.) Vanity not simply but superlatively. Let us believe him, and lay hold on that in which there is no vanity, in which there is truth; and what is based upon a solid rock, where there is no old age, nor decline, but all things bloom and flourish, without decay, or waxing old, or approaching dissolution. Let us, I beseech you, love God with genuine affection, not from fear of hell, but from desire of the kingdom. For what is comparable to seeing Christ? Surely nothing! What to the enjoyment of those good things? Surely nothing! Well may there be nothing; for "eye hath not seen, nor ear heard, neither have entered into the heart of man the things which God hath prepared for them that love Him." (1 Cor. ii. 9.) Let us be anxious to

---

[1] The construction is too involved for such a passage; a slight change would refer the whole latter clause to the Judgment, or to the destruction of the cities of the plain.

[2] i.e. the deluge.

[3] See Hom. xx. on St. Matt. fin., where he says the end of the world might now come at any time.

obtain those things, and let us despise all these. Are we not continually complaining that human life is nothing? Why art thou solicitous for what is nothing? Why dost thou sustain such toils, for what is nothing? Thou seest splendid houses, does the sight of them delude thee? Look up to heaven. Raise thy view from pillars of stone to that beautiful fabric, compared with which the others are as the works of ants and pismires. Learn philosophy from that spectacle, ascend to heavenly things, and look thence upon our splendid buildings, and see that they are nothing, the mere toys of little children. Seest thou not how much finer, how much lighter, how much purer, how much more translucent, is the air the higher thou ascendest? There have they that do alms their mansions and their tabernacles. These that are here are dissolved at the resurrection, or rather before the resurrection destroyed by the stroke of time. Nay, often in their most flourishing state and period an earthquake overthrows, or fire entirely ruins them. For not only the bodies of men, but their very buildings are liable to untimely deaths. Nay, sometimes things decayed by time stand firm under the shock of an earthquake, whilst glittering edifices, firmly fixed, and newly constructed, are struck but by lightning and perish. And this, I believe, is the interposition of God, that we may not take pride in our buildings.

Would you again have another ground for cheerfulness? Go to the public buildings, in which you share equally with others. For the most magnificent private houses, after all, are less splendid than the public edifices. There you may remain, as long as you please. They belong to you as much as to others, since they are common to you with others; they are common, and not private. But those, you say, delight you not. They delight you not, partly because you are familiar with them, and partly from your covetousness. So the pleasantness is not in the beauty, but in the appropriating! So the pleasure is in greediness, and in the wish to make every man's goods your own! How long are we to be nailed to these things? How long are we to be fastened to the earth, and grovel, like worms, in the dirt? God hath given us a body of earth, that we might carry it with us up to heaven, not that we should draw our soul down with it to earth. Earthy it is, but if we please, it may be heavenly. See how highly God has honored us, in committing to us so excellent a frame. I made heaven and earth, He says, and to you I give the power of creation. Make your earth heaven. For it is in thy power. "I am He that maketh and transformeth all things" (Amos v. 8, Sept.), saith God of Himself. And He hath given to men a similar

power; as a painter, being an affectionate father, teaches his own art to his son. I formed thy body beautiful, he says, but I give thee the power of forming something better. Make thy soul beautiful. I said, "Let the earth bring forth grass, and every fruitful tree." (Gen. i. 11.) Do thou also say, Let this earth [1] bring forth its proper fruit, and what thou willest to produce will be produced. "I make the summer and the cloud. I create the lightning and the wind." (Amos iv. 13; Ps. lxxiv. 17.) I formed the dragon, that is, the devil,[2] to make sport with him. (Ps. civ. 26.) Nor have I grudged thee the like power. Thou, if thou wilt, canst sport with him, and bind him as thou wouldest a sparrow. I make the sun to rise upon the evil and the good: do thou imitate Me, by imparting of that is thine to the good and the evil. When mocked I bear with it, and do good to those who mock Me: do thou imitate Me, as thou canst. I do good, not to be requited; do thou imitate Me, and do good, not to be repaid. I have lighted luminaries in the heavens. Do thou light others brighter than these, for thou canst, by enlightening those that are in error. For to know Me is a greater benefit than to behold the sun. Thou canst not create a man, but thou canst make him just and acceptable to God. I formed his substance, do thou beautify his will. See how I love thee, and have given thee the power in the greater things.

Beloved, see how we are honored! yet some are so unreasonable and so ungrateful as to say, "Why are we endowed with free will?" But how in all the particulars which we have mentioned could we have imitated God, if there had been no free will? I rule Angels, He says, and so dost thou, through Him who is the First-fruits. (1 Cor. xv. 23.) I sit on a royal throne, and thou art seated with Me in Him who is the First-fruits. As it is said, "He hath raised us up together and made us sit together in heavenly places in Christ Jesus." (Eph. ii. 6.) Through Him who is the First-fruits, Cherubim and Seraphim adore thee, with all the heavenly host, principalities and powers, thrones and dominions. Disparage not thy body, to which such high honors appertain, that the unbodied Powers tremble at it.

But what shall I say? It is not in this way only that I have shown My love to thee, but by what I have suffered. For thee I was spit upon, I was scourged. I emptied myself of glory, I left My Father and came to thee, who dost hate Me, and turn from Me, and art loath to hear My Name. I pursued thee, I ran after thee, that I might overtake thee. I united and joined

---

[1] i.e. the body.
[2] So St. Aug. on Ps. 103. Vulg. taking "formed" of his degradation.

thee to myself, "eat Me, drink Me," I said. Above I hold thee, and below I embrace thee. Is it not enough for thee that I have thy First-fruits above? Doth not this satisfy thy affection? I descended below: I not only am mingled with thee, I am entwined in thee. I am masticated,[1] broken into minute particles, that the interspersion,[2] and commixture, and union may be more complete. Things united remain yet in their own limits, but I am interwoven with thee. I would have no more any division between us. I will that we both be one.

Therefore knowing these things and remembering His abundant care for us, let us do all things which may prove us not unworthy of His great gift, which God grant that we may all obtain, through the grace and lovingkindness of Christ Jesus our Lord, with whom, &c.

HOMILY XVI.

1 Timothy v. 21–23.

"I charge thee before God and the Lord Jesus Christ and the elect angels, that thou observe these things without preferring one before another, doing nothing by partiality. Lay hands hastily on no man, neither be partaker of other men's sins: keep thyself pure. Drink no longer water, but use a little wine for thy stomach's sake and thine often infirmities."

HAVING spoken of Bishops and Deacons, of men, and women, of widows and elders, and of all others, and having shown how great was the authority of a Bishop, now he was speaking of judgment, he has added, "I charge thee before God and the Lord Jesus Christ and the elect angels, that thou observe these things without preferring one before another, doing nothing by partiality." Thus fearfully he charges him. For though Timothy was his beloved son, he did not therefore stand in awe of him. For as he was not ashamed to say of himself, "Lest by any means when I have preached to others, I myself should be a cast-away" (1 Cor. ix. 27); much less would he be afraid or ashamed in the case of Timothy. He called the Father and the Son to witness. But wherefore the elect Angels? From great moderation, as Moses said, "I call heaven and earth to witness" (Deut. iv. 26); and again, "Hear ye, O mountains, and strong foundations of the earth." (Mic. vi. 2.) He calls the Father and the Son to witness what he has said, making his appeal to Them against that future Day, that if anything should be done that ought not to be done, he was clear from the guilt of it.

"That thou observe these things without preferring one before another, doing nothing by partiality." That is, that thou deal impartially and equally between those who are upon trial and are to be judged by thee, that no one may pre-occupy thy mind, or gain thee over to his side beforehand.

But who are the elect Angels? It is because there are some not elect. As Jacob calls to witness God and the heap (Gen. xxxi. 45), so we often take at once superior and inferior persons to witness; so great a thing is testimony. As if he had said, I call to witness God and His Son and His servants, that I have charged thee: so before them I charge thee. He impresses Timothy with fear; after which he adds, what was most vital,[3] and bears most on the maintenance of the Church, the matter of Ordinations. "Lay hands," he says, "suddenly on no man, neither be partaker of other men's sins." What is "suddenly"? Not upon a first, nor a second, nor a third trial, but after frequent and strict examination and circumspection. For it is an affair of no common peril. For thou wilt be responsible for the sins committed by him, as well his past as his future sins, because thou hast delegated to him this power. For if thou overlook the past unduly, thou art answerable for the future also, as being the cause of them, by placing him in that station, and of the past too, for not leaving him to mourn over them, and to be in compunction. For as thou art a partaker of his good actions, so art thou of his sins.

"Keep thyself pure." This he says with reference to chastity.

"Drink no longer water, but use a little wine for thy stomach's sake and thy often infirmities." If one who had practiced fasting to such an extent, and used only water, so long that he had brought on "infirmities" and "frequent infirmities," is thus commanded to be chaste, and does not refuse the admonition, much less ought we to be offended when we receive an admonition from any one. But why did not Paul restore strength to his stomach? Not because he could not — for he whose garment had raised the dead

---

[1] τρώγομαι.   [2] ἀνάκρασις.   [3] Or "seasonable."

was clearly able to do this too, — but because he had a design of importance in withholding such aid. What then was his purpose?[1] That even now, if we see great and virtuous men afflicted with infirmities, we may not be offended, for this was a profitable visitation. If indeed to Paul himself a "messenger of Satan" was sent that he should not be "exalted above measure" (2 Cor. xii. 11), much more might it be so with Timothy. For the miracles he wrought were enough to have rendered him arrogant. For this reason he is left to be subject to the rules of medicine, that he may be humbled, and others may not be offended, but may learn that they who performed such excellent actions were men of the same nature as themselves. In other respects also Timothy seems to have been subject to disease, which is implied by that expression, "Thy often infirmities," as well of other parts as of the stomach. He does not however allow him to indulge freely in wine, but as much as was for health and not for luxury.[2]

Ver. 24. "Some men's sins are open beforehand, going before to judgment; and some they follow after."

In speaking of ordination, he had said, "Be not partaker of other men's sins." But what, he might say, if I be ignorant of them? Why, "some men's sins are open beforehand, going before them to judgment, and some they follow after." Some men's, he means, are manifest, because they go before, whilst others' are unknown, because they follow after.

Ver. 25. "Likewise also the good works of some are manifest beforehand, and they that are otherwise cannot be hid."

Chap. vi. ver. 1. "Let as many servants as are under the yoke count their masters worthy of all honor, that the Name of God and His doctrine be not blasphemed."

Let them count them "worthy of all honor," he says; for do not suppose, because thou art a believer, that thou art therefore a free man: since thy freedom is to serve the more faithfully. For if the unbeliever sees slaves conducting themselves insolently on account of their faith, he will blaspheme, as if the Doctrine produced insubordination. But when he sees them obedient, he will be more inclined to believe, and will the rather attend to our words. But God, and the Gospel we preach, will be blasphemed, if they are disobedient. But what if their own master be an unbeliever? Even in that case they ought to submit, for God's Name's sake.

Ver. 2. "And they that have believing masters, let them not despise them because they are brethren, but rather do them service, because they are faithful and beloved partakers of the benefit."

As though he had said, If ye are thought worthy of so great a benefit, as to have your masters for your brethren, on this account ye ought more especially to submit.

"Going before to judgment." This he had said, implying that of evil actions here some are concealed, and some are not; but there neither the good nor the bad can be concealed. And what is that going before to judgment? When one commits offenses that already condemn him, or when he is incorrigible, and when one thinks to set him right and cannot succeed. What then? What is the use of mentioning this? Because if here any escape detection, they will not hereafter. There all things are laid open; and this is the greatest consolation to those who do well.

Then because he had said, "Do nothing by partiality," as if under the necessity of interpreting it, he adds, "As many servants as are under the yoke." But you will say, What has a Bishop to do with this? Much surely, for it is his office to exhort and to teach these too. And here he makes excellent regulations with respect to them. For we see him everywhere commanding the servants rather than their masters, showing them the ways of submission, and treating them with great regard.[3] He exhorts them therefore to submit with great meekness. But the masters he recommends to forbear the use of terror. "Forbearing threatening" (Eph. vi. 9), he says. And why does he thus command? In the case of unbelievers, naturally, because it would have been unreasonable to address those who would pay no heed to him; but where believers were concerned, what was his reason? Because masters contribute greater benefits to their servants, than servants to their masters. For the former furnish the money to purchase for them sufficient food and clothing; and bestow much care upon them in other respects, so that the masters pay them the larger service, which is here intimated, when he says, "they are faithful and beloved, partakers of the benefit."[4] They suffer much toil and trouble for your repose, ought they not in return to receive much honor from their servants?

Moral. But if he exhorts servants to render such implicit obedience, consider what ought to be our disposition towards our Master, who brought us into existence out of nothing, and who feeds and clothes us. If in no other way then, let us render Him service at least as our

---

[1] A Paris MS. adds, "in not curing him," and is stated to vary much in this passage, but its readings are not given.
[2] This whole passage is treated more at length in the first Homily on the Statues, where most of these remarks are expanded and illustrated.

[3] Or making a great point of them, i.e. of the ways of submission.
[4] The words οἱ τῆς εὐεργεσίας ἀντιλαμβανόμενοι may mean, "such as set themselves to confer benefits."

servants render it to us. Do not they order their whole lives to afford rest to their masters, and is it not their work and their life to take care of their concerns? Are they not all day long engaged in their masters' work, and only a small portion of the evening in their own? But we, on the contrary, are ever engaged in our own affairs, in our Master's hardly at all, and that too, though He needs not our services, as masters need those of their servants, but those very acts redound to our own benefit. In their case the master is benefited by the ministry of the servant, but in ours the ministry of the servant profits not the Master, but is beneficial on the other hand to the servant. As the Psalmist says, "My goods are nothing unto Thee." (Ps. xvi. 2.) For say, what advantage is it to God, that I am just, or what injury, that I am unjust? Is not His nature incorruptible, incapable of injury, superior to all suffering? Servants having nothing of their own, all is their masters', however rich they may be. But we have many things of our own.

And it is not merely so great honor,[1] that we enjoy from the King of the universe. What master ever gave his own son for his servant? No one, but all would rather choose to give their servants for their sons. Here on the contrary, "He spared not His own Son, but gave Him up for us all," for His enemies who hated Him. Servants, though very hard service is exacted of them, are not impatient; at least, not the well-disposed. But how many times do we utter discontent?[2] The master promises to his servants nothing like what God promises to us; but what? Freedom here, which is often worse than bondage; for it is often embittered by famine beyond slavery itself.[3] Yet this is their greatest boon. But with God there is nothing temporal, nothing mortal; but what? wouldest thou learn? Listen then, He says, "Henceforth I call you not servants. Ye are my friends." (John xv. 13, 14.)

Beloved, let us be ashamed, let us fear. Let us only serve our Master, as our servants serve us. Rather not even[4] the smallest portion of service do we render! Necessity makes them philosophers. They have only food and lodging; but we, possessing much and expecting more, insult our Benefactor with our luxury. If from nothing else, from them at least let us learn the rules of philosophy. The Scripture is wont to send men not even to servants, but to irra-

tional creatures, as when it bids us imitate the bee and the ant. But I advise you but to imitate servants: only so much as they do from fear of their masters, let us do from the fear of God; for I cannot find that you do even this. They receive many insults from fear of us, and endure them in silence with the patience of philosophers. Justly or unjustly they are exposed to our violence, and they do not resist, but entreat us, though often they have done nothing wrong. They are contented to receive no more and often less than they need; with straw[5] for their bed, and only bread for their food, they do not complain or murmur at their hard living, but through fear of us are restrained from impatience. When they are intrusted with money, they restore it all. For I am not speaking of the worthless, but of the moderately good. If we threaten them, they are at once awed.

Is not this philosophy? For say not they are under necessity, when thou too art under a necessity in the fear of hell. And yet dost thou not learn wisdom, nor render to God as much honor, as thou receivest from thy servants. Of thy servants each has the apartment assigned to him by thy rules, and he does not invade that of his neighbor, nor do any injury from a desire of more than he has. This forbearance the fear of their master enforces among domestics, and seldom will you see a servant robbing or injuring a fellow-servant. But among free men it is quite the reverse. We bite and devour one another. We fear not our Master: we rob and plunder our fellow-servants, we strike them in His very sight. This the servant will not do; if he strikes, it is not when his master sees him; if he reviles, it is not when his master hears him. But we dare do anything, though God sees and hears it all.

The fear of their master is ever before their eyes, the fear of our Master never before ours. Hence the subversion of all order, hence all is confusion and destruction. And we never take into consideration the offenses we have committed, but if our servants do amiss, we call them to a rigorous account for everything, even to the least misdemeanor. I say not this to make servants remiss, but to chide our supineness, to rouse us from our sloth, that we may serve our God with as much zeal as servants do their master; our Maker, as faithfully as our fellow-creatures[6] serve us, from whom they have received no such gift. For they too are free by nature. To them also it was said, "Let them have dominion over the fishes." (Gen. i. 26.) For this slavery is not from nature: it is the result of some particular cause, or circumstances. Yet, notwithstanding, they pay us great honor;

---

[1] Or, "and it is not without reason that we enjoy so great honor": and so Old Lat. and Ben. that in the text seems more intelligible. The other might be explained by the sequel. See Rom. viii. 32.

[2] ἀποδυσπετοῦμεν.

[3] The slaves, as he had said before, were wholly provided for by their masters, and so suffer less in a scarcity than if they had been independent.

[4] The negative is added in Colb. and B. The sense requires it.

[5] στιβάδος.

[6] ὁμοούσιοι.

and we with great strictness exact services from them, whilst to God we hardly render the smallest portion, though the advantage of it would redound to ourselves. For the more zealously we serve God, the greater gainers we shall be. Let us not then deprive ourselves of such important benefits. For God is self-sufficient, and wants nothing; the recompense and the advantage reverts altogether to us. Let us therefore, I beseech you, be so affected, as serving not God but ourselves, and with fear and trembling let us serve Him, that we may obtain the promised blessings, through Jesus Christ our Lord, with whom, &c.

HOMILY XVII.

1 Timothy vi. 2–7.

"These things teach and exhort. If any man teach otherwise, and consent not to wholesome words, even the words of our Lord Jesus Christ, and to the doctrine which is according to godliness; he is proud, knowing nothing, but doting about questions and strifes of words, whereof cometh envy, strife, railings, evil surmisings, perverse disputings of men of corrupt minds, and destitute of the truth, supposing that gain is godliness: from such withdraw thyself. But godliness with contentment is great gain. For we brought nothing into this world, and it is certain we can carry nothing out."

A TEACHER has need not only of authority, but of gentleness, and not only of gentleness, but of authority. And all these the blessed Paul teaches, at one time saying, "These things command and teach" (1 Tim. iv. 11); at another, "These things teach and exhort."[1] For if physicians entreat the sick, not for the benefit of their own health, but that they may relieve their sickness, and restore their prostrate strength, much more ought we to observe this method, of entreating those whom we teach. For the blessed Paul does not refuse to be their servant: "We preach not ourselves," he says, "but Christ Jesus the Lord; and ourselves your servants for Jesus' sake" (2 Cor. iv. 5); and again, "All things are yours, whether Paul or Apollos." (1 Cor. iii. 12.) And in this service he serves with alacrity, for it is not slavery, but superior to freedom. For He says, "Whoever committeth sin is the servant of sin." (John viii. 34.)

"If any man teach otherwise, and consent not to wholesome words, even the words of our Lord Jesus Christ, and to the doctrine which is according to godliness, he is proud, knowing nothing." Presumption therefore arises not from knowledge, but from "knowing nothing." For he that knows the doctrines of godliness is also the most disposed to moderation. He who knows sound words, is not unsound. For what inflammation is in the body, that pride is in the soul. And as we do not in the first case say that the inflamed part is sound, so neither do we here consider the arrogant. It is possible then to be knowing, and yet to know nothing. For he that knows not what he ought to know, knows nothing. And that pride arises from knowing nothing is manifest from hence. Christ "made Himself of no reputation" (Phil. ii. 7), he therefore who knows this will not be high-minded. Man hath nothing except from God, therefore he will not be high-minded. "For what hast thou that thou didst not receive?" (1 Cor. iv. 7.) He washed the feet of His disciples, how can he who knows this be setting himself up? Therefore He says, "When ye have done all, say we are unprofitable servants." (Luke xvii. 10.) The publican was accepted only from his humility, the Pharisee perished by his boastfulness. He who is puffed up knoweth none of these things. Again, Christ Himself says, "If I have spoken evil, bear witness of the evil; but if well, why smitest thou me?" (John xviii. 23.)

"Doting[2] about questions." To question then is to dote. "And strifes of words"; this is justly said. For when the soul is fevered with reasonings, and stormy, then it questions, but when it is in a sound state, it does not question, but receives the faith. But from questionings and strifes of words nothing can be discovered. For when the things which faith only promises are received by an inquisitive spirit, it neither demonstrates them, nor suffers us to understand them. If one should close his eyes, he would not be able to find anything he sought: or if, again with his eyes open, he should bury himself, and exclude the sun, he would be unable to find anything, thus seeking. So without faith nothing can be discerned, but contentions must needs arise. "Whereof come railings, evil surmisings"; that is, erroneous opinions and doctrines arising from questionings. For when we begin to question, then we surmise concerning God things that we ought not.

---

[1] Or "entreat."

[2] νοσῶν.

" Perverse disputings," [1] that is, leisure or conversation, or he may mean intercommunication, and that as infected sheep by contact [2] communicate disease to the sound, so do these bad men.

" Destitute of the truth, thinking that gain is godliness." Observe what evils are produced by strifes of words. The love of gain, ignorance, and pride ; for pride is engendered by ignorance.

" From such withdraw thyself." He does not say, engage and contend with them, but " withdraw thyself," turn away from them ; as elsewhere he says, " A man that is an heretic after the first and second admonition reject." (Tit. iii. 10.) He shows that they do not so much err from ignorance, as they owe their ignorance to their indolence. Those who are contentious for the sake of money you will never persuade. They are only to be persuaded, so long as you give, and even so you will never satisfy their desires. For it is said, " The covetous man's eye is not satisfied with a portion." (Ecclus. xiv. 9.) From such then, as being incorrigible, it is right to turn away. And if he who had much obligation to fight for the truth, is advised not to engage in contention with such men, much more should we [3] avoid it, who are in the situation of disciples.

Having said, " They think that godliness is a means of gain," he adds : " But godliness with contentment is great gain," not when it possesses wealth, but when it has it not. For that he may not despond on account of his poverty, he encourages and revives his spirit. They think, he says, that godliness is a means of gain, [4] and so it is ; only not in their way, but in a much higher. Then having demolished theirs, he extols the other. For that worldly gain is nothing, is manifest, because it is left behind, and does not attend us, or go along with us at our departure. Whence is this plain? Because we had nothing when we came into this world, therefore we shall have nothing when we depart from it. For nature came naked into the world, and naked she will go out of it. Therefore we want no superfluities ; if we brought nothing with us, and shall take nothing away with us.

Ver. 8. " And having food and raiment, let us be therewith content."

Such things, and so much ought we to eat, as will suffice to nourish us, and such things should we put on, as will cover us, and clothe our nakedness, and nothing more ; and a common garment will answer this purpose. Then he urges them from the consideration of things here, saying,

Ver. 9. " But they that will be rich " ; not those that are rich, but those who wish to be. For a man may have money and make a good use of it, not overvaluing it, but bestowing it upon the poor. Such therefore he does not blame, but the covetous.

" They that will be rich fall into temptation and a snare, and into many foolish and hurtful lusts, which drown men in destruction and perdition."

He has justly said, " they drown men," since they cannot be raised from that depth. " In destruction and perdition."

Ver. 10. " For the love of money is the root of all evil ; which while some coveted after, they have erred from the faith, and pierced themselves through with many sorrows."

Two things he mentions, and that which to them might seem the more weighty he places last, their " many sorrows." And to learn how true this is, the only way is to sojourn with the rich, to see how many are their sorrows, how bitter their complaints.

Ver. 11. " But thou, O man of God."

This is a title of great dignity. For we are all men of God, but the righteous peculiarly so, not by right of creation only, but by that of appropriation. [5] If then thou art a " man of God," seek not superfluous things, which lead thee not to God, but

" Flee these things, and follow after righteousness." Both expressions are emphatic ; he does not say turn from one, and approach the other, but " flee these things, pursue righteousness," so as not to be covetous.

" Godliness," that is, soundness in doctrines. [6]

" Faith," which is opposed to questionings.

" Love," patience, meekness.

Ver. 12. " Fight the good fight of faith, lay hold on eternal life." Lo, there is thy reward, " whereunto thou art also called, and hast professed a good profession," in hope of eternal life, " before many witnesses."

That is, do not put that confidence to shame. Why dost thou labor to no profit? But what is the " temptation and snare," which he says, those that would be rich fall into? It causes them to err from the faith, it involves them in dangers, it renders them less intrepid. " Foolish desires," he says. And is it not a foolish desire, when men like to keep idiots and dwarfs, not from benevolent motives, but for their pleasure, when they have receptacles for fishes in their halls, when they bring up wild beasts, when they give their time to dogs, and dress up horses, and are as fond of them as of their chil-

---

[1] διαπαρατριβαί, rec. παραδιατριβαί.
[2] παρατριβόμενα.
[3] This he would hardly have said at Constantinople, when he was Bishop.
[4] This is undoubtedly the true sense, as the article is attached to " godliness."
[5] οἰκειώσεως.
[6] See on Stat. Hom. iv. 3.

dren? All these things are foolish and super-fluous, nowise necessary, nowise useful.

"Foolish and hurtful lusts!" What are hurtful lusts? When men live unlawfully, when they desire what is their neighbor's, when they do their utmost in[1] luxury, when they long for drunkenness, when they desire the murder and destruction of others. From these desires many have aimed at tyranny, and perished. Surely to labor with such views is both foolish and hurtful. And well has he said, "They have erred from the faith." Covetousness attracting their eyes to herself, and gradually stealing away their minds, suffers them not to see their way. For as one walking on the straight road, with his mind intent on something else, proceeds on his way indeed, but, often without knowing it, passes by the very city to which he was hastening, his feet plying on at random and to no purpose : such like a thing is covetousness. "They have pierced themselves through with many sorrows." Dost thou see what he means by that word "pierced"? What he means to express by the allusion[2] is this. Desires are thorns, and as when one touches thorns, he gores his hand, and gets him wounds, so he that falls into these lusts will be wounded by them, and pierce his soul with griefs. And what cares and troubles attend those who are thus pierced, it is not possible to express. Therefore he says, "Flee these things, and follow after righteousness, godliness, faith, love, patience, meekness." For meekness springs from love.

Ver. 12. "Fight the good fight."

Here he commends his boldness and manliness, that before all he confidently "made profession," and he reminds him of his early instruction.

"Lay hold on eternal life."

There is need not only of profession, but of patience also to persevere in that profession, and of vehement contention, and of numberless toils, that you be not overthrown. For many are the stumbling-blocks, and impediments, therefore the way is "strait and narrow." (Matt. vii. 14.) It is necessary therefore to be self-collected,[3] and well girt on every side. All around appear pleasures attracting the eyes of the soul. Those of beauty, of wealth, of luxury, of indolence, of glory, of revenge, of power, of dominion, and these are all fair and lovely in appearance, and able to captivate those who are unsteady, and who do not love the truth. For truth has but a severe and uninviting countenance. And why? Because the pleasures that she promises are all future, whereas the others hold out present honors and delights, and repose ; though all are false and counterfeit. To these therefore adhere gross, effeminate, unmanly minds, indisposed to the toils of virtue. As in the games of the heathens, he who does not earnestly covet the crown, may from the first give himself up to revellings and drunkenness, and so do in fact the cowardly and unmanly combatants, whilst those who look steadfastly to the crown sustain blows without number. For they are supported and roused to action by the hope of future reward.

MORAL. Let us then flee from this root of all evils, and we shall escape them all. "The love of money," he says, "is the root ; " thus says Paul, or rather Christ by Paul, and let us see how this is. The actual experience of the world testifies it. For what evil is not caused by wealth, or rather not by wealth, but by the wicked will of those who know not how to use it? For it is possible to use wealth in well doing, and even through means of it to inherit the kingdom. But now what was given us for the relief of the poor, to make amends for our past sins, to win a good report, and to please God, this we employ against the poor and wretched, or rather against our own souls, and to the high displeasure of God. For as for the other, a man robs him of his wealth, and reduces him to poverty, but himself to death ; and him he causes to pine in penury here, but himself in that eternal punishment. Are they equal sufferers, think you?

What evils then does it not cause ! what fraudulent practices, what robberies ! what miseries, enmities, contentions, battles ! Does it not stretch forth its hand even to the dead, nay, to fathers, and brethren? Do not they who are possessed by this passion violate the laws of nature, and the commandments of God? in short everything? Is it not this that renders our courts of justice necessary? Take away therefore the love of money, and you put an end to war, to battle, to enmity, to strife and contention. Such men ought therefore to be banished from the world, as wolves and pests. For as opposing and violent winds, sweeping over a calm sea, stir it up from its foundations, and mingle the sands of the deep with the waves above, so the lovers of wealth confound and unsettle everything. The covetous man never knows a friend : a friend, did I say? he knows not God Himself, driven mad, as he is, by the passion of avarice. Do ye not see the Titans going forth sword in hand? This is a representation of madness. But the lovers of money do not counterfeit, they are really mad, and beside themselves ; and if you could lay bare their souls, you would find them armed in this way not with one or two swords, but with thousands,

---

[1] προσπαλαίωσιν, lit. wrestle with.
[2] ἐμφάσεως, a form of speech implying something not directly expressed.
[3] συνεστράφθαι.

acknowledging no one, but turning their rage against all; flying and snarling at all, slaughtering not dogs,[1] but the souls of men, and uttering blasphemies against heaven itself. By these men all things are subverted, and ruined by their madness after wealth.

For whom indeed, whom I should accuse, I know not! It is a plague that so seizes all, some more, some less, but all in a degree. Like a fire catching a wood, that desolates and destroys all around, this passion has laid waste the world. Kings, magistrates, private persons, the poor, women, men, children, are all alike affected by it. As if a gross darkness had overspread the earth, no one is in his sober senses. Yet we hear, both in public and private, many declamations[2] against covetousness, but no one is mended by them.

What then is to be done? How shall we extinguish this flame? For though it has risen up to heaven itself, it is to be extinguished. We have only to be willing, and we shall be able to master the conflagration. For as by our will it has got head, so it may be brought under by our will. Did not our own choice cause it, and will not the same choice avail to extinguish it? Only let us be willing. But how shall that willingness be engendered? If we consider the vanity and the unprofitableness of wealth, that it cannot depart hence with us, that even here it forsakes us, and that whilst it remains behind, it inflicts upon us wounds that depart along with us. If we see that there are riches There, compared to which the wealth of this world is more despicable than dung. If we consider that it is attended with numberless dangers, with pleasure that is temporary, pleasure mingled with sorrow. If we contemplate aright the true riches of eternal life, we shall be able to despise worldly wealth. If we remember that it profits nothing either to glory, or health, or any other thing; but on the contrary drowns men in destruction and perdition. If thou consider that here thou art rich, and hast many under thee, but that when thou departest hence, thou wilt go naked and solitary. If we often represent[3] these things to ourselves, and listen to them from others, there will perhaps be a return to a sound mind, and a deliverance from this dreadful punishment.

Is a pearl beautiful? yet consider, it is but sea water, and was once cast away in the bosom of the deep. Are gold and silver beautiful? yet they were and are but dust and ashes. Are silken vestments beautiful? yet they are nothing but the spinning of worms. This beauty is but in opinion, in human prejudice, not in the nature of the things. For that which possesses beauty from nature, need not any to point it out. If you see a coin of brass that is but gilded over, you admire it at first, fancying that it is gold; but when the cheat is shown to you by one who understands it, your wonder vanishes with the deceit. The beauty therefore was not in the nature of the thing. Neither is it in silver; you may admire tin for silver, as you admired brass for gold, and you need some one to inform you what you should admire. Thus our eyes are not sufficient to discern the difference. It is not so with flowers, which are much more beautiful. If you see a rose, you need no one to inform you, you can of yourself distinguish an anemone, and a violet, or a lily, and every other flower. It is nothing therefore but prejudice. And to show, that this destructive passion is but a prejudice; tell me, if the Emperor were pleased to ordain that silver should be of more value than gold, would you not transfer your love and admiration to the former? Thus we are everywhere under the influence of covetousness and opinion.[4] And that it is so, and that a thing is valued for its rarity, and not for its nature, appears hence. The fruits that are held cheap among us are in high esteem among the Cappadocians, and among the Serians[5] even more valuable than the most precious among us, from which country these garments are brought; and many such instances might be given in Arabia and India, where spices are produced, and where precious stones are found. Such preference therefore is nothing but prejudice, and human opinion. We act not from judgment, but at random, and as accident determines. But let us recover from this intoxication, let us fix our view upon that which is truly beautiful, beautiful in its own nature, upon godliness and righteousness; that we may obtain the promised blessings, through the grace and lovingkindness of Jesus Christ our Lord, with whom, &c.

---

[1] There was a heathen festival at Argos, called Cynophontis (Athenæus, l. 3, Cas. p. 99), in which dogs met abroad were killed; but whether this was done in the warlike dance called Titanes (which was practiced even by persons of rank, Lucian, de Salt. § 21, p. 37 and 79) does not appear.

[2] See Libanius, Or. 7.

[3] ἐπάδωμεν.

[4] πλεονεξίας καὶ ὑπονοίας. The latter is literally suspicion, but in ver. 4 he seems to render it opinions, in the sense of imaginations bred by selfishness.

[5] Seres, a people on the borders of China. In Tac. Ann. ii. 33, A.D. 16, we find a law at Rome against men wearing silk, vestris Serica.

HOMILY XVIII.

1 TIMOTHY vi. 13–16.

"I give thee charge in the sight of God, Who quickeneth all things, and before Christ Jesus, Who before Pontius Pilate witnessed a good confession; that thou keep this commandment without spot, unrebukable, until the appearing of our Lord Jesus Christ: which in his times He shall show, Who is the blessed and only Potentate, the King of kings, and Lord of lords; Who only hath immortality, dwelling in the light which no man can approach unto; Whom no man hath seen, nor can see; to Whom be honor and power everlasting. Amen."

AGAIN he calls God to witness, as he had done a little before, at once to increase his disciple's awe, and to secure his safety, and to show that these were not human commandments, that receiving the commandment as from the Lord Himself, and ever bearing in mind the Witness[1] before Whom he heard it, he may have it more fearfully impressed upon his mind.

"I charge thee," he says, "before God, Who quickeneth all things."

Here is at once consolation in the dangers which awaited him, and a remembrance of the resurrection awakened in him.

"And before Jesus Christ, Who before Pontius Pilate witnessed a good confession."

The exhortation again is derived from the example of his Master, and what he means is this; as He had done, so ought ye to do, for for this cause He "witnessed" (1 Pet. ii. 21), that we might tread in His steps.

"A good confession."[2] What he does in his Epistle to the Hebrews,—"Looking unto Jesus, the Author and Finisher of our faith; Who for the joy that was set before Him endured the cross, despising the shame, and is set down at the right hand of the throne of God. For consider Him that endured such contradiction of sinners against Himself, lest ye be wearied and faint in your minds" (Heb. xii. 2, 3),—that he now does to his disciple Timothy. As if he had said, Fear not death, since thou art the servant of God, Who can give life to all things.

But to what "good confession" does he allude? To that which He made when Pilate asked, "Art thou a King?" "To this end," He said, "was I born." And again, "I came, that I might bear witness to the Truth. Behold, these have heard Me." (John xviii. 37.) He may mean this, or that when asked, "Art thou the Son of God?" He answered, "Thou sayest, that I am (the Son of God)." (Luke xxii. 70.) And many other testimonies and confessions did He make.

Ver. 14. "That thou keep this commandment without spot, unrebukable, until the appearing of our Lord Jesus Christ."

That is, till thy end, thy departure hence, though he does not so express it, but that he may the more arouse him, says, "till His appearing." But what is "to keep the commandment without spot"? To contract no defilement, either of doctrine or of life.

Ver. 15. "Which in His times He shall show, Who is the blessed and only Potentate, King of kings, and Lord of lords, Who only hath immortality, dwelling in the light which no man can approach unto."

Of whom are these things said? Of the Father, or of the Son? Of the Son, undoubtedly: and it is said for the consolation of Timothy, that he may not fear nor stand in awe of the kings of the earth.

"In His times," that is, the due and fitting times, that he may not be impatient, because it has not yet come. And whence is it manifest, that He will show it? Because He is the Potentate, the "only Potentate." He then will show it, Who is "blessed," nay blessedness itself; and this is said, to show that in that appearing there is nothing painful or uneasy.

But he says, "only," either in contradistinction to men, or because He was unoriginated,[3] or as we sometimes speak of a man whom we wish to extol.

"Who only hath immortality." What then? hath not the Son immortality? Is He not immortality itself? How should not He, who is of the same substance with the Father, have immortality?

"Dwelling in the light which no man can approach unto." Is He then Himself one Light, and is there another in which He dwells? is He then circumscribed by place? Think not of it. By this expression is represented the Incomprehensibleness of the Divine Nature. Thus he speaks of God, in the best way he is able. Observe, how when the tongue would utter something great, it fails in power.

"Whom no man hath seen nor can see." As, indeed, no one hath seen the Son, nor can see Him.[4]

---

[1] Edd. ἀφ' οὗ, "from whom"; but B. has ἐφ' οὗ, and Old Lat. *sub quo*, which is much better.

[2] Savile's punctuation. Ben. joins this to the preceding clause, but so it is scarcely grammatical.

[3] ἀγέννητον.

[4] That is, in His divine nature, considered apart from the human.

"To whom be honor and power everlasting. Amen." Thus properly, and much to the purpose, has he spoken of God. For as he had called Him to witness, he speaks much of that Witness, that his disciple may be in the greater awe. In these terms he ascribes glory to Him, and this is all we can do, or say. We must not enquire too curiously, who He is. If power everlasting is His, fear not. Yea though now it take not place,[1] to Him is honor, to Him is power evermore.

Ver. 17. "Charge them that are rich in this world that they be not high-minded."

He has well said, "rich in this world." For there are others rich in the future world. And this advice he gives, knowing that nothing so generally produces pride and arrogance as wealth. To abate this, therefore, he immediately adds, "Nor trust in uncertain riches"; since that was the source of pride; inasmuch as he who hopes in God, is not elated. Why dost thou place thy hopes upon what is instantly transferable? For such is wealth! and why hopest thou on that of which thou canst not be confident? But you say, how can they avoid being high-minded? By considering the instability and uncertainty of riches, and that hope in God is infinitely more valuable; God being the Author of wealth itself.

Ver. 17. "But in the living God," he says, "who giveth us richly all things to enjoy."

This "all things richly" is justly spoken, in reference to the changes of the year, to air, light, water, and other gifts. For how richly and ungrudgingly are all these bestowed! If thou seekest riches, seek those that are stable and enduring, and which are the fruit of good works. He shows that this is his meaning by what follows.

Ver. 18. "That they do good," he says, "that they be rich in good works, ready to distribute, willing to communicate."

The first phrase refers to wealth, the second to charity. For to be willing to communicate, implies that they are sociable and kind.

Ver. 19. "Laying up in store for themselves a good foundation against the time to come."

There nothing is uncertain, for the foundation being firm, there is no instability, all is firm, fixed, immovable, fast, and enduring.

Ver. 19. "That they may lay hold," he says, "on eternal life."

For the doing of good works can secure the enjoyment of eternal life.

Ver. 20. "O Timothy, keep that which is committed to thy trust."

Let it not suffer diminution. It is not thy own. Thou art intrusted with the property of another, do not lessen it.

Ver. 20. "Avoiding profane and vain babblings, and oppositions of science falsely so called."

Well did he thus call it. For where there is not faith, there is not knowledge; when anything springs from our reasonings, it is not knowledge. Or perhaps he says this, because some then assumed the name of Gnostics, as knowing more than others.

Ver. 21. "Which some professing have erred concerning the faith."

You see how again he commands Timothy not even to meet them. "Avoiding opposition." There are therefore oppositions to which we ought not to vouchsafe an answer, because they turn men from faith, and do not suffer one to be firmly established or fixed in it. Let us not then pursue this science, but adhere to faith, that unshaken rock. For neither floods nor winds assailing will be able to harm us, since we stand on the rock immovable. Thus even in this life, if we choose Him, Who is truly the foundation, we stand, and no harm assails us. For what can hurt him who hath chosen the riches, the honor, the glory, the pleasure of the life to come? They are all firm, in them there is no variableness; all things here subject to reverse, and are for ever changing. For what wouldest thou have? glory? The Psalmist says, "His glory shall not descend after him." (Ps. xlix. 17.) And often it abides not with him whilst he lives. But it is not so with virtue, all things which pertain to her are permanent. Here, he who obtains glory from his office, upon another succeeding to his office, becomes a private man and inglorious. The rich man is reduced to poverty by the attack of robbers, or the snares of sycophants and knaves. It is not so with Christians. The temperate man, if he take heed to himself, will not be robbed of his virtue. He who rules himself, cannot become a common man and a subject.

And that this rule is superior to any other, will appear upon examination. For of what advantage, tell me, is it to reign over nations of our fellow-men, and to be the slaves of our own passions? Or what are we the worse for having no one under our rule, if we are superior to the tyranny of the passions? That indeed is Freedom, that is Rule, that is Royalty and Sovereignty. The contrary is slavery, though a man be invested with countless diadems. For when a multitude of masters sway him from within, the love of money, the love of pleasure, and anger, and other passions, what avails his

---

See on Phil. ii. 5-11, Hom. vii. p. 78, and note g, and compare John i. 14-18; vi. 46; xiv. 7, 9; Luke xxiv. 39; John iv. 24; 2 Cor. iii. 17; 1 Tim. iii. 16; 1 John iii. 2.

[1] μὴ γένηται. He either means that though not yet fully *come*, His Kingdom, when come, shall be eternal, or puts γένεσθαι, "to take place," in opposition to εἶναι, "to be." The former word refers to events in time, the latter to the real constitution of things. Phil. ii. 10; Heb. ii. 8.

diadem? The tyranny of those passions is more severe, when not even his crown has power to deliver him from their subjection. As if one who had been a king should be reduced to slavery by barbarians, and they wishing to show their power the more absolutely, should not strip him of his purple robe and his diadem, but oblige him to work in them, and to perform all menial offices, to draw water, and to cook their food, that his disgrace and their honor might be the more apparent: so do our passions domineer over us more barbarously than any barbarians. For he that despises them can despise the barbarians too; but he that submits to them, will suffer more severely than from barbarians. The barbarian, when his power prevails, may afflict the body, but these passions torture the soul, and lacerate it all over. When the barbarian has prevailed, he delivers one to temporal death, but these to that which is to come. So that he alone is the free man, who has his freedom in himself; and he who submits to these unreasonable passions, is the slave.

No master, however inhuman, imposes such severe and inhuman commands. They say to him, in effect, "Disgrace thy soul without end or object, — offend thy God, — be deaf to the claims of nature; though it be thy father or thy mother, be not ashamed to set thyself against them." Such are the commands of avarice. "Sacrifice to me, she says, not calves, but men." The prophet indeed says, "Sacrifice men, for the calves have failed." (Hosea xiii. 2, Sept.) But avarice says, "Sacrifice men, though there are yet calves. Sacrifice those who have never injured thee, yea slay them, though they have been thy benefactors." Or again, "Be at war, and go about as the common enemy of all, of nature herself, and of God. Heap up gold, not that thou mayest enjoy it, but that thou mayest keep it, and work greater torture to thyself." For it is not possible that the lover of money should be able to enjoy it, since he fears lest his gold should be diminished, lest his hoards should fail. "Be watchful," it says, "be suspicious of every one, even domestics and friends. Have an eye to the goods of other men. Though you see the poor man perishing with hunger, give him nothing; but strip him, if it be possible, even of his skin. Break thine oaths, lie, swear. Be an accuser, a false informer. Refuse not, if it be necessary, to rush into fire, to submit to a thousand deaths, to perish with hunger, to struggle with disease." Does not avarice impose these laws? "Be offensive and impudent, shameless and bold, villainous and wicked, ungrateful, unfeeling, unfriendly, faithless, devoid of affection, a parricide, a beast rather than a man. Surpass the serpent in bitterness, the wolf in rapacity. Exceed in brutality even the beast, nay should it be necessary to proceed even to the malignity of the devil, refuse not. Be a stranger to thy benefactor."

Does not avarice say all this, and is it not listened to? God on the contrary says, Be a friend to all, be gentle, beloved by all, give offense causelessly to no one. "Honor thy father and thy mother." Win an honorable reputation. Be not a man, but an angel. Utter nothing immodest, nothing false, nor even think of it. Relieve the poor. Bring not trouble on thyself, by ravaging others. Be not bold nor insolent. God says this, but no one hearkens. Is not hell then justly threatened, and the fire, and the worm that dieth not? How long are we thus to thrust ourselves down the precipice? How long are we to walk upon thorns, and pierce ourselves with nails, and be grateful for it? We subject ourselves to cruel tyrants, and refuse the gentle Master, who imposes nothing grievous, nor barbarous, nor burdensome, nor unprofitable, but all things such as are useful, and valuable, and beneficial. Let us then arouse ourselves, and be self-collected, and gather our forces. Let us love God as we ought, that we may obtain the blessings promised to those that love Him, through the grace and mercy of our Lord Jesus Christ, with whom, to the Father, &c.

HOMILIES OF ST. JOHN CHRYSOSTOM,

ARCHBISHOP OF CONSTANTINOPLE,

ON THE

SECOND EPISTLE OF ST. PAUL THE APOSTLE

TO

TIMOTHY.

HOMILY I

2 TIMOTHY i. 1, 2.

" Paul, an apostle of Jesus Christ by the will of God, according to the promise of life which is in Jesus Christ, to Timothy, my dearly beloved son: Grace, mercy, and peace, from God the Father and Christ Jesus our Lord."

WHAT is the reason of his writing this second Epistle to Timothy? He had said, " I hope to come unto thee shortly" (1 Tim. iii. 14), and as this had not taken place, instead of coming to him, he consoles him by a letter, when he was grieving perhaps for his absence, and oppressed by the cares of the government, which he had now taken in hand. For even great men, when they are placed at the helm, and are charged with the direction of the Church, feel the strangeness of their position, and are overwhelmed, as it were, by the waves of business. This was particularly the case when the Gospel was first preached, when the ground was everywhere unturned, and all was opposition and hostility. There were, besides, heresies commencing from the Jewish teachers, as he has shown in his former Epistle. Nor does he only comfort him by letters, he invites him to come to him: " Do thy diligence," he says, " to come shortly unto me," and, " when thou comest, bring with thee the books, but especially the parchments." (2 Tim. iv. 9 and 13.) And he seems to have written this Epistle when his end

was approaching. For he says, " I am now ready to be offered up " ; and again, " At my first answer no man stood with me." (2 Tim. iv. 6 and 16.) To set all this right, he both offers consolation from his own trials, and also says,

" Paul, an apostle of Jesus Christ by the will of God, according to the promise of life which is in Christ Jesus."

Thus at the very commencement he raises up his mind. Tell me not, he says, of the dangers here. These obtain for us eternal life, where there is no peril, where grief and mourning flee away. For He hath not made us Apostles only that we might encounter dangers, but that we might even suffer and die.[1] And as it would not be a consolation to recount to him his own troubles, but rather an increase of his grief, he begins immediately with offering comfort, saying, " According to the promise of life which is in Jesus Christ." But if it is a " promise," seek it not here. For, " hope that is seen is not hope." (Rom. viii. 24.)

Ver. 2. " To Timothy, my dearly beloved son."

Not merely his " son," but, " dearly beloved " ; since it is possible for sons not to be beloved.

---

[1] If the reading is correct, πάσχωμεν must be emphatic, meaning " actually " suffer, for it is harsh to render it of the good things to come.

Not such, he means, art thou; I call thee not merely a son, but a "dearly beloved son." As he calls the Galatians his children, but at the same time complains of them; "My little children," he says, "of whom I travail in birth again." (Gal. iv. 19.) And he bears particular testimony to his virtue by calling him "beloved." For where love does not arise from nature, it must arise from the merit of the object. Those who are born of us, are loved not only on account of their virtue, but from the force of nature; but when those who are of the faith are beloved, it is on account of nothing but their merit, for what else can it be? And this especially in the case of Paul, who never acted from partiality. And further, he shows by calling him his "beloved son," that it was not because he was offended with him, or despised him, or condemned him; that he did not come to him.

Ver. 2. "Grace, mercy, and peace, from God the Father, and Christ Jesus our Lord."

These things which he before prayed for, he again invokes upon him. And observe how, at the very beginning, he excuses himself for not having come to him, nor seen him. For his words, "Till I come," and, "Hoping to come to thee shortly," had led Timothy to expect his coming soon. For this he excuses himself, but he does not immediately mention the cause of his not coming, lest he should grieve him mightily. For he was detained in prison by the emperor. But when at the end of the Epistle he invited him to come to him, then he informed him of it. He does not at the outset plunge him into sorrow, but encourages the hope that he shall see him. "Greatly desiring to see thee," and "Do thy diligence to come unto me shortly." (2 Tim. i. 4, and iv. 9.) Immediately therefore he raises him up, and proceeds to praise him.

Ver. 3, 4. "I thank God, whom I serve from my forefathers with pure conscience, that without ceasing I have remembrance of thee in my prayers night and day; greatly desiring to see thee, being mindful of thy tears, that I might be filled with joy."

"'I thank God,' he says, 'that I remember thee,' so much do I love thee." This is a mark of excessive love, when a man glories in his affection from loving so much. "I thank God," he says, "Whom I serve": and how? "With a pure conscience," for he had not violated his conscience. And here he speaks of his blameless life, for he everywhere calls his life his conscience. Or because I never gave up any good that I purposed, for any human cause, not even when I was a persecutor. Wherefore he says, "I obtained mercy, because I did it ignorantly in unbelief" (1 Tim. i. 13); all but saying, "Do

not suspect that it was done of wickedness." He properly commends his own disposition, that his love may appear sincere. For what he says is in fact, "I am not false, I do not think one thing and profess another." So in the book of Acts we read he was compelled to praise himself. For when they slandered him as a seditious man and an innovator, he said in his own defense, "Ananias said to me, The God of our fathers hath chosen thee that thou shouldest know His will, and see that Just One, and shouldest hear the voice of His mouth. For thou shalt be His witness unto all men of what thou hast seen and heard." (Acts xxii. 14, 15.) In the same manner here, that he may not, as if he had been forgetful, have the character of one void of friendship and conscience, he justly praises himself, saying, that "without ceasing I have remembrance of thee," and not simply that, but "in my prayers." That is, it is the business of my prayers, that which I constantly continue to perform. For this he shows by saying, "For this I besought God day and night, desiring to see thee." Mark his fervent desire, the intensity[1] of his love. And again, his humility, how he apologizes to his disciples, and then he shows that it was not on light or vain grounds; and this he had shown us before, but again gives proof of it. "Being mindful of thy tears." It was natural for Timothy, when parting from him,[2] to mourn and weep, more than a child torn away from the milk and from the breast of its mother. "That I may be filled with joy; greatly desiring to see thee." I would not willingly have deprived myself of so great a pleasure, though I had been of an unfeeling and brutal nature, for those tears coming to my remembrance would have been enough to soften me. But such is not my character. I am one of those who serve God purely; so that many strong motives urged me to come to thee. So then he wept. And he mentions another cause, and that of a consolatory kind.

Ver. 5. "When I call to remembrance the unfeigned faith that is in thee."

This is another commendation, that Timothy came not of Gentiles, nor of unbelievers, but of a family that served Christ from the first. (Acts xvi. 1, 3.)

"Which dwelt first in thy grandmother Lois, and thy mother Eunice."

For Timothy, it says, "was the son of a certain woman which was a Jewess, and believed." How a Jewess? how believing? Because she was not of the Gentiles, "but on account of his father, who was a Greek, and of the Jews that

---

[1] μανίαν. Lit. "madness."
[2] The present tense implies that it was at the time of parting. Mr. Greswell supposes that St. Paul had been recently apprehended in the presence of Timothy; see his work on the Harmony of the Gospels, Vol. 2, Diss. 1, pp. 97, 98.

were in those quarters, he took and circumcised him." Thus, as these mixtures of Jews and Gentiles took place, the Law began gradually to be dissolved. And mark in how many ways he shows that he did not despise him. "I serve God," he says, "I have a true conscience" for my part, and thou hast thy "tears," and not thy tears only, but for "thy faith," because thou art a laborer for the Truth, because there is no deceit in thee. As therefore thou showest thyself worthy of love, being so affectionate, so genuine a disciple of Christ; and as I am not one of those who are devoid of affection, but of those who earnestly pursue the Truth; what hindered me from coming to thee?

"And I am persuaded that in thee also."

From the beginning, he means, thou hast had this excellency. Thou receivedst from thy forefathers the faith unfeigned. For the praises of our ancestors, when we share in them, redound also to us. Otherwise they avail nothing, but rather condemn us; wherefore he has said, "I am persuaded that in thee also." It is not a conjecture, he means, it is my persuasion; I am fully assured of it. If therefore from no human motive thou hast embraced it, nothing will be able to shake thy faith.

Ver. 6. "Wherefore I put thee in remembrance that thou stir up the gift of God, which is in thee by the putting on of my hands."

You see how greatly dispirited and dejected he considers him to be. He almost says, "Think not that I despise thee, but be assured that I do not condemn thee, nor have I forgotten thee. Consider, at any rate, thy mother and thy grandmother. It is because I know that thou hast unfeigned faith that I put thee in remembrance." For it requires much zeal to stir up the gift of God. As fire requires fuel, so grace requires our alacrity, that it may be ever fervent. "I put thee in remembrance that thou stir up the gift of God, that is in thee by the putting on of my hands," that is, the grace of the Spirit, which thou hast received, for presiding over the Church, for the working of miracles, and for every service. For this grace it is in our power to kindle or to extinguish; wherefore he elsewhere says, "Quench not the Spirit." (1 Thess. v. 19.) For by sloth and carelessness it is quenched, and by watchfulness and diligence it is kept alive. For it is in thee indeed, but do thou render it more vehement, that is, fill it with confidence, with joy and delight. Stand manfully.

Ver. 7. "For God hath not given us the spirit of fear, but of power, and of love, and of a sound mind."

That is, we did not receive the Spirit, that we should shrink from exertion, but that we may speak with boldness. For to many He gives a spirit of fear, as we read in the wars of the Kings.

"A spirit of fear fell upon them." (Ex. xv. 16?) That is, he infused terror into them. But to thee He has given, on the contrary, a spirit of power, and of love toward Himself. This, then, is of grace, and yet not merely of grace, but when we have first performed our own parts. For the Spirit that maketh us cry, "Abba, Father," inspires us with love both towards Him, and towards our neighbor, that we may love one another. For love arises from power, and from not fearing. For nothing is so apt to dissolve love as fear, and a suspicion of treachery.

"For God hath not given us the spirit of fear, but of power, and of love, and of a sound mind":[1] he calls a healthy state of the soul a sound mind, or it may mean sobriety of mind, or else a sobering of the mind, that we may be sober-minded, and that if any evil befall us, it may sober us, and cut off superfluities.

Moral. Let us then not be distressed at the evils that happen to us. This is sobriety of mind. "In the season of temptation," he says, "make not haste." (Ecclus. ii. 2.) Many have their several griefs at home, and we share in each other's sorrows, though not in their sources. For one is unhappy on account of his wife, another on account of his child, or his domestic, another of his friend, another of his enemy, another of his neighbor, another from some loss. And various are the causes of sorrow, so that we can find no one free from trouble and unhappiness of some kind or other, but some have greater sorrows and some less. Let us not therefore be impatient, nor think ourselves only to be unhappy.

For there is no such thing in this mortal life as being exempt from sorrow. If not to-day, yet to-morrow; if not to-morrow, yet some later day trouble comes. For as one cannot sail, I mean, over a long sea, and not feel disquietude, so it is not possible to pass through this life, without experience of sorrow, yea though you name a rich man; for in that he is rich, he hath many occasions of inordinate desires,[2] yea, though the king himself, since he too is ruled by many, and cannot do all that he would. Many favors he grants contrary to his wishes, and more than all men is obliged to do what he would not. How so? Because he has many about him who wish to receive his gifts. And just think how[3] great is his chagrin, when he is desirous to effect something, but is unable, either from fear or suspicion, or hindered by enemies or by friends. Often when he has succeeded in achieving some end, he loses all the pleasure of it, from many becoming at enmity

---

[1] σωφρονισμοῦ.
[2] B. and Sav. Mar. ἀθυμιῶν, "of dejections." Edd. ἐπιθυμιῶν.
[3] Sav. Tr. "and how great."

with him. Again, do you think that they are free from grief, who live a life of ease? It is impossible. As a man cannot escape death, so neither can he escape sorrow. How many troubles must they endure, which we cannot express in words, and which they only can know by experience! How many have prayed a thousand times to die, in the midst of their wealth and luxury! For luxury by no means puts men out of the reach of grief: it is rather the very thing to produce sorrows, diseases, and uneasiness, often when there is no real ground for it. For when such is the habit of the soul, it is apt to grieve even without a cause. Physicians say that from a weak state of the stomach arise sorrows[1] without any occasion; and does not the like happen to ourselves, to feel uneasy, without knowing any cause for it? In short, we can find no one who is exempted from sorrow. And if he has less occasion for grief than ourselves, yet he thinks otherwise, for he feels his own sorrows, more than those of other men. As they who suffer pain in any part of their bodies, think that their sufferings exceed their neighbor's. He that has a disease of the eye, thinks there is nothing so painful, and he that has a disorder in the stomach, considers that the sorest of diseases, and each thinks that the heaviest of sufferings, with which he is himself afflicted. So it is with sorrow, each thinks his own present grief the most severe. For of this he judges by his own experience. He that is childless considers nothing so sad as to be without children; he that is poor, and has many children, complains of the extreme evils of a large family. He who has but one, looks upon this as the greatest misery, because that one, being set too much store by, and never corrected, becomes willful, and brings grief upon his father. He who has a beautiful wife, thinks nothing so bad as having a beautiful wife, because it is the occasion of jealousy and intrigue. He who has an ugly one, thinks nothing worse than having a plain wife, because it is constantly disagreeable. The private man thinks nothing more mean, more useless, than his mode of life. The soldier declares that nothing is more toilsome, more perilous, than warfare; that it would be better to live on bread and water than endure such hardships. He that is in power thinks there can be no greater burden than to attend to the necessities of others. He that is subject to that power, thinks nothing more servile than living at the beck of others. The married man considers nothing worse than a wife, and the cares of marriage. The unmarried declares there is nothing so wretched as being unmarried, and wanting the repose of a home. The mer-

chant thinks the husbandman happy in his security. The husbandman thinks the merchant so in his wealth. In short, all mankind are somehow hard to please, and discontented and impatient. When condemning the whole race, he saith, "Man is a thing of nought" (Ps. cxliv. 4), implying that the whole kind is a wretched unhappy creature. How many long for old age! How many think youth a happy time! Thus each different period has its unhappiness. When we find ourselves censured on account of our youth, we say, why are we not old? and when our heads are hoary, we ask whither has our youth flown? Numberless, in short, are the occasions of sorrow. There is one path only by which this unevenness can be escaped. It is the path of virtue. Yet that too has its sorrows, only they are sorrows not unprofitable, but productive of gain and advantage. For if any one has sinned, he washes away his sin by the compunction that comes of his sorrow. Or, if he has grieved in sympathizing with a fallen brother, this is not without its recompense. For sympathy with those that are in misery gives us great confidence towards God.

Hear therefore what philosophy is taught by the example of Job in holy Scripture! Hear also what Paul saith: "Weep with them that weep"; and again, "Condescend to men of low estate." (Rom. xii. 15, 16.) For, by the communication of sorrow, the extreme burden of it is lightened. For as in the case of a heavy load, he that bears part of the weight relieves him who was bearing it alone, so it is in all other things.

But now, when any one of our relatives dies, there are many who sit by and console us. Nay, we often raise up even an ass that has fallen; but when the souls of our brethren are falling, we overlook them and pass by, as if they were of less value than an ass. And if we see any one entering into a tavern indecently; nay, if we see him drunk, or guilty of any other unseemly action, we do not restrain him, we rather join him in it. Whence Paul has said: "They not only do these things, but have pleasure in them that do them." (Rom. i. 32.) The greater part even form associations[2] for the purposes of drunkenness. But do thou, O man, form associations to restrain the madness of inebriety. Such friendly doings are beneficial to those who are in bonds or in affliction. Something of this kind Paul enjoined to the Corinthians, alluding to which he says, "That there be no gatherings when I come." (1 Cor. xvi. 2.) But now everything is done with a view to luxury, reveling, and pleasure. We have a common seat, a common table, we have wine in common, and com-

---

[1] Or, "pains."

[2] συμμορίας. See on Stat. Hom. xi. fin. See also St. Chrysostom's advice to Clubs, on Rom. xiii. 14, Hom. xxiv. 14.

mon expenses, but we have no community of alms. Such were the friendly doings in the time of the Apostles; they brought all their goods into the common stock. Now I do not require you to bestow all, but some part. "Let each lay by him in store on the first day of the week, as God has prospered him," and lay it down as a tribute for the seven days. In this way give alms, whether more or less. "For thou shalt not appear before the Lord empty." (Ex. xxiii. 15.) This was said to the Jews, how much more then to us. For this cause the poor stand before the doors, that no one may enter empty, but each may do alms at his entrance. Thou enterest to implore mercy. First show mercy. He that comes later owes the more. For when we have been first, he that is second pays down more.[1] Make God thy debtor, and then offer thy prayers. Lend to Him, and then ask a return, and thou shalt receive it with usury. God wills this, and does not retract. If thou ask with alms, He holds himself obliged. If thou ask with alms, thou lendest and receivest interest. Yes, I beseech you! It is not for stretching out thy hands thou shalt be heard! stretch forth thy hands, not to heaven, but to the poor. If thou stretch forth thy hand to the hands of the poor, thou hast reached the very summit of heaven. For He who sits there receives thine alms. But if thou liftest them up without a gift, thou gainest nothing. If the king, arrayed in purple, should come to thee and ask an alms, wouldest thou not readily give all that thou hast? But now when thou art entreated through the poor, not by an earthly but a heavenly King, dost thou stand regardless, and defer thy gift? What punishment then dost thou not deserve? For the being heard depends not upon the lifting up of thy hands, nor on the multitude of thy words, but upon thy works. For hear the prophet, "When ye" spread "forth your hands, I will hide mine eyes from you: yea, when ye make many prayers, I will not hear." (Isa. i. 15.) For he ought to be silent, who needs mercy, and not even to look up to heaven; he that hath confidence may say[3] much. But what says the Scripture, "Judge for the fatherless, plead for the widow, learn to do good." (Isa. i. 17.) In this way we shall be heard, though we lift not up our hands, nor utter a word, nor make request. In these things then let us be zealous, that we may obtain the promised blessings, through grace and lovingkindness, &c.

HOMILY II.

2 TIMOTHY i. 8–10.

"Be not thou therefore ashamed of the testimony of our Lord, nor of me His prisoner: but be thou partaker of the afflictions of the Gospel according to the power of God; Who hath saved us, and called us with an holy calling, not according to our works, but according to His own purpose and grace, which was given us in Christ Jesus before the world began; but is now made manifest by the appearing of our Saviour Jesus Christ."

THERE is nothing worse than that man should measure and judge of divine things by human reasonings. For thus he will fall from that rock[2] a vast distance, and be deprived of the light. For if he who wishes with human eyes to apprehend the rays of the sun will not only not apprehend them, but, besides this failure, will sustain great injury; so, but in a higher degree, is he in a way to suffer this, and abusing the gift of God, who would by human reasonings gaze intently on that Light. Observe accordingly how Marcion, and Manes, and Valentinus, and others who introduced their heresies and pernicious doctrines[4] into the Church of God, measuring divine things by human reasonings, became ashamed of the Divine economy. Yet it was not a subject for shame, but rather for glorying; I speak of the Cross of Christ. For there is not so great a sign of the love of God for mankind, not heaven, nor sea, nor earth, nor the creation of all things out of nothing, nor all else beside, as the Cross. Hence it is the boast of Paul, "God forbid that I should glory, save in the Cross of our Lord Jesus Christ." (Gal. vi. 14.) But natural men, and those who attribute to God no more than to human beings, stumble, and become ashamed. Wherefore Paul from the first exhorts his disciple, and through him all others, in these words: "Be not thou ashamed of the testimony of our Lord," that is,[5] "Be not ashamed, that thou preachest One that was cru-

---

[1] He means in human transactions, where money *advanced* always has a certain value beyond a *deferred* payment.

[2] πέτρας, the rock of faith, but one suspects πείρας, "that endeavor," to be the true reading.

[3] Gr. "says," but he means "with propriety," for παρρησίαν ἔχων is the usual expression for one who has real claims. B. reads ὁ δὲ ὡς παρ., "but this man, as if he had claims."

[4] B. "those who gave birth to the other heresies, and introduced pernicious doctrines."

[5] B. "He means the death of Christ." The word "Testimony" might be rendered "Martyrdom," and such is the original idea of Martyrdom: see Euseb. Eccl. Hist. v. 2.

cified, but rather glory in it." For in themselves death and imprisonment and chains are matters of shame and reproach. But when the cause is added before us, and the mystery viewed aright, they will appear full of dignity, and matter for boasting. For it was that death which saved the world, when it was perishing. That death connected earth with heaven, that death destroyed the power of the devil, and made men angels, and sons of God : that death raised our nature to the kingly throne. Those chains were the conversion of many. "Be not" therefore "ashamed," he says, "of the testimony of our Lord, nor of me His prisoner : but be thou partaker of the afflictions of the Gospel " ; that is, though thou shouldest suffer the same things, be not thou ashamed. For that this is implied appears from what he said above ; " God hath given us a spirit of power, and of love, and of a sound mind " ; and by what follows, " Be thou partaker of the sufferings of the Gospel " : not merely be not ashamed of them, but be not ashamed even to experience them.

And he does not say, " Do not fear," but, the more to encourage him, " be not ashamed," as if there were no further danger, if he could overcome the shame. For shame is only then oppressive, when one is overcome by it. Be not therefore ashamed, if I, who raised the dead, who wrought miracles, who traversed the world, am now a prisoner. For I am imprisoned, not as a malefactor, but for the sake of Him who was crucified. If my Lord was not ashamed of the Cross, neither am I of chains. And with great propriety, when he exhorts him not to be ashamed, he reminds him of the Cross. If thou art not ashamed of the Cross, he means, neither be thou of chains ; if our Lord and Master endured the Cross, much more should we chains. For he who is ashamed of what He endured, is ashamed of Him that was crucified. Now it is not on my own account that I bear these chains ; therefore do not give way to human feelings, but bear thy part in these sufferings. " Be partaker of the afflictions of the Gospel." He says not this, as if the Gospel could suffer injury, but to excite his disciple to suffer for it.

" According to the power of God ; Who hath saved us, and called us with a holy calling, not according to our works, but according to His own purpose and grace, which was given us in Christ Jesus before the world began."

More especially because it was a hard thing to say, " Be partakers of afflictions," he again consoles him.[1] Reckon that thou sustainest these things, not by thine own power, but by the power of God. For it is thy part to choose and to be zealous, but God's to alleviate sufferings and bid them cease.[2] He then shows him the proofs of His power. Consider how thou wast saved, how thou wast called. As he elsewhere says, "According to His power that worketh in us." (Eph. iii. 20.) So much was it a greater exercise of power to persuade the world to believe, than to make the Heavens. But how was he " called with a holy calling "?[3] This means, He made them saints, who were sinners and enemies. " And this not of ourselves, it was the gift of God." If then He is mighty in calling us, and good, in that He hath done it of grace and not of debt, we ought not to fear. For He Who, when we should have perished,[4] saved us, though enemies, by grace, will He not much more cooperate with us, when He sees us working? " Not according to our own works," he says, " but according to his own purpose and grace," that is, no one compelling, no one counseling Him, but of His own purpose, from the impulse of His own goodness, He saved us ; for this is the meaning of " according to His own purpose." " Which was given us before the world began." That is, it was determined without beginning that these things should be done in Christ Jesus. This is no light consideration, that from the first He willed it. It was not an after-thought. How then is not the Son eternal? for He also willed it from the beginning.

Ver. 10. " But is now made manifest by the appearing of our Saviour Jesus Christ, Who hath abolished death, and hath brought life and immortality to light by the Gospel."

Thou seest the power, thou seest the gift bestowed not by works, but through the Gospel. These are objects of hope : for both were wrought in His Body. And how will they be wrought in ours? " By the Gospel."

Ver. 11. "Whereunto I am appointed a preacher and an Apostle, and a teacher of the Gentiles."

Why does he so constantly repeat this, and call himself a teacher of the Gentiles? Because he wishes to persuade them that they also ought to draw close to the Gentiles. Be not therefore dismayed at my sufferings. The sinews of death are unstrung. It is not as a malefactor that I suffer, but because I am " a teacher of the Gentiles." At the same time he makes his discourse worthy of credit.

Ver. 12. " For the which cause I also suffer these things, nevertheless I am not ashamed. For I know Whom I have believed, and am persuaded that He is able to keep that which I have committed unto Him against that day."

" I am not ashamed," he says. For are chains, are sufferings, a matter for shame ? Be

---

[1] Thus Old Lat. and B. The printed copies add, " by saying, ' Not according to our works,' that is," which is not to the purpose.

[2] B. omits " but," &c.
[3] Sav. How was he called ? " With a holy calling."
[4] So B. Edd. " when we needed to be saved."

not then ashamed! Thou seest how he illustrates his teaching by his works. "These
things," he says, "I suffer": I am cast into
prison, I am banished; "For I know Whom I
have believed, and am persuaded that He is
able to keep that which I have committed to
Him[1] against That Day." What is[2] "that which
is committed"?[3] The faith, the preaching of
the Gospel. He, who committed this to him,
he says, will preserve it unimpaired. I suffer
everything, that I may not be despoiled of this
treasure, and I am not ashamed at these things,
so long as it is preserved uninjured. Or he calls
the Faithful the charge which God committed
to him, or which he committed to God. For
he says, "Now I commit you to the Lord."
(Acts xx. 32.) That is, these things will not be
unprofitable to me. And in Timothy is seen the
fruit of the charge thus "committed." You see
that he is insensible to sufferings, from the hope
that he entertains of his disciples.

MORAL. Such ought a Teacher to be, so to
regard his disciples, to think them everything.
"Now we live," he says, "if ye stand fast in the
Lord." And again, "What is our hope, or joy,
or crown of rejoicing? are not even ye in the
presence of our Lord Jesus Christ?" (1 Thess.
iii. 8, and ii. 19.) You see his anxiety in
this matter, his regard for the good of his disciples, not less than for his own.[4] For teachers ought to surpass natural parents, to be more
zealous than they. And it becomes their children to be kindly affectioned towards them.
For he says, "Obey them that have the rule
over you, and submit yourselves: for they watch
for your souls as they that must give account."
(Heb. xiii. 17.) For say, is he subject to so
dangerous a responsibility, and art thou not willing to obey him, and that too, for thy own benefit? For though his own state should be good,
yet as long as thou art in a bad condition his
anxiety continues, he has a double account to
render. And consider what it is to be responsible and anxious for each of those who are
under his rule. What honor wouldest thou have
reckoned equal, what service, in requital of such
dangers? Thou canst not offer an equivalent.
For thou hast not yet devoted thy soul for him,
but he lays down his life for thee, and if he lays
it not down here, when the occasion requires it,
he loses it There. But thou art not willing to
submit even in words. This is the prime cause
of all these evils, that the authority of rulers is
neglected, that there is no reverence, no fear.
He says, "Obey them that have the rule over
you, and submit yourselves." But now all is

turned upside down and confounded. And this
I say not for the sake of the rulers; (for what
benefit will they have of the honor they receive
from us,[5] except so far as we are rendered
obedient;) but I say it for your advantage.
For with respect to the future, they will not be
benefited by the honor done them, but receive
the greater condemnation, neither will they be
injured as to the future by ill treatment, but will
have the more excuse. But all this I desire to
be done for your own sakes. For when rulers
are honored by their people, this too is reckoned
against them; as in the case of Eli it is said,
"Did I not choose him out of his father's
house?" (1 Sam. ii. 27.) But when they are
insulted, as in the instance of Samuel, God said,
"They have not rejected thee, but they have
rejected Me." (1 Sam. viii. 7.) Therefore insult is their gain, honor their burden. What I
say, therefore, is for your sakes, not for theirs.
He that honors the Priest, will honor God also;
and he who has learnt to despise the Priest, will
in process of time insult God. "He that receiveth you," He saith, "receiveth Me." (Matt.
x. 40.) "Hold my priests in honor" (Ecclus.
vii. 31?), He says. The Jews learned to despise
God, because they despised Moses, and would
have stoned him. For when a man is piously
disposed towards the Priest, he is much more so
towards God. And even if the Priest be wicked,
God seeing that thou respectest him, though
unworthy of honor, through reverence to Him,
will Himself reward thee. For if "he that receiveth a prophet in the name of a prophet shall
receive a prophet's reward" (Matt. x. 41); then
he who honoreth and submitteth and giveth way
to the Priest shall certainly be rewarded. For
if in the case of hospitality, when thou knowest
not the guest, thou receivest so high a recompense, much more wilt thou be requited, if thou
obeyest him whom He requires thee to obey.
"The Scribes and Pharisees," He says, "sit in
Moses' seat; all therefore, whatsoever they bid
you observe, that observe and do, but do not ye
after their works." (Matt. xxiii. 2, 3.) Knowest thou not what the Priest is? He is an Angel[6]
of the Lord. Are they his own words that he
speaks? If thou despisest him, thou despisest
not him, but God that ordained him. But how
does it appear, thou askest, that he is ordained of
God? Nay, if thou suppose it otherwise, thy hope
is rendered vain. For if God worketh nothing
through his means, thou neither hast any Laver,
nor art partaker of the Mysteries, nor of the benefit of Blessings; thou art therefore not a Christian.
What then, you say, does God ordain all, even the
unworthy? God indeed doth not ordain all, but
He worketh through all, though they be them-

---

[1] Lit. "my deposit."
[2] Sav. has τί σὴ π., Ben. τί ἔστι, B. τίς ἡ, which last is best.
[3] παρακαταθήκη.
[4] al. "no less than for his own kindred."

[5] This expression shows that he was not yet Bishop.
[6] Or, "a messenger."

selves unworthy, that the people may be saved. For if He spoke, for the sake of the people, by an ass, and by Balaam, a most wicked man, much more will He speak by the mouth of the Priest. What indeed will not God do or say for our salvation? By whom doth He not act? For if He wrought through Judas and those other that "prophesied," to whom He will say, "I never knew you; depart from Me, ye workers of iniquity" (Matt. vii. 22, 23); and if others "cast out devils" (Ps. vi. 8); will He not much more work through the Priests? Since if we were to make inquisition into the lives of our rulers, we should then become the ordainers [1] of our own teachers, and all would be confusion; the feet would be uppermost, the head below. Hear Paul saying, "But with me it is a very small thing that I should be judged of you, or of man's judgment." (1 Cor. iv. 3.) And again, "Why dost thou judge thy brother?" (Rom. xiv. 10.) For if we may not judge our brother, much less our teacher. If God commands this indeed, thou doest well, and sinnest if thou do it not; but if the contrary, dare not do it, nor attempt to go beyond the lines that are marked out. After Aaron had made the golden calf, Corah, Dathan, and Abiram raised an insurrection against him. And did they not perish? Let each attend to his own department. For if he teach perverted doctrine, though he be an Angel, obey him not; but if he teach the truth, take heed not to his life, but to his words. Thou hast Paul to instruct thee in what is right both by words and works. But thou sayest, "He gives not to the poor, he does not govern well." Whence knowest thou this? Blame not, before thou art informed. Be afraid of the great account. Many judgments are formed upon mere opinion. Imitate thy Lord, who said, "I will go down now, and see whether they have done altogether according to the cry of it, and if not, I will know." (Gen. xviii. 21.) But if thou hast enquired, and informed thyself, and seen; yet await the Judge, and usurp not the office of Christ. To Him it belongs, and not to thee, to make this inquisition. Thou art an inferior servant, not a master. Thou art a sheep, be not curious concerning the shepherd, lest thou have to give account of thy accusations against him. But you say, How does he teach me that which he does not practice himself? It is not he that speaks to thee. If it be he whom thou obeyest, thou hast no reward. It is Christ that thus admonishes thee. And what do I say? Thou oughtest not to obey even Paul, if he speaks of himself, or anything human, but the Apostle, that has Christ speaking in him. Let not us judge one another's conduct, but each his own. Examine thine own life.

But thou sayest, "He ought to be better than I." Wherefore? "Because he is a Priest." And is he not superior to thee in his labors, his dangers, his anxious conflicts and troubles? But if he is not better, oughtest thou therefore to destroy thyself? These are the words of arrogance.[2] For how is he not better than thyself? He steals, thou sayest, and commits sacrilege! How knowest thou this? Why dost thou cast thyself down a precipice? If thou shouldest hear it said that such an one hath a purple robe,[3] though thou knewest it to be true, and couldest convict him, thou declinest to do it, and pretendest ignorance, not being willing to run into unnecessary danger. But in this case thou art so far from being backward, that even without cause thou exposest thyself to the danger. Nor think thou art not responsible for these words. Hear what Christ says, "Every idle word that men shall speak, they shall give account thereof in the day of judgment." (Matt. xii. 36.) And dost thou think thyself better than another, and dost thou not groan, and beat thy breast, and bow down thy head, and imitate the Publican?

And then thou destroyest thyself, though thou be better. Be silent, that thou cease not to be better. If thou speak of it, thou hast done away the merit; if thou thinkest it, I do not say so; if thou dost not think it, thou hast added much. For if a notorious sinner, when he confessed, "went home justified," he who is a sinner in a less degree, and is conscious of it, how will he not be rewarded? Examine thy own life. Thou dost not steal; but thou art rapacious, and overbearing, and guilty of many other such things. I say not this to defend theft; God forbid! I deeply lament if there is any one really guilty of it, but I do not believe it. How great an evil is sacrilege, it is impossible to say. But I spare you. For I would not that our virtue should be rendered vain by accusing others. What was worse than the Publican? For it is true that he was a publican, and guilty of many offenses, yet because the Pharisee only said, "I am not as this publican," he destroyed all his merit. I am not, thou sayest, like this sacrilegious Priest. And dost not thou make all in vain?

This I am compelled to say, and to enlarge upon in my discourse, not so much because I am concerned for them, but because I fear for you, lest you should render your virtue vain by this boasting of yourselves, and condemnation of others. For hear the exhortation of Paul, "Let every one prove his own work, and then shall he have rejoicing in himself alone, and not in another." (Gal. vi. 4.)

---

[1] χειροτονηται.

[2] Or, "desperation," if it be taken with the preceding sentence.
[3] This was treason in a subject. See Gibbon, c. xl.

If you had a wound, tell me, and should go to a physician, would you stay him from salving and dressing your own wound, and be curious to enquire whether the physician had a wound, or not? and if he had, would you mind it? Or because he had it, would you forbear dressing your own, and say, A physician ought to be in sound health, and since he is not so, I shall let my wound go uncured? For will it be any palliation[1] for him that is under rule, that his Priest is wicked? By no means. He will suffer the destined punishment, and you too will meet with that which is your due. For the Teacher now only fills a place. For "it is written, They shall all be taught of God." (John vi. 45; Isa. liv. 13.) "Neither shall they say, Know the Lord. For all shall know Me from the least to the greatest." (Jer. xxxi. 34.) Why then, you will say, does he preside? Why is he set over us? I beseech you, let us not speak ill of our teachers, nor call them to so strict an account, lest we bring evil upon ourselves. Let us examine ourselves, and we shall not speak ill of others. Let us reverence that day, on which he enlightened[2] us. He who has a father, whatever faults he has, conceals them all. For it is said, "Glory not in the dishonor of thy father; for thy father's dishonor is no glory unto thee. And if his understanding fail, have patience with him." (Ecclus. iii. 10–12.) And if this be said of our natural fathers, much more of our spiritual fathers. Reverence him, in that he every day ministers to thee, causes the Scriptures to be read, sets the house in order for thee, watches for thee, prays for thee, stands imploring God on thy behalf, offers supplications for thee, for thee is all his worship. Reverence all this, think of this, and approach him with pious respect. Say not, he is wicked. What of that? He that is not wicked,[3] doth he of himself bestow upon thee these great benefits? By no means. Everything worketh according to thy faith. Not even the righteous man can benefit thee, if thou art unfaithful, nor the unrighteous harm thee, if thou art faithful. God, when He would save His people, wrought for the ark by Oxen.[4] Is it the good life or the virtue of the Priest that confers so much on thee? The gifts which God bestows are not such as to be effects of the virtue of the Priest. All is of grace. His part is but to open his mouth, while God worketh all: the Priest only performs a symbol.[5] Consider how wide was the distance between John and Jesus. Hear John saying, "I have need to be baptized of Thee?" (Matt. iii. 14), and, "Whose shoe's latchet I am not worthy to unloose." (John i. 27.) Yet notwithstanding this difference, the Spirit descended. Which John had not. For "of His fullness," it is said, "we all have received." (John i. 16.) Yet nevertheless, It descended not till He was baptized. But neither was it John who caused It to descend. Why then is this done? That thou mayest learn that the Priest performs a symbol.[6] No man differs so widely from another man, as John from Jesus, and yet with him[7] the Spirit descended, that we may learn, that it is God who worketh all, that all is God's doing. I am about to say what may appear strange, but be not astonished nor startled at it. The Offering is the same, whether a common man, or Paul or Peter offer it. It is the same which Christ gave to His disciples, and which the Priests now minister. This is nowise inferior to that, because it is not men that sanctify even this, but the Same who sanctified the one sanctifies the other also. For as the words which God spake are the same which the Priest now utters, so is the Offering the same, and the Baptism, that which He gave. Thus the whole is of faith. The Spirit immediately fell upon Cornelius, because he had previously fulfilled his part, and contributed his faith. And this is His Body, as well as that. And he who thinks the one inferior to the other, knows not that Christ even now is present, even now operates. Knowing therefore these things, which we have not said without reason, but that we may conform your minds in what is right, and render you more secure for the future, keep carefully in mind what has been spoken. For if we are always hearers, and never doers, we shall reap no advantage from what is said. Let us therefore attend diligently to the things spoken. Let us imprint them upon our minds. Let us have them ever engraved upon our consciences, and let us continually ascribe glory to the Father, and to the Son, and to the Holy Ghost.

---

[1] παραμυθία.
[2] i.e. baptized.
[3] Sav. mar. "he that is wicked," which supposes the objection to be somewhat differently put.
[4] 1 Sam. vi. 12.

[5] σύμβολον. This is said evidently of the act of the Priest considered *in itself*, and as distinct from the accompanying grace. For St. Chrysostom's view of the Priest's responsibility, see his Treatise on the Priesthood, and his comments on 1 Tim. iii. 1, &c., &c.
[6] Suicer collects passages on this word. It may mean "a pledge," but certainly has also the sense of "symbol." It seems to be used of the material elements before and after consecration.
[7] ἐπ' αὐτοῦ.

HOMILY III.

2 Timothy i. 13-18.

"Hold fast the form of sound words, which thou hast heard of me, in faith and love which is in Christ Jesus. That good thing which was committed unto thee keep by the Holy Ghost Which dwelleth in us. This thou knowest, that all they which are in Asia be turned away from me; of whom are Phygellus and Hermogenes. The Lord give mercy unto the house of Onesiphorus; for he oft refreshed me, and was not ashamed of my chain: but, when he was in Rome, he sought me out very diligently, and found me. The Lord grant unto him that he may find mercy of the Lord in that day: and in how many things he ministered unto me at Ephesus, thou knowest very well."

Not by letters alone did Paul instruct his disciple in his duty, but before by words also; which he shows, both in many other passages, as where he says, "whether by word or our Epistle" (2 Thess. ii. 15), and especially here. Let us not therefore suppose that anything relating to doctrine was spoken imperfectly. For many things he delivered to him without writing. Of these therefore he reminds him, when he says, "Hold fast the form of sound words, which thou hast heard of me." After the manner of artists, I have impressed on thee the image of virtue, fixing in thy soul a sort of rule, and model, and outline of all things pleasing to God. These things then hold fast, and whether thou art meditating any matter of faith or love, or of a sound mind, form from hence your ideas of them. It will not be necessary to have recourse to others for examples, when all has been deposited within thyself.

"That good thing which was committed unto thee keep," — how? — "by the Holy Ghost which dwelleth in us." For it is not in the power of a human soul, when instructed with things so great, to be sufficient for the keeping of them. And why? Because there are many robbers, and thick darkness, and the devil still at hand to plot against us; and we know not what is the hour, what the occasion for him to set upon us. How then, he means, shall we be sufficient for the keeping of them? "By the Holy Ghost"; that is if we have the Spirit[1] with us, if we do not expel grace, He will stand by us. For, "Except the Lord build the house, they labor in vain that build it. Except the Lord keep the city, the watchman waketh but in vain." (Ps. cxxvii. 1.) This is our wall, this our castle, this our refuge. If therefore It dwelleth in us, and is Itself our guard, what need of the commandment? That

we may hold It fast, may keep It, and not banish It by our evil deeds.

Then he describes his trials and temptations, not to depress his disciple, but to elevate him, that if he should ever fall into the same, he may not think it strange, when he looks back and remembers what things happened to his Teacher. What then says he? Since it was probable that Timothy might be apprehended, and be deserted, and be relieved by no friendly attention, or influence, or assistance, but be abandoned even by his friends and the faithful themselves, hear what he says, "This thou knowest, that all they which are in Asia be turned away from me." It seems that there were then in Rome many persons from the regions of Asia. "But no one stood by me," he says, no one acknowledged me, all were alienated. And observe the philosophy of his soul. He only mentions their conduct, he does not curse them, but he praises him that showed kindness to him, and invokes a thousand blessings upon him, without any curse on them. "Of whom is Phygellus and Hermogenes. The Lord give mercy to the house of Onesiphorus, for he oft refreshed me, and was not ashamed of my chain. But, when he was in Rome, he sought me out diligently and found me." Observe how he everywhere speaks of the shame, and not of the danger, lest Timothy should be alarmed. And yet it was a thing that was full of peril. For he gave offense to Nero by making friends with one of his prisoners.[2] But when he was in Rome, he says, he not only did not shun intercourse with me, but "sought me out very diligently, and found me."

"The Lord grant unto him that he may find mercy of the Lord in that day: and in how many things he ministered unto me at Ephesus, thou knowest very well."

Such ought the faithful to be. Neither fear, nor threats, nor disgrace, should deter them from assisting one another, standing by them and succoring them as in war. For they do not so much benefit those who are in danger, as themselves, by the service they render to them, making themselves partakers of the crowns due to them. For example, is any one of those who are devoted to God visited with affliction and distress, and maintaining the conflict with great fortitude; whilst thou art not yet brought[3] to this conflict? It is in thy power if thou wilt,

---

[1] B. and Sav. mar. add "abiding."

[2] τινὰ τῶν ἀνακειμενῶν αὐτῷ οἰκειωσάμενος. "quod quendam ex familiaribusque sibi attraxipet." — Montf.

[3] εἰλκύσθης, "drawn." See on Stat. Hom. i. 8.

without entering into the course, to be a sharer of the crowns reserved for him, by standing by him, preparing his mind,[1] and animating and exciting him. Hence it is that Paul elsewhere says, "Ye have done well that ye did communicate with my affliction. For even in Thessalonica ye sent once and again unto my necessity." (Phil. iv. 14, 16.) And how could they that were far off share in the affliction of him that was not with them? How? He says, "ye sent once and again unto my necessities." Again he says, speaking of Epaphroditus, "Because he was nigh unto death, not regarding his life, that he might supply your lack of service toward me." (Phil. ii. 30.) For as in the service of kings, not only those who fight the battle, but those who guard the baggage, share in the honor; and not merely so, but frequently even have an equal portion of the spoils, though they have not imbrued their hands in blood, nor stood in array, nor even seen the ranks of the enemy; so it is in these conflicts. For he who relieves the combatant, when wasted with hunger, who stands by him, encouraging him by words, and rendering him every service, he is not inferior to the combatant.

For do not suppose Paul the combatant, that irresistible and invincible one, but some one of the many, who, if he had not received much consolation and encouragement, would not perhaps have stood, would not have contended. So those who are out of the contest may perchance be the cause of victory to him, who is engaged in it, and may be partakers of the crowns reserved for the victor. And what wonder, if he who communicates to the living is thought worthy of the same rewards with those who contend, since it is possible to communicate after death even with the departed, with those who are asleep, who are already crowned, who want for nothing. For hear Paul saying, "Partaking in the memories of the Saints."[2] And how may this be done? When thou admirest a man,[3] when thou doest any of those acts for which he was crowned, thou art evidently a sharer in his labors, and in his crowns.

"The Lord grant unto him that he may find mercy of the Lord in that day." He had compassion on me, he says, he shall therefore have the like return in that terrible Day, when we shall have need of much mercy. "The Lord grant him to find mercy from the Lord." Are there two Lords then? By no means. But "to us there is one Lord Christ Jesus, and one God." (1 Cor. viii. 6.) Here those who are infected with the heresy of Marcion assail this expres-

sion; but let them learn that this mode of speech is not uncommon in Scripture; as when it is said, "The Lord said unto my Lord" (Ps. cx. 1); and again, "I said unto the Lord, Thou art my Lord" (Ps. xvi. 2); and, "The Lord rained fire from the Lord." (Gen. xix. 24.) This indicates that the Persons are of the same substance, not that there is a distinction of nature. For we are not to understand that there are two substances differing from each other, but two Persons, each being of the same substance.

Observe too, that he says, "The Lord grant him mercy." For as he himself had obtained mercy from Onesiphorus, so he wished him to obtain the same from God. MORAL. And if Onesiphorus, who exposed himself to danger, is saved by mercy, much more are we also saved by the same. For terrible indeed, terrible is that account, and such as needs great love for mankind, that we may not hear that awful sentence, "Depart from me . . . I never knew you, ye that work iniquity" (Matt. vii. 23); or that fearful word, "Depart, ye cursed, into everlasting fire, prepared for the devil and his angels" (Matt. xxv. 40): that we may not hear, "Between us and you there is a great gulf fixed" (Luke xvi. 16): that we may not hear that voice full of horror, "Take him away, and cast him into outer darkness": that we may not hear those words full of terror, "Thou wicked and slothful servant." (Matt. xxii. 13, and xxv. 26.) For awful truly and terrible is that tribunal. And yet God is gracious and merciful. He is called a God "of mercies and a God of comfort" (2 Cor. i. 3); good as none else is good, and kind, and gentle, and full of pity, Who "willeth not the death of a sinner, but that he should be converted and live." (Ez. xviii. 24; xxxiii. 11.) Whence then, whence is that Day so full of agony and anguish? A stream of fire is rolling before His face. The books of our deeds are opened. The day itself is burning as an oven, the angels are flying around, and many furnaces are prepared. How then is He good and merciful, and full of lovingkindness to man? Even herein is He merciful, and He shows in these things the greatness of His lovingkindness. For He holds forth to us these terrors, that being constrained by them, we may be awakened to the desire of the kingdom.

And observe how, besides commending Onesiphorus, he specifies his kindness, "he oft refreshed me"; like a wearied wrestler overcome by heat, he refreshed and strengthened him in his tribulations. And in how many things he ministered to me at Ephesus, thou knowest very well. Not only at Ephesus, but here also he refreshed me. For such ought to be the conduct of one on the watch and awakened to good

---

[1] ἀλείφοντι.
[2] Rom. xii. 13, where some read μνείαις. On the passage, however, he reads χρείαις, "necessities," as E. V.; see on Rom. Hom. xxi.
[3] B. adds, "when thou buildest his monument."

actions, not to work once, or twice, or thrice, but through the whole of life. For as our body is not fed once for all, and so provided with sustenance for a whole life, but needs also daily food, so in this too, godliness requires to be supported every day by good works. For we ourselves have need of great mercy. It is on account of our sins that God, the Friend of man, does all these things, not that He needs them Himself, but He does all for us. For therefore it is that He has revealed them all, and made them known to us, and not merely told us of them, but given us assurance of them by what He has done. Though He was worthy of credit upon His word only, that no one may think it is said hyperbolically, or in the way of threatening merely, we have further assurance by His works. How? By the punishments which He has inflicted both publicly and privately. And that thou mayest learn by the very examples, at one time he punished Pharaoh, at another time He brought a flood of water upon the earth, and that utter destruction, and again at another time a flood of fire: and even now we see in many instances the wicked suffering vengeance, and punishments, which things are figures of Hell.

For lest we should slumber and be slothful, and forget His word, He awakens our minds by deeds; showing us, even here, courts of justice, judgment seats, and trials. Is there then among men so great a regard for justice, and doth God, whose ordinance even these things are, make no account of it? Is this credible? In a house, in a market-place, there is a court of justice. The master daily sits in judgment upon his slaves, calls them to account for their offenses, punishes some and pardons others. In the country, the husbandman and his wife are daily at law. In a ship, the master is judge, and in a camp the general over his soldiers, and everywhere one may see judicial proceedings. In trades, the master judges the learner. In short all, publicly and privately, are judges to one another. In nothing is the consideration of justice overlooked, and all in every place give account of their actions. And is the inquisition for justice here thus spread through cities, through houses, and among individuals; and is there no regard for what is justice there, where "the right hand of God is full of righteousness" (Ps. xlviii. 10), and "His righteousness is as the mountains of God"? (Ps. xxxvi. 6.)

How is it then that God, "the righteous Judge, strong and patient" (Ps. vii. 11, Sept.), bears thus with men, and does not exact punishment? Here thou hast the cause, He is longsuffering, and thereby would lead thee to repentance. But if thou continuest in sin, thou "after thy hardness and impenitent heart treasurest up unto thyself wrath." (Rom. ii. 5.) If then He

is just, He repays according to desert, and does not overlook those who suffer wrongfully, but avenges them. For this is the part of one who is just. If He is powerful, He requites after death, and at the Resurrection: for this belongs to him who is powerful. And if because He is longsuffering He bears with men, let us not be disturbed, nor ask, why He does not prosecute vengeance here? For if this were done, the whole human race before this would have been swept away, if every day He should call us to account for our transgressions, since there is not, there is not indeed, a single day pure from sin, but in something greater or less we offend; so that we should not one of us have arrived at our twentieth year, but for His great longsuffering, and His goodness, that grants us a longer space for repentance, that we may put off our past transgressions.

Let each therefore, with an upright conscience, entering into a review of what he has done, and bringing his whole life before him, consider, whether he is not deserving of chastisements and punishments without number? And when he is indignant that some one, who has been guilty of many bad actions, escapes with impunity; let him consider his own faults, and his indignation will cease. For those crimes appear great, because they are in great and notorious matters; but if he will enquire into his own, he will perhaps find them more numerous. For to rob and to defraud is the same thing, whether it be done for gold or silver; since both proceed from the same mind. He that will steal a little would not refuse to steal much, if it fell in his way; and that it does not, is not his own choice, but an accidental circumstance. A poor man, who robs a poorer, would not hesitate to rob the rich if he could. His forbearance arises from weakness, and not from choice. Such an one, you say, is a ruler; and takes away the property of those who are under his rule. And say, dost not thou steal? For tell me not that he steals talents, and you as many[1] pence. In giving alms, some cast in gold, while the widow threw in two mites, yet she contributed not less than they. Wherefore? Because the intention is considered, and not the amount of the gift. And then, in the case of alms, thou wilt have God judge thus, and wouldest, because of thy poverty, receive no less a reward for giving two mites than he who lays down many talents of gold? and is not the same rule applicable to wrongful dealings? How is this consistent? As she who contributed two mites was considered equal to the greatest givers, because of her good intention, so thou, who

---
[1] δέκα.

stealest two mites, art as culpable as those mightier robbers. Nay, if I may give utterance to something strange, thou art a worse robber than they. For a man would be equally an adulterer, whether he committed the sin with the wife of a king, or of a poor man, or of a slave: since the offense is not judged by the quality of the persons, but by the wickedness of his will who commits it; so is it likewise in this case. Nay, I should call him who committed the sin with an inferior perhaps more guilty, than him who intrigued with the queen herself. For in this case, wealth, and beauty, and other attractions might be pleaded, none of which exist in the other. Therefore the other is the worse adulterer. Again, he seems to me a more determined drunkard, who commits that excess with bad wine; so he is a worse defrauder, who does not despise small thefts; for he who commits great robberies, would perhaps not stoop to petty thefts, whereas he who steals little things would never forbear greater, therefore he is the greater thief of the two. For how should he despise gold, who does not despise silver? So that when we accuse our rulers, let us recount our own faults, and we shall find ourselves more given to wrong and robbery than they; unless we judge of right and wrong rather by the act, than by the intention of the mind, as we ought to judge. If one should be convicted of having stolen the goods of a poor man, another those of a rich man, will they not both be punished alike? Is not a man equally a murderer, whether he murder a poor and deformed, or a rich and handsome, man? When therefore we say that such an one has seized upon another person's land, let us reflect upon our own faults, and then we shall not condemn other men, but we shall admire the longsuffering of God. We shall not be indignant that judgment does not fall upon them, but we shall be more slow to commit wickedness ourselves. For when we perceive ourselves liable to the same punishment, we shall no longer feel such discontent, and shall desist from offenses, and shall obtain the good things to come, through the grace and lovingkindness of our Lord Jesus Christ, to whom with the Father, &c.

HOMILY IV.

2 TIMOTHY ii. 1–7.

" Thou therefore, my son, be strong in the grace that is in Christ Jesus. And the things that thou hast heard of me among many witnesses, the same commit thou to faithful men, who shall be able to teach others also. Thou therefore endure hardness, as a good soldier of Jesus Christ. No man that warreth entangleth himself with the affairs of this life; that he may please him who hath chosen him to be a soldier. And if a man also strive for masteries, yet is he not crowned, except he strive lawfully. The husbandman that laboreth must be first partaker of the fruits. Consider what I say; and the Lord give thee understanding in all things."

THE young sailor at sea is inspired with great confidence, if the Master of the ship has been preserved in a shipwreck. For he will not consider that it is from his inexperience that he is exposed to the storm, but from the nature of things; and this has no little effect upon his mind. In war also the Captain, who sees his General wounded and recovered again, is much encouraged. And thus it produces some consolation to the faithful, that the Apostle should have been exposed to great sufferings, and not rendered weak by the utmost of them. And had it not been so, he would not have related his sufferings. For when Timothy heard, that he who possessed so great powers, who had conquered the whole world, is a prisoner, and afflicted, yet is not impatient, nor discontented upon the desertion of his friends; he, if ever exposed to the same sufferings himself, would not consider that it proceeded from human weakness, nor from the circumstance of his being a disciple, and inferior to Paul, since his teacher too suffered the like, but that all this happened from the natural course of things. For Paul himself did this,[1] and related what had befallen him, that he might strengthen Timothy, and renew his courage. And he shows that it was for this reason he mentioned his trials and afflictions, in that he has added, "Thou, therefore, my son, be strong in the grace that is in Christ Jesus." What sayest thou? Thou hast shaken us with terrors, thou hast told us that thou art in chains, in afflictions, that all have forsaken thee, and, as if thou hadst said thou hadst not suffered anything, nor been abandoned by any, thou addest, "Thou therefore, my son, be strong"? — And justly too. For these things

---

[1] So B. Sav. " these things," but with a mark of authority for omitting " did these things, and."

were to thy strengthening more than to his.[1] For if I, Paul, endure these things, much more oughtest thou to bear them. If the master, much more the disciple. And this exhortation he introduces with much affection, calling him "son," and not only so, but "my son." If thou art a son, he means, imitate thy father. If thou art a son, be strong in consideration of the things which I have said, or rather be strong, not merely from what I have told you, but "of God." "Be strong," he says, "in the grace that is in Christ Jesus"; that is, "through the grace of Christ." That is, stand firmly. Thou knowest the battle. For elsewhere he says, "We wrestle not against flesh and blood." (Eph. vi. 12.) And this he says not to depress but to excite them. Be sober therefore, he means, and watch, have the grace of the Lord coöperating with thee, and aiding thee in thy contest, contribute thy own part with much alacrity and resolution. "And the things that thou hast heard of me among many witnesses, the same commit thou to faithful men"; to "faithful" men, not to questioners nor to reasoners, to "faithful." How faithful? Such as betray not the Gospel they should preach. "The things which thou hast heard," not which thou hast searched out. For "faith cometh by hearing, and hearing by the word of God." (Rom. x. 17.) But wherefore, "among many witnesses"? As if he had said: Thou hast not heard in secret, nor apart, but in the presence of many, with all openness of speech. Nor does he say, Tell, but "commit," as a treasure committed is deposited in safety. Again he alarms his disciple, both from things above and things below. But he says not only "commit to faithful men"; for of what advantage is it that one is faithful, if he is not able to convey his doctrine to others? when he does not indeed betray the faith; but does not render others faithful? The teacher therefore ought to have two qualities, to be both faithful, and apt to teach; wherefore he says, "who shall be able to teach others also."

"Thou therefore endure hardness as a good soldier of Jesus Christ." Oh, how great a dignity is this, to be a soldier of Jesus Christ! Observe the kings on earth, how great an honor it is esteemed to serve under them. If therefore the soldier of the king ought to endure hardness, not to endure hardness is not the part of any soldier. So that it behooves thee not to complain, if thou endurest hardness, for that is the part of a soldier; but to complain, if thou dost not endure hardness.

"No man that warreth entangleth himself with the affairs of this life, that he may please him who hath chosen him to be a soldier. And if a man also strive for masteries, yet is he not crowned except he strive lawfully."

These things are said indeed to Timothy, but through him they are addressed to every teacher and disciple. Let no one therefore of those who hold the office of a Bishop disdain to hear these things, but let him be ashamed not to do them. "If any one strive for masteries," he says, "he is not crowned, except he strive lawfully." What is meant by "lawfully"? It is not enough that he enters into the lists, that he is anointed, and even engages, unless he comply with all the laws of the exercise, with respect to diet, to temperance and sobriety, and all the rules of the wrestling school, unless, in short, he go through all that is befitting for a wrestler,[2] he is not crowned. And observe the wisdom of Paul. He mentions wrestlers and soldiers, the one to prepare him for slaughter and blood, the other with reference to endurance, that he might bear everything with fortitude, and be ever in exercise.

"The husbandman that laboreth must be first partaker of the fruits."

He had first spoken from his own example as a teacher. He now speaks from those that are more common, as wrestlers and soldiers, and in their case he sets before him the rewards. First, that he may please him who hath chosen him to be a soldier; secondly, that he may be crowned; now he proposes a third example that more particularly suits himself. For the instance of the soldier and the wrestler corresponds to those who are under rule, but that of the husbandman to the Teacher. (Strive) not as a soldier or a wrestler only, but as a husbandman too. The husbandman takes care not of himself alone, but of the fruits of the earth. That is, no little reward of his labors is enjoyed by the husbandman.

Here he both shows, that to God nothing is wanting, and that there is a reward for Teaching, which he shows by a common instance. As the husbandman, he says, does not labor without profit, but enjoys before others the fruits of his own toils, so is it fit that the teacher should do: either he means this, or he is speaking of the honor to be paid to teachers, but this is less consistent. For why does he not say the husbandman simply, but him "that laboreth"? not only that worketh, but that is worn with toil? And here with reference to the delay of reward, that no one may be impatient, he says, thou reapest the fruit already, or there is a reward in the labor itself. When therefore he has set before him the examples of soldiers, of wrestlers, and husbandmen, and all figuratively, "No one," he says, "is crowned

---

[1] So Edd., but B. has ἐκεῖνα for ἐκεῖνον, "more than the other," and Old Lat. paraphrases it, "more than if I had suffered nothing."

[2] See Hom. iii. on Stat.

except he strive lawfully." And having observed that "the husbandman who laboreth must first be partaker of the fruits," he adds,

"Consider what I say, and the Lord give thee understanding in all things."

It is on this account that he has spoken these things in proverb and parable. Then again to show his affectionate disposition, he ceases not to pray for him, as fearing for his own son, and he says,

Ver. 8, 9. "Remember that Jesus Christ, of the seed of David, was raised from the dead, according to my Gospel. Wherein I suffer trouble as an evil-doer, even unto bonds."

On what account is this mentioned? It is directed chiefly against the heretics, at the same time to encourage Timothy, by showing the advantage of sufferings, since Christ, our Master, Himself overcame death by suffering. Remember this, he says, and thou wilt have sufficient comfort. "Remember that Jesus Christ, of the seed of David, was raised from the dead." For upon that point many had already begun to subvert the dispensation, being ashamed at the immensity of God's love to mankind. For of such a nature are the benefits which God has conferred upon us, that men were ashamed to ascribe them to God, and could not believe He had so far condescended. "According to my Gospel." Thus he everywhere speaks in his Epistles, saying "according to my Gospel,"[1] either because they were bound to believe him, or because there were some who preached "another Gospel." (Gal. i. 6.)

"Wherein I suffer trouble," he says, "as an evil-doer, even unto bonds." Again he introduces consolation and encouragement from himself, and he prepares[2] his hearer's mind with these two things; first, that he should know him to endure hardness; and, secondly, that he did not so but for a useful purpose, for in this case he will gain, in the other will even suffer harm. For what advantage is it, that you can show that a Teacher has exposed himself to hardship, but not for any useful purpose? But if it is for any benefit, if for the profit of those who are taught, then it is worthy of admiration.[3]

"But the word of God is not bound." That is, if we were soldiers of this world, and waged an earthly warfare, the chains that confine our hands would avail. But now God has made us such that nothing can subdue us. For our hands are bound, but not our tongue, since nothing can bind the tongue but cowardice and unbelief alone; and where these are not, though you fas-

ten chains upon us, the preaching of the Gospel is not bound. If indeed you bind a husbandman, you prevent his sowing, for he sows with his hand: but if you bind a Teacher, you hinder not the word, for it is sown with his tongue, not with his hand. Our word therefore is not subjected to bonds. For though we are bound, that is free, and runs its course. How? Because though bound, behold, we preach. This is for the encouragement of those that are free. For if we that are bound preach, much more does it behoove you that are loose to do so. You have heard that I suffer these things, as an evil-doer. Be not dejected. For it is a great wonder, that being bound I do the work of those that are free, that being bound I overcome all, that being bound I prevail over those that bound me. For it is the word of God, not ours. Human chains cannot bind the word of God. "These things I suffer on account of the elect."

Ver. 10. "Therefore I endure all things," he says, "for the elect's sake, that they may also obtain the salvation which is in Christ Jesus with eternal glory."

Behold another incentive. I endure these things, he says, not for myself, but for the salvation of others. It was in my power to have lived free from danger; to have suffered none of these things, if I had consulted my own interest. On what account then do I suffer these things? For the good of others, that others may obtain eternal life. What then dost thou promise thyself? He has not said, simply on account of these particular persons; but "for the elect's sake." If God has chosen them, it becomes us to suffer everything for their sakes. "That they also may obtain salvation." By saying, "they also," he means, as well as we. For God hath chosen us also; and as God suffered for our sakes, so should we suffer for their sakes. Thus it is a matter of retribution, not of favor. On the part of God it was grace, for He having received no previous benefit, hath done us good: but on our parts it is retribution, we having previously received benefits from God, suffer for these, for whom we suffer, in order "that they may obtain salvation." What sayest thou? What salvation? Art thou who wast not the author of salvation to thyself, but wast destroying thyself, art thou the author of salvation to others? Surely not, and therefore he adds, "salvation that is in Christ Jesus"; that which is truly salvation, "with eternal glory." Present things are afflictive, but they are but on earth. Present things are ignominious, but they are temporary. They are full of bitterness and pain; but they last only to-day and to-morrow.

Such is not the nature of the good things, they are eternal, they are in heaven. That is true glory, this is dishonor.

---

[1] As Rom. ii. 16; xvi. 25. Other phrases to the same purpose occur, 1 Cor. xv. 1; 1 Tim. i. 11, &c.

[2] Lit. "oils."

[3] B. and Sav. mar. read this passage differently, and Old Lat. differently from them; no one of the readings seems right, unless perhaps this.

Moral. For observe, I pray, beloved, that is not glory which is on earth, the true glory is in heaven. But if any one would be glorified, let him be dishonored. If he would obtain rest, let him suffer affliction. If any one would be forever illustrious, would enjoy pleasure, let him despise temporal things. And that dishonor is glory, and glory dishonor, let us now set before us to the best of our power, that we may see what is real glory. It is not possible to be glorified upon earth; if thou wouldest be glorified, it must be through dishonor. And let us prove this in the examples of two persons, Nero and Paul. The one had the glory of this world, the other the dishonor. How? The first was a tyrant, had obtained great success, had raised many trophies, had wealth ever flowing in, numerous armies everywhere; he had the greater part of the world and the imperial city subject to his sway, the whole senate crouching to him, and his palace too [1] was advancing with splendid show. When he must be armed, he went forth arrayed in gold and precious stones. When he was to sit still in peace, he sat clothed in robes of purple. He was surrounded by numerous guards and attendants. He was called Lord of land and sea, Emperor,[2] Augustus, Cæsar, King, and other such high-sounding names as implied[3] flattery and courtship; and nothing was wanting that might tend to glory. Even wise men and potentates and sovereigns trembled at him. For beside all this, he was said to be a cruel and violent man. He even wished to be thought a god, and he despised both all the idols, and the very God Who is over all. He was worshiped as a god. What greater glory than this? Or rather what greater dishonor? For — I know not how — my tongue is carried away by the force of truth, and passes sentence before judgment. Meanwhile let us examine the matter according to the opinion of the multitude, and of unbelievers, and the estimation of flattery.

What is greater in the common estimation of glory than to be reputed a god? It is indeed a great disgrace that any human being should be so mad, but for the present let us consider the matter according to the opinion of the multitude. Nothing then was wanting to him, that contributes to human glory, but he was worshiped by all as a god. Now in opposition to him, let us consider Paul. He was a Cilician, and the difference between Rome and Cilicia, all know. He was a tent-maker, a poor man, unskilled in the wisdom of those without, knowing only the Hebrew tongue, a language despised by all, especially by the Italians. For they do not so much despise the barbarian, the Greek, or any other tongue as the Syriac, and this has affinity with the Hebrew. Nor wonder at this, for if they despised the Greek, which is so admirable and beautiful, much more the Hebrew. He was a man that often lived in hunger, often went to bed without food, a man that was naked, and had not clothes to put on; "in cold, and nakedness," as he says of himself. (1 Cor. xi. 27.) Nor was this all; but he was cast into prison at the command of Nero himself, and confined with robbers, with impostors, with grave-breakers, with murderers, and he was, as he himself says, scourged as a malefactor. Who then is the more illustrious? The name of the one the greater part have never heard of. The other is daily celebrated by Greeks, and Barbarians, and Scythians, and those who inhabit the extremities of the earth.

But let us not yet consider what is the case now, but even at that time who was the more illustrious, who the more glorious, he that was in chains, and dragged bound from prison, or he that was clothed in a purple robe, and walked forth from a palace? The prisoner certainly. For the other, who had armies at his command, and sat arrayed in purple, was not able to do what he would. But the prisoner, that was like a malefactor, and in mean attire, could do everything with more authority. How? The one said, "Do not disseminate the word of God." The other said, "I cannot forbear; 'the word of God is not bound.'" Thus the Cilician, the prisoner, the poor tent-maker, who lived in hunger, despised the Roman, rich as he was, and emperor, and ruling over all, who enriched so many thousands; and with all his armies he availed nothing. Who then was illustrious? who venerable? He that in chains was a conqueror, or he that in a purple robe was conquered? He that standing below, smote, or he that sitting above, was smitten? He that commanded and was despised, or he who was commanded and made no account of the commands? He who being alone was victorious, or he who with numerous armies was defeated? The king therefore so came off, that his prisoner triumphed over him. Tell me then on whose side you would be? For do not look to what comes afterwards, but to what was then their state. Would you be on the side of Nero, or of Paul? I speak not according to the estimate of faith, for that is manifest; but according to the estimate of glory, and reverence, and preëminence. Any man of right understanding would say, on the side of Paul. For if to conquer is more illustrious than to be conquered, he is more glorious. And this is not yet much, that he conquered, but that being in so mean a state he

---

[1] One suspects the stops. Read, "and the palace itself, He walked in splendid attire."

[2] Αὐτοκράτωρ.

[3] Gr. "devised," whence it seems that "flattery," &c. should be in the nominative.

conquered one in so exalted a condition. For I say, and will not cease to repeat it, though bound with a chain, yet he smote him that was invested with a diadem.

Such is the power of Christ. The chain surpassed the kingly crown, and this apparel was shown more brilliant than that. Clothed in filthy rags, as the inhabitant of a prison, he turned all eyes upon the chains that hung on him, rather than on the purple robe. He stood on earth bound down and stooping low, and all left the tyrant mounted on a golden chariot to gaze on him. And well they might. For it was customary to see a king with white horses, but it was a strange and unwonted sight to behold a prisoner conversing with a king with as much confidence as a king would converse with a pitiful and wretched slave. The surrounding multitude were all slaves of the king, yet they admired not their lord, but him who was superior to their lord. And he before whom all feared and trembled, was trampled upon by one solitary man. See then how great was the brightness of these very chains !

And what need to mention what followed after these things ? The tomb of the one is nowhere to be seen; but the other lies in the royal city itself, in greater splendor than any king, even there where he conquered, where he raised his trophy. If mention is made of the one, it is with reproach, even among his kindred, for he is said to have been profligate. But the memory of the other is everywhere accompanied with a good report, not among[1] us only, but among his enemies. For when truth shines forth, it puts to shame even one's enemies, and if they admire him not for his faith, yet they admire him for his boldness and his manly freedom. The one is proclaimed by all mouths, as one that is crowned, the other is loaded with reproaches and accusations. Which then is the real splendor ?

And yet I am but praising the lion for his talons, when I ought to be speaking of his real honors. And what are these ? Those in the heavens. How will he come in a shining vesture with the King of Heaven ! How will Nero stand then, mournful and dejected ! And if what I say seems to thee incredible and ridiculous, thou art ridiculous for deriding that which is no subject for laughter. For if thou disbelievest the future, be convinced from what is past. The season for being crowned is not yet come, and yet how great honor has the combatant gained ! What honor then will he not obtain, when the Distributor of the prizes shall come ! He was among foreigners, "a stranger and a sojourner" (Heb. xi. 13), and thus is he admired : what good will he not enjoy, when he is amongst his own ? Now " our life is hid with Christ in God " (Col. iii. 3) ; yet he who is dead worketh more and is more honored than the living. When that our life shall come, what will he not participate ? What will he not attain ?

On this account God made him enjoy these honors, not because he wanted them. For if when in the body he despised popular glory, much more will he despise it now that he is delivered from the body. Nor only on this account has He caused him to enjoy honor, but that those who disbelieve the future may be convinced from the present. I say that when the Resurrection shall be, Paul will come with the King of Heaven, and will enjoy infinite blessings. But the unbeliever will not be convinced. Let him believe then from the present. The tent-maker is more illustrious, more honored than the king. No emperor of Rome ever enjoyed so great honor. The emperor is cast out, and lies, no one knows where. The tent-maker occupies the midst of the city, as if he were a king, and living. From these things believe, even with respect to the future. If he enjoys so great honor here, where he was persecuted and banished, what will he not be when he shall come hereafter ? If when he was a tent-maker, he was so illustrious, what will he be when he shall come rivaling the beams of the sun ? If in so much meanness he overcame such magnificence, to whom, at his coming, will he not be superior ? Can we avoid the conclusion ? Who is not moved by the fact, that a tent-maker became more honorable than the most honored of kings ? If here things happen so beyond the course of nature, much more will it be so hereafter. If thou wilt not believe the future, O man, believe the present. If thou wilt not believe invisible things, believe things that are seen : or rather believe things which are seen, for so thou wilt believe things which are invisible. But if thou wilt not, we may fitly say with the Apostle, "We are pure from your blood " (Acts xx. 26) : for we have testified to you of all things, and have left out nothing that we should have said. Blame yourselves therefore, and to yourselves[2] will ye impute the punishment of Hell. But let us, my beloved children, be imitators of Paul, not in his faith only, but in his life, that we may attain to heavenly glory, and trample upon that glory that is here. Let not any things present attract us. Let us despise visible things, that we may obtain heavenly things, or rather may[3] through these obtain the others, but let it be our aim preëminently to obtain those, of which God grant that we may be all accounted worthy, through the grace and lovingkindness, &c.

---

[1] B. reads παρ' for γὰρ, as the sense requires. Perhaps οἰκείων (rendered " kindred " just before) may mean " fellow-idolaters."

[2] Such must be the meaning, though the construction seems to require filling up. The change of tense may be rhetorical.

[3] B. " rather we shall."

HOMILY V.

2 TIMOTHY ii. 11–14.

"It is a faithful saying: for if we be dead with Him, we shall also live with Him: if we suffer, we shall also reign with Him: if we deny Him, He also will deny us: if we believe not, yet He abideth faithful: He cannot deny Himself. Of these things put them in remembrance, charging them before the Lord, that they strive not about words to no profit, but to the subverting of the hearers."

MANY of the weaker sort of men give up the effort of faith, and do not endure the deferring of their hope. They seek things present, and form from these their judgment of the future. When therefore their lot here was death, torments, and chains, and yet he says, they shall come to eternal life, they would not have believed, but would have said, "What sayest thou? When I live, I die; and when I die, I live? Thou promisest nothing on earth, and dost thou give it in heaven? Little things thou dost not bestow; and dost thou offer great things?" That none therefore may argue thus, he places beyond doubt the proof of these things, laying it down beforehand already, and giving certain signs. For, "remember," he says, "that Jesus Christ was raised from the dead"; that is, rose again after death. And now showing the same thing he says, "It is a faithful saying," that he who has attained a heavenly life, will attain eternal life also. Whence is it "faithful"? Because, he says, "If we be dead with Him, shall also live with Him." For say, shall we partake with Him in things laborious and painful; and shall we not in things beneficial? But not even a man would act thus, nor, if one had chosen to suffer affliction and death with him, would he refuse to him a share in his rest, if he had attained it. But how are we "dead with Him"? This death he means both of that in the Laver, and that in sufferings. For he says, "Bearing about in the body the dying of the Lord Jesus" (2 Cor. iv. 10); and, "We are buried with Him by baptism into death" (Rom. vi. 4); and, "Our old man is crucified with Him"; and, "We have been planted together in the likeness of His death." (Rom. vi. 5, 6.) But he also speaks here of death by trials: and that more especially, for he was also suffering trials when he wrote it. And this is what he says, "If we have suffered death on His account, shall we not live on His account? This is not to be doubted. 'If we suffer, we shall also reign with Him,'" not absolutely, we shall reign, but "if we suffer," showing that it is not

enough to die once, (the blessed man himself died daily,) but there was need of much patient endurance; and especially Timothy had need of it. For tell me not, he says, of your first sufferings, but that you continue to suffer.

Then on the other side he exhorts him, not from the good, but from the evil. For if wicked men were to partake of the same things, this would be no consolation. And if having endured they were to reign with Him, but not having endured were not indeed to reign with Him, but were to suffer no worse evil, though this were terrible, yet it would not be enough to affect most men with concern. Wherefore he speaks of something more dreadful still. If we deny Him, He will also deny us. So then there is a retribution not of good things only, but of the contrary. And consider what it is probable that he will suffer, who is denied in that kingdom. "Whosoever shall deny Me, him will I also deny." (Matt. x. 33.) And the retribution is not equal, though it seems so expressed. For we who deny Him are men, but He who denies us is God; and how great is the distance between God and man, it is needless to say.

Besides, we injure ourselves; Him we cannot injure. And to show this, he has added, "If we believe not, He abideth faithful: He cannot deny Himself": that is, if we believe not that He rose again, He is not injured by it. He is faithful and unshaken, whether we say so or not. If then He is not at all injured by our denying Him, it is for nothing else than for our benefit that He desires our confession. For He abideth the same, whether we deny Him or not. He cannot deny Himself, that is, His own Being. We may say that He is not; though such is not the fact. It is not in His nature, it is not possible for Him not to be, that is, to go into nonentity.[1] His subsistence always abides, always is. Let us not therefore be so affected, as if we could gratify or could injure Him. But lest any one should think that Timothy needed this advice, he has added,

"Of these things put them in remembrance, charging them before the Lord, that they strive

---

[1] MS. Aug. has ἡμεῖς κἂν λέγωμεν ὅτι οὐκ ἔστιν (εἰ καὶ πρᾶγμα οὕτως ἔχει οὐδὲ γὰρ οἴδαμεν τί τὴν οὐσίαν ἐστὶν) ὅμως οὐκ ἔχει φύσιν μὴ εἶναι· τουτέστιν, οὐ δυνατὸν εἰς τὸ μὴ εἶναι χωρῆσαι, which may be thus rendered by reading τὴν οὐσίαν τί for τί τὴν οὐσίαν. "Though we may say that He is not, if such statement means anything, (for we do not know what 'being' is,) yet He hath it not in His nature not to be, that is, He cannot pass into nonentity." Or reading only τὸ πρᾶγμα, "if the case is really so, (in some sense,) in that we do not know what He is in essence," &c. But Hales was perhaps right in finding no meaning in the words.

not about words to no profit, but to the subverting of the hearers." It is an overawing thing to call God to witness what we say, for if no one would dare to set at nought the testimony of man when appealed to, much less when the appeal is to God. If any one, for instance, entering into a contract, or making his will, chooses to call witnesses worthy of credit, would any transfer the things to those who are not included? Surely not. And even if he wishes it, yet fearing the credibility of the witnesses, he avoids it. What is "charging them before the Lord"? he calls God to witness both what was said, and what was done.

"That they strive not about words to no profit;" and not merely so, but "to the subverting of the hearers." Not only is there no gain from it, but much harm. "Of these things then put them in remembrance," and if they despise thee, God will judge them. But why does he admonish them not to strive about words? He knows that it is a dainty[1] thing, and that the human soul is ever prone to contend and to dispute about words. To guard against this, he has not only charged them "not to strive about words," but to render his discourse more alarming, he adds, "to the subverting of the hearers."

Ver. 15. "Study to show thyself approved unto God, a workman that needeth not to be ashamed, rightly dividing the word of truth."

Everywhere this "not being ashamed"! And why is he ever so careful to guard him against shame? Because it was natural for many to be ashamed both of Paul himself, as being a tentmaker, and of the preaching, since its teachers perished. For Christ had been crucified, himself was about to be beheaded, Peter was crucified with his head downwards, and these things they suffered from audacious and despicable men. Because such men were in power, he says, "Be not ashamed"; that is, fear not to do anything tending to godliness, though it be necessary to submit to slavery or any other suffering. For how does any one become approved? By being "a workman that needeth not to be ashamed." As the workman is not ashamed of any work, so neither should he be ashamed who labors in the Gospel. He should submit to anything.

"Rightly dividing the word of truth."

This he hath well said. For many distort it, and pervert it in every way, and many additions are made to it. He has not said directing it, but "rightly dividing," that is, cut away what is spurious, with much vehemence assail it, and extirpate it. With the sword of the Spirit cut off from your preaching, as from a thong, whatever is superfluous and foreign to it.

Ver. 16. "And shun profane novelties of speech."[2]

For they will not stop there. For when anything new has been introduced, it is ever producing innovations, and the error of him who has once left the safe harbor is infinite, and never stops.

"For they will increase unto more ungodliness," he says,

Ver. 17. "And their word will eat as doth a canker."

It is an evil not to be restrained, not curable by any medicine, it destroys the whole frame. He shows that novelty of doctrine is a disease, and worse than a disease. And here he implies that they are incorrigible, and that they erred not weakly but willfully.

"Of whom is Hymeneus and Philetus,"

Ver. 18. "Who concerning the truth have erred, saying that the resurrection is past already, and overthrow the faith of some."

He has well said, "They will increase unto more ungodliness." For it appears indeed to be a solitary evil, but see what evils spring out of it. For if the Resurrection is already past, not only do we suffer loss in being deprived of that great glory, but because judgment is taken away, and retribution also. For if the Resurrection is past, retribution also is past. The good therefore have reaped persecutions and afflictions, and the wicked have not been punished, nay verily, they live in great pleasure.[3] It were better to say that there is no resurrection, than that it is already past.

"And overthrow," he says, "the faith of some."

"Of some," not of all. For if there is no resurrection, faith is subverted. Our preaching is vain, nor is Christ risen; and if He is not risen, neither was He born, nor has He ascended into heaven. Observe how this error, while it seems to oppose the doctrine of the Resurrection, draws after it many other evils. What then, says one, ought we to do nothing for those who are subverted?[4]

Ver. 19. "Nevertheless," he says, "the foundation of God standeth sure, having this seal, The Lord knoweth them that are His. And, Let every one that nameth the name of the Lord[5] depart from iniquity."

He shows that even before they were subverted, they were not firm. For otherwise, they

---

[1] λύχνον.

[2] Gr. καινοφωνίας, for κενοφωνίας.

[3] Old Lat. here has, "so then the just have suffered tribulations and griefs in vain. But that is so far from being the truth, that contrariwise even in this life the good are fed with their own hopes, and have a foretaste of eternal felicity, persevering always with a serene and tranquil spirit, and the wicked, persecuted by the scourge of their own conscience, begin to suffer even here what they are to suffer for ever." But this seems an interpolation. See, however, on Rom. v. 5, Hom. ix.

[4] al. "Thus much of those who are subverted; but of those who are not so, what says he?"

[5] E. V. "of Christ."

would not have been overthrown at the first attack, as Adam [1] was firm before the commandment. For those who are fixed not only are not harmed through deceivers, but are even admired.

And he calls it "sure," and a "foundation"; so ought we to adhere to the faith; "having this seal, The Lord knoweth them that are His." What is this? He has taken it from Deuteronomy; [2] that is, Firm souls stand fixed and immovable. But whence are they manifest? From having these characters inscribed upon their actions, from their being known by God, and not perishing with the world, and from their departing from iniquity.

"Let every one," he says, "that nameth the name of the Lord depart from iniquity."

These are the distinguishing marks of the foundation. As [3] a foundation is shown to be firm, and as letters are inscribed upon a stone that the letters may be significant. But these letters are shown by works, "Having," he says, "this seal" fixed thereon, "Let every one that nameth the name of the Lord depart from iniquity." Thus if any one is unrighteous, he is not of the foundation. So that this too is of the seal, not to do iniquity.

MORAL. Let us not therefore put off from us the royal seal and token, that we may not be of those who are not sealed, that we may not be unsound, that we may be firmly grounded, that we may be of the foundation, and not carried to and fro. This marks them that are of God, that they depart from iniquity. For how can any one be of God Who is just, if he does iniquity, if by his works he opposes Him, if he insults Him by his misdeeds? Again we are speaking against injustice, and again we have many that are hostile to us. For this affection, like a tyrant, has seized upon the souls of all, and, what is worse, not by necessity nor violence, but by persuasion and gentle insinuation, and they are grateful for their slavery. And this is indeed the misery; for if they were held by constraint and not by love, they would soon depart. And whence is it, that a thing which is most bitter, appears to be sweet? whence is it that righteousness, which is a most sweet thing, becomes bitter? It is the fault of our senses. Thus some have thought honey bitter, and have taken with pleasure other things that were noxious. And the cause is not in the nature of things, but in the perverseness of the sufferers.

The judging faculty of the soul [4] is disordered. [5] Just as a balance, if its beam be unsteady, [6] moves round, and does not show accurately the weight of things placed in it; so the soul, if it has not the beam of its own thoughts fixed, and firmly riveted to the law of God, being carried round and drawn down, will not be able to judge aright of actions.

For if any one will examine carefully, he will perceive the great bitterness of injustice, not to those who suffer it, but to those who practice it, and to these more than to the others. And let us not speak of things future, but for the present of things here. Hath it not battles, judgments, condemnation, ill will, abuse? what is more bitter than these? Hath it not enmities, and wars, and accusations? what is more bitter than these? Hath it not conscience continually scourging and gnawing us? If it were possible, I could wish to draw out from the body the soul of the unrighteous man, and you would see it pale and trembling, ashamed, hiding its head, anxiously fearful, and self-condemned. For should we sink down into the very depths of wickedness, the judging faculty of the mind [7] is not destroyed, but remains unbribed. And no one pursues injustice thinking it to be good, but he invents excuses, and has recourse to every artifice of words to shift off the accusation. But he cannot get it off his conscience. Here indeed the speciousness of words, the corruption of rulers, and multitudes of flatterers, is often able to throw justice into the shade, but within, the conscience [8] has nothing of this sort, there are no flatterers there, no wealth to corrupt the judge. For the faculty of judging is naturally implanted in us by God, and what comes from God cannot be so corrupted. But uneasy slumbers, thick-coming fancies, and the frequent recollections of guilt, destroy our repose. Has any one, for instance, unjustly deprived another of his house? not only is he that is robbed rendered unhappy, but the man who robbed him. If he is persuaded of a future judgment, (if indeed any one is so persuaded,) he groans exceedingly, and is in misery. But if he believes not in futurity, yet he blushes for shame; or rather there is no man, whether Greek, Jew, or heretic, who is not afraid of a judgment to come.

---

[1] So Sav., but B. and one Lat., "as neither Adam." Another Lat. has "neither was Adam before the attack"; as he says on Rom. vii. 9, Hom. xii. "neither was the Tree the cause."

[2] Num. xvi. 5?

[3] Downes prefers the reading of MS. Aug., "Such an one, as a foundation, is firmly fixed, having this seal stamped on him. Well said he, 'seal.' For as when one writes on a stone, one writes that the characters may signify somewhat, so he that hath these characters in himself is made manifest by works. 'And let,'" &c., which seems better.

[4] ψυχῆς.

[5] B. reads Νοσεῖ, which Hales had conjectured. Sav. has Νόει, "consider the judging faculty."

[6] παρασαλευομένην. He seems to mean, "liable to slip toward one side."

[7] τοῦ νοῦ, which he seems here to distinguish from the soul. See Rom. vii. 23; 1 Cor. ii. 14.

[8] "In the corrupted currents of this world
Offense's gilded hand may shove by justice,
And oft 'tis seen, the wicked prize itself
Buys out the law: but 'tis not so above —
There is no shuffling — there the action lies
In its true nature — and we ourselves compell'd
E'en in the teeth and forehead of offense
To give in evidence."— Hamlet, Act iii. sc. 3.

And although he is not a philosopher with respect to futurity; yet he fears and trembles at what may befall him here, lest he may have some retribution in his property, his children, his family, or his life. For many such visitations God inflicts. For since the doctrine of the Resurrection is not sufficient to bring all men to reason, He affords even here many proofs of His righteous judgment, and exhibits them to the world. One who has gained wrongfully is without children, another falls in war, another is maimed in his body, another loses his son. He considers these things, on these his imagination dwells, and he lives in continual fear.

Know you not what the unrighteous suffer? Is there no bitterness in these things? And were there nothing of this sort, do not all condemn him, and hate and abhor him, and think him less rational than a beast, even those who are themselves unrighteous? For if they condemn themselves, much more do they condemn another, calling him rapacious, fraudulent, a pestilent fellow. What pleasure then can he enjoy? He has only the heavier care and anxiety to preserve his gains, and the being more anxious and troubled. For the more wealth any one gets about him, the more painful watchfulness does he store up for himself. Then what are the curses of those whom he has wronged, their pleadings against him?[1] And what, if sickness should befall him? For it is impossible for one, who has fallen into sickness, however atheistically he may be inclined, not to be anxious about these things, not to be thoughtful, when he is unable to do anything. For as long as we are here, the soul enjoying itself, does not tolerate painful thoughts: but when it is about to take its flight from the body, then a greater fear constrains it, as entering into the very portals of judgment. Even robbers, whilst they are in prison, live without fear, but when they are brought to the very curtain of the court,[2] they sink with terror. For when the fear of death is urgent, like a fire consuming all things besides, it obliges the soul to philosophize, and to take thought for futurity. The desire of wealth, the love of gain, and of bodily pleasures, no longer possesses it. These things passing away like clouds, leave the judging faculty clear, and grief entering in softens the hard heart. For nothing is so opposite to philosophy, as a life of pleasure; nor, on the other hand, is anything so favorable to philosophy as affliction. Consider what the covetous man will then be. For, "an hour of affliction," it is said, "maketh a man forget much pleasure." (Ecclus. ii. 27.) What will then be his state, when he considers those whom he has robbed, and injured, and defrauded, when he sees others reaping the fruits of his grasping, and himself going to pay the penalty? For it cannot, indeed it cannot be, that when fallen into sickness he should not reflect upon these things. For often the soul of itself is distracted with agony and terror. What a bitterness is this, tell me! And with every sickness these things must be endured. And what will he not suffer when he sees others punished or put to death?

These things await him here. And as to what he must undergo hereafter, it is not possible to say what punishment, what vengeance, what torments, what racks are reserved for him There. These things we declare. "He that hath ears to hear, let him hear." (Luke viii. 8.) We are for ever discoursing of these things, not willingly, but of necessity. For we could wish there were no obligation to mention such things at all. But since it must be, we would at least, by a little medicine, deliver you from your disease, and restore you to health. But whilst you remain in this sickness, it would show a mean and weak spirit, not to say cruelty and inhumanity, to desist from the healing treatment. For if when physicians despair of our bodies, we beseech them not to neglect us, not to cease to our last breath applying whatever is in their power, shall we not much more exhort ourselves? For perhaps when we have come to the very gates of Hell, the vestibule of wickedness itself, it may be possible to recover, to renew our strength, to lay hold on eternal life! How many, who have heard ten times and remained insensible, have afterwards at one hearing been converted! Or rather, not at one hearing; for though they seemed insensible at the ten discourses, yet they gained something, and afterwards showed all at once abundant fruit. For as a tree may receive ten strokes, and not fall; then afterwards be brought down all at once by a single blow: yet it is not done by that one blow, but by the ten which made that last successful. And this is known to him who sees the root, though he who takes his view of the trunk above knows it not. So it is in this case. And thus often, when physicians have applied many remedies, no benefit is perceived; but afterwards some one comes in and effects an entire cure. Yet it is not the work of him alone, but of these who have already reduced the disorder. So that, if now we do not bring forth the fruits of hearing the word, yet hereafter we shall. For that we shall bring them forth, I am fully persuaded. For it is not, indeed it is not possible that such eager desire, such a love of hearing, should fail of its effect. God forbid! But may we all, having become worthy of the admonitions of Christ, obtain the everlasting blessings, &c.

---

[1] ἐντυχίαι.   [2] παραπέτασμα.

HOMILY VI.

2 TIMOTHY ii. 20, 21.

" But in a great house there are not only vessels of gold and of silver, but also of wood and of earth; and some to honor, and some to dishonor. If a man therefore purge himself from these, he shall be a vessel unto honor, sanctified, and meet for the master's use, and prepared unto every good work."

MANY men are still even now perplexed to account for the fact, that the wicked are suffered to remain, and are not yet destroyed. Now doubtless various reasons may be assigned for this, as, that they may be converted, or that by their punishment they may be made an example to the multitude. But Paul here mentions a similar case. For he says,
" In a great house there are not only vessels of gold and silver, but also of wood and earth." Showing by this, that as in a great house it is likely there should be a great difference of vessels, so here also, in the whole world, for he speaks not of the Church only, but of the world at large. For think not, I pray, that he means it of the Church ; for there he would not have any vessels of wood or of earth, but all of gold or silver, where is the body of Christ, where is that "pure virgin, without spot, or wrinkle, or any such thing." (Eph. v. 27.) And this is what he means to say : Let it not disturb thee that there are corrupt and wicked men. For in a great house there are such vessels. But what then? they do not receive the same honor. But some are to honor and some to dishonor. " Nay," says one, " in a house they may be of some use, but not at all in the world." Though God employs them not for such honorable service, he makes use of them for other purposes. For instance, the vainglorious man builds much, so does the covetous man, the merchant, the tradesman, the magistrate ; there are certain works in the world suited to these. But the golden vessel is not of such a nature. It is employed about the royal table. He does not say however that wickedness is a necessary thing, (for how should it be ?) but that the wicked also have their work. For if all were of gold or of silver, there would be no need of the viler sort. For instance, if all were hardy, there would be no need of houses ; if all were free from luxury, there would be no need of dainties. If all were careful only for necessaries, there would be no need of splendid building.
" If therefore a man purge himself from these, he shall be a vessel unto honor, sanctified." Seest thou that it is not of nature, nor of the

necessity of matter, to be a vessel of gold or of earth, but of our own choice? For otherwise the earthen could not become gold, nor could the golden descend to the vileness of the other. But in this case there is much change, and alteration of state. Paul was an earthen vessel, and became a golden one. Judas was a golden vessel, and became an earthen one. The earthen vessels, therefore, are such from uncleanness. The fornicator and the covetous man become earthen vessels. " But how then does he say elsewhere, ' We have this treasure in earthen vessels,' so that he does not despise but honor the earthen vessel, speaking of it as the recipient of the treasure?" There he shows the nature itself, and not the form of the material. For he means to say that our body is an earthen vessel. For as earthenware is nothing else but baked clay, so is our body nothing but clay consolidated by the heat of the soul ; for that it is earthen, is evident. For as such a vessel is often by falling broken and dashed to pieces, so our body falls and is dissolved by death. For how do our bones differs from a potsherd, hard and dry as they are? or our flesh from clay, being, like it, composed of water? But, as I said, how is it that he does not speak contemptuously of it? Because there he is discoursing of its nature, here of our choice. " If a man," he says, " purge himself from these," not merely " cleanse," but " cleanse out," [1] that is, cleanse himself perfectly, " he shall be a vessel unto honor, sanctified, and meet for the Master's use." The others therefore are useless for any good purpose, though some use is made of them. " And prepared [2] unto every good work." Even though he do it not, he is fit for it, and has a capacity for it. We ought therefore to be prepared for everything, even for death, for martyrdom, for a life of virginity, or for all these.
Ver. 22. " Flee also youthful lusts."
Not only the lust of fornication, but every inordinate desire is a youthful lust. Let the aged learn that they ought not to do the deeds of the youthful. If one be given to insolence, or a lover of power, of riches, of bodily pleasures, it is a youthful lust, and foolish. These things must proceed from a heart not yet established, from a mind not deeply grounded, but in a wavering state. What then does he advise in order

---

[1] ἐκκαθάρῃ.
[2] B. " They are not, however, ' prepared,' " &c.

that none may be captivated by these things? "Flee youthful" imaginations, "but

"Follow righteousness, faith, charity, peace, with them that call on the Lord out of a pure heart."

He calls virtue in general, "righteousness": godliness of life, "faith, meekness, charity."

What is meant by "those that call upon the Lord out of a pure heart"? It is as if he said, Rejoice not in those who only call upon the Lord; but those who call upon Him sincerely and unfeignedly, who have nothing of deceit about them, who approach Him in peace, who are not contentious. With these associate thyself. But with others be not easy, but only as far as lies in you, be peaceable.

Ver. 23. "But foolish and unlearned questions avoid, knowing that they do gender strifes."

Do you see how he everywhere draws him off from questions; not that he was not able to overthrow them; for he was well able. For had he not been able he would have said, Be diligent, that thou mayest be able to refute them; as when he says, "Give attendance to reading, for by so doing thou shalt both save thyself and them that hear thee." (1 Tim. iv. 13, 16.) But he knew that it was useless to enter at all into these disputes, that there will be no end of it, save contentions, enmities, insults, and reproaches. These "questions" therefore "avoid"; so that there are other questions, some relating to the Scriptures, some to other things.

Ver. 24. "And the servant of the Lord must not strive."

Not even in questions ought he to strive, for the servant of the Lord must keep far from strife, since God is the God of peace, and what should the servant of the God of peace have to do with strife?

"But be gentle unto all men."

How is it then he says, "Rebuke with all authority" (Tit. ii. 15); and again, "Let no man despise thy youth" (1 Tim. iv. 12): and again, "Rebuke them sharply"? (Tit. i. 13.) Because this is consistent with meekness. For a strong rebuke, if it be given with gentleness, is most likely to wound deeply: for it is possible, indeed it is, to touch more effectually by gentleness, than one overawes by boldness.

"Apt to teach"; that is, those who are willing to be taught. For "a man that is an heretic," he says, "after the first and second admonition reject." (Tit. iii. 10.) "Patient." He has well added this, for it is a quality which a teacher above all things ought to possess. All things are vain without it. And if fishermen do not despair, though often they cast their nets for a whole day without catching anything, much more should not we. For see what is the result. From constant teaching, it often hap-

pens that the plow of the word, descending to the depth of the soul, roots out the evil passion that troubled it. For he that hears often will at length be affected. A man cannot go on hearing continually without some effect being produced. Sometimes therefore, when he was on the point of being persuaded, he is lost by our becoming weary. For the same thing occurs, as if an unskillful husbandman should in the first year dig about the vine he had planted, and seeking to reap some fruit in the second year, and again in the third, and gathering nothing, should after three years despair, and in the fourth year, when he was about to receive the recompense of his labors, abandon his vine. And having said, "Patient," he is not satisfied, but goes on to say,

Ver. 25. "In meekness instructing those that oppose themselves."

For he that teaches must be especially careful to do it with meekness. For a soul that wishes to learn cannot gain any useful instruction from harshness and contention. For when it would apply, being thus thrown into perplexity, it will learn nothing. He who would gain any useful knowledge ought above all things to be well disposed towards his teacher, and if this be not previously attained, nothing that is requisite or useful can be accomplished. And no one can be well disposed towards him who is violent and overbearing. How is it then that he says, "A man that is an heretic, after the first and second admonition, reject"? He speaks there of one incorrigible, of one whom he knows to be diseased beyond the possibility of cure.

"If God peradventure will give them repentance to the acknowledging of the truth."

Ver. 26. "And that they may recover themselves out of the snare of the devil."

What he says amounts to this. Perhaps there will be a reformation. Perhaps! for it is uncertain. So that we ought to withdraw only from those, of whom we can show plainly, and concerning whom we are fully persuaded, that whatever be done, they will not be reformed. "In meekness," he says. In this temper, you see, we ought to address ourselves to those who are willing to learn, and never cease from conversing with them till we have come to the demonstration.[1]

"Who are taken captive by him at his will."

It is truly said, "Who are taken captive,"[2] for meanwhile they float in error. Observe here how he teaches to be humble-minded. He has not said, if peradventure you should be able, but, "if peradventure God should grant them a recovery"; if anything be done, therefore, all

---

[1] That is, we ought not to be provoked by their slowness of apprehension to break off.
[2] ἐζωγρημένοι, "taken alive," applied to fish enclosed in a net.

is of the Lord. Thou plantest, thou waterest, but He soweth and maketh it produce fruit. Let us not therefore be so affected, as if we ourselves wrought the persuasion, even if we should persuade any one. "Taken captive by him," he says, "to His will."[1] This no one will say relates to doctrine, but to life. For "His will" is that we live rightly. But some are in the snare of the devil by reason of their life, we ought not therefore to be weary even with respect to these.

"If peradventure," he says, "they may recover, that are taken captive, unto His will." Now "If peradventure," implies much longsuffering. For not to do the will of God is a snare of the devil.

For as a sparrow, though it be not wholly enclosed, but only caught by the foot, is still under the power of him who set the snare; so though we be not wholly subverted, both in faith and life, but in life only, we are under the power of the devil. For, "Not every one that saith unto me, Lord, Lord, shall enter into the kingdom of heaven"; and again, "I know you not; depart from me, ye that work iniquity." (Matt. vii. 21–23.) You see there is no advantage from our faith, when our Lord knows us not: and to the virgins he says the same, "I know you not." (Matt. xxv. 12.) What then is the benefit of virginity, or of many labors, when the Lord knows us not? And in many places we find men not blamed for their faith, but punished for their evil life only; as elsewhere, not reproved for evil lives, but perishing for their pravity of doctrine. For these things hold together.[2] You see that when we do not the will of God, we are under the snare of the devil. And often not only from a bad life, but from one defect, we enter into Hell, where there are not good qualities to counterbalance it, since the virgins were not accused of fornication or adultery, nor of envy or ill-will, nor of drunkenness, nor of unsound faith, but of a failure of oil, that is, they failed in almsgiving, for that is the oil meant.[3] And those who were pronounced accursed in the words, "Depart from me, ye cursed, into everlasting fire," were not accused of any such crimes, but because they had not fed Christ.

Moral. Seest thou that a failure in almsgiving is enough to cast a man into hell fire? For where will he avail who does not give alms? Dost thou fast every day? So also did those virgins, but it availed them nothing. Dost thou pray? What of that? prayer without almsgiving is unfruitful, without that all things are unclean and unprofitable. The better part of virtue is destroyed. "He that loveth not his brother," it is said, "knoweth not God." (1 John iv. 8.) And how dost thou love him, when thou dost not even impart to him of these poor worthless things? Tell me, therefore, dost thou observe chastity? On what account? From fear of punishment? By no means. It is of a natural endowment that thou observest it, since if thou wast chaste from fear of punishment, and didst violence to nature in submitting to so severe a rule, much more oughtest thou to do alms. For to govern the desire of wealth, and of bodily pleasures, is not the same thing. The latter is much more difficult to restrain. And wherefore? Because the pleasure is natural, and the desire of it is innate and of natural growth in the body. It is not so with riches. Herein we are able to resemble God, in showing mercy and pity. When therefore we have not this quality, we are devoid of all good. He has not said, "ye shall be like unto your Father, if ye fast," nor "if ye be virgins," nor "if ye pray," hath He said, "ye shall be like unto your Father," for none of these things can be applied to God, nor are they His acts. But what? "Be ye merciful, as your Father in Heaven is merciful." (Luke vi. 36.) This is the work of God. If therefore thou hast not this, what hast thou? He says: "I will have mercy, and not sacrifice." (Hosea vi. 6.) God made Heaven, and earth, and sea. Great works these, and worthy of His wisdom! But by none of these has He so powerfully attracted human nature to Himself, as by mercy and the love of mankind. For that indeed is the work of power and wisdom and goodness. But it is far more so that He became a servant. Do we not for this more especially admire Him? are we not for this still more amazed at Him? Nothing attracts God to us so much as mercy. And the prophets from beginning to end discourse upon this subject. But I speak not of mercy that is accompanied with covetousness. That is not mercy. For it is not the root of the thorn but of the olive that produces the oil[4]; so it is not the root of covetousness, of iniquity, or of rapine, that produces mercy. Do not put a slander on almsgiving. Do not cause it to be evil spoken of by all. If thou committest robbery for this, that thou mayest give alms, nothing is more wicked than thy almsgiving. For when it is produced by rapine, it is not almsgiving, it is inhumanity, it is cruelty, it is an insult to God. If Cain so offended, by offering inferior gifts of his own, shall he not

---

[1] Gr. "To His will." As αὐτοῦ and ἐκείνου must refer to two different persons, the meaning probably is, "that they who are taken captive by the devil may be recovered to the will of God." And so he takes it.

[2] Sav. ἀλλήλων ἔχεται. Ben. ἔρχεται, which would be hardly Greek even with a preposition.

[3] So he takes it on Matt. xxv. Hom. lxxviii. al. lxxix. See also on Phil. i. 30, Hom. iv. 15, and notes, and on Rom. xi. 6, and on Rom. xiv. 13. St. Jerome and St. Aug. take the oil more generally of good works, with allusion to Matt. v. 16.

[4] He plays, as elsewhere, on the words ἔλεον and ἔλαιον.

offend, who offers the goods of another? An offering is nothing else but a sacrifice, a purification, not a pollution. And thou who darest not to pray with unclean hands, dost thou offer the dirt and filth of robbery, and think thou doest nothing wrong? Thou sufferest not thy hands to be full of dirt and filth, but having first cleansed these, thou offerest. Yet that filth is no charge against thee, while the other deserves reproach and blame. Let it not therefore be our consideration, how we may offer prayers and oblations with clean hands, but how the things offered may be pure. If one, after having washed a vessel clean, should fill it with unclean gifts, would it not be ridiculous mockery? Let the hands be clean; and they will be so, if we wash them not with water only, but first with righteousness. This is the purifier of the hands. But if they be full of unrighteousness, though they be washed a thousand times, it avails nothing. "Wash you, make you clean" (Isa. i. 16), He says, but does He add, "Go to the baths, the lakes, the rivers"? No; but what? "Put away the evil of your doings from your souls." This is to be clean.[1] This it is to be cleansed from defilement. This is real purity. The other is of little use; but this bestows upon us confidence towards God. The one may be obtained by adulterers, thieves, murderers, by worthless, and dissolute, and effeminate persons, and especially the latter. For they are ever careful of the cleanliness of their bodies, and scented with perfumes, cleansing their sepulcher.[2] For their body[3] is but a sepulcher, since the soul is dead within it. This cleanness therefore may be theirs,[4] but not that which is inward.

To wash the body is no great matter. That is a Jewish purification, senseless[5] and unprofitable, where purity within is wanting. Suppose one to labor under a putrefying sore, or consuming ulcer; let him wash his body ever so much, it is of no advantage. And if the putrefaction of the body receives no benefit from cleansing and disguising the outward appearance; when the soul is infected with rottenness, what is gained by the purity of the body? Nothing! Our prayers ought to be pure, and pure they cannot be, if they are sent forth from a corrupt soul, and nothing so corrupts the soul as avarice and rapine. But there are some who after committing numberless sins during the day, wash themselves in the evening and enter the churches, holding up their hands with much confidence, as if by the washing of the bath they had put off all their guilt. And if this were the case, it would be a vast advantage to use the bath daily! I would not myself cease to frequent the baths,[6] if it made us pure, and cleansed us from our sins! But these things are trifling and ridiculous, the toys of children. It is not the filth of the body, but the impurity of the soul, to which God is averse. For He says, "Blessed are the pure"—does He say in body? No—"in heart: for they shall see God." (Matt. v. 8.) And what says the Prophet: "Create in me a clean heart, O God." (Ps. li. 10.) And again, "Wash my heart from wickedness." (Jer. iv. 14.)

It is of great use to be in the habit of doing good actions. See how trifling and unprofitable these washings are. But when the soul is prepossessed by a habit, it does not depart from it, nor does it venture to draw nigh in prayer, till it has fulfilled these ceremonies. For instance, we have brought ourselves to a habit of washing and praying, and without washing we do not think it right to pray. And we do not willingly pray with unwashed hands, as if we should offend God, and violate our conscience. Now if this trifling custom has so great power over us, and is observed every day; if we had brought ourselves to a habit of almsgiving, and had determined so constantly to observe it, as never to enter a house of prayer with empty hands, the point would be gained. For great is the power of habit both in good things and in evil, and when this carries us on, there will be little trouble. Many are in the habit of crossing[7] themselves continually, and they need no one to remind them of it, but often when the mind is wandering after other things, the hand is involuntarily drawn by custom, as by some living teacher, to make the sign. Some have brought themselves into a habit of not swearing at all, and therefore neither willingly nor unwillingly do they ever do it. Let us then bring ourselves into such a habit of almsgiving.

What labors were it worth to us to discover such a remedy. For say, were there not the relief of almsgiving, while we still by our numberless sins rendered ourselves liable to Divine vengeance, should we not have lamented sadly? Should we not have said, O that it were possible by our wealth to wash away our sins, and we would have parted with it all! O that by our riches we could put away the wrath of God, then we would not spare our substance? For if we do this in sickness, and at the point of death we say, "If it were possible to buy off death, such an one would give all his possessions"; much more in this matter. For see how great is the love of God for man. He has granted us power to buy off not temporal but

---

[1] B., though usually here far inferior to the printed text, seems best in these words. Sav. has, "That is, be clean: this it is that cleanses," &c.
[2] σῆμα.
[3] σῶμα.
[4] B. reads μετεῖναι, for μετιέναι.
[5] Sav. "useless."

[6] This was thought too luxurious for persons of devout life. See Euseb. ii. 23, and St. Clem. Al. Pædag. iii. 9, who recommends providing for cleanliness by other means.
[7] σφραγίζειν.

eternal death. Do not purchase, He says, this short life, but that life that is everlasting. It is that I sell thee, not the other: I do not mock thee. Didst thou gain the present life, thou hadst gained nothing. I know the worth of that which I offer thee. The bargainers and traffickers in worldly goods do not act thus. They, when they can[1] impose on whom they will, give a little to receive a great deal. It is not so with God. He gives the greater by far for the less.

Tell me, if you were to go to a merchant, and he were to set before you two stones, one of little worth,[2] and the other very precious, and sure to fetch a large amount of wealth; if he allowed you for the price of the cheap one to carry off the more costly, should you complain of him? No! You would rather admire his liberality. So now, two lives are set before us, the one temporal, the other eternal. These God offers us for sale, but He would sell us the latter rather than the former. Why do we complain, like silly children, that we receive the more precious?[3] Is it possible then to purchase life for money? Yes, when what we bestow is our own, and not the property of another; when we do not practice an imposture. But, you say, henceforth the goods are mine. They are not thine after rapine. They are still thy neighbor's, though thou wert a thousand times the master of them. For if thou shouldest receive a deposit, it would not be thine own even for the short season that the depositor was traveling, though it might be laid up with thee. If therefore that is not ours, which we received with the consent and thanks of those who deposited it, even for the short period that we retain it, much less is that ours, which we plundered against the will of its owner. He is the master of it, however long thou mayest withhold it. But Virtue is[4] really our own; as for money, even our own is not strictly ours, much less that of others. To-day it is ours, to-morrow it belongs to another. What is of virtue is our own possession. This does not suffer loss, like other things, but is entirely possessed by all who have it. This therefore let us acquire, and let us despise riches, that we may be able to attain those real goods, of which God grant that we may be thought worthy to partake, through the grace and loving-kindness, &c.

HOMILY VII.

2 TIMOTHY iii. 1–7.

"This know also, that in the last days perilous times shall come. For men shall be lovers of their own selves, covetous, boasters, proud, blasphemers, disobedient to parents, unthankful, unholy, Without natural affection, truce-breakers, false accusers, incontinent, fierce, despisers of those that are good, Traitors, heady, high-minded, lovers of pleasure more than lovers of God; Having a form of godliness, but denying the power thereof; from such turn away. For of this sort are they, which creep into houses, and lead captive silly women laden with sins, led away with divers lusts and pleasures, Ever learning, and never able to come to the knowledge of the truth."

HE had said in the former Epistle, that "the Spirit speaketh expressly, that in the latter times some shall depart from the faith" (1 Tim. iv. 1, 2); and elsewhere in this Epistle he foretells that something of this kind will afterwards happen; and here again he does the same thing: "This know, that in the last days perilous times shall come." And this he pronounces not only from the future, but from the past; "As Jannes and Jambres withstood Moses." And again from reasoning; "In a great house there are not only vessels of gold and of silver." But why does he do this? In order that Timothy may not be troubled, nor any one of us, when there are evil men. If there were such in the time of Moses, and will be hereafter, it is no wonder that there are such in our times.

"In the last days perilous times shall come," he says, that is, exceeding bad times. How shall times be perilous?[5] He says it not blaming the days, nor the times, but the men of those times. For thus it is customary with us to speak of good times or evil times, from the events that happen in them, caused by men. Immediately he sets down the root and fountain, whence these and all other evils spring, that is, overweeningness. He that is seized with this passion is careless even of his own interests. For when a man overlooks the concerns of his neighbor, and is careless of them, how should he regard his own? For as he that looks to his neighbor's affairs will in them order his own

---

1 B. ἐξῇ for ἐξῆν.   2 B. counterfeit.
3 B. reads ὄψει for ὅτι. "We take the value by sight."
4 B. "those other things are."
5 B. adds, "that is," &c.

to advantage, so he that looks down upon his neighbor's concerns will neglect his own. For if we are members one of another, the welfare of our neighbor is not his concern only, but that of the whole body, and the injury of our neighbor is not confined to him, but distracts with pains all else as well.[1] If we are a building, whatever part is weakened, it affects the whole, whilst that which is solid gives strength and support to the rest. So also in the Church, if thou hast slighted thy neighbor, thou has injured thyself. How? In that one of thy own members hath suffered no small hurt. And if he, who does not impart of his possessions, goes into Hell, much more will he be condemned, who sees a neighbor suffering severer evils, and does not stretch out his hand, since in this case the loss is more grievous.

"For men shall be lovers of their own selves."

He that loves himself may be said not to love himself, but he that loves his brother, loves himself in the truest sense. From self-love springs covetousness. For the wretched niggardly temper of self-love contracts that love which should be widely extended, and diffused on every side. "Covetous." From covetousness springs boastfulness, from boastfulness pride, from pride blasphemy, from blasphemy defiance and disobedience. For he who exalts himself against men, will easily do it against God. Thus sins are produced. Often they ascend from below. He that is pious towards men, is still more pious towards God. He who is meek to his fellow-servants, is more meek to his Master. He that despises his fellow-servants, will end with despising God Himself. Moral. Let us not then despise one another, for that is an evil training which teaches us to despise God. And indeed to despise one another is in effect to despise God, Who commanded us to show all regard to one another. And this may be otherwise manifested by an example. Cain despised his brother, and so, immediately after, he despised God. How despised Him? Mark his insolent answer to God; "Am I my brother's keeper?" (Gen. iv. 9.) Again, Esau despised his brother, and he too despised God. Wherefore God said, "Jacob have I loved, but Esau have I hated." (Rom. ix. 13; Mal. i. 2, 3.) Hence Paul says, "Lest there be any fornicator or profane person as Esau." (Heb. xii. 16.) The brethren of Joseph despised him, and they also despised God. The Israelites despised Moses, and they also despised God. So too the sons of Eli despised the people, and they too despised God. Would you see it also from the contrary? Abraham, who was tender of his brother's son, was obedient to God, as is manifest in his conduct with respect to his son Isaac, and in all his other virtues. Again, Abel was meek to his brother, and he also was pious towards God. Let us not therefore despise one another, lest we learn also to despise God. Let us honor one another, that we may learn also to honor God. He that is insolent with respect to men, will also be insolent with respect to God. But when covetousness and selfishness and insolence meet together, what is wanting to complete destruction? Everything is corrupted, and a foul flood of sins bursts in. "Unthankful," he says. For how can the covetous man be thankful? To whom will he feel gratitude? To no one. He considers all men his enemies, and desires the goods of all. Though you spend your whole substance upon him, he will feel no gratitude. He is angry that you have not more, that you might bestow it upon him. And if you made him master of the whole world, he would still be unthankful, and think that he had received nothing. This desire is insatiable. It is the craving of disease; and such is the nature of the cravings of disease.

He who has a fever can never be satisfied, but with constant desire of drinking, is never filled, but suffers a continual thirst; so he who is mad after wealth never knows the fulfillment of his desire; whatever is bestowed upon him, he is still unsatisfied, and will therefore never be thankful. For he will feel no gratitude to him, who does not give him as much as he wishes, and this no one can ever do. And as there is no limit to his wishes, he will feel no gratitude. Thus no one is so unthankful as the covetous, so insensible as the lover of money. He is the enemy of all the world. He is indignant that there are men. He would have all one vast desert, that he might have the property of all. And many wild imaginations does he form. "O that there were an earthquake," he says, "in the city, that all the rest being swallowed up, I might be left alone, to have, if possible, the possessions of all! O that a pestilence would come and destroy everything but gold! O that there might be a submersion, or an eruption of the sea!" Such are his imaginations. He prays for nothing good, but for earthquakes, and thunderbolts, for wars, and plagues, and the like. Well, tell me now, thou wretched man, more servile than any slave, if all things were gold, wouldest thou not be destroyed by thy gold,[2] and perish with hunger? If the world were swallowed up by an earthquake, thou also wouldest perish by thy fatal desire. For if there were no other men than thyself, the necessaries of life would fail thee. For suppose that the other inhabitants of the earth were destroyed at once, and that their gold and silver came of its

---

[1] ἅπαντα λοιπόν, qu.? ἅπαν τὸ λοιπόν, "all the rest of the body."

[2] Al. "be parted from thy gold."

own accord to thee. (For such men fancy to themselves absurdities, and impossibilities.) But if their gold and silver, their vests of silk and cloth of gold, came into thy hands, what would it profit thee? Death would only the more certainly overtake thee, when there were none to prepare bread or till the earth for thee; wild beasts would prowl around, and the devil agitate thy soul with fear. Many devils indeed now possess it, but then they would lead thee to desperation, and plunge thee at once into destruction. But you say, "I would wish there should be tilling of the land and men to prepare food." Then they would consume somewhat. "But I would not have them consume anything." So insatiable is this desire! For what can be more ridiculous than this? Seest thou the impossibility of the thing? He wishes to have many to minister to him, yet he grudges them their share of food, because it diminishes his substance! What then? Wouldest thou then have men of stone? This is all a mockery; and waves, and tempest, and huge billows, and violent agitation, and storm, overwhelm the soul. It is ever hungry, ever thirsty. Shall we not pity and mourn for him? Of bodily diseases this is thought a most painful one, and it is called by physicians bulimy,[1] when a man being filled, is yet always hungry. And is not the same disorder in the soul more lamentable? For avarice is the morbid hunger of the soul, which is always filling, never satisfied, but still craving. If it were necessary to drink hellebore, or submit to anything a thousand times worse, would it not be worth our while to undertake it readily, that we might be delivered from this passion? There is no abundance of riches that can fill the belly of greediness. And shall we not be ashamed, that men can be thus transported with the love of money, whilst we show not any proportion of such earnestness in love to God, and honor Him not as bullion is honored? For money men will undergo watchings, and journeyings and continual perils, and hatred, and hostility, and, in short, everything. But we do not venture to utter a mere word for God, nor incur an enmity, but if we are required to assist any of those who are persecuted, we abandon the injured person, withdrawing ourselves from the hatred of the powerful, and the danger it involves. And though God has given us power that we might succor him, yet we suffer him to perish, from our unwillingness to incur men's hatred and displeasure. And this many profess to justify, saying, "Be loved for nothing, but be not hated for nothing." But is this to be hated for nothing? Or what is better than such hatred? For to be hated on account of God is better than to be loved on His account: for

when we are loved for God's sake, we are debtors for the honor, but when we are hated for His sake, He is our debtor to reward us. The lovers of wealth know no limit to their love, be it never so great; but we, if we have done ever so little, think that we have fulfilled everything. We love not God as much, no, not by many times over so much, as they love gold. Their inordinate rage for gold is a heavy accusation against them. It is our condemnation that we are not so beside ourselves for God; that we do not bestow upon the Lord of all as much love as they bestow upon mere earth, for gold from the mine is no better.

Let us then behold their madness, and be ashamed of ourselves. For what though we are not inflamed with the love of gold, while we are not earnest in our prayers to God? For in their case men despise wife, children, substance, and their own safety, and that when they are not certain that they shall increase their substance. For often, in the very midst of their hopes, they lose at once their life and their labor. But we, though we know that, if we love Him as we ought to love Him, we shall obtain our desire, yet love Him not, but are altogether cold in our love both to our neighbor and to God; cold in our love to God, because cold in our love to our neighbor. For it is not, indeed it is not possible that a man, who is a stranger to the feeling of love, should have any generosity or manly spirit, since the foundation of all that is good is no other than love. "On this," it is said, "hang all the law and the prophets." (Matt. xxii. 40.) For as fire set to a forest is wont to clear away everything, so the fire of love, wherever it is received, consumes and makes way through everything that is hurtful to the divine harvest, and renders the soil pure and fit for the reception of the seed. Where there is love, all evils are removed. There is no love of money, the root of evil, there is no self-love[2]: there is no boasting; for why should one boast over his friend? Nothing makes a man so humble as love. We perform the offices of servants to our friends, and are not ashamed; we are even thankful for the opportunity of serving them. We spare not our property, and often not our persons; for dangers too are encountered at times for him that is loved. No envy, no calumny is there, where there is genuine love. We not only do not slander our friends, but we stop the mouth of slanderers. All is gentleness and mildness. Not a trace of strife and contention appears. Everything breathes peace. For "Love," it is said, "is this fulfilling of the law." (Rom. xiii. 10.) There is nothing offensive with it. How so?

---

[1] βουλιμία, from βοῦς and λίμος.

[2] Gr. "love of money," an evident mistake, as Downes has noted.

Because where love exists, all the sins of covetousness, rapine, envy, slander, arrogance, perjury, and falsehood are done away. For men perjure themselves, in order to rob, but no one would rob him whom he loved, but would rather give him his own possessions. For we are more obliged than if we received from him. Ye know this, all you that have friends, friends, I mean, in reality, not in name only, but whoever loves as men ought to love, whoever is really linked to another. And let those who are ignorant of it learn from those who know.

I will now cite you from the Scriptures a wonderful instance of friendship. Jonathan, the son of Saul, loved David, and his soul was so knit to him, that David in mourning over him says, "Thy love to me was wonderful, passing the love of women. Thou wast wounded unto death." (2 Sam. i. 25, 26.) What then? did he envy David? Not at all, though he had great reason. How? Because, by the events he perceived that the kingdom would pass from himself to him, yet he felt nothing of the kind. He did not say, "This is he that is depriving me of my paternal kingdom," but he favored his obtaining the sovereignty; and he spared not his father for the sake of his friend. Yet let not any one think him a parricide, for he did not injure his father, but restrained his unjust attempts. He rather spared than injured him. He did not permit him to proceed to an unjust murder. He was many times willing even to die for his friend, and far from accusing him, he restrained even his father's accusation. Instead of envying, he joined in obtaining the kingdom for him. Why do I speak of wealth? He even sacrificed his own life for him. For the sake of his friend, he did not even stand in awe of his father, since his father entertained unjust designs, but his conscience was free from all such. Thus justice was conjoined with friendship.

Such then was Jonathan. Let us now consider David. He had no opportunity of returning the recompense, for his benefactor was taken away before the reign of David, and slain before he whom he had served came to his kingdom. What then? As far as it was allowed him and left in his power, let us see how that righteous man manifested his friendship. "Very pleasant," he says, "hast thou been to me, Jonathan; thou wast wounded unto death." (2 Sam. i. 25, Gr.) Is this all? This indeed was no slight tribute, but he also frequently rescued from danger his son and his grandson, in remembrance of the kindness of the father, and he continued to support and protect his children, as he would have done those of his own son. Such friendship I would wish all to entertain both towards the living and the dead.

Let women listen to this (for it is on their account especially that I refer to the departed) who enter into a second marriage, and defile the bed of their deceased husband, though they have loved him.[1] Not that I forbid a second marriage, or pronounce it a proof of wantonness, for Paul does not allow me, stopping my mouth by saying to women, "If she marry she hath not sinned." (1 Cor. vii. 28 and 40.) Yet let us attend to what follows, "But she is happier if she so abide." This state is much better than the other. Wherefore? for many reasons. For if it is better not to marry at all than to marry, much more in this case. "But some, you say, could not endure widowhood, and have fallen into many misfortunes." Yes; because they know not what widowhood is. For it is not widowhood to be exempt from a second marriage, as neither is it virginity to be altogether unmarried. For as "that which is comely," and "that ye may attend upon the Lord without distraction," is the mark of the one state, so it is the mark of the other to be desolate, to "continue in supplications and prayers," to renounce luxury and pleasure. For "she that liveth in pleasure is dead whilst she liveth." (1 Tim. v. 6.) If remaining a widow, thou wouldest have the same pomp, the same show, the same attire, as thou hadst while thy husband was living, it were better for thee to marry. For it is not the union that is objectionable, but the multitude of cares that attend it. But that which is not wrong, thou dost not: but that which is not indifferent, which is liable to blame, in that thou involvest thyself. On this account "some have turned aside after Satan," because they have not been able to live properly as widows.

Wouldest thou know what a widow is, and what a widow's dignity, hear Paul's account of it. "If she have brought up children, if she have lodged strangers, if she have washed the Saints' feet, if she have relieved the afflicted, if she have diligently followed every good work." (1 Tim. v. 10.) But when after the death of thy husband, thou art arrayed in the same pomp of wealth, no wonder if thou canst not support widowhood. Transfer this wealth, therefore, to heaven, and thou wilt find the burden of widowhood tolerable. But, thou sayest, what if I have children to succeed to their father's inheritance? Instruct them also to despise riches. Transfer thy own possessions, reserving for them just a sufficiency. Teach them too to be superior to riches. But what if besides my silver and gold, I am surrounded by a crowd of slaves, oppressed by a multitude of affairs, how shall I be equal to the care of all these things, when deprived of the support of my husband? This is but an excuse, a pretense, as appears from many causes.

---

[1] Sav. mar. "having ceased to love him."

For if thou dost not deserve wealth, nor seek to increase thy present possessions, thy burden will be light. To get riches is much more laborious than to take care of them. If therefore thou cuttest off this one thing, accumulating, and suppliest the needy out of thy substance, God will hold over thee His protecting hand. And if thou sayest this from a real desire to preserve the inheritance of thy fatherless children, and art not, under this pretense, possessed with covetousness; He who searches the heart knows how to secure their riches, even He who commanded thee to bring up children.

For it is not possible, indeed it is not, that a house established by almsgiving should suffer any calamity. If it should be unfortunate for a time, in the end it will prosper. This will be more than spear and shield to all the household. Hear what the devil says concerning Job. "Hast not thou made an hedge about him and about his house, and about all that he hath on every side?" (Job i. 10.) Wherefore? Hear Job himself saying, "I was eyes to the blind, and feet was I to the lame. I was a father to the orphans." (Job xxix. 15.) As he who does not turn aside from the calamities of others, will not suffer even in his own misfortunes, because he has learnt to sympathize; so he who will not bear the griefs of sympathy, will learn all sorrow in his own person.[1] And, as in the case of a bodily disease, if, when the foot is mortified, the hand does not sympathize by cleansing the wound, washing away the discharge, and applying a plaster, it will suffer the like disease of its own; so she who will not minister to another when she is not herself afflicted, will have to bear sufferings of her own. For the evil spreading from the other part will reach to this also, and the question will not be of ministering to the other, but of its own cure and relief. So it is here also. He that will not relieve others, will be a sufferer himself. "Thou hast hedged him in," saith Satan, "within and without," and I dare not attack him! But he suffered afflictions, you say. True. But those afflictions were the occasion of great good. His substance was doubled, his reward increased, his righteousness enlarged, his crown was splendid, his prize glorious. Both his spiritual and temporal blessings were augmented. He lost his children, but he received, not these restored, but others in their room, and those too he had safe for the Resurrection. Had they been restored, the number would have been diminished, but now having given others in their stead, He will present them also at the Resurrection. All these things happened to him, because of his openhandedness in almsgiving. Let us then do likewise, that we may obtain the same rewards by the grace and lovingkindness of our Lord Jesus Christ. Amen.

HOMILY VIII.

2 TIMOTHY iii. 1–4.

"This know also, that in the last days perilous times shall come. For men shall be lovers of their own selves, covetous, boasters, proud, blasphemers, disobedient to parents, unthankful, unholy, without natural affection, truce-breakers, false accusers, incontinent, fierce, despisers of those that are good, Traitors, heady, high-minded, lovers of pleasures more than lovers of God."

IF any now takes offense at the existence of heretics, let him remember that it was so from the beginning, the devil always setting up error by the side of truth. God from the beginning promised good, the devil came too with a promise. God planted Paradise, the devil deceived, saying, "Ye shall be as gods." (Gen. iii. 5.) For as he could show nothing in actions, he made the more promises in words. Such is the character of deceivers. After this were Cain and Abel, then the sons of Seth and the daughters of men; afterwards Ham and Japhet, Abraham and Pharaoh, Jacob and Esau; and so it is even to the end, Moses and the magicians, the Prophets and the false prophets, the Apostles and the false apostles, Christ and Antichrist. Thus it was then, both before and at that time. Then there was Theudas, then Simon, then were the Apostles, then too this party of Hermogenes and Philetus. In short, there was no time when falsehood was not set up in opposition to truth. Let us not therefore be distressed. That it would be so, was foretold from the beginning. Therefore he says, "Know that in the last days perilous times shall come. For men shall be lovers of their own selves, covetous, boasters, proud, blasphemers, disobedient to parents, unthankful, unholy, without natural affection." The unthankful then is unholy, and this is natural, for what will he be to others, who is not grateful to his benefactor? The unthankful man is a truce-breaker, he is without natural affection.

---

[1] "The tender for another's pain,
Th' unfeeling for his own." — Gray.

" False accusers," that is, slanderers. For those who are conscious that they have no good in themselves, whilst they commit many sins and offenses, find consolation in defaming the characters of others.

" Incontinent," with respect both to their tongue and their appetite, and everything else.

" Fierce," hence their inhumanity and cruelty, when any one is covetous, selfish, ungrateful, licentious.

" Despisers of those that are good, traitors, heady." " Traitors," betrayers of friendship ; " heady," having no steadiness ; " high-minded," filled with arrogance. " Lovers of pleasures more than lovers of God."

Ver. 5. " Having a form of godliness, but denying the power thereof."

In the Epistle to the Romans, he says somewhat on this wise, " Having the form of knowledge and of the truth in the law " (Rom. ii. 20), where he speaks in commendation of it : but here he speaks of this sin as an evil beyond all other defects. And why is this ? Because he does not use the words in the same signification. For an image is often taken to signify a likeness ; but sometimes a thing without life, and worthless. Thus he says himself in his Epistle to the Corinthians, " A man ought not to cover his head, forasmuch as he is the image and glory of God." (1 Cor. xi. 7.) But the Prophet says, " Man walketh in an image." (Ps. xxxix. 9, Gr.) And the Scripture sometimes takes a lion to represent royalty, as, " He couched as a lion, and as a lion's whelp, who shall raise him up ? " (Gen. xlix. 9, Gr.) And sometimes to signify rapacity, as, " a ravening and a roaring lion." (Ps. xxii. 13.) And we ourselves do the same. For as things are compounded and varied in themselves, they are fitly adduced for various images and examples. As when we would express our admiration of a beautiful woman, we say, she is like a picture ; and when we admire a painting, we say that it speaks, that it breathes. But we do not mean to express the same thing, but in one case to mark likeness, in the other beauty. So here with respect to form, in the one passage, it means a model, or representation, a doctrine, or pattern of godliness ; in the other, something that is lifeless, a mere appearance, show, and hypocrisy. Faith therefore, without works, is fitly called a mere form without the power. For as a fair and florid body, when it has no strength, is like a painted figure, so is a right faith apart from works. For let us suppose any one to be " covetous, a traitor, heady," and yet to believe aright ; of what advantage is it, if he wants all the qualities becoming a Christian, if he does not the works that characterize godliness, but outdoes the Greeks in impiety, when he is a mischief to those

with whom he associates, causes God to be blasphemed, and the doctrine to be slandered by his evil deeds?

" From such turn away," he says. But how is this, if men are to be so "in the latter times " ? There were probably then such, in some degree at least, though not to the same excess. But, in truth, through him he warns all to turn away from such characters.

Ver. 6. " For of this sort are they which creep into houses, and lead captive silly women laden with sins, led away with divers lusts."

Ver. 7. " Ever learning, and never able to come to the knowledge of the truth."

Do you see them employing the artifice of that old deceiver, the weapons which the devil used against Adam? " Entering into houses," he says. Observe how he shows their impudence by this expression,[1] their dishonorable ways, their deceitfulness. " Leading captive silly women," so that he who is easy to be deceived is a " silly woman," and nothing like a man : for to be deceived is the part of silly women. " Laden with sins." See whence arises their persuasion, from their sins, from their being conscious to themselves of nothing good ! And with great propriety has he said " laden."[2] For this expression marks the multitude of their sins, and their state of disorder and confusion ; " led away with divers lusts." He does not accuse nature, for it is not women simply, but such women as these, that he blames. And why " divers lusts " ? by that are implied their various faults, their luxury, their disorderly conduct, their wantonness. " Divers lusts," he says, that is, of glory, of wealth, of pleasure, of self-will, of honor : and perchance other vile desires are implied.

" Ever learning, and never able to come to the knowledge of the truth." He does not say thus to excuse, but to threaten them severely ; for their understanding was callous, because they had weighed themselves down with lusts and sins.

Ver. 8. " Now as Jannes and Jambres withstood Moses, so do these also resist the truth."

Who are these?[3] The magicians in the time of Moses. But how is it their names are nowhere else introduced? Either they were handed down by tradition, or it is probable that Paul knew them by inspiration.

" Men of corrupt minds," he says, " reprobate concerning the faith."

Ver. 9. " But they shall proceed no further ; for their folly shall be manifested unto all men, as theirs also was."

" They shall proceed no further " ; how then

---

[1] Gr. " by saying *entering*, the word implies *entering covertly*."
[2] Lit. " heaped."
[3] B. has this punctuation.

does he say elsewhere, "They will increase unto more ungodliness"? (2 Tim. ii. 16.) He there means, that beginning to innovate and to deceive, they will not pause in their error, but will always invent new deceits and corrupt doctrines, for error is never stationary. But here he says, that they shall not be able to deceive, nor carry men away with them, for however at first they may seem to impose upon them, they will soon and easily be detected. For that he is speaking to this effect appears from what follows. "For their folly shall be manifest unto all." Whence? Every way — "as theirs also was." For if errors flourish at first, they do not continue to the end, for so it is with things that are not fair by nature, but fair in appearance; they flourish for a time, and then are detected, and come to nought. But not such are our doctrines, and of these thou art a witness, for in our doctrines there is no deceit, for who would choose to die for a deceit?

Ver. 10. "But thou hast fully known[1] my doctrine." Wherefore be strong; for thou wert not merely present, but didst follow closely. Here he seems to imply that the period had been long, in that he says, "Thou hast followed up my doctrine"; this refers to his discourse. "Manner of life"; this to his conduct. "Purpose"; this to his zeal, and the firmness of his soul. I did not say these things, he says, and not do them; nor was I a philosopher in words only. "Faith, longsuffering." He means, how none of these things troubled me. "Charity," which those men had not; "patience," nor yet this. Towards the heretics, he means, I show much longsuffering; "patience," that under persecution.

Ver. 11. "Persecutions, afflictions."

There are two things that disquiet a teacher, the number of heretics, and men's wanting fortitude to endure sufferings. And yet he has[2] said much about these, that such always have been, and always will be, and no age will be free from them, and that they will not be able to injure us, and that in the world there are vessels of gold and of silver. You see how he proceeds to discourse about his afflictions, "which came upon me at Antioch, at Iconium, at Lystra."

Why has he selected these instances out of many? Because the rest was known to Timothy, and these perhaps were new events, and he does not mention the former ones, for he is not enumerating them particularly, for he is not actuated by ambition or vainglory, but he recounts them for the consolation of his disciple, not from ostentation. And here he speaks of Antioch in Pisidia, and Lystra, whence Timothy himself

---

[1] Gr. "followed up."
[2] al. "I have."

was. "What persecutions I endured." There was twofold matter of consolation, that I displayed a generous zeal, and that I was not forsaken. It cannot be said, that God abandoned me, but He rendered my crown more radiant. "What persecutions I endured: but out of them all the Lord delivered me."

Ver. 12. "Yea, and all those that will live godly in Christ Jesus shall suffer persecution."

But why, he says, should I speak only of myself? Each one that will live godly will be persecuted. Here he calls afflictions and sorrows, "persecutions," for it is not possible that a man pursuing the course of virtue should not be exposed to grief, tribulation, and temptations. For how can he escape it who is treading in the strait and narrow way, and who has heard, that "in the world ye shall have tribulation"? (John xvi. 33.) If Job in his time said, "The life of man upon earth is a state of trial" (Job vii. 1, Gr.); how much more was it so in those days?

Ver. 13. "But evil men and seducers shall wax worse and worse, deceiving, and being deceived."

Let none of these things, he says, disturb thee, if they are in prosperity, and thou in trials. Such is the nature of the case. From my own instance thou mayest learn that it is impossible for man, in his warfare with the wicked, not to be exposed to tribulation. One cannot be in combat and live luxuriously, one cannot be wrestling and feasting. Let none therefore of those who are contending seek for ease or joyous living. Again, the present state is contest, warfare, tribulation, straits, and trials, and the very scene of conflicts. The season for rest is not now, this is the time for toil and labor. No one who has just stripped and anointed himself thinks of ease. If thou thinkest of ease, why didst thou strip, or prepare to fight? "But do I not maintain the fight?" you say. What, when thou dost not conquer thy desires, nor resist the evil bias of nature?

Ver. 14. "But continue thou in the things that thou hast learned and hast been assured of, knowing of whom thou hast learned them; And that from a child thou hast known the holy Scriptures, which are able to make thee wise unto salvation through the faith which is in Christ Jesus."

What is this? As the prophet David exhorted, saying, "Be not thou envious against the workers of iniquity" (Ps. xxxvii. 1), so Paul exhorts, "Continue thou in the things which thou hast learned," and not simply learned, but "hast been assured of," that is, hast believed. And what have I believed? That this is the Life. And if thou seest things happening contrary to thy belief, be not troubled. The same happened to Abraham, yet he was not affected at it. He had heard, "In Isaac shall thy seed be called" (Gen. xxi. 12) ; and he was commanded to sacrifice Isaac, yet he was not troubled nor dismayed. Let no one be offended because of the wicked. This the Scripture taught from the beginning.

What then, if the good be in prosperity, and the wicked be punished? The one is likely to happen, the other not so. For the wicked will possibly be punished, but the good cannot always be rejoicing. No one was equal to Paul, yet he passed all his life in afflictions, in tears and groanings night and day. "For the space of three years," he says, "I ceased not to warn every one night and day with tears." (Acts xx. 31.) And again: "That which cometh upon me daily." (1 Cor. xi. 28.) He did not rejoice to-day, and grieve to-morrow, but he ceased not daily to grieve. How then does he say, "Evil men shall wax worse and worse"? He has not said, they shall find rest, but "they shall wax worse and worse." Their progress is for the worse. He has not said, they shall be in prosperity. But if they are punished, they are punished that thou mayest not suppose their sins are unavenged. For since we are not deterred from wickedness by the fear of hell, in very tenderness He rouses us from our insensibility, and awakens us. If no wicked man was ever punished, no one would believe that God presides over human affairs. If all were punished, no one would expect a future resurrection, since all had received their due here. On this account He both punishes, and forbears to punish. On this account the righteous suffer tribulation here, because they are sojourners, and strangers, and are in a foreign country. The just therefore endure these things for the purpose of trial. For hear what God said to Job: "Thinkest thou that I have warned thee otherwise, than that thou mightest appear just?"[1] (Job xl. 3, Gr.) But sinners when they endure any affliction, suffer but the punishment of their sins. Under all circumstances, therefore, whether afflictive or otherwise, let us give thanks to God. For both are beneficial. He does nothing in hatred or enmity to us, but all things from care and consideration for us.

"Knowing that from a child thou hast known the sacred writings." The holy Scriptures he calls "sacred writings." In these thou wast nurtured, so that through them thy faith ought to be firm and unshaken. For the root was laid deep, and nourished by length of time,[2] nor will anything subvert it.

And speaking of the holy Scriptures, he has added, "Which are able to make thee wise," that is, they will not suffer thee to have any foolish feeling, such as most men have. For he who knows the Scriptures as he ought, is not offended at anything that happens ; he endures all things manfully, referring them partly to faith, and to the incomprehensible nature of the divine dispensation, and partly knowing reasons for them, and finding examples in the Scriptures. Since it is a great sign of knowledge not to be curious about everything, nor to wish to know all things. And if you will allow me, I will explain myself by an example. Let us suppose a river, or rather rivers, (I ask no allowance, I only speak of what rivers really are,) all are not of the same depth. Some have a shallow bed, others one deep enough to drown one unacquainted with it. In one part there are whirlpools, and not in another. It is good therefore to forbear to make trial of all,[3] and it is no small proof of knowledge not to wish to sound all the depths: whereas he that would venture on every part of the river, is really most ignorant of the peculiar nature of rivers, and will often be in danger of perishing, from venturing into the deeper parts with the same boldness with which he crossed the shallows. So it is in the things of God. He that will know all things, and ventures to intrude into everything, he it is that is most ignorant what God is. And of rivers indeed, the greater part is safe, and the depths and whirlpools few, but with respect to the things of God, the greater part is hidden, and it is not possible to trace out His works. Why then art thou bent on drowning thyself in those depths?

Know this, however, that God dispenses all things, that He provides for all, that we are free agents, that some things He works, and some things He permits ; that He wills nothing evil to be done ; that all things are not done by His will, but some by ours also ; all evil things by ours alone, all good things by our will conjointly with His influence ; and that nothing is without His knowledge. Therefore He worketh all things.[4] Thou then knowing this canst reckon what things are good, what are evil, and what are indifferent. Thus virtue is good, vice is evil ; but riches and poverty, life and death, are things indifferent. If thou knowest this, thou wilt know thereby, that the righteous are afflicted that they may be crowned, the wicked, that they may receive the punishment of their sins. But all sinners are not punished here, lest the generality

---

[1] This corresponds to Job xl. 8, in our version, which stands thus: "Wilt thou condemn Me, that thou mayest be righteous?" Still he was approved, c. xlii. 8.
[2] B. has ἐν for οὐ, which must be right.

[3] Instead of "It is good," &c., one MS. has, "So also of the questions concerning God, some are such as to present a solution at once to the enquirer, but others so secret and hidden as even to cause the destruction of those who are too curiously eager to get knowledge."
[4] i.e. even what He permits is, to us, His appointment.

should disbelieve the Resurrection; nor all the righteous afflicted, lest men should think that vice, and not virtue, is approved. These are the rules and limits. Bring what you will to the test of these, and you will not be perplexed with doubt. For as there is among calculators the number of six thousand, to which all things can be reduced, and everything can be divided and multiplied in the scale of six thousand, and this is known to all who are acquainted with arithmetic[1]; so he who knows those rules, which I will briefly recapitulate, will never be offended. And what are these? That virtue is a good, vice an evil; that diseases, poverty, ill-treatment, false accusations, and the like, are things indifferent; that the righteous are afflicted here, or if ever they are in prosperity, it is that virtue may not appear odious; that the wicked enjoy pleasure now that hereafter they may be punished, or if they are sometimes visited, it is that vice may not seem to be approved, nor their actions to go unpunished; that all are not punished, lest there should be a disbelief of the time of resurrection; that even of the good, some who have done bad actions are quit of them here; and of the wicked, some have good ones, and are rewarded for them here, that their wickedness may be punished hereafter (Matt. vi. 5); that the works of God are for the most part incomprehensible, and that the difference between us and Him is greater than can be expressed. If we reason on these grounds, nothing will be able to trouble or perplex us. If we listen to the Scriptures continually, we shall find many such examples.

"Which are able," he says, "to make thee wise unto salvation."

For the Scriptures suggest to us what is to be done, and what is not to be done. For hear this blessed one elsewhere saying, "Thou art confident that thou thyself art a guide of the blind, a light of them which are in darkness, an instructor of the foolish, a teacher of babes." (Rom. ii. 19, 20.) Thou seest that the Law is the light of them which are in darkness; and if that which showeth the letter, the letter which killeth, is light, what then is the Spirit which quickeneth? If the Old Covenant is light, what is the New, which contains so many, and so great revelations? where the difference is as great, as if any one should open heaven to those who only know the earth, and make all things there visible. There we learn concerning hell, heaven, and judgment. Let us not believe in things irrational. They are nothing but imposture. "What," you say, "when what they foretell comes to pass?" It

is because you believe it, if it does come to pass. The impostor has taken thee captive. Thy life is in his power, he manages thee as he will. If a captain of robbers should have under his power and disposal the son of a king, who had fled to him, preferring the desert, and his lawless company, would he be able to pronounce whether he would live or die? Assuredly he would, not because he knows the future, but because he is the disposer of his life or death, the youth having put himself in his power. For according to his own pleasure, he may either kill him, or spare his life, as he is become subject to him, and it is equally at his[2] disposal to say whether thou shalt be rich or poor. The greater part of the world have delivered themselves up into the hands of the devil.

And furthermore, it contributes much to favor the pretenses of these deceivers, that a man has accustomed himself to believe in them. For no one takes notice of their failures, but their lucky conjectures are observed. But if these men have any power of prognosticating, bring them to me, a believer. I say not this, as magnifying myself, (for it is no great honor to be superior to these things,) and indeed I am deep-laden with sins; but with respect to these matters, I will not be humble-minded; by the grace of God I despise them all. Bring me this pretender to magic; let him, if he has any power of prognosticating, tell me what will happen to me to-morrow. But he will not tell me. For I am under the power of the King, and he has no claim to my allegiance or submission. I am far from his holes and caverns. I war under the king. "But some one committed theft," you say, "and this man discovered it." This is not always true, certainly, but for the most part absurdities and falsehoods. For they know nothing. If indeed they know anything, they ought rather to speak of their own concerns, how the numerous offerings to their idols have been stolen, how so much of their gold has been melted. Why have they not informed their Priests? Even for the sake of money, they have not been able to give information when their idol-temples have been burnt, and many have perished with them.[3] Why do they not provide for their own safety? But it is altogether a matter of chance, if they have predicted anything. With us there are prophets, and they do not fail. They do not speak truth in one instance and falsehood in another, but always declare the truth; for this is the privilege of foreknowledge.

Cease, then, from this madness, I beseech

---

[1] γράμματα, lit. letters. The γραμματισταί taught reading, writing, and arithmetic. See Johannes a Wower de Polymathia, c. vi. Græv. tom. ix. Hales suspects the number 6000, but it may refer to computations of money, as the talent contains 600 denarii, or 6000 asses.

[2] i.e. Satan's.

[3] He may allude to the burning of Daphne, lamented by Libanius, Or. 61, which is preserved by St. Chrysostom in his work on St. Babylas, § 18, Ben. t. 2, p. 566, where he also mentions this inability to discover the cause.

you, if at least you believe in Christ; and if you believe not, why do you expose yourselves? Why do you deceive? "How long will ye halt on both your hips?" (1 Kings xviii. 21, Sept.) Why do you go to them? Why enquire of them? The instant you go to them, the instant you enquire, you put yourself in slavery to them. For you enquire, as if you believed. "No," you say, "I do not enquire, as believing, but making trial of them." But to make trial, whether they speak the truth, is the part not of one who believes that they are false, but of one who still doubts. Wherefore then dost thou enquire what will happen? For if they answered, "This will happen, but do so and so, and thou wilt escape it"; even in that case thou oughtest by no means to be an idolater; yet thy madness were not so great. But if they foretell future events,[1] he that listens to them will gain nothing more than unavailing sorrow. The event does not happen, but he suffers the uneasiness, and torments,[2] himself.

If it were for our good, God would not have grudged us this foreknowledge. He who has revealed to us things in heaven, would not have envied us. For, "All things," He says, "that I have heard of the Father I have made known unto you"; and, "I call you not servants, but friends. Ye are my friends." (John xv. 15.) Why then did He not make these things known unto us? Because He would not have us concerned about them. And as a proof that He does not envy us this knowledge, such things were revealed to the ancients, because they were babes, even about an ass,[4] and the like. But to us, because He would not have us concerned about such things, He has not cared to reveal them. But what do we learn? Things which they never knew, for little indeed were all those things of old. But what we are taught is this, that we shall rise again, that we shall be immortal, and incorruptible, that our life shall have no end, that all things will pass away, that we shall be caught up in the clouds, that the wicked shall suffer punishment, and numberless other things, and in all these there is no falsehood. Is it not better to know these than to hear that the ass that was lost is found? Lo, thou hast gotten thine ass! Lo, thou hast found him! What is thy gain? Will he not soon be lost again some other way? For if he leave thee not, at least thou wilt lose him in thy death. But the things which I have mentioned, if we will but hold them fast, we shall retain perpetually. These therefore let us pursue. To these stable and enduring goods let us attach ourselves. Let us not give heed to soothsayers, fortune-tellers, and jugglers, but to God who knoweth all things certainly, whose knowledge is universal. Thus we shall know all that it befits us to know, and shall obtain all good things, through the grace and lovingkindness, &c.

HOMILY IX.

2 TIMOTHY iii. 16, 17.

"All Scripture is given by inspiration of God, and is profitable for doctrine, for reproof, for correction, for instruction in righteousness: That the man of God may be perfect, thoroughly furnished unto all good works." [R. V.: Every Scripture inspired of God is also profitable, &c.]

HAVING offered much exhortation and consolation from other sources, he adds that which is more perfect, derived from the Scriptures; and he is reasonably full in offering consolation, because he has a great and sad thing to say. For if Elisha, who was with his master to his last breath, when he saw him departing as it were in death,[3] rent his garments for grief, what think you must this disciple suffer, so loving and so beloved, upon hearing that his master was about to die, and that he could not enjoy his company when he was near his death, which is above all things apt to be distressing? For we are less grateful for the past time, when we have been deprived of the more recent intercourse of those who are departed. For this reason when he had previously offered much consolation, he then discourses concerning his own death: and this in no ordinary way, but in words adapted to comfort him and fill him with joy; so as to have it considered as a sacrifice rather than a death; a migration, as in fact it was, and a removal to a better state. "For I am now ready to be offered up" (2 Tim. iv. 6), he says. For this reason he writes: "All Scripture is given by inspiration of God,[5] and is profitable for doctrine,

---

[1] Downes thinks it should be "events not to come," but the contrast is in the *form* of the prediction. The aorist would justify, "The event *perchance* does not happen."

[2] Lit. "pickles."

[3] ἐν τρόπῳ τελευτῆς ὁρῶν αὐτὸν τελευτῶντα. An Old Lat. has "by a new and strange manner of death." The present Greek is difficult and suspected.

[4] Referring to 1 Sam. ix. 20.　　[5] Or, "every Scripture inspired," &c.

for reproof, for correction, for instruction in righteousness." All what Scripture? all that sacred writing, he means, of which I was speaking. This is said of what he was discoursing of ; about which he said, " From a child thou hast known the holy Scriptures." All such, then, " is given by inspiration of God " ; therefore, he means, do not doubt ; and it is " profitable for doctrine, for reproof, for correction, for instruction in righteousness : that the man of God may be perfect, thoroughly furnished unto all good works."

" For doctrine." For thence we shall know, whether we ought to learn or to be ignorant of anything. And thence we may disprove what is false, thence we may be corrected and brought to a right mind, may be comforted and consoled, and if anything is deficient, we may have it added to us.

" That the man of God may be perfect." For this is the exhortation of the Scripture given, that the man of God may be rendered perfect by it ; without this therefore he cannot be perfect. Thou hast the Scriptures, he says, in place of me. If thou wouldest learn anything, thou mayest learn it from them. And if he thus wrote to Timothy, who was filled with the Spirit, how much more to us !

" Thoroughly furnished unto all good works " ; not merely taking part in them, he means, but " thoroughly furnished."

Chap. iv. 1. " I charge thee therefore before God, and the Lord Jesus Christ, Who shall judge the quick and the dead."

He either means the wicked and the just, or the departed and those that are still living ; for many will be left alive. In the former Epistle he raised his fears, saying, " I give thee charge in the sight of God, Who quickeneth all things " (1 Tim. vi. 13) : but here he sets before him what is more dreadful, " Who shall judge the quick and the dead," that is, Who shall call them to account " at His appearing and His kingdom." When shall He judge? at His appearing with glory, and in His kingdom. Either he says this to show that He will not come in the way that He now has come, or, " I call to witness His coming, and His kingdom." He calls Him to witness, showing that he had reminded Him of that appearing. Then teaching him how he ought to preach the word, he adds,

Ver. 2. " Preach the word : be instant in season, out of season ; reprove, rebuke, exhort with all longsuffering and doctrine."

What means " in season, out of season "? That is, have not any limited season : let it always be thy season, not only in peace and security, and when sitting in the Church. Whether thou be in danger, in prison, in chains, or going to thy death, at that very time reprove. Withhold not rebuke, for reproof is then most seasonable,

when thy rebuke will be most successful, when the reality is proved. " Exhort," he says. After the manner of physicians, having shown the wound, he gives the incision, he applies the plaster. For if you omit either of these, the other becomes useless. If you rebuke without convicting, you will seem to be rash, and no one will tolerate it, but after the matter is proved, he will submit to rebuke : before, he will be headstrong. And if you convict and rebuke, but vehemently, and do not apply exhortation,[1] all your labor will be lost. For conviction[2] is intolerable in itself, if consolation be not mingled with it. As if incision, though salutary in itself, have not plenty of lenitives to assuage the pain, the patient cannot endure cutting and hacking, so it is in this matter.

" With all longsuffering and doctrine." For he that reproves is required to be longsuffering, that he may not believe hastily, and rebuke needs consolation, that it may be received as it ought. And why to " longsuffering " does he add " doctrine "? " Not as in anger, not as in hatred, not as insulting over him, not as having caught an enemy. Far be these things from thee." But how? As loving, as sympathizing with him, as more distressed than himself at his grief, as melted at his sufferings? " With all longsuffering and doctrine." No ordinary teaching is implied.

Ver. 3. " For the time will come when they will not endure sound doctrine."

Before they grow stiffnecked,[3] preoccupy them all. For this reason he says, " in season, out of season " ; do everything, so as to have willing disciples.

" But after their own lusts," he says, " shall they heap to themselves teachers."

Nothing can be more expressive than these words. For by saying " they shall heap to themselves," he shows the indiscriminate multitude of the teachers, as also by their being elected by their disciples. " They shall heap to themselves teachers," he says, " having itching ears." Seeking for such as speak to gratify and delight their hearers.

Ver. 4. " And they shall turn away their ears from the truth, and be turned unto fables."

This he foretells, not as willing to throw him into despair, but to prepare him to bear it firmly, when it shall happen. As Christ also did in saying, " They will deliver you up, and they will scourge you, and bring you before the synagogues, for My name's sake." (Matt. x. 17.) And this blessed man elsewhere says, " For I know this, that after my departure shall grievous wolves enter in among you, not sparing the flock." (Acts

---

[1] Or, " comfort."
[2] The word translated " reproof."
[3] See on Stat. Hom. xii.

xx. 29.) But this he said that they might watch, and duly use the present opportunity.

Ver. 5. "But watch thou in all things, endure affliction."

It was for this, therefore, that he foretold these things; as Christ also toward the end predicted that there should be "false Christs and false prophets"; so he too, when he was about to depart, spoke of these things. "But watch thou in all things, endure affliction"; that is, labor, preoccupy their minds before this pestilence assails them; secure the safety of the sheep before the wolves enter in, everywhere endure hardship.

"Do the work of an evangelist, make full proof of thy ministry." Thus it was the work of an evangelist that he should endure hardship, both in himself, and from those without; "make full proof of" that is, fulfill "thy ministry." And behold another necessity for his enduring affliction,

Ver. 6. "For I am now ready to be poured out,[1] and the time of my departure is at hand."

He has not said of my sacrifice; but, what is much more, "of my being poured out." For the whole of the sacrifice was not offered to God, but the whole of the drink-offering was.

Ver. 7. "I have fought the good fight, I have finished the course, I have kept the faith."

Often, when I have taken the Apostle into my hands, and have considered this passage, I have been at a loss to understand why Paul here speaks so loftily: "I have fought the good fight." But now by the grace of God I seem to have found it out. For what purpose then does he speak thus? He is desirous to console the despondency of his disciple, and therefore bids him be of good cheer, since he was going to his crown, having finished all his work, and obtained a glorious end. Thou oughtest to rejoice, he says, not to grieve. And why? Because, "I have fought the good fight." As a father whose son was sitting by him, bewailing his orphan state, might console him, saying, Weep not, my son; we have lived a good life, we have arrived at old age, and now we leave thee. Our life has been irreproachable, we depart with glory, and thou mayest be held in admiration for our actions. Our king is much indebted to us. As if he had said, We have raised trophies, we have conquered enemies, and this not boastfully; God forbid; but to raise up his dejected son, and to encourage him by his praises to bear firmly what had happened, to entertain good hopes, and not to think it a matter grievous to be borne. For sad, sad indeed is separation; and hear Paul himself, saying, "We being bereaved of[2] you for a short time, in presence, not

in heart." (1 Thess. ii. 17.) If he then felt so much at being separated from his disciples, what thinkest thou were the feelings of Timothy? If on parting from him whilst living he wept, so that Paul says, "Being mindful of thy tears, that I may be filled with joy." (2 Tim. i. 4), how much more at his death? These things then he wrote to console him. Indeed the whole Epistle is full of consolation, and is a sort of Testament. "I have fought the good fight, I have finished my course, I have kept the faith." "A good fight," he says, therefore do thou engage in it. But is that a good fight, where there are imprisonment, chains, and death? Yea, he says, for it is fought in the cause of Christ, and great crowns are won in it. "The good fight"! There is no worthier than this contest. This crown is without end. This is not of olive leaves. It has not a human umpire. It has not men for spectators. The theater is crowded with Angels. There men labor many days, and suffer hardships, and for one hour they receive the crown, and immediately all the pleasure passes away. But here far otherwise, it continues for ever in brightness, glory, and honor. Henceforth we ought to rejoice. For I am entering on my rest, I am leaving the race. Thou hast heard that "it is better to depart and to be with Christ."

I have finished "the course." For it behooves us both to contend and to run; to contend, by enduring afflictions firmly, and to run, not vainly, but to some good end. It is truly a good fight, not only delighting, but benefiting the spectator: and the race does not end in nothing. It is not a mere display of strength and of rivalry. It draws all up to heaven. This race is brighter than the sun's, yea, this which Paul ran upon earth, than that which he runs in heaven. And how had he "finished his course"? He traversed the whole world, beginning from Galilee and Arabia, and advancing to the extremities of the earth, so that, as he says, "From Jerusalem and round about unto Illyricum I have fully preached the Gospel of Christ." (Rom. xv. 19.) He passed over the earth like a bird, or rather more swiftly than a bird: for a bird only flies over it, but he, having the wing of the Spirit, made his way through numberless impediments, dangers, deaths, and calamities, so that he was even fleeter than a bird. Had he been a mere bird, he might have alighted and been taken, but being upborne by the Spirit he soared above all snares, as a bird with a wing of fire.

"I have kept the faith," he says. There were many things that would have robbed him of it, not only human friendships, but menaces, and deaths, and countless other perils: but he stood firm against all. How? by being sober and watchful. This might have sufficed for the con-

---

[1] i.e. as the drink-offering. [So R. V. in margin.—P. S.]
[2] ἀπορφανισθέντες.

solation of his disciples, but he further adds the rewards. And what are these?

Ver. 8. "Henceforth there is laid up for me a crown of righteousness."

Here again he calls virtue in general righteousness. Thou shouldest not grieve that I shall depart, to be invested with that crown which will by Christ be placed upon my head. But if I continued here, truly thy mightest rather grieve, and fear lest I should fail and perish.

Ver. 8. "Which the Lord, the righteous Judge, shall give me at that day, and not to me only, but to all that love His appearing."

Here also he raises his mind. If "to all," much more to Timothy. But he did not say, "and to thee," but "to all"; meaning, if to all, much more to him.

MORAL. But how, it may be asked, is one to "love the appearing" (τὴν ἐπιφάνειαν) of Christ? By rejoicing at His coming; and he who rejoices at His coming, will perform works worthy of His joy; he will throw away his substance if need be, and even his life, so that he may obtain future blessings, that he may be thought worthy to behold that second coming in a fitting state, in confidence, in brightness and glory. This is to "love His appearing." He who loves His appearing will do everything to ensure, before His general coming, a particular coming to himself. And how, you will say, is this possible? Hear from Christ, who says, "If a man love Me, he will keep My words, and My Father and I will come unto him, and make Our abode with him." (John xiv. 23.) And think how great a privilege it is that He who will appear to all generally, should promise to come to us in particular: for He says, "We will come and make Our abode with him." If any man "love His appearing," he will do everything to invite Him to himself, and to hold Him, that the light may shine upon him. Let there be nothing unworthy of His coming, and He will soon take up His abode with us.

And it is called His "Epiphany,"[1] because He will appear above,[2] and shine forth from on high. Let us therefore "seek those things that are above," and we shall soon draw down those beams upon us. None of those who grovel below, and bury themselves in this lower earth, will be able to view the light of that Sun. None of those who defile themselves with worldly things will be able to behold that Sun of righteousness. He shines on none of those who are so occupied. Recover thyself a little, recover thyself from that depth, from the waves of a worldly life, if thou wouldest see the Sun, and enjoy His appearing. Then thou wilt see Him with great confidence. Be even now a philosopher. Let not a spirit of perverseness possess thee, lest He smite thee severely, and bring thee low. Let not thy heart be hardened; nor darkened, lest thou be shipwrecked there. Let there be no self-deceit. For the rocks beneath the sea cause the most fatal shipwrecks. Nourish no wild beasts, I mean evil passions, worse than wild beasts. Confide not in things ever flowing, that thou mayest be able to stand firmly. None can stand upon water, but upon a rock all find a secure footing. Worldly things are as water, as a torrent, that passes away. "The waters," he saith, "are come in unto my soul." (Ps. lxix. 1.) Spiritual things are as a rock. For he saith, "Thou hast set my feet upon a rock." (Ps. xl. 2.) Worldly things are as mire and clay; let us extricate ourselves from them. For so we shall be able to attain to the appearing of Christ. Whatever may befall us, let us endure. It is a sufficient consolation in all circumstances that we suffer for Christ. This divine incantation let us repeat, and it will charm away the pain of every wound.

And how can we suffer for Christ, you ask? If one accuse thee falsely in any case, not on account of Christ, yet if thou bearest it patiently, if thou givest thanks, if thou prayest for him, all this thou doest for Christ. But if thou curse him, if thou utter discontent, if thou attempt to revenge it, though thou shouldest not be able, it is not for Christ's sake; thou sufferest loss, and art deprived of thy reward on account of thy intention. For it rests with us either to profit, or to be injured, by afflictions. It depends not upon the nature of the affliction, but upon the disposition of our own minds. As, for instance, great were the sufferings of Job, yet he suffered with thankfulness; and he was justified, not because he suffered, but because in suffering he endured it thankfully. Another under the same sufferings, yet not the same, for none ever suffered like Job — but under lighter sufferings, exclaims, is impatient, curses the whole world, and complains against God. He is condemned and sentenced, not because he suffered, but because he blasphemed; and he blasphemed, not from any necessity arising from his afflictions, since if necessity arising from events were the cause, Job too must have blasphemed; but since he, who suffered more severely, did no such thing, it did not come to pass from this cause, but from the man's weakness of purpose. We want therefore strength of soul, and nothing will then appear grievous, but if our soul is weak, we find a grievance in everything.

According to our dispositions, all things become tolerable or intolerable. Let us strengthen our resolution, and we shall bear all things easily. The tree whose roots are fixed deep in the earth is not shaken by the utmost violence of the storm, but if it be set lightly in the surface of

<hr/>

[1] ἐπιφάνεια.　　　[2] ἐπάνω.

the ground, a slight gust of wind will tear it up from the roots. So it is with us; if our flesh be nailed down by the fear of God, nothing will be able to shake us; but if we merely intend well, a little shock will subvert and destroy us. Wherefore, I exhort, let us bear all with much cheerfulness, imitating the Prophet, who says, "My soul cleaveth to Thee"; observe, he says not, draweth nigh, but "cleaveth to Thee"; and again, "My soul thirsteth for Thee." (Ps. lxii. 3.) He said not merely "longeth," that he might by such words express the vehemence of his desire; and again, "Fix[1] my flesh in Thy fear." (Ps. cxix. 120, Sept.) For he wishes us so to cleave and be united to Him, that we may never be separated from Him. If thus we hold by God, if thus we rivet our thoughts upon Him, if we thirst with the love of Him, all that we desire will be ours, and we shall obtain the good things to come, in Jesus Christ our Lord, to whom with the Father and the Holy Ghost be glory, power, and honor, now and for ever. Amen.

HOMILY X.

2 Timothy iv. 9–13.

"Do thy diligence to come shortly unto me: For Demas hath forsaken me, having loved this present world, and is departed unto Thessalonica; Crescens to Galatia, Titus unto Dalmatia. Only Luke is with me. Take Mark, and bring him with thee: for he is profitable to me for the ministry. And Tychicus have I sent to Ephesus. The cloak that I left at Troas with Carpus, when thou comest, bring with thee, and the books, but especially the parchments."

It is worth while to enquire why he calls Timothy to him, inasmuch as he was intrusted with a Church, and a whole nation. It was not from arrogance. For Paul was ready to come to him; for we find him saying, "But if I tarry long, that thou mayest know how thou oughtest to behave thyself in the house of God." (1 Tim. iii. 15.) But he was withholden by a strong necessity. He was no longer master of his own movements. He was in prison, and had been confined by Nero, and was all but on the point of death. That this might not happen before he saw his disciple, he therefore sends for him, desiring to see him before he dies, and perhaps to deliver much in charge to him. Wherefore he says, "Hasten to come to me before the winter."

"For Demas hath forsaken me, having loved this present world." He does not say, "That I may see thee before I depart this life," which would have grieved him, but "because I am alone," he says, "and have no one to help or support me."

"For Demas hath forsaken me, having loved this present world, and is departed to Thessalonica"; that is, having loved his own ease and security from danger, he has chosen rather to live luxuriously at home, than to suffer hardships with me, and share my present dangers. He has blamed him alone, not for the sake of blaming him, but to confirm us, that we may not be effeminate in declining toils and dangers, for this is, "having loved this present world." At the same time he wishes to draw his disciple to him.

"Crescens to Galatia, Titus to Dalmatia."

These he does not censure. For Titus was one of the most admirable men, so that to him he intrusted the affairs of the island, no small island, I mean, but that great one of Crete.

"Only Luke is with me." For he adhered to him inseparably. It was he who wrote the Gospel, and the General[2] Acts; he was devoted to labors, and to learning, and a man of fortitude; of him Paul writes, "whose praise is in the Gospel[3] throughout all the Churches." (2 Cor. viii. 18.)

"Take Mark, and bring him with thee, for he is profitable to me for the ministry."

It is not for his own relief, but for the ministry of the Gospel that he wanted him. For though imprisoned, he did not cease to preach. So it was on the same account he sent for Timothy, not for his own, but for the Gospel's sake, that his death might occasion no disturbance to the faithful, when many of his own disciples were present to prevent tumults, and to console those who would scarce have endurance to bear up at his death. For it is probable that the believers at Rome were men of consequence.

"And Tychicus have I sent to Ephesus. The cloak that I left at Troas with Carpus, when thou comest bring with thee, and the books, but especially the parchments."

The word here translated "cloak"[4] may

---

[1] Lit. "nail"; compare Gal. v. 24.
[2] καθολικὰς.
[3] He takes this to allude to the written Gospel.
[4] φελόνην. Some make it an ecclesiastical vestment.

mean a garment, or, as some say, a bag, in which the books were contained. But what had he to do with books, who was about to depart and go to God? He needed them much, that he might deposit them in the hands of the faithful, who would retain them in place of his own teaching. All the faithful, then, would suffer a great blow, but particularly those who were present at his death, and then enjoyed his society. But the cloak he requires, that he might not be obliged to receive one from another. For we see him making a great point of avoiding this; and elsewhere, when he was addressing those from Ephesus, he says, "Ye know that these hands have ministered to my necessities, and to those that were with me" (Acts xx. 34, 35); and again, "It is more blessed to give than to receive."

Ver. 14. "Alexander the coppersmith did me much evil; the Lord reward him according to his works."

Here he again makes mention of his trial, not wishing merely to censure and accuse the man, but to prepare his disciple for the conflicts, that he might bear them firmly. Though they be mean and contemptible persons, and without honor, who cause these trials, they ought all, he says, to be borne with fortitude. For he who suffers wrong from any great personage, receives no little distinction from the superiority of him who does the wrong. But he who is injured by a vile and abject person, suffers the greater annoyance. "He did me much evil," he says, that is, he persecuted me in various ways. But these things will not go unpunished! For the Lord will reward him according to his works. As he said above: "What persecutions I endured, but out of them all the Lord delivered me." (2 Tim. iii. 11.) So also here he consoles his disciples by a double consideration, that he himself had suffered wrong, and that the other would be rewarded for his evil deeds. Not that the Saints rejoice in the punishment of their persecutors, but that the cause of the Gospel required it, and the weaker would derive consolation from it.

Ver. 15. "Of whom be thou ware also; for he hath greatly withstood our words."

That is, he is hostile to us, and opposes us. He has not said, Revenge, punish, expel him, although by the grace given him he might have so done, but he does no such thing; nor does he arm Timothy against him, but only commands him to avoid him, leaving vengeance to God, and for the consolation of the weaker he has said that He will reward him, which is a prophecy rather than an imprecation. And that he says these things to prepare the mind of his disciple, is manifest also from what follows. But see how he mentions other of his trials.

Ver. 16. "At my first answer," he says, "no man stood with me, but all men forsook me: I pray God that it may not be laid to their charge."

Do you see how he spares his friends, notwithstanding it was a grievous thing they had done? For it is not the same thing to be despised by aliens, as by our own friends. Do you see his intense dejection? It cannot be said, that I was assailed by those without, but had comfort in the attention and support of my friends; for these also betrayed me. "All men," he says, "forsook me." And this was no light offense. For if he that in war abandons one who is exposed to danger, and shrinks from meeting the hands of his enemies, is justly smitten by his friends, as having utterly betrayed their cause, much more in the case of the Gospel. But what "first answer," does he speak of? He had stood before Nero, and had escaped. But afterwards, because he had converted his cup-bearer, he was beheaded. And here again is encouragement for his disciple in what follows.

Ver. 17. "Notwithstanding, the Lord stood with me, and strengthened me."

Though deserted by man, God doth not permit him to suffer any harm. He strengthened me, he says, that is, He gave me boldness in speaking. He suffered me not to sink.

"That by me the preaching might be fully known."

That is, might be fulfilled. Observe his great humility. He does not say He strengthened me as deserving of His gift, but that "the preaching," with which I was intrusted, "might be fully known." As if any one should wear a purple robe and a diadem, and to that circumstance should owe his safety.

"And that all the Gentiles might hear."

What is this? That the luster of the Gospel, and the care of His Providence for me, might be known to all.

"And I was delivered out of the mouth of the lion."

Ver. 18. "And the Lord shall deliver me from every evil work."

See how near he had been to death. He had fallen into the very jaws of the lion. For he calls Nero a lion from his ferocity, and the violent and daring character of his government. "The Lord delivered me," he says, "and will deliver." But if he says, "He will deliver me," why does he say, "I am ready to be offered"? Attend to the expression, "He delivered me," he says, "from the lion's mouth"; and again, "He will deliver me," not from the lion's mouth, but "from every evil work." For then He delivered me from the danger; but now that enough has been done for the Gospel, He will yet again deliver me from every sin, that is, He will not suffer me to depart with condemnation. For that he should be able to "resist unto blood striving against sin" (Heb. xii. 4), and not yield, is a deliverance from another lion, even the devil, so that this preservation is greater than the former, when he seems to be given up.

"And will preserve me unto His heavenly kingdom; to Whom be glory for ever and ever. Amen."

This then is salvation, when we shine forth there. But what means, "He will preserve me unto His kingdom"? He will deliver me from all blame, and preserve me there. For this is to be preserved unto His kingdom, to die here on account of it. For "He that hateth his life in this world shall keep it unto life eternal." (John xii. 25.)

"To whom be glory." Lo, here is a doxology to the Son.

Ver. 19. "Salute Priscilla and Aquila, and the household of Onesiphorus."

For he was then in Rome, of whom he said "The Lord grant unto him that he may find mercy of the Lord in that day." (2 Tim. i. 18.) By this naming of him, he makes those of his household also more zealous in such good actions.

"Salute Priscilla and Aquila." These are they of whom he makes continual mention, with whom too he had lodged, and who had taken Apollos to them. He names the woman first, as being I suppose more zealous, and more faithful, for she had then received Apollos; or it might be done indifferently. And it was to them no slight consolation to be thus saluted.[1] It conveyed a demonstration of esteem and love, and a participation in much grace. For the bare salutation of that holy and blessed man was sufficient to fill with grace him who received it.

Ver. 20. "Erastus abode at Corinth: but Trophimus have I left at Miletum sick."

This Trophimus and Tychicus, we know from the book of the Acts, sailed away with him from Judea, and were everywhere his companions, perhaps as being more zealous than the rest.

"Trophimus I have left at Miletum sick." Why then didst thou not heal him, instead of leaving him? The Apostles could not do everything, or they did not dispense miraculous gifts upon all occasions, lest more should be ascribed to them than was right. The same thing is observable of those blessed and righteous men, who were before them, as in the case of Moses, whose voice was weak. Why was not this defect removed? Nay, he was often afflicted with grief and dejection, and he was not admitted into the Land of Promise.

For many things were permitted by God, that the weakness of human nature might be manifested. And if with these defects the insensible Jews could ask, Where is Moses who brought us out of the land of Egypt (Ex. xxxii. 1)? how would they not have been affected towards him if he had brought them also into the Land of Promise? If he had not been suffered to be overpowered by the fear of Pharaoh, would they not have thought him a God? We see that the people of Lystra were thus affected in the case of Paul and Barnabas, thinking them to be Gods, when they rent their clothes, and ran in among the people, crying out and saying, "Sirs, why do ye these things? we also are men of like passions with you." (Acts xiv. 14, 15.) Peter, again, when he had healed the man lame from his birth, when all were amazed at the miracle, answered and said, "Ye men of Israel, why marvel ye at this, or why look ye so earnestly on us, as though by our own power or holiness we had made this man to walk"? (Acts iii. 12.) Hear also the blessed Paul, saying, "There was given to me a thorn in the flesh, lest I should be exalted above measure." (2 Cor. xii. 7.) But this, you say, was an expression of humility. Far from it. The thorn was not sent him that he might be humble, nor does he say this only out of humility. There are other causes besides to be assigned for it. Observe therefore how God, accounting for it, says, "My grace is sufficient for thee"; not "that thou mayest not be exalted above measure," but what? "For my strength is made perfect in weakness." Two ends therefore were answered at once: what was doing was made clearly manifest, and the whole was ascribed to God. For this cause he has said elsewhere, "We carry this treasure in earthen vessels" (2 Cor. iv. 7); that is, in bodies weak and liable to suffering. Why? "That the excellency of the power may be of God, and not of us." If our bodies were not subject to infirmity, all would be ascribed to them. And elsewhere we see him grieving at the infirmity of Epaphroditus, concerning whom he writes, "He was sick nigh unto death, but God had mercy on him." (Phil. ii. 27.) And many other instances there are of his ignorance of events, which was profitable both for him and his disciples.

"Trophimus I have left at Miletum sick." Miletus was near Ephesus. Did this happen then when he sailed to Judea, or upon some other occasion? For after he had been in Rome, he returned to Spain, but whether he came thence again into these parts, we know not.[2] We see him however deserted by all. "For Demas," he says, "hath forsaken me. Crescens

---

[1] B. πρόσρησις, as had been before conjectured.

[2] This is, however, a strong presumption that he did. See p. 476, note.

is departed into Galatia, Titus to Dalmatia. Erastus abode at Corinth. Trophimus have I left at Miletum sick."

Ver. 21. "Do thy diligence to come before winter. Eubulus greeteth thee, and Pudens, and Linus, and Claudia."

This Linus, some say, was second [1] Bishop of the Church of Rome after Peter. "And Claudia." You see how zealous for the faith the women were, how ardent! Such was Priscilla and this Claudia, already crucified, already prepared for the battle! But why, when there were so many faithful, does he mention only these women? Manifestly because they in purpose had already withdrawn from worldly affairs, and were illustrious above others. For a woman, as such, meets not with any impediments. It is the work of divine grace, that this sex should be impeded only in the affairs of this life, or rather not even in them. For a woman undertakes no small share of the whole administration, being the keeper of the house. And without her not even political affairs could be properly conducted. For if their domestic concerns were in a state of confusion and disorder, those who are engaged in public affairs would be kept at home, and political business would be ill managed. So that neither in those matters, as neither in spiritual, is she inferior. For she is able, if so inclined, to endure a thousand deaths. Accordingly many women have suffered martyrdom. She is able to practice chastity even more than men, no such strong flame disturbing her; and to show forth modesty and gravity, and " holiness, without which no one shall see the Lord " (Heb. xii. 14) ; and contempt of wealth, if she will, and in short all other virtues.

"Do thy diligence to come before winter." See how he urges him, yet he does not say anything to grieve him. He does not say, " Before I die," lest he should afflict him; but, " Before winter," that thou be not detained.

"Eubulus," he says, "greeteth thee, and Pudens, and Linus, and Claudia, and all the brethren." He does not mention the rest by name. Seest thou that those were the most zealous?

Ver. 22. "The Lord Jesus Christ be with thy spirit."

There can be no better prayer than this. Grieve not for my departure. The Lord will be with thee. And he says, not " with thee," but " with thy spirit." Thus there is a twofold assistance, the grace of the Spirit,[2] and God helping it. And otherwise God will not be with us, if we have not spiritual grace. For if

we be deserted by grace, how shall He be with us?

" Grace be with us. Amen."

Thus he prays for himself too, that they may always be well-pleasing to Him, that they may have grace together with the spiritual gift, for where this is, nothing will be grievous. For as he who beholds the king, and is in favor with him, is sensible of no uneasiness ; so though our friends forsake us, though we be overtaken by calamity, we shall feel no distress, if that grace be with us and fortify us.

MORAL. But how shall we draw down grace upon us? By doing what is pleasing to God, and obeying Him in all things. In great houses do we not see those domestics in favor, who do not regard their own interest, but with all zeal and alacrity promote their masters', and who not from the compulsion of the master, but from their own affection and good disposition, order all things well. When they are always before their eyes, when they are engaged in the house, when they are not occupied in any private concerns, nor caring for their own, but rather consider their masters' concerns as their own. For he who makes what is his own his master's, does not really give up his own to his master, but makes his interest his own ; he commands even as himself in his affairs,[3] and rules equally with him. He is often as much feared by the domestics, and whatever he says his master says too, and he is henceforth dreaded by all his enemies.

And if he who in worldly concerns prefers his master's interests to his own, does not really neglect his own interest, but rather advance it the more ; much more is this the case in spiritual matters. Despise thine own concerns, and thou wilt receive those of God. This He Himself wills. Despise earth, and seize upon the kingdom of heaven. Dwell there, not here. Be formidable there, not here. If thou art formidable there, thou wilt be formidable not to men, but to demons, and even to the devil himself. But if thy dependence is on worldly wealth, thou wilt be contemptible to them, and often to men too. Whatever be thy riches, thou wilt be rich in servile things. But if thou despisest these, thou wilt be radiant in the house of the King.

Such were the Apostles, despising a servile house and worldly wealth! And see how they commanded in the affairs of their Master. "Let one," they said, "be delivered from disease, another from the possession of devils: bind this man, and loose that." This was done by them on earth, but it was fulfilled as in Heaven. For, "whatever ye shall bind on earth," said He,

---

[1] i.e. the next. See Euseb. iii. 2, and note in Reading's Ed.; also Cave Hist. Lit. Linus is thought not to have survived the persecution of Nero, and probably to have been Bishop in St. Peter's lifetime, and supplied his place when absent.

[2] i.e. the original Gift, without which he had been but a carnal person.

[3] See Gen. xl. 4, 22.

"shall be bound in Heaven." (Matt. xviii. 18.) And greater power than His own did He give them. And that I lie not, appears from His own words. "He that believeth in Me, greater works shall he do than these which I do." (John xiv. 12.) Why so? Because this honor is reflected upon the Master.[1] As in our own affairs, if the servant has great power, the master is the more admired, for if the servant is so powerful, much more is he who commands him. But if any man, neglecting his master's service thinks only of his wife, his son, or his servant, and seeks to be rich, and to lay up treasure there, by stealing and robbing his master of his possessions, he is presently ruined, and his wealth perishes with him.

Wherefore having these examples, I beseech you, let us not regard our possessions, that we may regard ourselves : nay, let us despise them, that we may obtain them. If we despise them, He will take care of them; if we take care of them, God will despise them. Let us labor in the concerns of God, not in our own, or rather really in our own, for His are our own. I speak not of heaven,[2] nor of earth, nor of the things of this world : these are unworthy of Him. And they belong alike to the faithful and the unbelievers. What then do I speak of as His? His glory and His kingdom. These are His, and ours for His sake. How? "If we be dead with Him," He says, "we shall also live with Him. If we suffer, we shall also reign with Him." (2 Tim. ii. 11.) We are become "joint heirs," and are called His "brethren." Why do we sink below, when He is drawing us upward towards Himself? How long shall we be poor, and beggarly? Heaven is set before us; and do we linger on earth? Is His kingdom opened to us, and do we choose such poverty as is here? Is life immortal offered us, and do we spend ourselves for lands, for wood and stones? Be truly rich. I would wish thee to be so. Be covetous and rapacious, I blame thee not for it. Here it is a fault not to be covetous, here it is blameworthy not to be grasping. What then is this? "The kingdom of Heaven suffereth violence, and the violent take it by force." (Matt. xi. 12.) There be thou violent! be grasping! It is not diminished by being seized upon. For neither is virtue divided, nor piety lessened, nor the kingdom of Heaven. Virtue is increased when thou seizest upon it, whilst temporal goods are lessened when they are seized upon. And this appears from hence : Let there be ten thousand men in a city; if all seize on virtue, it is multiplied, for they become righteous in ten

thousand things.[3] If no one seizes upon it, it is diminished, for it is nowhere to be found.

Thou seest then that good things are multiplied on being possessed by many, but earthly goods are rather diminished by seizing. Let us not therefore sit down content with poverty, but let us choose riches. God is then rich, when those who enjoy His kingdom are many. "For He is rich," it is said, "unto all that call upon Him." (Rom. x. 12.) Increase then His substance ; and thou wilt increase it by taking possession of it, by being covetous of it, by violently seizing it. And truly there is need of violence. Wherefore? Because there are so many impediments, as wives and children, cares and worldly business; besides those demons, and him who is the ruler of them, the devil. There is need then of violence, there is need of fortitude. He who takes by violence is exposed to toils. How? He endures all things, he contends against necessities. How? He almost attempts impossibilities. If such are those who take by violence, and we shrink from attempting even what is possible, how shall we ever win? or when shall we enjoy the things for which we strive? "The violent," it is said, "take" the kingdom of heaven "by force." Violence and rapacity are needed. For it is not simply set before us, and ready to our hands. He who seizes by violence, is ever sober and watchful, he is anxious and thoughtful, that he may make his seizure at a seasonable time. Dost thou not see that in war he who is about to make a seizure keeps watch and is under arms the whole night? If then they who aim at seizing upon worldly goods, watch and are armed all the night long, should we, who wish to seize upon spiritual things, sleep and snore in the day, and continue always naked and unarmed? For he who is engaged in sin is unarmed ; as he who practices righteousness is armed. We do not fortify ourselves with almsgiving. We do not prepare for ourselves lamps that are burning, we do not fence ourselves in spiritual armor. We do not learn the way that leads thither. We are not sober and watchful, and therefore we can seize no spoil.

If a man wishes to make an attempt on a kingdom, does he not set death before him in a thousand shapes? Is he not armed at all points, does he not practice the art of war, does he not do everything with this view, and so rush on to the attack? But we do not act thus. We wish to take the spoil while we are sleeping, and therefore we come off with empty hands. Dost thou not see plunderers, how they flee, how

---

[1] See Acts iv. 12, 13; v. 4. The power of our Lord, after He had received His kingdom, was exercised through them.
[2] i.e. the material heaven.

[3] Lit. "they become righteous in ten thousand"; but the true reading is perhaps ἐν γὰρ τοῖς μυρίοις γίνεται δικαίοις, "for it is formed in ten thousand righteous men," as has been conjectured from an Old Lat.

rapidly they move? how they force their way through everything? And there is need of expedition here. The devil is in pursuit of thee. He orders those before to detain thee. But if thou art strong, if thou art watchful, thou wilt spurn one, and thrust aside another, and escape from all, as a bird. Yea, if thou depart hence, if thou escape from the market and the tumult, I mean this life, and arrive at those higher regions beyond these, in the world to come. For there, as in a solitude, there is no tumult, no one to disturb, or to stay thy course.

Hast thou seized? Yet a little exertion is needed after the seizure, that what thou hast seized may not be taken from thee. If we run on, if we look to none of those things that are set before our eyes, if we consider nothing but how we may escape from those who would hinder us, we shall be able to retain with all security what we have seized. Hast thou seized on chastity? Tarry not; flee beyond the reach of the devil. If he sees that he cannot overtake thee, he will cease to pursue; as we, when we can no longer see those who have robbed us, despair of the pursuit, and do not pursue, nor call on others to stop thief, but suffer them to escape. So do thou run vigorously at the beginning, and when thou art beyond the reach of the devil, he will not afterwards attack thee, but thou wilt be in safety, securely enjoying those unspeakable blessings, which God grant that we may all obtain through Jesus Christ our Lord. To whom with the Father, and the Holy Ghost, be glory, power, honor, and worship, now and for ever, and world without end. Amen.

HOMILIES OF ST. JOHN CHRYSOSTOM,

ARCHBISHOP OF CONSTANTINOPLE,

ON THE

EPISTLE OF ST. PAUL THE APOSTLE

TO

TITUS.

HOMILY I

TITUS i. 1–4.

"Paul, a servant of God, and an Apostle of Jesus Christ, according to the faith of God's elect, and the acknowledging of the truth which is after godliness; In hope of eternal life, which God, that cannot lie, promised before the world began; But hath in due times manifested His word through preaching, which is committed unto me according to the commandment of God our Saviour; To Titus, mine own son after the common faith; Grace, mercy, and peace, from God the Father, and the Lord Jesus Christ our Saviour."

TITUS was an approved one of the companions of Paul; otherwise, he would not have committed to him the charge of that whole island, nor would he have commanded him to supply what was deficient, as he says, "That thou shouldest set in order the·things that are wanting." (Ver. 5.) He would not have given him jurisdiction over so many Bishops, if he had not placed great confidence in him. They say that he also was a young man, because he calls him his son, though this does not prove it. I think that there is mention made of him in the Acts.[1] Perhaps he was a Corinthian, unless there was some other of the same name. And he summons Zenas, and orders Apollos to be sent to him, never Titus. (Tit. iii. 13.) For he also

[1] In the Vulgate, Acts xviii. 7, there is mention of "Titus, surnamed Justus," at Corinth, and a few MSS. have the name. In the Syriac, which St. Chrysostom might know, "Titus" stands for "Justus." [W. and Hort. read: Τιτίου Ἰούστου. — P. S.]

attests their superior virtue and courage in the presence of the Emperor.

Some time seems to have since elapsed, and Paul, when he wrote this Epistle, appears to have been at liberty. For he says nothing about his trials, but dwells continually upon the grace of God, as being a sufficient encouragement to believers to persevere in virtue. For to learn what they had deserved, and to what state they had been transferred, and that by grace, and what had been vouchsafed them, was no little encouragement. He takes aim also against the Jews, and if he censures the whole nation, we need not wonder, for he does the same in the case of the Galatians, saying, "O foolish Galatians." (Gal. iii. 1.) And this does not proceed from a censorious temper, but from affection. For if it were done for his own sake, one might fairly blame him; but if from the fervor of his zeal for the Gospel, it was not done reproachfully. Christ too, on many occasions, reproached the Scribes and Pharisees, not on his own account, but because they were the ruin of all the rest.

And he writes a short Epistle, with good reason, and this is a proof of the virtue of Titus, that he did not require many words, but a short remembrance. But this Epistle seems to have been written before that to Timothy, for that he wrote as near his end and in prison, but here, as free and at liberty. For his saying, "I have determined to winter at Nicopolis" (Tit. iii. 12), is a proof that he was not yet in bonds, as when he wrote to Timothy.

Ver. 1. "Paul, a servant of God, and an Apostle of Jesus Christ, according to the faith of God's elect."

You observe how he uses these expressions indifferently, sometimes calling himself the "servant of God," and sometimes the "servant of Christ," thus making no difference between the Father and the Son.

"According to the faith of God's elect, and the acknowledging of the truth which is after godliness. In hope of eternal life."

"According to the faith of God's elect." It is because thou hast believed, or rather because thou wast intrusted? I think he meant, that he was intrusted with God's elect, that is, not for any achievements of mine, nor from my toils and labors, did I receive this dignity. It was wholly the effect of His goodness who intrusted me. Yet that the grace may not seem without reason, (for still the whole was not of Him, for why did He not intrust it to others?) he therefore adds, "And the acknowledging of the truth that is after godliness." For it was for this acknowledgment that I was intrusted, or rather it was of His grace that this too was intrusted to me, for He was the author of this also. Whence Christ Himself said, "Ye have not chosen Me, but I have chosen you." (John xv. 16.) And elsewhere this same blessed one writes, "I shall know, even as also I am known." (1 Cor. xiii. 12.) And again, "If I may apprehend that, for which also I am apprehended of Christ Jesus." (Phil. iii. 12.) First we are apprehended, and afterwards we know: [1] first we were called, and then we obeyed. But in saying, "according to the faith of the elect," all is reckoned to them, because on their account I am an Apostle, not for my worthiness, but "for the elect's sake." As he elsewhere says, "All things are yours, whether Paul, or Apollos." (1 Cor. iii. 21.)

"And the acknowledging the truth that is after godliness." For there is a truth in other things, that is not according to godliness; for knowledge in matters of agriculture, knowledge of the arts, is true knowledge; but this truth is after godliness. Or this, "according to faith," means that they believed, as the other elect believed, and acknowledged the truth. This acknowledging then is from faith, and not from reasonings.

"In hope of eternal life." He spoke of the present life, which is in the grace of God, and he also speaks of the future, and sets before us the rewards that follow the mercies which God has bestowed upon us. For He is willing to crown us because we have believed, and have been delivered from error. Observe how the introduction is full of the mercies of God, and this whole Epistle is especially of the same character, thus exciting the holy man himself, and his disciples also, to greater exertions. For nothing profits us so much as constantly to remember the mercies of God, whether public or private. And if our hearts are warmed when we receive the favors of our friends, or hear some kind word or deed of theirs, much more shall we be zealous in His service when we see into what dangers we had fallen, and that God has delivered us from them all.

"And the acknowledging of the truth." This he says with reference to the type. For that was an "acknowledging" and a "godliness," yet not of the Truth,[2] yet neither was it falsehood, it was godliness, but it was in type and figure. And he has well said, "In hope of eternal life." For the former was in hope of the present life. For it is said, "he that doeth these things shall live in them." (Rom. x. 5.) You see how at the beginning he sets forth the difference of grace. They are not the elect, but we. For if they were once called the elect, yet are they no longer called so.

Ver. 2. "Which God, that cannot lie, promised before the world began."

That is, not now upon a change of mind, but from the beginning it was so foreordained. This he often asserts, as when he says, "Separated unto the Gospel of God." (Rom. i. 1.) And again, "Whom He did foreknow, He also did predestinate." (Rom. viii. 29.) Thus showing our high origin, in that He did not love us now first, but from the beginning: and it is no little matter to be loved of old, and from the beginning.

"Which God, that cannot lie, promised." If He "cannot lie," what He has promised will assuredly be fulfilled. If He "cannot lie," we ought not to doubt it, though it be after death. "Which God, that cannot lie," he says, "promised before the world began"; by this also, "before the world began," he shows that it is worthy of our belief. It is not because the Jews have not come in, that these things are promised. It had been so planned from the first. Hear therefore what he says,

"But hath in His own [3] times manifested."

Wherefore then was the delay? From His

[1] al. "first we are apprehended, and afterwards we apprehend; first we are known, and then we know."

[2] Thus our Lord, speaking as a Jew, said (John iv. 22), "We know what we worship"; and yet v. 23, "The hour cometh, and now is, when the true worshipers shall worship the Father in spirit and in truth."

[3] Or, "its own," ἰδίοις, E. V. "due."

concern for men, and that it might be done at a seasonable time. "It is time for Thee, Lord, to work" (Ps. cxix. 125), says the Prophet. For by "His own[1] times" is meant the suitable times, the due, the fitting.

Ver. 3. "But hath in due times manifested His word through preaching, which is committed unto me."

That is, the preaching is committed unto me. For this included everything, the Gospel, and things present, and things future, life, and godliness, and faith, and all things at once. "Through preaching," that is, openly and with all boldness, for this is the meaning of "preaching." For as a herald proclaims[2] in the theater in the presence of all, so also we preach, adding nothing, but declaring the things which we have heard. For the excellence of a herald consists in proclaiming to all what has really happened, not in adding or taking away anything. If therefore it is necessary to preach, it is necessary to do it with boldness of speech. Otherwise, it is not preaching. On this account Christ did not say, Tell it "upon the housetops," but "preach upon the housetops" (Matt. x. 27); showing both by the place and by the manner what was to be done.

"Which is committed unto me according to the commandment of God our Saviour."

The expressions, "committed unto me," and "according to the commandment," show the matter to be worthy of credit, so that no one should think it discreditable, nor be hesitating about it, or discontented. If then it is a commandment, it is not at my disposal. I fulfill what is commanded. For of things to be done, some are in our power, others are not. For what He commands, that is not in our power, what He permits, is left to our choice. For instance, "Whosoever shall say to his brother, Thou fool, shall be in danger of hell fire." (Matt. v. 22.) This is a commandment. And again, "If thou bring thy gift to the altar, and there rememberest that thy brother hath aught against thee, leave there thy gift before the altar, and go thy way; first be reconciled to thy brother, and then come and offer thy gift." (Matt. v. 23, 24.) This also is a command. But when He says, "If thou wilt be perfect, go and sell all that thou hast" (Matt. xix. 21): and, "He that is able to receive it, let him receive it" (Matt. xix. 12): this is not a command, for He makes His hearer the disposer of the matter, and leaves him the choice, whether he will do it or not. For these things we may either do or not do. But commandments are not left to our choice, we must either perform them, or be punished for not doing so. This is

implied when he says, "Necessity is laid upon me; yea woe is unto me, if I preach not the Gospel." (1 Cor. ix. 16.) This I will state more plainly, that it may be manifest to all. For instance, He that is intrusted with the government of the Church, and honored with the office of a Bishop, if he does not declare to the people what they ought to do, will have to answer for it. But the layman is under no such obligation. On this account Paul also says, "According to the commandment of God our Saviour," I do this. And see how the epithets fit in to what I have said. For having said above, "God who cannot lie," here he says, "According to the commandment of God our Saviour." If then He is our Saviour, and He commanded these things with a view that we should be saved, it is not from a love of command. It is a matter of faith, and the commandment of God our Saviour.

"To Titus mine own[3] son," that is, my true son. For it is possible for men not to be true sons, as he of whom he says, "If any man that is called a brother be a fornicator, or covetous, or an idolater, or a railer, or a drunkard, with such an one no not to eat." (1 Cor. v. 11.) Here is a son,[4] but not a true son. A son indeed he is, because he has once received the grace, and has been regenerated: but he is not a true son, because he is unworthy of his Father, and a deserter to the usurped sovereignty of another. For in children by nature, the true and the spurious are determined by the father that begot, and the mother who bore them. But it is not so in this case, but it depends on the disposition. For one who was a true son may become spurious, and a spurious son may become a true one. For it is not the force of nature, but the power of choice, on which it depends, whence it is subject to frequent changes. Onesimus was a true son, but he was again not true, for he became "unprofitable"; then he again became a true son, so as to be called by the Apostle his "own bowels." (Philem. 12.)

Ver. 4. "To Titus, mine own son after the common faith."

What is "after the common faith"? After he had called him his own son, and assumed the dignity of a father, hear how it is that he lessens and lowers that honor. He adds, "After the common faith"; that is, with respect to the faith I have no advantage over thee; for it is common, and both thou and I were born by it. Whence then does he call him his son? Either only wishing to express his affection for him, or his priority in the Gospel, or to show that Titus had been enlightened by him. On this account he calls the faithful both children and brethren;

---

[1] Or, "its own," ἰδίοις, E.V. "due."
[2] κηρύττει, the same word as is used for preaching.
[3] γνησίῳ.
[4] τέκνον.

brethren, because they were born by the same faith ; children, because it was by his hands. By mentioning the common faith, therefore, he intimates their brotherhood.

Ver. 4. "Grace and peace from God the Father, and the Lord Jesus Christ our Saviour."

Because he had called him his son, he adds, "from God the Father," to elevate his mind by showing whose son he was, and by not only naming the common faith, but by adding " our Father," he implies that he has this honor equally with himself. MORAL. Observe also how he offers the same prayers for the Teacher, as for the disciples and the multitude. For indeed he needs such prayers as much, or rather more than they, by how much he has greater enmities to encounter, and is more exposed to the necessity of offending God. For the higher is the dignity, the greater are the dangers of the priestly office. For one good act in his episcopal office is sufficient to raise him to heaven, and one error to sink him to hell itself. For, to pass over all other cases of daily occurrence, if he happens, either from friendship or any other cause, to have advanced an unworthy person to a Bishopric, and have committed to him the rule of a great city, see to how great a flame he renders himself obnoxious. For not only will he have to account for the souls that are lost, for they are lost through the man's irreligion, but for all that is done amiss by the other. For he that is irreligious in a private station will be much more so when he is raised to power. It is much indeed, if a pious man continue such after his elevation to rule. For he is then more strongly assailed by vainglory, and the love of wealth, and self-will, when office gives him the power ; and by offenses, insults, and reproaches, and numberless other evils. If therefore any one be irreligious, he will become more so when raised to office ; and he who appoints such a ruler will be answerable for all the offenses committed by him, and for the whole people. But if it is said of him who gives offense to one soul, " It were better for him that a millstone were hanged about his neck, and that he were drowned in the depth of the sea " (Matt. xviii. 6) ; what will he have to suffer who offends so many souls, whole cities and populations, and multitudes of families,[1] men, women, children, citizens, and husbandmen, the inhabitants of the city itself, and of all places subject to it? To say thrice as much more is to say nothing, so severe is the vengeance and the punishment to which he will be obnoxious. So that a Bishop especially needs the grace and peace of God. For if without these he governs the people, all is ruined and lost, for want of those helms. And though he be skilled in the art of steering, he will sink the vessel and those that sail in it, if he has not these helms, " the grace and peace of God."

Hence I am struck with astonishment at those who desire so great a burden. Wretched and unhappy man, seest thou what it is thou desirest ? If thou art by thyself, unknown and undistinguished, though thou committest ten thousand faults, thou hast only one soul for which to give an account, and for it alone wilt thou be answerable. But when thou art raised to this office, consider for how many persons thou art obnoxious to punishment. Hear what Paul says, " Obey them that have the rule over you, and submit yourselves : for they watch for your souls as they that must give account." (Heb. xiii. 17.) But dost thou desire honor and power? But what pleasure is there in this honor? I confess, I see not. For to be a ruler indeed is not possible, since it depends upon those under thy rule to obey or not. And to any one who considers the matter closely, it will appear that a Bishop does not so much come to rule, as to serve a multitude of masters, who are of opposite desires and sentiments. For what one commends, another blames ; what this man censures, that admires. To whom therefore shall he listen, with whom shall he comply? It is impossible ! And the slave that is bought with money complains if his master's commands are contrary to each other. But shouldest thou grieve, when so many masters give the contrary orders, thou art condemned even for this, and all mouths are opened against thee. Tell me then, is this honor, is this rule, is this power?

One who holds the Episcopal office has required a contribution of money. He who is unwilling to contribute not only withholds it, but that he may not seem to withhold it from indifference, he accuses his Bishop. He is a thief, he says, a robber, he engulfs the goods of the poor, he devours the rights of the needy. Cease thy calumnies ! How long wilt thou say these things? Wilt thou not contribute? No one compels thee, there is no constraint. Why dost thou revile him who counsels and advises thee? Is any one reduced to need, and he from inability, or some other hindrance, has not lent a hand? No allowance is made for him, the reproaches in this case are worse than in the other. This then is government ! And he cannot avenge himself. For they are his own bowels, and as though the bowels be swollen, and though they give pain to the head and the rest of the body, we venture not on revenge, we cannot take a sword and pierce them ; so if one of those under our rule be of such sort, and create trouble and disorder by these accusations, we dare not avenge ourselves, for this would be far from the

---

[1] So Sav. mar. Edd. " souls."

disposition of a father, but we must endure the grief till he becomes sound and well.

The slave bought with money has an appointed work, which when he has performed, he is afterwards his own master. But the Bishop is distracted on every side, and is expected to do many things that are beyond his power. If he knows not how to speak, there is great murmuring ; and if he can speak, then he is accused of being vainglorious. If he cannot raise the dead, he is of no worth, they say: such an one is pious, but this man is not. If he eats a moderate meal, for this he is accused, he ought to be strangled, they say. If he is seen at the bath,[1] he is much censured. In short, he ought not to look upon the sun ! If he does the same things that I do, if he bathes, eats and drinks, and wears the same clothing, and has the care of a house and servants, on what account is he set over me ? But he has domestics to minister to him, and an ass to ride upon, why then is he set over me ? But say, ought he then to have no one to wait upon him ? Ought he himself to light his own fire, to draw water, to cleave wood, to go to market ? How great a degradation would this be ! Even the holy Apostles would not that any ministers of the word should attend upon the tables of the widows, but they considered it a business unworthy of them : and would you degrade them to the offices of your own domestics ? Why dost not thou, who commandest these things, come and perform these services ? Tell me, does not he minister to thee a better service than thine, which is bodily ? Why dost thou not send thy domestic to wait upon him ? Christ washed the feet of His disciples ; is it a great thing for thee to give this service to thy Teacher ? But thou art not willing to render it thyself, and thou grudgest it to him. Ought he then to draw his livelihood from heaven ? But God wills not so.

But you say, " Had the Apostles free men to serve them ? " Would you then hear how the Apostles lived ? They made long journeys, and free men and honorable women laid down their lives and souls for their relief. But hear this blessed Apostle thus exhorting ; " Hold such in reputation " (Phil. ii. 29, 30) : and again, " Because for the work of Christ he was nigh unto death, not regarding his life, to supply your lack of service toward me." See what he says ! but

[1] See above, p. 499.

thou hast not a word to throw away upon thy spiritual father, much less wilt thou submit to any danger in his behalf. But thou sayest, " He ought not to frequent the bath." And where is this forbidden ? there is nothing honorable in being unclean.

These are not the things we find blamed or applauded at all. For the qualities which a Bishop is required to possess are different, as to be blameless, sober, orderly, hospitable, apt to teach. These the Apostle requires, and these we ought to look for in a ruler of the Church, but nothing further. Thou art not more strict than Paul, or rather more strict than the Spirit. If he be a striker, or violent, or cruel, and unmerciful, accuse him. These things are unworthy of a Bishop. If he be luxurious, this also is censurable. But if he takes care of his body that he may minister to thee, if he attends to his health that he may be useful, ought he for this to be accused ? Knowest thou not that bodily infirmity no less than infirmity of soul injures both us and the Church ? Why, otherwise, does Paul attend to this matter, in writing to Timothy, " Use a little wine for thy stomach's sake, and thy often infirmities " ? (1 Tim. v. 23.) For if we could practice virtue with the soul alone, we need not take care of the body. And why then were we born at all ? But if this has contributed a great share, is it not the extreme of folly to neglect it ?

For suppose a man honored with the Bishopric, and intrusted with a public charge of the Church, and let him in other respects be virtuous, and have every quality, which a priest ought to possess, yet let him be always confined to his bed by reason of great infirmity, what service will he be able to render ? Upon what mission can he go ? what visitation can he undertake ? whom can he rebuke or admonish ? These things I say, that you may learn not causelessly to accuse him, but rather may receive him favorably ; as also that if any one desire rule in the Church, seeing the shower of abuse that attends it, he may quench that desire. Great indeed is the danger of such a station, and it requires " the grace and peace of God." Which that we may have abundantly, do you pray for us, and we for you, that practicing virtue aright we may so obtain the blessings promised, through Jesus Christ, with whom, &c.

HOMILY II.

TITUS i. 5, 6.

"For this cause left I thee in Crete, that thou shouldest set in order the things that are wanting, and ordain elders in every city as I had appointed thee: If any be blameless, the husband of one wife, having faithful children, not accused of riot, or unruly."

THE whole life of men in ancient times was one of action and contention; ours on the contrary is a life of indolence. They knew that they were brought into the world for this purpose, that they might labor according to the will of Him who brought them into it; but we, as if we had been placed here but to eat and drink, and lead a life of pleasure, we pay no regard to spiritual things. I speak not only of the Apostles, but of those that followed them. You see them accordingly traversing all places, and pursuing this as their only business, living altogether as in a foreign land, as those who had no city upon earth. Hear therefore what the blessed Apostle saith,

"For this cause left I thee in Crete."

As if the whole world had been one house, they divided it among themselves, administering its affairs everywhere, each taking care of his several portion of it.

"For this cause left I thee in Crete, that thou shouldest set in order the things that are [R. V. were] wanting."

He does not command this in an imperious manner; "that thou shouldest set in order," he says. Here we see a soul free from all envy, seeking everywhere the advantage of his disciples, not curiously solicitous, whether the good was done by himself or by another. For where there was a case of danger and great difficulty, he in his own person set it in order. But those things which were rather attended with honor and praise he committed to his disciple, as the ordination of Bishops, and such other things as required some farther arrangement,[1] or, so to speak, to be brought to greater perfection. What sayest thou? does he farther set in order thy work? and dost thou not think it a disgrace bringing shame upon thee? By no means; for I look only to the common good, and whether it be done by me, or by another, it makes no difference to me. Thus it becomes him to be affected who presides in the Church, not to seek his own honor, but the common good.

"And ordain elders in every city," here he is speaking of Bishops, as we have before said,[2]

"as I had appointed thee. If any is blameless." "In every city," he says, for he did not wish the whole island to be intrusted to one, but that each should have his own charge and care, for thus he would have less labor himself, and those under his rule would receive greater attention, if the Teacher had not to go about to[3] the presidency of many Churches, but was left to be occupied with one only, and to bring that into order.

Ver. 6. "If any be blameless, the husband of one wife, having faithful children, not accused of riot, or unruly."

Why does he bring forward such an one? To stop the mouths of those heretics, who comdemned marriage, showing that it is not an unholy thing in itself, but so far honorable, that a married man might ascend the holy throne; and at the same reproving the wanton, and not permitting their admission into this high office who contracted a second marriage. For he who retains no kind regard for her who is departed, how shall he be a good president? and what accusation would he not incur? For you all know, that though it is not forbidden by the laws to enter into a second marriage, yet it is a thing liable to many ill constructions. Wishing therefore a ruler to give no handle for reproach to those under his rule, he on this account says, "If any be blameless,"[4] that is, if his life be free from reproach, if he has given occasion to no one to assail his character. Hear what Christ says, "If the light that is in thee be darkness, how great is that darkness!" (Matt. vi. 23.)

"Having faithful children, not accused of riot, or unruly."

We should observe what care he bestows upon children. For he who cannot be the instructor of his own children, how should he be the Teacher of others? If he cannot keep in order those whom he has had with him from the beginning, whom he has brought up, and over whom he had power both by the laws, and by nature, how will he be able to benefit those without? For if the incompetency[5] of the father had not been great, he would not have allowed those to become bad whom from the first he had under his power. For it is not possible, indeed it is not, that one should turn out ill who is brought up with much care, and

---

[1] ἐπιδιορθώσεως.
[2] See on 1 Tim. iii. 7, Hom. x.

[3] Sav. mar. "were not to be distracted by."
[4] ἀνέγκλητος.
[5] ναθέια.

has received great attention. Sins are not so prevalent by nature, as to overcome so much previous care. But if, occupied in the pursuit of wealth, he has made his children a secondary concern, and not bestowed much care upon them, even so he is unworthy. For if when nature prompted, he was so void of affection or so senseless, that he thought more of his wealth than of his children, how should he be raised to the Episcopal throne, and so great rule? For if he was unable to restrain them, it is a great proof of his weakness; and if he was unconcerned, his want of affection is much to be blamed. He then that neglects his own children, how shall he take care of other men's? And he has not only said, "not riotous," but not even "accused of riot." There must not be an ill report, or such an opinion of them.

Ver. 7. "For a Bishop must be blameless, as the steward of God; not self-willed, not soon angry, not given to wine, no striker."

For a ruler without, as he rules by law and compulsion, perhaps does not consult the wishes of those under his rule. But he who ought to rule men with their own consent, and who will be thankful for his rule, if he so conduct himself as to do everything of his own will, and share counsels with no one, makes his presidency tyrannical rather than popular. For he must be "blameless, as the steward of God, not self-willed, not soon angry." For how shall he instruct others to rule that passion, who has not taught himself? For power leads on to many temptations, it makes a man more harsh and difficult to please, even him that was very mild, surrounding him with so many occasions of anger. If he have not previously practiced himself in this virtue, he will grow harsh, and will injure and destroy much that is under his rule.

"Not given to wine,[1] no striker." Here he is speaking of the insolent man. For he should do all things by admonition or rebuke, and not by insolence. What necessity, tell me, for insult? He ought to terrify, to alarm, to penetrate the soul with the threat of hell. But he that is insulted becomes more impudent, and rather despises him that insults him. Nothing produces contempt more than insult; it disgraces the insolent person, and prevents his being respected, as he ought to be. Their discourse ought to be delivered with much caution. In reproving sins they should bear in mind the future judgment, but keep clear of all insolence. Yet if any prevent them from doing their duty, they must prosecute the matter with all authority. "Not a striker," he says. The teacher is the physician of souls. But the physician does not strike, but heals and restores him that has stricken him. "Not given to filthy lucre."

Ver. 8. "But a lover of hospitality, a lover of good men, sober, just, holy, temperate."

Ver. 9. "Holding fast the faithful word as he has been taught."

You see what intensity of virtue he required. "Not given to filthy lucre," that is, showing great contempt for money. "A lover of hospitality, a lover of good men, sober, just, holy"; he means, giving away all his substance to them that need. "Temperate"; he speaks not here of one who fasts, but of one who commands his passions, his tongue, his hands, his eyes. For this is temperance, to be drawn aside by no passion.

"Holding fast the faithful word as he hath been taught." By "faithful" is here meant "true," or that which was delivered through faith, not requiring reasonings, or questionings.

"Holding fast," that is, having care of it, making it his business. What then, if he be ignorant of the learning that is without? For this cause, he says, "the faithful word, according to teaching."[2]

"That he may be able both to exhort, and to convince the gainsayers."

So that there is need not of pomp of words, but of strong minds, of skill in the Scriptures, and of powerful thoughts. Do you not see that Paul put to flight the whole world, that he was more powerful than Plato and all the rest? But it was by miracles, you say. Not by miracles only, for if you peruse the Acts of the Apostles, you will find him often prevailing by his teaching previously to his miracles.

"That he may be able by sound doctrine to exhort," that is, to retain his own people, and to overthrow the adversaries. "And to convince the gainsayers." For if this is not done, all is lost. He who knows not how to combat the adversaries, and to "bring every thought into captivity to the obedience of Christ," and to beat down reasonings, he who knows not what he ought to teach with regard to right doctrine, far from him be the Teacher's throne. For the other qualities may be found in those under his rule, such as to be "blameless, to have his children in subjection, to be hospitable, just, holy." But that which characterizes the Teacher is this, to be able to instruct in the word, to which no regard is now paid.

Ver. 10. "For there are many unruly and vain talkers, and deceivers, especially they of the circumcision;"

Ver. 11. "Whose mouths must be stopped."

Seest thou how he shows that they are such? From their not wishing to be ruled, but to rule. For he has glanced at this. When therefore thou canst not persuade them, do not give them charges, but stop their mouths, for the benefit of

---

[1] πάροινον, see p. 438, note.

[2] The Greek does not exclude the sense of teaching others.

others. But of what advantage will this be, if they will not obey, or are unruly? Why then should he stop their mouths? In order that others may be benefited by it.

"Who subvert whole houses, teaching things which they ought not for filthy lucre's sake."

For if he has undertaken the office of a Teacher, and is not able to combat these enemies, and to stop their mouths who are so shameless, he will become in each case the cause of their destruction who perish. And if some one has thus advised, "Seek not to be a judge, unless thou canst take away iniquity" (Ecclus. vii. 6); much more may we say here, "Seek not to be a Teacher, if thou art unequal to the dignity of the office; but though dragged to it, decline it." Dost thou see that the love of power,[1] the love of filthy lucre, is the cause of these evils? "Teaching things which they ought not," he says, "for filthy lucre's sake."

MORAL. For there is nothing which is not spoiled by these passions. But as when violent winds, falling on a calm sea, turn it up from its foundation, and mingle the sand with the waves, so these passions assailing the soul turn all upside down, and dim the clearness of the mental sight, but especially does the mad desire of glory. For a contempt for money any one may easily attain, but to despise the honor that proceeds from the multitude, requires a great effort, a philosophic temper, a certain angelic soul that reaches to the very summit of heaven. For there is no passion so tyrannical, so universally prevalent, in a greater or less degree indeed, but still everywhere. How then shall we subdue it, if not wholly, yet in some little part? By looking up to heaven, by setting God before our eyes, by entertaining thoughts superior to earthly things. Imagine, when thou desirest glory, that thou hast already attained it, and mark the end, and thou wilt find it to be nothing. Consider with what loss it is attended, of how many and how great blessings it will deprive thee. For thou wilt undergo the toils and dangers, yet be deprived of the fruits and rewards of them. Consider that the majority are bad, and despise their opinion. In the case of each individual, consider what the man is, and thou wilt see how ridiculous a thing is glory, that it is rather to be called shame.

And after this, lift up thy thoughts to the theater[2] above. When in doing any good thou considerest that it ought to be displayed to men, and thou seekest for some spectators of the action, and art in travail to be seen, reflect that God beholds thee, and all that desire will be extinguished. Retire from the earth, and look to that theater that is in Heaven. If men should

praise thee, yet hereafter they will blame thee, will envy thee, will assail thy character; or if they do not, yet their praise will not benefit thee. It is not so with God. He delights in praising our virtuous deeds. Hast thou spoken well, and obtained applause? What hast thou gained? For if those who applauded thee were benefited, changed in their minds, become better men, and had desisted from their evil deeds, then mightest thou indeed rejoice, not at the praises bestowed, but at the wonderful change for the better. But if they continue their praises, and loud plaudits, but gain no good by what they applaud, thou oughtest rather to grieve: for these things turn to their judgment and condemnation.[3] But thou obtainest glory for thy piety. If thou art truly pious, and conscious of no guilt, thou shouldest rejoice, not because thou are reputed pious, but because thou art so. But if, without being so, thou desirest the good opinion of the multitude, consider that they will not be thy judges at the last day, but He who knoweth perfectly the things that are hid. And if while conscious of guilt, thou art supposed by all to be pure, instead of rejoicing, thou shouldest grieve and mourn bitterly, keeping constantly in view that Day, in which all things will be revealed, in which the hidden things of darkness will be brought to light.

Dost thou enjoy honor? reject it, knowing that it renders thee a debtor. Does no one honor thee? thou oughtest to rejoice at it. For God will not lay[4] to thy charge this, among other things, that thou hast enjoyed honor. Seest thou not that God upbraids Israel with this among other things, by his prophet, "I took of your sons for Prophets, and of your young men for sanctification"? (Amos ii. 11, Sept.) Thou wilt therefore gain this advantage at least, that thou wilt not aggravate thy punishment. For he who is not honored in the present life, who is despised, and held in no consideration, but is insulted and scorned, gains this at least, if nothing else, that he has not to answer for being honored by his fellow-servants.[5] And on many other accounts he gains[6] by it. He is brought down and humbled, nor if he would, can he be high-minded, if[7] he takes the more heed to himself. But he, who enjoys more honor, besides being responsible for great debts, is lifted up into arrogance and vainglory, and becomes the slave of men; and as this tyranny increases, he is compelled to do many things which he would not.

Knowing therefore that it is better to want

---

[1] So B. and Sav. mar. Edd. "avarice."
[2] i.e. spectators.

[3] B. and Sav. mar. add, "and condemnation."
[4] One MS. "will lay." The sense is the same, as it refers to the contrary case.
[5] In this spirit Coleridge prays "to be forgiven for fame."
[6] B. "will gain." Ben. "has cause to rejoice."
[7] B. and Sav. mar. "but."

glory, than to possess it, let us not seek for honors, but evade them when they are offered, let us cast them from us, let us extinguish that desire. This we have said at once to the rulers of the Church, and to those under their rule. For a soul desirous of honor, and of being glorified, shall not see the kingdom of heaven. This is not my own saying. I speak not my own words, but those of the Spirit of God. He shall not see it, though he practice virtue. For he saith, "They have their reward." (Matt. vi. 5.) He then, who has no reward to receive, how shall he see the kingdom of heaven? I forbid thee not to desire glory, but I would wish it to be the true glory, that which proceeds from God. "Whose praise," it is said, "is not of men, but of God." (Rom. ii. 29.) Let us be pious in secret, not cumbered with parade, and show, and hypocrisy. Let us cast away the sheep's clothing, and rather let us become sheep. Nothing is more worthless than the glory of men. Should thou see a company of little children, mere sucklings, wouldest thou desire glory from them?[1] Be thus affected towards all men with respect to glory.

It is for this reason called vainglory. Dost thou see the masks worn by stage-players? how beautiful and splendid they are, fashioned to the extreme height of elegance. Canst thou show me any such real countenance? By no means. What then? didst thou ever fall in love with them? No. Wherefore? Because they are empty, imitating beauty, but not being really beautiful. Thus human glory is empty, and an imitation of glory: it is not true glory. That beauty only which is natural, which is within, is lasting: that which is put on externally often conceals deformity, conceals it from men until the evening. But when the theater breaks up, and the masks are taken off, each appears what he really is.

Let us therefore pursue truth, and not be as if we were on the stage and acting a part. For of what advantage is it, tell me, to be gazed at by a multitude? It is vainglory, and nothing else. For return to thy house, and solitude, and immediately all is gone. Thou hast gone to the market-place, thou hast turned upon thee the eyes of all present. What hast thou gained? Nothing. It vanished, and passed away like dissolving smoke. Do we then love things thus unsubstantial? How unreasonable is this! what madness! To one thing only let us look, to the praise of God. If this be our object, we shall never seek the praise of men; but if it falls to us, we shall despise, deride, and reject it. We shall be affected as those who desire gold, but receive clay. Let not any one praise thee, for it profits nothing; and if he blame thee, it harms thee not. But with God praise and blame are attended with real gain and loss, whilst all is vain that proceeds from men. And herein we are made like unto God, that He needs not glory from men. "I receive not," said Christ, "honor from men." (John v. 41.) Is this then a light thing, tell me? When thou art unwilling to despise glory, say, "By despising it, I shall resemble God," and immediately thou wilt despise it. But it is impossible that the slave of glory should not be a slave to all, more servile than slaves in reality. For we do not impose upon our slaves such tasks, as glory exacts from her captives. Base and shameful are the things she makes them say, and do,[2] and suffer, and when she sees them obedient, she is the more urgent in her commands.

Let us fly then, I entreat you, let us fly from this slavery. But how shall we be able? If we think seriously[3] of what is in this world, if we observe that things present are a dream, a shadow, and nothing better; we shall easily overcome this desire, and neither in little nor in great things shall be led captive by it. But if in little things we do not despise it, we shall easily be overcome by it in the most important. Let us therefore remove far from us the sources of it, and these are, folly, and meanness of mind, so that, if we assume a lofty spirit, we shall be able to look beyond honor from the multitude, and to extend our views to heaven, and obtain the good things there. Of which God grant that we may all be partakers, by the grace and lovingkindness of our Lord Jesus Christ, with whom, &c.

---

[1] Sav. mar. "No, thou sayest."

[2] So Old Lat. and as it seems two MSS., but the reading of the MSS. is not fully stated.

[3] φιλοσοφήσωμεν.

HOMILY III.

TITUS i. 12–14.

"One of themselves, even a prophet of their own, said, The Cretians are always liars, evil beasts, slow bellies. This witness is true. Wherefore rebuke them sharply, that they may be sound in the faith; Not giving heed to Jewish fables, and commandments of men, that turn from the truth."

THERE are several questions here. First, who it was that said this? Secondly, why Paul quoted it? Thirdly, why he brings forward a testimony that is not correct? Let us then offer a seasonable solution of these, having premised some other things. For when Paul was discoursing to the Athenians, in the course of his harangue he quoted these words, "To the Unknown God": and again, "For we also are His offspring, as certain also of your own poets have said." (Acts xvii. 23, 28.) It was Epimenides[1] who said this, himself a Cretan, and whence he was moved to say it is necessary to mention. It is this. The Cretans have a tomb of Jupiter, with this inscription. "Here lieth Zan, whom they call Jove." On account of this inscription, then, the poet ridiculing the Cretans as liars, as he proceeds, introduces, to increase the ridicule, this passage.

For even a tomb, O King, of thee
They made, who never diedst, but aye shalt be.

If then this testimony is true, observe what a difficulty! For if the poet is true who said that they spoke falsely, in asserting that Jupiter could die, as the Apostle says, it is a fearful thing! Attend, beloved, with much exactness. The poet said that the Cretans were liars for saying that Jupiter was dead. The Apostle confirmed his testimony: so, according to the Apostle, Jupiter is immortal: for he says, "this witness is true"! What shall we say then? Or rather how shall we solve this? The Apostle has not said this, but simply and plainly applied this testimony to their habit of falsehood. Else why has he not added, "For even a tomb, O king, of thee, they made"? So that the Apostle has not said this, but only that one had well said, "The Cretians are always liars." But it is not only from hence that we are confident that Jupiter is not a God. From many other arguments we are able to prove this, and not from the testimony of the Cretans. Besides, he has not said,

that in this they were liars. Nay and it is more probable that they were deceived as to this point too.[2] For they believed in other gods, on which account the Apostle calls them liars.

And as to the question, why does he cite the testimonies of the Greeks? It is because we put them most to confusion when we bring our testimonies and accusations from their own writers, when we make those their accusers, who are admired among themselves. For this reason he elsewhere quotes those words, "To the Unknown God." For the Athenians, as they did not receive all their gods from the beginning, but from time to time admitted some others, as those from the Hyperboreans, the worship of Pan, and the greater and the lesser mysteries, so these same, conjecturing that besides these there might be some other God, of whom they were ignorant, that they might be duly devout to him also, erected to him an altar, with this inscription, "To the Unknown God," thereby almost implying, "if there might be some God unknown to them." He therefore said to them, Him whom you have by anticipation acknowledged, I declare to you. But those words, "We also are His offspring," are quoted from Aratus, who having previously said, "Earth's paths are full of Jove, the sea is full"—adds, "For we too are His offspring," in which I conceive he shows that we are sprung from God. How then does Paul wrest what is said of Jupiter to the God of the universe? He has not transferred to God what belongs to Jupiter. But what is applicable to God, and was neither justly nor properly applied to Jupiter, this he restores to God, since the name of God belongs to Him alone, and is not lawfully bestowed upon idols.

And from what writers should he address them? From the Prophets? They would not have believed them. Since with the Jews too he does not argue from the Gospels, but from the Prophets. For this reason he says, "Unto the Jews I became as a Jew, to them that are without law, as without law, to those that are under the Law, as under the Law." (1 Cor. ix. 20, 21.) Thus does God too, as in the case of the wise men, He does not conduct them by an Angel, nor a Prophet, nor an Apostle, nor an Evangelist, but how? By a star. For as their art made them conversant with these, He made use of such

---

[1] The words here quoted are found in Callimachus, Hymn ad Jov. v. 8, to whom Theodoret ascribes them. The "evil beasts," &c., is found in Hesiod, Theogon. v. 26, applied to shepherds. Downes suggested that Epimenides may have borrowed from Hesiod, and Callimachus from him.

[2] He seems to mean in thinking Jupiter a God.

means to guide them. So in the case of the oxen, that drew the ark. "If it goeth up by the way of his own coast, then He hath done us this great evil" (1 Sam. vi. 9), as their prophets suggested. Do these prophets then speak the truth? No; but he refutes and confounds them out of their own mouths. Again, in the case of the witch, because Saul believed in her, he caused him to hear through her what was about to befall him. Why then did Paul stop the mouth of the spirit, that said, "These men are the servants of the most high God, which show unto us the way of salvation"? (Acts xvi. 17.) And why did Christ hinder the devils from speaking of Him? In this case there was reason, since the miracles were going on. For here it was not a star that proclaimed Him, but He Himself; and the demons again were not worshiped[1]; for it was not an image that spoke, that it should be forbidden. He also suffered Balaam to bless, and did not restrain him. Thus He everywhere condescends.

And what wonder? for He permitted opinions erroneous, and unworthy of Himself, to prevail, as that He was a body formerly,[2] and that He was visible. In opposition to which He says, " God is a Spirit." (John iv. 24.) Again, that He delighted in sacrifices, which is far from His nature. And He utters words at variance with His declarations of Himself, and many such things. For He nowhere considers His own dignity, but always what will be profitable to us. And if a father considers not his own dignity, but talks lispingly with his children, and calls their meat and drink not by their Greek names, but by some childish and barbarous words, much more doth God. Even in reproving He condescends, as when He speaks by the prophet, " Hath a nation changed their gods?" (Jer. ii. 11), and in every part of Scripture there are instances of His condescension both in words and actions.

Ver. 13. " Wherefore rebuke them sharply, that they may be sound in the faith."

This he says, because their disposition was froward, deceitful, and dissolute. They have these numberless bad qualities; and because they are prone to lying, deceiving, gluttonous, and slothful, severe reproof is necessary. For such characters will not be managed by mildness, "therefore rebuke them." He speaks not here of Gentiles, but of his own people. " Sharply." Give them, he says, a stroke that cuts deep. For one method is not to be employed with all, but they are to be differently dealt with, according to their various characters and dispositions. He does not here have recourse to exhortation. For as he who treats

with harshness the meek and ingenuous, may destroy them; so he who flatters one that requires severity, causes him to perish, and does not suffer him to be reclaimed.

" That they may be sound in the faith."

This then is soundness, to introduce nothing spurious, nor foreign. But if they who are scrupulous about meats are not sound, but are sick and weak; for, " Them that are weak," he says, " receive ye, but not to doubtful disputations " (Rom xiv. 1); what can be said of those who observe the same fasts, (with the Jews,) who keep the sabbaths, who frequent the places that are consecrated by them? I speak of that at Daphne,[3] of that which is called the cave of Matrona, and of that plain in Cilicia, which is called Saturn's. How are these sound? With them a heavier stroke is necessary. Why then does he not do the same with the Romans? Because their dispositions were different, they were of a nobler character.

Ver. 14. " Not giving heed," he says, " to Jewish fables."

The Jewish tenets were fables in two ways, because they were imitations, and because the thing was past its season, for such things become fables at last. For when a thing ought not to be done, and being done, is injurious, it is a fable even as it is useless. As then those[4] ought not to be regarded, so neither ought these. For this is not being sound. For if thou believest the Faith, why dost thou add other things, as if the faith were not sufficient to justify? Why dost thou enslave thyself by subjection to the Law? Hast thou no confidence in what thou believest? This is a mark of an unsound and unbelieving mind. For one who is faithful does not doubt, but such an one evidently doubts.

Ver. 15. " Unto the pure," he says, " all things are pure."

Thou seest that this is said to a particular purpose.

" But unto them that are defiled and unbelieving is nothing pure."

Things then are not clean or unclean from their own nature, but from the disposition of him who partakes of them.

" But even their mind and conscience is defiled."

Ver. 16. " They profess that they know God; but in works they deny Him, being abominable, and disobedient, and to every good work reprobate."

The swine therefore is clean. Why then was it forbidden as unclean? It was not unclean by nature; for, " all things are pure." Nothing is more unclean than a fish, inasmuch as it even

---

[1] i.e. by Saul. 1 Sam. xxviii. 8.
[2] This word seems to refer to the time when the opinions were allowed to prevail.

[3] See on Stat. Hom. xvii.
[4] i.e. heathen fables.

feeds upon human flesh. But it was permitted and considered clean. Nothing is more unclean than a bird, for it eats worms; or than a stag, which is said to have its name[1] from eating serpents. Yet all these were eaten. Why then was the swine forbidden, and many other things? Not because they were unclean, but to check excessive luxury. But had this been said, they would not have been persuaded; they were restrained therefore by the fear of uncleanness. For tell me, if we enquire nicely into these things, what is more unclean than wine; or than water, with which they mostly purified themselves? They touched not the dead, and yet they were cleansed by the dead, for the victim was dead, and with that they were cleansed. This therefore was a doctrine for children. In the composition of wine, does not dung form a part? For as the vine draws moisture from the earth, so does it from the dung that is thrown upon it. In short, if we wish to be very nice, everything is unclean, otherwise if we please not to be nice, nothing is unclean. Yet all things are pure. God made nothing unclean, for nothing is unclean, except sin only. For that reaches to the soul, and defiles it. Other uncleanness is human prejudice.

"But unto them that are defiled and unbelieving is nothing pure; but even their mind and conscience is defiled."

For how can there be anything unclean among the pure? But he that has a weak soul makes everything unclean, and if there be set abroad a scrupulous enquiry into what is clean or unclean, he will touch nothing. For even these things are not clean, I speak of fish, and other things, according to their notions; (for "their mind and conscience," he says, "is defiled,") but all are impure. Yet Paul says not so; he turns the whole matter upon themselves. For nothing is unclean, he says, but themselves, their mind and their conscience; and nothing is more unclean than these;[2] but an evil will is unclean.

"They profess that they know God, but in works they deny Him, being abominable and disobedient, and unto every good work reprobate."

ii. 1. "But speak thou the things that become sound doctrine."

This then is uncleanness. They are themselves unclean. But be not thou silent on that account. Do thy part, although they may not receive thee. Advise and counsel them, though they may not be persuaded. Here he censures them more severely. For they who are mad imagine that nothing stands still, yet this arises not from the objects that are seen, but from the eyes that see. Because they are unsteady and

giddy, they think that the earth turns round with them, which yet turns not, but stands firm. The derangement[3] is of their own state, not from any affection of the element. So it is here, when the soul is unclean, it thinks all things unclean. Therefore scrupulous observances are no mark of purity, but it is the part of purity to be bold in all things. For he that is pure by nature ventures upon all things, they that are defiled, upon nothing. This we may say against Marcion. Seest thou that it is a mark of purity to be superior to all defilement, to touch nothing implies impurity. This holds even with respect to God. That He assumed flesh is a proof of purity; if through fear He had not taken it, there would have been defilement. He who eats not things that seem unclean, is himself unclean and weak, he who eats, is neither. Let us not call such pure, they are the unclean. He is pure, who dares to feed upon all things. All this caution we ought to exercise towards the things that defile the soul. For that is uncleanness, that is defilement. None of these things is so. Those who have a vitiated palate think what is set before them is unclean, but this is the effect of their disorder. It becomes us therefore to understand the nature of things pure, and things unclean.

MORAL. What then is unclean? Sin, malice, covetousness, wickedness.[4] As it is written: "Wash you, make you clean, put away the evil of your doings." (Isa. i. 16.) "Create in me a clean heart, O God." (Ps. li. 10.) "Depart ye, depart ye, go ye out from thence, touch no unclean thing." (Isa. lii. 52.) These observances were emblems of purifications.[5] "Touch not a dead body," it is said. For sin is such, it is dead and offensive. "The leper is unclean." For sin is a leprosy, various and multiform. And that they had this meaning, appears from what follows. For if the leprosy is general, and overspreads the whole body, he is clean; if it is partial, he is unclean. Thus you see that what is various and changeable is the unclean thing. He again whose seed passes from him is unclean, consider one that is so in soul, casting away his seed. He who is uncircumcised is unclean. These things are not allegorical[6] but typical, for he who does not cut off the wickedness of his heart is the unclean person. He who worketh on the Sabbath is to be stoned, that is, he who is not at all times devoted to God, shall perish.[7] You see how many varieties

---

[1] ἔλαφος.
[2] B. "none of these things is unclean."

[3] al. "the notion," ὑπόνοια, and so B.; it is better than ἀπόνοια.
[4] Sav. "fornication," but πονηρία is repeated in the next quotation, and has most authority.
[5] al "of uncleannesses."
[6] This hardly makes sense. Read ἀληθεία for ἀλληγορία. "These things are not truth, but types," which is his usual way of speaking. Just above, Savile's text is followed.
[7] See on Stat. Hom. xii., where it appears that he does not exclude a reference to the Lord's Day.

of uncleanness there are. The woman in child-bed is unclean. Yet God made child-birth, and the seed of copulation. Why then is the woman unclean, unless something further was intimated? And what was this? He intended to produce piety in the soul, and to deter it from fornication. For if she is unclean who has borne a child, much more she who has committed fornication. If to approach his own wife is not altogether pure, much less to have intercourse with the wife of another. He who attends a funeral is unclean, much more he who has mixed in war and slaughter. And many kinds of uncleanness would be found, if it were necessary to recount them all. But these things are not now required of us. But all is transferred to the soul.

For bodily things are nearer to us, from these therefore he introduced instruction. But it is not so now. For we ought not to be confined to figures, and shadows, but to adhere to the truth, and to uphold it : sin is the unclean thing. From that let us flee, from that let us abstain. "If thou comest near it, it will bite[1] thee." (Ecclus. xxi. 2.) Nothing is more unclean than covetousness. Whence is this manifest? From the facts themselves. For what does it not defile? the hands, the soul, the very house where the ill-gotten treasure is laid up. But the Jews consider this as nothing. And yet Moses carried off the bones of Joseph. Samson drank from the jawbone of an ass, and ate honey from the lion, and Elijah was nourished by ravens, and by a widow woman. And tell me, if we were to be precise about these things, what can be more unclean than our books, which are

made of the skins of animals? The fornicator, then, is not the only one that is unclean, but others more than he, as the adulterer. But both the one and the other are unclean, not on account of the intercourse, (for according to that reasoning a man cohabiting with his own wife would be unclean,) but because of the wickedness of the act, and the injury done to his neighbor in his nearest interests. Dost thou see that it is wickedness that is unclean? He who had two wives was not unclean, and David who had many wives was not unclean. But when he had one unlawfully, he became unclean. Why? Because he had injured and defrauded his neighbor. And the fornicator is not unclean on account of the intercourse, but on account of the manner of it, because it injures the woman, and they injure one another, making the woman common, and subverting the laws of nature. For she ought to be the wife of one man, since it is said, "Male and female created He them." (Gen. i. 27.) And, "they twain shall be one flesh." Not "those many," but "they twain shall be one flesh." Here then is injustice, and therefore the act is wicked. Again, when anger exceeds due measure, it makes a man unclean, not in itself, but because of its excess. Since it is not said, "He that is angry," merely, but "angry without a cause." Thus every way to desire overmuch is unclean, for it proceeds from a greedy and irrational disposition. Let us therefore be sober, I beseech you, let us be pure, in that which is real purity, that we may be thought worthy to see God, through Jesus Christ our Lord, with whom, &c.

HOMILY IV.

TITUS ii. 2-5.

"That the aged men be sober, grave, temperate, sound in faith, in charity, in patience. The aged women likewise, that they be in behavior as becometh holiness, not false accusers, not given to much wine, teachers of good things; That they may teach the young women to be sober, to love their husbands, to love their children, To be discreet, chaste, keepers at home, good, obedient to their own husbands, that the word of God be not blasphemed."

THERE are some failings which age has, that youth has not. Some indeed it has in common with youth, but in addition it has[2] a slowness, a

timidity, a forgetfulness, an insensibility, and an irritability. For this reason he exhorts old men concerning these matters, "to be vigilant."[3] For there are many things which at this period make men otherwise than vigilant, especially what I mentioned, their general insensibility, and the difficulty of stirring or exciting them. Wherefore he also adds, "grave, temperate."[4] Here he means prudent. For temperance is named from the well-tempered[5] mind. For there are, indeed there are, among the old, some who rave and are beside themselves, some from wine, and some from sorrow. For old age makes them narrowminded.

---

[1] Sav. δήξεται, which reading Ben. unaccountably neglects, having δέξεται, and in Lat. *suscipiet.*
[2] MS. Colb. "And youth indeed has many faults, old age however has."

[3] νηφαλίους. E. V. "sober." [R. V. "temperate." — P.S.]
[4] [R. V. "soberminded." — P.S.]   [5] σωφροσύνη.

"Sound in faith, in charity [love], in patience."

He has well added "in patience," for this quality more especially befits old men.

Ver. 3. "The aged women likewise, that they be in behavior as becometh holiness."

That is, that in their very dress and carriage they exhibit modesty.

"Not false accusers, not given to much wine."

For this was particularly the vice of women and of old age. For from their natural coldness at that period of life arises the desire of wine, therefore he directs his exhortation to that point, to cut off all occasion of drunkenness, wishing them to be far removed from that vice, and to escape the ridicule that attends it. For the fumes mount more easily from beneath, and the membranes (of the brain) receive the mischief from their being impaired by age, and this especially causes intoxication. Yet wine is necessary at this age, because of its weakness, but much is not required. Nor do young women require much, though for a different reason, because it kindles the flame of lust.

"Teachers of good things."

And yet thou forbiddest a woman to teach; how dost thou command it here, when elsewhere thou sayest, "I suffer not a woman to teach"? (1 Tim. ii. 12.) But mark what he has added, "Nor to usurp authority over the man." For at the beginning it was permitted to men to teach both men and women. But to women it is allowed to instruct by discourse at home. But they are nowhere permitted to preside, nor to extend their speech to great length, wherefore he adds, "Nor to usurp authority over the man."

Ver. 4. "That they may teach the young women to be sober."

Observe how he binds the people together, how he subjects the younger women to the elder. For he is not speaking there of daughters, but merely in respect of age. Let each of the elder women, he means, teach any one that is younger to be sober.

"To love their husbands."

This is the chief point of all that is good in a household, "A man and his wife that agree together." (Ecclus. xxv. 1.) For where this exists, there will be nothing that is unpleasant. For where the head is in harmony with the body, and there is no disagreement between them, how shall not all the other members be at peace? For when the rulers are at peace, who is there to divide and break up concord? as on the other hand, where these are ill disposed to each other, there will be no good order in the house. This then is a point of the highest importance, and of more consequence than wealth, or rank, or power, or aught else. Nor has he said merely to be at peace, but "to love their husbands." For where love is, no discord will find admittance, far from it, other advantages too spring up.

"To love their children." This is well added, since she who loves the root, will much more love the fruit.

"To be discreet, chaste, keepers at home, good." All these spring from love. They become "good, and keepers at home," from affection to their husbands.

"Obedient to their own husbands, that the word of God be not blasphemed."

She who despises her husband, neglects also her house; but from love springs great soberness, and all contention is done away. And if he be a Heathen, he will soon be persuaded; and if he be a Christian, he will become a better man. Seest thou the condescension of Paul? He who in everything would withdraw us from worldly concerns, here bestows his consideration upon domestic affairs. For when these are well conducted, there will be room for spiritual things, but otherwise, they too will be marred. For she who keeps at home will be also sober, she that keeps at home will be also a prudent manager, she will have no inclination for luxury, unseasonable expenses, and other such things.

"That the word of God," he says, "be not blasphemed."

See how his first concern is for the preaching of the word, not for worldly things; for when he writes to Timothy, he says, "that we may lead a quiet and peaceable life in all godliness and honesty" (1 Tim. ii. 2); and here, "that the word of God," and the doctrine, "be not blasphemed." For if it should happen that a believing woman, married to an unbeliever, should not be virtuous, the blasphemy is usually carried on to God; but if she be of good character, the Gospel obtains glory from her, and from her virtuous actions. Let those women hearken who are united to wicked men or unbelievers; let them hear, and learn to lead them to godliness by their own example. For if thou gain nothing else, and do not attract thy husband to embrace right doctrines, yet thou hast stopped his mouth, and dost not allow him to blaspheme Christianity; and this is no mean thing, but great indeed, that the doctrine should be admired through our conversation.

Ver. 6. "Young men likewise exhort to be soberminded."

See how he everywhere recommends the observance of decorum. For he has committed to women the greater part in the instruction of women, having appointed the elder to teach the younger. But the whole instruction of men he assigns to Titus himself. For nothing is so difficult for that age as to overcome unlawful pleasures. For neither the love of wealth, nor the

desire of glory, or any other thing so much solic-
its the young, as fleshly lust. Therefore passing over other things, he directs his admonition
to that vital point. Not however that he would
have other things neglected ; for what says he ?

Ver. 7. " In all things showing thyself a pattern
of good works."

Let the elder women, he says, teach the
younger, but do thou thyself exhort young men
to be soberminded. And let the luster of thy
life be a common school of instruction, a pattern
of virtue to all, publicly exhibited, like some original model, containing in itself all beauties, affording examples whence those who are willing
may easily imprint upon themselves any of its
excellences.

Ver. 7, 8. " In [thy] doctrine showing uncorruptness, gravity, sincerity, Sound speech that
cannot be condemned ; that he that is of the
contrary part may be ashamed, having no evil
thing to say of you."

By " him that is of the contrary part," he
means the devil, and every one who ministers
to him. For when the life is illustrious, and the
discourse corresponds to it, being meek and
gentle, and affording no handle to the adversaries, it is of unspeakable advantage. Of great
use then is the ministry of the word, not any
common word, but that which is approved, and
cannot be condemned, affording no pretext to
those who are willing to censure it.

Ver. 9. " Exhort servants to be obedient to
their own masters, and to please them well in
all things."

Dost thou see what he has previously said,
" that he that is of the contrary part may be
ashamed, having no evil thing to say of you."
He therefore is deserving of condemnation, who
under pretense of continence separates wives
from their husbands, and he who under any
other pretext takes away servants from their
masters. This is not " speech that cannot be
condemned," but it gives great handle to the
unbelieving, and opens the mouths of all against
us.

" Not answering again."

Ver. 10. " Not purloining, but showing all
good fidelity, that they may adorn the doctrine
of God our Saviour in all things."

Thus he has well said in another place, " Doing
service as to the Lord, and not to men." For
if thou servest thy master with good will, yet the
occasion of this service proceeds from thy fear,[1]
and he who with so great fear renders Him service, shall receive the greater reward. For if
he restrain not his hand, or his unruly tongue,
how shall the Gentile admire the doctrine that
is among us? But if they see their slave, who

has been taught the philosophy of Christ, displaying more self-command than their own philosophers, and serving with all meekness and
good will, he will in every way admire the power
of the Gospel. For the Greeks judge not of
doctrines by the doctrine itself, but they make
the life and conduct the test of the doctrines.
Let women therefore and servants be their instructors by their conversation. For both among
themselves, and everywhere, it is admitted that
the race of servants is passionate, not open to
impression, intractable, and not very apt to receive instruction in virtue, not from their nature,
God forbid, but from their ill breeding,[2] and the
neglect of their masters. For those who rule
them care about nothing but their own service ;
or if they do sometimes attend to their morals,
they do it only to spare themselves the trouble
that would be caused them by their fornication,
their thefts, or their drunkenness, and being
thus neglected and having no one to concern
himself about them, they naturally sink into the
very depths of wickedness. For if under the
direction of a father and mother, a guardian, a
master, and teacher, with suitable companions,
with the honor of a free condition, and many
other advantages, it is difficult to escape inti-
macies with the wicked, what can we expect
from those who are destitute of all these, and
are mixed up with the wicked, and associate
fearlessly with whomsoever they will, no one
troubling herself about their friendships? What
sort of persons do we suppose they will be?
On this account it is difficult for any servant to
be good, especially when they have not the
benefit of instruction either from those without
or from ourselves. They do not converse with
free men of orderly conduct, who have a great
regard for their reputation. For all these reasons
it is a difficult and surprising thing that there
should ever be a good servant.

When therefore it is seen that the power of
religion, imposing a restraint upon a class naturally so self-willed, has rendered them singularly
well behaved and gentle, their masters, however
unreasonable they may be, will form a high
opinion of our doctrines. For it is manifest,
that having previously infixed in their souls a
fear of the Resurrection, of the Judgment, and
of all those things which we are taught by our
philosophy to expect after death, they have been
able to resist wickedness, having in their souls a
settled principle to counterbalance the pleasures
of sin. So that it is not by chance or without
reason, that Paul shows so much consideration
for this class of men : since the more wicked
they are, the more admirable is the power of
that preaching which reforms them. For we

---

[1] i.e. of God.

[2] Colb. " way of life."

then most admire a physician, when he restores to a healthy and sane state one who was despaired of, whom nothing benefited, who was unable to command his unreasonable desires, and wallowed in them. And observe what he most requires of them; the qualities which contribute most to their masters' ease.

"Not answering again, not purloining"; that is, to show all good will in matters intrusted to them, to be particularly faithful in their masters' concerns, and obedient to their commands.

MORAL. Do not therefore think that I enlarge upon this subject without a purpose. For the rest of my discourse will be addressed to servants. Look not to this, my good friend, that thou servest a man, but that thy service is to God, that thou adornest the Gospel. Then thou wilt undertake everything in obedience to thy master, bearing with him, though impatient, and angry without a cause. Consider that thou art not gratifying him, but fulfilling the commandment of God; then thou wilt easily submit to anything. And what I have said before, I repeat here, that when our spiritual state is right, the things of this life will follow. For a servant, so tractable and so well disposed, will not only be accepted by God, and made partaker of those glorious crowns, but his master himself, whom he serves so well, even though he be brutish and stone-hearted, inhuman and ferocious, will commend and admire him, and will honor him above all the rest, and will set him over their heads, though he be a Gentile.

And that servants are required to be thus disposed towards a Gentile master, I will show you by an example. Joseph, who was of a different religion from the Egyptian, was sold to the chief cook.[1] What then did he? When he saw the young man was virtuous, he did not consider the difference of their religion, but loved and favored and admired him, and committed the others to his superintendence, and knew nothing of the affairs of his own house because of him. Thus he was a second master, and even more of a master than his lord, for he knew more of his master's affairs than his master himself. And even afterwards, as it seems to me, when he believed the unjust accusation framed against him by his wife, yet from his former regard for him, retaining a respect for that just man, he satisfied his resentment with imprisonment. For if he had not greatly reverenced and esteemed him from his former conduct, he would have thrust his sword through his body, and dispatched him at once. "For jealousy is the rage of a man; therefore he will not regard any ransom, neither will he rest content, though thou givest many gifts." (Prov. vi. 34, 35.) And if such is the jealousy of men in general, much more violent must it have been with him, an Egyptian and barbarian, and injured as he thought by one whom he had honored. For you all know that injuries do not affect us in the same way from all persons, but that those grieve us most bitterly and deeply which proceed from those who were well-affected toward us, who had trusted us and whom we had trusted, and who had received many kindnesses from us. He did not consider with himself, nor say, What! have I taken a servant into my house, shared with him my substance, made him free, and even greater than myself, and is this the return that he makes me? He did not say this, so much was his mind prepossessed by his previous respect for him.

And what wonder if he enjoyed so much honor in the house, when we see what great regard he obtained even in a prison. You know how practiced in cruelty are the dispositions of those who have the custody of prisons. They profit by the misfortune of others, and harass those whom others support in their afflictions, making a gain of them that is truly deplorable, with a more than brutal cruelty. For they take advantage of those wretched circumstances which ought to excite their pity. And we may further observe, that they do not treat in the same manner all their prisoners; for those who are confined upon accusation only, and who are injuriously treated, they perhaps pity, but they punish with numberless inflictions those who are imprisoned for shameful and atrocious crimes. So that the keeper of the prison not only from the manner of such men might have been expected to be inhuman, but from the cause for which he was imprisoned. For who would not have been incensed against a young man, who having been raised to so great honor, was charged with requiting such favors by a base attempt upon master's wife. Would not the keeper, considering these things, the honor to which he had been raised, and the crime for which he was imprisoned, would he not have treated him with more than brutal cruelty? But he was raised above all these things by his hope in God. For the virtue of the soul can mollify even wild beasts. And by the same meekness which had gained his master, he captivated also the keeper of the prison. Thus Joseph was again a ruler, he ruled in the prison as he had ruled in the house. For since he was destined to reign, it was fit that he should learn to be governed, and while he was governed he became a governor, and presided in the house.

For if Paul requires this of one who is[2] promoted to a Church, saying, "If a man know not how to rule his own house, how shall he take

---

[1] So Sept., Gen. xxxix. 1; comp. on Stat. Hom. xix. 11.

[2] ἑλκόμενον, literally, "dragged"; see on Stat. Hom. i. 16.

care of the Church of God?" (1 Tim. iii. 5), it was fit that he who was to be a governor, should first be an excellent ruler of the house. He presided over the prison, not as over a prison, but as if it had been a house. For he alleviated the calamities of all, and took charge of those who were imprisoned as if they had been his own members, not only taking an interest in their misfortunes and consoling them, but if he saw any one absorbed in thought, he went to him and enquired the cause, and could not bear even to see any one dejected, or be easy till he had relieved his dejection. Such love as this, many a one has not shown even to his own children. And to these things may be traced the beginning of his good fortune. For our part must go before, and then the blessing of God will follow.

For that he did show this care and concern we learn from the story. He saw, it is said, two eunuchs who had been cast into prison by Pharaoh, his chief butler and chief baker, and he said, "Wherefore look ye so sadly to-day?" (Gen. xl. 7.) And not from this question only, but from the conduct of these men, we may discern his merit. For, though they were the officers of the king, they did not despise him, nor in their despair did they reject his services, but they laid open to him all their secret, as to a brother who could sympathize with them.

And all this has been said by me to prove, that though the virtuous man be in slavery, in captivity, in prison; though he be in the depth of the earth, nothing will be able to overcome him. This I have said to servants, that they may learn that though they have masters that are very brutes, as this Egyptian, or ferocious as the keeper of the prison, they may gain their regard, and though they be heathen as they were, or whatever they be, they may soon win them to gentleness. For nothing is more engaging than good manners, nothing more agreeable and delightful than meekness, gentleness, and obedience. A person of this character is suitable to all. Such an one is not ashamed of slavery, he does not avoid the poor, the sick, and the infirm. For virtue is superior, and prevails over everything. And if it has such power in slaves, how much more in those who are free? This then let us practice, whether bond or free, men or women. Thus we shall be loved both by God and men; and not only by virtuous men, but by the wicked; nay by them more especially, for they more especially honor and respect virtue. For as those who are under rule stand most in awe of the meek, so do the vicious most revere the virtuous, knowing from what they themselves have fallen. Since such then is the fruit of virtue, this let us pursue, and attain. If we adhere to this, nothing will be formidable, but all things easy and manageable. And though we pass through the fire and through the water, all things yield to virtue, even death itself. Let us then be zealous in the pursuit of it, that we may attain the good things to come, in Jesus Christ our Lord, with whom, &c.

HOMILY V.

TITUS ii. 11–14.

" For the grace of God that bringeth salvation hath appeared unto all men, Teaching them that, denying ungodliness and worldly lusts, we should live soberly, righteously, and godly, in this present world; Looking for that blessed hope, and the glorious appearing of the great God and our Saviour Jesus Christ; who gave Himself for us, that He might redeem us from all iniquity, and purify unto Himself a peculiar people, zealous of good works."

HAVING demanded from servants so great virtue, for it is great virtue to adorn the doctrine of our God and Saviour in all things, and charged them to give no occasion of offense to their masters, even in common matters, he adds the just cause, why servants should be such : " For the grace of God, that bringeth salvation, hath appeared." Those who have God for their Teacher,[1] may well be such as I have described, seeing their numberless sins have been forgiven to them. For you know that in addition to other considerations, this in no common degree awes and humbles the soul, that when it had innumerable sins to answer for, it received not punishment, but obtained pardon, and infinite favors. For if one, whose servant had committed many offenses, instead of scourging him with thongs, should grant him a pardon for all those, but should require an account of his future conduct, and bid him beware of falling into the same faults again, and should bestow high favors upon

---

[1] Colb. " a Divine Teacher."

him, who do you think would not be overcome at hearing of such kindness? But do not think that grace stops at the pardon of former sins — it secures us against them in future, for this also is of grace. Since if He were never to punish those who still do amiss, this would not be so much grace, as encouragement to evil and wickedness.

"For the grace of God," he says, "hath appeared, teaching us that, denying ungodliness and worldly lusts, we should live soberly, righteously, and godly in the present world ; looking for the blessed hope, and the glorious appearing of the great God and our Saviour Jesus Christ." See, how together with the rewards he places the virtue. And this is of grace, to deliver us from worldly things, and to lead us to Heaven. He speaks here of two appearings ; for there are two ; the first of grace, the second of retribution and justice.

"That denying ungodliness," he says, " and worldly lusts."

See here the foundation of all virtue. He has not said "avoiding," but "denying." Denying implies the greatest distance, the greatest hatred and aversion. With as much resolution and zeal as they turned from idols, with so much let them turn from vice itself, and worldly lusts. For these too are idols, that is, worldly lusts, and covetousness, and this he names idolatry. Whatever things are useful for the present life are worldly lusts,[1] whatever things perish with the present life are worldly lusts. Let us then have nothing to do with these. Christ came, "that we should deny ungodliness."[2] Ungodliness relates to doctrines, worldly lusts to a wicked life.

"And should live soberly, righteously, and godly in the present world."

Dost thou see, what I always affirm, that it is not sobriety only to abstain from fornication, but that we must be free from other passions. So then he who loves wealth is not sober. For as the fornicator loves women, so the other loves money, and even more inordinately, for he is not impelled by so strong a passion. And he is certainly a more powerless[3] charioteer who cannot manage a gentle horse, than he who cannot restrain a wild and unruly one. What then? says he, is the love of wealth weaker than the love of women? This is manifest from many reasons. In the first place, lust springs from the necessity of nature, and what arises from this necessity must be difficult to restrain, since it is implanted in our nature. Secondly, because the ancients had no regard for wealth, but for women they had great regard, in respect of their chastity.

And no one blamed him who cohabited with his wife according to law, even to old age, but all blamed him who hoarded money. And many of the Heathen philosophers despised money, but none of them were indifferent to women, so that this passion is more imperious than the other. But since we are addressing the Church, let us not take our examples from the Heathens, but from the Scriptures. This then the blessed Paul places almost in the rank of a command. "Having food and raiment, let us be therewith content."[4] (1 Tim. vi. 8.) But concerning women he says, "Defraud ye not one the other, except it be with consent " — and "come together again." (1 Cor. vii. 5.) And you see him often laying down rules for a lawful intercourse, and he permits the enjoyment of this desire, and allows of a second marriage, and bestows much consideration upon the matter, and never punishes on account of it. But he everywhere condemns him that is fond of money. Concerning wealth also Christ often commanded that we should avoid the corruption of it, but He says nothing about abstaining from a wife. For hear what He says concerning money; "Whosoever forsaketh not all that he hath " (Luke xiv. 33) ; but he nowhere says, "Whosoever forsaketh not his wife " ; for he knew how imperious that passion is. And the blessed Paul says, "Marriage is honorable in all, and the bed undefiled " (Heb. xiii. 4) ; but he has nowhere said that the care of riches is honorable, but the reverse. Thus he says to Timothy, "They that will be rich fall into temptation and a snare, and into many foolish and hurtful lusts." (1 Tim. vi. 9.) He says not, they that will be covetous, but, they that will be rich.

And that you may learn from the common notions the true state of this matter, it must be set before you generally. If a man were once for all deprived of money, he would no longer be tormented with the desire of it, for nothing so much causes the desire of wealth, as the possession of it. But it is not so with respect to lust, but many who have been made eunuchs have not been freed from the flame that burned within them, for the desire resides in other organs, being seated inwardly in our nature. To what purpose then is this said? Because the covetous is more intemperate than the fornicator, inasmuch as the former gives way to a weaker passion. Indeed it proceeds less from passion than from baseness of mind. But lust is natural, so that if a man does not approach a woman, nature performs her part and operation. But there is nothing of this sort in the case of avarice.

---

[1] Two MSS. add, " Whatever things go not with us to heaven are worldly lusts."

[2] ἀσέβειαν.

[3] ἀκρατής.

[4] Two MSS. and Old Lat. add, "And about virgins what says he? ' I have no commandment of the Lord.' " Which Montf. rejects with little reason.

"That we should live godly in this present world."

And what is this hope? what the reward of our labors?

"Looking for the blessed hope and the appearing."

For nothing is more blessed and more desirable than that appearing. Words are not able to represent it, the blessings thereof surpass our understanding.

"Looking for the blessed hope and glorious appearing of our great God and Saviour." [1]

Where are those who say that the Son is inferior to the Father?

"Our great God and Saviour." He who saved us when we were enemies. What will He not do then when He has us approved? [2]

"The great God." When he says great with respect to God, he says it not comparatively but absolutely, [3] after Whom no one is great, since it is relative. For if it is relative, He is great by comparison, not great by nature. But now He is incomparably great.

Ver. 14. "Who gave Himself for us, that He might redeem us from all iniquity, and purify unto Himself a peculiar people."

"Peculiar": that is, selected from the rest, and having nothing in common with them.

"Zealous of good works."

Dost thou see that our part is necessary, not merely works, but "zealous"; we should with all alacrity, with a becoming earnestness, go forward in virtue. For when we were weighed down with evils, and incurably diseased, it was of His lovingkindness that we were delivered. But what follows after this is our part as well as His.

Ver. 15. "These things speak and exhort, and rebuke with all authority."

"These things speak and exhort." Do you see how he charges Timothy? "Reprove, rebuke, exhort." But here, "Rebuke with all authority." For the manners of this people were more stubborn, wherefore he orders them to be rebuked more roughly, and with all authority. For there are some sins, which ought to be prevented by command. We may with persuasion advise men to despise riches, to be meek, and the like. But the adulterer, the fornicator, the defrauder, ought to be brought to a better course by command. And those who are addicted to augury and divination, and the like, should be corrected "with all authority." Observe how he would have him insist on these things with independence, and with entire freedom. [4]

"Let no man despise thee." But

Chap. iii. 1. "Put them in mind to be subject to principalities and powers, to obey magistrates, to be ready to every good work, to speak evil of no man, to be no brawlers."

What then? even when men do evil, may we not revile them? nay, but "to be ready to every good work, to speak evil of no man." Hear the exhortation, "To speak evil of no man." Our lips should be pure from reviling. For if our reproaches are true, it is not for us to utter them, but for the Judge to enquire into the matter. "For why," he says, "dost thou judge thy brother?" (Rom. xiv. 10.) But if they are not true, how great the fire. [5] Hear what the thief says to his fellow-thief. "For we are also in the same condemnation." (Luke xxiii. 40.) We are running the same hazard. [6] If thou revilest others, thou wilt soon fall into the same sins. Therefore the blessed Paul admonishes us: "Let him that standeth, take heed lest he fall." (1 Cor. x. 12.)

"To be no brawlers, but gentle, showing all meekness unto all men."

Unto Greeks and Jews, to the wicked and the evil. For when he says, "Let him that standeth take heed lest he fall," he wakens their fears from the future; but here, on the contrary, he exhorts them from the consideration of the past, and the same in what follows;

Ver. 3. "For we ourselves also were sometimes foolish."

Thus also he does in his Epistle to the Galatians, where he says, "Even so we, when we were children, were in bondage under the elements of the world." (Gal. iv. 4.) Therefore he says, Revile no one, for such also thou wast thyself.

"For we ourselves also were sometimes foolish, disobedient, deceived, serving divers lusts and pleasures, living in malice and envy, hateful, and hating one another."

Therefore we ought to be thus to all, to be gently disposed. For he who was formerly in such a state, and has been delivered from it, ought not to reproach others, but to pray, to be thankful to Him who has granted both to him and them deliverance from such evils. Let no one boast; for all have sinned. If then, doing well thyself, thou art inclined to revile others, consider thy own former life, and the uncertainty of the future, and restrain thy anger. [7] For if thou hast lived virtuously from thy earliest youth, yet nevertheless thou mayest have many sins; and if thou hast not, as thou thinkest, consider that this is not the effect of thy virtue, but of the

---

[1] This is the meaning, as Middleton has shown. The English Version, "The great God and our Saviour," is ambiguous.

[2] Edd. οὐκ εὐδοκιμοῦντας λαβών. The order does not admit the sense, "seeing He received us when not approved," so that this would be, "how will he not punish us if he finds us not approved"; but B. has not the negative, which Downes had rejected.

[3] ἀπολύτως. [4] ἐξουσίας.

[5] i.e. hereafter. See Hom. i. on Tit. i. 4, p. 522, "how great a flame."

[6] ἀγῶνα.

[7] Colb. and Old Lat. "impulse."

grace of God. For if He had not called thy forefathers, thou wouldest have been disobedient. See here how he mentions every sort of wickedness. How many things has not God dispensed by the Prophets and all other means? have we heard?

"For we," he says, "were once deceived."'

Ver. 4. "But after that the kindness and love of God our Saviour toward man appeared." How? "Not by works of righteousness which we have done, but according to His mercy He saved us, by the washing of regeneration, and renewing of the Holy Ghost."

Strange! How were we drowned[1] in wickedness, so that we could not be purified, but' needed a new birth? For this is implied by "Regeneration." For as when a house is in a ruinous state no one places props under it, nor makes any addition to the old building, but pulls it down to its foundations, and rebuilds it anew; so in our case, God has not repaired us, but has made us anew. For this is "the renewing of the Holy Ghost." He has made us new men. How? "By His Spirit"; and to show this further, he adds,

Ver. 6. "Which He shed on us abundantly through Jesus Christ our Saviour."

Thus we need the Spirit abundantly.

"That being justified by His grace" — again by grace and not by debt — "we may be made heirs according to the hope of eternal life."

At the same time there is an incitement to humility, and a hope for the future. For if when we were so abandoned, as to require to be born again, to be saved by grace, to have no good in us, if then He saved us, much more will He save us in the world to come.

For nothing was worse than the brutality of mankind before the coming of Christ. They were all affected towards each other as if enemies and at war. Fathers slew their own sons, and mothers were mad against their children. There was no order settled, no natural, no written law; everything was subverted. There were adulteries continually, and murders, and things if possible worse than murders, and thefts; indeed we are told by one of the heathen, that this practice was esteemed a point of virtue. And naturally, since they worshiped a god[2] of such character. Their oracles frequently required them to put such and such men to death. Let me tell you one of the stories of that time. One Androgeus, the son of Minos, coming to Athens, obtained a victory in wrestling, for which he was punished and put to death. Apollo therefore, remedying one evil by another, ordered twice seven youths to be executed on his account. What could be more savage than this

tyrannical command? And it was executed too. A man undertook to atone the mad rage of the demon, and slew these young men, because the deceit of the oracle prevailed with them. But afterwards, when the young men resisted and stood upon their defense, it was no longer done. If now it had been just, it ought not to have been prevented, but if unjust, as undoubtedly it was, it ought not to have been commanded at all. Then they worshiped boxers and wrestlers. They waged constant wars in perpetual succession, city by city, village by village, house by house. They were addicted to the love of boys, and one of their wise men made a law that Pædrasty, as well as anointing for wrestling,[3] should not be allowed to slaves, as if it was an honorable thing; and they had houses for this purpose, in which it was openly practiced. And if all that was done among them was related, it would be seen that they openly outraged nature, and there was none to restrain them. Then their dramas were replete with adultery, lewdness, and corruption of every sort. In their indecent nocturnal assemblies, women were admitted to the spectacle. There was seen the abomination of a virgin sitting in the theater during the night, amidst a drunken multitude of young men madly reveling. The very festival was the darkness, and the abominable deeds practiced by them. On this account he says, "For we ourselves also were sometimes foolish, disobedient, deceived, serving divers lusts and pleasures." One man loved his stepmother,[4] a woman her step-son, and in consequence hung herself. For as to their passion for boys, whom they called their "Pædica," it is not fit to be named. And would you see a son married to his mother? This too happened among them, and what is horrible, though it was done in ignorance, the god whom they worshiped did not prevent it, but permitted this outrage to nature to be committed, and that though she was a person of distinction. And if those, who, if for no other reason, yet for the sake of their reputation with the multitude, might have been expected to adhere to virtue; if they rushed thus headlong into vice, what is it likely was the conduct of the greater part, who lived in obscurity? What is more diversified than this pleasure? The wife of a certain one fell in love with another man, and with the help of her adulterer, slew her husband upon his return. The greater part of you probably know the story. The son of the murdered man killed the adulterer, and after him his mother, then he himself became mad, and was haunted by furies.

---

[1] βεβαπτισμένοι.
[2] Mercury.

[3] Lit. "dryly," i.e. without the bath, as in the case of wrestling, which was practiced by all that were free.
[4] Downes may be right in taking this of Phœnix, Il. ix. 452. What follows refers to Hippolytus, of whom Montfaucon seems to forget that this could not be said.

After this the madman himself slew another man, and took his wife. What can be worse than such calamities as these? But I mention these instances taken from the Heathens,[1] with this view, that I may convince the Gentiles, what evils then prevailed in the world. But we may show the same from our own writings. For it is said, "They sacrificed their sons and daughters unto devils." (Ps. cvi. 37.) Again, the Sodomites were destroyed for no other cause than their unnatural appetites. Soon after the coming of Christ, did not a king's daughter dance at a banquet in the presence of drunken men, and did she not ask as the reward of her dancing the murder and the head of a Prophet? "Who can utter the mighty acts of the Lord?" (Ps. vi. 2.)

"Hateful," he says, "and hating one another." For it must necessarily happen, when we let loose every pleasure on the soul, that there should be much hatred. For where love is, with virtue, no man overreacheth another in any matter. Mark also what Paul says, "Be not deceived, neither fornicators, nor idolaters, nor adulterers, nor effeminate, nor abusers of themselves with mankind, nor covetous, nor drunkards, nor revilers, shall inherit the kingdom of God. And such were some of you." (1 Cor. vi. 9, 10.) Dost thou see how every species of wickedness prevailed? It was a state of gross darkness, and the corruption of all that was right. For if those who had the advantage of prophecies, and who saw so many evils inflicted upon their enemies, and even upon themselves, nevertheless did not restrain themselves, but committed numberless foolish crimes, what would be the case with others? One of their lawgivers ordered that virgins should wrestle naked in the presence of men. Many blessings on you! that ye cannot endure the mention of it; but their philosophers were not ashamed of the actual practice. Another, the chief of their philosophers, approves of their going out to the war, and of their being common,[2] as if he were a pimp and pander to their lusts.

"Living in malice and envy."

For if those who professed philosophy among them made such laws, what shall we say of those who were not philosophers? If such were the maxims of those who wore a long beard, and assumed the grave cloak,[3] what can be said of others? Woman was not made for this, O man, to be prostituted as common. O ye subverters of all decency, who use men, as if they were women, and lead out women to war, as if they were men! This is the work of the devil, to subvert and confound all things, to overleap the boundaries that have been appointed from the beginning, and remove those which God has set to nature. For God assigned to woman the care of the house only, to man the conduct of public affairs. But you reduce the head to the feet, and raise the feet to the head. You suffer women to bear arms, and are not ashamed. But why do I mention these things? They introduce on the stage a woman that murders her own children, nor are they ashamed to stuff the ears of men with such abominable stories.

Ver. 4. "But after that the kindness and love of God our Saviour towards man appeared, Not by works of righteousness which we have done, but according to His mercy He saved us by the washing of regeneration, and renewing of the Holy Ghost, which He shed on us abundantly through Jesus Christ our Saviour, that being justified by His grace we should be made heirs according to the hope of eternal life."

What means, "according to the hope"? That, as we have hoped, so we shall enjoy eternal life, or because ye are even already heirs.

"This is a faithful saying."

Because he had been speaking of things future and not of the present, therefore he adds, that it is worthy of credit. These things are true, he says, and this is manifest from what has gone before. For He who has delivered us from such a state of iniquity, and from so many evils, will assuredly impart to us the good things to come, if we abide in grace. For all proceeds from the same kind concern.

MORAL. Let us then give thanks to God, and not revile them; nor accuse them, but rather let us beseech them, pray for them, counsel and advise them, though they should insult and spurn us. For such is the nature of those who are diseased.[4] But those who are concerned for the health of such persons do all things and bear all things, though it may not avail, that they may not have themselves to accuse of negligence. Know ye not that often, when a physician despairs of a sick man, some relative standing by addresses him, "Bestow further attendance, leave nothing undone, that I may not have to accuse myself, that I may incur no blame,[5] no self-reproach." Do you not see the great care that near kinsmen take of their relations, how much they do for them, both entreating the physicians to cure them, and sitting perseveringly beside them? Let us at least imitate them. And yet there is no comparison between the objects of our concern. For if any

---

[1] His object was probably to take familiar instances; these are chiefly from the Greek Drama.

[2] This is an unfair view of Plato's Republic, against which, however, it is a real objection that it sets aside a law of nature, though with political, and not sensual views. Some have seen a great truth allegorized in this, and it may be justly, but ordinary Greeks would be more likely to take it as St. Chrysostom does, and Plato perhaps hints that it would be so in practice, b. viii. init.

[3] τρίβωνα.

[4] νοσοῦντες.

[5] μηδὲν μέμφωμαι.

one had a son diseased in his body, he could not refuse to take a long journey to free him from his disease. But when the soul is in a bad state, no one concerns himself about it, but we all are indolent, all careless, all negligent, and overlook our wives, our children, and ourselves, when attacked[1] by this dangerous disease. But when it is too late, we become sensible of it. Consider how disgraceful and absurd it is to say afterwards, "we never looked for it, we never expected that this would be the event." And it is no less dangerous than disgraceful. For if in the present life it is the part of foolish men to make no provision for the future, much more must it be so with respect to the next life, when we hear many counseling us, and informing us what is to be done, and what not to be done. Let us then hold fast that hope.[2] Let us be careful of our salvation, let us in all things call upon God, that He may stretch forth His hand to us. How long will you be slothful? How long negligent? How long shall we be careless of ourselves and of our fellow-servants? He hath shed richly upon us the grace of His Spirit. Let us therefore consider how great is the grace he has bestowed upon us, and let us show as great earnestness ourselves, or, since this is not possible, some, although it be less. For if after this grace we are insensible, the heavier will be our punishment. "For if I," He says, "had not come and spoken unto them, they had not had sin, but now they have no cloak for their sin." (John xv. 22.) But God forbid that this should be said of us, and grant that we may all be thought worthy of the blessings promised to those who have loved Him, in Jesus Christ our Lord, &c.

HOMILY VI.

TITUS iii. 8–11.

"These things I will that thou affirm constantly, that they which have believed in God might be careful to maintain good works. These things are good and profitable unto men. But avoid foolish questions, and genealogies, and contentions, and strivings about the law, for they are unprofitable and vain. A man that is an heretic after the first and second admonition reject. Knowing that he that is such is subverted, and sinneth, being condemned of himself."

HAVING spoken of the love of God to man, of His ineffable regard for us, of what we were and what He has done for us, he has added, "These things I will that thou affirm constantly, that they which have believed in God might be careful to maintain good works"; that is, Discourse of these things, and from a consideration of them exhort to almsgiving. For what has been said will not only apply to humility, to the not being puffed up, and not reviling others, but to every other virtue. So also in arguing with the Corinthians, he says, "Ye know that our Lord being rich became poor, that we through His poverty might be rich." (2 Cor. viii. 9.) Having considered the care and exceeding love of God for man, he thence exhorts them to almsgiving, and that not in a common and slight manner, but "that they may be careful," he says, "to maintain good works," that is, both to succor the injured, not only by money, but by patronage and protection, and to defend the widows and orphans, and to afford a refuge to all that are afflicted. For this is to maintain good works. For these things, he says, are good and profitable unto men. "But avoid foolish questions, and genealogies, and contentions, and strivings about the law, for they are unprofitable and vain." What do these "genealogies" mean? For in his Epistle to Timothy he mentions "fables and endless genealogies." (1 Tim. i. 4.) [Perhaps both here and there glancing at the Jews, who, priding themselves on having Abraham for their forefather, neglected their own part. On this account he calls them both "foolish and unprofitable"; for it is the part of folly to confide in things unprofitable.[3]] "Contentions," he means, with heretics, in which he would not have us labor to no purpose, where nothing is to be gained, for they end in nothing. For when a man is perverted and predetermined not to change his mind, whatever may happen, why shouldest thou labor in vain, sowing upon a rock, when thou shouldest spend thy honorable toil upon thy own people, in discoursing with them upon almsgiving and every other virtue? How then does he elsewhere say, "If God peradventure will give them repentance" (2 Tim. ii. 25); but here, "A man that is an heretic after the first and second admonition reject, knowing

---

[1] al. "wasting."
[2] So Ben. from Colb. Sav. "this care."

[3] B., Colb., and Old Lat. omit the part in brackets.

that he that is such is subverted and sinneth, being condemned of himself"? In the former passage he speaks of the correction of those of whom he had hope, and who had simply made opposition. But when he is known and manifest to all, why dost thou contend[1] in vain? why dost thou beat the air? What means, "being condemned of himself"? Because he cannot say that no one has told him, no one admonished him; since therefore after admonition he continues the same, he is self-condemned.

Ver. 12. "When I shall send Artemas unto thee, or Tychicus; be diligent to come unto me to Nicopolis." What sayest thou? After having appointed him to preside over Crete, dost thou again summon him to thyself? It was not to withdraw him from that occupation,[2] but to discipline him the more for it. For that he does not call him to attend upon him, as if he took him everywhere with him as his follower, appears from what he adds:

"For I have determined there to winter."

Now Nicopolis[3] is a city of Thrace.

Ver. 14. "Bring Zenas the lawyer and Apollos on their journey diligently, that nothing be wanting unto them."

These were not of the number to whom Churches had been intrusted, but of the number of his companions. But Apollos was the more vehement, being "an eloquent man, and mighty in the Scriptures." (Acts xviii. 24.) But if Zenas was a lawyer, you say, he ought not to have been supported by others. But by a lawyer here is meant one versed in the laws of the Jews. And he seems to say, supply their wants abundantly, that nothing may be lacking to them.

Ver. 14, 15. "And let ours also learn to maintain good works for necessary uses, that they be not unfruitful. All that are with me salute thee. Greet them that love us in the faith."

That is, either those that love Paul himself,[4] or those men that are faithful.

"Grace be with you all. Amen."

How then dost thou command him to stop the mouths of gainsayers, if he must pass them by when they are doing everything to their own destruction?[5] He means that he should not do it principally for their advantage, for being once perverted in their minds, they would not profit by it. But if they injured others, it behooved him to withstand and contend with them; and manfully await[6] them, but if thou art reduced

to necessity, seeing them destroying others, be not silent, but stop their mouths, from regard to those whom they would destroy. It is not indeed possible for a zealous man of upright life to abstain from contention, but so do as I have said. For the evil arises from idleness and a vain philosophy, that one should be occupied about words only. For it is a great injury to be uttering a superfluity of words, when one ought to be teaching, or praying, or giving thanks. For it is not right to be sparing of our money but not sparing of our words; we ought rather to spare words than our money, and not to give ourselves up to all sorts of persons.

What means, "that they be careful to maintain good works"? That they wait not for those who are in want to come to them, but that they seek out those who need their assistance. Thus the considerate man shows his concern, and with great zeal will he perform this duty. For in doing good actions, it is not those who receive the kindness that are benefited, so much as those who do it that make gain and profit, for it gives them confidence towards God. But in the other case, there is no end of contention: therefore he calls the heretic incorrigible. For as to neglect those for whom there is a hope of conversion is the part of slothfulness, so to bestow pains upon those who are diseased past remedy is the extreme of folly and madness; for we render them more bold.

"And let ours," he says, "learn to maintain good works for necessary uses, that they be not unfruitful." You observe that he is more anxious for them than for those who are to receive their kindnesses. For they might probably have been brought on their way by many others, but I am concerned, he says, for our own friends. For what advantage would it be to them, if others should dig up treasures,[7] and maintain their teachers? This would be no benefit to them, for they remained unfruitful. Could not Christ then, Who with five loaves fed five thousand men, and with seven loaves fed four thousand, could not He have supported Himself and His disciples?

MORAL. For what reason then was He maintained by women? For women, it is said, followed Him, and ministered unto Him. (Mark xv. 41.) It was to teach us from the first that He is concerned for those who do good. Could not Paul, who supported others by his own hands, have maintained himself without assistance from others? But you see him receiving and requesting aid. And hear the reason for it. "Not because I desire a gift," he says, "but I desire fruit that may abound to your account."

---

[1] πυκτεύεις.

[2] σχολῆς.

[3] Montfaucon mentions two of this name in Thrace. Mr. Greswell takes this to be in Epirus.

[4] He means, perhaps, that "in faith" (which has not the article) may be applied to this.

[5] B. makes "When they undoing everything for mischief," part of the answer, omitting "their own," and adding αὐτόν in the sense of ultro. Other copies vary.

[6] περιίστασθαι, or as B. περιίστασο. Ed. Par. proposes προσίστασθαι, "to resist," but needlessly.

[7] He probably means their own stores.

(Phil. iv. 17.) And at the beginning too, when men sold all their possessions and laid them at the Apostles' feet, the Apostles, seest thou, were more concerned for them than for those who received their alms. For if their concern had only been that the poor might by any means be relieved, they would not have judged so severely of the sin of Ananias and Sapphira, when they kept back their money. Nor would Paul have charged men to give "not grudgingly nor of necessity." (2 Cor. ix. 7.) What sayest thou, Paul? dost thou discourage giving to the poor? No, he answers; but I consider not their advantage only, but the good of those who give. Dost thou see, that when the prophet gave that excellent counsel to Nebuchadnezzar, he did not merely consider the poor. For he does not content himself with saying, Give to the poor; but what? "Break off thy sins by almsdeeds,[1] and thine iniquities by showing mercy to the poor." (Dan. iv. 27.) Part with thy wealth, not that others may be fed, but that thou mayest escape punishment. And Christ again says, "Go.and sell that thou hast, and give to the poor . . . and come and follow Me." (Matt. xix. 21.) Dost thou see that the commandment was given that he might be induced to follow Him? For as riches are an impediment, therefore he commands them to be given to the poor, instructing the soul to be pitiful and merciful, to despise wealth, and to flee from covetousness. For he who has learnt to give to him that needs, will in time learn not to receive from those who have to give. This makes men like God. Yet virginity, and fasting, and lying on the ground, are more difficult than this, but nothing is so strong and powerful to extinguish the fire of our sins as almsgiving. It is greater than all other virtues. It places the lovers of it by the side of the King Himself, and justly. For the effect of virginity, of fasting, of lying on the ground, is confined to those who practice them, and no other is saved thereby. But almsgiving extends to all, and embraces the members of Christ, and actions that extend their effects to many are far greater than those which are confined to one.

For almsgiving is the mother of love, of that love, which is the characteristic of Christianity, which is greater than all miracles, by which the disciples of Christ are manifested. It is the medicine of our sins, the cleansing of the filth of our souls, the ladder fixed to heaven; it binds together the body of Christ. Would you learn how excellent a thing it is? In the time of the Apostles, men selling their possessions brought them to them, and they were distributed. For it is said, "Distribution was made unto every man according as he had need." (Acts

iv. 35.) For tell me how, setting aside the future, and not now considering the kingdom that is to come, let us see who in the present life are the gainers, those who received, or those who gave. The former murmured and quarreled with each other. The latter had one soul. "They were of one heart, and of one soul," it is said, "and grace was upon them all." (Acts iv. 32.) And they lived in great simplicity.[2] Dost thou see that they were gainers even by thus giving? Tell me now, with whom would you wish to be numbered, with those who gave away their possessions, and had nothing, or with those who received even the goods of others?

See the fruit of almsgiving, the separations and hindrances were removed, and immediately their souls were knit together. "They were all of one heart and of one soul." So that even setting aside almsgiving, the parting with riches is attended with gain. And these things I have said, that those who have not succeeded to an inheritance from their forefathers may not be cast down, as if they had less than those who are wealthy. For if they please they have more. For they will more readily incline to almsgiving, like the widow, and they will have no occasion for enmity towards their neighbor, and they will enjoy freedom in every respect. Such an one cannot be threatened with the confiscation of his goods, and he is superior to all wrongs. As those who fly unincumbered with clothes are not easily caught, but they who are incumbered with many garments and a long train are soon overtaken, so it is with the rich man and the poor. The one, though he be taken, will easily make his escape, whilst the other, though he be not detained, is incumbered by cords of his own, by numberless cares, distresses, passions, provocations, all which overwhelm the soul, and not these alone, but many other things which riches draw after them. It is much more difficult for a rich man to be moderate and to live frugally, than for the poor, more difficult for him to be free from passion. Then he, you say, will have the greater reward.—By no means.—What, not if he overcomes greater difficulties?—But these difficulties were of his own seeking. For we are not commanded to become rich, but the reverse. But he prepares for himself so many stumbling-blocks and impediments.

Others not only divest themselves of riches, but macerate their bodies, as travelers in the narrow way. Instead of doing this, thou heatest more intensely the furnace of thy passions, and gettest more about thee.[3] Go therefore into the broad way, for it is that which receives such as thee. But the narrow way is for those who are

---

[1] E. V. "righteousness."

[2] Edd. ὠφελείας, "utility," which makes little sense. B. τῆς ἀφελείας, which agrees with ἀφελότητι, Acts ii. 46.
[3] Two MSS. have the middle voice.

afflicted and straitened, who bear along with them nothing but those burdens, which they can carry through it, as almsgiving, love for mankind, goodness, and meekness. These if thou bearest, thou wilt easily find entrance, but if thou takest with thee arrogance, a soul inflamed with passions, and that load of thorns, wealth, there is need of wide room for thee to pass, nor wilt thou well be able to enter into the crowd without striking others, and coming down upon them on thy way. In this case a wide distance from others is required. But he who carries gold and silver, I mean the achievements of virtue, does not cause his neighbors to flee from him, but brings men nearer to him, even to link themselves with him.[1] But if riches in themselves are thorns, what must covetousness be? Why dost thou take that away with thee? Is it to make the flame greater by adding fuel to that fire? Is not the fire of hell sufficient? Consider how the Three Children overcame the furnace. Imagine that to be hell. With tribulation were they plunged into it, bound and fettered; but within they found large room; not so they that stood around without.

Something of this kind even now will be experienced, if we will manfully resist the trials that encompass us. If we have hope in God, we shall be in security, and have ample room, and those who bring us into these straits shall perish. For it is written, " Whoso diggeth a pit shall fall therein." (Ecclus. xxvi. 27.) Though they bind our hands and our feet, the affliction will have power to set us loose. For observe this miracle. Those whom men had bound, the fire set free. As if certain persons were delivered up to the servants of their friends, and the servants, from regard to the friendship of their master, instead of injuring them, should treat them with much respect; so the fire, when as it knew that the Three Children were the friends of its Lord, burst their fetters, set them free, and let them go, and became to them as a pavement, and was trodden under their feet. And justly, since they had been cast into it for the glory of God. Let us, as many of us as are afflicted, hold fast these examples.

But behold, they were delivered from their affliction, you say, and we are not. True, they were delivered, and justly; since they did not enter into that furnace expecting deliverance, but as if to die outright. For hear what they say: "There is a God in Heaven, Who will de-

liver us. But if not, be it known unto thee, O King, that we will not serve thy gods, nor worship the golden image which thou hast set up." (Dan. iii. 17, 18.) But we, as if bargaining on the chastisements of the Lord, even fix a time, saying, " If He does not show mercy till this time." Therefore it is that we are not delivered. Surely Abraham did not leave his home expecting again to receive his son, but as prepared to sacrifice him; and it was contrary to his expectation that he received him again safe. And thou, when thou fallest into tribulation, be not in haste to be delivered,[2] prepare thy mind for all endurance, and speedily thou shalt be delivered from thy affliction. For God brings it upon thee for this end, that He may chasten thee. When therefore from the first we learn to bear it patiently, and do not sink into despair, He presently relieves us, as having effected the whole matter.

I should like to tell you an instructive story, which has much of profit in it. What then is it? Once, when a persecution arose, and a severe war was raging against the Church, two men were apprehended. The one was ready to suffer anything whatever; the other was prepared to submit with firmness to be beheaded, but with fear and trembling shrunk from other tortures. Observe then the dispensation towards these men. When the judge was seated, he ordered the one who was ready to endure anything, to be beheaded. The other he caused to be hung up and tortured, and that not once or twice, but from city to city. Now why was this permitted? That he might recover through torments that quality of mind which he had neglected, that he might shake off all cowardice, and be no longer afraid to endure anything. Joseph too, when he was urgent to escape from prison, was left to remain there. For hear him saying, " Indeed I was stolen away out of the land of the Hebrews; but do thou make mention of me to the king." (Gen. xl. 14, 15.) And for this he was suffered to remain, that he might learn not to place hope or confidence in men, but to cast all upon God. Knowing these things therefore let us give thanks to God, and let us do all things that are expedient for us, that we may obtain the good things to come, through Jesus Christ our Lord, with whom to the Father be glory, with the Holy Ghost, now and ever, and world without end. Amen.

---

[1] Edd. συνδιαζῶντας, " to spend their lives with "; but New Par. from Colb. συνδυάζοντας, and so B.

[2] Two MSS. quote Ecclus. ii. 2, " Make not haste in time of trouble."

HOMILIES OF ST. JOHN CHRYSOSTOM,

ARCHBISHOP OF CONSTANTINOPLE,

ON THE

EPISTLE OF ST. PAUL THE APOSTLE

TO

PHILEMON

ARGUMENT.

FIRST, it is necessary to state the argument of the Epistle, then also the matters that are questioned respecting it. What then is the argument? Philemon was a man of admirable and noble character. That he was an admirable man is evident from the fact, that his whole household was of believers,[1] and of such believers as even to be called a Church: therefore he says in this Epistle, "And to the Church that is in thy house." (v. 2.) He bears witness also to his great obedience, and that "the bowels of the Saints are refreshed in him." (v. 7.) And he himself in this Epistle commanded him to prepare him a lodging. (v. 22.) It seems to me therefore that his house was altogether[2] a lodging for the Saints. This excellent[3] man, then, had a certain slave named Onesimus. This Onesimus, having stolen something from his master, had run away. For that he had stolen, hear what he says: "If he hath wronged thee, or oweth thee aught, I will repay thee." (v. 18, 19.) Coming therefore to Paul at Rome, and having found him in prison, and having enjoyed the benefit of his teaching, he there also received Baptism. For that he obtained there the gift of Baptism is manifest from his saying, "Whom I have begotten in my bonds." (v. 10.) Paul therefore writes, recommending

him to his master, that on every account he should forgive him, and receive him as one now regenerate.[4]

But because some say, that it was superfluous that this Epistle should be annexed, since he is making a request about a small matter in behalf of one man, let them learn who make these objections, that they are themselves deserving of very many censures. For it was not only proper that these small Epistles, in behalf of things so necessary, should have been inscribed,[5] but I wish that it were possible to meet with one who could deliver to us the history of the Apostles, not only all they wrote and spoke of, but of the rest of their conversation, even what they ate, and when they ate, when they walked, and where they sat,[6] what they did every day, in what parts they were, into what house they entered, and where they lodged[7]—to relate everything with minute exactness, so replete with advantage is all that was done by them. But the greater part, not knowing the benefit that would result thence, proceed to censure it.

For if only seeing those places where they sat or where they were imprisoned, mere lifeless spots, we often transport our minds thither, and imagine their virtue, and are excited by it,

---

[1] B. and a Venice MS. read πιστῶν. Edd. πιστὴν, which applies to the household as one.
[2] πάντων ἔνεκεν. The phrase occurs again in a few lines, where it is translated, "on every account."
[3] θαυμαστὸς as before.

[4] B. and Ven. here add, "And on this score forgive him everything. And so much for the argument. Now let us proceed to the solution of the questions. Inasmuch as some venture to say," &c. and presently, "For I say not only this, that it was proper, . . . but add this also, that I wish."
[5] He means in the Canon, as before by the word "annexed."
[6] So B. and Ven. Edd. "where they sat and when they walked."
[7] Lat. "landed," but κατήχθησαν bears the other sense, and he means evidently, "in what part of the house." B. and Ven. have, "I would not have been weary of relating."

and become more zealous, much more would this be the case, if we heard their words and their other actions. But concerning a friend a man enquires, where he lives, what he is doing, whither he is going: and say, should we not make these enquiries[1] about these the general instructors of the world? For when a man leads a spiritual life, the habit, the walk, the words and the actions of such an one, in short, all that relates to him, profits the hearers, and nothing is a hindrance or impediment.

But it is useful for you to learn that this Epistle was sent upon necessary matters. Observe therefore how many things are rectified thereby. We have this one thing first, that in all things it becomes one to be in earnest. For if Paul bestows so much concern upon a runaway, a thief, and a robber, and does not refuse nor is ashamed to send him back with such commendations; much more does it become us not to be negligent in such matters. Secondly, that we ought not to abandon the race of slaves, even if they have proceeded to extreme wickedness. For if a thief and a runaway become so virtuous that Paul was willing to make him a companion, and says in this Epistle, " that in thy stead he might have ministered unto me " (v. 13), much more ought we not to abandon the free. Thirdly, that we ought not to withdraw slaves from the service of their masters. For if Paul, who had such confidence in Philemon, was unwilling to detain Onesimus, so useful and serviceable to minister to himself, without the consent of his master, much less ought we so to act. For if the servant is so excellent, he ought by all means to continue in that service, and to acknowledge the authority of his master, that he may be the occasion of benefit to all in that house. Why dost thou take the candle from the candlestick to place it in the bushel?

I wish it were possible to bring into the cities those (servants) who are without. " What," say you, " if he also should become corrupt." And why should he, I beseech you? Because he has come into the city? But consider, that being without he will be much more corrupt. For he who is corrupt being within, will be much more so being without. For here he will be delivered from necessary care, his master taking that care upon himself; but there the concern about those things will draw him off perhaps even from things more necessary, and more spiritual. On this account the blessed Paul, when giving them the best counsel, said, " Art thou called, being a servant? care not for it: but if even thou mayest be made free, use it rather " (1 Cor. vii. 21); that is, abide in slavery.[2] But what is more important than all, that the word of God be not blasphemed, as he himself says in one of his Epistles. " Let as many servants as are under the yoke count their own masters worthy of all honor, that the name of God and His doctrine be not blasphemed." (1 Tim. vi. 1.) For the Gentiles also will say, that even one who is a slave can be well pleasing to God. But now many are reduced to the necessity of blasphemy, and of saying Christianity has been introduced into life for the subversion of everything, masters having their servants taken from them, and it is a matter of violence.

Let me also say one other thing. He teaches us not to be ashamed of our domestics, if they are virtuous. For if Paul, the most admirable of men, speaks thus much in favor of this one, much more should we speak favorably of ours. There being then so many good effects — and yet we have not mentioned all — does any one think it superfluous that this Epistle was inserted? And would not this be extreme folly? Let us then, I beseech you, apply to the Epistle written by the Apostle. For having gained already so many advantages from it, we shall gain more from the text.[3]

---

[1] B. and Ven. ἐρωτῶντας.

[2] So also he says on the place, and Theodoret too, although he calls it a hyperbole. Εἰ καὶ is properly "if even," but the καὶ may be taken with the *following* word, as "also"; see Kühner, § 824, anm. 1, who quotes Eur. Andr. 1080, and Xen. Mem. i. c. 6, § 12.

[3] τῆς ὑφῆς.

[NOTE. — The views of the Fathers on Slavery and Emancipation were very conservative, as slavery was interwoven with the whole structure of the Roman empire and could not be suddenly abolished without a radical social revolution. But the spirit of Christianity always suggested and encouraged individual emancipation and the ultimate abolition of the institution by teaching the universal love of God, the common redemption and brotherhood of men, and the sacredness of personality. Comp. Bishop Lightfoot's Commentary on *Colossians and Philemon*, and Schaff's *Church History*, I. 793–798; II. 347–354; III. 115–122. Möhler, in his *Vermischte Schriften*, II. 896 sqq., has collected the views of St. Chrysostom on slavery, and says that since the time of the Apostle Paul no one has done more valuable service to slaves than St. Chrysostom. — P. S.]

HOMILY I.

PHILEMON i. 1–3.

"Paul, a prisoner of Jesus Christ, and Timothy our
brother, unto Philemon our dearly beloved, and fellow-laborer, And to our beloved Apphia, and Archippus our fellow-soldier, and to the Church in thy
house: Grace to you, and peace, from God our
Father and the Lord Jesus Christ."

THESE things are said to a master in behalf of
a servant. Immediately at the outset, he has
pulled down his spirit, and not suffered him to
be ashamed, he has quenched his anger; calling
himself a prisoner, he strikes him with compunction, and makes him collect himself, and makes
it appear that present things are nothing. For
if a chain for Christ's sake is not a shame but a
boast, much more is slavery not to be considered
a reproach. And this he says, not exalting himself, but for a good purpose doing this, showing
thence that he was worthy of credit; and this
he does not for his own sake, but that he may
more readily obtain the favor. As if he had
said, "It is on your account that I am invested
with this chain." As he also has said elsewhere,
there indeed showing his concern, but here his
trustworthiness.

Nothing is greater than this boast, to be called
"the stigmatized[1] of Christ." "For I bear in
my body the marks of the Lord Jesus." (Gal.
vi. 17.)

"The prisoner of the Lord." For he had
been bound on His account. Who would not
be struck with awe, who would not be humbled
when he hears of the chains of Christ? Who
would not be ready to give up even his own life,
much less one domestic?

"And Timothy our brother."

He joins another also with himself, that he,
being entreated by many, may the more readily
yield and grant the favor.

"Unto Philemon our dearly beloved, and fellow-laborer."

If "beloved," then his confidence is not boldness nor forwardness, but a proof of much affection. If a "fellow-laborer," then not only may
he be instructed in such a matter, but he ought
to acknowledge it as a favor. For he is gratifying himself, he is building up the same work.
So that apart from any request, he says, thou
hast another necessity for granting the favor.
For if he is profitable to the Gospel, and thou
art anxious to promote the Gospel, then oughtest thou not to be entreated, but to entreat.

Ver. 2. "And to our beloved Apphia."

It seems to me that she was his partner in
life. Observe the humility of Paul; he both
joins Timothy with him in his request, and asks
not only the husband, but the wife also, and
some one else, perhaps a friend.

"And Archippus," he says, "our fellow-soldier."

Not wishing to effect such things by command, and not taking it ill, if he did not immediately comply with his request; but he begs
them to do what a stranger might have done[2] to
aid his request. For not only the being requested by many, but the petition being urged
to many, contributes to its being granted. And
on this account he says, "And Archippus our
fellow-soldier." If thou art a fellow-soldier,
thou oughtest also to take a concern in these
things. But this is the Archippus, about whom
he says in his Epistle to the Colossians, "Say to
Archippus, Take heed to the ministry which
thou hast received in the Lord, that thou fulfill
it." (Col. iv. 17.) It seems to me too, that he,
whom he joins with him in this request, was also
one of the Clergy. And he calls him his fellow-
soldier, that he may by all means coöperate with
him.

"And to the Church in thy house."

Here he has not omitted even the slaves.
For he knew that often even the words of slaves
have power to overthrow their master; and
more especially when his request was in behalf
of a slave. And perhaps it was they particularly
who exasperated him. He does not suffer them
therefore to fall into envy,[3] having honored them
by including them in a salutation with their
masters. And neither does he allow the master
to take offense. For if he had made mention
of them by name, perhaps he would have been
angry. And if he had not mentioned them at
all, he[4] might have been displeased. Observe
therefore how prudently he has found a way by
his manner of mentioning them, both to honor
them by his mention of them, and not to wound
him. For the name of the "Church" does not
suffer masters to be angry, even though they are
reckoned together with their servants. For the
Church knows not the distinction of master and
servant. By good actions and by sins she defines the one and the other. If then it is a

---

[1] στιγματίας. Literally, "branded slave."

[2] He may mean a stranger to Onesimus.
[3] i.e. of Onesimus.
[4] Some suggest the plural, "they," but there is no MS. authority
for it. The last editor defends the singular, as the expression used
would please Philemon.

Church, be not displeased that thy slave is saluted with thee. "For in Christ Jesus there is neither bond nor free." (Gal. iii. 28.)

"Grace to you, and peace."

By mentioning "grace," he brings his own sins to his remembrance. Consider, he says, how great things God has pardoned in thee, how by grace thou art saved. Imitate thy Lord. And he prays for "peace" to him; and naturally: for it comes then when we imitate Him, then grace abides. Since even that servant who was unmerciful to his fellow-servants, until he demanded the hundred pence, had the grace of his master abiding on him. But when he made that demand, it was taken from him, and he was delivered to the tormentors.

MORAL. Considering these things, then, let us also be merciful and forgiving towards those who have trespassed against us. The offenses against us here are a hundred pence, but those from us against God are ten thousand talents. But you know that offenses are also judged by the quality of the persons: for instance, he who has insulted a private person has done wrong, but not so much as he who has insulted a magistrate, and he who has offended a greater magistrate offends in a higher degree, and he who offends an inferior one in a lower degree; but he who insults the king offends much more. The injury indeed is the same, but it becomes greater by the excellence of the person. And if he who insults a king receives intolerable punishment, on account of the superiority[1] of the person; for how many talents will he be answerable who insults God? so that even if we should commit the same offenses against God, that we do against men, even so it is not an equal thing: but as great as is the difference between God and men, so great is that between the offenses against Him and them.

But now I find also that the offenses exceed, not only in that they become great by the eminence of the person, but by their very nature. And it is a horrible saying that I am about to utter, and truly awful, but it is necessary to be said, that it may even so shake our minds and strike them with terror, showing that we fear men much more than God, and we honor men much more than God. For consider, he that commits adultery knows that God sees him, yet he disregards Him; but if a man see him, he restrains his lust. Does not such a one not only honor men above God, not only insult God, but, which is even much more dreadful, whilst he fears them, despise Him? For if he sees them, he restrains the flame of lust, but rather what flame? it is not a flame, but a willfulness. For

if indeed it was not lawful to have intercourse with a woman, the matter perhaps would be a flame, but now[2] it is insult and wantonness. For if he should see men, he desists from his mad passion, but for the longsuffering of God he has less regard. Again, another who steals, is conscious that he is committing robbery, and endeavors to deceive men, and defends himself against those who accuse him, and clothes his apology with a fair show; but though he cannot thus prevail with God, he does not regard Him, nor stand in awe of Him, nor honor Him. And if the king indeed commands us to abstain from other men's goods, or even to give away our own, all readily contribute, but when God commands not to rob, nor to gather other men's goods, we do not forbear.

Do you see then that we honor men more than God? It is a sad and grievous saying, a heavy charge. But show that it is grievous; flee from the fact! But if you fear not the fact, how can I believe you when you say, We fear your words, you lay a burden on us! It is you that by the deed lay a burden on yourselves, and not our words. And if I but name the words of which you do the deeds, you are offended. And is not this absurd?

May the thing spoken by me prove false! I would rather myself in That Day bear the imputation of ill language, as having vainly and causelessly reproached you, than see you accused of such things.

But not only do you honor men more than God, but you compel others to do so likewise. Many have thus compelled their domestics and slaves. Some have drawn them into marriage against their will, and others have forced them to minister to disgraceful services, to infamous love, to acts of rapine, and fraud, and violence: so that the accusation is twofold, and neither can they obtain pardon upon the plea of necessity. For if you yourself do wrong things unwillingly, and on account of the command of the ruler, not even so is it by any means a sufficient excuse: but the offense becomes heavier, when you compel them also to fall into the same sins. For what pardon can there be any more for such an one?

These things I have said, not from a wish to condemn you, but to show in how many things we are debtors to God. For if by honoring men even equally with God, we insult God, how much more, when we honor men above Him? But if those offenses that are committed against men are shown to be much greater against God; how much more when the actual offense is greater and more grievous in its own quality.

Let any one examine himself, and he will see

---

[1] Edd. ἀξιοπιστίαν, literally, "worthiness of credit," but in later Greek "of consideration." Sav. mar. B. and Ven. have ὑπεροχήν.

[2] Sav. mar. B. and Ven. "but now, with most men, what is lawful is despised," and, "but what is forbidden made much of, it is all," &c.

that he does everything on account of men. Exceedingly blessed we should be, if we did as many things for the sake of God, as we do for the sake of men, and of the opinion of men, and for the dread or the respect of men. If then we have so many things to answer for, we ought with all alacrity to forgive those who injure us, who defraud us, and not to bear malice. For there is a way to the forgiveness of our sins that needs no labors, nor expense of wealth, nor any other things, but merely our own choice. We have no need to set out upon our travels, nor go beyond the boundaries of our country, nor submit to dangers and toils, but only to will.

What excuse, tell me, shall we have in things that appear difficult,[1] when we do not do even a light thing, attended too with so much gain and so much benefit, and no trouble? Canst thou not despise wealth? Canst thou not spend thy substance on the needy? Canst thou not will anything that is good? Canst thou not forgive him that has injured thee? For if thou hadst not so many things to answer for, and God had only commanded thee to forgive, oughtest thou not to do it? But now having so many things to answer for, dost thou not forgive? and that too, knowing that thou art required to do it on account of things which thou hast from Him? If indeed we go to our debtor, he knowing it, receives us courteously, and shows us honor, and pays us every attention in a liberal way; and that though he is not paying off his debt, but because he wishes to render us merciful in our demand of payment: and thou, who owest so much to God, and art commanded to forgive that thou mayest receive in return, dost not thou forgive? And wherefore not, I beseech you? Woe is me! How much of goodness do we receive, and what wickedness do we show in return! What sleepiness! what indolence! How easy a thing is virtue, attended too with much advantage; and how laborious a thing is vice! But we, flying from that which is so light, pursue that which is heavier than lead.

Here there is no need of bodily strength, nor of wealth, nor possessions, nor of power, nor of friendship, nor of any other thing; but it is sufficient only to will, and all is accomplished. Hath some one grieved thee, and insulted thee, and mocked thee? But consider, how often thou hast done such things to others, and even to the Lord Himself; and forbear, and forgive him it. Consider that thou sayest, "Forgive us

our debts, as we also forgive our debtors." (Matt. vi. 13.) Consider, that if thou dost not forgive, thou wilt not be able to say this with confidence: but if thou forgivest, thou demandest the matter as a debt, not by reason of the nature of the thing, but on account of the lovingkindness of Him that hath granted it. And wherein is it equal, that one who forgives his fellow-servants should receive remission of the sins committed against the Lord? but nevertheless we do receive such great lovingkindness, because He is rich in mercy and pity.

And that I may show that even without these things, and without the remission, thou art a gainer by forgiving, consider how many friends such a person has, how the praises of such an one are everywhere sounded by men who go about saying, "This is a good man, he is easily reconciled, he knows not to bear malice, he is no sooner stricken than he is healed." When such an one falls into any misfortune, who will not pity him? when he has offended, who will not pardon him? When he asks a favor of others, who will not grant it to him? Who will not be willing to be the friend and servant of so good a soul? Yea, I entreat you, let us do all things for Him,[2] not to our friends, not to our relations only, but even to our domestics. For He says, "Forbearing threatening, knowing that your Master also is in heaven." (Eph. vi. 9.)

If we forgive our neighbors their trespasses, ours will be forgiven to us, if we bestow alms, if we be humble. For this also taketh away sins. For if the publican, only for saying, "God be merciful to me a sinner" (Luke xviii. 13), went down justified, much more we also, if we be humble and contrite, shall be able to obtain abundant lovingkindness. If we confess our own sins and condemn ourselves, we shall be cleansed from the most of our defilement. For there are many ways that purify. Let us therefore in every way war against the devil. I have said nothing difficult, nothing burdensome. Forgive him that has injured thee, have pity on the needy, humble thy soul, and though thou be a grievous sinner, thou wilt be able to obtain the kingdom, by these means purging off thy sins themselves, and wiping off their stain. And God grant that we all, having purified ourselves here by confession from all the filth of our sins, may there obtain the blessings promised in Christ Jesus our Lord, &c.

---

[1] Raphelius (ap. Par.) notes that he means "what presumption is there that we would do them if we could?"

[2] Or, "to this purpose," as the Latin. But it seems to be an unexpected turn upon the last clause. Compare the general argument of Bp. Butler's Sermons on the Love of God.

HOMILY II.

PHILEMON i. 4–6.

"I thank my God, making mention of thee always in my prayers, Hearing of thy love and faith, which thou hast towards the Lord Jesus, and toward all saints. That the communication of thy faith may become effectual by the acknowledging [in the knowledge] of every good thing which is in us,[1] in Christ Jesus."

HE does not immediately at the commencement ask the favor, but having first admired the man, and having praised him for his good actions, and having shown no small proof of his love, that he always made mention of him in his prayers, and having said that many are refreshed by him, and that he is obedient and complying in all things; then he puts it last of all, by this particularly putting him to the blush.[2] For if others obtain the things which they ask, much more Paul. If coming before others, he was worthy to obtain, much more when he comes after others, and asks a thing not pertaining to himself, but in behalf of another. Then, that he may not seem to have written on this account only, and that no one may say, "If it were not for Onesimus thou wouldest not have written," see how he assigns other causes also of his Epistle. In the first place manifesting his love, then also desiring that a lodging may be prepared for him.

"Hearing," he says, "of thy love."

This is wonderful, and much greater than if being present he had seen it when he[3] was present. For it is plain that from its being excessive it had become manifest, and had reached even to Paul. And yet the distance between Rome and Phrygia was not small. For he seems to have been there from the mention of Archippus. For the Colossians were of Phrygia, writing to whom he said, "When this Epistle is read among you, cause that it be read also in the Church of the Laodiceans, and that ye likewise read the Epistle from Laodicea." (Col. iv. 16.) And this is a city of Phrygia.

I pray, he says, "that the communication of thy faith may become effectual in the knowledge of every good thing which is in Christ Jesus." Dost thou see him first giving, before he receives, and before he asks a favor himself bestowing a much greater one of his own? "That the communication of thy faith," he says, "may become effectual by the acknowledging of every good thing which is in you in Christ Jesus"; that is, that thou mayest attain all virtue, that

nothing may be deficient. For so faith becomes effectual, when it is accompanied with works. For "without works faith is dead." (Jas. ii. 26.) And he has not said, "Thy faith," but "the communication of thy faith," connecting it with himself, and showing that it is one body, and by this particularly making him ashamed to refuse. If thou art a partaker, he says, with respect to the faith, thou oughtest to communicate also with respect to other things.

Ver. 7. "For we have [I had] great joy and consolation in thy love, because the bowels [hearts] of the Saints are refreshed by thee, brother."

Nothing so shames us into giving, as to bring forward the kindnesses bestowed on others, and particularly when a man is more entitled to respect than they. And he has not said, "If you do it to others, much more to me"; but he has insinuated the same thing, though he has contrived to do it in another and a more gracious manner.

"I had joy," that is, thou hast given me confidence from the things which thou hast done to others. "And consolation," that is, we are not only gratified, but we are also comforted. For they are members of us. If then there ought to be such an agreement, that in the refreshing of any others who are in affliction, though we obtain nothing, we should be delighted on their account, as if it were one body that was benefited; much more if you shall refresh us also. And he has not said, "Because thou yieldest, and compliest," but even more vehemently and emphatically, "because the bowels of the Saints," as if it were for a darling child fondly loved by its parents, so that this love and affection shows that he also is exceedingly beloved by them.

Ver. 8. "Wherefore, though I might be much bold in Christ to enjoin thee that which is convenient [befitting]."

Observe how cautious he is, lest any of the things which were spoken even from exceeding love should so strike the hearer, as that he should be hurt. For this reason before he says, "to enjoin thee," since it was offensive, although, as spoken out of love, it was more proper to soothe him, yet nevertheless from an excess of delicacy, he as it were corrects it by saying, "Having confidence," by which he implies that Philemon was a great man,[4] that is "Thou hast given

---

[1] E. V. "in you." [The R. V. reads "in you," ἐν ὑμῖν, and puts "us," ἡμῖν, in the margin. — P. S.]
[2] δυσωπῶν.
[3] Philemon, as it is παρόντος.

[4] i.e. a man of high Christian character, who would admit such claims as his.

confidence to us." And not only that, but adding the expression " in Christ," by which he shows that it was not that he was more illustrious in the world, not that he was more powerful, but it was on account of his faith in Christ, — then he also adds, " to enjoin thee," and not that only, but " that which is convenient," that is, a reasonable action. And see out of how many things he brings proof for this. Thou doest good to others, he says, and to me, and for Christ's sake, and that the thing is reasonable, and that love giveth, wherefore also he adds,

Ver. 9. " Yet for love's sake, I rather beseech thee."

As if he had said, I know indeed that I can effect it by commanding with much authority, from things which have already taken place. But because I am very solicitous about this matter, " I beseech thee." He shows both these things at once ; that he has confidence in him, for he commands him ;[1] and that he is exceedingly concerned about the matter, wherefore he beseeches him.

" Being such an one," he says, " as Paul the aged." Strange ! how many things are here to shame him into compliance ! Paul, from the quality of his person, from his age, because he was old, and from what was more just than all, because he was also " a prisoner of Jesus Christ."

For who would not receive with open arms a combatant who had been crowned ? Who seeing him bound for Christ's sake, would not have granted him ten thousand favors ? By so many considerations having previously soothed his mind, he has not immediately introduced the name, but defers making so great a request. For you know what are the minds of masters towards slaves that have run away ; and particularly when they have done this with robbery, even if they have good masters, how their anger is increased. This anger then having taken all these pains to soothe, and having first persuaded him readily to serve him in anything whatever, and having prepared his soul to all obedience, then he introduces his request, and says, " I beseech thee," and with the addition of praises, " for my son whom I have begotten in my bonds."

Again the chains are mentioned to shame him into compliance, and then the name. For he has not only extinguished his anger, but has caused him to be delighted. For I would not have called him my son, he says, if he were not especially profitable. What I called Timothy, that I call him also. And repeatedly showing his affection, he urges him by the very period of his new birth, " I have begotten him in my bonds," he says, so that on this account also he was worthy to obtain much honor, because he

was begotten in his very conflicts, in his trials in the cause of Christ.

" Onesimus,"

Ver. 11. " Which in time past was to thee unprofitable."

See how great is his prudence, how he confesses the man's faults, and thereby extinguishes his anger. I know, he says, that he was unprofitable.

" But now " he will be " profitable to thee and to me."

He has not said he will be useful to thee, lest he should contradict it, but he has introduced his own person, that his hopes may seem worthy of credit, " But now," he says, " profitable to thee and to me." For if he was profitable to Paul, who required so great strictness, much more would he be so to his master.

Ver. 12. " Whom I have sent again to thee."

By this also he has quenched his anger, by delivering him up. For masters are then most enraged, when they are entreated for the absent, so that by this very act he mollified him the more.

Ver. 12. " Thou therefore receive him, that is mine own bowels."

And again he has not given the bare name, but uses with it a word that might move him, which is more affectionate than son. He has said, " son," he has said, " I have begotten " him,[2] so that it was probable[3] he would love him much, because he begot him in his trials. For it is manifest that we are most inflamed with affection for those children, who have been born to us in dangers which we have escaped, as when the Scripture saith, " Woe, Barochabel ! "[4] and again when Rachel names Benjamin, " the son of my sorrow." (Gen. xxxv. 18.)

" Thou therefore," he says, " receive him, that is mine own bowels." He shows the greatness of his affection. He has not said, Take him back,[5] he has not said, Be not angry,[6] but " receive him " ; that is, he is worthy not only of pardon, but of honor. Why ? Because he is become the son of Paul.

Ver. 13. " Whom I would have retained with me, that in thy stead he might have ministered unto me in the bonds of the Gospel."

Dost thou see after how much previous preparation, he has at length brought him honorably before his master, and observe with how much wisdom he has done this. See for how much he makes him answerable, and how much he honors the other. Thou hast found, he says, a way by which thou mayest through him

---

[1] He means that his words would be felt as a command, and were really not *less*, but *more*.

[2] Old Lat. adds, " in my bonds," which the sense requires.
[3] B. and Ven. " so as to show that he loved him especially."
[4] The last Paris edition has a note from Raphelius and Hemsterhusius which curiously illustrates the variation of names. This οὐαιβαροχαβὴλ is in Sept. 1 Sam. iv. 21, οὐαιβαρχαβὼθ, Vat. Οὐαιχαβὼθ Alex., Or. Hex. οὐαὶ ἰοχαβὴδ, E. V. " Ichabod."
[5] ἀπόδεξαι.
[6] προσλαβοῦ.

repay thy service to me. Here he shows that he has considered his advantage more than that of his slave, and that he respects him exceedingly.

Ver. 14. "But without thy mind," he says, "would I do nothing; that thy benefit should not be, as it were, of necessity, but willingly."

This particularly flatters the person asked, when the thing being profitable in itself, it is brought out with his concurrence. For two good effects are produced thence, the one person gains, and the other is rendered more secure. And he has not said, That it should not be of necessity, but "as it were of necessity." For I knew, he says, that not having learnt[1] it, but coming to know it at once, thou wouldest not have been angry, but nevertheless out of an excess of consideration, that it should "not be as it were of necessity."

Ver. 15, 16. "For perhaps he was therefore parted from thee for a season that thou shouldest have him for ever; no longer as a bond-servant."

He has well said, "perhaps," that the master may yield. For since the flight arose from perverseness, and a corrupt mind, and not from such intention, he has said, "perhaps." And he has not said, therefore he fled, but, therefore he was "separated,"[2] by a more fair sounding expression softening him the more. And he has not said, He separated himself, but, "he was separated." For it was not his own arrangement that he should depart either for this purpose or for that. Which also Joseph says, in making excuse for his brethren, "For God did send me hither" (Gen. xlv. 5), that is, He made use of their wickedness for a good end. "Therefore," he says, "he was parted for a season."[3] Thus he contracts the time, acknowledges the offense, and turns it all to a providence.[4] "That thou shouldest receive him," he says, "for ever," not for the present season only, but even for the future, that thou mightest always have him, no longer a slave, but more honorable than a slave. For thou wilt have a slave abiding with thee, more well-disposed than a brother, so that thou hast gained both in time, and in the quality of thy slave. For hereafter he will not run away. "That thou shouldest receive him," he says, "for ever," that is, have him again.

"No longer as a bond-servant, but more than a bond-servant, a brother beloved, especially to me."

Thou hast lost a slave for a short time, but thou wilt find a brother for ever, not only thy brother, but mine also. Here also there is much virtue. But if he is my brother, thou also wilt not be ashamed of him. By calling him his son, he hath shown his natural affection; and by calling him his brother, his great good will for him, and his equality in honor.

MORAL. These things are not written without an object, but that we masters may not despair of our servants, nor press too hard on them, but may learn to pardon the offenses of such servants, that we may not be always severe, that we may not from their servitude be ashamed to make them partakers with us in all things when they are good. For if Paul was not ashamed to call one "his son, his own bowels, his brother, his beloved," surely we ought not to be ashamed. And why do I say Paul? The Master of Paul is not ashamed to call our servants His own brethren; and are we ashamed? See how He honors us; He calls our servants His own brethren, friends, and fellow-heirs. See to what He has descended! What therefore having done, shall we have accomplished our whole duty? We shall never in any wise do it; but to whatever degree of humility we have come, the greater part of it is still left behind. For consider, whatever thou doest, thou doest to a fellow-servant, but thy Master hath done it to thy servants. Hear and shudder! Never be elated at thy humility!

Perhaps you laugh at the expression, as if humility could puff up. But be not surprised at it, it puffs up, when it is not genuine. How, and in what manner? When it is practiced to gain the favor of men, and not of God, that we may be praised, and be high-minded. For this also is diabolical. For as many are vainglorious on account of their not being vainglorious,[5] so are they elated on account of their humbling themselves, by reason of their being high-minded. For instance, a brother has come, or even a servant thou hast received him, thou hast washed his feet; immediately thou thinkest highly of thyself. I have done, thou sayest, what no other has done. I have achieved humility. How then may any one continue in humility? If he remembers the command of Christ, which says, "When ye shall have done all things, say, We are unprofitable servants." (Luke xvii. 10.) And again the Teacher of the world, saying, "I count not myself to have apprehended." (Phil. iii. 13.) He who has persuaded himself that he has done no great thing, however many things he may have done, he alone can be humble-minded, he who thinks that he has not reached perfection.

Many are elated on account of their humility; but let not us be so affected. Hast thou done any act of humility? be not proud of it, otherwise all the merit of it is lost. Such was the Pharisee, he was puffed up because he gave his tythes to the poor, and he lost all the merit of

1 i.e. by previous explanation, μαθών.
2 Gr. ἐχωρίσθη. [R. V. "he was parted *from thee*."—P.S.]
3 ὥραν, lit. "an hour."   4 οἰκονομίαν.

5 "Proud of his periods leveled against pride."—Anon.

it. (Luke xviii. 12.) But not so the publican. Hear Paul again saying, "I know nothing by myself, yet am I not hereby justified." (1 Cor. iv. 4.) Seest thou that he does not exalt himself, but by every means abases and humbles himself, and that too when he had arrived at the very summit. And the Three Children were in the fire, and in the midst of the furnace, and what said they? "We have sinned and committed iniquity with our fathers." (Song, v. 6, in Sept.; Dan. iii. 29, 30; v. 16.) This it is to have a contrite heart; on this account they could say, "Nevertheless in a contrite heart and a humble spirit let us be accepted." Thus even after they had fallen into the furnace they were exceedingly humbled, even more so than they were before. For when they saw the miracle that was wrought, thinking themselves unworthy of that deliverance, they were brought lower in humility. For when we are persuaded that we have received great benefits beyond our desert, then we are particularly grieved. And yet what benefit had they received beyond their desert? They had given themselves up to the furnace; they had been taken captive for the sins of others; for they were still young; and they murmured not, nor were indignant, nor did they say, What good is it to us that we serve God, or what advantage have we in worshiping Him? This man is impious, and is become our lord. We are punished with the idolatrous by an idolatrous king. We have been led into captivity. We are deprived of our country, our freedom, all our paternal goods, we are become prisoners and slaves, we are enslaved to a barbarous king. None of these things did they say. But what? "We have sinned and committed iniquity." And not for themselves but for others they offer prayers. Because, say they, "Thou hast delivered us to a hateful and a wicked king." Again, Daniel, being a second time cast into the pit, said, "For God hath remembered me." Wherefore should He not remember[1] thee, O Daniel, when thou didst glorify Him before the king, saying, "Not for any wisdom that I have"? (Dan. ii. 30.) But when thou wast cast into the den of lions, because thou didst not obey that most wicked decree, wherefore should He not remember thee? For this very reason surely should He.[2] Wast thou not cast into it on His account? "Yea truly," he says, "but I am a debtor for many things." And if he said such things after having displayed so great virtue, what should we say after this? But hear what David says, "If He thus say, I have no delight in thee, behold here am I, let Him do to me as seemeth good unto Him." (2 Sam. xv. 26.) And yet

he had an infinite number of good things to speak of. And Eli also says, "It is the Lord: let Him do what seemeth Him good." (1 Sam. iii. 18.)

This is the part of well-disposed servants, not only in His mercies, but in His corrections, and in punishments wholly to submit to Him. For how is it not absurd,[3] if we bear with masters beating their servants, knowing that they will spare them, because they are their own;[4] and yet suppose that God in punishing will not spare? This also Paul has intimated, saying, "Whether we live or die, we are the Lord's." (Rom. xiv. 8.) A man, we say, wishes not his property to be diminished, he knows how he punishes, he is punishing his own servants. But surely no one of us spares more than He Who brought us into being out of nothing, Who maketh the sun to rise, Who causeth rain; Who breathed our life into us, Who gave His own Son for us.

But as I said before, and on which account I have said all that I have said, let us be humble-minded as we ought, let us be moderate as we ought. Let it not be to us an occasion of being puffed up. Art thou humble, and humbler than all men? Be not high-minded on that account, neither reproach others, lest thou lose thy boast. For this very cause thou art humble, that thou mayest be delivered from the madness of pride; if therefore through thy humility thou fallest into that madness, it were better for thee not to be humble. For hear Paul saying, "Sin worketh death in me by that which is good, that sin by the commandment might become exceeding sinful." (Rom. vii. 13.) When it enters into thy thought to admire thyself because thou art humble, consider thy Master, to what He descended, and thou wilt no longer admire thyself, nor praise thyself, but wilt deride thyself as having done nothing. Consider thyself altogether to be a debtor. Whatever thou hast done, remember that parable, "Which of you having a servant . . . will say unto him, when he is come in, Sit down to meat? . . . I say unto you, Nay . . . but stay and serve me." (From Luke xvii. 7, 8.) Do we return thanks to our servants, for waiting upon us? By no means. Yet God is thankful to us, who serve not Him, but do that which is expedient for ourselves.

But let not us be so affected, as if He owed us thanks, that He may owe us the more, but as if we were discharging a debt. For the matter truly is a debt, and all that we do is of debt. For if when we purchase slaves with our money, we wish them to live altogether for us, and whatever they have to have it for ourselves, how

---

[1] B. "didst thou not remember," and presently, "did I not remember." The construction in either case is so elliptical as to be difficult.

[2] Bel and Dragon, verse 38 [ὁ δὲ κύριος ὁ θεὸς ἐμνήσθη τοῦ Δανιήλ.—P. S.]

[3] B. and Ven. add, "for us to be well disposed while we are favored, but discontented when we are chastised; tell me now."

[4] Such seems the principle in Ex. xxi. 21.

much more must it be so with Him, who brought us out of nothing into being, who after this bought us with His precious Blood, who paid down such a price for us as no one would endure to pay for his own son, who shed His own Blood for us? If therefore we had ten thousand souls, and should lay them all down for Him, should we make Him an equal return? By no means. And why? Because He did this, owing us nothing, but the whole was a matter of grace. But we henceforth are debtors : and being God Himself, He became a servant, and not being subject to death, subjected Himself to death in the flesh. We, if we do not lay down our lives for Him, by the law of nature must certainly lay them down, and a little later shall be separated from it,[1] however unwillingly. So also in the case of riches, if we do not bestow them for His sake, we shall render them up from necessity at our end. So it is also with humility. Although we are not humble for His sake, we shall be made humble by tribulations, by calamities, by over-ruling powers. Seest thou therefore how great is the grace ! He hath not said, "What great things do the Martyrs do? Although they die not for Me, they certainly will die." But He owns Himself much indebted to them, because they voluntarily resign that which in the course of nature they were about to resign shortly against their will. He hath not said, "What great thing do they, who give away their riches? Even against their will they will have to surrender them." But He owns Himself much indebted to them too, and is not ashamed to confess before all that He, the Master, is nourished by His slaves.

For this also is the glory of a Master, to have grateful slaves. And this is the glory of a Master, that He should thus love His slaves. And this is the glory of a Master, to claim for His own what is theirs. And this is the glory of a Master, not to be ashamed to confess them before all. Let us therefore be stricken with awe at this so great love of Christ. Let us be inflamed with this love-potion. Though a man be low and mean, yet if we hear that he loves us, we are above all things warmed with love towards him, and honor him exceedingly. And do we then love? and when our Master loveth us so much, we are not excited? Let us not, I beseech you, let us not be so indifferent with regard to the salvation of our souls, but let us love Him according to our power, and let us spend all upon His love, our life, our riches, our glory, everything, with delight, with joy, with alacrity, not as rendering anything to Him, but to ourselves. For such is the law of those who love. They think that they are receiving favors, when they are suffering wrong for the sake of their beloved. Therefore let us be so affected towards our Lord, that we [3] also may partake of the good things to come in Christ Jesus our Lord.

HOMILY III.

PHILEMON i. 17–19.

"If thou count me therefore a partner, receive him as myself. If he hath wronged thee at all, or oweth thee aught, put that to mine account; I Paul write it with mine own hand, I will repay it : that I say not to thee how thou owest unto me even thine own self besides."

No procedure is so apt to gain a hearing,[2] as not to ask for everything at once. For see after how many praises, after how much preparation he hath introduced this great matter. After having said that he is " my son," that he is a partaker of the Gospel, that he is " my bowels," that thou receivest him back " as a brother," and " hold him as a brother," then he has added " as myself." And Paul was not ashamed to do this. For he who was not ashamed to be called the servant of the faithful, but confesses that he was such, much more would he not refuse this. But what he says is to this effect. If thou art of the same mind with me, if thou runnest upon the same terms,[4] if thou considerest me a friend, receive him as myself.

" If he hath wronged thee at all." See where and when he has introduced the mention of the injury ; last, after having said so many things in his behalf. For since the loss of money is particularly apt to annoy men, that he might not accuse him of this, (for it was most likely that it was spent,) then he brings in this, and says, " If he hath wronged thee." He does not say, If he has stolen anything ; but what? " If

[1] The sense naturally leads to this transition to the singular, which is not uncommon in St. Chrysostom.
[2] παραινεῖν.

[3] B. and Ven. add, "May both obtain His help here, and."
[4] ἐπὶ τοῖς αὐτοῖς, perhaps " for the same prize."

he hath wronged thee." At the same time he both confessed the offense, and not as if it were the offense of a servant, but of a friend against a friend, making use of the expression of "wrong" rather than of theft.

"Put that to mine account," he says, that is, reckon the debt to me, "I will repay it." Then also with that spiritual pleasantry,

"I Paul write[1] it with mine own hand." At once movingly and pleasantly; if when Paul did not refuse to execute a bond for him, he should refuse to receive him! This would both shame Philemon into compliance, and bring Onesimus out of trouble. "I write it," he says, "with mine own hand." Nothing is more affectionate than these "bowels," nothing more earnest, nothing more zealous. See what[2] great concern he bestows in behalf of one man. "Albeit I do not say to thee how thou owest unto me even thine own self besides." Then that it might not appear insulting to him, whom he requests, if he had not the confidence to ask and obtain in behalf of a theft, he in some measure relieves this, saying, "That I say not unto thee how thou owest to me even thine own self besides." Not only thine own things, but thyself also. And this proceeded from love, and was according to the rule of friendship, and was a proof of his great confidence. See how he everywhere provides for both, that he may ask with great security, and that this may not seem a sign of too little[3] confidence in him.

Ver. 20. "Yea, brother."

What is, "Yea, brother"? Receive him, he says. For this we must understand though unexpressed. For dismissing all pleasantry, he again pursues his former considerations, that is, serious ones. And yet even these are serious. For the things that proceed from Saints are of themselves serious, even when they are pleasantry.

"Yea, brother, let me have joy of thee in the Lord, refresh my heart in Christ."[4]

That is, thou grantest the favor to the Lord, not to me. "My heart," that is, toward thyself.

Ver. 21. "Having confidence in thy obedience, I write unto thee."

What stone would not these things have softened? What wild beast would not these things have rendered mild, and prepared to receive him heartily? After having borne witness to him by so many great testimonies of his goodness,

he is not ashamed again to excuse himself. He says, Not barely requesting it, nor as commanding it, nor arbitrarily, but "having confidence in thy obedience I wrote unto thee." What he had said at the beginning, "having confidence," that he also says here in the sealing up of his letter.

"Knowing that thou wilt also do more than I say."

At the same time in saying this he excited him. For he would have been ashamed, though for nothing else, if having such credit with him as this, that he would do more than he said, — he should not do so much.

Ver. 22. "But withal prepare me also a lodging: for I trust that through your prayers I shall be given unto you."

This also was the part of one who was exceedingly confident — or rather this too was in behalf of Onesimus, that not being indifferent, but knowing that he upon his return would know the things relating to him, they might lay aside all remembrance of the wrong, and might the rather grant the favor. For great was the influence and the honor of Paul residing among them, of Paul in his age, of Paul after imprisonment. Again, it is a proof of their love that he says that they pray; and to attribute to them so much as that they pray for "him." For although I be now in danger, yet nevertheless you will see me if ye pray for it.

Ver. 23. "Epaphras, my fellow-prisoner in Christ Jesus, saluteth thee."

He was sent by the Colossians, so that from this it appears that Philemon was also at Colossæ. And he calls him his "fellow-prisoner," showing that he also was in much tribulation, so that if not on his own account, yet on account of the other, it was right that he should be heard. For he that is in tribulation, and overlooks himself, and is concerned for others, deserves to be heard.

And he puts him to shame from another consideration, if his countryman is a fellow-prisoner with Paul and suffers affliction with him, and he himself does not grant him a favor in behalf of his own servant. And he has added, "my fellow-prisoner in Christ Jesus," instead of on account of Christ.

Ver. 24. "Mark, Aristarchus, Demas, Luke, my fellow-workers."

Why then does he put Luke last? And yet he elsewhere says, "Only Luke is with me" (2 Tim. iv. 11), and "Demas," he says, was one of those who "forsook him, having loved the present world." (2 Tim. iv. 10.) All these things, although they are mentioned elsewhere, yet nevertheless ought not to be passed over here without enquiry, nor ought we merely to hear them as things of course. But how comes he to say that he who forsook him salutes them? For

---

[1] [ἔγραψα, the epistolary aorist.—P. S.]

[2] Colb. "what entreaty he makes."

[3] The Editor has ventured to insert μὴ from Raphelius' conjecture. Old Lat. omits the former negative. If the common text ("too much confidence") is right, "security" means confidence in Philemon, but that is indifferent Greek.

[4] So the best MSS. and most Fathers for ἐνκυρίῳ. Hemsterhusius quoted in New Par. defends the Vulgate *Ego te fruar in Domino* for the former clause, giving it a general sense; Beza has *hunc fructum.* [A. V. "my bowels in the Lord"; R. V. "my heart in Christ."—P. S.]

"Erastus," he says, "abode at Corinth." (2 Tim. iv. 20.) He adds Epaphras, both as known to them, and being of their country. And Mark, as being himself also an admirable man. Why then does he number Demas with these? Perhaps it was after this that he became more remiss, when he saw the dangers multiplied. But Luke being last became first. And from these indeed he salutes him, urging him the more to obedience, and calls them his fellow-laborers, and in this way shames him into granting the request.

Ver. 25. "The grace of our Lord Jesus Christ be with your spirit. Amen."

Moral. He hath closed his Epistle with a prayer. And indeed prayer is a great good, salutary, and preservative of our souls. But it is great when we do things worthy of it, and do not render ourselves unworthy. And thou too, therefore, when thou goest to the priest, and he shall say to thee, "The Lord will have mercy on thee, my son," do not confide in the word only, but add also works. Do acts worthy of mercy, God will bless thee, my son, if indeed thou doest things worthy of blessing. He will bless thee, if thou showest mercy to thy neighbor. For the things which we wish to obtain from God, of those we ought first to impart to our neighbors. But if we deprive our neighbors of them, how can we wish to obtain them? "Blessed," He says, "are the merciful: for they shall obtain mercy." (Matt. v. 7.) For if men show mercy to such, much more will God, but to the unmerciful by no means. "For he shall have judgment without mercy to him that hath showed no mercy." (Jas. ii. 13.)

An excellent thing is mercy! Why then hast thou not done it to another? Dost thou wish to be pardoned, when thou offendest? why then dost thou not thyself pardon him who has offended thee? But thou comest to God, asking of Him the kingdom of heaven, and thou thyself dost not give money when it is begged of thee. For this cause we do not obtain mercy, because we do not show mercy. But why? you say. Is not this also a part of mercy, to show mercy to the unmerciful? Nay![1] For he that treated with the greatest kindness the hard-hearted cruel man, that had done numberless ills to his neighbor, how should he be merciful? What then, say you? Hath not the Laver saved us, who had committed infinite evils? It hath delivered us from them, not that we should commit them again, but that we may not commit them. For "how shall we," it is said, "that are dead to sin, live any longer therein"? (Rom. vi. 2.)

"What then? shall we sin because we are not

under the law? God forbid." (v. 15.) For this cause God hath delivered thee from those sins that thou mightest no more run back to that dishonor. Since even physicians relieve their feverish patients from their heat, not that they may abuse their health to their injury and disorder, (since it would be better to be sick, if one was about to use his health only that he might confine himself again to his bed,) but having learnt the evils that arise from sickness, they may no longer fall into the same, that they may the more securely preserve their health, that they may do everything that conduces to its preservation.

How then? you say: what is the lovingkindness of God, if He is not about to save the bad? For oftentimes I hear many talking in this way, that He is the Friend of man, and will by all means save all. That we may not therefore vainly deceive ourselves, (for I remember that I made a promise of this kind to you,) come let us to-day move this argument. I lately discoursed with you about Hell, and I deferred my argument upon the lovingkindness of God. It is proper therefore to-day to resume it. That there will, then, be a hell, we have, as I think, sufficiently proved, bringing forward the deluge, and former evils, and arguing that it is not possible that He who performed these things should leave the men of the present age unpunished. For if thus He chastised those who sinned before the Law, He will not let those go unpunished who after grace have committed greater wickedness. It has been questioned therefore how is He good? how merciful to man, if at least He punishes? and we have deferred the argument, that we might not overwhelm your ears with a multitude of words.

Come, to-day let us discharge the debt, and show how good is God, even in punishing. For this discourse would be suitable for us in opposition to the heretics. Let us therefore pay earnest heed to it. God, standing in no need of anything from us, yet created us. For that He stood in need of us, is manifest from His having made us after a long time. For He might have made us long ago, if He had needed us. For if He Himself was, even without us, and we were made in later times, He made us, not needing us.

He made the Heaven, the earth, the sea, all things that exist, for our sake. Tell me, are not these marks of goodness? And many things one might mention. But to cut short the matter, "He maketh the sun to rise on the evil and the good, and sendeth rain on the just and on the unjust." (Matt. v. 45.) Is not this a mark of goodness? No, you say. For I said once in conversing with a Marcionite, Are not these things a mark of goodness? and he answered, If

---

[1] The negative is understood in "for."

He did not call men to account for their sins, it were a mark of goodness. But if He calls them to account, it is not goodness. That man, however, is not now present. But come, let us repeat what was then said, and more beside. For I, out of my superfluity, show that if He did not call men to account, He would not be good; but because He does call them to account, therefore He is good.

For, say, if He did not call us to account, would human life then have endured? Should we not then have fallen into the state of beasts? For if when there is this fear impending over us, and the giving account, and judgments, we have gone beyond fishes in devouring one another, we have thrown wolves and lions into the shade in ravaging one another's possessions; if He did not call us to account, and we were persuaded of this, with how great tumult and confusion would life be filled? What would be the fabled labyrinth after this, compared with the perplexities of the world? Would you not see numberless indecencies and disorders? For who then would have respected his father any more? Or who would have spared his mother? Who would have left unattempted any pleasure, any wickedness? And that the matter is so, I will endeavor to show you from one house only. How? You who raise these questions and who have servants; if I could make it manifest to these, that if they should destroy the family of their masters,[1] if they should insult their persons, if they should plunder everything, if they should turn things upside down, if they should treat them as enemies, they would not threaten them, nor correct them, nor punish them, nor even grieve them with a word, would this be any proof of goodness? I maintain that this is the extreme of cruelty, not only because the wife and children are betrayed by this unreasonable kindness, but because the slaves themselves are destroyed before them. For they will be drunkards, wanton, dissolute, and more irrational than any beasts. Is this, tell me, a proof of goodness, to trample upon the noble nature of the soul, and to destroy both themselves and others beside? Seest thou that to call men to account is a proof of great goodness? But why do I speak of slaves, who more readily fall into these sins?

But let a man have sons, and let him permit them to do everything they will, and let him not punish them; will they not be worse than anything? tell me. In the case of men then, it is a mark of goodness to punish, and of cruelty not to punish, and is it not so in the case of God? So that because He is good, therefore He has prepared a hell.

And do you wish that I should speak of another instance of God's goodness? It is not only this, but that He does not suffer the good to become bad. For if they were destined to meet with the same things, they would all be bad. But now this also does not a little console the good. For hear the Prophet, saying, "The righteous shall rejoice when he seeth the vengeance upon the ungodly, he shall wash his hands in the blood of the sinner." (Ps. lviii. 10.) Not rejoicing on account of it, God forbid! but fearing lest he should suffer the same things, he will render his own life more pure. This then is a mark of His great care. Yes, you say, but He ought only to threaten, and not to punish also. But if He does punish, and still you say it is a matter of threat, and on that account become more slothful, if it were really but a threat, would you not become more supine? If the Ninevites had known it was a matter of threat, they would not have repented. But because they repented, they cause the threat to stop at words only. Dost thou wish it to be a threat only? Thou hast the disposal of that matter. Become a better man, and it stops only at the threat. But if, which be far from thee! thou despiseth the threat, thou wilt come to the experience of it. The men before[2] the flood, if they had feared the threat, would not have experienced the execution of it. And we, if we fear the threat, shall not expose ourselves to experience the reality. God forbid we should. And may the merciful God grant that we all henceforth, having been brought to sound mind, may obtain those unspeakable blessings. Of which may we all be thought worthy, through the grace and lovingkindness of our Lord Jesus Christ, with whom to the Father, together with the Holy Ghost, be glory, power, and honor, now and for ever and ever. Amen.

---

[1] δεσποτείαν.

[2] So Sav. al. "of."

INDEXES

HOMILIES ON GALATIANS AND EPHESIANS.

INDEX OF SUBJECTS.

Christians, in all conditions called saints and faithful, 49; their blessings spiritual, 50; how chosen in Christ, 51; in order to be unblamable, 51; ought to be like Angels, 55, 62, 100; how sealed by the Spirit, 56, 120; their privilege in having Christ for their head, 62; are members of His body, 62; partakers of His body in the Eucharist, 63; are made to sit in heavenly places, 67; are created unto good works, 68; may not live in the flesh, but in heaven, 74; are given what elder saints toiled after, 75; are collectively and severally the temple of God, 75; are bound as one body by mutual ties, 102; all equal in Christ, 102; alike in grace, differ in gifts, 103; how light in the Lord, 133; cannot serve God and mammon, 135; must walk circumspectly and not give offense, 137; must put on the whole armor of God, 160; their conflict with the devil, 161; must stand well and be braced up for the fight, 163; how they are to keep the Passover, 165; their warfare ceases in the land of promise, 166; are here in a pilgrimage or campaign, 166.

Chrysostom, St., did not preach to please, 79; calls to public humiliation, 102; offers to resign his dignity for the sake of unity, 108; his times, manifold vices of, 78, 79 (and note); neglect of Communion, 64; degeneracy of teachers, 78; Church offices salable, *ib.;* the Church in conflagration through pride, 100; treatment of slaves, 123.

Church, name of, implies unity, 4; divided into a thousand parties, 8; represented by Sarah, 34; its exaltation as the body of Christ, 62; is Christ's fullness, 62; shall continue till He comes, 76, 82; is one body in Him, 99; binds all together by mutual good offices, *ib.;* is like a house built of men's souls, 100, 101; set on fire by pride, *ib.;* ought not to seek the support of bad men, 107; is the spouse of Christ, 144; her condition when He took her, *ib.*

Circumcision, brings us under the Law, 37; observed by St. Paul, not preached, 38.

Clamor, forbidden, 123; is the vehicle of anger, a special fault of women, *ib.*

Commandments, the Ten, the order of them, 153.

Communicants, unworthy, 79; careless and formal, 108; must refrain from reviling, and why, 120.

Communion, Church, not to be expanded to take in bad men, 107.

Concession, and command, difference between, 15; condescension of the Apostles to the Judaists, 1–15.

Corner-stone. See *Christ.*

Corruption, various meanings of the word, 171.

Courtezans, 151.

Covenants, old and new proceeded both from the Father and the Son, 6.

Covetousness is idolatry in Christians, 133–34; leads to the death of the soul, 134.

Cross, destroys the need of the Law, 3; removes the curse, 27; the boast of Christians, 46; raises them above the old Dispensation as well as above the world, 46.

Curiosity, generally misdirected and misplaced, 141.

Damsels, devoted to monastic life, 115–16.

David, a guileless character, 123.

Deacon, his office in dismissing the congregation, 64 (and note).

Death, of the soul, what it is, 134; the second death, 172.

Devil, why called the prince of this world, 66; why of the power of the air, *ib.;* takes advantage of men's quarrels, 119; and of their covetousness, 162; his wiles, 159; his forces, 160; may be overcome, 160; but is not to be wrestled with so much as trampled on, 162; his fiery darts are doubts, 169; and evil desires and sharp sorrows, 169; to be slain by keeping the commandments, 169.

Dispensation of grace, 76.

Drunkenness, excludes from Heaven, 69; its temporal ill effects, 138.

Earnest, the meaning of the word explained, 56; see *Spirit.*

Economy, of the Apostles about the Law, 15; to be beneficial to the objects of it, must be concealed from them, 16; of St. Paul in circumcising Timothy, 16.

Education in Scripture remedies that in the Classics, 154; consists in nurture, see *Children.*

Eli, 154.

Elisha, 95.

Ephesus, the metropolis of [Proconsular] Asia, 49; the abode of St. John and of Timothy, and a great resort of philosophers, *ib.;* its inhabitants advanced in knowledge, 49.

Epiphany, the great festival of the Greek Church in remembrance of our Lord's Baptism and Birth, 63 (note); a season for Communicating, *ib.*

Equality of ranks, inconsistent with peace, 147; Christian equality, 102; civil slavery not inconsistent with it, 142; mutual service, 158.

Eucharist, called the flesh of Christ, 41; Christ's body and blood partaken in it, 63; the preparation for it, 63; profanation of it, 64; neglect of it, *ib.;* formalism of Communicating only at the seasons, danger of unworthy Communicating, 63; inconsistency of coming to Service and not Communicating, 64; unfitness not the fault of nature but of indolence, 65; Christ specially present in the Eucharist, 65; allusions to the Eucharistic Service, 120–21; see *Sacrifice.*

Evidences, of the Gospel, 9.

Evil, not necessarily connected with this life, 5; not in our bodily substance but our will, 42.

Faith, vitiated by a slight adulteration, 7; to be defended in slight matters, 8; slight perversion of, invalidates the ministerial authority, 8; anterior to the Law, 26–27; justifies without the Law, 26; but not without love, 37; ever sees Christ, 24; gains miraculous and spiritual powers, 25; as no force if the Law be added, 25; makes us sons of God, 30; always joined with love by St. Paul, 60; will not save without works, 67; a shield to protect ready believers, 169.

Faithful, the, bear about the form of Christ, 30; the body of Christ, 41.

Falsehood, an instance of willful sin, 58.

Fasting, a means of intercession, 101.

Father and Son, one in will, 4; one in act, 6; reveal each other, 11, 146.

Fathers, their duties in the nurture of their children, 154.

Faults, to be mildly corrected, 43.

Fetters and bonds, gloried in by St. Paul, 84, &c.

Fireworshipers, 110.

Flesh, means not the body, but the depraved will, 41.

Forgiveness, motives for it, 128–29.

Foundation, *καταβολή*, a beautiful allusion contained in the word, 51; Christ the foundation, 75.

"Fullness of the times" was Christ's coming, 54.

"Fullness of Christ" is the Church, 62.

"Fullness of God" explained, 82.

Galatians, nature of their error, 2; feared to forsake the Law, 6; justly called "foolish," 23; sons of Abraham as Isaac was, 34; misled by party spirit, 40.

"Gather together into one," the meaning of the expression, 54.

Gentile customs, 8.

Gentiles, raised above the privileges of the Jews, 71; their calling a mystery, 80; the vanity of their worship as directed to the creatures, 110; it flattered men's evil passions, 111.

God, loves us for His own Name's sake, 56; a just apprehension of Him forbids us to doubt or rationalize, 60; the knowledge of Him derived from His Spirit, *ib.;* His goodness not to be presumed upon, 69; kind to the unthankful, 139; no respecter of persons, 159.

Good-pleasure, the meaning of the word, 52.

Government, in its origin paternal, 82; must be centered in one, 146; exemplified in a household, 159.

Gospels, one in substance, though fourfold in form, 7; easily perverted, 7.

Gospel, no afterthought, 51, 55; may be in itself an offense, in the manner of preaching it should not be, 137.

Grace, sets us free, makes us new, heirs and sons, 30; the great change it produces in Christians, 52; arrays the soul in spiritual beauty, 53.

Guilelessness, 123.

Habit, one sinful one may ruin us, 68; evil ones must be cured by cultivating their opposites, 125–26.

Hagar, 149.

Hannah, an example to mothers, 154; of watchfulness and prayer, 170; her reverence and contrition, 170.

Harlots, their treatment of their lovers, 83.

Heretics, denied the Co-equality of the Father and the Son, 4; considered this life essentially evil, 5.

Herod, judgment upon, 90.

Holiness in teachers more influential than miracles, 77.

Holy children, as examples of triumph over affliction, 93.

Hospitality, to be shown to the poor, 151.

Household, the mistress's duty in the conduct of, 124; when well ordered sheds a fragrance around, 143; is a little city and its head a prince, 159.

Husbands, to love their wives as Christ loved the Church, 144–45; the husband the head of the family, 146; the importance of him to the household, 148; character of a good one, 149; must show all forbearance, 150; and wean his wife from the world, *ib.*

Hymn, the Angelic Hymn, "Holy, Holy, Holy," sung in the Eucharistic service, 64 (and note), 121, 165.

Idolatry of Christians is covetousness, 134; its origin, 135.

Ignorance, to profess it more wise than to profess knowledge, 141.

Incarnation, effects of, 30.

Inheritance, by lot, according to a purpose, 55.

Israelites, how they kept the Passover, 164; how they fell, 165; their history is a mystery or type, *ib.*

Jailer at Philippi, conversion of, 87.

James the Less, not the Lord's brother, though so called, 13.

Jeremiah in prison, 94.

Jericho, 166.

Jerusalem, earthly and heavenly, 166.

Jesting, forbidden to Christians, 130; the character of one given to it, 131; enormous when extended to Scripture, 131–32.

Jesus, the Son of Nave, the type of Jesus the Son of God, 166.

Jews, the hindrance to their conversion, 4; their blessings earthly, 50; how of old chosen by God, 51; their privileges how stated by St. Paul, 71; how Jews and Gentiles are made one, 71.

Job, an example of protracted suffering, 172.

John Baptist in prison, 94.

Joseph in prison, 94.

Judaizers opposed St. Paul, 2; their ambition, 42; in St. Chrysostom's day, 8, 21; heresy of, 11.

Judgments, temporal, a call to repentance, 79.

Julian, St., a recluse, his character, 156.

Laver, of Baptism. See *Baptism.*

Law the, not evil, but weak and dangerous, 20; death to, different meanings of, 22; causes faith not to avail, 25; curse of removed by the Cross, 27; partially restrains sin, 28; provided for self-knowledge and self-restraint, 29; once led to, now leads from Christ, 29; sometimes means Genesis, often the Old Testament, 33; obedience to part of, subjects to the whole, 36; abolished to make room for a higher rule of life, 39, 42; fulfilled by the various gifts of the faithful, 43; the ceremonies of, abolished in Christ, 72.

Lent-season, 63.

Light, detects darkness by its own shining, 133, 136.

Lot, inheritance by lot implies that we are not chosen by merit, 55 (and note).

Love, God's love the cause of our being chosen, 52; how to understand its extent, 82; its effects and obligations upon man, 98; always combined with faith, 60, 171; towards enemies enforced, 82, 127–129; its fruit unity and mutual confidence, 97–98; is the condition of our receiving the Spirit, 105; love between husband and wife, 149.

Lowliness, the ground of all graces, 96.

Man, the wonderful exaltation of his nature in Christ, 61; his littleness and greatness, 62; a fourfold consideration of him, 114.

Manichees, considered the world essentially evil, 5 (note); and the body, 39; paid divine honors to the heavenly bodies, 5.

Manichees, 139 (and note).

Marcionites, allowed one Gospel only, 7, 139 (and note).

Marks of the Cross, 47.

Marriage, &c., some heretics forbade it, 147; rules for, 151.

Masters, their duties, 158.

Mildness in correcting enjoined, 43.

Minister, in what sense not applied to the Son, 54 (and note).

Ministers of the Gospel to be obeyed though wicked, 8; unless they vitiate the faith, 8; maintained by their disciples, 44; mutual benefits of this, 45; contrast in the case of Heathen teachers, 45 (note).

Monks, 165 (note); their self-denial, 248.

Moses, an example of love to enemies, 83.

Murder, an instance of voluntary sin, 57.

Mystery, "of His will," 53; the calling of the Gentiles so called, 77; of the Gospel made known to angels by the Church, 80; the union of Christ and the Church so called, 146.

Natural, what acts are so called, 73.

Nature, does not force man to sin, 57.

Necessity, not to be pleaded in excuse for sin, 57.

Nineveh, its repentance an example to us, 101–2.

Novatians, denied repentance to the lapsed, 25 (note).

Oaths, not necessary to beget confidence, 62.

Obedience, slight breach of, punishable, 7.

Passover, its historical and mystical meaning, 165; how kept by Israelites, how to be kept by Christians, 165.

Paul, St., followed Christ's example in his mode of preaching, 1; his divine calling and commission, 2; suddenness of his conversion a proof of its being divine, 10; sincerity of his motives, 10; his opposition to Christianity on religious motives, *ib.;* called on account of his capacity, 10; reason of his first journey from Antioch to Jerusalem, 11; reason of his second journey, 14; his fervency and humility, 12; equal in dignity to St. Peter, 12; his humility shown in his visit to St. Peter, 12; his doctrine approved by the Apostles, 17; his tenderness and skill, 31–2; observed,

HOMILIES ON GALATIANS AND EPHESIANS.

INDEX OF TEXTS.

HOMILIES

ON

PHILIPPIANS, COLOSSIANS, AND THESSALONIANS.

INDEX OF SUBJECTS.

HOMILIES

ON

PHILIPPIANS, COLOSSIANS, AND THESSALONIANS.

INDEX OF TEXTS.*

* [The Oxford edition includes all texts merely *quoted*, which are very numerous. Only those are here given which Chrysostom has to some extent *explained*. — J. A. B.]

HOMILIES

ON

THE EPISTLES TO TIMOTHY, TITUS, AND PHILEMON.

INDEX OF SUBJECTS.

HOMILIES

ON

THE EPISTLES TO TIMOTHY, TITUS, AND PHILEMON.

INDEX OF TEXTS.